THE ACADEMY AWARDS INDEX

THE ACADEMY AWARDS INDEX

The Complete Categorical and Chronological Record

Compiled with an Introduction
by RICHARD SHALE

Foreword by Robert Wise

Greenwood Press
Westport, Connecticut • London

Library of Congress Cataloging-in-Publication Data

Shale, Richard.
The Academy Awards index : the complete categorical and chronological record / compiled with an introduction by Richard Shale ; foreword by Robert Wise.
p. cm.
Includes bibliographical references and index.
ISBN 0–313–27738–9 (alk. paper)
1. Academy Award (Motion pictures) I. Title.
PN1993.92.S53 1993
791.43′079—dc20 92–40226

British Library Cataloguing in Publication Data is available.

Library of Congress Catalog Card Number: 92–40226
ISBN: 0–313–27738–9

First published in 1993

Greenwood Press, 88 Post Road West, Westport, CT 06881
An imprint of Greenwood Publishing Group, Inc.

Printed in the United States of America

The paper used in this book complies with the Permanent Paper Standard issued by the National Information Standards Organization (Z39.48–1984).

10 9 8 7 6 5 4 3 2 1

To my mother, Virginia Shale,
and to the memory of my father, Don Shale.

Contents

Foreword by Robert Wise ix
Introduction xi
Acknowledgments xiii
The Academy: How It Started, What It Is, What It Does 1

I. Listing by Academy Award Categories 15

Annual Awards 17
  Best Picture 17
  Actor 31
  Actress 42
  Supporting Actor 53
  Supporting Actress 62
  Directing 71
  Writing 82
  Cinematography 110
  Art Direction/Set Decoration 126
  Sound 148
  Film Editing 165
  Music: Scoring 176
  Music: Best Original Song 199
  Costume Design 216
  Make-up 228
  Visual Effects 231
  Sound Effects Editing 234
  Short Films 236
  Documentary 258
  Foreign Language Film Award 277

Other Awards 285
  Honorary Awards 285
  Special Achievement Awards 295
  Irving G. Thalberg Memorial Award 297
  Jean Hersholt Humanitarian Award 299
  Gordon E. Sawyer Award 301
  Scientific or Technical Awards 302

Discontinued Categories 335
  Unique and Artistic Picture 335
  Engineering Effects 336
  Assistant Director 337
  Dance Direction 339
  Special Effects 341
  Special Visual Effects 346
  Sound Effects 348

II. Chronological Index of Academy Awards 349

Appendix I: Academy Founders 701
Appendix II: Academy Presidents 705
Appendix III: Directors of Best Picture 707
Selected Bibliography 709
Index 723

Photo section follows page 348.

Foreword

As of this writing the Academy of Motion Picture Arts and Sciences is in its 66th year. Over the course of those years literally hundreds of theatrical films have been nominated for awards of excellence in various dramatic categories as well as the scientific awards of filmmaking.

Richard Shale's *Academy Awards Index: The Complete Categorical and Chronological Record* not only lists all these nominations year by year but also tells us the final winners in every category. This comprehensive index allows the reader to find quickly the information wanted, not only by picture title but also by individuals' names.

In addition, the book gives a short history of the Academy. It also briefly gives the backgrounds for the awards given in the various branches of the Academy and for the honorary awards the Academy gives out.

Shale's book is an absolutely first-rate reference for scholars and film buffs alike. Browsing through it reminds the reader of all the fine movies made over the years and the outstanding creative work done by the artists who made them. The book itself is worthy of a golden "Oscar."

Robert Wise
Academy Award Winner
Director-Producer

Robert Wise began his film career as an editor at RKO. After editing several films including Orson Welles' *Citizen Kane* and *The Magnificent Ambersons*, he graduated to directing and later to producing. He has received four Oscars for directing and producing Best Picture winners *West Side Story* and *The Sound of Music*. In 1967 Mr. Wise received the Irving G. Thalberg Memorial Award.

Introduction

There is a fascinating parallel between the history of film and the evolution of the Oscars over the past sixty-five years. The advent of talkies, the age of the Hollywood musical, and the growing popularity of color, for example, have all been reflected by changes in the award categories. Those who examine movies through the awards of the Academy of Motion Picture Arts and Sciences literally will find a story with a cast of thousands, and this index has been compiled to make more accessible the names of those performers, craftsmen, and scientists—all artists in their respective fields—and the films they created.

To underscore when each category was established and when those no longer in existence were discontinued, the first major section of the book is indexed according to award category, each introduced by a brief explanation of its history and voting procedure. The same information is repeated, in chronological arrangement, in the second major section of the book. Names of winning nominees are indicated throughout by large capital letters and a star in front of the entry; other nominees are indicated by small capital letters.

Some critics of the Academy argue that the awards are self-serving and that the competition is meaningless since comparisons of different roles and different films are impossible. The complaints that a comedy cannot be judged against a dramatic picture, that no single achievement can be judged "best," and that the winners do not always coincide with the public's choice seem to me to miss the point. The Oscars are and always have been a means by which film industry people recognize their fellow workers, and few would deny that politics and sentiment have sometimes influenced the voting.

The awards have attained a popularity and significance far beyond the dreamiest expectations of the Academy founders. Vincent Canby, film critic for the *New York Times*, writes, "More than any other program of its kind, the annual Oscar telecast epitomizes American show biz and where show biz happens to be at that particular moment. It has to do not only with movies and the state of that so-called popular art, but also with television, with business, and especially with the American civilization, as it is and as it wants to see itself."

It is not my intention in this volume to debate the validity of the Oscars but to record the results. Those who wish to defend or attack the choices of the Academy voters may find the ammunition for their arguments in these pages. My aim is to offer a complete account of the Academy Awards and to provide easy access to the names of the nominees and winners.

Acknowledgments

This book could not have been completed without the help of many people. I was greatly assisted by Hildegard Schnuttgen's staff of reference librarians at Youngstown State University's Maag Library and the reference department of the Youngstown Public Library, who were helpful in countless ways. My research was aided considerably by a grant from Youngstown State University's University Research Council; I am most grateful for that support.

My special gratitude goes to the excellent staff of the Academy of Motion Picture Arts and Sciences' Margaret Herrick Library and Patrick Stockstill, the Academy historian, who responded with friendliness and efficiency to my seemingly endless questions.

I am particularly grateful to Robert Wise for providing the foreword to this book and to my editors at Greenwood Press. Marilyn Brownstein, George Butler, and Penny Sippel all offered encouragement and guidance. Lynn Wheeler's copyediting saved me from many a slip. I thank them for their patience, friendliness, and editorial skills.

Thanks also to Stan Hochman for help at the beginning and to my research assistant Bob Hackley for help at the end. I am especially grateful to my wife Deborah for her assistance in compiling the alphabetical index. For permission to use photographs, I thank Katharine Hepburn, the Roy Export Company, *American Cinematographer*, and especially Kristine Krueger of the Academy of Motion Picture Arts and Sciences and Kathy Lendech of Turner Entertainment Company.

To my wife Deborah and son Rennie go my love and thanks for their patience, understanding, and moral support.

The Academy: How It Started, What It Is, What It Does

To the general public, the Academy of Motion Picture Arts and Sciences simply means the Oscars. But to the founders sixty-five years ago and to the five thousand active members, the Academy has always meant much more. To place the birth of the Oscars in proper perspective, it is necessary first to examine the Academy itself and its many other important activities in addition to the annual awards.

Origins of the Academy

When the idea for an Academy of Motion Picture Arts and Sciences (AMPAS) was developed in the late 1920s, the movie industry was in the midst of its greatest period of change. Potentially revolutionary experiments in sound had begun which would seriously threaten and finally doom the silent picture. Repercussions from scandals that had rocked Hollywood earlier in the decade were still being felt, and the industry, particularly sensitive to outside attacks and cries for censorship, searched for a manageable way to protect itself.

Less known to the public but of great concern within the industry was the growing mood of unionism. There had been a strike by studio craftsmen in 1918, and by the mid-twenties the labor struggle had intensified. Los Angeles was a stronghold of the open shop and, as such, presented a challenge to organized labor. On November 29, 1926, nine major studios and five unions signed the Studio Basic Agreement, and the motion picture industry became unionized after a ten-year struggle. The pact, however, covered only stagehands, carpenters, musicians, electricians, and painters; the major talent groups were still without bargaining power, and the producers could only anticipate that the actors, writers, and directors would also soon press for standardized contracts.

In such a climate the seeds of the Academy were sown. During the first week of January 1927, five weeks after the Studio Basic Agreement was signed, the idea for a new organization was suggested over dinner at the home of MGM chief Louis B. Mayer. Present as Mayer's guests were actor Conrad Nagel and director Fred Niblo. Several sources also claim Fred Beetson of the Association of Motion Picture Producers was present, and Beetson himself later wrote in an *Academy Bulletin* of his good fortune "to be one of the original four to discuss the value to the industry of forming an organization for the benefit of all in the industry." The prospect of such an institution prompted the men to plan a dinner the following week to which they would invite representatives from all creative branches of the motion picture industry.

On January 11, 1927, thirty-six people gathered at the Ambassador Hotel in Los Angeles and enthusiastically endorsed the idea of an association which would be mutually beneficial. These persons became the founders of the Academy of Motion Picture Arts and Sciences (see Appendix I). By March 19, 1927, articles of incorporation had been presented and the first officers elected. Douglas Fairbanks was chosen as president, with Fred Niblo as vice-president, M. C. Levee as treasurer, and Frank Woods as secretary. The Academy was granted a charter as a non-profit corporation by the State of California on May 4, 1927, and a week later on May 11, an organizational banquet was held at the Biltmore Hotel. Three hundred persons attended, and, according to the Academy's 1929 *Annual Report*, 231 people joined the new Academy that night.

Because it was not limited to a single studio or to a specific talent group, the newly created organization had great potential as a forum for exchanging ideas and settling differences. "Each of the talent classes had grievances with no medium for their adjustment," wrote Frank Woods. "But more than this and of greater importance as some of us viewed it, the screen and all its people were under a great and alarming cloud of public censure and contempt. . . . Some constructive action seemed imperative to halt the attacks and establish the industry in the public mind as a respectable, legitimate institution, and its people as reputable individuals."

Shortly after the organizational banquet, the Academy published on June 20, 1927, a statement of aims which read in part:

> The Academy will take aggressive action in meeting outside attacks that are unjust.
>
> It will promote harmony and solidarity among the membership and among the different branches.
>
> It will reconcile internal differences that may exist or arise.
>
> It will adopt such ways and means as are proper to further the welfare and protect the honor and good repute of the profession.
>
> It will encourage the improvement and advancement of the arts and sciences of the profession by the interchange of constructive ideas and by awards of merit for distinctive achievements.
>
> It will take steps to develop the greater power and influence of the screen.
>
> In a word, the Academy proposes to do for the motion picture profession in all its branches what other great national and international bodies have done for other arts and sciences and industries.

Labor Relations

Despite the positive and nobly stated purposes of the Academy, critics would later charge that the organization was nothing more than a company union conceived by the wily Mayer as a means by which the producers could control the talent groups and forestall unionization. Murray Ross wrote in *Stars and Strikes*, his 1941 study of Hollywood's labor struggle: "The founding of the Academy was a master stroke of producer ingenuity; its successful operation resulted from actor acquiescence in its policies." Others vehemently denied the charges and pointed out that the structure of the Academy offered equal representation to all. The producers constituted only one of the five branches of the Academy—actors, directors, technicians, and writers had equal status—and the Board of Directors which ran the organization was made up of three representatives from each branch.

A labor dispute became the first order of business for the new Academy. In the summer of 1927 the studios, claiming pressure from their New York bankers, tried to impose a 10 percent salary cut as a response to charges of financial mismanagement and extravagance. When the talent groups protested loudly and threatened to strike, the studios quickly suggested that the producers' branch of the Academy hold conferences with the other branches to air grievances and suggest ways of cutting costs. The sessions were held, and the result was a decision to withdraw the proposed salary cut. But when this announcement was made at an Academy dinner on July 28, 1927, the producers let the other branches accept the blame for soaring motion picture costs. The talent branches felt double-crossed, and though the Academy claimed credit for averting the salary cut, this episode marked the beginning for many of a distrust of the Academy's impartiality in labor-management disputes.

The realization that sound pictures would become more than a passing fad prompted many legitimate stage actors to come to Hollywood and switch to film work. Many of these stage players belonged to the Actors' Equity Association which had won a closed shop on Broadway in 1919, and a controversy soon developed over who should represent film actors. In December 1927 the Academy announced the successful negotiation of a contract for free-lance actors, which was the first standard actor-producer agreement in the history of Hollywood. For the next two years Equity battled the Academy for the right to represent actors, but AMPAS gained the advantage after a 1929 strike by Equity failed to generate sufficient support.

The novelty of talking pictures had sustained movie box-office receipts after the crash of 1929, but in 1931 the depression caught up with the film industry. By 1933 Paramount was bankrupt, RKO and Universal were in receivership, and Fox had been forced to reorganize. The crisis came in March 1933 when President Roosevelt declared a nationwide bank holiday. Hollywood reeled. Some studios immediately suspended salaries; others talked of closing, and production schedules were suddenly uncertain. The Academy quickly formed an Emergency Committee which suggested temporary 50 percent pay cuts as an alternative to a complete shutdown. The committee worked out a scale making the cuts more equitable for low income workers, and no salary cuts were to last longer than the eight-week period from March 6th to April 30th. Many studios restored salaries immediately; others were to resume full pay on a timetable worked out by the Academy committee.

The Academy was given the right to inspect the studios' financial records, and Price Waterhouse and Company was hired to conduct the audits. (Three years later the firm would be retained by the Academy on a permanent basis to tabulate the Academy Award voting.) The stumbling block arose when Warner Brothers refused to restore salaries on the date set by the Academy. Darryl Zanuck, then with Warners, had promised his employees that the studio would abide by the Academy decision, and when it refused, Zanuck resigned his $5,000-a-week job in protest.

The Warners controversy also precipitated the resignation of Conrad Nagel as Academy president when his actions met with the disapproval of the Board. The Los Angeles *Times* quoted Nagel as saying he worked through Will Hays to persuade Harry Warner to accept the Academy decision, but another paper claimed Nagel supported Warner's stand and in doing so drew a vote of no confidence from the Academy directors. The Academy issued a statement simply saying "the intensive struggle within the industry within the last few weeks has resulted in many questions of Academy policy with some of which Mr. Nagel felt he could not agree."

The Academy survived this crisis but with a further erosion of its reputation because the salary waiver plan had not been popular with the talent groups. Despite the Academy's attempt to deal equitably with a difficult situation, "it marked," one labor historian noted, "the beginning of the end of the usefulness of the AMPAS in the labor relations field."

J. T. Reed replaced Nagel as president and immediately speeded up work on a new constitution that would reorganize the Academy. After less than a month in office Reed sent "An Open Letter to Every Member of the Academy" in which he outlined the changes in structure and policy. "Every effort has been made," he wrote, "to guarantee that both the election system and the Academy as a whole will be free from politics, and from any taint of self-preservation in office."

Further trouble erupted that summer. Already pressured by internal strife and the growing militancy of Hollywood unionization, the Academy nearly capsized in the troubled waters of the National Recovery Administration. On June 16, 1933, Roosevelt signed the National Industrial Recovery Act which suspended anti-trust laws and allowed industries to regulate themselves through "codes of fair competition." The NRA Motion Picture Code became the longest of more than six hundred industry codes drawn up. Though J. T. Reed was a member of the code committee, the Academy lacked enough internal unity to be much of a factor in the code hearings. The studios saw the code as a first step toward government control of the industry, and the talent groups saw it as a tool for further producer dominance.

Convinced that the Academy was not acting in their best interests, several actors quit to form the Screen Actors Guild in July 1933, and the new group gained further impetus that fall when the provisions of the code became known. As Murray Ross noted: "The final draft of the NRA code published in September contained the agency-licensing, salary-control, and antiraiding provisions which aroused instant and widespread indignation. The knowledge that Reed, the president of the Academy, was a member of the committee which drafted the obnoxious provisions intensified the actors' resentment."

Thus began an exodus of actors. In October, fourteen prominent stars, including James Cagney, Gary Cooper, Fredric March, Frank Morgan, Paul Muni, and George Raft, resigned from the Academy. By November the fledgling Screen Actors Guild had over a thousand members. A rejuvenated Screen Writers Guild, whose aims were similar, joined with the actors and jointly published *The Screen Guild's Magazine*, which constantly editorialized against the Academy and called it a company union.

At issue was the power struggle for the right to represent the talent groups in negotiations with the producers. "Hidden behind the mask of an arbiter of taste," the Screen Actors Guild charged, "and obscured under the cloak of research, what the Academy is really trying to do is destroy the possibility of an honest actor organization—of, by, and for actors. . . . The Guild is not going to be destroyed. But the Academy cannot exist and claim jurisdiction over actors without throwing a constant harpoon into Guild efforts for betterment of actor conditions."

On May 27, 1935, the U.S. Supreme Court unanimously declared that Roosevelt's National Recovery Administration was unconstitutional. The removal of the controversial Code of Fair Competition left labor relations in Hollywood even more chaotic than before. And so the battle raged.

The low point in Academy-Guild relations came at the Eighth Awards banquet held March 5, 1936. A few days before the dinner the Screen Guilds sent their members the following telegram:

> You have probably been asked by your producer to go to the Academy dinner stop we find that this is a concerted move to make people think that Guild members are supporting the Academy stop the Board feels that since the Academy is definitely inimical to the best interests of the Guilds you should not attend.

The boycott was successful, and only a handful of actors and writers attended the Oscar ceremony. Dudley Nichols, a militant member of the Screen Writers Guild who had resigned from the Academy three years earlier, won the Oscar for Best Screenplay and became the first person to refuse an Academy Award. "I realize," Nichols wrote, "the awards were voted by a generous membership who had no thought of personal partiality or political interest. But a writer who accepts an Academy award tacitly supports the Academy, and I believe it to be the duty of every screen writer to stand with his own, and to strengthen the Guild."

In 1937 the Academy rewrote its by-laws and withdrew completely from labor-movement negotiations. W. S. Van Dyke, who chaired the Academy's Reorganization Committee, pointed out that the change allowed the Academy "to return to its first principles and be non-economic and non-political in theory and in fact."

Though finally divisive, the Academy's ten-year involvement with labor problems was by no means a complete failure. In the early days the Conciliation Committee had successfully settled a number of disputes between individuals of different branches, and the Academy's efforts in negotiating provided a foundation on which the Guilds could later build. In their detailed study of the labor movement in Los Angeles, Louis and Richard Perry concluded:

> The AMPAS had been an innovation in industrial relations, and seemed to be a reasonable idea for successful industry-wide employee representation. Through the Academy a number of talent groups obtained standard contracts and developed codes covering various practices which worked to their benefit. Although the AMPAS was not a true union, it introduced the principle of collective bargaining. Thus when opportunities to develop labor unions came along, the talent groups were able to use the experience gained in Academy relationships to good advantage in establishing collective bargaining through various guilds.

Only once after 1937 did the Academy reenter the stormy world of politics, and that occurred during the blacklist period of the 1950s. On February 6, 1957, the Academy enacted the following rule: "Any person who, before any duly constituted Federal legislative committee or body, shall have admitted that he is a member of the Communist Party (and has not since publicly renounced the party) or who shall have refused to answer whether or not he is, or was, a member of the Communist Party or shall have refused to respond to a subpoena to appear before such a committee or body, shall be ineligible for any Academy Award so long as he persists in such a refusal."

One person affected by the rule was screenwriter Michael Wilson, who had won an Oscar for *A Place in the Sun* (1951) before being blacklisted. He appeared certain to be nominated for *Friendly Persuasion* (which was released in 1956 without screenplay credit), but when the nominations were announced February 18th the film was listed without Wilson's name. That same year blacklisted writer Dalton Trumbo won an Oscar for writing *The Brave One* but was unable to claim it since he had written the film under the pseudonym Robert Rich.

Late in 1958 several Academy members, including George Seaton and Valentine

Davies, began a campaign to repeal the rule. Among that year's possible nominations for Best Story and Screenplay was *The Defiant Ones*, written by Nathan E. Douglas and Harold Jacob Smith. Smith was "clean" but Douglas (a pseudonym for blacklisted screenwriter Ned Young) had once taken the Fifth Amendment. The Academy, faced with the embarrassing prospect of having to declare half of a writing team ineligible, revoked the rule on January 12, 1959, six weeks before the 1958 nominations were announced. Denying any specific connection to *The Defiant Ones* (for which Douglas and Smith did win Oscars), the Board of Governors issued a statement calling the rule "unworkable and impractical to administer and enforce." In the future the Academy would simply "honor achievements as presented."

Dalton Trumbo hailed the Academy decision as the equivalent of an official end to the blacklist. In a letter to Michael Wilson he wrote, "How can an industry officially rescind a blacklist which legally it cannot admit the existence of? There *was*, however, the Academy rule. Revocation of the Academy rule was the nearest thing to an official rescission of the blacklist that could or will occur."

In 1975 Trumbo finally received his 1956 Oscar after Frank and Maurice King, producers of *The Brave One*, sent the Academy an affidavit verifying that the mysterious Robert Rich was in fact Trumbo. In 1985 two more blacklisted writers received overdue recognition. Carl Foreman and Michael Wilson, screenwriters for *The Bridge on the River Kwai*, had been denied onscreen credit, which instead went to Pierre Boulle, author of the novel on which the screenplay was based. Boulle received the 1957 Oscar for a screenplay he had not written. In 1985 the Academy set the record straight and awarded posthumous Oscars to the families of Foreman and Wilson.

Technical Activities

The Academy's role in technical research was far more successful and harmonious than its labor relations. The advent of talking pictures required an enormous amount of technical study, for not only sound but lighting, camera operation, and set construction were affected. From January through April 1928 the Academy's technicians' branch co-sponsored with the American Society of Cinematographers and the Association of Motion Picture Producers a series of lectures on incandescent lighting. The demonstrations and papers read approximated the scholarly function of a true academy, and 150 cinematographers received training. A similar school in sound fundamentals was organized in 1929, and over nine hundred persons were instructed in the latest techniques.

The Academy could draw upon the talent of all studios, and many technical problems were first handled by special committees such as the Aperture Committee and the Screen Illumination Committee, but in 1929 these groups were consolidated into the Academy Producers-Technicians Joint Committee. In January 1930 the Technical Bureau of the Association of Motion Picture Producers, which duplicated many of the Joint Committee's activities, was transferred to Academy jurisdiction. It was absorbed into the Producers-Technicians Committee but continued to receive financial support from the producers' association. A further indication of the Academy's growing involvement in research was the establishment of a category for Scientific or Technical achievement for the third year of awards.

In 1932 the Academy reorganized its technical activities into a Research Council which included members from all five branches and representatives from the major companies manufacturing motion picture equipment. Under the reorganization of the Academy following the 1933 bank holiday crisis, the companies and studios engaged in production became Corporate (non-voting) Members of the Academy, and their dues were used solely to finance the work of the Research Council.

The Research Council became quite prominent during World War II. The Academy had maintained a training course for Signal Corps officers since 1930, and during World War II the Council sponsored a series of schools for motion-picture cameramen and still photographers in the Signal Corps and the Marines. Even before war was declared, the Signal Corps turned to Hollywood for help in preparing training films. Under the leadership of Darryl Zanuck, the Research Council in October 1940 volunteered to negotiate the contracts for government films. The studios and guilds pledged their support, and by November 1940 the Council had become the body that would distribute the projects to the studios. The agreement was to assign the projects alphabetically, but frequent exceptions were made, and smaller producers not a party to the Research Council's plan complained they were being frozen out. As Harry Truman's Senate committee on the war effort discovered in 1943, the assignments had not always been parceled out evenly—of the $1.4 million spent by the government in this period more than 70 percent went to four major studios: Paramount, Twentieth-Century-Fox, MGM, and RKO. The Research Council delivered 330 reels to the War Department before the contract was canceled in December 1942.

The Research Council was also responsible for determining officers' commissions for motion picture people who joined the Armed Forces. The Military Personnel Selection Committee considered over fifteen hundred applicants, recommending 105 for commissions and 610 for enlistment.

The invaluable work performed during the war was the last major activity of the Academy's Research Council. To facilitate its acceptance of funding from commercial companies, the Council was transferred to the Association of Motion Picture Producers in January 1948 and renamed the Motion Picture Research Council.

Publications and Educational Activities

When the Academy was founded in 1927 no one could imagine that the annual awards would eventually overshadow all of the organization's other activities. That these other projects are less publicized than the Oscar does not diminish their importance. The record in the field of education, for instance, is nearly as old as the Academy itself.

The early investigations in lighting resulted in the Academy's first book, *Report on Incandescent Illumination*, published in 1928, and the sound school resulted in two volumes: *Recording Sound for Motion Pictures* in 1931 and the updated, more authoritative *Motion Picture Sound Engineering* in 1938.

The College Affairs Committee had cooperated with the University of Southern California in 1928 to present a film course, and these lectures were published the following year as *Introduction to the Photoplay*. Several universities began their cinema departments with help from the Academy, and the practice of assisting college students and faculty members is continued today by the National Film Information Service, a mail service to researchers, and the Visiting Artists Program.

The Academy has made four attempts to publish a magazine. The first effort, *Motion Picture Arts and Sciences*, which lasted for only a single issue, was published in November 1927 and circulated only to Academy members. It featured articles, Academy news, a lithograph by Cedric Gibbons, and an artistic photograph by Karl Struss. The following year the Board signed a contract to purchase an existing periodical called *Hollywood*, but when it became apparent that the magazine could not be turned into a national publication the contract was canceled by mutual consent. A third try in 1939 was titled *Montage*. Intended as a monthly, only one issue was printed. According to Academy executive secretary Donald Gledhill, it was to have contained film information "upon a level comparable to the academic and professional journals in other fields." The most recent attempt at an Academy magazine came in 1972. *Academy Leader* offered a mix of film news and reviews and featured excellent reproductions of stills. Intended as a quarterly, it ceased publication after three issues.

Several other Academy publications have been more lasting. *The Screen Achievements Records Bulletin* began in 1933 as a list of film productions and credits for writers and directors. Known since 1978 as the *Annual Index of Motion Picture Credits*, this document now provides an authoritative list of credits in ten craft areas.

Equally important to the industry is the *Academy Players Directory*, published three times a year, which serves as a casting director's bible. Pictures of the player and the name of the player's agent are included, and everyone gets the same amount of space, regardless of rank or reputation. The publication, begun in 1937 as an alternative to the many private casting directories that exploited actors, now includes approximately twenty thousand entries.

In 1970 the Academy and the Writers Guild of America jointly published *Who Wrote the Movie and What Else Did He Write?*, a comprehensive directory of screenwriting credits from 1936 through 1969.

The Academy Foundation was created in the early 1940s to oversee educational and cultural activities of the motion picture industry. First discussed in September 1942 by Charles Coburn, George Stevens, Farciot Edouart, Walter Wanger, and Darryl Zanuck, the Foundation filed articles of incorporation on January 31, 1944. It is incorporated separately from the Academy in order to qualify for certain tax exemption privileges and to receive state, federal, and private funding.

One of the first and most valuable projects of the Foundation was the restoration of the Library of Congress Paper Prints Collection. Motion pictures made between 1894 and 1912 were copyrighted as a series of still photographs by reproducing a paper print of the celluloid original. Approximately 2.5 million feet of these prints were stored and forgotten in Washington until discovered in the early 1940s by Howard Walls, then working for the Copyright Office. Walls subsequently was appointed Curator of the Motion Picture Collection of the Library of Congress, and he set about to find a means of transferring the paper prints back to film. With the help of Carl Gregory he started the restoration process but was forced to stop in 1947 when Congress voted to discontinue the Motion Picture Division. The Academy Foundation was persuaded to undertake the project, and Walls was hired as curator of the film archives. After Walls left the Academy in the early 1950s, Kemp Niver took over the restoration work and successfully devised an economical way of transferring the priceless paper prints to 16mm film. When the Academy's funds for the project ran out after two and a half years, Senator Thomas Kuchel (R-Calif.) successfully pushed through a government appropriation to complete the work. Niver received an Honorary Oscar in 1954 for his Renovare process which made possible the completion of the ten-year project.

The Academy encourages film study in a number of ways. Scholarships and grants are given both in the United States and abroad to encourage the development of film schools, and the Visiting Artists Program sends industry professionals to college campuses as speakers. The Don and Gee Nicholl Fellowships in Screenwriting provide financial remuneration for aspiring screenwriters. For almost twenty years the Academy has honored young filmmakers with the Student Film Awards. The Academy Foundation sponsors seminars on aspects of filmmaking as well as four specific annual lectures: the Marvin Borowsky Lecture on Screenwriting (begun in 1973), the George Pal Lecture on Fantasy in Film (begun in 1980), the Jack Oakie Lecture on Comedy in Film (begun in 1981), and the George Stevens Lecture on Directing (begun in 1982).

The Academy headquarters in Beverly Hills houses the 1,111-seat Samuel Goldwyn Theater, a custom-designed facility capable of handling every known projection and sound system. It sets the standard for the industry and is regarded as one of the technically finest movie theaters in the world.

The Margaret Herrick Library is named for the woman who served as executive director of the Academy from 1943 until 1970 when she retired. The research facility, begun in 1931, is open to the public and holds one of the world's most complete collections of film-related material.

On January 28, 1991, the Academy opened its Center for Motion Picture Study in the renovated Beverly Hills Waterworks building on La Cienega Boulevard. The Center houses the Margaret Herrick Library and the Academy Film Archive.

The Academy Awards

When the Academy of Motion Picture Arts and Sciences was organized in 1927, among the several general committees formed was one named Awards of Merit. The original seven members of this group were Sid Grauman, Bess Meredyth, J. Stuart Blackton, Richard Barthelmess, D. W. Griffith, and Henry King, with Cedric Gibbons as chairman. (Charles Rosher and George Fawcett subsequently replaced Griffith, Gibbons, and Barthelmess.) An awards presentation was considered by this committee, and a 1928 *Academy Bulletin* reported that "a partial plan was worked out, but, in the press of other business, no definite action was taken by the Board."

By May 1928 interest in the awards had been revived, and that summer the procedure for nominations was worked out. In July the Academy Board authorized awards in twelve categories and, anticipating that the contest would become a yearly event, decided to limit the nominations to achievements in pictures released in a specific twelve-month period. August 1, 1927, to July 31, 1928, was declared the period of eligibility, and the studios happily furnished the Academy with a list of pictures released within those dates. To refresh the memories of its members, the Academy sent this reminder list of eligible films to everyone, a practice that has been maintained to the present.

Five Boards of Judges—one for each Academy branch—were appointed to consider the nominations made by the general membership, and by the August 15, 1928, deadline nearly one thousand nominations had been received. The rules stated "no national or Academy membership distinctions are to be considered."

A list of the ten achievements in each category receiving the highest number of votes was turned over to the Boards of Judges which narrowed the ten choices down to three recommendations for each award. A Central Board of Judges consisting of one member from each branch examined these three finalists in each class and decided who was to receive the first place and honorable mentions. The five men who decided these first awards were: Alec Francis, representing the Actors Branch; Frank Lloyd, Directors; Sid Grauman, Producers; Tom Geraghty, Writers; and A. George Volck, Technicians. The results were announced immediately, though the presentations were not made until three months later at the Academy's second anniversary banquet.

The period of eligibility remained August 1st to July 31st for the next four years but was changed to the calendar year for the Sixth Awards. The adjustment required the addition of five months to the eligibility period, so the 1932/33 Awards covered August 1, 1932, to December 31, 1933. Since 1934 the eligibility period has remained January 1st to December 31st. (Short Films, Documentaries, and the Foreign Language Film Award have different eligibility periods and are exceptions to the general rule.)

The selection of winners by Branch and Central Boards of Judges was used again for the Second Awards, though the number of categories was pared to seven and the practice of awarding honorable mentions was dropped. Sound pictures were eligible for the first time, having been excluded from consideration the first year because their development was too recent to insure competitive results.

The selection process was broadened the following year, and for the Third through the Eighth Awards nominations and final voting were by the full Academy membership. In 1936 (9th year) nominations were made by a special Awards Nominating Committee appointed by the Academy president, but the final vote was retained by the full membership.

The problems in labor relations that plagued the Academy in the mid-thirties had resulted in the resignation of nearly half of the members, so, in an attempt to get a more representative vote and also to appear more democratic, nominating and final voting privileges were extended to the motion picture guilds and unions as well as to Academy members. This expansion of eligible voters remained in effect from 1937 (10th year) through 1945 (18th year). Class B of the Screen Actors' Guild—the extras—was dropped in 1944, and in 1946 (19th year) the final vote was again limited to Academy members. Guilds and unions continued to vote for nominees until 1957 (30th year) when the current rule of nominating and final voting by Academy members only was put back into effect.

Each branch of the Academy makes its own rules. Most achievements are not "entered" in competition; they are simply eligible if they have met the following general rule:

> Academy Awards of Merit shall be bestowed for achievements in connection with feature-length motion pictures (defined as motion pictures over 30 minutes in running time) first publicly exhibited by means of 35mm or 70mm film for paid admission (previews excluded) in a commercial motion picture theater in the Los Angeles area, defined as Los Angeles, West Los Angeles, or Beverly Hills, between January 1, [year] and midnight of December 31, [year], such exhibition being for a consecutive run of not less than a week after an opening prior to midnight of December 31st, following normal exploitation and advertising utilized by the producer for his or her other pictures within the dates specified.

Four categories allow exceptions to this general rule: Documentaries and Short Films are entered by their producers, and Music Awards require the creator of the achievement to file an Official Submission Form. Foreign Language Films are submitted by each country's equivalent to AMPAS (limit: one film per country). (The three current exceptions to the location rule are Documentaries, Short Films, and the entries for the Foreign Language Film Award.)

Rules are sometimes created or clarified as a result of a controversy or confusion. Many Academy members, for instance, felt Bette Davis's 1934 performance in *Of Human Bondage* was the best of the year, and a furor erupted when her name was not listed among the nominees for Best Actress. The Academy was forced to accept write-in candidates, but the confusion eventually brought about a rule prohibiting write-ins.

With the creation of the Supporting Actor and Actress categories in 1936, it was only a matter of time before clarifying rules would be needed. Paulette Goddard's 1943 nomination for Supporting Actress in *So Proudly We Hail* left many members asking if she really belonged under Best Actress since she had received co-star billing for the role. The following year Barry Fitzgerald, who co-starred with Bing Crosby in *Going My Way*, found himself nominated in two categories for the same role. (He lost the Best Actor award to Crosby but won the Supporting Actor Oscar.) The Academy finally asked the studios to designate which category the performance belonged in, and thereafter the yearly reminder lists to members carried a designation distinguishing the leads from the supporting roles. In 1964 the Academy Board of Governors voted to omit this differentiation, and the rule now in effect says the "determination as to whether a role is a lead or a support shall be made individually by members of the [Actors'] branch at the time of balloting."

An actor or actress can no longer be nominated in both categories for the same performance, but the rules have never prevented a nomination in lead and supporting categories for two different roles. This happened to Fay Bainter in 1938, Teresa Wright in 1942, Jessica Lange in 1982, Sigourney Weaver in 1988, and Al Pacino in 1992. (Bainter, Wright, and Lange lost the Best Actress award but won for Supporting Actress; Pacino won Best Actor but lost in the Supporting Actor category; Weaver lost in both categories.) Nor can actors and actresses compete against themselves. Should two different performances by the same person receive enough votes for a nomination, only one will be accepted.

For several years it was possible for a film to be eligible for both Documentary Short Subject and Short Subject–Live Action, but when *Sentinels of Silence* won the 1971 Oscars in *both* categories the rule was changed to allow a film to compete in *either* but not both classifications. The choice was then left to the producer. Present rules, however, prohibit documentary films from being entered in the Short Films competition.

One cannot, it appears, refuse Academy recognition. Actor George C. Scott declined his 1970 Best Actor nomination for *Patton*, just as he had done in 1961 for a Supporting Actor nomination in *The Hustler*. Daniel Taradash, president of the Academy, tersely explained that it was Scott's *performance*, not Scott, that was involved and that the nomination would stand. It did, and Scott won. Two years later Marlon Brando refused his Best Actor award won for *The Godfather* on the grounds that Hollywood had not treated the American Indian fairly in its pictures. Neither Scott's nor Brando's action was without precedent, since Dudley Nichols had previously refused a 1935 Oscar for writing *The Informer*. Despite such refusals, all men are still listed as winners.

Oscars have occasionally been awarded to persons who have died before their achievements could be recognized. The most recent posthumous award went to the late Howard Ashman, lyricist for "Beauty and the Beast," winner of the 1991 Best Song award. Peter Finch died before being named Best Actor for his 1976 role in *Network*. The practice of posthumous awards goes all the way back to the first awards ceremony when an honorable mention for Title Writing was presented to Gerald Duffy who had died some months before. Due to unusual circumstances, composer Raymond Rasch didn't win his Oscar until eight years after he died. Rasch, Larry Russell (who had also died before winning the award), and Charlie Chaplin had collaborated on the musical score of Chaplin's 1952 film *Limelight*. The film was never released in the Los Angeles area until 1972 when it qualified for and won the award for Best Original Dramatic Score.

Price Waterhouse and Company, the firm of certified public accountants which had first worked with the Academy during the 1933 bank moratorium salary crisis, began counting Oscar ballots in 1936, the year a preferential system of voting was begun:

> Under the preferential system of voting, each member has one vote, which may be expressed in several alternate choices, in the order of his preference. If his first choice agrees with that of a sufficient majority, that achievement becomes one of the nominations. However, should his first choice be in the minority, his vote is applied to his second choice, or his third, and so on until the voter has helped to select one of the achievements. In this way, the entire voting group has a voice in the ultimate selections. Voters are not obligated to list more choices than they really have, but if only one choice is expressed, and it is in the minority, the ballot becomes void and cannot help in the selection of another achievement.

For the first twelve years of the Academy Awards, the final results of the balloting were released to the press prior to the ceremony to accommodate newspaper deadlines, but when one paper broke the pledge not to print the winners' names until after the ceremony the practice of advance notice ended. With the 1940 Awards came sealed envelopes and secrecy. From 1940 to 1955 the names of *all* winners were withheld until the actual awards presentation. Since the 29th Awards in 1956, the annual awards voted by the entire Academy membership have remained secret until the presentation. The "other" awards voted by the Board of Governors are announced in advance. These include Honorary, Special Achievement, and Scientific or Technical Awards as well as the Thalberg, Hersholt, and Sawyer awards.

The Academy Award statuette was designed in 1928 by MGM Art Director Cedric Gibbons. Once his sketches (which, contrary to the popular myth, were not first drawn on the tablecloth during an Academy banquet) were approved by the Academy Board, Los Angeles sculptor George Stanley created the trophy. The figure represents a knight holding a crusader's sword standing on a reel of film whose spokes represent the five original branches of the Academy—Actors, Directors, Producers, Technicians, and Writers. The nickname Oscar dates from the early 1930s, and several people, including Margaret Herrick (then the Academy's librarian, later Executive Director), actress Bette Davis, and Hollywood columnist Sidney Skolsky, have claimed credit for the nickname. Verification of who really named Oscar is not possible, but the nickname won immediate approval. The Oscar is thirteen and a half inches tall and weighs eight and a half pounds. It is made of britannium and is gold plated. The statuettes have been numbered since 1949 (starting with #501).

Academy Awards may take several forms. Recipients of all annual awards, Special

Achievement awards, Scientific or Technical Awards of Merit, Hersholt, and Sawyer awards receive Oscar statuettes. Recipients of the Scientific and Engineering Award receive Academy plaques, and the Technical Achievement Award winners receive certificates. The Irving G. Thalberg Memorial Award is a bronze head of Thalberg. Honorary Awards may be a statuette, scroll, life membership, or any design ordered by the Board of Governors. Walt Disney, for example, received one large statuette and seven miniatures for *Snow White and the Seven Dwarfs*, and Edgar Bergen got a wooden statuette when honored for the creation of Charlie McCarthy. On the eleven occasions when an Honorary Juvenile Award was given, the winner received a miniature statuette. All nominees receive Certificates of Nomination.

World War II produced one temporary change in the Oscar: plaster statuettes were awarded in 1942, 1943, and 1944 when all metals were needed for the war effort. These ersatz Oscars were replaced by the genuine metal ones after the war. Another tradition, however, ended permanently during World War II. The Academy banquet, a yearly event since the first organizational dinner in 1927, was discontinued in 1944. A banquet seemed inappropriate during wartime, especially in a country that was rationing its food, and, more practically, the crowds had grown too large to be comfortably accommodated at a dinner.

After alternating between the Ambassador and Biltmore Hotels for several years, the awards ceremony switched to a theater setting in 1944 when the banquet was discontinued. After three years at Grauman's Chinese Theatre, two at the Shrine Auditorium, and one at the Academy's own Academy Awards Theatre, the Oscar ceremony settled in for eleven straight years at RKO's Pantages Theatre. In 1961 (33rd year) the ceremony moved to the Santa Monica Civic Auditorium where it remained until 1969 when it switched to the Dorothy Chandler Pavilion of the Los Angeles County Music Center. Here the ceremony has remained except for three years (the 60th Awards in 1988, the 61st Awards in 1989, and the 63rd Awards in 1991) when the presentations returned after a forty-year absence to the Shrine Civic Auditorium.

The publicity achieved through radio and television has helped immeasurably to popularize the Oscar and the people who win them. The first awards drew little coverage, but the second awards caused enough interest to prompt Los Angeles radio station KNX to broadcast an hour of the ceremonies. The entire ceremony was broadcast for the first time in 1945 over the ABC network and the Armed Forces Radio Service. Such exposure may be one reason why the Academy has frequently asked a comedian to host the presentations. Will Rogers and humorist Irvin S. Cobb were among the hosts during the first decade of awards. Bob Hope served as master of ceremonies a dozen and a half times between 1940 and 1978, and Johnny Carson assumed those duties five times between 1979 and 1984. Billy Crystal has hosted the last four Oscar presentations.

The Academy had always depended upon the Hollywood studios to underwrite the cost of the awards presentations, but in 1949 the studios announced the end of their financial support. Some said the pullout was due to the British film *Hamlet* being named Best Picture in 1948, but *Newsweek* reported that the decision had been reached months before the 1948 winners were announced. By the early 1950s the Academy faced a financial crisis but ironically was rescued by television, a medium then regarded with great suspicion by Hollywood. RCA Victor agreed to sponsor the 1952 Awards which NBC would televise for the first time. *Life* magazine noted wryly that television ''bought the rights to the ceremony for $100,000, used it for a one-and-a-half-hour show which presumably kept millions of TV-viewers from going to the movies that night.'' Despite criticisms that the awards had been tainted by commercialism, the marriage of Oscar and television was successful, and *Variety* headlined ''1st MAJOR PIX-TV WEDDING BIG CLICK.'' The national TV hookup allowed the Academy to experiment with simultaneous ceremonies in Los Angeles and New York; viewers would be switched back and forth according to which city the winner was in. For five years, 1953 through 1957, this practice of holding presentations on both coasts was continued. The Oscar ceremonies were telecast in color for the first time in 1966 (by ABC); radio broadcasts were dropped in favor of television coverage only in 1969.

In its first sixty-five years, the Academy of Motion Picture Arts and Sciences has grown from thirty-six founders (see Appendix I) to an organization of over fifty-four hundred members. Of this total, five thousand are active and life members, and the remaining are non-voting associate members. Dues for all are $200. For many years the fee remained $100 a year. Dues were raised to $150 in 1985 and to the present rate in 1993.

I

LISTING BY ACADEMY AWARD CATEGORIES

(1927–1992)

ANNUAL AWARDS

Best Picture

The Best Picture is one of the original categories established for the 1927/28 awards. Only three times, in 1928/29, 1931/32, and 1935, has the film named Best Picture failed to win any other awards. *Ben Hur*, named Best Picture in 1959, holds the record for the most awards with eleven Oscars out of twelve nominations. *West Side Story* (1961) with ten awards and *Gigi* (1958) and *The Last Emperor* (1987) with nine are the closest runners-up. *All About Eve* (1950) holds the record for the most nominations with fourteen.

The Best Picture award is the only category in which the nominations are voted by the entire Academy membership.

1927/28 First Year

THE RACKET, The Caddo Company, Paramount Famous Lasky. Howard Hughes, Producer.

7TH HEAVEN, Fox. William Fox, Producer.

★ WINGS, Paramount Famous Lasky. Lucien Hubbard, Producer.

1928/29 Second Year

ALIBI, Art Cinema, UA. Roland West, Producer.

★ BROADWAY MELODY, Metro-Goldwyn-Mayer. Harry Rapf, Producer.

HOLLYWOOD REVUE, Metro-Goldwyn-Mayer. Harry Rapf, Producer.

IN OLD ARIZONA, Fox. Winfield Sheehan, Studio Head.

THE PATRIOT, Paramount. Ernst Lubitsch, Producer.

1929/30 Third Year

★ ALL QUIET ON THE WESTERN FRONT, Universal. Carl Laemmle, Jr., Producer.

THE BIG HOUSE, Cosmopolitan Metro-Goldwyn-Mayer. Irving Thalberg, Producer.

DISRAELI, Warner Bros. Darryl F. Zanuck, Producer.

THE DIVORCEE, Metro-Goldwyn-Mayer. Robert Z. Leonard, Producer.

THE LOVE PARADE, Paramount Famous Lasky. Ernst Lubitsch, Producer.

1930/31 Fourth Year

★ CIMARRON, RKO Radio. William LeBaron, Producer.

EAST LYNNE, Fox. Winfield Sheehan, Studio Head.

THE FRONT PAGE, Caddo, UA. Howard Hughes, Producer.

SKIPPY, Paramount Publix. Adolph Zukor, Studio Head.

TRADER HORN, Metro-Goldwyn-Mayer. Irving Thalberg, Producer.

1931/32 Fifth Year

ARROWSMITH, Goldwyn, UA. Samuel Goldwyn, Producer.

BAD GIRL, Fox. Winfield Sheehan, Studio Head.

THE CHAMP, Metro-Goldwyn-Mayer. King Vidor, Producer.

FIVE STAR FINAL, First National. Hal B. Wallis, Producer.

★ GRAND HOTEL, Metro-Goldwyn-Mayer. Irving Thalberg, Producer.

ONE HOUR WITH YOU, Paramount Publix. Ernst Lubitsch, Producer.

SHANGHAI EXPRESS, Paramount Publix. Adolph Zukor, Studio Head.

SMILING LIEUTENANT, Paramount Publix. Ernst Lubitsch, Producer.

1932/33 Sixth Year

★ CAVALCADE, Fox. Winfield Sheehan, Studio Head.

A FAREWELL TO ARMS, Paramount. Adolph Zukor, Studio Head.

42ND STREET, Warner Bros. Darryl F. Zanuck, Producer.

I AM A FUGITIVE FROM A CHAIN GANG, Warner Bros. Hal B. Wallis, Producer.

LADY FOR A DAY, Columbia. Frank Capra, Producer.

LITTLE WOMEN, RKO Radio. Merian C. Cooper, Producer, with Kenneth MacGowan.

THE PRIVATE LIFE OF HENRY VIII, London Films, UA (British). Alexander Korda, Producer.

SHE DONE HIM WRONG, Paramount. William LeBaron, Producer.

SMILIN' THRU, Metro-Goldwyn-Mayer. Irving Thalberg, Producer.

STATE FAIR, Fox. Winfield Sheehan, Studio Head.

1934 Seventh Year

THE BARRETTS OF WIMPOLE STREET, Metro-Goldwyn-Mayer. Irving Thalberg, Producer.

CLEOPATRA, Paramount. Cecil B. DeMille, Producer.

FLIRTATION WALK, First National. Jack L. Warner and Hal B. Wallis, Producers, with Robert Lord.

THE GAY DIVORCEE, RKO Radio. Pandro S. Berman, Producer.

HERE COMES THE NAVY, Warner Bros. Lou Edelman, Producer.

THE HOUSE OF ROTHSCHILD, 20th Century, UA. Darryl F. Zanuck, Producer, with William Goetz and Raymond Griffith.

IMITATION OF LIFE, Universal. John M. Stahl, Producer.

★ IT HAPPENED ONE NIGHT, Columbia. Harry Cohn, Producer.

ONE NIGHT OF LOVE, Columbia. Harry Cohn, Producer, with Everett Riskin.

THE THIN MAN, Metro-Goldwyn-Mayer. Hunt Stromberg, Producer.

VIVA VILLA, Metro-Goldwyn-Mayer. David O. Selznick, Producer.

THE WHITE PARADE, Fox. Jesse L. Lasky, Producer.

1935 Eighth Year

ALICE ADAMS, RKO Radio. Pandro S. Berman, Producer.

BROADWAY MELODY OF 1936, Metro-Goldwyn-Mayer. John W. Considine, Jr., Producer.

CAPTAIN BLOOD, Warner Bros.-Cosmopolitan. Hal Wallis, Producer, with Harry Joe Brown and Gordon Hollingshead.

DAVID COPPERFIELD, Metro-Goldwyn-Mayer. David O. Selznick, Producer.

THE INFORMER, RKO Radio. Cliff Reid, Producer.

LES MISERABLES, 20th Century, UA. Darryl F. Zanuck, Producer.

LIVES OF A BENGAL LANCER, Paramount. Louis D. Lighton, Producer.

A MIDSUMMER NIGHT'S DREAM, Warner Bros. Henry Blanke, Producer.

★ MUTINY ON THE BOUNTY, Metro-Goldwyn-Mayer. Irving Thalberg, Producer, with Albert Lewin.

NAUGHTY MARIETTA, Metro-Goldwyn-Mayer. Hunt Stromberg, Producer.

RUGGLES OF RED GAP, Paramount. Arthur Hornblow, Jr., Producer.

TOP HAT, RKO Radio. Pandro S. Berman, Producer.

1936 Ninth Year

ANTHONY ADVERSE, Warner Bros. Henry Blanke, Producer.

DODSWORTH, Goldwyn, UA. Samuel Goldwyn, Producer, with Merritt Hulbert.

★ THE GREAT ZIEGFELD. Metro-Goldwyn-Mayer. Hunt Stromberg, Producer.

LIBELED LADY, Metro-Goldwyn-Mayer. Lawrence Weingarten, Producer.

MR. DEEDS GOES TO TOWN, Columbia. Frank Capra, Producer.

ROMEO AND JULIET, Metro-Goldwyn-Mayer. Irving Thalberg, Producer.

SAN FRANCISCO, Metro-Goldwyn-Mayer. John Emerson and Bernard H. Hyman, Producers.

THE STORY OF LOUIS PASTEUR, Warner Bros. Henry Blanke, Producer.

A TALE OF TWO CITIES, Metro-Goldwyn-Mayer. David O. Selznick, Producer.

THREE SMART GIRLS, Universal. Joseph Pasternak, Producer, with Charles R. Rogers.

1937 Tenth Year

THE AWFUL TRUTH, Columbia. Leo McCarey, Producer, with Everett Riskin.

CAPTAINS COURAGEOUS, Metro-Goldwyn-Mayer. Louis D. Lighton, Producer.

DEAD END, Goldwyn, UA. Samuel Goldwyn, Producer, with Merritt Hulbert.

THE GOOD EARTH, Metro-Goldwyn-Mayer. Irving Thalberg, Producer, with Albert Lewin.

IN OLD CHICAGO, 20th Century-Fox. Darryl F. Zanuck, Producer, with Kenneth MacGowan.

★ THE LIFE OF EMILE ZOLA, Warner Bros. Henry Blanke, Producer.

LOST HORIZON, Columbia. Frank Capra, Producer.

100 MEN AND A GIRL, Universal. Charles R. Rogers, Producer, with Joe Pasternak.

STAGE DOOR, RKO Radio. Pandro S. Berman, Producer.

A STAR IS BORN, Selznick International, UA. David O. Selznick, Producer.

1938 Eleventh Year

THE ADVENTURES OF ROBIN HOOD, Warner Bros. Hal B. Wallis, Producer, with Henry Blanke.

ALEXANDER'S RAGTIME BAND, 20th Century-Fox. Darryl F. Zanuck, Producer, with Harry Joe Brown.

BOYS TOWN, Metro-Goldwyn-Mayer. John W. Considine, Jr., Producer.

THE CITADEL, Metro-Goldwyn-Mayer (British). Victor Saville, Producer.

FOUR DAUGHTERS, Warner Bros.-First National. Hal B. Wallis, Producer, with Henry Blanke.

GRAND ILLUSION, R.A.O., World Pictures (French). Frank Rollmer and Albert Pinkovitch, Producers.

JEZEBEL, Warner Bros. Hal B. Wallis, Producer, with Henry Blanke.

PYGMALION, Metro-Goldwyn-Mayer (British). Gabriel Pascal, Producer.

TEST PILOT, Metro-Goldwyn-Mayer. Louis D. Lighton, Producer.

★ YOU CAN'T TAKE IT WITH YOU, Columbia. Frank Capra, Producer.

1939 Twelfth Year

DARK VICTORY, Warner Bros. David Lewis, Producer.

★ GONE WITH THE WIND, Selznick, M-G-M. David O. Selznick, Producer.

GOODBYE, MR. CHIPS, Metro-Goldwyn-Mayer (British). Victor Saville, Producer.

LOVE AFFAIR, RKO Radio. Leo McCarey, Producer.

MR. SMITH GOES TO WASHINGTON, Columbia. Frank Capra, Producer.
NINOTCHKA, Metro-Goldwyn-Mayer. Sidney Franklin, Producer.
OF MICE AND MEN, Roach, UA. Lewis Milestone, Producer.
STAGECOACH, Wanger, UA. Walter Wanger, Producer.
WIZARD OF OZ, Metro-Goldwyn-Mayer. Mervyn LeRoy, Producer.
WUTHERING HEIGHTS, Goldwyn, UA. Samuel Goldwyn, Producer.

1940 Thirteenth Year

ALL THIS, AND HEAVEN TOO, Warner Bros. Jack L. Warner and Hal B. Wallis, Producers, with David Lewis.
FOREIGN CORRESPONDENT, Wanger, UA. Walter Wanger, Producer.
THE GRAPES OF WRATH, 20th Century-Fox. Darryl F. Zanuck, Producer, with Nunnally Johnson.
THE GREAT DICTATOR, Chaplin, UA. Charles Chaplin, Producer.
KITTY FOYLE, RKO Radio. David Hempstead, Producer.
THE LETTER, Warner Bros. Hal B. Wallis, Producer.
THE LONG VOYAGE HOME, Argosy-Wanger, UA. John Ford, Producer.
OUR TOWN, Lesser, UA. Sol Lesser, Producer.
THE PHILADELPHIA STORY, Metro-Goldwyn-Mayer. Joseph L. Mankiewicz, Producer.
★ REBECCA, Selznick International, UA. David O. Selznick, Producer.

1941 Fourteenth Year

BLOSSOMS IN THE DUST, Metro-Goldwyn-Mayer. Irving Asher, Producer.
CITIZEN KANE, Mercury, RKO Radio. Orson Welles, Producer.
HERE COMES MR. JORDAN, Columbia. Everett Riskin, Producer.
HOLD BACK THE DAWN, Paramount. Arthur Hornblow, Jr., Producer.
★ HOW GREEN WAS MY VALLEY, 20th Century-Fox. Darryl F. Zanuck, Producer.
THE LITTLE FOXES, Goldwyn, RKO Radio. Samuel Goldwyn, Producer.
THE MALTESE FALCON, Warner Bros. Hal B. Wallis, Producer.
ONE FOOT IN HEAVEN, Warner Bros. Hal B. Wallis, Producer.
SERGEANT YORK, Warner Bros. Jesse L. Lasky and Hal B. Wallis, Producers.
SUSPICION, RKO Radio. Produced by RKO Radio.

1942 Fifteenth Year

THE INVADERS, Ortus, Columbia (British). Michael Powell, Producer.
KINGS ROW, Warner Bros. Hal B. Wallis, Producer.
THE MAGNIFICENT AMBERSONS, Mercury, RKO Radio. Orson Welles, Producer.
★ MRS. MINIVER, Metro-Goldwyn-Mayer. Sidney Franklin, Producer.
THE PIED PIPER, 20th Century-Fox. Nunnally Johnson, Producer.
THE PRIDE OF THE YANKEES, Goldwyn, RKO Radio. Samuel Goldwyn, Producer.
RANDOM HARVEST, Metro-Goldwyn-Mayer. Sidney Franklin, Producer.
THE TALK OF THE TOWN, Columbia. George Stevens, Producer.
WAKE ISLAND, Paramount. Joseph Sistrom, Producer.
YANKEE DOODLE DANDY, Warner Bros. Jack L. Warner and Hal B. Wallis, Producers, with William Cagney.

1943 Sixteenth Year

★ CASABLANCA, Warner Bros. Hal B. Wallis, Producer.
FOR WHOM THE BELL TOLLS, Paramount. Sam Wood, Producer.
HEAVEN CAN WAIT, 20th Century-Fox. Ernst Lubitsch, Producer.

THE HUMAN COMEDY, Metro-Goldwyn-Mayer. Clarence Brown, Producer.

IN WHICH WE SERVE, Two Cities, UA (British). Noel Coward, Producer.

MADAME CURIE, Metro-Goldwyn-Mayer. Sidney Franklin, Producer.

THE MORE THE MERRIER, Columbia. George Stevens, Producer.

THE OX-BOW INCIDENT, 20th Century-Fox. Lamar Trotti, Producer.

THE SONG OF BERNADETTE, 20th Century-Fox. William Perlberg, Producer.

WATCH ON THE RHINE, Warner Bros. Hal B. Wallis, Producer.

1944 Seventeenth Year

DOUBLE INDEMNITY, Paramount. Joseph Sistrom, Producer.

GASLIGHT, Metro-Goldwyn-Mayer. Arthur Hornblow, Jr., Producer.

★ GOING MY WAY, Paramount. Leo McCarey, Producer.

SINCE YOU WENT AWAY, Selznick International, UA. David O. Selznick, Producer.

WILSON, 20th Century-Fox. Darryl F. Zanuck, Producer.

1945 Eighteenth Year

ANCHORS AWEIGH, Metro-Goldwyn-Mayer. Joe Pasternak, Producer.

THE BELLS OF ST. MARY'S, Rainbow, RKO Radio. Leo McCarey, Producer.

★ THE LOST WEEKEND, Paramount. Charles Brackett, Producer.

MILDRED PIERCE, Warner Bros. Jerry Wald, Producer.

SPELLBOUND, Selznick International, UA. David O. Selznick, Producer.

1946 Nineteenth Year

★ THE BEST YEARS OF OUR LIVES, Goldwyn, RKO Radio. Samuel Goldwyn, Producer.

HENRY V, Rank-Two-Cities, UA (British). Laurence Olivier, Producer.

IT'S A WONDERFUL LIFE, Liberty, RKO Radio. Frank Capra, Producer.

THE RAZOR'S EDGE, 20th Century-Fox. Darryl F. Zanuck, Producer.

THE YEARLING, Metro-Goldwyn-Mayer. Sidney Franklin, Producer.

1947 Twentieth Year

THE BISHOP'S WIFE, Goldwyn, RKO Radio. Samuel Goldwyn, Producer.

CROSSFIRE, RKO Radio. Adrian Scott, Producer.

★ GENTLEMAN'S AGREEMENT, 20th Century-Fox. Darryl F. Zanuck, Producer.

GREAT EXPECTATIONS, Rank-Cineguild, U-I (British). Ronald Neame, Producer.

MIRACLE ON 34TH STREET, 20th Century-Fox. William Perlberg, Producer.

1948 Twenty-first Year

★ HAMLET, Rank-Two Cities, U-I (British). Laurence Olivier, Producer.

JOHNNY BELINDA, Warner Bros. Jerry Wald, Producer.

THE RED SHOES, Rank-Archers, Eagle-Lion (British). Michael Powell and Emeric Pressburger, Producers.

THE SNAKE PIT, 20th Century-Fox. Anatole Litvak and Robert Bassler, Producers.

TREASURE OF SIERRA MADRE, Warner Bros. Henry Blanke, Producer.

1949 Twenty-second Year

★ ALL THE KING'S MEN, Rossen, Columbia. Robert Rossen, Producer.

BATTLEGROUND, Metro-Goldwyn-Mayer. Dore Schary, Producer.

THE HEIRESS, Paramount. William Wyler, Producer.

A LETTER TO THREE WIVES, 20th Century-Fox. Sol C. Siegel, Producer.

TWELVE O'CLOCK HIGH, 20th Century-Fox. Darryl F. Zanuck, Producer.

1950 Twenty-third Year

★ ALL ABOUT EVE, 20th Century-Fox. Darryl F. Zanuck, Producer.

BORN YESTERDAY, Columbia. S. Sylvan Simon, Producer.

FATHER OF THE BRIDE, Metro-Goldwyn-Mayer. Pandro S. Berman, Producer.

KING SOLOMON'S MINES, Metro-Goldwyn-Mayer. Sam Zimbalist, Producer.

SUNSET BOULEVARD, Paramount. Charles Brackett, Producer.

1951 Twenty-fourth Year

★ AN AMERICAN IN PARIS, Metro-Goldwyn-Mayer. Arthur Freed, Producer.

DECISION BEFORE DAWN, 20th Century-Fox. Anatole Litvak and Frank McCarthy, Producers.

A PLACE IN THE SUN, Paramount. George Stevens, Producer.

QUO VADIS, Metro-Goldwyn-Mayer. Sam Zimbalist, Producer.

A STREETCAR NAMED DESIRE, Charles K. Feldman Group Prods., Warner Bros. Charles K. Feldman, Producer.

1952 Twenty-fifth Year

★ THE GREATEST SHOW ON EARTH, Cecil B. DeMille, Paramount. Cecil B. DeMille, Producer.

HIGH NOON, Stanley Kramer Prods., UA. Stanley Kramer, Producer.

IVANHOE, Metro-Goldwyn-Mayer. Pandro S. Berman, Producer.

MOULIN ROUGE, Romulus Films, UA. John Huston, Producer.

THE QUIET MAN, Argosy Pictures Corp., Republic. John Ford and Merian C. Cooper, Producers.

1953 Twenty-sixth Year

★ FROM HERE TO ETERNITY, Columbia. Buddy Adler, Producer.

JULIUS CAESAR, Metro-Goldwyn-Mayer. John Houseman, Producer.

THE ROBE, 20th Century-Fox. Frank Ross, Producer.

ROMAN HOLIDAY, Paramount. William Wyler, Producer.

SHANE, Paramount. George Stevens, Producer.

1954 Twenty-seventh Year

THE CAINE MUTINY, A Stanley Kramer Prod., Columbia. Stanley Kramer, Producer.

THE COUNTRY GIRL, Perlberg-Seaton, Paramount. William Perlberg, Producer.

★ ON THE WATERFRONT, Horizon-American Corp., Columbia. Sam Spiegel, Producer.

SEVEN BRIDES FOR SEVEN BROTHERS, Metro-Goldwyn-Mayer. Jack Cummings, Producer.

THREE COINS IN THE FOUNTAIN, 20th Century-Fox. Sol C. Siegel, Producer.

1955 Twenty-eighth Year

LOVE IS A MANY-SPLENDORED THING, 20th Century-Fox. Buddy Adler, Producer.

★ MARTY, Hecht and Lancaster's Steven Prods., UA. Harold Hecht, Producer.

MISTER ROBERTS, An Orange Prod., Warner Bros. Leland Hayward, Producer.

PICNIC, Columbia. Fred Kohlmar, Producer.

THE ROSE TATTOO, Hal Wallis, Paramount. Hal B. Wallis, Producer.

1956 Twenty-ninth Year

★ AROUND THE WORLD IN 80 DAYS, The Michael Todd Co., Inc., UA. Michael Todd, Producer.

FRIENDLY PERSUASION, Allied Artists. William Wyler, Producer.

GIANT, Giant Prod., Warner Bros.

George Stevens and Henry Ginsberg, Producers.

THE KING AND I, 20th Century-Fox. Charles Brackett, Producer.

THE TEN COMMANDMENTS, Motion Picture Assocs., Inc., Paramount. Cecil B. DeMille, Producer.

1957 Thirtieth Year

★ THE BRIDGE ON THE RIVER KWAI, A Horizon Picture, Columbia. Sam Spiegel, Producer.

PEYTON PLACE, Jerry Wald Prods., Inc., 20th Century-Fox. Jerry Wald, Producer.

SAYONARA, William Goetz, Prod., Warner Bros. William Goetz, Producer.

12 ANGRY MEN, Orion-Nova Prod., UA. Henry Fonda and Reginald Rose, Producers.

WITNESS FOR THE PROSECUTION, Edward Small-Arthur Hornblow Prod., UA. Arthur Hornblow, Jr., Producer.

1958 Thirty-first Year

AUNTIE MAME, Warner Bros. Jack L. Warner, Studio head.

CAT ON A HOT TIN ROOF, Avon Prods., Inc., M-G-M. Lawrence Weingarten, Producer.

THE DEFIANT ONES, Stanley Kramer, UA. Stanley Kramer, Producer.

★ GIGI, Arthur Freed Prods., Inc., M-G-M. Arthur Freed, Producer.

SEPARATE TABLES, Clifton Prods., Inc., UA. Harold Hecht, Producer.

1959 Thirty-second Year

ANATOMY OF A MURDER, Otto Preminger, Columbia. Otto Preminger, Producer.

★ BEN-HUR, Metro-Goldwyn-Mayer. Sam Zimbalist, Producer.

THE DIARY OF ANNE FRANK, 20th Century-Fox. George Stevens, Producer.

THE NUN'S STORY, Warner Bros. Henry Blanke, Producer.

ROOM AT THE TOP, Romulus Films, Ltd., Continental Distr., Inc. (British). John and James Woolf, Producers.

1960 Thirty-third Year

THE ALAMO, Batjac Prod., UA. John Wayne, Producer.

★ THE APARTMENT, The Mirisch Co., Inc., UA. Billy Wilder, Producer.

ELMER GANTRY, Burt Lancaster-Richard Brooks Prod., UA. Bernard Smith, Producer.

SONS AND LOVERS, Company of Artists, Inc., 20th Century-Fox. Jerry Wald, Producer.

THE SUNDOWNERS, Warner Bros. Fred Zinnemann, Producer.

1961 Thirty-fourth Year

FANNY, Mansfield Prod., Warner Bros. Joshua Logan, Producer.

THE GUNS OF NAVARONE, Carl Foreman Prod., Columbia. Carl Foreman, Producer.

THE HUSTLER, Robert Rossen Prod., 20th Century-Fox. Robert Rossen, Producer.

JUDGMENT AT NUREMBERG, Stanley Kramer Prod., UA. Stanley Kramer, Producer.

★ WEST SIDE STORY, Mirisch Pictures, Inc., and B and P Enterprises, Inc., UA. Robert Wise, Producer.

1962 Thirty-fifth Year

★ LAWRENCE OF ARABIA, Horizon Pictures (G.B.), Ltd.-Sam Spiegel-David Lean Prod., Columbia. Sam Spiegel, Producer.

THE LONGEST DAY, Darryl F. Zanuck Prod., 20th Century-Fox. Darryl F. Zanuck, Producer.

THE MUSIC MAN, Warner Bros. Morton Da Costa, Producer.

MUTINY ON THE BOUNTY, Arcola Prod., M-G-M. Aaron Rosenberg, Producer.

TO KILL A MOCKINGBIRD, Universal-International-Pakula-Mulligan-Brentwood Prod., U-I. Alan J. Pakula, Producer.

1963 Thirty-sixth Year

AMERICA AMERICA, Athena Enterprises Prod., Warner Bros. Elia Kazan, Producer.

CLEOPATRA, 20th Century-Fox Ltd.-MCL Films S.A.-WALWA Films S.A. Prod., 20th Century-Fox. Walter Wanger, Producer.

HOW THE WEST WAS WON, Metro-Goldwyn-Mayer and Cinerama. Bernard Smith, Producer.

LILIES OF THE FIELD, Rainbow Prod., UA. Ralph Nelson, Producer.

★ TOM JONES, Woodfall Prod., UA-Lopert Pictures. Tony Richardson, Producer.

1964 Thirty-seventh Year

BECKET, Hal Wallis Prod., Paramount. Hal B. Wallis, Producer.

DR. STRANGELOVE OR: HOW I LEARNED TO STOP WORRYING AND LOVE THE BOMB, Hawk Films, Ltd. Prod., Columbia. Stanley Kubrick, Producer.

MARY POPPINS, Walt Disney Prods. Walt Disney and Bill Walsh, Producers.

★ MY FAIR LADY, Warner Bros. Jack L. Warner, Producer.

ZORBA THE GREEK, Rochley, Ltd. Prod., International Classics. Michael Cacoyannis, Producer.

1965 Thirty-eighth Year

DARLING, Anglo-Amalgamated, Ltd. Prod., Embassy. Joseph Janni, Producer.

DOCTOR ZHIVAGO, Sostar S.A.-Metro-Goldwyn-Mayer British Studios, Ltd. Prod., M-G-M. Carlo Ponti, Producer.

SHIP OF FOOLS, Columbia. Stanley Kramer, Producer.

★ THE SOUND OF MUSIC, Argyle Enterprises Prod., 20th Century-Fox. Robert Wise, Producer.

A THOUSAND CLOWNS, Harrell Prod., United Artists. Fred Coe, Producer.

1966 Thirty-ninth Year

ALFIE, Sheldrake Films, Ltd. Prod., Paramount. Lewis Gilbert, Producer.

★ A MAN FOR ALL SEASONS, Highland Films, Ltd. Prod., Columbia. Fred Zinnemann, Producer

THE RUSSIANS ARE COMING! THE RUSSIANS ARE COMING!, Mirisch Corp. of Delaware Prod., U.A. Norman Jewison, Producer.

THE SAND PEBBLES, Argyle-Solar Prod., 20th Century-Fox. Robert Wise, Producer.

WHO'S AFRAID OF VIRGINIA WOOLF?, Chenault Prod., Warner Bros. Ernest Lehman, Producer.

1967 Fortieth Year

BONNIE AND CLYDE, Tatira-Hiller Prod., Warner Bros.-Seven Arts. Warren Beatty, Producer.

DOCTOR DOLITTLE, Apjac Prods., 20th Century-Fox. Arthur P. Jacobs, Producer.

THE GRADUATE, Mike Nichols-Lawrence Turman Prod., Embassy. Lawrence Turman, Producer.

GUESS WHO'S COMING TO DINNER, Columbia. Stanley Kramer, Producer.

★ IN THE HEAT OF THE NIGHT, Mirisch Corp. Prod., United Artists. Walter Mirisch, Producer.

1968 Forty-first Year

FUNNY GIRL, Rastar Prods., Columbia. Ray Stark, Producer.

THE LION IN WINTER, Haworth Prods., Avco Embassy. Martin Poll, Producer.

★ OLIVER!, Romulus Films, Columbia. John Woolf, Producer.

RACHEL, RACHEL, Kayos Prod., Warner Bros.-Seven Arts. Paul Newman, Producer.

ROMEO AND JULIET, B.H.E. Film-Verona Prod.-Dino De Laurentiis Cinematografica Prod., Paramount. Anthony Havelock-Allan and John Brabourne, Producers.

1969 Forty-second Year

ANNE OF THE THOUSAND DAYS, Hal B. Wallis-Universal Pictures, Ltd. Production, Universal. Hal B. Wallis, Producer.

BUTCH CASSIDY AND THE SUNDANCE KID, George Roy Hill-Paul Monash Prod., 20th Century-Fox. John Foreman, Producer.

HELLO, DOLLY!, Chenault Productions, 20th Century-Fox. Ernest Lehman, Producer.

★ MIDNIGHT COWBOY, Jerome Hellman-John Schlesinger Production, United Artists. Jerome Hellman, Producer.

Z, Reggane Films-O.N.C.I.C. Production, Cinema V. Jacques Perrin and Hamed Rachedi, Producers.

1970 Forty-third Year

AIRPORT, Ross-Hunter-Universal Prod., Universal. Ross Hunter, Producer.

FIVE EASY PIECES, BBS Prods., Columbia. Bob Rafelson and Richard Wechsler, Producers.

LOVE STORY, The Love Story Company Prod., Paramount. Howard G. Minsky, Producer.

MASH, Aspen Prods., 20th Century-Fox. Ingo Preminger, Producer.

★ PATTON, 20th Century-Fox. Frank McCarthy, Producer.

1971 Forty-fourth Year

A CLOCKWORK ORANGE, A Hawks Films, Ltd. Prod., Warner Bros. Stanley Kubrick, Producer.

FIDDLER ON THE ROOF, Mirisch-Cartier Prods., UA. Norman Jewison, Producer.

★ THE FRENCH CONNECTION, A Philip D'Antoni Prod. in association with Schine-Moore Prods., 20th Century-Fox. Philip D'Antoni, Producer.

THE LAST PICTURE SHOW, BBS Prods., Columbia. Stephen J. Friedman, Producer.

NICHOLAS AND ALEXANDRA, A Horizon Pictures Prod., Columbia. Sam Spiegel, Producer.

1972 Forty-fifth Year

CABARET, An ABC Pictures Production, Allied Artists. Cy Feuer, Producer.

DELIVERANCE, Warner Bros. John Boorman, Producer.

THE EMIGRANTS, A Svensk Filmindustri Production, Warner Bros. Bengt Forslund, Producer.

★ THE GODFATHER, An Albert S. Ruddy Production, Paramount. Albert S. Ruddy, Producer.

SOUNDER, Radnitz/Mattel Productions, 20th Century-Fox. Robert B. Radnitz, Producer.

1973 Forty-sixth Year

AMERICAN GRAFFITI, A Universal-Lucasfilm, Ltd.-Coppola Company Prod., Universal. Francis Ford Coppola, Producer; Gary Kurtz, Co-Producer

CRIES AND WHISPERS, A Svenka Filminstitutet-Cinematograph AB Prod., New World Pictures. Ingmar Bergman, Producer.

THE EXORCIST, Hoya Prods., Warner Bros. William Peter Blatty, Producer.

★ THE STING, A Universal-Bill/Phillips-George Roy Hill Film Prod., Zanuck/Brown Presentation, Universal. Tony Bill, Michael and Julia Phillips, Producers.

A TOUCH OF CLASS, Brut Prods., Avco Embassy. Melvin Frank, Producer.

1974 Forty-seventh Year

CHINATOWN, A Robert Evans Production, Paramount. Robert Evans, Producer.

THE CONVERSATION, A Directors Company Production, Paramount. Francis Ford Coppola, Producer. Fred Roos, Co-Producer.

★ THE GODFATHER PART II, A Coppola Company Production, Paramount. Francis Ford Coppola, Producer; Gray Frederickson and Fred Roos, Co-Producers.

LENNY, A Marvin Worth Production, United Artists. Marvin Worth, Producer.

THE TOWERING INFERNO, An Irwin Allen Production, 20th Century-Fox/Warner Bros. Irwin Allen, Producer.

1975 Forty-eighth Year

BARRY LYNDON, A Hawk Films, Ltd., Production, Warner Bros. Stanley Kubrick, Producer.

DOG DAY AFTERNOON, Warner Bros. Martin Bregman and Martin Elfand, Producers.

JAWS, A Universal-Zanuck/Brown Production, Universal. Richard D. Zanuck and David Brown, Producers.

NASHVILLE, An ABC Entertainment-Jerry Weintraub-Robert Altman Production, Paramount. Robert Altman, Producer.

★ ONE FLEW OVER THE CUCKOO'S NEST, A Fantasy Films Production, United Artists. Saul Zaentz and Michael Douglas, Producers.

1976 Forty-ninth Year

ALL THE PRESIDENT'S MEN, A Wildwood Enterprises Production, Warner Bros. Walter Coblenz, Producer.

BOUND FOR GLORY, The Bound for Glory Company Production, United Artists. Robert F. Blumofe and Harold Leventhal, Producers.

NETWORK, A Howard Gottfried/Paddy Chayefsky Production, Metro-Goldwyn-Mayer/United Artists. Howard Gottfried, Producer.

★ ROCKY, A Robert Chartoff-Irwin Winkler Production, United Artists. Irwin Winkler and Robert Chartoff, Producers.

TAXI DRIVER, A Bill/Phillips Production of a Martin Scorsese Film, Columbia Pictures. Michael Phillips and Julia Phillips, Producers.

1977 Fiftieth Year

★ ANNIE HALL, Jack Rollins-Charles H. Joffe Productions, United Artists. Charles H. Joffe, Producer.

THE GOODBYE GIRL, A Ray Stark Production, Metro-Goldwyn-Mayer/Warner Bros. Ray Stark, Producer.

JULIA, A Twentieth Century-Fox Production, 20th Century-Fox. Richard Roth, Producer.

STAR WARS, A Twentieth Century-Fox Production, 20th Century-Fox. Gary Kurtz, Producer.

THE TURNING POINT, Hera Productions, 20th Century-Fox. Herbert Ross and Arthur Laurents, Producers.

1978 Fifty-first Year

COMING HOME, A Jerome Hellman Enterprises Production, United Artists. Jerome Hellman, Producer.

★ THE DEER HUNTER, An EMI

Films/Michael Cimino Film Production, Universal. Barry Spikings, Michael Deeley, Michael Cimino, and John Peverall, Producers.

HEAVEN CAN WAIT, Dogwood Productions, Paramount. Warren Beatty, Producer.

MIDNIGHT EXPRESS, A Casablanca-Filmworks Production, Columbia. Alan Marshall and David Puttnam, Producers.

AN UNMARRIED WOMAN, A Twentieth Century-Fox Production, 20th Century-Fox. Paul Mazursky and Tony Ray, Producers.

1979 Fifty-second Year

ALL THAT JAZZ, A Columbia/Twentieth Century-Fox Production, 20th Century-Fox. Robert Alan Aurthur, Producer.

APOCALYPSE NOW, An Omni Zoetrope Production, United Artists. Francis Coppola, Producer; Fred Roos, Gray Frederickson, and Tom Sternberg, Co-Producers.

BREAKING AWAY, A Twentieth Century-Fox Production, 20th Century-Fox. Peter Yates, Producer.

★ KRAMER VS. KRAMER, Stanley Jaffe Productions, Columbia. Stanley R. Jaffe, Producer.

NORMA RAE, A Twentieth Century-Fox Production, 20th Century-Fox. Tamara Asseyev and Alex Rose, Producers.

1980 Fifty-third Year

COAL MINER'S DAUGHTER, A Bernard Schwartz-Universal Pictures Production, Universal. Bernard Schwartz, Producer.

THE ELEPHANT MAN, A Brooksfilms, Ltd., Production, Paramount. Jonathan Sanger, Producer.

★ ORDINARY PEOPLE, A Wildwood Enterprises Production, Paramount. Ronald L. Schwary, Producer.

RAGING BULL, A Robert Chartoff-Irwin Winkler Production, United Artists. Irwin Winkler and Robert Chartoff, Producers.

TESS, A Renn-Burrill Co-production with the participation of the Société Française de Production (S.F.P.), Columbia. Claude Berri, Producer; Timothy Burrill, Co-Producer.

1981 Fifty-fourth Year

ATLANTIC CITY, An International Cinema Corporation Production, Paramount. Denis Heroux, Producer.

★ CHARIOTS OF FIRE, Enigma Productions Limited, The Ladd Company/Warner Bros. David Puttnam, Producer.

ON GOLDEN POND, An ITC Films/IPC Films Production, Universal. Bruce Gilbert, Producer.

RAIDERS OF THE LOST ARK, A Lucasfilm Production, Paramount. Frank Marshall, Producer.

REDS, A.J.R.S. Production, Paramount. Warren Beatty, Producer.

1982 Fifty-fifth Year

E.T. THE EXTRA-TERRESTRIAL, A Universal Pictures Production, Universal. Steven Spielberg and Kathleen Kennedy, Producers.

★ GANDHI, An Indo-British Films Production, Columbia. Richard Attenborough, Producer.

MISSING, A Universal Pictures/Polygram Pictures Presentation of an Edward Lewis Production, Universal. Edward Lewis and Mildred Lewis, Producers.

TOOTSIE, A Mirage/Punch Production, Columbia. Sydney Pollack and Dick Richards, Producers.

THE VERDICT, A Fox-Zanuck/Brown Production, Twentieth Century-Fox.

Richard D. Zanuck and David Brown, Producers.

1983 Fifty-sixth Year

THE BIG CHILL, A Carson Productions Group Production, Columbia. Michael Shamberg, Producer.

THE DRESSER, A Goldcrest Films/ Television Limited/World Film Services Production, Columbia. Peter Yates, Producer.

THE RIGHT STUFF, A Robert Chartoff-Irwin Winkler Production, The Ladd Company through Warner Bros. Irwin Winkler and Robert Chartoff, Producers.

TENDER MERCIES, An EMI Presentation of an Antron Media Production, Universal/AFD. Philip S. Hobel, Producer.

★ TERMS OF ENDEARMENT, A James L. Brooks Production, Paramount. James L. Brooks, Producer.

1984 Fifty-seventh Year

★ AMADEUS, A Saul Zaentz Company Production, Orion. Saul Zaentz, Producer.

THE KILLING FIELDS, A Goldcrest Films and Television/International Film Investors L.P. Production, Warner Bros. David Puttnam, Producer.

A PASSAGE TO INDIA, A G. W. Films Limited Production, Columbia. John Brabourne and Richard Goodwin, Producers.

PLACES IN THE HEART, A Tri-Star Pictures Production, Tri-Star. Arlene Donovan, Producer.

A SOLDIER'S STORY, A Caldix Films Production, Columbia. Norman Jewison, Ronald L. Schwary, and Patrick Palmer, Producers.

1985 Fifty-eighth Year

THE COLOR PURPLE, A Warner Bros. Production, Warner Bros. Steven Spielberg, Kathleen Kennedy, Frank Marshall, and Quincy Jones, Producers.

KISS OF THE SPIDER WOMAN, An H. B. Filmes Production in Association with Sugarloaf Films, Island Alive. David Weisman, Producer.

★ OUT OF AFRICA, A Universal Pictures Limited Production, Universal. Sydney Pollack, Producer.

PRIZZI'S HONOR, An ABC Motion Pictures Production, 20th Century-Fox. John Foreman, Producer.

WITNESS, An Edward S. Feldman Production, Paramount. Edward S. Feldman, Producer.

1986 Fifty-ninth Year

CHILDREN OF A LESSER GOD, A Burt Sugarman Production, Paramount. Burt Sugarman and Patrick Palmer, Producers.

HANNAH AND HER SISTERS, A Jack Rollins and Charles H. Joffe Production, Orion. Robert Greenhut, Producer.

THE MISSION, A Warner Bros./ Goldcrest and Kingsmere Production, Warner Bros. Fernando Ghia and David Puttnam, Producers.

★ PLATOON, A Hemdale Film Production, Orion. Arnold Kopelson, Producer.

A ROOM WITH A VIEW, A Merchant Ivory Production, Cinecom. Ismail Merchant, Producer.

1987 Sixtieth Year

BROADCAST NEWS, A 20th Century-Fox Production, 20th Century Fox. James L. Brooks, Producer.

FATAL ATTRACTION, A Jaffe/Lansing Production, Paramount. Stanley R. Jaffe and Sherry Lansing, Producers.

HOPE AND GLORY, A Davros Production Services Limited Production, Columbia. John Boorman, Producer.

★ THE LAST EMPEROR, A Hemdale Film Production, Columbia. Jeremy Thomas, Producer.

MOONSTRUCK, A Patrick Palmer and Norman Jewison Production, M-G-M. Patrick Palmer and Norman Jewison, Producers.

1988 Sixty-first Year

THE ACCIDENTAL TOURIST, A Warner Bros. Production, Warner Bros. Lawrence Kasdan, Charles Okun, and Michael Grillo, Producers.

DANGEROUS LIAISONS, A Lorimar Production, Warner Bros. Norma Heyman and Hank Moonjean, Producers.

MISSISSIPPI BURNING, A Frederick Zollo Production, Orion. Frederick Zollo and Robert F. Colesberry, Producers.

★ RAIN MAN, A Guber-Peters Company Production, United Artists. Mark Johnson, Producer.

WORKING GIRL, A 20th Century-Fox Production, 20th Century-Fox. Douglas Wick, Producer.

1989 Sixty-second Year

BORN ON THE FOURTH OF JULY, An A. Kitman Ho and Ixtlan Production, Universal. A. Kitman Ho and Oliver Stone, Producers.

DEAD POETS SOCIETY, A Touchstone Pictures Production in Association with Silver Screen Partners IV, Buena Vista. Steven Haft, Paul Junger Witt, and Tony Thomas, Producers.

★ DRIVING MISS DAISY, A Zanuck Company Production, Warner Bros. Richard D. Zanuck and Lili Fini Zanuck, Producers.

FIELD OF DREAMS, A Gordon Company Production, Universal. Lawrence Gordon and Charles Gordon, Producers.

MY LEFT FOOT, A Ferndale Films Production, Miramax. Noel Pearson, Producer.

1990 Sixty-third Year

AWAKENINGS, A Columbia Pictures Production, Columbia. Walter F. Parkes and Lawrence Lasker, Producers.

★ DANCES WITH WOLVES, A Tig Production, Orion. Jim Wilson and Kevin Costner, Producers.

GHOST, A Howard W. Koch Production, Paramount. Lisa Weinstein, Producer.

THE GODFATHER, PART III, A Zoetrope Studios Production, Paramount. Francis Ford Coppola, Producer.

GOODFELLAS, A Warner Bros. Production, Warner Bros. Irwin Winkler, Producer.

1991 Sixty-fourth Year

BEAUTY AND THE BEAST, A Walt Disney Pictures Production, Buena Vista. Don Hahn, Producer.

BUGSY, A Tri-Star Pictures Production, Tri-Star. Mark Johnson, Barry Levinson, and Warren Beatty, Producers.

JFK, A Camelot Production, Warner Bros. A. Kitman Ho and Oliver Stone, Producers.

THE PRINCE OF TIDES, A Barwood/Longfellow Production, Columbia. Barbra Streisand and Andrew Karsh, Producers.

★ THE SILENCE OF THE LAMBS, A Strong Heart/Demme Production, Orion. Edward Saxon, Kenneth Utt, and Ron Bozman, Producers.

1992 Sixty-fifth Year

THE CRYING GAME, A Palace Pictures Production, Miramax. Stephen Woolley, Producer.

A FEW GOOD MEN, A Castle Rock Entertainment Production,

Columbia. David Brown, Rob Reiner, and Andrew Scheinman, Producers.

HOWARDS END, A Merchant Ivory Production, Sony Pictures Classics. Ismail Merchant, Producer.

SCENT OF A WOMAN, A Universal Pictures Production, Universal. Martin Brest, Producer.

★ UNFORGIVEN, A Warner Bros. Production, Warner Bros. Clint Eastwood, Producer.

Actor

When nominations for the first acting awards were solicited in 1928, Academy members were asked to name the actor and actress who "gave the best performance in acting, with special reference to character portrayal and effectiveness of dramatic or comedy rendition." Emil Jannings won the first Actor award, effectively demonstrating that one need not be an Academy member or even an American to win.

Four actors have won the award twice: Spencer Tracy (1937, 1938), Fredric March (1931/32, 1946), Gary Cooper (1941, 1952), and Marlon Brando (1954, 1972). Tracy and Laurence Olivier have the highest number of Best Actor nominations with nine followed by Brando and Jack Lemmon with seven. (Olivier, Brando, and Lemmon also have received Best Supporting Actor nominations.) A tie occurred during the fifth year of competition. Wallace Beery came within a vote of Fredric March, and, in those days before an independent accounting firm tabulated the votes, when a nominee came within three votes of another a tie was declared. In 1944 Barry Fitzgerald was nominated for Best Actor and Best Supporting Actor for the same performance. The rules now prevent this, although an actor may still be nominated in both categories for two different roles. The present rules also limit an actor to one nomination per category.

Achievements in this category are nominated by members of the Academy Actors Branch who decide individually at the time of balloting whether a role is a lead or support.

1927/28 First Year

RICHARD BARTHELMESS in *The Noose* and *The Patent Leather Kid*, First National.

★ EMIL JANNINGS in *The Last Command* and *The Way of All Flesh*, Paramount Famous Lasky.

1928/29 Second Year

GEORGE BANCROFT in *Thunderbolt*, Paramount Famous Lasky.

★ WARNER BAXTER in *In Old Arizona*, Fox.

CHESTER MORRIS in *Alibi*, Art Cinema, UA.

PAUL MUNI in *The Valiant*, Fox.

LEWIS STONE in *The Patriot*, Paramount Famous Lasky.

1929/30 Third Year

★ GEORGE ARLISS in *Disraeli*,* WARNER BROS.

GEORGE ARLISS in *The Green Goddess*, Warner Bros.

WALLACE BEERY in *The Big House*, Cosmopolitan, Metro-Goldwyn-Mayer.

*George Arliss was nominated for work in two films, but his award specified only his performance in *Disraeli*.

MAURICE CHEVALIER in *The Big Pond*, Paramount Publix.

MAURICE CHEVALIER in *The Love Parade*, Paramount Famous Lasky.

RONALD COLMAN in *Bulldog Drummond*, Goldwyn, UA.

RONALD COLMAN in *Condemned*, Goldwyn, UA.

LAWRENCE TIBBETT in *The Rogue Song*, Metro-Goldwyn-Mayer.

1930/31 Fourth Year

★ LIONEL BARRYMORE in *A Free Soul*, Metro-Goldwyn-Mayer.

JACKIE COOPER in *Skippy*, Paramount Publix.

RICHARD DIX in *Cimarron*, RKO Radio.

FREDRIC MARCH in *The Royal Family of Broadway*, Paramount Publix.

ADOLPHE MENJOU in *The Front Page*, Caddo, UA.

1931/32 Fifth Year

Tie

★ WALLACE BEERY in *The Champ*, Metro-Goldwyn-Mayer.

ALFRED LUNT in *The Guardsman*, Metro-Goldwyn-Mayer.

★ FREDRIC MARCH in *Dr. Jekyll and Mr. Hyde*, Paramount Publix.

1932/33 Sixth Year

LESLIE HOWARD in *Berkeley Square*, Fox.

★ CHARLES LAUGHTON in *The Private Life of Henry VIII*, London Films, UA. (British)

PAUL MUNI in *I Am a Fugitive from a Chain Gang*, Warner Bros.

1934 Seventh Year

★ CLARK GABLE in *It Happened One Night*, Columbia.

FRANK MORGAN in *Affairs of Cellini*, 20th Century, UA.

WILLIAM POWELL in *The Thin Man*, Metro-Goldwyn-Mayer.

1935 Eighth Year

CLARK GABLE in *Mutiny on the Bounty*, Metro-Goldwyn-Mayer.

CHARLES LAUGHTON in *Mutiny on the Bounty*, Metro-Goldwyn-Mayer.

★ VICTOR MCLAGLEN in *The Informer*, RKO Radio.

FRANCHOT TONE in *Mutiny on the Bounty*, Metro-Goldwyn-Mayer.

1936 Ninth Year

GARY COOPER in *Mr. Deeds Goes to Town*, Columbia.

WALTER HUSTON in *Dodsworth*, Goldwyn, UA.

★ PAUL MUNI in *The Story of Louis Pasteur*, Warner Bros.

WILLIAM POWELL in *My Man Godfrey*, Universal.

SPENCER TRACY in *San Francisco*, Metro-Goldwyn-Mayer.

1937 Tenth Year

CHARLES BOYER in *Conquest*, Metro-Goldwyn-Mayer.

FREDRIC MARCH in *A Star Is Born*, Selznick, UA.

ROBERT MONTGOMERY in *Night Must Fall*, Metro-Goldwyn-Mayer.

PAUL MUNI in *The Life of Emile Zola*, Warner Bros.

★ SPENCER TRACY in *Captains Courageous*, Metro-Goldwyn-Mayer.

1938 Eleventh Year

CHARLES BOYER in *Algiers*, Wanger, UA.

JAMES CAGNEY in *Angels with Dirty Faces*, Warner Bros.

ROBERT DONAT in *The Citadel*, Metro-Goldwyn-Mayer. (British)

LESLIE HOWARD in *Pygmalion*, Metro-Goldwyn-Mayer. (British)

★ SPENCER TRACY in *Boys Town*, Metro-Goldwyn-Mayer.

1939 Twelfth Year

★ ROBERT DONAT in *Goodbye, Mr. Chips*, Metro-Goldwyn-Mayer. (British)

CLARK GABLE in *Gone with the Wind*, Selznick, M-G-M.

LAURENCE OLIVIER in *Wuthering Heights*, Goldwyn, UA.

MICKEY ROONEY in *Babes in Arms*, Metro-Goldwyn-Mayer.

JAMES STEWART in *Mr. Smith Goes to Washington*, Columbia.

1940 Thirteenth Year

CHARLES CHAPLIN in *The Great Dictator*, Chaplin, UA.

HENRY FONDA in *The Grapes of Wrath*, 20th Century-Fox.

RAYMOND MASSEY in *Abe Lincoln in Illinois*, RKO Radio.

LAURENCE OLIVIER in *Rebecca*, Selznick-UA.

★ JAMES STEWART in *The Philadelphia Story*, Metro-Goldwyn-Mayer.

1941 Fourteenth Year

★ GARY COOPER in *Sergeant York*, Warner Bros.

CARY GRANT in *Penny Serenade*, Columbia.

WALTER HUSTON in *All That Money Can Buy*, RKO Radio.

ROBERT MONTGOMERY in *Here Comes Mr. Jordan*, Columbia.

ORSON WELLES in *Citizen Kane*, Mercury, RKO Radio.

1942 Fifteenth Year

★ JAMES CAGNEY in *Yankee Doodle Dandy*, Warner Bros.

RONALD COLMAN in *Random Harvest*, Metro-Goldwyn-Mayer.

GARY COOPER in *The Pride of the Yankees*, Goldwyn, RKO Radio.

WALTER PIDGEON in *Mrs. Miniver*, Metro-Goldwyn-Mayer.

MONTY WOOLLEY in *The Pied Piper*, 20th Century-Fox.

1943 Sixteenth Year

HUMPHREY BOGART in *Casablanca*, Warner Bros.

GARY COOPER in *For Whom the Bell Tolls*, Paramount.

★ PAUL LUKAS in *Watch on the Rhine*, Warner Bros.

WALTER PIDGEON in *Madame Curie*, Metro-Goldwyn-Mayer.

MICKEY ROONEY in *The Human Comedy*, Metro-Goldwyn-Mayer.

1944 Seventeenth Year

CHARLES BOYER in *Gaslight*, Metro-Goldwyn-Mayer.

★ BING CROSBY in *Going My Way*, Paramount.

BARRY FITZGERALD in *Going My Way*, Paramount.

CARY GRANT in *None but the Lonely Heart*, RKO Radio.

ALEXANDER KNOX in *Wilson*, 20th Century-Fox.

1945 Eighteenth Year

BING CROSBY in *The Bells of St. Mary's*, Rainbow, RKO Radio.

GENE KELLY in *Anchors Aweigh*, Metro-Goldwyn-Mayer.

★ RAY MILLAND in *The Lost Weekend*, Paramount.

GREGORY PECK in *The Keys of the Kingdom*, 20th Century-Fox.

CORNEL WILDE in *A Song to Remember*, Columbia.

1946 Nineteenth Year

★ FREDRIC MARCH in *The Best Years of Our Lives*, Goldwyn, RKO Radio.

LAURENCE OLIVIER in *Henry V*, J. Arthur Rank-Two Cities, UA. (British)

LARRY PARKS in *The Jolson Story*, Columbia.

GREGORY PECK in *The Yearling*, Metro-Goldwyn-Mayer.

JAMES STEWART in *It's a Wonderful Life*, Liberty Films, RKO Radio.

1947 Twentieth Year

★ RONALD COLMAN in *A Double Life*, Kanin, U-I.

JOHN GARFIELD in *Body and Soul*, Enterprise, UA.

GREGORY PECK in *Gentleman's Agreement*, 20th Century-Fox.

WILLIAM POWELL in *Life with Father*, Warner Bros.

MICHAEL REDGRAVE in *Mourning Becomes Electra*, RKO Radio.

1948 Twenty-first Year

LEW AYRES in *Johnny Belinda*, Warner Bros.

MONTGOMERY CLIFT in *The Search*, Praesens Films, M-G-M. (Swiss)

DAN DAILEY in *When My Baby Smiles at Me*, 20th Century-Fox.

★ LAURENCE OLIVIER in *Hamlet*, J. Arthur Rank-Two Cities, U-I. (British)

CLIFTON WEBB in *Sitting Pretty*, 20th Century-Fox.

1949 Twenty-second Year

★ BRODERICK CRAWFORD in *All the King's Men*, Robert Rossen, Columbia.

KIRK DOUGLAS in *Champion*, Screen Plays Corp., UA.

GREGORY PECK in *Twelve O'Clock High*, 20th Century-Fox.

RICHARD TODD in *The Hasty Heart*, Warner Bros.

JOHN WAYNE in *Sands of Iwo Jima*, Republic.

1950 Twenty-third Year

LOUIS CALHERN in *The Magnificent Yankee*, Metro-Goldwyn-Mayer.

★ JOSE FERRER in *Cyrano de Bergerac*, Stanley Kramer, UA.

WILLIAM HOLDEN in *Sunset Boulevard*, Paramount.

JAMES STEWART in *Harvey*, Universal-International.

SPENCER TRACY in *Father of the Bride*, Metro-Goldwyn-Mayer.

1951 Twenty-fourth Year

★ HUMPHREY BOGART in *The African Queen*, Horizon, UA.

MARLON BRANDO in *A Streetcar Named Desire*, Charles K. Feldman Group Prods., Warner Bros.

MONTGOMERY CLIFT in *A Place in the Sun*, Paramount.

ARTHUR KENNEDY in *Bright Victory*, Universal-International.

FREDRIC MARCH in *Death of a Salesman*, Stanley Kramer, Columbia.

1952 Twenty-fifth Year

MARLON BRANDO in *Viva Zapata!*, 20th Century-Fox.

★ GARY COOPER in *High Noon*, Stanley Kramer, UA.

KIRK DOUGLAS in *The Bad and the Beautiful*, Metro-Goldwyn-Mayer.

JOSE FERRER in *Moulin Rouge*, Romulus Films, UA.

ALEC GUINNESS in *The Lavender Hill Mob*, J. Arthur Rank Presentation-Ealing Studios, U-I. (British)

1953 Twenty-sixth Year

MARLON BRANDO in *Julius Caesar*, Metro-Goldwyn-Mayer.

RICHARD BURTON in *The Robe*, 20th Century-Fox.

MONTGOMERY CLIFT in *From Here to Eternity*, Columbia.

★ WILLIAM HOLDEN in *Stalag 17*, Paramount.

BURT LANCASTER in *From Here to Eternity*, Columbia.

1954 Twenty-seventh Year

HUMPHREY BOGART in *The Caine Mutiny*, Kramer, Columbia.

★ MARLON BRANDO in *On the Waterfront*, Horizon-American, Columbia.

BING CROSBY in *The Country Girl*, Perlberg-Seaton, Paramount.

JAMES MASON in *A Star Is Born*, Transcona, Warner Bros.

DAN O'HERLIHY in *Adventures of Robinson Crusoe*, Dancigers-Ehrlich, UA.

1955 Twenty-eighth Year

★ ERNEST BORGNINE in *Marty*, Hecht and Lancaster's Steven Prods., UA.

JAMES CAGNEY in *Love Me or Leave Me*, Metro-Goldwyn-Mayer.

JAMES DEAN in *East of Eden*, Warner Bros.

FRANK SINATRA in *The Man with the Golden Arm*, Preminger, UA.

SPENCER TRACY in *Bad Day at Black Rock*, Metro-Goldwyn-Mayer.

1956 Twenty-ninth Year

★ YUL BRYNNER in *The King and I*, 20th Century-Fox.

JAMES DEAN in *Giant*, Giant Prod., Warner Bros.

KIRK DOUGLAS in *Lust for Life*, Metro-Goldwyn-Mayer.

ROCK HUDSON in *Giant*, Giant Prod., Warner Bros.

SIR LAURENCE OLIVIER in *Richard III*, Laurence Olivier Prod., Lopert Films Dist. Corp. (British)

1957 Thirtieth Year

MARLON BRANDO in *Sayonara*, William Goetz Prod., Warner Bros.

ANTHONY FRANCIOSA in *A Hatful of Rain*, 20th Century-Fox.

★ ALEC GUINNESS in *The Bridge on the River Kwai*, A Horizon Picture, Columbia.

CHARLES LAUGHTON in *Witness for the Prosecution*, Edward Small-Arthur Hornblow Prod., UA.

ANTHONY QUINN in *Wild Is the Wind*, A Hal Wallis Prod., Paramount.

1958 Thirty-first Year

TONY CURTIS in *The Defiant Ones*, Stanley Kramer, UA.

PAUL NEWMAN in *Cat on a Hot Tin Roof*, Avon Prods., Inc., M-G-M.

★ DAVID NIVEN in *Separate Tables*, Clifton Prods., Inc., UA.

SIDNEY POITIER in *The Defiant Ones*, Stanley Kramer, UA.

SPENCER TRACY in *The Old Man and the Sea*, Leland Hayward, Warner Bros.

1959 Thirty-second Year

LAURENCE HARVEY in *Room at the Top*, Romulus Films, Ltd., Continental Dist., Inc. (British)

★ CHARLTON HESTON in *Ben-Hur*, Metro-Goldwyn-Mayer.

JACK LEMMON in *Some Like It Hot*, Ashton Prods. and The Mirisch Co., UA.

PAUL MUNI in *The Last Angry Man*, Fred Kohlmar Prods., Columbia.

JAMES STEWART in *Anatomy of a Murder*, Otto Preminger, Columbia.

1960 Thirty-third Year

TREVOR HOWARD in *Sons and Lovers*, Company of Artists, Inc., 20th Century-Fox.

★ BURT LANCASTER in *Elmer Gantry*, Burt Lancaster-Richard Brooks Prod., UA.

JACK LEMMON in *The Apartment*, The Mirisch Company, Inc., UA.

LAURENCE OLIVIER in *The Entertainer*, Woodfall Prod., Continental Dist., Inc. (British)

SPENCER TRACY in *Inherit the Wind*, Stanley Kramer, UA.

1961 Thirty-fourth Year

CHARLES BOYER in *Fanny*, Mansfield Prod., Warner Bros.

PAUL NEWMAN in *The Hustler*, Robert Rossen Prod., 20th Century-Fox.

★ MAXIMILIAN SCHELL in *Judgment at Nuremberg*, Stanley Kramer Prod., UA.

SPENCER TRACY in *Judgment at Nuremberg*, Stanley Kramer Prod., UA.

STUART WHITMAN in *The Mark*, Raymond Stross-Sidney Buchman Prod., Continental Dist., Inc. (British)

1962 Thirty-fifth Year

BURT LANCASTER in *Bird Man of Alcatraz*, Harold Hecht Prod., UA.

JACK LEMMON in *Days of Wine and Roses*, Martin Manulis-Jalem Prod., Warner Bros.

MARCELLO MASTROIANNI in *Divorce—Italian Style*, Lux-Vides-Galatea Film Prod., Embassy Pictures.

PETER O'TOOLE in *Lawrence of Arabia*, Horizon Pictures (G.B.), Ltd.-Sam Spiegel-David Lean Prod., Columbia.

★ GREGORY PECK in *To Kill a Mockingbird*, Universal-International-Pakula-Mulligan-Brentwood Prod., U-I.

1963 Thirty-sixth Year

ALBERT FINNEY in *Tom Jones*, Woodfall Prod., UA-Lopert Pictures.

RICHARD HARRIS in *This Sporting Life*, Julian Wintle-Leslie Parkyn Prod., Walter Reade-Sterling-Continental Dist.

REX HARRISON in *Cleopatra*, 20th Century-Fox Ltd.-MCL Films S.A.-WALWA Films S.A. Prod., 20th Century-Fox.

PAUL NEWMAN in *Hud*, Salem-Dover Prod., Paramount.

★ SIDNEY POITIER in *Lilies of the Field*, Rainbow Prod., UA.

1964 Thirty-seventh Year

RICHARD BURTON in *Becket*, Hal Wallis Prod., Paramount.

★ REX HARRISON in *My Fair Lady*, Warner Bros.

PETER O'TOOLE in *Becket*, Hal Wallis Prod., Paramount.

ANTHONY QUINN in *Zorba the Greek*, Rochley, Ltd. Prod., International Classics.

PETER SELLERS in *Dr. Strangelove or: How I Learned to Stop Worrying and Love the Bomb*, Hawk Films, Ltd. Prod., Columbia.

1965 Thirty-eighth Year

RICHARD BURTON in *The Spy Who Came in from the Cold*, Salem Films, Ltd. Prod., Paramount.

★ LEE MARVIN in *Cat Ballou*, Harold Hecht Prod., Columbia.

LAURENCE OLIVIER in *Othello*, B.H.E. Prod., Warner Bros.

ROD STEIGER in *The Pawnbroker*, Ely Landau Prod., American Intl.

OSKAR WERNER in *Ship of Fools*, Columbia.

1966 Thirty-ninth Year

ALAN ARKIN in *The Russians Are Coming! The Russians Are Coming!*, Mirisch Corp. of Delaware Prod., UA.

RICHARD BURTON in *Who's Afraid of Virginia Woolf?*, Chenault Prod., Warner Bros.

MICHAEL CAINE in *Alfie*, Sheldrake Films, Ltd. Prod., Paramount.

STEVE MC QUEEN in *The Sand Pebbles*, Argyle-Solar Prod., 20th Century-Fox.

★ PAUL SCOFIELD in *A Man for All Seasons*, Highland Films, Ltd. Prod., Columbia.

1967 Fortieth Year

WARREN BEATTY in *Bonnie and Clyde*, Tatira-Hiller Prod., Warner Bros.-Seven Arts.

DUSTIN HOFFMAN in *The Graduate*, Mike Nichols-Lawrence Turman Prod., Embassy.

PAUL NEWMAN in *Cool Hand Luke*, Jalem Prod., Warner Bros.-Seven Arts.

★ ROD STEIGER in *In the Heat of the Night*, Mirisch Corp. Prod., United Artists.

SPENCER TRACY in *Guess Who's Coming to Dinner*, Columbia.

1968 Forty-first Year

ALAN ARKIN in *The Heart Is a Lonely Hunter*, Warner Bros.-Seven Arts.

ALAN BATES in *The Fixer*, John Frankenheimer-Edward Lewis Prods., Metro-Goldwyn-Mayer.

RON MOODY in *Oliver!*, Romulus Films, Ltd., Columbia.

PETER O'TOOLE in *The Lion in Winter*, Haworth Prods., Ltd., Avco Embassy.

★ CLIFF ROBERTSON in *Charly*, American Broadcasting Companies-Selmur Pictures Prod., Cinerama.

1969 Forty-second Year

RICHARD BURTON in *Anne of the Thousand Days*, Hal B. Wallis-Universal Pictures, Ltd. Prod., Universal.

DUSTIN HOFFMAN in *Midnight Cowboy*, Jerome Hellman-John Schlesinger Prod., United Artists.

PETER O'TOOLE in *Goodbye, Mr. Chips*, APJAC Prod., Metro-Goldwyn-Mayer.

JON VOIGHT in *Midnight Cowboy*, Jerome Hellman-John Schlesinger Prod., United Artists.

★ JOHN WAYNE in *True Grit*, Hal Wallis Prod., Paramount.

1970 Forty-third Year

MELVYN DOUGLAS in *I Never Sang for My Father*, Jamel Prods., Columbia.

JAMES EARL JONES in *The Great White Hope*, Lawrence Turman Films Prod., 20th Century-Fox.

JACK NICHOLSON in *Five Easy Pieces*, BBS Prods., Columbia.

RYAN O'NEAL in *Love Story*, The Love Story Company Prod., Paramount.

★ GEORGE C. SCOTT in *Patton*, 20th Century-Fox.

1971 Forty-fourth Year

PETER FINCH in *Sunday Bloody Sunday*, A Joseph Janni Prod., UA.

★ GENE HACKMAN in *The French Connection*, A Philip D'Antoni Prod. in association with Schine-Moore Prods., 20th Century-Fox.

WALTER MATTHAU in *Kotch*, A Kotch Company Prod., ABC Pictures Presentation, Cinerama.

GEORGE C. SCOTT in *The Hospital*, A Howard Gottfried-Paddy Chayefsky Prod. in association with Arthur Hiller, UA.

TOPOL in *Fiddler on the Roof*, A Mirisch-Cartier Prod., UA.

1972 Forty-fifth Year

★ MARLON BRANDO in *The Godfather*, An Albert S. Ruddy Production, Paramount.

MICHAEL CAINE in *Sleuth*, A Palomar Pictures International Production, 20th Century-Fox.

LAURENCE OLIVIER in *Sleuth*, A Palomar Pictures International Production, 20th Century-Fox.

PETER O'TOOLE in *The Ruling Class*, A Keep Films, Ltd. Production, Avco Embassy.

PAUL WINFIELD in *Sounder*, Radnitz/Mattel Productions, 20th Century-Fox.

1973 Forty-sixth Year

MARLON BRANDO in *Last Tango in Paris*, A PEA Produzioni Europee Associate S.A.S.-Les Productions Artistes Associes S.A. Prod., UA.

★ JACK LEMMON in *Save the Tiger*, Filmways-Jalem-Cirandinha Prods., Paramount.

JACK NICHOLSON in *The Last Detail*, An Acrobat Films Prod., Columbia.

AL PACINO in *Serpico*, A Produzioni De Laurentiis International Manufacturing Company S.p.A. Prod., Paramount.

ROBERT REDFORD in *The Sting*, A Universal-Bill/Phillips-George Roy Hill Film Production, Zanuck/Brown Presentation, Universal.

1974 Forty-seventh Year

★ ART CARNEY in *Harry and Tonto*, 20th Century-Fox.

ALBERT FINNEY in *Murder on the Orient Express*, A G.W. Films, Ltd., Production, Paramount.

DUSTIN HOFFMAN in *Lenny*, A Marvin Worth Production, United Artists.

JACK NICHOLSON in *Chinatown*, A Robert Evans Production, Paramount.

AL PACINO in *The Godfather Part II*, A Coppola Company Production, Paramount.

1975 Forty-eighth Year

WALTER MATTHAU in *The Sunshine Boys*, A Ray Stark Production, Metro-Goldwyn-Mayer.

★ JACK NICHOLSON in *One Flew over the Cuckoo's Nest*, A Fantasy Films Production, United Artists.

AL PACINO in *Dog Day Afternoon*, Warner Bros.

MAXIMILIAN SCHELL in *The Man in the Glass Booth*, An Ely Landau Organization Production, AFT Distributing.

JAMES WHITMORE in *Give 'em Hell, Harry!*, A Theatrovision Production, Avco Embassy.

1976 Forty-ninth Year

ROBERT DE NIRO in *Taxi Driver*, A Bill/Phillips Production of a Martin Scorsese Film, Columbia Pictures.

★ PETER FINCH in *Network*, A Howard Gottfried/Paddy Chayefsky Production, Metro-Goldwyn-Mayer/United Artists.

GIANCARLO GIANNINI in *Seven Beauties*, A Medusa Distribuzione Production, Cinema 5, Ltd.

WILLIAM HOLDEN in *Network*, A Howard Gottfried/Paddy Chayefsky Production, Metro-Goldwyn-Mayer/United Artists.

SYLVESTER STALLONE in *Rocky*, A Robert Chartoff-Irwin Winkler Production, United Artists.

1977 Fiftieth Year

WOODY ALLEN in *Annie Hall*, Jack Rollins-Charles H. Joffe Productions, United Artists.

RICHARD BURTON in *Equus*, A Winkast Company, Ltd./P.B., Ltd. Production, United Artists.

★ RICHARD DREYFUSS in *The Goodbye Girl*, A Ray Stark Production, Metro-Goldwyn-Mayer/Warner Bros.

MARCELLO MASTROIANNI in *A Special Day*, A Canafox Films Production, Cinema 5, Ltd.

JOHN TRAVOLTA in *Saturday Night Fever*, A Robert Stigwood Production, Paramount.

1978 Fifty-first Year

WARREN BEATTY in *Heaven Can Wait*, Dogwood Productions, Paramount.

GARY BUSEY in *The Buddy Holly Story*, An Innovisions-ECA Production, Columbia.

ROBERT DE NIRO in *The Deer Hunter*, An EMI Films/Michael Cimino Film Production, Universal.

LAURENCE OLIVIER in *The Boys from Brazil*, An ITC Entertainment Production, 20th Century-Fox.

★ JON VOIGHT in *Coming Home*, A Jerome Hellman Enterprises Production, United Artists.

1979 Fifty-second Year

★ DUSTIN HOFFMAN in *Kramer vs. Kramer*, Stanley Jaffe Productions, Columbia.

JACK LEMMON in *The China Syndrome*, A Michael Douglas/IPC Films Production, Columbia.

AL PACINO in *. . . And Justice for All*, A Malton Films Limited Production, Columbia.

ROY SCHEIDER in *All That Jazz*, A Columbia/Twentieth Century-Fox Production, 20th Century-Fox.

PETER SELLERS in *Being There*, A Lorimar Film-Und Fernsehproduktion GmbH Production, United Artists.

1980 Fifty-third Year

★ ROBERT DE NIRO in *Raging Bull*, A Robert Chartoff-Irwin Winkler Production, United Artists.

ROBERT DUVALL in *The Great Santini*, An Orion Pictures-Bing Crosby Production, Orion Pictures.

JOHN HURT in *The Elephant Man*, A Brooksfilms, Ltd., Production, Paramount.

JACK LEMMON in *Tribute*, A Lawrence Turman-David Foster Presentation of a Joel B. Michaels-Garth H. Drabinsky Production, 20th Century-Fox.

PETER O'TOOLE in *The Stunt Man*, Melvin Simon Productions, 20th Century-Fox.

1981 Fifty-fourth Year

WARREN BEATTY in *Reds*, A J.R.S. Production, Paramount.

★ HENRY FONDA in *On Golden Pond*, An ITC Films/IPC Films Production, Universal.

BURT LANCASTER in *Atlantic City*, An International Cinema Corporation Production, Paramount.

DUDLEY MOORE in *Arthur*, A Rollins, Joffe, Morra, and Brezner Production, Orion.

PAUL NEWMAN in *Absence of Malice*, A Mirage Enterprises Production, Columbia.

1982 Fifty-fifth Year

DUSTIN HOFFMAN in *Tootsie*, A Mirage/Punch Production, Columbia.

★ BEN KINGSLEY in *Gandhi*, An Indo-British Films Production, Columbia.

JACK LEMMON in *Missing*, A Universal Pictures/Polygram Pictures Presentation of an Edward Lewis Production, Universal.

PAUL NEWMAN in *The Verdict*, A Fox-Zanuck/Brown Production, 20th Century-Fox.

PETER O'TOOLE in *My Favorite Year*, A Metro-Goldwyn-Mayer/Brooksfilm/Michael Gruskoff Production, M-G-M/UA.

1983 Fifty-sixth Year

MICHAEL CAINE in *Educating Rita*, An Acorn Pictures Limited Production, Columbia.

TOM CONTI in *Reuben, Reuben*, A Saltair/Walter Shenson Production presented by The Taft Entertainment Co., 20th Century-Fox International Classics.

TOM COURTENAY in *The Dresser*, A Goldcrest Films/Television Limited/World Film Services Production, Columbia.

★ ROBERT DUVALL in *Tender Mercies*, An EMI Presentation of an Antron Media Production, Universal/AFD.

ALBERT FINNEY in *The Dresser*, A Goldcrest Films/Television Limited/World Film Services Production, Columbia.

1984 Fifty-seventh Year

★ F. MURRAY ABRAHAM in *Amadeus*, A Saul Zaentz Company Production, Orion.

JEFF BRIDGES in *Starman*, A Columbia Pictures Production, Columbia.
ALBERT FINNEY in *Under the Volcano*, An Ithaca Enterprises Production, Universal.
TOM HULCE in *Amadeus*, A Saul Zaentz Company Production, Orion.
SAM WATERSTON in *The Killing Fields*, A Goldcrest Films and Television/ International Film Investors L.P. Production, Warner Bros.

1985 Fifty-eighth Year

HARRISON FORD in *Witness*, an Edward S. Feldman Production, Paramount.
JAMES GARNER in *Murphy's Romance*, a Fogwood Films Production, Columbia.
⋆ WILLIAM HURT in *Kiss of the Spider Woman*, an H. B. Filmes Production in Association with Sugarloaf Films, Island Alive.
JACK NICHOLSON in *Prizzi's Honor*, an ABC Motion Pictures Production, 20th Century-Fox.
JON VOIGHT in *Runaway Train*, a Cannon Films Production, Cannon.

1986 Fifty-ninth Year

DEXTER GORDON in *'Round Midnight*, An Irwin Winkler Production, Warner Bros.
BOB HOSKINS in *Mona Lisa*, A Palace/ Handmade Production, Island Pictures.
WILLIAM HURT in *Children of a Lesser God*, A Burt Sugarman Production, Paramount.
⋆ PAUL NEWMAN in *The Color of Money*, A Touchstone Pictures Production in association with Silver Screen Partners II, Buena Vista.
JAMES WOODS in *Salvador*, a Helmdale Film Production, Hemdale Releasing.

1987 Sixtieth Year

⋆ MICHAEL DOUGLAS in *Wall Street*, An Oaxatal Production, 20th Century-Fox.
WILLIAM HURT in *Broadcast News*, A Twentieth Century-Fox Production, 20th Century-Fox.
MARCELLO MASTROIANNI in *Dark Eyes*, An Excelsior TV and RAI Uno Production, Island Pictures.
JACK NICHOLSON in *Ironweed*, A Taft Entertainment Pictures/Keith Barish Production, Tri-Star.
ROBIN WILLIAMS in *Good Morning, Vietnam*, A Touchstone Pictures Production in association with Silver Screen Partners III, Buena Vista.

1988 Sixty-first Year

GENE HACKMAN in *Mississippi Burning*, A Frederick Zollo Production, Orion.
TOM HANKS in *Big*, A Twentieth Century-Fox Production, 20th Century-Fox.
⋆ DUSTIN HOFFMAN in *Rain Man*, A Guber-Peters Company Production, United Artists.
EDWARD JAMES OLMOS in *Stand and Deliver*, A Mendez/Musca and Olmos Production, Warner Bros.
MAX VON SYDOW in *Pelle the Conqueror*, A Per Holst/Kaerne Films Production, Miramax Films.

1989 Sixty-second Year

KENNETH BRANAGH in *Henry V*, A Renaissance Films Production in association with BBC, Samuel Goldwyn Company.
TOM CRUISE in *Born on the Fourth of July*, An A. Kitman Ho and Ixtlan Production, Universal.
MORGAN FREEMAN in *Driving Miss Daisy*, A Zanuck Company Production, Warner Bros.
⋆ DANIEL DAY LEWIS in *My Left Foot*, A Ferndale Films Production, Miramax.
ROBIN WILLIAMS in *Dead Poets Society*, A Touchstone Pictures Production in association with Silver Screen Partners IV, Buena Vista.

1990 Sixty-third Year

KEVIN COSTNER in *Dances with Wolves*, A Tig Production, Orion.

ROBERT DE NIRO in *Awakenings*, A Columbia Pictures Production, Columbia.

GERARD DEPARDIEU in *Cyrano de Bergerac*, A Hachette Premiere Production, Orion Classics.

RICHARD HARRIS in *The Field*, A Granada Production, Avenue Pictures.

★ JEREMY IRONS in *Reversal of Fortune*, A Reversal Films Production, Warner Bros.

1991 Sixty-fourth Year

WARREN BEATTY in *Bugsy*, A Tri-Star Pictures Production, Tri-Star.

ROBERT DE NIRO in *Cape Fear*, An Amblin Entertainment Production in association with Cappa Films and Tribeca Productions, Universal.

★ ANTHONY HOPKINS in *The Silence of the Lambs*, A Strong Heart/Demme Production, Orion.

NICK NOLTE in *The Prince of Tides*, A Barwood/Longfellow Production, Columbia.

ROBIN WILLIAMS in *The Fisher King*, A Tri-Star Pictures Production, Tri-Star.

1992 Sixty-fifth Year

ROBERT DOWNEY, JR. in *Chaplin*, A Carolco Pictures Production, Tri-Star.

CLINT EASTWOOD in *Unforgiven*, A Warner Bros. Production, Warner Bros.

★ AL PACINO in *Scent of a Woman*, A Universal Pictures Production, Universal.

STEPHEN REA in *The Crying Game*, A Palace Pictures Production, Miramax.

DENZEL WASHINGTON in *Malcolm X*, A By Any Means Necessary Cinema Production, Warner Bros.

Actress

The rules governing actors also apply to the Best Actress category. A tie for Best Actress occurred in 1968, but, unlike the 1931/32 tie between actors, the rules now required Katharine Hepburn and Barbra Streisand to compile identical vote totals. It was Hepburn's third Oscar in this category (1932/33, 1967, 1968). Her record fourth Oscar came in 1981. Ten other actresses have won twice: Luise Rainer (1936, 1937), Bette Davis (1935, 1938), Vivien Leigh (1939, 1951), Olivia DeHavilland (1946, 1949), Ingrid Bergman (1944, 1956, plus a 1974 Supporting Actress award), Elizabeth Taylor (1960, 1966), Glenda Jackson (1970, 1973), Jane Fonda (1971, 1978), Sally Field (1979, 1984), and Jodie Foster (1988, 1991). The actresses with the most nominations are Katharine Hepburn with twelve and Bette Davis with ten.

Achievements in this category are nominated by members of the Academy Actors Branch who decide individually at the time of balloting whether a role is a lead or support.

1927/28 First Year

LOUISE DRESSER in *A Ship Comes In*, DeMille Pictures, Pathé.

★ JANET GAYNOR in *7th Heaven*, *Street Angel*, and *Sunrise*, Fox.

GLORIA SWANSON in *Sadie Thompson*, Gloria Swanson Productions, UA.

1928/29 Second Year

RUTH CHATTERTON in *Madame X*, Metro-Goldwyn-Mayer.

BETTY COMPSON in *The Barker*, First National.

JEANNE EAGELS in *The Letter*, Paramount Famous Lasky.

CORRINNE GRIFFITH in *The Divine Lady*, First National.

BESSIE LOVE in *Broadway Melody*, Metro-Goldwyn-Mayer.

★ MARY PICKFORD in *Coquette*, Pickford, UA.

1929/30 Third Year

NANCY CARROLL in *The Devil's Holiday*, Paramount.

RUTH CHATTERTON in *Sarah and Son*, Paramount Famous Lasky.

GRETA GARBO in *Anna Christie*, Metro-Goldwyn-Mayer.

GRETA GARBO in *Romance*, Metro-Goldwyn-Mayer.

★ NORMA SHEARER in *The Divorcee*,* Metro-Goldwyn-Mayer.

NORMA SHEARER in *Their Own Desire*, Metro-Goldwyn-Mayer.

GLORIA SWANSON in *The Trespasser*, Kennedy, UA.

1930/31 Fourth Year

MARLENE DIETRICH in *Morocco*, Paramount Publix.

★ MARIE DRESSLER in *Min and Bill*, Metro-Goldwyn-Mayer.

*Norma Shearer was nominated for work in two films, but her award specified only her performance in *The Divorcee*.

IRENE DUNNE in *Cimarron*, RKO Radio.
ANN HARDING in *Holiday*, Pathe.
NORMA SHEARER in *A Free Soul*, Metro-Goldwyn-Mayer.

1931/32 Fifth Year

MARIE DRESSLER in *Emma*, Metro-Goldwyn-Mayer.
LYNN FONTANNE in *The Guardsman*, Metro-Goldwyn-Mayer.
★ HELEN HAYES in *The Sin of Madelon Claudet*, Metro-Goldwyn-Mayer.

1932/33 Sixth Year

★ KATHARINE HEPBURN in *Morning Glory*, RKO Radio.
MAY ROBSON in *Lady for a Day*, Columbia.
DIANA WYNYARD in *Cavalcade*, Fox.

1934 Seventh Year

★ CLAUDETTE COLBERT in *It Happened One Night*, Columbia.
GRACE MOORE in *One Night of Love*, Columbia.
NORMA SHEARER in *The Barretts of Wimpole Street*, Metro-Goldwyn-Mayer.

1935 Eighth Year

ELISABETH BERGNER in *Escape Me Never*, British & Dominions, UA. (British)
CLAUDETTE COLBERT in *Private Worlds*, Paramount.
★ BETTE DAVIS in *Dangerous*, Warner Bros.
KATHARINE HEPBURN in *Alice Adams*, RKO Radio.
MIRIAM HOPKINS in *Becky Sharp*, Pioneer, RKO Radio.
MERLE OBERON in *The Dark Angel*, Goldwyn, UA.

1936 Ninth Year

IRENE DUNNE in *Theodora Goes Wild*, Columbia.
GLADYS GEORGE in *Valiant Is the Word for Carrie*, Paramount.
CAROLE LOMBARD in *My Man Godfrey*, Universal.
★ LUISE RAINER in *The Great Ziegfeld*, Metro-Goldwyn-Mayer.
NORMA SHEARER in *Romeo and Juliet*, Metro-Goldwyn-Mayer.

1937 Tenth Year

IRENE DUNNE in *The Awful Truth*, Columbia.
GRETA GARBO in *Camille*, Metro-Goldwyn-Mayer.
JANET GAYNOR in *A Star Is Born*, Selznick, UA.
★ LUISE RAINER in *The Good Earth*, Metro-Goldwyn-Mayer.
BARBARA STANWYCK in *Stella Dallas*, Goldwyn, UA.

1938 Eleventh Year

FAY BAINTER in *White Banners*, Warner Bros.
★ BETTE DAVIS in *Jezebel*, Warner Bros.
WENDY HILLER in *Pygmalion*, Metro-Goldwyn-Mayer. (British)
NORMA SHEARER in *Marie Antoinette*, Metro-Goldwyn-Mayer.
MARGARET SULLAVAN in *Three Comrades*, Metro-Goldwyn-Mayer.

1939 Twelfth Year

BETTE DAVIS in *Dark Victory*, Warner Bros.
IRENE DUNNE in *Love Affair*, RKO Radio.
GRETA GARBO in *Ninotchka*, Metro-Goldwyn-Mayer.
GREER GARSON in *Goodbye, Mr. Chips*, Metro-Goldwyn-Mayer. (British)
★ VIVIEN LEIGH in *Gone with the Wind*, Selznick, Metro-Goldwyn-Mayer.

1940 Thirteenth Year

BETTE DAVIS in *The Letter*, Warner Bros.

JOAN FONTAINE in *Rebecca*, Selznick, UA.

KATHARINE HEPBURN in *The Philadelphia Story*, Metro-Goldwyn-Mayer.

★ GINGER ROGERS in *Kitty Foyle*, RKO Radio.

MARTHA SCOTT in *Our Town*, Lesser, UA.

1941 Fourteenth Year

BETTE DAVIS in *The Little Foxes*, Goldwyn, RKO Radio.

OLIVIA DE HAVILLAND in *Hold Back the Dawn*, Paramount.

★ JOAN FONTAINE in *Suspicion*, RKO Radio.

GREER GARSON in *Blossoms in the Dust*, Metro-Goldwyn-Mayer.

BARBARA STANWYCK in *Ball of Fire*, Goldwyn, RKO Radio.

1942 Fifteenth Year

BETTE DAVIS in *Now, Voyager*, Warner Bros.

★ GREER GARSON in *Mrs. Miniver*, Metro-Goldwyn-Mayer.

KATHARINE HEPBURN in *Woman of the Year*, Metro-Goldwyn-Mayer.

ROSALIND RUSSELL in *My Sister Eileen*, Columbia.

TERESA WRIGHT in *The Pride of the Yankees*, Goldwyn, RKO Radio.

1943 Sixteenth Year

JEAN ARTHUR in *The More the Merrier*, Columbia.

INGRID BERGMAN in *For Whom the Bell Tolls*, Paramount.

JOAN FONTAINE in *The Constant Nymph*, Warner Bros.

GREER GARSON in *Madame Curie*, Metro-Goldwyn-Mayer.

★ JENNIFER JONES in *The Song of Bernadette*, 20th Century-Fox.

1944 Seventeenth Year

★ INGRID BERGMAN in *Gaslight*, Metro-Goldwyn-Mayer.

CLAUDETTE COLBERT in *Since You Went Away*, Selznick, UA.

BETTE DAVIS in *Mr. Skeffington*, Warner Bros.

GREER GARSON in *Mrs. Parkington*, Metro-Goldwyn-Mayer.

BARBARA STANWYCK in *Double Indemnity*, Paramount.

1945 Eighteenth Year

INGRID BERGMAN in *The Bells of St. Mary's*, Rainbow, RKO Radio.

★ JOAN CRAWFORD in *Mildred Pierce*, Warner Bros.

GREER GARSON in *The Valley of Decision*, Metro-Goldwyn-Mayer.

JENNIFER JONES in *Love Letters*, Wallis, Paramount.

GENE TIERNEY in *Leave Her to Heaven*, 20th Century-Fox.

1946 Nineteenth Year

★ OLIVIA DE HAVILLAND in *To Each His Own*, Paramount.

CELIA JOHNSON in *Brief Encounter*, Rank, U-I. (British)

JENNIFER JONES in *Duel in the Sun*, Selznick International.

ROSALIND RUSSELL in *Sister Kenny*, RKO Radio.

JANE WYMAN in *The Yearling*, Metro-Goldwyn-Mayer.

1947 Twentieth Year

JOAN CRAWFORD in *Possessed*, Warner Bros.

SUSAN HAYWARD in *Smash Up—The Story of a Woman*, Wanger U-I.

DOROTHY MCGUIRE in *Gentleman's Agreement*, 20th Century-Fox.

ROSALIND RUSSELL in *Mourning Becomes Electra*, RKO Radio.

★ LORETTA YOUNG in *The Farmer's Daughter*, RKO Radio.

1948 Twenty-first Year

INGRID BERGMAN in *Joan of Arc*, Sierra, RKO Radio.

OLIVIA DE HAVILLAND in *The Snake Pit*, 20th Century-Fox.
IRENE DUNNE in *I Remember Mama*, RKO Radio.
BARBARA STANWYCK in *Sorry, Wrong Number*, Wallis, Paramount.
★ JANE WYMAN in *Johnny Belinda*, Warner Bros.

1949 Twenty-second Year

JEANNE CRAIN in *Pinky*, 20th Century-Fox.
★ OLIVIA DE HAVILLAND in *The Heiress*, Paramount.
SUSAN HAYWARD in *My Foolish Heart*, Goldwyn, RKO Radio.
DEBORAH KERR in *Edward, My Son*, Metro-Goldwyn-Mayer.
LORETTA YOUNG in *Come to the Stable*, 20th Century-Fox.

1950 Twenty-third Year

ANNE BAXTER in *All about Eve*, 20th Century-Fox.
BETTE DAVIS in *All about Eve*, 20th Century-Fox.
★ JUDY HOLLIDAY in *Born Yesterday*, Columbia.
ELEANOR PARKER in *Caged*, Warner Bros.
GLORIA SWANSON in *Sunset Boulevard*, Paramount.

1951 Twenty-fourth Year

KATHARINE HEPBURN in *The African Queen*, Horizon, UA.
★ VIVIEN LEIGH in *A Streetcar Named Desire*, Charles K. Feldman Group Prods., Warner Bros.
ELEANOR PARKER in *Detective Story*, Paramount.
SHELLEY WINTERS in *A Place in the Sun*, Paramount.
JANE WYMAN in *The Blue Veil*, Wald-Krasna, RKO Radio.

1952 Twenty-fifth Year

★ SHIRLEY BOOTH in *Come Back, Little Sheba*, Hal Wallis, Paramount.
JOAN CRAWFORD in *Sudden Fear*, Joseph Kaufman Prods., RKO Radio.
BETTE DAVIS in *The Star*, Bert E. Friedlob, 20th Century-Fox.
JULIE HARRIS in *The Member of the Wedding*, Stanley Kramer, Columbia.
SUSAN HAYWARD in *With a Song in My Heart*, 20th Century-Fox.

1953 Twenty-sixth Year

LESLIE CARON in *Lili*, Metro-Goldwyn-Mayer.
AVA GARDNER in *Mogambo*, Metro-Goldwyn-Mayer.
★ AUDREY HEPBURN in *Roman Holiday*, Paramount.
DEBORAH KERR in *From Here to Eternity*, Columbia.
MAGGIE MCNAMARA in *The Moon Is Blue*, Preminger-Herbert, UA.

1954 Twenty-seventh Year

DOROTHY DANDRIDGE in *Carmen Jones*, Otto Preminger, 20th Century-Fox.
JUDY GARLAND in *A Star Is Born*, Transcona, Warner Bros.
AUDREY HEPBURN in *Sabrina*, Paramount.
★ GRACE KELLY in *The Country Girl*, Perlberg-Seaton, Paramount.
JANE WYMAN in *The Magnificent Obsession*, Universal-International.

1955 Twenty-eighth Year

SUSAN HAYWARD in *I'll Cry Tomorrow*, Metro-Goldwyn-Mayer.
KATHARINE HEPBURN in *Summertime*, Ilya Lopert-David Lean, UA. (Anglo-American)
JENNIFER JONES in *Love Is a Many-Splendored Thing*, 20th Century-Fox.
★ ANNA MAGNANI in *The Rose Tattoo*, Hal B. Wallis, Paramount.
ELEANOR PARKER in *Interrupted Melody*, Metro-Goldwyn-Mayer.

1956 Twenty-ninth Year

CARROLL BAKER in *Baby Doll*, A Newtown Prod., Warner Bros.

★ INGRID BERGMAN in *Anastasia*, 20th Century-Fox.

KATHARINE HEPBURN in *The Rainmaker*, Hal Wallis Prods., Paramount.

NANCY KELLY in *The Bad Seed*, Warner Bros.

DEBORAH KERR in *The King and I*, 20th Century-Fox.

1957 Thirtieth Year

DEBORAH KERR in *Heaven Knows, Mr. Allison*, 20th Century-Fox.

ANNA MAGNANI in *Wild Is the Wind*, Hal Wallis Prod., Paramount.

ELIZABETH TAYLOR in *Raintree County*, Metro-Goldwyn-Mayer.

LANA TURNER in *Peyton Place*, Jerry Wald Prods. Inc., 20th Century-Fox.

★ JOANNE WOODWARD in *The Three Faces of Eve*, 20th Century-Fox.

1958 Thirty-first Year

★ SUSAN HAYWARD in *I Want to Live!*, Figaro, Inc., UA.

DEBORAH KERR in *Separate Tables*, Clifton Prods., Inc., UA.

SHIRLEY MACLAINE in *Some Came Running*, Sol C. Siegel Prods., Inc., M-G-M.

ROSALIND RUSSELL in *Auntie Mame*, Warner Bros.

ELIZABETH TAYLOR in *Cat on a Hot Tin Roof*, Avon Prods., Inc., M-G-M.

1959 Thirty-second Year

DORIS DAY in *Pillow Talk*, Arwin Prods., Inc., U-I.

AUDREY HEPBURN in *The Nun's Story*, Warner Bros.

KATHARINE HEPBURN in *Suddenly, Last Summer*, Horizon Prod., Columbia.

★ SIMONE SIGNORET in *Room at the Top*, Romulus Films, Ltd., Continental Dist., Inc. (British)

ELIZABETH TAYLOR in *Suddenly, Last Summer*, Horizon Prod., Columbia.

1960 Thirty-third Year

GREER GARSON in *Sunrise at Campobello*, Schary Prod., Warner Bros.

DEBORAH KERR, in *The Sundowners*, Warner Bros.

SHIRLEY MACLAINE in *The Apartment*, The Mirisch Co., Inc., UA.

MELINA MERCOURI in *Never on Sunday*, Melinafilm Prod., Lopert Pictures Corp. (Greek)

★ ELIZABETH TAYLOR in *Butterfield 8*, Afton-Linebrook Prod., M-G-M.

1961 Thirty-fourth Year

AUDREY HEPBURN in *Breakfast at Tiffany's*, Jurow-Shepherd Prod., Paramount.

PIPER LAURIE in *The Hustler*, Robert Rossen Prod., 20th Century-Fox.

★ SOPHIA LOREN in *Two Women*, Champion-Les Films Marceau-Cocinor and Société Generale de Cinematographie Prod., Embassy Pictures Corp. (Italo-French)

GERALDINE PAGE in *Summer and Smoke*, Hal Wallis Prod., Paramount.

NATALIE WOOD in *Splendor in the Grass*, NBI Prod., Warner Bros.

1962 Thirty-fifth Year

★ ANNE BANCROFT in *The Miracle Worker*, Playfilms Prod., UA.

BETTE DAVIS in *What Ever Happened To Baby Jane?*, Seven Arts-Associates & Aldrich Co. Prod., Warner Bros.

KATHARINE HEPBURN in *Long Day's Journey into Night*, Ely Landau Prods., Embassy Pictures.

GERALDINE PAGE in *Sweet Bird of Youth*, Roxbury Prod., M-G-M.

LEE REMICK in *Days of Wine and Roses*, Martin Manulis-Jalem Prod., Warner Bros.

1963 Thirty-sixth Year

LESLIE CARON in *The L-Shaped Room*, Romulus Prods., Ltd., Columbia.

SHIRLEY MACLAINE in *Irma La Douce*, Mirisch-Phalanx Prod., UA.

★ PATRICIA NEAL in *Hud*, Salem-Dover Prod., Paramount.

RACHEL ROBERTS in *This Sporting Life*, Julian Wintle-Leslie Parkyn Prod., Walter Reade-Sterling-Continental Dist.

NATALIE WOOD in *Love with the Proper Stranger*, Boardwalk-Rona Prod., Paramount.

1964 Thirty-seventh Year

★ JULIE ANDREWS in *Mary Poppins*, Walt Disney Prods.

ANNE BANCROFT in *The Pumpkin Eater*, Romulus Films, Ltd. Prod., Royal Films International.

SOPHIA LOREN in *Marriage Italian Style*, Champion-Concordia Prod., Embassy Pictures.

DEBBIE REYNOLDS in *The Unsinkable Molly Brown*, Marten Prod., M-G-M.

KIM STANLEY in *Seance on a Wet Afternoon*, Richard Attenborough-Bryan Forbes Prod., Artixo Prods., Ltd.

1965 Thirty-eighth Year

JULIE ANDREWS in *The Sound of Music*, Argyle Enterprises Prod., 20th Century-Fox.

★ JULIE CHRISTIE in *Darling*, Anglo-Amalgamated, Ltd. Prod., Embassy.

SAMANTHA EGGAR in *The Collector*, The Collector Company, Columbia.

ELIZABETH HARTMAN in *A Patch of Blue*, Pandro S. Berman-Guy Green Prod., M-G-M.

SIMONE SIGNORET in *Ship of Fools*, Columbia.

1966 Thirty-ninth Year

ANOUK AIMEE in *A Man and a Woman*, Les Films 13 Prod., Allied Artists.

IDA KAMINSKA in *The Shop on Main Street*, Ceskoslovensky Film Company Prod., Prominent Films.

LYNN REDGRAVE in *Georgy Girl*, Everglades Prods., Ltd., Columbia.

VANESSA REDGRAVE in *Morgan!*, Quintra Films, Ltd. Prod., Cinema V.

★ ELIZABETH TAYLOR in *Who's Afraid of Virginia Woolf?*, Chenault Prod., Warner Bros.

1967 Fortieth Year

ANNE BANCROFT in *The Graduate*, Mike Nichols-Lawrence Turman Prod., Embassy.

FAYE DUNAWAY in *Bonnie and Clyde*, Tatira-Hiller Prod., Warner Bros.-Seven Arts.

DAME EDITH EVANS in *The Whisperers*, Seven Pines Prods., Ltd., United Artists.

AUDREY HEPBURN in *Wait until Dark*, Warner Bros.-Seven Arts.

★ KATHARINE HEPBURN in *Guess Who's Coming to Dinner*, Columbia.

1968 Forty-first Year

Tie

★ KATHARINE HEPBURN in *The Lion in Winter*, Haworth Prods., Ltd., Avco Embassy.

PATRICIA NEAL in *The Subject Was Roses*, Metro-Goldwyn-Mayer.

VANESSA REDGRAVE in *Isadora*, Robert and Raymond Hakim-Universal, Ltd. Prod., Universal.

★ BARBRA STREISAND in *Funny Girl*, Rastar Prods., Columbia.

JOANNE WOODWARD in *Rachel, Rachel*, Kayos Prod., Warner Bros.-Seven Arts.

1969 Forty-second Year

GENEVIEVE BUJOLD in *Anne of the Thousand Days*, Hal B. Wallis-Universal Pictures, Ltd. Prod., Universal.

JANE FONDA in *They Shoot Horses, Don't They?*, Chartoff-Winkler-Pollack Prod., ABC Pictures Presentation, Cinerama.

LIZA MINNELLI in *The Sterile Cuckoo*, Boardwalk Prods., Paramount.

JEAN SIMMONS in *The Happy Ending*, Pax Films Prod., United Artists.

★ MAGGIE SMITH in *The Prime of Miss Jean Brodie*, 20th Century-Fox Prods., Ltd., 20th Century-Fox.

1970 Forty-third Year

JANE ALEXANDER in *The Great White Hope*, Lawrence Turman Films Prod., 20th Century-Fox.

★ GLENDA JACKSON in *Women in Love*, Larry Kramer-Martin Rosen Prod., United Artists.

ALI MACGRAW in *Love Story*, The Love Story Company Prod., Paramount.

SARAH MILES in *Ryan's Daughter*, Faraway Prods., Metro-Goldwyn-Mayer.

CARRIE SNODGRESS in *Diary of a Mad Housewife*, Frank Perry Films Prod., Universal.

1971 Forty-fourth Year

JULIE CHRISTIE in *McCabe & Mrs. Miller*, A Robert Altman-David Foster Prod., Warner Bros.

★ JANE FONDA in *Klute*, A Gus Prod., Warner Bros.

GLENDA JACKSON in *Sunday Bloody Sunday*, A Joseph Janni Prod., UA.

VANESSA REDGRAVE in *Mary, Queen of Scots*, A Hal Wallis-Universal Pictures, Ltd. Prod., Universal.

JANET SUZMAN in *Nicholas and Alexandra*, A Horizon Pictures Prod., Columbia.

1972 Forty-fifth Year

★ LIZA MINNELLI in *Cabaret*, An ABC Pictures Production, Allied Artists.

DIANA ROSS in *Lady Sings the Blues*, A Motown-Weston-Furie Production, Paramount.

MAGGIE SMITH in *Travels with My Aunt*, Robert Fryer Productions, Metro-Goldwyn-Mayer.

CICELY TYSON in *Sounder*, Radnitz/Mattel Productions, 20th Century-Fox.

LIV ULLMANN in *The Emigrants*, A Svensk Filmindustri Production, Warner Bros.

1973 Forty-sixth Year

ELLEN BURSTYN in *The Exorcist*, Hoya Prods., Warner Bros.

★ GLENDA JACKSON in *A Touch of Class*, Brut Prods., Avco Embassy.

MARSHA MASON in *Cinderella Liberty*, A Sanford Prod., 20th Century-Fox.

BARBRA STREISAND in *The Way We Were*, Rastar Prods., Columbia.

JOANNE WOODWARD in *Summer Wishes, Winter Dreams*, A Rastar Pictures Prod., Columbia.

1974 Forty-seventh Year

★ ELLEN BURSTYN in *Alice Doesn't Live Here Anymore*, Warner Bros.

DIAHANN CARROLL in *Claudine*, Third World Cinema Productions in association with Joyce Selznick and Tina Pine, 20th Century-Fox.

FAYE DUNAWAY in *Chinatown*, A Robert Evans Production, Paramount.

VALERIE PERRINE in *Lenny*, A Marvin Worth Production, United Artists.

GENA ROWLANDS in *A Woman under the Influence*, A Faces International Films Production.

1975 Forty-eighth Year

ISABELLE ADJANI in *The Story of Adele H.*, A Les Films du Carrosse-Les Productions Artistes Associés Production, New World Pictures.

ANN-MARGRET in *Tommy*, A Robert

Stigwood Organisation, Ltd. Production, Columbia.

★ LOUISE FLETCHER in *One Flew over the Cuckoo's Nest*, A Fantasy Films Production, United Artists.

GLENDA JACKSON in *Hedda*, A Royal Shakespeare-Brut Productions-George Barrie/Robert Enders Film Production, Brut Productions.

CAROL KANE in *Hester Street*, Midwest Film Productions.

1976 Forty-ninth Year

MARIE-CHRISTINE BARRAULT in *Cousin, Cousine*, Les Films Pomereu-Gaumont Production, Northal Film Distributors Ltd.

★ FAYE DUNAWAY in *Network*, A Howard Gottfried/Paddy Chayefsky Production, Metro-Goldwyn-Mayer/United Artists.

TALIA SHIRE in *Rocky*, A Robert Chartoff-Irwin Winkler Production, United Artists.

SISSY SPACEK in *Carrie*, A Redbank Films Production, United Artists.

LIV ULLMANN in *Face to Face*, A Cinematograph A.B. Production, Paramount.

1977 Fiftieth Year

ANNE BANCROFT in *The Turning Point*, Hera Productions, 20th Century-Fox.

JANE FONDA in *Julia*, A Twentieth Century-Fox Production, 20th Century-Fox.

★ DIANE KEATON in *Annie Hall*, Jack Rollins-Charles H. Joffe Productions, United Artists.

SHIRLEY MACLAINE in *The Turning Point*, Hera Productions, 20th Century-Fox.

MARSHA MASON in *The Goodbye Girl*, A Ray Stark Production, M-G-M/Warner Bros.

1978 Fifty-first Year

INGRID BERGMAN in *Autumn Sonata*, A Personafilm GmbH Production, Sir Lew Grade-Martin Starger-ITC Entertainment Presentation, New World Pictures.

ELLEN BURSTYN in *Same Time, Next Year*, A Walter Mirisch-Robert Mulligan Production, Mirisch Corporation/Universal Pictures Presentation, Universal.

JILL CLAYBURGH in *An Unmarried Woman*, A Twentieth Century-Fox Production, 20th Century-Fox.

★ JANE FONDA in *Coming Home*, A Jerome Hellman Enterprises Production, United Artists.

GERALDINE PAGE in *Interiors*, A Jack Rollins-Charles H. Joffe Production, United Artists.

1979 Fifty-second Year

JILL CLAYBURGH in *Starting Over*, An Alan J. Pakula/James L. Brooks Production, Paramount.

★ SALLY FIELD in *Norma Rae*, A Twentieth Century-Fox Production, 20th Century-Fox.

JANE FONDA in *The China Syndrome*, A Michael Douglas/IPC Films Production, Columbia.

MARSHA MASON in *Chapter Two*, A Ray Stark Production, Columbia.

BETTE MIDLER in *The Rose*, A Twentieth Century-Fox Production, 20th Century-Fox.

1980 Fifty-third Year

ELLEN BURSTYN in *Resurrection*, A Universal Pictures Production, Universal.

GOLDIE HAWN in *Private Benjamin*, A Warner Bros. Production, Warner Bros.

MARY TYLER MOORE in *Ordinary People*, A Wildwood Enterprises Production, Paramount.

GENA ROWLANDS in *Gloria*, A Columbia Pictures Production, Columbia.

★ SISSY SPACEK in *Coal Miner's Daughter*, A Bernard Schwartz-

Universal Pictures Production, Universal.

1981 Fifty-fourth Year

★ KATHARINE HEPBURN in *On Golden Pond*, An ITC Films/IPC Films Production, Universal.

DIANE KEATON, in *Reds*, A J.R.S. Production, Paramount.

MARSHA MASON in *Only When I Laugh*, A Columbia Pictures Production, Columbia.

SUSAN SARANDON in *Atlantic City*, An International Cinema Corporation Production, Paramount.

MERYL STREEP in *The French Lieutenant's Woman*, A Parlon Production, United Artists.

1982 Fifty-fifth Year

JULIE ANDREWS in *Victor/Victoria*, A Metro-Goldwyn-Mayer Production, M-G-M/UA.

JESSICA LANGE in *Frances*, A Brooksfilm/EMI Production, Universal/A.F.D.

SISSY SPACEK in *Missing*, A Universal Pictures/Polygram Pictures Presentation of an Edward Lewis Production, Universal.

★ MERYL STREEP in *Sophie's Choice*, An ITC Entertainment Presentation of a Pakula-Barish Production, Universal/A.F.D.

DEBRA WINGER in *An Officer and a Gentleman*, A Lorimar Production in association with Martin Elfand, Paramount.

1983 Fifty-sixth Year

JANE ALEXANDER in *Testament*, An Entertainment Events Production in association with American Playhouse, Paramount.

★ SHIRLEY MACLAINE in *Terms of Endearment*, A James L. Brooks Production, Paramount.

MERYL STREEP in *Silkwood*, An ABC Motion Pictures Production, 20th Century-Fox.

JULIE WALTERS in *Educating Rita*, An Acorn Pictures Limited Production, Columbia.

DEBRA WINGER in *Terms of Endearment*, A James L. Brooks Production, Paramount.

1984 Fifty-seventh Year

JUDY DAVIS in A *Passage to India*, A G. W. Films Limited Production, Columbia.

★ SALLY FIELD in *Places in the Heart*, a Tri-Star Pictures Production, Tri-Star.

JESSICA LANGE in *Country*, A Touchstone Films Production, Buena Vista.

VANESSA REDGRAVE in *The Bostonians*, A Merchant Ivory Production, Almi Pictures.

SISSY SPACEK in *The River*, A Universal Pictures Production, Universal.

1985 Fifty-eighth Year

ANNE BANCROFT in *Agnes of God*, a Columbia Pictures Production, Columbia.

WHOOPI GOLDBERG in *The Color Purple*, a Warner Bros. Production, Warner Bros.

JESSICA LANGE in *Sweet Dreams*, an HBO Pictures Production in association with Silver Screen Partners, Tri-Star.

★ GERALDINE PAGE in *The Trip to Bountiful*, a Bountiful Production, Island Pictures.

MERYL STREEP in *Out of Africa*, a Universal Pictures Limited Production, Universal.

1986 Fifty-ninth Year

JANE FONDA in *The Morning After*, A Lorimar Motion Pictures Production, 20th Century-Fox.

★ MARLEE MATLIN in *Children of a*

Lesser God, A Burt Sugarman Production, Paramount.

SISSY SPACEK in *Crimes of the Heart*, A Crimes of the Heart Production, De Laurentiis Entertainment Group.

KATHLEEN TURNER in *Peggy Sue Got Married*, A Rastar Production, Tri-Star.

SIGOURNEY WEAVER in *Aliens*, A Twentieth Century-Fox Film Production, 20th Century-Fox.

1987 Sixtieth Year

★ CHER in *Moonstruck*, A Patrick Palmer and Norman Jewison Production, MGM.

GLENN CLOSE in *Fatal Attraction*, A Jaffe/Lansing Production, Paramount.

HOLLY HUNTER in *Broadcast News*, A Twentieth Century-Fox Production, 20th Century-Fox.

SALLY KIRKLAND in *Anna*, A Magnus Films Production, Vestron.

MERYL STREEP in *Ironweed*, A Taft Entertainment Pictures/Keith Barish Production, Tri-Star.

1988 Sixty-first Year

GLENN CLOSE in *Dangerous Liaisons*, A Lorimar Production, Warner Bros.

★ JODIE FOSTER in *The Accused*, A Jaffe/Lansing Production, Paramount.

MELANIE GRIFFITH in *Working Girl*, A Twentieth Century-Fox Production, 20th Century-Fox.

MERYL STREEP in *A Cry in the Dark*, A Cannon Entertainment/Golan-Globus Production, Warner Bros.

SIGOURNEY WEAVER in *Gorillas in the Mist*, A Warner Bros. Production, Warner Bros./Universal.

1989 Sixty-second Year

ISABELLE ADJANI in *Camille Claudel*, A Films Christian Fechner-Lilith Films-Gaumont-A2 TV France-Films A2-DD Production, Orion Classics.

PAULINE COLLINS in *Shirley Valentine*, A Lewis Gilbert/Willy Russell Production, Paramount.

JESSICA LANGE in *Music Box*, A Carolco Pictures Production, Tri-Star.

MICHELLE PFEIFFER in *The Fabulous Baker Boys*, A Gladden Entertainment Presentation of a Mirage Production, 20th Century-Fox.

★ JESSICA TANDY in *Driving Miss Daisy*, A Zanuck Company Production, Warner Bros.

1990 Sixty-third Year

★ KATHY BATES in *Misery*, A Castle Rock Entertainment Production, Columbia.

ANJELICA HUSTON in *The Grifters*, A Martin Scorsese Production, Miramax.

JULIA ROBERTS in *Pretty Woman*, A Touchstone Pictures Production, Buena Vista.

MERYL STREEP in *Postcards from the Edge*, A Columbia Pictures Production, Columbia.

JOANNE WOODWARD in *Mr. & Mrs. Bridge*, A Merchant Ivory Production, Miramax.

1991 Sixty-fourth Year

GEENA DAVIS in *Thelma & Louise*, A Pathé Entertainment Production, M-G-M.

LAURA DERN in *Rambling Rose*, A Carolco Pictures Production, Seven Arts/New Line.

★ JODIE FOSTER in *The Silence of the Lambs*, A Strong Heart/Demme Production, Orion.

BETTE MIDLER in *For the Boys*, A Twentieth Century-Fox Production, 20th Century-Fox.

SUSAN SARANDON in *Thelma & Louise*, A Pathé Entertainment Production, M-G-M.

1992 Sixty-fifth Year

CATHERINE DENEUVE in *Indochine*, A Paradis Films/La Générale d'Images/BAC Films/Orly Films/Cine Cinq Production, Sony Pictures Classics.

MARY MCDONNELL in *Passion Fish*, An Atchafalaya Films Production, Miramax.

MICHELLE PFEIFFER in *Love Field*, A Sanford/Pillsbury Production, Orion.

SUSAN SARANDON in *Lorenzo's Oil*, A Kennedy Miller Films Production, Universal.

★ EMMA THOMPSON in *Howards End*, A Merchant Ivory Production, Sony Pictures Classics.

Supporting Actor

In 1936 the acting awards were expanded to recognize supporting roles. Within five years Walter Brennan had won three Oscars, and no one has since matched this total in the Supporting Actor category.

Confusion eventually developed over the distinction between a lead and a supporting role, and for several years the studios decided to which category an acting performance belonged. This designation was announced prior to balloting in the Academy's annual reminder lists. In 1964 the Academy Board of Governors voted to eliminate the designation and leave the decision up to each voter.

Achievements in this category are nominated by members of the Academy Actors Branch who decide individually at the time of balloting whether a role is a lead or support.

1936 Ninth Year

MISCHA AUER in *My Man Godfrey*, Universal.

★ WALTER BRENNAN in *Come and Get It*, Goldwyn, UA.

STUART ERWIN in *Pigskin Parade*, 20th Century-Fox.

BASIL RATHBONE in *Romeo and Juliet*, Metro-Goldwyn-Mayer.

AKIM TAMIROFF in *The General Died at Dawn*, Paramount.

1937 Tenth Year

RALPH BELLAMY in *The Awful Truth*, Columbia.

THOMAS MITCHELL in *Hurricane*, Goldwyn, UA.

★ JOSEPH SCHILDKRAUT in *The Life of Emile Zola*, Warner Bros.

H. B. WARNER in *Lost Horizon*, Columbia.

ROLAND YOUNG in *Topper*, Roach, Metro-Goldwyn-Mayer.

1938 Eleventh Year

★ WALTER BRENNAN in *Kentucky*, 20th Century-Fox.

JOHN GARFIELD in *Four Daughters*, Warner Bros.

GENE LOCKHART in *Algiers*, Wanger, UA.

ROBERT MORLEY in *Marie Antoinette*, Metro-Goldwyn-Mayer.

BASIL RATHBONE in *If I Were King*, Paramount.

1939 Twelfth Year

BRIAN AHERNE in *Juarez*, Warner Bros.

HARRY CAREY in *Mr. Smith Goes to Washington*, Columbia.

BRIAN DONLEVY in *Beau Geste*, Paramount.

★ THOMAS MITCHELL in *Stagecoach*, Wanger, UA.

CLAUDE RAINS in *Mr. Smith Goes to Washington*, Columbia.

1940 Thirteenth Year

ALBERT BASSERMANN in *Foreign Correspondent*, Wanger, UA.

★ WALTER BRENNAN in *The Westerner*, Goldwyn, UA.

WILLIAM GARGAN in *They Knew What They Wanted*, RKO Radio.

JACK OAKIE in *The Great Dictator*, Chaplin, UA.

JAMES STEPHENSON in *The Letter*, Warner Bros.

1941 Fourteenth Year

WALTER BRENNAN in *Sergeant York*, Warner Bros.

CHARLES COBURN in *The Devil and Miss Jones*, RKO Radio.

★ DONALD CRISP in *How Green Was My Valley*, 20th Century-Fox.

JAMES GLEASON in *Here Comes Mr. Jordan*, Columbia.

SYDNEY GREENSTREET in *The Maltese Falcon*, Warner Bros.

1942 Fifteenth Year

WILLIAM BENDIX in *Wake Island*, Paramount.

★ VAN HEFLIN in *Johnny Eager*, Metro-Goldwyn-Mayer.

WALTER HUSTON in *Yankee Doodle Dandy*, Warner Bros.

FRANK MORGAN in *Tortilla Flat*, Metro-Goldwyn-Mayer.

HENRY TRAVERS in *Mrs. Miniver*, Metro-Goldwyn-Mayer.

1943 Sixteenth Year

CHARLES BICKFORD in *The Song of Bernadette*, 20th Century-Fox.

★ CHARLES COBURN in *The More the Merrier*, Columbia.

J. CARROL NAISH in *Sahara*, Columbia.

CLAUDE RAINS in *Casablanca*, Warner Bros.

AKIM TAMIROFF in *For Whom the Bell Tolls*, Paramount.

1944 Seventeenth Year

HUME CRONYN in *The Seventh Cross*, Metro-Goldwyn-Mayer.

★ BARRY FITZGERALD in *Going My Way*, Paramount.

CLAUDE RAINS in *Mr. Skeffington*, Warner Bros.

CLIFTON WEBB in *Laura*, 20th Century-Fox.

MONTY WOOLLEY in *Since You Went Away*, Selznick, UA.

1945 Eighteenth Year

MICHAEL CHEKHOV in *Spellbound*, Selznick, UA.

JOHN DALL in *The Corn Is Green*, Warner Bros.

★ JAMES DUNN in *A Tree Grows in Brooklyn*, 20th Century-Fox.

ROBERT MITCHUM in *G. I. Joe*, Cowan, UA.

J. CARROL NAISH in *A Medal for Benny*, Paramount.

1946 Nineteenth Year

CHARLES COBURN in *The Green Years*, Metro-Goldwyn-Mayer.

WILLIAM DEMAREST in *The Jolson Story*, Columbia.

CLAUDE RAINS in *Notorious*, RKO Radio.

★ HAROLD RUSSELL in *The Best Years of Our Lives*, Goldwyn, RKO Radio.

CLIFTON WEBB in *The Razor's Edge*, 20th Century-Fox.

1947 Twentieth Year

CHARLES BICKFORD in *The Farmer's Daughter*, RKO Radio.

THOMAS GOMEZ in *Ride the Pink Horse*, Universal-International.

★ EDMUND GWENN in *Miracle on 34th Street*, 20th Century-Fox.

ROBERT RYAN in *Crossfire*, RKO Radio.

RICHARD WIDMARK in *Kiss of Death*, 20th Century-Fox.

1948 Twenty-first Year

CHARLES BICKFORD in *Johnny Belinda*, Warner Bros.

JOSE FERRER in *Joan of Arc*, Sierra, RKO Radio.

OSCAR HOMOLKA in *I Remember Mama*, RKO Radio.

★ WALTER HUSTON in *Treasure of Sierra Madre*, Warner Bros.
CECIL KELLAWAY in *The Luck of the Irish*, 20th Century-Fox.

1949 Twenty-second Year

JOHN IRELAND in *All the King's Men*, Rossen, Columbia.
★ DEAN JAGGER in *Twelve O'Clock High*, 20th Century-Fox.
ARTHUR KENNEDY in *Champion*, Screen Plays Corp., UA.
RALPH RICHARDSON in *The Heiress*, Paramount.
JAMES WHITMORE in *Battleground*, Metro-Goldwyn-Mayer.

1950 Twenty-third Year

JEFF CHANDLER in *Broken Arrow*, 20th Century-Fox.
EDMUND GWENN in *Mister 880*, 20th Century-Fox.
SAM JAFFE in *The Asphalt Jungle*, Metro-Goldwyn-Mayer.
★ GEORGE SANDERS in *All about Eve*, 20th Century-Fox.
ERICH VON STROHEIM in *Sunset Boulevard*, Paramount.

1951 Twenty-fourth Year

LEO GENN in *Quo Vadis*, Metro-Goldwyn-Mayer.
★ KARL MALDEN in *A Streetcar Named Desire*, Charles K. Feldman Group Prods., Warner Bros.
KEVIN MCCARTHY in *Death of a Salesman*, Kramer, Columbia.
PETER USTINOV in *Quo Vadis*, Metro-Goldwyn-Mayer.
GIG YOUNG in *Come Fill the Cup*, Warner Bros.

1952 Twenty-fifth Year

RICHARD BURTON in *My Cousin Rachel*, 20th Century-Fox.
ARTHUR HUNNICUTT in *The Big Sky*, Winchester, RKO Radio.
VICTOR MCLAGLEN in *The Quiet Man*, Argosy, Republic.
JACK PALANCE in *Sudden Fear*, Kaufman, RKO Radio.
★ ANTHONY QUINN in *Viva Zapata!*, 20th Century-Fox.

1953 Twenty-sixth Year

EDDIE ALBERT in *Roman Holiday*, Paramount.
BRANDON DE WILDE in *Shane*, Paramount.
JACK PALANCE in *Shane*, Paramount.
★ FRANK SINATRA in *From Here to Eternity*, Columbia.
ROBERT STRAUSS in *Stalag 17*, Paramount.

1954 Twenty-seventh Year

LEE J. COBB in *On the Waterfront*, Horizon-American, Columbia.
KARL MALDEN in *On the Waterfront*, Horizon-American, Columbia.
★ EDMOND O'BRIEN in *The Barefoot Contessa*, Figaro, UA.
ROD STEIGER in *On the Waterfront*, Horizon-American, Columbia.
TOM TULLY in *The Caine Mutiny*, Kramer, Columbia

1955 Twenty-eighth Year

ARTHUR KENNEDY in *Trial*, Metro-Goldwyn-Mayer.
★ JACK LEMMON in *Mister Roberts*, An Orange Prod., Warner Bros.
JOE MANTELL in *Marty*, Hecht & Lancaster's Steven Prods., UA.
SAL MINEO in *Rebel without a Cause*, Warner Bros.
ARTHUR O'CONNELL in *Picnic*, Columbia.

1956 Twenty-ninth Year

DON MURRAY in *Bus Stop*, 20th Century-Fox.
ANTHONY PERKINS in *Friendly Persuasion*, Allied Artists.

★ ANTHONY QUINN in *Lust for Life*, Metro-Goldwyn-Mayer.

MICKEY ROONEY in *The Bold and the Brave*, Filmakers Releasing Org., RKO Radio.

ROBERT STACK in *Written on the Wind*, Universal-International.

1957 Thirtieth Year

★ RED BUTTONS in *Sayonara*, William Goetz Prod., Warner Bros.

VITTORIO DE SICA in *A Farewell to Arms*, The Selznick Co., Inc., 20th Century-Fox.

SESSUE HAYAKAWA in *The Bridge on the River Kwai*, A Horizon Picture, Columbia.

ARTHUR KENNEDY in *Peyton Place*, Jerry Wald Prods., Inc., 20th Century-Fox.

RUSS TAMBLYN in *Peyton Place*, Jerry Wald Prods., Inc., 20th Century-Fox.

1958 Thirty-first Year

THEODORE BIKEL in *The Defiant Ones*, Stanley Kramer, UA.

LEE J. COBB in *The Brothers Karamazov*, Avon Prods., Inc., M-G-M.

★ BURL IVES in *The Big Country*, Anthony-Worldwide Prods., UA.

ARTHUR KENNEDY in *Some Came Running*, Sol C. Siegel Prods., Inc., M-G-M.

GIG YOUNG in *Teacher's Pet*, Perlberg-Seaton, Paramount.

1959 Thirty-second Year

★ HUGH GRIFFITH in *Ben-Hur*, Metro-Goldwyn-Mayer.

ARTHUR O'CONNELL in *Anatomy of a Murder*, Otto Preminger, Columbia.

GEORGE C. SCOTT in *Anatomy of a Murder*, Otto Preminger, Columbia.

ROBERT VAUGHN in *The Young Philadelphians*, Warner Bros.

ED WYNN in *The Diary of Anne Frank*, 20th Century-Fox.

1960 Thirty-third Year

PETER FALK in *Murder, Inc.*, 20th Century-Fox.

JACK KRUSCHEN in *The Apartment*, The Mirisch Co., Inc., UA.

SAL MINEO in *Exodus*, Carlyle-Alpina S.A. Prod., UA.

★ PETER USTINOV in *Spartacus*, Bryna Prods., Inc., U-I.

CHILL WILLS in *The Alamo*, Batjac Prod., UA.

1961 Thirty-fourth Year

★ GEORGE CHAKIRIS in *West Side Story*, Mirisch Pictures, Inc., and B and P Enterprises, Inc., UA.

MONTGOMERY CLIFT in *Judgment at Nuremberg*, Stanley Kramer Prod., UA.

PETER FALK in *Pocketful of Miracles*, Franton Prod., UA.

JACKIE GLEASON in *The Hustler*, Robert Rossen Prod., 20th Century-Fox.

GEORGE C. SCOTT in *The Hustler*, Robert Rossen Prod., 20th Century-Fox.

1962 Thirty-fifth Year

★ ED BEGLEY in *Sweet Bird of Youth*, Roxbury Prod., M-G-M.

VICTOR BUONO in *What Ever Happened to Baby Jane?*, Seven Arts-Associates & Aldrich Co. Prod., Warner Bros.

TELLY SAVALAS in *Bird Man of Alcatraz*, Harold Hecht Prod., UA.

OMAR SHARIF in *Lawrence of Arabia*, Horizon Pictures (G.B.), Ltd.-Sam Spiegel-David Lean Prod., Columbia.

TERENCE STAMP in *Billy Budd*, Harvest Prods., Allied Artists.

1963 Thirty-sixth Year

NICK ADAMS in *Twilight of Honor*, Perlberg-Seaton Prod., M-G-M.

BOBBY DARIN in *Captain Newman, M.D.*, Universal-Brentwood-Reynard Prod., Universal.

★ MELVYN DOUGLAS in *Hud*, Salem-Dover Prod., Paramount.

HUGH GRIFFITH in *Tom Jones*, Woodfall Prod., UA-Lopert Pictures.

JOHN HUSTON in *The Cardinal*, Gamma Prod., Columbia.

1964 Thirty-seventh Year

JOHN GIELGUD in *Becket*, Hal Wallis Prod., Paramount.

STANLEY HOLLOWAY in *My Fair Lady*, Warner Bros.

EDMOND O'BRIEN in *Seven Days in May*, Joel Prods., Paramount.

LEE TRACY in *The Best Man*, Millar-Turman Prod., United Artists.

★ PETER USTINOV in *Topkapi*, Filmways Prod., United Artists.

1965 Thirty-eighth Year

★ MARTIN BALSAM in *A Thousand Clowns*, Harrell Prod., United Artists.

IAN BANNEN in *The Flight of the Phoenix*, Associates & Aldrich Company Prod., 20th Century-Fox.

TOM COURTENAY in *Doctor Zhivago*, Sostar S.A.-Metro-Goldwyn-Mayer British Studios, Ltd. Prod. M-G-M.

MICHAEL DUNN in *Ship of Fools*, Columbia.

FRANK FINLAY in *Othello*, B.H.E. Prod., Warner Bros.

1966 Thirty-ninth Year

MAKO in *The Sand Pebbles*, Argyle-Solar Prod., 20th Century-Fox.

JAMES MASON in *Georgy Girl*, Everglades Prods., Ltd., Columbia.

★ WALTER MATTHAU in *The Fortune Cookie*, Phalanx-Jalem-Mirisch Corp. of Delaware Prod., UA.

GEORGE SEGAL in *Who's Afraid of Virginia Woolf?*, Chenault Prod., Warner Bros.

ROBERT SHAW in *A Man for All Seasons*, Highland Films, Ltd., Prod., Columbia.

1967 Fortieth Year

JOHN CASSAVETES in *The Dirty Dozen*, MKH Prods., Ltd., M-G-M.

GENE HACKMAN in *Bonnie and Clyde*, Tatira-Hiller Prod., Warner Bros.-Seven Arts.

CECIL KELLAWAY in *Guess Who's Coming to Dinner*, Columbia.

★ GEORGE KENNEDY in *Cool Hand Luke*, Jalem Prod., Warner Bros.-Seven Arts.

MICHAEL J. POLLARD in *Bonnie and Clyde*, Tatira-Hiller Prod., Warner Bros.-Seven Arts.

1968 Forty-first Year

★ JACK ALBERTSON in *The Subject Was Roses*, M-G-M.

SEYMOUR CASSEL in *Faces*, John Cassavetes Prod., Walter Reade-Continental Distributing.

DANIEL MASSEY in *Star!*, Robert Wise Prod., 20th Century-Fox.

JACK WILD in *Oliver!*, Romulus Films, Ltd., Columbia.

GENE WILDER in *The Producers*, Sidney Glazier Prod., Avco Embassy.

1969 Forty-second Year

RUPERT CROSSE in *The Reivers*, Irving Ravetch-Arthur Kramer-Solar Prods., Cinema Center Films Presentation, National General.

ELLIOTT GOULD in *Bob & Carol & Ted & Alice*, Frankovich Prods., Columbia.

JACK NICHOLSON in *Easy Rider*, Pando-Raybert Prod., Columbia.

ANTHONY QUAYLE in *Anne of the Thousand Days*, Hal B. Wallis-Universal Pictures, Ltd., Prod., Universal.

★ GIG YOUNG in *They Shoot Horses, Don't They?*, Chartoff-Winkler-

Pollack Prod., ABC Pictures Presentation, Cinerama.

1970 Forty-third Year

RICHARD CASTELLANO in *Lovers and Other Strangers*, ABC Pictures Prod., Cinerama.

CHIEF DAN GEORGE in *Little Big Man*, Hiller Prods., Ltd.-Stockbridge Prods., Cinema Center Films Presentation, National General.

GENE HACKMAN in *I Never Sang for My Father*, Jamel Prods., Columbia.

JOHN MARLEY in *Love Story*, The Love Story Company Prod., Paramount.

★ JOHN MILLS in *Ryan's Daughter*, Faraway Prods., M-G-M.

1971 Forty-fourth Year

JEFF BRIDGES in *The Last Picture Show*, BBS Prods., Columbia.

LEONARD FREY in *Fiddler on the Roof*, Mirisch-Cartier Prods., UA.

RICHARD JAECKEL in *Sometimes a Great Notion*, A Universal-Newman-Foreman Company Prod., Universal.

★ BEN JOHNSON in *The Last Picture Show*, BBS Prods., Columbia.

ROY SCHEIDER in *The French Connection*, A Philip D'Antoni Prod. in association with Schine-Moore Prods., 20th Century-Fox.

1972 Forty-fifth Year

EDDIE ALBERT in *The Heartbreak Kid*, A Palomar Pictures International Production, 20th Century-Fox.

JAMES CAAN in *The Godfather*, An Albert S. Ruddy Production, Paramount.

ROBERT DUVALL in *The Godfather*, An Albert S. Ruddy Production, Paramount.

★ JOEL GREY in *Cabaret*, An ABC Pictures Production, Allied Artists.

AL PACINO in *The Godfather*, An Albert S. Ruddy Production, Paramount.

1973 Forty-sixth Year

VINCENT GARDENIA in *Bang the Drum Slowly*, A Rosenfield Production, Paramount.

JACK GILFORD in *Save the Tiger*, Filmways-Jalem-Cirandinha Productions, Paramount.

★ JOHN HOUSEMAN in *The Paper Chase*, Thompson-Paul Productions, 20th Century-Fox.

JASON MILLER in *The Exorcist*, Hoya Productions, Warner Bros.

RANDY QUAID in *The Last Detail*, An Acrobat Films Prod., Columbia.

1974 Forty-seventh Year

FRED ASTAIRE in *The Towering Inferno*, An Irwin Allen Production, 20th Century-Fox/Warner Bros.

JEFF BRIDGES in *Thunderbolt and Lightfoot*, A Malpaso Company Film Production, United Artists.

★ ROBERT DE NIRO in *The Godfather Part II*, A Coppola Company Production, Paramount.

MICHAEL V. GAZZO in *The Godfather Part II*, A Coppola Company Production, Paramount.

LEE STRASBERG in *The Godfather Part II*, A Coppola Company Production, Paramount.

1975 Forty-eighth Year

★ GEORGE BURNS in *The Sunshine Boys*, A Ray Stark Production, M-G-M.

BRAD DOURIF in *One Flew over the Cuckoo's Nest*, A Fantasy Films Production, United Artists.

BURGESS MEREDITH in *The Day of the Locust*, A Jerome Hellman Production, Paramount.

CHRIS SARANDON in *Dog Day Afternoon*, Warner Bros.

JACK WARDEN in *Shampoo*, Rubeeker Productions, Columbia.

1976 Forty-ninth Year

NED BEATTY in *Network*, A Howard Gottfried/Paddy Chayefsky Production, M-G-M/UA.

BURGESS MEREDITH in *Rocky*, A Robert Chartoff-Irwin Winkler Production, United Artists.

LAURENCE OLIVIER in *Marathon Man*, A Robert Evans-Sidney Beckerman Production, Paramount.

★ JASON ROBARDS in *All the President's Men*, A Wildwood Enterprises Production, Warner Bros.

BURT YOUNG in *Rocky*, A Robert Chartoff-Irwin Winkler Production, United Artists.

1977 Fiftieth Year

MIKHAIL BARYSHNIKOV in *The Turning Point*, Hera Productions, 20th Century-Fox.

PETER FIRTH in *Equus*, A Winkast Company, Ltd./P.B., Ltd. Production, United Artists.

ALEC GUINNESS in *Star Wars*, A Twentieth Century-Fox Production, 20th Century-Fox.

★ JASON ROBARDS in *Julia*, A Twentieth Century-Fox Production, 20th Century-Fox.

MAXIMILIAN SCHELL in *Julia*, A Twentieth Century-Fox Production, 20th Century-Fox.

1978 Fifty-first Year

BRUCE DERN in *Coming Home*, A Jerome Hellman Enterprises Production, United Artists.

RICHARD FARNSWORTH in *Comes a Horseman*, A Robert Chartoff-Irwin Winkler Production, United Artists.

JOHN HURT in *Midnight Express*, A Casablanca-Filmworks Production, Columbia.

★ CHRISTOPHER WALKEN in *The Deer Hunter*, An EMI Films/Michael Cimino Film Production, Universal.

JACK WARDEN in *Heaven Can Wait*, Dogwood Productions, Paramount.

1979 Fifty-second Year

★ MELVYN DOUGLAS in *Being There*, A Lorimar Film-Und Fernsehproduktion GmbH Production, United Artists.

ROBERT DUVALL in *Apocalypse Now*, An Omni Zoetrope Production, United Artists.

FREDERIC FORREST in *The Rose*, A Twentieth Century-Fox Production, 20th Century-Fox.

JUSTIN HENRY in *Kramer vs. Kramer*, Stanley Jaffe Productions, Columbia.

MICKEY ROONEY in *The Black Stallion*, An Omni Zoetrope Production, United Artists.

1980 Fifty-third Year

JUDD HIRSCH in *Ordinary People*, A Wildwood Enterprises Production, Paramount.

★ TIMOTHY HUTTON in *Ordinary People*, A Wildwood Enterprises Production, Paramount.

MICHAEL O'KEEFE in *The Great Santini*, An Orion Pictures-Bing Crosby Production, Orion Pictures.

JOE PESCI in *Raging Bull*, A Robert Chartoff-Irwin Winkler Production, United Artists.

JASON ROBARDS in *Melvin and Howard*, A Linson/Phillips/ Demme-Universal Pictures Production, Universal.

1981 Fifty-fourth Year

JAMES COCO in *Only When I Laugh*, A Columbia Pictures Production, Columbia.

★ JOHN GIELGUD in *Arthur*, A Rollins, Joffe, Morra, and Brezner Production, Orion.

IAN HOLM in *Chariots of Fire*, Enigma Productions Limited, The Ladd Company/Warner Bros.

JACK NICHOLSON in *Reds*, A J.R.S. Production, Paramount.

HOWARD E. ROLLINS, JR., in *Ragtime*, A Ragtime Production, Paramount.

1982 Fifty-fifth Year

CHARLES DURNING in *The Best Little Whorehouse in Texas*, A Universal and RKO Pictures Presentation of a Miller-Milkis-Boyett Production, Universal.

★ LOUIS GOSSETT, JR., in *An Officer and a Gentleman*, A Lorimar Production in association with Martin Elfand, Paramount.

JOHN LITHGOW in *The World According to Garp*, A Warner Bros. Production, Warner Bros.

JAMES MASON in *The Verdict*, A Fox-Zanuck/Brown Production, 20th Century-Fox.

ROBERT PRESTON in *Victor/Victoria*, A Metro-Goldwyn-Mayer Production, M-G-M/UA.

1983 Fifty-sixth Year

CHARLES DURNING in *To Be or Not to Be*, A Brooksfilms Production, 20th Century-Fox.

JOHN LITHGOW in *Terms of Endearment*, A James L. Brooks Production, Paramount.

★ JACK NICHOLSON in *Terms of Endearment*, A James L. Brooks Production, Paramount.

SAM SHEPARD in *The Right Stuff*, A Robert Chartoff-Irwin Winkler Production, The Ladd Company through Warner Bros.

RIP TORN in *Cross Creek*, A Robert B. Radnitz/Martin Ritt/Thorn EMI Films Production, Universal.

1984 Fifty-seventh Year

ADOLPH CAESAR in *A Soldier's Story*, A Caldix Films Production, Columbia.

JOHN MALKOVICH in *Places in the Heart*, A Tri-Star Pictures Production, Tri-Star.

NORIYUKI "PAT" MORITA in *The Karate Kid*, A Columbia Pictures Production, Columbia.

★ HAING S. NGOR in *The Killing Fields*, A Goldcrest Films and Television/International Film Investors L.P. Production, Warner Bros.

RALPH RICHARDSON in *Greystoke: The Legend of Tarzan, Lord of the Apes*, A Warner Bros. Production, Warner Bros.

1985 Fifty-eighth Year

★ DON AMECHE in *Cocoon*, a Fox/Zanuck-Brown Production, 20th Century-Fox.

KLAUS MARIA BRANDAUER in *Out of Africa*, a Universal Pictures Limited Production, Universal.

WILLIAM HICKEY in *Prizzi's Honor*, an ABC Motion Pictures Production, 20th Century-Fox.

ROBERT LOGGIA in *Jagged Edge*, a Columbia Pictures Production, Columbia.

ERIC ROBERTS in *Runaway Train*, a Cannon Films Production, Cannon.

1986 Fifty-ninth Year

TOM BERENGER in *Platoon*, A Hemdale Film Production, Orion.

★ MICHAEL CAINE in *Hannah and Her Sisters*, A Jack Rollins and Charles H. Joffe Production, Orion.

WILLEM DAFOE in *Platoon*, A Hemdale Film Production, Orion.

DENHOLM ELLIOTT in *A Room with a View*, A Merchant Ivory Production, Cinecom.

DENNIS HOPPER in *Hoosiers*, A Carter De Haven Production, Orion.

1987 Sixtieth Year

ALBERT BROOKS in *Broadcast News*, A Twentieth Century-Fox Production, 20th Century-Fox.

★ SEAN CONNERY in *The Untouchables*, An Art Linson Production, Paramount.

MORGAN FREEMAN in *Street Smart*, A Cannon Films Production, Cannon.
VINCENT GARDENIA in *Moonstruck*, A Patrick Palmer and Norman Jewison Production, M-G-M.
DENZEL WASHINGTON in *Cry Freedom*, A Marble Arch Production, Universal.

1988 Sixty-first Year

ALEC GUINNESS in *Little Dorrit*, A Sands Films Production, Cannon.
★ KEVIN KLINE in *A Fish Called Wanda*, A Michael Shamberg-Prominent Features Production, M-G-M.
MARTIN LANDAU in *Tucker: the Man and His Dream*, A Lucasfilm Production, Paramount.
RIVER PHOENIX in *Running on Empty*, A Lorimar Production, Warner Bros.
DEAN STOCKWELL in *Married to the Mob*, A Mysterious Arts-Demme Production, Orion.

1989 Sixty-second Year

DANNY AIELLO in *Do the Right Thing*, A Forty Acres and a Mule Filmworks Production, Universal.
DAN AYKROYD in *Driving Miss Daisy*, A Zanuck Company Production, Warner Bros.
MARLON BRANDO in *A Dry White Season*, A Metro-Goldwyn-Mayer Presentation of a Paula Weinstein Production, M-G-M.
MARTIN LANDAU in *Crimes and Misdemeanors*, A Jack Rollins and Charles H. Joffe Production, Orion.
★ DENZEL WASHINGTON in *Glory*, A Tri-Star Pictures Production, Tri-Star.

1990 Sixty-third Year

BRUCE DAVISON in *Longtime Companion*, An American Playhouse Production, Samuel Goldwyn Company.
ANDY GARCIA in *The Godfather, Part III*, A Zoetrope Studios Production, Paramount.
GRAHAM GREENE in *Dances with Wolves*, A Tig Production, Orion.
AL PACINO in *Dick Tracy*, A Touchstone Pictures Production, Buena Vista.
★ JOE PESCI in *GoodFellas*, A Warner Bros. Production, Warner Bros.

1991 Sixty-fourth Year

TOMMY LEE JONES in *JFK*, A Camelot Production, Warner Bros.
HARVEY KEITEL in *Bugsy*, A Tri-Star Pictures Production, Tri-Star.
BEN KINGSLEY in *Bugsy*, A Tri-Star Pictures Production, Tri-Star.
MICHAEL LERNER in *Barton Fink*, A Barton Circle Production, 20th Century-Fox.
★ JACK PALANCE in *City Slickers*, A Castle Rock Entertainment Production, Columbia.

1992 Sixty-fifth Year

JAYE DAVIDSON in *The Crying Game*, A Palace Pictures Production, Miramax.
★ GENE HACKMAN in *Unforgiven*, A Warner Bros. Production, Warner Bros.
JACK NICHOLSON in *A Few Good Men*, A Castle Rock Entertainment Production, Columbia.
AL PACINO in *Glengarry Glen Ross*, A Stephanie Lynn Production, New Line.
DAVID PAYMER in *Mr. Saturday Night*, A Castle Rock Entertainment Production, Columbia.

Supporting Actress

The Supporting Actress category, created in 1936 with the Supporting Actor award, is marked by a surprising lack of multiple winners. Only Shelley Winters, with Oscars in 1959 and 1965, has received more than one Supporting Actress award, though Ingrid Bergman and Helen Hayes have won acting awards in both the lead and supporting categories. Ten-year-old Tatum O'Neal, 1973's Best Supporting Actress, is the youngest to win an award in *any* of the acting categories. In 1938 Fay Bainter was nominated for Best Actress and Best Supporting Actress for two different roles, as were Teresa Wright in 1942, Jessica Lange in 1982, and Sigourney Weaver in 1988.

Achievements in this category are nominated by members of the Academy Actors Branch who decide individually at the time of balloting whether a role is a lead or support.

1936 Ninth Year

BEULAH BONDI in *The Gorgeous Hussy*, Metro-Goldwyn-Mayer.

ALICE BRADY in *My Man Godfrey*, Universal.

BONITA GRANVILLE in *These Three*, Goldwyn, UA.

MARIA OUSPENSKAYA in *Dodsworth*, Goldwyn, UA.

★ GALE SONDERGAARD in *Anthony Adverse*, Warner Bros.

1937 Tenth Year

★ ALICE BRADY in *In Old Chicago*, 20th Century-Fox.

ANDREA LEEDS in *Stage Door*, RKO Radio.

ANNE SHIRLEY in *Stella Dallas*, Goldwyn, UA.

CLAIRE TREVOR in *Dead End*, Goldwyn, UA.

DAME MAY WHITTY in *Night Must Fall*, M-G-M.

1938 Eleventh Year

★ FAY BAINTER in *Jezebel*, Warner Bros.

BEULAH BONDI in *Of Human Hearts*, M-G-M.

BILLIE BURKE in *Merrily We Live*, Roach, M-G-M.

SPRING BYINGTON in *You Can't Take It with You*, Columbia.

MILIZA KORJUS in *The Great Waltz*, M-G-M.

1939 Twelfth Year

OLIVIA DE HAVILLAND in *Gone with the Wind*, Selznick, M-G-M.

GERALDINE FITZGERALD in *Wuthering Heights*, Goldwyn, UA.

★ HATTIE McDANIEL in *Gone with the Wind*, Selznick, M-G-M.

EDNA MAY OLIVER in *Drums along the Mohawk*, 20th Century-Fox.

MARIA OUSPENSKAYA in *Love Affair*, RKO Radio.

1940 Thirteenth Year

JUDITH ANDERSON in *Rebecca*, Selznick, UA.

★ JANE DARWELL in *The Grapes of Wrath*, 20th Century-Fox.

RUTH HUSSEY in *The Philadelphia Story*, M-G-M.

BARBARA O'NEIL in *All This, and Heaven Too*, Warner Bros.
MARJORIE RAMBEAU in *Primrose Path*, RKO Radio.

1941 Fourteenth Year

SARA ALLGOOD in *How Green Was My Valley*, 20th Century-Fox.
★ MARY ASTOR in *The Great Lie*, Warner Bros.
PATRICIA COLLINGE in *The Little Foxes*, Goldwyn, RKO Radio.
TERESA WRIGHT in *The Little Foxes*, Goldwyn, RKO Radio.
MARGARET WYCHERLY in *Sergeant York*, Warner Bros.

1942 Fifteenth Year

GLADYS COOPER in *Now, Voyager*, Warner Bros.
AGNES MOOREHEAD in *The Magnificent Ambersons*, Mercury, RKO Radio.
SUSAN PETERS in *Random Harvest*, M-G-M.
DAME MAY WHITTY in *Mrs. Miniver*, M-G-M.
★ TERESA WRIGHT in *Mrs. Miniver*, M-G-M.

1943 Sixteenth Year

GLADYS COOPER in *The Song of Bernadette*, 20th Century-Fox.
PAULETTE GODDARD in *So Proudly We Hail*, Paramount.
★ KATINA PAXINOU in *For Whom the Bell Tolls*, Paramount.
ANNE REVERE in *The Song of Bernadette*, 20th Century-Fox.
LUCILE WATSON in *Watch on the Rhine*, Warner Bros.

1944 Seventeenth Year

★ ETHEL BARRYMORE in *None but the Lonely Heart*, RKO Radio.
JENNIFER JONES in *Since You Went Away*, Selznick, UA.
ANGELA LANSBURY in *Gaslight*, M-G-M.
ALINE MACMAHON in *Dragon Seed*, M-G-M.
AGNES MOOREHEAD in *Mrs. Parkington*, M-G-M.

1945 Eighteenth Year

EVE ARDEN in *Mildred Pierce*, Warner Bros.
ANN BLYTH in *Mildred Pierce*, Warner Bros.
ANGELA LANSBURY in *The Picture of Dorian Gray*, M-G-M.
JOAN LORRING in *The Corn Is Green*, Warner Bros.
★ ANNE REVERE in *National Velvet*, M-G-M.

1946 Nineteenth Year

ETHEL BARRYMORE in *The Spiral Staircase*, RKO Radio.
★ ANNE BAXTER in *The Razor's Edge*, 20th Century-Fox.
LILLIAN GISH in *Duel in the Sun*, Selznick International.
FLORA ROBSON in *Saratoga Trunk*, Warner Bros.
GALE SONDERGAARD in *Anna and the King of Siam*, 20th Century-Fox.

1947 Twentieth Year

ETHEL BARRYMORE in *The Paradine Case*, Selznick.
GLORIA GRAHAME in *Crossfire*, RKO Radio.
★ CELESTE HOLM in *Gentleman's Agreement*, 20th Century-Fox.
MARJORIE MAIN in *The Egg and I*, Universal-International.
ANNE REVERE in *Gentleman's Agreement*, 20th Century-Fox.

1948 Twenty-first Year

BARBARA BEL GEDDES in *I Remember Mama*, RKO Radio.
ELLEN CORBY in *I Remember Mama*, RKO Radio.
AGNES MOOREHEAD in *Johnny Belinda*, Warner Bros.

JEAN SIMMONS in *Hamlet*, Rank-Two Cities, U-I. (British)

★ CLAIRE TREVOR in *Key Largo*, Warner Bros.

1949 Twenty-second Year

ETHEL BARRYMORE in *Pinky*, 20th Century-Fox.

CELESTE HOLM in *Come to the Stable*, 20th Century-Fox.

ELSA LANCHESTER in *Come to the Stable*, 20th Century-Fox.

★ MERCEDES McCAMBRIDGE in *All the King's Men*, Rossen, Columbia.

ETHEL WATERS in *Pinky*, 20th Century-Fox.

1950 Twenty-third Year

HOPE EMERSON in *Caged*, Warner Bros.

CELESTE HOLM in *All about Eve*, 20th Century-Fox.

★ JOSEPHINE HULL in *Harvey*, Universal-International.

NANCY OLSON in *Sunset Boulevard*, Paramount.

THELMA RITTER in *All about Eve*, 20th Century-Fox.

1951 Twenty-fourth Year

JOAN BLONDELL in *The Blue Veil*, Wald-Krasna, RKO Radio.

MILDRED DUNNOCK in *Death of a Salesman*, Kramer, Columbia.

LEE GRANT in *Detective Story*, Paramount.

★ KIM HUNTER in *A Streetcar Named Desire*, Charles K. Feldman Group Prods, Warner Bros.

THELMA RITTER in *The Mating Season*, Paramount.

1952 Twenty-fifth Year

★ GLORIA GRAHAME in *The Bad and the Beautiful*, M-G-M.

JEAN HAGEN in *Singin' in the Rain*, M-G-M.

COLETTE MARCHAND in *Moulin Rouge*, Romulus, UA.

TERRY MOORE in *Come Back, Little Sheba*, Wallis, Paramount.

THELMA RITTER in *With a Song in My Heart*, 20th Century-Fox.

1953 Twenty-sixth Year

GRACE KELLY in *Mogambo*, M-G-M.

GERALDINE PAGE in *Hondo*, Wayne-Fellows, Warner Bros.

MARJORIE RAMBEAU in *Torch Song*, M-G-M.

★ DONNA REED in *From Here to Eternity*, Columbia.

THELMA RITTER in *Pickup on South Street*, 20th Century-Fox.

1954 Twenty-seventh Year

NINA FOCH in *Executive Suite*, M-G-M.

KATY JURADO in *Broken Lance*, 20th Century-Fox.

★ EVA MARIE SAINT in *On the Waterfront*, Horizon-American, Columbia.

JAN STERLING in *The High and the Mighty*, Wayne-Fellows, Warner Bros.

CLAIRE TREVOR in *The High and the Mighty*, Wayne-Fellows, Warner Bros.

1955 Twenty-eighth Year

BETSY BLAIR in *Marty*, Hecht & Lancaster's Steven Prods., UA.

PEGGY LEE in *Pete Kelly's Blues*, A Mark VIII Ltd. Prod., Warner Bros.

MARISA PAVAN in *The Rose Tattoo*, Hal Wallis, Paramount.

★ JO VAN FLEET in *East of Eden*, Warner Bros.

NATALIE WOOD in *Rebel Without A Cause*, Warner Bros.

1956 Twenty-ninth Year

MILDRED DUNNOCK in *Baby Doll*, A Newtown Prod., Warner Bros.

EILEEN HECKART in *The Bad Seed*, Warner Bros.

MERCEDES MCCAMBRIDGE in *Giant*, Giant Prod., Warner Bros.
PATTY MCCORMACK in *The Bad Seed*, Warner Bros.
★ DOROTHY MALONE in *Written on the Wind*, Universal-International.

1957 Thirtieth Year

CAROLYN JONES in *The Bachelor Party*, Norma Prod., UA.
ELSA LANCHESTER in *Witness for the Prosecution*, Edward Small-Arthur Hornblow Prod., UA.
HOPE LANGE in *Peyton Place*, Jerry Wald Prods., Inc., 20th Century-Fox.
★ MIYOSHI UMEKI in *Sayonara*, William Goetz Prod., Warner Bros.
DIANE VARSI in *Peyton Place*, Jerry Wald Prods., Inc., 20th Century-Fox.

1958 Thirty-first Year

PEGGY CASS in *Auntie Mame*, Warner Bros.
★ WENDY HILLER in *Separate Tables*, Clifton Prods., Inc., UA.
MARTHA HYER in *Some Came Running*, Sol C. Siegel Prods., Inc., M-G-M.
MAUREEN STAPLETON in *Lonelyhearts*, Schary Prods., Inc., UA.
CARA WILLIAMS in *The Defiant Ones*, Stanley Kramer, UA.

1959 Thirty-second Year

HERMIONE BADDELEY in *Room at the Top*, Romulus Films, Ltd., Continental Distributing, Inc. (British)
SUSAN KOHNER in *Imitation of Life*, Universal-International.
JUANITA MOORE in *Imitation of Life*, Universal-International.
THELMA RITTER in *Pillow Talk*, Arwin Prods., Inc., U-I.
★ SHELLEY WINTERS in *The Diary of Anne Frank*, 20th Century-Fox.

1960 Thirty-third Year

GLYNIS JOHNS in *The Sundowners*, Warner Bros.
★ SHIRLEY JONES in *Elmer Gantry*, Burt Lancaster-Richard Brooks Prod., UA.
SHIRLEY KNIGHT in *The Dark at the Top of the Stairs*, Warner Bros.
JANET LEIGH in *Psycho*, Alfred J. Hitchcock Prods., Paramount.
MARY URE in *Sons and Lovers*, Company of Artists, Inc., 20th Century-Fox.

1961 Thirty-fourth Year

FAY BAINTER in *The Children's Hour*, Mirisch-Worldwide Prod., UA.
JUDY GARLAND in *Judgment at Nuremberg*, Stanley Kramer Prod., UA.
LOTTE LENYA in *The Roman Spring of Mrs. Stone*, Seven Arts Presentation, Warner Bros.
UNA MERKEL in *Summer and Smoke*, Hal Wallis Prod., Paramount.
★ RITA MORENO in *West Side Story*, Mirisch Pictures, Inc., and B and P Enterprises, Inc., UA.

1962 Thirty-fifth Year

MARY BADHAM in *To Kill a Mockingbird*, Universal-International-Pakula-Mulligan-Brentwood Prod., U-I.
★ PATTY DUKE in *The Miracle Worker*, Playfilms Prod., UA.
SHIRLEY KNIGHT in *Sweet Bird of Youth*, Roxbury Prod., M-G-M.
ANGELA LANSBURY in *The Manchurian Candidate*, M. C. Prod., UA.
THELMA RITTER in *Bird Man of Alcatraz*, Harold Hecht Prod., UA.

1963 Thirty-sixth Year

DIANE CILENTO in *Tom Jones*, Woodfall Prod., UA-Lopert Pictures.
DAME EDITH EVANS in *Tom Jones*, Woodfall Prod., UA-Lopert Pictures.
JOYCE REDMAN in *Tom Jones*, Woodfall Prod., UA-Lopert Pictures.

★ MARGARET RUTHERFORD in *The V.I.P.s*, M-G-M.

LILIA SKALA in *Lilies of the Field*, Rainbow Prod., UA.

1964 Thirty-seventh Year

GLADYS COOPER in *My Fair Lady*, Warner Bros.

DAME EDITH EVANS in *The Chalk Garden*, Quota Rentals, Ltd.-Ross Hunter Prod., Universal.

GRAYSON HALL in *The Night of the Iguana*, Seven Arts Prod., M-G-M.

★ LILA KEDROVA in *Zorba the Greek*, Rochley, Ltd. Prod., International Classics.

AGNES MOOREHEAD in *Hush . . . Hush, Sweet Charlotte*, Associates & Aldrich Co. Prod., 20th Century-Fox.

1965 Thirty-eighth Year

RUTH GORDON in *Inside Daisy Clover*, Park Place Prod., Warner Bros.

JOYCE REDMAN in *Othello*, B.H.E. Prod., Warner Bros.

MAGGIE SMITH in *Othello*, B.H.E. Prod., Warner Bros.

★ SHELLEY WINTERS in *A Patch of Blue*, Pandro S. Berman-Guy Green Prod., M-G-M.

PEGGY WOOD in *The Sound of Music*, Argyle Enterprises Prod., 20th Century-Fox.

1966 Thirty-ninth Year

★ SANDY DENNIS in *Who's Afraid of Virginia Woolf?*, Chenault Prod., Warner Bros.

WENDY HILLER in *A Man for All Seasons*, Highland Films, Ltd. Prod., Columbia.

JOCELYNE LAGARDE in *Hawaii*, Mirisch Corp. of Delaware Prod., UA.

VIVIEN MERCHANT in *Alfie*, Sheldrake Films, Ltd. Prod., Paramount.

GERALDINE PAGE in *You're a Big Boy Now*, Seven Arts.

1967 Fortieth Year

CAROL CHANNING in *Thoroughly Modern Millie*, Ross Hunter-Universal Prod., Universal.

MILDRED NATWICK in *Barefoot in the Park*, Hal Wallis Prod., Paramount.

★ ESTELLE PARSONS in *Bonnie and Clyde*, Tatira-Hiller Prod., Warner Bros.-Seven Arts.

BEAH RICHARDS in *Guess Who's Coming to Dinner*, Columbia.

KATHARINE ROSS in *The Graduate*, Mike Nichols-Lawrence Turman Prod., Embassy.

1968 Forty-first Year

LYNN CARLIN in *Faces*, John Cassavetes Prod., Walter Reade-Continental Distributing.

★ RUTH GORDON in *Rosemary's Baby*, William Castle Enterprises Prod., Paramount.

SONDRA LOCKE in *The Heart Is a Lonely Hunter*, Warner Bros.-Seven Arts.

KAY MEDFORD in *Funny Girl*, Rastar Prods., Columbia.

ESTELLE PARSONS in *Rachel, Rachel*, Kayos Prod., Warner Bros.-Seven Arts.

1969 Forty-second Year

CATHERINE BURNS in *Last Summer*, Frank Perry-Alsid Prod., Allied Artists.

DYAN CANNON in *Bob & Carol & Ted & Alice*, Frankovich Prods., Columbia.

★ GOLDIE HAWN in *Cactus Flower*, Frankovich Prods., Columbia.

SYLVIA MILES in *Midnight Cowboy*, A Jerome Hellman-John Schlesinger Prod., United Artists.

SUSANNAH YORK in *They Shoot Horses, Don't They?*, Chartoff-Winkler-Pollack Prod., ABC Pictures Presentation, Cinerama.

1970 Forty-third Year

KAREN BLACK in *Five Easy Pieces*, BBS Prods., Columbia.

LEE GRANT in *The Landlord*, A Mirisch-Cartier II Prod., United Artists.

★ HELEN HAYES in *Airport*, Ross-Hunter-Universal Prod., Universal.

SALLY KELLERMAN in *MASH*, Aspen Prods., 20th Century-Fox.

MAUREEN STAPLETON in *Airport*, Ross-Hunter-Universal Prod., Universal.

1971 Forty-fourth Year

ELLEN BURSTYN in *The Last Picture Show*, BBS Prods., Columbia.

BARBARA HARRIS in *Who Is Harry Kellerman, and Why Is He Saying Those Terrible Things about Me?*, A Who Is Harry Kellerman Company Prod., Cinema Center Films Presentation, National General.

★ CLORIS LEACHMAN in *The Last Picture Show*, BBS Prods., Columbia.

MARGARET LEIGHTON in *The Go-Between*, A World Film Services, Ltd. Prod., Columbia.

ANN-MARGRET in *Carnal Knowledge*, Icarus Prods., Avco Embassy.

1972 Forty-fifth Year

JEANNIE BERLIN in *The Heartbreak Kid*, A Palomar Pictures International Production, 20th Century-Fox.

★ EILEEN HECKART in *Butterflies Are Free*, Frankovich Productions, Columbia.

GERALDINE PAGE in *Pete 'n' Tillie*, A Universal-Martin Ritt-Julius J. Epstein Production, Universal.

SUSAN TYRRELL in *Fat City*, Rastar Productions, Columbia.

SHELLEY WINTERS in *The Poseidon Adventure*, An Irwin Allen Production, 20th Century-Fox.

1973 Forty-sixth Year

LINDA BLAIR in *The Exorcist*, Hoya Prods., Warner Bros.

CANDY CLARK in *American Graffiti*, A Universal-Lucasfilm, Ltd.-Coppola Company Prod., Universal.

MADELINE KAHN in *Paper Moon*, A Directors Company Prod., Paramount.

★ TATUM O'NEAL in *Paper Moon*, A Directors Company Prod., Paramount.

SYLVIA SIDNEY in *Summer Wishes, Winter Dreams*, A Rastar Pictures Prod., Columbia.

1974 Forty-seventh Year

★ INGRID BERGMAN in *Murder on the Orient Express*, A G. W. Films, Ltd., Production, Paramount.

VALENTINA CORTESE in *Day for Night*, A Les Films Du Carrosse and P.E.C.F., Paris; P.I.C., Rome Prod., Warner Bros.

MADELINE KAHN in *Blazing Saddles*, Warner Bros.

DIANE LADD in *Alice Doesn't Live Here Anymore*, Warner Bros.

TALIA SHIRE in *The Godfather Part II*, A Coppola Company Prod., Paramount.

1975 Forty-eighth Year

RONEE BLAKLEY in *Nashville*, An ABC Entertainment-Jerry Weintraub-Robert Altman Production, Paramount.

★ LEE GRANT in *Shampoo*, Rubeeker Productions, Columbia.

SYLVIA MILES in *Farewell, My Lovely*, An Elliott Kastner-ITC Production, Avco Embassy.

LILY TOMLIN in *Nashville*, An ABC Entertainment-Jerry Weintraub-Robert Altman Production, Paramount.

BRENDA VACCARO in *Jacqueline Susann's Once Is Not Enough*, A

Howard W. Koch Production, Paramount.

1976 Forty-ninth Year

JANE ALEXANDER in *All the President's Men*, A Wildwood Enterprises Production, Warner Bros.

JODIE FOSTER in *Taxi Driver*, A Bill/Phillips Production of a Martin Scorsese Film, Columbia Pictures.

LEE GRANT in *Voyage of the Damned*, An ITC Entertainment Production, Avco Embassy.

PIPER LAURIE in *Carrie*, A Redbank Films Production, United Artists.

★ BEATRICE STRAIGHT in *Network*, A Howard Gottfried/Paddy Chayefsky Production, M-G-M/UA.

1977 Fiftieth Year

LESLIE BROWNE in *The Turning Point*, Hera Productions, 20th Century-Fox.

QUINN CUMMINGS in *The Goodbye Girl*, A Ray Stark Production, M-G-M/Warner Bros.

MELINDA DILLON in *Close Encounters of the Third Kind*, Close Encounter Productions, Columbia.

★ VANESSA REDGRAVE in *Julia*, A Twentieth Century-Fox Production, 20th Century-Fox.

TUESDAY WELD in *Looking for Mr. Goodbar*, A Freddie Fields Production, Paramount.

1978 Fifty-first Year

DYAN CANNON in *Heaven Can Wait*, Dogwood Productions, Paramount.

PENELOPE MILFORD in *Coming Home*, A Jerome Hellman Enterprises Production, United Artists.

★ MAGGIE SMITH in *California Suite*, A Ray Stark Production, Columbia.

MAUREEN STAPLETON in *Interiors*, A Jack Rollins-Charles H. Joffe Production, United Artists.

MERYL STREEP in *The Deer Hunter*, An EMI Films/Michael Cimino Film Production, Universal.

1979 Fifty-second Year

JANE ALEXANDER in *Kramer vs. Kramer*, Stanley Jaffe Productions, Columbia.

BARBARA BARRIE in *Breaking Away*, A Twentieth Century-Fox Production, 20th Century-Fox.

CANDICE BERGEN in *Starting Over*, An Alan J. Pakula/James L. Brooks Production, Paramount.

MARIEL HEMINGWAY in *Manhattan*, A Jack Rollins-Charles H. Joffe Production, United Artists.

★ MERYL STREEP in *Kramer vs. Kramer*, Stanley Jaffe Productions, Columbia.

1980 Fifty-third Year

EILEEN BRENNAN in *Private Benjamin*, A Warner Bros. Production, Warner Bros.

EVA LE GALLIENNE in *Resurrection*, A Universal Pictures Production, Universal.

CATHY MORIARTY in *Raging Bull*, A Robert Chartoff-Irwin Winkler Production, United Artists.

DIANA SCARWID in *Inside Moves*, A Goodmark Production, A.F.D. (Associated Film Distribution).

★ MARY STEENBURGEN in *Melvin and Howard*, A Linson/Phillips/Demme-Universal Pictures Production, Universal.

1981 Fifty-fourth Year

MELINDA DILLON in *Absence of Malice*, A Mirage Enterprises Production, Columbia.

JANE FONDA in *On Golden Pond*, An ITC Films/IPC Films Production, Universal.

JOAN HACKETT in *Only When I Laugh*, A Columbia Pictures Production, Columbia.

ELIZABETH MCGOVERN in *Ragtime*, A Ragtime Production, Paramount.

★ MAUREEN STAPLETON in *Reds*, A J.R.S. Production, Paramount.

1982 Fifty-fifth Year

GLENN CLOSE in *The World According to Garp*, A Warner Bros. Production, Warner Bros.

TERI GARR in *Tootsie*, A Mirage/Punch Production, Columbia.

★ JESSICA LANGE in *Tootsie*, A Mirage/Punch Production, Columbia.

KIM STANLEY in *Frances*, A Brooksfilm/ EMI Production, Universal/A.F.D.

LESLEY ANN WARREN in *VICTOR/ VICTORIA*, A Metro-Goldwyn-Mayer Production, M-G-M/UA.

1983 Fifty-sixth Year

CHER in *Silkwood*, An ABC Motion Pictures Production, 20th Century-Fox.

GLENN CLOSE in *The Big Chill*, A Carson Productions Group Production, Columbia.

★ LINDA HUNT in *The Year of Living Dangerously*, A Freddie Fields Presentation of a Metro-Goldwyn-Mayer Production, M-G-M/UA.

AMY IRVING in *Yentl*, A United Artists/ Ladbroke Feature/Barwood Production, M-G-M/UA.

ALFRE WOODARD in *Cross Creek*, A Robert B. Radnitz/Martin Ritt/Thorn EMI Films Production, Universal.

1984 Fifty-seventh Year

★ PEGGY ASHCROFT in *A Passage to India*, A G. W. Films Limited Production, Columbia.

GLENN CLOSE in *The Natural*, A Tri-Star Pictures Production, Tri-Star.

LINDSAY CROUSE in *Places in the Heart*, A Tri-Star Pictures Production, Tri-Star.

CHRISTINE LAHTI in *Swing Shift*, A Warner Bros. Production, Warner Bros.

GERALDINE PAGE in *The Pope of Greenwich Village*, A United Artists-Koch/Kirkwood Production, M-G-M/ UA.

1985 Fifty-eighth Year

MARGARET AVERY in *The Color Purple*, a Warner Bros. Production, Warner Bros.

★ ANJELICA HUSTON in *Prizzi's Honor*, an ABC Motion Pictures Production, 20th Century-Fox.

AMY MADIGAN in *Twice in a Lifetime*, a Yorkin Company Production, Bud Yorkin Productions.

MEG TILLY in *Agnes of God*, a Columbia Pictures Production, Columbia.

OPRAH WINFREY in *The Color Purple*, a Warner Bros. Production, Warner Bros.

1986 Fifty-ninth Year

TESS HARPER in *Crimes of the Heart*, A Crimes of the Heart Production, De Laurentiis Entertainment Group.

PIPER LAURIE in *Children of a Lesser God*, A Burt Sugarman Production, Paramount.

MARY ELIZABETH MASTRANTONIO in *The Color of Money*, A Touchstone Pictures Production in association with Silver Screen Partners II, Buena Vista.

MAGGIE SMITH in *A Room with a View*, A Merchant Ivory Production, Cinecom.

★ DIANNE WIEST in *Hannah and Her Sisters*, A Jack Rollins and Charles H. Joffe Production, Orion.

1987 Sixtieth Year

NORMA ALEANDRO in *Gaby—a True Story*, A G. Brimmer Production, Tri-Star.

ANNE ARCHER in *Fatal Attraction*, A Jaffe/Lansing Production, Paramount.

★ OLYMPIA DUKAKIS in *Moonstruck*, A Patrick Palmer and Norman Jewison Production, M-G-M.

ANNE RAMSEY in *Throw Momma from the Train*, A Rollins, Morra, and Brezner Production, Orion.

ANN SOTHERN in *The Whales of August*, An Alive Films Production with Circle Associates, Alive Films.

1988 Sixty-first Year

JOAN CUSACK in *Working Girl*, A Twentieth Century-Fox Production, 20th Century-Fox.

★ GEENA DAVIS in *The Accidental Tourist*, A Warner Bros. Production, Warner Bros.

FRANCES MCDORMAND in *Mississippi Burning*, A Frederick Zollo Production, Orion.

MICHELLE PFEIFFER in *Dangerous Liaisons*, A Lorimar Production, Warner Bros.

SIGOURNEY WEAVER in *Working Girl*, A Twentieth Century-Fox Production, 20th Century-Fox.

1989 Sixty-second Year

★ BRENDA FRICKER in *My Left Foot*, A Ferndale Films Production, Miramax.

ANJELICA HUSTON in *Enemies, a Love Story*, A Morgan Creek Production, 20th Century-Fox.

LENA OLIN in *Enemies, a Love Story*, A Morgan Creek Production, 20th Century-Fox.

JULIA ROBERTS in *Steel Magnolias*, A Rastar Production, Tri-Star.

DIANNE WIEST in *Parenthood*, An Imagine Entertainment Production, Universal.

1990 Sixty-third Year

ANNETTE BENING in *The Grifters*, A Martin Scorsese Production, Miramax.

LORRAINE BRACCO in *GoodFellas*, A Warner Bros. Production, Warner Bros.

★ WHOOPI GOLDBERG in *Ghost*, A Howard W. Koch Production, Paramount.

DIANE LADD in *Wild at Heart*, A Polygram/Propaganda Films Production, Samuel Goldwyn Company.

MARY MCDONNELL in *Dances with Wolves*, A Tig Production, Orion.

1991 Sixty-fourth Year

DIANE LADD in *Rambling Rose*, A Carolco Pictures Production, Seven Arts/New Line.

JULIETTE LEWIS in *Cape Fear*, An Amblin Entertainment Production in association with Cappa Films and Tribeca Productions, Universal.

KATE NELLIGAN in *The Prince of Tides*, A Barwood/Longfellow Production, Columbia.

★ MERCEDES RUEHL in *The Fisher King*, A Tri-Star Pictures Production, Tri-Star.

JESSICA TANDY in *Fried Green Tomatoes*, An Act III Communications in association with Electric Shadow Production, Universal.

1992 Sixty-fifth Year

JUDY DAVIS in *Husbands and Wives*, A Tri-Star Pictures Production, Tri-Star.

JOAN PLOWRIGHT in *Enchanted April*, A BBC Films Production in association with Greenpoint Films, Miramax.

VANESSA REDGRAVE in *Howards End*, A Merchant Ivory Production, Sony Pictures Classics.

MIRANDA RICHARDSON in *Damage*, A SKREBA/Damage/NEF/Le Studio Canal + Production, New Line.

★ MARISA TOMEI in *My Cousin Vinny*, A 20th Century-Fox Production, 20th Century-Fox.

Directing

The category for Directing was begun in 1927/28, and for that year only there were two awards, one for direction of a dramatic film, another for comedy direction. The latter was dropped the following year. John Ford with four Oscars (1935, 1940, 1941, 1952) and Frank Capra (1934, 1936, 1938) and William Wyler (1942, 1946, 1959) with three each are the most frequent winners in this category. Though the categories are completely separate, voting patterns indicate a correlation between the Best Picture and Directing awards. Only two times in the last twenty years (1981, 1989) has the film voted Best Picture not been directed by the person named Best Director.

Achievements in this category are nominated by members of the Directors Branch.

1927/28 First Year

Comedy Picture (Not given after this year)

★ LEWIS MILESTONE for *Two Arabian Knights*, The Caddo Company, UA.

TED WILDE for *Speedy*, Harold Lloyd Corp., Paramount Famous Lasky.

Dramatic Picture

★ FRANK BORZAGE for *7th Heaven*, Fox.

HERBERT BRENON for *Sorrell and Son*, Art Cinema, UA.

KING VIDOR for *The Crowd*, Metro-Goldwyn-Mayer.

1928/29 Second Year

LIONEL BARRYMORE for *Madame X*, Metro-Goldwyn-Mayer.

HARRY BEAUMONT for *Broadway Melody*, Metro-Goldwyn-Mayer.

IRVING CUMMINGS for *In Old Arizona*, Fox.

★ FRANK LLOYD for *The Divine Lady*, First National.*

FRANK LLOYD for *Weary River* and *Drag*, First National.

ERNST LUBITSCH for *The Patriot*, Paramount Famous Lasky.

1929/30 Third Year

CLARENCE BROWN for *Anna Christie*, Metro-Goldwyn-Mayer.

CLARENCE BROWN for *Romance*, Metro-Goldwyn-Mayer.

ROBERT LEONARD for *The Divorcee*, Metro-Goldwyn-Mayer.

ERNST LUBITSCH for *The Love Parade*, Paramount Famous Lasky.

★ LEWIS MILESTONE for *All Quiet on the Western Front*, Universal.

KING VIDOR for *Hallelujah*, Metro-Goldwyn-Mayer.

1930/31 Fourth Year

CLARENCE BROWN for *A Free Soul*, Metro-Goldwyn-Mayer.

LEWIS MILESTONE for *The Front Page*, Caddo, UA.

WESLEY RUGGLES for *Cimarron*, RKO Radio.

*Frank Lloyd was nominated for more than one achievement, but his award specified only his work on *The Divine Lady*.

★ NORMAN TAUROG for *Skippy*, Paramount Publix.
JOSEPH VON STERNBERG for *Morocco*, Paramount Publix.

1931/32 Fifth Year

★ FRANK BORZAGE for *Bad Girl*, Fox.
KING VIDOR for *The Champ*, Metro-Goldwyn-Mayer.
JOSEF VON STERNBERG for *Shanghai Express*, Paramount Publix.

1932/33 Sixth Year

FRANK CAPRA for *Lady for a Day*, Columbia.
GEORGE CUKOR for *Little Women*, RKO Radio.
★ FRANK LLOYD for *Cavalcade*, Fox.

1934 Seventh Year

★ FRANK CAPRA for *It Happened One Night*, Columbia.
VICTOR SCHERTZINGER for *One Night of Love*, Columbia.
W. S. VAN DYKE for *The Thin Man*, Metro-Goldwyn-Mayer.

1935 Eighth Year

★ JOHN FORD for *The Informer*, RKO Radio.
HENRY HATHAWAY for *Lives of a Bengal Lancer*, Paramount.
FRANK LLOYD for *Mutiny on the Bounty*, Metro-Goldwyn-Mayer.

1936 Ninth Year

★ FRANK CAPRA for *Mr. Deeds Goes to Town*, Columbia.
GREGORY LA CAVA for *My Man Godfrey*, Universal.
ROBERT Z. LEONARD for *The Great Ziegfeld*, Metro-Goldwyn-Mayer.
W. S. VAN DYKE for *San Francisco*, Metro-Goldwyn-Mayer.
WILLIAM WYLER for *Dodsworth*, Goldwyn, UA.

1937 Tenth Year

WILLIAM DIETERLE for *The Life of Emile Zola*, Warner Bros.
SIDNEY FRANKLIN for *The Good Earth*, Metro-Goldwyn-Mayer.
GREGORY LA CAVA for *Stage Door*, RKO Radio.
★ LEO McCAREY for *The Awful Truth*, Columbia.
WILLIAM WELLMAN for *A Star Is Born*, Selznick, UA.

1938 Eleventh Year

★ FRANK CAPRA for *You Can't Take It with You*, Columbia.
MICHAEL CURTIZ for *Angels with Dirty Faces*, Warner Bros.
MICHAEL CURTIZ for *Four Daughters*, Warner Bros.
NORMAN TAUROG for *Boys Town*, Metro-Goldwyn-Mayer.
KING VIDOR for *The Citadel*, Metro-Goldwyn-Mayer.

1939 Twelfth Year

FRANK CAPRA for *Mr. Smith Goes to Washington*, Columbia.
★ VICTOR FLEMING for *Gone with the Wind*, Selznick, M-G-M.
JOHN FORD for *Stagecoach*, Wanger, UA.
SAM WOOD for *Goodbye, Mr. Chips*, Metro-Goldwyn-Mayer. (British)
WILLIAM WYLER for *Wuthering Heights*, Goldwyn, UA.

1940 Thirteenth Year

GEORGE CUKOR for *The Philadelphia Story*, Metro-Goldwyn-Mayer.
★ JOHN FORD for *The Grapes of Wrath*, 20th Century-Fox.
ALFRED HITCHCOCK for *Rebecca*, Selznick, UA.
SAM WOOD for *Kitty Foyle*, RKO Radio.
WILLIAM WYLER for *The Letter*, Warner Bros.

1941 Fourteenth Year

★ JOHN FORD for *How Green Was My Valley*, 20th Century-Fox.
ALEXANDER HALL for *Here Comes Mr. Jordan*, Columbia.
HOWARD HAWKS for *Sergeant York*, Warner Bros.
ORSON WELLES for *Citizen Kane*, Mercury, RKO Radio.
WILLIAM WYLER for *The Little Foxes*, Goldwyn, RKO Radio.

1942 Fifteenth Year

MICHAEL CURTIZ for *Yankee Doodle Dandy*, Warner Bros.
JOHN FARROW for *Wake Island*, Paramount.
MERVYN LEROY for *Random Harvest*, Metro-Goldwyn-Mayer.
SAM WOOD for *Kings Row*, Warner Bros.
★ WILLIAM WYLER for *Mrs. Miniver*, Metro-Goldwyn-Mayer.

1943 Sixteenth Year

CLARENCE BROWN for *The Human Comedy*, Metro-Goldwyn-Mayer.
★ MICHAEL CURTIZ for *Casablanca*, Warner Bros.
HENRY KING for *The Song of Bernadette*, 20th Century-Fox.
ERNST LUBITSCH for *Heaven Can Wait*, 20th Century-Fox.
GEORGE STEVENS for *The More the Merrier*, Columbia.

1944 Seventeenth Year

ALFRED HITCHCOCK for *Lifeboat*, 20th Century-Fox.
HENRY KING for *Wilson*, 20th Century-Fox.
★ LEO McCAREY for *Going My Way*, Paramount.
OTTO PREMINGER for *Laura*, 20th Century-Fox.
BILLY WILDER for *Double Indemnity*, Paramount.

1945 Eighteenth Year

CLARENCE BROWN for *National Velvet*, Metro-Goldwyn-Mayer.
ALFRED HITCHCOCK for *Spellbound*, Selznick, UA.
LEO MCCAREY for *The Bells of St. Mary's*, Rainbow, RKO Radio.
JEAN RENOIR for *The Southerner*, Loew-Hakim, UA.
★ BILLY WILDER for *The Lost Weekend*, Paramount.

1946 Nineteenth Year

CLARENCE BROWN for *The Yearling*, Metro-Goldwyn-Mayer.
FRANK CAPRA for *It's a Wonderful Life*, Liberty, RKO Radio.
DAVID LEAN for *Brief Encounter*, Rank, U-I. (British)
ROBERT SIODMAK for *The Killers*, Hellinger, Universal.
★ WILLIAM WYLER for *The Best Years of Our Lives*, Goldwyn, RKO Radio.

1947 Twentieth Year

GEORGE CUKOR for *A Double Life*, Kanin, U-I.
EDWARD DMYTRYK for *Crossfire*, RKO Radio.
★ ELIA KAZAN for *Gentleman's Agreement*, 20th Century-Fox.
HENRY KOSTER for *The Bishop's Wife*, Goldwyn, RKO Radio.
DAVID LEAN for *Great Expectations*, Rank-Cineguild, U-I. (British)

1948 Twenty-first Year

★ JOHN HUSTON for *Treasure of Sierra Madre*, Warner Bros.
ANATOLE LITVAK for *The Snake Pit*, 20th Century-Fox.
JEAN NEGULESCO for *Johnny Belinda*, Warner Bros.
LAURENCE OLIVIER for *Hamlet*, Rank-Two Cities, U-I. (British)
FRED ZINNEMANN for *The Search*, Praesens Films, M-G-M. (Swiss)

1949 Twenty-second Year

★ JOSEPH L. MANKIEWICZ for *A Letter to Three Wives*, 20th Century-Fox.

CAROL REED for *The Fallen Idol*, London Films, SRO. (British)

ROBERT ROSSEN for *All the King's Men*, Rossen, Columbia.

WILLIAM A. WELLMAN for *Battleground*, Metro-Goldwyn-Mayer.

WILLIAM WYLER for *The Heiress*, Paramount.

1950 Twenty-third Year

GEORGE CUKOR for *Born Yesterday*, Columbia.

JOHN HUSTON for *The Asphalt Jungle*, Metro-Goldwyn-Mayer.

★ JOSEPH L. MANKIEWICZ for *All about Eve*, 20th Century-Fox.

CAROL REED for *The Third Man*, Selznick-London Films, SRO. (British)

BILLY WILDER for *Sunset Boulevard*, Paramount.

1951 Twenty-fourth Year

JOHN HUSTON for *The African Queen*, Horizon, UA.

ELIA KAZAN for *A Streetcar Named Desire*, Charles K. Feldman Group Prods., Warner Bros.

VINCENTE MINNELLI for *An American in Paris*, Metro-Goldwyn-Mayer.

★ GEORGE STEVENS for *A Place in the Sun*, Paramount.

WILLIAM WYLER for *Detective Story*, Paramount.

1952 Twenty-fifth Year

CECIL B. DEMILLE for *The Greatest Show on Earth*, Cecil B. DeMille, Paramount.

★ JOHN FORD for *The Quiet Man*, Argosy, Republic.

JOHN HUSTON for *Moulin Rouge*, Romulus Films, UA.

JOSEPH L. MANKIEWICZ for *Five Fingers*, 20th Century-Fox.

FRED ZINNEMANN for *High Noon*, Stanley Kramer, UA.

1953 Twenty-sixth Year

GEORGE STEVENS for *Shane*, Paramount.

CHARLES WALTERS for *Lili*, Metro-Goldwyn-Mayer.

BILLY WILDER for *Stalag 17*, Paramount.

WILLIAM WYLER for *Roman Holiday*, Paramount.

★ FRED ZINNEMANN for *From Here to Eternity*, Columbia.

1954 Twenty-seventh Year

ALFRED HITCHCOCK for *Rear Window*, Patron, Inc., Paramount.

★ ELIA KAZAN for *On the Waterfront*, Horizon-American, Columbia.

GEORGE SEATON for *The Country Girl*, Perlberg-Seaton, Paramount.

WILLIAM WELLMAN for *The High and the Mighty*, Wayne-Fellows, Warner Bros.

BILLY WILDER for *Sabrina*, Paramount.

1955 Twenty-eighth Year

ELIA KAZAN for *East of Eden*, Warner Bros.

DAVID LEAN for *Summertime*, Ilya Lopert-David Lean, UA. (Anglo-American)

JOSHUA LOGAN for *Picnic*, Columbia.

★ DELBERT MANN for *Marty*, Hecht & Lancaster's Steven Prods., UA.

JOHN STURGES for *Bad Day at Black Rock*, Metro-Goldwyn-Mayer.

1956 Twenty-ninth Year

MICHAEL ANDERSON for *Around the World in 80 Days*, The Michael Todd Co., Inc., UA.

WALTER LANG for *The King and I*, 20th Century-Fox.

★ GEORGE STEVENS for *Giant*, Giant Prod., Warner Bros.
KING VIDOR for *War and Peace*, A Ponti-DeLaurentiis Prod., Paramount. (Italo-American)
WILLIAM WYLER for *Friendly Persuasion*, Allied Artists.

1957 Thirtieth Year

★ DAVID LEAN for *The Bridge on the River Kwai*, A Horizon Picture, Columbia.
JOSHUA LOGAN for *Sayonara*, William Goetz Prod., Warner Bros.
SIDNEY LUMET for *12 Angry Men*, Orion-Nova Prod., UA.
MARK ROBSON for *Peyton Place*, Jerry Wald Prods., Inc., 20th Century-Fox.
BILLY WILDER for *Witness for the Prosecution*, Edward Small-Arthur Hornblow Prod., UA.

1958 Thirty-first Year

RICHARD BROOKS for *Cat on a Hot Tin Roof*, Avon Prods., Inc., M-G-M.
STANLEY KRAMER for *The Defiant Ones*, Stanley Kramer, UA.
★ VINCENTE MINNELLI for *Gigi*, Arthur Freed Prods., Inc., M-G-M.
MARK ROBSON for *The Inn of the Sixth Happiness*, 20th Century-Fox.
ROBERT WISE for *I Want To Live!*, Figaro, Inc., UA.

1959 Thirty-second Year

JACK CLAYTON for *Room at the Top*, Romulus Films, Ltd., Continental Dist. Inc. (British)
GEORGE STEVENS for *The Diary of Anne Frank*, 20th Century-Fox.
BILLY WILDER for *Some Like It Hot*, Ashton Prods. & The Mirisch Co., UA.
★ WILLIAM WYLER for *Ben-Hur*, Metro-Goldwyn-Mayer.
FRED ZINNEMANN for *The Nun's Story*, Warner Bros.

1960 Thirty-third Year

JACK CARDIFF for *Sons and Lovers*, Company of Artists, Inc., 20th Century-Fox.
JULES DASSIN for *Never on Sunday*, Melinafilm Prod., Lopert Pictures Corp. (Greek)
ALFRED HITCHCOCK for *Psycho*, Alfred J. Hitchcock Prods., Paramount.
★ BILLY WILDER for *The Apartment*, The Mirisch Co., Inc., UA.
FRED ZINNEMANN for *The Sundowners*, Warner Bros.

1961 Thirty-fourth Year

FEDERICO FELLINI for *La Dolce Vita*, Riama Film Prod., Astor Pictures, Inc. (Italian)
STANLEY KRAMER for *Judgment at Nuremberg*, Stanley Kramer Prod., UA.
ROBERT ROSSEN for *The Hustler*, Robert Rossen Prod., 20th Century-Fox.
J. LEE THOMPSON for *The Guns of Navarone*, Carl Foreman Prod., Columbia.
★ ROBERT WISE and JEROME ROBBINS for *West Side Story*, Mirisch Pictures, Inc., and B and P Enterprises, Inc., UA.

1962 Thirty-fifth Year

PIETRO GERMI for *Divorce—Italian Style*, Lux-Vides-Galatea Film Prod., Embassy Pictures.
★ DAVID LEAN for *Lawrence of Arabia*, Horizon Pictures (G.B.), Ltd.-Sam Spiegel-David Lean Prod., Columbia.
ROBERT MULLIGAN for *To Kill a Mockingbird*, Universal-International-Pakula-Mulligan-Brentwood Prod., U-I.
ARTHUR PENN for *The Miracle Worker*, Playfilms Prod., UA.
FRANK PERRY for *David and Lisa*, Heller-Perry Prods., Continental Dist.

1963 Thirty-sixth Year

FEDERICO FELLINI for *Federico Fellini's 8½*, Cineriz Prod., Embassy Pictures.

ELIA KAZAN for *America America*, Athena Enterprises Prod., Warner Bros.

OTTO PREMINGER for *The Cardinal*, Gamma Prod., Columbia.

★ TONY RICHARDSON for *Tom Jones*, Woodfall Prod., UA-Lopert Pictures.

MARTIN RITT for *Hud*, Salem-Dover Prod., Paramount.

1964 Thirty-seventh Year

MICHAEL CACOYANNIS for *Zorba the Greek*, Rochley, Ltd. Prod., Intl. Classics.

★ GEORGE CUKOR for *My Fair Lady*, Warner Bros.

PETER GLENVILLE for *Becket*, Hal Wallis Prod., Paramount.

STANLEY KUBRICK for *Dr. Strangelove or: How I Learned to Stop Worrying and Love the Bomb*, Hawk Films, Ltd. Prod., Columbia.

ROBERT STEVENSON for *Mary Poppins*, Walt Disney Prods.

1965 Thirty-eighth Year

DAVID LEAN for *Doctor Zhivago*, Sostar S.A.-Metro-Goldwyn-Mayer British Studios, LTD. Prod., M-G-M.

JOHN SCHLESINGER for *Darling*, Anglo-Amalgamated, Ltd. Prod., Embassy.

HIROSHI TESHIGAHARA for *Woman in the Dunes*, Teshigahara Prod., Pathe Contemporary Films.

★ ROBERT WISE for *The Sound of Music*, Argyle Enterprises Prod., 20th Century-Fox.

WILLIAM WYLER for *The Collector*, The Collector Company, Columbia.

1966 Thirty-ninth Year

MICHELANGELO ANTONIONI for *Blow-Up*, Carlo Ponti Prod., Premier Productions.

RICHARD BROOKS for *The Professionals*, Pax Enterprises Prod., Columbia.

CLAUDE LELOUCH for *A Man and a Woman*, Les Films 13 Prod., Allied Artists.

MIKE NICHOLS for *Who's Afraid of Virginia Woolf?*, Chenault Prod., Warner Bros.

★ FRED ZINNEMANN for *A Man for All Seasons*, Highland Films, Ltd. Prod., Columbia.

1967 Fortieth Year

RICHARD BROOKS for *In Cold Blood*, Pax Enterprises Prod., Columbia.

NORMAN JEWISON for *In the Heat of the Night*, Mirisch Corp. Prod., United Artists.

STANLEY KRAMER for *Guess Who's Coming to Dinner*, Columbia.

★ MIKE NICHOLS for *The Graduate*, Mike Nichols-Lawrence Turman Prod., Embassy.

ARTHUR PENN for *Bonnie and Clyde*, Tatira-Hiller Prod., Warner Bros.-Seven Arts.

1968 Forty-first Year

ANTHONY HARVEY for *The Lion in Winter*, Haworth Prods., Avco Embassy.

STANLEY KUBRICK for *2001: A Space Odyssey*, Polaris Prod., Metro-Goldwyn-Mayer.

GILLO PONTECORVO for *The Battle of Algiers*, Igor-Casbah Film Prod., Allied Artists.

★ CAROL REED for *Oliver!*, Romulus Films, Columbia.

FRANCO ZEFFIRELLI for *Romeo & Juliet*, B.H.E. Film-Verona Prod.-Dino De Laurentiis Cinematografica Prod., Paramount.

1969 Forty-second Year

COSTA-GAVRAS for *Z*, Reggane Films-O.N.C.I.C. Prod., Cinema V.

GEORGE ROY HILL for *Butch Cassidy*

and the Sundance Kid, George Roy Hill-Paul Monash Prod., 20th Century-Fox.

ARTHUR PENN for *Alice's Restaurant*, Florin Prod., United Artists.

SYDNEY POLLACK for *They Shoot Horses, Don't They?*, Chartoff-Winkler-Pollack Prod., ABC Pictures Presentation, Cinerama.

★ JOHN SCHLESINGER for *Midnight Cowboy*, Jerome Hellman-John Schlesinger Prod., United Artists.

1970 Forty-third Year

ROBERT ALTMAN for *MASH*, Aspen Prods., 20th Century-Fox.

FEDERICO FELLINI for *Fellini Satyricon*, Alberto Grimaldi Prod., United Artists.

ARTHUR HILLER for *Love Story*, The Love Story Company Prod., Paramount.

KEN RUSSELL for *Women in Love*, Larry Kramer-Martin Rosen Prod., United Artists.

★ FRANKLIN J. SCHAFFNER for *Patton*, 20th Century-Fox.

1971 Forty-fourth Year

PETER BOGDANOVICH for *The Last Picture Show*, BBS Prods., Columbia.

★ WILLIAM FRIEDKIN for *The French Connection*, A Philip D'Antoni Prod. in association with Schine-Moore Prods., 20th Century-Fox.

NORMAN JEWISON for *Fiddler on the Roof*, Mirisch-Cartier Prods., UA.

STANLEY KUBRICK for *A Clockwork Orange*, A Hawks Films, Ltd., Prod., Warner Bros.

JOHN SCHLESINGER for *Sunday Bloody Sunday*, A Joseph Janni Prod., UA.

1972 Forty-fifth Year

JOHN BOORMAN for *Deliverance*, Warner Bros.

FRANCIS FORD COPPOLA for *The Godfather*, An Albert S. Ruddy Production, Paramount.

★ BOB FOSSE for *Cabaret*, An ABC Pictures Production, Allied Artists.

JOSEPH L. MANKIEWICZ for *Sleuth*, A Palomar Pictures International Production, 20th Century-Fox.

JAN TROELL for *The Emigrants*, A Svensk Filmindustri Production, Warner Bros.

1973 Forty-sixth Year

INGMAR BERGMAN for *Cries and Whispers*, A Svenska Filminstitutet-Cinematograph AB Prod., New World Pictures.

BERNARDO BERTOLUCCI for *Last Tango in Paris*, A PEA Produzioni Europée Associate S.A.S.-Les Productions Artistes Associés S.A. Prod., UA.

WILLIAM FRIEDKIN for *The Exorcist*, Hoya Prods., Warner Bros.

★ GEORGE ROY HILL for *The Sting*, A Universal-Bill/Phillips-George Roy Hill Film Prod., Zanuck/Brown Presentation, Universal.

GEORGE LUCAS for *American Graffiti*, A Universal-Lucasfilm, Ltd.-Coppola Company Prod., Universal.

1974 Forty-seventh Year

JOHN CASSAVETES for *A Woman under the Influence*, A Faces International Films Prod.

★ FRANCIS FORD COPPOLA for *The Godfather Part II*, A Coppola Company Prod., Paramount.

BOB FOSSE for *Lenny*, A Marvin Worth Prod., United Artists.

ROMAN POLANSKI for *Chinatown*, A Robert Evans Prod., Paramount.

FRANCOIS TRUFFAUT for *Day for Night*, A Les Films Du Carrosse and P.E.C.F., Paris; P.I.C., Rome Prod., Warner Bros.

1975 Forty-eighth Year

ROBERT ALTMAN for *Nashville*, An ABC Entertainment-Jerry Weintraub-Robert Altman Production, Paramount.

FEDERICO FELLINI for *Amarcord*, An F.C. Productions-P.E.C.F. Production, New World Pictures.

★ MILOS FORMAN for *One Flew over the Cuckoo's Nest*, A Fantasy Films Production, United Artists.

STANLEY KUBRICK for *Barry Lyndon*, A Hawk Films, Ltd. Production, Warner Bros.

SIDNEY LUMET for *Dog Day Afternoon*, Warner Bros.

1976 Forty-ninth Year

★ JOHN G. AVILDSEN for *Rocky*, A Robert Chartoff-Irwin Winkler Production, United Artists.

INGMAR BERGMAN for *Face to Face*, A Cinematograph A.B. Production, Paramount.

SIDNEY LUMET for *Network*, A Howard Gottfried/Paddy Chayefsky Production, Metro-Goldwyn-Mayer/United Artists.

ALAN J. PAKULA for *All the President's Men*, A Wildwood Enterprises Production, Warner Bros.

LINA WERTMULLER for *Seven Beauties*, A Medusa Distribuzione Production, Cinema 5, Ltd.

1977 Fiftieth Year

★ WOODY ALLEN for *Annie Hall*, Jack Rollins/Charles H. Joffe Productions, United Artists.

GEORGE LUCAS for *Star Wars*, A Twentieth Century-Fox Production, 20th Century-Fox.

HERBERT ROSS for *The Turning Point*, Hera Productions, 20th Century-Fox.

STEVEN SPIELBERG for *Close Encounters of the Third Kind*, Close Encounter Productions, Columbia.

FRED ZINNEMAN for *Julia*, A Twentieth Century-Fox Production, 20th Century-Fox.

1978 Fifty-first Year

WOODY ALLEN for *Interiors*, A Jack Rollins-Charles H. Joffe Production, United Artists.

HAL ASHBY for *Coming Home*, A Jerome Hellman Enterprises Production, United Artists.

WARREN BEATTY and BUCK HENRY for *Heaven Can Wait*, Dogwood Productions, Paramount.

★ MICHAEL CIMINO for *The Deer Hunter*, An EMI Films/Michael Cimino Film Production, Universal.

ALAN PARKER for *Midnight Express*, A Casablanca-Filmworks Production, Columbia.

1979 Fifty-second Year

★ ROBERT BENTON for *Kramer vs. Kramer*, Stanley Jaffe Productions, Columbia.

FRANCIS COPPOLA for *Apocalypse Now*, An Omni Zoetrope Production, United Artists.

BOB FOSSE for *All That Jazz*, A Columbia/Twentieth Century-Fox Production, 20th Century-Fox.

EDOUARD MOLINARO for *La Cage aux Folles*, A Les Productions Artistes Associés De Ma Produzione SPA Production, United Artists.

PETER YATES for *Breaking Away*, A Twentieth Century-Fox Production, 20th Century-Fox.

1980 Fifty-third Year

DAVID LYNCH for *The Elephant Man*, A Brooksfilms, Ltd. Production, Paramount.

ROMAN POLANSKI for *Tess*, A Renn-Burrill Co-production with the participation of the Société Française de Production (S.F.P.), Columbia.

★ ROBERT REDFORD for *Ordinary*

People, A Wildwood Enterprises Production, Paramount.

RICHARD RUSH for *The Stunt Man*, Melvin Simon Productions, 20th Century-Fox.

MARTIN SCORSESE for *Raging Bull*, A Robert Chartoff-Irwin Winkler Production, United Artists.

1981 Fifty-fourth Year

★ WARREN BEATTY for *Reds*, A J.R.S. Production, Paramount.

HUGH HUDSON for *Chariots of Fire*, Enigma Productions Limited, The Ladd Company/Warner Bros.

LOUIS MALLE for *Atlantic City*, An International Cinema Corporation Production, Paramount.

MARK RYDELL for *On Golden Pond*, An ITC Films/IPC Films Production, Universal.

STEVEN SPIELBERG for *Raiders of the Lost Ark*, A Lucasfilm Production, Paramount.

1982 Fifty-fifth Year

★ RICHARD ATTENBOROUGH for *Gandhi*, An Indo-British Films Production, Columbia.

SIDNEY LUMET for *The Verdict*, A Fox-Zanuck/Brown Production, 20th Century-Fox.

WOLFGANG PETERSEN for *Das Boot*, A Bavaria Atelier GmbH Production, Columbia.

SYDNEY POLLACK for *Tootsie*, a Mirage/Punch Production, Columbia.

STEVEN SPIELBERG for *E.T. the Extra-Terrestrial*, A Universal Pictures Production, Universal.

1983 Fifty-sixth Year

BRUCE BERESFORD for *Tender Mercies*, An EMI Presentation of an Antron Media Production, Universal/AFD.

INGMAR BERGMAN for *Fanny and Alexander*, A Cinematograph AB for the Swedish Film Institute/the Swedish Television SVT 1, Sweden/Gaumont, France/Personafilm, and Tobias Filmkunst, BRD Production, Embassy.

★ JAMES L. BROOKS for *Terms of Endearment*, A James L. Brooks Production, Paramount.

MIKE NICHOLS for *Silkwood*, An ABC Motion Pictures Production, 20th Century-Fox.

PETER YATES for *The Dresser*, A Goldcrest Film/Television Limited/World Film Services Production, Columbia.

1984 Fifty-seventh Year

WOODY ALLEN for *Broadway Danny Rose*, A Jack Rollins and Charles H. Joffe Production, Orion.

ROBERT BENTON for *Places in the Heart*, A Tri-Star Pictures Production, Tri-Star.

★ MILOS FORMAN for *Amadeus*, A Saul Zaentz Company Production, Orion.

ROLAND JOFFE for *The Killing Fields*, A Goldcrest Films & Television/International Film Investors L.P. Production, Warner Bros.

DAVID LEAN for *A Passage To India*, A G. W. Films Limited Production, Columbia.

1985 Fifty-eighth Year

HECTOR BABENCO for *Kiss of the Spider Woman*, An H. B. Filmes Production in association with Sugarloaf Films, Island Alive.

JOHN HUSTON for *Prizzi's Honor*, An ABC Motion Pictures Production, 20th Century-Fox.

AKIRA KUROSAWA for *Ran*, A Greenwich Film/Nippon Herald Films/Herald Ace Production, Orion Classics.

★ SYDNEY POLLACK for *Out of Africa*, A Universal Pictures Limited Production, Universal.

PETER WEIR for *Witness*, An Edward S. Feldman Production, Paramount.

1986 Fifty-ninth Year

WOODY ALLEN for *Hannah and Her Sisters*, A Jack Rollins and Charles H. Joffe Production, Orion.

JAMES IVORY for *A Room with a View*, A Merchant Ivory Production, Cinecom.

ROLAND JOFFE for *The Mission*, A Warner Bros./Goldcrest and Kingsmere Production, Warner Bros.

DAVID LYNCH for *Blue Velvet*, A Blue Velvet S. A. Production, De Laurentiis Entertainment Group.

★ OLIVER STONE for *Platoon*, A Hemdale Film Production, Orion.

1987 Sixtieth Year

★ BERNARDO BERTOLUCCI for *The Last Emperor*, A Hemdale Film Production, Columbia.

JOHN BOORMAN for *Hope and Glory*, A Davros Production Services Limited Production, Columbia.

LASSE HALLSTROM for *My Life as a Dog*, A Svensk Filmindustri/ Filmteknik Production, Skouras Pictures.

NORMAN JEWISON for *Moonstruck*, A Patrick Palmer and Norman Jewison Production, M-G-M.

ADRIAN LYNE for *Fatal Attraction*, A Jaffe/Lansing Production, Paramount.

1988 Sixty-first year

CHARLES CRICHTON for *A Fish Called Wanda*, A Michael Shamberg-Prominent Features Production, M-G-M.

★ BARRY LEVINSON for *Rain Man*, A Guber-Peters Company Production, United Artists.

MIKE NICHOLS for *Working Girl*, A Twentieth Century-Fox Production, 20th Century-Fox.

ALAN PARKER for *Mississippi Burning*, A Frederick Zollo Production, Orion.

MARTIN SCORSESE for *The Last Temptation of Christ*, A Testament Production, Universal/Cineplex Odeon.

1989 Sixty-second Year

WOODY ALLEN for *Crimes and Misdemeanors*, A Jack Rollins and Charles H. Joffe Production, Orion.

KENNETH BRANAGH for *Henry V*, A Renaissance Films Production in association with BBC, Samuel Goldwyn Company.

JIM SHERIDAN for *My Left Foot*, A Ferndale Films Production, Miramax.

★ OLIVER STONE for *Born on the Fourth of July*, An A. Kitman Ho and Ixtlan Production, Universal.

PETER WEIR for *Dead Poets Society*, A Touchstone Pictures Production in association with Silver Screen Partners IV, Buena Vista.

1990 Sixty-third Year

FRANCIS FORD COPPOLA for *The Godfather, Part III*, A Zoetrope Studios Production, Paramount.

★ KEVIN COSTNER for *Dances With Wolves*, A Tig Production, Orion.

STEPHEN FREARS for *The Grifters*, A Martin Scorsese Production, Miramax.

BARBET SCHROEDER for *Reversal of Fortune*, A Reversal Films Production, Warner Bros.

MARTIN SCORSESE for *GoodFellas*, A Warner Bros. Production, Warner Bros.

1991 Sixty-fourth Year

★ JONATHAN DEMME for *The Silence of the Lambs*, A Strong Heart/Demme Production, Orion.

BARRY LEVINSON for *Bugsy* A Tri-Star Pictures Production, Tri-Star.

RIDLEY SCOTT for *Thelma & Louise*, A

Pathé Entertainment Production, M-G-M.

JOHN SINGLETON for *Boyz N the Hood*, A Columbia Pictures Production, Columbia.

OLIVER STONE for *JFK*, A Camelot Production, Warner Bros.

1992 Sixty-fifth Year

ROBERT ALTMAN for *The Player*, An Avenue Pictures Production, Fine Line.

MARTIN BREST for *Scent of a Woman*, A Universal Pictures Production, Universal.

★ CLINT EASTWOOD for *Unforgiven*, A Warner Bros. Production, Warner Bros.

JAMES IVORY for *Howards End*, A Merchant Ivory Production, Sony Pictures Classics.

NEIL JORDAN for *The Crying Game*, A Palace Pictures Production, Miramax.

Writing

Established as one of the original categories in 1927/28, the Writing awards have undergone considerable changes in the past fifty years. An award for Title Writing was added at the last minute in 1927/28, but the rapid demise of silent films rendered the job of the title writer obsolete, and the category was dropped after the first awards. A single Writing award was given the second and third years, but since 1930/31 at least two and for several years three awards have been made annually. The division of the category has usually depended upon whether a screenplay was original or adapted, and the wording of these divisions has changed frequently. The present rule allows two awards: Best Screenplay Written Directly for the Screen—based on factual material or on story material not previously published or produced—and Best Screenplay—based on material from another medium.

The Writing awards have been marked by occasional controversy. Dudley Nichols, embroiled in a dispute between the Academy and the Screen Writers' Guild, refused a 1935 Oscar for *The Informer*. Blacklisted writer Dalton Trumbo won a 1956 Oscar under the pseudonym Robert Rich, and the same year another blacklisted writer, Michael Wilson, a previous Oscar winner, was declared ineligible for political reasons. Two films with the same title caused further confusion in 1956. Both pictures were titled *High Society:* one was a Cole Porter musical from MGM, the other a low-budget Bowery Boys film from Allied Artists. Edward Bernds and Elwood Ullman, the writers of the Allied Artists film, asked that their names be withdrawn when it became apparent that members of the Writers branch and the Writers Guild had meant to nominate the other film. Even so, MGM's *High Society* would have been eligible not for an original but for an adapted screenplay.

Achievements in this category are nominated by members of the Academy Writers Branch.

1927/28 First Year

Adaptation

ALFRED COHN, *The Jazz Singer*, Warner Bros.

ANTHONY COLDEWAY, *Glorious Betsy*, Warner Bros.

★ BENJAMIN GLAZER, *7th Heaven*, Fox.

Original Story

LAJOS BIRO, *The Last Command*, Paramount Famous Lasky.

★ BEN HECHT, *Underworld*, Paramount Famous Lasky.

Title Writing (Not given after this year)

GERALD DUFFY, *The Private Life of Helen of Troy*, First National.

★ JOSEPH FARNHAM

GEORGE MARION, JR.

1928/29 Second Year

TOM BARRY, *The Valiant* and *In Old Arizona*, Fox.

ELLIOTT CLAWSON, *The Leatherneck*,

Ralph Block, Pathé; *Sal of Singapore*, Pathé; *Skyscraper* and *The Cop*, DeMille Pictures, Pathé.

★ HANS KRALY, *The Patriot*, Paramount Famous Lasky.*

HANS KRALY, *The Last of Mrs. Cheyney*, Metro-Goldwyn-Mayer.

JOSEPHINE LOVETT, *Our Dancing Daughters*, Cosmopolitan, Metro-Goldwyn-Mayer.

BESS MEREDYTH, *Wonder of Women* and *A Woman of Affairs*, Metro-Goldwyn-Mayer.

1929/30 Third Year†

ALL QUIET ON THE WESTERN FRONT, Universal (George Abbott, Maxwell Anderson, Del Andrews).

★ THE BIG HOUSE, Cosmopolitan, Metro-Goldwyn-Mayer, FRANCES MARION.

DISRAELI, Warner Bros. (Julian Josephson).

THE DIVORCEE, Metro-Goldwyn-Mayer (John Meehan).

STREET OF CHANCE, Paramount Famous Lasky (Howard Estabrook).

1930/31 Fourth Year

Adaptation

★ CIMARRON, RKO Radio: HOWARD ESTABROOK.

THE CRIMINAL CODE, Columbia: SETON MILLER and FRED NIBLO, JR.

HOLIDAY, Pathé: HORACE JACKSON.

LITTLE CAESAR, Warner Bros.: FRANCIS FARAGOH and ROBERT N. LEE.

SKIPPY, Paramount: Publix: JOSEPH MANKIEWICZ and SAM MINTZ.

Original Story

★ THE DAWN PATROL, Warner Bros.-First National: JOHN MONK SAUNDERS.

DOORWAY TO HELL, Warner Bros.-First National: ROWLAND BROWN.

LAUGHTER, Paramount Publix: HARRY D'ABBADIE D'ARRAST, DOUGLAS DOTY, and DONALD OGDEN STEWART.

THE PUBLIC ENEMY, Warner Bros. National: JOHN BRIGHT and KUBEC GLASMON.

SMART MONEY, Warner Bros.: LUCIEN HUBBARD and JOSEPH JACKSON.

1931/32 Fifth Year

Adaptation

ARROWSMITH, Goldwyn, UA: SIDNEY HOWARD.

★ BAD GIRL, Fox: EDWIN BURKE.

DR. JEKYLL AND MR. HYDE, Paramount Publix: PERCY HEATH and SAMUEL HOFFENSTEIN.

Original Story

★ THE CHAMP, Metro-Goldwyn-Mayer: FRANCES MARION.

LADY AND GENT, Paramount Publix: GROVER JONES and WILLIAM SLAVENS MCNUTT.

STAR WITNESS, Warner Bros.: LUCIEN HUBBARD.

WHAT PRICE HOLLYWOOD, RKO Radio: ADELA ROGERS ST. JOHN and JANE MURFIN.

1932/33 Sixth Year

Adaptation

LADY FOR A DAY, Columbia: ROBERT RISKIN.

★ LITTLE WOMEN, RKO Radio:

*Hans Kraly was nominated for more than one achievement, but his award specified only his work on *The Patriot*.

†Nominations this year were by film title, and only the individual associated with the winning film was announced. The people who worked on the other nominated films are listed parenthetically to indicate that they received no official public nomination.

VICTOR HEERMAN and SARAH Y. MASON.

STATE FAIR, Fox: PAUL GREEN and SONYA LEVIEN.

Original Story

★ ONE WAY PASSAGE, Warner Bros.: ROBERT LORD.

THE PRIZEFIGHTER AND THE LADY, Metro-Goldwyn-Mayer: FRANCES MARION.

RASPUTIN AND THE EMPRESS, Metro-Goldwyn-Mayer: CHARLES MACARTHUR.

1934 Seventh Year

Adaptation

★ IT HAPPENED ONE NIGHT, Columbia: ROBERT RISKIN.

THE THIN MAN, Metro-Goldwyn-Mayer: FRANCES GOODRICH and ALBERT HACKETT.

VIVA VILLA, Metro-Goldwyn-Mayer: BEN HECHT.

Original Story

HIDE-OUT, Metro-Goldwyn-Mayer: MAURI GRASHIN.

★ MANHATTAN MELODRAMA, Metro-Goldwyn-Mayer: ARTHUR CAESAR.

THE RICHEST GIRL IN THE WORLD, RKO Radio: NORMAN KRASNA.

1935 Eighth Year

Original Story

BROADWAY MELODY OF 1936, Metro-Goldwyn-Mayer: MOSS HART.

THE GAY DECEPTION, Lasky, Fox: DON HARTMAN and STEPHEN AVERY.

★ THE SCOUNDREL, Paramount: BEN HECHT and CHARLES MACARTHUR.

Screenplay

★ THE INFORMER, RKO Radio: DUDLEY NICHOLS.

LIVES OF A BENGAL LANCER, Paramount: ACHMED ABDULLAH, JOHN L. BALDERSTON, GROVER JONES, WILLIAM SLAVENS MCNUTT, and WALDEMAR YOUNG.

MUTINY ON THE BOUNTY, Metro-Goldwyn-Mayer: JULES FURTHMAN, TALBOT JENNINGS, and CAREY WILSON.

1936 Ninth Year

Original Story

FURY, Metro-Goldwyn-Mayer: NORMAN KRASNA.

THE GREAT ZIEGFELD, Metro-Goldwyn-Mayer: WILLIAM ANTHONY MCGUIRE.

SAN FRANCISCO, Metro-Goldwyn-Mayer: ROBERT HOPKINS.

★ THE STORY OF LOUIS PASTEUR, Warner Bros.: PIERRE COLLINGS and SHERIDAN GIBNEY.

THREE SMART GIRLS, Universal: ADELE COMMANDINI.

Screenplay

AFTER THE THIN MAN, Metro-Goldwyn-Mayer: FRANCES GOODRICH and ALBERT HACKETT.

DODSWORTH, Goldwyn, UA: SIDNEY HOWARD.

MR. DEEDS GOES TO TOWN, Columbia: ROBERT RISKIN.

MY MAN GODFREY, Universal: ERIC HATCH and MORRIS RYSKIND.

★ THE STORY OF LOUIS PASTEUR, Warner Bros.: PIERRE COLLINGS and SHERIDAN GIBNEY.

1937 Tenth Year

Original Story

BLACK LEGION, Warner Bros.: ROBERT LORD.

IN OLD CHICAGO, 20th Century-Fox: NIVEN BUSCH.

THE LIFE OF EMILE ZOLA, Warner Bros.: HEINZ HERALD, and GEZA HERCZEG.

100 MEN AND A GIRL, Universal: HANS KRALY.

★ A STAR IS BORN, Selznick, UA: WILLIAM A. WELLMAN and ROBERT CARSON.

Screenplay

THE AWFUL TRUTH, Columbia: VIÑA DELMAR.

CAPTAINS COURAGEOUS, Metro-Goldwyn-Mayer: MARC CONNOLLY, JOHN LEE MAHIN, and DALE VAN EVERY.

★ THE LIFE OF EMILE ZOLA, Warner Bros.: HEINZ HERALD, GEZA HERCZEG, and NORMAN REILLY RAINE.

STAGE DOOR, RKO Radio: MORRIS RYSKIND and ANTHONY VEILLER.

A STAR IS BORN, Selznick, UA: ALAN CAMPBELL, ROBERT CARSON, and DOROTHY PARKER.

1938 Eleventh Year

Original Story

ALEXANDER'S RAGTIME BAND, 20th Century-Fox: IRVING BERLIN.

ANGELS WITH DIRTY FACES, Warner Bros.: ROWLAND BROWN.

BLOCKADE, Wanger, UA: JOHN HOWARD LAWSON.

★ BOYS TOWN, Metro-Goldwyn-Mayer: ELEANORE GRIFFIN and DORE SCHARY.

MAD ABOUT MUSIC, Universal: MARCELLA BURKE and FREDERICK KOHNER.

TEST PILOT, Metro-Goldwyn-Mayer: FRANK WEAD.

Screenplay

BOYS TOWN, Metro-Goldwyn-Mayer: JOHN MEEHAN and DORE SCHARY.

THE CITADEL, Metro-Goldwyn-Mayer (British): IAN DALRYMPLE, ELIZABETH HILL, and FRANK WEAD.

FOUR DAUGHTERS, Warner Bros.: LENORE COFFEE and JULIUS J. EPSTEIN.

★ PYGMALION, Metro-Goldwyn-Mayer (British): GEORGE BERNARD SHAW, Adaptation by IAN DALRYMPLE, CECIL LEWIS, and W. P. LIPSCOMB.

YOU CAN'T TAKE IT WITH YOU, Columbia: ROBERT RISKIN.

1939 Twelfth Year

Original Story

BACHELOR MOTHER, RKO Radio: FELIX JACKSON.

LOVE AFFAIR, RKO Radio: MILDRED CRAM and LEO MCCAREY.

★ MR. SMITH GOES TO WASHINGTON, Columbia: LEWIS R. FOSTER.

NINOTCHKA, Metro-Goldwyn-Mayer: MELCHIOR LENGYEL.

YOUNG MR. LINCOLN, 20th Century-Fox: LAMAR TROTTI.

Screenplay

★ GONE WITH THE WIND, Selznick, M-G-M: SIDNEY HOWARD.

GOODBYE, MR. CHIPS, Metro-Goldwyn-Mayer (British): ERIC MASCHWITZ, R. C. SHERRIFF, and CLAUDINE WEST.

MR. SMITH GOES TO WASHINGTON, Columbia: SIDNEY BUCHMAN.

NINOTCHKA, Metro-Goldwyn-Mayer: CHARLES BRACKETT, WALTER REISCH, and BILLY WILDER.

WUTHERING HEIGHTS, Goldwyn, UA: BEN HECHT and CHARLES MACARTHUR.

1940 Thirteenth Year

Original Story

★ ARISE, MY LOVE, Paramount: BENJAMIN GLAZER and JOHN S. TOLDY.

COMRADE X, Metro-Goldwyn-Mayer: WALTER REISCH.

EDISON THE MAN, Metro-Goldwyn-

Mayer: HUGO BUTLER and DORE SCHARY.

MY FAVORITE WIFE, RKO Radio: LEO MCCAREY, BELLA SPEWACK, and SAMUEL SPEWACK.

THE WESTERNER, Goldwyn, UA: STUART N. LAKE.

Original Screenplay

ANGELS OVER BROADWAY, Columbia: BEN HECHT.

DR. EHRLICH'S MAGIC BULLET, Warner Bros.: NORMAN BURNSIDE, HEINZ HERALD, and JOHN HUSTON.

FOREIGN CORRESPONDENT, Wanger, UA: CHARLES BENNETT and JOAN HARRISON.

THE GREAT DICTATOR, Chaplin, UA: CHARLES CHAPLIN.

★ THE GREAT McGINTY, Paramount: PRESTON STURGES.

Screenplay

THE GRAPES OF WRATH, 20th Century-Fox: NUNNALLY JOHNSON.

KITTY FOYLE, RKO Radio: DALTON TRUMBO.

THE LONG VOYAGE HOME, Argosy-Wanger, UA: DUDLEY NICHOLS.

★ THE PHILADELPHIA STORY, Metro-Goldwyn-Mayer: DONALD OGDEN STEWART.

REBECCA, Selznick, UA: ROBERT E. SHERWOOD and JOAN HARRISON.

1941 Fourteenth Year

Original Story

BALL OF FIRE, Goldwyn, RKO Radio: THOMAS MONROE and BILLY WILDER.

★ HERE COMES MR. JORDAN, Columbia: HARRY SEGALL.

THE LADY EVE, Paramount: MONCKTON HOFFE.

MEET JOHN DOE, Warner Bros.: RICHARD CONNELL and ROBERT PRESNELL.

NIGHT TRAIN, 20th Century-Fox: GORDON WELLESLEY.

Original Screenplay

★ CITIZEN KANE, Mercury, RKO Radio: HERMAN J. MANKIEWICZ and ORSON WELLES.

THE DEVIL AND MISS JONES, RKO Radio: NORMAN KRASNA.

SERGEANT YORK, Warner Bros: HARRY CHANDLEE, ABEM FINKEL, JOHN HUSTON, and HOWARD KOCH.

TALL, DARK AND HANDSOME, 20th Century-Fox: KARL TUNBERG and DARRELL WARE.

TOM, DICK AND HARRY, RKO Radio: PAUL JARRICO.

Screenplay

★ HERE COMES MR. JORDAN, Columbia: SIDNEY BUCHMAN and SETON I. MILLER.

HOLD BACK THE DAWN, Paramount: CHARLES BRACKETT and BILLY WILDER.

HOW GREEN WAS MY VALLEY, 20th Century-Fox: PHILIP DUNNE.

THE LITTLE FOXES, Goldwyn, RKO Radio: LILLIAN HELLMAN.

THE MALTESE FALCON, Warner Bros: JOHN HUSTON.

1942 Fifteenth Year

Original Story

HOLIDAY INN, Paramount: IRVING BERLIN.

★ THE INVADERS, Ortus, Columbia (British): EMERIC PRESSBURGER.

THE PRIDE OF THE YANKEES, Goldwyn, RKO Radio: PAUL GALLICO.

THE TALK OF THE TOWN, Columbia: SIDNEY HARMON.

YANKEE DOODLE DANDY, Warner Bros: ROBERT BUCKNER.

Original Screenplay

ONE OF OUR AIRCRAFT IS MISSING, Powell, UA (British): MICHAEL POWELL and EMERIC PRESSBURGER.

THE ROAD TO MOROCCO, Paramount: FRANK BUTLER and DON HARTMAN.

WAKE ISLAND, Paramount: W. R. BURNETT and FRANK BUTLER.

THE WAR AGAINST MRS. HADLEY, Metro-Goldwyn-Mayer: GEORGE OPPENHEIMER.

★ WOMAN OF THE YEAR, Metro-Goldwyn-Mayer: MICHAEL KANIN and RING LARDNER, JR.

Screenplay

THE INVADERS, Ortus, Columbia (British): RODNEY ACKLAND and EMERIC PRESSBURGER.

★ MRS. MINIVER, Metro-Goldwyn-Mayer: GEORGE FROESCHEL, JAMES HILTON, CLAUDINE WEST, and ARTHUR WIMPERIS.

THE PRIDE OF THE YANKEES, Goldwyn, RKO Radio: HERMAN J. MANKIEWICZ and JO SWERLING.

RANDOM HARVEST, Metro-Goldwyn-Mayer: GEORGE FROESCHEL, CLAUDINE WEST, and ARTHUR WIMPERIS.

THE TALK OF THE TOWN, Columbia: SIDNEY BUCHMAN and IRWIN SHAW.

1943 Sixteenth Year

Original Story

ACTION IN THE NORTH ATLANTIC, Warner Bros: GUY GILPATRIC.

DESTINATION TOKYO, Warner Bros: STEVE FISHER.

★ THE HUMAN COMEDY, Metro-Goldwyn-Mayer: WILLIAM SAROYAN.

THE MORE THE MERRIER, Columbia: FRANK ROSS and ROBERT RUSSELL.

SHADOW OF A DOUBT, Universal: GORDON MCDONNELL.

Original Screenplay

AIR FORCE, Warner Bros: DUDLEY NICHOLS.

IN WHICH WE SERVE, Two Cities, UA (British): NOEL COWARD.

THE NORTH STAR, Goldwyn, RKO Radio: LILLIAN HELLMAN.

★ PRINCESS O'ROURKE, Warner Bros: NORMAN KRASNA.

SO PROUDLY WE HAIL, Paramount: ALLAN SCOTT.

Screenplay

★ CASABLANCA, Warner Bros: JULIUS J. EPSTEIN, PHILIP G. EPSTEIN, and HOWARD KOCH.

HOLY MATRIMONY, 20th Century-Fox: NUNNALLY JOHNSON.

THE MORE THE MERRIER, Columbia: RICHARD FLOURNOY, LEWIS R. FOSTER, FRANK ROSS, and ROBERT RUSSELL.

THE SONG OF BERNADETTE, 20th Century-Fox: GEORGE SEATON.

WATCH ON THE RHINE, Warner Bros.: DASHIELL HAMMETT.

1944 Seventeenth Year

Original Story

★ GOING MY WAY, Paramount: LEO McCAREY.

A GUY NAMED JOE, Metro-Goldwyn-Mayer: DAVID BOEHM and CHANDLER SPRAGUE.

LIFEBOAT, 20th Century-Fox: JOHN STEINBECK.

NONE SHALL ESCAPE, Columbia: ALFRED NEUMANN and JOSEPH THAN.

THE SULLIVANS, 20th Century-Fox: EDWARD DOHERTY and JULES SCHERMER.

Original Screenplay

HAIL THE CONQUERING HERO, Paramount: PRESTON STURGES.

THE MIRACLE OF MORGAN'S CREEK, Paramount: PRESTON STURGES.

TWO GIRLS AND A SAILOR, Metro-Goldwyn-Mayer: RICHARD CONNELL and GLADYS LEHMAN.

★ WILSON, 20th Century-Fox: LAMAR TROTTI.

WING AND A PRAYER, 20th Century-Fox: JEROME CADY.

Screenplay

DOUBLE INDEMNITY, Paramount: RAYMOND CHANDLER and BILLY WILDER.

GASLIGHT, Metro-Goldwyn-Mayer: JOHN L. BALDERSTON, WALTER REISCH, and JOHN VAN DRUTEN.

★ GOING MY WAY, Paramount: FRANK BUTLER and FRANK CAVETT.

LAURA, 20th Century-Fox: JAY DRATLER, SAMUEL HOFFENSTEIN, and BETTY REINHARDT.

MEET ME IN ST. LOUIS, Metro-Goldwyn-Mayer: IRVING BRECHER and FRED F. FINKELHOFFE.

1945 Eighteenth Year

Original Story

THE AFFAIRS OF SUSAN, Wallis, Paramount: LASZLO GOROG and THOMAS MONROE.

★ THE HOUSE ON 92ND STREET, 20th Century-Fox: CHARLES G. BOOTH.

A MEDAL FOR BENNY, Paramount: JOHN STEINBECK and JACK WAGNER.

OBJECTIVE-BURMA, Warner Bros: ALVAH BESSIE.

A SONG TO REMEMBER, Columbia: ERNST MARISCHKA.

Original Screenplay

DILLINGER, Monogram: PHILIP YORDAN.

★ MARIE-LOUISE, Praesens Films (Swiss): RICHARD SCHWEIZER.

MUSIC FOR MILLIONS, Metro-Goldwyn-Mayer: MYLES CONNOLLY.

SALTY O'ROURKE, Paramount: MILTON HOLMES.

WHAT NEXT, CORPORAL HARGROVE?, Metro-Goldwyn-Mayer: HARRY KURNITZ.

Screenplay

G. I. JOE, Cowan, UA: LEOPOLD ATLAS, GUY ENDORE, and PHILIP STEVENSON.

★ THE LOST WEEKEND, Paramount: CHARLES BRACKETT and BILLY WILDER.

MILDRED PIERCE, Warner Bros: RANALD MACDOUGALL.

PRIDE OF THE MARINES, Warner Bros: ALBERT MALTZ.

A TREE GROWS IN BROOKLYN, 20th Century-Fox: FRANK DAVIS and TESS SLESINGER.

1946 Nineteenth Year

Original Story

THE DARK MIRROR, Universal-International: VLADIMIR POZNER.

THE STRANGE LOVE OF MARTHA IVERS, Wallis, Paramount: JACK PATRICK.

THE STRANGER, International, RKO Radio: VICTOR TRIVAS.

TO EACH HIS OWN, Paramount: CHARLES BRACKETT.

★ VACATION FROM MARRIAGE, London Films, M-G-M (British): CLEMENCE DANE.

Original Screenplay

THE BLUE DAHLIA, Paramount: RAYMOND CHANDLER.

CHILDREN OF PARADISE, Pathé-Cinema, Tricolore (French): JACQUES PREVERT.

NOTORIOUS, RKO Radio: BEN HECHT.

THE ROAD TO UTOPIA, Paramount: NORMAN PANAMA and MELVIN FRANK.

★ THE SEVENTH VEIL, Rank, Universal (British): MURIEL BOX and SYDNEY BOX.

Screenplay

ANNA AND THE KING OF SIAM, 20th Century-Fox: SALLY BENSON and TALBOT JENNINGS.

★ THE BEST YEARS OF OUR LIVES, Goldwyn, RKO Radio: ROBERT E. SHERWOOD.

BRIEF ENCOUNTER, Rank, U-I (British): ANTHONY HAVELOCK-ALLAN, DAVID LEAN, and RONALD NEAME.

THE KILLERS, Hellinger, U-I: ANTHONY VEILLER.
OPEN CITY, Minerva Films (Italian): SERGIO AMIDEI and F. FELLINI.

1947 Twentieth Year

Original Story

A CAGE OF NIGHTINGALES, Gaumont, Lopert Films (French): GEORGES CHAPEROT and RENE WHEELER.
IT HAPPENED ON FIFTH AVENUE, Roy Del Ruth, Allied Artists: HERBERT CLYDE LEWIS and FREDERICK STEPHANI.
KISS OF DEATH, 20th Century-Fox: ELEAZAR LIPSKY.
★ MIRACLE ON 34TH STREET, 20th Century-Fox: VALENTINE DAVIES.
SMASH-UP—THE STORY OF A WOMAN, Wanger, U-I: DOROTHY PARKER and FRANK CAVETT.

Original Screenplay

★ THE BACHELOR AND THE BOBBY-SOXER, RKO Radio: SIDNEY SHELDON.
BODY AND SOUL, Enterprise, UA: ABRAHAM POLONSKY.
A DOUBLE LIFE, Kanin Prod., U-I: RUTH GORDON and GARSON KANIN.
MONSIEUR VERDOUX, Chaplin, UA: CHARLES CHAPLIN.
SHOE-SHINE, Lopert Films (Italian): SERGIO AMIDEI, ADOLFO FRANCI, C. G. VIOLA, and CESARE ZAVATTINI.

Screenplay

BOOMERANG!, 20th Century-Fox: RICHARD MURPHY.
CROSSFIRE, RKO Radio: JOHN PAXTON.
GENTLEMAN'S AGREEMENT, 20th Century-Fox: MOSS HART.
GREAT EXPECTATIONS, Rank-Cineguild, U-I (British): DAVID LEAN, RONALD NEAME, and ANTHONY HAVELOCK-ALLAN.
★ MIRACLE ON 34TH STREET, 20th Century-Fox: GEORGE SEATON.

1948 Twenty-first Year

Motion Picture Story

THE LOUISIANA STORY, Robert Flaherty, Lopert: FRANCES FLAHERTY and ROBERT FLAHERTY.
THE NAKED CITY, Hellinger, U-I: MALVIN WALD.
RED RIVER, Monterey Productions, UA: BORDEN CHASE.
THE RED SHOES, Rank-Archers, Eagle-Lion (British): EMERIC PRESSBURGER.
★ THE SEARCH, Praesens Films, M-G-M (Swiss): RICHARD SCHWEIZER and DAVID WECHSLER.

Screenplay

A FOREIGN AFFAIR, Paramount: CHARLES BRACKETT, BILLY WILDER, and RICHARD L. BREEN.
JOHNNY BELINDA, Warner Bros.: IRMGARD VON CUBE and ALLEN VINCENT.
THE SEARCH, Praesens Films, M-G-M (Swiss): RICHARD SCHWEIZER and DAVID WECHSLER.
THE SNAKE PIT, 20th Century-Fox: FRANK PARTOS and MILLEN BRAND.
★ TREASURE OF SIERRA MADRE, Warner Bros.: JOHN HUSTON.

1949 Twenty-second Year

Motion Picture Story

COME TO THE STABLE, 20th Century-Fox: CLARE BOOTHE LUCE.
IT HAPPENS EVERY SPRING, 20th Century-Fox: SHIRLEY W. SMITH and VALENTINE DAVIES.
SANDS OF IWO JIMA, Republic: HARRY BROWN.
★ THE STRATTON STORY, Metro-Goldwyn-Mayer: DOUGLAS MORROW.

WHITE HEAT, Warner Bros.: VIRGINIA KELLOGG.

Screenplay

ALL THE KING'S MEN, a Robert Rossen Prod., Columbia: ROBERT ROSSEN.

THE BICYCLE THIEF, De Sica, Mayer-Burstyn (Italian): CESARE ZAVATTINI.

CHAMPION, Screen Plays Corp., UA: CARL FOREMAN.

THE FALLEN IDOL, London Films, SRO (British): GRAHAM GREENE.

★ A LETTER TO THREE WIVES, 20th Century-Fox: JOSEPH L. MANKIEWICZ.

Story and Screenplay

★ BATTLEGROUND, Metro-Goldwyn-Mayer: ROBERT PIROSH.

JOLSON SINGS AGAIN, Columbia: SIDNEY BUCHMAN.

PAISAN, Roberto Rossellini, Mayer-Burstyn (Italian): ALFRED HAYES, FEDERICO FELLINI, SERGIO AMIDEI, MARCELLO PAGLIERO, and ROBERTO ROSSELLINI.

PASSPORT TO PIMLICO, Rank-Ealing, Eagle-Lion (British): T.E.B. CLARKE.

THE QUIET ONE, Film Documents, Mayer-Burstyn: HELEN LEVITT, JANICE LOEB, and SIDNEY MEYERS.

1950 Twenty-third Year

Motion Picture Story

BITTER RICE, Lux Films (Italian): GIUSEPPE DE SANTIS and CARLO LIZZANI.

THE GUNFIGHTER, 20th Century-Fox: WILLIAM BOWERS and ANDRE DE TOTH.

MYSTERY STREET, Metro-Goldwyn-Mayer: LEONARD SPIGELGASS.

★ PANIC IN THE STREETS, 20th Century-Fox: EDNA ANHALT and EDWARD ANHALT.

WHEN WILLIE COMES MARCHING HOME, 20th Century-Fox: SY GOMBERG.

Screenplay

★ ALL ABOUT EVE, 20th Century-Fox: JOSEPH L. MANKIEWICZ.

THE ASPHALT JUNGLE, Metro-Goldwyn-Mayer: BEN MADDOW and JOHN HUSTON.

BORN YESTERDAY, Columbia: ALBERT MANNHEIMER.

BROKEN ARROW, 20th Century-Fox: MICHAEL BLANKFORT*.

FATHER OF THE BRIDE, Metro-Goldwyn-Mayer: FRANCES GOODRICH and ALBERT HACKETT.

Story and Screenplay

ADAM'S RIB, Metro-Goldwyn-Mayer: RUTH GORDON and GARSON KANIN.

CAGED, Warner Bros: VIRGINIA KELLOGG and BERNARD C. SCHOENFELD.

THE MEN, Kramer, UA: CARL FOREMAN.

NO WAY OUT, 20th Century-Fox: JOSEPH L. MANKIEWICZ and LESSER SAMUELS.

★ SUNSET BOULEVARD, Paramount: CHARLES BRACKETT, BILLY WILDER, and D. M. MARSHMAN, JR.

1951 Twenty-fourth Year

Motion Picture Story

BULLFIGHTER AND THE LADY, Republic: BUDD BOETTICHER and RAY NAZARRO.

THE FROGMEN, 20th Century-Fox: OSCAR MILLARD.

HERE COMES THE GROOM, Paramount: ROBERT RISKIN and LIAM O'BRIEN.

★ SEVEN DAYS TO NOON, Boulting

*The Writers Guild of America West now credits blacklisted writer Albert Maltz with the screenplay for *Broken Arrow*. Michael Blankfort, who fronted for Maltz, received the nomination at the time and continues to be listed as the official nominee.

Bros., Mayer-Kingsley-Distinguished Films (British): PAUL DEHN and JAMES BERNARD.

TERESA, Metro-Goldwyn-Mayer: ALFRED HAYES and STEWART STERN.

Screenplay

THE AFRICAN QUEEN, Horizon, UA: JAMES AGEE and JOHN HUSTON.

DETECTIVE STORY, Paramount: PHILIP YORDAN and ROBERT WYLER.

LA RONDE, Sacha Gordine, Commercial Pictures (French): JACQUES NATANSON and MAX OPHULS.

★ A PLACE IN THE SUN, Paramount: MICHAEL WILSON and HARRY BROWN.

A STREETCAR NAMED DESIRE, Charles K. Feldman Group Prods., Warner Bros: TENNESSEE WILLIAMS.

Story and Screenplay

★ AN AMERICAN IN PARIS, Metro-Goldwyn-Mayer: ALAN JAY LERNER.

THE BIG CARNIVAL, Paramount: BILLY WILDER, LESSER SAMUELS, and WALTER NEWMAN.

DAVID AND BATHSHEBA, 20th Century-Fox: PHILIP DUNNE.

GO FOR BROKE!, Metro-Goldwyn-Mayer: ROBERT PIROSH.

THE WELL, Popkin, UA: CLARENCE GREENE and RUSSELL ROUSE.

1952 Twenty-fifth Year

Motion Picture Story

★ THE GREATEST SHOW ON EARTH, DeMille, Paramount: FREDERIC M. FRANK, THEODORE ST. JOHN, and FRANK CAVETT.

MY SON JOHN, Rainbow, Paramount: LEO MCCAREY.

THE NARROW MARGIN, RKO Radio: MARTIN GOLDSMITH and JACK LEONARD.

THE PRIDE OF ST. LOUIS, 20th Century-Fox: GUY TROSPER.

THE SNIPER, Kramer, Columbia: EDNA ANHALT and EDWARD ANHALT.

Screenplay

★ THE BAD AND THE BEAUTIFUL, Metro-Goldwyn-Mayer: CHARLES SCHNEE.

FIVE FINGERS, 20th Century-Fox: MICHAEL WILSON.

HIGH NOON, Kramer, UA: CARL FOREMAN.

THE MAN IN THE WHITE SUIT, Rank-Ealing, U-I (British): ROGER MACDOUGALL, JOHN DIGHTON, and ALEXANDER MACKENDRICK.

THE QUIET MAN, Argosy, Republic: FRANK S. NUGENT.

Story and Screenplay

THE ATOMIC CITY, Paramount: SYDNEY BOEHM.

BREAKING THE SOUND BARRIER, London Films, UA (British): TERENCE RATTIGAN.

★ THE LAVENDER HILL MOB, Rank-Ealing, U-I (British): T.E.B. CLARKE.

PAT AND MIKE, Metro-Goldwyn-Mayer: RUTH GORDON and GARSON KANIN.

VIVA ZAPATA!, 20th Century-Fox: JOHN STEINBECK.

1953 Twenty-sixth Year

Motion Picture Story

ABOVE AND BEYOND, Metro-Goldwyn-Mayer: BEIRNE LAY, JR..

THE CAPTAIN'S PARADISE, London Films, Lopert-UA (British): ALEC COPPEL.

LITTLE FUGITIVE, Little Fugitive Prod. Co., Joseph Burstyn, Inc.: RAY ASHLEY, MORRIS ENGEL, and RUTH ORKIN.

★ ROMAN HOLIDAY, Paramount: IAN MCLELLAN HUNTER.*

Screenplay

THE CRUEL SEA, Rank-Ealing, U-I (British): ERIC AMBLER.

★ FROM HERE TO ETERNITY, Columbia: DANIEL TARADASH.

LILI, Metro-Goldwyn-Mayer: HELEN DEUTSCH.

ROMAN HOLIDAY, Paramount: IAN MCLELLAN HUNTER and JOHN DIGHTON.

SHANE, Paramount: A. B. GUTHRIE, JR.

Story and Screenplay

THE BAND WAGON, Metro-Goldwyn-Mayer: BETTY COMDEN and ADOLPH GREEN.

THE DESERT RATS, 20th Century-Fox: RICHARD MURPHY.

THE NAKED SPUR, Metro-Goldwyn-Mayer: SAM ROLFE and HAROLD JACK BLOOM.

TAKE THE HIGH GROUND, Metro-Goldwyn-Mayer: MILLARD KAUFMAN.

★ TITANIC, 20th Century-Fox: CHARLES BRACKETT, WALTER REISCH, and RICHARD BREEN.

1954 Twenty-seventh Year

Motion Picture Story

BREAD, LOVE AND DREAMS, Titanus, I.F.E. Releasing Corp. (Italian): ETTORE MARGADONNA.

★ BROKEN LANCE, 20th Century-Fox: PHILIP YORDAN.

FORBIDDEN GAMES, Silver Films, Times Film Corp. (French): FRANÇOIS BOYER.

NIGHT PEOPLE, 20th Century-Fox: JED HARRIS and TOM REED.

THERE'S NO BUSINESS LIKE SHOW BUSINESS, 20th Century-Fox: LAMAR TROTTI.

Screenplay

THE CAINE MUTINY, A Stanley Kramer Prod., Columbia: STANLEY ROBERTS.

★ THE COUNTRY GIRL, Perlberg-Seaton, Paramount: GEORGE SEATON.

REAR WINDOW, Patron Inc., Paramount: JOHN MICHAEL HAYES.

SABRINA, Paramount: BILLY WILDER, SAMUEL TAYLOR, and ERNEST LEHMAN.

SEVEN BRIDES FOR SEVEN BROTHERS, Metro-Goldwyn-Mayer: ALBERT HACKETT, FRANCES GOODRICH, and DOROTHY KINGSLEY.

Story and Screenplay

THE BAREFOOT CONTESSA, A Figaro, Inc., Prod. UA: JOSEPH MANKIEWICZ.

GENEVIEVE, A J. Arthur Rank Presentation-Sirius Prods., Ltd., U-I (British): WILLIAM ROSE.

THE GLENN MILLER STORY, Universal-International: VALENTINE DAVIES and OSCAR BRODNEY.

KNOCK ON WOOD, Dena Prods., Paramount: NORMAN PANAMA and MELVIN FRANK.

★ ON THE WATERFRONT, Horizon-American Corp., Columbia: BUDD SCHULBERG.

1955 Twenty-eighth Year

Motion Picture Story

★ LOVE ME OR LEAVE ME, Metro-Goldwyn-Mayer: DANIEL FUCHS.

THE PRIVATE WAR OF MAJOR BENSON, U-I: JOE CONNELLY and BOB MOSHER.

REBEL WITHOUT A CAUSE, Warner Bros.: NICHOLAS RAY.

THE SHEEP HAS 5 LEGS, Raoul Ploquin, United Motion Picture Organization (French): JEAN MARSAN, HENRY

*The Writers Guild of America West now credits blacklisted writer Dalton Trumbo with the story for *Roman Holiday*. The Oscar was awarded to Ian McLellan Hunter, who acted as a front for Trumbo.

TROYAT, JACQUES PERRET, HENRI VERNEUIL, and RAOUL PLOQUIN.

STRATEGIC AIR COMMAND, Paramount: BEIRNE LAY, JR.

Screenplay

BAD DAY AT BLACK ROCK, Metro-Goldwyn-Mayer: MILLARD KAUFMAN.

BLACKBOARD JUNGLE, Metro-Goldwyn-Mayer: RICHARD BROOKS.

EAST OF EDEN, Warner Bros.: PAUL OSBORN.

LOVE ME OR LEAVE ME, Metro-Goldwyn-Mayer: DANIEL FUCHS and ISOBEL LENNART.

★ MARTY, Hecht and Lancaster's Steven Prods., UA: PADDY CHAYEFSKY.

Story and Screenplay

THE COURT-MARTIAL OF BILLY MITCHELL, A United States Pictures Prod., Warner Bros.: MILTON SPERLING and EMMET LAVERY.

★ INTERRUPTED MELODY, Metro-Goldwyn-Mayer: WILLIAM LUDWIG and SONYA LEVIEN.

IT'S ALWAYS FAIR WEATHER, Metro-Goldwyn-Mayer: BETTY COMDEN and ADOLPH GREEN.

MR. HULOT'S HOLIDAY, Fred Orain Prod., GBD International Releasing Corp. (French): JACQUES TATI and HENRI MARQUET.

THE SEVEN LITTLE FOYS, Hope Enterprises, Inc., and Scribe Prods.: MELVILLE SHAVELSON and JACK ROSE.

1956 Twenty-ninth Year

Motion Picture Story

★ THE BRAVE ONE, King Bros. Prods., Inc., RKO Radio: ROBERT RICH (pseudonym for DALTON TRUMBO).*

THE EDDY DUCHIN STORY, Columbia: LEO KATCHER.

HIGH SOCIETY, Allied Artists: EDWARD BERNDS and ELWOOD ULLMAN (withdrawn from final ballot).

THE PROUD AND THE BEAUTIFUL, La Compagnie Industrielle Commerciale Cinematographique, Kingsley International (French): JEAN-PAUL SARTRE.

UMBERTO D., Rizzoli-De Sica-Amato Prod. Harrison and Davidson (Italian): CESARE ZAVATTINI.

Best Screenplay—adapted

★ AROUND THE WORLD IN 80 DAYS, The Michael Todd Co., Inc., UA: JAMES POE, JOHN FARROW, and S. J. PERELMAN.

BABY DOLL, A Newtown Prod., Warner Bros.: TENNESSEE WILLIAMS.

FRIENDLY PERSUASION, Allied Artists: (Writer MICHAEL WILSON ineligible for nomination under Academy bylaws.)

GIANT, Giant Prod., Warner Bros.: FRED GUIOL and IVAN MOFFAT.

LUST FOR LIFE, Metro-Goldwyn-Mayer: NORMAN CORWIN.

Best Screenplay—original

THE BOLD AND THE BRAVE, Filmakers Releasing Organization, RKO Radio: ROBERT LEWIN.

JULIE, Arwin Prods., M-G-M: ANDREW L. STONE.

LA STRADA, Ponti-De Laurentiis Prod., Trans-Lux Dist. Corp. (Italian): FEDERICO FELLINI and TULLIO PINELLI.

THE LADY KILLERS, Ealing Studios Ltd., Continental Dist., Inc. (British): WILLIAM ROSE.

★ THE RED BALLOON, Films

*Blacklisted screenwriter Trumbo, who wrote the screenplay for *The Brave One* under the pseudonym of Robert Rich, officially received his Oscar on May 2, 1975.

Montsouris, Lopert Films Dist. Corp. (French): ALBERT LAMORISSE.

1957 Thirtieth Year*

Screenplay—based on material from another medium

★ THE BRIDGE ON THE RIVER KWAI, A Horizon Picture, Columbia: PIERRE BOULLE,† CARL FOREMAN, and MICHAEL WILSON.

HEAVEN KNOWS, MR. ALLISON, 20th Century-Fox: JOHN LEE MAHIN and JOHN HUSTON.

PEYTON PLACE, Jerry Wald Prods., Inc., 20th Century-Fox: JOHN MICHAEL HAYES.

SAYONARA, William Goetz Prod., Warner Bros.: PAUL OSBORN.

12 ANGRY MEN, Orion-Nova Prod., UA: REGINALD ROSE.

Story and Screenplay—written directly for the screen

★ DESIGNING WOMAN, Metro-Goldwyn-Mayer: GEORGE WELLS.

FUNNY FACE, Paramount: LEONARD GERSHE.

I VITELLONI, Peg Films/Cite Films, API-Janus Films (Italian): Story by FEDERICO FELLINI, ENNIO FLAIANO, and TULLIO PINELLI; screenplay by FEDERICO FELLINI and ENNIO FLAIANO.

MAN OF A THOUSAND FACES, Universal-International: Story by RALPH WHEELRIGHT; screenplay by R. WRIGHT CAMPBELL, IVAN GOFF, and BEN ROBERTS.

THE TIN STAR, The Perlberg-Seaton Prod., Paramount: Story by BARNEY SLATER and JOEL KANE; screenplay by DUDLEY NICHOLS.

1958 Thirty-first Year

Screenplay—based on material from another medium

CAT ON A HOT TIN ROOF, Avon Prods., Inc., M-G-M: RICHARD BROOKS and JAMES POE.

★ GIGI, Arthur Freed Prods., Inc., M-G-M: ALAN JAY LERNER.

THE HORSE'S MOUTH, Knightsbridge, UA (British): ALEC GUINNESS.

I WANT TO LIVE!, Figaro, Inc., UA: NELSON GIDDING and DON MANKIEWICZ.

SEPARATE TABLES, Clifton Prods., Inc., UA: TERENCE RATTIGAN and JOHN GAY.

Story and Screenplay—written directly for the screen

★ THE DEFIANT ONES, Stanley Kramer, UA: NATHAN E. DOUGLAS‡ and HAROLD JACOB SMITH.

THE GODDESS, Carnegie Prods., Inc., Columbia: PADDY CHAYEFSKY.

HOUSEBOAT, Paramount and Scribe, Paramount: MELVILLE SHAVELSON and JACK ROSE.

THE SHEEPMAN, Metro-Goldwyn-Mayer: Story by JAMES EDWARD GRANT; screenplay by WILLIAM BOWERS and JAMES EDWARD GRANT.

TEACHER'S PET, Perlberg-Seaton, Paramount: FAY KANIN and MICHAEL KANIN.

*Rules changed this year to two awards for Writing instead of three awards previously given.

†Boulle, the author of the original novel, neither read nor wrote English but received credit for the screenplay. Foreman and Wilson were the actual screenwriters but were blacklisted at the time and denied onscreen credit; in 1985 the Academy officially recognized their contributions and awarded Oscars to their widows.

‡A pseudonym for blacklisted writer Ned Young.

1959 Thirty-second Year

Screenplay—based on material from another medium

ANATOMY OF A MURDER, Otto Preminger, Columbia: WENDELL MAYES.

BEN-HUR, Metro-Goldwyn-Mayer: KARL TUNBERG.

THE NUN'S STORY, Warner Bros.: ROBERT ANDERSON.

★ ROOM AT THE TOP, Romulus Films, Ltd., Continental Dist., Inc. (British): NEIL PATERSON.

SOME LIKE IT HOT, Ashton Prods. and The Mirisch Co., UA: BILLY WILDER and I.A.L. DIAMOND.

Story and Screenplay—written directly for the screen

THE 400 BLOWS, Les Films du Carrosse and SEDIF, Zenith International (French): FRANÇOIS TRUFFAUT and MARCEL MOUSSY.

NORTH BY NORTHWEST, Metro-Goldwyn-Mayer: ERNEST LEHMAN.

OPERATION PETTICOAT, Granart Co., U-I: Story by PAUL KING and JOSEPH STONE; screenplay by STANLEY SHAPIRO and MAURICE RICHLIN.

★ PILLOW TALK, Arwin Prods., Inc., U-I: Story by RUSSELL ROUSE and CLARENCE GREENE; screenplay by STANLEY SHAPIRO and MAURICE RICHLIN.

WILD STRAWBERRIES, Svensk Filmindustri, Janus Films (Swedish): INGMAR BERGMAN.

1960 Thirty-third Year

Screenplay—based on material from another medium

★ ELMER GANTRY, Burt Lancaster-Richard Brooks Prod., UA: RICHARD BROOKS.

INHERIT THE WIND, Stanley Kramer Prod., UA: NATHAN E. DOUGLAS and HAROLD JACOB SMITH.

SONS AND LOVERS, Company of Artists, Inc., 20th Century-Fox: GAVIN LAMBERT and T.E.B. CLARKE.

THE SUNDOWNERS, Warner Bros.: ISOBEL LENNART.

TUNES OF GLORY, H. M. Films Limited Prod., Lopert Pictures Corp. (British): JAMES KENNAWAY.

Story and Screenplay—written directly for the screen

THE ANGRY SILENCE, Beaver Films Limited Prod., Joseph Harris-Sig Shore (British): Story by RICHARD GREGSON and MICHAEL CRAIG; screenplay by BRYAN FORBES.

★ THE APARTMENT, The Mirisch Co., Inc., UA: BILLY WILDER and I.A.L. DIAMOND.

THE FACTS OF LIFE, Panama and Frank Prod., UA: NORMAN PANAMA and MELVIN FRANK.

HIROSHIMA, MON AMOUR, Argos Films-Como Films-Daiei Pictures, Ltd.-Pathé Overseas Prod., Zenith International Film Corp. (French-Japanese): MARGUERITE DURAS.

NEVER ON SUNDAY, Melinafilm Prod., Lopert Pictures Corp. (Greek): JULES DASSIN.

1961 Thirty-fourth Year

Screenplay—based on material from another medium

BREAKFAST AT TIFFANY'S, Jurow-Shepherd Prod., Paramount: GEORGE AXELROD.

THE GUNS OF NAVARONE, Carl Foreman Prod., Columbia: CARL FOREMAN.

THE HUSTLER, Robert Rossen Prod., 20th Century-Fox: SIDNEY CARROLL and ROBERT ROSSEN.

★ JUDGMENT AT NUREMBERG, Stanley Kramer Prod., UA: ABBY MANN.

WEST SIDE STORY, Mirisch Pictures, Inc., and B and P Enterprises, Inc., UA: ERNEST LEHMAN.

Story and Screenplay—written directly for the screen

BALLAD OF A SOLDIER, Mosfilm Studio Prod., Kingsley International-M.J.P. Enterprises, Inc. (Russian): VALENTIN YOSHOV and GRIGORI CHUKHRAI.

GENERAL DELLA ROVERE, Zebra and S.N.E. Gaumont Prod., Continental Dist., Inc. (Italian): SERGIO AMIDEI, DIEGO FABBRI, and INDRO MONTANELLI.

LA DOLCE VITA, Riama Film Prod., Astor Pictures, Inc. (Italian): FEDERICO FELLINI, TULLIO PINELLI, ENNIO FLAIANO, and BRUNELLO RONDI.

LOVER COME BACK, Universal-International-The 7 Pictures Corp., Nob Hill Prods., Inc., Arwin Prods., Inc., U-I: STANLEY SHAPIRO and PAUL HENNING.

★ SPLENDOR IN THE GRASS, NBI Prod., Warner Bros.: WILLIAM INGE.

1962 Thirty-fifth Year

Screenplay—based on material from another medium

DAVID AND LISA, Heller-Perry Prods., Continental Distributing: ELEANOR PERRY.

LAWRENCE OF ARABIA, Horizon Pictures (G.B.), Ltd.-Sam Spiegel-David Lean Prod., Columbia: ROBERT BOLT.

LOLITA, Seven Arts Prods., M-G-M: VLADIMIR NABOKOV.

THE MIRACLE WORKER, Playfilms Prod., UA: WILLIAM GIBSON.

★ TO KILL A MOCKINGBIRD, Universal-International-Pakula-Mulligan-Brentwood Prod., U-I: HORTON FOOTE.

Story and Screenplay—written directly for the screen

★ DIVORCE—ITALIAN STYLE, Lux-Vides-Galatea Film Prod., Embassy Pictures: ENNIO DE CONCINI, ALFREDO GIANNETTI, and PIETRO GERMI.

FREUD, Universal-International-John Huston Prod., U-I: Story by CHARLES KAUFMAN. Screenplay by CHARLES KAUFMAN and WOLFGANG REINHARDT.

LAST YEAR AT MARIENBAD, Preceitel-Terra Film Prod., Astor Pictures: ALAIN ROBBE-GRILLET.

THAT TOUCH OF MINK, Universal-International-Granley-Arwin-Nob Hill Prod., U-I: STANLEY SHAPIRO and NATE MONASTER.

THROUGH A GLASS DARKLY, Svensk Filmindustri Prod., Janus Films: INGMAR BERGMAN.

1963 Thirty-sixth Year

Screenplay—based on material from another medium

CAPTAIN NEWMAN, M.D., Universal-Brentwood-Reynard Prod., Universal: RICHARD L. BREEN, PHOEBE EPHRON, and HENRY EPHRON.

HUD, Salem-Dover Prod., Paramount: IRVING RAVETCH and HARRIET FRANK, JR.

LILIES OF THE FIELD, Rainbow Prod., UA: JAMES POE.

SUNDAYS AND CYBELE, Terra-Fides-Orsay-Films Trocadero Prods., Columbia: SERGE BOURGUIGNON and ANTOINE TUDAL.

★ TOM JONES, Woodfall Prod., UA-Lopert Pictures: JOHN OSBORNE.

Story and Screenplay—written directly for the screen

AMERICA AMERICA, Athena Enterprises Prod., Warner Bros.: ELIA KAZAN.

FEDERICO FELLINI'S 8 1/2, Cineriz Prod., Embassy Pictures: FEDERICO FELLINI, ENNIO FLAIANO, TULLIO PINELLI, and BRUNELLO RONDI.

THE FOUR DAYS OF NAPLES, Titanus Prod., M-G-M: Story by PASQUALE FESTA CAMPANILE, MASSIMO

FRANCIOSA, NANNI LOY, and VASCO PRATOLINI. Screenplay by CARLO BERNARI, PASQUALE FESTA CAMPANILE, MASSIMO FRANCIOSA, and NANNI LOY.

★ HOW THE WEST WAS WON, Metro-Goldwyn-Mayer and Cinerama: JAMES R. WEBB.

LOVE WITH THE PROPER STRANGER, Boardwalk-Rona Prod., Paramount: ARNOLD SCHULMAN.

1964 Thirty-seventh Year

Screenplay—based on material from another medium

★ BECKET, Hal Wallis Prod., Paramount: EDWARD ANHALT.

DR. STRANGELOVE OR: HOW I LEARNED TO STOP WORRYING AND LOVE THE BOMB, Hawk Films, Ltd. Prod., Columbia: STANLEY KUBRICK, PETER GEORGE, and TERRY SOUTHERN.

MARY POPPINS, Walt Disney Prods.: BILL WALSH and DON DAGRADI.

MY FAIR LADY, Warner Bros.: ALAN JAY LERNER.

ZORBA THE GREEK, Rochley, Ltd. Prod., International Classics: MICHAEL CACOYANNIS.

Story and Screenplay—written directly for the screen

★ FATHER GOOSE, Universal-Granox Prod., Universal: Story by S. H. BARNETT; screenplay by PETER STONE and FRANK TARLOFF.

A HARD DAY'S NIGHT, Walter Shenson Prod., United Artists: ALUN OWEN.

ONE POTATO, TWO POTATO, Bawalco Picture Prod., Cinema V Distributing: Story by ORVILLE H. HAMPTON; screenplay by RAPHAEL HAYES and ORVILLE H. HAMPTON.

THE ORGANIZER, Lux-Vides-Mediterranee Cinema Prod., Walter Reade-Sterling-Continental Distributing: AGE, SCARPELLI, and MARIO MONICELLI.

THAT MAN FROM RIO, Ariane-Les Artistes Prod., Lopert Pictures: JEAN-PAUL RAPPENEAU, ARIANE MNOUCHKINE, DANIEL BOULANGER, and PHILIPPE DE BROCA.

1965 Thirty-eighth Year

Screenplay—based on material from another medium

CAT BALLOU, Harold Hecht Prod., Columbia: WALTER NEWMAN and FRANK R. PIERSON.

THE COLLECTOR, The Collector Company, Columbia: STANLEY MANN and JOHN KOHN.

★ DOCTOR ZHIVAGO, Sostar S.A.-Metro-Goldwyn-Mayer British Studios, Ltd. Prod., M-G-M: ROBERT BOLT.

SHIP OF FOOLS, Columbia: ABBY MANN.

A THOUSAND CLOWNS, Harrell Prod., United Artists: HERB GARDNER.

Story and Screenplay—written directly for the screen

CASANOVA '70, C. C. Champion-Les Films Concordia Prod., Embassy: AGE, SCARPELLI, MARIO MONICELLI, TONINO GUERRA, GIORGIO SALVIONI, and SUSO CECCHI D'AMICO.

★ DARLING, Anglo-Amalgamated, Ltd. Prod., Embassy: FREDERIC RAPHAEL.

THOSE MAGNIFICENT MEN IN THEIR FLYING MACHINES, 20th Century-Fox, Ltd. Prod., 20th Century-Fox: JACK DAVIES and KEN ANNAKIN.

THE TRAIN, Les Prods. Artistes Associés, United Artists: FRANKLIN COEN and FRANK DAVIS.

THE UMBRELLAS OF CHERBOURG, Parc-Madeleine Films Prod., American International: JACQUES DEMY.

1966 Thirty-ninth Year

Screenplay—based on material from another medium

ALFIE, Sheldrake Films, Ltd. Prod., Paramount: BILL NAUGHTON.

★ A MAN FOR ALL SEASONS, Highland Films, Ltd. Prod., Columbia: ROBERT BOLT.

THE PROFESSIONALS, Pax Enterprises Prod., Columbia: RICHARD BROOKS.

THE RUSSIANS ARE COMING! THE RUSSIANS ARE COMING!, Mirisch Corp. of Delaware Prod., UA: WILLIAM ROSE.

WHO'S AFRAID OF VIRGINIA WOOLF?, Chenault Prod., Warner Bros.: ERNEST LEHMAN.

Story and Screenplay—written directly for the screen

BLOW-UP, Carlo Ponti Prod., Premier Productions: Story by MICHELANGELO ANTONIONI; screenplay by MICHELANGELO ANTONIONI, TONINO GUERRA, and EDWARD BOND.

THE FORTUNE COOKIE, Phalanx-Jalem-Mirisch Corp. of Delaware Prod., UA: BILLY WILDER and I.A.L. DIAMOND.

KHARTOUM, Julian Blaustein Prod., UA: ROBERT ARDREY.

★ A MAN AND A WOMAN, Les Films 13 Prod., Allied Artists: Story by CLAUDE LELOUCH; screenplay by PIERRE UYTTERHOEVEN and CLAUDE LELOUCH.

THE NAKED PREY, Theodora Prod., Paramount: CLINT JOHNSTON and DON PETERS.

1967 Fortieth Year

Screenplay—based on material from another medium

COOL HAND LUKE, Jalem Prod., Warner Bros.-Seven Arts.: DONN PEARCE and FRANK R. PIERSON.

THE GRADUATE, Mike Nichols/ Lawrence Turman Prod., Embassy: CALDER WILLINGHAM and BUCK HENRY.

IN COLD BLOOD, Pax Enterprises Prod., Columbia: RICHARD BROOKS.

★ IN THE HEAT OF THE NIGHT, Mirisch Corp. Prod., United Artists: STIRLING SILLIPHANT.

ULYSSES, Walter Reade, Jr.-Joseph Strick Prod., Walter Reade-Continental Distributing: JOSEPH STRICK and FRED HAINES.

Story and Screenplay—written directly for the screen

BONNIE AND CLYDE, Tatira-Hiller Prod., Warner Bros.-Seven Arts: DAVID NEWMAN and ROBERT BENTON.

DIVORCE AMERICAN STYLE, Tandem Prods. for National General Prods., Columbia: Story by ROBERT KAUFMAN; screenplay by NORMAN LEAR.

★ GUESS WHO'S COMING TO DINNER, Columbia: WILLIAM ROSE.

LA GUERRE EST FINIE, Sofracima and Europa-Film Prod., Brandon Films: JORGE SEMPRUN.

TWO FOR THE ROAD, Stanley Donen Films Prod., 20th Century-Fox: FREDERIC RAPHAEL.

1968 Forty-first Year

Screenplay—based on material from another medium

★ THE LION IN WINTER, Haworth Prods., Avco Embassy: JAMES GOLDMAN.

THE ODD COUPLE, Howard W. Koch Prod., Paramount: NEIL SIMON.

OLIVER!, Romulus Films, Columbia: VERNON HARRIS.

RACHEL, RACHEL, Kayos Prod., Warner Bros.-Seven Arts: STEWART STERN.

ROSEMARY'S BABY, William Castle

Enterprises Prod., Paramount: ROMAN POLANSKI.

Story and Screenplay—written directly for the screen

THE BATTLE OF ALGIERS, Igor-Casbah Film Prod., Allied Artists: FRANCO SOLINAS and GILLO PONTECORVO.

FACES, John Cassavetes Prod., Walter Reade-Continental Dist.: JOHN CASSAVETES.

HOT MILLIONS, Mildred Freed Albert Prod., Metro-Goldwyn-Mayer: IRA WALLACH and PETER USTINOV.

★ THE PRODUCERS, Sidney Glazier Prod., Avco Embassy: MEL BROOKS.

2001: A SPACE ODYSSEY, Polaris Prod., Metro-Goldwyn-Mayer: STANLEY KUBRICK and ARTHUR C. CLARKE.

1969 Forty-second Year

Screenplay—based on material from another medium

ANNE OF THE THOUSAND DAYS, Hal B. Wallis-Universal Pictures, Ltd. Prod., Universal: JOHN HALE and BRIDGET BOLAND; adaptation by RICHARD SOKOLOVE.

GOODBYE, COLUMBUS, Willow Tree Prods., Paramount: ARNOLD SCHULMAN.

★ MIDNIGHT COWBOY, Jerome Hellman-John Schlesinger Prod., United Artists: WALDO SALT.

THEY SHOOT HORSES, DON'T THEY?, Chartoff-Winkler-Pollack Prod., ABC Pictures Presentation, Cinerama: JAMES POE and ROBERT E. THOMPSON.

Z, Reggane Films-O.N.C.I.C. Prod., Cinema V: JORGE SEMPRUN and COSTA-GAVRAS.

Story and Screenplay—based on material not previously published or produced

BOB & CAROL & TED & ALICE, Frankovich Prods., Columbia: PAUL MAZURSKY and LARRY TUCKER.

★ BUTCH CASSIDY AND THE SUNDANCE KID, George Roy Hill-Paul Monash Prod., 20th Century-Fox: WILLIAM GOLDMAN.

THE DAMNED, Pegaso-Praesidens Film Prod., Warner Bros.: Story by NICOLA BADALUCCO; screenplay by NICOLA BADALUCCO, ENRICO MEDIOLI, and LUCHINO VISCONTI.

EASY RIDER, Pando-Raybert Prods., Columbia: PETER FONDA, DENNIS HOPPER, and TERRY SOUTHERN.

THE WILD BUNCH, Phil Feldman Prod., Warner Bros.: Story by WALON GREEN and ROY N. SICKNER; screenplay by WALON GREEN and SAM PECKINPAH.

1970 Forty-third Year

Screenplay—based on material from another medium

AIRPORT, Ross Hunter-Universal Prod., Universal: GEORGE SEATON.

I NEVER SANG FOR MY FATHER, Jamel Prods., Columbia: ROBERT ANDERSON.

LOVERS AND OTHER STRANGERS, ABC Pictures Prod., Cinerama: RENEE TAYLOR, JOSEPH BOLOGNA, and DAVID ZELAG GOODMAN.

★ MASH, Aspen Prods., 20th Century-Fox: RING LARDNER, JR.

WOMEN IN LOVE, Larry Kramer-Martin Rosen Prod., UA: LARRY KRAMER.

Story and Screenplay—based on factual material or material not previously published or produced

FIVE EASY PIECES, BBS Prods., Columbia: Story by BOB RAFELSON and ADRIEN JOYCE; screenplay by ADRIEN JOYCE.

JOE, Cannon Group Prod., Cannon Releasing: NORMAN WEXLER.

LOVE STORY, The Love Story Company Prod., Paramount: ERICH SEGAL.

MY NIGHT AT MAUD'S, Films du

Losange-Carrosse-Renn-Deux Mondes-La Gueville-Simar-La Pleiade-F.F.P. Prod., Pathe Contemporary: ERIC ROHMER.

★ PATTON, 20th Century-Fox: FRANCIS FORD COPPOLA and EDMUND H. NORTH.

1971 Forty-fourth Year

Screenplay—based on material from another medium

A CLOCKWORK ORANGE, A Hawks Films, Ltd. Prod., Warner Bros.: STANLEY KUBRICK.

THE CONFORMIST, Mars Film Produzione, S.P.A.-Marianne Prods., Paramount: BERNARDO BERTOLUCCI.

★ THE FRENCH CONNECTION, A Philip D'Antoni Prod. in association with Schine-Moore Prods., 20th Century-Fox: ERNEST TIDYMAN.

THE GARDEN OF THE FINZI-CONTINIS, A Gianni Hecht Lucari-Arthur Cohn Prod., Cinema 5, Ltd.: UGO PIRRO and VITTORIO BONICELLI.

THE LAST PICTURE SHOW, BBS Prods., Columbia: LARRY MCMURTRY and PETER BOGDANOVICH.

Story and Screenplay—based on factual material or material not previously published or produced

★ THE HOSPITAL, A Howard Gottfried-Paddy Chayefsky Prod. in association with Arthur Hiller, UA: PADDY CHAYEFSKY.

INVESTIGATION OF A CITIZEN ABOVE SUSPICION, A Vera Films, S.P.A. Prod., Columbia: ELIO PETRI and UGO PIRRO.

KLUTE, A Gus Prod., Warner Bros.: ANDY LEWIS and DAVE LEWIS.

SUMMER OF '42, A Robert Mulligan-Richard Alan Roth Prod., Warner Bros.: HERMAN RAUCHER.

SUNDAY BLOODY SUNDAY, A Joseph Janni Prod., UA: PENELOPE GILLIATT.

1972 Forty-fifth Year

Screenplay—based on material from another medium

CABARET, An ABC Pictures Prod., Allied Artists: JAY ALLEN.

THE EMIGRANTS, A Svensk Filmindustri Prod., Warner Bros.: JAN TROELL and BENGT FORSLUND.

★ THE GODFATHER, An Albert S. Ruddy Prod., Paramount: MARIO PUZO and FRANCIS FORD COPPOLA.

PETE 'N' TILLIE, A Universal-Martin Ritt-Julius J. Epstein Prod., Universal: JULIUS J. EPSTEIN.

SOUNDER, Radnitz/Mattel Prods., 20th Century-Fox: LONNE ELDER III.

Story and Screenplay—based on factual material or material not previously published or produced

★ THE CANDIDATE, A Redford-Ritchie Prod., Warner Bros.: JEREMY LARNER.

THE DISCREET CHARM OF THE BOURGEOISIE, A Serge Silberman Prod., 20th Century-Fox: LUIS BUÑUEL in collaboration with JEAN-CLAUDE CARRIÈRE.

LADY SINGS THE BLUES, A Motown-Weston-Furie Prod., Paramount: TERENCE MCCLOY, CHRIS CLARK, and SUZANNE DE PASSE.

MURMUR OF THE HEART, A Nouvelles Editions De Films-Marianne Productions-Vides Cinematografica-Franz Seitz Filmproduktion, Continental Distributing: LOUIS MALLE.

YOUNG WINSTON, An Open Road Films, Ltd. Prod., Columbia: CARL FOREMAN.

1973 Forty-sixth Year

Screenplay—based on material from another medium

★ THE EXORCIST, Hoya Prods., Warner Bros.: WILLIAM PETER BLATTY.

THE LAST DETAIL, An Acrobat Films Prod., Columbia: ROBERT TOWNE.

THE PAPER CHASE, Thompson-Paul Prods., 20th Century-Fox: JAMES BRIDGES.

PAPER MOON, A Directors Company Prod., Paramount: ALVIN SARGENT.

SERPICO, A Produzioni De Laurentiis International Manufacturing Company S.p.A. Prod., Paramount: WALDO SALT and NORMAN WEXLER.

Story and Screenplay—based on factual material or material not previously published or produced

AMERICAN GRAFFITI, A Universal-Lucasfilm, Ltd.-Coppola Company Prod., Universal: GEORGE LUCAS, GLORIA KATZ, and WILLARD HUYCK.

CRIES AND WHISPERS, A Svenska Filminstitutet-Cinematograph AB Prod., New World Pictures: INGMAR BERGMAN.

SAVE THE TIGER, Filmways-Jalem-Cirandinha Prods., Paramount: STEVE SHAGAN.

★ THE STING, A Universal-Bill/Phillips-George Roy Hill Film Prod., Zanuck/Brown Presentation, Universal: DAVID S. WARD.

A TOUCH OF CLASS, Brut Productions, Avco Embassy: MELVIN FRANK and JACK ROSE.

1974 Forty-seventh Year

Original Screenplay

ALICE DOESN'T LIVE HERE ANYMORE, Warner Bros.: ROBERT GETCHELL.

★ CHINATOWN, A Robert Evans Production, Paramount: ROBERT TOWNE.

THE CONVERSATION, A Directors Company Production, Paramount: FRANCIS FORD COPPOLA.

DAY FOR NIGHT, A Les Films Du Carrosse and P.E.C.F., Paris; P.I.C., Rome Production, Warner Bros.: FRANÇOIS TRUFFAUT, JEAN-LOUIS RICHARD, and SUZANNE SCHIFFMAN.

HARRY AND TONTO, 20th Century-Fox: PAUL MAZURSKY and JOSH GREENFELD.

Screenplay adapted from other material

THE APPRENTICESHIP OF DUDDY KRAVITZ, An International Cinemedia Centre, Ltd. Prod., Paramount: MORDECAI RICHLER; adaptation by LIONEL CHETWYND.

★ THE GODFATHER PART II, A Coppola Company Prod., Paramount: FRANCIS FORD COPPOLA and MARIO PUZO.

LENNY, A Marvin Worth Production, United Artists: JULIAN BARRY.

MURDER ON THE ORIENT EXPRESS, A G. W. Films, Ltd. Prod., Paramount: PAUL DEHN.

YOUNG FRANKENSTEIN, A Gruskoff/Venture Films-Crossbow Prods.-Jouer, Ltd. Production, 20th Century-Fox: GENE WILDER and MEL BROOKS.

1975 Forty-eighth Year

Original Screenplay

AMARCORD, An F. C. Productions-P.E.C.F. Production, New World Pictures: FEDERICO FELLINI and TONINO GUERRA.

AND NOW MY LOVE, A Rizzoli Film-Les Films 13 Production, Avco Embassy: CLAUDE LELOUCH and PIERRE UYTTERHOEVEN.

★ DOG DAY AFTERNOON, Warner Bros.: FRANK PIERSON.

LIES MY FATHER TOLD ME, Pentimento Productions, Ltd.-Pentacle VIII Productions, Ltd., Columbia: TED ALLAN.

SHAMPOO, Rubeeker Productions, Columbia: ROBERT TOWNE and WARREN BEATTY.

Screenplay adapted from other material

BARRY LYNDON, A Hawk Films, Ltd. Production, Warner Bros.: STANLEY KUBRICK.

THE MAN WHO WOULD BE KING, An Allied Artists-Columbia Pictures Production, Allied Artists: JOHN HUSTON and GLADYS HILL.

★ ONE FLEW OVER THE CUCKOO'S NEST, A Fantasy Films Production, United Artists: LAWRENCE HAUBEN and BO GOLDMAN.

SCENT OF A WOMAN, A Dean Film Production, 20th Century-Fox: RUGGERO MACCARI and DINO RISI.

THE SUNSHINE BOYS, A Ray Stark Production, Metro-Goldwyn-Mayer: NEIL SIMON.

1976 Forty-ninth Year

Screenplay Written Directly for the Screen

COUSIN, COUSINE, Les Films Pomereu-Gaumont Production, Northal Film Distributors Ltd.: JEAN-CHARLES TACCHELLA; adaptation by DANIELE THOMPSON.

THE FRONT, Columbia Pictures: WALTER BERNSTEIN.

★ NETWORK, A Howard Gottfried/Paddy Chayefsky Production, Metro-Goldwyn-Mayer/United Artists: PADDY CHAYEFSKY.

ROCKY, A Robert Chartoff-Irwin Winkler Production, United Artists: SYLVESTER STALLONE.

SEVEN BEAUTIES, A Medusa Distribuzione Production, Cinema 5, Ltd.: LINA WERTMULLER.

Screenplay Based on Material from Another Medium

★ ALL THE PRESIDENT'S MEN, A Wildwood Enterprises Production, Warner Bros.: WILLIAM GOLDMAN.

BOUND FOR GLORY, The Bound for Glory Company Production, United Artists: ROBERT GETCHELL.

FELLINI'S CASANOVA, A P.E.A.-Produzioni Europee Associate S.p.A. Production, Universal: FEDERICO FELLINI and BERNADINO ZAPPONI.

THE SEVEN PERCENT SOLUTION, A Herbert Ross Film/Winitsky-Sellers Production, A Universal Release: NICHOLAS MEYER.

VOYAGE OF THE DAMNED, An ITC Entertainment Production, Avco Embassy: STEVE SHAGAN and DAVID BUTLER.

1977 Fiftieth Year

Screenplay Written Directly for the Screen

★ ANNIE HALL, Jack Rollins-Charles H. Joffe Productions, United: WOODY ALLEN and MARSHALL BRICKMAN.

THE GOODBYE GIRL, A Ray Stark Production, Metro-Goldwyn-Mayer/Warner Bros.: NEIL SIMON.

THE LATE SHOW, A Lion's Gate Film Production, Warner Bros.: ROBERT BENTON.

STAR WARS, A Twentieth Century-Fox Production, 20th Century-Fox: GEORGE LUCAS.

THE TURNING POINT, Hera Productions, 20th Century-Fox: ARTHUR LAURENTS.

Screenplay based on material from another medium

EQUUS, A Winkast Company, Ltd./P.B., Ltd. Production, United Artists: PETER SHAFFER.

I NEVER PROMISED YOU A ROSE GARDEN, A Scherick/Blatt Production, New World Pictures: GAVIN LAMBERT and LEWIS JOHN CARLINO.

★ JULIA, A Twentieth Century-Fox Production, 20th Century-Fox: ALVIN SARGENT.

OH, GOD!, A Warner Bros. Production, Warner Bros.: LARRY GELBART.

THAT OBSCURE OBJECT OF DESIRE, A Greenwich-Les Films Galaxie-In Cine Production, First Artists: LUIS BUÑUEL and JEAN-CLAUDE CARRIÈRE.

1978 Fifty-first Year

Screenplay Written Directly for the Screen

AUTUMN SONATA, A Personafilm GmbH Production, Sir Lew Grade-Martin Starger-ITC Entertainment Presentation, New World Pictures: INGMAR BERGMAN.

★ COMING HOME, A Jerome Hellman Enterprises Production, United Artists: Story by NANCY DOWD; screenplay by WALDO SALT and ROBERT C. JONES.

THE DEER HUNTER, An EMI Films/ Michael Cimino Film Production, Universal: Story by MICHAEL CIMINO, DERIC WASHBURN, LOUIS GARFINKLE, and QUINN K. REDEKER; screenplay by DERIC WASHBURN.

INTERIORS, A Jack Rollins-Charles H. Joffe Production, United Artists: WOODY ALLEN.

AN UNMARRIED WOMAN; A Twentieth Century-Fox Production, 20th Century-Fox: PAUL MAZURSKY.

Screenplay Based on Material from Another Medium

BLOODBROTHERS, A Warner Bros. Production, Warner Bros.: WALTER NEWMAN.

CALIFORNIA SUITE; A Ray Stark Production, Columbia: NEIL SIMON.

HEAVEN CAN WAIT, Dogwood Productions, Paramount: ELAINE MAY and WARREN BEATTY.

★ MIDNIGHT EXPRESS, A Casablanca-Filmworks Production, Columbia: OLIVER STONE.

SAME TIME, NEXT YEAR, A Walter Mirisch-Robert Mulligan Production, Mirisch Corporation/Universal Pictures Presentation, Universal: BERNARD SLADE.

1979 Fifty-second Year

Screenplay Written Directly for the Screen

ALL THAT JAZZ, A Columbia/Twentieth Century-Fox Production, 20th Century-Fox: ROBERT ALAN AURTHUR and BOB FOSSE.

. . . AND JUSTICE FOR ALL, A Malton Films Limited Production, Columbia: VALERIE CURTIN and BARRY LEVINSON.

★ BREAKING AWAY, A Twentieth Century-Fox Production, 20th Century-Fox: STEVE TESICH.

THE CHINA SYNDROME, A Michael Douglas / IPC Films Production, Columbia: MIKE GRAY, T. S. COOK, and JAMES BRIDGES.

MANHATTAN, A Jack Rollins-Charles H. Joffe Production, United Artists: WOODY ALLEN and MARSHALL BRICKMAN.

Screenplay Based on Material from Another Medium

APOCALYPSE NOW, An Omni Zoetrope Production, United Artists: JOHN MILIUS and FRANCIS COPPOLA.

★ KRAMER VS. KRAMER, Stanley Jaffe Productions, Columbia: ROBERT BENTON.

LA CAGE AUX FOLLES, A Les Productions Artistes Associés De Ma Produzione SPA Production, United Artists: FRANCIS VEBER, EDOUARD MOLINARO, MARCELLO DANON, and JEAN POIRET.

A LITTLE ROMANCE, A Pan Arts Associates Production, Orion Pictures Company: ALLAN BURNS.

NORMA RAE, A Twentieth Century-Fox Production, 20th Century-Fox: IRVING RAVETCH and HARRIET FRANK, JR.

1980 Fifty-third Year

Screenplay Written Directly for the Screen

BRUBAKER, A Twentieth Century-Fox Production, 20th Century-Fox: W. D. RICHTER; story by W. D. RICHTER and ARTHUR ROSS.

FAME, A Metro-Goldwyn-Mayer

Production, Metro-Goldwyn-Mayer: CHRISTOPHER GORE.

★ MELVIN AND HOWARD, A Linson/Phillips/Demme-Universal Pictures Production, Universal: BO GOLDMAN.

MON ONCLE D'AMERIQUE, A Philippe Dussart-Andrea Films T.F. 1 Production, New World Pictures: JEAN GRUAULT.

PRIVATE BENJAMIN, A Warner Bros. Production, Warner Bros.: NANCY MEYERS, CHARLES SHYER, and HARVEY MILLER.

Screenplay Based on Material from Another Medium

BREAKER MORANT, Produced in association with the Australian Film Commission, the South Australian Film Corporation, and the Seven Network and Pact Productions, New World Pictures/Quartet/ Films Incorporated: JONATHAN HARDY, DAVID STEVENS, and BRUCE BERESFORD.

COAL MINER'S DAUGHTER, A Bernard Schwartz-Universal Pictures Production, Universal: TOM RICKMAN.

THE ELEPHANT MAN, A Brooksfilms, Ltd. Production, Paramount: CHRISTOPHER DEVORE, ERIC BERGREN, and DAVID LYNCH.

★ ORDINARY PEOPLE, A Wildwood Enterprises Production, Paramount: ALVIN SARGENT.

THE STUNT MAN, Melvin Simon Productions, 20th Century-Fox: LAWRENCE B. MARCUS; adaptation by RICHARD RUSH.

1981 Fifty-fourth Year

Screenplay Written Directly for the Screen

ABSENCE OF MALICE, A Mirage Enterprises Production, Columbia: KURT LUEDTKE.

ARTHUR, A Rollins, Joffe, Morra, and Brezner Production, Orion: STEVE GORDON.

ATLANTIC CITY, An International Cinema Corporation Production, Paramount: JOHN GUARE.

★ CHARIOTS OF FIRE, Enigma Productions Limited, The Ladd Company/Warner Bros.: COLIN WELLAND.

REDS, A J.R.S. Production, Paramount: WARREN BEATTY and TREVOR GRIFFITHS.

Screenplay Based on Material from Another Medium

THE FRENCH LIEUTENANT'S WOMAN, A Parlon Production, United Artists: HAROLD PINTER.

★ ON GOLDEN POND, An ITC Films/ IPC Films Production, Universal: ERNEST THOMPSON.

PENNIES FROM HEAVEN, A Metro-Goldwyn-Mayer/Herbert Ross/Hera Production, Metro-Goldwyn-Mayer: DENNIS POTTER.

PRINCE OF THE CITY, An Orion Pictures/ Warner Bros. Production, Orion/ Warner Bros.: JAY PRESSON ALLEN and SIDNEY LUMET.

RAGTIME, A Ragtime Production, Paramount: MICHAEL WELLER.

1982 Fifty-fifth Year

Screenplay Written Directly for the Screen

DINER, A Jerry Weintraub Production, M-G-M/UA: BARRY LEVINSON.

E.T. THE EXTRA-TERRESTRIAL, A Universal Pictures Production, Universal: MELISSA MATHISON.

★ GANDHI, An Indo-British Films Production, Columbia: JOHN BRILEY.

AN OFFICER AND A GENTLEMAN, A Lorimar Production in association with Martin Elfand, Paramount: DOUGLAS DAY STEWART.

TOOTSIE, A Mirage/Punch Production, Columbia: Story by DON MCGUIRE and LARRY GELBART; screenplay by LARRY GELBART and MURRAY SCHISGAL.

Screenplay Based on Material from Another Medium

DAS BOOT, A Bavaria Atelier GmbH Production, Columbia: WOLFGANG PETERSEN.

★ MISSING, A Universal Pictures/Polygram Pictures Presentation of an Edward Lewis Production, Universal: COSTA-GAVRAS and DONALD STEWART.

SOPHIE'S CHOICE, An ITC Entertainment Presentation of a Pakula-Barish Production, Universal/A.F.D.: ALAN J. PAKULA.

THE VERDICT, A Fox-Zanuck/Brown Production, 20th Century-Fox: DAVID MAMET.

VICTOR/VICTORIA, A Metro-Goldwyn-Mayer Production, M-G-M/UA: BLAKE EDWARDS.

1983 Fifty-sixth Year

Screenplay Written Directly for the Screen

THE BIG CHILL, A Carson Productions Group Production, Columbia: LAWRENCE KASDAN and BARBARA BENEDEK.

FANNY AND ALEXANDER, A Cinematograph AB for the Swedish Film Institute/the Swedish Television SVT 1, Sweden/Gaumont, France/Personafilm and Tobis Filmkunst, BRD Production, Embassy: INGMAR BERGMAN.

SILKWOOD, An ABC Motion Pictures Production, 20th Century-Fox: NORA EPHRON and ALICE ARLEN.

★ TENDER MERCIES, An EMI Presentation of an Antron Media Production, Universal/A.F.D.: HORTON FOOTE.

WARGAMES, A United Artists Presentation of a Leonard Goldberg Production, M-G-M/UA: LAWRENCE LASKER and WALTER F. PARKES.

Screenplay Based on Material from Another Medium

BETRAYAL, A Horizon Film Production, 20th Century-Fox International Classics: HAROLD PINTER.

THE DRESSER, A Goldcrest Films/Television Limited/World Film Services Production, Columbia: RONALD HARWOOD.

EDUCATING RITA, An Acorn Pictures Limited Production, Columbia: WILLY RUSSELL.

REUBEN, REUBEN, A Saltair/Walter Shenson Production presented by the Taft Entertainment Co., 20th Century-Fox International Classics: JULIUS J. EPSTEIN.

★ TERMS OF ENDEARMENT, A James L. Brooks Production, Paramount: JAMES L. BROOKS.

1984 Fifty-seventh Year

Screenplay Written Directly for the Screen

BEVERLY HILLS COP, A Don Simpson/Jerry Bruckheimer Production in association with Eddie Murphy Productions, Paramount: Story by DANILO BACH and DANIEL PETRIE, JR.; screenplay by DANIEL PETRIE, JR.

BROADWAY DANNY ROSE, A Jack Rollins and Charles H. Joffe Production, Orion: WOODY ALLEN.

EL NORTE, An Independent Production, Cinecom International/Island Alive: GREGORY NAVA and ANNA THOMAS.

★ PLACES IN THE HEART, A Tri-Star Pictures Production, Tri-Star: ROBERT BENTON.

SPLASH, A Touchstone Films Production, Buena Vista: Screen story by BRUCE JAY FRIEDMAN; screenplay by LOWELL GANZ, BABALOO MANDEL and BRUCE JAY FRIEDMAN; based on a story by BRIAN GRAZER.

Screenplay Based on Material from Another Medium

★ AMADEUS, A Saul Zaentz Company Production, Orion: PETER SHAFFER.

GREYSTOKE: THE LEGEND OF TARZAN, LORD OF THE APES, A Warner Bros. Production, Warner Bros.: P. H. VAZAK and MICHAEL AUSTIN.

THE KILLING FIELDS, A Goldcrest Films and Television/International Film Investors L.P. Production, Warner Bros.: BRUCE ROBINSON.

A PASSAGE TO INDIA, A G. W. Films Limited Production, Columbia: DAVID LEAN.

A SOLDIER'S STORY, A Caldix Films Production, Columbia: CHARLES FULLER.

1985 Fifty-eighth Year

Screenplay Written Directly for the Screen

BACK TO THE FUTURE, an Amblin Entertainment/Universal Pictures Production, Universal: ROBERT ZEMECKIS and BOB GALE.

BRAZIL, an Embassy International Pictures Production, Universal: TERRY GILLIAM, TOM STOPPARD, and CHARLES MCKEOWN.

THE OFFICIAL STORY, a Historias Cinematograficas/Cinemania and Progress Communications Production, Almi Pictures: LUIS PUENZO and AIDA BORTNIK.

THE PURPLE ROSE OF CAIRO, a Jack Rollins and Charles H. Joffe Production, Orion: WOODY ALLEN.

★ WITNESS, an Edward S. Feldman Production, Paramount: Story by WILLIAM KELLEY, PAMELA WALLACE, and EARL W. WALLACE; screenplay by EARL W. WALLACE and WILLIAM KELLEY.

Screenplay Based on Material from Another Medium

THE COLOR PURPLE, a Warner Bros. Production, Warner Bros.: MENNO MEYJES.

KISS OF THE SPIDER WOMAN, an H.B. Filmes Production in association with Sugarloaf Films, Island Alive: LEONARD SCHRADER.

★ OUT OF AFRICA, a Universal Pictures Limited Production, Universal: KURT LUEDTKE.

PRIZZI'S HONOR, an ABC Motion Pictures Production, 20th Century-Fox: RICHARD CONDON and JANET ROACH.

THE TRIP TO BOUNTIFUL, a Bountiful Production, Island Pictures: HORTON FOOTE.

1986 Fifty-ninth Year

Screenplay Written Directly for the Screen

"CROCODILE" DUNDEE, A Rimfire Films Ltd. Production: Story by PAUL HOGAN; PAUL HOGAN, KEN SHADIE, and JOHN CORNELL.

★ HANNAH AND HER SISTERS, A Jack Rollins and Charles H. Joffe Production, Orion: WOODY ALLEN.

MY BEAUTIFUL LAUNDRETTE, A Working Title Ltd./SAF Production for Film Four International, Orion Classics: HANIF KUREISHI.

PLATOON, A Hemdale Film Production, Orion: OLIVER STONE.

SALVADOR, A Hemdale Film Production, Hemdale Releasing: OLIVER STONE and RICHARD BOYLE.

Screenplay Based on Material from Another Medium

CHILDREN OF A LESSER GOD, A Burt Sugarman Production, Paramount: HESPER ANDERSON and MARK MEDOFF.

THE COLOR OF MONEY, A Touchstone

Pictures Production in association with Silver Screen Partners II, Buena Vista: RICHARD PRICE.

CRIMES OF THE HEART, A Crimes of the Heart Production, De Laurentiis Entertainment Group: BETH HENLEY.

★ A ROOM WITH A VIEW, A Merchant Ivory Production, Cinecom: RUTH PRAWER JHABVALA.

STAND BY ME, An Act III Production, Columbia: RAYNOLD GIDEON, and BRUCE A. EVANS.

1987 Sixtieth Year

Screenplay Written Directly for the Screen

AU REVOIR LES ENFANTS (Goodbye, Children), An NEF (Paris) Production, Orion Classics: LOUIS MALLE.

BROADCAST NEWS, A Twentieth Century-Fox Production, 20th Century-Fox: JAMES L. BROOKS.

HOPE AND GLORY, A Davros Production Services Limited Production, Columbia: JOHN BOORMAN.

★ MOONSTRUCK, A Patrick Palmer and Norman Jewison Production, M-G-M: JOHN PATRICK SHANLEY.

RADIO DAYS, A Jack Rollins and Charles H. Joffe Production, Orion: WOODY ALLEN.

Screenplay Based on Material from Another Medium

THE DEAD, A Liffey Films Production, Vestron: TONY HUSTON.

FATAL ATTRACTION, A Jaffe/Lansing Production, Paramount: JAMES DEARDEN.

FULL METAL JACKET, A Natant Production, Warner Bros.: STANLEY KUBRICK, MICHAEL HERR, and GUSTAV HASFORD.

★ THE LAST EMPEROR, A Hemdale Film Production, Columbia: MARK PEPLOE and BERNARDO BERTOLUCCI.

MY LIFE AS A DOG, A Svensk Filmindustri/Filmteknik Production, Skouras Pictures: LASSE HALLSTRÖM, REIDAR JÖNSSOM, BRASSE BRÄNNSTRÖM, and PER BERGLUND.

1988 Sixty-first Year

Screenplay Written Directly for the Screen

BIG, A Twentieth Century-Fox Production, 20th Century-Fox: GARY ROSS and ANNE SPIELBERG.

BULL DURHAM, A Mount Company Production, Orion: RON SHELTON.

A FISH CALLED WANDA, A Michael Shamberg-Prominent Features Production, M-G-M: Story by JOHN CLEESE and CHARLES CRICHTON; screenplay by JOHN CLEESE.

★ RAIN MAN, A Guber-Peters Company Production, United Artists: Story by BARRY MORROW; screenplay by RONALD BASS and BARRY MORROW.

RUNNING ON EMPTY, A Lorimar Production, Warner Bros.: NAOMI FONER.

Screenplay Based on Material from Another Medium

THE ACCIDENTAL TOURIST, A Warner Bros. Production, Warner Bros.: FRANK GALATI and LAWRENCE KASDAN.

★ DANGEROUS LIAISONS, A Lorimar Production, Warner Bros.: CHRISTOPHER HAMPTON.

GORILLAS IN THE MIST, A Warner Bros. Production, Warner Bros./Universal: Story by ANNA HAMILTON PHELAN and TAB MURPHY; screenplay by ANNA HAMILTON PHELAN.

LITTLE DORRIT, A Sands Films Production, Cannon: CHRISTINE EDZARD.

THE UNBEARABLE LIGHTNESS OF BEING, A Saul Zaentz Company Production, Orion: JEAN-CLAUDE CARRIÈRE and PHILIP KAUFMAN.

1989 Sixty-second Year

Screenplay Written Directly for the Screen

CRIMES AND MISDEMEANORS, A Jack Rollins and Charles H. Joffe Production, Orion: WOODY ALLEN.

★ DEAD POETS SOCIETY, A Touchstone Pictures Production in association with Silver Screen Partners IV, Buena Vista: TOM SCHULMAN.

DO THE RIGHT THING, A Forty Acres and a Mule Filmworks Production, Universal: SPIKE LEE.

SEX, LIES, AND VIDEOTAPE, An Outlaw Production, Miramax: STEVEN SODERBERGH.

WHEN HARRY MET SALLY . . . , A Castle Rock Production, Columbia: NORA EPHRON.

Screenplay Based on Material from Another Medium

BORN ON THE FOURTH OF JULY, An A. Kitman Ho and Ixtlan Production, Universal: OLIVER STONE and RON KOVIC.

★ DRIVING MISS DAISY, A Zanuck Company Production, Warner Bros.: ALFRED UHRY.

ENEMIES, A LOVE STORY, A Morgan Creek Production, 20th Century-Fox: ROGER L. SIMON and PAUL MAZURSKY.

FIELD OF DREAMS, A Gordon Company Production, Universal: PHIL ALDEN ROBINSON.

MY LEFT FOOT, A Ferndale Films Production, Miramax: JIM SHERIDAN and SHANE CONNAUGHTON.

1990 Sixty-third Year

Screenplay Written Directly for the Screen

ALICE, A Jack Rollins and Charles H. Joffe Production, Orion: WOODY ALLEN.

AVALON, A Tri-Star Production, Tri-Star: BARRY LEVINSON.

★ GHOST, A Howard W. Koch Production, Paramount: BRUCE JOEL RUBIN.

GREEN CARD, A Green Card Company Production, Buena Vista: PETER WEIR.

METROPOLITAN, A Westerly Film-Video Production, New Line: WHIT STILLMAN.

Screenplay Based on Material from Another Medium

AWAKENINGS, A Columbia Pictures Production, Columbia: STEVEN ZAILLIAN.

★ DANCES WITH WOLVES, A Tig Production, Orion: MICHAEL BLAKE.

GOODFELLAS, A Warner Bros. Production, Warner Bros.: NICHOLAS PILEGGI and MARTIN SCORSESE.

THE GRIFTERS, A Martin Scorsese Production, Miramax: DONALD E. WESTLAKE.

REVERSAL OF FORTUNE, A Reversal Films Production, Warner Bros.: NICHOLAS KAZAN.

1991 Sixty-fourth Year

Screenplay Written Directly for the Screen

BOYZ N THE HOOD, A Columbia Pictures Production, Columbia: JOHN SINGLETON.

BUGSY, A Tri-Star Pictures Production, Tri-Star: JAMES TOBACK.

THE FISHER KING, A Tri-Star Pictures Production, Tri-Star: RICHARD LA GRAVENESE.

GRAND CANYON, A Twentieth Century-Fox Production, 20th Century-Fox: LAWRENCE KASDAN and MEG KASDAN.

★ THELMA & LOUISE, A Pathé Entertainment Production, M-G-M: CALLIE KHOURI.

Screenplay Based on Material Previously Produced or Published

EUROPA, EUROPA, A CCC-Filmkunst and Les Films du Losange Production, Orion Classics: AGNIESZKA HOLLAND.

FRIED GREEN TOMATOES, An Act III Communications in association with Electric Shadow Production, Universal: FANNIE FLAGG and CAROL SOBIESKI.

JFK, A Camelot Production, Warner Bros.: OLIVER STONE and ZACHARY SKLAR.

THE PRINCE OF TIDES, A Barwood/ Longfellow Production, Columbia: PAT CONROY and BECKY JOHNSTON.

★ THE SILENCE OF THE LAMBS, A Strong Heart/Demme Production, Orion: TED TALLY.

1992 Sixty-fifth Year

Screenplay Written Directly for the Screen

★ THE CRYING GAME, A Palace Pictures Production, Miramax: NEIL JORDAN.

HUSBANDS AND WIVES, A Tri-Star Pictures Production, Tri-Star: WOODY ALLEN.

LORENZO'S OIL, A Kennedy Miller Films Production, Universal: GEORGE MILLER and NICK ENRIGHT.

PASSION FISH, An Atchafalaya Films Production, Miramax: JOHN SAYLES.

UNFORGIVEN, A Warner Bros. Production, Warner Bros.: DAVID WEBB Peoples.

Screenplay Based on Material Previously Produced or Published

ENCHANTED APRIL, A BBC Films Production in association with Greenpoint Films, Miramax: PETER BARNES.

★ HOWARDS END, A Merchant Ivory Production, Sony Pictures Classics: RUTH PRAWER JHABVALA.

THE PLAYER, An Avenue Pictures Production, Fine Line: MICHAEL TOLKIN.

A RIVER RUNS THROUGH IT, A Columbia Pictures Production, Columbia: RICHARD FRIEDENBERG.

SCENT OF A WOMAN, A Universal Pictures Production, Universal: BO GOLDMAN.

Cinematography

Cinematography is one of three categories (with Costume Design and Art Direction-Set Decoration) that has in certain years been split into separate awards for black-and-white films and color films. When the category was begun at the first awards, color cinematography was still in an experimental stage. By the mid-1930s, however, Technicolor had perfected its three-color process, and the use of color became more widespread. Special awards for color cinematography were given by the Academy in 1936, 1937, and 1938, and in 1939 the Cinematography award was officially divided into black-and-white and color categories. Except for 1957, the practice of giving separate awards continued through 1966. As late as 1964 black-and-white films outnumbered color by a narrow margin among the year's eligible pictures, but within three years only one film in five was made in black and white. In 1967 the Academy voted to eliminate the separate categories and give only a single award.

Achievements in this category are nominated by the members of the Academy Cinematographers Branch.

1927/28 First Year

Tie

GEORGE BARNES, *The Devil Dancer* and *The Magic Flame*, Samuel Goldwyn, UA, and *Sadie Thompson*, Gloria Swanson Productions, UA.

★ CHARLES ROSHER, *Sunrise*, Fox.

★ KARL STRUSS, *Sunrise*, Fox.

1928/29 Second Year

GEORGE BARNES, *Our Dancing Daughters*, Cosmopolitan, Metro-Goldwyn-Mayer.

★ CLYDE DEVINNA, *White Shadows in the South Seas*, Cosmopolitan, Metro-Goldwyn-Mayer.

ARTHUR EDESON, *In Old Arizona*, Fox.

ERNEST PALMER, *Four Devils* and *Street Angel*, Fox.

JOHN SEITZ, *The Divine Lady*, First National.

*1929/30 Third Year**

ALL QUIET ON THE WESTERN FRONT, Universal (ARTHUR EDESON).

ANNA CHRISTIE, Metro-Goldwyn-Mayer (WILLIAM DANIELS).

HELL'S ANGELS, The Caddo Company, UA (GAETANO GAUDIO and HARRY PERRY).

THE LOVE PARADE, Paramount Famous Lasky (VICTOR MILNER).

★ WITH BYRD AT THE SOUTH POLE, Paramount Publix, JOSEPH T. RUCKER and WILLARD VAN DER VEER.

*Nominations this year were by film title, and only the individuals associated with the winning film were announced. The people who worked on the other nominated films are listed parenthetically to indicate that they received no official public nomination.

1930/31 Fourth Year

CIMARRON, RKO Radio: EDWARD CRONJAGER.

MOROCCO, Paramount Publix: LEE GARMES.

THE RIGHT TO LOVE, Paramount Publix: CHARLES LANG.

SVENGALI, Warners-First National: BARNEY "CHICK" MCGILL.

★ TABU, Paramount Publix: FLOYD CROSBY.

1931/32 Fifth Year

ARROWSMITH, Goldwyn, UA: RAY JUNE.

DR. JEKYLL AND MR. HYDE, Paramount: KARL STRUSS.

★ SHANGHAI EXPRESS, Paramount: LEE GARMES.

1932/33 Sixth Year

★ A FAREWELL TO ARMS, Paramount: CHARLES BRYANT LANG, JR.

REUNION IN VIENNA, Metro-Goldwyn-Mayer: GEORGE J. FOLSEY, JR.

SIGN OF THE CROSS, Paramount: KARL STRUSS.

1934 Seventh Year

THE AFFAIRS OF CELLINI, 20th Century, UA: CHARLES ROSHER.

★ CLEOPATRA, Paramount: VICTOR MILNER.

OPERATION 13, Metro-Goldwyn-Mayer: GEORGE FOLSEY.

1935 Eighth Year

BARBARY COAST, Goldwyn, UA: RAY JUNE.

THE CRUSADES, Paramount: VICTOR MILNER.

LES MISERABLES, 20th Century, UA: GREGG TOLAND.

★ A MIDSUMMER NIGHT'S DREAM, Warner Bros.: HAL MOHR.*

1936 Ninth Year

★ ANTHONY ADVERSE, Warner Bros.: GAETANO GAUDIO.

THE GENERAL DIED AT DAWN, Paramount: VICTOR MILNER.

THE GORGEOUS HUSSY, Metro-Goldwyn-Mayer: GEORGE FOLSEY.

1937 Tenth Year

DEAD END, Goldwyn, UA: GREGG TOLAND.

★ THE GOOD EARTH, Metro-Goldwyn-Mayer: KARL FREUND.

WINGS OVER HONOLULU, Universal: JOSEPH VALENTINE.

1938 Eleventh Year

ALGIERS, Wanger, UA: JAMES WONG HOWE.

ARMY GIRL, Republic: ERNEST MILLER and HARRY WILD.

THE BUCCANEER, Paramount: VICTOR MILNER.

★ THE GREAT WALTZ, Metro-Goldwyn-Mayer: JOSEPH RUTTENBERG.

JEZEBEL, Warner Bros.: ERNEST HALLER.

MAD ABOUT MUSIC, Universal: JOSEPH VALENTINE.

MERRILY WE LIVE, Roach, Metro-Goldwyn-Mayer: NORBERT BRODINE.

SUEZ, 20th Century-Fox: PEVERELL MARLEY.

VIVACIOUS LADY, RKO Radio: ROBERT DE GRASSE.

YOU CAN'T TAKE IT WITH YOU, Columbia: JOSEPH WALKER.

THE YOUNG IN HEART, Selznick, UA: LEON SHAMROY.

**A Midsummer Night's Dream* was not one of the official nominees. Hal Mohr became the first and only person to win an award as a write-in candidate. The rules were changed the following year to prohibit write-in votes.

1939 Twelfth Year

Black and White

STAGECOACH, Wanger, UA: BERT GLENNON.

★ WUTHERING HEIGHTS, Goldwyn, UA: GREGG TOLAND.

Color

★ GONE WITH THE WIND, Selznick, M-G-M: ERNEST HALLER and RAY RENNAHAN.

THE PRIVATE LIVES OF ELIZABETH AND ESSEX, Warner Bros.: SOL POLITO and W. HOWARD GREENE.

1940 Thirteenth Year

Black and White

ABE LINCOLN IN ILLINOIS, RKO Radio: JAMES WONG HOWE.

ALL THIS, AND HEAVEN TOO, Warner Bros.: ERNEST HALLER.

ARISE, MY LOVE, Paramount: CHARLES B. LANG, JR.

BOOM TOWN, Metro-Goldwyn-Mayer: HAROLD ROSSON.

FOREIGN CORRESPONDENT, Wanger, UA: RUDOLPH MATE.

THE LETTER, Warner Bros.: GAETANO GAUDIO.

THE LONG VOYAGE HOME, Argosy-Wanger, UA: GREGG TOLAND.

★ REBECCA, Selznick, UA: GEORGE BARNES.

SPRING PARADE, Universal: JOSEPH VALENTINE.

WATERLOO BRIDGE, Metro-Goldwyn-Mayer: JOSEPH RUTTENBERG.

Color

BITTER SWEET, Metro-Goldwyn-Mayer: OLIVER T. MARSH and ALLEN DAVEY.

THE BLUE BIRD, 20th Century-Fox: ARTHUR MILLER and RAY RENNAHAN.

DOWN ARGENTINE WAY, 20th Century-Fox: LEON SHAMROY and RAY RENNAHAN.

NORTH WEST MOUNTED POLICE, Paramount: VICTOR MILNER and W. HOWARD GREENE.

NORTHWEST PASSAGE, Metro-Goldwyn-Mayer: SIDNEY WAGNER and WILLIAM V. SKALL.

★ THE THIEF OF BAGDAD, Korda, UA (British): GEORGE PERINAL.

1941 Fourteenth Year

Black and White

THE CHOCOLATE SOLDIER, Metro-Goldwyn-Mayer: KARL FREUND.

CITIZEN KANE, Mercury, RKO Radio: GREGG TOLAND.

DR. JEKYLL AND MR. HYDE, Metro-Goldwyn-Mayer: JOSEPH RUTTENBERG.

HERE COMES MR. JORDAN, Columbia: JOSEPH WALKER.

HOLD BACK THE DAWN, Paramount: LEO TOVER.

★ HOW GREEN WAS MY VALLEY, 20th Century-Fox: ARTHUR MILLER.

SERGEANT YORK, Warner Bros.: SOL POLITO.

SUN VALLEY SERENADE, 20th Century-Fox: EDWARD CRONJAGER.

SUNDOWN, Wanger, UA: CHARLES LANG.

THAT HAMILTON WOMAN, Korda, UA: RUDOLPH MATE.

Color

ALOMA OF THE SOUTH SEAS, Paramount: WILFRED M. CLINE, KARL STRUSS, and WILLIAM SNYDER.

BILLY THE KID, Metro-Goldwyn-Mayer: WILLIAM V. SKALL and LEONARD SMITH.

★ BLOOD AND SAND, 20th Century-Fox: ERNEST PALMER and RAY RENNAHAN.

BLOSSOMS IN THE DUST, Metro-Goldwyn-Mayer: KARL FREUND and W. HOWARD GREENE.

DIVE BOMBER, Warner Bros.: BERT GLENNON.

LOUISIANA PURCHASE, Paramount: HARRY HALLENBERGER and RAY RENNAHAN.

1942 Fifteenth Year

Black and White

KINGS ROW, Warner Bros.: JAMES WONG HOWE.

THE MAGNIFICENT AMBERSONS, Mercury, RKO Radio: STANLEY CORTEZ.

MOONTIDE, 20th Century-Fox: CHARLES CLARKE.

★ MRS. MINIVER, Metro-Goldwyn-Mayer: JOSEPH RUTTENBERG.

THE PIED PIPER, 20th Century-Fox: EDWARD CRONJAGER.

THE PRIDE OF THE YANKEES, Goldwyn, RKO Radio: RUDOLPH MATE.

TAKE A LETTER, DARLING, Paramount: JOHN MESCALL.

THE TALK OF THE TOWN, Columbia: TED TETZLAFF.

TEN GENTLEMEN FROM WEST POINT, 20th Century-Fox: LEON SHAMROY.

THIS ABOVE ALL, 20th Century-Fox: ARTHUR MILLER.

Color

ARABIAN NIGHTS, Wanger, Universal: MILTON KRASNER, WILLIAM V. SKALL, and W. HOWARD GREENE.

★ THE BLACK SWAN, 20th Century-Fox: LEON SHAMROY.

CAPTAINS OF THE CLOUDS, Warner Bros.: SOL POLITO.

JUNGLE BOOK, Korda, UA: W. HOWARD GREENE.

REAP THE WILD WIND, Paramount: VICTOR MILNER and WILLIAM V. SKALL.

TO THE SHORES OF TRIPOLI, 20th Century-Fox: EDWARD CRONJAGER and WILLIAM V. SKALL.

1943 Sixteenth Year

Black and White

AIR FORCE, Warner Bros.: JAMES WONG HOWE, ELMER DYER, and CHARLES MARSHALL.

CASABLANCA, Warner Bros.: ARTHUR EDESON.

CORVETTE K-225, Universal: TONY GAUDIO.

FIVE GRAVES TO CAIRO, Paramount: JOHN SEITZ.

THE HUMAN COMEDY, Metro-Goldwyn-Mayer: HARRY STRADLING.

MADAME CURIE, Metro-Goldwyn-Mayer: JOSEPH RUTTENBERG.

THE NORTH STAR, Goldwyn, RKO Radio: JAMES WONG HOWE.

SAHARA, Columbia: RUDOLPH MATE.

SO PROUDLY WE HAIL, Paramount: CHARLES LANG.

★ THE SONG OF BERNADETTE, 20th Century-Fox: ARTHUR MILLER.

Color

FOR WHOM THE BELL TOLLS, Paramount: RAY RENNAHAN.

HEAVEN CAN WAIT, 20th Century-Fox: EDWARD CRONJAGER.

HELLO, FRISCO, HELLO, 20th Century-Fox; CHARLES G. CLARKE and ALLEN DAVEY.

LASSIE COME HOME, Metro-Goldwyn-Mayer: LEONARD SMITH.

★ PHANTOM OF THE OPERA, Universal: HAL MOHR and W. HOWARD GREENE.

THOUSANDS CHEER, Metro-Goldwyn-Mayer: GEORGE FOLSEY.

1944 Seventeenth Year

Black and White

DOUBLE INDEMNITY, Paramount: JOHN SEITZ.

DRAGON SEED, Metro-Goldwyn-Mayer: SIDNEY WAGNER.

GASLIGHT, Metro-Goldwyn-Mayer: JOSEPH RUTTENBERG.

GOING MY WAY, Paramount: LIONEL LINDON.

★ LAURA, 20th Century-Fox: JOSEPH LaSHELLE.

LIFEBOAT, 20th Century-Fox: GLEN MACWILLIAMS.

SINCE YOU WENT AWAY, Selznick, UA: STANLEY CORTEZ and LEE GARMES.

THIRTY SECONDS OVER TOKYO, Metro-Goldwyn-Mayer: ROBERT SURTEES and HAROLD ROSSON.

THE UNINVITED, Paramount: CHARLES LANG.

THE WHITE CLIFFS OF DOVER, Metro-Goldwyn-Mayer: GEORGE FOLSEY.

Color

COVER GIRL, Columbia: RUDY MATE and ALLEN M. DAVEY.

HOME IN INDIANA, 20th Century-Fox: EDWARD CRONJAGER.

KISMET, Metro-Goldwyn-Mayer: CHARLES ROSHER.

LADY IN THE DARK, Paramount: RAY RENNAHAN.

MEET ME IN ST. LOUIS, Metro-Goldwyn-Mayer: GEORGE FOLSEY.

★ WILSON, 20th Century-Fox: LEON SHAMROY.

1945 Eighteenth Year

Black and White

THE KEYS OF THE KINGDOM, 20th Century-Fox: ARTHUR MILLER.

THE LOST WEEKEND, Paramount: JOHN F. SEITZ.

MILDRED PIERCE, Warner Bros.: ERNEST HALLER.

★ THE PICTURE OF DORIAN GRAY, Metro-Goldwyn-Mayer: HARRY STRADLING.

SPELLBOUND, Selznick, UA: GEORGE BARNES.

Color

ANCHORS AWEIGH, Metro-Goldwyn-Mayer: ROBERT PLANCK and CHARLES BOYLE.

★ LEAVE HER TO HEAVEN, 20th Century-Fox: LEON SHAMROY.

NATIONAL VELVET, Metro-Goldwyn-Mayer: LEONARD SMITH.

A SONG TO REMEMBER, Columbia: TONY GAUDIO and ALLEN M. DAVEY.

THE SPANISH MAIN, RKO Radio: GEORGE BARNES.

1946 Nineteenth Year

Black and White

★ ANNA AND THE KING OF SIAM, 20th Century-Fox: ARTHUR MILLER.

THE GREEN YEARS, Metro-Goldwyn-Mayer: GEORGE FOLSEY.

Color

THE JOLSON STORY, Columbia: JOSEPH WALKER.

★ THE YEARLING, Metro-Goldwyn-Mayer: CHARLES ROSHER, LEONARD SMITH, and ARTHUR ARLING.

1947 Twentieth Year

Black and White

THE GHOST AND MRS. MUIR, 20th Century-Fox: CHARLES LANG, JR.

★ GREAT EXPECTATIONS, Rank-Cineguild, U-I (British): GUY GREEN.

GREEN DOLPHIN STREET, Metro-Goldwyn-Mayer: GEORGE FOLSEY.

Color

★ BLACK NARCISSUS, Rank-Archers, U-I (British): JACK CARDIFF.

LIFE WITH FATHER, Warner Bros.: PEVERELL MARLEY and WILLIAM V. SKALL.

MOTHER WORE TIGHTS, 20th Century-Fox: HARRY JACKSON.

1948 Twenty-first Year

Black and White

A FOREIGN AFFAIR, Paramount: CHARLES B. LANG, JR.

I REMEMBER MAMA, RKO Radio: NICHOLAS MUSURACA.

JOHNNY BELINDA, Warner Bros.: TED MCCORD.

★ THE NAKED CITY, Hellinger, U-I: WILLIAM DANIELS.

PORTRAIT OF JENNIE, The Selznick Studio: JOSEPH AUGUST.

Color

GREEN GRASS OF WYOMING, 20th Century-Fox: CHARLES G. CLARKE.

★ JOAN OF ARC, Sierra Pictures, RKO Radio: JOSEPH VALENTINE, WILLIAM V. SKALL, and WINTON HOCH.

THE LOVES OF CARMEN, Beckworth Corporation, Columbia: WILLIAM SNYDER.

THE THREE MUSKETEERS, Metro-Goldwyn-Mayer: ROBERT PLANCK.

1949 Twenty-second Year

Black and White

★ BATTLEGROUND, Metro-Goldwyn-Mayer: PAUL C. VOGEL.

CHAMPION, Screen Plays Corp., UA: FRANK PLANER.

COME TO THE STABLE, 20th Century-Fox: JOSEPH LASHELLE.

THE HEIRESS, Paramount: LEO TOVER.

PRINCE OF FOXES, 20th Century-Fox: LEON SHAMROY.

Color

THE BARKLEYS OF BROADWAY, Metro-Goldwyn-Mayer: HARRY STRADLING.

JOLSON SINGS AGAIN, Columbia: WILLIAM SNYDER.

LITTLE WOMEN, Metro-Goldwyn-Mayer: ROBERT PLANCK and CHARLES SCHOENBAUM.

SAND, 20th Century-Fox: CHARLES G. CLARKE.

★ SHE WORE A YELLOW RIBBON, Argosy, RKO Radio: WINTON HOCH.

1950 Twenty-third Year

Black and White

ALL ABOUT EVE, 20th Century-Fox: MILTON KRASNER.

THE ASPHALT JUNGLE, Metro-Goldwyn-Mayer: HAROLD ROSSON.

THE FURIES, Wallis, Paramount: VICTOR MILNER.

SUNSET BOULEVARD, Paramount: JOHN F. SEITZ.

★ THE THIRD MAN, Selznick-London Films, SRO (British): ROBERT KRASKER.

Color

ANNIE GET YOUR GUN, Metro-Goldwyn-Mayer: CHARLES ROSHER.

BROKEN ARROW, 20th Century-Fox: ERNEST PALMER.

THE FLAME AND THE ARROW, Norma-F.R., Warner Bros.: ERNEST HALLER.

★ KING SOLOMON'S MINES, Metro-Goldwyn-Mayer: ROBERT SURTEES.

SAMSON AND DELILAH, DeMille, Paramount: GEORGE BARNES.

1951 Twenty-fourth Year

Black and White

DEATH OF A SALESMAN, Kramer, Columbia: FRANK PLANER.

THE FROGMEN, 20th Century-Fox: NORBERT BRODINE.

★ A PLACE IN THE SUN, Paramount: WILLIAM C. MELLOR.

STRANGERS ON A TRAIN, Warner Bros.: ROBERT BURKS.

A STREETCAR NAMED DESIRE, Charles K. Feldman Group Prods., Warner Bros.: HARRY STRADLING.

Color

★ AN AMERICAN IN PARIS, Metro-Goldwyn-Mayer: ALFRED GILKS; ballet photographed by JOHN ALTON.

DAVID AND BATHSHEBA, 20th Century-Fox: LEON SHAMROY.

QUO VADIS, Metro-Goldwyn-Mayer: ROBERT SURTEES and WILLIAM V. SKALL.

SHOW BOAT, Metro-Goldwyn-Mayer: CHARLES ROSHER.

WHEN WORLDS COLLIDE, Paramount: JOHN F. SEITZ and W. HOWARD GREENE.

1952 Twenty-fifth Year

Black and White

★ THE BAD AND THE BEAUTIFUL, Metro-Goldwyn-Mayer: ROBERT SURTEES.

THE BIG SKY, Winchester, RKO Radio: RUSSELL HARLAN.

MY COUSIN RACHEL, 20th Century-Fox: JOSEPH LASHELLE.

NAVAJO, Bartlett-Foster, Lippert: VIRGIL E. MILLER.

SUDDEN FEAR, Joseph Kaufman, RKO Radio: CHARLES B. LANG, JR.

Color

HANS CHRISTIAN ANDERSEN, Goldwyn, RKO Radio: HARRY STRADLING.

IVANHOE, Metro-Goldwyn-Mayer: F. A. YOUNG.

MILLION DOLLAR MERMAID, Metro-Goldwyn-Mayer: GEORGE J. FOLSEY.

★ THE QUIET MAN, Argosy, Republic: WINTON C. HOCH and ARCHIE STOUT.

THE SNOWS OF KILIMANJARO, 20th Century-Fox: LEON SHAMROY.

1953 Twenty-sixth Year

Black and White

THE FOUR POSTER, Kramer, Columbia: HAL MOHR.

★ FROM HERE TO ETERNITY, Columbia: BURNETT GUFFEY.

JULIUS CAESAR, Metro-Goldwyn-Mayer: JOSEPH RUTTENBERG.

MARTIN LUTHER, Louis de Rochemont Associates: JOSEPH C. BRUN.

ROMAN HOLIDAY, Paramount: FRANK PLANER and HENRY ALEKAN.

Color

ALL THE BROTHERS WERE VALIANT, Metro-Goldwyn-Mayer: GEORGE FOLSEY.

BENEATH THE TWELVE-MILE REEF, 20th Century-Fox: EDWARD CRONJAGER.

LILI, Metro-Goldwyn-Mayer: ROBERT PLANCK.

THE ROBE, 20th Century-Fox: LEON SHAMROY.

★ SHANE, Paramount: LOYAL GRIGGS.

1954 Twenty-seventh Year

Black and White

THE COUNTRY GIRL, Perlberg-Seaton, Paramount: JOHN F. WARREN.

EXECUTIVE SUITE, Metro-Goldwyn-Mayer: GEORGE FOLSEY.

★ ON THE WATERFRONT, Horizon-American Corp., Columbia: BORIS KAUFMAN.

ROGUE COP, Metro-Goldwyn-Mayer: JOHN SEITZ.

SABRINA, Paramount: CHARLES LANG, JR.

Color

THE EGYPTIAN, 20th Century-Fox: LEON SHAMROY.

REAR WINDOW, Patron Inc., Paramount: ROBERT BURKS.

SEVEN BRIDES FOR SEVEN BROTHERS, Metro-Goldwyn-Mayer: GEORGE FOLSEY.

THE SILVER CHALICE, A Victor Saville Prod., Warner Bros.: WILLIAM V. SKALL.

★ THREE COINS IN THE

FOUNTAIN, 20th Century-Fox: MILTON KRASNER.

1955 Twenty-eighth Year

Black and White

BLACKBOARD JUNGLE, Metro-Goldwyn-Mayer: RUSSELL HARLAN.

I'LL CRY TOMORROW, Metro-Goldwyn-Mayer: ARTHUR E. ARLING.

MARTY, Hecht and Lancaster's Steven Prods., UA: JOSEPH LASHELLE.

QUEEN BEE, Columbia: CHARLES LANG.

★ THE ROSE TATTOO, Hal Wallis, Paramount: JAMES WONG HOWE.

Color

GUYS AND DOLLS, Samuel Goldwyn Prods., Inc., M-G-M: HARRY STRADLING.

LOVE IS A MANY-SPLENDORED THING, 20th Century-Fox: LEON SHAMROY.

A MAN CALLED PETER, 20th Century-Fox: HAROLD LIPSTEIN.

OKLAHOMA!, Rodgers & Hammerstein Pictures, Inc., Magna Theatre Corp.: ROBERT SURTEES.

★ TO CATCH A THIEF, Paramount: ROBERT BURKS.

1956 Twenty-ninth Year

Black and White

BABY DOLL, A Newtown Prod., Warner Bros.: BORIS KAUFMAN.

THE BAD SEED, Warner Bros.: HAL ROSSON.

THE HARDER THEY FALL, Columbia: BURNETT GUFFEY.

★ SOMEBODY UP THERE LIKES ME, Metro-Goldwyn-Mayer: JOSEPH RUTTENBERG.

STAGECOACH TO FURY, Regal Films, Inc. Prod., 20th Century-Fox: WALTER STRENGE.

Color

★ AROUND THE WORLD IN 80 DAYS, The Michael Todd Co., Inc., UA: LIONEL LINDON.

THE EDDY DUCHIN STORY, Columbia: HARRY STRADLING.

THE KING AND I, 20th Century-Fox: LEON SHAMROY.

THE TEN COMMANDMENTS, Motion Picture Assoc., Paramount: LOYAL GRIGGS.

WAR AND PEACE, A Ponti-De Laurentiis Prod., Paramount (Italo-American): JACK CARDIFF.

*1957 Thirtieth Year**

AN AFFAIR TO REMEMBER, Jerry Wald Prods., Inc., 20th Century-Fox: MILTON KRASNER.

★ THE BRIDGE ON THE RIVER KWAI, A Horizon Picture, Columbia: JACK HILDYARD.

FUNNY FACE, Paramount: RAY JUNE.

PEYTON PLACE, Jerry Wald Prods., Inc., 20th Century-Fox: WILLIAM MELLOR.

SAYONARA, William Goetz Prod., Warner Bros.: ELLSWORTH FREDERICKS.

1958 Thirty-first Year†

Black and White

★ THE DEFIANT ONES, Stanley Kramer, UA: SAM LEAVITT.

DESIRE UNDER THE ELMS, Don Hartman, Paramount: DANIEL L. FAPP.

I WANT TO LIVE!, Figaro, Inc., UA: LIONEL LINDON.

SEPARATE TABLES, Clifton Prods., Inc., UA: CHARLES LANG, JR.

THE YOUNG LIONS, 20th Century-Fox: JOE MACDONALD.

*Rules changed this year to one award for Cinematography instead of separate awards for black-and-white and color films.

†Rules changed this year to two awards for Cinematography: one for black and white and one for color.

Color

AUNTIE MAME, Warner Bros.: HARRY STRADLING, SR.

CAT ON A HOT TIN ROOF, Avon Prods., Inc., M-G-M: WILLIAM DANIELS.

★ GIGI, Arthur Freed Prods., Inc., M-G-M: JOSEPH RUTTENBERG.

THE OLD MAN AND THE SEA, Leland Hayward, Warner Bros.: JAMES WONG HOWE.

SOUTH PACIFIC, South Pacific Enterprises, Inc., Magna Theatre Corp.: LEON SHAMROY.

1959 Thirty-second Year

Black and White

ANATOMY OF A MURDER, Otto Preminger, Columbia: SAM LEAVITT.

CAREER, Hal Wallis Prods., Paramount: JOSEPH LASHELLE.

★ THE DIARY OF ANNE FRANK, 20th Century-Fox: WILLIAM C. MELLOR.

SOME LIKE IT HOT, Ashton Prods. and The Mirisch Co., UA: CHARLES LANG, JR.

THE YOUNG PHILADELPHIANS, Warner Bros.: HARRY STRADLING, SR.

Color

★ BEN-HUR, Metro-Goldwyn-Mayer: ROBERT L. SURTEES.

THE BIG FISHERMAN, Rowland V. Lee Prods., Buena Vista Film Dist. Co., Inc.: LEE GARMES.

THE FIVE PENNIES, Dena Prod., Paramount: DANIEL L. FAPP.

THE NUN'S STORY, Warner Bros.: FRANZ PLANER.

PORGY AND BESS, Samuel Goldwyn Prods., Columbia: LEON SHAMROY.

1960 Thirty-third Year

Black and White

THE APARTMENT, The Mirisch Co., UA: JOSEPH LASHELLE.

THE FACTS OF LIFE, Panama and Frank Prod., UA: CHARLES B. LANG, JR.

INHERIT THE WIND, Stanley Kramer Prod., UA: ERNEST LASZLO.

PSYCHO, Alfred J. Hitchcock Prods., Paramount: JOHN L. RUSSELL.

★ SONS AND LOVERS, Company of Artists, Inc., 20th Century-Fox: FREDDIE FRANCIS.

Color

THE ALAMO, Batjac Prod., UA: WILLIAM H. CLOTHIER.

BUTTERFIELD 8, Afton-Linebrook Prod., M-G-M: JOSEPH RUTTENBERG and CHARLES HARTEN.

EXODUS, Carlyle-Alpina S. A. Prod., UA: SAM LEAVITT.

PEPE, G. S.-Posa Films International Prod., Columbia: JOE MACDONALD.

★ SPARTACUS, Bryna Prods., Inc., U-I: RUSSELL METTY.

1961 Thirty-fourth Year

Black and White

THE ABSENT MINDED PROFESSOR, Walt Disney Prods., Buena Vista Distribution Co., Inc.: EDWARD COLMAN.

THE CHILDREN'S HOUR, Mirisch-Worldwide Prod., UA: FRANZ F. PLANER.

★ THE HUSTLER, Robert Rossen Prod., 20th Century-Fox: EUGEN SHUFTAN.

JUDGMENT AT NUREMBERG, Stanley Kramer Prod., UA: ERNEST LASZLO.

ONE, TWO, THREE, Mirisch Company, Inc., in association with Pyramid Prods., A. G., UA: DANIEL L. FAPP.

Color

FANNY, Mansfield Prod., Warner Bros.: JACK CARDIFF.

FLOWER DRUM SONG, Universal-International-Ross Hunter Prod. in association with Joseph Fields, U-I: RUSSELL METTY.

A MAJORITY OF ONE, Warner Bros.: HARRY STRADLING, SR.

ONE-EYED JACKS, Pennebaker Prod., Paramount: CHARLES LANG, JR.

★ WEST SIDE STORY, Mirisch Pictures, Inc., and B and P Enterprises Inc., UA: DANIEL L. FAPP.

1962 Thirty-fifth Year

Black and White

BIRD MAN OF ALCATRAZ, Harold Hecht Prod., UA: BURNETT GUFFEY.

★ THE LONGEST DAY, Darryl F. Zanuck Prods., 20th Century-Fox: JEAN BOURGOIN and WALTER WOTTITZ.

TO KILL A MOCKINGBIRD, Universal-International-Pakula-Mulligan-Brentwood Prod., U-I: RUSSELL HARLAN.

TWO FOR THE SEESAW, Mirisch-Argyle-Talbot Prod., in association with Seven Arts Prods., UA: TED MCCORD.

WHAT EVER HAPPENED TO BABY JANE?, Seven Arts-Associates and Aldrich Co. Prod., Warner Bros.: ERNEST HALLER.

Color

GYPSY, Warner Bros.: HARRY STRADLING, SR.

HATARI!, Malabar Prods., Paramount: RUSSELL HARLAN.

★ LAWRENCE OF ARABIA, Horizon Pictures (G.B.), Ltd.-Sam Spiegel-David Lean Prod., Columbia: FRED A. YOUNG.

MUTINY ON THE BOUNTY, Arcola Prod., M-G-M: ROBERT L. SURTEES.

THE WONDERFUL WORLD OF THE BROTHERS GRIMM, Metro-Goldwyn-Mayer and Cinerama: PAUL C. VOGEL.

1963 Thirty-sixth Year

Black and White

THE BALCONY, Walter Reade-Sterling-Allen-Hodgdon Prod., Walter Reade-Sterling-Continental Dist.: GEORGE FOLSEY.

THE CARETAKERS, Hall Bartlett Prod., UA: LUCIEN BALLARD.

★ HUD, Salem-Dover Prod., Paramount: JAMES WONG HOWE.

LILIES OF THE FIELD, Rainbow Prod., UA: ERNEST HALLER.

LOVE WITH THE PROPER STRANGER, Boardwalk-Rona Prod., Paramount: MILTON KRASNER.

Color

THE CARDINAL, Gamma Prod., Columbia: LEON SHAMROY.

★ CLEOPATRA, 20th Century-Fox Ltd.-MCL Films S.A.-WALWA Films S.A. Prod., 20th Century-Fox: LEON SHAMROY.

HOW THE WEST WAS WON, Metro-Goldwyn-Mayer and Cinerama: WILLIAM H. DANIELS, MILTON KRASNER, CHARLES LANG, JR., and JOSEPH LASHELLE.

IRMA LA DOUCE, Mirisch-Phalanx Prod., UA: JOSEPH LASHELLE.

IT'S A MAD, MAD, MAD, MAD WORLD, Casey Prod., UA: ERNEST LASZLO.

1964 Thirty-seventh Year

Black and White

THE AMERICANIZATION OF EMILY, Martin Ransohoff Prod., M-G-M: PHILIP H. LATHROP.

FATE IS THE HUNTER, Arcola Pictures Prod., 20th Century-Fox: MILTON KRASNER.

HUSH . . . HUSH, SWEET CHARLOTTE, Associates and Aldrich Prod., 20th Century-Fox: JOSEPH BIROC.

THE NIGHT OF THE IGUANA, Seven Arts Prod., M-G-M: GABRIEL FIGUEROA.

★ ZORBA THE GREEK, Rochley, Ltd. Prod., International Classics: WALTER LASSALLY.

Color

BECKET, Hal Wallis Prod., Paramount: GEOFFREY UNSWORTH.

CHEYENNE AUTUMN, John Ford-Bernard Smith Prod., Warner Bros.: WILLIAM H. CLOTHIER.

MARY POPPINS, Walt Disney Prods.: EDWARD COLMAN.

★ MY FAIR LADY, Warner Bros.: HARRY STRADLING.

THE UNSINKABLE MOLLY BROWN, Marten Prod., M-G-M: DANIEL L. FAPP.

1965 Thirty-eighth Year

Black and White

IN HARM'S WAY, Sigma Prods., Paramount: LOYAL GRIGGS.

KING RAT, Coleytown Prod., Columbia: BURNETT GUFFEY.

MORITURI, Arcola-Colony Prod., 20th Century-Fox: CONRAD HALL.

A PATCH OF BLUE, Pandro S. Berman-Guy Green Prod., M-G-M: ROBERT BURKS.

★ SHIP OF FOOLS, Columbia: ERNEST LASZLO.

Color

THE AGONY AND THE ECSTASY, International Classics Prod., 20th Century-Fox: LEON SHAMROY.

★ DOCTOR ZHIVAGO, Sostar S.A.-Metro-Goldwyn-Mayer British Studios, Ltd. Prod., M-G-M: FREDDIE YOUNG.

THE GREAT RACE, Patricia-Jalem-Reynard Prod., Warner Bros.: RUSSELL HARLAN.

THE GREATEST STORY EVER TOLD, George Stevens Prod., UA: WILLIAM C. MELLOR and LOYAL GRIGGS.

THE SOUND OF MUSIC, Argyle Enterprises Prod., 20th Century-Fox: TED MCCORD.

1966 Thirty-ninth Year

Black and White

THE FORTUNE COOKIE, Phalanx-Jalem-Mirisch Corp. of Delaware Prod., U.S.: JOSEPH LASHELLE.

GEORGY GIRL, Everglades Prods., Ltd., Columbia: KEN HIGGINS.

IS PARIS BURNING?, Transcontinental Films-Marianne Prod., Paramount: MARCEL GRIGNON.

SECONDS, The Seconds Company, Paramount: JAMES WONG HOWE.

★ WHO'S AFRAID OF VIRGINIA WOOLF?, Chenault Prod., Warner Bros.: HASKELL WEXLER.

Color

FANTASTIC VOYAGE, 20th Century-Fox: ERNEST LASZLO.

HAWAII, Mirisch Corp. of Delaware Prod., UA: RUSSELL HARLAN.

★ A MAN FOR ALL SEASONS, Highland Films, Ltd. Prod., Columbia: TED MOORE.

THE PROFESSIONALS, Pax Enterprises Prod., Columbia: CONRAD HALL.

THE SAND PEBBLES, Argyle-Solar Prod., 20th Century-Fox: JOSEPH MACDONALD.

*1967 Fortieth Year**

★ BONNIE AND CLYDE, Tatira-Hiller Prod., Warner Bros.-Seven Arts: BURNETT GUFFEY.

*Rules changed this year to one award for Cinematography instead of separate awards for black and white and color.

CAMELOT, Warner Bros.-Seven Arts: RICHARD H. KLINE.

DOCTOR DOLITTLE, Apjac Prods., 20th Century-Fox: ROBERT SURTEES.

THE GRADUATE, Mike Nichols-Lawrence Turman Prod., Embassy: ROBERT SURTEES.

IN COLD BLOOD, Pax Enterprises Prod., Columbia: CONRAD HALL.

1968 Forty-first Year

FUNNY GIRL, Rastar Prods., Columbia: HARRY STRADLING.

ICE STATION ZEBRA, Filmways Prod., Metro-Goldwyn-Mayer: DANIEL L. FAPP.

OLIVER!, Romulus Films, Columbia: OSWALD MORRIS.

★ ROMEO & JULIET, B.H.E. Film-Verona Prod.-Dino De Laurentiis Cinematografica Prod., Paramount: PASQUALINO DE SANTIS.

STAR!, Robert Wise Prod., 20th Century-Fox: ERNEST LASZLO.

1969 Forty-second Year

ANNE OF THE THOUSAND DAYS, Hal B. Wallis-Universal Pictures, Ltd. Prod., Universal: ARTHUR IBBETSON.

BOB & CAROL & TED & ALICE, Frankovich Prods., Columbia: CHARLES B. LANG.

★ BUTCH CASSIDY AND THE SUNDANCE KID, George Roy Hill-Paul Monash Prod., 20th Century-Fox: CONRAD HALL.

HELLO, DOLLY!, Chenault Prods., 20th Century-Fox: HARRY STRADLING.

MAROONED, Frankovich-Sturges Prod., Columbia: DANIEL FAPP.

1970 Forty-third Year

AIRPORT, Ross Hunter-Universal Prod., Universal: ERNEST LASZLO.

PATTON, 20th Century-Fox: FRED KOENEKAMP.

★ RYAN'S DAUGHTER, Faraway Prods., Metro-Goldwyn-Mayer: FREDDIE YOUNG.

TORA! TORA! TORA!, 20th Century-Fox: CHARLES F. WHEELER, OSAMI FURUYA, SINSAKU HIMEDA and MASAMICHI SATOH.

WOMEN IN LOVE, Larry Kramer-Martin Rosen Prod., UA: BILLY WILLIAMS.

1971 Forty-fourth Year

★ FIDDLER ON THE ROOF, Mirisch-Cartier Prods., UA: OSWALD MORRIS.

THE FRENCH CONNECTION, A Philip D'Antoni Prod., in association with Schine-Moore Prods., 20th Century-Fox: OWEN ROIZMAN.

THE LAST PICTURE SHOW, BBS Prods., Columbia: ROBERT SURTEES.

NICHOLAS AND ALEXANDRA, A Horizon Pictures Prod., Columbia: FREDDIE YOUNG.

SUMMER OF '42, A Robert Mulligan-Richard Alan Roth Prod., Warner Bros.: ROBERT SURTEES.

1972 Forty-fifth Year

BUTTERFLIES ARE FREE, Frankovich Productions, Columbia: CHARLES B. LANG.

★ CABARET, An ABC Pictures Production, Allied Artists: GEOFFREY UNSWORTH.

THE POSEIDON ADVENTURE, An Irwin Allen Production, 20th Century-Fox: HAROLD E. STINE.

1776, A Jack L. Warner Production, Columbia: HARRY STRADLING, JR.

TRAVELS WITH MY AUNT, Robert Fryer Productions, Metro-Goldwyn-Mayer: DOUGLAS SLOCOMBE.

1973 Forty-sixth Year

★ CRIES AND WHISPERS, A Svenska Filminstitutet-

Cinematograph AB Prod., New World Pictures: SVEN NYKVIST.

THE EXORCIST, Hoya Prods., Warner Bros.: OWEN ROIZMAN.

JONATHAN LIVINGSTON SEAGULL, A JLS Limited Partnership Prod., Paramount: JACK COUFFER.

THE STING, A Universal-Bill/Phillips-George Roy Hill Film Prod., Zanuck/Brown Presentation, Universal: ROBERT SURTEES.

THE WAY WE WERE, Rastar Prods., Columbia: HARRY STRADLING, JR.

1974 Forty-seventh Year

CHINATOWN, A Robert Evans Prod., Paramount: JOHN A. ALONZO.

EARTHQUAKE, A Universal-Mark Robson-Filmakers Group Prod., Universal: PHILIP LATHROP.

LENNY, A Marvin Worth Prod., UA: BRUCE SURTEES.

MURDER ON THE ORIENT EXPRESS, A G. W. Films, Ltd. Prod., Paramount: GEOFFREY UNSWORTH.

⋆ THE TOWERING INFERNO, An Irwin Allen Prod., 20th Century-Fox/Warner Bros.: FRED KOENEKAMP and JOSEPH BIROC.

1975 Forty-eighth Year

⋆ BARRY LYNDON, A Hawk Films, Ltd. Production, Warner Bros.: JOHN ALCOTT.

THE DAY OF THE LOCUST, A Jerome Hellman Production, Paramount: CONRAD HALL.

FUNNY LADY, A Rastar Pictures Production, Columbia: JAMES WONG HOWE.

THE HINDENBURG, A Robert Wise-Filmakers Group-Universal Production, Universal: ROBERT SURTEES.

ONE FLEW OVER THE CUCKOO'S NEST, A Fantasy Films Production, United Artists: HASKELL WEXLER and BILL BUTLER.

1976 Forty-ninth Year

⋆ BOUND FOR GLORY, The Bound for Glory Company Production, United Artists: HASKELL WEXLER.

KING KONG, A Dino De Laurentiis Production, Paramount: RICHARD H. KLINE.

LOGAN'S RUN, A Saul David Production, Metro-Goldwyn-Mayer: ERNEST LASZLO.

NETWORK, A Howard Gottfried/Paddy Chayefsky Production, Metro-Goldwyn-Mayer/United Artists: OWEN ROIZMAN.

A STAR IS BORN, A Barwood/Jon Peters Production, First Artists Presentation, Warner Bros.: ROBERT SURTEES.

1977 Fiftieth Year

⋆ CLOSE ENCOUNTERS OF THE THIRD KIND, Close Encounter Productions, Columbia: VILMOS ZSIGMOND.

ISLANDS IN THE STREAM, A Peter Bart/Max Palevsky Production, Paramount: FRED J. KOENEKAMP.

JULIA, A Twentieth Century-Fox Production, 20th Century-Fox: DOUGLAS SLOCOMBE.

LOOKING FOR MR. GOODBAR, A Freddie Fields Production, Paramount: WILLIAM A. FRAKER.

THE TURNING POINT, Hera Productions, 20th Century-Fox: ROBERT SURTEES.

1978 Fifty-first Year

⋆ DAYS OF HEAVEN, An OP Production, Paramount: NESTOR ALMENDROS.

THE DEER HUNTER, An EMI Films/Michael Cimino Film Production, Universal: VILMOS ZSIGMOND.

HEAVEN CAN WAIT, Dogwood

Productions, Paramount: WILLIAM A. FRAKER.

SAME TIME, NEXT YEAR, A Walter Mirisch-Robert Mulligan Production, Mirisch Corporation/Universal Pictures Presentation, Universal: ROBERT SURTEES.

THE WIZ, A Motown/Universal Pictures Production, Universal: OSWALD MORRIS.

1979 Fifty-second Year

ALL THAT JAZZ, A Columbia/Twentieth Century-Fox Production, 20th Century-Fox: GIUSEPPE ROTUNNO.

★ APOCALYPSE NOW, An Omni Zoetrope Production, United Artists: VITTORIO STORARO.

THE BLACK HOLE, Walt Disney Productions, Buena Vista Distribution Co.: FRANK PHILLIPS.

KRAMER VS. KRAMER, Stanley Jaffe Productions, Columbia: NESTOR ALMENDROS.

1941, An A-Team/Steven Spielberg Film Production, Universal-Columbia Presentation, Universal: WILLIAM A. FRAKER.

1980 Fifty-third Year

THE BLUE LAGOON, A Columbia Pictures Production, Columbia: NESTOR ALMENDROS.

COAL MINER'S DAUGHTER, A Bernard Schwartz-Universal Pictures Production, Universal: RALF D. BODE.

THE FORMULA, A Metro-Goldwyn-Mayer Production, Metro-Goldwyn-Mayer: JAMES CRABE.

RAGING BULL, A Robert Chartoff-Irwin Winkler Production, United Artists: MICHAEL CHAPMAN.

★ TESS, A Renn-Burrill Co-production with the participation of the Société Française de Production (S.F.P.), Columbia: GEOFFREY UNSWORTH and GHISLAIN CLOQUET.

1981 Fifty-fourth Year

EXCALIBUR, An Orion Pictures Production, Orion: ALEX THOMSON.

ON GOLDEN POND, An ITC Films/IPC Films Production, Universal: BILLY WILLIAMS.

RAGTIME, A Ragtime Production, Paramount: MIROSLAV ONDRICEK.

RAIDERS OF THE LOST ARK, A Lucasfilm Production, Paramount: DOUGLAS SLOCOMBE.

★ REDS, A J.R.S. Production, Paramount: VITTORIO STORARO.

1982 Fifty-fifth Year

DAS BOOT, A Bavaria Atelier GmbH Production, Columbia: JOST VACANO.

E.T. THE EXTRA-TERRESTRIAL, A Universal Pictures Production, Universal: ALLEN DAVIAU.

★ GANDHI, An Indo-British Films Production, Columbia: BILLY WILLIAMS and RONNIE TAYLOR.

SOPHIE'S CHOICE, An ITC Entertainment Presentation of a Pakula-Barish Production, Universal/A.F.D.: NESTOR ALMENDROS.

TOOTSIE, A Mirage/Punch Production, Columbia: OWEN ROIZMAN.

1983 Fifty-sixth Year

★ FANNY and ALEXANDER, A Cinematograph AB for the Swedish Film Institute/the Swedish Television SVT 1, Sweden/Gaumont, France/Personafilm and Tobis Filmkunst, BRD Production, Embassy: SVEN NYKVIST.

FLASHDANCE, A Polygram Pictures Production, Paramount: DON PETERMAN.

THE RIGHT STUFF, A Robert Chartoff-Irwin Winkler Production, The Ladd Company through Warner Bros.: CALEB DESCHANEL.

WARGAMES, A United Artists Presentation of a Leonard Goldberg

Production, M-G-M/UA: WILLIAM A. FRAKER.

ZELIG, A Jack Rollins and Charles H. Joffe Production, Orion through Warner Bros.: GORDON WILLIS.

1984 Fifty-seventh Year

AMADEUS, A Saul Zaentz Company Production, Orion: MIROSLAV ONDRICEK.

★ THE KILLING FIELDS, A Goldcrest Films and Television/ International Film Investors L.P. Production, Warner Bros.: CHRIS MENGES.

THE NATURAL, A Tri-Star Pictures Production, Tri-Star: CALEB DESCHANEL.

A PASSAGE TO INDIA, A G. W. Films Limited Production, Columbia: ERNEST DAY.

THE RIVER, A Universal Pictures Production, Universal: VILMOS ZSIGMOND.

1985 Fifty-eighth Year

THE COLOR PURPLE, A Warner Bros. Production, Warner Bros.: ALLEN DAVIAU.

MURPHY'S ROMANCE, A Fogwood Films Production, Columbia: WILLIAM A. FRAKER.

★ OUT OF AFRICA, A Universal Pictures Limited Production, Universal: DAVID WATKIN.

RAN, A Greenwich Film/Nippon Herald Films/Herald Ace Production, Orion Classics: TAKAO SAITO, MASAHARU UEDA, and ASAKAZU NAKAI.

WITNESS, An Edward S. Feldman Production, Paramount: JOHN SEALE.

1986 Fifty-ninth Year

★ THE MISSION, A Warner Bros./ Goldcrest and Kingsmere Production, Warner Bros.: CHRIS MENGES.

PEGGY SUE GOT MARRIED, A Rastar Production, Tri-Star: JORDAN CRONENWETH.

PLATOON, A Hemdale Production, Orion: ROBERT RICHARDSON.

A ROOM WITH A VIEW, A Merchant Ivory Production, Cinecom: TONY PIERCE-ROBERTS.

STAR TREK IV: THE VOYAGE HOME, A Harve Bennett Production, Paramount: DON PETERMAN.

1987 Sixtieth Year

BROADCAST NEWS, A Twentieth Century-Fox Production, 20th Century-Fox: MICHAEL BALLHAUS.

EMPIRE OF THE SUN, A Warner Bros. Production, Warner Bros.: ALLEN DAVIAU.

HOPE AND GLORY, A Davros Production Services Limited Production, Columbia: PHILIPPE ROUSSELOT.

★ THE LAST EMPEROR, A Hemdale Film Production, Columbia: VITTORIO STORARO.

MATEWAN, A Red Dog Films Production, Cinecom Pictures: HASKELL WEXLER.

1988 Sixty-first Year

★ MISSISSIPPI BURNING, A Frederick Zollo Production, Orion: PETER BIZIOU.

RAIN MAN, A Guber-Peters Company Production, United Artists: JOHN SEALE.

TEQUILA SUNRISE, A Mount Company Production, Warner Bros.: CONRAD L. HALL.

THE UNBEARABLE LIGHTNESS OF BEING, A Saul Zaentz Company Production, Orion: SVEN NYKVIST.

WHO FRAMED ROGER RABBIT, An Amblin Entertainment and

Touchstone Pictures Production, Buena Vista: DEAN CUNDEY.

1989 Sixty-second Year

THE ABYSS, A Twentieth Century-Fox Production, 20th Century-Fox: MIKAEL SALOMON.

BLAZE, A Touchstone Pictures Production in association with Silver Screen Partners IV, Buena Vista: HASKELL WEXLER.

BORN ON THE FOURTH OF JULY, An A. Kitman Ho and Ixtlan Production, Universal: ROBERT RICHARDSON.

THE FABULOUS BAKER BOYS, A Gladden Entertainment Presentation of a Mirage Production, 20th Century-Fox: MICHAEL BALLHAUS.

* GLORY, A Tri-Star Pictures Production, Tri-Star: FREDDIE FRANCIS.

1990 Sixty-third Year

AVALON, A Tri-Star Production, Tri-Star: ALLEN DAVIAU.

* DANCES WITH WOLVES, A Tig Production, Orion: DEAN SEMLER.

DICK TRACY, A Touchstone Pictures Production, Buena Vista: VITTORIO STORARO.

THE GODFATHER PART III, A Zoetrope Studios Production, Paramount: GORDON WILLIS.

HENRY & JUNE, A Walrus and Associates Production, Universal: PHILIPPE ROUSSELOT.

1991 Sixty-fourth Year

BUGSY, A Tri-Star Pictures Production, Tri-Star: ALLEN DAVIAU.

* JFK, A Camelot Production, Warner Bros.: ROBERT RICHARDSON.

THE PRINCE OF TIDES, A Barwood/Longfellow Production, Columbia: STEPHEN GOLDBLATT.

TERMINATOR 2: JUDGMENT DAY, A Carolco Production, Tri-Star: ADAM GREENBURG.

THELMA & LOUISE, A Pathé Entertainment Production, M-G-M: ADRIAN BIDDLE.

1992 Sixty-fifth Year

HOFFA, A 20th Century-Fox Production, 20th Century-Fox: STEPHEN H. BURUM.

HOWARDS END, A Merchant Ivory Production, Sony Pictures Classics: TONY PIERCE-ROBERTS.

THE LOVER, A Renn Production/Burrill Productions/Films A2, MGM/UA: ROBERT FRAISSE.

* A RIVER RUNS THROUGH IT, A Columbia Pictures Production, Columbia: PHILIPPE ROUSSELOT.

UNFORGIVEN, A Warner Bros. Production, Warner Bros: JACK N. GREEN.

Art Direction/Set Decoration

An art director not only designs the sets and backgrounds but works with the director, cinematographer, and costume designer to create the visual character of a film. A set decorator supplies the appropriate decor for a set—furniture, draperies, and decorative details for the interiors.

Art Direction is one of the original categories begun with the first awards. As originally defined, the award honored "the best achievement in set designing, with special reference to art quality, correct detail, story application, and originality." In 1941 the rules were changed to provide an award for the interior decorator as well as the art director, but this was not considered a new category since the two winners must work together on the same film. In 1947 the name was changed from Art Direction-Interior Decoration to Art Direction-Set Decoration.

For twenty-five years (1940–67 except for 1957–58), this category was divided into separate awards for black-and-white films and color films. The most frequent winners in this category are Cedric Gibbons, with eleven awards for Art Direction, and Edwin B. Willis, who worked with Gibbons, with eight Set Decoration Oscars.

Achievements in this category are nominated by all members of the Academy Art Directors Branch except the Costume Designers.

1927/28 First Year

ROCHUS GLIESE, *Sunrise*, Fox.

★ WILLIAM CAMERON MENZIES, *The Dove*, Joseph M. Schenck Productions, UA, and *Tempest*, Art Cinema, UA.

HARRY OLIVER, *7th Heaven*, Fox.

1928/29 Second Year

HANS DREIER, *The Patriot*, Paramount Famous Lasky.

★ CEDRIC GIBBONS, *The Bridge of San Luis Rey* and other pictures, Metro-Goldwyn-Mayer.

MITCHELL LEISEN, *Dynamite*, Pathé, Metro-Goldwyn-Mayer.

WILLIAM CAMERON MENZIES, *Alibi*, Art Cinema, UA, and *The Awakening*, Samuel Goldwyn, UA.

HARRY OLIVER, *Street Angel*, Fox.

*1929/30 Third Year**

BULLDOG DRUMMOND, Samuel Goldwyn, UA (WILLIAM CAMERON MENZIES).

★ KING OF JAZZ, Universal: HERMAN ROSSE.

THE LOVE PARADE, Paramount Famous Lasky (HANS DREIER).

SALLY, First National (JACK OKEY).

THE VAGABOND KING, Paramount Publix (HANS DREIER).

*Nominations this year were by film title, and only the individual associated with the winning film was announced. The people who worked on the other nominated films are listed parenthetically to indicate that they received no official public nomination.

1930/31 Fourth Year

★ CIMARRON, RKO Radio: MAX REE.

JUST IMAGINE, Fox: STEPHEN GOOSSON and RALPH HAMMERAS.

MOROCCO, Paramount Publix: HANS DREIER.

SVENGALI, Warner Bros.: ANTON GROT.

WHOOPEE, Goldwyn, UA: RICHARD DAY.

1931/32 Fifth Year

A NOUS LA LIBERTÉ (French): LAZARE MEERSON.

ARROWSMITH, Goldwyn, UA: RICHARD DAY.

★ TRANSATLANTIC, Fox: GORDON WILES.

1932/33 Sixth Year

★ CAVALCADE, Fox: WILLIAM S. DARLING.

A FAREWELL TO ARMS, Paramount: HANS DREIER and ROLAND ANDERSON.

WHEN LADIES MEET, Metro-Goldwyn-Mayer: CEDRIC GIBBONS.

1934 Seventh Year

THE AFFAIRS OF CELLINI, 20th Century, UA: RICHARD DAY.

THE GAY DIVORCEE, RKO Radio: VAN NEST POLGLASE and CARROLL CLARK.

★ THE MERRY WIDOW, Metro-Goldwyn-Mayer: CEDRIC GIBBONS and FREDERIC HOPE.

1935 Eighth Year

★ THE DARK ANGEL, Goldwyn, UA: RICHARD DAY.

LIVES OF A BENGAL LANCER, Paramount: HANS DREIER and ROLAND ANDERSON.

TOP HAT, RKO Radio: CARROLL CLARK and VAN NEST POLGLASE.

1936 Ninth Year

ANTHONY ADVERSE, Warner Bros.: ANTON GROT.

★ DODSWORTH, Goldwyn, UA: RICHARD DAY.

THE GREAT ZIEGFELD, Metro-Goldwyn-Mayer: CEDRIC GIBBONS, EDDIE IMAZU, and EDWIN B. WILLIS.

LLOYDS OF LONDON, 20th Century-Fox: WILLIAM S. DARLING.

THE MAGNIFICENT BRUTE, Universal: ALBERT S. D'AGOSTINO and JACK OTTERSON.

ROMEO AND JULIET, Metro-Goldwyn-Mayer: CEDRIC GIBBONS, FREDERIC HOPE, and EDWIN B. WILLIS.

WINTERSET, RKO Radio: PERRY FERGUSON.

1937 Tenth Year

CONQUEST, Metro-Goldwyn-Mayer: CEDRIC GIBBONS and WILLIAM HORNING.

A DAMSEL IN DISTRESS, RKO Radio: CARROLL CLARK.

DEAD END, Goldwyn, UA: RICHARD DAY.

EVERY DAY'S A HOLIDAY, Major Prods., Paramount: WIARD IHNEN.

THE LIFE OF EMILE ZOLA, Warner Bros.: ANTON GROT.

★ LOST HORIZON, Columbia: STEPHEN GOOSSON.

MANHATTAN MERRY-GO-ROUND, Republic: JOHN VICTOR MACKAY.

THE PRISONER OF ZENDA, Selznick, UA: LYLE WHEELER.

SOULS AT SEA, Paramount: HANS DREIER and ROLAND ANDERSON.

VOGUES OF 1938, Wanger, UA: ALEXANDER TOLUBOFF.

WEE WILLIE WINKIE, 20th Century-Fox: WILLIAM S. DARLING and DAVID HALL.

YOU'RE A SWEETHEART, Universal: JACK OTTERSON.

1938 Eleventh Year

★ ADVENTURES OF ROBIN HOOD, Warner Bros.: CARL J. WEYL.

ADVENTURES OF TOM SAWYER, Selznick, UA: LYLE WHEELER.

ALEXANDER'S RAGTIME BAND, 20th Century-Fox: BERNARD HERZBRUN and BORIS LEVEN.
ALGIERS, Wanger, UA: ALEXANDER TOLUBOFF.
CAREFREE, RKO Radio: VAN NEST POLGLASE.
GOLDWYN FOLLIES, Goldwyn, UA: RICHARD DAY.
HOLIDAY, Columbia: STEPHEN GOOSSON and LIONEL BANKS.
IF I WERE KING, Paramount: HANS DREIER and JOHN GOODMAN.
MAD ABOUT MUSIC, Universal: JACK OTTERSON.
MARIE ANTOINETTE, Metro-Goldwyn-Mayer: CEDRIC GIBBONS.
MERRILY WE LIVE, Roach, M-G-M: CHARLES D. HALL.

1939 Twelfth Year

BEAU GESTE, Paramount: HANS DREIER and ROBERT ODELL.
CAPTAIN FURY, Roach, UA: CHARLES D. HALL.
FIRST LOVE, Universal: JACK OTTERSON and MARTIN OBZINA.
★ GONE WITH THE WIND, Selznick, M-G-M: LYLE WHEELER.
LOVE AFFAIR, RKO Radio: VAN NEST POLGLASE and AL HERMAN.
MAN OF CONQUEST, Republic: JOHN VICTOR MACKAY.
MR. SMITH GOES TO WASHINGTON, Columbia: LIONEL BANKS.
THE PRIVATE LIVES OF ELIZABETH AND ESSEX, Warner Bros.: ANTON GROT.
THE RAINS CAME, 20th Century-Fox: WILLIAM DARLING and GEORGE DUDLEY.
STAGECOACH, Wanger, UA: ALEXANDER TOLUBOFF.
THE WIZARD OF OZ, Metro-Goldwyn-Mayer: CEDRIC GIBBONS and WILLIAM A. HORNING.
WUTHERING HEIGHTS, Goldwyn, UA: JAMES BASEVI.

1940 Thirteenth Year

Black and White

ARISE, MY LOVE, Paramount: HANS DREIER and ROBERT USHER.
ARIZONA, Columbia: LIONEL BANKS and ROBERT PETERSON.
THE BOYS FROM SYRACUSE, Universal: JOHN OTTERSON.
DARK COMMAND, Republic: JOHN VICTOR MACKAY.
FOREIGN CORRESPONDENT, Wanger, UA: ALEXANDER GOLITZEN.
LILLIAN RUSSELL, 20th Century-Fox: RICHARD DAY and JOSEPH C. WRIGHT.
MY FAVORITE WIFE, RKO Radio: VAN NEST POLGLASE and MARK-LEE KIRK.
MY SON, MY SON, Small, UA: JOHN DUCASSE SCHULZE.
OUR TOWN, Lesser, UA: LEWIS J. RACHMIL.
★ PRIDE AND PREJUDICE, Metro-Goldwyn-Mayer: CEDRIC GIBBONS and PAUL GROESSE.
REBECCA, Selznick, UA: LYLE WHEELER.
SEA HAWK, Warner Bros.: ANTON GROT.
THE WESTERNER, Goldwyn, UA: JAMES BASEVI.

Color

BITTER SWEET, Metro-Goldwyn-Mayer: CEDRIC GIBBONS and JOHN S. DETLIE.
DOWN ARGENTINE WAY, 20th Century-Fox: RICHARD DAY and JOSEPH C. WRIGHT.
NORTH WEST MOUNTED POLICE, Paramount: HANS DREIER and ROLAND ANDERSON.
★ THE THIEF OF BAGDAD, Korda, UA: VINCENT KORDA.

*1941 Fourteenth Year**

Black and White

CITIZEN KANE, Mercury, RKO Radio: PERRY FERGUSON and VAN NEST POLGLASE; Interior Decoration: AL FIELDS and DARRELL SILVERA.

FLAME OF NEW ORLEANS, Universal: MARTIN OBZINA and JACK OTTERSON; Interior Decoration: RUSSELL A. GAUSMAN.

HOLD BACK THE DAWN, Paramount: HANS DREIER and ROBERT USHER; Interior Decoration: SAM COMER.

★ HOW GREEN WAS MY VALLEY, 20th Century-Fox: RICHARD DAY and NATHAN JURAN; Interior Decoration: THOMAS LITTLE.

LADIES IN RETIREMENT, Columbia: LIONEL BANKS; Interior Decoration: GEORGE MONTGOMERY.

THE LITTLE FOXES, Goldwyn, RKO Radio: STEPHEN GOOSSON; Interior Decoration: HOWARD BRISTOL.

SERGEANT YORK, Warner Bros.: JOHN HUGHES; Interior Decoration: FRED MACLEAN.

SON OF MONTE CRISTO, Small, UA: JOHN DUCASSE SCHULZE; Interior Decoration: EDWARD G. BOYLE.

SUNDOWN, Wanger, UA: ALEXANDER GOLITZEN; Interior Decoration: RICHARD IRVINE.

THAT HAMILTON WOMAN, Korda, UA: VINCENT KORDA; Interior Decoration: JULIA HERON.

WHEN LADIES MEET, Metro-Goldwyn-Mayer: CEDRIC GIBBONS and RANDALL DUELL; Interior Decoration: EDWIN B. WILLIS.

Color

BLOOD AND SAND, 20th Century-Fox: RICHARD DAY and JOSEPH C. WRIGHT; Interior Decoration: THOMAS LITTLE.

★ BLOSSOMS IN THE DUST, Metro-Goldwyn-Mayer: CEDRIC GIBBONS and URIE McCLEARY; Interior Decoration: EDWIN B. WILLIS.

LOUISIANA PURCHASE, Paramount: RAOUL PENE DU BOIS; Interior Decoration: STEPHEN A. SEYMOUR.

1942 Fifteenth Year

Black and White

GEORGE WASHINGTON SLEPT HERE, Warner Bros.: MAX PARKER and MARK-LEE KIRK; Interior Decoration: CASEY ROBERTS.

THE MAGNIFICENT AMBERSONS, Mercury, RKO Radio: ALBERT S. D' AGOSTINO; Interior Decoration: AL FIELDS and DARRELL SILVERA.

THE PRIDE OF THE YANKEES, Goldwyn, RKO Radio: PERRY FERGUSON; Interior Decoration: HOWARD BRISTOL.

RANDOM HARVEST, Metro-Goldwyn-Mayer: CEDRIC GIBBONS and RANDALL DUELL; Interior Decoration: EDWIN B. WILLIS and JACK MOORE.

THE SHANGHAI GESTURE, Arnold, UA: BORIS LEVEN; Interior Decoration: BORIS LEVEN.

SILVER QUEEN, Sherman, UA: RALPH BERGER; Interior Decoration: EMILE KURI.

THE SPOILERS, Universal: JOHN B. GOODMAN and JACK OTTERSON; Interior Decoration: RUSSELL A. GAUSMAN and EDWARD R. ROBINSON.

TAKE A LETTER, DARLING, Paramount: HANS DREIER and ROLAND ANDERSON; Interior Decoration: SAM COMER.

THE TALK OF THE TOWN, Columbia: LIONEL BANKS and RUDOLPH

*Category name changed from Art Direction to Art Direction-Interior Decoration.

STERNAD; Interior Decoration: FAY BABCOCK.

★ THIS ABOVE ALL, 20th Century-Fox: RICHARD DAY and JOSEPH WRIGHT; Interior Decoration: THOMAS LITTLE.

Color

ARABIAN NIGHTS, Universal: ALEXANDER GOLITZEN and JACK OTTERSON; Interior Decoration: RUSSELL A. GAUSMAN and IRA S. WEBB.

CAPTAINS OF THE CLOUDS, Warner Bros.: TED SMITH; Interior Decoration: CASEY ROBERTS.

JUNGLE BOOK, Korda, UA: VINCENT KORDA; Interior Decoration: JULIA HERON.

★ MY GAL SAL, 20th Century-Fox: RICHARD DAY and JOSEPH WRIGHT; Interior Decoration: THOMAS LITTLE.

REAP THE WILD WIND, Paramount: HANS DREIER and ROLAND ANDERSON; Interior Decoration: GEORGE SAWLEY.

1943 Sixteenth Year

Black and White

FIVE GRAVES TO CAIRO, Paramount: HANS DREIER and ERNST FEGTE; Interior Decoration: BERTRAM GRANGER.

FLIGHT FOR FREEDOM, RKO Radio: ALBERT S. D'AGOSTINO and CARROLL CLARK; Interior Decoration: DARRELL SILVERA and HARLEY MILLER.

MADAME CURIE, Metro-Goldwyn-Mayer: CEDRIC GIBBONS and PAUL GROESSE; Interior Decoration: EDWIN B. WILLIS and HUGH HUNT.

MISSION TO MOSCOW, Warner Bros.: CARL WEYL; Interior Decoration: GEORGE J. HOPKINS.

THE NORTH STAR, Goldwyn, RKO Radio: PERRY FERGUSON; Interior Decoration: HOWARD BRISTOL.

★ THE SONG OF BERNADETTE, 20th Century-Fox: JAMES BASEVI and WILLIAM DARLING; Interior Decoration: THOMAS LITTLE.

Color

FOR WHOM THE BELL TOLLS, Paramount: HANS DREIER and HALDANE DOUGLAS; Interior Decoration: BERTRAM GRANGER.

THE GANG'S ALL HERE, 20th Century-Fox: JAMES BASEVI and JOSEPH C. WRIGHT; Interior Decoration: THOMAS LITTLE.

★ PHANTOM OF THE OPERA, Universal: ALEXANDER GOLITZEN and JOHN B. GOODMAN; Interior Decoration: RUSSELL A. GAUSMAN and IRA S. WEBB.

THIS IS THE ARMY, Warner Bros.: JOHN HUGHES and LT. JOHN KOENIG; Interior Decoration: GEORGE J. HOPKINS.

THOUSANDS CHEER, Metro-Goldwyn-Mayer: CEDRIC GIBBONS and DANIEL CATHCART; Interior Decoration: EDWIN B. WILLIS and JACQUES MERSEREAU.

1944 Seventeenth Year

Black and White

ADDRESS UNKNOWN, Columbia: LIONEL BANKS and WALTER HOLSCHER; Interior Decoration: JOSEPH KISH.

THE ADVENTURES OF MARK TWAIN, Warner Bros.: JOHN J. HUGHES; Interior Decoration: FRED MACLEAN.

CASANOVA BROWN, International, RKO Radio: PERRY FERGUSON; Interior Decoration: JULIA HERON.

★ GASLIGHT, Metro-Goldwyn-Mayer: CEDRIC GIBBONS and WILLIAM FERRARI; Interior Decoration: EDWIN B. WILLIS and PAUL HULDSCHINSKY.

LAURA, 20th Century-Fox: LYLE

WHEELER and LELAND FULLER; Interior Decoration: THOMAS LITTLE.

NO TIME FOR LOVE, Paramount: HANS DREIER and ROBERT USHER; Interior Decoration: SAM COMER.

SINCE YOU WENT AWAY, Selznick, UA: MARK-LEE KIRK; Interior Decoration: VICTOR A. GANGELIN.

STEP LIVELY, RKO Radio: ALBERT S. D'AGOSTINO and CARROLL CLARK; Interior Decoration: DARRELL SILVERA and CLAUDE CARPENTER.

Color

THE CLIMAX, Universal: JOHN B. GOODMAN and ALEXANDER GOLITZEN; Interior Decoration: RUSSELL A. GAUSMAN and IRA S. WEBB.

COVER GIRL, Columbia: LIONEL BANKS and CARY ODELL; Interior Decoration: FAY BABCOCK.

THE DESERT SONG, Warner Bros.: CHARLES NOVI; Interior Decoration: JACK MCCONAGHY.

KISMET, Metro-Goldwyn-Mayer: CEDRIC GIBBONS and DANIEL B. CATHCART; Interior Decoration: EDWIN B. WILLIS and RICHARD PEFFERLE.

LADY IN THE DARK, Paramount: HANS DREIER and RAOUL PENE DU BOIS; Interior Decoration: RAY MOYER.

THE PRINCESS AND THE PIRATE, Goldwyn, RKO Radio: ERNST FEGTE; Interior Decoration: HOWARD BRISTOL.

★ WILSON, 20th Century-Fox: WIARD IHNEN; Interior Decoration: THOMAS LITTLE.

1945 Eighteenth Year

Black and White

★ BLOOD ON THE SUN, Cagney, UA: WIARD IHNEN; Interior Decoration: A. ROLAND FIELDS.

EXPERIMENT PERILOUS, RKO Radio: ALBERT S. D'AGOSTINO and JACK OKEY; Interior Decoration: DARRELL SILVERA and CLAUDE CARPENTER.

THE KEYS OF THE KINGDOM, 20th Century-Fox: JAMES BASEVI and WILLIAM DARLING; Interior Decoration: THOMAS LITTLE and FRANK E. HUGHES.

LOVE LETTERS, Hal Wallis, Paramount: HANS DREIER and ROLAND ANDERSON; Interior Decoration: SAM COMER and RAY MOYER.

THE PICTURE OF DORIAN GRAY, Metro-Goldwyn-Mayer: CEDRIC GIBBONS and HANS PETERS; Interior Decoration: EDWIN B. WILLIS, JOHN BONAR, and HUGH HUNT.

Color

★ FRENCHMAN'S CREEK, Paramount: HANS DREIER and ERNST FEGTE; Interior Decoration: SAM COMER.

LEAVE HER TO HEAVEN, 20th Century-Fox: LYLE WHEELER and MAURICE RANSFORD; Interior Decoration: THOMAS LITTLE.

NATIONAL VELVET, Metro-Goldwyn-Mayer: CEDRIC GIBBONS and URIE MCCLEARY; Interior Decoration: EDWIN B. WILLIS and MILDRED GRIFFITHS.

SAN ANTONIO, Warner Bros.: TED SMITH; Interior Decoration: JACK MCCONAGHY.

A THOUSAND AND ONE NIGHTS, Columbia: STEPHEN GOOSSON and RUDOLPH STERNAD; Interior Decoration: FRANK TUTTLE.

1946 Nineteenth Year

Black and White

★ ANNA AND THE KING OF SIAM, 20th Century-Fox: LYLE WHEELER and WILLIAM DARLING; Interior Decoration: THOMAS LITTLE and FRANK E. HUGHES.

KITTY, Paramount: HANS DREIER and

WALTER TYLER; Interior Decoration: SAM COMER and RAY MOYER.

THE RAZOR'S EDGE, 20th Century-Fox: RICHARD DAY and NATHAN JURAN; Interior Decoration: THOMAS LITTLE and PAUL S. FOX.

Color

CAESAR AND CLEOPATRA, Rank, UA (British): JOHN BRYAN; Interior Decoration: No credits listed.

HENRY V, Rank, UA (British): PAUL SHERIFF and CARMEN DILLON; Interior Decoration: No credits listed.

★ THE YEARLING, Metro-Goldwyn-Mayer: CEDRIC GIBBONS and PAUL GROESSE; Interior Decoration: EDWIN B. WILLIS.

1947 Twentieth Year*

Black and White

THE FOXES OF HARROW, 20th Century-Fox: LYLE WHEELER and MAURICE RANSFORD; Set Decoration: THOMAS LITTLE and PAUL S. FOX.

★ GREAT EXPECTATIONS, Rank-Cineguild, U-I (British): JOHN BRYAN; Set Decoration: WILFRED SHINGLETON.

Color

★ BLACK NARCISSUS, Rank-Archers, U-I (British): ALFRED JUNGE; Set Decoration: ALFRED JUNGE.

LIFE WITH FATHER, Warner Bros.: ROBERT M. HAAS; Set Decoration: GEORGE JAMES HOPKINS.

1948 Twenty-first Year

Black and White

★ HAMLET, Rank-Two Cities, U-I (British): ROGER K. FURSE; Set Decoration: CARMEN DILLON.

JOHNNY BELINDA, Warner Bros.: ROBERT HAAS; Set Decoration: WILLIAM WALLACE.

Color

JOAN OF ARC, Sierra Pictures, RKO Radio: RICHARD DAY; Set Decoration: EDWIN CASEY ROBERTS and JOSEPH KISH.

★ THE RED SHOES, Rank-Archers, Eagle-Lion (British): HEIN HECKROTH; Set Decoration: ARTHUR LAWSON.

1949 Twenty-second Year

Black and White

COME TO THE STABLE, 20th Century-Fox: LYLE WHEELER and JOSEPH C. WRIGHT; Set Decoration: THOMAS LITTLE and PAUL S. FOX.

★ THE HEIRESS, Paramount: JOHN MEEHAN and HARRY HORNER; Set Decoration: EMILE KURI.

MADAME BOVARY, Metro-Goldwyn-Mayer: CEDRIC GIBBONS and JACK MARTIN SMITH; Set Decoration: EDWIN B. WILLIS and RICHARD A. PEFFERLE.

Color

ADVENTURES OF DON JUAN, Warner Bros.: EDWARD CARRERE; Set Decoration: LYLE REIFSNIDER.

★ LITTLE WOMEN, Metro-Goldwyn-Mayer: CEDRIC GIBBONS and PAUL GROESSE; Set Decoration: EDWIN B. WILLIS and JACK D. MOORE.

SARABAND, Rank-Ealing, Eagle-Lion (British): JIM MORAHAN, WILLIAM KELLNER, and MICHAEL RELPH; Set Decoration: No credits listed.

1950 Twenty-third Year

Black and White

ALL ABOUT EVE, 20th Century-Fox: LYLE WHEELER and GEORGE DAVIS;

*Category name changed from Art Direction-Interior Decoration to Art Direction-Set Decoration.

Set Decoration: THOMAS LITTLE and WALTER M. SCOTT.

THE RED DANUBE, Metro-Goldwyn-Mayer: CEDRIC GIBBONS and HANS PETERS; Set Decoration: EDWIN B. WILLIS and HUGH HUNT.

★ SUNSET BOULEVARD, Paramount: HANS DREIER and JOHN MEEHAN; Set Decoration: SAM COMER and RAY MOYER.

Color

ANNIE GET YOUR GUN, Metro-Goldwyn-Mayer: CEDRIC GIBBONS and PAUL GROESSE; Set Decoration: EDWIN B. WILLIS and RICHARD A. PEFFERLE.

DESTINATION MOON, George Pal, Eagle-Lion Classics: ERNST FEGTE; Set Decoration: GEORGE SAWLEY.

★ SAMSON AND DELILAH, DeMille-Paramount: HANS DREIER and WALTER TYLER; Set Decoration: SAM COMER and RAY MOYER.

1951 Twenty-fourth Year

Black and White

FOURTEEN HOURS, 20th Century-Fox: LYLE WHEELER and LELAND FULLER; Set Decoration: THOMAS LITTLE and FRED J. RODE.

HOUSE ON TELEGRAPH HILL, 20th Century-Fox: LYLE WHEELER and JOHN DECUIR; Set Decoration: THOMAS LITTLE and PAUL S. FOX.

LA RONDE, Sacha Gordine Prod., Commercial Pictures (French): D'EAUBONNE; Set Decoration: No credits listed.

★ A STREETCAR NAMED DESIRE, Chas. K. Feldman Group Prods., Warner Bros.: RICHARD DAY; Set Decoration: GEORGE JAMES HOPKINS.

TOO YOUNG TO KISS, Metro-Goldwyn-Mayer: CEDRIC GIBBONS and PAUL GROESSE; Set Decoration: EDWIN B. WILLIS and JACK D. MOORE.

Color

★ AN AMERICAN IN PARIS, Metro-Goldwyn-Mayer: CEDRIC GIBBONS and PRESTON AMES; Set Decoration: EDWIN B. WILLIS and KEOGH GLEASON.

DAVID AND BATHSHEBA, 20th Century-Fox: LYLE WHEELER and GEORGE DAVIS; Set Decoration: THOMAS LITTLE and PAUL S. FOX.

ON THE RIVIERA, 20th Century-Fox: LYLE WHEELER and LELAND FULLER; Musical Settings: JOSEPH C. WRIGHT; Set Decoration: THOMAS LITTLE and WALTER M. SCOTT.

QUO VADIS, Metro-Goldwyn-Mayer: WILLIAM A. HORNING, CEDRIC GIBBONS, and EDWARD CARFAGNO; Set Decoration: HUGH HUNT.

TALES OF HOFFMAN, Powell-Pressburger, Lopert (British): HEIN HECKROTH; Set Decoration: No credits listed.

1952 Twenty-fifth Year

Black and White

★ THE BAD AND THE BEAUTIFUL, Metro-Goldwyn-Mayer: CEDRIC GIBBONS and EDWARD CARFAGNO; Set Decoration: EDWIN B. WILLIS and KEOGH GLEASON.

CARRIE, Paramount: HAL PEREIRA and ROLAND ANDERSON; Set Decoration: EMILE KURI.

MY COUSIN RACHEL, 20th Century-Fox: LYLE WHEELER AND JOHN DECUIR; Set Decoration: WALTER M. SCOTT.

RASHOMON, Daiei, RKO Radio (Japanese): MATSUYAMA; Set Decoration: H. MOTSUMOTO.

VIVA ZAPATA!, 20th Century-Fox: LYLE WHEELER and LELAND FULLER; Set Decoration: THOMAS LITTLE and CLAUDE CARPENTER.

Color

HANS CHRISTIAN ANDERSEN, Goldwyn, RKO Radio: RICHARD DAY and

CLAVE; Set Decoration: HOWARD BRISTOL.

THE MERRY WIDOW, Metro-Goldwyn-Mayer: CEDRIC GIBBONS and PAUL GROESSE; Set Decoration: EDWIN B. WILLIS and ARTHUR KRAMS.

★ MOULIN ROUGE, Romulus Films, UA: PAUL SHERIFF; Set Decoration: MARCEL VERTES.

THE QUIET MAN, Argosy, Republic: FRANK HOTALING; Set Decoration: JOHN MCCARTHY, JR., and CHARLES THOMPSON.

THE SNOWS OF KILIMANJARO, 20th Century-Fox; LYLE WHEELER and JOHN DECUIR; Set Decoration: THOMAS LITTLE and PAUL S. FOX.

1953 Twenty-sixth Year

Black and White

★ JULIUS CAESAR, Metro-Goldwyn-Mayer: CEDRIC GIBBONS and EDWARD CARFAGNO; Set Decoration: EDWIN B. WILLIS and HUGH HUNT.

MARTIN LUTHER, Louis de Rochemont Assocs.: FRITZ MAURISCHAT and PAUL MARKWITZ; Set Decoration: No credits listed.

THE PRESIDENT'S LADY, 20th Century-Fox: LYLE WHEELER and LELAND FULLER; Set Decoration: PAUL S. FOX.

ROMAN HOLIDAY, Paramount: HAL PEREIRA and WALTER TYLER; Set Decoration: No credits listed.

TITANIC, 20th Century-Fox: LYLE WHEELER and MAURICE RANSFORD; Set Decoration: STUART REISS.

Color

KNIGHTS OF THE ROUND TABLE, Metro-Goldwyn-Mayer: ALFRED JUNGE and HANS PETERS; Set Decoration: JOHN JARVIS.

LILI, Metro-Goldwyn-Mayer: CEDRIC GIBBONS and PAUL GROESSE; Set Decoration: EDWIN B. WILLIS and ARTHUR KRAMS.

★ THE ROBE, 20th Century-Fox: LYLE WHEELER and GEORGE W. DAVIS; Set Decoration: WALTER M. SCOTT and PAUL S. FOX.

THE STORY OF THREE LOVES, Metro-Goldwyn-Mayer: CEDRIC GIBBONS, PRESTON AMES, EDWARD CARFAGNO, and GABRIEL SCOGNAMILLO; Set Decoration: EDWIN B. WILLIS, KEOGH GLEASON, ARTHUR KRAMS, and JACK D. MOORE.

YOUNG BESS, Metro-Goldwyn-Mayer: CEDRIC GIBBONS and URIE MCCLEARY; Set Decoration: EDWIN B. WILLIS and JACK D. MOORE.

1954 Twenty-seventh Year

Black and White

THE COUNTRY GIRL, Perlberg-Seaton, Paramount: HAL PEREIRA and ROLAND ANDERSON; Set Decoration: SAM COMER and GRACE GREGORY.

EXECUTIVE SUITE, Metro-Goldwyn-Mayer: CEDRIC GIBBONS and EDWARD CARFAGNO; Set Decoration: EDWIN B. WILLIS and EMILE KURI.

LE PLAISIR, Stera Film-CCFC Prod., Arthur Meyer-Edward Kingsley (French): MAX OPHULS; Set Decoration: No credits listed.

★ ON THE WATERFRONT, Horizon-American Corp., Columbia: RICHARD DAY; Set Decoration: No credits listed.

SABRINA, Paramount: HAL PEREIRA and WALTER TYLER; Set Decoration: SAM COMER and RAY MOYER.

Color

BRIGADOON, Metro-Goldwyn-Mayer: CEDRIC GIBBONS and PRESTON AMES; Set Decoration: EDWIN B. WILLIS and KEOGH GLEASON.

DESIREE, 20th Century-Fox: LYLE WHEELER and LELAND FULLER; Set

Decoration: WALTER M. SCOTT and PAUL S. FOX.

RED GARTERS, Paramount: HAL PEREIRA and ROLAND ANDERSON; Set Decoration: SAM COMER and RAY MOYER.

A STAR IS BORN, A Transcona Enterprises Prod., Warner Bros.: MALCOLM BERT, GENE ALLEN, and IRENE SHARAFF; Set Decoration: GEORGE JAMES HOPKINS.

★ 20,000 LEAGUES UNDER THE SEA, Walt Disney Prods., Buena Vista Film Dist. Co., Inc.: JOHN MEEHAN; Set Decoration: EMILE KURI.

1955 Twenty-eighth Year

Black and White

BLACKBOARD JUNGLE, Metro-Goldwyn-Mayer: CEDRIC GIBBONS and RANDALL DUELL; Set Decoration: EDWIN B. WILLIS and HENRY GRACE.

I'LL CRY TOMORROW, Metro-Goldwyn-Mayer: CEDRIC GIBBONS and MALCOLM BROWN; Set Decoration: EDWIN B. WILLIS and HUGH B. HUNT.

THE MAN WITH THE GOLDEN ARM, Otto Preminger Prod., UA: JOSEPH C. WRIGHT; Set Decoration: DARRELL SILVERA.

MARTY, Hecht and Lancaster's Steven Prods., UA: EDWARD S. HAWORTH and WALTER SIMONDS; Set Decoration: ROBERT PRIESTLEY.

★ THE ROSE TATTOO, Hal Wallis, Paramount: HAL PEREIRA and TAMBI LARSEN; Set Decoration: SAM COMER and ARTHUR KRAMS.

Color

DADDY LONG LEGS, 20th Century-Fox: LYLE WHEELER and JOHN DECUIR; Set Decoration: WALTER M. SCOTT and PAUL S. FOX.

GUYS AND DOLLS, Samuel Goldwyn Prods., Inc., M-G-M: OLIVER SMITH and JOSEPH C. WRIGHT; Set Decoration: HOWARD BRISTOL.

LOVE IS A MANY-SPLENDORED THING, 20th Century-Fox: LYLE WHEELER and GEORGE W. DAVIS; Set Decoration: WALTER M. SCOTT and JACK STUBBS.

★ PICNIC, Columbia: WILLIAM FLANNERY and JO MIELZINER; Set Decoration: ROBERT PRIESTLEY.

TO CATCH A THIEF, Paramount: HAL PEREIRA and JOSEPH MCMILLAN JOHNSON; Set Decoration: SAM COMER and ARTHUR KRAMS.

1956 Twenty-ninth Year

Black and White

THE MAGNIFICENT SEVEN (a.k.a. THE SEVEN SAMURAI), A Toho Prod., Kingsley International (Japanese): TAKASHI MATSUYAMA; Set Decoration: No credits listed.

THE PROUD AND THE PROFANE, The Perlberg-Seaton Prod., Paramount: HAL PEREIRA and A. EARL HEDRICK; Set Decoration: SAMUEL M. COMER and FRANK R. MCKELVY.

THE SOLID GOLD CADILLAC, Columbia: ROSS BELLAH; Set Decoration: WILLIAM R. KIERNAN and LOUIS DIAGE.

★ SOMEBODY UP THERE LIKES ME, Metro-Goldwyn-Mayer: CEDRIC GIBBONS and MALCOLM F. BROWN; Set Decoration: EDWIN B. WILLIS and F. KEOGH GLEASON.

TEENAGE REBEL, 20th Century-Fox: LYLE R. WHEELER and JACK MARTIN SMITH; Set Decoration: WALTER M. SCOTT and STUART A. REISS.

Color

AROUND THE WORLD IN 80 DAYS, The Michael Todd Co., Inc., UA: JAMES W. SULLIVAN and KEN ADAM; Set Decoration: ROSS J. DOWD.

GIANT, Giant Prod., Warner Bros.: BORIS LEVEN; Set Decoration: RALPH S. HURST.

★ THE KING AND I, 20th Century-Fox: LYLE R. WHEELER and JOHN DeCUIR; Set Decoration: WALTER M. SCOTT and PAUL S. FOX.

LUST FOR LIFE, Metro-Goldwyn-Mayer: CEDRIC GIBBONS, HANS PETERS, and PRESTON AMES; Set Decoration: EDWIN B. WILLIS and F. KEOGH GLEASON.

THE TEN COMMANDMENTS, Motion Picture Assocs., Inc., Paramount: HAL PEREIRA, WALTER H. TYLER, and ALBERT NOZAKI; Set Decoration: SAM M. COMER and RAY MOYER.

*1957 Thirtieth Year**

FUNNY FACE, Paramount: HAL PEREIRA and GEORGE W. DAVIS; Set Decoration: SAM COMER and RAY MOYER.

LES GIRLS, Sol C. Siegel Prods., Inc., M-G-M: WILLIAM A. HORNING and GENE ALLEN; Set Decoration: EDWIN B. WILLIS and RICHARD PEFFERLE.

PAL JOEY, Essex-George Sidney Prod., Columbia: WALTER HOLSCHER; Set Decoration: WILLIAM KIERNAN and LOUIS DIAGE.

RAINTREE COUNTY, Metro-Goldwyn-Mayer: WILLIAM A. HORNING and URIE MCCLEARY; Set Decoration: EDWIN B. WILLIS and HUGH HUNT.

★ SAYONARA, William Goetz Prod., Warner Bros.: TED HAWORTH; Set Decoration: ROBERT PRIESTLEY.

1958 Thirty-first Year

AUNTIE MAME, Warner Bros.: MALCOLM BERT; Set Decoration: GEORGE JAMES HOPKINS.

BELL, BOOK AND CANDLE, Phoenix Prods., Inc., Columbia: CARY ODELL; Set Decoration: LOUIS DIAGE.

A CERTAIN SMILE, 20th Century-Fox: LYLE R. WHEELER and JOHN DECUIR; Set Decoration: WALTER M. SCOTT and PAUL S. FOX.

★ GIGI, Arthur Freed Prods., Inc., M-G-M: WILLIAM A. HORNING and PRESTON AMES; Set Decoration: HENRY GRACE and KEOGH GLEASON.

VERTIGO, Alfred J. Hitchcock Prods., Inc., Paramount: HAL PEREIRA and HENRY BUMSTEAD; Set Decoration: SAM COMER and FRANK MCKELVY.

1959 Thirty-second Year†

Black and White

CAREER, Hal Wallis Prods., Paramount: HAL PEREIRA and WALTER TYLER; Set Decoration: SAM COMER and ARTHUR KRAMS.

★ THE DIARY OF ANNE FRANK, 20th Century-Fox: LYLE R. WHEELER and GEORGE W. DAVIS; Set Decoration: WALTER M. SCOTT and STUART A. REISS.

THE LAST ANGRY MAN, Fred Kohlmar Prods., Columbia: CARL ANDERSON; Set Decoration: WILLIAM KIERNAN.

SOME LIKE IT HOT, Ashton Prods. and The Mirisch Co., UA: TED HAWORTH; Set Decoration: EDWARD G. BOYLE.

SUDDENLY, LAST SUMMER, Horizon Prod., Columbia: OLIVER MESSELL and WILLIAM KELLNER; Set Decoration: SCOT SLIMON.

Color

★ BEN-HUR, Metro-Goldwyn-Mayer: WILLIAM A. HORNING and EDWARD CARFAGNO; Set Decoration: HUGH HUNT.

*Rules changed this year to one award for Art Direction instead of separate awards for black and white and color.

†Rules changed this year to two awards for Art Direction: one for black and white and one for color.

THE BIG FISHERMAN, Rowland V. Lee Prods., Buena Vista Film Dist. Co., Inc.: JOHN DECUIR; Set Decoration: JULIA HERON.

JOURNEY TO THE CENTER OF THE EARTH, Joseph M. Schenck Enterprises, Inc. and Cooga Mooga Film Prods., Inc., 20th Century-Fox: LYLE R. WHEELER, FRANZ BACHELIN, and HERMAN A. BLUMENTHAL; Set Decoration: WALTER M. SCOTT and JOSEPH KISH.

NORTH BY NORTHWEST, Metro-Goldwyn-Mayer: WILLIAM A. HORNING, ROBERT BOYLE, and MERRILL PYE; Set Decoration: HENRY GRACE and FRANK MCKELVY.

PILLOW TALK, Arwin Prods., Inc., U-I: RICHARD H. RIEDEL; Set Decoration: RUSSELL A. GAUSMAN and RUBY R. LEVITT.

1960 Thirty-third Year

Black and White

★ THE APARTMENT, The Mirisch Co., Inc., UA: ALEXANDER TRAUNER; Set Decoration: EDWARD G. BOYLE.

THE FACTS OF LIFE, Panama and Frank Prod., UA: JOSEPH MCMILLAN JOHNSON and KENNETH A. REID; Set Decoration: ROSS DOWD.

PSYCHO, Alfred J. Hitchcock Prods., Paramount: JOSEPH HURLEY and ROBERT CLATWORTHY; Set Decoration: GEORGE MILO.

SONS AND LOVERS, Company of Artists, Inc., 20th Century-Fox: TOM MORAHAN; Set Decoration: LIONEL COUCH.

VISIT TO A SMALL PLANET, Hal Wallis Prods., Paramount: HAL PEREIRA and WALTER TYLER; Set Decoration: SAM COMER and ARTHUR KRAMS.

Color

CIMARRON, Metro-Goldwyn-Mayer: GEORGE W. DAVIS and ADDISON HEHR; Set Decoration: HENRY GRACE, HUGH HUNT, and OTTO SIEGEL.

IT STARTED IN NAPLES, Paramount and Capri Prod., Paramount: HAL PEREIRA and ROLAND ANDERSON; Set Decoration: SAM COMER and ARRIGO BRESCHI.

PEPE, G.S.-Posa Films International Prod., Columbia: TED HAWORTH; Set Decoration: WILLIAM KIERNAN.

★ SPARTACUS, Bryna Prods., Inc., U-I: ALEXANDER GOLITZEN and ERIC ORBOM; Set Decoration: RUSSELL A. GAUSMAN and JULIA HERON.

SUNRISE AT CAMPOBELLO, Schary Prod., Warner Bros.: EDWARD CARRERE; Set Decoration: GEORGE JAMES HOPKINS.

1961 Thirty-fourth Year

Black and White

THE ABSENT MINDED PROFESSOR, Walt Disney Prod., Buena Vista Distribution Co., Inc.: CARROLL CLARK; Set Decoration: EMILE KURI and HAL GAUSMAN.

THE CHILDREN'S HOUR. Mirisch-Worldwide Prod., UA: FERNANDO CARRERE; Set Decoration: EDWARD G. BOYLE.

★ THE HUSTLER, Robert Rossen Prod., 20th Century-Fox: HARRY HORNER; Set Decoration: GENE CALLAHAN.

JUDGMENT AT NUREMBERG, Stanley Kramer Prod., UA: RUDOLPH STERNAD; Set Decoration: GEORGE MILO.

LA DOLCE VITA, Riama Film Prod., Astor Pictures, Inc. (Italian): PIERO GHERARDI.

Color

BREAKFAST AT TIFFANY'S, Jurow-Shepherd Prod., Paramount: HAL PEREIRA and ROLAND ANDERSON; Set

Decoration: SAM COMER and RAY MOYER.

EL CID, Samuel Bronston Prod., in association with Dear Film Prod., Allied Artists: VENIERO COLASANTI and JOHN MOORE.

FLOWER DRUM SONG, Universal-International-Ross Hunter Prod., in association with Joseph Fields, U-I: ALEXANDER GOLITZEN and JOSEPH WRIGHT; Set Decoration: HOWARD BRISTOL.

SUMMER AND SMOKE, Hal Wallis Prod., Paramount: HAL PEREIRA and WALTER TYLER; Set Decoration: SAM COMER and ARTHUR KRAMS.

★ WEST SIDE STORY, Mirisch Pictures, Inc., and B and P Enterprises, Inc., UA: BORIS LEVEN; Set Decoration: VICTOR A. GANGELIN.

1962 Thirty-fifth Year

Black and White

DAYS OF WINE AND ROSES, Martin Manulis-Jalem Prod., Warner Bros.: JOSEPH WRIGHT; Set Decoration: GEORGE JAMES HOPKINS.

THE LONGEST DAY, Darryl F. Zanuck Prods., 20th Century-Fox: TED HAWORTH, LEON BARSACQ, and VINCENT KORDA; Set Decoration: GABRIEL BECHIR.

PERIOD OF ADJUSTMENT, Marten Prod., M-G-M: GEORGE W. DAVIS and EDWARD CARFAGNO; Set Decoration: HENRY GRACE and DICK PEFFERLE.

THE PIGEON THAT TOOK ROME, Llenroc Prods., Paramount: HAL PEREIRA and ROLAND ANDERSON; Set Decoration: SAM COMER and FRANK R. MCKELVY.

★ TO KILL A MOCKINGBIRD, Universal-International-Pakula-Mulligan-Brentwood Prod., U-I: ALEXANDER GOLITZEN and HENRY BUMSTEAD; Set Decoration: OLIVER EMERT.

Color

★ LAWRENCE OF ARABIA, Horizon Pictures (G.B.), Ltd.-Sam Spiegel-David Lean Prod., Columbia: JOHN BOX and JOHN STOLL; Set Decoration: DARIO SIMONI.

THE MUSIC MAN, Warner Bros.: PAUL GROESSE; Set Decoration: GEORGE JAMES HOPKINS.

MUTINY ON THE BOUNTY, Arcola Prod., M-G-M: GEORGE W. DAVIS and J. MCMILLAN JOHNSON; Set Decoration: HENRY GRACE and HUGH HUNT.

THAT TOUCH OF MINK, Universal-International-Granley-Arwin-Nob Hill Prod., U-I: ALEXANDER GOLITZEN and ROBERT CLATWORTHY; Set Decoration: GEORGE MILO.

THE WONDERFUL WORLD OF THE BROTHERS GRIMM, Metro-Goldwyn-Mayer and Cinerama: GEORGE W. DAVIS and EDWARD CARFAGNO; Set Decoration: HENRY GRACE and DICK PEFFERLE.

1963 Thirty-sixth Year

Black and White

★ AMERICA AMERICA, Athena Enterprises Prod., Warner Bros.: GENE CALLAHAN.

FEDERICO FELLINI'S 8½, Cineriz Prod., Embassy Pictures: PIERO GHERARDI.

HUD, Salem-Dover Prod., Paramount: HAL PEREIRA and TAMBI LARSEN; Set Decoration: SAM COMER and ROBERT BENTON.

LOVE WITH THE PROPER STRANGER, Boardwalk-Rona Prod., Paramount: HAL PEREIRA and ROLAND ANDERSON; Set Decoration: SAM COMER and GRACE GREGORY.

TWILIGHT OF HONOR, Perlberg-Seaton Prod., M-G-M: GEORGE W. DAVIS and

PAUL GROESSE; Set Decoration: HENRY GRACE and HUGH HUNT.

Color

THE CARDINAL, Gamma Production, Columbia: LYLE WHEELER; Set Decoration: GENE CALLAHAN.

★ CLEOPATRA, 20th Century-Fox Ltd.-MCL Films S.A.-WALWA Films S.A. Prod., 20th Century Fox: JOHN DeCUIR, JACK MARTIN SMITH, HILYARD BROWN, HERMAN BLUMENTHAL, ELVEN WEBB, MAURICE PELLING, and BORIS JURAGA; Set Decoration: WALTER M. SCOTT, PAUL S. FOX, and RAY MOYER.

COME BLOW YOUR HORN, Essex-Tandem Enterprises Prod., Paramount: HAL PEREIRA and ROLAND ANDERSON; Set Decoration: SAM COMER and JAMES PAYNE.

HOW THE WEST WAS WON, Metro-Goldwyn-Mayer and Cinerama: GEORGE W. DAVIS, WILLIAM FERRARI, and ADDISON HEHR; Set Decoration: HENRY GRACE, DON GREENWOOD, JR., and JACK MILLS.

TOM JONES, Woodfall Production, UA-Lopert Pictures: RALPH BRINTON, TED MARSHALL, and JOCELYN HERBERT; Set Decoration: JOSIE MACAVIN.

1964 Thirty-seventh Year

Black and White

THE AMERICANIZATION OF EMILY, Martin Ransohoff Prod., M-G-M: GEORGE W. DAVIS, HANS PETERS, and ELLIOT SCOTT; Set Decoration: HENRY GRACE and ROBERT R. BENTON.

HUSH . . . HUSH, SWEET CHARLOTTE, Associates and Aldrich Prod., 20th Century-Fox: WILLIAM GLASGOW; Set Decoration: RAPHAEL BRETTON.

THE NIGHT OF THE IGUANA, Seven Arts Prod., M-G-M: STEPHEN GRIMES.

SEVEN DAYS IN MAY, Joel Prods., Paramount: CARY ODELL; Set Decoration: EDWARD G. BOYLE.

★ ZORBA THE GREEK, Rochley, Ltd. Prod., International Classics: VASSILIS FOTOPOULOS.

Color

BECKET, Hal Wallis Prod., Paramount: JOHN BRYAN and MAURICE CARTER; Set Decoration: PATRICK MCLOUGHLIN and ROBERT CARTWRIGHT.

MARY POPPINS, Walt Disney Prods.: CARROLL CLARK and WILLIAM H. TUNTKE; Set Decoration: EMILE KURI and HAL GAUSMAN.

★ MY FAIR LADY, Warner Bros.: GENE ALLEN and CECIL BEATON; Set Decoration: GEORGE JAMES HOPKINS.

THE UNSINKABLE MOLLY BROWN, Marten Prod., M-G-M: GEORGE W. DAVIS and PRESTON AMES; Set Decoration: HENRY GRACE and HUGH HUNT.

WHAT A WAY TO GO, Apjac-Orchard Prod., 20th Century-Fox: JACK MARTIN SMITH and TED HAWORTH; Set Decoration: WALTER M. SCOTT and STUART A. REISS.

1965 Thirty-eighth Year

Black and White

KING RAT, Coleytown Prod., Columbia: ROBERT EMMET SMITH; Set Decoration: FRANK TUTTLE.

A PATCH OF BLUE, Pandro S. Berman-Guy Green Prod., M-G-M: GEORGE W. DAVIS and URIE MCCLEARY; Set Decoration: HENRY GRACE and CHARLES S. THOMPSON.

★ SHIP OF FOOLS, Columbia: ROBERT CLATWORTHY; Set Decoration: JOSEPH KISH.

THE SLENDER THREAD, Paramount: HAL PEREIRA and JACK POPLIN; Set Decoration: ROBERT BENTON and JOSEPH KISH.

THE SPY WHO CAME IN FROM THE COLD, Salem Films, Ltd. Prod., Paramount: HAL PEREIRA, TAMBI LARSEN, and EDWARD MARSHALL; Set Decoration: JOSIE MACAVIN.

Color

THE AGONY AND THE ECSTASY, International Classics Prod., 20th Century-Fox: JOHN DECUIR and JACK MARTIN SMITH; Set Decoration: DARIO SIMONI.

★ DOCTOR ZHIVAGO, Sostar S.A.-Metro-Goldwyn-Mayer British Studios, Ltd. Prod., M-G-M: JOHN BOX and TERRY MARSH; Set Decoration: DARIO SIMONI.

THE GREATEST STORY EVER TOLD, George Stevens Prod., United Artists: RICHARD DAY, WILLIAM CREBER, and DAVID HALL; Set Decoration: RAY MOYER, FRED MACLEAN, and NORMAN ROCKETT.

INSIDE DAISY CLOVER, Park Place Prod., Warner Bros.: ROBERT CLATWORTHY; Set Decoration: GEORGE JAMES HOPKINS.

THE SOUND OF MUSIC, Argyle Enterprises Prod., 20th Century-Fox: BORIS LEVEN; Set Decoration: WALTER M. SCOTT and RUBY LEVITT.

1966 Thirty-ninth Year

Black and White

THE FORTUNE COOKIE, Phalanx-Jalem-Mirisch Corp. of Delaware Prod., U.A.: ROBERT LUTHARDT; Set Decoration: EDWARD G. BOYLE.

THE GOSPEL ACCORDING TO ST. MATTHEW, Arco-Lux Cie Cinematografique de France Prod., Walter Reade-Continental Distributing: LUIGI SCACCIANOCE.

IS PARIS BURNING?, Transcontinental Films-Marianne Prod., Paramount: WILLY HOLT; Set Decoration: MARC FREDERIX and PIERRE GUFFROY.

MISTER BUDDWING, DDD-Cherokee Prod., M-G-M: GEORGE W. DAVIS and PAUL GROESSE; Set Decoration: HENRY GRACE and HUGH HUNT.

★ WHO'S AFRAID OF VIRGINIA WOOLF?, Chenault Prod., Warner Bros.: RICHARD SYLBERT; Set Decoration: GEORGE JAMES HOPKINS.

Color

★ FANTASTIC VOYAGE, 20th Century-Fox: JACK MARTIN SMITH and DALE HENNESY; Set Decoration: WALTER M. SCOTT and STUART A. REISS.

GAMBIT, Universal: ALEXANDER GOLITZEN and GEORGE C. WEBB; Set Decoration: JOHN MCCARTHY and JOHN AUSTIN.

JULIET OF THE SPIRITS, Rizzoli Films S.P.A. Prod., Rizzoli Films: PIERO GHERARDI.

THE OSCAR, Greene-Rouse Prod., Embassy: HAL PEREIRA and ARTHUR LONERGAN; Set Decoration: ROBERT BENTON and JAMES PAYNE.

THE SAND PEBBLES, Argyle-Solar Prod., 20th Century-Fox: BORIS LEVEN; Set Decoration: WALTER M. SCOTT, JOHN STURTEVANT, and WILLIAM KIERNAN.

*1967 Fortieth Year**

★ CAMELOT, Warner Bros.-Seven Arts: JOHN TRUSCOTT and EDWARD CARRERE; Set Decoration: JOHN W. BROWN.

DOCTOR DOLITTLE, Apjac Prods., 20th Century-Fox: MARIO CHIARI, JACK

*Rules changed this year to one award for Art Direction instead of separate awards for black and white and color.

MARTIN SMITH, and ED GRAVES; Set Decoration: WALTER M. SCOTT and STUART A. REISS.

GUESS WHO'S COMING TO DINNER, Columbia: ROBERT CLATWORTHY; Set Decoration: FRANK TUTTLE.

THE TAMING OF THE SHREW, Royal Films International-Films Artistici Internazionali S.r.L. Prod., Columbia: RENZO MONGIARDINO, JOHN DECUIR, ELVEN WEBB, and GIUSEPPE MARIANI; Set Decoration: DARIO SIMONI and LUIGI GERVASI.

THOROUGHLY MODERN MILLIE, Ross Hunter-Universal Prod., Universal: ALEXANDER GOLITZEN and GEORGE C. WEBB; Set Decoration: HOWARD BRISTOL.

1968 Forty-first Year

★ OLIVER!, Romulus Films, Ltd., Columbia. JOHN BOX and TERENCE MARSH; Set Decoration: VERNON DIXON and KEN MUGGLESTON.

THE SHOES OF THE FISHERMAN, George Englund Prod., Metro-Goldwyn-Mayer: GEORGE W. DAVIS and EDWARD CARFAGNO.

STAR!, Robert Wise Prod., 20th Century-Fox: BORIS LEVEN; Set Decoration: WALTER M. SCOTT and HOWARD BRISTOL.

2001: A SPACE ODYSSEY, Polaris Prod., Metro-Goldwyn-Mayer: TONY MASTERS, HARRY LANGE, and ERNIE ARCHER.

WAR AND PEACE, Mosfilm Prod., Walter Reade-Continental Dist.: MIKHAIL BOGDANOV and GENNADY MYASNIKOV; Set Decoration: G. KOSHELEV and V. UVAROV.

1969 Forty-second Year

ANNE OF THE THOUSAND DAYS, Hal B. Wallis-Universal Pictures, Ltd. Prod., Universal: MAURICE CARTER and LIONEL COUCH; Set Decoration: PATRICK MCLOUGHLIN.

GAILY, GAILY, Mirisch-Cartier Prod., United Artists: ROBERT BOYLE and GEORGE B. CHAN; Set Decoration: EDWARD BOYLE and CARL BIDDISCOMBE.

★ HELLO, DOLLY!, Chenault Prods., 20th Century-Fox: JOHN DeCUIR, JACK MARTIN SMITH, and HERMAN BLUMENTHAL; Set Decoration: WALTER M. SCOTT, GEORGE HOPKINS, and RAPHAEL BRETTON.

SWEET CHARITY, Universal: ALEXANDER GOLITZEN and GEORGE C. WEBB; Set Decoration: JACK D. MOORE.

THEY SHOOT HORSES, DON'T THEY?, Chartoff-Winkler-Pollack Prod., ABC Pictures Presentation, Cinerama: HARRY HORNER; Set Decoration: FRANK MCKELVEY.

1970 Forty-third Year

AIRPORT, Ross Hunter-Universal Prod., Universal: ALEXANDER GOLITZEN and E. PRESTON AMES; Set Decoration: JACK D. MOORE and MICKEY S. MICHAELS.

THE MOLLY MAGUIRES, Tamm Prods., Paramount: TAMBI LARSEN; Set Decoration: DARRELL SILVERA.

★ PATTON, 20th Century-Fox: URIE McCLEARY and GIL PARRONDO; Set Decoration: ANTONIO MATEOS and PIERRE-LOUIS THEVENET.

SCROOGE, Waterbury Films, Ltd. Prod., Cinema Center Films Presentation, National General: TERRY MARSH and BOB CARTWRIGHT; Set Decoration: PAMELA CORNELL.

TORA! TORA! TORA!, 20th Century-Fox: JACK MARTIN SMITH, YOSHIRO MURAKI, RICHARD DAY, and TAIZOH KAWASHIMA; Set Decoration: WALTER M. SCOTT, NORMAN ROCKETT, and CARL BIDDISCOMBE.

1971 Forty-fourth Year

THE ANDROMEDA STRAIN, A Universal-Robert Wise Prod., Universal: BORIS LEVEN and WILLIAM TUNTKE; Set Decoration: RUBY LEVITT.

BEDKNOBS AND BROOMSTICKS, Walt Disney Prods., Buena Vista Distribution Company: JOHN B. MANSBRIDGE and PETER ELLENSHAW; Set Decoration: EMILE KURI and HAL GAUSMAN.

FIDDLER ON THE ROOF, Mirisch-Cartier Prods., UA: ROBERT BOYLE and MICHAEL STRINGER; Set Decoration: PETER LAMONT.

MARY, QUEEN OF SCOTS, Hal Wallis-Universal Pictures, Ltd. Prod., Universal: TERENCE MARSH and ROBERT CARTWRIGHT; Set Decoration: PETER HOWITT.

★ NICHOLAS AND ALEXANDRA, A Horizon Pictures Prod., Columbia: JOHN BOX, ERNEST ARCHER, JACK MAXSTED, and GIL PARRONDO; Set Decoration: VERNON DIXON.

1972 Forty-fifth Year

★ CABARET, An ABC Pictures Production, Allied Artists: ROLF ZEHETBAUER and JURGEN KIEBACH; Set Decoration: HERBERT STRABEL.

LADY SINGS THE BLUES, A Motown-Weston-Furie Production, Paramount: CARL ANDERSON; Set Decoration: REG ALLEN.

THE POSEIDON ADVENTURE, An Irwin Allen Production, 20th Century-Fox: WILLIAM CREBER; Set Decoration: RAPHAEL BRETTON.

TRAVELS WITH MY AUNT, Robert Fryer Productions, Metro-Goldwyn-Mayer: JOHN BOX, GIL PARRONDO, and ROBERT W. LAING.

YOUNG WINSTON, An Open Road Films, Ltd. Production, Columbia: DON ASHTON, GEOFFREY DRAKE, JOHN GRAYSMARK, and WILLIAM HUTCHINSON; Set Decoration: PETER JAMES.

1973 Forty-sixth Year

BROTHER SUN SISTER MOON, Euro International Films-Vic Film (Prods.), Ltd., Paramount: LORENZO MONGIARDINO and GIANNI QUARANTA; Set Decoration: CARMELO PATRONO.

THE EXORCIST, Hoya Prods., Warner Bros.: BILL MALLEY; Set Decoration: JERRY WUNDERLICH.

★ THE STING, A Universal-Bill/Phillips-George Roy Hill Film Prod., Zanuck/Brown Presentation, Universal: HENRY BUMSTEAD; Set Decoration: JAMES PAYNE.

TOM SAWYER, An Arthur P. Jacobs Prod., Reader's Digest Presentation, UA: PHILIP JEFFERIES; Set Decoration: ROBERT DE VESTEL.

THE WAY WE WERE, Rastar Prods., Columbia: STEPHEN GRIMES; Set Decoration: WILLIAM KIERNAN.

1974 Forty-seventh Year

CHINATOWN, A Robert Evans Prod., Paramount: RICHARD SYLBERT and W. STEWART CAMPBELL; Set Decoration: RUBY LEVITT.

EARTHQUAKE, A Universal-Mark Robson-Filmakers Group Prod., Universal: ALEXANDER GOLITZEN and E. PRESTON AMES; Set Decoration: FRANK MCKELVY.

★ THE GODFATHER PART II, A Coppola Company Prod., Paramount: DEAN TAVOULARIS and ANGELO GRAHAM; Set Decoration: GEORGE R. NELSON.

THE ISLAND AT THE TOP OF THE WORLD, Walt Disney Prods., Buena Vista Distribution Company: PETER ELLENSHAW, JOHN B. MANSBRIDGE, WALTER TYLER, and AL ROELOFS; Set Decoration: HAL GAUSMAN.

THE TOWERING INFERNO, An Irwin Allen Prod., 20th Century-Fox/ Warner Bros.: WILLIAM CREBER and WARD PRESTON; Set Decoration: RAPHAEL BRETTON.

1975 Forty-eighth Year

★ BARRY LYNDON, A Hawk Films, Ltd. Production, Warner Bros.: KEN ADAM and ROY WALKER; Set Decoration: VERNON DIXON.

THE HINDENBURG, A Robert Wise-Filmakers Group-Universal Production, Universal: EDWARD CARFAGNO; Set Decoration: FRANK MCKELVY.

THE MAN WHO WOULD BE KING, An Allied Artists-Columbia Pictures Production, Allied Artists: ALEXANDER TRAUNER and TONY INGLIS; Set Decoration: PETER JAMES.

SHAMPOO, Rubeeker Productions, Columbia: RICHARD SYLBERT and W. STEWART CAMPBELL; Set Decoration: GEORGE GAINES.

THE SUNSHINE BOYS, A Ray Stark Production, Metro-Goldwyn-Mayer: ALBERT BRENNER; Set Decoration: MARVIN MARCH.

1976 Forty-ninth Year

★ ALL THE PRESIDENT'S MEN, A Wildwood Enterprises Production, Warner Bros.: GEORGE JENKINS; Set Decoration: GEORGE GAINES.

THE INCREDIBLE SARAH, A Helen M. Strauss-Reader's Digest Films, Ltd. Production, Seymour Borde and Associates: ELLIOT SCOTT and NORMAN REYNOLDS.

THE LAST TYCOON, A Sam Spiegel-Elia Kazan Film Production, Paramount: GENE CALLAHAN and JACK COLLIS; Set Decoration: JERRY WUNDERLICH.

LOGAN'S RUN, A Saul David Production, Metro-Goldwyn-Mayer: DALE HENNESY; Set Decoration: ROBERT DE VESTEL.

THE SHOOTIST, A Frankovich/Self Production, Dino De Laurentiis Presentation, Paramount: ROBERT F. BOYLE; Set Decoration: ARTHUR JEPH PARKER.

1977 Fiftieth Year

AIRPORT '77, A Jennings Lang Production, Universal: GEORGE C. WEBB; Set Decoration: MICKEY S. MICHAELS.

CLOSE ENCOUNTERS OF THE THIRD KIND, Close Encounter Productions, Columbia: JOE ALVES and DAN LOMINO; Set Decoration: PHIL ABRAMSON.

THE SPY WHO LOVED ME, Eon Productions, United Artists: KEN ADAM and PETER LAMONT; Set Decoration: HUGH SCAIFE.

★ STAR WARS, A Twentieth Century-Fox Production, 20th Century-Fox: JOHN BARRY, NORMAN REYNOLDS, and LESLIE DILLEY; Set Decoration: ROGER CHRISTIAN.

THE TURNING POINT, Hera Productions, 20th Century-Fox: ALBERT BRENNER; Set Decoration: MARVIN MARCH.

1978 Fifty-first Year

THE BRINK'S JOB, A William Friedkin Film/Universal Production, Dino De Laurentiis Presentation, Universal: DEAN TAVOULARIS and ANGELO GRAHAM; Set Decoration: GEORGE R. NELSON.

CALIFORNIA SUITE, A Ray Stark Production, Columbia: ALBERT BRENNER; Set Decoration: MARVIN MARCH.

★ HEAVEN CAN WAIT, Dogwood Productions, Paramount: PAUL SYLBERT and EDWIN O'DONOVAN; Set Decoration: GEORGE GAINES.

INTERIORS, A Jack Rollins-Charles H. Joffe Production, United Artists: MEL

BOURNE; Set Decoration: DANIEL ROBERT.

THE WIZ, A Motown/Universal Pictures Production, Universal: TONY WALTON and PHILIP ROSENBERG; Set Decoration: EDWARD STEWART and ROBERT DRUMHELLER.

1979 Fifty-second Year

ALIEN, Twentieth Century-Fox Productions Limited, 20th Century-Fox: MICHAEL SEYMOUR, LES DILLEY, and ROGER CHRISTIAN; Set Decoration: IAN WHITTAKER.

★ ALL THAT JAZZ, A Columbia/ Twentieth Century-Fox Production, 20th Century-Fox: PHILIP ROSENBERG and TONY WALTON; Set Decoration: EDWARD STEWART and GARY BRINK.

APOCALYPSE NOW, An Omni Zoetrope Production, UA: DEAN TAVOULARIS and ANGELO GRAHAM; Set Decoration: GEORGE R. NELSON.

THE CHINA SYNDROME, A Michael Douglas/IPC Films Production, Columbia: GEORGE JENKINS; Set Decoration: ARTHUR JEPH PARKER.

STAR TREK—THE MOTION PICTURE, A Century Associates Production, Paramount: HAROLD MICHELSON, JOE JENNINGS, LEON HARRIS, and JOHN VALLONE; Set Decoration: LINDA DESCENNA.

1980 Fifty-third Year

COAL MINER'S DAUGHTER, A Bernard Schwartz-Universal Pictures Production, Universal: JOHN W. CORSO; Set Decoration: JOHN M. DWYER.

THE ELEPHANT MAN, A Brooksfilms, Ltd. Production, Paramount: STUART CRAIG and BOB CARTWRIGHT; Set Direction: HUGH SCAIFE.

THE EMPIRE STRIKES BACK, A Lucasfilm, Ltd. Production, 20th Century-Fox: NORMAN REYNOLDS, LESLIE DILLEY, HARRY LANGE, and ALAN TOMKINS; Set Decoration: MICHAEL FORD.

KAGEMUSHA (THE SHADOW WARRIOR), A Toho Co., Ltd.-Kurosawa Productions, Ltd.: Co-production, 20th Century-Fox: YOSHIRO MURAKI.

★ TESS, A Renn-Burrill Co-production with the participation of the Société Française de Production (S.F.P.), Columbia: PIERRE GUFFROY and JACK STEVENS.

1981 Fifty-fourth Year

THE FRENCH LIEUTENANT'S WOMAN, A Parlon Production, UA: ASSHETON GORTON; Set Decoration: ANN MOLLO.

HEAVEN'S GATE, Partisan Productions, Ltd., UA: TAMBI LARSEN; Set Decoration: JIM BERKEY.

RAGTIME, A Ragtime Production, Paramount: JOHN GRAYSMARK, PATRIZIA VON BRANDENSTEIN, and ANTHONY READING; Set Decoration: GEORGE DE TITTA, SR., GEORGE DE TITTA, JR., and PETER HOWITT.

★ RAIDERS OF THE LOST ARK, A Lucasfilm Production, Paramount: NORMAN REYNOLDS and LESLIE DILLEY; Set Decoration: MICHAEL FORD.

REDS, A J.R.S. Production, Paramount: RICHARD SYLBERT; Set Decoration: MICHAEL SEIRTON.

1982 Fifty-fifth Year

ANNIE, A Rastar Films Production, Columbia: DALE HENNESY; Set Decoration: MARVIN MARCH.

BLADE RUNNER, A Michael Deeley-Ridley Scott Production, The Ladd Company/Sir Run Run Shaw: LAWRENCE G. PAULL and DAVID L. SNYDER; Set Decoration: LINDA DESCENNA.

★ GANDHI, An Indo-British Films

Production, Columbia: STUART CRAIG and BOB LAING; Set Decoration: MICHAEL SEIRTON.

LA TRAVIATA, An Accent Films B.V. Production in association with RAI-Radiotelevisione Italiana, Producers Sales Organization: FRANCO ZEFFIRELLI; Set Decoration: GIANNI QUARANTA.

VICTOR/VICTORIA, A Metro-Goldwyn-Mayer Production, M-G-M/UA: RODGER MAUS, TIM HUTCHINSON, and WILLIAM CRAIG SMITH; Set Decoration: HARRY CORDWELL.

1983 Fifty-sixth Year

★ FANNY and ALEXANDER, A Cinematograph AB for the Swedish Film Institute/the Swedish Television SVT 1, Sweden/Gaumont, France/ Personafilm and Tobis Filmkunst, BRD Production, Embassy: ANNA ASP.

RETURN OF THE JEDI, A Lucasfilm Production, 20th Century-Fox: NORMAN REYNOLDS, FRED HOLE, and JAMES SCHOPPE; Set Decoration: MICHAEL FORD.

THE RIGHT STUFF, A Robert Chartoff-Irwin Winkler Production, The Ladd Company through Warner Bros.: GEOFFREY KIRKLAND, RICHARD J. LAWRENCE, W. STEWART CAMPBELL, and PETER ROMERO; Set Decoration: PAT PENDING and GEORGE R. NELSON.

TERMS OF ENDEARMENT, A James L. Brooks Production, Paramount: POLLY PLATT and HAROLD MICHELSON; Set Decoration: TOM PEDIGO and ANTHONY MONDELLO.

YENTL, A United Artists/Ladbroke Feature/Barwood Production, M-G-M/UA: ROY WALKER and LESLIE TOMKINS; Set Decoration: TESSA DAVIES.

1984 Fifty-seventh Year

★ AMADEUS, A Saul Zaentz Company Production, Orion: PATRIZIA VON BRANDENSTEIN; Set Decoration: KAREL CERNY.

THE COTTON CLUB, A Totally Independent Production, Orion: RICHARD SYLBERT; Set Decoration: GEORGE GAINES and LES BLOOM.

THE NATURAL, A Tri-Star Pictures Production, Tri-Star: ANGELO GRAHAM, MEL BOURNE, JAMES J. MURAKAMI, and SPEED HOPKINS; Set Decoration: BRUCE WEINTRAUB.

A PASSAGE TO INDIA, A G. W. Films Limited Production, Columbia: JOHN BOX and LESLIE TOMKINS; Set Decoration: HUGH SCAIFE.

2010, A Metro-Goldwyn-Mayer Presentation of a Peter Hyams Film Production, M-G-M/UA: ALBERT BRENNER; Set Decoration: RICK SIMPSON.

1985 Fifty-eighth Year

BRAZIL, an Embassy International Pictures Production, Universal: NORMAN GARWOOD; Set Decoration: MAGGIE GRAY.

THE COLOR PURPLE, a Warner Bros. Production, Warner Bros.: J. MICHAEL RIVA; Set Decoration: LINDA DE SCENNA.

★ OUT OF AFRICA, a Universal Pictures Limited Production, Universal: STEPHEN GRIMES; Set Decoration: JOSIE MACAVIN.

RAN, a Greenwich Film/Nippon Herald Films/Herald Ace Production, Orion Classics: YOSHIRO MURAKI and SHINOBU MURAKI.

WITNESS, an Edward S. Feldman Production, Paramount: STAN JOLLEY; Set Decoration: JOHN ANDERSON.

1986 Fifty-ninth Year

ALIENS, A Twentieth Century-Fox Film Production, 20th Century-Fox: PETER LAMONT; Set Decoration: CRISPIAN SALLIS.

THE COLOR OF MONEY, A Touchstone Pictures Production in association with Silver Screen Partners II, Buena Vista: BORIS LEVEN; Set Decoration: KAREN A. O'HARA.

HANNAH AND HER SISTERS, A Jack Rollins and Charles H. Joffe Production, Orion: STUART WURTZEL; Set Decoration: CAROL JOFFE.

THE MISSION, A Warner Bros./ Goldcrest and Kingsmere Production, Warner Bros.: STUART CRAIG; Set Decoration: JACK STEPHENS.

★ A ROOM WITH A VIEW, A Merchant Ivory Production, Cinecom: GIANNI QUARANTA and BRIAN ACKLAND-SNOW; Set Decoration: BRIAN SAVEGAR and ELIO ALTRAMURA.

1987 Sixtieth Year

EMPIRE OF THE SUN, A Warner Bros. Production, Warner Bros.: NORMAN REYNOLDS; Set Decoration: HARRY CORDWELL.

HOPE AND GLORY, A Davros Production Services Limited Production, Columbia: ANTHONY PRATT; Set Decoration: JOAN WOOLLARD.

★ THE LAST EMPEROR, A Hemdale Film Production, Columbia: FERDINANDO SCARFIOTTI; Set Decoration: BRUNO CESARI, and OSVALDO DESIDERI.

RADIO DAYS, A Jack Rollins and Charles H. Joffe Production, Orion: SANTO LOQUASTO; Set Decoration: CAROL JOFFE, LES BLOOM, and GEORGE DETITTA, JR.

THE UNTOUCHABLES, An Art Linson Production, Paramount: PATRIZIA VON BRANDENSTEIN; Set Decoration: HAL GAUSMAN.

1988 Sixty-first Year

BEACHES, A Touchstone Pictures Production in association with Silver Screen Partners III, Buena Vista: ALBERT BRENNER; Set Decoration: GARRETT LEWIS.

★ DANGEROUS LIAISONS, A Lorimar Production, Warner Bros.: STUART CRAIG; Set Decoration: GERARD JAMES.

RAIN MAN, A Guber-Peters Company Production, UA: IDA RANDOM; Set Decoration: LINDA DESCENNA.

TUCKER: THE MAN AND HIS DREAM, A Lucasfilm Production, Paramount: DEAN TAVOULARIS; Set Decoration: ARMIN GANZ.

WHO FRAMED ROGER RABBIT, An Amblin Entertainment and Touchstone Pictures Production, Buena Vista: ELLIOT SCOTT; Set Decoration: PETER HOWITT.

1989 Sixty-second Year

THE ABYSS, A Twentieth Century-Fox Production, 20th Century-Fox: LESLIE DILLEY; Set Decoration: ANNE KULJIAN.

THE ADVENTURES OF BARON MUNCHAUSEN, A Prominent Features and Laura Film Production, Columbia: DANTE FERRETTI; Set Decoration: FRANCESCA LO SCHIAVO.

★ BATMAN, A Warner Bros. Production, Warner Bros.: ANTON FURST; Set Decoration: PETER YOUNG.

DRIVING MISS DAISY, A Zanuck Company Production, Warner Bros.: BRUNO RUBEO; Set Decoration: CRISPIAN SALLIS.

GLORY, A Tri-Star Pictures Production, Tri-Star: NORMAN GARWOOD; Set Decoration: GARRETT LEWIS.

1990 Sixty-third Year

CYRANO DE BERGERAC, A Hachette Premiere Production, Orion Classics: EZIO FRIGERIO; Set Decoration: JACQUES ROUXEL.

DANCES WITH WOLVES, A Tig Production, Orion: JEFFREY

BEECROFT; Set Decoration: LISA DEAN.

★ DICK TRACY, A Touchstone Pictures Production, Buena Vista: RICHARD SYLBERT; Set Decoration: RICK SIMPSON.

THE GODFATHER PART III, A Zoetrope Studios Production, Paramount: DEAN TAVOULARIS; Set Decoration: GARY FETTIS.

HAMLET, An Icon Production, Warner Bros.: DANTE FERRETTI; Set Decoration: FRANCESCA LO SCHIAVO.

1991 Sixty-fourth Year

BARTON FINK, A Barton Circle Production, 20th Century-Fox: DENNIS GASSNER; Set Decoration: NANCY HAIGH.

★ BUGSY, a Tri-Star Pictures Production, Tri-Star: DENNIS GASSNER; Set Decoration: NANCY HAIGH.

THE FISHER KING, A Tri-Star Pictures Production, Tri-Star: MEL BOURNE; Set Decoration: CINDY CARR.

HOOK, A Tri-Star Pictures Production, Tri-Star: NORMAN GARWOOD; Set Decoration: GARRETT LEWIS.

THE PRINCE OF TIDES, A Barwood/Longfellow Production, Columbia: PAUL SYLBERT; Set Decoration: CARYL HELLER.

1992 Sixty-fifth Year

BRAM STOKER'S DRACULA, A Columbia Pictures Production, Columbia: THOMAS SANDERS; Set Decoration: GARRETT LEWIS.

CHAPLIN, A Carolco Pictures Production, Tri-Star: STUART CRAIG; Set Decoration: CHRIS A. BUTLER.

★ HOWARDS END, A Merchant Ivory Production, Sony Pictures Classics: LUCIANA ARRIGHI; Set Decoration: IAN WHITTAKER.

TOYS, A 20th Century-Fox Production, 20th Century-Fox: FERDINANDO SCARFIOTTI; Set Decoration: LINDA DeSCENNA.

UNFORGIVEN, A Warner Bros. Production, Warner Bros.: HENRY BUMSTEAD; Set Decoration: JANICE BLACKIE-GOODINE.

Sound

The Academy recognized the tremendous significance of sound at the first awards ceremony by giving a special award to Warner Brothers for producing *The Jazz Singer*. No other sound pictures won an award, however, because none were eligible. Sound was judged too recent a development to permit fair competition, so the first awards were limited to silent films. By the second year, sound pictures were allowed to compete, and they swept the awards. The third year, a new category called Sound Recording was established. Until 1969 the Sound Recording award, or simply Sound award as it was called after 1957, went to a studio's sound department. It was accepted by the head of the department who usually carried the title Sound Director. Since 1969 the award has gone to the re-recording mixers (not to exceed three) and the production mixer who actually do the work on the film being honored. The change was made at the request of the Academy Sound Branch which pointed out that recording conditions had changed and soundtracks could now be the work of more than one studio sound department or could represent the work of non-studio technicians.

Achievements in this category are nominated by members of the Academy Sound Branch.

*1929/30 Third Year**

★ THE BIG HOUSE, Cosmopolitan, Metro-Goldwyn-Mayer: DOUGLAS SHEARER for MGM STUDIO SOUND DEPARTMENT.

THE CASE OF SERGEANT GRISCHA, RKO Radio (JOHN TRIBBY for the RKO RADIO STUDIO SOUND DEPARTMENT).

THE LOVE PARADE, Paramount Famous Lasky (FRANKLIN HANSEN for the PARAMOUNT FAMOUS LASKY STUDIO SOUND DEPARTMENT).

RAFFLES, Samuel Goldwyn, UA (OSCAR LAGERSTROM for the UNITED ARTISTS STUDIO SOUND DEPARTMENT).

SONG OF THE FLAME, First National (GEORGE GROVES for the FIRST NATIONAL STUDIO SOUND DEPARTMENT).

1930/31 Fourth Year

METRO-GOLDWYN-MAYER STUDIO SOUND DEPARTMENT.

★ PARAMOUNT PUBLIX STUDIO SOUND DEPARTMENT.

RKO RADIO STUDIO SOUND DEPARTMENT.

SAMUEL GOLDWYN SOUND DEPARTMENT.

1931/32 Fifth Year

M-G-M STUDIO SOUND DEPARTMENT.

★ PARAMOUNT PUBLIX STUDIO SOUND DEPARTMENT.

RKO RADIO STUDIO SOUND DEPARTMENT.

*Nominations this year were by film title, and only the Sound Department associated with the winning film was announced. The Sound Departments that worked on the other nominated films are listed parenthetically to indicate that they received no official public nomination.

WARNER BROS.-FIRST NATIONAL STUDIO SOUND DEPARTMENT.

1932/33 Sixth Year

★ A FAREWELL TO ARMS, Paramount, PARAMOUNT STUDIO SOUND DEPARTMENT, FRANKLIN B. HANSEN, Sound Director.

42ND STREET, Warner Bros., WARNER BROS. STUDIO SOUND DEPARTMENT, NATHAN LEVINSON, Sound Director.

GOLDIGGERS OF 1933, Warner Bros., WARNER BROS. STUDIO SOUND DEPARTMENT, NATHAN LEVINSON. Sound Director.

I AM A FUGITIVE FROM A CHAIN GANG, Warner Bros., WARNER BROS. STUDIO SOUND DEPARTMENT, NATHAN LEVINSON, Sound Director.

1934 Seventh Year

THE AFFAIRS OF CELLINI, 20th Century, UA: UNITED ARTISTS STUDIO SOUND DEPARTMENT, THOMAS T. MOULTON, Sound Director.

CLEOPATRA, Paramount: PARAMOUNT STUDIO SOUND DEPARTMENT, FRANKLIN HANSEN, Sound Director.

FLIRTATION WALK, First National: WARNER BROS.-FIRST NATIONAL STUDIO SOUND DEPARTMENT, NATHAN LEVINSON, Sound Director.

THE GAY DIVORCEE, RKO Radio: RKO RADIO STUDIO SOUND DEPARTMENT, CARL DREHER, Sound Director.

IMITATION OF LIFE, Universal: UNIVERSAL STUDIO SOUND DEPARTMENT, THEODORE SODERBERG, Sound Director.

★ ONE NIGHT OF LOVE, Columbia: COLUMBIA STUDIO SOUND DEPARTMENT, JOHN LIVADARY, Sound Director.

VIVA VILLA, Metro-Goldwyn-Mayer: MGM STUDIO SOUND DEPARTMENT, DOUGLAS SHEARER, Sound Director.

THE WHITE PARADE, Jesse L. Lasky, Fox: FOX STUDIO SOUND DEPARTMENT, E. H. HANSEN, Sound Director.

1935 Eighth Year

THE BRIDE OF FRANKENSTEIN, Universal: UNIVERSAL STUDIO SOUND DEPARTMENT, GILBERT KURLAND, Sound Director.

CAPTAIN BLOOD, Warner Bros.: WARNER BROS.-FIRST NATIONAL STUDIO SOUND DEPARTMENT, NATHAN LEVINSON, Sound Director.

THE DARK ANGEL, Goldwyn, UA: UNITED ARTISTS STUDIO SOUND DEPARTMENT, THOMAS T. MOULTON. Sound Director.

I DREAM TOO MUCH, RKO Radio: RKO RADIO STUDIO SOUND DEPARTMENT, CARL DREHER, Sound Director.

LIVES OF A BENGAL LANCER, Paramount: PARAMOUNT STUDIO SOUND DEPARTMENT, FRANKLIN HANSEN, Sound Director.

LOVE ME FOREVER, Columbia: COLUMBIA STUDIO SOUND DEPARTMENT, JOHN LIVADARY, Sound Director.

★ NAUGHTY MARIETTA, Metro-Goldwyn-Mayer: M-G-M STUDIO SOUND DEPARTMENT, DOUGLAS SHEARER. Sound Director.

THANKS A MILLION, 20th Century-Fox: 20TH CENTURY-FOX STUDIO SOUND DEPARTMENT, E. H. HANSEN, Sound Director.

1,000 DOLLARS A MINUTE, Republic: REPUBLIC STUDIO SOUND DEPARTMENT.

1936 Ninth Year

BANJO ON MY KNEE, 20th Century-Fox: 20TH CENTURY-FOX STUDIO SOUND DEPARTMENT, E. H. HANSEN, Sound Director.

THE CHARGE OF THE LIGHT BRIGADE, Warner Bros.: WARNER BROS. STUDIO

SOUND DEPARTMENT, NATHAN LEVINSON, Sound Director.

DODSWORTH, Goldwyn, UA: UNITED ARTISTS STUDIO SOUND DEPARTMENT, THOMAS T. MOULTON, Sound Director.

GENERAL SPANKY, Roach, M-G-M: HAL ROACH STUDIO SOUND DEPARTMENT, ELMER A. RAGUSE, Sound Director.

MR. DEEDS GOES TO TOWN, Columbia: COLUMBIA STUDIO SOUND DEPT., JOHN LIVADARY, Sound Director.

★ SAN FRANCISCO, Metro-Goldwyn-Mayer: M-G-M STUDIO SOUND DEPARTMENT, DOUGLAS SHEARER, Sound Director.

THE TEXAS RANGERS, Paramount: PARAMOUNT STUDIO SOUND DEPARTMENT, FRANKLIN HANSEN, Sound Director.

THAT GIRL FROM PARIS, RKO Radio: RKO RADIO STUDIO SOUND DEPARTMENT, J. O. AALBERG, Sound Director.

THREE SMART GIRLS, Universal: UNIVERSAL STUDIO SOUND DEPARTMENT, HOMER G. TASKER, Sound Director.

1937 Tenth Year

THE GIRL SAID NO, Grand National: GRAND NATIONAL STUDIO SOUND DEPARTMENT, A. E. KAYE, Sound Director.

HITTING A NEW HIGH. RKO Radio: RKO RADIO STUDIO SOUND DEPARTMENT, JOHN AALBERG, Sound Director.

★ THE HURRICANE, Goldwyn, UA: UNITED ARTISTS STUDIO SOUND DEPARTMENT, THOMAS T. MOULTON, Sound Director.

IN OLD CHICAGO, 20th Century-Fox: 20TH CENTURY-FOX STUDIO SOUND DEPARTMENT, E. H. HANSEN, Sound Director.

THE LIFE OF EMILE ZOLA, Warner Bros.: WARNER BROS. STUDIO SOUND DEPARTMENT, NATHAN LEVINSON, Sound Director.

LOST HORIZON, Columbia: COLUMBIA STUDIO SOUND DEPARTMENT, JOHN LIVADARY, Sound Director.

MAYTIME, Metro-Goldwyn-Mayer: M-G-M STUDIO SOUND DEPARTMENT, DOUGLAS SHEARER, Sound Director.

100 MEN AND A GIRL, Universal: UNIVERSAL STUDIO SOUND DEPARTMENT, HOMER TASKER, Sound Director.

TOPPER, Roach, M-G-M: HAL ROACH STUDIO SOUND DEPARTMENT, ELMER RAGUSE, Sound Director.

WELLS FARGO, Paramount: PARAMOUNT STUDIO SOUND DEPARTMENT, L. L. RYDER, Sound Director.

1938 Eleventh Year

ARMY GIRL, Republic: REPUBLIC STUDIO SOUND DEPARTMENT, CHARLES LOOTENS, Sound Director.

★ THE COWBOY AND THE LADY, Goldwyn, UA: UNITED ARTISTS STUDIO SOUND DEPARTMENT, THOMAS MOULTON, Sound Director.

FOUR DAUGHTERS. Warner Bros.: WARNER BROS. STUDIO SOUND DEPARTMENT, NATHAN LEVINSON, Sound Director.

IF I WERE KING, Paramount: PARAMOUNT STUDIO SOUND DEPARTMENT, L. L. RYDER, Sound Director.

MERRILY WE LIVE, Roach, M-G-M: HAL ROACH STUDIO SOUND DEPARTMENT, ELMER RAGUSE, Sound Director.

SUEZ, 20th Century-Fox: 20TH CENTURY-FOX STUDIO SOUND DEPARTMENT, EDMUND HANSEN, Sound Director.

SWEETHEARTS, Metro-Goldwyn-Mayer: M-G-M STUDIO SOUND DEPARTMENT, DOUGLAS SHEARER, Sound Director.

THAT CERTAIN AGE, Universal: UNIVERSAL STUDIO SOUND

DEPARTMENT, BERNARD B. BROWN, Sound Director.

VIVACIOUS LADY, RKO Radio: RKO RADIO STUDIO SOUND DEPARTMENT, JAMES WILKINSON, Sound Director.

YOU CAN'T TAKE IT WITH YOU, Columbia: COLUMBIA STUDIO SOUND DEPARTMENT, JOHN LIVADARY, Sound Director.

1939 Twelfth Year

BALALAIKA, Metro-Goldwyn-Mayer: M-G-M STUDIO SOUND DEPARTMENT, DOUGLAS SHEARER, Sound Director.

GONE WITH THE WIND, Selznick. M-G-M: SAMUEL GOLDWYN STUDIO SOUND DEPARTMENT, THOMAS T. MOULTON, Sound Director.

GOODBYE, MR. CHIPS, Metro-Goldwyn-Mayer (British): DENHAM STUDIO SOUND DEPARTMENT, A. W. WATKINS, Sound Director.

THE GREAT VICTOR HERBERT, Paramount: PARAMOUNT STUDIO SOUND DEPARTMENT, LOREN RYDER, Sound Director.

THE HUNCHBACK OF NOTRE DAME, RKO Radio: RKO RADIO STUDIO SOUND DEPARTMENT, JOHN AALBERG, Sound Director.

MAN OF CONQUEST, Republic: REPUBLIC STUDIO SOUND DEPARTMENT, C. L. LOOTENS, Sound Director.

MR. SMITH GOES TO WASHINGTON, Columbia: COLUMBIA STUDIO SOUND DEPARTMENT, JOHN LIVADARY, Sound Director.

OF MICE AND MEN, Roach, M-G-M: HAL ROACH STUDIO SOUND DEPARTMENT, ELMER RAGUSE, Sound Director.

THE PRIVATE LIVES OF ELIZABETH AND ESSEX, Warner Bros.: WARNER BROS. STUDIO SOUND DEPARTMENT, NATHAN LEVINSON, Sound Director.

THE RAINS CAME, 20th Century-Fox: 20TH CENTURY-FOX STUDIO SOUND DEPARTMENT, E. H. HANSEN, Sound Director.

★ WHEN TOMORROW COMES, Universal: UNIVERSAL STUDIO SOUND DEPARTMENT, BERNARD B. BROWN, Sound Director.

1940 Thirteenth Year

BEHIND THE NEWS, Republic: REPUBLIC STUDIO SOUND DEPARTMENT, CHARLES LOOTENS, Sound Director.

CAPTAIN CAUTION, Roach, UA: HAL ROACH STUDIO SOUND DEPARTMENT, ELMER RAGUSE, Sound Director.

THE GRAPES OF WRATH, 20th Century-Fox: 20TH CENTURY-FOX STUDIO SOUND DEPARTMENT, E. H. HANSEN, Sound Director.

THE HOWARDS OF VIRGINIA, Columbia: GENERAL SERVICE STUDIO SOUND DEPARTMENT, JACK WHITNEY, Sound Director.

KITTY FOYLE. RKO Radio: RKO RADIO STUDIO SOUND DEPARTMENT, JOHN AALBERG, Sound Director.

NORTH WEST MOUNTED POLICE, Paramount: PARAMOUNT STUDIO SOUND DEPARTMENT, LOREN RYDER, Sound Director.

OUR TOWN, Lesser, UA: SAMUEL GOLDWYN STUDIO SOUND DEPARTMENT, THOMAS MOULTON, Sound Director.

THE SEA HAWK, Warner Bros.: WARNER BROS. STUDIO SOUND DEPARTMENT, NATHAN LEVINSON, Sound Director.

SPRING PARADE, Universal: UNIVERSAL STUDIO SOUND DEPARTMENT, BERNARD B. BROWN, Sound Director.

★ STRIKE UP THE BAND, Metro-Goldwyn-Mayer: M-G-M STUDIO SOUND DEPARTMENT, DOUGLAS SHEARER, Sound Director.

TOO MANY HUSBANDS, Columbia: COLUMBIA STUDIO SOUND DEPARTMENT, JOHN LIVADARY, Sound Director.

1941 Fourteenth Year

APPOINTMENT FOR LOVE, Universal: UNIVERSAL STUDIO SOUND DEPARTMENT, BERNARD B. BROWN, Sound Director.

BALL OF FIRE, Goldwyn, RKO Radio: SAMUEL GOLDWYN STUDIO SOUND DEPARTMENT, THOMAS MOULTON, Sound Director.

THE CHOCOLATE SOLDIER, Metro-Goldwyn-Mayer: M-G-M STUDIO SOUND DEPARTMENT, DOUGLAS SHEARER, Sound Director.

CITIZEN KANE, Mercury, RKO Radio: RKO RADIO STUDIO SOUND DEPARTMENT, JOHN AALBERG, Sound Director.

THE DEVIL PAYS OFF, Republic: REPUBLIC STUDIO SOUND DEPARTMENT, CHARLES LOOTENS, Sound Director.

HOW GREEN WAS MY VALLEY, 20th Century-Fox: 20TH CENTURY-FOX STUDIO SOUND DEPARTMENT, E. H. HANSEN, Sound Director.

THE MEN IN HER LIFE, Columbia: COLUMBIA STUDIO SOUND DEPARTMENT, JOHN LIVADARY, Sound Director.

SERGEANT YORK, Warner Bros.: WARNER BROS. STUDIO SOUND DEPARTMENT, NATHAN LEVINSON, Sound Director.

SKYLARK, Paramount: PARAMOUNT STUDIO SOUND DEPARTMENT, LOREN RYDER, Sound Director.

★ THAT HAMILTON WOMAN, Korda, UA: GENERAL SERVICE STUDIO SOUND DEPARTMENT, JACK WHITNEY, Sound Director.

TOPPER RETURNS, Roach, UA: HAL ROACH STUDIO SOUND DEPARTMENT, ELMER RAGUSE, Sound Director.

1942 Fifteenth Year

ARABIAN NIGHTS, Universal: UNIVERSAL STUDIO SOUND DEPARTMENT, BERNARD B. BROWN, Sound Director.

BAMBI, Disney, RKO Radio: WALT DISNEY STUDIO SOUND DEPARTMENT, SAM SLYFIELD, Sound Director.

FLYING TIGERS, Republic: REPUBLIC STUDIO SOUND DEPARTMENT, DANIEL BLOOMBERG, Sound Director.

FRIENDLY ENEMIES, Small, UA: SOUND SERVICE, INC., JACK WHITNEY, Sound Director.

THE GOLD RUSH, Chaplin, UA: RCA SOUND, JAMES FIELDS, Sound Director.

MRS. MINIVER, Metro-Goldwyn-Mayer: M-G-M STUDIO SOUND DEPARTMENT, DOUGLAS SHEARER, Sound Director.

ONCE UPON A HONEYMOON, RKO Radio: RKO RADIO STUDIO SOUND DEPARTMENT, STEVE DUNN, Sound Director.

THE PRIDE OF THE YANKEES, Goldwyn, RKO Radio: SAMUEL GOLDWYN STUDIO SOUND DEPARTMENT, THOMAS MOULTON, Sound Director.

ROAD TO MOROCCO, Paramount: PARAMOUNT STUDIO SOUND DEPARTMENT, LOREN RYDER, Sound Director.

THIS ABOVE ALL, 20th Century-Fox: 20TH CENTURY-FOX STUDIO SOUND DEPARTMENT, E. H. HANSEN, Sound Director.

★ YANKEE DOODLE DANDY, Warner Bros.: WARNER BROS. STUDIO SOUND DEPARTMENT, NATHAN LEVINSON, Sound Director.

YOU WERE NEVER LOVELIER, Columbia: COLUMBIA STUDIO SOUND DEPARTMENT, JOHN LIVADARY, Sound Director.

1943 Sixteenth Year

HANGMEN ALSO DIE, Pressburger, UA: SOUND SERVICE, INC., JACK WHITNEY, Sound Director.

IN OLD OKLAHOMA, Republic: REPUBLIC STUDIO SOUND DEPARTMENT, DANIEL J. BLOOMBERG, Sound Director.

MADAME CURIE, Metro-Goldwyn-Mayer: M-G-M STUDIO SOUND DEPARTMENT, DOUGLAS SHEARER, Sound Director.

THE NORTH STAR, Goldwyn, RKO Radio: SAMUEL GOLDWYN STUDIO SOUND DEPARTMENT, THOMAS MOULTON, Sound Director.

THE PHANTOM OF THE OPERA, Universal: UNIVERSAL STUDIO SOUND DEPARTMENT, BERNARD B. BROWN, Sound Director.

RIDING HIGH, Paramount: PARAMOUNT STUDIO SOUND DEPARTMENT, LOREN L. RYDER, Sound Director.

SAHARA, Columbia: COLUMBIA STUDIO SOUND DEPARTMENT, JOHN LIVADARY, Sound Director.

SALUDOS AMIGOS, Disney, RKO Radio: WALT DISNEY STUDIO SOUND DEPARTMENT, C. O. SLYFIELD, Sound Director.

SO THIS IS WASHINGTON, Votion, RKO Radio: RCA SOUND, J. L. FIELDS, Sound Director.

THE SONG OF BERNADETTE, 20th Century-Fox: 20TH CENTURY-FOX STUDIO SOUND DEPARTMENT, E. H. HANSEN, Sound Director.

THIS IS THE ARMY, Warner Bros.: WARNER BROS. STUDIO SOUND DEPARTMENT, NATHAN LEVINSON, Sound Director.

★ THIS LAND IS MINE, RKO Radio: RKO RADIO STUDIO SOUND DEPARTMENT, STEPHEN DUNN, Sound Director.

1944 Seventeenth Year

BRAZIL, Republic: REPUBLIC STUDIO SOUND DEPARTMENT, DANIEL J. BLOOMBERG, Sound Director.

CASANOVA BROWN, International, RKO Radio: SAMUEL GOLDWYN STUDIO SOUND DEPARTMENT, THOMAS T. MOULTON, Sound Director.

COVER GIRL, Columbia: COLUMBIA STUDIO SOUND DEPARTMENT, JOHN LIVADARY, Sound Director.

DOUBLE INDEMNITY, Paramount: PARAMOUNT STUDIO SOUND DEPARTMENT, LOREN RYDER, Sound Director.

HIS BUTLER'S SISTER, Universal: UNIVERSAL STUDIO SOUND DEPARTMENT, BERNARD B. BROWN, Sound Director.

HOLLYWOOD CANTEEN, Warner Bros.: WARNER BROS. STUDIO SOUND DEPARTMENT, NATHAN LEVINSON, Sound Director.

IT HAPPENED TOMORROW, Arnold, UA: SOUND SERVICES, INC., JACK WHITNEY, Sound Director.

KISMET, Metro-Goldwyn-Mayer: M-G-M STUDIO SOUND DEPARTMENT, DOUGLAS SHEARER, Sound Director.

MUSIC IN MANHATTAN, RKO Radio: RKO RADIO STUDIO SOUND DEPARTMENT, STEPHEN DUNN, Sound Director.

VOICE IN THE WIND, Ripley-Monter, UA: RCA SOUND, W. M. DALGLEISH, Sound Director.

★ WILSON, 20th Century-Fox: 20TH CENTURY-FOX STUDIO SOUND DEPARTMENT, E. H. HANSEN, Sound Director.

1945 Eighteenth Year

★ THE BELLS OF ST. MARY'S, Rainbow, RKO Radio: RKO RADIO STUDIO SOUND DEPARTMENT, STEPHEN DUNN, Sound Director.

THE FLAME OF THE BARBARY COAST, Republic: REPUBLIC STUDIO SOUND DEPARTMENT, DANIEL J. BLOOMBERG, Sound Director.

LADY ON A TRAIN, Universal: UNIVERSAL STUDIO SOUND DEPARTMENT, BERNARD B. BROWN, Sound Director.

LEAVE HER TO HEAVEN, 20th Century-Fox: 20TH CENTURY-FOX STUDIO

SOUND DEPARTMENT, THOMAS T. MOULTON, Sound Director.

RHAPSODY IN BLUE, Warner Bros.: WARNER BROS. STUDIO SOUND DEPARTMENT, NATHAN LEVINSON, Sound Director.

A SONG TO REMEMBER, Columbia: COLUMBIA STUDIO SOUND DEPARTMENT, JOHN LIVADARY, Sound Director.

THE SOUTHERNER, Loew-Hakim, UA: SOUND SERVICES, INC., JACK WHITNEY, Sound Director.

THEY WERE EXPENDABLE, Metro-Goldwyn-Mayer: M-G-M STUDIO SOUND DEPARTMENT, DOUGLAS SHEARER, Sound Director.

THE THREE CABALLEROS, Disney, RKO Radio: WALT DISNEY STUDIO SOUND DEPARTMENT, C. O. SLYFIELD, Sound Director.

THREE IS A FAMILY, Master Productions, UA: RCA SOUND, W. V. WOLFE, Sound Director.

THE UNSEEN, Paramount: PARAMOUNT STUDIO SOUND DEPARTMENT, LOREN L. RYDER, Sound Director.

WONDER MAN, Goldwyn, RKO Radio: SAMUEL GOLDWYN STUDIO SOUND DEPARTMENT, GORDON SAWYER, Sound Director.

1946 Nineteenth Year

THE BEST YEARS OF OUR LIVES, Goldwyn, RKO Radio: SAMUEL GOLDWYN STUDIO SOUND DEPARTMENT, GORDON SAWYER, Sound Director.

IT'S A WONDERFUL LIFE, Liberty, RKO Radio: RKO RADIO STUDIO SOUND DEPARTMENT, JOHN AALBERG, Sound Director.

★ THE JOLSON STORY, Columbia: COLUMBIA STUDIO SOUND DEPARTMENT, JOHN LIVADARY, Sound Director.

1947 Twentieth Year

★ THE BISHOP'S WIFE, Goldwyn, RKO Radio: SAMUEL GOLDWYN STUDIO SOUND DEPARTMENT, GORDON SAWYER, Sound Director.

GREEN DOLPHIN STREET, Metro-Goldwyn-Mayer: M-G-M STUDIO SOUND DEPARTMENT, DOUGLAS SHEARER, Sound Director.

T-MEN, Reliance Pictures, Eagle-Lion: SOUND SERVICES, INC., JACK WHITNEY, Sound Director.

1948 Twenty-first Year

JOHNNY BELINDA, Warner Bros.: WARNER BROS. SOUND DEPARTMENT.

MOONRISE, Marshall Grant Prods., Republic: REPUBLIC SOUND DEPARTMENT.

★ THE SNAKE PIT, 20th Century-Fox: 20TH CENTURY-FOX SOUND DEPARTMENT.

1949 Twenty-second Year

ONCE MORE, MY DARLING, Neptune Films, U-I: UNIVERSAL-INTERNATIONAL SOUND DEPARTMENT.

SANDS OF IWO JIMA, Republic: REPUBLIC SOUND DEPARTMENT.

★ TWELVE O'CLOCK HIGH, 20th Century-Fox: 20TH CENTURY-FOX SOUND DEPARTMENT.

1950 Twenty-third Year

★ ALL ABOUT EVE, 20th Century-Fox: 20TH CENTURY-FOX SOUND DEPARTMENT.

CINDERELLA, Disney, RKO Radio: DISNEY SOUND DEPARTMENT.

LOUISA, Universal-International: UNIVERSAL-INTERNATIONAL SOUND DEPARTMENT.

OUR VERY OWN, Goldwyn, RKO Radio: GOLDWYN SOUND DEPARTMENT.

TRIO, Rank-Sydney Box: PARAMOUNT (British) SOUND DEPARTMENT.

1951 Twenty-fourth Year

BRIGHT VICTORY, Universal-International: LESLIE I. CAREY, Sound Director.

★ THE GREAT CARUSO, Metro-Goldwyn-Mayer: DOUGLAS SHEARER, Sound Director.

I WANT YOU, Samuel Goldwyn Prods., Inc., RKO Radio: GORDON SAWYER, Sound Director.

A STREETCAR NAMED DESIRE, Charles K. Feldman Group Prods., Warner Bros.: COL. NATHAN LEVINSON, Sound Director.

TWO TICKETS TO BROADWAY, RKO Radio: JOHN O. AALBERG, Sound Director.

1952 Twenty-fifth Year

★ BREAKING THE SOUND BARRIER, London Films, UA (British): LONDON FILM SOUND DEPARTMENT.

HANS CHRISTIAN ANDERSEN, Goldwyn, RKO Radio: GOLDWYN SOUND DEPARTMENT, GORDON SAWYER, Sound Director.

THE PROMOTER, Rank, Ronald Neame, U-I (British): PINEWOOD STUDIOS SOUND DEPARTMENT.

THE QUIET MAN, Argosy, Republic: REPUBLIC SOUND DEPARTMENT, DANIEL J. BLOOMBERG, Sound Director.

WITH A SONG IN MY HEART, 20th Century-Fox: 20TH CENTURY-FOX SOUND DEPARTMENT, THOMAS T. MOULTON, Sound Director.

1953 Twenty-sixth Year

CALAMITY JANE, Warner Bros.: WARNER BROS. SOUND DEPARTMENT, WILLIAM A. MUELLER, Sound Director.

★ FROM HERE TO ETERNITY, Columbia: COLUMBIA SOUND DEPARTMENT, JOHN P. LIVADARY, Sound Director.

KNIGHTS OF THE ROUND TABLE, Metro-Goldwyn-Mayer: A. W. WATKINS, Sound Director.

THE MISSISSIPPI GAMBLER, Universal-International: UNIVERSAL-INTERNATIONAL SOUND DEPARTMENT, LESLIE I. CAREY, Sound Director.

THE WAR OF THE WORLDS, Paramount: PARAMOUNT SOUND DEPARTMENT, LOREN L. RYDER, Sound Director.

1954 Twenty-seventh Year

BRIGADOON, Metro-Goldwyn-Mayer: WESLEY C. MILLER, Sound Director.

THE CAINE MUTINY, Columbia: JOHN P. LIVADARY, Sound Director.

★ THE GLENN MILLER STORY, Universal-International: LESLIE I. CAREY, Sound Director.

REAR WINDOW, Paramount: LOREN L. RYDER, Sound Director.

SUSAN SLEPT HERE, RKO Radio: JOHN O. AALBERG, Sound Director.

1955 Twenty-eighth Year

LOVE IS A MANY-SPLENDORED THING, 20TH CENTURY-FOX STUDIO SOUND DEPARTMENT: CARL W. FAULKNER, Sound Director.

LOVE ME OR LEAVE ME, Metro-GOLDWYN-MAYER STUDIO SOUND DEPARTMENT: WESLEY C. MILLER, Sound Director.

MISTER ROBERTS, WARNER BROS. STUDIO SOUND DEPARTMENT: WILLIAM A. MUELLER, Sound Director.

NOT AS A STRANGER, RADIO CORPORATION OF AMERICA SOUND DEPARTMENT: WATSON JONES, SOUND DIRECTOR.

★ OKLAHOMA!, TODD-AO SOUND DEPARTMENT: FRED HYNES, Sound Director.

1956 Twenty-ninth Year

THE BRAVE ONE, King Bros. Productions, Inc.: JOHN MYERS, Sound Director.

THE EDDY DUCHIN STORY, COLUMBIA STUDIO SOUND DEPARTMENT: JOHN LIVADARY, Sound Director.

FRIENDLY PERSUASION, Allied Artists, WESTREX SOUND SERVICES, INC.: GORDON R. GLENNAN, Sound

Director; and SAMUEL GOLDWYN STUDIO SOUND DEPARTMENT: GORDON SAWYER, Sound Director.

★ THE KING AND I, 20TH CENTURY-FOX STUDIO SOUND DEPARTMENT: CARL FAULKNER, Sound Director.

THE TEN COMMANDMENTS, PARAMOUNT STUDIO SOUND DEPARTMENT: LOREN L. RYDER, Sound Director.

*1957 Thirtieth Year**

GUNFIGHT AT THE O.K. CORRAL, PARAMOUNT STUDIO SOUND DEPARTMENT: GEORGE DUTTON, Sound Director.

LES GIRLS, METRO-GOLDWYN-MAYER STUDIO SOUND DEPARTMENT: DR. WESLEY C. MILLER, Sound Director.

PAL JOEY, COLUMBIA STUDIO SOUND DEPARTMENT: JOHN P. LIVADARY, Sound Director.

★ SAYONARA, WARNER BROS. STUDIO SOUND DEPARTMENT: GEORGE GROVES, Sound Director.

WITNESS FOR THE PROSECUTION, SAMUEL GOLDWYN STUDIO SOUND DEPARTMENT: GORDON SAWYER, Sound Director.

1958 Thirty-first Year

I WANT TO LIVE!, SAMUEL GOLDWYN STUDIO SOUND DEPARTMENT: GORDON E. SAWYER, Sound Director.

★ SOUTH PACIFIC, TODD-AO SOUND DEPARTMENT: FRED HYNES, Sound Director.

A TIME TO LOVE AND A TIME TO DIE, UNIVERSAL-INTERNATIONAL STUDIO SOUND DEPARTMENT: LESLIE I. CAREY, Sound Director.

VERTIGO, PARAMOUNT STUDIO SOUND DEPARTMENT: GEORGE DUTTON, Sound Director.

THE YOUNG LIONS, 20TH CENTURY-FOX STUDIO SOUND DEPARTMENT: CARL FAULKNER, Sound Director.

1959 Thirty-second Year

★ BEN-HUR, METRO-GOLDWYN-MAYER STUDIO SOUND DEPARTMENT: FRANKLIN E. MILTON, Sound Director.

JOURNEY TO THE CENTER OF THE EARTH, 20TH CENTURY-FOX STUDIO SOUND DEPARTMENT: CARL FAULKNER, Sound Director.

LIBEL!, METRO-GOLDWYN-MAYER LONDON SOUND DEPARTMENT (BRITISH): A. W. WATKINS, Sound Director.

THE NUN'S STORY, WARNER BROS. STUDIO SOUND DEPARTMENT: GEORGE R. GROVES, Sound Director.

PORGY AND BESS, SAMUEL GOLDWYN STUDIO SOUND DEPARTMENT: GORDON E. SAWYER, Sound Director; and TODD-AO SOUND DEPARTMENT: FRED HYNES, Sound Director.

1960 Thirty-third Year

★ THE ALAMO, SAMUEL GOLDWYN STUDIO SOUND DEPARTMENT: GORDON E. SAWYER, Sound Director; and TODD-AO SOUND DEPARTMENT: FRED HYNES, Sound Director.

THE APARTMENT, SAMUEL GOLDWYN STUDIO SOUND DEPARTMENT: GORDON E. SAWYER, Sound Director.

CIMARRON, METRO-GOLDWYN-MAYER STUDIO SOUND DEPARTMENT: FRANKLIN E. MILTON, Sound Director.

PEPE, COLUMBIA STUDIO SOUND DEPARTMENT: CHARLES RICE, Sound Director.

SUNRISE AT CAMPOBELLO, WARNER BROS. STUDIO SOUND DEPARTMENT: GEORGE R. GROVES, Sound Director.

*Name of category changed from Sound Recording to Sound.

1961 Thirty-fourth Year

THE CHILDREN'S HOUR, SAMUEL GOLDWYN STUDIO SOUND DEPARTMENT: GORDON E. SAWYER, Sound Director.

FLOWER DRUM SONG, REVUE STUDIO SOUND DEPARTMENT: WALDON O. WATSON, Sound Director.

THE GUNS OF NAVARONE, SHEPPERTON STUDIO SOUND DEPARTMENT: JOHN COX, Sound Director.

THE PARENT TRAP, WALT DISNEY STUDIO SOUND DEPARTMENT: ROBERT O. COOK, Sound Director.

★ WEST SIDE STORY, TODD-AO SOUND DEPARTMENT: FRED HYNES, Sound Director; and SAMUEL GOLDWYN STUDIO SOUND DEPARTMENT: GORDON E. SAWYER, Sound Director.

1962 Thirty-fifth Year

BON VOYAGE, WALT DISNEY STUDIO SOUND DEPARTMENT: ROBERT O. COOK, Sound Director.

★ LAWRENCE OF ARABIA, SHEPPERTON STUDIO SOUND DEPARTMENT: JOHN COX, Sound Director.

THE MUSIC MAN, WARNER BROS. STUDIO SOUND DEPARTMENT: GEORGE R. GROVES, Sound Director.

THAT TOUCH OF MINK, UNIVERSAL CITY STUDIO SOUND DEPARTMENT: WALDON O. WATSON, Sound Director.

WHAT EVER HAPPENED TO BABY JANE?, GLEN GLENN SOUND DEPARTMENT: JOSEPH KELLY, Sound Director.

1963 Thirty-sixth Year

BYE BYE BIRDIE, COLUMBIA STUDIO SOUND DEPARTMENT: CHARLES RICE, Sound Director.

CAPTAIN NEWMAN, M.D., UNIVERSAL CITY STUDIO SOUND DEPARTMENT: WALDON O. WATSON, Sound Director.

CLEOPATRA, 20TH CENTURY-FOX STUDIO SOUND DEPARTMENT: JAMES P. CORCORAN, Sound Director; and TODD A-O SOUND DEPARTMENT: FRED HYNES, Sound Director.

★ HOW THE WEST WAS WON, METRO-GOLDWYN-MAYER STUDIO SOUND DEPARTMENT: FRANKLIN E. MILTON, Sound Director.

IT'S A MAD, MAD, MAD, MAD WORLD, SAMUEL GOLDWYN STUDIO SOUND DEPARTMENT: GORDON E. SAWYER, Sound Director.

1964 Thirty-seventh Year

BECKET, SHEPPERTON STUDIO SOUND DEPARTMENT: JOHN COX, Sound Director.

FATHER GOOSE, UNIVERSAL CITY STUDIO SOUND DEPARTMENT: WALDON O. WATSON, Sound Director.

MARY POPPINS, WALT DISNEY STUDIO SOUND DEPARTMENT: ROBERT O. COOK, Sound Director.

★ MY FAIR LADY, WARNER BROS. STUDIO SOUND DEPARTMENT: GEORGE R. GROVES, Sound Director.

THE UNSINKABLE MOLLY BROWN, METRO-GOLDWYN-MAYER STUDIO SOUND DEPARTMENT: FRANKLIN E. MILTON, Sound Director.

1965 Thirty-eighth Year

THE AGONY AND THE ECSTASY, 20THECENTURY-FOX STUDIO SOUND DEPARTMENT: JAMES P. CORCORAN, Sound Director.

DOCTOR ZHIVAGO, METRO-GOLDWYN-MAYER BRITISH STUDIO SOUND DEPARTMENT: A. W. WATKINS, Sound Director; and METRO-GOLDWYN-MAYER STUDIO SOUND DEPARTMENT: FRANKLIN E. MILTON, Sound Director.

THE GREAT RACE, WARNER BROS. STUDIO SOUND DEPARTMENT: GEORGE R. GROVES, Sound Director.

SHENANDOAH, UNIVERSAL CITY STUDIO

SOUND DEPARTMENT: WALDON O. WATSON, Sound Director.

★ THE SOUND OF MUSIC, 20TH CENTURY-FOX STUDIO SOUND DEPARTMENT: JAMES P. CORCORAN, Sound Director; and TODD-AO SOUND DEPARTMENT: FRED HYNES, Sound Director.

1966 Thirty-ninth Year

GAMBIT, UNIVERSAL CITY STUDIO SOUND DEPARTMENT: WALDON O. WATSON, Sound Director.

★ GRAND PRIX, METRO-GOLDWYN-MAYER STUDIO SOUND DEPARTMENT: FRANKLIN E. MILTON, Sound Director.

HAWAII, SAMUEL GOLDWYN STUDIO SOUND DEPARTMENT: GORDON E. SAWYER, Sound Director.

THE SAND PEBBLES, 20TH CENTURY-FOX STUDIO SOUND DEPARTMENT: JAMES P. CORCORAN, Sound Director.

WHO'S AFRAID OF VIRGINIA WOOLF?, WARNER BROS. STUDIO SOUND DEPARTMENT: GEORGE R. GROVES, Sound Director.

1967 Fortieth Year

CAMELOT, WARNER BROS.-SEVEN ARTS STUDIO SOUND DEPARTMENT.

THE DIRTY DOZEN, METRO-GOLDWYN-MAYER STUDIO SOUND DEPARTMENT.

DOCTOR DOLITTLE, 20TH CENTURY-FOX STUDIO SOUND DEPARTMENT.

★ IN THE HEAT OF THE NIGHT, SAMUEL GOLDWYN STUDIO SOUND DEPARTMENT.

THOROUGHLY MODERN MILLIE, UNIVERSAL CITY STUDIO SOUND DEPARTMENT.

1968 Forty-first Year

BULLITT, WARNER BROS.-SEVEN ARTS STUDIO SOUND DEPARTMENT.

FINIAN'S RAINBOW, WARNER BROS.-SEVEN ARTS STUDIO SOUND DEPARTMENT.

FUNNY GIRL, COLUMBIA STUDIO SOUND DEPARTMENT.

★ OLIVER!, SHEPPERTON STUDIO SOUND DEPARTMENT.

STAR!, 20TH CENTURY-FOX STUDIO SOUND DEPARTMENT.

1969 Forty-second Year

ANNE OF THE THOUSAND DAYS, Hal B. Wallis-Universal Pictures, Ltd. Production, Universal: JOHN ALDRED.

BUTCH CASSIDY AND THE SUNDANCE KID, George Roy Hill-Paul Monash Prod., 20th Century-Fox: WILLIAM EDMUNDSON and DAVID DOCKENDORF.

GAILY, GAILY, Mirisch-Cartier Production, United Artists: ROBERT MARTIN and CLEM PORTMAN.

★ HELLO, DOLLY!, Chenault Productions, 20th Century-Fox: JACK SOLOMON and MURRAY SPIVACK.

MAROONED, Frankovich-Sturges Production, Columbia: LES FRESHOLTZ and ARTHUR PIANTADOSI.

1970 Forty-third Year

AIRPORT, Ross Hunter-Universal Prod., Universal: RONALD PIERCE and DAVID MORIARTY.

★ PATTON, 20th Century-Fox: DOUGLAS WILLIAMS and DON BASSMAN.

RYAN'S DAUGHTER, Faraway Prods., Metro-Goldwyn-Mayer: GORDON K. MCCALLUM and JOHN BRAMALL.

TORA! TORA! TORA!, 20th Century-Fox: MURRAY SPIVACK and HERMAN LEWIS.

WOODSTOCK, Wadleigh-Maurice, Ltd. Prod., Warner Bros: DAN WALLIN and LARRY JOHNSON.

1971 Forty-fourth Year

DIAMONDS ARE FOREVER, An Albert R. Broccoli-Harry Saltzman Prod., UA: GORDON K. MCCALLUM, JOHN MITCHELL, and ALFRED J. OVERTON.

★ FIDDLER ON THE ROOF, Mirisch-

Cartier Prods., UA: GORDON K. MCCALLUM and DAVID HILDYARD.

THE FRENCH CONNECTION, A Philip D'Antoni Prod., in association with Schine-Moore Prods., 20th Century-Fox: THEODORE SODERBERG and CHRISTOPHER NEWMAN.

KOTCH, A Kotch Prod., ABC Pictures Presentation, Cinerama: RICHARD PORTMAN and JACK SOLOMON.

MARY, QUEEN OF SCOTS, A Hal Wallis-Universal Pictures, Ltd. Prod., Universal: BOB JONES and JOHN ALDRED.

1972 Forty-fifth Year

BUTTERFLIES ARE FREE, Frankovich Prods., Columbia: ARTHUR PIANTADOSI and CHARLES KNIGHT.

⋆ CABARET, An ABC Pictures Production, Allied Artists: ROBERT KNUDSON and DAVID HILDYARD.

THE CANDIDATE, A Redford-Ritchie Prod., Warner Bros.: RICHARD PORTMAN and GENE CANTAMESSA.

THE GODFATHER, An Albert S. Ruddy Prod., Paramount: BUD GRENZBACH, RICHARD PORTMAN, and CHRISTOPHER NEWMAN.

THE POSEIDON ADVENTURE, An Irwin Allen Prod., 20th Century-Fox: THEODORE SODERBERG and HERMAN LEWIS.

1973 Forty-sixth Year

THE DAY OF THE DOLPHIN, Icarus Prods., Avco Embassy: RICHARD PORTMAN and LAWRENCE O. JOST.

⋆ THE EXORCIST, Hoya Prods., Warner Bros.: ROBERT KNUDSON and CHRIS NEWMAN.

THE PAPER CHASE, Thompson-Paul Prods., 20th Century-Fox: DONALD O. MITCHELL and LAWRENCE O. JOST.

PAPER MOON, A Directors Company Prod., Paramount: RICHARD PORTMAN and LES FRESHOLTZ.

THE STING, A Universal-Bill/Phillips-George Roy Hill Film Prod., Zanuck/Brown Presentation, Universal: RONALD K. PIERCE and ROBERT BERTRAND.

1974 Forty-seventh Year

CHINATOWN, A Robert Evans Production, Paramount: BUD GRENZBACH and LARRY JOST.

THE CONVERSATION, A Directors Company Production, Paramount: WALTER MURCH and ARTHUR ROCHESTER.

⋆ EARTHQUAKE, A Universal-Mark Robson-Filmakers Group Production, Universal: RONALD PIERCE and MELVIN METCALFE, SR.

THE TOWERING INFERNO, An Irwin Allen Production, 20th Century-Fox/Warner Bros.: THEODORE SODERBERG and HERMAN LEWIS.

YOUNG FRANKENSTEIN, A Gruskoff/Venture Films-Crossbow Prods.-Jouer, Ltd. Production, 20th Century-Fox; RICHARD PORTMAN and GENE CANTAMESSA.

1975 Forty-eighth Year

BITE THE BULLET, A Pax Enterprises Production, Columbia: ARTHUR PIANTADOSI, LES FRESHOLTZ, RICHARD TYLER, and AL OVERTON, JR.

FUNNY LADY, A Rastar Pictures Production, Columbia: RICHARD PORTMAN, DON MACDOUGALL, CURLY THIRLWELL, and JACK SOLOMON.

THE HINDENBURG, A Robert Wise-Filmakers Group-Universal Production, Universal: LEONARD PETERSON, JOHN A. BOLGER, JR., JOHN MACK, and DON K. SHARPLESS.

⋆ JAWS, A Universal-Zanuck/Brown Production, Universal: ROBERT L. HOYT, ROGER HEMAN, EARL MADERY, and JOHN CARTER.

THE WIND AND THE LION, A Herb Jaffe Production, Metro-Goldwyn-Mayer: HARRY W. TETRICK, AARON ROCHIN,

WILLIAM MCCAUGHEY, and ROY CHARMAN.

1976 Forty-ninth Year

★ ALL THE PRESIDENT'S MEN, A Wildwood Enterprises Production, Warner Bros.: ARTHUR PIANTADOSI, LES FRESHOLTZ, DICK ALEXANDER, and JIM WEBB.

KING KONG, A Dino De Laurentiis Production, Paramount: HARRY WARREN TETRICK, WILLIAM MCCAUGHEY, AARON ROCHIN, and JACK SOLOMON.

ROCKY, A Robert Chartoff-Irwin Winkler Production, United Artists: HARRY WARREN TETRICK, WILLIAM MCCAUGHEY, LYLE BURBRIDGE, and BUD ALPER.

SILVER STREAK, A Frank Yablans Presentations Production, 20th Century-Fox: DONALD MITCHELL, DOUGLAS WILLIAMS, RICHARD TYLER, and HAL ETHERINGTON.

A STAR IS BORN, A Barwood/Jon Peters Production, First Artists Presentation, Warner Bros.: ROBERT KNUDSON, DAN WALLIN, ROBERT GLASS, and TOM OVERTON.

1977 Fiftieth Year

CLOSE ENCOUNTERS OF THE THIRD KIND, Close Encounter Productions, Columbia: ROBERT KNUDSON, ROBERT J. GLASS, DON MACDOUGALL, and GENE S. CANTAMESSA.

THE DEEP, A Casablanca Filmworks Production, Columbia: WALTER GOSS, DICK ALEXANDER, TOM BECKERT, and ROBIN GREGORY.

SORCERER, A William Friedkin Film Production, Paramount-Universal: ROBERT KNUDSON, ROBERT J. GLASS, RICHARD TYLER, and JEAN-LOUIS DUCARME.

★ STAR WARS, A Twentieth Century-Fox Production, 20th Century-Fox: DON MacDOUGALL, RAY WEST, BOB MINKLER, and DEREK BALL.

THE TURNING POINT, Hera Productions, 20th Century-Fox: THEODORE SODERBERG, PAUL WELLS, DOUGLAS O. WILLIAMS, and JERRY JOST.

1978 Fifty-first Year

THE BUDDY HOLLY STORY, An Innovisions-ECA Production, Columbia: TEX RUDLOFF, JOEL FEIN, CURLY THIRLWELL, and WILLIE BURTON.

DAYS OF HEAVEN, An OP Production, Paramount: JOHN K. WILKINSON, ROBERT W. GLASS, JR., JOHN T. REITZ, and BARRY THOMAS.

★ THE DEER HUNTER, an EMI Films/Michael Cimino Film Production, Universal: RICHARD PORTMAN, WILLIAM McCAUGHEY, AARON ROCHIN, and DARRIN KNIGHT.

HOOPER, A Warner Bros. Production, Warner Bros.: ROBERT KNUDSON, ROBERT J. GLASS, DON MACDOUGALL, and JACK SOLOMON.

SUPERMAN, A Dovemead, Ltd. Production, Alexander Salkind Presentation, Warner Bros.: GORDON K. MCCALLUM, GRAHAM HARTSTONE, NICOLAS LE MESSURIER, and ROY CHARMAN.

1979 Fifty-second Year

★ APOCALYPSE NOW, An Omni Zoetrope Production, United Artists: WALTER MURCH, MARK BERGER, RICHARD BEGGS, and NAT BOXER.

THE ELECTRIC HORSEMAN, Rastar Films/ Wildwood Enterprises/S. Pollack Productions, Columbia: ARTHUR PIANTADOSI, LES FRESHOLTZ, MICHAEL MINKLER, and AL OVERTON.

METEOR, Meteor Productions, American International Pictures:

WILLIAM MCCAUGHEY, AARON ROCHIN, MICHAEL J. KOHUT, and JACK SOLOMON.

1941, An A-Team/Steven Spielberg Film Production, Universal-Columbia Presentation, Universal: ROBERT KNUDSON, ROBERT J. GLASS, DON MACDOUGALL, and GENE S. CANTAMESSA.

THE ROSE, A Twentieth Century-Fox Production, 20th Century-Fox: THEODORE SODERBERG, DOUGLAS WILLIAMS, PAUL WELLS, and JIM WEBB.

1980 Fifty-third Year

ALTERED STATES, A Warner Bros. Production, Warner Bros.: ARTHUR PIANTADOSI, LES FRESHOLTZ, MICHAEL MINKLER, and WILLIE D. BURTON.

COAL MINER'S DAUGHTER, A Bernard Schwartz-Universal Pictures Production, Universal: RICHARD PORTMAN, ROGER HEMAN, and JIM ALEXANDER.

★ THE EMPIRE STRIKES BACK, A Lucasfilm, Ltd. Production, 20th Century-Fox: BILL VARNEY, STEVE MASLOW, GREGG LANDAKER, and PETER SUTTON.

FAME, A Metro-Goldwyn-Mayer Production, Metro-Goldwyn-Mayer: MICHAEL J. KOHUT, AARON ROCHIN, JAY M. HARDING, and CHRIS NEWMAN.

RAGING BULL, A Robert Chartoff-Irwin Winkler Production, United Artists: DONALD O. MITCHELL, BILL NICHOLSON, DAVID J. KIMBALL, and LES LAZAROWITZ.

1981 Fifty-fourth Year

ON GOLDEN POND, An ITC Films/IPC Films Production, Universal: RICHARD PORTMAN and DAVID RONNE.

OUTLAND, A Ladd Company Production, The Ladd Company: JOHN K. WILKINSON, ROBERT W. GLASS, JR., ROBERT M. THIRLWELL, and ROBIN GREGORY.

PENNIES FROM HEAVEN, A Metro-Goldwyn-Mayer/Herbert Ross/Hera Production, Metro-Goldwyn-Mayer: MICHAEL J. KOHUT, JAY M. HARDING, RICHARD TYLER, and AL OVERTON.

★ RAIDERS OF THE LOST ARK, A Lucasfilm Production, Paramount: BILL VARNEY, STEVE MASLOW, GREGG LANDAKER, and ROY CHARMAN.

REDS, A. J.R.S. Production, Paramount: DICK VORISEK, TOM FLEISCHMAN, and SIMON KAYE.

1982 Fifty-fifth Year

DAS BOOT, A Bavaria Atelier GmbH Production, Columbia: MILAN BOR, TREVOR PYKE, and MIKE LE-MARE.

★ E.T. THE EXTRA-TERRESTRIAL, A Universal Pictures Production, Universal: ROBERT KNUDSON, ROBERT GLASS, DON DIGIROLAMO, and GENE CANTAMESSA.

GANDHI, An Indo-British Films Production, Columbia: GERRY HUMPHREYS, ROBIN O'DONOGHUE, JONATHAN BATES, and SIMON KAYE.

TOOTSIE, A Mirage/Punch Production, Columbia: ARTHUR PIANTADOSI, LES FRESHOLTZ, DICK ALEXANDER, and LES LAZAROWITZ.

TRON, A Walt Disney Production, Buena Vista Distribution: MICHAEL MINKLER, BOB MINKLER, LEE MINKLER, and JIM LA RUE.

1983 Fifty-sixth Year

NEVER CRY WOLF, A Walt Disney Production, Buena Vista: ALAN R. SPLET, TODD BOEKELHEIDE, RANDY THOM, and DAVID PARKER.

RETURN OF THE JEDI, A Lucasfilm Production, 20th Century-Fox: BEN

BURTT, GARY SUMMERS, RANDY THOM, and TONY DAWE.

★ THE RIGHT STUFF, A Robert Chartoff-Irwin Winkler Production, The Ladd Company through Warner Bros.: MARK BERGER, TOM SCOTT, RANDY THOM, and DAVID MACMILLAN.

TERMS OF ENDEARMENT, A James L. Brooks Production, Paramount: DONALD O. MITCHELL, RICK KLINE, KEVIN O'CONNELL, and JIM ALEXANDER.

WARGAMES, A United Artists Presentation of a Leonard Goldberg Production, M-G-M/UA: MICHAEL J. KOHUT, CARLOS DE LARIOS, AARON ROCHIN, and WILLIE D. BURTON.

1984 Fifty-seventh Year

★ AMADEUS, A Saul Zaentz Company Production, Orion: MARK BERGER, TOM SCOTT, TODD BOEKELHEIDE, and CHRIS NEWMAN.

DUNE, A Dino De Laurentiis Corporation Production, Universal: BILL VARNEY, STEVE MASLOW, KEVIN O'CONNELL, and NELSON STOLL.

A PASSAGE TO INDIA, A G. W. Films Limited Production, Columbia: GRAHAM V. HARTSTONE, NICOLAS LE MESSURIER, MICHAEL A. CARTER, and JOHN MITCHELL.

THE RIVER, A Universal Pictures Production, Universal: NICK ALPHIN, ROBERT THIRLWELL, RICHARD PORTMAN, and DAVID RONNE.

2010, A Metro-Goldwyn-Mayer Presentation of a Peter Hyams Film Production, M-G-M/UA: MICHAEL J. KOHUT, AARON ROCHIN, CARLOS DE LARIOS, and GENE S. CANTAMESSA.

1985 Fifty-eighth Year

BACK TO THE FUTURE, an Amblin Entertainment/Universal Pictures Production, Universal: BILL VARNEY, B. TENNYSON SEBASTIAN II, ROBERT THIRLWELL, and WILLIAM B. KAPLAN.

A CHORUS LINE, an Embassy Films Associates and Polygram Pictures Production, Columbia: DONALD O. MITCHELL, MICHAEL MINKLER, GERRY HUMPHREYS, and CHRIS NEWMAN.

LADYHAWKE, a Warner Bros. and 20th Century-Fox Production, Warner Bros.: LES FRESHOLTZ, DICK ALEXANDER, VERN POORE, and BUD ALPER.

★ OUT OF AFRICA, a Universal Pictures Limited Production, Universal: CHRIS JENKINS, GARY ALEXANDER, LARRY STENSVOLD, and PETER HANDFORD.

SILVERADO, a Columbia Pictures Production, Columbia: DONALD O. MITCHELL, RICK KLINE, KEVIN O'CONNELL, and DAVID RONNE.

1986 Fifty-ninth Year

ALIENS, A Twentieth Century-Fox Film Production, 20th Century-Fox: GRAHAM V. HARTSTONE, NICOLAS LE MESSURIER, MICHAEL A. CARTER, and ROY CHARMAN.

HEARTBREAK RIDGE, A Warner Bros. Production, Warner Bros.: LES FRESHOLTZ, DICK ALEXANDER, VERN POORE, and WILLIAM NELSON.

★ PLATOON, A Hemdale Film Production, Orion: JOHN (DOC) WILKINSON, RICHARD ROGERS, CHARLES (BUD) GRENZBACH, and SIMON KAYE.

STAR TREK IV: THE VOYAGE HOME, A Harvé Bennett Production, Paramount: TERRY PORTER, DAVE HUDSON, MEL METCALFE, and GENE S. CANTAMESSA.

TOP GUN, A Don Simpson/Jerry Bruckheimer Production, Paramount: DONALD O. MITCHELL, KEVIN O'CONNELL, RICK KLINE, and WILLIAM B. KAPLAN.

1987 Sixtieth Year

EMPIRE OF THE SUN, A Warner Bros. Production, Warner Bros.: ROBERT KNUDSON, DON DIGIROLAMO, JOHN BOYDE, and TONY DAWE.

★ THE LAST EMPEROR, A Hemdale Film Production, Columbia: BILL ROWE and IVAN SHARROCK.

LETHAL WEAPON, A Warner Bros. Production, Warner Bros.: LES FRESHOLTZ, DICK ALEXANDER, VERN POORE, and BILL NELSON.

ROBOCOP, A Tobor Pictures Production, Orion: MICHAEL J. KOHUT, CARLOS DE LARIOS, AARON ROCHIN, and ROBERT WALD.

THE WITCHES OF EASTWICK, A Warner Bros. Production, Warner Bros.: WAYNE ARTMAN, TOM BECKERT, TOM DAHL, and ART ROCHESTER.

1988 Sixty-first Year

★ BIRD, A Malpaso Production, Warner Bros.: LES FRESHOLTZ, DICK ALEXANDER, VERN POORE, and WILLIE D. BURTON.

DIE HARD, A Twentieth Century-Fox Production, 20th Century-Fox: DON BASSMAN, KEVIN F. CLEARY, RICHARD OVERTON, and AL OVERTON.

GORILLAS IN THE MIST, A Warner Bros. Production, Warner Bros./Universal: ANDY NELSON, BRIAN SAUNDERS, and PETER HANDFORD.

MISSISSIPPI BURNING, A Frederick Zollo Production, Orion: ROBERT LITT, ELLIOT TYSON, RICHARD C. KLINE, and DANNY MICHAEL.

WHO FRAMED ROGER RABBIT, An Amblin Entertainment and Touchstone Pictures Production, Buena Vista: ROBERT KNUDSON, JOHN BOYD, DON DIGIROLAMO, and TONY DAWE.

1989 Sixty-second Year

THE ABYSS, A Twentieth Century-Fox Film Production, 20th Century-Fox: DON BASSMAN, KEVIN F. CLEARY, RICHARD OVERTON, and LEE ORLOFF.

★ BLACK RAIN, A Jaffe/Lansing Production in association with Michael Douglas, Paramount: DONALD O. MITCHELL, KEVIN O'CONNELL, GREG RUSSELL, and KEITH A. WESTER.

BORN ON THE FOURTH OF JULY, An A. Kitman Ho and Ixtlan Production, Universal: MICHAEL MINKLER, GREGORY H. WATKINS, WYLIE STATEMAN, and TOD A. MAITLAND.

GLORY, A Tri-Star Pictures Production, Tri-Star: DONALD O. MITCHELL, GREGG C. RUDLOFF, ELLIOT TYSON, and RUSSELL WILLIAMS II.

INDIANA JONES AND THE LAST CRUSADE, A Lucasfilm Ltd. Production, Paramount: BEN BURTT, GARY SUMMERS, SHAWN MURPHY, and TONY DAWE.

1990 Sixty-third Year

★ DANCES WITH WOLVES, A Tig Production, Orion: RUSSELL WILLIAMS II, JEFFREY PERKINS, BILL W. BENTON, and GREG WATKINS.

DAYS OF THUNDER, A Don Simpson and Jerry Bruckheimer Production, Paramount: CHARLES WILBORN, DONALD O. MITCHELL, RICK KLINE, and KEVIN O'CONNELL.

DICK TRACY, A Touchstone Pictures Production, Buena Vista: THOMAS CAUSEY, CHRIS JENKINS, DAVID E. CAMPBELL, and D. M. HEMPHILL.

THE HUNT FOR RED OCTOBER, A Mace Neufeld/Jerry Sherlock Production, Paramount: RICHARD BRYCE GOODMAN, RICHARD OVERTON, KEVIN F. CLEARY, and DON BASSMAN.

TOTAL RECALL, A Carolco Pictures Production, Tri-Star: NELSON STOLL, MICHAEL J. KOHUT, CARLOS DE LARIOS, and AARON ROCHIN.

1991 Sixty-fourth Year

BACKDRAFT, A Trilogy Entertainment Group/Brian Grazer Production, Universal: GARY SUMMERS, RANDY THOM, GARY RYDSTROM, and GLENN WILLIAMS.

BEAUTY AND THE BEAST, A Walt Disney Pictures Production, Buena Vista: TERRY PORTER, MEL METCALFE, DAVID J. HUDSON, and DOC KANE.

JFK, A Camelot Production, Warner Bros.: MICHAEL MINKLER, GREGG LANDAKER, and TOD A. MAITLAND.

THE SILENCE OF THE LAMBS, A Strong Heart/Demme Production, Orion: TOM FLEISHMAN and CHRISTOPHER NEWMAN.

★ TERMINATOR 2: JUDGMENT DAY, A Carolco Production, Tri-Star: TOM JOHNSON, GARY RYDSTROM, GARY SUMMERS, and LEE ORLOFF.

1992 Sixty-fifth Year

ALADDIN, A Walt Disney Pictures Production, Buena Vista: TERRY PORTER, MEL METCALFE, DAVID J. HUDSON, and DOC KANE.

A FEW GOOD MEN, A Castle Rock Entertainment Production, Columbia: KEVIN O'CONNELL, RICK KLINE, and BOB EBER.

★ THE LAST OF THE MOHICANS, A 20th Century-Fox Production, 20th Century-Fox: CHRIS JENKINS, DOUG HEMPHILL, MARK SMITH, and SIMON KAYE.

UNDER SIEGE, A Northwest Production, Warner Bros.: DON MITCHELL, FRANK A. MONTANO, RICK HART, and SCOTT SMITH.

UNFORGIVEN, A Warner Bros. Production, Warner Bros.: LES FRESHOLTZ, VERN POORE, DICK ALEXANDER, and ROB YOUNG.

Film Editing

Few persons would argue that the role of the film editor is as much creative as it is technical. By taking raw footage through a first cut to the final cut, a film editor faces a series of artistic decisions that shape the rhythm and style of the completed film and contribute substantially to how successfully the film meets the original expectations of the director.

Film editors who joined the Academy originally were assigned to the Technicians Branch. In the early 1930s they formed their own section within that branch, but it was not until 1946 that the Film Editors Branch was created.

The award for Film Editing was established in 1934. Ralph Dawson (1935, 1936, 1938) and Daniel Mandell (1942, 1946, 1960) with three awards each are the most frequent winners in this category.

Achievements in this category are nominated by members of the Academy Film Editors Branch.

1934 Seventh Year

CLEOPATRA, Paramount: ANNE BAUCHENS.

★ ESKIMO, Metro-Goldwyn-Mayer: CONRAD NERVIG.

ONE NIGHT OF LOVE, Columbia: GENE MILFORD.

1935 Eighth Year

DAVID COPPERFIELD, Metro-Goldwyn-Mayer: ROBERT J. KERN.

THE INFORMER, RKO Radio: GEORGE HIVELY.

LES MISERABLES, 20th Century, UA: BARBARA MCLEAN.

LIVES OF A BENGAL LANGER, Paramount: ELLSWORTH HOAGLAND.

★ A MIDSUMMER NIGHT'S DREAM, Warner Bros.: RALPH DAWSON.

MUTINY ON THE BOUNTY, Metro-Goldwyn-Mayer: MARGARET BOOTH.

1936 Ninth Year

★ ANTHONY ADVERSE, Warner Bros.: RALPH DAWSON.

COME AND GET IT, Goldwyn, UA: EDWARD CURTISS.

THE GREAT ZIEGFELD, Metro-Goldwyn-Mayer: WILLIAM S. GRAY.

LLOYDS OF LONDON, 20th Century-Fox: BARBARA MCLEAN.

A TALE OF TWO CITIES, Metro-Goldwyn-Mayer: CONRAD A. NERVIG.

THEODORA GOES WILD, Columbia: OTTO MEYER.

1937 Tenth Year

THE AWFUL TRUTH, Columbia: AL CLARK.

CAPTAINS COURAGEOUS, Metro-Goldwyn-Mayer: ELMO VERNON.

THE GOOD EARTH, Metro-Goldwyn-Mayer: BASIL WRANGELL.

★ LOST HORIZON, Columbia: GENE HAVLICK and GENE MILFORD.

100 MEN AND A GIRL, Universal: BERNARD W. BURTON.

1938 Eleventh Year

★ THE ADVENTURES OF ROBIN HOOD, Warner Bros.: RALPH DAWSON.

ALEXANDER'S RAGTIME BAND, 20th Century-Fox: BARBARA MCLEAN.

THE GREAT WALTZ, Metro-Goldwyn-Mayer: TOM HELD.

TEST PILOT, Metro-Goldwyn-Mayer: TOM HELD.

YOU CAN'T TAKE IT WITH YOU, Columbia: GENE HAVLICK.

1939 Twelfth Year

★ GONE WITH THE WIND, Selznick, M-G-M: HAL C. KERN and JAMES E. NEWCOM.

GOODBYE, MR. CHIPS, Metro-Goldwyn-Mayer (British): CHARLES FREND.

MR. SMITH GOES TO WASHINGTON, Columbia: GENE HAVLICK and AL CLARK.

THE RAINS CAME, 20th Century-Fox: BARBARA MCLEAN.

STAGECOACH, Wanger, UA: OTHO LOVERING and DOROTHY SPENCER.

1940 Thirteenth Year

THE GRAPES OF WRATH, 20th Century-Fox: ROBERT E. SIMPSON.

THE LETTER, Warner Bros.: WARREN LOW.

THE LONG VOYAGE HOME, Argosy-Wanger, UA: SHERMAN TODD.

★ NORTH WEST MOUNTED POLICE, Paramount: ANNE BAUCHENS.

REBECCA, Selznick, UA: HAL C. KERN.

1941 Fourteenth Year

CITIZEN KANE, Mercury-RKO Radio: ROBERT WISE.

DR. JEKYLL AND MR. HYDE, Metro-Goldwyn-Mayer: HAROLD F. KRESS.

HOW GREEN WAS MY VALLEY, 20th Century-Fox: JAMES B. CLARK.

THE LITTLE FOXES, Goldwyn-RKO Radio: DANIEL MANDELL.

★ SERGEANT YORK, Warner Bros.: WILLIAM HOLMES.

1942 Fifteenth Year

MRS. MINIVER, Metro-Goldwyn-Mayer: HAROLD F. KRESS.

★ THE PRIDE OF THE YANKEES, Goldwyn, RKO Radio: DANIEL MANDELL.

THE TALK OF THE TOWN, Columbia: OTTO MEYER.

THIS ABOVE ALL, 20th Century-Fox: WALTER THOMPSON.

YANKEE DOODLE DANDY, Warner Bros.: GEORGE AMY.

1943 Sixteenth Year

★ AIR FORCE, Warner Bros.: GEORGE AMY.

CASABLANCA, Warner Bros.: OWEN MARKS.

FIVE GRAVES TO CAIRO, Paramount: DOANE HARRISON.

FOR WHOM THE BELL TOLLS, Paramount: SHERMAN TODD and JOHN LINK.

THE SONG OF BERNADETTE, 20th Century-Fox: BARBARA MCLEAN.

1944 Seventeenth Year

GOING MY WAY, Paramount: LEROY STONE.

JANIE, Warner Bros.: OWEN MARKS.

NONE BUT THE LONELY HEART, RKO Radio: ROLAND GROSS.

SINCE YOU WENT AWAY, Selznick, UA: HAL C. KERN and JAMES E. NEWCOM.

★ WILSON, 20th Century-Fox: BARBARA McLEAN.

1945 Eighteenth Year

THE BELLS OF ST. MARY'S, Rainbow, RKO Radio: HARRY MARKER.

THE LOST WEEKEND, Paramount: DOANE HARRISON.

★ NATIONAL VELVET, Metro-Goldwyn-Mayer: ROBERT J. KERN.

OBJECTIVE-BURMA, Warner Bros.: GEORGE AMY.

A SONG TO REMEMBER, Columbia: CHARLES NELSON.

1946 Nineteenth Year

★ THE BEST YEARS OF OUR LIVES, Goldwyn, RKO Radio: DANIEL MANDELL.

IT'S A WONDERFUL LIFE, Liberty, RKO Radio: WILLIAM HORNBECK.

THE JOLSON STORY, Columbia: WILLIAM LYON.

THE KILLERS, Hellinger, Universal: ARTHUR HILTON.

THE YEARLING, Metro-Goldwyn-Mayer: HAROLD KRESS.

1947 Twentieth Year

THE BISHOP'S WIFE, Goldwyn, RKO Radio: MONICA COLLINGWOOD.

★ BODY AND SOUL, Enterprise, UA: FRANCIS LYON and ROBERT PARRISH.

GENTLEMAN'S AGREEMENT, 20th Century-Fox: HARMON JONES.

GREEN DOLPHIN STREET, Metro-Goldwyn-Mayer: GEORGE WHITE.

ODD MAN OUT, Rank-Two Cities, U-I (British): FERGUS MCDONNELL.

1948 Twenty-first Year

JOAN OF ARC, Sierra Pictures, RKO Radio: FRANK SULLIVAN.

JOHNNY BELINDA, Warner Bros.: DAVID WEISBART.

★ THE NAKED CITY, Hellinger, U-I: PAUL WEATHERWAX.

RED RIVER, Monterey Prods., UA: CHRISTIAN NYBY.

THE RED SHOES, Rank-Archers, Eagle-Lion (British): REGINALD MILLS.

1949 Twenty-second Year

ALL THE KING'S MEN, Rossen Prod., Columbia: ROBERT PARRISH and AL CLARK.

BATTLEGROUND, Metro-Goldwyn-Mayer: JOHN DUNNING.

★ CHAMPION, Screen Plays Corp., UA: HARRY GERSTAD.

SANDS OF IWO JIMA, Republic: RICHARD L. VAN ENGER.

THE WINDOW, RKO Radio: FREDERIC KNUDTSON.

1950 Twenty-third Year

ALL ABOUT EVE, 20th Century-Fox: BARBARA MCLEAN.

ANNIE GET YOUR GUN, Metro-Goldwyn-Mayer: JAMES E. NEWCOM.

★ KING SOLOMON'S MINES, Metro-Goldwyn-Mayer: RALPH E. WINTERS and CONRAD A. NERVIG.

SUNSET BOULEVARD, Paramount: ARTHUR SCHMIDT and DOANE HARRISON.

THE THIRD MAN, Selznick-London Films, SRO (British): OSWALD HAFENRICHTER.

1951 Twenty-fourth Year

AN AMERICAN IN PARIS, Metro-Goldwyn-Mayer: ADRIENNE FAZAN.

DECISION BEFORE DAWN, 20th Century-Fox: DOROTHY SPENCER.

★ A PLACE IN THE SUN, Paramount: WILLIAM HORNBECK.

QUO VADIS, Metro-Goldwyn-Mayer: RALPH E. WINTERS.

THE WELL, Popkin, UA: CHESTER SCHAEFFER.

1952 Twenty-fifth Year

COME BACK, LITTLE SHEBA, Wallis, Paramount: WARREN LOW.

FLAT TOP, Monogram: WILLIAM AUSTIN.

THE GREATEST SHOW ON EARTH, DeMille, Paramount: ANNE BAUCHENS.

★ HIGH NOON, Kramer, UA: ELMO WILLIAMS and HARRY GERSTAD.

MOULIN ROUGE, Romulus, UA: RALPH KEMPLEN.

1953 Twenty-sixth Year

CRAZYLEGS, Bartlett, Republic: IRVINE (COTTON) WARBURTON.

★ FROM HERE TO ETERNITY, Columbia: WILLIAM LYON.

THE MOON IS BLUE, Preminger-Herbert, UA: OTTO LUDWIG.

ROMAN HOLIDAY, Paramount: ROBERT SWINK.

WAR OF THE WORLDS, Paramount: EVERETT DOUGLAS.

1954 Twenty-seventh Year

THE CAINE MUTINY, A Stanley Kramer Prod., Columbia: WILLIAM A. LYON and HENRY BATISTA.

THE HIGH AND THE MIGHTY, Wayne-Fellows Prod., Inc., Warner Bros.: RALPH DAWSON.

★ ON THE WATERFRONT, Horizon-American Corp., Columbia: GENE MILFORD.

SEVEN BRIDES FOR SEVEN BROTHERS, Metro-Goldwyn-Mayer: RALPH E. WINTERS.

20,000 LEAGUES UNDER THE SEA, Walt Disney Prods., Buena Vista Film Dist. Co., Inc.: ELMO WILLIAMS.

1955 Twenty-eighth Year

BLACKBOARD JUNGLE, Metro-Goldwyn-Mayer: FERRIS WEBSTER.

THE BRIDGES AT TOKO-RI, Perlberg-Seaton, Paramount: ALMA MACRORIE.

OKLAHOMA!, Rodgers & Hammerstein Pictures, Inc., Magna Theatre Corp.: GENE RUGGIERO and GEORGE BOEMLER.

★ PICNIC, Columbia: CHARLES NELSON and WILLIAM A. LYON.

THE ROSE TATTOO, Hal Wallis, Paramount: WARREN LOW.

1956 Twenty-ninth Year

★ AROUND THE WORLD IN 80 DAYS, The Michael Todd Co., Inc., UA: GENE RUGGIERO and PAUL WEATHERWAX.

THE BRAVE ONE, King Bros. Prods., Inc., RKO Radio: MERRILL G. WHITE.

GIANT, Giant Prod., Warner Bros.: WILLIAM HORNBECK, PHILIP W. ANDERSON, and FRED BOHANAN.

SOMEBODY UP THERE LIKES ME, Metro-Goldwyn-Mayer: ALBERT AKST.

THE TEN COMMANDMENTS, Motion Picture Assocs., Inc., Paramount: ANNE BAUCHENS.

1957 Thirtieth Year

★ THE BRIDGE ON THE RIVER KWAI, A Horizon Picture, Columbia: PETER TAYLOR.

GUNFIGHT AT THE O.K. CORRAL, A Hal Wallis Prod., Paramount: WARREN LOW.

PAL JOEY, Essex-George Sidney Prod., Columbia: VIOLA LAWRENCE and JEROME THOMS.

SAYONARA, William Goetz Prod., Warner Bros.: ARTHUR P. SCHMIDT and PHILIP W. ANDERSON.

WITNESS FOR THE PROSECUTION, Edward Small-Arthur Hornblow Prod., UA: DANIEL MANDELL.

1958 Thirty-first Year

AUNTIE MAME, Warner Bros.: WILLIAM ZIEGLER.

COWBOY, Phoenix Pictures, Columbia: WILLIAM A. LYON and AL CLARK.

THE DEFIANT ONES, Stanley Kramer, UA: FREDERIC KNUDTSON.

★ GIGI, Arthur Freed Prods., Inc., M-G-M: ADRIENNE FAZAN.

I WANT TO LIVE!, Figaro, Inc., UA: WILLIAM HORNBECK.

1959 Thirty-second Year

ANATOMY OF A MURDER, Otto Preminger, Columbia: LOUIS R. LOEFFLER.

★ BEN-HUR, Metro-Goldwyn-Mayer: RALPH E. WINTERS and JOHN D. DUNNING.

NORTH BY NORTHWEST, Metro-Goldwyn-Mayer: GEORGE TOMASINI.
THE NUN'S STORY, Warner Bros.: WALTER THOMPSON.
ON THE BEACH, Lomitas Prods., UA: FREDERIC KNUDTSON.

1960 Thirty-third Year

THE ALAMO, Batjac Prod., UA: STUART GILMORE.
★ THE APARTMENT, The Mirisch Co., UA: DANIEL MANDELL.
INHERIT THE WIND, Stanley Kramer Prod., UA: FREDERIC KNUDTSON.
PEPE, G. S.-Posa Films International Prod., Columbia: VIOLA LAWRENCE and AL CLARK.
SPARTACUS, Bryna Prods., Inc., U-I: ROBERT LAWRENCE.

1961 Thirty-fourth Year

FANNY, Mansfield Prod., Warner Bros.: WILLIAM H. REYNOLDS.
THE GUNS OF NAVARONE, Carl Foreman Prod., Columbia: ALAN OSBISTON.
JUDGMENT AT NUREMBERG, Stanley Kramer Prod., UA: FREDERIC KNUDTSON.
THE PARENT TRAP, Walt Disney Prods., Buena Vista Dist. Co., Inc.: PHILIP W. ANDERSON.
★ WEST SIDE STORY, Mirisch Pictures, Inc., and B and P Enterprises, Inc., UA: THOMAS STANFORD.

1962 Thirty-fifth Year

★ LAWRENCE OF ARABIA, Horizon Pictures (G.B.), Ltd.-Sam Spiegel-David Lean Prod., Columbia: ANNE COATES.
THE LONGEST DAY, Darryl F. Zanuck Prods., 20th Century-Fox: SAMUEL E. BEETLEY.
THE MANCHURIAN CANDIDATE, M.C. Prod., UA: FERRIS WEBSTER.
THE MUSIC MAN, Warner Bros.: WILLIAM ZIEGLER.
MUTINY ON THE BOUNTY, Arcola Prod., M-G-M: JOHN MCSWEENEY, JR.

1963 Thirty-sixth Year

THE CARDINAL, Gamma Prod., Columbia: LOUIS R. LOEFFLER.
CLEOPATRA, 20th Century-Fox Ltd.-MCL Films S.A.-WALWA Films S.A. Prod., 20th Century-Fox: DOROTHY SPENCER.
THE GREAT ESCAPE, Mirisch-Alpha Picture Prod., UA: FERRIS WEBSTER.
★ HOW THE WEST WAS WON, Metro-Goldwyn-Mayer and Cinerama: HAROLD F. KRESS.
IT'S A MAD, MAD, MAD, MAD WORLD, Casey Prod., UA: FREDERIC KNUDTSON, ROBERT C. JONES, and GENE FOWLER, JR.

1964 Thirty-seventh Year

BECKET, Hal Wallis Prod., Paramount: ANNE COATES.
FATHER GOOSE, Universal-Granox Prod., Universal: TED J. KENT.
HUSH . . . HUSH, SWEET CHARLOTTE, Associates and Aldrich Prod., 20th Century-Fox: MICHAEL LUCIANO.
★ MARY POPPINS, Walt Disney Prods.: COTTON WARBURTON.
MY FAIR LADY, Warner Bros.: WILLIAM ZIEGLER.

1965 Thirty-eighth Year

CAT BALLOU, Harold Hecht Prod., Columbia: CHARLES NELSON.
DOCTOR ZHIVAGO, Sostar S.A.-Metro-Goldwyn-Mayer British Studios, Ltd. Prod., M-G-M: NORMAN SAVAGE.
THE FLIGHT OF THE PHOENIX, Associates and Aldrich Company Prod., 20th Century-Fox: MICHAEL LUCIANO.
THE GREAT RACE, Patricia-Jalem-Reynard Prod., Warner Bros.: RALPH E. WINTERS.
★ THE SOUND OF MUSIC, Argyle

Enterprises Prod., 20th Century-Fox: WILLIAM REYNOLDS.

1966 Thirty-ninth Year

FANTASTIC VOYAGE, 20th Century-Fox: WILLIAM B. MURPHY.

* GRAND PRIX, Douglas-Lewis-John Frankenheimer-Cherokee Prod., M-G-M: FREDRIC STEINKAMP, HENRY BERMAN, STEWART LINDER, and FRANK SANTILLO.

THE RUSSIANS ARE COMING! THE RUSSIANS ARE COMING!, Mirisch Corp. of Delaware Prod., United Artists: HAL ASHBY and J. TERRY WILLIAMS.

THE SAND PEBBLES, Argyle-Solar Prod., 20th Century-Fox: WILLIAM REYNOLDS.

WHO'S AFRAID OF VIRGINIA WOOLF?, Chenault Prod., Warner Bros.: SAM O'STEEN.

1967 Fortieth Year

BEACH RED, Theodora Prods., United Artists: FRANK P. KELLER.

THE DIRTY DOZEN, MKH Prods., Ltd., M-G-M: MICHAEL LUCIANO.

DOCTOR DOLITTLE, Apjac Prods., 20th Century-Fox: SAMUEL E. BEETLEY and MARJORIE FOWLER.

GUESS WHO'S COMING TO DINNER, Columbia: ROBERT C. JONES.

* IN THE HEAT OF THE NIGHT, Mirisch Corp. Prod., United Artists: HAL ASHBY.

1968 Forty-first Year

* BULLITT, Solar Prod., Warner Bros.-Seven Arts.: FRANK P. KELLER.

FUNNY GIRL, Rastar Prods., Columbia: ROBERT SWINK, MAURY WINETROBE, and WILLIAM SANDS.

THE ODD COUPLE, Howard W. Koch Prod., Paramount: FRANK BRACHT.

OLIVER!, Romulus Films, Columbia: RALPH KEMPLEN.

WILD IN THE STREETS, American International: FRED FEITSHANS and EVE NEWMAN.

1969 Forty-second Year

HELLO, DOLLY!, Chenault Prods., 20th Century-Fox: WILLIAM REYNOLDS.

MIDNIGHT COWBOY, Jerome Hellman-John Schlesinger Prod., United Artists: HUGH A. ROBERTSON.

THE SECRET OF SANTA VITTORIA, Stanley Kramer Company Prod., United Artists: WILLIAM LYON and EARLE HERDAN.

THEY SHOOT HORSES, DON'T THEY?, Chartoff-Winkler-Pollack Prod., ABC Pictures Presentation Cinerama: FREDRIC STEINKAMP.

* Z, Reggane Films-O.N.C.I.C. Prod., Cinema V: FRANÇOISE BONNOT.

1970 Forty-third Year

AIRPORT, Ross Hunter-Universal Prod., Universal: STUART GILMORE.

MASH, Aspen Prods., 20th Century-Fox: DANFORD B. GREENE.

* PATTON, 20th Century-Fox: HUGH S. FOWLER.

TORA! TORA! TORA!, 20th Century-Fox: JAMES E. NEWCOM, PEMBROKE J. HERRING, and INOUE CHIKAYA.

WOODSTOCK, Wadleigh-Maurice, Ltd. Prod., Warner Bros.: THELMA SCHOONMAKER.

1971 Forty-fourth Year

THE ANDROMEDA STRAIN, A Universal-Robert Wise Prod., Universal: STUART GILMORE and JOHN W. HOLMES.

A CLOCKWORK ORANGE, A Hawks Films, Ltd., Prod., Warner Bros.: BILL BUTLER.

* THE FRENCH CONNECTION, A Philip D'Antoni Prod., in association with Schine-Moore Prods., 20th Century-Fox: JERRY GREENBERG.

KOTCH, A Kotch Company Prod., ABC

Pictures Presentation, Cinerama: RALPH E. WINTERS.

SUMMER OF '42, A Robert Mulligan-Richard Alan Roth Prod., Warner Bros.: FOLMAR BLANGSTED.

1972 Forty-fifth Year

★ CABARET, An ABC Pictures Production, Allied Artists: DAVID BRETHERTON.

DELIVERANCE, Warner Bros.: TOM PRIESTLEY.

THE GODFATHER, An Albert S. Ruddy Production, Paramount: WILLIAM REYNOLDS and PETER ZINNER.

THE HOT ROCK, A Landers-Roberts Production, 20th Century-Fox: FRANK P. KELLER and FRED W. BERGER.

THE POSEIDON ADVENTURE, An Irwin Allen Production, 20th Century-Fox: HAROLD F. KRESS.

1973 Forty-sixth Year

AMERICAN GRAFFITI, A Universal-Lucasfilm, Ltd.-Coppola Company Prod., Universal: VERNA FIELDS and MARCIA LUCAS.

THE DAY OF THE JACKAL, Warwick Film Prods., Ltd.-Universal Prods. France S.A., Universal: RALPH KEMPLEN.

THE EXORCIST, Hoya Prods., Warner Bros.: JORDAN LEONDOPOULOS, BUD SMITH, EVAN LOTTMAN, and NORMAN GAY.

JONATHAN LIVINGSTON SEAGULL, A JLS Limited Partnership Prod., Paramount: FRANK P. KELLER and JAMES GALLOWAY.

★ THE STING, A Universal-Bill/Phillips-George Roy Hill Film Prod., Zanuck/Brown Presentation, Universal: WILLIAM REYNOLDS.

1974 Forty-seventh Year

BLAZING SADDLES, Warner Bros.: JOHN C. HOWARD and DANFORD GREENE.

CHINATOWN, A Robert Evans Prod., Paramount: SAM O'STEEN.

EARTHQUAKE, A Universal-Mark Robson-Filmakers Group Prod., Universal: DOROTHY SPENCER.

THE LONGEST YARD, An Albert S. Ruddy Prod., Paramount: MICHAEL LUCIANO.

★ THE TOWERING INFERNO, An Irwin Allen Prod., 20th Century-Fox/Warner Bros.: HAROLD F. KRESS and CARL KRESS.

1975 Forty-eighth Year

DOG DAY AFTERNOON, Warner Bros.: DEDE ALLEN.

★ JAWS, A Universal-Zanuck/Brown Production, Universal: VERNA FIELDS.

THE MAN WHO WOULD BE KING, An Allied Artists-Columbia Pictures Production, Allied Artists: RUSSELL LLOYD.

ONE FLEW OVER THE CUCKOO'S NEST, A Fantasy Films Production, United Artists: RICHARD CHEW, LYNZEE KLINGMAN, and SHELDON KAHN.

THREE DAYS OF THE CONDOR, A Dino De Laurentiis Production, Paramount: FREDRIC STEINKAMP and DON GUIDICE.

1976 Forty-ninth Year

ALL THE PRESIDENT'S MEN, A Wildwood Enterprises Production, Warner Bros.: ROBERT L. WOLFE.

BOUND FOR GLORY, The Bound for Glory Company Production, United Artists: ROBERT JONES and PEMBROKE J. HERRING.

NETWORK, A Howard Gottfried/Paddy Chayefsky Production, Metro-Goldwyn-Mayer/United Artists: ALAN HEIM.

★ ROCKY, A Robert Chartoff-Irwin Winkler Production, United Artists: RICHARD HALSEY and SCOTT CONRAD.

TWO-MINUTE WARNING, A Filmways/Larry Peerce-Edward S. Feldman Film Production, Universal: EVE NEWMAN and WALTER HANNEMANN.

1977 Fiftieth Year

CLOSE ENCOUNTERS OF THE THIRD KIND, Close Encounter Productions, Columbia: MICHAEL KAHN.

JULIA, A Twentieth Century-Fox Production, 20th Century-Fox: WALTER MURCH and MARCEL DURHAM.

SMOKEY AND THE BANDIT, A Universal/Rastar Production, Universal: WALTER HANNEMANN and ANGELO ROSS.

★ STAR WARS, A Twentieth Century-Fox Production, 20th Century-Fox: PAUL HIRSCH, MARCIA LUCAS, and RICHARD CHEW.

THE TURNING POINT, Hera Productions, 20th Century-Fox: WILLIAM REYNOLDS.

1978 Fifty-first Year

THE BOYS FROM BRAZIL, An ITC Entertainment Production, 20th Century-Fox: ROBERT E. SWINK.

COMING HOME, A Jerome Hellman Enterprises Production, United Artists: DON ZIMMERMAN.

★ THE DEER HUNTER, An EMI Films/Michael Cimino Film Production, Universal: PETER ZINNER.

MIDNIGHT EXPRESS, A Casablanca-Filmworks Production, Columbia: GERRY HAMBLING.

SUPERMAN, A Dovemead, Ltd. Production, Alexander Salkind Presentation, Warner Bros.: STUART BAIRD.

1979 Fifty-second Year

★ ALL THAT JAZZ, A Columbia/Twentieth Century-Fox Production, 20th Century-Fox: ALAN HEIM.

APOCALYPSE NOW, An Omni Zoetrope Production, UA: RICHARD MARKS, WALTER MURCH, GERALD B. GREENBERG, and LISA FRUCHTMAN.

THE BLACK STALLION, An Omni Zoetrope Production, UA: ROBERT DALVA.

KRAMER VS. KRAMER, Stanley Jaffe Productions, Columbia: JERRY GREENBERG.

THE ROSE, A Twentieth Century-Fox Production, 20th Century-Fox: ROBERT L. WOLFE and C. TIMOTHY O'MEARA.

1980 Fifty-third Year

COAL MINER'S DAUGHTER, A Bernard Schwartz-Universal Pictures Production, Universal: ARTHUR SCHMIDT.

THE COMPETITION, A Rastar Films Production, Columbia: DAVID BLEWITT.

THE ELEPHANT MAN, A Brooksfilms, Ltd. Production, Paramount: ANNE V. COATES.

FAME, A Metro-Goldwyn-Mayer Production, M-G-M: GERRY HAMBLING.

★ RAGING BULL, A Robert Chartoff-Irwin Winkler Production, United Artists: THELMA SCHOONMAKER.

1981 Fifty-fourth Year

CHARIOTS OF FIRE, Enigma Productions Limited. The Ladd Company/Warner Bros.: TERRY RAWLINGS.

THE FRENCH LIEUTENANT'S WOMAN, A Parlon Production, UA: JOHN BLOOM.

ON GOLDEN POND, An ITC Films/IPC Films Production, Universal: ROBERT L. WOLFE.

★ RAIDERS OF THE LOST ARK, A Lucasfilm Production, Paramount: MICHAEL KAHN.

REDS, A J.R.S. Production, Paramount: DEDE ALLEN and CRAIG MCKAY.

1982 Fifty-fifth Year

DAS BOOT, A Bavaria Atelier GmbH Production, Columbia: HANNES NIKEL.

E.T. THE EXTRA-TERRESTRIAL, A Universal Pictures Production, Universal: CAROL LITTLETON.

★ GANDHI, An Indo-British Films Production, Columbia: JOHN BLOOM.

AN OFFICER AND A GENTLEMAN, A Lorimar Production in association with Martin Elfand, Paramount: PETER ZINNER.

TOOTSIE, A Mirage/Punch Production, Columbia: FREDRIC STEINKAMP and WILLIAM STEINKAMP.

1983 Fifty-sixth Year

BLUE THUNDER, A Rastar Features Production, Columbia: FRANK MORRISS and EDWARD ABROMS.

FLASHDANCE, A Polygram Pictures Production, Paramount: BUD SMITH and WALT MULCONERY.

★ THE RIGHT STUFF, A Robert Chartoff-Irwin Winkler Production, The Ladd Company through Warner Bros.: GLENN FARR, LISA FRUCHTMAN, STEPHEN A. ROTTER, DOUGLAS STEWART, and TOM ROLF.

SILKWOOD, An ABC Motion Pictures Production, 20th Century-Fox: SAM O'STEEN.

TERMS OF ENDEARMENT, A James L. Brooks Production, Paramount: RICHARD MARKS.

1984 Fifty-seventh Year

AMADEUS, A Saul Zaentz Company Production, Orion: NENA DANEVIC and MICHAEL CHANDLER.

THE COTTON CLUB, A Totally Independent Production, Orion: BARRY MALKIN and ROBERT Q. LOVETT.

★ THE KILLING FIELDS, A Goldcrest Films and Television/ International Film Investors L.P. Production, Warner Bros.: JIM CLARK.

A PASSAGE TO INDIA, A G. W. Films Limited Production, Columbia: DAVID LEAN.

ROMANCING THE STONE, An El Corazon Producciones S.A. Production, 20th Century-Fox: DONN CAMBERN and FRANK MORRISS.

1985 Fifty-eighth Year

A CHORUS LINE, An Embassy Films Associates and Polygram Pictures Production, Columbia: JOHN BLOOM.

OUT OF AFRICA, A Universal Pictures Limited Production, Universal: FREDRIC STEINKAMP, WILLIAM STEINKAMP, PEMBROKE HERRING, and SHELDON KAHN.

PRIZZI'S HONOR, An ABC Motion Pictures Production, 20th Century-Fox: RUDI FEHR and KAJA FEHR.

RUNAWAY TRAIN, A Cannon Films Production, Cannon: HENRY RICHARDSON.

★ WITNESS, An Edward S. Feldman Production, Paramount: THOM NOBLE.

1986 Fifty-ninth Year

ALIENS, A Twentieth Century-Fox Film Production, 20th Century-Fox: RAY LOVEJOY.

HANNAH AND HER SISTERS, A Jack Rollins and Charles H. Joffe Production, Orion: SUSAN E. MORSE.

THE MISSION, A Warner Bros./ Goldcrest and Kingsmere Production, Warner Bros.: JIM CLARK.

★ PLATOON, A Hemdale Film Production, Orion: CLAIRE SIMPSON.

TOP GUN, A Don Simpson/Jerry Bruckheimer Production, Paramount: BILLY WEBER and CHRIS LEBENZON.

1987 Sixtieth Year

BROADCAST NEWS, A Twentieth Century-Fox Production, 20th Century-Fox: RICHARD MARKS.

EMPIRE OF THE SUN, A Warner Bros. Production, Warner Bros.: MICHAEL KAHN.

FATAL ATTRACTION, A Jaffe/Lansing Production, Paramount: MICHAEL KAHN and PETER E. BERGER.

★ THE LAST EMPEROR, A Hemdale Film Production, Columbia: GABRIELLA CRISTIANI.

ROBOCOP, A Tobor Pictures Production, Orion: FRANK J. URIOSTE.

1988 Sixty-first Year

DIE HARD, A Twentieth Century-Fox Production, 20th Century-Fox: FRANK J. URIOSTE and JOHN F. LINK.

GORILLAS IN THE MIST, A Warner Bros. Production, Warner Bros./Universal: STUART BAIRD.

MISSISSIPPI BURNING, A Frederick Zollo Production, Orion: GERRY HAMBLING.

RAIN MAN, A Guber-Peters Company Production, United Artists: STU LINDER.

★ WHO FRAMED ROGER RABBIT, An Amblin Entertainment and Touchstone Pictures Production, Buena Vista: ARTHUR SCHMIDT.

1989 Sixty-second Year

THE BEAR, A Renn Production, Tri-Star: NÖELLE BOISSON.

★ BORN ON THE FOURTH OF JULY, An A. Kitman Ho and Ixtlan Production, Universal: DAVID BRENNER and JOE HUTSHING.

DRIVING MISS DAISY, A Zanuck Company Production, Warner Bros.: MARK WARNER.

THE FABULOUS BAKER BOYS, A Gladden Entertainment Presentation of a Mirage Production, 20th Century-Fox: WILLIAM STEINKAMP.

GLORY, A Tri-Star Pictures Production, Tri-Star: STEVEN ROSENBLUM.

1990 Sixty-third Year

★ DANCES WITH WOLVES, A Tig Production, Orion: NEIL TRAVIS.

GHOST, A Howard W. Koch Production, Paramount: WALTER MURCH.

THE GODFATHER PART III, A Zoetrope Studios Production, Paramount: BARRY MALKIN, LISA FRUCHTMAN, and WALTER MURCH.

GOODFELLAS, A Warner Bros. Production, Warner Bros.: THELMA SCHOONMAKER.

THE HUNT FOR RED OCTOBER, A Mace Neufeld/Jerry Sherlock Production, Paramount: DENNIS VIRKLER and JOHN WRIGHT.

1991 Sixty-fourth Year

THE COMMITMENTS, A Beacon Communications Production, 20th Century-Fox: GERRY HAMBLING.

★ JFK, A Camelot Production, Warner Bros.: JOE HUTSHING and PIETRO SCALIA.

THE SILENCE OF THE LAMBS, A Strong Heart/Demme Production, Orion: CRAIG MCKAY.

TERMINATOR 2: JUDGMENT DAY, A Carolco Production, Tri-Star: CONRAD BUFF, MARK GOLDBLATT, and RICHARD A. HARRIS.

THELMA & LOUISE, A Pathé Entertainment Production, M-G-M: THOM NOBLE.

1992 Sixty-fifth Year

BASIC INSTINCT, A Carolco Production, Tri-Star: FRANK J. URIOSTE.

THE CRYING GAME, A Palace Pictures Production, Miramax: KANT PAN.

A FEW GOOD MEN, A Castle Rock Entertainment Production, Columbia: ROBERT LEIGHTON.

THE PLAYER, An Avenue Pictures Production, Fine Line: GERALDINE PERONI.

★ UNFORGIVEN, A Warner Bros. Production, Warner Bros.: JOEL COX.

Music: Scoring

The Music Award for Scoring was established in 1934, and for the first four years it was a Music Department Achievement with the Oscar going to the head of the studio's music department rather than to the composer. In 1938 rule changes gave the composer the award and split the category into two parts, Best Score and Original Score. Three years later these designations were changed again; this time the categories depended upon whether the film was dramatic or musical. Since then the names of the category divisions have changed several times. The present designations are Original Score and Original Song Score. The latter has had few nominations in recent years. The Academy defines a song score as a work consisting of "not fewer than five original songs by the same writer or team of writers used either as voice-overs on the soundtrack or visually performed. . . . The score's chief emphasis must be the dramatic usage of these five or more songs. What is simply a group of songs unrelated to the story line of the film will not be considered a valid song score."

Entries in this category are submitted by the creators of the achievement and are screened by members of the Academy Music Branch who determine the five nominees. If fewer than twenty-five qualified works are submitted, the nominations may be limited to three.

1934 Seventh Year

Score

THE GAY DIVORCEE, RKO Radio Studio Music Department: MAX STEINER, Head; Score by KENNETH WEBB and SAMUEL HOFFENSTEIN.

THE LOST PATROL, RKO Radio Studio Music Department: MAX STEINER, Head; Score by MAX STEINER.

★ ONE NIGHT OF LOVE, Columbia Studio Music Department: LOUIS SILVERS, Head; Thematic music by VICTOR SCHERTZINGER and GUS KAHN.

1935 Eighth Year

Score

★ THE INFORMER, RKO Radio Studio Music Department: MAX STEINER, Head; Score by MAX STEINER.

MUTINY ON THE BOUNTY, Metro-Goldwyn-Mayer Studio Music Department: NAT W. FINSTON, Head; Score by HERBERT STOTHART.

PETER IBBETSON, Paramount Studio Music Department: IRVIN TALBOT, Head; Score by ERNST TOCH.

1936 Ninth Year

Score

★ ANTHONY ADVERSE, Warner Bros. Studio Music Department: LEO FORBSTEIN, Head; Score by ERICH WOLFGANG KORNGOLD.

THE CHARGE OF THE LIGHT BRIGADE, Warner Bros. Studio Music Department: LEO FORBSTEIN, Head; Score by MAX STEINER.

THE GARDEN OF ALLAH, Selznick International Pictures Music Department: MAX STEINER, Head; Score by MAX STEINER.

THE GENERAL DIED AT DAWN, Paramount Studio Music Department: BORIS MORROS, Head; Score by WERNER JANSSEN.

WINTERSET, RKO Radio Studio Music Department: NATHANIEL SHILKRET, Head; Score by NATHANIEL SHILKRET.

1937 Tenth Year

Score

THE HURRICANE, Samuel Goldwyn Studio Music Department: ALFRED NEWMAN, Head; Score by ALFRED NEWMAN.

IN OLD CHICAGO, 20th Century-Fox Studio Music Department: LOUIS SILVERS, Head; Score: No composer credit.

THE LIFE OF EMILE ZOLA, Warner Bros. Studio Music Department: LEO FORBSTEIN, Head; Score by MAX STEINER.

LOST HORIZON, Columbia Studio Music Department: MORRIS STOLOFF, Head; Score by DIMITRI TIOMKIN.

MAKE A WISH, Principal Productions: DR. HUGO RIESENFELD, Musical Director; Score by DR. HUGO RIESENFELD.

MAYTIME, Metro-Goldwyn-Mayer Studio Music Department: NAT W. FINSTON, Head; Score by HERBERT STOTHART.

★ 100 MEN AND A GIRL, Universal Studio Music Department: CHARLES PREVIN, Head; Score: No composer credit.

PORTIA ON TRIAL, Republic Studio Music Department: ALBERTO COLOMBO, Head; Score by ALBERTO COLOMBO.

THE PRISONER OF ZENDA, Selznick International Pictures Music Department: ALFRED NEWMAN, Musical Director; Score by ALFRED NEWMAN.

QUALITY STREET, RKO Radio Studio Music Department: ROY WEBB, Musical Director; Score by ROY WEBB.

SNOW WHITE AND THE SEVEN DWARFS, Walt Disney Studio Music Department: LEIGH HARLINE, Head; Score by FRANK CHURCHILL, LEIGH HARLINE, and PAUL J. SMITH.

SOMETHING TO SING ABOUT, Grand National Studio Music Department: C. BAKALEINIKOFF, Musical Director; Score by VICTOR SCHERTZINGER.

SOULS AT SEA, Paramount Studio Music Department: BORIS MORROS, Head; Score by W. FRANKE HARLING and MILAN RODER.

WAY OUT WEST, Hal Roach Studio Music Department: MARVIN HATLEY, Head; Score by MARVIN HATLEY.

1938 Eleventh Year

Scoring

★ ALEXANDER'S RAGTIME BAND, 20th Century-Fox: ALFRED NEWMAN.

CAREFREE, RKO Radio: VICTOR BARAVALLE.

GIRLS SCHOOL, Columbia: MORRIS STOLOFF and GREGORY STONE.

GOLDWYN FOLLIES, Goldwyn, UA: ALFRED NEWMAN.

JEZEBEL, Warner Bros.: MAX STEINER.

MAD ABOUT MUSIC, Universal: CHARLES PREVIN and FRANK SKINNER.

STORM OVER BENGAL, Republic: CY FEUER.

SWEETHEARTS, Metro-Goldwyn-Mayer: HERBERT STOTHART.

THERE GOES MY HEART, Hal Roach, UA: MARVIN HATLEY.

TROPIC HOLIDAY, Paramount: BORIS MORROS.

THE YOUNG IN HEART, Selznick, UA: FRANZ WAXMAN.

Original Score

★ THE ADVENTURES OF ROBIN HOOD, Warner Bros.: ERICH WOLFGANG KORNGOLD.

ARMY GIRL, Republic: VICTOR YOUNG.

BLOCKADE, Walter Wanger, UA: WERNER JANSSEN.

BLOCKHEADS, Hal Roach, UA: MARVIN HATLEY.

BREAKING THE ICE, RKO Radio: VICTOR YOUNG.

THE COWBOY AND THE LADY, Goldwyn, UA: ALFRED NEWMAN.

IF I WERE KING, Paramount: RICHARD HAGEMAN.

MARIE ANTOINETTE, Metro-Goldwyn-Mayer: HERBERT STOTHART.

PACIFIC LINER, RKO Radio: RUSSELL BENNETT.

SUEZ, 20th Century-Fox: LOUIS SILVERS.

THE YOUNG IN HEART, Selznick, UA: FRANZ WAXMAN.

1939 Twelfth Year

Scoring

BABES IN ARMS, Metro-Goldwyn-Mayer: ROGER EDENS and GEORGE E. STOLL.

FIRST LOVE, Universal: CHARLES PREVIN.

THE GREAT VICTOR HERBERT, Paramount: PHIL BOUTELJE and ARTHUR LANGE.

THE HUNCHBACK OF NOTRE DAME, RKO Radio: ALFRED NEWMAN.

INTERMEZZO, Selznick, UA: LOU FORBES.

MR. SMITH GOES TO WASHINGTON, Columbia: DIMITRI TIOMKIN.

OF MICE AND MEN, Roach, UA: AARON COPLAND.

THE PRIVATE LIVES OF ELIZABETH AND ESSEX, Warner Bros.: ERICH WOLFGANG KORNGOLD.

SHE MARRIED A COP, Republic: CY FEUER.

★ STAGECOACH, Walter Wanger, UA: RICHARD HAGEMAN, FRANK HARLING, JOHN LEIPOLD, and LEO SHUKEN.

SWANEE RIVER, 20th Century-Fox: LOUIS SILVERS.

THEY SHALL HAVE MUSIC, Goldwyn, UA: ALFRED NEWMAN.

WAY DOWN SOUTH, Lesser, RKO Radio: VICTOR YOUNG.

Original Score

DARK VICTORY, Warner Bros.: MAX STEINER.

ETERNALLY YOURS, Walter Wanger, UA: WERNER JANSSEN.

GOLDEN BOY, Columbia: VICTOR YOUNG.

GONE WITH THE WIND, Selznick, M-G-M: MAX STEINER.

GULLIVER'S TRAVELS, Paramount: VICTOR YOUNG.

THE MAN IN THE IRON MASK, Small, UA: LUD GLUSKIN and LUCIEN MORAWECK.

MAN OF CONQUEST, Republic: VICTOR YOUNG.

NURSE EDITH CAVELL, RKO Radio: ANTHONY COLLINS.

OF MICE AND MEN, Roach, UA: AARON COPLAND.

THE RAINS CAME, 20th Century-Fox: ALFRED NEWMAN.

★ THE WIZARD OF OZ, Metro-Goldwyn-Mayer: HERBERT STOTHART.

WUTHERING HEIGHTS, Goldwyn, UA: ALFRED NEWMAN.

1940 Thirteenth Year

Scoring

ARISE, MY LOVE, Paramount: VICTOR YOUNG.

HIT PARADE OF 1941, Republic: CY FEUER.

IRENE, Imperadio, RKO Radio: ANTHONY COLLINS.

OUR TOWN, Sol Lesser, UA: AARON COPLAND.

THE SEA HAWK, Warner Bros.: ERICH WOLFGANG KORNGOLD.

SECOND CHORUS, Paramount: ARTIE SHAW.

SPRING PARADE, Universal: CHARLES PREVIN.

STRIKE UP THE BAND, Metro-Goldwyn-Mayer: GEORGIE STOLL and ROGER EDENS.

★ TIN PAN ALLEY, 20th Century-Fox: ALFRED NEWMAN.

Original Score

ARIZONA, Columbia: VICTOR YOUNG.

THE DARK COMMAND, Republic: VICTOR YOUNG.

THE FIGHT FOR LIFE, U.S. Government-Columbia: LOUIS GRUENBERG.

THE GREAT DICTATOR, Chaplin, UA: MEREDITH WILLSON.

THE HOUSE OF SEVEN GABLES, Universal: FRANK SKINNER.

THE HOWARDS OF VIRGINIA, Columbia: RICHARD HAGEMAN.

THE LETTER, Warner Bros.: MAX STEINER.

THE LONG VOYAGE HOME, Argosy-Wanger, UA: RICHARD HAGEMAN.

THE MARK OF ZORRO, 20th Century-Fox: ALFRED NEWMAN.

MY FAVORITE WIFE, RKO Radio: ROY WEBB.

NORTH WEST MOUNTED POLICE, Paramount: VICTOR YOUNG.

ONE MILLION B.C., Hal Roach, UA: WERNER HEYMANN.

OUR TOWN, Sol Lesser, UA: AARON COPLAND.

★ PINOCCHIO, Disney, RKO Radio: LEIGH HARLINE, PAUL J. SMITH, and NED WASHINGTON.

REBECCA, Selznick, UA: FRANZ WAXMAN.

THE THIEF OF BAGDAD, Korda, UA: MIKLOS ROZSA.

WATERLOO BRIDGE, Metro-Goldwyn-Mayer: HERBERT STOTHART.

1941 Fourteenth Year

Scoring of a Dramatic Picture

★ ALL THAT MONEY CAN BUY, RKO Radio: BERNARD HERRMANN.

BACK STREET, Universal: FRANK SKINNER.

BALL OF FIRE, Goldwyn, RKO Radio: ALFRED NEWMAN.

CHEERS FOR MISS BISHOP, Rowland, UA: EDWARD WARD.

CITIZEN KANE, Mercury, RKO Radio: BERNARD HERRMANN.

DR. JEKYLL AND MR. HYDE, Metro-Goldwyn-Mayer: FRANZ WAXMAN.

HOLD BACK THE DAWN, Paramount: VICTOR YOUNG.

HOW GREEN WAS MY VALLEY, 20th Century-Fox: ALFRED NEWMAN.

KING OF THE ZOMBIES, Monogram: EDWARD KAY.

LADIES IN RETIREMENT, Columbia: MORRIS STOLOFF and ERNST TOCH.

THE LITTLE FOXES, Goldwyn, RKO Radio: MEREDITH WILLSON.

LYDIA, Korda, UA: MIKLOS ROZSA.

MERCY ISLAND, Republic: CY FEUER and WALTER SCHARF.

SERGEANT YORK, Warner Bros.: MAX STEINER.

SO ENDS OUR NIGHT, Loew-Lewin, UA: LOUIS GRUENBERG.

SUNDOWN, Walter Wanger, UA: MIKLOS ROZSA.

SUSPICION, RKO Radio: FRANZ WAXMAN.

TANKS A MILLION, Roach, UA: EDWARD WARD.

THAT UNCERTAIN FEELING, Lubitsch, UA: WERNER HEYMANN.

THIS WOMAN IS MINE, Universal: RICHARD HAGEMAN.

Scoring of a Musical Picture

ALL AMERICAN CO-ED, Roach, UA: EDWARD WARD.

BIRTH OF THE BLUES, Paramount: ROBERT EMMETT DOLAN.

BUCK PRIVATES, Universal: CHARLES PREVIN.

THE CHOCOLATE SOLDIER, Metro-Goldwyn-Mayer: HERBERT STOTHART and BRONISLAU KAPER.

★ DUMBO, Disney, RKO Radio: FRANK CHURCHILL and OLIVER WALLACE.

ICE CAPADES, Republic: CY FEUER.

THE STRAWBERRY BLONDE, Warner Bros.: HEINZ ROEMHELD.

SUN VALLEY SERENADE, 20th Century-Fox: EMIL NEWMAN.

SUNNY, RKO Radio: ANTHONY COLLINS.

YOU'LL NEVER GET RICH, Columbia: MORRIS STOLOFF.

1942 Fifteenth Year

Scoring of a Dramatic or Comedy Picture

ARABIAN NIGHTS, Universal: FRANK SKINNER.

BAMBI, Disney, RKO Radio: FRANK CHURCHILL and EDWARD PLUMB.

THE BLACK SWAN, 20th Century-Fox: ALFRED NEWMAN.

THE CORSICAN BROTHERS, Small, UA: DIMITRI TIOMKIN.

FLYING TIGERS, Republic: VICTOR YOUNG.

THE GOLD RUSH, Chaplin, UA: MAX TERR.

I MARRIED A WITCH, Cinema Guild, UA: ROY WEBB.

JOAN OF PARIS, RKO Radio: ROY WEBB.

JUNGLE BOOK, Korda, UA: MIKLOS ROZSA.

KLONDIKE FURY, Monogram: EDWARD KAY.

★ NOW, VOYAGER, Warner Bros.: MAX STEINER.

THE PRIDE OF THE YANKEES, Goldwyn, RKO Radio: LEIGH HARLINE.

RANDOM HARVEST, Metro-Goldwyn-Mayer: HERBERT STOTHART.

THE SHANGHAI GESTURE, Arnold, UA: RICHARD HAGEMAN.

SILVER QUEEN, Sherman, UA: VICTOR YOUNG.

TAKE A LETTER, DARLING, Paramount: VICTOR YOUNG.

THE TALK OF THE TOWN, Columbia: FREDERICK HOLLANDER and MORRIS STOLOFF.

TO BE OR NOT TO BE, Lubitsch, UA: WERNER HEYMANN.

Scoring of a Musical Picture

FLYING WITH MUSIC, Roach, UA: EDWARD WARD.

FOR ME AND MY GAL, Metro-Goldwyn-Mayer: ROGER EDENS and GEORGIE STOLL.

HOLIDAY INN, Paramount: ROBERT EMMETT DOLAN.

IT STARTED WITH EVE, Universal: CHARLES PREVIN and HANS SALTER.

JOHNNY DOUGHBOY, Republic: WALTER SCHARF.

MY GAL SAL, 20th Century-Fox: ALFRED NEWMAN.

★ YANKEE DOODLE DANDY, Warner Bros.: RAY HEINDORF and HEINZ ROEMHELD.

YOU WERE NEVER LOVELIER, Columbia: LEIGH HARLINE.

1943 Sixteenth Year

Scoring of a Dramatic or Comedy Picture

THE AMAZING MRS. HOLLIDAY, Universal: HANS J. SALTER and FRANK SKINNER.

CASABLANCA, Warner Bros.: MAX STEINER.

THE COMMANDOS STRIKE AT DAWN, Columbia: LOUIS GRUENBERG and MORRIS STOLOFF.

THE FALLEN SPARROW, RKO Radio: C. BAKALEINIKOFF and ROY WEBB.

FOR WHOM THE BELL TOLLS, Paramount: VICTOR YOUNG.
HANGMEN ALSO DIE, Arnold, UA: HANNS EISLER.
HI DIDDLE DIDDLE, Stone, UA: PHIL BOUTELJE.
IN OLD OKLAHOMA, Republic: WALTER SCHARF.
JOHNNY COME LATELY, Cagney, UA: LEIGH HARLINE.
THE KANSAN, Sherman, UA: GERARD CARBONARA.
LADY OF BURLESQUE, Stromberg, UA: ARTHUR LANGE.
MADAME CURIE, Metro-Goldwyn-Mayer: HERBERT STOTHART.
THE MOON AND SIXPENCE, Loew-Lewin, UA: DIMITRI TIOMKIN.
THE NORTH STAR, Goldwyn, RKO Radio: AARON COPLAND.
★ THE SONG OF BERNADETTE, 20th Century-Fox: ALFRED NEWMAN.
VICTORY THROUGH AIR POWER, Disney, UA: EDWARD H. PLUMB, PAUL J. SMITH, and OLIVER G. WALLACE.

Scoring of a Musical Picture

CONEY ISLAND, 20th Century-Fox: ALFRED NEWMAN.
HIT PARADE OF 1943, Republic: WALTER SCHARF.
THE PHANTOM OF THE OPERA, Universal: EDWARD WARD.
SALUDOS AMIGOS, Disney, RKO Radio: EDWARD H. PLUMB, PAUL J. SMITH, and CHARLES WOLCOTT.
THE SKY'S THE LIMIT, RKO Radio: LEIGH HARLINE.
SOMETHING TO SHOUT ABOUT, Columbia: MORRIS STOLOFF.
STAGE DOOR CANTEEN, Lesser, UA: FREDERIC E. RICH.
STAR SPANGLED RHYTHM, Paramount: ROBERT EMMETT DOLAN.
★ THIS IS THE ARMY, Warner Bros.: RAY HEINDORF.
THOUSANDS CHEER, Metro-Goldwyn-Mayer: HERBERT STOTHART.

1944 Seventeenth Year

Scoring of a Dramatic or Comedy Picture

ADDRESS UNKNOWN, Columbia: MORRIS STOLOFF and ERNST TOCH.
THE ADVENTURES OF MARK TWAIN, Warner Bros.: MAX STEINER.
THE BRIDGE OF SAN LUIS REY, Bogeaus, UA: DIMITRI TIOMKIN.
CASANOVA BROWN, International, RKO Radio: ARTHUR LANGE.
CHRISTMAS HOLIDAY, Universal: H. J. SALTER.
DOUBLE INDEMNITY, Paramount: MIKLOS ROZSA.
THE FIGHTING SEABEES, Republic: WALTER SCHARF and ROY WEBB.
THE HAIRY APE, Levey, UA: MICHEL MICHELET and EDWARD PAUL.
IT HAPPENED TOMORROW, Arnold, UA: ROBERT STOLZ.
JACK LONDON, Bronston, UA: FREDERIC E. RICH.
KISMET, Metro-Goldwyn-Mayer: HERBERT STOTHART.
NONE BUT THE LONELY HEART, RKO Radio: C. BAKALEINIKOFF and HANNS EISLER.
THE PRINCESS AND THE PIRATE, Regent, RKO Radio: DAVID ROSE.
★ SINCE YOU WENT AWAY, Selznick, UA: MAX STEINER.
SUMMER STORM, Angelus, UA: KARL HAJOS.
THREE RUSSIAN GIRLS, R and F Prods., UA: FRANKE HARLING.
UP IN MABEL'S ROOM, Small, UA: EDWARD PAUL.
VOICE IN THE WIND, Ripley-Monter, UA: MICHEL MICHELET.
WILSON, 20th Century-Fox: ALFRED NEWMAN.
WOMAN OF THE TOWN, Sherman, UA: MIKLOS ROZSA.

Scoring of a Musical Picture

BRAZIL, Republic: WALTER SCHARF.

★ COVER GIRL, Columbia: CARMEN DRAGON and MORRIS STOLOFF.

HIGHER AND HIGHER, RKO Radio: C. BAKALEINIKOFF.

HOLLYWOOD CANTEEN, Warner Bros.: RAY HEINDORF.

IRISH EYES ARE SMILING, 20th Century-Fox: ALFRED NEWMAN.

KNICKERBOCKER HOLIDAY, RCA, UA: WERNER R. HEYMANN and KURT WEILL.

LADY IN THE DARK, Paramount: ROBERT EMMETT DOLAN.

LADY LET'S DANCE, Monogram: EDWARD KAY.

MEET ME IN ST. LOUIS, Metro-Goldwyn-Mayer: GEORGIE STOLL.

THE MERRY MONAHANS, Universal: H. J. SALTER.

MINSTREL MAN, PRC: LEO ERDODY and FERDE GROFÉ.

SENSATIONS OF 1945, Stone, UA: MAHLON MERRICK.

SONG OF THE OPEN ROAD, Rogers, UA: CHARLES PREVIN.

UP IN ARMS, Avalon, RKO Radio: LOUIS FORBES and RAY HEINDORF.

1945 Eighteenth Year

Scoring of a Dramatic or Comedy Picture

THE BELLS OF ST. MARY'S, Rainbow, RKO Radio: ROBERT EMMETT DOLAN.

BREWSTER'S MILLIONS, Small, UA: LOU FORBES.

CAPTAIN KIDD, Bogeaus, UA: WERNER JANSSEN.

ENCHANTED COTTAGE, RKO Radio: ROY WEBB.

FLAME OF THE BARBARY COAST, Republic: DALE BUTTS and MORTON SCOTT.

G. I. HONEYMOON, Monogram: EDWARD J. KAY.

G. I. JOE, Cowan, UA: LOUIS APPLEBAUM and ANN RONELL.

GUEST IN THE HOUSE, Guest in the House, Inc., UA: WERNER JANSSEN.

GUEST WIFE, Greentree Prods., UA: DANIELE AMFITHEATROF.

THE KEYS OF THE KINGDOM, 20th Century-Fox: ALFRED NEWMAN.

THE LOST WEEKEND, Paramount: MIKLOS ROZSA.

LOVE LETTERS, Wallis, Paramount: VICTOR YOUNG.

MAN WHO WALKED ALONE, PRC: KARL HAJOS.

OBJECTIVE-BURMA, Warner Bros.: FRANZ WAXMAN.

PARIS-UNDERGROUND, Bennett, UA: ALEXANDER TANSMAN.

A SONG TO REMEMBER, Columbia: MIKLOS ROZSA and MORRIS STOLOFF.

THE SOUTHERNER, Loew-Hakim, UA: WERNER JANSSEN.

★ SPELLBOUND, Selznick, UA: MIKLOS ROZSA.

THIS LOVE OF OURS, Universal: H. J. SALTER.

VALLEY OF DECISION, Metro-Goldwyn-Mayer: HERBERT STOTHART.

WOMAN IN THE WINDOW, International, RKO Radio: HUGO FRIEDHOFER and ARTHUR LANGE.

Scoring of a Musical Picture

★ ANCHORS AWEIGH, Metro-Goldwyn-Mayer: GEORGIE STOLL.

BELLE OF THE YUKON, International, RKO Radio: ARTHUR LANGE.

CAN'T HELP SINGING, Universal: JEROME KERN and H. J. SALTER.

HITCHHIKE TO HAPPINESS, Republic: MORTON SCOTT.

INCENDIARY BLONDE, Paramount: ROBERT EMMETT DOLAN.

RHAPSODY IN BLUE, Warner Bros.: RAY HEINDORF and MAX STEINER.

STATE FAIR, 20th Century-Fox: CHARLES HENDERSON and ALFRED NEWMAN.

SUNBONNET SUE, Monogram: EDWARD J. KAY.

THREE CABALLEROS, Disney-RKO Radio: EDWARD PLUMB, PAUL J. SMITH, and CHARLES WOLCOTT.

TONIGHT AND EVERY NIGHT, Columbia: MARLIN SKILES and MORRIS STOLOFF.

WHY GIRLS LEAVE HOME, PRC: WALTER GREENE.

WONDER MAN, Beverly, RKO Radio: LOU FORBES and RAY HEINDORF.

1946 Nineteenth Year

Scoring of a Dramatic or Comedy Picture

ANNA AND THE KING OF SIAM, 20th Century-Fox: BERNARD HERRMANN.

★ THE BEST YEARS OF OUR LIVES, Goldwyn, RKO Radio: HUGO FRIEDHOFER.

HENRY V, Rank, UA (British): WILLIAM WALTON.

HUMORESQUE, Warner Bros.: FRANZ WAXMAN.

THE KILLERS, Universal: MIKLOS ROZSA.

Scoring of a Musical Picture

BLUE SKIES, Paramount: ROBERT EMMETT DOLAN.

CENTENNIAL SUMMER, 20th Century-Fox: ALFRED NEWMAN.

THE HARVEY GIRLS, Metro-Goldwyn-Mayer: LENNIE HAYTON.

★ THE JOLSON STORY, Columbia: MORRIS STOLOFF.

NIGHT AND DAY, Warner Bros.: RAY HEINDORF and MAX STEINER.

1947 Twentieth Year

Scoring of a Dramatic or Comedy Picture

THE BISHOP'S WIFE, Goldwyn, RKO Radio: HUGO FRIEDHOFER.

CAPTAIN FROM CASTILE, 20th Century-Fox: ALFRED NEWMAN.

★ A DOUBLE LIFE, Kanin, U-I: MIKLOS ROZSA.

FOREVER AMBER, 20th Century-Fox: DAVID RAKSIN.

LIFE WITH FATHER, Warner Bros.: MAX STEINER.

Scoring of a Musical Picture

FIESTA, Metro-Goldwyn-Mayer: JOHNNY GREEN.

★ MOTHER WORE TIGHTS, 20th Century-Fox: ALFRED NEWMAN.

MY WILD IRISH ROSE, Warner Bros.: RAY HEINDORF and MAX STEINER.

ROAD TO RIO, Hope-Crosby, Paramount: ROBERT EMMETT DOLAN.

SONG OF THE SOUTH, Disney, RKO Radio: DANIELE AMFITHEATROF, PAUL J. SMITH, and CHARLES WOLCOTT.

1948 Twenty-first Year

Scoring of a Dramatic or Comedy Picture

HAMLET, Rank-Two Cities, U-I (British): WILLIAM WALTON.

JOAN OF ARC, Sierra Pictures, RKO Radio: HUGO FRIEDHOFER.

JOHNNY BELINDA, Warner Bros.: MAX STEINER.

★ THE RED SHOES, Rank-Archers-Eagle-Lion (British): BRIAN EASDALE.

THE SNAKE PIT, 20th Century-Fox: ALFRED NEWMAN.

Scoring of a Musical Picture

★ EASTER PARADE, Metro-Goldwyn-Mayer: JOHNNY GREEN and ROGER EDENS.

THE EMPEROR WALTZ, Paramount: VICTOR YOUNG.

THE PIRATE, Metro-Goldwyn-Mayer: LENNIE HAYTON.

ROMANCE ON THE HIGH SEAS, Curtiz, Warner Bros.: RAY HEINDORF.

WHEN MY BABY SMILES AT ME, 20th Century-Fox: ALFRED NEWMAN.

1949 Twenty-second Year

Scoring of a Dramatic or Comedy Picture

BEYOND THE FOREST, Warner Bros.: MAX STEINER.

CHAMPION, Screen Plays Corp., UA: DIMITRI TIOMKIN.
★ THE HEIRESS, Paramount: AARON COPLAND.

Scoring of a Musical Picture

JOLSON SINGS AGAIN, Sidney Buchman, Columbia: MORRIS STOLOFF and GEORGE DUNING.
LOOK FOR THE SILVER LINING, Warner Bros.: RAY HEINDORF.
★ ON THE TOWN, Metro-Goldwyn-Mayer: ROGER EDENS and LENNIE HAYTON.

1950 Twenty-third Year

Scoring of a Dramatic or Comedy Picture

ALL ABOUT EVE, 20th Century-Fox: ALFRED NEWMAN.
THE FLAME AND THE ARROW, Norma-F.R., Warner Bros.: MAX STEINER.
NO SAD SONGS FOR ME, Columbia: GEORGE DUNING.
SAMSON AND DELILAH, Paramount: VICTOR YOUNG.
★ SUNSET BOULEVARD, Paramount: FRANZ WAXMAN.

Scoring of a Musical Picture

★ ANNIE GET YOUR GUN, Metro-Goldwyn-Mayer: ADOLPH DEUTSCH and ROGER EDENS.
CINDERELLA, Disney, RKO Radio: OLIVER WALLACE and PAUL J. SMITH.
I'LL GET BY, 20th Century-Fox: LIONEL NEWMAN.
THREE LITTLE WORDS, Metro-Goldwyn-Mayer: ANDRÉ PREVIN.
THE WEST POINT STORY, Warner Bros.: RAY HEINDORF.

1951 Twenty-fourth Year

Scoring of a Dramatic or Comedy Picture

DAVID AND BATHSHEBA, 20th Century-Fox: ALFRED NEWMAN.
DEATH OF A SALESMAN, Kramer, Columbia: ALEX NORTH.
★ A PLACE IN THE SUN, Paramount: FRANZ WAXMAN.
QUO VADIS, Metro-Goldwyn-Mayer: MIKLOS ROZSA.
A STREETCAR NAMED DESIRE, Charles K. Feldman Prods., Warner Bros.: ALEX NORTH.

Scoring of a Musical Picture

ALICE IN WONDERLAND, Disney, RKO Radio: OLIVER WALLACE.
★ AN AMERICAN IN PARIS, Metro-Goldwyn-Mayer: JOHNNY GREEN and SAUL CHAPLIN.
THE GREAT CARUSO, Metro-Goldwyn-Mayer: PETER HERMAN ADLER and JOHNNY GREEN.
ON THE RIVIERA, 20th Century-Fox: ALFRED NEWMAN.
SHOW BOAT, Metro-Goldwyn-Mayer: ADOLPH DEUTSCH and CONRAD SALINGER.

1952 Twenty-fifth Year

Scoring of a Dramatic or Comedy Picture

★ HIGH NOON, Kramer, UA: DIMITRI TIOMKIN.
IVANHOE, Metro-Goldwyn-Mayer: MIKLOS ROZSA.
MIRACLE OF FATIMA, Warner Bros.: MAX STEINER.
THE THIEF, Fran Prods., UA: HERSCHEL BURKE GILBERT.
VIVA ZAPATA!, 20th Century-Fox: ALEX NORTH.

Scoring of a Musical Picture

HANS CHRISTIAN ANDERSEN, Goldwyn, RKO Radio: WALTER SCHARF.
THE JAZZ SINGER, Warner Bros.: RAY HEINDORF and MAX STEINER.
THE MEDIUM, Transfilm-Lopert (Italian): GIAN-CARLO MENOTTI.
SINGIN' IN THE RAIN, Metro-Goldwyn-Mayer: LENNIE HAYTON.
★ WITH A SONG IN MY HEART, 20th Century-Fox: ALFRED NEWMAN.

1953 Twenty-sixth Year

Scoring of a Dramatic or Comedy Picture

ABOVE AND BEYOND, Metro-Goldwyn-Mayer: HUGO FRIEDHOFER.

FROM HERE TO ETERNITY, Columbia: MORRIS STOLOFF and GEORGE DUNING.

JULIUS CAESAR, Metro-Goldwyn-Mayer: MIKLOS ROZSA.

⋆ LILI, Metro-Goldwyn-Mayer: BRONISLAU KAPER.

THIS IS CINERAMA, Cinerama Prods. Corp.: LOUIS FORBES.

Scoring of a Musical Picture

THE BANDWAGON, Metro-Goldwyn-Mayer: ADOLPH DEUTSCH.

CALAMITY JANE, Warner Bros.: RAY HEINDORF.

⋆ CALL ME MADAM, 20th Century-Fox: ALFRED NEWMAN.

5,000 FINGERS OF DR. T., Kramer-Columbia: FREDERICK HOLLANDER and MORRIS STOLOFF.

KISS ME KATE, Metro-Goldwyn-Mayer: ANDRÉ PREVIN and SAUL CHAPLIN.

1954 Twenty-seventh Year

Scoring of a Dramatic or Comedy Picture

THE CAINE MUTINY, A Stanley Kramer Prod., Columbia: MAX STEINER.

GENEVIEVE, A J. Arthur Rank Presentation—Sirius Prods. Ltd., U-I (British): MUIR MATHIESON.*

⋆ THE HIGH AND THE MIGHTY, Wayne-Fellows Prods., Inc., Warner Bros.: DIMITRI TIOMKIN.

ON THE WATERFRONT, Horizon-American Corp., Columbia: LEONARD BERNSTEIN.

THE SILVER CHALICE, A Victor Saville Prod., Warner Bros.: FRANZ WAXMAN.

Scoring of a Musical Picture

CARMEN JONES, Otto Preminger, 20th Century-Fox: HERSCHEL BURKE GILBERT.

THE GLENN MILLER STORY, Universal-International: JOSEPH GERSHENSON and HENRY MANCINI.

⋆ SEVEN BRIDES FOR SEVEN BROTHERS, Metro-Goldwyn-Mayer: ADOLPH DEUTSCH and SAUL CHAPLIN.

A STAR IS BORN, A Transcona Enterprises Prod., Warner Bros.: RAY HEINDORF.

THERE'S NO BUSINESS LIKE SHOW BUSINESS, 20th Century-Fox: ALFRED NEWMAN and LIONEL NEWMAN.

1955 Twenty-eighth Year

Scoring of a Dramatic or Comedy Picture

BATTLE CRY, Warner Bros.: MAX STEINER.

⋆ LOVE IS A MANY-SPLENDORED THING, 20th Century-Fox: ALFRED NEWMAN.

THE MAN WITH THE GOLDEN ARM, Otto Preminger Prod., UA: ELMER BERNSTEIN.

PICNIC, Columbia: GEORGE DUNING.

THE ROSE TATTOO, Hal Wallis, Paramount: ALEX NORTH.

Scoring of a Musical Picture

DADDY LONG LEGS, 20th Century-Fox: ALFRED NEWMAN.

GUYS AND DOLLS, Samuel Goldwyn Prods., Inc., M-G-M: JAY BLACKTON and CYRIL J. MOCKRIDGE.

IT'S ALWAYS FAIR WEATHER, Metro-Goldwyn-Mayer: ANDRÉ PREVIN.

LOVE ME OR LEAVE ME, Metro-Goldwyn-Mayer: PERCY FAITH and GEORGE STOLL.

⋆ OKLAHOMA!, Rogers &

*The Academy now recognizes Larry Adler as the composer of *Genevieve*. Adler was blacklisted at the time, and Muir Mathieson was given screen credit for the achievement that earned a nomination.

Hammerstein Pictures, Inc., Magna Theatre Corp.: ROBERT RUSSELL BENNETT, JAY BLACKTON, and ADOLPH DEUTSCH.

1956 Twenty-ninth Year

Scoring of a Dramatic or Comedy Picture

ANASTASIA, 20th Century-Fox: ALFRED NEWMAN.

★ AROUND THE WORLD IN 80 DAYS, The Michael Todd Co., Inc., UA: VICTOR YOUNG.

BETWEEN HEAVEN AND HELL, 20th Century-Fox: HUGO FRIEDHOFER.

GIANT, Giant Prod., Warner Bros.: DIMITRI TIOMKIN.

THE RAINMAKER, A Hal Wallis Prod., Paramount: ALEX NORTH.

Scoring of a Musical Picture

THE BEST THINGS IN LIFE ARE FREE, 20th Century-Fox: LIONEL NEWMAN.

THE EDDY DUCHIN STORY, Columbia: MORRIS STOLOFF and GEORGE DUNING.

HIGH SOCIETY, Sol C. Spiegel Prod., M-G-M: JOHNNY GREEN and SAUL CHAPLIN.

★ THE KING AND I, 20th Century-Fox: ALFRED NEWMAN and KEN DARBY.

MEET ME IN LAS VEGAS, Metro-Goldwyn-Mayer: GEORGE STOLL and JOHNNY GREEN.

*1957 Thirtieth Year**

AN AFFAIR TO REMEMBER (Dramatic or Comedy), Jerry Wald Prods., Inc., 20th Century-Fox: HUGO FRIEDHOFER.

BOY ON A DOLPHIN (Dramatic or Comedy), 20th Century-Fox: HUGO FRIEDHOFER.

★ THE BRIDGE ON THE RIVER KWAI (Dramatic or Comedy), A Horizon Picture, Columbia: MALCOLM ARNOLD.

PERRI (Dramatic or Comedy), Walt Disney Prods., Buena Vista Film Dist. Co., Inc.: PAUL SMITH.

RAINTREE COUNTY (Dramatic or Comedy), Metro-Goldwyn-Mayer: JOHNNY GREEN.

1958 Thirty-first Year†

Scoring of a Dramatic or Comedy Picture

THE BIG COUNTRY, Anthony-Worldwide Prods., UA: JEROME MOROSS.

★ THE OLD MAN AND THE SEA, Leland Hayward, Warner Bros.: DIMITRI TIOMKIN.

SEPARATE TABLES, Clifton Prods., Inc., UA: DAVID RAKSIN.

WHITE WILDERNESS, Walt Disney Prods., Buena Vista Film Dist. Co., Inc.: OLIVER WALLACE.

THE YOUNG LIONS, 20th Century-Fox: HUGO FRIEDHOFER.

Scoring of a Musical Picture

THE BOLSHOI BALLET, A Rank Organization Presentation-Harmony Film, Rank Film Distributors of America, Inc. (British): YURI FAIER and G. ROZHDESTVENSKY.

DAMN YANKEES, Warner Bros.: RAY HEINDORF.

★ GIGI, Arthur Freed Prods., Inc., M-G-M: ANDRÉ PREVIN.

MARDI GRAS, Jerry Wald Prods., Inc., 20th Century-Fox: LIONEL NEWMAN.

SOUTH PACIFIC, South Pacific Enterprises, Inc., Magna Theatre Corp.: ALFRED NEWMAN and KEN DARBY.

*Rules changed this year to one award for Music Scoring instead of separate awards for Scoring of a Dramatic or Comedy Picture and Scoring of a Musical Picture.

†Rules changed this year to two awards—one award for Scoring of a Dramatic or Comedy Picture and one award for Scoring of a Musical Picture.

1959 Thirty-second Year

Scoring of a Dramatic or Comedy Picture

★ BEN-HUR, Metro-Goldwyn-Mayer: MIKLOS ROZSA.

THE DIARY OF ANNE FRANK, 20th Century-Fox: ALFRED NEWMAN.

THE NUN'S STORY, Warner Bros.: FRANZ WAXMAN.

ON THE BEACH, Lomitas Prods., Inc., UA: ERNEST GOLD.

PILLOW TALK, Arwin Prods., Inc., U-I: FRANK DEVOL.

Scoring of a Musical Picture

THE FIVE PENNIES, Dena Prod., Paramount: LEITH STEVENS.

LI'L ABNER, Panama and Frank, Paramount: NELSON RIDDLE and JOSEPH J. LILLEY.

★ PORGY AND BESS, Samuel Goldwyn Prods., Columbia: ANDRÉ PREVIN and KEN DARBY.

SAY ONE FOR ME, Bing Crosby Prods., 20th Century-Fox: LIONEL NEWMAN.

SLEEPING BEAUTY, Walt Disney Prods., Buena Vista Film Dist. Co., Inc.: GEORGE BRUNS.

1960 Thirty-third Year

Scoring of a Dramatic or Comedy Picture

THE ALAMO, Batjac Prod., UA: DIMITRI TIOMKIN.

ELMER GANTRY, Burt Lancaster-Richard Brooks Prod., UA: ANDRÉ PREVIN.

★ EXODUS, Carlyle-Alpina S.A. Prod., UA: ERNEST GOLD.

THE MAGNIFICENT SEVEN, Mirisch-Alpha Prod., UA: ELMER BERNSTEIN.

SPARTACUS, Bryna Prods., Inc., U-I: ALEX NORTH.

Scoring of a Musical Picture

BELLS ARE RINGING, Arthur Freed Prod., M-G-M: ANDRÉ PREVIN.

CAN-CAN, Suffolk-Cummings Prods., 20th Century-Fox: NELSON RIDDLE.

LET'S MAKE LOVE, Company of Artists, Inc., 20th Century-Fox: LIONEL NEWMAN and EARLE H. HAGEN.

PEPE, G. S.-Posa Films International Prod., Columbia: JOHNNY GREEN.

★ SONG WITHOUT END, Goetz-Vidor Pictures Prod., Columbia: MORRIS STOLOFF and HARRY SUKMAN.

1961 Thirty-fourth Year

Scoring of a Dramatic or Comedy Picture

★ BREAKFAST AT TIFFANY'S, Jurow-Shepherd Prod., Paramount: HENRY MANCINI.

EL CID, Samuel Bronston Prod., in association with Dear Film Prod., Allied Artists: MIKLOS ROZSA.

FANNY, Mansfield Prod., Warner Bros.: MORRIS STOLOFF and HARRY SUKMAN.

THE GUNS OF NAVARONE, Carl Foreman Prod., Columbia: DIMITRI TIOMKIN.

SUMMER AND SMOKE, Hal Wallis Prod., Paramount: ELMER BERNSTEIN.

Scoring of a Musical Picture

BABES IN TOYLAND, Walt Disney Prod., Buena Vista Dist. Co., Inc.: GEORGE BRUNS.

FLOWER DRUM SONG, Universal-International-Ross Hunter Prod., in association with Joseph Fields, U-I: ALFRED NEWMAN and KEN DARBY.

KHOVANSHCHINA, Mosfilm Studios, Artkino Pictures (Russian): DIMITRI SHOSTAKOVICH.

PARIS BLUES, Pennebaker, Inc., UA: DUKE ELLINGTON.

★ WEST SIDE STORY, Mirisch Pictures, Inc., and B and P Enterprises, Inc., UA: SAUL CHAPLIN, JOHNNY GREEN, SID RAMIN, and IRWIN KOSTAL.

1962 Thirty-fifth Year

Music Score—substantially original

FREUD, Universal-International-John Huston Prod., U-I: JERRY GOLDSMITH.

★ LAWRENCE OF ARABIA, Horizon Pictures (G.B.), Ltd.-Sam Spiegel-David Lean Prod., Columbia: MAURICE JARRE.

MUTINY OF THE BOUNTY, Arcola Prod., M-G-M: BRONISLAU KAPER.

TARAS BULBA, Harold Hecht Prod., UA: FRANZ WAXMAN.

TO KILL A MOCKINGBIRD, Universal-International-Pakula-Mulligan-Brentwood Prod., U-I: ELMER BERNSTEIN.

Scoring of Music—adaptation or treatment

BILLY ROSE'S JUMBO, Euterpe-Arwin Prod., M-G-M: GEORGE STOLL.

GIGOT, Seven Arts Prods., 20th Century-Fox: MICHEL MAGNE.

GYPSY, Warner Bros.: FRANK PERKINS.

★ THE MUSIC MAN, Warner Bros.: RAY HEINDORF.

THE WONDERFUL WORLD OF THE BROTHERS GRIMM, Metro-Goldwyn-Mayer and Cinerama: LEIGH HARLINE.

1963 Thirty-sixth Year

Music Score—substantially original

CLEOPATRA, 20th Century-Fox Ltd.-MCL Films S.A.-WALWA Films S.A. Prod., 20th Century-Fox: ALEX NORTH.

55 DAYS AT PEKING, Samuel Bronston Prod., Allied Artists: DIMITRI TIOMKIN.

HOW THE WEST WAS WON, Metro-Goldwyn-Mayer and Cinerama: ALFRED NEWMAN and KEN DARBY.

IT'S A MAD, MAD, MAD, MAD WORLD, Casey Prod., UA: ERNEST GOLD.

★ TOM JONES, Woodfall Prod., UA-Lopert Pictures: JOHN ADDISON.

Scoring of Music—adaptation or treatment

BYE BYE BIRDIE, Kohlmar-Sidney Prod., Columbia: JOHN GREEN.

★ IRMA LA DOUCE, Mirisch-Phalanx Prod., UA: ANDRÉ PREVIN.

A NEW KIND OF LOVE, Llenroc Prods., Paramount: LEITH STEVENS.

SUNDAYS AND CYBELE, Terra-Fides-Orsay-Films Trocadero Prod., Columbia: MAURICE JARRE.

THE SWORD IN THE STONE, Walt Disney Prods., Buena Vista Distribution Co.: GEORGE BRUNS.

1964 Thirty-seventh Year

Music Score—substantially original

BECKET, Hal Wallis Prod., Paramount: LAURENCE ROSENTHAL.

THE FALL OF THE ROMAN EMPIRE, Bronston-Roma Prod., Paramount: DIMITRI TIOMKIN.

HUSH . . . HUSH, SWEET CHARLOTTE, Associates and Aldrich Prod., 20th Century-Fox: FRANK DEVOL.

★ MARY POPPINS, Walt Disney Prods.: RICHARD M. SHERMAN and ROBERT B. SHERMAN.

THE PINK PANTHER, Mirisch-G-E-Prod., United Artists: HENRY MANCINI.

Scoring of Music—adaptation or treatment

A HARD DAY'S NIGHT, Walter Shenson Prod., United Artists: GEORGE MARTIN.

MARY POPPINS, Walt Disney Prods.: IRWIN KOSTAL.

★ MY FAIR LADY, Warner Bros.: ANDRÉ PREVIN.

ROBIN AND THE 7 HOODS, P-C Prod., Warner Bros.: NELSON RIDDLE.

THE UNSINKABLE MOLLY BROWN, Marten Prod., M-G-M: ROBERT ARMBRUSTER, LEO ARNAUD, JACK

ELLIOTT, JACK HAYES, CALVIN JACKSON, and LEO SHUKEN.

1965 Thirty-eighth Year

Music Score—substantially original

THE AGONY AND THE ECSTASY, International Classics Prods., 20th Century-Fox: ALEX NORTH.

★ DOCTOR ZHIVAGO, Sostar S.A.-Metro-Goldwyn-Mayer British Studios, Ltd. Prod., M-G-M: MAURICE JARRE.

THE GREATEST STORY EVER TOLD, George Stevens Prod., United Artists: ALFRED NEWMAN.

A PATCH OF BLUE, Pandro S. Berman-Guy Green Prod., M-G-M: JERRY GOLDSMITH.

THE UMBRELLAS OF CHERBOURG, Parc-Madeleine Films Prod., American Intl.: MICHEL LEGRAND and JACQUES DEMY.

Scoring of Music—adaptation or treatment

CAT BALLOU, Harold Hecht Prod., Columbia: DEVOL.

THE PLEASURE SEEKERS, 20th Century-Fox: LIONEL NEWMAN and ALEXANDER COURAGE.

★ THE SOUND OF MUSIC, Argyle Enterprises Prod., 20th Century-Fox: IRWIN KOSTAL.

A THOUSAND CLOWNS, Harrell Prod., United Artists: DON WALKER.

THE UMBRELLAS OF CHERBOURG, Parc-Madeleine Films Prod., American Intl.: MICHEL LEGRAND.

1966 Thirty-ninth Year

Original Music Score

THE BIBLE, Thalia-A.G. Prod., 20th Century-Fox: TOSHIRO MAYUZUMI.

★ BORN FREE, Open Road Films, Ltd.-Atlas Films, Ltd. Prod., Columbia: JOHN BARRY.

HAWAII, Mirisch Corp. of Delaware Prod., UA: ELMER BERNSTEIN.

THE SAND PEBBLES, Argyle-Solar Prod., 20th Century-Fox: JERRY GOLDSMITH.

WHO'S AFRAID OF VIRGINIA WOOLF?, Chenault Prod., Warner Bros.: ALEX NORTH.

Scoring of Music—adaptation or treatment

★ A FUNNY THING HAPPENED ON THE WAY TO THE FORUM, Melvin Frank Prod., United Artists: KEN THORNE.

THE GOSPEL ACCORDING TO ST. MATTHEW, Arco-Lux Cie Cinematografique de France Prod., Walter Reade-Continental Distributing: LUIS ENRIQUE BACALOV.

RETURN OF THE SEVEN, Mirisch Prod., United Artists: ELMER BERNSTEIN.

THE SINGING NUN, Metro-Goldwyn-Mayer: HARRY SUKMAN.

STOP THE WORLD—I WANT TO GET OFF, Warner Bros. Prods., Ltd., Warner Bros.: AL HAM.

1967 Fortieth Year

Original Music Score

COOL HAND LUKE, Jalem Prod., Warner Bros.-Seven Arts: LALO SCHIFRIN.

DOCTOR DOLITTLE, Apjac Prods., 20th Century-Fox: LESLIE BRICUSSE.

FAR FROM THE MADDING CROWD, Appia Films, Ltd. Prod., M-G-M: RICHARD RODNEY BENNETT.

IN COLD BLOOD, Pax Enterprises Prod., Columbia: QUINCY JONES.

★ THOROUGHLY MODERN MILLIE, Ross Hunter-Universal Prod., Universal: ELMER BERNSTEIN.

Scoring of Music—adaptation or treatment

★ CAMELOT, Warner Bros.-Seven Arts: ALFRED NEWMAN and KEN DARBY.

DOCTOR DOLITTLE, Apjac Productions, 20th Century-Fox: LIONEL NEWMAN and ALEXANDER COURAGE.

GUESS WHO'S COMING TO DINNER, Columbia: DEVOL.

THOROUGHLY MODERN MILLIE, Ross Hunter-Universal Production, Universal: ANDRÉ PREVIN and JOSEPH GERSHENSON.

VALLEY OF THE DOLLS, Red Lion Prods., 20th Century-Fox: JOHN WILLIAMS.

1968 Forty-first Year

Original Score—for a motion picture (not a musical)

THE FOX, Raymond Stross-Motion Pictures International Prod., Claridge Pictures: LALO SCHIFRIN.

★ THE LION IN WINTER, Haworth Prods., Ltd., Avco Embassy: JOHN BARRY.

PLANET OF THE APES, Apjac Prods., 20th Century-Fox: JERRY GOLDSMITH.

THE SHOES OF THE FISHERMAN, George Englund Prod., Metro-Goldwyn-Mayer: ALEX NORTH.

THE THOMAS CROWN AFFAIR, Mirisch-Simkoe-Solar Prod., United Artists: MICHEL LEGRAND.

Score of a Musical Picture—original or adaptation

FINIAN'S RAINBOW, Warner Bros.-Seven Arts: Adapted by RAY HEINDORF.

FUNNY GIRL, Rastar Prods., Columbia: Adapted by WALTER SCHARF.

★ OLIVER!, Romulus Films, Columbia: Adapted by JOHN GREEN.

STAR!, Robert Wise Prod., 20th Century-Fox: Adapted by LENNIE HAYTON.

THE YOUNG GIRLS OF ROCHEFORT, Mag Bodard-Gilbert de Goldschmidt-Parc Film-Madeleine Films Prod., Warner Bros.-Seven Arts: MICHEL LEGRAND and JACQUES DEMY.

1969 Forty-second Year

Original Score—for a motion picture (not a musical)

ANNE OF THE THOUSAND DAYS, Hal B. Wallis-Universal Pictures, Ltd. Prod., Universal: GEORGES DELERUE.

★ BUTCH CASSIDY AND THE SUNDANCE KID, George Roy Hill-Paul Monash Prod., 20th Century-Fox: BURT BACHARACH.

THE REIVERS, Irving Ravetch-Arthur Kramer-Solar Prods., Cinema Center Films Presentation, National General: JOHN WILLIAMS.

THE SECRET OF SANTA VITTORIA, Stanley Kramer Company Prod., United Artists: ERNEST GOLD.

THE WILD BUNCH, Phil Feldman Prod., Warner Bros.: JERRY FIELDING.

Score of a Musical Picture—original or adaptation

GOODBYE, MR. CHIPS, Apjac Prod., Metro-Goldwyn-Mayer: Music and lyrics by LESLIE BRICUSSE; Adapted by JOHN WILLIAMS.

★ HELLO DOLLY!, Chenault Prods., 20th Century-Fox: Adapted by LENNIE HAYTON and LIONEL NEWMAN.

PAINT YOUR WAGON, Alan Jay Lerner Prod., Paramount: Adapted by NELSON RIDDLE.

SWEET CHARITY, Universal: Adapted by CY COLEMAN.

THEY SHOOT HORSES, DON'T THEY?, Chartoff-Winkler-Pollack Prod., ABC Pictures Presentation, Cinerama: Adapted by JOHN GREEN and ALBERT WOODBURY.

1970 Forty-third Year

Original Score

AIRPORT, Ross Hunter-Universal Prod., Universal: ALFRED NEWMAN.

CROMWELL, Irving Allen, Ltd. Prod., Columbia: FRANK CORDELL.

★ LOVE STORY, The Love Story Company Prod., Paramount: FRANCIS LAI.

PATTON, 20th Century-Fox: JERRY GOLDSMITH.

SUNFLOWER, Sostar Prod., Avco Embassy: HENRY MANCINI.

Original Song Score

THE BABY MAKER, Robert Wise Prod., National General: Music by FRED KARLIN; Lyrics by TYLWYTH KYMRY.

A BOY NAMED CHARLIE BROWN, Lee Mendelson-Melendez Features Prod., Cinema Center Films Presentation, National General: Music by ROD MCKUEN and JOHN SCOTT TROTTER; Lyrics by ROD MCKUEN, BILL MELENDEZ, and AL SHEAN; Adapted by VINCE GUARALDI.

DARLING LILI, Geoffrey Prods., Paramount: Music by HENRY MANCINI; Lyrics by JOHNNY MERCER.

★ LET IT BE, Beatles-Apple Prod., UA: Music and lyrics by THE BEATLES.

SCROOGE, Waterbury Films, Ltd. Prod., Cinema Center Films Presentation, National General: Music and lyrics by LESLIE BRICUSSE; Adapted by IAN FRASER and HERBERT W. SPENCER.

1971 Forty-fourth Year

Original Dramatic Score

MARY, QUEEN OF SCOTS, A Hal Wallis-Universal Pictures, Ltd. Prod., Universal: JOHN BARRY.

NICHOLAS AND ALEXANDRA, A Horizon Pictures Prod., Columbia: RICHARD RODNEY BENNETT.

SHAFT, Shaft Prods., Ltd., M-G-M: ISAAC HAYES.

STRAW DOGS, A Talent Associates, Ltd.-Amerbroco Films, Ltd. Prod., ABC Pictures Presentation, Cinerama: JERRY FIELDING.

★ SUMMER OF '42, A Robert Mulligan-Richard Alan Roth Prod., Warner Bros.: MICHEL LEGRAND.

Scoring: Adaptation and Original Song Score

BEDKNOBS AND BROOMSTICKS, Walt Disney Prods., Buena Vista Distribution Company: Song Score by RICHARD M. SHERMAN and ROBERT B. SHERMAN; Adapted by IRWIN KOSTAL.

THE BOY FRIEND, A Russflix, Ltd. Prod., M-G-M: Adapted by PETER MAXWELL DAVIES and PETER GREENWELL.

★ FIDDLER ON THE ROOF, Mirisch-Cartier Prods., UA: Adapted by JOHN WILLIAMS.

TCHAIKOVSKY, A Dimitri Tiomkin-Mosfilm Studios Prod.: Adapted by DIMITRI TIOMKIN.

WILLY WONKA AND THE CHOCOLATE FACTORY, A Wolper Pictures, Ltd. Prod., Paramount: Song Score by LESLIE BRICUSSE and ANTHONY NEWLEY; Adapted by WALTER SCHARF.

1972 Forty-fifth Year

Original Dramatic Score

IMAGES, A Hemdale Group, Ltd.-Lion's Gate Films Prod., Columbia: JOHN WILLIAMS.

★ LIMELIGHT, A Charles Chaplin Prod., Columbia: CHARLES CHAPLIN, RAYMOND RASCH, and LARRY RUSSELL.*

NAPOLEON AND SAMANTHA, A Walt Disney Prods., Buena Vista

*Academy Award eligibility rules require a film to be commercially exhibited in a Los Angeles theatre to qualify for Oscar consideration. *Limelight* was made in 1952 but not shown in Los Angeles until 1972. Thus, its eligibility year fell two decades after its actual year of production.

Distribution Company: BUDDY BAKER.

THE POSEIDON ADVENTURE, An Irwin Allen Prod., 20th Century-Fox: JOHN WILLIAMS.

SLEUTH, A Palomar Pictures International Prod., 20th Century-Fox: JOHN ADDISON.

Scoring: Adaptation and Original Song Score

★ CABARET, An ABC Pictures Prod., Allied Artists: Adapted by RALPH BURNS.

LADY SINGS THE BLUES, A Motown-Weston-Furie Prod., Paramount: Adapted by GIL ASKEY.

MAN OF LA MANCHA, A PEA Produzioni Europee Associate Prod., UA: Adapted by LAURENCE ROSENTHAL.

1973 Forty-sixth Year

Original Dramatic Score

CINDERELLA LIBERTY, A Sanford Prod., 20th Century-Fox: JOHN WILLIAMS.

THE DAY OF THE DOLPHIN, Icarus Prods., Avco Embassy: GEORGES DELERUE.

PAPILLON, A Corona-General Production Company Prod., Allied Artists: JERRY GOLDSMITH.

A TOUCH OF CLASS, Brut Prods., Avco Embassy: JOHN CAMERON.

★ THE WAY WE WERE, Rastar Prods., Columbia: MARVIN HAMLISCH.

Scoring: Original Song Score and/or Adaptation

JESUS CHRIST SUPERSTAR, A Universal-Norman Jewison-Robert Stigwood Prod., Universal: Adapted by ANDRÉ PREVIN, HERBERT SPENCER, and ANDREW LLOYD WEBBER.

★ THE STING, A Universal-Bill/Phillips-George Roy Hill Film Prod., Zanuck/Brown Presentation, Universal: Adapted by MARVIN HAMLISCH.

TOM SAWYER, An Arthur P. Jacobs Prod., Reader's Digest Presentation, UA: Song Score by RICHARD M. SHERMAN and ROBERT B. SHERMAN; Adapted by JOHN WILLIAMS.

1974 Forty-seventh Year

Original Dramatic Score

CHINATOWN, A Robert Evans Prod., Paramount: JERRY GOLDSMITH.

★ THE GODFATHER PART II, A Coppola Company Prod., Paramount: NINO ROTA and CARMINE COPPOLA.

MURDER ON THE ORIENT EXPRESS, A G. W. Films, Ltd. Prod., Paramount: RICHARD RODNEY BENNETT.

SHANKS, William Castle Prods., Paramount: ALEX NORTH.

THE TOWERING INFERNO, An Irwin Allen Prod., 20th Century-Fox/Warner Bros.: JOHN WILLIAMS.

Scoring: Original Song Score and/or Adaptation

★ THE GREAT GATSBY, A David Merrick Prod., Paramount: Adapted by NELSON RIDDLE.

THE LITTLE PRINCE, A Stanley Donen Enterprises, Ltd. Prod., Paramount: Song Score by ALAN JAY LERNER and FREDERICK LOEWE; Adapted by ANGELA MORLEY and DOUGLAS GAMLEY.

PHANTOM OF THE PARADISE, Harbor Prods., 20th Century-Fox: Song Score by PAUL WILLIAMS; Adapted by PAUL WILLIAMS and GEORGE ALICESON TIPTON.

1975 Forty-eighth Year

Original Score

BIRDS DO IT, BEES DO IT, A Wolper Pictures Production, Columbia: GERALD FRIED.

BITE THE BULLET, A Pax Enterprises Production, Columbia: ALEX NORTH.

★ JAWS, A Universal-Zanuck/Brown Production, Universal: JOHN WILLIAMS.

ONE FLEW OVER THE CUCKOO'S NEST, A Fantasy Films Production, United Artists: JACK NITZSCHE.

THE WIND AND THE LION, A Herb Jaffe Production, Metro-Goldwyn-Mayer: JERRY GOLDSMITH.

Scoring: Original Song Score and/or Adaptation

★ BARRY LYNDON, A Hawk Films, Ltd. Production, Warner Bros.: Adapted by LEONARD ROSENMAN.

FUNNY LADY, A Rastar Pictures Production, Columbia: Adapted by PETER MATZ.

TOMMY, A Robert Stigwood Organisation, Ltd. Production, Columbia: Adapted by PETER TOWNSHEND.

1976 Forty-ninth Year

Original Score

OBSESSION, George Litto Productions, Columbia Pictures: BERNARD HERRMANN.

★ THE OMEN, 20th Century-Fox Productions, Ltd., 20th Century-Fox: JERRY GOLDSMITH.

THE OUTLAW JOSEY WALES, A Malpaso Company Production, Warner Bros.: JERRY FIELDING.

TAXI DRIVER, A Bill/Phillips Production of a Martin Scorsese Film, Columbia Pictures: BERNARD HERRMANN.

VOYAGE OF THE DAMNED, An ITC Entertainment Production, Avco Embassy: LALO SCHIFRIN.

Original Song Score and Its Adaptation or Best Adaptation Score

★ BOUND FOR GLORY, The Bound for Glory Company Production, United Artists: Adapted by LEONARD ROSENMAN.

BUGSY MALONE, A Goodtimes Enterprises, Ltd. Production, Paramount: Song Score and Its Adaptation by PAUL WILLIAMS.

A STAR IS BORN, A Barwood/Jon Peters Production, First Artists Presentation, Warner Bros.: Adapted by ROGER KELLAWAY.

1977 Fiftieth Year

Original Score

CLOSE ENCOUNTERS OF THE THIRD KIND, Close Encounter Productions, Columbia: JOHN WILLIAMS.

JULIA, A Twentieth Century-Fox Production, 20th Century-Fox: GEORGES DELERUE.

MOHAMMAD-MESSENGER OF GOD, A Filmco International Production, Irwin Yablans Company: MAURICE JARRE.

THE SPY WHO LOVED ME, Eon Productions, United Artists: MARVIN HAMLISCH.

★ STAR WARS, A Twentieth Century-Fox Production, 20th Century-Fox: JOHN WILLIAMS.

Original Song Score and Its Adaptation or Best Adaptation Score

★ A LITTLE NIGHT MUSIC, A Sascha-Wien Film Production in association with Elliott Kastner, New World Pictures: Adapted by JONATHAN TUNICK.

PETE'S DRAGON, Walt Disney Productions, Buena Vista Distribution Company: Song Score by AL KASHA and JOEL HIRSCHHORN; Adapted by IRWIN KOSTAL.

THE SLIPPER AND THE ROSE—THE STORY OF CINDERELLA, Paradine Co-Productions, Ltd., Universal: Song Score by RICHARD M. SHERMAN and

ROBERT B. SHERMAN; Adapted by ANGELA MORLEY.

1978 Fifty-first Year

Original Score

THE BOYS FROM BRAZIL, An ITC Entertainment Production, 20th Century-Fox: JERRY GOLDSMITH.

DAYS OF HEAVEN, An OP Production, Paramount: ENNIO MORRICONE.

HEAVEN CAN WAIT, Dogwood Productions, Paramount: DAVE GRUSIN.

★ MIDNIGHT EXPRESS, A Casablanca-Filmworks Production, Columbia: GIORGIO MORODER.

SUPERMAN, A Dovemead, Ltd. Production, Alexander Salkind Presentation, Warner Bros.: JOHN WILLIAMS.

Original Song Score and Its Adaptation or Best Adaptation Score

★ THE BUDDY HOLLY STORY, An Innovisions-ECA Production, Columbia: Adaptation Score by JOE RENZETTI.

PRETTY BABY, A Louis Malle Film Production, Paramount: Adaptation Score by JERRY WEXLER.

THE WIZ, A Motown/Universal Pictures Production, Universal: Adaptation Score by QUINCY JONES.

1979 Fifty-second Year

Original Score

THE AMITYVILLE HORROR, An American International/Professional Films Production, American International Pictures: LALO SCHIFRIN.

THE CHAMP, A Metro-Goldwyn-Mayer Production, Metro-Goldwyn-Mayer: DAVE GRUSIN.

★ A LITTLE ROMANCE, A Pan Arts Associates Production, Orion Pictures Company: GEORGES DELERUE.

STAR TREK—THE MOTION PICTURE, A Century Associates Production, Paramount: JERRY GOLDSMITH.

10, Geoffrey Productions, Orion Pictures Company: HENRY MANCINI.

Original Song Score and Its Adaptation or Best Adaptation Score

★ ALL THAT JAZZ, A Columbia/ Twentieth Century-Fox Production, 20th Century-Fox: Adaptation Score by RALPH BURNS.

BREAKING AWAY, A Twentieth Century-Fox Production, 20th Century-Fox: Adaptation Score by PATRICK WILLIAMS.

THE MUPPET MOVIE, A Jim Henson Production, Lord Grade/Martin Starger Presentation, Associated Film Distribution: Original Song Score by PAUL WILLIAMS and KENNY ASCHER; Adapted by PAUL WILLIAMS.

1980 Fifty-third Year

Original Score

ALTERED STATES, A Warner Bros. Production, Warner Bros.: JOHN CORIGLIANO.

THE ELEPHANT MAN, A Brooksfilms, Ltd. Production, Paramount: JOHN MORRIS.

THE EMPIRE STRIKES BACK, A Lucasfilm, Ltd. Production, Twentieth Century-Fox: JOHN WILLIAMS.

★ FAME, A Metro-Goldwyn-Mayer Production, Metro-Goldwyn-Mayer: MICHAEL GORE.

TESS, A Renn-Burrill Co-production with the participation of the Societé Française de Production (S.F.P.), Columbia: PHILIPPE SARDE.

Original Song Score and Its Adaptation or Best Adaptation Score

No nominations.

1981 Fifty-fourth Year

Original Score

★ CHARIOTS OF FIRE, Enigma Productions Limited, The Ladd

Company/Warner Bros.: VANGELIS.

DRAGONSLAYER, A Barwood/Robbins Production, Paramount: ALEX NORTH.

ON GOLDEN POND, An ITC Films/IPC Films Production, Universal: DAVE GRUSIN.

RAGTIME, A Ragtime Production, Paramount: RANDY NEWMAN.

RAIDERS OF THE LOST ARK, A Lucasfilm Production, Paramount: JOHN WILLIAMS.

Original Song Score and Its Adaptation or Best Adaptation Score

No nominations.

1982 Fifty-fifth Year

Original Score

★ E.T. THE EXTRA-TERRESTRIAL, A Universal Pictures Production, Universal: JOHN WILLIAMS.

GANDHI, An Indo-British Films Production, Columbia: RAVI SHANKAR and GEORGE FENTON.

AN OFFICER AND A GENTLEMAN, A Lorimar Production in association with Martin Elfand, Paramount: JACK NITZSCHE.

POLTERGEIST, A Metro-Goldwyn-Mayer/Steven Spielberg Production, M-G-M/UA: JERRY GOLDSMITH.

SOPHIE'S CHOICE, An ITC Entertainment Presentation of a Pakula-Barish Production, Universal/A.F.D.: MARVIN HAMLISCH.

Original Song Score and Its Adaptation or Best Adaptation Score

ANNIE, A Rastar Films Production, Columbia: Adaptation Score by RALPH BURNS.

ONE FROM THE HEART, A Zoetrope Studios Production, Columbia: Song Score by TOM WAITS.

★ VICTOR/VICTORIA, A Metro-Goldwyn-Mayer Production, M-G-M/UA: Song Score by HENRY MANCINI and LESLIE BRICUSSE; Adapted by HENRY MANCINI.

1983 Fifty-sixth Year

Original Score

CROSS CREEK, A Robert B. Radnitz/Martin Ritt/Thorn EMI Films Production, Universal: LEONARD ROSENMAN.

RETURN OF THE JEDI, A Lucasfilm Production, 20th Century-Fox: JOHN WILLIAMS.

★ THE RIGHT STUFF, A Robert Chartoff-Irwin Winkler Production, The Ladd Company through Warner Bros.: BILL CONTI.

TERMS OF ENDEARMENT, A James L. Brooks Production, Paramount: MICHAEL GORE.

UNDER FIRE, A Lions Gate Films Production, Orion: JERRY GOLDSMITH.

Original Song Score and Its Adaptation or Best Adaptation Score

THE STING II, A Jennings Lang/Universal Pictures Production, Universal: Adaptation Score by LALO SCHIFRIN.

TRADING PLACES, An Aaron Russo Production, Paramount: Adaptation Score by ELMER BERNSTEIN.

★ YENTL, A United Artists/Ladbroke Feature/Barwood Production, MGM/UA: Original Song Score by MICHAEL LEGRAND, ALAN BERGMAN, and MARILYN BERGMAN.

1984 Fifty-seventh Year

Original Score

INDIANA JONES AND THE TEMPLE OF DOOM, A Lucasfilm Production, Paramount: JOHN WILLIAMS.

THE NATURAL, A Tri-Star Pictures Production, Tri-Star: RANDY NEWMAN.

★ A PASSAGE TO INDIA, A G. W.

Films Limited Production, Columbia: MAURICE JARRE.

THE RIVER, A Universal Pictures Production, Universal: JOHN WILLIAMS.

UNDER THE VOLCANO, An Ithaca Enterprises Production, Universal: ALEX NORTH.

Original Song Score and Its Adaptation or Best Adaptation Score

THE MUPPETS TAKE MANHATTAN, A Tri-Star Pictures Production, Tri-Star: JEFF MOSS.

★ PURPLE RAIN, A Purple Films Company Production, Warner Bros.: PRINCE.

SONGWRITER, A Tri-Star Pictures Production, Tri-Star: KRIS KRISTOFFERSON.

1985 Fifty-eighth Year

Original Score

AGNES OF GOD, a Columbia Pictures Production, Columbia: GEORGES DELERUE.

THE COLOR PURPLE, a Warner Bros. Production, Warner Bros.: QUINCY JONES, JEREMY LUBBOCK, ROD TEMPERTON, CAIPHUS SEMENYA, ANDRAE CROUCH, CHRIS BOARDMAN, JORGE CALANDRELLI, JOEL ROSENBAUM, FRED STEINER, JACK HAYES, JERRY HEY, and RANDY KERBER.

★ OUT OF AFRICA, a Universal Pictures Limited Production, Universal: JOHN BARRY.

SILVERADO, a Columbia Pictures Production, Columbia: BRUCE BROUGHTON.

WITNESS, an Edward S. Feldman Production, Paramount: MAURICE JARRE.

Original Song Score

No nominations.

1986 Fifty-ninth Year

Original Score

ALIENS, A Twentieth Century-Fox Film Production, 20th Century-Fox: JAMES HORNER.

HOOSIERS, A Carter De Haven Production, Orion: JERRY GOLDSMITH.

THE MISSION, A Warner Bros./ Goldcrest and Kingsmere Production, Warner Bros.: ENNIO MORRICONE.

★ 'ROUND MIDNIGHT, An Irwin Winkler Production, Warner Bros.: HERBIE HANCOCK.

STAR TREK VI: THE UNDISCOVERED COUNTRY, A Harve Bennett Production, Paramount: LEONARD ROSENMAN.

Original Song Score

No nominations.

1987 Sixtieth Year

Original Score

CRY FREEDOM, A Marble Arch Production, Universal: GEORGE FENTON and JONAS GWANGWA.

EMPIRE OF THE SUN, A Warner Bros. Production, Warner Bros.: JOHN T. WILLIAMS.

★ THE LAST EMPEROR, A Hemdale Film Production, Columbia: RYUICHI SAKAMOTO, DAVID BYRNE, and CONG SU.

THE UNTOUCHABLES, An Art Linson Production, Paramount: ENNIO MORRICONE.

THE WITCHES OF EASTWICK, A Warner Bros. Production, Warner Bros.: JOHN T. WILLIAMS.

Original Song Score

No nominations.

1988 Sixty-first Year

Original Score

THE ACCIDENTAL TOURIST, A Warner Bros. Production, Warner Bros.: JOHN WILLIAMS.

DANGEROUS LIAISONS, A Lorimar Production, Warner Bros.: GEORGE FENTON.

GORILLAS IN THE MIST, A Warner Bros. Production, Warner Bros./Universal: MAURICE JARRE.

★ THE MILAGRO BEANFIELD WAR, A Robert Redford/Moctesuma Esparza Production, Universal: DAVE GRUSIN.

RAIN MAN, A Guber-Peters Company Production, United Artists: HANS ZIMMER.

Original Song Score

No nominations.

1989 Sixty-second Year

Original Score

BORN ON THE FOURTH OF JULY, An A. Kitman Ho and Ixtlan Production, Universal: JOHN WILLIAMS.

THE FABULOUS BAKER BOYS, A Gladden Entertainment Presentation of a Mirage Production, 20th Century-Fox: DAVID GRUSIN.

FIELD OF DREAMS, A Gordon Company Production, Universal: JAMES HORNER.

INDIANA JONES AND THE LAST CRUSADE, A Lucasfilm Ltd. Production, Paramount: JOHN WILLIAMS.

★ THE LITTLE MERMAID, A Walt Disney Pictures Production in association with Silver Screen Partners IV, Buena Vista: ALAN MENKEN.

Original Song Score

No nominations.

1990 Sixty-third Year

Original Score

AVALON, A Tri-Star Production, Tri-Star: RANDY NEWMAN.

★ DANCES WITH WOLVES, A Tig Production, Orion: JOHN BARRY.

GHOST, A Howard W. Koch Production, Paramount: MAURICE JARRE.

HAVANA, A Universal Pictures Limited Production, Universal: DAVID GRUSIN.

HOME ALONE, A 20th Century-Fox Production, 20th Century-Fox: JOHN WILLIAMS.

Original Song Score

No nominations.

1991 Sixty-fourth Year

Original Score

★ BEAUTY AND THE BEAST, A Walt Disney Pictures Production, Buena Vista: ALAN MENKEN.

BUGSY, A Tri-Star Pictures Production, Tri-Star: ENNIO MORRICONE.

THE FISHER KING, A Tri-Star Pictures Production, Tri-Star: GEORGE FENTON.

JFK, A Camelot Production, Warner Bros.: JOHN WILLIAMS.

THE PRINCE OF TIDES, A Barwood/Longfellow Production, Columbia: JAMES NEWTON HOWARD.

Original Song Score

No nominations.

1992 Sixty-fifth Year

Original Score

★ ALADDIN, A Walt Disney Pictures Production, Buena Vista: ALAN MENKEN.

BASIC INSTINCT, A Carolco Production, Tri-Star: JERRY GOLDSMITH.

CHAPLIN, A Carolco Pictures Production, Tri-Star: JOHN BARRY.

HOWARDS END, A Merchant Ivory Production, Sony Pictures Classics: RICHARD ROBBINS.

A RIVER RUNS THROUGH IT, A Columbia Pictures Production, Columbia: MARK ISHAM.

Original Song Score

No nominations.

Music: Best Original Song

In 1934 an award for Best Song was created along with the Music Scoring award. The category has remained relatively unchanged except for a name change in 1975 to Best Original Song. According to Academy rules, "There must be a substantive rendition (not necessarily visual) of both lyric and melody (clearly audible, intelligible, and recognizably performed as a song) in the film."

Like the Scoring awards, entries for Best Original Song are submitted by the creators of the achievement and are screened by members of the Academy Music Branch who determine the nominees.

1934 Seventh Year

CARIOCA from *Flying Down to Rio*, RKO Radio: Music by VINCENT YOUMANS; Lyrics by EDWARD ELISCU and GUS KAHN.

★ THE CONTINENTAL from *The Gay Divorcee*, RKO Radio: Music by CON CONRAD; Lyrics by HERB MAGIDSON.

LOVE IN BLOOM from *She Loves Me Not*, Paramount: Music by RALPH RAINGER; Lyrics by LEO ROBIN.

1935 Eighth Year

CHEEK TO CHEEK from *Top Hat*, RKO Radio: Music and Lyrics by IRVING BERLIN.

LOVELY TO LOOK AT from *Roberta*, RKO Radio: Music by JEROME KERN; Lyrics by DOROTHY FIELDS and JIMMY MCHUGH.

★ LULLABY OF BROADWAY from *Gold Diggers of 1935*, Warner Bros.: Music by HARRY WARREN; Lyrics by AL DUBIN.

1936 Ninth Year

DID I REMEMBER from *Suzy*, Metro-Goldwyn-Mayer: Music by WALTER DONALDSON; Lyrics by HAROLD ADAMSON.

I'VE GOT YOU UNDER MY SKIN from *Born to Dance*, Metro-Goldwyn-Mayer: Music and Lyrics by COLE PORTER.

A MELODY FROM THE SKY from *Trail of the Lonesome Pine*, Paramount: Music by LOUIS ALTER; Lyrics by SIDNEY MITCHELL.

PENNIES FROM HEAVEN from *Pennies from Heaven*, Columbia: Music by ARTHUR JOHNSTON; Lyrics by JOHNNY BURKE.

★ THE WAY YOU LOOK TONIGHT from *Swing Time*, RKO Radio: Music by JEROME KERN; Lyrics by DOROTHY FIELDS.

WHEN DID YOU LEAVE HEAVEN from *Sing Baby Sing*, 20th Century-Fox: Music by RICHARD A. WHITING; Lyrics by WALTER BULLOCK.

1937 Tenth Year

REMEMBER ME from *Mr. Dodd Takes the Air*, Warner Bros.: Music by HARRY WARREN; Lyrics by AL DUBIN.

★ SWEET LEILANI from *Waikiki Wedding*, Paramount: Music and Lyrics by HARRY OWENS.

THAT OLD FEELING from *Vogues of*

1938, Wanger, UA: Music by SAMMY FAIN; Lyrics by LEW BROWN.

THEY CAN'T TAKE THAT AWAY FROM ME from *Shall We Dance*, RKO Radio: Music by GEORGE GERSHWIN; Lyrics by IRA GERSHWIN.

WHISPERS IN THE DARK from *Artists and Models*, Paramount: Music by FREDERICK HOLLANDER; Lyrics by LEO ROBIN.

1938 Eleventh Year

ALWAYS AND ALWAYS from *Mannequin*, Metro-Goldwyn-Mayer: Music by EDWARD WARD; Lyrics by CHET FORREST and BOB WRIGHT.

CHANGE PARTNERS AND DANCE WITH ME from *Carefree*, RKO Radio: Music and Lyrics by IRVING BERLIN.

COWBOY AND THE LADY from *The Cowboy and the Lady*, Goldwyn, UA: Music by LIONEL NEWMAN; Lyrics by ARTHUR QUENZER.

DUST from *Under Western Stars*, Republic: Music and Lyrics by JOHNNY MARVIN.

JEEPERS CREEPERS from *Going Places*, Warner Bros.: Music by HARRY WARREN; Lyrics by JOHNNY MERCER.

MERRILY WE LIVE from *Merrily We Live*, Roach, M-G-M: Music by PHIL CRAIG; Lyrics by ARTHUR QUENZER.

A MIST OVER THE MOON from *The Lady Objects*, Columbia: Music by BEN OAKLAND; Lyrics by OSCAR HAMMERSTEIN II.

MY OWN from *That Certain Age*, Universal: Music by JIMMY MCHUGH; Lyrics by HAROLD ADAMSON.

NOW IT CAN BE TOLD from *Alexander's Ragtime Band*, 20th Century-Fox: Music and Lyrics by IRVING BERLIN.

★ THANKS FOR THE MEMORY from *Big Broadcast of 1938*, Paramount: Music by RALPH RAINGER; Lyrics by LEO ROBIN.

1939 Twelfth Year

FAITHFUL FOREVER from *Gulliver's Travels*, Paramount: Music by RALPH RAINGER; Lyrics by LEO ROBIN.

I POURED MY HEART INTO A SONG from *Second Fiddle*, 20th Century-Fox: Music and Lyrics by IRVING BERLIN.

★ OVER THE RAINBOW from *The Wizard of Oz*, Metro-Goldwyn-Mayer: Music by HAROLD ARLEN; Lyrics by E. Y. HARBURG.

WISHING from *Love Affair*, RKO Radio: Music and Lyrics by BUDDY DE SYLVA.

1940 Thirteenth Year

DOWN ARGENTINE WAY from *Down Argentine Way*, 20th Century-Fox: Music by HARRY WARREN; Lyrics by MACK GORDON.

I'D KNOW YOU ANYWHERE from *You'll Find Out*, RKO Radio: Music by JIMMY MCHUGH; Lyrics by JOHNNY MERCER.

IT'S A BLUE WORLD from *Music in My Heart*, Columbia: Music and Lyrics by CHET FORREST and BOB WRIGHT.

LOVE OF MY LIFE from *Second Chorus*, Paramount: Music by ARTIE SHAW; Lyrics by JOHNNY MERCER.

ONLY FOREVER from *Rhythm on the River*, Paramount: Music by JAMES MONACO; Lyrics by JOHN BURKE.

OUR LOVE AFFAIR from *Strike up the Band*, Metro-Goldwyn-Mayer: Music and Lyrics by ROGER EDENS and GEORGIE STOLL.

WALTZING IN THE CLOUDS from *Spring Parade*, Universal: Music by ROBERT STOLZ; Lyrics by GUS KAHN.

★ WHEN YOU WISH UPON A STAR from *Pinocchio*, Disney, RKO Radio: Music by LEIGH HARLINE; Lyrics by NED WASHINGTON.

WHO AM I? from *Hit Parade of 1941*,

Republic: Music by JULE STYNE; Lyrics by WALTER BULLOCK.

1941 Fourteenth Year

BABY MINE from *Dumbo*, Disney, RKO Radio: Music by FRANK CHURCHILL; Lyrics by NED WASHINGTON.

BE HONEST WITH ME from *Ridin' on a Rainbow*, Republic: Music and Lyrics by GENE AUTRY and FRED ROSE.

BLUES IN THE NIGHT from *Blues in the Night*, Warner Bros.: Music by HAROLD ARLEN; Lyrics by JOHNNY MERCER.

BOOGIE WOOGIE BUGLE BOY OF COMPANY B from *Buck Privates*, Universal: Music by HUGH PRINCE; Lyrics by DON RAYE.

CHATTANOOGA CHOO CHOO from *Sun Valley Serenade*, 20th Century-Fox: Music by HARRY WARREN; Lyrics by MACK GORDON.

DOLORES from *Las Vegas Nights*, Paramount: Music by LOU ALTER; Lyrics by FRANK LOESSER.

★ THE LAST TIME I SAW PARIS from *Lady Be Good*, Metro-Goldwyn-Mayer: Music by JEROME KERN; Lyrics by OSCAR HAMMERSTEIN II.

OUT OF THE SILENCE from *All American Co-Ed*, Roach, UA: Music and Lyrics by LLOYD B. NORLIND.

SINCE I KISSED MY BABY GOODBYE from *You'll Never Get Rich*, Columbia: Music and Lyrics by COLE PORTER.

1942 Fifteenth Year

ALWAYS IN MY HEART from *Always in My Heart*, Warner Bros.: Music by ERNESTO LECUONA; Lyrics by KIM GANNON.

DEARLY BELOVED from *You Were Never Lovelier*, Columbia: Music by JEROME KERN; Lyrics by JOHNNY MERCER.

HOW ABOUT YOU? from *Babes on Broadway*, Metro-Goldwyn-Mayer: Music by BURTON LANE; Lyrics by RALPH FREED.

IT SEEMS I HEARD THAT SONG BEFORE from *Youth on Parade*, Republic: Music by JULE STYNE; Lyrics by SAMMY CAHN.

I'VE GOT A GAL IN KALAMAZOO from *Orchestra Wives*, 20th Century-Fox: Music by HARRY WARREN; Lyrics by MACK GORDON.

LOVE IS A SONG from *Bambi*, Disney, RKO Radio: Music by FRANK CHURCHILL; Lyrics by LARRY MOREY.

PENNIES FOR PEPPINO from *Flying with Music*, Roach, UA: Music by EDWARD WARD; Lyrics by CHET FORREST and BOB WRIGHT.

PIG FOOT PETE from *Hellzapoppin*, Universal: Music by GENE DE PAUL; Lyrics by DON RAYE.

THERE'S A BREEZE ON LAKE LOUISE from *The Mayor of 44th Street*, RKO Radio: Music by HARRY REVEL; Lyrics by MORT GREENE.

★ WHITE CHRISTMAS from *Holiday Inn*, Paramount: Music and Lyrics by IRVING BERLIN.

1943 Sixteenth Year

CHANGE OF HEART from *Hit Parade of 1943*, Republic: Music by JULE STYNE; Lyrics by HAROLD ADAMSON.

HAPPINESS IS A THING CALLED JOE from *Cabin in the Sky*, Metro-Goldwyn-Mayer: Music by HAROLD ARLEN; Lyrics by E. Y. HARBURG.

MY SHINING HOUR from *The Sky's the Limit*, RKO Radio: Music by HAROLD ARLEN; Lyrics by JOHNNY MERCER.

SALUDOS AMIGOS from *Saludos Amigos*, Disney, RKO Radio: Music by CHARLES WOLCOTT; Lyrics by NED WASHINGTON.

SAY A PRAYER FOR THE BOYS OVER

THERE from *Hers to Hold*, Universal: Music by JIMMY MCHUGH; Lyrics by HERB MAGIDSON.

THAT OLD BLACK MAGIC from *Star Spangled Rhythm*, Paramount: Music by HAROLD ARLEN; Lyrics by JOHNNY MERCER.

THEY'RE EITHER TOO YOUNG OR TOO OLD from *Thank Your Lucky Stars*, Warner Bros.: Music by ARTHUR SCHWARTZ; Lyrics by FRANK LOESSER.

WE MUSTN'T SAY GOOD BYE from *Stage Door Canteen*, Lesser, UA: Music by JAMES MONACO; Lyrics by AL DUBIN.

YOU'D BE SO NICE TO COME HOME TO from *Something to Shout About*, Columbia: Music and Lyrics by COLE PORTER.

⋆ YOU'LL NEVER KNOW from *Hello, Frisco, Hello*, 20th Century-Fox: Music by HARRY WARREN; Lyrics by MACK GORDON.

1944 Seventeenth Year

I COULDN'T SLEEP A WINK LAST NIGHT from *Higher and Higher*, RKO Radio: Music by JIMMY MCHUGH; Lyrics by HAROLD ADAMSON.

I'LL WALK ALONE from *Follow the Boys*, Universal: Music by JULE STYNE; Lyrics by SAMMY CAHN.

I'M MAKING BELIEVE from *Sweet and Lowdown*, 20th Century-Fox: Music by JAMES V. MONACO; Lyrics by MACK GORDON.

LONG AGO AND FAR AWAY from *Cover Girl*, Columbia: Music by JEROME KERN; Lyrics by IRA GERSHWIN.

NOW I KNOW from *Up in Arms*, Avalon, RKO Radio: Music by HAROLD ARLEN; Lyrics by TED KOEHLER.

REMEMBER ME TO CAROLINA from *Minstrel Man*, PRC: Music by HARRY REVEL; Lyrics by PAUL WEBSTER.

RIO DE JANEIRO from *Brazil*, Republic: Music by ARY BARROSO; Lyrics by NED WASHINGTON.

SILVER SHADOWS AND GOLDEN DREAMS from *Lady Let's Dance*, Monogram: Music by LEW POLLACK; Lyrics by CHARLES NEWMAN.

SWEET DREAMS SWEETHEART from *Hollywood Canteen*, Warner Bros.: Music by M. K. JEROME; Lyrics by TED KOEHLER.

⋆ SWINGING ON A STAR from *Going My Way*, Paramount: Music by JAMES VAN HEUSEN; Lyrics by JOHNNY BURKE.

TOO MUCH IN LOVE from *Song of the Open Road*, Rogers, UA: Music by WALTER KENT; Lyrics by KIM GANNON.

THE TROLLEY SONG from *Meet Me in St. Louis*, Metro-Goldwyn-Mayer: Music and Lyrics by RALPH BLANE and HUGH MARTIN.

1945 Eighteenth Year

ACCENTUATE THE POSITIVE from *Here Come the Waves*, Paramount: Music by HAROLD ARLEN; Lyrics by JOHNNY MERCER.

ANYWHERE from *Tonight and Every Night*, Columbia: Music by JULE STYNE; Lyrics by SAMMY CAHN.

AREN'T YOU GLAD YOU'RE YOU from *The Bells of St. Mary's*, Rainbow, RKO Radio: Music by JAMES VAN HEUSEN; Lyrics by JOHNNY BURKE.

THE CAT AND THE CANARY from *Why Girls Leave Home*, PRC: Music by JAY LIVINGSTON; Lyrics by RAY EVANS.

ENDLESSLY from *Earl Carroll Vanities*, Republic: Music by WALTER KENT; Lyrics by KIM GANNON.

I FALL IN LOVE TOO EASILY from *Anchors Aweigh*, Metro-Goldwyn-Mayer: Music by JULE STYNE; Lyrics by SAMMY CAHN.

I'LL BUY THAT DREAM from *Sing Your Way Home*, RKO Radio: Music by

ALLIE WRUBEL; Lyrics by HERB MAGIDSON.

★ IT MIGHT AS WELL BE SPRING from *State Fair*, 20th Century-Fox: Music by RICHARD RODGERS; Lyrics by OSCAR HAMMERSTEIN II.

LINDA from *G. I. Joe*, Cowan, UA: Music and Lyrics by ANN RONELL.

LOVE LETTERS from *Love Letters*, Wallis, Paramount: Music by VICTOR YOUNG; Lyrics by EDWARD HEYMAN.

MORE AND MORE from *Can't Help Singing*, Universal: Music by JEROME KERN; Lyrics by E. Y. HARBURG.

SLEIGHRIDE IN JULY from *Belle of the Yukon*, International, RKO Radio: Music by JAMES VAN HEUSEN; Lyrics by JOHNNY BURKE.

SO IN LOVE from *Wonder Man*, Beverly Prods., RKO Radio: Music by DAVID ROSE; Lyrics by LEO ROBIN.

SOME SUNDAY MORNING from *San Antonio*, Warner Bros.: Music by RAY HEINDORF and M. K. JEROME; Lyrics by TED KOEHLER.

1946 Nineteenth Year

ALL THROUGH THE DAY from *Centennial Summer*, 20th Century-Fox: Music by JEROME KERN; Lyrics by OSCAR HAMMERSTEIN II.

I CAN'T BEGIN TO TELL YOU from *The Dolly Sisters*, 20th Century-Fox: Music by JAMES MONACO; Lyrics by MACK GORDON.

OLE BUTTERMILK SKY from *Canyon Passage*, Wanger, Universal: Music by HOAGY CARMICHAEL; Lyrics by JACK BROOKS.

★ ON THE ATCHISON, TOPEKA AND SANTA FE from *The Harvey Girls*, Metro-Goldwyn-Mayer: Music by HARRY WARREN; Lyrics by JOHNNY MERCER.

YOU KEEP COMING BACK LIKE A SONG from *Blue Skies*, Paramount: Music and Lyrics by IRVING BERLIN.

1947 Twentieth Year

A GAL IN CALICO from *The Time, Place and the Girl*, Warner Bros.: Music by ARTHUR SCHWARTZ; Lyrics by LEO ROBIN.

I WISH I DIDN'T LOVE YOU SO from *The Perils of Pauline*, Paramount: Music and Lyrics by FRANK LOESSER.

PASS THAT PEACE PIPE from *Good News*, Metro-Goldwyn-Mayer: Music and Lyrics by RALPH BLANE, HUGH MARTIN, and ROGER EDENS.

YOU DO from *Mother Wore Tights*, 20th Century-Fox: Music by JOSEF MYROW; Lyrics by MACK GORDON.

★ ZIP-A-DEE-DOO-DAH from *Song of the South*, Disney-RKO Radio: Music by ALLIE WRUBEL; Lyrics by RAY GILBERT.

1948 Twenty-first Year

★ BUTTONS AND BOWS from *The Paleface*, Paramount: Music and Lyrics by JAY LIVINGSTON and RAY EVANS.

FOR EVERY MAN THERE'S A WOMAN from *Casbah*, Marston Pictures, U-I: Music by HAROLD ARLEN; Lyrics by LEO ROBIN.

IT'S MAGIC from *Romance on the High Seas*, Curtiz, Warner Bros.: Music by JULE STYNE; Lyrics by SAMMY CAHN.

THIS IS THE MOMENT from *That Lady in Ermine*, 20th Century-Fox: Music by FREDERICK HOLLANDER; Lyrics by LEO ROBIN.

THE WOODY WOODPECKER SONG from *Wet Blanket Policy*, Walter Lantz, UA (Cartoon): Music and Lyrics by RAMEY IDRISS and GEORGE TIBBLES.

1949 Twenty-second Year

★ BABY, IT'S COLD OUTSIDE from *Neptune's Daughter*, Metro-Goldwyn-Mayer: Music and Lyrics by FRANK LOESSER.

IT'S A GREAT FEELING from *It's a Great*

Feeling, Warner Bros.: Music by JULE STYNE; Lyrics by SAMMY CAHN.

LAVENDER BLUE from *So Dear to My Heart*, Disney-RKO Radio: Music by ELIOT DANIEL; Lyrics by LARRY MOREY.

MY FOOLISH HEART from *My Foolish Heart*, Goldwyn-RKO Radio: Music by VICTOR YOUNG; Lyrics by NED WASHINGTON.

THROUGH A LONG AND SLEEPLESS NIGHT from *Come to the Stable*, 20th Century-Fox: Music by ALFRED NEWMAN; Lyrics by MACK GORDON.

1950 Twenty-third Year

BE MY LOVE from *The Toast of New Orleans*, Metro-Goldwyn-Mayer: Music by NICHOLAS BRODSZKY; Lyrics by SAMMY CAHN.

BIBBIDY-BOBBIDI-BOO from *Cinderella*, Disney, RKO Radio: Music and Lyrics by MACK DAVID, AL HOFFMAN, and JERRY LIVINGSTON.

⋆ MONA LISA from *Captain Carey, USA*, Paramount: Music and Lyrics by RAY EVANS and JAY LIVINGSTON.

MULE TRAIN from *Singing Guns*, Palomar Pictures, Republic: Music and Lyrics by FRED GLICKMAN, HY HEATH, and JOHNNY LANGE.

WILHELMINA from *Wabash Avenue*, 20th Century-Fox: Music by JOSEF MYROW; Lyrics by MACK GORDON.

1951 Twenty-fourth Year

⋆ IN THE COOL, COOL, COOL OF THE EVENING from *Here Comes the Groom*, Paramount: Music by HOAGY CARMICHAEL; Lyrics by JOHNNY MERCER.

A KISS TO BUILD A DREAM ON from *The Strip*, Metro-Goldwyn-Mayer: Music and Lyrics by BERT KALMAR, HARRY RUBY, and OSCAR HAMMERSTEIN II.

NEVER from *Golden Girl*, 20th Century-Fox: Music by LIONEL NEWMAN; Lyrics by ELIOT DANIEL.

TOO LATE NOW from *Royal Wedding*, Metro-Goldwyn-Mayer: Music by BURTON LANE; Lyrics by ALAN JAY LERNER.

WONDER WHY from *Rich, Young and Pretty*, Metro-Goldwyn-Mayer: Music by NICHOLAS BRODSZKY; Lyrics by SAMMY CAHN.

1952 Twenty-fifth Year

AM I IN LOVE from *Son of Paleface*, Paramount: Music and Lyrics by JACK BROOKS.

BECAUSE YOU'RE MINE from *Because You're Mine*, Metro-Goldwyn-Mayer: Music by NICHOLAS BRODSZKY; Lyrics by SAMMY CAHN.

⋆ HIGH NOON (DO NOT FORSAKE ME, OH MY DARLIN') from *High Noon*, Kramer, UA: Music by DIMITRI TIOMKIN; Lyrics by NED WASHINGTON.

THUMBELINA from *Hans Christian Andersen*, Goldwyn, RKO Radio: Music and Lyrics by FRANK LOESSER.

ZING A LITTLE ZONG from *Just for You*, Paramount: Music by HARRY WARREN; Lyrics by LEO ROBIN.

1953 Twenty-sixth Year

THE MOON IS BLUE from *The Moon Is Blue*, Preminger-Herbert Prod., UA: Music by HERSCHEL BURKE GILBERT; Lyrics by SYLVIA FINE.

MY FLAMING HEART from *Small Town Girl*, Metro-Goldwyn-Mayer: Music by NICHOLAS BRODSZKY; Lyrics by LEO ROBIN.

SADIE THOMPSON'S SONG (BLUE PACIFIC BLUES) from *Miss Sadie Thompson*, Beckworth, Columbia: Music by LESTER LEE; Lyrics by NED WASHINGTON.

⋆ SECRET LOVE from *Calamity Jane*, Warner Bros.: Music by SAMMY

FAIN; Lyrics by PAUL FRANCIS WEBSTER.

THAT'S AMORE from *The Caddy*, York Pictures, Paramount: Music by HARRY WARREN; Lyrics by JACK BROOKS.

1954 Twenty-seventh Year

COUNT YOUR BLESSINGS INSTEAD OF SHEEP from *White Christmas*, Paramount: Music and Lyrics by IRVING BERLIN.

THE HIGH AND THE MIGHTY from *The High and the Mighty*, Wayne-Fellows Prods., Inc., Warner Bros.: Music by DIMITRI TIOMKIN; Lyrics by NED WASHINGTON.

HOLD MY HAND from *Susan Slept Here*, RKO Radio: Music and Lyrics by JACK LAWRENCE and RICHARD MYERS.

THE MAN THAT GOT AWAY from *A Star Is Born*, A Transcona Enterprises Prod., Warner Bros.: Music by HAROLD ARLEN; Lyrics by IRA GERSHWIN.

★ THREE COINS IN THE FOUNTAIN from *Three Coins in the Fountain*, 20th Century-Fox: Music by JULE STYNE; Lyrics by SAMMY CAHN.

1955 Twenty-eighth Year

I'LL NEVER STOP LOVING YOU from *Love Me or Leave Me*, Metro-Goldwyn-Mayer: Music by NICHOLAS BRODSZKY; Lyrics by SAMMY CAHN.

★ LOVE IS A MANY-SPLENDORED THING from *Love Is a Many-Splendored Thing*, 20th Century-Fox: Music by SAMMY FAIN; Lyrics by PAUL FRANCIS WEBSTER.

SOMETHING'S GOTTA GIVE from *Daddy Long Legs*, 20th Century-Fox: Music and Lyrics by JOHNNY MERCER.

(LOVE IS) THE TENDER TRAP from *The Tender Trap*, Metro-Goldwyn-Mayer: Music by JAMES VAN HEUSEN; Lyrics by SAMMY CAHN.

UNCHAINED MELODY from *Unchained*, Hall Bartlett Prods., Inc., Warner Bros.: Music by ALEX NORTH; Lyrics by HY ZARET.

1956 Twenty-ninth Year

FRIENDLY PERSUASION (THEE I LOVE) from *Friendly Persuasion*, Allied Artists: Music by DIMITRI TIOMKIN; Lyrics by PAUL FRANCIS WEBSTER.

JULIE from *Julie*, Arwin Prods., M-G-M: Music by LEITH STEVENS; Lyrics by TOM ADAIR.

TRUE LOVE from *High Society*, Sol C. Siegel Prod., M-G-M: Music and Lyrics by COLE PORTER.

★ WHATEVER WILL BE, WILL BE (QUE SERA, SERA) from *The Man Who Knew Too Much*, Hitchcock Prod., Paramount: Music and Lyrics by JAY LIVINGSTON and RAY EVANS.

WRITTEN ON THE WIND from *Written on the Wind*, Universal-International: Music by VICTOR YOUNG; Lyrics by SAMMY CAHN.

1957 Thirtieth Year

AN AFFAIR TO REMEMBER from *An Affair to Remember*, Jerry Wald Prods., Inc., 20th Century-Fox: Music by HARRY WARREN; Lyrics by HAROLD ADAMSON and LEO MCCAREY.

★ ALL THE WAY from *The Joker Is Wild*, A.M.B.L. Prod., Paramount: Music by JAMES VAN HEUSEN; Lyrics by SAMMY CAHN.

APRIL LOVE from *April Love*, 20th Century-Fox: Music by SAMMY FAIN; Lyrics by PAUL FRANCIS WEBSTER.

TAMMY from *Tammy and the Bachelor*, Universal-International: Music and Lyrics by RAY EVANS and JAY LIVINGSTON.

WILD IS THE WIND from *Wild Is the Wind*, A Hal Wallis Prod., Paramount: Music by DIMITRI

TIOMKIN; Lyrics by NED WASHINGTON.

1958 Thirty-first Year

ALMOST IN YOUR ARMS (LOVE SONG FROM "HOUSEBOAT") from *Houseboat*, Paramount and Scribe, Paramount: Music and Lyrics by JAY LIVINGSTON and RAY EVANS.

A CERTAIN SMILE from A *Certain Smile*, 20th Century-Fox: Music by SAMMY FAIN; Lyrics by PAUL FRANCIS WEBSTER.

★ GIGI from *Gigi*, Arthur Freed Prods., M-G-M: Music by FREDERICK LOEWE; Lyrics by ALAN JAY LERNER.

TO LOVE AND BE LOVED from *Some Came Running*, Sol C. Siegel Prods., Inc., M-G-M: Music by JAMES VAN HEUSEN; Lyrics by SAMMY CAHN.

A VERY PRECIOUS LOVE from *Marjorie Morningstar*, Beachwold Pictures, Warner Bros.: Music by SAMMY FAIN; Lyrics by PAUL FRANCIS WEBSTER.

1959 Thirty-second Year

THE BEST OF EVERYTHING from *The Best of Everything*, Company of Artists, Inc., 20th Century-Fox: Music by ALFRED NEWMAN; Lyrics by SAMMY CAHN.

THE FIVE PENNIES from *The Five Pennies*, Dena Prod., Paramount: Music and Lyrics by SYLVIA FINE.

THE HANGING TREE from *The Hanging Tree*, Baroda Prods., Inc., Warner Bros.: Music by JERRY LIVINGSTON; Lyrics by MACK DAVID.

★ HIGH HOPES from *A Hole in the Head*, Sincap Prods., UA: Music by JAMES VAN HEUSEN; Lyrics by SAMMY CAHN.

STRANGE ARE THE WAYS OF LOVE from *The Young Land*, C. V. Whitney Pictures, Inc., Columbia: Music by DIMITRI TIOMKIN; Lyrics by NED WASHINGTON.

1960 Thirty-third Year

THE FACTS OF LIFE from *The Facts of Life*, Panama and Frank Prod., UA: Music and Lyrics by JOHNNY MERCER.

FARAWAY PART OF TOWN from *Pepe*, G.S.-Posa Films International Prod., Columbia: Music by ANDRÉ PREVIN; Lyrics by DORY LANGDON.

THE GREEN LEAVES OF SUMMER from *The Alamo*, Batjac Prod., UA: Music by DIMITRI TIOMKIN; Lyrics by PAUL FRANCIS WEBSTER.

★ NEVER ON SUNDAY from *Never on Sunday*, Melinafilm Prod., Lopert Pictures Corp. (Greek): Music and Lyrics by MANOS HADJIDAKIS.

THE SECOND TIME AROUND from *High Time*, Bing Crosby Prods., 20th Century-Fox: Music by JAMES VAN HEUSEN; Lyrics by SAMMY CAHN.

1961 Thirty-fourth Year

BACHELOR IN PARADISE from *Bachelor in Paradise*, Ted Richmond Prod., M-G-M: Music by HENRY MANCINI; Lyrics by MACK DAVID.

LOVE THEME FROM EL CID (THE FALCON AND THE DOVE) from *El Cid*, Samuel Bronston Prod., in association with Dear Film Prod., Allied Artists: Music by MIKLOS ROZSA; Lyrics by PAUL FRANCIS WEBSTER.

★ MOON RIVER from *Breakfast at Tiffany's* Jurow-Shepherd Prod., Paramount: Music by HENRY MANCINI; Lyrics by JOHNNY MERCER.

POCKETFUL OF MIRACLES from *Pocketful of Miracles*, Franton Prod., UA: Music by JAMES VAN HEUSEN; Lyrics by SAMMY CAHN.

TOWN WITHOUT PITY from *Town without Pity*, Mirisch Company in association with Gloria Films, UA: Music by DIMITRI TIOMKIN; Lyrics by NED WASHINGTON.

1962 Thirty-fifth Year

★ DAYS OF WINE AND ROSES from *Days of Wine and Roses*, Martin Manulis-Jalem Prod., Warner Bros.: Music by HENRY MANCINI: Lyrics by JOHNNY MERCER.

LOVE SONG FROM MUTINY ON THE BOUNTY (FOLLOW ME) from *Mutiny on the Bounty*, Arcola Prod., M-G-M: Music by BRONISLAU KAPER; Lyrics by PAUL FRANCIS WEBSTER.

SONG FROM TWO FOR THE SEESAW (SECOND CHANCE) from *Two for the Seesaw*, Mirisch-Argyle-Talbot Prod., in association with Seven Arts Productions, UA: Music by ANDRÉ PREVIN; Lyrics by DORY LANGDON.

TENDER IS THE NIGHT from *Tender Is the Night*, 20th Century-Fox: Music by SAMMY FAIN; Lyrics by PAUL FRANCIS WEBSTER.

WALK ON THE WILD SIDE from *Walk on the Wild Side*, Famous Artists Prods., Columbia: Music by ELMER BERNSTEIN; Lyrics by MACK DAVID.

1963 Thirty-sixth Year

★ CALL ME IRRESPONSIBLE from *Papa's Delicate Condition*, Amro Prods., Paramount: Music by JAMES VAN HEUSEN; Lyrics by SAMMY CAHN.

CHARADE from *Charade*, Universal-Stanley Donen Prod., Universal: Music by HENRY MANCINI; Lyrics by JOHNNY MERCER.

IT'S A MAD, MAD, MAD, MAD WORLD from *It's a Mad, Mad, Mad, Mad, World*, Casey Prod., UA: Music by ERNEST GOLD; Lyrics by MACK DAVID.

MORE from *Mondo Cane*, Cineriz Prod., Times Film: Music by RIZ ORTOLANI and NINO OLIVIERO; Lyrics by NORMAN NEWELL.

SO LITTLE TIME from *55 Days at Peking*, Samuel Bronston Prod., Allied Artists: Music by DIMITRI TIOMKIN; Lyrics by PAUL FRANCIS WEBSTER.

1964 Thirty-seventh Year

★ CHIM CHIM CHER-EE from *Mary Poppins*, Walt Disney Prods.: Music and Lyrics by RICHARD M. SHERMAN and ROBERT B. SHERMAN.

DEAR HEART from *Dear Heart*, W.B.-Out-of-Towners Prod., Warner Bros.: Music by HENRY MANCINI; Lyrics by JAY LIVINGSTON and RAY EVANS.

HUSH . . . HUSH, SWEET CHARLOTTE from *Hush . . . Hush, Sweet Charlotte*, Associates and Aldrich Prod., 20th Century-Fox: Music by FRANK DEVOL; Lyrics by MACK DAVID.

MY KIND OF TOWN from *Robin and the 7 Hoods*, P-C Prod., Warner Bros.: Music by JAMES VAN HEUSEN; Lyrics by SAMMY CAHN.

WHERE LOVE HAS GONE from *Where Love Has Gone*, Paramount-Embassy Pictures Prod., Paramount: Music by JAMES VAN HEUSEN; Lyrics by SAMMY CAHN.

1965 Thirty-eighth Year

THE BALLAD OF CAT BALLOU from *Cat Ballou*, Harold Hecht Prod., Columbia: Music by JERRY LIVINGSTON; Lyrics by MACK DAVID.

I WILL WAIT FOR YOU from *The Umbrellas of Cherbourg*, Parc-Madeleine Films Prod., American Intl.: Music by MICHEL LEGRAND; Lyrics by JACQUES DEMY.

★ THE SHADOW OF YOUR SMILE from *The Sandpiper*, Filmways-Venice Prod., M-G-M: Music by JOHNNY MANDEL; Lyrics by PAUL FRANCIS WEBSTER.

THE SWEETHEART TREE from *The Great Race*, Patricia-Jalem-Reynard Prod.,

Warner Bros.: Music by HENRY MANCINI; Lyrics by JOHNNY MERCER.

WHAT'S NEW PUSSYCAT? from *What's New Pussycat?*, Famous Artists-Famartists Prod., United Artists: Music by BURT BACHARACH; Lyrics by HAL DAVID.

1966 Thirty-ninth Year

ALFIE from *Alfie*, Sheldrake Films, Ltd. Prod., Paramount: Music by BURT BACHARACH; Lyrics by HAL DAVID.

★ BORN FREE from *Born Free*, Open Road Films, Ltd.-Atlas Films, Ltd. Prod., Columbia: Music by JOHN BARRY; Lyrics by DON BLACK.

GEORGY GIRL from *Georgy Girl*, Everglades Prods., Ltd., Columbia: Music by TOM SPRINGFIELD; Lyrics by JIM DALE.

MY WISHING DOLL from *Hawaii*, Mirisch Corp. of Delaware Prod., UA: Music by ELMER BERNSTEIN; Lyrics by MACK DAVID.

A TIME FOR LOVE from *An American Dream*, Warner Bros.: Music by JOHNNY MANDEL; Lyrics by PAUL FRANCIS WEBSTER.

1967 Fortieth Year

THE BARE NECESSITIES from *The Jungle Book*, Walt Disney Prods., Buena Vista Distribution Co.: Music and Lyrics by TERRY GILKYSON.

THE EYES OF LOVE from *Banning*, Universal: Music by QUINCY JONES; Lyrics by BOB RUSSELL.

THE LOOK OF LOVE from *Casino Royale*, Famous Artists Prods., Ltd., Columbia: Music by BURT BACHARACH; Lyrics by HAL DAVID.

★ TALK TO THE ANIMALS from *Doctor Dolittle*, Apjac Prods., 20th Century-Fox: Music and Lyrics by LESLIE BRICUSSE.

THOROUGHLY MODERN MILLIE from *Thoroughly Modern Millie*, Ross Hunter-Universal Prod., Universal: Music and Lyrics by JAMES VAN HEUSEN and SAMMY CAHN.

1968 Forty-first Year

CHITTY CHITTY BANG BANG from *Chitty Chitty Bang Bang*, Warfield Prods., United Artists: Music and Lyrics by RICHARD M. SHERMAN and ROBERT B. SHERMAN.

FOR LOVE OF IVY from *For Love of Ivy*, American Broadcasting Companies-Palomar Pictures International Prod., Cinerama: Music by QUINCY JONES; Lyrics by BOB RUSSELL.

FUNNY GIRL from *Funny Girl*, Rastar Prods., Columbia: Music by JULE STYNE; Lyrics by BOB MERRILL.

STAR! from *Star!*, Robert Wise Prod., 20th Century-Fox: Music by JIMMY VAN HEUSEN; Lyrics by SAMMY CAHN.

★ THE WINDMILLS OF YOUR MIND from *The Thomas Crown Affair*, Mirisch-Simkoe-Solar Prod., United Artists: Music by MICHEL LEGRAND; Lyrics by ALAN BERGMAN and MARILYN BERGMAN.

1969 Forty-second Year

COME SATURDAY MORNING from *The Sterile Cuckoo*, Boardwalk Prods., Parmount: Music by FRED KARLIN; Lyrics by DORY PREVIN.

JEAN from *The Prime of Miss Jean Brodie*, 20th Century-Fox Prods., Ltd., 20th Century-Fox: Music and Lyrics by ROD MCKUEN.

★ RAINDROPS KEEP FALLIN' ON MY HEAD from *Butch Cassidy and the Sundance Kid*, George Roy Hill-Paul Monash Prod., 20th Century-Fox: Music by BURT BACHARACH; Lyrics by HAL DAVID.

TRUE GRIT from *True Grit*, Hal Wallis Prod., Paramount: Music by ELMER BERNSTEIN; Lyrics by DON BLACK.

WHAT ARE YOU DOING THE REST OF YOUR LIFE? from *The Happy Ending*, Pax Films Prod., United Artists: Music by MICHEL LEGRAND; Lyrics by ALAN BERGMAN and MARILYN BERGMAN.

1970 Forty-third Year

★ FOR ALL WE KNOW from *Lovers and Other Strangers*, ABC Pictures Prod., Cinerama: Music by FRED KARLIN; Lyrics by ROBB ROYER and JAMES GRIFFIN a.k.a. ROBB WILSON and ARTHUR JAMES.

PIECES OF DREAMS from *Pieces of Dreams*, RFB Enterprises Prod., United Artists: Music by MICHEL LEGRAND; Lyrics by ALAN BERGMAN and MARILYN BERGMAN.

THANK YOU VERY MUCH from *Scrooge*, Waterbury Films, Ltd. Prod., Cinema Center Films Presentation, National General: Music and Lyrics by LESLIE BRICUSSE.

TILL LOVE TOUCHES YOUR LIFE from *Madron*, Edric-Isracine-Zev Braun Prods., Four Star-Excelsior Releasing: Music by RIZ ORTOLANI; Lyrics by ARTHUR HAMILTON.

WHISTLING AWAY THE DARK from *Darling Lili*, Geoffrey Prods., Paramount: Music by HENRY MANCINI; Lyrics by JOHNNY MERCER.

1971 Forty-fourth Year

THE AGE OF NOT BELIEVING from *Bedknobs and Broomsticks*, Walt Disney Prods., Buena Vista Distribution Company: Music and Lyrics by RICHARD M. SHERMAN and ROBERT B. SHERMAN.

ALL HIS CHILDREN from *Sometimes a Great Notion*, A Universal-Newman-Foreman Company Prod., Universal: Music by HENRY MANCINI; Lyrics by ALAN BERGMAN and MARILYN BERGMAN.

BLESS THE BEASTS AND CHILDREN from *Bless the Beasts and Children*, Columbia: Music and Lyrics by BARRY DEVORZON and PERRY BOTKIN, JR..

LIFE IS WHAT YOU MAKE IT from *Kotch*, A Kotch Company Production, ABC Pictures Presentation, Cinerama: Music by MARVIN HAMLISCH; Lyrics by JOHNNY MERCER.

★ THEME FROM SHAFT from *Shaft*, Shaft Prods., Ltd., M-G-M: Music and Lyrics by ISAAC HAYES.

1972 Forty-fifth Year

BEN from *Ben*, BCP Productions, Cinerama: Music by WALTER SCHARF; Lyrics by DON BLACK.

COME FOLLOW, FOLLOW ME from *The Little Ark*, Robert Radnitz Productions, Ltd., Cinema Center Films Presentation, National General: Music by FRED KARLIN; Lyrics by MARSHA KARLIN.

MARMALADE, MOLASSES & HONEY from *The Life and Times of Judge Roy Bean*, A First Artists Production Company, Ltd. Production, National General: Music by MAURICE JARRE; Lyrics by MARILYN BERGMAN and ALAN BERGMAN.

★ THE MORNING AFTER from *The Poseidon Adventure*, An Irwin Allen Production, 20th Century-Fox: Music and Lyrics by AL KASHA and JOEL HIRSCHHORN.

STRANGE ARE THE WAYS OF LOVE from *The Stepmother*, Magic Eye of Hollywood Productions, Crown International: Music by SAMMY FAIN; Lyrics by PAUL FRANCIS WEBSTER.

1973 Forty-sixth Year

ALL THAT LOVE WENT TO WASTE from *A Touch of Class*, Brut Prods., Avco Embassy: Music by GEORGE BARRIE; Lyrics by SAMMY CAHN.

LIVE AND LET DIE from *Live and Let Die*, Eon Prods., UA: Music and

Lyrics by PAUL MCCARTNEY and LINDA MCCARTNEY.

LOVE from *Robin Hood*, Walt Disney Prods., Buena Vista Distribution Company: Music by GEORGE BRUNS; Lyrics by FLOYD HUDDLESTON.

NICE TO BE AROUND from *Cinderella Liberty*, A Sanford Prod., 20th Century-Fox: Music by JOHN WILLIAMS; Lyrics by PAUL WILLIAMS.

★ THE WAY WE WERE from *The Way We Were*, Rastar Prods., Columbia: Music by MARVIN HAMLISCH; Lyrics by ALAN BERGMAN and MARILYN BERGMAN.

1974 Forty-seventh Year

BENJI'S THEME (I FEEL LOVE) from *Benji*, Mulberry Square: Music by EUEL BOX; Lyrics by BETTY BOX.

BLAZING SADDLES from *Blazing Saddles*, Warner Bros.: Music by JOHN MORRIS; Lyrics by MEL BROOKS.

LITTLE PRINCE from *The Little Prince*, A Stanley Donen Enterprises, Ltd. Prod., Paramount: Music by FREDERICK LOEWE; Lyrics by ALAN JAY LERNER.

★ WE MAY NEVER LOVE LIKE THIS AGAIN from *The Towering Inferno*, An Irwin Allen Production, 20th Century-Fox/Warner Bros.: Music and Lyrics by AL KASHA and JOEL HIRSCHHORN.

WHEREVER LOVE TAKES ME from *Gold*, Avton Film Productions, Ltd., Allied Artists: Music by ELMER BERNSTEIN; Lyrics by DON BLACK.

*1975 Forty-eighth Year**

HOW LUCKY CAN YOU GET from *Funny Lady*, A Rastar Pictures Production, Columbia: Music and Lyrics by FRED EBB and JOHN KANDER.

★ I'M EASY from *Nashville*, An ABC Entertainment-Jerry Weintraub-Robert Altman Production, Paramount: Music and Lyrics by KEITH CARRADINE.

NOW THAT WE'RE IN LOVE from *Whiffs*, Brut Productions, 20th Century-Fox: Music by GEORGE BARRIE; Lyrics by SAMMY CAHN.

RICHARD'S WINDOW from *The Other Side of the Mountain*, A Filmways-Larry Peerce-Universal Production, Universal: Music by CHARLES FOX; Lyrics by NORMAN GIMBEL.

THEME FROM MAHOGANY (DO YOU KNOW WHERE YOU'RE GOING TO) from *Mahogany*, A Jobete Film Production, Paramount: Music by MICHAEL MASSER; Lyrics by GERRY GOFFIN.

1976 Forty-ninth Year

AVE SATANI from *The Omen*, 20th Century-Fox Productions, Ltd., 20th Century Fox: Music and Lyrics by JERRY GOLDSMITH.

COME TO ME from *The Pink Panther Strikes Again*, Amjo Productions, Ltd., United Artists: Music by HENRY MANCINI; Lyrics by DON BLACK.

★ EVERGREEN (LOVE THEME FROM A STAR IS BORN) from *A Star Is Born*, A Barwood/Jon Peters Production, First Artists Presentation, Warner Bros.: Music by BARBRA STREISAND; Lyrics by PAUL WILLIAMS.

GONNA FLY NOW from *Rocky*, a Robert Chartoff-Irwin Winkler Production, United Artists: Music by BILL CONTI; Lyrics by CAROL CONNORS and AYN ROBBINS.

A WORLD THAT NEVER WAS from *Half a House*, Lenro Productions, First American Films: Music by SAMMY FAIN; Lyrics by PAUL FRANCIS WEBSTER.

*Name of category changed from Best Song to Best Original Song.

1977 Fiftieth Year

Best Original Song

CANDLE ON THE WATER from *Pete's Dragon*, Walt Disney Productions, Buena Vista Distribution Company: Music and Lyrics by AL KASHA and JOEL HIRSCHHORN.

NOBODY DOES IT BETTER from *The Spy Who Loved Me*, Eon Productions, United Artists: Music by MARVIN HAMLISCH; Lyrics by CAROLE BAYER SAGER.

THE SLIPPER AND THE ROSE WALTZ (HE DANCED WITH ME/SHE DANCED WITH ME) from *The Slipper and the Rose—The Story of Cinderella*, Paradine Co-Productions, Ltd., Universal: Music and Lyrics by RICHARD M. SHERMAN and ROBERT B. SHERMAN.

SOMEONE'S WAITING FOR YOU from *The Rescuers*, Walt Disney Productions, Buena Vista Distribution Company: Music by SAMMY FAIN; Lyrics by CAROL CONNORS and AYN ROBBINS.

★ YOU LIGHT UP MY LIFE from *You Light up My Life*, The Session Company Production, Columbia: Music and Lyrics by JOSEPH BROOKS.

1978 Fifty-first Year

HOPELESSLY DEVOTED TO YOU from *Grease*, A Robert Stigwood/Allan Carr Production, Paramount: Music and Lyrics by JOHN FARRAR.

★ LAST DANCE from *Thank God It's Friday*, A Casablanca-Motown Production, Columbia: Music and Lyrics by PAUL JABARA.

THE LAST TIME I FELT LIKE THIS from *Same Time, Next Year*, A Walter Mirisch-Robert Mulligan Production, Mirisch Corporation/Universal Pictures Presentation, Universal: Music by MARVIN HAMLISCH; Lyrics by ALAN BERGMAN and MARILYN BERGMAN.

READY TO TAKE A CHANCE AGAIN from *Foul Play*, A Miller-Milkis/Colin Higgins Picture Production, Paramount: Music by CHARLES FOX; Lyrics by NORMAN GIMBEL.

WHEN YOU'RE LOVED from *The Magic of Lassie*, Lassie Productions, The International Picture Show Company: Music and Lyrics by RICHARD M. SHERMAN and ROBERT B. SHERMAN.

1979 Fifty-second Year

★ IT GOES LIKE IT GOES from *Norma Rae*, A Twentieth Century-Fox Production, 20th Century-Fox: Music by DAVID SHIRE; Lyrics by NORMAN GIMBEL.

THE RAINBOW CONNECTION from *The Muppet Movie*, A Jim Henson Production, Lord Grade/Martin Starger Presentation, AFD (Associated Film Distribution): Music and Lyrics by PAUL WILLIAMS and KENNY ASCHER.

SONG FROM 10 (IT'S EASY TO SAY) from *10*, Geoffrey Productions, Orion Pictures Company: Music by HENRY MANCINI; Lyrics by ROBERT WELLS.

THEME FROM ICE CASTLES (THROUGH THE EYES OF LOVE) from *Ice Castles*, An International Cinemedia Center Production, Columbia: Music by MARVIN HAMLISCH; Lyrics by CAROLE BAYER SAGER.

THEME FROM THE PROMISE (I'LL NEVER SAY "GOODBYE") from *The Promise*, A Fred Weintraub-Paul Heller Presentation/Universal Production, Universal: Music by DAVID SHIRE; Lyrics by ALAN BERGMAN and MARILYN BERGMAN.

1980 Fifty-third Year

★ FAME from *Fame*, A Metro-Goldwyn-Mayer Production, Metro-Goldwyn-Mayer: Music by MICHAEL GORE; Lyrics by DEAN PITCHFORD.

NINE TO FIVE from *Nine to Five*, A Twentieth Century-Fox Production, 20th Century-Fox: Music and Lyrics by DOLLY PARTON.

ON THE ROAD AGAIN from *Honeysuckle Rose*, A Warner Bros. Production, Warner Bros.: Music and Lyrics by WILLIE NELSON.

OUT HERE ON MY OWN from *Fame*, A Metro-Goldwyn-Mayer Production, Metro-Goldwyn-Mayer: Music by MICHAEL GORE; Lyrics by LESLEY GORE.

PEOPLE ALONE from *The Competition*, A Rastar Films Production, Columbia: Music by LALO SCHIFRIN; Lyrics by WILBUR JENNINGS.

1981 Fifty-fourth Year

★ ARTHUR'S THEME (BEST THAT YOU CAN DO) from *Arthur*, A Rollins, Joffe, Morra, and Brezner Production, Orion: Music and Lyrics by BURT BACHARACH, CAROLE BAYER SAGER, CHRISTOPHER CROSS, and PETER ALLEN.

ENDLESS LOVE from *Endless Love*, A Polygram/Universal Pictures/ Keith Barish/Dyson Lovell Production, Universal: Music and Lyrics by LIONEL RICHIE.

THE FIRST TIME IT HAPPENS from *The Great Muppet Caper*, A Jim Henson/ ITC Film Entertainment Limited Production, Universal: Music and Lyrics by JOE RAPOSO.

FOR YOUR EYES ONLY from *For Your Eyes Only*, An EON Production, United Artists: Music by BILL CONTI; Lyrics by MICK LEESON.

ONE MORE HOUR from *Ragtime*, A Ragtime Production, Paramount: Music and Lyrics by RANDY NEWMAN.

1982 Fifty-fifth Year

EYE OF THE TIGER from *Rocky III*, A Robert Chartoff-Irwin Winkler/ United Artists Production, M-G-M/ UA: Music and Lyrics by JIM PETERIK and FRANKIE SULLIVAN III.

HOW DO YOU KEEP THE MUSIC PLAYING? from *Best Friends*, A Timberlane Films Production, Warner Bros.: Music by MICHEL LEGRAND; Lyrics by ALAN BERGMAN and MARILYN BERGMAN.

IF WE WERE IN LOVE from *Yes, Giorgio*, A Metro-Goldwyn-Mayer Production, M-G-M/UA: Music by JOHN WILLIAMS; Lyrics by ALAN BERGMAN and MARILYN BERGMAN.

IT MIGHT BE YOU from *Tootsie*, A Mirage/Punch Production, Columbia: Music by DAVE GRUSIN; Lyrics by ALAN BERGMAN and MARILYN BERGMAN.

★ UP WHERE WE BELONG from *An Officer and a Gentleman*, A Lorimar Production in association with Martin Elfand, Paramount: Music by JACK NITZSCHE and BUFFY SAINTE-MARIE; Lyrics by WILL JENNINGS.

1983 Fifty-sixth Year

★ FLASHDANCE . . . WHAT A FEELING from *Flashdance*, A Polygram Pictures Production, Paramount: Music by GIORGIO MORODER; Lyrics by KEITH FORSEY and IRENE CARA.

MANIAC from *Flashdance*, A Polygram Pictures Production, Paramount: Music and Lyrics by MICHAEL SEMBELLO and DENNIS MATKOSKY.

OVER YOU from *Tender Mercies*, An EMI Presentation of an Antron Media Production, Universal/AFD: Music and Lyrics by AUSTIN ROBERTS and BOBBY HART.

PAPA, CAN YOU HEAR ME? from *Yentl*, A United Artists/Ladbroke Feature/ Barwood Production, M-G-M/UA: Music by MICHEL LEGRAND; Lyrics by ALAN BERGMAN and MARILYN BERGMAN.

THE WAY HE MAKES ME FEEL from *Yentl*, A United Artists/Ladbroke Feature/Barwood Production, M-G-M/UA: Music by MICHEL LEGRAND; Lyrics by ALAN BERGMAN and MARILYN BERGMAN.

1984 Fifty-seventh Year

AGAINST ALL ODDS (TAKE A LOOK AT ME NOW) from *Against All Odds*, A New Visions Production, Columbia: Music and Lyrics by PHIL COLLINS.

FOOTLOOSE from *Footloose*, A Daniel Melnick Production, Paramount: Music and Lyrics by KENNY LOGGINS and DEAN PITCHFORD.

GHOSTBUSTERS from *Ghostbusters*, A Columbia Pictures Production, Columbia: Music and Lyrics by RAY PARKER, JR.

★ I JUST CALLED TO SAY I LOVE YOU from *The Woman in Red*, A Woman in Red Production, Orion: Music and Lyrics by STEVIE WONDER.

LET'S HEAR IT FOR THE BOY from *Footloose*, A Daniel Melnick Production, Paramount: Music and Lyrics by TOM SNOW and DEAN PITCHFORD.

1985 Fifty-eighth Year

MISS CELIE'S BLUES (SISTER) from *The Color Purple*, A Warner Bros. Production, Warner Bros.: Music by QUINCY JONES and ROD TEMPERTON; Lyrics by QUINCY JONES, ROD TEMPERTON, and LIONEL RICHIE.

POWER OF LOVE from *Back to the Future*, An Amblin Entertainment/ Universal Pictures Production, Universal: Music by CHRIS HAYES and JOHNNY COLLA; Lyrics by HUEY LEWIS.

★ SAY YOU, SAY ME from *White Nights*, A New Visions Production, Columbia: Music and Lyrics by LIONEL RICHIE.

SEPARATE LIVES (LOVE THEME FROM WHITE NIGHTS) from *White Nights*, A New Visions Production, Columbia: Music and Lyrics by STEPHEN BISHOP.

SURPRISE, SURPRISE from *A Chorus Line*, An Embassy Films Associates and Polygram Pictures Production, Columbia: Music by MARVIN HAMLISCH; Lyrics by EDWARD KLEBAN.

1986 Fifty-ninth Year

GLORY OF LOVE from *The Karate Kid Part II*, Columbia Pictures Production, Columbia: Music by PETER CETERA and DAVID FOSTER; Lyrics by PETER CETERA and DIANE NINI.

LIFE IN A LOOKING GLASS from *That's Life!*, A Paradise Cove/Ubilam Production, Columbia: Music by HENRY MANCINI; Lyrics by LESLIE BRICUSSE.

MEAN GREEN MOTHER FROM OUTER SPACE from *Little Shop of Horrors*, A Geffen Company Production, Geffen Company through Warner Bros.: Music by ALAN MENKEN; Lyrics by HOWARD ASHMAN.

SOMEWHERE OUT THERE from *An American Tail*, An Amblin Entertainment Production, Universal: Music by JAMES HORNER and BARRY MANN; Lyrics by CYNTHIA WEIL.

★ TAKE MY BREATH AWAY from *Top Gun*, A Don Simpson/Jerry Bruckheimer Production, Paramount: Music by GIORGIO MORODER; Lyrics by TOM WHITLOCK.

1987 Sixtieth Year

CRY FREEDOM from *Cry Freedom*, a Marble Arch Production, Universal: Music and Lyrics by GEORGE FENTON and JONAS GWANGWA.

★ (I'VE HAD) THE TIME OF MY LIFE from *Dirty Dancing*, A Vestron

Pictures Production in association with Great American Films Limited Partnership, Vestron: Music by FRANKE PREVITE, JOHN DeNICOLA, and DONALD MARKOWITZ; Lyrics by FRANKE PREVITE.

NOTHING'S GONNA STOP US NOW from *Mannequin*, A Gladden Entertainment Production, 20th Century-Fox: Music and Lyrics by ALBERT HAMMOND and DIANE WARREN.

SHAKEDOWN from *Beverly Hills Cop II*, A Don Simpson and Jerry Bruckheimer Production in association with Eddie Murphy Productions, Paramount: Music by HAROLD FALTERMEYER and KEITH FORSEY; Lyrics by HAROLD FALTERMEYER, KEITH FORSEY, and BOB SEGER.

STORYBOOK LOVE from *The Princess Bride*, An Act III Communications Production, 20th Century-Fox: Music and Lyrics by WILLY DEVILLE.

1988 Sixty-first Year

CALLING YOU from *Bagdad Cafe*, A Pelemele Film Production, Island: Music and Lyrics by BOB TELSON.

★ LET THE RIVER RUN from *Working Girl*, A 20th Century-Fox Production, 20th Century-Fox: Music and Lyrics by CARLY SIMON.

TWO HEARTS from *Buster*, An N.F.H. Production, Hemdale: Music by LAMONT DOZIER; Lyrics by PHIL COLLINS.

1989 Sixty-second Year

AFTER ALL from *Chances Are*, A Tri-Star Pictures Production, Tri-Star: Music by TOM SNOW; Lyrics by DEAN PITCHFORD.

THE GIRL WHO USED TO BE ME from *Shirley Valentine*, A Lewis Gilbert/ Willy Russell Production, Paramount: Music by MARVIN HAMLISCH; Lyrics by ALAN BERGMAN and MARILYN BERGMAN.

I LOVE TO SEE YOU SMILE from *Parenthood*, An Imagine Entertainment Production, Universal: Music and Lyrics by RANDY NEWMAN.

KISS THE GIRL from *The Little Mermaid*, A Walt Disney Pictures Production in association with Silver Screen Partners IV, Buena Vista: Music by ALAN MENKEN; Lyrics by HOWARD ASHMAN.

★ UNDER THE SEA from *The Little Mermaid*, A Walt Disney Pictures Production in association with Silver Screen Partners IV, Buena Vista: Music by ALAN MENKEN; Lyrics by HOWARD ASHMAN.

1990 Sixty-third Year

BLAZE OF GLORY from *Young Guns II*, A Morgan Creek Production, 20th Century-Fox: Music and Lyrics by JON BON JOVI.

I'M CHECKIN' OUT from *Postcards from the Edge*, A Columbia Pictures Production, Columbia: Music and Lyrics by SHEL SILVERSTEIN.

PROMISE ME YOU'LL REMEMBER from *The Godfather Part III*, A Zoetrope Studios Production, Paramount: Music by CARMINE COPPOLA; Lyrics by JOHN BETTIS.

SOMEWHERE IN MY MEMORY from *Home Alone*, A 20th Century-Fox Production, 20th Century-Fox: Music by JOHN WILLIAMS; Lyrics by LESLIE BRICUSSE.

★ SOONER OR LATER (I ALWAYS GET MY MAN) from *Dick Tracy*, A Touchstone Pictures Production, Buena Vista: Music and Lyrics by STEPHEN SONDHEIM.

1991 Sixty-fourth Year

★ BEAUTY AND THE BEAST from *Beauty and the Beast*, A Walt Disney

Pictures Production, Buena Vista: Music by ALAN MENKEN; Lyrics by HOWARD ASHMAN.

BELLE from *Beauty and the Beast*, A Walt Disney Pictures Production, Buena Vista: Music by ALAN MENKEN; Lyrics by HOWARD ASHMAN.

BE OUR GUEST from *Beauty and the Beast*, A Walt Disney Pictures Production, Buena Vista: Music by ALAN MENKEN; Lyrics by HOWARD ASHMAN.

(EVERYTHING I DO) I DO IT FOR YOU from *Robin Hood: Prince of Thieves*, A Morgan Creek Production, Warner Bros.: Music by MICHAEL KAMEN; Lyrics by BRYAN ADAMS and ROBERT JOHN LANGE.

WHEN YOU'RE ALONE from *Hook*, A Tri-Star Pictures Production, Tri-Star: Music by JOHN WILLIAMS; Lyrics by LESLIE BRICUSSE.

1992 Sixty-fifth Year

BEAUTIFUL MARIA OF MY SOUL from *The Mambo Kings*, A Northwest Production, Warner Bros.: Music by ROBERT KRAFT; Lyrics by ARNE GLIMCHER.

FRIEND LIKE ME from *Aladdin*, A Walt Disney Pictures Production, Buena Vista: Music by ALAN MENKEN; Lyrics by HOWARD ASHMAN.

I HAVE NOTHING from *The Bodyguard*, A Warner Bros. Production, Warner Bros.: Music by DAVID FOSTER; Lyrics by LINDA THOMPSON.

RUN TO YOU from *The Bodyguard*, A Warner Bros. Production, Warner Bros.: Music by JUD FRIEDMAN; Lyrics by ALLAN RICH.

★ WHOLE NEW WORLD from *Aladdin*, A Walt Disney Pictures Production, Buena Vista: Music by ALAN MENKEN; Lyrics by TIM RICE.

Costume Design

A costume designer dresses not only the actors but, in effect, the picture itself. And though costume design is frequently associated only with dressy spectacles like *Cleopatra* or *Gigi*, one must remember that all films require costumes. "More difficult, and far less likely to win applause," says Oscar-winning costume designer Julie Harris, "are the films which require dressing down, rather than dressing up."

The Academy Award for Costume Design was begun in 1948 with separate awards given for black-and-white films and color films. With the exception of 1957 and 1958, this division was retained until 1967 when the lack of black-and-white films made two separate awards impractical.

Edith Head, with an astonishing thirty-four nominations and eight Oscars, has dominated the category, though several other designers including Irene Sharaff, Orry-Kelly, Dorothy Jeakins, Charles LeMaire, and Anthony Powell have each won three or more awards.

Achievements in this category are nominated by the Costume Designer members of the Academy Art Directors Branch.

1948 Twenty-first Year

Black and White

B. F.'S DAUGHTER, Metro-Goldwyn-Mayer: IRENE.

★ HAMLET, Rank-Two Cities, U-I (British): ROGER K. FURSE.

Color

THE EMPEROR WALTZ, Paramount: EDITH HEAD and GILE STEELE.

★ JOAN OF ARC, Sierra, RKO Radio: DOROTHY JEAKINS and KARINSKA.

1949 Twenty-second Year

Black and White

★ THE HEIRESS, Paramount: EDITH HEAD and GILE STEELE.

PRINCE OF FOXES, 20th Century-Fox: VITTORIO NINO NOVARESE.

Color

★ ADVENTURES OF DON JUAN, Warner Bros.: LEAH RHODES, TRAVILLA, and MARJORIE BEST.

MOTHER IS A FRESHMAN, 20th Century-Fox: KAY NELSON.

1950 Twenty-third Year

Black and White

★ ALL ABOUT EVE, 20th Century-Fox: EDITH HEAD and CHARLES LEMAIRE.

BORN YESTERDAY, Columbia: JEAN LOUIS.

THE MAGNIFICENT YANKEE, Metro-Goldwyn-Mayer: WALTER PLUNKETT.

Color

THE BLACK ROSE, 20th Century-Fox: MICHAEL WHITTAKER.

★ SAMSON AND DELILAH, DeMille, Paramount: EDITH HEAD, DOROTHY JEAKINS, ELOIS JENSSEN, GILE STEELE, and GWEN WAKELING.

THAT FORSYTE WOMAN, Metro-Goldwyn-Mayer: WALTER PLUNKETT and VALLES.

1951 Twenty-fourth Year

Black and White

KIND LADY, Metro-Goldwyn-Mayer: WALTER PLUNKETT and GILE STEELE.

THE MODEL AND THE MARRIAGE BROKER, 20th Century-Fox: CHARLES LEMARIE and RENIE.

THE MUDLARK, 20th Century-Fox: EDWARD STEVENSON and MARGARET FURSE.

★ A PLACE IN THE SUN, Paramount: EDITH HEAD.

A STREETCAR NAMED DESIRE, Charles K. Feldman Group Prods., Warner Bros.: LUCINDA BALLARD.

Color

★ AN AMERICAN IN PARIS, Metro-Goldwyn-Mayer: ORRY-KELLY, WALTER PLUNKETT, and IRENE SHARAFF.

DAVID AND BATHSHEBA, 20th Century-Fox: CHARLES LEMAIRE and EDWARD STEVENSON.

THE GREAT CARUSO, Metro-Goldwyn-Mayer: HELEN ROSE and GILE STEELE.

QUO VADIS, Metro-Goldwyn-Mayer: HERSCHEL MCCOY.

TALES OF HOFFMANN, Powell-Pressburger, Lopert (British): HEIN HECKROTH.

1952 Twenty-fifth Year

Black and White

AFFAIR IN TRINIDAD, Beckworth, Columbia: JEAN LOUIS.

★ THE BAD AND THE BEAUTIFUL, Metro-Goldwyn-Mayer: HELEN ROSE.

CARRIE, Paramount: EDITH HEAD.

MY COUSIN RACHEL, 20th Century-Fox: CHARLES LEMAIRE and DOROTHY JEAKINS.

SUDDEN FEAR, Joseph Kaufman, RKO Radio: SHEILA O'BRIEN.

Color

THE GREATEST SHOW ON EARTH, DeMille, Paramount: EDITH HEAD, DOROTHY JEAKINS, and MILES WHITE.

HANS CHRISTIAN ANDERSEN, Goldwyn, RKO Radio: CLAVE, MARY WILLS, and MADAME KARINSKA.

THE MERRY WIDOW, Metro-Goldwyn-Mayer: HELEN ROSE and GILE STEELE.

★ MOULIN ROUGE, Romulus, UA: MARCEL VERTES.

WITH A SONG IN MY HEART, 20th Century-Fox: CHARLES LEMAIRE.

1953 Twenty-sixth Year

Black and White

THE ACTRESS, Metro-Goldwyn-Mayer: WALTER PLUNKETT.

DREAM WIFE, Metro-Goldwyn-Mayer: HELEN ROSE and HERSCHEL MCCOY.

FROM HERE TO ETERNITY, Columbia: JEAN LOUIS.

THE PRESIDENT'S LADY, 20th Century-Fox: CHARLES LEMAIRE and RENIE.

★ ROMAN HOLIDAY, Paramount: EDITH HEAD.

Color

THE BAND WAGON, Metro-Goldwyn-Mayer: MARY ANN NYBERG.

CALL ME MADAM, 20th Century-Fox: IRENE SHARAFF.

HOW TO MARRY A MILLIONAIRE, 20th Century-Fox: CHARLES LEMAIRE and TRAVILLA.

★ THE ROBE, 20th Century-Fox:

CHARLES LeMAIRE and EMILE SANTIAGO.

YOUNG BESS, Metro-Goldwyn-Mayer: WALTER PLUNKETT.

1954 Twenty-seventh Year

Black and White

THE EARRINGS OF MADAME DE . . . , Franco-London Prods., Arlan Pictures (French): GEORGES ANNENKOV and ROSINE DELAMARE.

EXECUTIVE SUITE, Metro-Goldwyn-Mayer: HELEN ROSE.

INDISCRETION OF AN AMERICAN WIFE, A Vittorio DeSica Prod., Columbia: CHRISTIAN DIOR.

IT SHOULD HAPPEN TO YOU, Columbia: JEAN LOUIS.

★ SABRINA, Paramount: EDITH HEAD.

Color

BRIGADOON, Metro-Goldwyn-Mayer: IRENE SHARAFF.

DESIREE, 20th Century-Fox: CHARLES LEMAIRE and RENE HUBERT.

★ GATE OF HELL, A Daiei Prod., Edward Harrison (Japanese): SANZO WADA.

A STAR IS BORN, A Transcona Enterprises Prod., Warner Bros.: JEAN LOUIS, MARY ANN NYBERG, and IRENE SHARAFF.

THERE'S NO BUSINESS LIKE SHOW BUSINESS, 20th Century-Fox: CHARLES LEMAIRE, TRAVILLA, and MILES WHITE.

1955 Twenty-eighth Year

Black and White

★ I'LL CRY TOMORROW, Metro-Goldwyn-Mayer: HELEN ROSE.

THE PICKWICK PAPERS, Renown Prod., Kingsley International Pictures (British): BEATRICE DAWSON.

QUEEN BEE, Columbia: JEAN LOUIS.

THE ROSE TATTOO, Hal Wallis, Paramount: EDITH HEAD.

UGETSU, Daiei Motion Picture Co., Edward Harrison (Japanese): TADAOTO KAINOSCHO.

Color

GUYS AND DOLLS, Samuel Goldwyn Prods., Inc., M-G-M: IRENE SHARAFF.

INTERRUPTED MELODY, Metro-Goldwyn-Mayer: HELEN ROSE.

★ LOVE IS A MANY-SPLENDORED THING, 20th Century-Fox: CHARLES LeMAIRE.

TO CATCH A THIEF, Paramount: EDITH HEAD.

THE VIRGIN QUEEN, 20th Century-Fox: CHARLES LEMAIRE and MARY WILLS.

1956 Twenty-ninth Year

Black and White

THE MAGNIFICENT SEVEN (a.k.a. THE SEVEN SAMURAI), A Toho Prod., Kingsley International (Japanese): KOHEI EZAKI.

THE POWER AND THE PRIZE, Metro-Goldwyn-Mayer: HELEN ROSE.

THE PROUD AND THE PROFANE, The Perlberg-Seaton Prod., Paramount: EDITH HEAD.

★ THE SOLID GOLD CADILLAC, Columbia: JEAN LOUIS.

TEENAGE REBEL, 20th Century-Fox: CHARLES LEMAIRE and MARY WILLS.

Color

AROUND THE WORLD IN 80 DAYS, The Michael Todd Co., Inc., UA: MILES WHITE.

GIANT, Giant Prod., Warner Bros.: MOSS MABRY and MARJORIE BEST.

★ THE KING AND I, 20th Century-Fox: IRENE SHARAFF.

THE TEN COMMANDMENTS, Motion Picture Assoc., Inc., Paramount: EDITH HEAD, RALPH JESTER, JOHN

JENSEN, DOROTHY JEAKINS, and ARNOLD FRIBERG.

WAR AND PEACE, A Ponti-De Laurentiis Prod., Paramount (Italo-American): MARIE DE MATTEIS.

*1957 Thirtieth Year**

AN AFFAIR TO REMEMBER, Jerry Wald Prods., Inc., 20th Century-Fox: CHARLES LEMAIRE.

FUNNY FACE, Paramount: EDITH HEAD and HUBERT DE GIVENCHY.

★ LES GIRLS, Sol C. Siegel Prods., Inc., M-G-M: ORRY-KELLY.

PAL JOEY, Essex-George Sidney Prod., Columbia: JEAN LOUIS.

RAINTREE COUNTY, Metro-Goldwyn-Mayer: WALTER PLUNKETT.

1958 Thirty-first Year

BELL, BOOK AND CANDLE, Phoenix Prods., Inc., Columbia: JEAN LOUIS.

THE BUCCANEER, Cecil B. DeMille, Paramount: RALPH JESTER, EDITH HEAD, and JOHN JENSEN.

A CERTAIN SMILE, 20th Century-Fox: CHARLES LEMAIRE and MARY WILLS.

★ GIGI, Arthur Freed Prods., Inc., M-G-M: CECIL BEATON.

SOME CAME RUNNING, Sol C. Siegel Prods., Inc., M-G-M: WALTER PLUNKETT.

1959 Thirty-second Year†

Black and White

CAREER, Hal Wallis Prods., Paramount: EDITH HEAD.

THE DIARY OF ANNE FRANK, 20th Century-Fox: CHARLES LEMAIRE and MARY WILLS.

THE GAZEBO, Avon Prod., M-G-M: HELEN ROSE.

★ SOME LIKE IT HOT, Ashton Prods. & The Mirisch Co., UA: ORRY-KELLY.

THE YOUNG PHILADELPHIANS, Warner Bros.: HOWARD SHOUP.

Color

★ BEN-HUR, Metro-Goldwyn-Mayer: ELIZABETH HAFFENDEN.

THE BEST OF EVERYTHING, Company of Artists, Inc., 20th Century-Fox: ADELE PALMER.

THE BIG FISHERMAN, Rowland V. Lee Prods., Buena Vista Film Dist. Co., Inc.: RENIE.

THE FIVE PENNIES, Dena Prod., Paramount: EDITH HEAD.

PORGY AND BESS, Samuel Goldwyn Prods., Columbia: IRENE SHARAFF.

1960 Thirty-third Year

Black and White

★ THE FACTS OF LIFE, Panama and Frank Prod., UA: EDITH HEAD and EDWARD STEVENSON.

NEVER ON SUNDAY, Melinafilm Prod., Lopert Pictures Corp. (Greek): DENNY VACHLIOTI.

THE RISE AND FALL OF LEGS DIAMOND, United States Prod., Warner Bros.: HOWARD SHOUP.

SEVEN THIEVES, 20th Century-Fox: BILL THOMAS.

THE VIRGIN SPRING, Svensk Filmindustri Prod., Janus Films, Inc. (Swedish): MARIK VOS.

Color

CAN-CAN, Suffolk-Cummings Prods., 20th Century-Fox: IRENE SHARAFF.

*Rules changed this year to one award for Costume Design instead of separate awards for black-and-white and color films.

†Rules changed this year to two awards for Costume Design: one for black-and-white films and one for color films.

MIDNIGHT LACE, Ross Hunter-Arwin Prod., U-I: IRENE.

PEPE, G.S.-Posa Films International Prod., Columbia: EDITH HEAD.

★ SPARTACUS, Bryna Prods., Inc., U-I: VALLES and BILL THOMAS.

SUNRISE AT CAMPOBELLO, Schary Prod., Warner Bros.: MARJORIE BEST.

1961 Thirty-fourth Year

Black and White

THE CHILDREN'S HOUR, Mirisch-Worldwide Prod., UA: DOROTHY JEAKINS.

CLAUDELLE INGLISH, Warner Bros.: HOWARD SHOUP.

JUDGMENT AT NUREMBERG, Stanley Kramer Prod., UA: JEAN LOUIS.

★ LA DOLCE VITA, Riama Film Prod., Astor Pictures, Inc. (Italian): PIERO GHERARDI.

YOJIMBO, Toho Company, Ltd. and Kurosawa Prod., Toho Company, Ltd. (Japanese): YOSHIRO MURAKI.

Color

BABES IN TOYLAND, Walt Disney Prods., Buena Vista Distribution Co., Inc.: BILL THOMAS.

BACK STREET, Universal-International-Ross Hunter Prods., Inc.-Carrollton, Inc., U-I: JEAN LOUIS.

FLOWER DRUM SONG, Universal-International-Ross Hunter Prod., in association with Joseph Fields, U-I: IRENE SHARAFF.

POCKETFUL OF MIRACLES, Franton Prod., UA: EDITH HEAD and WALTER PLUNKETT.

★ WEST SIDE STORY, Mirisch Pictures, Inc., and B and P Enterprises, Inc., UA: IRENE SHARAFF.

1962 Thirty-fifth Year

Black and White

DAYS OF WINE AND ROSES, Martin Manulis-Jalem Prod., Warner Bros.: DON FELD.

THE MAN WHO SHOT LIBERTY VALANCE, John Ford Prod., Paramount: EDITH HEAD.

THE MIRACLE WORKER, Playfilms Prod., UA: RUTH MORLEY.

PHAEDRA, Jules Dassin-Melinafilm Prod., Lopert Pictures: DENNY VACHLIOTI.

★ WHAT EVER HAPPENED TO BABY JANE?, Seven Arts-Associates and Aldrich Co. Prod., Warner Bros.: NORMA KOCH.

Color

BON VOYAGE, Walt Disney Prod., Buena Vista Distribution Co.: BILL THOMAS.

GYPSY, Warner Bros.: ORRY-KELLY.

THE MUSIC MAN, Warner Bros.: DOROTHY JEAKINS.

MY GEISHA, Sachiko Prod., Paramount: EDITH HEAD.

★ THE WONDERFUL WORLD OF THE BROTHERS GRIMM, Metro-Goldwyn-Mayer and Cinerama: MARY WILLS.

1963 Thirty-sixth Year

Black and White

★ FEDERICO FELLINI'S 8½, Cineriz Prod., Embassy Pictures: PIERO GHERARDI.

LOVE WITH THE PROPER STRANGER, Boardwalk-Rona Prod., Paramount: EDITH HEAD.

THE STRIPPER, Jerry Wald Prods., 20th Century-Fox: TRAVILLA.

TOYS IN THE ATTIC, Mirisch-Claude Prod., UA: BILL THOMAS.

WIVES AND LOVERS, Hal Wallis Prod., Paramount: EDITH HEAD.

Color

THE CARDINAL, Gamma Prod., Columbia: DONALD BROOKS.

★ CLEOPATRA, 20th Century-Fox Ltd.-MCL Films S.A.-WALWA Films S.A. Prod., 20th Century-Fox:

IRENE SHARAFF, VITTORIO NINO NOVARESE, and RENIE.

HOW THE WEST WAS WON, Metro-Goldwyn-Mayer and Cinerama: WALTER PLUNKETT.

THE LEOPARD, Titanus Prod., 20th Century-Fox: PIERO TOSI.

A NEW KIND OF LOVE, Llenroc Prods., Paramount: EDITH HEAD.

1964 Thirty-seventh Year

Black and White

A HOUSE IS NOT A HOME, Clarence Greene-Russell Rouse Prod., Embassy Pictures: EDITH HEAD.

HUSH . . . HUSH, SWEET CHARLOTTE, Associates and Aldrich Prod., 20th Century-Fox: NORMA KOCH.

KISSES FOR MY PRESIDENT, Pearlayne Prod., Warner Bros.: HOWARD SHOUP.

★ THE NIGHT OF THE IGUANA, Seven Arts Prod., M-G-M: DOROTHY JEAKINS.

THE VISIT, Cinecitta-Dear Film-Les Films du Siècle-P.E.C.S. Prod., 20th Century-Fox: RENE HUBERT.

Color

BECKET, Hal Wallis Prod., Paramount: MARGARET FURSE.

MARY POPPINS, Walt Disney Prods.: TONY WALTON.

★ MY FAIR LADY, Warner Bros.: CECIL BEATON.

THE UNSINKABLE MOLLY BROWN, Marten Prod., M-G-M: MORTON HAACK.

WHAT A WAY TO GO, Apjac-Orchard Prod., 20th Century-Fox: EDITH HEAD and MOSS MABRY.

1965 Thirty-eighth Year

Black and White

★ DARLING, Anglo-Amalgamated, Ltd. Prod., Embassy: JULIE HARRIS.

MORITURI, Arcola-Colony Prod., 20th Century-Fox: MOSS MABRY.

A RAGE TO LIVE, Mirisch Corp. of Delaware-Araho Prod., United Artists: HOWARD SHOUP.

SHIP OF FOOLS, Columbia: BILL THOMAS and JEAN LOUIS.

THE SLENDER THREAD, Paramount: EDITH HEAD.

Color

THE AGONY AND THE ECSTASY, International Classics Prod., 20th Century-Fox: VITTORIO NINO NOVARESE.

★ DOCTOR ZHIVAGO, Sostar S.A.-Metro-Goldwyn-Mayer British Studios, Ltd. Prod., M-G-M: PHYLLIS DALTON.

THE GREATEST STORY EVER TOLD, George Stevens Prod., United Artists: VITTORIO NINO NOVARESE and MARJORIE BEST.

INSIDE DAISY CLOVER, Park Place Prod., Warner Bros.: EDITH HEAD and BILL THOMAS.

THE SOUND OF MUSIC, Argyle Enterprises Prod., 20th Century-Fox: DOROTHY JEAKINS.

1966 Thirty-ninth Year

Black and White

THE GOSPEL ACCORDING TO ST. MATTHEW, Arco-Lux Cie Cinematografique de France Prod., Walter Reade-Continental Distributing: DANILO DONATI.

MANDRAGOLA, Europix-Consolidated: DANILO DONATI.

MISTER BUDDWING, DDD-Cherokee Prod., M-G-M: HELEN ROSE.

MORGAN!, Quintra Films, Ltd. Prod., Cinema V: JOCELYN RICKARDS.

★ WHO'S AFRAID OF VIRGINIA WOOLF?, Chenault Prod., Warner Bros.: IRENE SHARAFF.

Color

GAMBIT, Universal: JEAN LOUIS.

HAWAII, Mirisch Corp. of Delaware

Prod., United Artists: DOROTHY JEAKINS.

JULIET OF THE SPIRITS, Rizzoli Films S.P.A. Prod., Rizzoli Films: PIERO GHERARDI.

★ A MAN FOR ALL SEASONS, Highland Films, Ltd. Prod., Columbia: ELIZABETH HAFFENDEN and JOAN BRIDGE.

THE OSCAR, Greene-Rouse Prod., Embassy: EDITH HEAD.

*1967 Fortieth Year**

BONNIE AND CLYDE, Tatira-Hiller Prod., Warner Bros.-Seven Arts: THEADORA VAN RUNKLE.

★ CAMELOT, Warner Bros.-Seven Arts: JOHN TRUSCOTT.

THE HAPPIEST MILLIONAIRE, Walt Disney Prods., Buena Vista Dist. Co.: BILL THOMAS.

THE TAMING OF THE SHREW, Royal Films International-Films Artistici Internazionali S.r.L. Prod., Columbia: IRENE SHARAFF and DANILO DONATI.

THOROUGHLY MODERN MILLIE, Ross Hunter-Universal Prod., Universal: JEAN LOUIS.

1968 Forty-first Year

THE LION IN WINTER, Haworth Prods., Avco Embassy: MARGARET FURSE.

OLIVER!, Romulus Films, Columbia: PHYLLIS DALTON.

PLANET OF THE APES, APJAC Prods., 20th Century-Fox: MORTON HAACK.

★ ROMEO & JULIET, B.H.E. Film-Verona Prod.-Dino De Laurentiis Cinematografica Prod., Paramount: DANILO DONATI.

STAR!, Robert Wise Prod., 20th Century-Fox: DONALD BROOKS.

1969 Forty-second Year

★ ANNE OF THE THOUSAND DAYS, Hal B. Wallis-Universal Pictures, Ltd. Prod., Universal: MARGARET FURSE.

GAILY, GAILY, Mirisch-Cartier Prod., United Artists: RAY AGHAYAN.

HELLO, DOLLY!, Chenault Prods., 20th Century-Fox: IRENE SHARAFF.

SWEET CHARITY, Universal: EDITH HEAD.

THEY SHOOT HORSES, DON'T THEY?, Chartoff-Winkler-Pollack Prod., ABC Pictures Presentation, Cinerama: DON-FELD.

1970 Forty-third Year

AIRPORT, Ross Hunter-Universal Prod., Universal: EDITH HEAD.

★ CROMWELL, Irving Allen, Ltd. Prod., Columbia: NINO NOVARESE.

DARLING LILI, Geoffrey Prods., Paramount: DONALD BROOKS and JACK BEAR.

THE HAWAIIANS, Mirisch Prods., United Artists: BILL THOMAS.

SCROOGE, Waterbury Films, Ltd. Prod., Cinema Center Films Presentation, National General: MARGARET FURSE.

1971 Forty-fourth Year

BEDKNOBS AND BROOMSTICKS, Walt Disney Prods., Buena Vista Distribution Company: BILL THOMAS.

DEATH IN VENICE, An Alfa Cinematografica-P.E.C.F. Prod., Warner Bros.: PIERO TOSI.

MARY, QUEEN OF SCOTS, A Hal Wallis-Universal Pictures, Ltd. Prod., Universal: MARGARET FURSE.

★ NICHOLAS AND ALEXANDRA, A Horizon Pictures Prod., Columbia:

*Rules changed this year to one award for Costume Design instead of separate awards for black-and-white and color films.

YVONNE BLAKE and ANTONIO CASTILLO.

WHAT'S THE MATTER WITH HELEN?, A Filmways-Raymax Prod., UA: MORTON HAACK.

1972 Forty-fifth Year

THE GODFATHER, An Albert S. Ruddy Prod., Paramount: ANNA HILL JOHNSTONE.

LADY SINGS THE BLUES, A Motown-Weston-Furie Prod., Paramount: BOB MACKIE, RAY AGHAYAN, and NORMA KOCH.

THE POSEIDON ADVENTURE, An Irwin Allen Prod., 20th Century-Fox: PAUL ZASTUPNEVICH.

★ TRAVELS WITH MY AUNT, Robert Fryer Prods., Metro-Goldwyn-Mayer: ANTHONY POWELL.

YOUNG WINSTON, An Open Road Films, Ltd. Prod., Columbia: ANTHONY MENDLESON.

1973 Forty-sixth Year

CRIES AND WHISPERS, A Svenska Filminstitutet-Cinematograph AB Prod., New World Pictures: MARIK VOS.

LUDWIG, A Mega Film S.p.A. Prod., Metro-Goldwyn-Mayer: PIERO TOSI.

★ THE STING, A Universal-Bill/Phillips-George Roy Hill Film Prod., Zanuck/Brown Presentation, Universal: EDITH HEAD.

TOM SAWYER, An Arthur P. Jacobs Prod., Reader's Digest Presentation, UA: DONFELD.

THE WAY WE WERE, Rastar Prods., Columbia: DOROTHY JEAKINS and MOSS MABRY.

1974 Forty-seventh Year

CHINATOWN, A Robert Evans Prod., Paramount: ANTHEA SYLBERT.

DAISY MILLER, A Directors Company Prod., Paramount: JOHN FURNESS.

THE GODFATHER PART II, A Coppola Company Prod., Paramount: THEADORA VAN RUNKLE.

★ THE GREAT GATSBY, A David Merrick Prod., Paramount: THEONI V. ALDREDGE.

MURDER ON THE ORIENT EXPRESS, A G. W. Films, Ltd. Prod., Paramount: TONY WALTON.

1975 Forty-eighth Year

★ BARRY LYNDON, A Hawk Films, Ltd. Production, Warner Bros.: ULLA-BRITT SODERLUND and MILENA CANONERO.

THE FOUR MUSKETEERS, A Film Trust S.A. Production, 20th Century-Fox: YVONNE BLAKE and RON TALSKY.

FUNNY LADY, A Rastar Pictures Production, Columbia: RAY AGHAYAN and BOB MACKIE.

THE MAGIC FLUTE, A Sveriges Radio A.B. Production, Surrogate Releasing: HENNY NOREMARK and KARIN ERSKINE.

THE MAN WHO WOULD BE KING, An Allied Artists-Columbia Pictures Production, Allied Artists: EDITH HEAD.

1976 Forty-ninth Year

BOUND FOR GLORY, The Bound for Glory Company Production, United Artists: WILLIAM THEISS.

★ FELLINI'S CASANOVA, A P.E.A.-Produzioni Europee Associate S.p.A. Production, Universal: DANILO DONATI.

THE INCREDIBLE SARAH, A Helen M. Strauss-Reader's Digest Films, Ltd. Production, Seymour Borde and Associates: ANTHONY MENDLESON.

THE PASSOVER PLOT, Coast Industries-Golan-Globus Productions, Ltd., Atlas Films: MARY WILLS.

THE SEVEN PERCENT SOLUTION, A Herbert Ross Film/Winitsky-Sellers Production, A Universal Release: ALAN BARRETT.

1977 Fiftieth Year

AIRPORT '77, A Jennings Lang Production, Universal: EDITH HEAD and BURTON MILLER.

JULIA, A Twentieth Century-Fox Production, 20th Century-Fox: ANTHEA SYLBERT.

A LITTLE NIGHT MUSIC, A Sascha-Wien Film Production in association with Elliott Kastner, New World Pictures: FLORENCE KLOTZ.

THE OTHER SIDE OF MIDNIGHT, A Frank Yablans Presentations Production, 20th Century-Fox: IRENE SHARAFF.

★ STAR WARS, A Twentieth Century-Fox Production, 20th Century-Fox: JOHN MOLLO.

1978 Fifty-first Year

CARAVANS, An Ibex Films-F.I.D.C.I. Production, Universal: RENIE CONLEY.

DAYS OF HEAVEN, An OP Production, Paramount: PATRICIA NORRIS.

★ DEATH ON THE NILE, A John Brabourne-Richard Goodwin Production, Paramount: ANTHONY POWELL.

THE SWARM, A Warner Bros. Production, Warner Bros.: PAUL ZASTUPNEVICH.

THE WIZ, A Motown/Universal Pictures Production, Universal: TONY WALTON.

1979 Fifty-second Year

AGATHA, A Sweetwall Production in association with Casablanca Filmworks. First Artists Presentation, Warner Bros.: SHIRLEY RUSSELL.

★ ALL THAT JAZZ, A Columbia/ Twentieth Century-Fox Production, 20th Century-Fox: ALBERT WOLSKY.

BUTCH AND SUNDANCE: THE EARLY DAYS, A Twentieth Century-Fox Production, 20th Century-Fox: WILLIAM THEISS.

THE EUROPEANS, Merchant Ivory Productions, Levitt-Pickman: JUDY MOORCROFT.

LA CAGE AUX FOLLES, A Les Productions Artistes Associés De Ma Produzione SPA Production, United Artists: PIERO TOSI and AMBRA DANON.

1980 Fifty-third Year

THE ELEPHANT MAN, A Brooksfilms, Ltd. Production, Paramount: PATRICIA NORRIS.

MY BRILLIANT CAREER, A Margaret Fink Films Pty., Ltd. Production, Analysis Film Releasing: ANNA SENIOR.

SOMEWHERE IN TIME, A Rastar-Stephen Deutsch-Universal Pictures Production, Universal: JEAN-PIERRE DORLEAC.

★ TESS, A Renn-Burrill Co-production with the participation of the Société Française de Production (S.F.P.), Columbia: ANTHONY POWELL.

WHEN TIME RAN OUT, A Warner Bros. Production, Warner Bros.: PAUL ZASTUPNEVICH.

1981 Fifty-fourth Year

★ CHARIOTS OF FIRE, Enigma Productions Limited, The Ladd Company/Warner Bros.: MILENA CANONERO.

THE FRENCH LIEUTENANT'S WOMAN, A Parlon Production, United Artists: TOM RAND.

PENNIES FROM HEAVEN, A Metro-Goldwyn-Mayer/Herbert Ross/Hera Production, Metro-Goldwyn-Mayer: BOB MACKIE.

RAGTIME, A Ragtime Production, Paramount: ANNA HILL JOHNSTONE.

REDS, A J.R.S. Production, Paramount: SHIRLEY RUSSELL.

1982 Fifty-fifth Year

★ GANDHI, An Indo-British Films Production, Columbia: JOHN MOLLO and BHANU ATHAIYA.

LA TRAVIATA, An Accent Films B.V. Production in association with RAI-Radiotelevisione Italiana, Producers Sales Organization: PIERO TOSI.

SOPHIE'S CHOICE, An ITC Entertainment Presentation of a Pakula-Barish Production, Universal/ A.F.D.: ALBERT WOLSKY.

TRON, A Walt Disney Production, Buena Vista Distribution: ELOIS JENSSEN and ROSANNA NORTON.

VICTOR/VICTORIA, A Metro-Goldwyn-Mayer Production, M-G-M/UA: PATRICIA NORRIS.

1983 Fifty-sixth Year

CROSS CREEK, A Robert B. Radnitz/ Martin Ritt/Thorn EMI Films Production, Universal: JOE I. TOMPKINS.

★ FANNY AND ALEXANDER, A Cinematograph AB for the Swedish Film Institute/the Swedish Television SVT 1, Sweden/Gaumont, France/ Personafilm and Tobis Filmkunst, BRD Production, Embassy: MARIK VOS.

HEART LIKE A WHEEL, An Aurora Film Partners/Twentieth Century-Fox Production, 20th Century-Fox: WILLIAM WARE THEISS.

THE RETURN OF MARTIN GUERRE, A Société Française de Production Cinematographique/ Société de Productions des Films Marcel Dassault—FR 3 Production, European International Distribution: ANNE-MARIE MARCHAND.

ZELIG, A Jack Rollins and Charles H. Joffe Production, Orion through Warner Bros.: SANTO LOQUASTO.

1984 Fifty-seventh Year

★ AMADEUS, A Saul Zaentz Company Production, Orion: THEODOR PISTEK.

THE BOSTONIANS, A Merchant Ivory Production, Almi Pictures: JENNY BEAVAN and JOHN BRIGHT.

A PASSAGE TO INDIA, A G. W. Films Limited Production, Columbia: JUDY MOORCROFT.

PLACES IN THE HEART, A Tri-Star Pictures Production, Tri-Star: ANN ROTH.

2010, A Metro-Goldwyn-Mayer Presentation of a Peter Hyams Film Production, M-G-M/UA: PATRICIA NORRIS.

1985 Fifty-eighth Year

THE COLOR PURPLE, a Warner Bros. Production, Warner Bros.: AGGIE GUERARD RODGERS.

THE JOURNEY OF NATTY GANN, a Walt Disney Pictures and Silver Screen Partners II Production, Buena Vista: ALBERT WOLSKY.

OUT OF AFRICA, a Universal Pictures Limited Production, Universal: MILENA CANONERO.

PRIZZI'S HONOR, an ABC Motion Pictures Production, 20th Century-Fox: DONFELD.

★ RAN, a Greenwich Film/Nippon Herald Films/Herald Ace Production, Orion Classics: EMI WADA.

1986 Fifty-ninth Year

THE MISSION, A Warner Bros./ Goldcrest and Kingsmere Production, Warner Bros.: ENRICO SABBATINI.

OTELLO, A Cannon Production, Cannon: ANNA ANNI.

PEGGY SUE GOT MARRIED, A Rastar Production, Tri-Star: THEADORA VAN RUNKLE.

PIRATES, A Carthago Films Production in association with Accent Cominco, Cannon: ANTHONY POWELL.

★ A ROOM WITH A VIEW, A Merchant Ivory Production, Cinecom JENNY BEAVAN and JOHN BRIGHT.

1987 Sixtieth Year

THE DEAD, A Liffey Films Production, Vestron: DOROTHY JEAKINS.

EMPIRE OF THE SUN, A Warner Bros. Production, Warner Bros.: BOB RINGWOOD.

★ THE LAST EMPEROR, A Hemdale Film Production, Columbia: JAMES ACHESON.

MAURICE, A Merchant Ivory Production, Cinecom Pictures: JENNY BEAVAN and JOHN BRIGHT.

THE UNTOUCHABLES, An Art Linson Production, Paramount: MARILYN VANCE-STRAKER.

1988 Sixty-first Year

COMING TO AMERICA, An Eddie Murphy Production, Paramount: DEBORAH NADOOLMAN.

★ DANGEROUS LIAISONS, A Lorimar Production, Warner Bros.: JAMES ACHESON.

A HANDFUL OF DUST, A Stage Screen Production, New Line: JANE ROBINSON.

SUNSET, A Hudson Hawk Production, Tri-Star: PATRICIA NORRIS.

TUCKER: THE MAN AND HIS DREAM, A Lucasfilm Production, Paramount: MILENA CANONERO.

1989 Sixty-second Year

THE ADVENTURES OF BARON MUNCHAUSEN, A Prominent Features and Laura Film Production, Columbia: GABRIELLA PESCUCCI.

DRIVING MISS DAISY, A Zanuck Company Production, Warner Bros.: ELIZABETH MCBRIDE.

HARLEM NIGHTS, An Eddie Murphy Production, Paramount: JOE I. TOMPKINS.

★ HENRY V, A Renaissance Films Production, Samuel Goldwyn Company: PHYLLIS DALTON.

VALMONT, A Claude Berri and Renn Production, Orion: THEODOR PISTEK.

1990 Sixty-third Year

AVALON, A Tri-Star Production, Tri-Star: GLORIA GRESHAM.

★ CYRANO DE BERGERAC, A Hachette Premiere Production, Orion Classics: FRANCA SQUARCIAPINO.

DANCES WITH WOLVES, A Tig Production, Orion: ELSA ZAMPARELLI.

DICK TRACY, A Touchstone Pictures Production, Buena Vista: MILENA CANONERO.

HAMLET, An Icon Production, Warner Bros.: MAURIZIO MILLENOTTI.

1991 Sixty-fourth Year

THE ADDAMS FAMILY, A Scott Rudin Production, Paramount: RUTH MYERS.

BARTON FINK, A Barton Circle Production, Twentieth Century-Fox: RICHARD HORNUNG.

★ BUGSY, A Tri-Star Pictures Production, Tri-Star: ALBERT WOLSKY.

HOOK, A Tri-Star Pictures Production, Tri-Star: ANTHONY POWELL.

MADAME BOVARY, An MK2/C.E.D./FR3 Films Production, Samuel Goldwyn Company: CORRINE JORY.

1992 Sixty-fifth Year

★ BRAM STOKER'S DRACULA, A Columbia Pictures Production, Columbia: EIKO ISHIOKA.

ENCHANTED APRIL, A BBC Films Production in association with

Greenpoint Films, Miramax: SHEENA NAPIER.

HOWARDS END, A Merchant Ivory Production, Sony Pictures Classics: JENNY BEAVAN and JOHN BRIGHT.

MALCOLM X, A By Any Means Necessary Cinema Production, Warner Bros.: RUTH CARTER.

TOYS, A 20th Century-Fox Production, 20th Century-Fox.: ALBERT WOLSKY.

Make-up

Prior to the establishment of a Make-up Award for the 1981 Oscars, distinguished achievements in this field were recognized by Honorary Awards. (William Tuttle in 1964 and John Chambers in 1968 received such recognition for make-up work.)

The rules for this new award require the president of the Academy to appoint a committee of three which in turn forms a Make-up Award Committee made up of qualified make-up artists, hair stylists, art directors, cinematographers, and other experts in the field of make-up technology.

Make-up and hair stylist members of the Academy select achievements from the year's eligible films. The producers of the films chosen for further balloting (up to a maximum of seven films) provide the name of the person principally responsible for make-up achievement and furnish to the Academy a film clip (not to exceed ten minutes) that demonstrates the work.

Members of the Make-up Award Committee screen these clips and vote according to a predetermined point system. The committee has three options:

1. If no films achieve a satisfactory score, the Committee may recommend to the Academy Board of Governors that no award be given.
2. If only one film achieves a satisfactory score, the Committee shall recommend that a Special Achievement Award for make-up be given.
3. If two or more films achieve satisfactory scores, the Committee shall recommend up to three films to be nominated for the Make-up Award. In this case, the winner is determined by the entire membership of the Academy.

1981 Fifty-fourth Year

★ AN AMERICAN WEREWOLF IN LONDON, A Lycanthrope/ Polygram/Universal Pictures Production, Universal: RICK BAKER.

HEARTBEEPS, A Michael Phillips/ Universal Pictures Production, Universal: STAN WINSTON.

1982 Fifty-fifth Year

GANDHI, An Indo-British Films Production, Columbia: TOM SMITH.

★ QUEST FOR FIRE, An International Cinema Corporation Production, 20th Century-Fox: SARAH MONZANI and MICHÈLE BURKE.

1983 Fifty-sixth Year

None.

1984 Fifty-seventh Year

★ AMADEUS, A Saul Zaentz Company Production, Orion: PAUL LEBLANC and DICK SMITH.

GREYSTOKE: THE LEGEND OF TARZAN, LORD OF THE APES, A Warner Bros. Production, Warner Bros.: RICK BAKER and PAUL ENGELEN.

2010, A Metro-Goldwyn-Mayer

Presentation of a Peter Hyams Film Production, M-G-M/UA: MICHAEL WESTMORE.

1985 Fifty-eighth Year

THE COLOR PURPLE, a Warner Bros. Production, Warner Bros.: KEN CHASE.

★ MASK, a Universal Pictures Production, Universal: MICHAEL WESTMORE and ZOLTAN.

REMO WILLIAMS: THE ADVENTURE BEGINS, a Dick Clark/Larry Spiegel/ Mel Bergman Production, Orion: CARL FULLERTON.

1986 Fifty-ninth Year

THE CLAN OF THE CAVE BEAR, A Warner Bros. and PSO Production, Warner Bros.: MICHAEL G. WESTMORE and MICHÈLE BURKE.

★ THE FLY, A Brooksfilm Ltd. Production, 20th Century-Fox: CHRIS WALAS and STEPHAN DUPUIS.

LEGEND, A Legend Company Production, Universal: ROB BOTTIN, and PETER ROBB-KING.

1987 Sixtieth Year

HAPPY NEW YEAR, A Columbia Pictures Production, Columbia: BOB LADEN.

★ HARRY AND THE HENDERSONS, A Universal/ Amblin Entertainment Production, Universal: RICK BAKER.

1988 Sixty-first Year

★ BEETLEJUICE, A Geffen Film Company Production, Geffen/Warner Bros.: VE NEILL, STEVE LA PORTE, and ROBERT SHORT.

COMING TO AMERICA, An Eddie Murphy Production, Paramount: RICK BAKER.

SCROOGED, An Art Linson Production, Paramount: TOM BURMAN and BARI DRIEBAND-BURMAN.

1989 Sixty-second Year

THE ADVENTURES OF BARON MUNCHAUSEN, A Prominent Features and Laura Film Production, Columbia: MAGGIE WESTON and FABRIZIO SFORZA.

DAD, A Universal Pictures/Amblin Entertainment Production, Universal: DICK SMITH, KEN DIAZ, and GREG NELSON.

★ DRIVING MISS DAISY, A Zanuck Company Production, Warner Bros.: MANLIO ROCCHETTI, LYNN BARBER, and KEVIN HANEY.

1990 Sixty-third Year

CYRANO DE BERGERAC, A Hachette Premiere Production, Orion Classics: MICHÈLE BURKE and JEAN-PIERRE EYCHENNE.

★ DICK TRACY, A Touchstone Pictures Production, Buena Vista: JOHN CAGLIONE, JR., and DOUG DREXLER.

EDWARD SCISSORHANDS, A 20th Century-Fox Production, 20th Century-Fox: VE NEILL and STAN WINSTON.

1991 Sixty-fourth Year

HOOK, A Tri-Star Pictures Production, Tri-Star: CHRISTINA SMITH, MONTAGUE WESTMORE, and GREG CANNOM.

STAR TREK VI: THE UNDISCOVERED COUNTRY, A Paramount Pictures Production, Paramount: MICHAEL MILLS, EDWARD FRENCH, and RICHARD SNELL.

★ TERMINATOR 2: JUDGMENT DAY, A Carolco Production, Tri-Star: STAN WINSTON and JEFF DAWN.

1992 Sixty-fifth Year

BATMAN RETURNS, A Warner Bros. Production, Warner Bros.: VE NEILL, RONNIE SPECTER, and STAN WINSTON.

★ BRAM STOKER'S DRACULA, A Columbia Pictures Production, Columbia: GREG CANNOM, MICHÈLE BURKE, and MATTHEW W. MUNGLE.

HOFFA, A 20th Century-Fox Production, 20th Century-Fox: VE NEILL, GREG CANNOM, and JOHN BLAKE.

Visual Effects

Visual effects have been recognized by the Academy under a variety of category names. From 1939 through 1962, the Special Effects category honored both visual and sound effects. In 1963 the Academy separated this category into Special Visual Effects and Sound Effects. The former was an annual award through 1971; the latter through 1967. Visual effects were recognized by Special Achievement Awards from 1972 until 1977 when the present annual award category was established.

When a single achievement in visual effects is recommended for recognition by the Visual Effects Award Committee, the Academy Board of Governors may vote a Special Achievement Award. When two or three films are nominated by the committee, present rules call for these nominees to be placed in an annual award category called Visual Effects. As with all annual awards, the winner is chosen by the entire Academy membership.

Achievements in this field are judged "on the basis of:

(a) consideration of the contribution the visual effects make to the overall production and
(b) the artistry, skill and fidelity with which the visual illusions are achieved."

1977 Fiftieth Year

CLOSE ENCOUNTERS OF THE THIRD KIND, Close Encounter Productions, Columbia: ROY ARBOGAST, DOUGLAS TRUMBULL, MATTHEW YURICICH, GREGORY JEIN, and RICHARD YURICICH.

★ STAR WARS, A Twentieth Century-Fox Production, 20th Century-Fox: JOHN STEARS, JOHN DYKSTRA, RICHARD EDLUND, GRANT McCUNE, and ROBERT BLALACK.

1978 Fifty-first Year

None. Visual Effects this year were recognized by a Special Achievement Award rather than an annual award.

1979 Fifty-second Year

★ ALIEN, Twentieth Century-Fox Productions Limited, 20th Century-Fox: H. R. GIGER, CARLO RAMBALDI, BRIAN JOHNSON, NICK ALLDER, and DENYS AYLING.

THE BLACK HOLE, Walt Disney Productions, Buena Vista Distribution Co.: PETER ELLENSHAW, ART CRUICKSHANK, EUSTACE LYCETT, DANNY LEE, HARRISON ELLENSHAW, and JOE HALE.

MOONRAKER, Eon Productions Ltd., United Artists: DEREK MEDDINGS, PAUL WILSON, and JOHN EVANS.

1941, An A-Team/Steven Spielberg Film Production, Universal-Columbia Presentation, Universal: WILLIAM A. FRAKER, A. D. FLOWERS, and GREGORY JEIN.

STAR TREK—THE MOTION PICTURE, A Century Associates Production, Paramount: DOUGLAS TRUMBULL,

JOHN DYKSTRA, RICHARD YURICICH, ROBERT SWARTHE, DAVE STEWART, and GRANT MCCUNE.

1980 Fifty-third Year

None. Visual Effects this year were recognized by a Special Achievement Award rather than an annual award.

1981 Fifty-fourth Year

DRAGONSLAYER, A Barwood/Robbins Production, Paramount: DENNIS MUREN, PHIL TIPPETT, KEN RALSTON, and BRIAN JOHNSON.

★ RAIDERS OF THE LOST ARK, A Lucasfilm Production, Paramount: RICHARD EDLUND, KIT WEST, BRUCE NICHOLSON, and JOE JOHNSTON.

1982 Fifty-fifth Year

BLADE RUNNER, A Michael Deeley-Ridley Scott Production, The Ladd Company/Sir Run Run Shaw: DOUGLAS TRUMBULL, RICHARD YURICICH, and DAVID DRYER.

★ E.T. THE EXTRA-TERRESTRIAL, A Universal Pictures Production, Universal: CARLO RAMBALDI, DENNIS MUREN, and KENNETH F. SMITH.

POLTERGEIST, A Metro-Goldwyn-Mayer/Steven Spielberg Production, M-G-M/UA: RICHARD EDLUND, MICHAEL WOOD, and BRUCE NICHOLSON.

1983 Fifty-sixth Year

None. Visual Effects this year were recognized by a Special Achievement Award rather than an annual award.

1984 Fifty-seventh Year

GHOSTBUSTERS, A Columbia Pictures Production, Columbia: RICHARD EDLUND, JOHN BRUNO, MARK VARGO, and CHUCK GASPAR.

★ INDIANA JONES AND THE TEMPLE OF DOOM, A Lucasfilm Production, Paramount: DENNIS MUREN, MICHAEL McALISTER, LORNE PETERSON, and GEORGE GIBBS.

2010, A Metro-Goldwyn-Mayer Presentation of a Peter Hyams Film Production, M-G-M/UA: RICHARD EDLUND, NEIL KREPELA, GEORGE JENSON, and MARK STETSON.

1985 Fifty-eighth Year

★ COCOON, A Fox/Zanuck-Brown Production, 20th Century-Fox: KEN RALSTON, RALPH McQUARRIE, SCOTT FARRAR, and DAVID BERRY.

RETURN TO OZ, A Walt Disney Pictures and Silver Screen Partners II Production, Buena Vista: WILL VINTON, IAN WINGROVE, ZORAN PERISIC, and MICHAEL LLOYD.

YOUNG SHERLOCK HOLMES, An Amblin Entertainment Production in association with Henry Winkler/Roger Birnbaum, Paramount: DENNIS MUREN, KIT WEST, JOHN ELLIS, and DAVID ALLEN.

1986 Fifty-ninth Year

★ ALIENS. A Twentieth Century-Fox Film Production, 20th Century-Fox: ROBERT SKOTAK, STAN WINSTON, JOHN RICHARDSON, and SUZANNE BENSON.

LITTLE SHOP OF HORRORS, A Geffen Company Production, Geffen Company through Warner Bros.: LYLE CONWAY, BRAN FERREN, and MARTIN GUTTERIDGE.

POLTERGEIST II: THE OTHER SIDE, A Victor-Grais Production, M-G-M: RICHARD EDLUND, JOHN BRUNO, GARRY WALLER, and WILLIAM NEIL.

1987 Sixtieth Year

★ INNERSPACE, A Warner Bros. Production, Warner Bros.: DENNIS

MUREN, WILLIAM GEORGE, HARLEY JESSUP, and KENNETH SMITH.

PREDATOR, A 20th Century-Fox Production, 20th Century-Fox: JOEL HYNEK, ROBERT M. GREENBERG, RICHARD GREENBERG, and STAN WINSTON.

1988 Sixty-first Year

DIE HARD, A 20th Century-Fox Production, 20th Century-Fox: RICHARD EDLUND, AL DISARRO, BRENT BOATES, and THAINE MORRIS.

★ WHO FRAMED ROGER RABBIT, An Amblin Entertainment and Touchstone Pictures Production, Buena Vista: KEN RALSTON, RICHARD WILLIAMS, EDWARD JONES, and GEORGE GIBBS.

WILLOW, A Lucasfilm Production in association with Imagine Entertainment Production, M-G-M: DENNIS MUREN, MICHAEL MCALISTER, PHIL TIPPETT, and CHRIS EVANS.

1989 Sixty-second Year

★ THE ABYSS, A 20th Century-Fox Film Production, 20th Century-Fox: JOHN BRUNO, DENNIS MUREN, HOYT YEATMAN, and DENNIS SKOTAK.

THE ADVENTURES OF BARON MUNCHAUSEN, A Prominent Features and Laura Film Production, Columbia: RICHARD CONWAY and KENT HOUSTON.

BACK TO THE FUTURE PART II, A Universal Pictures/Amblin Entertainment Production, Universal: KEN RALSTON, MICHAEL LANTIERI, JOHN BELL, and STEVE GAWLEY.

1990 Sixty-third Year

None. Visual Effects this year were recognized by a Special Achievement Award rather than an annual award.

1991 Sixty-fourth Year

BACKDRAFT, A Trilogy Entertainment Group/Brian Grazer Production, Universal: MIKAEL SALOMON, ALLEN HALL, CLAY PINNEY, and SCOTT FARRAR.

HOOK, A Tri-Star Pictures Production, Tri-Star: ERIC BREVIG, HARLEY JESSUP, MARK SULLIVAN, and MICHAEL LANTIERI.

★ TERMINATOR 2: JUDGMENT DAY, A Carolco Production, Tri-Star: DENNIS MUREN, STAN WINSTON, GENE WARREN, JR., and ROBERT SKOTAK.

1992 Sixty-fifth Year

ALIEN^3, A 20th Century-Fox Production, 20th Century-Fox: RICHARD EDLUND, ALEC GILLIS, TOM WOODRUFF, JR., and GEORGE GIBBS.

BATMAN RETURNS, A Warner Bros. Production, Warner Bros.: MICHAEL FINK, CRAIG BARRON, JOHN BRUNO, and DENNIS SKOTAK.

★ DEATH BECOMES HER, A Universal Pictures Production, Universal: KEN RALSTON, DOUG CHIANG, DOUG SMYTHE, and TOM WOODRUFF.

Sound Effects Editing

The Sound Effects Editing category, established as an annual award in 1982, has its origins in the Special Effects award, which, from 1939 to 1962, honored visual and audible achievements.

In 1963 the Academy split this category into Special Visual Effects and Sound Effects, and the latter was an annual award from 1963 to 1967. Present rules allow the Sound Effects Editing Award Committee three options:

1. If at least two but not more than three candidates are deemed worthy, the nominated achievements will be voted by the entire Academy membership as an annual award.
2. If only one achievement is deemed worthy, the committee may recommend to the Board of Governors that a Special Achievement award for Sound Effects Editing be given.
3. If no achievements receive sufficient scores in preliminary balloting, the committee may recommend that no award be given.

The award is generally given to the Supervising Sound Editor who is responsible for the "planning, creation, supervision, and execution of the sound effects editing" for the nominated film. In rare cases two individuals may be honored for a single achievement.

1982 Fifty-fifth Year

DAS BOOT, A Bavaria Atelier GmbH Production, Columbia: MIKE LE-MARE.

★ E.T. THE EXTRA-TERRESTRIAL, A Universal Pictures Production, Universal: CHARLES L. CAMPBELL and BEN BURTT.

POLTERGEIST, A Metro-Goldwyn-Mayer/Steven Spielberg Production, M-G-M/UA: STEPHEN HUNTER FLICK and RICHARD L. ANDERSON.

1983 Fifty-sixth Year

RETURN OF THE JEDI, A Lucasfilm Production, 20th Century-Fox: BEN BURTT.

★ THE RIGHT STUFF, A Robert Chartoff-Irwin Winkler Production, The Ladd Company through Warner Bros.: JAY BOEKELHEIDE.

1984 Fifty-seventh Year

None. Sound Effects Editing this year was recognized by a Special Achievement Award rather than an annual award.

1985 Fifty-eighth Year

★ BACK TO THE FUTURE, An Amblin Entertainment/Universal Pictures Production, Universal: CHARLES L. CAMPBELL and ROBERT RUTLEDGE.

LADYHAWKE, A Warner Bros. and 20th Century-Fox Production, Warner

Bros.: BOB HENDERSON and ALAN MURRAY.

RAMBO: FIRST BLOOD PART II, An Anabasis Investments Production, Tri-Star: FREDERICK J. BROWN.

1986 Fifty-ninth Year

★ ALIENS, A Twentieth Century-Fox Film Production, 20th Century-Fox: DON SHARPE.

STAR TREK IV: THE VOYAGE HOME, A Harve Bennett Production, Paramount: MARK MANGINI.

TOP GUN, A Don Simpson/Jerry Bruckheimer Production, Paramount: CECELIA HALL and GEORGE WATTERS II.

1987 Sixtieth Year

None. Sound Effects Editing this year was recognized by a Special Achievement Award rather than an annual award.

1988 Sixty-first Year

DIE HARD, A 20th Century-Fox Production, 20th Century-Fox: STEPHEN H. FLICK and RICHARD SHORR.

★ WHO FRAMED ROGER RABBIT, An Amblin Entertainment and Touchstone Pictures Production, Buena Vista: CHARLES L. CAMPBELL and LOUIS L. EDEMANN.

WILLOW, A Lucasfilm Production in association with Imagine Entertainment Production, M-G-M: BEN BURTT and RICHARD HYMNS.

1989 Sixty-second Year

BLACK RAIN, A Jaffe/Lansing Production in association with Michael Douglas, Paramount: MILTON C. BURROW and WILLIAM L. MANGER.

★ INDIANA JONES AND THE LAST CRUSADE, A Lucasfilm Ltd. Production, Paramount: BEN BURTT and RICHARD HYMNS.

LETHAL WEAPON 2, A Warner Bros. Production, Warner Bros.: ROBERT HENDERSON and ALAN ROBERT MURRAY.

1990 Sixty-third Year

FLATLINERS, A Stonebridge Entertainment Production, Columbia: CHARLES L. CAMPBELL and RICHARD FRANKLIN.

★ THE HUNT FOR RED OCTOBER, A Mace Neufeld/Jerry Sherlock Production, Paramount: CECELIA HALL and GEORGE WATTERS II.

TOTAL RECALL, A Carolco Pictures Production, Tri-Star: STEPHEN H. FLICK.

1991 Sixty-fourth Year

BACKDRAFT, A Trilogy Entertainment Group/Brian Grazer Production, Universal: GARY RYDSTROM and RICHARD HYMNS.

STAR TREK VI: THE UNDISCOVERED COUNTRY, A Paramount Pictures Production, Paramount: GEORGE WATTERS II and F. HUDSON MILLER.

★ TERMINATOR 2: JUDGMENT DAY, A Carolco Production, Tri-Star: GARY RYDSTROM and GLORIA S. BORDERS.

1992 Sixty-fifth Year

ALADDIN, A Walt Disney Pictures Production, Buena Vista: MARK MANGINI.

★ BRAM STOKER'S DRACULA, A Columbia Pictures Production, Columbia: TOM C. MCCARTHY and DAVID E. STONE.

UNDER SIEGE, A Northwest Production, Warner Bros.: JOHN LEVEQUE and BRUCE STAMBLER.

Short Films

The fifth annual Academy Awards covering 1931/32 saw the introduction of a Short Subjects category. The popularity of Walt Disney's Mickey Mouse and Silly Symphony films may have played a part in the establishment of the new category, and Disney's *Flowers and Trees*, the first film ever made in three-color Technicolor, was the first winner in the cartoon division. Ten of the first eleven cartoon awards went to Disney films.

For the first four years the category was divided into cartoon, comedy, and novelty, but in 1936, spurred by the innovative use of color in short subjects, these divisions were changed to cartoon, one-reel, two-reel, and color. Within two years, however, the widespread use of Technicolor made the latter division superfluous, and it was dropped. The divisions were changed once again in 1957 to their present form: cartoon and live action. (The words "animated film" were substituted for cartoon in 1971.) The category's name was changed from Short Subjects to Short Films in 1974. Films must not exceed thirty minutes in running time.

The distinction between Short Films—Live Action and Documentary Short Subject was for many years imprecise. In 1971 *Sentinels of Silence* won in both categories. The rules were changed to permit eligible films to be entered in one or the other category but not both. A later rule change made Documentary short subjects ineligible for consideration in the Short Films categories. The category of Live Action Short Film was discontinued after the 1992 Awards.

Entries in this category are submitted by the creators of the achievement and are screened by members of the Academy Short Films Branch who determine the nominees. Final voting is restricted to Academy members who attend a special screening of the nominated films.

1931/32 Fifth Year

Cartoons

★ FLOWERS AND TREES, Walt Disney, UA.

IT'S GOT ME AGAIN, Leon Schlesinger, Warner Bros.

MICKEY'S ORPHANS, Walt Disney, Columbia.

Comedy

THE LOUD MOUTH, Mack Sennett.

★ THE MUSIC BOX, Hal Roach, M-G-M (Laurel and Hardy).

SCRATCH-AS-CATCH-CAN, RKO Radio.

Novelty

SCREEN SOUVENIRS, Paramount.

SWING HIGH, Metro-Goldwyn-Mayer. (Sport Champion)

★ WRESTLING SWORDFISH, Mack Sennett, Educational. (Cannibals of the Deep)

1932/33 Sixth Year

Cartoons

BUILDING A BUILDING, Walt Disney, UA.

THE MERRY OLD SOUL, Walter Lantz, Universal.
★ THE THREE LITTLE PIGS, Walt Disney, UA.

Comedy

MISTER MUGG, Universal. (Comedies)
A PREFERRED LIST, Louis Brock, RKO Radio. (Headliner Series #5)
★ SO THIS IS HARRIS, Louis Brock, RKO Radio. (Special)

Novelty

★ KRAKATOA, Joe Rock, Educational. (Three-reel special)
MENU, Pete Smith, M-G-M. (Oddities)
THE SEA, Educational. (Battle for Life)

1934 Seventh Year

Cartoons

HOLIDAY LAND, Charles Mintz, Columbia.
JOLLY LITTLE ELVES, Universal.
★ THE TORTOISE AND THE HARE, Walt Disney, UA.

Comedy

★ LA CUCARACHA, RKO Radio. (Special)
MEN IN BLACK, Columbia. (Broadway Comedies)
WHAT, NO MEN!, Warner Bros. (Broadway Brevities)

Novelty

BOSOM FRIENDS, Educational. (Treasure Chest)
★ CITY OF WAX, Educational. (Battle for Life)
STRIKES AND SPARES, Metro-Goldwyn-Mayer. (Oddities)

1935 Eighth Year

Cartoons

THE CALICO DRAGON, Harman-Ising, M-G-M.
★ THREE ORPHAN KITTENS, Walt Disney, UA.
WHO KILLED COCK ROBIN?, Walt Disney, UA.

Comedy

★ HOW TO SLEEP, Metro-Goldwyn-Mayer. (Miniature)
OH, MY NERVES, Columbia. (Broadway Comedies)
TIT FOR TAT, Hal Roach, M-G-M. (Laurel and Hardy)

Novelty

AUDIOSCOPIKS, Metro-Goldwyn-Mayer. (Special)
CAMERA THRILLS, Universal. (Special)
★ WINGS OVER MT. EVEREST, Educational. (Special)

1936 Ninth Year

Cartoons

★ COUNTRY COUSIN, Walt Disney, UA.
OLD MILL POND, Harman-Ising, M-G-M.
SINBAD THE SAILOR, Paramount.

One Reel

★ BORED OF EDUCATION, Hal Roach, M-G-M. (Our Gang)
MOSCOW MOODS, Paramount. (Headliners)
WANTED, A MASTER, Pete Smith, M-G-M. (Pete Smith Specialties)

Two Reels

DOUBLE OR NOTHING, Warner Bros. (Broadway Brevities)
DUMMY ACHE, RKO Radio. (Edgar Kennedy Comedies)
★ THE PUBLIC PAYS, Metro-Goldwyn-Mayer. (Crime Doesn't Pay)

Color

★ GIVE ME LIBERTY, Warner Bros. (Broadway Brevities)
LA FIESTA DE SANTA BARBARA, Metro-Goldwyn-Mayer. (Musical Revues)
POPULAR SCIENCE J-6-2, Paramount.

1937 Tenth Year

Cartoons

EDUCATED FISH, Paramount.
THE LITTLE MATCH GIRL, Charles Mintz, Columbia.
★ THE OLD MILL, Walt Disney, RKO Radio.

One Reel

A NIGHT AT THE MOVIES, Metro-Goldwyn-Mayer. (Robert Benchley)
★ PRIVATE LIFE OF THE GANNETS, Educational.
ROMANCE OF RADIUM, Pete Smith, M-G-M. (Pete Smith Specialties)

Two Reels

DEEP SOUTH, RKO Radio. (Radio Musical Comedies)
SHOULD WIVES WORK, RKO Radio. (Leon Errol Comedies)
★ TORTURE MONEY, Metro-Goldwyn-Mayer. (Crime Doesn't Pay)

Color

THE MAN WITHOUT A COUNTRY, Warner Bros. (Broadway Brevities)
★ PENNY WISDOM, Pete Smith, M-G-M. (Pete Smith Specialties)
POPULAR SCIENCE J-7-1, Paramount.

1938 Eleventh Year

Cartoons

BRAVE LITTLE TAILOR, Walt Disney, RKO Radio.
★ FERDINAND THE BULL, Walt Disney, RKO Radio.
GOOD SCOUTS, Walt Disney, RKO Radio.
HUNKY AND SPUNKY, Paramount.
MOTHER GOOSE GOES HOLLYWOOD, Walt Disney, RKO Radio.

One Reel

THE GREAT HEART, Metro-Goldwyn-Mayer. (Miniature)
★ THAT MOTHERS MIGHT LIVE, Metro-Goldwyn-Mayer. (Miniature)
TIMBER TOPPERS, 20th Century-Fox. (Ed Thorgensen-Sports)

Two Reels

★ DECLARATION OF INDEPENDENCE, Warner Bros. (Historical Featurette)
SWINGTIME IN THE MOVIES, Warner Bros. (Broadway Brevities)
THEY'RE ALWAYS CAUGHT, Metro-Goldwyn-Mayer. (Crime Doesn't Pay)

1939 Twelfth Year

Cartoons

DETOURING AMERICA, Warner Bros.
PEACE ON EARTH, Metro-Goldwyn-Mayer.
THE POINTER, Walt Disney, RKO Radio.
★ THE UGLY DUCKLING, Walt Disney, RKO Radio.

One Reel

★ BUSY LITTLE BEARS, Paramount. (Paragraphics)
INFORMATION PLEASE, RKO Radio.
PROPHET WITHOUT HONOR, Metro-Goldwyn-Mayer. (Miniature)
SWORD FISHING, Warner Bros. (Vitaphone Varieties)

Two Reels

DRUNK DRIVING, Metro-Goldwyn-Mayer. (Crime Doesn't Pay)
FIVE TIMES FIVE, RKO Radio. (Special)
★ SONS OF LIBERTY, Warner Bros. (Historical Featurette)

1940 Thirteenth Year

Cartoons

★ MILKY WAY, Metro-Goldwyn-Mayer. (Rudolph Ising Series)
PUSS GETS THE BOOT, Metro-Goldwyn-Mayer. (Cat and Mouse Series)
A WILD HARE, Leon Schlesinger, Warner Bros.

One Reel

LONDON CAN TAKE IT, Warner Bros. (Vitaphone Varieties)

MORE ABOUT NOSTRADAMUS, Metro-Goldwyn-Mayer.

★ QUICKER 'N A WINK, Pete Smith, M-G-M.

SIEGE, RKO Radio. (Reelism)

Two Reels

EYES OF THE NAVY, Metro-Goldwyn-Mayer. (Crime Doesn't Pay)

SERVICE WITH THE COLORS, Warner Bros. (National Defense Series)

★ TEDDY, THE ROUGH RIDER, Warner Bros. (Historical Featurette)

1941 Fourteenth Year

Cartoons

BOOGIE WOOGIE BUGLE BOY OF COMPANY B, Walter Lantz, Universal.

HIAWATHA'S RABBIT HUNT, Leon Schlesinger, Warner Bros.

HOW WAR CAME, Columbia, (Raymond Gram Swing Series)

★ LEND A PAW, Walt Disney, RKO Radio.

THE NIGHT BEFORE CHRISTMAS, Metro-Goldwyn-Mayer. (Tom and Jerry Series)

RHAPSODY IN RIVETS, Leon Schlesinger, Warner Bros.

RHYTHM IN THE RANKS, Paramount. (George Pal Puppetoon Series)

THE ROOKIE BEAR, Metro-Goldwyn-Mayer. (Bear Series)

SUPERMAN NO. 1, Paramount.

TRUANT OFFICER DONALD, Walt Disney, RKO Radio.

One Reel

ARMY CHAMPIONS, Pete Smith, M-G-M. (Pete Smith Specialties)

BEAUTY AND THE BEACH, Paramount. (Headliner Series)

DOWN ON THE FARM, Paramount. (Speaking of Animals)

FORTY BOYS AND A SONG, Warner Bros. (Melody Master Series)

KINGS OF THE TURF, Warner Bros. (Color Parade Series)

★ OF PUPS AND PUZZLES, Metro-Goldwyn-Mayer. (Passing Parade Series)

SAGEBRUSH AND SILVER, 20th Century-Fox. (Magic Carpet Series)

Two Reels

ALIVE IN THE DEEP, Woodard Productions, Inc.

FORBIDDEN PASSAGE, Metro-Goldwyn-Mayer. (Crime Doesn't Pay)

THE GAY PARISIAN, Warner Bros. (Miniature Featurette Series)

★ MAIN STREET ON THE MARCH, Metro-Goldwyn-Mayer. (Two-Reel Special)

THE TANKS ARE COMING, Warner Bros. (National Defense Series)

1942 Fifteenth Year

Cartoons

ALL OUT FOR V, 20th Century-Fox.

THE BLITZ WOLF, Metro-Goldwyn-Mayer.

★ DER FUEHRER'S FACE, Walt Disney, RKO Radio.

JUKE BOX JAMBOREE, Walt Lantz, Universal.

PIGS IN A POLKA, Leon Schlesinger, Warner Bros.

TULIPS SHALL GROW, Paramount. (George Pal Puppetoon)

One Reel

DESERT WONDERLAND, 20th Century-Fox. (Magic Carpet Series)

MARINES IN THE MAKING, Metro-Goldwyn-Mayer. (Pete Smith Specialties)

★ SPEAKING OF ANIMALS AND THEIR FAMILIES, Paramount. (Speaking of Animals)

UNITED STATES MARINE BAND, Warner Bros. (Melody Master Bands)

Two Reels

★ BEYOND THE LINE OF DUTY, Warner Bros. (Broadway Brevities)

DON'T TALK, Metro-Goldwyn-Mayer. (Two-Reel Special)

PRIVATE SMITH OF THE U.S.A., RKO Radio. (This Is America Series)

1943 Sixteenth Year

Cartoons

THE DIZZY ACROBAT, Walter Lantz, Universal: WALTER LANTZ, Producer.

THE FIVE HUNDRED HATS OF BARTHOLOMEW CUBBINS, Paramount. (George Pal Puppetoon)

GREETINGS, BAIT, Warner Bros.: LEON SCHLESINGER, Producer.

IMAGINATION, Columbia: DAVE FLEISCHER Producer.

REASON AND EMOTION, Walt Disney, RKO Radio: WALT DISNEY, Producer.

★ YANKEE DOODLE MOUSE, Metro-Goldwyn-Mayer: FREDERICK QUIMBY, Producer.

One Reel

★ AMPHIBIOUS FIGHTERS, Paramount: GRANTLAND RICE, Producer.

CAVALCADE OF THE DANCE WITH VELOZ AND YOLANDA, Warner Bros.: (Melody Master Bands) GORDON HOLLINGSHEAD, Producer.

CHAMPIONS CARRY ON, 20th Century-Fox: (Sports Reviews) EDMUND REEK, Producer.

HOLLYWOOD IN UNIFORM, Columbia: (Screen Snapshots #1, Series 22) RALPH STAUB, Producer.

SEEING HANDS, Metro-Goldwyn-Mayer. (Pete Smith Specialty)

Two Reels

★ HEAVENLY MUSIC, Metro-Goldwyn-Mayer: JERRY BRESLER and SAM COSLOW, Producers.

LETTER TO A HERO, RKO Radio: (This Is America) FRED ULLMAN, Producer.

MARDI GRAS, Paramount: (Musical Parade) WALTER MACEWEN, Producer.

WOMEN AT WAR, Warner Bros.: (Technicolor Special) GORDON HOLLINGSHEAD, Producer.

1944 Seventeenth Year

Cartoons

AND TO THINK I SAW IT ON MULBERRY STREET, Paramount. (George Pal Puppetoon)

THE DOG, CAT AND CANARY, Columbia. (Screen Gems)

FISH FRY, Universal: WALTER LANTZ, Producer.

HOW TO PLAY FOOTBALL, Walt Disney, RKO Radio: WALT DISNEY, Producer.

★ MOUSE TROUBLE, Metro-Goldwyn-Mayer: FREDERICK C. QUIMBY, Producer.

MY BOY, JOHNNY, 20th Century-Fox: PAUL TERRY, Producer.

SWOONER CROONER, Warner Bros.

One Reel

BLUE GRASS GENTLEMEN, 20th Century-Fox: (Sports Review) EDMUND REEK, Producer.

50TH ANNIVERSARY OF MOTION PICTURES, Columbia: (Screen Snapshots #9, Series 23) RALPH STAUB, Producer.

JAMMIN' THE BLUES, Warner Bros.: (Melody Master Bands) GORDON HOLLINGSHEAD, Producer.

MOVIE PESTS, Metro-Goldwyn-Mayer. (Pete Smith Specialty)

★ WHO'S WHO IN ANIMAL LAND, Paramount: (Speaking of Animals) JERRY FAIRBANKS, Producer.

Two Reels

BOMBALERA, Paramount: (Musical Parade) LOUIS HARRIS, Producer.

★ I WON'T PLAY, Warner Bros.: (Featurette) GORDON HOLLINGSHEAD, Producer.

MAIN STREET TODAY, Metro-Goldwyn-Mayer: (Two-Reel Special) JERRY BRESLER, Producer.

1945 Eighteenth Year

Cartoons

DONALD'S CRIME, Walt Disney, RKO Radio: (Donald Duck) WALT DISNEY, Producer.

JASPER AND THE BEANSTALK, Paramount: (Pal Puppetoon-Jasper Series) GEORGE PAL, Producer.

LIFE WITH FEATHERS, Warner Bros.: (Merrie Melodies) EDDIE SELZER, Producer.

MIGHTY MOUSE IN GYPSY LIFE, 20th Century-Fox: (Terrytoon) PAUL TERRY, Producer.

POET AND PEASANT, Universal: (Lantz Technicolor Cartune) WALTER LANTZ, Producer.

★ QUIET PLEASE, Metro-Goldwyn-Mayer: (Tom and Jerry Series) FREDERICK QUIMBY, Producer.

RIPPLING ROMANCE, Columbia. (Color Rhapsodies)

One Reel

ALONG THE RAINBOW TRAIL, 20th Century-Fox: (Movietone Adventure) EDMUND REEK, Producer.

SCREEN SNAPSHOTS 25TH ANNIVERSARY, Columbia: (Screen Snapshots) RALPH STAUB, Producer.

★ STAIRWAY TO LIGHT, Metro-Goldwyn-Mayer: (John Nesbitt Passing Parade) HERBERT MOULTON, Producer.

STORY OF A DOG, Warner Bros.: (Vitaphone Varieties) GORDON HOLLINGSHEAD, Producer.

WHITE RHAPSODY, Paramount: (Sportlights) GRANTLAND RICE, Producer.

YOUR NATIONAL GALLERY, Universal: (Variety Views) JOSEPH O'BRIEN and THOMAS MEAD, Producers.

Two Reels

A GUN IN HIS HAND, Metro-Goldwyn-Mayer: (Crime Does Not Pay) CHESTER FRANKLIN, Producer.

THE JURY GOES ROUND 'N' ROUND, Columbia: (All Star Comedies) JULES WHITE, Producer.

THE LITTLE WITCH, Paramount: (Musical Parade) GEORGE TEMPLETON, Producer.

★ STAR IN THE NIGHT, Warner Bros.: (Broadway Brevities) GORDON HOLLINGSHEAD, Producer.

1946 Nineteenth Year

Cartoons

★ THE CAT CONCERTO, Metro-Goldwyn-Mayer: (Tom and Jerry) FREDERICK QUIMBY, Producer.

CHOPIN'S MUSICAL MOMENTS, Universal: (Musical Miniatures) WALTER LANTZ, Producer.

JOHN HENRY AND THE INKY POO, Paramount: (Puppetoon) GEORGE PAL, Producer.

SQUATTER'S RIGHTS, Disney-RKO Radio: (Mickey Mouse) WALT DISNEY, Producer.

WALKY TALKY HAWKY, Warner Bros.: (Merrie Melodies) EDWARD SELZER, Producer.

One Reel

DIVE-HI CHAMPS, Paramount: (Sportlights) JACK EATON, Producer.

★ FACING YOUR DANGER, Warner Bros.: (Sports Parade) GORDON HOLLINGSHEAD, Producer.

GOLDEN HORSES, 20th Century-Fox: (Movietone Sports Review) EDMUND REEK, Producer.

SMART AS A FOX, Warner Bros.: (Varieties) GORDON HOLLINGSHEAD, Producer.

SURE CURES, Metro-Goldwyn-Mayer:

(Pete Smith Specialty) PETE SMITH, Producer.

Two Reels

★ A BOY AND HIS DOG, Warner Bros.: (Featurettes) GORDON HOLLINGSHEAD, Producer.

COLLEGE QUEEN, Paramount: (Musical Parade) GEORGE TEMPLETON, Producer.

HISS AND YELL, Columbia: (All Star Comedies) JULES WHITE, Producer.

THE LUCKIEST GUY IN THE WORLD, Metro-Goldwyn-Mayer: (Two-Reel Special) JERRY BRESLER, Producer.

1947 Twentieth Year

Cartoons

CHIP AN' DALE, Walt Disney, RKO Radio: (Donald Duck) WALT DISNEY, Producer.

DR. JEKYLL AND MR. MOUSE, Metro-Goldwyn-Mayer: (Tom and Jerry) FREDERICK QUIMBY, Producer.

PLUTO'S BLUE NOTE, Walt Disney, RKO Radio: (Pluto) WALT DISNEY, Producer.

TUBBY THE TUBA, Paramount: (George Pal Puppetoon) GEORGE PAL, Producer.

★ TWEETIE PIE, Warner Bros.: (Merrie Melodies) EDWARD SELZER, Producer.

One Reel

BROOKLYN, U.S.A.., Universal-International: (Variety Series) THOMAS MEAD, Producer.

★ GOODBYE MISS TURLOCK, Metro-Goldwyn-Mayer: (John Nesbitt Passing Parade) HERBERT MOULTON, Producer.

MOON ROCKETS, Paramount: (Popular Science) JERRY FAIRBANKS, Producer.

NOW YOU SEE IT, Metro-Goldwyn-Mayer: PETE SMITH, Producer.

SO YOU WANT TO BE IN PICTURES, Warner Bros.: (Joe McDoakes) GORDON HOLLINGSHEAD, Producer.

Two Reels

CHAMPAGNE FOR TWO, Paramount: (Musical Parade Featurette) HARRY GREY, Producer.

★ CLIMBING THE MATTERHORN, Monogram: (Color) IRVING ALLEN, Producer.

FIGHT OF THE WILD STALLIONS, Universal-International: (Special) THOMAS MEAD, Producer.

GIVE US THE EARTH, Metro-Goldwyn-Mayer: (Special) HERBERT MORGAN, Producer.

A VOICE IS BORN, Columbia: (Musical Featurette) BEN BLAKE, Producer.

1948 Twenty-first Year

Cartoons

★ THE LITTLE ORPHAN, Metro-Goldwyn-Mayer: (Tom and Jerry) FRED QUIMBY, Producer.

MICKEY AND THE SEAL, Walt Disney, RKO Radio: (Pluto) WALT DISNEY, Producer.

MOUSE WRECKERS, Warner Bros.: (Looney Tunes) EDWARD SELZER, Producer.

ROBIN HOODLUM, United Productions of America, Columbia: (Fox and Crow) UNITED PRODUCTIONS OF AMERICA, Producer.

TEA FOR TWO HUNDRED, Walt Disney, RKO Radio: (Donald Duck) WALT DISNEY, Producer.

One Reel

ANNIE WAS A WONDER, Metro-Goldwyn-Mayer: (John Nesbitt Passing Parade) HERBERT MOULTON, Producer.

CINDERELLA HORSE, Warner Bros.: (Sports Parade) GORDON HOLLINGSHEAD, Producer.

SO YOU WANT TO BE ON THE RADIO, Warner Bros.: (Joe McDoakes) GORDON HOLLINGSHEAD, Producer.

★ SYMPHONY OF A CITY, 20th Century-Fox: (Movietone Specialty) EDMUND H. REEK, Producer.

YOU CAN'T WIN, Metro-Goldwyn-Mayer: (Pete Smith Specialty) PETE SMITH, Producer.

Two Reels

CALGARY STAMPEDE, Warner Bros.: (Technicolor Special) GORDON HOLLINGSHEAD, Producer.

GOING TO BLAZES, Metro-Goldwyn-Mayer: (Special) HERBERT MORGAN, Producer.

SAMBA-MANIA, Paramount: (Musical Parade) HARRY GREY, Producer.

★ SEAL ISLAND, Walt Disney, RKO Radio: (True Life Adventure Series) WALT DISNEY, Producer.

SNOW CAPERS, Universal-International: (Special Series) THOMAS MEAD, Producer.

1949 Twenty-second Year

Cartoons

★ FOR SCENT-IMENTAL REASONS, Warner Bros.: (Looney Tunes) EDWARD SELZER, Producer.

HATCH UP YOUR TROUBLES, Metro-Goldwyn-Mayer: (Tom and Jerry) FRED QUIMBY, Producer.

MAGIC FLUKE, United Productions of America, Columbia: (Fox and Crow) STEPHEN BOSUSTOW, Producer.

TOY TINKERS, Walt Disney, RKO Radio: WALT DISNEY, Producer.

One Reel

★ AQUATIC HOUSE-PARTY, Paramount: (Grantland Rice Sportlights) JACK EATON, Producer.

ROLLER DERBY GIRL, Paramount: (Pacemaker) JUSTIN HERMAN, Producer.

SO YOU THINK YOU'RE NOT GUILTY, Warner Bros.: (Joe McDoakes) GORDON HOLLINGSHEAD, Producer.

SPILLS AND CHILLS, Warner Bros.: (Black-and-White Sports Review) WALTON C. AMENT, Producer.

WATER TRIX, Metro-Goldwyn-Mayer: (Pete Smith Specialty) PETE SMITH, Producer.

Two Reels

BOY AND THE EAGLE, RKO Radio: WILLIAM LASKY, Producer.

CHASE OF DEATH, Irving Allen Productions: (Color Series) IRVING ALLEN, Producer.

THE GRASS IS ALWAYS GREENER, Warner Bros.: (Black and White) GORDON HOLLINGSHEAD, Producer.

SNOW CARNIVAL, Warner Bros.: (Technicolor) GORDON HOLLINGSHEAD, Producer.

★ VAN GOGH, Canton-Weiner: GASTON DIEHL and ROBERT HAESSENS, Producers.

1950 Twenty-third Year

Cartoons

★ GERALD McBOING-BOING, United Productions of America, Columbia: (Jolly Frolics Series) STEPHEN BOSUSTOW, Executive Producer.

JERRY'S COUSIN, Metro-Goldwyn-Mayer: (Tom and Jerry) FRED QUIMBY, Producer.

TROUBLE INDEMNITY, United Productions of America, Columbia: (Mr. Magoo Series) STEPHEN BOSUSTOW, Executive Producer.

One Reel

BLAZE BUSTERS, Warner Bros.: (Vitaphone Novelties) ROBERT YOUNGSON, Producer.

★ GRANDAD OF RACES, Warner Bros.: (Sports Parade) GORDON HOLLINGSHEAD, Producer.

WRONG WAY BUTCH, Metro-Goldwyn-Mayer: PETE SMITH, Producer.

Two Reels

★ BEAVER VALLEY, Walt Disney, RKO Radio: (True-Life Adventure) WALT DISNEY, Producer.

GRANDMA MOSES, Falcon Films, Inc., A.F. Films: FALCON FILMS, INC., Producer.

MY COUNTRY 'TIS OF THEE, Warner Bros.: (Featurette Series) GORDON HOLLINGSHEAD, Producer.

1951 Twenty-fourth Year

Cartoons

LAMBERT, THE SHEEPISH LION, Walt Disney, RKO Radio: (Special) WALT DISNEY, Producer.

ROOTY TOOT TOOT, United Productions of America, Columbia: (Jolly Frolics) STEPHEN BOSUSTOW, Executive Producer.

★ TWO MOUSEKETEERS, Metro-Goldwyn-Mayer: (Tom and Jerry) FRED QUIMBY, Producer.

One Reel

RIDIN' THE RAILS, Paramount: (Sportlights) JACK EATON, Producer.

THE STORY OF TIME, A Signal Films Production by ROBERT G. LEFFINGWELL, Cornell Film Company (British).

★ WORLD OF KIDS, Warner Bros.: (Vitaphone Novelties) ROBERT YOUNGSON, Producer.

Two Reels

BALZAC, Les Films du Compass, A.F. Films, Inc. (French): LES FILMS DU COMPASS, Producer.

DANGER UNDER THE SEA, Universal-International, TOM MEAD, Producer.

★ NATURE'S HALF ACRE, Walt Disney, RKO Radio: (True-Life Adventure) WALT DISNEY, Producer.

1952 Twenty-fifth Year

Cartoons

★ JOHANN MOUSE, Metro-Goldwyn-Mayer: (Tom and Jerry) FRED QUIMBY, Producer.

LITTLE JOHNNY JET, Metro-Goldwyn-Mayer: (M-G-M Series) FRED QUIMBY, Producer.

MADELINE, UPA, Columbia: (Jolly Frolics) STEPHEN BOSUSTOW, Executive Producer.

PINK AND BLUE BLUES, UPA, Columbia: (Mister Magoo) STEPHEN BOSUSTOW, Executive Producer.

ROMANCE OF TRANSPORTATION, National Film Board of Canada (Canadian): TOM DALY, Producer.

One Reel

ATHLETES OF THE SADDLE, Paramount: (Sportlights Series) JACK EATON, Producer.

DESERT KILLER, Warner Bros.: (Sports Parade) GORDON HOLLINGSHEAD, Producer.

★ LIGHT IN THE WINDOW, Art Films Prods., 20th Century-Fox: (Art Series) BORIS VERMONT, Producer.

NEIGHBOURS, National Film Board of Canada (Canadian): NORMAN MCLAREN, Producer.

ROYAL SCOTLAND, Crown Film Unit, BRITISH INFORMATION SERVICES (British).

Two Reels

BRIDGE OF TIME, A London Film Prod., BRITISH INFORMATION SERVICES (British).

DEVIL TAKE US, A Theatre of Life Prod.: (Theatre of Life Series) HERBERT MORGAN, Producer.

THAR SHE BLOWS!, Warner Bros.: (Technicolor Special) GORDON HOLLINGSHEAD, Producer.

★ WATER BIRDS, Walt Disney, RKO

Radio: (True-Life Adventure) WALT DISNEY, Producer.

1953 Twenty-sixth Year

Cartoons

CHRISTOPHER CRUMPET, UPA, Columbia: (Jolly Frolics) STEPHEN BOSUSTOW, Producer.

FROM A TO Z-Z-Z-Z, Warner Bros. Cartoons, Inc., Warner Bros.: (Looney Tunes) EDWARD SELZER, Producer.

RUGGED BEAR, Walt Disney, RKO Radio: (Donald Duck) WALT DISNEY, Producer.

THE TELL TALE HEART, UPA, Columbia: (UPA Cartoon Special) STEPHEN BOSUSTOW, Producer.

★ TOOT, WHISTLE, PLUNK AND BOOM, Walt Disney, Buena Vista Film Distribution Co., Inc.: (Special Music Series) WALT DISNEY, Producer.

One Reel

CHRIST AMONG THE PRIMITIVES, IFE Releasing Corp. (Italian): VINCENZO LUCCI-CHIARISSI, Producer.

HERRING HUNT, NATIONAL FILM BOARD OF CANADA, RKO Pathe, Inc. (Canadian). (Canada Carries on Series)

JOY OF LIVING, Art Film Prods., 20th Century-Fox: (Art Film Series) BORIS VERMONT, Producer.

★ THE MERRY WIVES OF WINDSOR OVERTURE, Metro-Goldwyn-Mayer: (Overture Series) JOHNNY GREEN, Producer.

WEE WATER WONDERS, Paramount: (Grantland Rice Sportlights Series) JACK EATON, Producer.

Two Reels

★ BEAR COUNTRY, Walt Disney, RKO Radio: (True-Life Adventure) WALT DISNEY, Producer.

BEN AND ME, Walt Disney, Buena Vista Film Distribution Co., Inc.: (Cartoon Special Series) WALT DISNEY, Producer.

RETURN TO GLENNASCAUL, DUBLIN GATE THEATRE PROD., Mayor-Kingsley Inc.

VESUVIUS EXPRESS, 20th Century-Fox: (CinemaScope Shorts Series) OTTO LANG, Producer.

WINTER PARADISE, Warner Bros.: (Technicolor Special) CEDRIC FRANCIS, Producer.

1954 Twenty-seventh Year

Cartoons

CRAZY MIXED UP PUP, Walter Lantz Prods., U-I: WALTER LANTZ, Producer.

PIGS IS PIGS, Walt Disney Prods., RKO Radio: WALT DISNEY, Producer.

SANDY CLAWS, Warner Bros. Cartoons, Inc.: EDWARD SELZER, Producer.

TOUCHE, PUSSY CAT, Metro-Goldwyn-Mayer: FRED QUIMBY, Producer.

★ WHEN MAGOO FLEW, United Productions of America, Columbia: STEPHEN BOSUSTOW, Producer.

One Reel

THE FIRST PIANO QUARTETTE, 20th Century-Fox: OTTO LANG, Producer.

THE STRAUSS FANTASY, Metro-Goldwyn-Mayer: JOHNNY GREEN, Producer.

★ THIS MECHANICAL AGE, Warner Bros.: ROBERT YOUNGSON, Producer.

Two Reels

BEAUTY AND THE BULL, Warner Bros.: CEDRIC FRANCIS, Producer.

JET CARRIER, 20th Century-Fox: OTTO LANG, Producer.

SIAM, Walt Disney Prods., Buena Vista Film Distribution Co., Inc.: WALT DISNEY, Producer.

★ A TIME OUT OF WAR, Carnival Prods.: DENIS SANDERS and TERRY SANDERS, Producers.

1955 Twenty-eighth Year

Cartoons

GOOD WILL TO MEN, Metro-Goldwyn-Mayer: FRED QUIMBY, WILLIAM HANNA, and JOSEPH BARBERA, Producers.

THE LEGEND OF ROCK-A-BYE-POINT, Walter Lantz Prods., U-I: WALTER LANTZ, Producer.

NO HUNTING, Walt Disney Prods., RKO Radio: WALT DISNEY, Producer.

★ SPEEDY GONZALES, Warner Bros. Cartoons, Inc.: EDWARD SELZER, Producer.

One Reel

GADGETS GALORE, Warner Bros.: ROBERT YOUNGSON, Producer.

★ SURVIVAL CITY, 20th Century-Fox: EDMUND REEK, Producer.

3RD AVE. EL, Carson Davidson Prods., Ardee Films: CARSON DAVIDSON, Producer.

THREE KISSES, Paramount: JUSTIN HERMAN, Producer.

Two Reels

THE BATTLE OF GETTYSBURG, Metro-Goldwyn-Mayer: DORE SCHARY, Producer.

★ THE FACE OF LINCOLN, University of Southern California Presentation, Cavalcade Pictures, Inc.: WILBUR T. BLUME, Producer.

ON THE TWELFTH DAY . . . , Go Pictures, Inc., George Brest and Assocs.: GEORGE K. ARTHUR, Producer.

SWITZERLAND, Walt Disney Prods., Buena Vista Film Distribution Co., Inc.: WALT DISNEY, Producer.

24 HOUR ALERT, Warner Bros.: CEDRIC FRANCIS, Producer.

1956 Twenty-ninth Year

Cartoons

GERALD MCBOING-BOING ON PLANET MOO, UPA Pictures, Columbia: STEPHEN BOSUSTOW, Producer.

THE JAYWALKER, UPA Pictures, Columbia: STEPHEN BOSUSTOW, Producer.

★ MISTER MAGOO'S PUDDLE JUMPER, UPA Pictures, Columbia: STEPHEN BOSUSTOW, Producer.

One Reel

★ CRASHING THE WATER BARRIER, Warner Bros.: KONSTANTIN KALSER, Producer.

I NEVER FORGET A FACE, Warner Bros.: ROBERT YOUNGSON, Producer.

TIME STOOD STILL, Warner Bros.: CEDRIC FRANCIS, Producer.

Two Reels

★ THE BESPOKE OVERCOAT, Romulus Films: GEORGE K. ARTHUR, Producer.

COW DOG, Walt Disney Prods., Buena Vista Film Distribution Co., Inc.: LARRY LANSBURGH, Producer.

THE DARK WAVE, 20th Century-Fox: JOHN HEALY, Producer.

SAMOA, Walt Disney Prods., Buena Vista Film Distribution Co., Inc.: WALT DISNEY, Producer.

*1957 Thirtieth Year**

Cartoons

★ BIRDS ANONYMOUS, Warner Bros.: EDWARD SELZER, Producer.

ONE DROOPY KNIGHT, Metro-Goldwyn-Mayer: WILLIAM HANNA and JOSEPH BARBERA, Producers.

TABASCO ROAD, Warner Bros.: EDWARD SELZER, Producer.

TREES AND JAMAICA DADDY, UPA

*Rules changed this year to two awards for Short Subjects instead of three as previously given.

Pictures, Columbia: STEPHEN BOSUSTOW, Producer.

THE TRUTH ABOUT MOTHER GOOSE, Walt Disney Prods., Buena Vista Film Distribution Co., Inc.: WALT DISNEY, Producer.

Live-Action Subjects

A CHAIRY TALE, National Film Board of Canada, Kingsley International Pictures Corp.: NORMAN MCLAREN, Producer.

CITY OF GOLD, National Film Board of Canada, Kingsley International Pictures Corp.: TOM DALY, Producer.

FOOTHOLD ON ANTARCTICA, World Wide Pictures, Lester A. Schoenfeld Films: JAMES CARR, Producer.

PORTUGAL, Walt Disney Prods., Buena Vista Film Distribution Co., Inc.: BEN SHARPSTEEN, Producer.

★ THE WETBACK HOUND, Walt Disney Prods., Buena Vista Film Distribution Co., Inc.: LARRY LANSBURGH, Producer.

1958 Thirty-first Year

Cartoons

★ KNIGHTY KNIGHT BUGS, Warner Bros.: JOHN W. BURTON, Producer.

PAUL BUNYAN, Walt Disney Prods., Buena Vista Film Distribution Co., Inc.: WALT DISNEY, Producer.

SIDNEY'S FAMILY TREE, Terrytoons, 20th Century-Fox: WILLIAM M. WEISS, Producer.

Live-Action Subjects

★ GRAND CANYON, Walt Disney Prods., Buena Vista Film Distribution Co., Inc.: WALT DISNEY, Producer.

JOURNEY INTO SPRING, British Transport Films, Lester A. Schoenfeld Films: IAN FERGUSON, Producer.

THE KISS, Cohay Prods., Continental Distributing, Inc.: JOHN PATRICK HAYES, Producer.

SNOWS OF AORANGI, New Zealand Screen Board: GEORGE BREST ASSOCIATES.

T IS FOR TUMBLEWEED, Continental Distributing, Inc.: JAMES A. LEBENTHAL, Producer.

1959 Thirty-second Year

Cartoons

MEXICALI SHMOES, Warner Bros.: JOHN W. BURTON, Producer.

★ MOONBIRD, Storyboard, Inc.: EDWARD HARRISON and JOHN HUBLEY, Producers.

NOAH'S ARK, Walt Disney Prods., Buena Vista Film Distribution Co., Inc.: WALT DISNEY, Producer.

THE VIOLINIST, Pintoff Prods., Inc., Kingsley International Pictures Corp.: ERNEST PINTOFF, Producer.

Live-Action Subjects

BETWEEN THE TIDES, British Transport Films, Lester A. Schoenfeld Films (British): IAN FERGUSON, Producer.

★ THE GOLDEN FISH, Les Requins Associés, Columbia (French): JACQUES-YVES COUSTEAU, Producer.

MYSTERIES OF THE DEEP, Walt Disney Prods., Buena Vista Film Distribution Co., Inc.: WALT DISNEY, Producer.

THE RUNNING, JUMPING AND STANDING-STILL FILM, Lion International Films, Ltd., Kingsley-Union Films (British): PETER SELLERS, Producer.

SKYSCRAPER, Joseph Burstyn Film Enterprises, Inc.: SHIRLEY CLARKE, WILLARD VAN DYKE, and IRVING JACOBY, Producers.

1960 Thirty-third Year

Cartoons

GOLIATH II, Walt Disney Prods., Buena Vista Distribution Co., Inc.: WALT DISNEY, Producer.

HIGH NOTE, Warner Bros.

MOUSE AND GARDEN, Warner Bros.

★ MUNRO, Rembrandt Films, Film Representations, Inc.: WILLIAM L. SNYDER, Producer.

A PLACE IN THE SUN, George K. Arthur-Go Pictures, Inc. (Czechoslovakian): FRANTISEK VYSTRECIL, Producer.

Live-Action Subjects

THE CREATION OF WOMAN, Trident Films, Inc., Sterling World Distributors Corp. (Indian): CHARLES F. SCHWEP and ISMAIL MERCHANT, Producers.

★ DAY OF THE PAINTER, Little Movies, Kingsley-Union Films: EZRA R. BAKER, Producer.

ISLANDS OF THE SEA, Walt Disney Prods., Buena Vista Distribution Co., Inc.: WALT DISNEY, Producer.

A SPORT IS BORN, Paramount: LESLIE WINIK, Producer.

1961 Thirty-fourth Year

Cartoons

AQUAMANIA, Walt Disney Prods., Buena Vista Distribution Co., Inc.: WALT DISNEY, Producer.

BEEP PREPARED, Warner Bros.: CHUCK JONES, Producer.

★ ERSATZ (THE SUBSTITUTE), ZAGREB FILM, Herts-Lion International Corp.

NELLY'S FOLLY, Warner Bros.: CHUCK JONES, Producer.

PIED PIPER OF GUADALUPE, Warner Bros.: FRIZ FRELENG, Producer.

Live-Action Subjects

BALLON VOLE (PLAY BALL!), CINÉ-DOCUMENTS, Kingsley International Pictures Corp.

THE FACE OF JESUS, Dr. John D. Jennings, Harry Stern, Inc.: DR. JOHN D. JENNINGS, Producer.

ROOFTOPS OF NEW YORK, McCarty-Rush Prod., in association with ROBERT GAFFNEY, Columbia.

★ SEAWARDS THE GREAT SHIPS, Templar Film Studios: LESTER A. SCHOENFELD FILMS.

VERY NICE, VERY NICE, National Film Board of Canada: KINGSLEY INTERNATIONAL PICTURES CORP.

1962 Thirty-fifth Year

Cartoons

★ THE HOLE, Storyboard Inc., Brandon Films, Inc.: JOHN HUBLEY and FAITH HUBLEY, Producers.

ICARUS MONTGOLFIER WRIGHT, Format Films, United Artists: JULES ENGEL, Producer.

NOW HEAR THIS, Warner Bros.

SELF DEFENSE—FOR COWARDS, Rembrandt Films, Film Representations, Inc.: WILLIAM L. SNYDER, Producer.

SYMPOSIUM ON POPULAR SONGS, Walt Disney Prods., Buena Vista Distribution Co.: WALT DISNEY, Producer.

Live-Action Subjects

BIG CITY BLUES, Mayfair Pictures Company: MARTINA and CHARLES HUGUENOT VAN DER LINDEN, Producers.

THE CADILLAC, United Producers Releasing Org.: ROBERT CLOUSE, Producer.

THE CLIFF DWELLERS (formerly titled "ONE PLUS ONE"), Group II Film Prods.: Lester A. Schoenfeld Films: HAYWARD ANDERSON, Producer.

★ HEUREUX ANNIVERSAIRE (HAPPY ANNIVERSARY), CAPAC Prods., Atlantic Pictures Corp.: PIERRE ETAIX and J. C. CARRIERE, Producers.

PAN, Mayfair Picture Company: HERMAN VAN DER HORST, Producer.

1963 Thirty-sixth Year

Cartoons

AUTOMANIA 2000, Halas and Batchelor Prod., Pathe Contemporary Films: JOHN HALAS, Producer.

★ THE CRITIC, Pintoff-Crossbow Prods., Columbia: ERNEST PINTOFF, Producer.

THE GAME (INGRA), Zagreb Film, Rembrandt Films-Film Representations: DUSAN VUKOTIC, Producer.

MY FINANCIAL CAREER, National Film Board of Canada, Walter Reade-Sterling-Continental Distributing: COLIN LOW and TOM DALY, Producers.

PIANISSIMO, Cinema 16: CARMEN D'A VINO, Producer.

Live-Action Subjects

THE CONCERT, James A. King Corp., George K. Arthur-Go Pictures: EZRA BAKER, Producer.

HOME-MADE CAR, BP (North America) Ltd., Lester A. Schoenfeld Films: JAMES HILL, Producer.

★ AN OCCURRENCE AT OWL CREEK BRIDGE, Films du Centaure-Filmartic, Cappagariff-Janus Films: PAUL DE ROUBAIX and MARCEL ICHAC, Producers.

SIX-SIDED TRIANGLE, Milesian Film Prod. Ltd., Lion International Films: CHRISTOPHER MILES, Producer.

THAT'S ME, Stuart Prods., Pathe Contemporary Films: WALKER STUART, Producer.

1964 Thirty-seventh Year

Cartoons

CHRISTMAS CRACKER, NATIONAL FILM BOARD OF CANADA, Favorite Films of California.

HOW TO AVOID FRIENDSHIP, Rembrandt Films, Film Representations: WILLIAM L. SNYDER, Producer.

NUDNIK #2, Rembrandt Films, Film Representations: WILLIAM L. SNYDER, Producer.

★ THE PINK PHINK, Mirisch-Geoffrey Prods., UA: DAVID H. DePATIE and FRIZ FRELENG, Producers.

Live-Action Subjects

★ CASALS CONDUCTS: 1964, Thalia Films, Beckman Film Corp.: EDWARD SCHREIBER, Producer.

HELP! MY SNOWMAN'S BURNING DOWN, Carson Davidson Prods., Pathe Contemporary Films: CARSON DAVIDSON, Producer.

THE LEGEND OF JIMMY BLUE EYES, Robert Clouse Associates, Topaz Film Corp.: ROBERT CLOUSE, Producer.

1965 Thirty-eighth Year

Cartoons

CLAY OR THE ORIGIN OF SPECIES, Harvard University, Pathe Contemporary Films: ELIOT NOYES, JR., Producer.

★ THE DOT AND THE LINE, Metro-Goldwyn-Mayer: CHUCK JONES and LES GOLDMAN, Producers.

THE THIEVING MAGPIE (LA GAZZA LADRA), Giulio Gianini-Emanuele Luzzati, Allied Artists: EMANUELE LUZZATI, Producer.

Live-Action Subjects

★ THE CHICKEN (LE POULET), Renn Prods., Pathe Contemporary Films: CLAUDE BERRI, Producer.

FORTRESS OF PEACE, Lothar Wolff Prods. for Farner-Looser Films, Cinerama: LOTHAR WOLFF, Producer.

SKATERDATER, Byway Prods., United Artists: MARSHAL BACKLAR and NOEL BLACK, Producers.

SNOW, British Transport Films in association with Geoffrey Jones

(Films) Ltd., Manson Distributing: EDGAR ANSTEY, Producer.

TIME PIECE, Muppets, Inc., Pathe Contemporary Films: JIM HENSON, Producer.

1966 Thirty-ninth Year

Cartoons

THE DRAG, National Film Board of Canada, Favorite Films: WOLF KOENIG and ROBERT VERRALL, Producers.

★ HERB ALPERT AND THE TIJUANA BRASS DOUBLE FEATURE, Hubley Studio, Paramount: JOHN HUBLEY and FAITH HUBLEY, Producers.

THE PINK BLUEPRINT, Mirisch-Geoffrey-DePatie-Freleng, UA: DAVID H. DEPATIE and FRIZ FRELENG, Producers.

Live-Action Subjects

TURKEY THE BRIDGE, Samaritan Prods., Lester A. Schoenfeld Films: DEREK WILLIAMS, Producer.

★ WILD WINGS, British Transport Films, Manson Distributing: EDGAR ANSTEY, Producer.

THE WINNING STRAIN, Winik Films, Paramount: LESLIE WINIK, Producer.

1967 Fortieth Year

Cartoons

★ THE BOX, Murakami-Wolf Films, Brandon Films: FRED WOLF, Producer.

HYPOTHESE BETA, Films Orzeaux, Pathe Contemporary Films: JEAN-CHARLES MEUNIER, Producer.

WHAT ON EARTH!, National Film Board of Canada, Columbia: ROBERT VERRALL and WOLF KOENIG, Producers.

Live-Action Subjects

PADDLE TO THE SEA, National Film Board of Canada, Favorite Films: JULIAN BIGGS, Producer.

★ A PLACE TO STAND, T.D.F. Prod. for the Ontario Department of Economics and Development, Columbia: CHRISTOPHER CHAPMAN, Producer.

SKY OVER HOLLAND, John Ferno Prod. for The Netherlands, Seneca International: JOHN FERNO, Producer.

STOP, LOOK AND LISTEN, Metro-Goldwyn-Mayer: LEN JANSON and CHUCK MENVILLE, Producers.

1968 Forty-first Year

Cartoons

THE HOUSE THAT JACK BUILT, National Film Board of Canada, Columbia: WOLF KOENIG and JIM MACKAY, Producers.

THE MAGIC PEAR TREE, Murakami-Wolf Prods., Bing Crosby Prods.: JIMMY MURAKAMI, Producer.

WINDY DAY, Hubley Studios, Paramount: JOHN HUBLEY and FAITH HUBLEY, Producers.

★ WINNIE THE POOH AND THE BLUSTERY DAY, Walt Disney Prods., Buena Vista Dist.: WALT DISNEY, Producer.

Live-Action Subjects

THE DOVE, Coe-Davis, Schoenfeld Film Dist.: GEORGE COE, SIDNEY DAVIS, and ANTHONY LOVER, Producers.

DUO, NATIONAL FILM BOARD OF CANADA, COLUMBIA.

PRELUDE, Prelude Company, Excelsior Dist.: JOHN ASTIN, Producer.

★ ROBERT KENNEDY REMEMBERED, Guggenheim Prods., National General: CHARLES GUGGENHEIM, Producer.

1969 Forty-second Year

Cartoons

★ IT'S TOUGH TO BE A BIRD, Walt Disney Prods., Buena Vista Dist.: WARD KIMBALL, Producer.

OF MEN AND DEMONS, Hubley Studios, Paramount: JOHN HUBLEY and FAITH HUBLEY, Producers.

WALKING, National Film Board of Canada, Columbia: RYAN LARKIN, Producer.

Live-Action Subjects

BLAKE, National Film Board of Canada, Vaudeo Inc.: DOUG JACKSON, Producer.

★ THE MAGIC MACHINES, Fly-by-Night Prods., Manson Distributing: JOAN KELLER STERN, Producer.

PEOPLE SOUP, Pangloss Prods., Columbia: MARC MERSON, Producer.

1970 Forty-third Year

Cartoons

THE FURTHER ADVENTURES OF UNCLE SAM: PART TWO, The Haboush Company, Goldstone Films: ROBERT MITCHELL and DALE CASE, Producers.

★ IS IT ALWAYS RIGHT TO BE RIGHT?, Stephen Bosustow Prods., Lester A. Schoenfeld Films: NICK BOSUSTOW, Producer.

THE SHEPHERD, Cameron Guess and Associates, Brandon Films: CAMERON GUESS, Producer.

Live-Action Subjects

★ THE RESURRECTION OF BRONCHO BILLY, University of Southern California, Dept. of Cinema, Universal: JOHN LONGENECKER, Producer.

SHUT UP... I'M CRYING, Robert Siegler Prods., Lester A. Schoenfeld Films: ROBERT SIEGLER, Producer.

STICKY MY FINGERS... FLEET MY FEET, The American Film Institute, Lester A. Schoenfeld Films: JOHN HANCOCK, Producer.

*1971 Forty-fourth Year**

Animated

★ THE CRUNCH BIRD, Maxwell-Petok-Petrovich Prods., Regency Film Distributing Corp.: TED PETOK, Producer.

EVOLUTION, National Film Board of Canada, Columbia: MICHAEL MILLS, Producer.

THE SELFISH GIANT, Potterton Prods., Pyramid Films: PETER SANDER and MURRAY SHOSTAK, Producers.

Live Action

GOOD MORNING, E/G Films, Seymour Borde and Associates: DENNY EVANS and KEN GREENWALD, Producers.

THE REHEARSAL, A Cinema Verona Prod., Schoenfeld Film Distributing Corp.: STEPHEN F. VERONA, Producer.

★ SENTINELS OF SILENCE, Producciones Concord, Paramount: MANUEL ARANGO and ROBERT AMRAM, Producers.

1972 Forty-fifth Year

Animated

★ A CHRISTMAS CAROL, A Richard Williams Production, American Broadcasting Company Film Services: RICHARD WILLIAMS, Producer.

KAMA SUTRA RIDES AGAIN, Bob Godfrey Films, Ltd., Lion International Films: BOB GODFREY, Producer.

TUP TUP, A Zagreb Film-Corona Cinematografica Production, Manson Distributing Corp.: NEDELJKO DRAGIC, Producer.

Live Action

FROG STORY, Gidron Productions, Schoenfeld Film Distributing Corp.:

*The designation of this category was changed from "Cartoons" to "Animated Films."

RON SATLOF and RAY GIDEON, Producers.

★ NORMAN ROCKWELL'S WORLD . . . AN AMERICAN DREAM, A Concepts Unlimited Production, Columbia: RICHARD BARCLAY, Producer.

SOLO, Pyramid Films, United Artists: DAVID ADAMS, Producer.

1973 Forty-sixth Year

Animated

★ FRANK FILM, A Frank Mouris Production: FRANK MOURIS, Producer.

THE LEGEND OF JOHN HENRY, A Stephen Bosustow-Pyramid Films Prod.: NICK BOSUSTOW and DAVID ADAMS, Producers.

PULCINELLA, A Luzzati-Gianini Prod.: EMANUELE LUZZATI and GUILIO GIANINI, Producers.

Live Action

★ THE BOLERO, An Allan Miller Production: ALLAN MILLER and WILLIAM FERTIK, Producers.

CLOCKMAKER, James Street Prods. Ltd.: RICHARD GAYER, Producer.

LIFE TIMES NINE, Insight Prods.: PEN DENSHAM and JOHN WATSON, Producers.

*1974 Forty-seventh Year**

Animated

★ CLOSED MONDAYS, Lighthouse Productions: WILL VINTON and BOB GARDINER, Producers.

THE FAMILY THAT DWELT APART, National Film Board of Canada: YVON MALLETTE and ROBERT VERRALL, Producers.

HUNGER, National Film Board of Canada: PETER FOLDES and RENÉ JODOIN, Producers.

VOYAGE TO NEXT, The Hubley Studio: FAITH HUBLEY and JOHN HUBLEY, Producers.

WINNIE THE POOH AND TIGGER TOO, Walt Disney Productions: WOLFGANG REITHERMAN, Producer.

Live Action

CLIMB, Dewitt Jones Productions: DEWITT JONES, Producer.

THE CONCERT, The Black and White Colour Film Company, Ltd.: JULIAN CHAGRIN and CLAUDE CHAGRIN, Producers.

★ ONE-EYED MEN ARE KINGS, C.A.P.A.C. Productions (Paris): PAUL CLAUDON and EDMOND SECHAN, Producers.

PLANET OCEAN, Graphic Films: GEORGE V. CASEY, Producer.

THE VIOLIN, A Sincinkin, Ltd. Production: ANDREW WELSH and GEORGE PASTIC, Producers.

1975 Forty-eighth Year

Animated

★ GREAT, Grantstern Ltd. and British Lion Films Ltd.: BOB GODFREY, Producer.

KICK ME, Robert Swarthe Productions: ROBERT SWARTHE, Producer.

MONSIEUR POINTU, National Film Board of Canada: RENÉ JODOIN, BERNARD LONGPRÉ, and ANDRÉ LEDUC, Producers.

SISYPHUS, Hungarofilms: MARCELL JANKOVICS, Producer.

Live Action

★ ANGEL AND BIG JOE, Bert Salzman Productions: BERT SALZMAN, Producer.

CONQUEST OF LIGHT, Louis Marcus Films Ltd.: LOUIS MARCUS, Producer.

DAWN FLIGHT, Lawrence M. Lansburgh Productions: LAWRENCE M.

*Name of category changed from "Short Subjects" to "Short Films."

LANSBURGH and BRIAN LANSBURGH, Producers.

A DAY IN THE LIFE OF BONNIE CONSOLO, Barr Films: BARRY SPINELLO, Producer.

DOUBLETALK, Beattie Productions: ALAN BEATTIE, Producer.

1976 Forty-ninth Year

Animated

DEDALO, A Cineteam Realizzazioni Production: MANFREDO MANFREDI, Producer.

★ LEISURE, A Film Australia Production: SUZANNE BAKER, Producer.

THE STREET, National Film Board of Canada: CAROLINE LEAF and GUY GLOVER, Producers.

Live Action

★ IN THE REGION OF ICE, An American Film Institute Production: ANDRE GUTTFREUND and PETER WERNER, Producers.

KUDZU, A Short Production: MARJORIE ANNE SHORT, Producer.

THE MORNING SPIDER, The Black and White Colour Film Company: JULIAN CHAGRIN and CLAUDE CHAGRIN, Producers.

NIGHTLIFE, Opus Films, Ltd.: CLAIRE WILBUR and ROBIN LEHMAN, Producers.

NUMBER ONE, Number One Productions: DYAN CANNON and VINCE CANNON, Producers.

1977 Fiftieth Year

Animated

THE BEAD GAME, National Film Board of Canada: ISHU PATEL, Producer.

THE DOONESBURY SPECIAL, The Hubley Studio: JOHN HUBLEY, FAITH HUBLEY, and GARRY TRUDEAU, Producers.

JIMMY THE C, A Motionpicker Production: JIMMY PICKER and ROBERT GROSSMAN, Producers.

★ SAND CASTLE, National Film Board of Canada: CO HOEDEMAN, Producer.

Live Action

THE ABSENT-MINDED WAITER, The Aspen Film Society: WILLIAM E. MCEUEN, Producer.

FLOATING FREE, A Trans World International Production: JERRY BUTTS, Producer.

★ I'LL FIND A WAY, National Film Board of Canada: BEVERLY SHAFFER and YUKI YOSHIDA, Producers.

NOTES ON THE POPULAR ARTS, Saul Bass Films: SAUL BASS, Producer.

SPACEBORNE, A Lawrence Hall of Science Production for the Regents of the University of California with the cooperation of NASA: PHILIP DAUBER, Producer.

1978 Fifty-first Year

Animated

OH MY DARLING, Nico Crama Productions: NICO CRAMA, Producer.

RIP VAN WINKLE, A Will Vinton/Billy Budd Film, Will Vinton Productions: WILL VINTON, Producer.

★ SPECIAL DELIVERY, National Film Board of Canada: EUNICE MACAULAY and JOHN WELDON, Producers.

Live Action

A DIFFERENT APPROACH, A Jim Belcher/Brookfield Production: JIM BELCHER and FERN FIELD, Producers.

MANDY'S GRANDMOTHER, Illumination Films: ANDREW SUGERMAN, Producer.

STRANGE FRUIT, The American Film Institute: SETH PINSKER, Producer.

★ TEENAGE FATHER, New Visions Inc. for the Children's Home Society of California: TAYLOR HACKFORD, Producer.

1979 Fifty-second Year

Animated

DREAM DOLL, Bob Godfrey Films/ Zagreb Films/Halas and Batchelor, FilmWright: BOB GODFREY and ZLATKO GRGIC, Producers.

★ EVERY CHILD, National Film Board of Canada: DEREK LAMB, Producer.

IT'S SO NICE TO HAVE A WOLF AROUND THE HOUSE, AR&T Productions for Learning Corporation of America: PAUL FIERLINGER, Producer.

Live Action

★ BOARD AND CARE, Ron Ellis Films: SARAH PILLSBURY and RON ELLIS, Producers.

BRAVERY IN THE FIELD, National Film Board of Canada: ROMAN KROITOR and STEFAN WODOSLAWSKY, Producers.

OH BROTHER, MY BROTHER, Ross Lowell Productions, Pyramid Films, Inc.: CAROL LOWELL and ROSS LOWELL, Producers.

THE SOLAR FILM, Wildwood Enterprises Inc.: SAUL BASS and MICHAEL BRITTON, Producers.

SOLLY'S DINER, Mathias/Zukerman/ Hankin Productions: HARRY MATHIAS, JAY ZUKERMAN, and LARRY HANKIN, Producers.

1980 Fifty-third Year

Animated

ALL NOTHING, Radio Canada: FREDERIC BACK, Producer.

★ THE FLY, Pannonia Film, Budapest: FERENC ROFUSZ, Producer.

HISTORY OF THE WORLD IN THREE MINUTES FLAT, Michael Mills Productions Ltd.: MICHAEL MILLS, Producer.

Live Action

★ THE DOLLAR BOTTOM, Rocking Horse Films Limited, Paramount: LLOYD PHILLIPS, Producer.

FALL LINE, Sports Imagery, Inc.: BOB CARMICHAEL and GREG LOWE, Producers.

A JURY OF HER PEERS, Sally Heckel Productions: SALLY HECKEL, Producer.

1981 Fifty-fourth Year

Animated

★ CRAC, Société Radio-Canada: FREDERIC BACK, Producer.

THE CREATION, Will Vinton Productions: WILL VINTON, Producer.

THE TENDER TALE OF CINDERELLA PENGUIN, National Film Board of Canada: JANET PERLMAN, Producer.

Live Action

COUPLES AND ROBBERS, Flamingo Pictures Ltd.: CHRISTINE OESTREICHER, Producer.

FIRST WINTER, National Film Board of Canada: JOHN N. SMITH, Producer.

★ VIOLET, The American Film Institute: PAUL KEMP and SHELLEY LEVINSON, Producers.

1982 Fifty-fifth Year

Animated

THE GREAT COGNITO, Will Vinton Productions: WILL VINTON, Producer.

THE SNOWMAN, Snowman Enterprises Ltd.: JOHN COATES, Producer.

★ TANGO, Film Polski: ZBIGNIEW RYBCZYNAKI, Producer.

Live Action

BALLET ROBOTIQUE, Bob Rogers and Company: BOB ROGERS, Producer.

★ A SHOCKING ACCIDENT, Flamingo Pictures Ltd.: CHRISTINE OESTREICHER, Producer.

THE SILENCE, The American Film

Institute: MICHAEL TOSHIYUKI UNO and JOSEPH BENSON, Producers.

SPLIT CHERRY TREE, Learning Corporation of America: JAN SAUNDERS, Producer.

SREDNI VASHTAR, Laurentic Film Productions Ltd.: ANDREW BIRKIN, Producer.

1983 Fifty-sixth Year

Animated

MICKEY'S CHRISTMAS CAROL, Walt Disney Productions: BURNY MATTINSON, Producer.

SOUND OF SUNSHINE—SOUND OF RAIN, Hallinan Plus!: EDA GODEL HALLINAN, Producer.

★ SUNDAE IN NEW YORK, Motionpicker Productions: JIMMY PICKER, Producer.

Live Action

★ BOYS AND GIRLS, Atlantis Films Ltd.: JANICE L. PLATT, Producer.

GOODIE-TWO-SHOES, Timeless Films, Paramount Pictures: IAN EMES, Producer.

OVERNIGHT SENSATION, A Bloom Film Production: JON N. BLOOM, Producer.

1984 Fifty-seventh Year

Animated

★ CHARADE, A Sheridan College Production: JON MINNIS, Producer.

DOCTOR DESOTO, Michael Sporn Animation, Inc.: MORTON SCHINDEL and MICHAEL SPORN, Producers.

PARADISE, National Film Board of Canada: ISHU PATEL, Producer.

Live Action

THE PAINTED DOOR, Atlantis Films Limited in association with the National Film Board of Canada: MICHAEL MACMILLAN and JANICE L. PLATT, Producers.

TALES OF MEETING AND PARTING, The American Film Institute—Directing Workshop for Women: SHARON ORECK and LESLI LINKA GLATTER, Producers.

★ UP, Pyramid Films: MIKE HOOVER, Producer.

1985 Fifty-eighth Year

Animated

★ ANNA & BELLA, The Netherlands: CILIA VAN DIJK, Producer.

THE BIG SNIT, National Film Board of Canada: RICHARD CONDIE and MICHAEL SCOTT, Producers.

SECOND CLASS MAIL, National Film and Television School: ALISON SNOWDEN, Producer.

Live Action

GRAFFITI, The American Film Institute: DIANNA COSTELLO, Producer.

★ MOLLY'S PILGRIM, Phoenix Films: JEFF BROWN, Producer.

RAINBOW WAR, Bob Rogers and Company: BOB ROGERS, Producer.

1986 Fifty-ninth Year

Animated

THE FROG, THE DOG, AND THE DEVIL, New Zealand National Film Unit: HUGH MACDONALD and MARTIN TOWNSEND, Producers.

★ A GREEK TRAGEDY, CineTe pvba: LINDA VAN TULDEN and WILLEM THIJSSEN, Producers.

LUXO JR., Pixar Productions: JOHN LASSETER and WILLIAM REEVES, Producers.

Live Action

EXIT, RAI Radiotelevisione Italian/RAI-UNO: STEFANO REALI and PINO QUARTUILO, Producers.

LOVE STRUCK, Rainy Day Productions: FREDDA WEISS, Producer.

★ PRECIOUS IMAGES, Calliope Films Inc.: CHUCK WORKMAN, Producer.

1987 Sixtieth Year

Animated

GEORGE AND ROSEMARY, National Film Board of Canada: EUNICE MACAULAY, Producer.

★ THE MAN WHO PLANTED TREES, Société Radio-Canada/ Canadian Broadcasting Corporation: FREDERIC BACK, Producer.

YOUR FACE, Bill Plympton Productions: BILL PLYMPTON, Producer.

Live Action

MAKING WAVES, The Production Pool Ltd.: ANN WINGATE, Producer.

★ RAY'S MALE HETEROSEXUAL DANCE HALL, Chanticleer Films: JONATHAN SANGER and JANA SUE MEMEL, Producers.

SHOESHINE, Tom Abrams Productions: ROBERT A. KATZ, Producer.

1988 Sixty-first Year

Animated

THE CAT CAME BACK, National Film Board of Canada: CORDELL BARKER, Producer.

TECHNOLOGICAL THREAT, Kroyer Films, Inc.: BILL KROYER, Producer.

★ TIN TOY, Pixar: JOHN LASSETER, Producer.

Live Action

★ THE APPOINTMENTS OF DENNIS JENNINGS, Schooner Productions, Inc.: DEAN PARISOT and STEVEN WRIGHT, Producers.

CADILLAC DREAMS, Cadillac Dreams Production: MATIA KARRELL, Producer.

GULLAH TALES, Georgia State University: GARY MOSS, Producer.

1989 Sixty-second Year

Animated

★ BALANCE, A Lauenstein Production: CHRISTOPH LAUENSTEIN and WOLFGANG LAUENSTEIN, Producers.

COW, The "Pilot" Co-op Animated Film Studio with VPTO Videofilm: ALEXANDER PETROV, Producer.

THE HILL FARM, National Film and Television School: MARK BAKER, Producer.

Live Action

AMAZON DIARY, Determined Productions, Inc.: ROBERT NIXON, Producer.

THE CHILDEATER, Stephen-Tammuz Productions, Ltd.: JONATHAN TAMMUZ, Producer.

★ WORK EXPERIENCE, North Inch Production Ltd.: JAMES HENDRIE, Producer.

1990 Sixty-third Year

Animated

★ CREATURE COMFORTS, An Aardman Animations Limited Production: NICK PARK, Producer.

A GRAND DAY OUT, A National Film and Television School Production: NICK PARK, Producer.

GRASSHOPPERS (CAVALLETTE), A Bruno Bozzetto Production: BRUNO BOZZETTO, Producer.

Live Action

BRONX CHEERS, An American Film Institute Production: RAYMOND DE FELITTA and MATTHEW GROSS, Producers.

DEAR ROSIE, A World's End Production: PETER CATTANEO and BARNABY THOMPSON, Producers.

★ THE LUNCH DATE, An Adam Davidson Production: ADAM DAVIDSON, Producer.

SENZENI NA? (WHAT HAVE WE DONE?) An American Film Institute Production: BERNARD JOFFA and ANTHONY E. NICHOLAS, Producers.

12:01 PM, A Chanticleer Films

Production: HILLARY RIPPS and JONATHAN HEAP, Producers.

1991 Sixty-fourth Year

Animated

BLACKFLY, A National Film Board of Canada Production: CHRISTOPHER HINTON, Producer.

★ MANIPULATION, A Tandem Films Production: DANIEL GREAVES, Producer.

STRINGS, A National Film Board of Canada Production: WENDY TILBY, Producer.

Live Action

BIRCH STREET GYM, Chanticleer Films Production: STEPHEN KESSLER and T. R. CONROY, Producers.

LAST BREEZE OF SUMMER, American Film Institute Production: DAVID M. MASSEY, Producer.

★ SESSION MAN, Chanticleer Films Production: SETH WINSTON and ROB FRIED, Producers.

1992 Sixty-fifth Year

Animated

ADAM, An Aardman Animations Ltd. Production: PETER LORD, Producer.

★ MONA LISA DESCENDING A STAIRCASE, A Joan C. Gratz Production: JOAN C. GRATZ, Producer.

ŘEČI, ŘEČI, ŘEČI . . . (WORDS, WORDS, WORDS), A Krátky Film Production: MICHAELA PAVLÁTOVÁ, Producer.

THE SANDMAN, A Batty Berry Mackinnon Production: PAUL BERRY, Producer.

SCREEN PLAY, A Bare Boards Film Production: BARRY J.C. PURVES, Producer.

Live Action

Not given after this year.

CONTACT, A Chanticleer Films, Inc. Production: JONATHAN DARBY and JANA SUE MEMEL, Producers.

CRUISE CONTROL, A Palmieri Pictures Production: MATT PALMIERI, Producer.

THE LADY IN WAITING, A Taylor Made Films Production: CHRISTIAN M. TAYLOR, Producer.

★ OMNIBUS, A Lazennec tout court/ Le C.R.R.A.V. Production: SAM KARMANN, Producer.

SWAN SONG, A Renaissance Films PLC Production: KENNETH BRANAGH, Producer.

Documentary

The Academy honored a nonfiction film for the first time in 1936 when it voted a special award to *The March of Time*, but it was not until 1941 that a separate category for documentary film was established. The Academy defines documentary films as "those dealing creatively with cultural, artistic, historical, social, scientific, economic or other significant subjects, photographed in actual occurrence or re-enacted, produced in animation, stop-motion, or any other technique, and wherein the emphasis is on factual content and not on fiction. The purely technical instructional film will not be considered."

World War II brought a terrific expansion in nonfiction film—newsreels, training films, and documentaries—and the 1942 Documentary awards listed four co-winners chosen from twenty-five nominations. The category was divided the following year so that feature films would not compete against short subjects. Present rules define features as films with running times exceeding thirty minutes.

In 1969, for the first and only time, an Oscar had to be withdrawn. When the 1968 Documentary Feature winner *Young Americans* was declared ineligible, the runner-up *Journey into Self* was awarded an Oscar in a private ceremony at Academy headquarters. In 1971 *Sentinels of Silence* won both Documentary Short Subject and Short Subject—Live Action. The rules were then changed to permit eligible films to be entered in one or the other category but not both. A later rule change excluded documentary films from the Short Films category. In 1992 the Academy voted to discontinue the category of Documentary Short Subject.

Films eligible for this award are entered by their producers and are screened by a Documentary Awards Committee which determines the nominees. Final voting is restricted to Academy members who have seen *all* nominated films.

1941 Fourteenth Year

ADVENTURES IN THE BRONX, Film Assocs.

BOMBER, U.S. Office for Emergency Management Film Unit.

CHRISTMAS UNDER FIRE, British Ministry of Information, Warner Bros.

★ CHURCHILL'S ISLAND, Canadian Film Board, UA.

LETTER FROM HOME, British Ministry of Information.

LIFE OF A THOROUGHBRED, 20th Century-Fox.

NORWAY IN REVOLT, March of Time, RKO Radio.

SOLDIERS OF THE SKY, 20th Century-Fox.

WAR CLOUDS IN THE PACIFIC, Canadian Film Board.

*1942 Fifteenth Year**

AFRICA, PRELUDE TO VICTORY, March of Time, 20th Century-Fox.

*Four winners were selected this year.

★ BATTLE OF MIDWAY, U.S. Navy, 20th Century-Fox.
COMBAT REPORT, U.S. Army Signal Corps.
CONQUER BY THE CLOCK, Office of War Information, RKO Pathe: FREDERIC ULLMAN, JR., Producer.
THE GRAIN THAT BUILT A HEMISPHERE, Coordinator's Office, Motion Picture Society for the Americas: WALT DISNEY, Producer.
HENRY BROWNE, FARMER, U.S. Department of Agriculture, Republic.
HIGH OVER THE BORDERS, Canadian National Film Board.
HIGH STAKES IN THE EAST, Netherlands Information Bureau.
INSIDE FIGHTING CHINA, Canadian National Film Board.
IT'S EVERYBODY'S WAR, Office of War Information, 20th Century-Fox.
★ KOKODA FRONT LINE, Australian News and Information Bureau.
LISTEN TO BRITAIN, British Ministry of Information.
LITTLE BELGIUM, Belgian Ministry of Information.
LITTLE ISLES OF FREEDOM, Warner Bros.: VICTOR STOLOFF and EDGAR LOEW, Producers.
★ MOSCOW STRIKES BACK, Artkino (Russian).
MR. BLABBERMOUTH, Office of War Information, M-G-M.
MR. GARDENIA JONES, Office of War Information, M-G-M.
NEW SPIRIT, U.S. Treasury Department: WALT DISNEY, Producer.
★ PRELUDE TO WAR, U.S. Army Special Services.
THE PRICE OF VICTORY, Office of War Information, Paramount: PINE-THOMAS.
A SHIP IS BORN, U.S. Merchant Marine, Warner Bros.
TWENTY-ONE MILES, British Ministry of Information.
WE REFUSE TO DIE, Office of War Information, Paramount: WILLIAM C. THOMAS, Producer.
WHITE EAGLE, Cocanen Films.
WINNING YOUR WINGS, U.S. Army Air Force, Warner Bros.

1943 Sixteenth Year

Short Subjects

CHILDREN OF MARS, This Is America Series, RKO Radio.
★ DECEMBER 7TH, U.S. Navy, Field Photographic Branch, Office of Strategic Services.
PLAN FOR DESTRUCTION, Metro-Goldwyn-Mayer.
SWEDES IN AMERICA, Office of War Information, Overseas Motion Picture Bureau.
TO THE PEOPLE OF THE UNITED STATES, U.S. Public Health Service, Walter Wanger Prods.
TOMORROW WE FLY, U.S. Navy, Bureau of Aeronautics.
YOUTH IN CRISIS, March of Time, 20th Century-Fox.

Features

BAPTISM OF FIRE, U.S. Army, Fighting Men Series.
BATTLE OF RUSSIA, Special Service Division of the War Department.
★ DESERT VICTORY, British Ministry of Information.
REPORT FROM THE ALEUTIANS, U.S. Army Pictorial Service, Combat Film Series.
WAR DEPARTMENT REPORT, Field Photographic Branch, Office of Strategic Services.

1944 Seventeenth Year

Short Subjects

ARTURO TOSCANINI, Motion Picture Bureau, Overseas Branch, Office of War Information.
NEW AMERICANS, This Is America Series, RKO Radio.

★ WITH THE MARINES AT TARAWA, U.S. Marine Corps.

Features

★ THE FIGHTING LADY, 20th Century-Fox and U.S. Navy.

RESISTING ENEMY INTERROGATION, U.S. Army Air Force.

1945 Eighteenth Year

Short Subjects

★ HITLER LIVES?, Warner Bros.

LIBRARY OF CONGRESS, Overseas Motion Picture Bureau, Office of War Information.

TO THE SHORES OF IWO JIMA, U.S. Marine Corps.

Features

THE LAST BOMB, U.S. Army Air Force.

★ THE TRUE GLORY, Governments of Great Britain and the United States of America.

1946 Nineteenth Year

Short Subjects

ATOMIC POWER, 20th Century-Fox.

LIFE AT THE ZOO, Artkino.

PARAMOUNT NEWS ISSUE #37, Paramount.

★ SEEDS OF DESTINY, U.S. War Department.

TRAFFIC WITH THE DEVIL, Metro-Goldwyn-Mayer.

Features

No Features were nominated this year.

1947 Twentieth Year

Short Subjects

★ FIRST STEPS, United Nations Division of Films and Visual Education.

PASSPORT TO NOWHERE, RKO Radio: (This Is America Series) FREDERIC ULLMAN, JR., Producer.

SCHOOL IN THE MAILBOX, Australian News and Information Bureau.

Features

★ DESIGN FOR DEATH, RKO Radio: SID ROGELL, Executive Producer; THERON WARTH and RICHARD O. FLEISCHER, Producers.

JOURNEY INTO MEDICINE, U.S. Department of State, Office of Information and Educational Exchange.

THE WORLD IS RICH, British Information Services: PAUL ROTHA, Producer.

1948 Twenty-first Year

Short Subjects

HEART TO HEART, Fact Film Organization: HERBERT MORGAN, Producer.

OPERATION VITTLES, U.S. Army Air Force.

★ TOWARD INDEPENDENCE, U.S. Army.

Features

THE QUIET ONE, Mayer-Burstyn: JANICE LOEB, Producer.

★ THE SECRET LAND, U.S. Navy, M-G-M: O. O. DULL, Producer.

1949 Twenty-second Year

Short Subjects (Tie)

★ A CHANCE TO LIVE, March of Time, 20th Century-Fox: RICHARD DE ROCHEMONT, Producer.

1848, A. F. Films, Inc.: FRENCH CINEMA GENERAL COOPERATIVE, Producer.

THE RISING TIDE, National Film Board of Canada: ST. FRANCIS-XAVIER UNIVERSITY (Nova Scotia), Producer.

★ SO MUCH FOR SO LITTLE, Warner Bros. Cartoons, Inc.: EDWARD SELZER, Producer.

Features

★ DAYBREAK IN UDI, British Information Services: CROWN FILM UNIT, Producer.

KENJI COMES HOME, A Protestant Film Commission Prod.: PAUL F. HEARD, Producer.

1950 Twenty-third Year

Short Subjects

THE FIGHT: SCIENCE AGAINST CANCER, NATIONAL FILM BOARD OF CANADA in cooperation with the Medical Film Institute of the Association of American Medical Colleges.

THE STAIRS, Film Documents, Inc.

* WHY KOREA?, 20th Century-Fox Movietone: EDMUND REEK, Producer.

Features

* THE TITAN: STORY OF MICHELANGELO, Michelangelo Co., Classics Pictures, Inc.: ROBERT SNYDER, Producer.

WITH THESE HANDS, Promotional Films Co., Inc.: JACK ARNOLD and LEE GOODMAN, Producers.

1951 Twenty-fourth Year

Short Subjects

* BENJY, Made by FRED ZINNEMANN with the cooperation of Paramount Pictures Corp. for the Los Angeles Orthopaedic Hospital.

ONE WHO CAME BACK: OWEN CRUMP, Producer. (Film sponsored by the Disabled American Veterans, in cooperation with the United States Department of Defense and the Association of Motion Picture Producers.)

THE SEEING EYE, Warner Bros.: GORDON HOLLINGSHEAD, Producer.

Features

I WAS A COMMUNIST FOR THE F.B.I., Warner Bros.: BRYAN FOY, Producer.

* KON-TIKI, An Artfilm Prod., RKO Radio (Norwegian): OLLE NORDEMAR, Producer.

1952 Twenty-fifth Year

Short Subjects

DEVIL TAKE US, Theatre of Life Prod.: HERBERT MORGAN, Producer.

THE GARDEN SPIDER (EPEIRA DIADEMA), Cristallo Films, I.F.E. Releasing Corp. (Italian): ALBERTO ANCILOTTO, Producer.

MAN ALIVE!, Made by United Productions of America for the American Cancer Society: STEPHEN BOSUSTOW, Executive Producer.

* NEIGHBOURS, National Film Board of Canada, Arthur Mayer-Edward Kingsley, Inc. (Canadian): NORMAN McLAREN, Producer.

Features

THE HOAXTERS, Metro-Goldwyn-Mayer: DORE SCHARY, Producer.

NAVAJO, Bartlett-Foster Prod., Lippert Pictures, Inc.: HALL BARTLETT, Producer.

* THE SEA AROUND US, RKO Radio: IRWIN ALLEN, Producer.

1953 Twenty-sixth Year

Short Subjects

* THE ALASKAN ESKIMO, Walt Disney Prods., RKO Radio: WALT DISNEY, Producer.

THE LIVING CITY, Encyclopaedia Britannica Films, Inc.: JOHN BARNES, Producer.

OPERATION BLUE JAY, U.S. Army Signal Corps.

THEY PLANTED A STONE, World Wide Pictures, British Information Services (British): JAMES CARR, Producer.

THE WORD, 20th Century-Fox: JOHN HEALY and JOHN ADAMS, Producers.

Features

THE CONQUEST OF EVEREST, Countryman Films, Ltd. and Group 3 Ltd., UA (British): JOHN TAYLOR,

LEON CLORE, and GRAHAME THARP, Producers.

★ THE LIVING DESERT, Walt Disney Prods., Buena Vista Film Dist. Co., Inc.: WALT DISNEY, Producer.

A QUEEN IS CROWNED, J. Arthur Rank Organization, Ltd., U-I (British): CASTLETON KNIGHT, Producer.

1954 Twenty-seventh Year

Short Subjects

JET CARRIER, 20th Century-Fox: OTTO LANG, Producer.

REMBRANDT: A SELF-PORTRAIT, Distributors Corp. of America: MORRIE ROIZMAN, Producer.

★ THURSDAY'S CHILDREN, British Information Services (British): WORLD WIDE PICTURES AND MORSE FILMS, Producers.

Features

THE STRATFORD ADVENTURE, National Film Board of Canada, Continental Dist., Inc. (Canadian): GUY GLOVER, Producer.

★ THE VANISHING PRAIRIE, Walt Disney Prods., Buena Vista Film Dist. Co., Inc.: WALT DISNEY, Producer.

1955 Twenty-eighth Year

Short Subjects

THE BATTLE OF GETTYSBURG, Metro-Goldwyn-Mayer: DORE SCHARY, Producer.

THE FACE OF LINCOLN, University of Southern California Presentation, Cavalcade Pictures, Inc.: WILBER T. BLUME, Producer.

★ MEN AGAINST THE ARCTIC, Walt Disney Prods., Buena Vista Film Dist. Co., Inc.: WALT DISNEY, Producer.

Features

HEARTBREAK RIDGE, René Risacher Prod., Tudor Pictures (French): RENÉ RISACHER, Producer.

★ HELEN KELLER IN HER STORY, Nancy Hamilton Presentation: NANCY HAMILTON, Producer.

1956 Twenty-ninth Year

Short Subjects

A CITY DECIDES, Charles Guggenheim and Assocs., Inc. Prod.

THE DARK WAVE, 20th Century-Fox: JOHN HEALY, Producer.

THE HOUSE WITHOUT A NAME, Universal-International: VALENTINE DAVIES, Producer.

MAN IN SPACE, Walt Disney Prods., Buena Vista Film Dist. Co., Inc.: WARD KIMBALL, Producer.

★ THE TRUE STORY OF THE CIVIL WAR, Camera Eye Pictures, Inc.: LOUIS CLYDE STOUMEN, Producer.

Features

THE NAKED EYE, Camera Eye Pictures, Inc.: LOUIS CLYDE STOUMEN, Producer.

★ THE SILENT WORLD, A Filmad-F.S.J.Y.C. Prod., Columbia (French): JACQUES-YVES COUSTEAU, Producer.

WHERE MOUNTAINS FLOAT, Brandon Films, Inc. (Danish): THE GOVERNMENT FILM COMMITTEE OF DENMARK, Producer.

1957 Thirtieth Year

Short Subjects

No Short Subject Documentary nominations were voted this year.

Features

★ ALBERT SCHWEITZER, Hill and Anderson Prod., Louis de

Rochemont Assocs.: JEROME HILL, Producer.

ON THE BOWERY, Lionel Rogosin Prods., Film Representations, Inc.: LIONEL ROGOSIN, Producer.

TORERO!, Producciones Barbachano Ponce, Columbia (Mexican): MANUEL BARBACHANO PONCE, Producer.

1958 Thirty-first Year

Short Subjects

★ AMA GIRLS, Walt Disney Prods., Buena Vista Film Dist. Co., Inc.: BEN SHARPSTEEN, Producer.

EMPLOYEES ONLY, Hughes Aircraft Co.: KENNETH G. BROWN, Producer.

JOURNEY INTO SPRING, British Transport Films, Lester A. Schoenfeld Films: IAN FERGUSON, Producer.

THE LIVING STONE, National Film Board of Canada: TOM DALY, Producer.

OVERTURE, United Nations Film Service: THOROLD DICKINSON, Producer.

Features

ANTARCTIC CROSSING, World Wide Pictures, Lester A. Schoenfeld Films: JAMES CARR, Producer.

THE HIDDEN WORLD, Small World Co.: ROBERT SNYDER, Producer.

PSYCHIATRIC NURSING, Dynamic Films, Inc.: NATHAN ZUCKER, Producer.

★ WHITE WILDERNESS, Walt Disney Prods., Buena Vista Film Dist. Co., Inc.: BEN SHARPSTEEN, Producer.

1959 Thirty-second Year

Short Subjects

DONALD IN MATHMAGIC LAND, Walt Disney Prods., Buena Vista Film Dist. Co., Inc.: WALT DISNEY, Producer.

FROM GENERATION TO GENERATION, Cullen Assocs., Maternity Center Assoc.: EDWARD F. CULLEN, Producer.

★ GLASS, Netherlands Government, George K. Arthur-Go Pictures, Inc. (The Netherlands): BERT HAANSTRA, Producer.

Features

THE RACE FOR SPACE, Wolper, Inc.: DAVID L. WOLPER, Producer.

★ SERENGETI SHALL NOT DIE, Okapia-Film Prod., Transocean Film (German): BERNHARD GRZIMEK, Producer.

1960 Thirty-third Year

Short Subjects

BEYOND SILENCE, United States Information Agency.

A CITY CALLED COPENHAGEN, Statens Filmcentral, Danish Government Film Office (Danish).

GEORGE GROSZ' INTERREGNUM, Educational Communications Corp.: CHARLES CAREY and ALTINA CAREY, Producers.

★ GIUSEPPINA, James Hill Prod., Lester A. Schoenfeld Films (British): JAMES HILL, Producer.

UNIVERSE, National Film Board of Canada, Lester A. Schoenfeld Films (Canadian): COLIN LOW, Producer.

Features

★ THE HORSE WITH THE FLYING TAIL, Walt Disney Prods., Buena Vista Dist. Co., Inc.: LARRY LANSBURGH, Producer.

REBEL IN PARADISE, Tiare Co.: ROBERT D. FRASER, Producer.

1961 Thirty-fourth Year

Short Subjects

BREAKING THE LANGUAGE BARRIER, United States Air Force.

CRADLE OF GENIUS, Plough Prods., An Irving M. Lesser Film Presentation (Irish): JIM O'CONNOR and TOM HAYES, Producers.

KAHL, Dido-Film-GmbH., AEG-Filmdienst (German).

L'UOMO IN GRIGIO (THE MAN IN GRAY), (Italian): BENEDETTO BENEDETTI, Producer.

★ PROJECT HOPE, MacManus, John and Adams, Inc., Ex-Cell-O Corp., A Klaeger Film Production: FRANK P. BIBAS, Producer.

Features

LA GRANDE OLIMPIADE (OLYMPIC GAMES 1960), dell'Istituto Nazionale Luce, Comitato Organizzatore dei Giochi della XVII Olimpiade, Cineriz (Italian).

★ LE CIEL ET LA BOUE (SKY ABOVE AND MUD BENEATH), Ardennes Films and Michael Arthur Film Prods., Rank Film Distrs., Ltd. (French): ARTHUR COHN and RENÉ LAFUITE, Producers.

1962 Thirty-fifth Year

Short Subjects

★ DYLAN THOMAS, TWW Ltd., Janus Films (Welsh): JACK HOWELLS, Producer.

THE JOHN GLENN STORY, Department of the Navy, Warner Bros.: WILLIAM L. HENDRICKS, Producer.

THE ROAD TO THE WALL, CBS Films, Inc., Department of Defense: ROBERT SAUDEK, Producer.

Features

ALVORADA (BRAZIL'S CHANGING FACE), MW Filmproduktion (German): HUGO NIEBELING, Producer.

★ BLACK FOX, Image Prods., Inc., Heritage Films, Inc.: LOUIS CLYDE STOUMEN, Producer.

1963 Thirty-sixth Year

Short Subjects

★ CHAGALL, Auerbach Film Enterprises, Ltd.-Flag Films: SIMON SCHIFFRIN, Producer.

THE FIVE CITIES OF JUNE, United States Information Agency: GEORGE STEVENS, JR., Producer.

THE SPIRIT OF AMERICA, Spotlite News: ALGERNON G. WALKER, Producer.

THIRTY MILLION LETTERS, British Transport Films: EDGAR ANSTEY, Producer.

TO LIVE AGAIN, Wilding Inc.: MEL LONDON, Producer.

Features

LE MAILLON ET LA CHAINE (THE LINK AND THE CHAIN), Films du Centaure-Filmartic: PAUL DE ROUBAIX, Producer.

★ ROBERT FROST: A LOVER'S QUARREL WITH THE WORLD, WGBH Educational Foundation: ROBERT HUGHES, Producer.

THE YANKS ARE COMING, David L. Wolper Prods.: MARSHALL FLAUM, Producer.

1964 Thirty-seventh Year

Short Subjects

BREAKING THE HABIT, American Cancer Society, Modern Talking Picture Service: HENRY JACOBS and JOHN KORTY, Producers.

CHILDREN WITHOUT, National Education Association, Guggenheim Productions.

KENOJUAK, National Film Board of Canada.

★ NINE FROM LITTLE ROCK, United States Information Agency, Guggenheim Productions.

140 DAYS UNDER THE WORLD, New Zealand National Film Unit, Rank Film Distributors of New Zealand:

GEOFFREY SCOTT and OXLEY HUGHAN, Producers.

Features

THE FINEST HOURS, Le Vien Films, Ltd., Columbia: JACK LE VIEN, Producer.
FOUR DAYS IN NOVEMBER, David L. Wolper Prods., UA: MEL STUART, Producer.
THE HUMAN DUTCH, Haanstra Filmproductie: BERT HAANSTRA, Producer.
★ JACQUES-YVES COUSTEAU'S WORLD WITHOUT SUN, Filmad-Les Requins Associés-Orsay-CEIAP, Columbia: JACQUES-YVES COUSTEAU, Producer.
OVER THERE, 1914–18, Zodiac Prods., Pathe Contemporary Films: JEAN AUREL, Producer.

1965 Thirty-eighth Year

Short Subjects

MURAL ON OUR STREET, Henry Street Settlement, Pathe Contemporary Films: KIRK SMALLMAN, Producer.
OUVERTURE, Mafilm Prods., HUNGAROFILM-PATHE CONTEMPORARY FILMS.
POINT OF VIEW, Vision Associates Prod., National Tuberculosis Assoc.
★ TO BE ALIVE!, Johnson Wax: FRANCIS THOMPSON, INC., Producer.
YEATS COUNTRY, Aengus Films Ltd. for the Dept. of External Affairs of Ireland: PATRICK CAREY and JOE MENDOZA, Producers.

Features

THE BATTLE OF THE BULGE ... THE BRAVE RIFLES, Mascott Prods.: LAURENCE E. MASCOTT, Producer.
★ THE ELEANOR ROOSEVELT STORY, Sidney Glazier Prod., American Intl.: SIDNEY GLAZIER, Producer.
THE FORTH ROAD BRIDGE, Random Film Prods., Ltd., Shell-Mex and B.P. Film Library: PETER MILLS, Producer.
LET MY PEOPLE GO, Wolper Prods.: MARSHALL FLAUM, Producer.
TO DIE IN MADRID, Ancinex Prods., Altura Films Intl.: FREDERIC ROSSIF, Producer.

1966 Thirty-ninth Year

Short Subjects

ADOLESCENCE, M.K. Prods.: MARIN KARMITZ and VLADIMIR FORGENCY, Producers.
COWBOY, United States Information Agency: MICHAEL AHNEMANN and GARY SCHLOSSER, Producers.
THE ODDS AGAINST, Vision Associates Prod. for the American Foundation Institute of Corrections: LEE R. BOBKER and HELEN KRISTT RADIN, Producers.
SAINT MATTHEW PASSION, Mafilm Studio, HUNGAROFILM.
★ A YEAR TOWARD TOMORROW, Sun Dial Films, Inc. Prod. for Office of Economic Opportunity: EDMOND A. LEVY, Producer.

Features

THE FACE OF GENIUS, WBZ-TV, Group W, Boston: ALFRED R. KELMAN, Producer.
HELICOPTER CANADA, Centennial Commission, National Film Board of Canada: PETER JONES and TOM DALY, Producers.
LE VOLCAN INTERDIT (THE FORBIDDEN VOLCANO), Cine Documents Tazieff, Athos Films: HAROUN TAZIEFF, Producer.

THE REALLY BIG FAMILY, David L. Wolper Prod.: ALEX GRASSHOFF, Producer.

★ THE WAR GAME, BBC Prod. for the British Film Institute, Pathe Contemporary Films: PETER WATKINS, Producer.

1967 Fortieth Year

Short Subjects

MONUMENT TO THE DREAM, Guggenheim Prods.: CHARLES E. GUGGENHEIM, Producer.

A PLACE TO STAND, T.D.F. Prod. for the Ontario Dept. of Economics and Development: CHRISTOPHER CHAPMAN, Producer.

★ THE REDWOODS, King Screen Prods.: MARK HARRIS and TREVOR GREENWOOD, Producers.

SEE YOU AT THE PILLAR, Associated British-Pathe Prod.: ROBERT FITCHETT, Producer.

WHILE I RUN THIS RACE, Sun Dial Films for VISTA, an Economic Opportunity Program: CARL V. RAGSDALE, Producer.

Features

★ THE ANDERSON PLATOON, French Broadcasting System: PIERRE SCHOENDOERFFER, Producer.

FESTIVAL, Patchke Prods.: MURRAY LERNER, Producer.

HARVEST, United States Information Agency: CARROLL BALLARD, Producer.

A KING'S STORY, Jack Le Vien Prod.: JACK LE VIEN, Producer.

A TIME FOR BURNING, Quest Prods. for Lutheran Film Associates: WILLIAM C. JERSEY, Producer.

1968 Forty-first Year

Short Subjects

THE HOUSE THAT ANANDA BUILT, Films Division, Government of India: FALI BILIMORIA, Producer.

THE REVOLVING DOOR, Vision Associates for the American Foundation Institute of Corrections: LEE R. BOBKER, Producer.

A SPACE TO GROW, Office of Economic Opportunity for Project Upward Bound: THOMAS P. KELLY, JR., Producer.

A WAY OUT OF THE WILDERNESS, John Sutherland Prods.: DAN E. WEISBURD, Producer.

★ WHY MAN CREATES, Saul Bass and Associates: SAUL BASS, Producer.

Features

A FEW NOTES ON OUR FOOD PROBLEM, United States Information Agency: JAMES BLUE, Producer.

★ JOURNEY INTO SELF, Western Behavioral Sciences Institute: BILL McGAW, Producer.

THE LEGENDARY CHAMPIONS, Turn of the Century Fights: WILLIAM CAYTON, Producer.

OTHER VOICES, DHS Films: DAVID H. SAWYER, Producer.

YOUNG AMERICANS, The Young Americans Prod.: ROBERT COHN and ALEX GRASSHOFF, Producers.*

1969 Forty-second Year

Short Subjects

★ CZECHOSLOVAKIA 1968, Sanders-Fresco Film Makers for United

**Young Americans* won the award but was later declared ineligible because it had been released prior to the eligibility year. On May 8, 1969, the first runner-up, *Journey into Self*, was declared the winner.

States Information Agency: DENIS SANDERS and ROBERT M. FRESCO, Producers.

AN IMPRESSION OF JOHN STEINBECK: WRITER, Donald Wrye Prods. for United States Information Agency: DONALD WRYE, Producer.

JENNY IS A GOOD THING, ACI Prod. for Project Head Start: JOAN HORVATH, Producer.

LEO BEUERMAN, Centron Prod.: ARTHUR H. WOLF and RUSSELL A. MOSSER, Producers.

THE MAGIC MACHINES, Fly-by-Night Prods.: JOAN KELLER STERN, Producer.

Features

★ ARTHUR RUBINSTEIN—THE LOVE OF LIFE, Midem Prod.: BERNARD CHEVRY, Producer.

BEFORE THE MOUNTAIN WAS MOVED, Robert K. Sharpe Prods. for the Office of Economic Opportunity: ROBERT K. SHARPE, Producer.

IN THE YEAR OF THE PIG, Emile de Antonio Prod.: EMILE DE ANTONIO, Producer.

THE OLYMPICS IN MEXICO, Film Section of the Organizing Committee for the XIX Olympic Games.

THE WOLF MEN, MGM Documentary: IRWIN ROSTEN, Producer.

1970 Forty-third Year

Short Subjects

THE GIFTS, Richter-McBride Prods. for the Water Quality Office of the Environmental Protection Agency: ROBERT MCBRIDE, Producer.

★ INTERVIEWS WITH MY LAI VETERANS, Laser Film Corp.: JOSEPH STRICK, Producer.

A LONG WAY FROM NOWHERE, Robert Aller Prods.: BOB ALLER, Producer.

OISIN, An Aengus Film: VIVIEN CAREY and PATRICK CAREY, Producers.

TIME IS RUNNING OUT, Gesellschaft fur bildende Filme: HORST DALLMAYR and ROBERT MENEGOZ, Producers.

Features

CHARIOTS OF THE GODS, Terra-Filmkunst GmbH.: DR. HARALD REINL, Producer.

JACK JOHNSON, The Big Fights: JIM JACOBS, Producer.

KING: A FILMED RECORD . . . MONTGOMERY TO MEMPHIS, Commonwealth United Prod.: ELY LANDAU, Producer.

SAY GOODBYE, A Wolper Prod.: DAVID H. VOWELL, Producer.

★ WOODSTOCK, A Wadleigh-Maurice Ltd. Prod.: BOB MAURICE, Producer.

1971 Forty-fourth Year

Short Subjects

ADVENTURES IN PERCEPTION, Han van Gelder Filmproduktie for Netherlands Information Service: HAN VAN GELDER, Producer.

ART IS . . . , Henry Strauss Associates for Sears Roebuck Foundation: JULIAN KRAININ and DEWITT L. SAGE, JR., Producers.

THE NUMBERS START WITH THE RIVER, A WH Picture for United States Information Agency: DONALD WRYE, Producer.

★ SENTINELS OF SILENCE, Producciones Concord, Paramount: MANUEL ARANGO and ROBERT AMRAM, Producers.

SOMEBODY WAITING, Snider Prods. for University of California Medical Film Library: HAL RINEY, DICK SNIDER, and SHERWOOD OMENS, Producers.

Features

ALASKA WILDERNESS LAKE, Alan Landsburg Prods.: ALAN LANDSBURG, Producer.

★ THE HELLSTROM CHRONICLE,

David L. Wolper Prods., Cinema 5, Ltd.: WALON GREEN, Producer.

ON ANY SUNDAY, Bruce Brown Films-Solar Prods., Cinema 5, Ltd.: BRUCE BROWN, Producer.

THE RA EXPEDITIONS, Swedish Broadcasting Company, Interwest Film Corp.: LENNART EHRENBORG and THOR HEYERDAHL, Producers.

THE SORROW AND THE PITY, Television Rencontre-Norddeutscher Rundfunk-Television Swiss Romande, Cinema 5, Ltd.: MARCEL OPHULS, Producer.

1972 Forty-fifth Year

Short Subjects

HUNDERTWASSER'S RAINY DAY, An Argos Films-Peter Schamoni Film Prod.: PETER SCHAMONI, Producer.

K-Z, A Nexus Film Production: GIORGIO TREVES, Producer.

SELLING OUT, A Unit Productions Film: TADEUSZ JAWORSKI, Producer.

★ THIS TINY WORLD, A Charles Huguenot van der Linden Production: CHARLES and MARTINA HUGENOT VAN DER LINDEN, Producers.

THE TIDE OF TRAFFIC, A BP-Greenpark Production: HUMPHREY SWINGLER, Producer.

Features

APE AND SUPER-APE, A Bert Haanstra Film Production, Netherlands Ministry of Culture, Recreation and Social Welfare: BERT HAANSTRA, Producer.

MALCOLM X, A Marvin Worth Production, Warner Bros.: MARVIN WORTH and ARNOLD PERL, Producers.

MANSON, Merrick International Pictures: ROBERT HENDRICKSON and LAURENCE MERRICK, Producers.

★ MARJOE, A Cinema X Production, Cinema 5, Ltd.: HOWARD SMITH and SARAH KERNOCHAN, Producers.

THE SILENT REVOLUTION, A Leonaris Film Production: ECKEHARD MUNCK, Producer.

1973 Forty-sixth Year

Short Subjects

BACKGROUND, D'Avino and Fucci-Stone Prods.: CARMEN D'AVINO, Producer.

CHILDREN AT WORK (Paisti Ag Obair), Gael-Linn Films: LOUIS MARCUS, Producer.

CHRISTO'S VALLEY CURTAIN, A Maysles Films Prod.: ALBERT MAYSLES and DAVID MAYSLES, Producers.

FOUR STONES FOR KANEMITSU, A Tamarind Prod.: (Producer credit in controversy).

★ PRINCETON: A SEARCH FOR ANSWERS, Krainin-Sage Prods.: JULIAN KRAININ and DEWITT L. SAGE, JR., Producers.

Features

ALWAYS A NEW BEGINNING, Goodell Motion Pictures: JOHN D. GOODELL, Producer.

BATTLE OF BERLIN, Chronos Film: BENGT VON ZUR MUEHLEN, Producer.

★ THE GREAT AMERICAN COWBOY, Keith Merrill Associates-Rodeo Film Prods.: KEITH MERRILL, Producer.

JOURNEY TO THE OUTER LIMITS, National Geographic Society and Wolper Prods.: ALEX GRASSHOFF, Producer.

WALLS OF FIRE, Mentor Prods.: GERTRUDE ROSS MARKS and EDMUND F. PENNEY, Producers.

1974 Forty-seventh Year

Short Subjects

CITY OUT OF WILDERNESS, Francis Thompson Inc.: FRANCIS THOMPSON, Producer.

★ DON'T, R. A. Films: ROBIN LEHMAN, Producer.

EXPLORATORIUM, A Jon Boorstin Prod.: JON BOORSTIN, Producer.

JOHN MUIR'S HIGH SIERRA, Dewitt Jones Prods.: DEWITT JONES and LESLEY FOSTER, Producers.

NAKED YOGA, A Filmshop Prod.: RONALD S. KASS and MERVYN LLOYD, Producers.

Features

ANTONIA: A PORTRAIT OF THE WOMAN, Rocky Mountain Prods.: JUDY COLLINS and JILL GODMILOW, Producers.

THE CHALLENGE... A TRIBUTE TO MODERN ART, A World View Prod.: HERBERT KLINE, Producer.

THE 81ST BLOW, A Film by Ghetto Fighters House: JACQUOT EHRLICH, DAVID BERGMAN, and HAIM GOURI, Producers.

★ HEARTS AND MINDS, A Touchstone-Audjeff-BBS Prod., Howard Zucker/Henry Jaglom-Rainbow Pictures Presentation: PETER DAVIS and BERT SCHNEIDER, Producers.

THE WILD AND THE BRAVE, ESJ Prods., in association with Tomorrow Entertainment Inc. and Jones/Howard Ltd.: NATALIE R. JONES and EUGENE S. JONES, Producers.

1975 Forty-eighth Year

Short Subjects

ARTHUR AND LILLIE, Department of Communication, Stanford University: JON ELSE, STEVEN KOVACS, and KRISTINE SAMUELSON, Producers.

★ THE END OF THE GAME, Opus Films Limited: CLAIRE WILBUR and ROBIN LEHMAN, Producers.

MILLIONS OF YEARS AHEAD OF MAN, BASF.: MANFRED BAIER, Producer.

PROBES IN SPACE, Graphic Films: GEORGE V. CASEY, Producer.

WHISTLING SMITH, National Film Board of Canada: BARRIE HOWELLS and MICHAEL SCOTT, Producers.

Features

THE CALIFORNIA REICH, Yasny Talking Pictures: WALTER F. PARKES and KEITH F. CRITCHLOW, Producers.

FIGHTING FOR OUR LIVES, A Farm Worker Film: GLEN PEARCY, Producer.

THE INCREDIBLE MACHINE, National Geographic Society and Wolper Prods.: IRWIN ROSTEN, Producer.

★ THE MAN WHO SKIED DOWN EVEREST, A Crawley Films Presentation: F. R. CRAWLEY, JAMES HAGER, and DALE HARTLEBEN, Producers.

THE OTHER HALF OF THE SKY: A CHINA MEMOIR, MacLaine Productions: SHIRLEY MacLAINE, Producer.

1976 Forty-ninth Year

Short Subjects

AMERICAN SHOESHINE, Titan Films: SPARKY GREENE, Producer.

BLACKWOOD, National Film Board of Canada: TONY IANZELO and ANDY THOMPSON, Producers.

THE END OF THE ROAD, Pelican Films: JOHN ARMSTRONG, Producer.

★ NUMBER OUR DAYS, Community Television of Southern California: LYNNE LITTMAN, Producer.

UNIVERSE, Graphic Films Corp. for NASA: LESTER NOVROS, Producer.

Features

★ HARLAN COUNTY, U.S.A., Cabin Creek Films: BARBARA KOPPLE, Producer.

HOLLYWOOD ON TRIAL, October Films/Cinema Associates Production: JAMES GUTMAN and DAVID HELPERN, JR., Producers.

OFF THE EDGE, Pentacle Films: MICHAEL FIRTH, Producer.

PEOPLE OF THE WIND, Elizabeth E. Rogers Productions: ANTHONY HOWARTH and DAVID KOFF, Producers.

VOLCANO: AN INQUIRY INTO THE LIFE AND DEATH OF MALCOLM LOWRY, National Film Board of Canada: DONALD BRITTAIN and ROBERT DUNCAN, Producers.

1977 Fiftieth Year

Short Subjects

AGUEDA MARTINEZ: OUR PEOPLE, OUR COUNTRY, A Moctesuma Esparza Production: MOCTESUMA ESPARZA, Producer.

FIRST EDITION, D. L. Sage Productions: HELEN WHITNEY and DEWITT L. SAGE, JR., Producers.

★ GRAVITY IS MY ENEMY, A John Joseph Production: JOHN JOSEPH and JAN STUSSY, Producers.

OF TIME, TOMBS AND TREASURE, A Charlie/Papa Production: JAMES R. MESSENGER, Producer.

THE SHETLAND EXPERIENCE, Balfour Films: DOUGLAS GORDON, Producer.

Features

THE CHILDREN OF THEATRE STREET, Mack-Vaganova Company: ROBERT DORNHELM and EARLE MACK, Producers.

HIGH GRASS CIRCUS, National Film Board of Canada: BILL BRIND, TORBEN SCHIOLER, and TONY IANZELO, Producers.

HOMAGE TO CHAGALL—THE COLOURS OF LOVE, A CBC Production: HARRY RASKY, Producer.

UNION MAIDS, A Klein, Reichert, Mogulescu Production: JAMES KLEIN, JULIA REICHERT, and MILES MOGULESCU, Producers.

★ WHO ARE THE DEBOLTS? AND WHERE DID THEY GET NINETEEN KIDS?, Korty Films and Charles M. Schulz Creative Associates in association with Sanrio Films: JOHN KORTY, DAN McCANN, and WARREN L. LOCKHART, Producers.

1978 Fifty-first Year

Short Subjects

THE DIVIDED TRAIL, A Jerry Aronson Production: JERRY ARONSON, Producer.

AN ENCOUNTER WITH FACES, Films Division, Government of India: K. KAPIL, Producer.

★ THE FLIGHT OF THE GOSSAMER CONDOR, A Shedd Production: JACQUELINE PHILLIPS SHEDD, Producer.

GOODNIGHT MISS ANN, An August Cinquegrana Films Production: AUGUST CINQUEGRANA, Producer.

SQUIRES OF SAN QUENTIN, The J. Gary Mitchell Film Company: J. GARY MITCHELL, Producer.

Features

THE LOVERS' WIND, Ministry of Culture and Arts of Iran: ALBERT LAMORISSE, Producer.

MYSTERIOUS CASTLES OF CLAY, A Survival Anglia Ltd. Production: ALAN ROOT, Producer.

RAONI, A Franco-Brazilian Production: MICHEL GAST, BARRY WILLIAMS, and JEAN-PIERRE DUTILLEUX, Producers.

★ SCARED STRAIGHT!, A Golden West Television Production: ARNOLD SHAPIRO, Producer.

WITH BABIES AND BANNERS: STORY OF THE WOMEN'S EMERGENCY BRIGADE, A Women's Labor History Film Project Production: ANNE BOHLEN, LYN GOLDFARB, and LORRAINE GRAY, Producers.

1979 Fifty-second Year

Short Subjects

DAE, Vardar Film/Skopje.

KORYO CELADON, Charlie/Papa Productions, Inc.

NAILS, National Film Board of Canada.

★ PAUL ROBESON: TRIBUTE TO AN ARTIST, Janus Films, Inc.

REMEMBER ME, Dick Young Productions, Ltd.: DICK YOUNG, Producer.

Features

★ BEST BOY, Only Child Motion Pictures, Inc.: IRA WOHL, Producer.

GENERATION ON THE WIND, More Than One Medium: DAVID A. VASSAR, Producer.

GOING THE DISTANCE, National Film Board of Canada.

THE KILLING GROUND, ABC News Closeup Unit: STEVE SINGER and TOM PRIESTLEY, Producers.

THE WAR AT HOME, Catalyst Films/ Madison Film Production Co.: GLENN SILBER and BARRY ALEXANDER BROWN, Producers.

1980 Fifty-third Year

Short Subjects

DON'T MESS WITH BILL, John Watson and Pen Densham's Insight Productions Inc.: JOHN WATSON and PEN DENSHAM, Producers.

THE ERUPTION OF MOUNT ST. HELENS, Graphic Films Corporation: GEORGE CASEY, Producer.

IT'S THE SAME WORLD, Dick Young Productions, Ltd.: DICK YOUNG, Producer.

★ KARL HESS: TOWARD LIBERTY, Hallé/Ladue, Inc.: PETER W. LADUE and ROLAND HALLÉ, Producers.

LUTHER METKE AT 94, UCLA Ethnographic Film Program: RICHARD HAWKINS and JORGE PRELORAN, Producers.

Features

AGEE, James Agee Film Project: ROSS SPEARS, Producer.

THE DAY AFTER TRINITY, Jon Else Productions: JON ELSE, Producer.

★ FROM MAO TO MOZART: ISAAC STERN IN CHINA, Hopewell Foundation: MURRAY LERNER, Producer.

FRONT LINE, David Bradbury Productions: DAVID BRADBURY, Producer.

THE YELLOW STAR—THE PERSECUTION OF EUROPEAN JEWS 1933–45, Chronos Films: BENGT VON ZUR MUEHLEN, Producer.

1981 Fifty-fourth Year

Short Subjects

AMERICAS IN TRANSITION, Americas in Transition, Inc.: OBIE BENZ, Producer.

★ CLOSE HARMONY, A Noble Enterprise: NIGEL NOBLE, Producer.

JOURNEY FOR SURVIVAL, Dick Young Productions, Inc.: DICK YOUNG, Producer.

SEE WHAT I SAY, Michigan Women Filmmakers Productions: LINDA CHAPMAN, PAM LEBLANC, and FREDDI STEVENS, Producers.

URGE TO BUILD, Roland Hallé Productions, Inc.: ROLAND HALLÉ and JOHN HOOVER, Producers.

Features

AGAINST WIND AND TIDE: A CUBAN ODYSSEY, Seven League Productions, Inc.: SUSANNE BAUMAN and PAUL NESHAMKIN, Producers.

BROOKLYN BRIDGE, Florentine Films: KEN BURNS, Producer.

EIGHT MINUTES TO MIDNIGHT: A PORTRAIT OF DR. HELEN CALDICOTT, The Caldicott Project: MARY BENJAMIN, SUSANNE SIMPSON, and BOYD ESTUS, Producers.

EL SALVADOR: ANOTHER VIETNAM, Catalyst Media Productions: GLENN SILBER and TETE VASCONCELLOS, Producers.

★ GENOCIDE, Arnold Schwartzman Productions, Inc.: ARNOLD SCHWARTZMAN and RABBI MARVIN HIER, Producers.

1982 Fifty-fifth Year

Short Subjects

GODS OF METAL, A Richter Productions Film: ROBERT RICHTER, Producer.

★ IF YOU LOVE THIS PLANET, National Film Board of Canada: EDWARD LE LORRAIN, Producer.

THE KLAN: A LEGACY OF HATE IN AMERICA, Guggenheim Productions, Inc.: CHARLES GUGGENHEIM and WERNER SCHUMANN, Producers.

TO LIVE OR LET DIE, American Film Foundation: FREIDA LEE MOCK, Producer.

TRAVELING HOPEFULLY, Arnuthfonyus Films, Inc.: JOHN G. AVILDSEN, Producer.

Features

AFTER THE AXE, National Film Board of Canada: STURLA GUNNARSSON and STEVE LUCAS, Producers.

BEN'S MILL, Public Broadcasting Associates—ODYSSEY: JOHN KAROL and MICHEL CHALUFOUR, Producers.

IN OUR WATER, A Foresight Films Production: MEG SWITZGABLE, Producer.

★ JUST ANOTHER MISSING KID, Canadian Broadcasting Corporation: JOHN ZARITSKY, Producer.

A PORTRAIT OF GISELLE, Wishupon Productions: JOSEPH WISHY, Producer.

1983 Fifty-sixth Year

Short Subjects

★ FLAMENCO AT 5:15, National Film Board of Canada: CYNTHIA SCOTT and ADAM SYMANSKY, Producers.

IN THE NUCLEAR SHADOW: WHAT CAN THE CHILDREN TELL US?, Impact Productions: VIVIENNE VERDON-ROE and ERIC THIERMANN, Producers.

SEWING WOMAN, DeepFocus Productions: ARTHUR DONG, Producer.

SPACES: THE ARCHITECTURE OF PAUL RUDOLPH, Eisenhardt Productions Inc.: ROBERT EISENHARDT, Producer.

YOU ARE FREE (IHR ZENT FREI), A Brokman/Landis Production: DEA BROKMAN and ILENE LANDIS, Producers.

Features

CHILDREN OF DARKNESS, "Children of Darkness" Productions: RICHARD KOTUK and ARA CHEKMAYAN, Producers.

FIRST CONTACT, Arundel Productions: BOB CONNOLLY and ROBIN ANDERSON, Producers.

★ HE MAKES ME FEEL LIKE DANCIN', Edgar J. Scherick Associates Production: EMILE ARDOLINO, Producer.

THE PROFESSION OF ARMS (War Series Film #3), National Film Board of Canada: MICHAEL BRYANS and TINA VILJOEN, Producers.

SEEING RED, Heartland Productions: JAMES KLEIN and JULIA REICHERT, Producers.

1984 Fifty-seventh Year

Short Subjects

THE CHILDREN OF SOONG CHING LING, UNICEF and the Soong Ching Ling

Foundation: GARY BUSH and PAUL T. K. LIN, Producers.

CODE GRAY: ETHICAL DILEMMAS IN NURSING, The Nursing Ethics Project/Fanlight Productions: BEN ACHTENBERG and JOAN SAWYER, Producers.

THE GARDEN OF EDEN, Florentine Films: LAWRENCE R. HOTT and ROGER M. SHERMAN, Producers.

RECOLLECTIONS OF PAVLOVSK, Leningrad Documentary Film Studio: IRINA KALININA, Producer.

★ THE STONE CARVERS, Paul Wagner Productions: MARJORIE HUNT and PAUL WAGNER, Producers.

Features

HIGH SCHOOLS, Guggenheim Productions, Inc.: CHARLES GUGGENHEIM and NANCY SLOSS, Producers.

IN THE NAME OF THE PEOPLE, Pan American Films: ALEX W. DREHSLER and FRANK CHRISTOPHER, Producers.

MARLENE, Zev Braun Pictures, Inc./ OKO Film Produktion: KAREL DIRKA and ZEV BRAUN, Producers.

STREETWISE, Bear Creek Productions, Inc.: CHERYL MCCALL, Producer.

★ THE TIMES OF HARVEY MILK, Black Sand Educational Productions, Inc.: ROBERT EPSTEIN and RICHARD SCHMIECHEN, Producers.

1985 Fifty-eighth Year

Short Subjects

THE COURAGE TO CARE, A United Way Production: ROBERT GARDNER, Producer.

KEATS AND HIS NIGHTINGALE: A BLIND DATE, A Production of the Rhode Island Committee for the Humanities: MICHAEL CROWLEY and JAMES WOLPAW, Producers.

MAKING OVERTURES—THE STORY OF A COMMUNITY ORCHESTRA, A Rhombus Media, Inc. Production: BARBARA WILLIS SWEETE, Producer.

★ WITNESS TO WAR: DR. CHARLIE CLEMENTS, A Skylight Picture Production: DAVID GOODMAN, Producer.

THE WIZARD OF THE STRINGS, A Seventh Hour Production: ALAN EDELSTEIN, Producer.

Features

★ BROKEN RAINBOW, An Earthworks Films Production: MARIA FLORIO and VICTORIA MUDD, Producers.

LAS MADRES—THE MOTHERS OF PLAZA DE MAYO, Sponsored by Film Arts Foundation: SUSAN A MUÑOZ and LOURDES PORTILLO, Producers.

SOLDIERS IN HIDING, A Filmworks, Inc. Production: JAPHET ASHER, Producer.

THE STATUE OF LIBERTY, A Florentine Films Production: KEN BURNS and BUDDY SQUIRES, Producers.

UNFINISHED BUSINESS, A Mouchette Films Production: STEVEN OKAZAKI, Producer.

1986 Fifty-ninth Year

Short Subjects

DEBONAIR DANCERS, An Alison Nigh-Strelich Production: ALISON NIGH-STRELICH, Producer.

THE MASTERS OF DISASTER, Indiana University Audio Visual Center: SONYA FRIEDMAN, Producer.

RED GROOMS: SUNFLOWER IN A HOTHOUSE, A Polaris Entertainment Production: THOMAS L. NEFF and MADELINE BELL, Producers.

SAM, A Film by Aaron D. Weisblatt: AARON D. WEISBLATT, Producer.

★ WOMEN—FOR AMERICA, FOR THE WORLD, An Educational Film and Video Project: VIVIENNE VERDON-ROE, Producer.

Features (Tie)

★ ARTIE SHAW: TIME IS ALL YOU'VE GOT, A Bridge Film Production: BRIGITTE BERMAN, Producer.

CHILE: HASTA CUANDO?, A David Bradbury Production: DAVID BRADBURY, Producer.

★ DOWN AND OUT IN AMERICA, A Joseph Feury Production: JOSEPH FEURY and MILTON JUSTICE, Producers.

ISAAC IN AMERICA: A JOURNEY WITH ISAAC BASHEVIS SINGER, Film by Amram Nowak Associates: KIRK SIMON, Producer.

WITNESS TO APARTHEID, A Production of Developing News, Inc.: SHARON I. SOPHER, Producer.

1987 Sixtieth Year

Short Subjects

FRANCES STELOFF: MEMOIRS OF A BOOKSELLER, A Winterlude Films, Inc. Production: DEBORAH DICKSON, Producer.

IN THE WEE WEE HOURS . . . , University of Southern California School of Cinema/TV: UNIVERSITY OF SOUTHERN CALIFORNIA SCHOOL OF CINEMA/TV.

LANGUAGE SAYS IT ALL, A Tripod Production: MEGAN WILLIAMS, Producer.

SILVER INTO GOLD, Department of Communications, Stanford University: LYNN MUELLER, Producer.

★ YOUNG AT HEART A Sue Marx Films, Inc. Production: SUE MARX and PAMELA CONN, Producers.

Features

EYES ON THE PRIZE: AMERICA'S CIVIL RIGHTS YEARS/BRIDGE TO FREEDOM 1965, A Blackside, Inc. Production: CALLIE CROSSLEY and JAMES A. DEVINNEY, Producers.

HELLFIRE: A JOURNEY FROM HIROSHIMA, JOHN JUNKERMAN and JOHN W. DOWER, Producers.

RADIO BIKINI, A Production of Crossroads Film Project, Ltd.: ROBERT STONE, Producer.

A STITCH FOR TIME, A Production of Peace Quilters Production Company, Inc.: BARBARA HERBICH and CYRIL CHRISTO, Producers.

★ THE TEN-YEAR LUNCH: THE WIT AND LEGEND OF THE ALGONQUIN ROUND TABLE, An Aviva Films Production: AVIVA SLESIN, Producer.

1988 Sixty-first Year

Short Subjects

THE CHILDREN'S STOREFRONT, A Simon and Goodman Picture Company Production: KAREN GOODMAN, Producer.

FAMILY GATHERING, A Lise Yasui Production: LISE YASUI and ANN TEGNELL, Producers.

GANG COPS, Center for Visual Anthropology at the University of Southern California: THOMAS B. FLEMING and DANIEL J. MARKS, Producers.

PORTRAIT OF IMOGEN, A Pacific Pictures Production: NANCY HALE and MEG PARTRIDGE, Producers.

★ YOU DON'T HAVE TO DIE, A Tiger Rose Production in Association with Filmworks, Inc.: WILLIAM GUTTENTAG and MALCOLM CLARKE, Producers.

Features

THE CRY OF REASON—BEYERS NAUDE: AN AFRIKANER SPEAKS OUT, A Production of Worldwide Documentaries, Inc.: ROBERT BILHEIMER and RONALD MIX, Producers.

★ HOTEL TERMINUS: THE LIFE AND TIMES OF KLAUS BARBIE, A Production of The Memory Pictures Company: MARCEL OPHULS, Producer.

LET'S GET LOST, A Production of Little Bear Films, Inc.: BRUCE WEBER and NAN BUSH, Producers.

PROMISES TO KEEP, A Production of Durrin Productions, Inc.: GINNY DURRIN, Producer.

WHO KILLED VINCENT CHIN?, A Production of Film News Now Foundation and Detroit Educational Television Foundation: RENEE TAJIMA and CHRISTINE CHOY, Producers.

1989 Sixty-second Year

Short Subjects

FINE FOOD, FINE PASTRIES, OPEN 6 TO 9, A Production of David Petersen Productions: DAVID PETERSEN, Producer.

★ THE JOHNSTOWN FLOOD, A Production of Guggenheim Productions, Inc.: CHARLES GUGGENHEIM, Producer.

YAD VASHEM: PRESERVING THE PAST TO ENSURE THE FUTURE, A Ray Errol Fox Production: RAY ERROL FOX, Producer.

Features

ADAM CLAYTON POWELL, A Production of RKB Productions: RICHARD KILBERG and YVONNE SMITH, Producers.

★ COMMON THREADS: STORIES FROM THE QUILT, A Telling Pictures and the Couturie Company Production: ROBERT EPSTEIN and BILL COUTURIE, Producers.

CRACK USA: COUNTY UNDER SIEGE, A Production of Half-Court Productions, Ltd.: VINCE DIPERSIO and WILLIAM GUTTENTAG, Producers.

FOR ALL MANKIND, A Production of Apollo Associates/FAM Productions Inc.: AL REINERT and BETSY BROYLES BREIR, Producers.

SUPER CHIEF: THE LIFE AND LEGACY OF EARL WARREN, A Quest Production: JUDITH LEONARD and BILL JERSEY, Producers.

1990 Sixty-third Year

Short Subjects

BURNING DOWN TOMORROW, An Interscope Communications Inc. Production: KIT THOMAS, Producer.

CHIMPS: SO LIKE US, A Simon and Goodman Picture Company Production: KAREN GOODMAN and KIRK SIMON, Producers.

★ DAYS OF WAITING, A Mouchette Films Production: STEVEN OKAZAKI, Producer.

JOURNEY INTO LIFE: THE WORLD OF THE UNBORN, An ABC/Kane Productions International, Inc. Production: DEREK BROMHALL, Producer.

ROSE KENNEDY: A LIFE TO REMEMBER, A Production of Sanders and Mock Productions and American Film Foundation: FREIDA LEE MOCK and TERRY SANDERS, Producers.

Features

★ AMERICAN DREAM, A Cabin Creek Films Production: BARBARA KOPPLE and ARTHUR COHN, Producers.

BERKELEY IN THE SIXTIES, A Production of Berkeley in the Sixties Production Partnership: MARK KITCHELL, Producer.

BUILDING BOMBS, A Mori/Robinson Production: MARK MORI and SUSAN ROBINSON, Producers.

FOREVER ACTIVISTS: STORIES FROM THE VETERANS OF THE ABRAHAM LINCOLN BRIGADE, A Judith Montell Production: JUDITH MONTELL, Producer.

WALDO SALT: A SCREENWRITER'S JOURNEY, A Waldo Productions, Inc.

Production: ROBERT HILLMANN, Producer.

1991 Sixty-fourth Year

Short Subjects

BIRDNESTERS OF THAILAND (a.k.a. SHADOW HUNTERS), Antenne 2/ National Geographic Society/M.D.I./ Wind Horse Production: ERIC VALLI and ALAIN MAJANI, Producers.

★ DEADLY DECEPTION: GENERAL ELECTRIC, NUCLEAR WEAPONS AND OUR ENVIRONMENT, Women's Educational Media Inc. Production: DEBRA CHASNOFF, Producer.

A LITTLE VICIOUS, Film and Video Workshop Inc. Production: IMMY HUMES, Producer.

THE MARK OF THE MAKER, McGowan Film and Video Inc.: DAVID MCGOWAN, Producer.

MEMORIAL: LETTERS FROM AMERICAN SOLDIERS, Couturie Co. Production: BILL COUTURIE and BERNARD EDELMAN, Producers.

Features

DEATH ON THE JOB, Half-Court Pictures Ltd. Production: VINCE DIPERSIO and WILLIAM GUTTENTAG, Producers.

DOING TIME: LIFE INSIDE THE BIG HOUSE, Video Verité Production: ALAN RAYMOND and SUSAN RAYMOND, Producers.

★ IN THE SHADOW OF THE STARS, Light-Saraf Films Production: ALLIE LIGHT and IRVING SARAF, Producers. (First Run Features)

THE RESTLESS CONSCIENCE: RESISTANCE TO HITLER WITHIN GERMANY 1933–1945, Hava Kohav Beller Production: HAVA KOHAV BELLER, Producer.

WILD BY LAW, Florentine Films Production: LAWRENCE HOTT and DIANE GAREY, Producers.

1992 Sixty-fifth Year

Short Subjects (Not given after this year)

AT THE EDGE OF CONQUEST: THE JOURNEY OF CHIEF WAI-WAI, A Realis Pictures, Inc. Production: GEOFFREY O'CONNOR, Producer.

BEYOND IMAGINING: MARGARET ANDERSON AND THE "LITTLE REVIEW," A Wendy L. Weinberg Production: WENDY L. WEINBERG, Producer.

THE COLOURS OF MY FATHER: A PORTRAIT OF SAM BORENSTEIN, An Imageries P.B. Ltd. Production in coproduction with the National Film Board of Canada: RICHARD ELSON and SALLY BOCHNER, Producers.

★ EDUCATING PETER, A State of the Art, Inc. Production: THOMAS C. GOODWIN AND GERARDINE WURZBURG, Producers.

WHEN ABORTION WAS ILLEGAL: UNTOLD STORIES, A Concentric Media Production: DOROTHY FADIMAN, Producer.

Features

CHANGING OUR MINDS: THE STORY OF DR. EVELYN HOOKER, An Intrepid Production: DAVID HAUGLAND, Producer.

FIRES OF KUWAIT, A Black Sun Films, Ltd./IMAX Corporation Production: SALLY DUNDAS, Producer.

LIBERATORS: FIGHTING ON TWO FRONTS IN WORLD WAR II, A Miles Educational Film Productions, Inc. Production: WILLIAM MILES and NINA ROSENBLUM, Producers.

MUSIC FOR THE MOVIES: BERNARD HERRMANN, An Alternate Current Inc./Les Films d'Ici Production: MARGARET SMILOV AND ROMA BARAN, Producers.

★ THE PANAMA DECEPTION, An Empowerment Project Production: BARBARA TRENT and DAVID KASPER, Producers.

Foreign Language Film Award

When the Academy was founded in 1927, Conrad Nagel proposed that it be named the Academy of Motion Picture Arts and Sciences International. Though the last word of his suggestion was dropped, the Academy would eventually recognize the worldwide nature of film through a foreign film award. By the end of World War II some groups such as the National Board of Review and the New York Film Critics had been recognizing foreign films for over a decade, and a special Oscar in 1946 to Laurence Olivier for *Henry V* prompted *Variety* to speculate that the Academy too would soon set up an international award. The 1947 ceremonies included a special award to the Italian neo-realist film *Shoeshine*, and Academy president Jean Hersholt called for an annual award for foreign language films. "An international award, if properly planned and carefully administered," he added, "would promote a closer relationship between American film craftsmen and those of other countries." The Academy Board of Governors continued to give honorary Oscars to foreign language films each year until 1956 when a new category was officially established, and the Best Foreign Language Film became an annual award. In 1957 the rules changed to give the award to the production company rather than to the individual producers. Present rules clearly state that the Oscar will be awarded "to the picture and not to any one individual."

To be eligible, a film must have a soundtrack in the original language and carry English subtitles. Each country decides what film to submit to the Academy, and only one film is accepted annually from each country. To date more than sixty countries have submitted entries. The entries are screened by a Foreign Language Film Award Committee which determines the five nominees. Final voting is restricted to Academy members who have seen all nominated films.

Italy has received nine awards out of twenty-four nominations. France also has nine wins from a record twenty-eight nominations.

1956 Twenty-ninth Year

THE CAPTAIN OF KÖPENICK, Real-Film (Germany): GYULA TREBITSCH and WALTER KOPPEL, Producers.

GERVAISE, Agnes Delahaie Productions Cinematographiques and Silver Film (France): ANNIE DORFMANN, Producer.

HARP OF BURMA, Nikkatsu Corporation (Japan): MASAYUKI TAKAGI, Producer.

★ LA STRADA, A Ponti-De Laurentiis Production (Italy): DINO DE LAURENTIIS and CARLO PONTI, Producers.

QIVITOQ, A/S Nordisk Films Kompagni (Denmark): O. DALSGAARD-OLSEN, Producer.

1957 Thirtieth Year

THE DEVIL CAME AT NIGHT, Gloria Film (Germany).

GATES OF PARIS, Filmsonor S.A. Production (France).

MOTHER INDIA, Mehboob Productions (India).

★ THE NIGHTS OF CABIRIA, Dino De Laurentiis Production (Italy).

NINE LIVES, Nordsjofilm (Norway).

1958 Thirty-first Year

ARMS AND THE MAN, H.R. Sokal-P. Goldbaum Production, Bavaria Filmkunst A.G. (Germany).

LA VENGANZA, Guion Producciones Cinematograficas (Spain).

★ MY UNCLE, Specta-Gray-Alter Films in association with Films du Centaure (France).

THE ROAD A YEAR LONG, Jadran Film (Yugoslavia).

THE USUAL UNIDENTIFIED THIEVES, Lux-Vides-Cinecitta (Italy).

1959 Thirty-second Year

★ BLACK ORPHEUS, Dispatfilm and Gemma Cinematografica (France).

THE BRIDGE, Fono Film (Germany).

THE GREAT WAR, Dino De Laurentiis Cinematografica (Italy).

PAW, Laterna Film (Denmark).

THE VILLAGE ON THE RIVER, N.V. Nationale Filmproductie Maatschappij (The Netherlands).

1960 Thirty-third Year

KAPO, Vides-Zebrafilm-Cineriz (Italy).

LA VERITÉ, Han Productions (France).

MACARIO, Clasa Films Mundiales, S.A. (Mexico).

THE NINTH CIRCLE, Jadran Film Production (Yugoslavia).

★ THE VIRGIN SPRING, AB Svensk Filmindustri (Sweden).

1961 Thirty-fourth Year

HARRY AND THE BUTLER, Bent Christensen Production (Denmark).

IMMORTAL LOVE, Shochiku Co., Ltd. (Japan).

THE IMPORTANT MAN, Peliculas Rodriguez, S.A. (Mexico).

PLACIDO, Jet Films (Spain).

★ THROUGH A GLASS DARKLY, AB Svensk Filmindustri (Sweden).

1962 Thirty-fifth Year

ELECTRA, A Michael Cacoyannis Production (Greece).

THE FOUR DAYS OF NAPLES, Titanus-Metro (Italy).

KEEPER OF PROMISES (THE GIVEN WORD), Cinedistri (Brazil).

★ SUNDAYS AND CYBELE, Terra-Fides-Orsay-Trocadero Films (France).

TLAYUCAN, Producciones Matouk, S.A. (Mexico).

1963 Thirty-sixth Year

★ FEDERICO FELLINI'S 8½, A Cineriz Production (Italy).

KNIFE IN THE WATER, A Kamera Unit of Film Polski Production (Poland).

LOS TARANTOS, Tecisa-Films R.B. (Spain).

THE RED LANTERNS, Th. Damaskinos and V. Michaelides A.E. (Greece).

TWIN SISTERS OF KYOTO, Shochiku Co., Ltd. (Japan).

1964 Thirty-seventh Year

RAVEN'S END, AB Europa Film (Sweden).

SALLAH, A Sallah Film Ltd. Production (Israel).

THE UMBRELLAS OF CHERBOURG, A Parc-Madeleine-Beta Films Production (France).

WOMAN IN THE DUNES, A Teshigahara Production (Japan).

★ YESTERDAY, TODAY AND TOMORROW, A Champion-Concordia Production (Italy).

1965 Thirty-eighth Year

BLOOD ON THE LAND, Th. Damaskinos and V. Michaelides, A.E.-Finos Film (Greece).

DEAR JOHN, AB Sandrew-Ateljeerna (Sweden).

KWAIDAN, A Toho Company, Ltd. Production (Japan).

MARRIAGE ITALIAN STYLE, A Champion-Concordia Production (Italy).

★ THE SHOP ON MAIN STREET, A Ceskoslovensky Film Production (Czechoslovakia).

1966 Thirty-ninth Year

THE BATTLE OF ALGIERS, Igor Film-Casbah Film Production (Italy).

LOVES OF A BLONDE, Barrandov Film Production (Czechoslovakia).

★ A MAN AND A WOMAN, Les Films 13 Production (France).

PHARAOH, Kadr Film Unit Production (Poland).

THREE, Avala Film Production (Yugoslavia).

1967 Fortieth Year

★ CLOSELY WATCHED TRAINS, Barrandov Film Studio Production (Czechoslovakia).

EL AMOR BRUJO, Films R.B., S.A. Production (Spain).

I EVEN MET HAPPY GYPSIES, Avala Film Production (Yugoslavia).

LIVE FOR LIFE, Les Films Ariane-Les Productions Artistes Associés-Vides Films Production (France).

PORTRAIT OF CHIEKO, Shochiku Co., Ltd. Production (Japan).

1968 Forty-first Year

THE BOYS OF PAUL STREET, Bohgros Films-Mafilm Studio I Production (Hungary).

THE FIREMEN'S BALL, Barrandov Film Studio Production (Czechoslovakia).

THE GIRL WITH THE PISTOL, Documento Film Production (Italy).

STOLEN KISSES, Les Films du Carrosse-Les Productions Artistes Associés Production (France).

★ WAR AND PEACE, Mosfilm Production (U.S.S.R.).

1969 Forty-second Year

ADALEN '31, AB Svensk Filmindustri Production (Sweden).

THE BATTLE OF NERETVA, United Film Producers-Igor Film-Eichberg Film-Commonwealth United Production (Yugoslavia).

THE BROTHERS KARAMAZOV, Mosfilm Production (U.S.S.R.).

MY NIGHT AT MAUD'S, Films du Losange-F.F.P.-Films du Carrosse-Films des Deux Mondes-Films de la Pleiade-Gueville-Renn-Simar Films Production (France).

★ Z, Reggane-O.N.C.I.C. Production (Algeria).

1970 Forty-third Year

FIRST LOVE, Alfa Prods.-Seitz Film Prod. (Switzerland).

HOA-BINH, Madeleine-Parc-La Gueville-C.A.P.A.C. Prod. (France).

★ INVESTIGATION OF A CITIZEN ABOVE SUSPICION, Vera Films Prod. (Italy).

PAIX SUR LES CHAMPS, Philippe Collette-E.G.C. Prod. (Belgium).

TRISTANA, Forbes Films, Ltd.-United Cineworld-Epoca Films-Talia Film-Les Films Corona-Selenia Cinematografica Prod. (Spain).

1971 Forty-fourth Year

DODES'KA-DEN, A Toho Company, Ltd.-Yonki no Kai Prod. (Japan).

THE EMIGRANTS, A Svensk Filmindustri Prod. (Sweden).

★ THE GARDEN OF THE FINZI-CONTINIS, A Gianni Hecht Lucari-Arthur Cohn Prod. (Italy).

THE POLICEMAN, An Ephi-Israeli Motion Picture Studios Prod. (Israel).

TCHAIKOVSKY, A Dimitri Tiomkin-Mosfilm Studios Prod. (U.S.S.R.).

1972 Forty-fifth Year

THE DAWNS HERE ARE QUIET, A Gorky Film Studios Prod. (U.S.S.R.).

★ THE DISCREET CHARM OF THE BOURGEOISIE, A Serge Silberman Prod. (France).

I LOVE YOU ROSA, A Noah Films Ltd. Prod. (Israel).

MY DEAREST SEÑORITA, An El Iman Prod. (Spain).

THE NEW LAND, A Svensk Filmindustri Prod. (Sweden).

1973 Forty-sixth Year

★ DAY FOR NIGHT, A Les Films du Carrosse-P.E.C.F. (Paris)-P.I.C. (Rome) Prod. (France).

THE HOUSE ON CHELOUCHE STREET, A Noah Films Prod. (Israel).

L'INVITATION, A Groupe 5 Geneve-Television Suisse Romande-Citel Films-Planfilm (Paris) Prod. (Switzerland).

THE PEDESTRIAN, An ALFA Glarus-MFG-Seitz-Zev Braun Prod. (Federal Republic of Germany).

TURKISH DELIGHT, A Rob Houwer Film Prod. (The Netherlands).

1974 Forty-seventh Year

★ AMARCORD, An F.C. (Rome)-P.E.C.F. (Paris) Prod. (Italy).

CATSPLAY, A Hunnia Studio Prod. (Hungary).

THE DELUGE, A Film Polski Prod. (Poland).

LACOMBE, LUCIEN, An NEF-UPF (Paris)-Vides Film (Rome)-Hallelujah Film (Munich) Prod. (France).

THE TRUCE, A Tamames-Zemborain Prod. (Argentina).

1975 Forty-eighth Year

★ DERSU UZALA, A Mosfilms Studios Production (U.S.S.R).

LAND OF PROMISE, A Film Polski Production (Poland).

LETTERS FROM MARUSIA, A Conacine Production (Mexico).

SANDAKAN NO. 8, A Toho-Haiyuza Production (Japan).

SCENT OF A WOMAN, A Dean Film Production (Italy).

1976 Forty-ninth Year

★ BLACK AND WHITE IN COLOR, An Arthur Cohn Production/Société Ivoirienne de Cinema (Ivory Coast).

COUSIN, COUSINE, Les Films Pomereu-Gaumont Production (France).

JACOB, THE LIAR, A VEB/DEFA Production (German Democratic Republic).

NIGHTS AND DAYS, A Polish Corporation for Film-"KADR" Film Unit Production (Poland).

SEVEN BEAUTIES, A Medusa Distribuzione Production (Italy).

1977 Fiftieth Year

IPHIGENIA, A Greek Film Centre Production (Greece).

★ MADAME ROSA, A Lira Films Production (France).

OPERATION THUNDERBOLT, A Golan-Globus Production (Israel).

A SPECIAL DAY, A Canafox Films Production (Italy).

THAT OBSCURE OBJECT OF DESIRE, A Greenwich-Les Films Galaxie-In Cine Production (Spain).

1978 Fifty-first Year

★ GET OUT YOUR HANDKERCHIEFS, A Les Films Ariane-C.A.P.A.C. Production (France).

THE GLASS CELL, A Roxy Film Production (Federal Republic of Germany).

HUNGARIANS, A Dialong Studio Production (Hungary).

VIVA ITALIA!, A Dean Film Production (Italy).

WHITE BIM BLACK EAR, A Central

Studio of Films for Children and Youth Production (U.S.S.R.).

1979 Fifty-second Year

THE MAIDS OF WILKO, A Polish Corporation for Film Production (Poland).

MAMA TURNS A HUNDRED, Elias Querejeta P.C. Production (Spain).

A SIMPLE STORY, A Renn Productions/Sara Films/F.R. 3/Rialto Films Production, Quartet Films (France).

★ THE TIN DRUM, A Franz Seitz Film/Bioskop Film/Artemis Film/Hallelujah Film/GGB 14.KG/Argos Films Production (Federal Republic of Germany).

TO FORGET VENICE, A Rizzoli Film/Action Film Production, Quartet Films (Italy).

1980 Fifty-third Year

CONFIDENCE, A Mafilm Studios Production (Hungary).

KAGEMUSHA (THE SHADOW WARRIOR), A Toho Co., Ltd.-Kurosawa Productions, Ltd. Co-production (Japan).

THE LAST METRO, A Les Films du Carrosse Production (France).

★ MOSCOW DOES NOT BELIEVE IN TEARS, A Mosfilm Studio Production (U.S.S.R.).

THE NEST, An A. Punto E.L. S.A. Production (Spain).

1981 Fifty-fourth Year

THE BOAT IS FULL, A Limbo Film AG Production (Switzerland).

MAN OF IRON, A Polish Corporation for Film, Unit "X" Production (Poland).

★ MEPHISTO, A Mafilm-Objektiv Studio and Manfred Durniok Production (Hungary).

MUDDY RIVER, A Kimura Production (Japan).

THREE BROTHERS, An Iter Film (Rome)/Gaumont (Paris) Production (Italy).

1982 Fifty-fifth Year

ALSINO AND THE CONDOR, A Nicaraguan Film Institute Production (Nicaragua).

COUP DE TORCHON (CLEAN SLATE), A Films de la Tour Production (France).

THE FLIGHT OF THE EAGLE, A Bold Productions for the Swedish Film Institute, the Swedish Television SVT 2, Svensk Filmindustri and Norsk Film A/S Production (Sweden).

PRIVATE LIFE, A Mosfilm Studio Production (U.S.S.R.).

★ VOLVER A EMPEZAR (TO BEGIN AGAIN), A Nickel Odeon, S.A. Production (Spain).

1983 Fifty-sixth Year

CARMEN, An Emiliano Piedra Production (Spain).

ENTRE NOUS, A Partners Production (France).

★ FANNY AND ALEXANDER, A Cinematograph AB for the Swedish Film Institute/the Swedish Television SVT 1, Sweden/Gaumont, France/Personafilm and Tobis Filmkunst, BRD Production (Sweden).

JOB'S REVOLT, A Mafilm Tarsulas Studio/Hungarian Television (Budapest)/ZDF (Mainz) Production (Hungary).

LE BAL, A Cineproduction S.A.-Films A2 (Paris)/Massfilm (Rome)/O.N.C.I.C. (Alger) Production (Algeria).

1984 Fifty-seventh Year

BEYOND THE WALLS, An April Films Ltd. Production (Israel).

CAMILA, A GEA Cinematografica S.R.L. Production (Argentina).

★ DANGEROUS MOVES, An Arthur Cohn Production (Switzerland).

DOUBLE FEATURE, A Nickel Odeon, S.A. Production (Spain).

WARTIME ROMANCE, An Odessa Film Studio Production (U.S.S.R.).

1985 Fifty-eighth Year

ANGRY HARVEST, A CCC-Filmkunst GmbH/Admiral Film Production (Federal Republic of Germany).

COLONEL REDL, A Mafilm-Objektiv Studio/Manfred Durniok/ORF/ZDF Production (Hungary).

★ THE OFFICIAL STORY, A Historias Cinematograficas/ Cinemania and Progress Communications Production (Argentina).

3 MEN AND A CRADLE, A Flach Film Production (France).

WHEN FATHER WAS AWAY ON BUSINESS, A Forum Film Production (Yugoslavia).

1986 Fifty-ninth Year

★ THE ASSAULT, A Fons Rademakers Production B.V. for Cannon Group Holland, Cannon (The Netherlands).

BETTY BLUE, A Gaumont Presentation of a Constellation/Cargo Production, Alive Films (France).

THE DECLINE OF THE AMERICAN EMPIRE, A Corporation Image M & M/ National Film Board of Canada Production, Cineplex Odeon (Canada).

MY SWEET LITTLE VILLAGE, A Barrandov Film Studios Production, Circle Films (Czechoslovakia).

38, An Arabella Film/Satel Film Production (Austria).

1987 Sixtieth Year

AU REVOIR LES ENFANTS (GOODBYE, CHILDREN), An NEF (Paris) Production (France).

★ BABETTE'S FEAST, A Panorama Film International Production in Cooperation with Nordisk Film and the Danish Film Institute (Denmark).

COURSE COMPLETED, A Nickel Odeon Dos Production (Spain).

THE FAMILY, A Massfilm-Cinecittà-Les Films Ariane-Cinemax Prodûction (Italy).

PATHFINDER, A Filmkameratene Production (Norway).

1988 Sixty-first Year

HANUSSEN, An Objektiv Studio/CCC Filmkunst/ ZDF/Hungarofilm/ MOKEP Production (Hungary).

THE MUSIC TEACHER, An RTBF/K2 One Production (Belgium).

★ PELLE THE CONQUEROR, A Per Holst/Kaerne Films Production (Denmark).

SALAAM BOMBAY!, A Mirabai Production (India).

WOMEN ON THE VERGE OF A NERVOUS BREAKDOWN, An El Deseo/ Laurenfilm Production (Spain).

1989 Sixty-second Year

CAMILLE CLAUDEL, A Films Christian Fechner-Lilith Films-Gaumont-A2 TV France-Films A2-DD Production (France).

★ CINEMA PARADISO, A Cristaldifilm/Films Ariane Production (Italy).

JESUS OF MONTREAL, A Max Films/ Gérard Mital Production (Canada).

SANTIAGO, THE STORY OF HIS NEW LIFE, A Dios los Cría Producciones/ Pedro Muñiz Production (Puerto Rico).

WALTZING REGITZE, A Nordisk Film/ Danish Film Institute Production (Denmark).

1990 Sixty-third Year

CYRANO DE BERGERAC, A Hachette Premiere Production (France).

★ JOURNEY OF HOPE, A Catpics/ Condor Features Production (Switzerland).

JU DOU, A China Film Co-Production Corporation/Tokuma Shoten

Publishing Production (People's Republic of China).

THE NASTY GIRL, A Production of Sentana Filmproduktion (Germany).

OPEN DOORS, An Erre Produzioni/ Istituto Luce Production (Italy).

1991 Sixty-fourth Year

CHILDREN OF NATURE, An Icelandic Film Corp. Ltd./Max Film (Berlin)/ Metro Film (Oslo) Production (Iceland).

THE ELEMENTARY SCHOOL, A Barrandov Film Studio Production (Czechoslovakia).

★ MEDITERRANEO, A Pentafilm S.p.A./A.M.A. Film S.r.l. Film Production, Miramax (Italy).

THE OX, A Sweetland Films AB/Jean Doumanian Production (Sweden).

RAISE THE RED LANTERN, An ERA Intl. (HK) Ltd. Presentation in association with China Film Co-production Corp. Production, Orion Classics (Hong Kong).

1992 Sixty-fifth Year

CLOSE TO EDEN, A Camera One-Hachette premiere et Compagnie/ UGC Images (France)/ Studio Trite (URSS) Production (Russia).

DAENS, A Favourite Films/Films Dérives/ Titane & Shooting Star Filmcompany Production (Belgium).

★ INDOCHINE, A Paradis Films/La Générale d'Images/BAC Films/Orly Films/ Ciné Cinq Production (France).

A PLACE IN THE WORLD, An Adolfo Aristarain/Osvaldo Papaleo/Mirna Rosales Production (Uruguay).*

SCHTONK, A Bavaria Film GmbH Production (Germany).

*Disqualified after the nominations were announced.

OTHER AWARDS

Honorary Awards

The Honorary Awards, known as Special Awards until 1950, are not limited to achievements from a single year and thus provide a flexibility not permitted in the annual awards. People such as D. W. Griffith, Charlie Chaplin, Lillian Gish, and Mack Sennett, whose greatest achievements in film came before the Academy Awards were established, were recognized by the Academy through Honorary Awards.

Outstanding achievement in fields that fall outside the annual award categories may also be recognized through Honorary Oscars. The Board of Governors has used this category to reward service to the Academy and to honor persons whose entire career is more distinguished than single, yearly achievements that may have been overlooked by the voters.

Several annual award categories such as Make-up, Special Effects, Documentary, Color Cinematography, and Foreign Language Film began as Honorary Awards.

Honorary Awards are voted by the Academy Board of Governors. Present rules prohibit posthumous awards. Unless otherwise noted, the award took the form of an Oscar statuette.

1927/28 First Year

WARNER BROS. for producing *The Jazz Singer*, the pioneer outstanding talking picture, which has revolutionized the industry.

CHARLES CHAPLIN for versatility and genius in writing, acting, directing, and producing *The Circus*.*

1928/29 Second Year

No Special Awards were given this year.

1929/30 Third Year

No Special Awards were given this year.

1930/31 Fourth Year

No Special Awards were given this year.

1931/32 Fifth Year

WALT DISNEY for the creation of Mickey Mouse.

1933 Sixth Year

No Special Awards were given this year.

1934 Seventh Year

SHIRLEY TEMPLE in grateful recognition of her outstanding contribution to screen entertainment

*The Academy Board of Judges voted unanimously to withdraw Chaplin's name from the competitive categories in order to honor him with a Special Award.

during the year 1934. (Miniature statuette)

1935 Eighth Year

DAVID WARK GRIFFITH for his distinguished creative achievements as director and producer and his invaluable initiative and lasting contributions to the progress of the motion picture arts.

1936 Ninth Year

MARCH OF TIME for its significance to motion pictures and for having revolutionized one of the most important branches of the industry—the newsreel.

W. HOWARD GREENE and HAROLD ROSSON for the color cinematography of the Selznick International Production, *The Garden of Allah*. (Plaques)

1937 Tenth Year

MACK SENNETT "for his lasting contribution to the comedy technique of the screen, the basic principles of which are as important today as when they were first put into practice, the Academy presents a Special Award to that master of fun, discoverer of stars, sympathetic, kindly, understanding comedy genius—Mack Sennett."

EDGAR BERGEN for his outstanding comedy creation, Charlie McCarthy. (Wooden statuette)

THE MUSEUM OF MODERN ART FILM LIBRARY for its significant work in collecting films dating from 1895 to the present and for the first time making available to the public the means of studying the historical and aesthetic development of the motion picture as one of the major arts. (Scroll certificate)

W. HOWARD GREENE for the color photography of *A Star Is Born*. (This Award was recommended by a committee of leading cinematographers after viewing all the color pictures made during the year.) (Plaque)

1938 Eleventh Year

DEANNA DURBIN and MICKEY ROONEY for their significant contribution in bringing to the screen the spirit and personification of youth and as juvenile players setting a high standard of ability and achievement. (Miniature statuette trophies)

HARRY M. WARNER in recognition of patriotic service in the production of historical short subjects presenting significant episodes in the early struggle of the American people for liberty. (Scroll)

WALT DISNEY for *Snow White and the Seven Dwarfs*, recognized as a significant screen innovation that has charmed millions and pioneered a great new entertainment field for the motion picture cartoon. (One statuette—seven miniature statuettes)

OLIVER MARSH and ALLEN DAVEY for the color cinematography of the Metro-Goldwyn-Mayer production, *Sweethearts*. (Plaques)

For outstanding achievement in creating Special Photographic and Sound Effects in the Paramount production, *Spawn of the North*. Special Effects by GORDON JENNINGS, assisted by JAN DOMELA, DEV JENNINGS, IRMIN ROBERTS, and ART SMITH. Transparencies by FARCIOT EDOUART, assisted by LOYAL GRIGGS. Sound Effects by LOREN RYDER, assisted by HARRY MILLS, LOUIS H. MESENKOP, and WALTER OBERST. (Plaques)

J. ARTHUR BALL for his outstanding

contributions to the advancement of color in Motion Picture Photography. (Scroll)

1939 Twelfth Year

DOUGLAS FAIRBANKS (Commemorative Award)—recognizing the unique and outstanding contribution of Douglas Fairbanks, first president of the Academy, to the international development of the motion picture.

MOTION PICTURE RELIEF FUND—acknowledging the outstanding services to the industry during the past year of the Motion Picture Relief Fund and its progressive leadership. Presented to JEAN HERSHOLT, president; RALPH MORGAN, chairman of the Executive Committee; RALPH BLOCK, first vice president; CONRAD NAGEL. (Plaques)

JUDY GARLAND for her outstanding performance as a screen juvenile during the past year. (Miniature statuette)

WILLIAM CAMERON MENZIES for outstanding achievement in the use of color for the enhancement of dramatic mood in the production of *Gone with the Wind*. (Plaque)

TECHNICOLOR COMPANY for its contributions in successfully bringing three-color feature production to the screen.

1940 Thirteenth Year

BOB HOPE in recognition of his unselfish services to the Motion Picture Industry. (Special silver plaque)

COLONEL NATHAN LEVINSON for his outstanding service to the industry and the U.S. Army during the past nine years, which has made possible the present efficient mobilization of the motion picture industry facilities for the production of Army Training Films.

1941 Fourteenth Year

REY SCOTT for his extraordinary achievement in producing *Kukan*, the film record of China's struggle, including its photography with a 16mm camera under the most difficult and dangerous conditions. (Certificate)

THE BRITISH MINISTRY OF INFORMATION for its vivid and dramatic presentation of the heroism of the RAF in the documentary film, *Target for Tonight*. (Certificate)

LEOPOLD STOKOWSKI and his associates for their unique achievement in the creation of a new form of visualized music in Walt Disney's production *Fantasia*, thereby widening the scope of the motion picture as entertainment and as an art form. (Certificate)

WALT DISNEY, WILLIAM GARITY, JOHN N. A. HAWKINS, and the RCA MANUFACTURING COMPANY for their outstanding contribution to the advancement of the use of sound in motion pictures through the production of *Fantasia*. (Certificates)

1942 Fifteenth Year

CHARLES BOYER for his progressive cultural achievement in establishing the French Research Foundation in Los Angeles as a source of reference for the Hollywood Motion Picture Industry. (Certificate)

NOEL COWARD for his outstanding production achievement in *In Which We Serve*. (Certificate)

METRO-GOLDWYN-MAYER STUDIO for its achievement in representing the American Way of Life in the production of the *Andy Hardy* series of films. (Certificate)

1943 Sixteenth Year

GEORGE PAL for the development of novel methods and techniques in the production of short subjects known as Puppetoons. (Plaque)

1944 Seventeenth Year

MARGARET O'BRIEN, outstanding child actress of 1944. (Miniature statuette)

BOB HOPE, for his many services to the Academy, a Life Membership in the Academy of Motion Picture Arts and Sciences.

1945 Eighteenth Year

WALTER WANGER for his six years of service as president of the Academy of Motion Picture Arts and Sciences. (Special plaque)

PEGGY ANN GARNER, outstanding child actress of 1945. (Miniature statuette)

THE HOUSE I LIVE IN, tolerance short subject; produced by Frank Ross and Mervyn LeRoy; directed by Mervyn LeRoy; screenplay by Albert Maltz; song "The House I Live In," music by Earl Robinson, lyrics by Lewis Allen; starring Frank Sinatra; released by RKO Radio.

REPUBLIC STUDIO, DANIEL J. BLOOMBERG and the REPUBLIC SOUND DEPARTMENT for the building of an outstanding musical scoring auditorium that provides optimum recording conditions and combines all elements of acoustic and engineering design. (Certificates)

1946 Nineteenth Year

LAURENCE OLIVIER for his outstanding achievement as actor, producer, and director in bringing *Henry V* to the screen.

HAROLD RUSSELL for bringing hope and courage to his fellow veterans through his appearance in *The Best Years of Our Lives*.

ERNST LUBITSCH for his distinguished contributions to the art of the motion picture. (Scroll)

CLAUDE JARMAN, JR., outstanding child actor of 1946. (Miniature statuette)

1947 Twentieth Year

JAMES BASKETTE for his able and heart-warming characterization of Uncle Remus, friend and storyteller to the children of the world.

BILL AND COO, in which artistry and patience blended in a novel and entertaining use of the medium of motion pictures. (Plaque)

SHOE-SHINE—the high quality of this motion picture, brought to eloquent life in a country scarred by war, is proof to the world that the creative spirit can triumph over adversity.

COLONEL WILLIAM N. SELIG, ALBERT E. SMITH, THOMAS ARMAT, and GEORGE K. SPOOR, (one of) the small group of pioneers whose belief in a new medium, and whose contributions to its development, blazed the trail along which the motion picture has progressed, in their lifetime, from obscurity to worldwide acclaim.

1948 Twenty-first Year

MONSIEUR VINCENT (French)—voted by the Academy Board of Governors as the most outstanding foreign language film released in the United States during 1948.

IVAN JANDL, for the outstanding juvenile performance of 1948 in *The Search*. (Miniature statuette)

SID GRAUMAN, master showman, who raised the standard of the exhibition of motion pictures.

ADOLPH ZUKOR, a man who has been called the father of the feature film in America, for his services to the industry over a period of forty years.

WALTER WANGER for distinguished service to the industry in adding to its moral stature in the world community by his production of the picture *Joan of Arc*.

1949 Twenty-second Year

THE BICYCLE THIEF (Italian)—voted by the Academy Board of Governors as the most outstanding foreign language film released in the United States during 1949.

BOBBY DRISCOLL, as the outstanding juvenile actor of 1949. (Miniature statuette)

FRED ASTAIRE for his unique artistry and his contributions to the technique of musical pictures.

CECIL B. DEMILLE, distinguished motion picture pioneer, for thirty-seven years of brilliant showmanship.

JEAN HERSHOLT, for distinguished service to the motion picture industry.

*1950 Twenty-third Year**

GEORGE MURPHY for his services in interpreting the film industry to the country at large.

LOUIS B. MAYER for distinguished service to the motion picture industry.

THE WALLS OF MALAPAGA (Franco-Italian)—voted by the Board of Governors as the most outstanding foreign language film released in the United States in 1950.

1951 Twenty-fourth Year

GENE KELLY in appreciation of his versatility as an actor, singer, director, and dancer, and specifically for his brilliant achievements in the art of choreography on film.

RASHOMON (Japanese)—voted by the Board of Governors as the most outstanding foreign language film released in the United States during 1951.

1952 Twenty-fifth Year

GEORGE ALFRED MITCHELL for the design and development of the camera that bears his name and for his continued and dominant presence in the field of cinematography.

JOSEPH M. SCHENCK for long and distinguished service to the motion picture industry.

MERIAN C. COOPER for his many innovations and contributions to the art of motion pictures.

HAROLD LLOYD, master comedian and good citizen.

BOB HOPE for his contribution to the laughter of the world, his service to the motion picture industry, and his devotion to the American premise.

FORBIDDEN GAMES (French)—Best Foreign Language Film first released in the United States during 1952.

1953 Twenty-sixth Year

PETE SMITH for his witty and pungent observations on the American scene in his series of *Pete Smith Specialties*.

20TH CENTURY-FOX FILM CORPORATION in recognition of their imagination, showmanship, and foresight in introducing the revolutionary process known as CinemaScope.

JOSEPH I. BREEN for his conscientious, open-minded, and dignified management of the Motion Picture Production Code.

BELL AND HOWELL COMPANY

*Name of category changed from Special Awards to Honorary Awards.

for their pioneering and basic achievements in the advancement of the motion picture industry.

1954 Twenty-seventh Year

BAUSCH & LOMB OPTICAL COMPANY for their contributions to the advancement of the motion picture industry.

KEMP R. NIVER for the development of the Renovare Process which has made possible the restoration of the Library of Congress Paper Film Collection.

GRETA GARBO for her unforgettable screen performances.

DANNY KAYE for his unique talents, and his service to the Academy, the motion picture industry, and the American people.

JON WHITELEY for his outstanding juvenile performance in *The Little Kidnappers*. (Miniature statuette)

VINCENT WINTER for his outstanding juvenile performance in *The Little Kidnappers*. (Miniature statuette)

GATE OF HELL (Japanese)—Best Foreign Language Film first released in the United States during 1954.

1955 Twenty-eighth Year

SAMURAI, THE LEGEND OF MUSASHI (Japanese)—Best Foreign Language Film first released in the United States during 1955.

1956 Twenty-ninth Year

EDDIE CANTOR for distinguished service to the film industry.

1957 Thirtieth Year

CHARLES BRACKETT for outstanding service to the Academy.

B. B. KAHANE for distinguished service to the motion picture industry.

GILBERT M. ("BRONCHO BILLY") ANDERSON, motion picture pioneer, for his contributions to the development of motion pictures as entertainment.

THE SOCIETY OF MOTION PICTURE AND TELEVISION ENGINEERS for their contributions to the advancement of the motion picture industry.

1958 Thirty-first Year

MAURICE CHEVALIER for his contributions to the world of entertainment for more than half a century.

1959 Thirty-second Year

LEE DE FOREST for his pioneering inventions which brought sound to the motion picture.

BUSTER KEATON for his unique talents which brought immortal comedies to the screen.

1960 Thirty-third Year

GARY COOPER for his many memorable screen performances and the international recognition he, as an individual, has gained for the motion picture industry.

STAN LAUREL for his creative pioneering in the field of cinema comedy. (Statuette)

HAYLEY MILLS for *Pollyanna*, the most outstanding juvenile performance during 1960. (Miniature statuette)

1961 Thirty-fourth Year

WILLIAM L. HENDRICKS for his outstanding patriotic service in the conception, writing, and production of the Marine Corps film, *A Force in Readiness*, which has brought honor to the Academy and the motion picture industry.

FRED L. METZLER for his dedication and outstanding service to the

Academy of Motion Picture Arts and Sciences.

JEROME ROBBINS for his brilliant achievements in the art of choreography on film.

1962 Thirty-fifth Year

No Honorary Awards were given this year.

1963 Thirty-sixth Year

No Honorary Awards were given this year.

1964 Thirty-seventh Year

WILLIAM TUTTLE for his outstanding make-up achievement for *7 Faces of Dr. Lao.*

1965 Thirty-eighth Year

BOB HOPE for unique and distinguished service to our industry and the Academy. (Gold medal)

1966 Thirty-ninth Year

Y. FRANK FREEMAN for unusual and outstanding service to the Academy during his thirty years in Hollywood.

YAKIMA CANUTT for achievements as a stunt man and for developing safety devices to protect stunt men everywhere.

1967 Fortieth Year

ARTHUR FREED for distinguished service to the Academy and the production of six top-rated Awards telecasts.

1968 Forty-first Year

JOHN CHAMBERS for his outstanding make-up achievement for *Planet of the Apes.*

ONNA WHITE for her outstanding choreography achievement for *Oliver!.*

1969 Forty-second Year

CARY GRANT for his unique mastery of the art of screen acting with the respect and affection of his colleagues.

1970 Forty-third Year

LILLIAN GISH for superlative artistry and for distinguished contribution to the progress of motion pictures.

ORSON WELLES for superlative artistry and versatility in the creation of motion pictures.

1971 Forty-fourth Year

CHARLES CHAPLIN for the incalculable effect he has had in making motion pictures the art form of this century.

1972 Forty-fifth Year

CHARLES S. BOREN, leader for thirty-eight years of the industry's enlightened labor relations and architect of its policy of nondiscrimination. With the respect and affection of all who work in films.

EDWARD G. ROBINSON, who achieved greatness as a player, a patron of the arts, and a dedicated citizen . . . in sum, a Renaissance man. From his friends in the industry he loves.

1973 Forty-sixth Year

HENRI LANGLOIS for his devotion to the art of film, his massive contributions in preserving its past, and his unswerving faith in its future.

GROUCHO MARX in recognition of his brilliant creativity and for the unequalled achievements of the Marx Brothers in the art of motion picture comedy.

1974 Forty-seventh Year

HOWARD HAWKS—A master American filmmaker whose creative efforts hold a distinguished place in world cinema.

JEAN RENOIR—a genius who, with grace, responsibility, and enviable devotion through silent film, sound film, feature, documentary, and television, has won the world's admiration.

1975 Forty-eighth Year

MARY PICKFORD in recognition of her unique contributions to the film industry and the development of film as an artistic medium.

1976 Forty-ninth Year

No Honorary Awards were given this year.

1977 Fiftieth Year

MARGARET BOOTH for sixty-two years of exceptionally distinguished service to the motion picture industry as a film editor.

Medals of Commendation

GORDON E. SAWYER and SIDNEY P. SOLOW in appreciation for outstanding service and dedication in upholding the high standards of the Academy of Motion Picture Arts and Sciences.

1978 Fifty-first Year

WALTER LANTZ for bringing joy and laughter to every part of the world through his unique animated motion pictures.

THE MUSEUM OF MODERN ART DEPARTMENT OF FILM for the contribution it has made to the public's perception of movies as an art form.

LAURENCE OLIVIER for the full body of his work, for the unique achievements of his entire career, and for his lifetime of contribution to the art of film.

KING VIDOR for his incomparable achievements as a cinematic creator and innovator.

Medals of Commendation

LINWOOD G. DUNN, LOREN L. RYDER, and WALDON O. WATSON in appreciation for outstanding service and dedication in upholding the high standards of the Academy of Motion Picture Arts and Sciences.

1979 Fifty-second Year

HAL ELIAS for his dedication and distinguished service to the Academy of Motion Picture Arts and Sciences.

ALEC GUINNESS for advancing the art of screen acting through a host of memorable and distinguished performances.

Medals of Commendation

JOHN O. AALBERG, CHARLES G. CLARKE, and JOHN G. FRAYNE in appreciation for outstanding service and dedication in upholding the high standards of the Academy of Motion Picture Arts and Sciences.

1980 Fifty-third Year

HENRY FONDA, the consummate actor, in recognition of his brilliant accomplishments and enduring contribution to the art of motion pictures.

Medal of Commendation

FRED HYNES in appreciation for outstanding service and dedication in upholding the high standards of the Academy of Motion Picture Arts and Sciences.

1981 Fifty-fourth Year

BARBARA STANWYCK, for superlative creativity and unique

contribution to the art of screen acting.

1982 Fifty-fifth Year

MICKEY ROONEY in recognition of his sixty years of versatility in a variety of memorable film performances.

1983 Fifty-sixth Year

HAL ROACH in recognition of his unparalleled record of distinguished contributions to the motion picture art form.

1984 Fifty-seventh Year

JAMES STEWART for his fifty years of memorable performances and for his high ideals both on and off the screen, with the respect and affection of his colleagues.

NATIONAL ENDOWMENT FOR THE ARTS in recognition of its twentieth anniversary and its dedicated commitment to fostering artistic and creative activity and excellence in every area of the arts.

1985 Fifty-eighth Year

PAUL NEWMAN in recognition of his many memorable and compelling screen performances and for his personal integrity and dedication to his craft.

ALEX NORTH in recognition of his brilliant artistry in the creation of memorable music for motion pictures.

Medal of Commendation

JOHN H. WHITNEY, SR., for cinematic pioneering.

1986 Fifty-ninth Year

RALPH BELLAMY for his unique artistry and his distinguished service to the profession of acting.

Medal of Commendation

E. M. (AL) LEWIS in appreciation for outstanding service and dedication in upholding the high standards of the Academy of Motion Picture Arts and Sciences.

1987 Sixtieth Year

No Honorary Awards were given this year.

1988 Sixty-first Year

EASTMAN KODAK in recognition of the company's fundamental contributions to the art of motion pictures during the first century of film history.

NATIONAL FILM BOARD OF CANADA in recognition of its fiftieth anniversary and its dedicated commitment to originate artistic, creative, and technological activity and excellence in every area of filmmaking.

1989 Sixty-second Year

AKIRA KUROSAWA for accomplishments that have inspired, delighted, enriched, and entertained audiences and influenced filmmakers throughout the world.

Special Commendation

The Academy of Motion Picture Arts and Sciences' Board of Governors commends the contributions of the MEMBERS OF THE ENGINEERING COMMITTEES OF THE SOCIETY OF MOTION PICTURE AND TELEVISION ENGINEERS (SMPTE). By establishing industry standards, they have greatly contributed to making film a primary form of international communication.

1990 Sixty-third year

SOPHIA LOREN, one of the genuine treasures of world cinema who, in a career rich with memorable performances, has added permanent luster to our art form.

MYRNA LOY in recognition of her extraordinary qualities both onscreen and off, with appreciation for a lifetime's worth of indelible performances.

Medals of Commendation

RODERICK T. RYAN, DON TRUMBULL, and GEOFFREY H. WILLIAMSON in appreciation for outstanding service and dedication in upholding the high standards of the Academy of Motion Picture Arts and Sciences.

1991 Sixty-fourth Year

SATYAJIT RAY for his rare mastery of the art of motion pictures and for his profound humanitarian outlook, which has had an indelible influence on filmmakers and audiences throughout the world.

Medals of Commendation

RICHARD J. STUMPF and JOSEPH WESTHEIMER in appreciation for outstanding service and dedication in upholding the high standards of the Academy of Motion Picture Arts and Sciences.

Award of Commendation (Special plaque)

PETE COMANDINI, RICHARD T. DAYTON, DONALD HAGANS, and RICHARD T. RYAN of YCM Laboratories for the creation and development of a motion picture film restoration process using liquid gate and registration correction on a contact printer.

1992 Sixty-fifth Year

FEDERICO FELLINI in appreciation of one of the screen's master storytellers.

Medal of Commendation

PETRO VLAHOS in appreciation for outstanding service and dedication in upholding the high standards of the Academy of Motion Picture Arts and Sciences.

Special Achievement Awards

Established in 1972, the Special Achievement Awards have been given most frequently for work previously recognized in the Special Effects, Special Visual Effects, and Sound Effects categories. Special Achievement Awards are classified as "other" rather than as annual awards. As such, they are voted by the Board of Governors rather than the Academy membership at large. Present rules state that Special Achievement Awards shall be given when an achievement "makes an exceptional contribution to the motion picture for which it was created, but for which there is no annual award category." A recent example is the 1988 award to Richard Williams for Animation Direction. The rules for three annual award categories—Make-up, Visual Effects, and Sound Effects Editing—specify that "in the event that there are fewer than two nominations, a Special Effects Award *may* be voted by the Board of Governors."

1972 Forty-fifth Year

Visual Effects: L. B. ABBOTT and A. D. FLOWERS for *The Poseidon Adventure*, An Irwin Allen Production, 20th Century-Fox.

1973 Forty-sixth Year

None.

1974 Forty-seventh Year

Visual Effects: FRANK BRENDEL, GLEN ROBINSON, and ALBERT WHITLOCK for *Earthquake*, A Universal-Mark Robson-Filmakers Group Production, Universal.

1975 Forty-eighth Year

Sound Effects: PETER BERKOS for *The Hindenburg*, A Robert Wise-Filmakers Group-Universal Production, Universal.

Visual Effects: ALBERT WHITLOCK and GLEN ROBINSON for *The Hindenburg*, A Robert Wise-Filmakers Group-Universal Production, Universal.

1976 Forty-ninth Year

Visual Effects: CARLO RAMBALDI, GLEN ROBINSON, and FRANK VAN DER VEER for *King Kong*, A Dino De Laurentiis Production, Paramount.

Visual Effects: L. B. ABBOTT, GLEN ROBINSON, and MATTHEW YURICICH for *Logan's Run*, A Saul David Production, Metro-Goldwyn-Mayer.

1977 Fiftieth Year

Sound Effects: BENJAMIN BURTT, JR., for the creation of the alien, creature, and robot voices in *Star Wars*, A Twentieth Century-Fox Production, Twentieth Century-Fox.

Sound Effects Editing Award: FRANK WARNER for *Close Encounters of the Third Kind*, Close Encounter Productions, Columbia.

1978 Fifty-first Year

Visual Effects: LES BOWIE, COLIN CHILVERS, DENYS COOP, ROY

FIELD, DEREK MEDDINGS, and ZORAN PERISIC for *Superman*, A Dovemead Ltd. Production, Alexander Salkind Presentation, Warner Bros.

1979 Fifty-second Year

Sound Editing: ALAN SPLET for *The Black Stallion*, An Omni Zoetrope Production, United Artists.

1980 Fifty-third Year

Visual Effects: BRIAN JOHNSON, RICHARD EDLUND, DENNIS MUREN, and BRUCE NICHOLSON for *The Empire Strikes Back*, A Lucasfilm, Ltd. Production, 20th Century-Fox.

1981 Fifty-fourth Year

Sound Effects Editing: BENJAMIN P. BURTT, JR., and RICHARD L. ANDERSON for *Raiders of the Lost Ark*, A Lucasfilm Production, Paramount.

1982 Fifty-fifth Year

None.

1983 Fifty-sixth Year

Visual Effects: RICHARD EDLUND, DENNIS MUREN, PHIL TIPPETT, and KEN RALSTON, for *Return of the Jedi*, A Lucasfilm Production, 20th Century-Fox.

1984 Fifty-seventh Year

Sound Effects Editing: KAY ROSE for *The River*, A Universal Pictures Production, Universal.

1985 Fifty-eighth Year

None.

1986 Fifty-ninth Year

None.

1987 Sixtieth Year

Sound Effects Editing: STEPHEN FLICK and JOHN POSPISIL for *Robocop*, A Tobor Pictures Production, Orion.

1988 Sixty-first Year

Animation Direction: RICHARD WILLIAMS for *Who Framed Roger Rabbit?*, An Amblin Entertainment and Touchstone Pictures Production, Buena Vista.

1989 Sixty-second Year

None.

1990 Sixty-third Year

Visual Effects: ERIC BREVIG, ROB BOTTIN, TIM MCGOVERN, and ALEX FUNKE for *Total Recall*, A Carolco Pictures Production, Tri-Star.

1991 Sixty-fourth Year

None.

1992 Sixty-fifth Year

None.

Irving G. Thalberg Memorial Award

Irving Thalberg (1899–1936) was a motion picture producer of extraordinary ability. He went to work for Carl Laemmle at Universal and was managing the studio by the time he was twenty-one. In 1923 he became head of production for Louis B. Mayer, and, after the merger which created Metro-Goldwyn-Mayer the following year, he became second only to Mayer in charge of production at the new studio. Thalberg guided the artistic policy of MGM in the 1920s and 1930s and helped make the studio among the most powerful in Hollywood. He died of pneumonia on September 14, 1936.

At the 1936 Academy Awards banquet, held on March 4, 1937, plans were announced for a memorial award to be inaugurated at the 1937 awards. The Irving G. Thalberg Memorial Award, given "to creative producers whose body of work reflects a consistently high quality of motion picture production," has been awarded thirty-one times in the past fifty-six years. Darryl F. Zanuck won it three times before the rules were changed limiting individuals to a single award. In 1990 Zanuck's son Richard was a co-recipient with David Brown, making him the first second-generation winner. It also marked the first time a team of producers was honored. Robert Benjamin won the award posthumously in 1979, but the rules now prevent posthumous or multiple awards. The Thalberg Award is not an Oscar statuette, but a head of Thalberg, and is voted by the Academy Board of Governors.

1937	Tenth Year	Darryl F. Zanuck
1938	Eleventh Year	Hal B. Wallis
1939	Twelfth Year	David O. Selznick
1940	Thirteenth Year	None
1941	Fourteenth Year	Walt Disney
1942	Fifteenth Year	Sidney Franklin
1943	Sixteenth Year	Hal B. Wallis
1944	Seventeenth Year	Darryl F. Zanuck
1945	Eighteenth Year	None
1946	Nineteenth Year	Samuel Goldwyn
1947	Twentieth Year	None
1948	Twenty-first Year	Jerry Wald
1949	Twenty-second Year	None
1950	Twenty-third Year	Darryl F. Zanuck
1951	Twenty-fourth Year	Arthur Freed
1952	Twenty-fifth Year	Cecil B. DeMille
1953	Twenty-sixth Year	George Stevens

1954	Twenty-seventh Year	None
1955	Twenty-eighth Year	None
1956	Twenty-ninth Year	Buddy Adler
1957	Thirtieth Year	None
1958	Thirty-first Year	Jack L. Warner
1959	Thirty-second Year	None
1960	Thirty-third Year	None
1961	Thirty-fourth Year	Stanley Kramer
1962	Thirty-fifth Year	None
1963	Thirty-sixth Year	Sam Spiegel
1964	Thirty-seventh Year	None
1965	Thirty-eighth Year	William Wyler
1966	Thirty-ninth Year	Robert Wise
1967	Fortieth Year	Alfred Hitchcock
1968	Forty-first Year	None
1969	Forty-second Year	None
1970	Forty-third Year	Ingmar Bergman
1971	Forty-fourth Year	None
1972	Forty-fifth Year	None
1973	Forty-sixth Year	Lawrence Weingarten
1974	Forty-seventh Year	None
1975	Forty-eighth Year	Mervyn LeRoy
1976	Forty-ninth Year	Pandro S. Berman
1977	Fiftieth Year	Walter Mirisch
1978	Fifty-first Year	None
1979	Fifty-second Year	Ray Stark
1980	Fifty-third Year	None
1981	Fifty-fourth Year	Albert R. "Cubby" Broccoli
1982	Fifty-fifth Year	None
1983	Fifty-sixth Year	None
1984	Fifty-seventh Year	None
1985	Fifty-eighth Year	None
1986	Fifty-ninth Year	Steven Spielberg
1987	Sixtieth Year	Billy Wilder
1988	Sixty-first Year	None
1989	Sixty-second Year	None
1990	Sixty-third Year	Richard Zanuck and David Brown
1991	Sixty-fourth Year	George Lucas
1992	Sixty-fifth Year	None

Jean Hersholt Humanitarian Award

The Jean Hersholt Humanitarian Award is named for an actor whose film career spanned fifty years and 453 films. Danish-born Jean Hersholt (1886–1956) began his film career in 1906 when he was twenty. He immigrated to the United States in 1913 and became an American citizen in 1920. Despite a prolific career as an actor, Hersholt's interests were not limited to film. He made the first complete English translation of Hans Christian Andersen's fairy tales, and in 1951 he donated to the Library of Congress the most complete collection of Andersen's works ever assembled outside of Denmark. Hersholt received honorary awards from the Academy in 1939 and 1949 and was knighted by the King of Denmark in 1946. Much of Hersholt's fame came as a result of a radio character named Dr. Christian which he played for eighteen years.

When he died of cancer in 1956, Jean Hersholt was remembered as much for his humanitarian work as for his acting. He had headed the Motion Picture Relief Fund for eighteen years and was one of the founders of the Motion Picture Country Day Home. The award named in his honor is given to individuals "in the motion picture industry whose humanitarian efforts have brought credit to the industry."

The Hersholt Award is voted by the Academy Board of Governors.

1956	Twenty-ninth Year	Y. Frank Freeman
1957	Thirtieth Year	Samuel Goldwyn
1958	Thirty-first Year	None
1959	Thirty-second Year	Bob Hope
1960	Thirty-third Year	Sol Lesser
1961	Thirty-fourth Year	George Seaton
1962	Thirty-fifth Year	Steve Broidy
1963	Thirty-sixth Year	None
1964	Thirty-seventh Year	None
1965	Thirty-eighth Year	Edmond L. DePatie
1966	Thirty-ninth Year	George Bagnall
1967	Fortieth Year	Gregory Peck
1968	Forty-first Year	Martha Raye
1969	Forty-second Year	George Jessel
1970	Forty-third Year	Frank Sinatra
1971	Forty-fourth Year	None
1972	Forty-fifth Year	Rosalind Russell
1973	Forty-sixth Year	Lew Wasserman
1974	Forty-seventh Year	Arthur B. Krim

1975	Forty-eighth Year	Jules C. Stein
1976	Forty-ninth Year	None
1977	Fiftieth Year	Charlton Heston
1978	Fifty-first Year	Leo Jaffe
1979	Fifty-second Year	Robert Benjamin
1980	Fifty-third Year	None
1981	Fifty-fourth Year	Danny Kaye
1982	Fifty-fifth Year	Walter Mirisch
1983	Fifty-sixth Year	M. J. Frankovich
1984	Fifty-seventh Year	David L. Wolper
1985	Fifty-eighth Year	Charles "Buddy" Rogers
1986	Fifty-ninth Year	None
1987	Sixtieth Year	None
1988	Sixty-first Year	None
1989	Sixty-second Year	Howard W. Koch
1990	Sixty-third Year	None
1991	Sixty-fourth Year	None
1992	Sixty-fifth Year	Audrey Hepburn and Elizabeth Taylor

Gordon E. Sawyer Award

The Gordon E. Sawyer Award, an Oscar statuette, is named for the veteran sound director of the Samuel Goldwyn Studios who died in 1981. Under his directorship, the Samuel Goldwyn Studios Sound Department won four Oscars for Sound, and at the 50th Awards Sawyer himself received an honorary Medal of Commendation "in appreciation for outstanding service and dedication in upholding the high standards of the Academy of Motion Picture Arts and Sciences." During his distinguished career, Sawyer served as a governor of the Academy for seventeen years. He was a member of the Scientific or Technical Awards Committee for forty-three years and served as its chairman for twelve years.

To honor individuals who have made significant contributions that advance the science or technology of motion pictures, the Academy Board of Governors established the Gordon E. Sawyer Award. Like the Thalberg and Hersholt Awards, it recognizes long-term accomplishments rather than single achievements and is given only in years when a worthy candidate is approved by the Academy Board of Governors.

1981	Fifty-fourth Year	Joseph B. Walker
1982	Fifty-fifth Year	John O. Aalberg
1983	Fifty-sixth Year	Dr. John G. Frayne
1984	Fifty-seventh Year	Linwood G. Dunn
1985	Fifty-eighth Year	None
1986	Fifty-ninth Year	None
1987	Sixtieth Year	Fred Hynes
1988	Sixty-first Year	Gordon Henry Cook
1989	Sixty-second Year	Pierre Angenieux
1990	Sixty-third Year	Stefan Kudelski
1991	Sixty-fourth Year	Ray Harryhausen
1992	Sixty-fifth Year	Erich Kaestner

Scientific or Technical Awards

The Academy has always been involved with the technical aspects of motion pictures, first through the Producers-Technicians Joint Committee and later through the Research Council. Among the earliest projects of the Academy were the sponsorships of studies on incandescent lighting and on motion picture sound engineering. The Scientific or Technical Awards were established in time for the 1930/31 ceremonies, and, according to the *Academy Bulletin*, nominations were solicited "from all Hollywood studios and from major manufacturing and development companies in the American motion picture industry." Then, as now, the category was divided into three classes.

In 1978 the Academy changed the names of the categories from Class I, Class II, and Class III to the following:

1. *Academy Award of Merit* (Academy statuette): For basic achievements that have a definite influence upon the advancement of the industry.
2. *Scientific and Engineering Award* (Academy plaque): For those achievements that exhibit a high level of engineering and are important to the progress of the industry.
3. *Technical Achievement Award* (Academy certificate): For those accomplishments that contribute to the progress of the industry.

The present rules state that awards may be given for "devices, methods, formulas, discoveries, or inventions of special and outstanding value to the arts and sciences of motion pictures and employed in the motion picture industry during the awards year."

Awards in this category are voted by the Academy Board of Governors on the recommendation of a Scientific or Technical Awards Committee appointed by the Academy president.

1930/31 Fourth Year

Class I

ELECTRICAL RESEARCH PRODUCTS, INC., RCA-PHOTOPHONE, INC., and RKO RADIO PICTURES, INC., for noise-reduction recording equipment.

DuPONT FILM MANUFACTURING CORP. and EASTMAN KODAK CO. for supersensitive panchromatic film.

Class II

FOX FILM CORP. for effective use of synchro-projection composite photography.

Class III

ELECTRICAL RESEARCH PRODUCTS, INC., for moving-coil microphone transmitters.

RKO RADIO PICTURES, INC., for reflex-type microphone concentrators.

RCA-PHOTOPHONE, INC., for ribbon microphone transmitters.

1931/32 Fifth Year

Class I

None.

Class II

TECHNICOLOR MOTION PICTURE CORP. for their color cartoon process.

Class III

EASTMAN KODAK CO. for the Type II-B Sensitometer.

1932/33 Sixth Year

Class I

None.

Class II

ELECTRICAL RESEARCH PRODUCTS, INC., for their wide-range recording and reproducing system.

RCA-VICTOR CO., INC., for their high-fidelity recording and reproducing system.

Class III

FOX FILM CORP., FRED JACKMAN and WARNER BROS. PICTURES, INC., and SIDNEY SANDERS of RKO Studios, Inc., for their development and effective use of the translucent cellulose screen in composite photography.

1934 Seventh Year

Class I

None.

Class II

ELECTRICAL RESEARCH PRODUCTS, INC., for their development of the vertical cut disc method of recording sound for motion pictures (hill-and-dale recording).

Class III

COLUMBIA PICTURES CORP. for their application of the vertical cut disc method (hill-and-dale recording) to actual studio production, with their recording of the sound on the picture, *One Night of Love*.

BELL AND HOWELL CO. for their development of the Bell and Howell fully automatic sound and picture printer.

1935 Eighth Year

Class I

None.

Class II

AGFA ANSCO CORP. for their development of the Agfa infrared film.

EASTMAN KODAK CO. for their development of the Eastman PolaScreen.

Class III

METRO-GOLDWYN-MAYER STUDIO for the development of antidirectional negative and positive development by means of jet turbulation, and the application of the method to all negative and print processing of the entire product of a major producing company.

WILLIAM A. MUELLER of Warner Bros.-First National Studio Sound Department for his method of dubbing, in which the level of the dialogue automatically controls the level of the accompanying music and sound effects.

MOLE-RICHARDSON CO. for their development of the "Solar-spot" spot lamps.

DOUGLAS SHEARER and METRO-GOLDWYN-MAYER STUDIO SOUND DEPARTMENT for their automatic control system for cameras and sound recording machines and auxiliary stage equipment.

ELECTRICAL RESEARCH PRODUCTS, INC., for their study and development of equipment to analyze and measure flutter resulting from the travel of the film through the mechanisms used in the recording and reproduction of sound.

PARAMOUNT PRODUCTIONS, INC., for the design and construction of the Paramount transparency air-turbine developing machine.

NATHAN LEVINSON, Director of Sound Recording for Warner Bros.-First National Studio, for the method of intercutting variable density and variable area sound tracks to secure an increase in the effective volume range of sound recorded for motion pictures.

1936 Ninth Year

Class I

DOUGLAS SHEARER and the METRO-GOLDWYN-MAYER STUDIO SOUND DEPARTMENT for the development of a practical two-way horn system and a biased Class A push-pull recording system.

Class II

E. C. WENTE and the BELL TELEPHONE LABORATORIES for their multicellular high-frequency horn and receiver.

RCA MANUFACTURING CO., INC., for their rotary stabilizer sound head.

Class III

RCA MANUFACTURING CO., INC., for their development of a method of recording and printing sound records utilizing a restricted spectrum (known as ultraviolet light recording).

ELECTRICAL RESEARCH PRODUCTS, INC., for the ERPI "Type Q" portable recording channel.

RCA MANUFACTURING CO., INC., for furnishing a practical design and specifications for a non-slip printer.

UNITED ARTISTS STUDIO CORP. for the development of a practical, efficient, and quiet wind machine.

1937 Tenth Year

Class I

AGFA ANSCO CORP. for Agfa Supreme and Agfa Ultra Speed pan motion picture negatives.

Class II

WALT DISNEY PRODS., LTD., for the design and application to production of the Multi-Plane Camera.

EASTMAN KODAK CO. for two fine-grain duplicating film stocks.

FARCIOT EDOUART and PARAMOUNT PICTURES, INC., for the development of the Paramount dual-screen transparency camera setup.

DOUGLAS SHEARER and the METRO-GOLDWYN-MAYER STUDIO SOUND DEPARTMENT for a method of varying the scanning width of variable density sound tracks (squeeze tracks) for the purpose of obtaining an increased amount of noise reduction.

Class III

JOHN ARNOLD and the METRO-GOLDWYN-MAYER STUDIO CAMERA DEPARTMENT for their improvement of the semiautomatic follow focus device and its application to all of the cameras used by the Metro-Goldwyn-Mayer Studio.

JOHN LIVADARY, Director of Sound Recording for Columbia Pictures Corp., for the application of the biplanar light valve to motion picture sound recording.

THOMAS T. MOULTON and the UNITED ARTISTS STUDIO SOUND DEPARTMENT for the application to motion picture sound recording of volume indicators that have peak reading response and linear decibel scales.

RCA MANUFACTURING CO., INC., for the introduction of the modulated high-frequency method of determining optimum photographic processing conditions for variable width sound tracks.

JOSEPH E. ROBBINS and PARAMOUNT PICTURES, INC., for an exceptional application of acoustic principles to the soundproofing of gasoline generators and water pumps.

DOUGLAS SHEARER and the METRO-GOLDWYN-MAYER STUDIO SOUND DEPARTMENT for the design of the film drive mechanism as incorporated in the ERPI 1010 reproducer.

1938 Eleventh Year

Class I

None.

Class II

None.

Class III

JOHN AALBERG and the RKO RADIO STUDIO SOUND DEPARTMENT for the application of compression to variable area recording in motion picture production.

BYRON HASKIN and the SPECIAL EFFECTS DEPARTMENT of WARNER BROS. STUDIO for pioneering the development and for the first practical application to motion picture production of the triple-head background projector.

1939 Twelfth Year

Class I

None.

Class II

None.

Class III

GEORGE ANDERSON of Warner Bros. Studio for an improved positive head for sun arcs.

JOHN ARNOLD of Metro-Goldwyn-Mayer Studio for the M-G-M mobile camera crane.

THOMAS T. MOULTON, FRED ALBIN, and the SOUND DEPARTMENT of the SAMUEL GOLDWYN STUDIO for the origination and application of the Delta db test to sound recording in motion pictures.

FARCIOT EDOUART, JOSEPH E. ROBBINS, WILLIAM RUDOLPH, and PARAMOUNT PICTURES, INC., for the design and construction of a quiet, portable treadmill.

EMERY HUSE and RALPH B. ATKINSON of Eastman Kodak Co. for their specifications for chemical analysis of photographic developers and fixing baths.

HAROLD NYE of Warner Bros. Studio for a miniature incandescent spot lamp.

A. J. TONDREAU of Warner Bros. Studio for the design and manufacture of an improved sound track printer.

Multiple Award for important contributions in cooperative development of new improved process projection equipment:

F. R. ABBOTT, HALLER BELT, ALAN COOK, and BAUSCH &

LOMB OPTICAL CO. for faster projection lenses.

MITCHELL CAMERA CO. for a new type process projection head.

MOLE-RICHARDSON CO. for a new type automatically controlled projection arc lamp.

CHARLES HANDLEY, DAVID JOY, and NATIONAL CARBON CO. for improved and more stable high-intensity carbons.

WINTON HOCH and TECHNICOLOR MOTION PICTURE CORP. for an auxiliary optical system.

DON MUSGRAVE and SELZNICK INTERNATIONAL PICTURES, INC., for pioneering in the use of coordinated equipment in the production *Gone with the Wind.*

1940 Thirteenth Year

Class I

20TH CENTURY-FOX FILM CORP. for the design and construction of the 20th Century Silenced Camera, developed by DANIEL CLARK, GROVER LAUBE, CHARLES MILLER, and ROBERT W. STEVENS.

Class II

None.

Class III

WARNER BROS. STUDIO ART DEPARTMENT and ANTON GROT for the design and perfection of the Warner Bros. water ripple and wave illusion machine.

1941 Fourteenth Year

Class I

None.

Class II

ELECTRICAL RESEARCH PRODUCTS DIVISION OF WESTERN ELECTRIC CO., INC., for the development of the precision integrating sphere densitometer.

RCA MANUFACTURING CO. for the design and development of the MI-3043 Uni-directional microphone.

Class III

RAY WILKINSON and the PARAMOUNT STUDIO LABORATORY for pioneering in the use of and for the first practical application to release printing of fine-grain positive stock.

CHARLES LOOTENS and the REPUBLIC STUDIO SOUND DEPARTMENT for pioneering the use of and for the first practical application to motion picture production of CLASS B push-pull variable area recording.

WILBUR SILVERTOOTH and the PARAMOUNT STUDIO ENGINEERING DEPARTMENT for the design and computation of a relay condenser system applicable to transparency process projection, delivering considerably more usable light.

PARAMOUNT PICTURES, INC., and 20TH CENTURY-FOX FILM CORP. for the development and first practical application to motion picture production of an automatic scene slating device.

DOUGLAS SHEARER and the METRO-GOLDWYN-MAYER STUDIO SOUND DEPARTMENT, and to LOREN RYDER and the PARAMOUNT STUDIO SOUND DEPARTMENT for pioneering the development of fine-grain emulsions for variable density original sound recording in studio production.

1942 Fifteenth Year

Class I

None.

Class II

CARROLL CLARK, F. THOMAS THOMPSON, and the RKO RADIO STUDIO ART and MINIATURE DEPARTMENTS for the design and construction of a moving cloud and horizon machine.

DANIEL B. CLARK and the 20TH CENTURY-FOX FILM CORP. for the development of a lens calibration system and the application of this system to exposure control in cinematography.

Class III

ROBERT HENDERSON and the PARAMOUNT STUDIO ENGINEERING and TRANSPARENCY DEPARTMENTS for the design and construction of adjustable light bridges and screen frames for transparency process photography.

DANIEL J. BLOOMBERG and the REPUBLIC STUDIO SOUND DEPARTMENT for the design and application to motion picture production of a device for marking action negatives for preselection purposes.

1943 Sixteenth Year

Class I

None.

Class II

FARCIOT EDOUART, EARLE MORGAN, BARTON THOMPSON, and the PARAMOUNT STUDIO ENGINEERING and TRANSPARENCY DEPARTMENTS for the development and practical application to motion picture production of a method of duplicating and enlarging natural color photographs, transferring the image emulsions to glass plates, and projecting these slides by especially designed stereopticon equipment.

PHOTO PRODUCTS DEPARTMENT, E. I. Du PONT de NEMOURS AND CO., INC., for the development of fine-grain motion picture films.

Class III

DANIEL J. BLOOMBERG and the REPUBLIC STUDIO SOUND DEPARTMENT for the design and development of an inexpensive method of converting Moviolas to Class B push-pull reproduction.

CHARLES GALLOWAY CLARKE and the 20TH CENTURY-FOX STUDIO CAMERA DEPARTMENT for the development and practical application of a device for composing artificial clouds into motion picture scenes during production photography.

FARCIOT EDOUART and the PARAMOUNT STUDIO TRANSPARENCY DEPARTMENT for an automatic electric transparency cueing timer.

WILLARD H. TURNER and the RKO RADIO STUDIO SOUND DEPARTMENT for the design and construction of the phono-cue starter.

1944 Seventeenth Year

Class I

None.

Class II

STEPHEN DUNN and the RKO RADIO STUDIO SOUND DEPARTMENT and RADIO CORPORATION OF AMERICA for the design and development of the electronic compressor-limiter.

Class III

LINWOOD DUNN, CECIL LOVE, and ACME TOOL MANUFACTURING CO. for the design and construction of the Acme-Dunn Optical Printer.

GROVER LAUBE and the 20TH CENTURY-FOX STUDIO CAMERA DEPARTMENT for the development of a continuous-loop projection device.

WESTERN ELECTRIC CO. for the design and construction of the 1126A Limiting Amplifier for variable density sound recording.

RUSSELL BROWN, RAY HINSDALE, and JOSEPH E. ROBBINS for the development and production use of the Paramount floating hydraulic boat rocker.

GORDON JENNINGS for the design and construction of the Paramount nodal point tripod.

RADIO CORPORATION OF AMERICA and the RKO RADIO STUDIO SOUND DEPARTMENT for the design and construction of the RKO reverberation chamber.

DANIEL J. BLOOMBERG and the REPUBLIC STUDIO SOUND DEPARTMENT for the design and development of a multi-interlock selector switch.

BERNARD B. BROWN and JOHN P. LIVADARY for the design and engineering of a separate soloist and chorus recording room.

PAUL ZEFF, S. J. TWINING, and GEORGE SEID of the Columbia Studio Laboratory for the formula and application to production of a simplified variable area sound negative developer.

PAUL LERPAE for the design and construction of the Paramount traveling matte projection and photographing device.

1945 Eighteenth Year

Class I

None.

Class II

None.

Class III

LOREN L. RYDER, CHARLES R. DAILY, and the PARAMOUNT STUDIO SOUND DEPARTMENT for the design, construction, and use of the first dial controlled step-by-step sound channel line-up and test circuit.

MICHAEL S. LESHING, BENJAMIN C. ROBINSON, ARTHUR B. CHATELAIN, and ROBERT C. STEVENS of 20th Century-Fox Studio and JOHN G. CAPSTAFF of Eastman Kodak Co. for the 20th Century-Fox film processing machine.

1946 Nineteenth Year

Class I

None.

Class II

None.

Class III

HARLAN L. BAUMBACH and the PARAMOUNT WEST COAST LABORATORY for an improved method for the quantitative determination of hydroquinone and metol in photographic developing baths.

HERBERT E. BRITT for the development and application of formulas and equipment for producing cloud and smoke effects.

BURTON F. MILLER and the WARNER BROS. STUDIO SOUND and ELECTRICAL DEPARTMENTS for the design and construction of a motion picture arc lighting generator filter.

CARL FAULKNER of the 20th Century-Fox Studio Sound Department for the reversed bias method, including a double bias method for light valve and galvanometer density recording.

MOLE-RICHARDSON CO. for the Type 450 superhigh-intensity carbon arc lamp.

ARTHUR F. BLINN, ROBERT O. COOK, C. O. SLYFIELD, and the WALT DISNEY STUDIO SOUND DEPARTMENT for the design and development of an audio finder and track viewer for checking and locating noise in sound tracks.

BURTON F. MILLER and the WARNER BROS. STUDIO SOUND DEPARTMENT for the design and application of an equalizer to eliminate relative spectral energy distortion in electronic compressors.

MARTY MARTIN and HAL ADKINS of the RKO Radio Studio Miniature Department for the design and construction of equipment providing visual bullet effects.

HAROLD NYE and the WARNER BROS. STUDIO ELECTRICAL DEPARTMENT for the development of the electronically controlled fire and gaslight effect.

1947 Twentieth Year

Class I

None.

Class II

C. C. DAVIS and ELECTRICAL RESEARCH PRODUCTS, DIVISION OF WESTERN ELECTRIC CO. for the development and application of an improved film drive filter mechanism.

C. R. DAILY and the PARAMOUNT STUDIO FILM LABORATORY, STILL and ENGINEERING DEPARTMENTS for the development and first practical application to motion picture and still photography of a method of increasing film speed as first suggested to the industry by E. I. duPont de Nemours & Co.

Class III

NATHAN LEVINSON and the WARNER BROS. STUDIO SOUND DEPARTMENT for the design and construction of a constant-speed sound editing machine.

FARCIOT EDOUART, C. R. DAILY, HAL CORL, H. G. CARTWRIGHT, and the PARAMOUNT STUDIO TRANSPARENCY and ENGINEERING DEPARTMENTS for the first application of a special antisolarizing glass to high-intensity background and spot arc projectors.

FRED PONEDEL of Warner Bros. Studio for pioneering the fabrication and practical application to motion picture color photography of large translucent photographic backgrounds.

KURT SINGER and the RCA-VICTOR DIVISION of the RADIO CORPORATION OF AMERICA for the design and development of a continuously variable band elimination filter.

JAMES GIBBONS of Warner Bros. Studio for the development and production of large dyed plastic filters for motion picture photography.

1948 Twenty-first Year

Class I

None.

Class II

VICTOR CACCIALANZA, MAURICE AYERS, and the PARAMOUNT STUDIO SET CONSTRUCTION DEPARTMENT for the development and application of "Paralite," a new lightweight plaster process for set construction.

NICK KALTEN, LOUIS J. WITTI, and the 20TH CENTURY-FOX STUDIO MECHANICAL EFFECTS DEPARTMENT for a process of preserving and flame-proofing foliage.

Class III

MARTY MARTIN, JACK LANNON, RUSSELL SHEARMAN, and the RKO RADIO STUDIO SPECIAL EFFECTS DEPARTMENT for the development of a new method of simulating falling snow on motion picture sets.

A. J. MORAN and the WARNER BROS. STUDIO ELECTRICAL DEPARTMENT for a method of remote control for shutters on motion picture arc lighting equipment.

1949 Twenty-second Year

Class I

EASTMAN KODAK CO. for the development and introduction of an improved safety base motion picture film.

Class II

None.

Class III

LOREN L. RYDER, BRUCE H. DENNEY, ROBERT CARR, and the PARAMOUNT STUDIO SOUND DEPARTMENT for the development and application of the supersonic playback and public address system.

M. B. PAUL for the first successful large-area seamless translucent backgrounds.

HERBERT BRITT for the development and application of formulas and equipment producing artificial snow and ice for dressing motion picture sets.

ANDRE COUTANT and JACQUES MATHOT for the design of the Eclair Camerette.

CHARLES R. DAILY, STEVE CSILLAG, and the PARAMOUNT STUDIO ENGINEERING, EDITORIAL, and MUSIC DEPARTMENTS for a new precision method of computing variable tempo-click tracks.

INTERNATIONAL PROJECTOR CORP. for a simplified and self-adjusting take-up device for projection machines.

ALEXANDER VELCOFF for the application to production of the infrared photographic evaluator.

1950 Twenty-third Year

Class I

None.

Class II

JAMES B. GORDON and the 20TH CENTURY-FOX STUDIO CAMERA DEPARTMENT for the design and development of a multiple-image film viewer.

JOHN PAUL LIVADARY, FLOYD CAMPBELL, L. W. RUSSELL, and the COLUMBIA STUDIO SOUND DEPARTMENT for the development of a multitrack magnetic rerecording system.

LOREN L. RYDER and the PARAMOUNT STUDIO SOUND DEPARTMENT for the first studio-wide application of magnetic sound recording to motion picture production.

Class III

None.

1951 Twenty-fourth Year

Class I

None.

Class II

GORDON JENNINGS, S. L. STANCLIFFE, and the PARAMOUNT STUDIO SPECIAL

PHOTOGRAPHIC and ENGINEERING DEPARTMENTS for the design, construction, and application of a servo-operated recording and repeating device.

OLIN L. DUPY of Metro-Goldwyn-Mayer Studio for the design, construction, and application of a motion picture reproducing system.

RADIO CORPORATION OF AMERICA, VICTOR DIVISION, for pioneering direct positive recording with anticipatory noise reduction.

Class III

RICHARD M. HAFF, FRANK P. HERRNFELD, GARLAND C. MISENER, and the ANSCO FILM DIVISION OF GENERAL ANILINE AND FILM CORP. for the development of the Ansco color scene tester.

FRED PONEDEL, RALPH AYRES, and GEORGE BROWN of Warner Bros. Studio for an air-driven water motor to provide flow, wake, and white water for marine sequences in motion pictures.

GLEN ROBINSON and the METRO-GOLDWYN-MAYER STUDIO CONSTRUCTION DEPARTMENT for the development of a new music wire and cable cutter.

JACK GAYLORD and the METRO-GOLDWYN-MAYER STUDIO CONSTRUCTION DEPARTMENT for the development of balsa falling snow.

CARLOS RIVAS of Metro-Goldwyn-Mayer Studio for the development of an automatic magnetic film splicer.

1952 Twenty-fifth Year

Class I

EASTMAN KODAK CO. for the introduction of Eastman color negative and Eastman color print film.

ANSCO DIVISION, GENERAL ANILINE AND FILM CORP. for the introduction of Ansco color negative and Ansco color print film.

Class II

TECHNICOLOR MOTION PICTURE CORP. for an improved method of color motion picture photography under incandescent light.

Class III

PROJECTION, STILL PHOTOGRAPHIC, and DEVELOPMENT ENGINEERING DEPARTMENTS of METRO-GOLDWYN-MAYER STUDIO for an improved method of projecting photographic backgrounds.

JOHN G. FRAYNE and R. R. SCOVILLE and WESTREX CORP. for a method of measuring distortion in sound reproduction.

PHOTO RESEARCH CORP. for creating the Spectra color temperature meter.

GUSTAV JIROUCH for the design of the Robot automatic film splicer.

CARLOS RIVAS of Metro-Goldwyn-Mayer Studio for the development of a sound reproducer for magnetic film.

1953 Twenty-sixth Year

Class I

PROFESSOR HENRI CHRETIEN and EARL SPONABLE, SOL HALPRIN, LORIN GRIGNON, HERBERT BRAGG, and CARL FAULKNER of 20th Century-Fox Studios for creating, developing, and engineering the equipment, processes, and techniques known as CinemaScope.

FRED WALLER for designing and developing the multiple photographic and projection systems that culminated in Cinerama.

Class II

REEVES SOUNDCRAFT CORP, for their development of a process of applying stripes of magnetic oxide to motion picture film for sound recording and reproduction.

Class III

WESTREX CORP. for the design and construction of a new film editing machine.

1954 Twenty-seventh Year

Class I

PARAMOUNT PICTURES, INC., LOREN L. RYDER, JOHN R. BISHOP, and all the members of the technical and engineering staff for developing a method of producing and exhibiting motion pictures known as VistaVision.

Class II

None.

Class III

DAVID S. HORSLEY and the UNIVERSAL-INTERNATIONAL STUDIO SPECIAL PHOTOGRAPHIC DEPARTMENT for a portable remote control device for process projectors.

KARL FREUND and FRANK CRANDELL of Photo Research Corp. for the design and development of a direct-reading brightness meter.

WESLEY C. MILLER, J. W. STAFFORD, K. M. FRIERSON, and the METRO-GOLDWYN-MAYER STUDIO SOUND DEPARTMENT for an electronic sound printing comparison device.

JOHN P. LIVADARY, LLOYD RUSSELL, and the COLUMBIA STUDIO SOUND DEPARTMENT for an improved limiting amplifier as applied to sound-level comparison devices.

ROLAND MILLER and MAX GOEPPINGER of Magnascope Corp. for the design and development of a cathode-ray magnetic sound track viewer.

CARLOS RIVAS, G. M. SPRAGUE, and the METRO-GOLDWYN-MAYER STUDIO SOUND DEPARTMENT for the design of a magnetic sound editing machine.

FRED WILSON of the Samuel Goldwyn Studio Sound Department for the design of a variable, multiple-band equalizer.

P. C. YOUNG of the Metro-Goldwyn-Mayer Studio Projection Department for the practical application of a variable focal length attachment to motion picture projector lenses.

FRED KNOTH and ORIEN ERNEST of the Universal-International Studio Technical Department for the development of a hand-portable, electric, dry oil-fog machine.

1955 Twenty-eighth Year

Class I

NATIONAL CARBON CO. for the development and production of a high-efficiency yellow flame carbon for motion picture color photography.

Class II

EASTMAN KODAK CO. for Eastman Tri-X panchromatic negative film.

FARCIOT EDOUART, HAL CORL, and the PARAMOUNT STUDIO TRANSPARENCY DEPARTMENT for the engineering and development of a double-frame, triple-head background projector.

Class III

20TH CENTURY-FOX STUDIO and BAUSCH & LOMB CO. for the new combination lenses for CinemaScope photography.

WALTER JOLLEY, MAURICE LARSON, and R. H. SPIES of 20th Century-Fox Studio for a spraying process that creates simulated metallic surfaces.

STEVE KRILANOVICH for an improved camera dolly incorporating multidirectional steering.

DAVE ANDERSON of 20th Century-Fox Studio for an improved spotlight capable of maintaining a fixed circle of light at constant intensity over varied distances.

LOREN L. RYDER, CHARLES WEST, HENRY FRACKER, and PARAMOUNT STUDIO for a projection film index to establish proper framing for various aspect ratios.

FARCIOT EDOUART, HAL CORL, and the PARAMOUNT STUDIO TRANSPARENCY DEPARTMENT for an improved dual-stereopticon background projector.

1956 Twenty-ninth Year

Class I

None.

Class II

None.

Class III

RICHARD H. RANGER of Rangertone, Inc., for the development of a synchronous recording and reproducing system for quarter-inch magnetic tape.

TED HIRSCH, CARL HAUGE, and EDWARD REICHARD of Consolidated Film Industries for an automatic scene counter for laboratory projection rooms.

THE TECHNICAL DEPARTMENTS of PARAMOUNT PICTURES CORP. for the engineering and development of the Paramount lightweight horizontal-movement VistaVision camera.

ROY C. STEWART AND SONS of Stewart-Trans Lux Corp., DR. C. R. DAILY, and the TRANSPARENCY DEPARTMENT of PARAMOUNT PICTURES CORP. for the engineering and development of the HiTrans and Para-HiTrans rear projection screens.

THE CONSTRUCTION DEPARTMENT of METRO-GOLDWYN-MAYER STUDIO for a new, hand-portable fog machine.

DANIEL J. BLOOMBERG, JOHN POND, WILLIAM WADE, and the ENGINEERING and CAMERA DEPARTMENTS of REPUBLIC STUDIO for the Naturama adaptation to the Mitchell camera.

1957 Thirtieth Year

Class I

TODD-AO CORP. and WESTREX CORP. for developing a method of producing and exhibiting wide-film motion pictures known as the Todd-AO System.

MOTION PICTURE RESEARCH COUNCIL for the design and development of a high-efficiency projection screen for drive-in theatres.

Class II

SOCIÉTÉ D'OPTIQUE ET DE MÉCANIQUE DE HAUTE PRECISION for the development of a high-speed vari-focal photographic lens.

HARLAN L. BAUMBACH, LORAND WARGO, HOWARD M. LITTLE, and the UNICORN ENGINEERING CORP. for the development of an automatic printer light selector.

Class III

CHARLES E. SUTTER, WILLIAM B. SMITH, PARAMOUNT

PICTURES CORP., and GENERAL CABLE CORP. for the engineering and application to studio use of aluminum lightweight electrical cable and connectors.

1958 Thirty-first Year

Class I

None.

Class II

DON W. PRIDEAUX, LEROY G. LEIGHTON, and the LAMP DIVISION of GENERAL ELECTRIC CO. for the development and production of an improved 10-kilowatt lamp for motion picture set lighting.

PANAVISION, INC., for the design and development of the Auto Panatar anamorphic photographic lens for 35mm CinemaScope photography.

Class III

WILLY BORBERG of the General Precision Laboratory, Inc., for the development of a high-speed intermittent movement for 35mm motion picture theatre projection equipment.

FRED PONEDEL, GEORGE BROWN, and CONRAD BOYE of the Warner Bros. Special Effects Department for the design and fabrication of a new rapid-fire marble gun.

1959 Thirty-second Year

Class I

None.

Class II

DOUGLAS G. SHEARER of Metro-Goldwyn-Mayer, Inc., and ROBERT E. GOTTSCHALK and JOHN R. MOORE of Panavision, Inc., for the development of a system of production and exhibiting wide-film motion pictures known as Camera 65.

WADSWORTH E. POHL, WILLIAM EVANS, WERNER HOPF, S. E. HOWSE, THOMAS P. DIXON, STANFORD RESEARCH INSTITUTE, and TECHNICOLOR CORP. for the design and development of the Technicolor electronic printing timer.

WADSWORTH E. POHL, JACK ALFORD, HENRY IMUS, JOSEPH SCHMIT, PAUL FASSNACHT, AL LOFQUIST, and TECHNICOLOR CORP. for the development and practical application of equipment for wet printing.

DR. HOWARD S. COLEMAN, DR. A. FRANCIS TURNER, HAROLD H. SCHROEDER, JAMES R. BENFORD, and HAROLD E. ROSENBERGER of the Bausch & Lomb Optical Co. for the design and development of the Balcold projection mirror.

ROBERT P. GUTTERMAN of General Kinetics, Inc., and the LIPSNER-SMITH CORP. for the design and development of the CF-2 Ultrasonic Film Cleaner.

Class III

UB IWERKS of Walt Disney Prods. for the design of an improved optical printer for special effects and matte shots.

E. L. STONES, GLEN ROBINSON, WINFIELD HUBBARD, and LUTHER NEWMAN of the Metro-Goldwyn-Mayer Studio Construction Department for the design of a multiple-cable remote-controlled winch.

1960 Thirty-third Year

Class I

None.

Class II

AMPEX PROFESSIONAL PRODUCTS CO. for the production of a well-engineered multipurpose sound system combining high standards of quality with convenience of control, dependable operation, and simplified emergency provisions.

Class III

ARTHUR HOLCOMB, PETRO VLAHOS, and COLUMBIA STUDIO CAMERA DEPARTMENT for a camera flicker indicating device.

ANTHONY PAGLIA and the 20TH CENTURY-FOX STUDIO MECHANICAL EFFECTS DEPARTMENT for the design and construction of a miniature flak gun and ammunition.

CARL HAUGE, ROBERT GRUBEL, and EDWARD REICHARD of Consolidated Film Industries for the development of an automatic developer replenisher system.

1961 Thirty-fourth Year

Class I

None.

Class II

SYLVANIA ELECTRIC PRODUCTS, INC., for the development of a hand-held high-power photographic lighting unit known as the Sun Gun Professional.

JAMES DALE, S. WILSON, H. E. RICE, JOHN RUDE, LAURIE ATKIN, WADSWORTH E. POHL, H. PEASGOOD, and TECHNICOLOR CORP. for a process of automatic selective printing.

20TH CENTURY-FOX RESEARCH DEPARTMENT, under the direction of E. I. SPONABLE and HERBERT E. BRAGG, and DELUXE LABORATORIES, INC., with the assistance of F. D. LESLIE, R. D. WHITMORE, A. A. ALDEN, ENDEL POOL, and JAMES B. GORDON, for a system of decompressing and recomposing CinemaScope pictures for conventional aspect ratios.

Class III

HURLETRON, INC., ELECTRIC EYE EQUIPMENT DIVISION, for an automatic light changing system for motion picture printers.

WADSWORTH E. POHL and TECHNICOLOR CORP. for an integrated sound and picture transfer process.

1962 Thirty-fifth Year

Class I

None.

Class II

RALPH CHAPMAN for the design and development of an advanced motion picture camera crane.

ALBERT S. PRATT, JAMES L. WASSELL, and HANS C. WOHLRAB of the Professional Division, Bell & Howell Co., for the design and development of a new and improved automatic motion picture additive color printer.

NORTH AMERICAN PHILIPS CO., INC., for the design and engineering of the Norelco Universal 70/35mm motion picture projector.

CHARLES E. SUTTER, WILLIAM BRYSON SMITH, and LOUIS C. KENNELL of Paramount Pictures Corp. for the engineering and application to motion picture production of a new system of electric power distribution.

Class III

ELECTRO-VOICE, INC., for a highly directional dynamic line microphone.

LOUIS G. MACKENZIE for a selective sound effects repeater.

1963 Thirty-sixth Year

Class I

None.

Class II

None.

Class III

DOUGLAS G. SHEARER and A. ARNOLD GILLESPIE of Metro-Goldwyn-Mayer Studios for the engineering of an improved background process projection system.

1964 Thirty-seventh Year

Class I

PETRO VLAHOS, WADSWORTH E. POHL, and UB IWERKS for the conception and perfection of techniques for color traveling matte composite cinematography.

Class II

SIDNEY P. SOLOW, EDWARD H. REICHARD, CARL W. HAUGE, and JOB SANDERSON of Consolidated Film Industries for the design and development of a versatile automatic 35mm composite color printer.

PIERRE ANGENIEUX for the development of a ten-to-one zoom lens for cinematography.

Class III

MILTON FORMAN, RICHARD B. GLICKMAN, and DANIEL J. PEARLMAN of ColorTran Industries for advancements in the design and application to motion picture photography of lighting units using quartz iodine lamps.

STEWART FILMSCREEN CORPORATION for a seamless, translucent blue screen for traveling matte color cinematography.

ANTHONY PAGLIA and the 20TH CENTURY-FOX STUDIO MECHANICAL EFFECTS DEPARTMENT for an improved method of producing explosion flash effects for motion pictures.

EDWARD H. REICHARD and CARL W. HAUGE of Consolidated Film Industries for the design of a proximity cue detector and its application to motion picture printers.

EDWARD H. REICHARD, LEONARD L. SOKOLOW, and CARL W. HAUGE of Consolidated Film Industries for the design and application to motion picture laboratory practice of a stroboscopic scene tester for color and black-and-white film.

NELSON TYLER for the design and construction of an improved helicopter camera system.

1965 Thirty-eighth Year

Class I

None.

Class II

ARTHUR J. HATCH of Strong Electric Corporation, subsidiary of General Precision Equipment Corporation, for the design and development of an air-blown carbon arc projection lamp.

STEFAN KUDELSKI for the design and development of the Nagra portable 1/4-inch tape recording system for motion picture sound recording.

Class III

None.

1966 Thirty-ninth Year

Class I

None.

Class II

MITCHELL CAMERA CORPORATION for the design and development of the Mitchell Mark II 35mm Portable Motion Picture Reflex Camera.

ARNOLD & RICHTER KG for the design and development of the Arriflex 35mm Portable Motion Picture Reflex Camera.

Class III

PANAVISION INCORPORATED for the design of the Panatron Power Inverter and its application to motion picture camera operation.

CARROLL KNUDSON for the production of a Composers Manual for Motion Picture Music Synchronization.

RUBY RAKSIN for the production of a Composers Manual for Motion Picture Music Synchronization.

1967 Fortieth Year

Class I

None.

Class II

None.

Class III

ELECTRO-OPTICAL DIVISION of the KOLLMORGEN CORPORATION for the design and development of a series of motion picture projection lenses.

PANAVISION INCORPORATED for a variable-speed motor for motion picture cameras.

FRED R. WILSON of the Samuel Goldwyn Studio Sound Department for an audio level clamper.

WALDON O. WATSON and the UNIVERSAL CITY STUDIO SOUND DEPARTMENT for new concepts in the design of a music scoring stage.

1968 Forty-first Year

Class I

PHILIP V. PALMQUIST of MINNESOTA MINING AND MANUFACTURING CO., DR. HERBERT MEYER of the Motion Picture and Television Research Center, and CHARLES D. STAFFELL of the Rank Organisation for the development of a successful embodiment of the reflex background projection system for composite cinematography.

EASTMAN KODAK COMPANY for the development and introduction of a color reversal intermediate film for motion pictures.

Class II

DONALD W. NORWOOD for the design and development of the Norwood photographic exposure meters.

EASTMAN KODAK COMPANY and PRODUCERS SERVICE COMPANY for the development of a new, high-speed, step-optical reduction printer.

EDMUND M. DiGIULIO, NIELS G. PETERSEN, and NORMAN S. HUGHES of the Cinema Product Development Company for the design and application of a conversion that makes available the reflex viewing system for motion picture cameras.

OPTICAL COATING LABORATORIES, INC., for the development of an improved antireflection coating for photographic and projection lens systems.

EASTMAN KODAK COMPANY for the introduction of a new, high-speed motion picture color negative film.

PANAVISION INCORPORATED for

the conception, design, and introduction of a 65mm hand-held motion picture camera.

TODD-AO COMPANY and the MITCHELL CAMERA COMPANY for the design and engineering of the Todd-AO hand-held motion picture camera.

Class III

CARL W. HAUGE and EDWARD H. REICHARD of Consolidated Film Industries and E. MICHAEL MEAHL and ROY J. RIDENOUR of Ramtronics for engineering an automatic exposure control for printing-machine lamps.

EASTMAN KODAK COMPANY for a new direct positive film and to CONSOLIDATED FILM INDUSTRIES for the application of this film to the making of postproduction work prints.

1969 Forty-second Year

Class I

None.

Class II

HAZELTINE CORPORATION for the design and development of the Hazeltine Color Film Analyzer.

FOUAD SAID for the design and introduction of the Cinemobile series of equipment trucks for location motion picture production.

JUAN DE LA CIERVA and DYNASCIENCES CORPORATION for the design and development of the Dynalens optical-image motion compensator.

Class III

OTTO POPELKA of Magna-Tech Electronics Co., Inc., for the development of an electronically controlled looping system.

FENTON HAMILTON of Metro-Goldwyn-Mayer Studios for the concept and engineering of a mobile battery power unit for location lighting.

PANAVISION INCORPORATED for the design and development of the Panaspeed Motion Picture Camera Motor.

ROBERT M. FLYNN and RUSSELL HESSY of Universal City Studios, Inc., for a machine-gun modification for motion picture photography.

1970 Forty-third Year

Class I

None.

Class II

LEONARD SOKOLOW and EDWARD H. REICHARD of Consolidated Film Industries for the concept and engineering of the Color Proofing Printer for motion pictures.

Class III

SYLVANIA ELECTRIC PRODUCTS, INC., for the development and introduction of a series of compact tungsten halogen lamps for motion picture production.

B. J. LOSMANDY for the concept, design, and application of microminiature solid-state amplifier modules used in motion picture recording equipment.

EASTMAN KODAK COMPANY and PHOTO ELECTRONICS CORPORATION for the design and engineering of an improved video color analyzer for motion picture laboratories.

ELECTRO SOUND INCORPORATED for the design and introduction of the Series 8000 Sound System for motion picture theatres.

1971 Forty-fourth Year

Class I

None.

Class II

JOHN N. WILKINSON of Optical Radiation Corporation for the development and engineering of a system of xenon arc lamphouses for motion picture projection.

Class III

THOMAS JEFFERSON HUTCHINSON, JAMES R. ROCHESTER, and FENTON HAMILTON for the development and introduction of the Sunbrute system of xenon arc lamps for location lighting in motion picture production.

PHOTO RESEARCH, a DIVISION OF KOLLMORGEN CORPORATION, for the development and introduction of the film-lens-balanced three-color meter.

ROBERT D. AUGUSTE and CINEMA PRODUCTS CO. for the development and introduction of a new crystal-controlled lightweight motor for the 35mm motion picture Arriflex camera.

PRODUCERS SERVICE CORPORATION and CONSOLIDATED FILM INDUSTRIES; and CINEMA RESEARCH CORPORATION and RESEARCH PRODUCTS, INC., for the engineering and implementation of fully automated blow-up motion picture printing systems.

CINEMA PRODUCTS CO. for a control motor to actuate zoom lenses on motion picture cameras.

1972 Forty-fifth Year

Class I

None.

Class II

JOSEPH E. BLUTH for research and development in the field of electronic photography and transfer of video tape to motion picture film.

EDWARD H. REICHARD and HOWARD T. LA ZARE of Consolidated Film Industries, and EDWARD EFRON of IBM for the engineering of a computerized light-valve monitoring system for motion picture printing.

PANAVISION INCORPORATED for the development and engineering of the Panaflex motion picture camera.

Class III

PHOTO RESEARCH, a DIVISION OF KOLLMORGEN CORPORATION, and PSC TECHNOLOGY INC., Acme Products Division, for the Spectra Film Gate Photometer for motion picture printers.

CARTER EQUIPMENT COMPANY, INC., and RAMTRONICS for the Ramtronics light-valve photometer for motion picture printers.

DAVID DEGENKOLB, HARRY LARSON, MANFRED MICHELSON, and FRED SCOBEY of DeLuxe General Incorporated for the development of a computerized motion picture printer and process control system.

JIRO MUKAI and RYUSHO HIROSE of Canon, Inc., and WILTON R. HOLM of the AMPTP Motion Picture and Television Research Center for development of the Canon Macro Zoom Lens for motion picture photography.

PHILIP V. PALMQUIST and LEONARD L. OLSON of the 3M Company and FRANK P. CLARK of the AMPTP Motion Picture and Television Research Center for development of Nextel simulated blood for motion picture color photography.

E. H. GEISSLER and G. M. BERGGREN of Wil-Kin, Inc., for engineering of the Ultra-Vision Motion Picture Theater Projection System.

1973 Forty-sixth Year

Class I

None.

Class II

JOACHIM GERB and ERICH KAESTNER of Arnold & Richter Company for the development and engineering of the Arriflex 35BL motion picture camera.

MAGNA-TECH ELECTRONIC CO., INC., for the engineering and development of a high-speed rerecording system for motion picture production.

WILLIAM W. VALLIANT of PSC Technology Inc., HOWARD F. OTT of Eastman Kodak Company, and GERRY DIEBOLD of Richmark Camera Service, Inc., for the development of a liquid-gate system for motion picture printers.

HAROLD A. SCHEIB, CLIFFORD H. ELLIS, and ROGER W. BANKS of Research Products Incorporated for the concept and engineering of the Model 2101 optical printer for motion picture optical effects.

Class III

ROSCO LABORATORIES, INC., for the technical advances and the development of a complete system of light-control materials for motion picture photography.

RICHARD H. VETTER of the Todd-AO Corporation for the design of an improved anamorphic focusing system for motion picture photography.

1974 Forty-seventh Year

Class I

None.

Class II

JOSEPH D. KELLY of Glen Glenn Sound for the design of new audio control consoles that have advanced the state of the art of sound recording and rerecording for motion picture production.

THE BURBANK STUDIOS SOUND DEPARTMENT for the design of new audio control consoles engineered and constructed by the Quad-Eight Sound Corporation.

SAMUEL GOLDWYN STUDIOS SOUND DEPARTMENT for the design of a new audio control console engineered and constructed by the Quad-Eight Sound Corporation.

QUAD-EIGHT SOUND CORPORATION for the engineering and construction of new audio control consoles designed by the Burbank Studios Sound Department and by the Samuel Goldwyn Studios Sound Department.

WALDON O. WATSON, RICHARD J. STUMPF, ROBERT J. LEONARD, and the UNIVERSAL CITY STUDIOS SOUND DEPARTMENT for the development and engineering of the Sensurround System for motion picture presentation.

Class III

ELEMACK COMPANY, Rome, Italy, for the design and development of the Spyder camera dolly.

LOUIS AMI of the Universal City Studios for the design and construction of a reciprocating camera platform used to photograph special visual effects for motion pictures.

1975 Forty-eighth Year

Class I

None.

Class II

CHADWELL O'CONNOR of the O'Connor Engineering Laboratories

for the concept and engineering of a fluid-damped camerahead for motion picture photography.

WILLIAM F. MINER of Universal City Studios, Inc., and the WESTINGHOUSE ELECTRIC CORPORATION for the development and engineering of a solid-state. 500-kilowatt, direct-current static rectifier for motion picture lighting.

Class III

LAWRENCE W. BUTLER and ROGER BANKS for the concept of applying low inertia and stepping electric motors to film transport systems and optical printers for motion picture production.

DAVID J. DEGENKOLB and FRED SCOBEY of Deluxe General Incorporated and JOHN C. DOLAN and RICHARD DUBOIS of the Akwaklame Company for the development of a technique for silver recovery from photographic wash-waters by ion exchange.

JOSEPH WESTHEIMER for the development of a device to obtain shadowed titles on motion picture films.

CARTER EQUIPMENT CO., INC., and RAMTRONICS for the engineering and manufacture of a computerized tape-punching system for programming laboratory printing machines.

THE HOLLYWOOD FILM COMPANY for the engineering and manufacture of a computerized tape-punching system for programming laboratory printing machines.

BELL & HOWELL for the engineering and manufacture of a computerized tape-punching system for programming laboratory printing machines.

FREDRIK SCHLYTER for the engineering and manufacture of a computerized tape-punching system for programming laboratory printing machines.

1976 Forty-ninth Year

Class I

None.

Class II

CONSOLIDATED FILM INDUSTRIES and the BARNEBEY-CHENEY COMPANY for the development of a system for the recovery of film-cleaning solvent vapors in a motion picture laboratory.

WILLIAM L. GRAHAM, MANFRED G. MICHELSON, GEOFFREY F. NORMAN, and SIEGFRIED SEIBERT of Technicolor for the development and engineering of a continuous high-speed, color motion picture printing system.

Class III

FRED BARTSCHER of the Kollmorgen Corporation and GLENN BERGGREN of the Schneider Corporation for the design and development of a single-lens magnifier for motion picture projection lenses.

PANAVISION INCORPORATED for the design and development of superspeed lenses for motion picture photography.

HIROSHI SUZUKAWA of Canon and WILTON R. HOLM of AMPTP Motion Picture and Television Research Center for the design and development of superspeed lenses for motion picture photography.

CARL ZEISS COMPANY for the design and development of superspeed lenses for motion picture photography.

PHOTO RESEARCH DIVISION of

the KOLLMORGEN CORPORATION for the engineering and manufacture of the spectra TriColor Meter.

1977 Fiftieth Year

Class I

GARRETT BROWN and the CINEMA PRODUCTS CORP. engineering staff, under the supervision of JOHN JURGENS, for the invention and development of Steadicam.

Class II

JOSEPH D. KELLY, BARRY K. HENLEY, HAMMOND H. HOLT, and GLEN GLENN SOUND for the concept and development of a post-production audio processing system for motion picture films.

PANAVISION, INCORPORATED, for the concept and engineering of the improvements incorporated in the Panaflex Motion Picture Camera.

N. PAUL KENWORTHY, JR., and WILLIAM R. LATADY for the invention and development of the Kenworthy Snorkel Camera System for motion picture photography.

JOHN C. DYKSTRA for the development of the Dykstraflex Camera and to ALVAH J. MILLER and JERRY JEFFRESS for the engineering of the Electronic Motion Control System used in concert for multiple-exposure visual effects motion picture photography.

The EASTMAN KODAK COMPANY for the development and introduction of a new duplicating film for motion pictures.

STEFAN KUDELSKI of Nagra Magnetic Recorders, Incorporated, for the engineering of the improvements incorporated in the Nagra 4.2L sound recorder for motion picture production.

Class III

ERNST NETTMANN of the Astrovision Division of Continental Camera Systems, Incorporated, for the engineering of its Snorkel Aerial Camera System.

EECO (ELECTRONIC ENGINEERING COMPANY OF CALIFORNIA) for developing a method for interlocking nonsprocketed film and tape media used in motion picture production.

DR. BERNHARD KUHL and WERNER BLOCK of OSRAM, GmbH, for the development of the HMI high-efficiency discharge lamp for motion picture lighting.

PANAVISION, INCORPORATED, for the design of Panalite, a camera-mounted controllable light for motion picture photography.

PANAVISION, INCORPORATED, for the engineering of the Panahead gearhead for motion picture cameras.

PICLEAR, INC., for originating and developing an attachment to motion picture projectors to improve screen image quality.

*1978 Fifty-first Year**

Academy Award of Merit (Academy statuette)

EASTMAN KODAK COMPANY for the research and development of a duplicating color film for motion pictures.

STEFAN KUDELSKI of Nagra Magnetic Recorders, Incorporated,

*In 1979 the Academy retitled the three categories of the Scientific or Technical Awards. The Class I designation was changed to Academy Award of Merit, Class II to Scientific and Engineering Award, and Class III to Technical Achievement Award.

for the continuing research, design, and development of the Nagra Production Sound Recorder for motion pictures.

PANAVISION, INCORPORATED, and its engineering staff, under the direction of Robert E. Gottschalk, for the concept, design, and continuous development of the Panaflex Motion Picture Camera System.

Scientific and Engineering Award (Academy plaque)

RAY M. DOLBY, IOAN R. ALLEN, DAVID P. ROBINSON, STEPHEN M. KATZ, and PHILIP S. J. BOOLE of Dolby Laboratories, Incorporated, for the development and implementation of an improved sound recording and reproducing system for motion picture production and exhibition.

Technical Achievement Award (Academy certificate)

KARL MACHER and GLENN M. BERGGREN of Isco Optische Werke for the development and introduction of the Cinelux-ULTRA lens for 35mm motion picture projection.

DAVID J. DEGENKOLB, ARTHUR L. FORD, and FRED J. SCOBEY of DeLuxe General, Incorporated, for the development of a method to recycle motion picture laboratory photographic wash-waters by ion exchange.

KIICHI SEKIGUCHI of CINE-FI International for the development of the CINE-FI Auto Radio Sound System for drive-in theaters.

LEONARD CHAPMAN of Leonard Equipment Company for the design and manufacture of a small, mobile, motion picture camera platform known as the Chapman Hustler Dolly.

JAMES L. FISHER of J. L. Fisher, Incorporated, for the design and manufacture of a small, mobile, motion picture camera platform known as the Fisher Model Ten Dolly.

ROBERT STINDT of Production Grip Equipment Company, for the design and manufacture of a small, mobile, motion picture camera platform known as the Stindt Dolly.

1979 Fifty-second Year

Academy Award of Merit (Academy statuette)

MARK SERRURIER for the progressive development of the Moviola from the 1924 invention of his father, Iwan Serrurier, to the present Series 20 sophisticated film editing equipment.

Scientific and Engineering Award (Academy plaque)

NEIMAN-TILLAR ASSOCIATES for the creative development and to MINI-MICRO SYSTEMS, INCORPORATED, for the design and engineering of an Automated Computer-Controlled Editing Sound System (ACCESS) for motion picture postproduction.

Technical Achievement Award (Academy certificate)

MICHAEL V. CHEWEY, WALTER G. EGGERS, and ALLEN HECHT of M-G-M Laboratories for the development of a computer-controlled paper-tape programmer system and its applications in the motion picture laboratory.

IRWIN YOUNG, PAUL KAUFMAN, and FREDRIK SCHLYTER of Du Art Film Laboratories, Incorporated, for the development of a computer-controlled paper-tape programmer system and its applications in the motion picture laboratory.

JAMES S. STANFIELD and PAUL W. TRESTER for the development and manufacture of a device for the repair or protection of sprocket holes in motion picture film.

ZORAN PERISIC of Courier Films, Limited, for the Zoptic Special Optical Effects Device for motion picture photography.

A. D. FLOWERS and LOGAN R. FRAZEE for the development of a device to control flight patterns of miniature airplanes during motion picture photography.

PHOTO RESEARCH DIVISION OF KOLLMORGEN CORPORATION for the development of the Spectra Series II Cine Special Exposure Meter for motion picture photography.

BRUCE LYON and JOHN LAMB for the development of a video animation system for testing motion picture animation sequences.

ROSS LOWELL of Lowel-Light Manufacturing, Incorporated, for the development of compact lighting equipment for motion picture photography.

1980 Fifty-third Year

Academy Award of Merit (Academy statuette)

LINWOOD G. DUNN, CECIL D. LOVE, and ACME TOOL AND MANUFACTURING COMPANY for the concept, engineering, and development of the Acme-Dunn Optical Printer for motion picture special effects.

Scientific and Engineering Award (Academy plaque)

JEAN-MARIE LAVALOU, ALAIN MASSERON, and DAVID SAMUELSON of Samuelson Alga Cinema S.A. and Samuelson Film Service, Limited, for the engineering and development of the Louma Camera Crane and remote control system for motion picture production.

EDWARD B. KRAUSE of Filmline Corporation for the engineering and manufacture of the microdemand drive for continuous motion picture film processors.

ROSS TAYLOR for the concept and development of a system of air guns for propelling objects used in special effects motion picture production.

DR. BERNARD KÜHL and DR. WERNER BLOCK of OSRAM GmbH for the progressive engineering and manufacture of the OSRAM HMI light source for motion picture color photography.

DAVID A. GRAFTON for the optical design and engineering of a telecentric anamorphic lens for motion picture optical effects printers.

Technical Achievement Award (Academy certificate)

CARTER EQUIPMENT COMPANY for the development of a continuous contact, total immersion, additive color motion picture printer.

HOLLYWOOD FILM COMPANY for the development of a continuous contact, total immersion, additive color motion picture printer.

ANDRÉ DEBRIE S.A. for the development of a continuous contact, total immersion, additive color motion picture printer.

CHARLES VAUGHN and EUGENE NOTTINGHAM of Cinetron Computer Systems, Incorporated, for the development of a versatile, general-purpose computer system for animation and optical effects motion picture photography.

JOHN W. LANG, WALTER HRASTNIK, and CHARLES J. WATSON of Bell and Howell Company for the development and manufacture of a modular, continuous contact motion picture film printer.

WORTH BAIRD of LaVezzi Machine Works, Incorporated, for the advanced design and manufacture of a film sprocket for motion picture projectors.

PETER A. REGLA and DAN SLATER of Elicon for the development of a follow focus system for motion picture optical effects printers and animation stands.

1981 Fifty-fourth Year

Academy Award of Merit (Academy statuette)

FUJI PHOTO FILM COMPANY, LTD., for the research, development, and introduction of a new ultrahigh-speed color negative film for motion pictures.

Scientific and Engineering Award (Academy plaque)

LEONARD SOKOLOW for the concept and design and HOWARD LAZARE for the development of the Consolidated Film Industries' Stroboscan motion picture film viewer.

RICHARD EDLUND and INDUSTRIAL LIGHT AND MAGIC, INCORPORATED, for the concept and engineering of a beam-splitter optical composite motion picture printer.

RICHARD EDLUND and INDUSTRIAL LIGHT AND MAGIC, INCORPORATED, for the engineering of the Empire Motion Picture Camera System.

EDWARD J. BLASKO and DR. RODERICK T. RYAN of the Eastman Kodak Company for the application of the Prostar Microfilm Processor for motion picture title and special optical effects production.

NELSON TYLER for the progressive development and improvement of the Tyler helicopter motion picture camera platform.

Technical Achievement Award (Academy certificate)

HAL LANDAKER for the concept and ALAN D. LANDAKER for the engineering of the Burbank Studios' Production Sound Department 24-frame color video system.

BILL HOGAN of Ruxton, Ltd., and RICHARD J. STUMPF and DANIEL R. BREWER of Universal City Studios' Production Sound Department for the engineering of a 24-frame color video system.

ERNST F. NETTMANN of Continental Camera Systems, Inc., for the development of a pitching lens for motion picture photography.

BILL TAYLOR of Universal Studios for the concept and specifications for a two-format, rotating-head, aerial image optical printer.

PETER D. PARKS of Oxford Scientific Films for the development of the OSF microscopic photography.

DR. LOUIS STANKIEWICZ and H. L. BLACHFORD for the development of Baryfol sound barrier materials.

DENNIS MUREN and STUART ZIFF of Industrial Light and Magic, Incorporated, for the development of a motion picture figure mover for animation photography.

JOHN DEMUTH for the engineering of a 24-frame video system.

1982 Fifty-fifth Year

Academy Award of Merit (Academy statuette)

AUGUST ARNOLD and ERICH KAESTNER of Arnold & Richter GmbH for the concept and engineering of the first operational 35mm, hand-held, spinning-mirror-reflex motion picture camera.

Scientific and Engineering Award (Academy plaque)

COLIN F. MOSSMAN and the RESEARCH AND DEVELOPMENT GROUP OF RANK FILM LABORATORIES, LONDON, for the engineering and implementation of a 4,000-meter printing system for motion picture laboratories.

SANTE ZELLI and SALVATORE ZELLI of Elemack Italia S.r.l., Rome, Italy, for the continuing engineering, design, and development that has resulted in the Elemack Camera Dolly Systems for motion picture production.

LEONARD CHAPMAN for the engineering design, development, and manufacture of the PeeWee Camera Dolly for motion picture production.

DR. MOHAMMAD S. NOZARI of Minnesota Mining and Manufacturing Company for the research and development of the 3M Photogard protective coating for motion picture film.

BRIANNE MURPHY and DONALD SCHISLER of Mitchell Insert Systems, Incorporated, for the concept, design, and manufacture of the MISI Camera Insert Car and Process Trailer.

JACOBUS L. DIMMERS for the engineering and manufacture of the Teccon Enterprises' magnetic transducer for motion picture sound recording and playback.

Technical Achievement Award (Academy certificate)

RICHARD W. DEATS for the design and manufacture of the Little Big Crane for motion picture production.

CONSTANT TRESFON and ADRIAAN DE ROOY of Egripment and ED PHILLIPS and CARLOS DE MATTOS of Matthews Studio Equipment, Incorporated, for the design and manufacture of the Tulip Crane for motion picture production.

BRAN FERREN of Associates and Ferren for the design and development of a computerized lightning effect system for motion picture photography.

CHRISTIE ELECTRIC CORPORATION and LAVEZZI MACHINE WORKS, INCORPORATED, for the design and manufacture of the Ultramittent film transport for Christie motion picture projectors.

1983 Fifty-sixth Year

Academy Award of Merit (Academy statuette)

DR. KURT LARCHE of OSRAM GmbH for the research and development of xenon short-arc discharge lamps for motion picture projection.

Scientific and Engineering Award (Academy plaque)

JONATHAN ERLAND and ROGER DORNEY of Apogee, Incorporated, for the engineering and development of a reverse bluescreen traveling matte process for special effects photography.

GERALD L. TURPIN of Lightflex International Limited for the design, engineering, and development of an on-camera device providing contrast control, sourceless fill light, and special effects for motion picture photography.

GUNNAR P. MICHELSON for the engineering and development of an improved, electronic, high-speed, precision light valve for use in motion picture printing machines.

Technical Achievement Award (Academy certificate)

WILLIAM G. KROKAUGGER of Mole-Richardson Company for the design and engineering of a portable, 12,000-watt, lighting-control dimmer for use in motion picture production.

CHARLES J. WATSON, LARRY L. LANGREHR, and JOHN H. STEINER for the development of the BHP (electromechanical) fader for use on continuous motion picture contact printers.

ELIZABETH D. DE LA MARE of De La Mare Engineering, Incorporated, for the progressive development and continuous research of special effects pyrotechnics originally designed by Glenn W. De La Mare for motion picture production.

DOUGLAS FRIES, JOHN LACEY, and MICHAEL SIGRIST for the design and engineering of a 35mm reflex conversion camera system for special effects photography.

JACK CASHIN of Ultra-Stereo Labs, Incorporated, for the engineering and development of a four-channel, stereophonic, decoding system for optical motion picture sound track reproduction.

DAVID J. DEGENKOLB for the design and development of an automated device used in the silver recovery process in motion picture laboratories.

1984 Fifty-seventh Year

Academy Award of Merit (Academy statuette)

None.

Scientific and Engineering Award (Academy plaque)

DONALD A. ANDERSON and DIANA REINERS of 3M Company for the development of "Cinetrak" Magnetic Film #350/351 for motion picture sound recording.

BARRY M. STULTZ, RUBEN AVILA, and WES KENNEDY of Film Processing Corporation for the development of FPC 200 PB Fullcoat Magnetic Film for motion picture sound recording.

BARRY M. STULTZ, RUBEN AVILA, and WES KENNEDY of Film Processing Corporation for the formulation and application of an improved sound track stripe to 70mm motion picture film, and to JOHN MOSELY for the engineering research involved therein.

KENNETH RICHTER of Richter Cine Equipment for the design and engineering of the R-2 Auto-Collimator for examining image quality at the focal plane of motion picture camera lenses.

GÜNTHER SCHAIDT and ROSCO LABORATORIES, INCORPORATED, for the development of an improved, nontoxic fluid for creating fog and smoke for motion picture production.

JOHN WHITNEY, JR., and GARY DEMOS of Digital Productions, Incorporated, for the practical simulation of motion picture photography by means of computer-generated images.

Technical Achievement Award (Academy certificate)

NAT TIFFEN of Tiffen Manufacturing Corporation for the production of high-quality, durable, laminated color filters for motion picture photography.

DONALD TRUMBULL, JONATHAN

ERLAND, STEPHEN FOG, and PAUL BURK of Apogee, Incorporated, for the design and development of the "Blue Max" high-power, blue-flux projector for traveling matte composite photography.

JONATHAN ERLAND and ROBERT BEALMEAR of Apogee, Incorporated, for an innovative design for front projection screens and an improved method for their construction.

HOWARD J. PRESTON of Preston Cinema Systems for the design and development of a variable-speed control device with automatic exposure compensation for motion picture cameras.

1985 Fifty-eighth Year

Academy Award of Merit (Academy statuette)

None.

Scientific and Engineering Award (Academy plaque)

IMAX SYSTEMS CORPORATION for a method of filming and exhibiting high-fidelity, large-format, wide-angle motion pictures.

ERNST NETTMANN of E. F. Nettmann & Associates for the invention and EDWARD PHILLIPS and CARLOS DeMATTOS of Matthews Studio Equipment, Inc., for the development of the Cam-Remote for motion picture photography.

MYRON GORDIN, JOE P. CROOKHAM, JIM DROST, and DAVID CROOKHAM of Musco Mobile Lighting, Ltd., for the invention of a method of transporting adjustable, high-intensity luminaires and their application to the motion picture industry.

Technical Achievement Award (Academy certificate)

DAVID W. SPENCER for the development of an Animation Photo Transfer (APT) process.

HARRISON & HARRISON, OPTICAL ENGINEERS, for the invention and development of Harrison Diffusion Filters for motion picture photography.

LARRY BARTON of Cinematography Electronics, Inc., for a precision speed, crystal-controlled device for motion picture photography.

ALAN LANDAKER of the Burbank Studios for the Mark III Camera Drive for motion picture photography.

1986 Fifty-ninth Year

Academy Award of Merit (Academy statuette)

None.

Scientific and Engineering Award (Academy plaque)

BRAN FERREN, CHARLES HARRISON, and KENNETH WISNER of Associates and Ferren for the concept and design of an advanced optical printer.

RICHARD BENJAMIN GRANT and RON GRANT of Auricle Control Systems for their invention of the Film Composer's Time Processor.

ANTHONY D. BRUNO and JOHN L. BAPTISTA of Metro-Goldwyn-Mayer Laboratories, Incorporated and MANFRED G. MICHELSON and BRUCE W. KELLER of Technical Film Systems, Incorporated, for the design and engineering of a continuous-feed printer.

ROBERT GREENBERG, JOEL HYNEK, and EUGENE MAMUT of R/Greenberg Associates,

Incorporated, and DR. ALFRED THUMIM, ELAN LIPSCHITZ, and DARRYL A. ARMOUR of the Oxberry Division of Richmark Camera Service, Incorporated, for the design and development of the RGA/Oxberry Compu-Quad Special Effects Optical Printer.

PROFESSOR FRITZ SENNHEISER of Sennheiser Electronic Corporation for the invention of an interference tube directional microphone.

RICHARD EDLUND, GENE WHITEMAN, DAVID GRAFTON, MARK WEST, JERRY JEFFRESS, and BOB WILCOX of Boss Film Corporation for the design and development of a Zoom Aerial (ZAP) 65mm Optical Printer.

WILLIAM L. FREDRICK and HAL NEEDHAM for the design and development of the Shotmaker Elite camera car and crane.

Technical Achievement Award (Academy certificate)

LEE ELECTRIC (LIGHTING) LIMITED for the design and development of an electronic, flicker-free, discharge lamp control system.

PETER D. PARKS of Oxford Scientific Films' Image Quest Division for the development of a live aero-compositor for special effects photography.

MATT SWEENEY and LUCINDA STRUB for the development of an automatic capsule gun for simulating bullet hits for motion picture special effects.

CARL HOLMES of Carl E. Holmes Company and ALEXANDER BRYCE of the Burbank Studios for the development of a mobile DC power supply unit for motion picture production photography.

BRAN FERREN of Associates and Ferren for the development of a laser synchro-cue system for applications in the motion picture industry.

JOHN L. BAPTISTA of Metro-Goldwyn-Mayer Laboratories, Inc., for the development and installation of a computerized silver recovery operation.

DAVID W. SAMUELSON for the development of programs incorporated into a pocket computer for motion picture cinematographers and WILLIAM B. POLLARD for contributing new algorithms on which the programs are based.

HAL LANDAKER and ALAN LANDAKER of the Burbank Studios for the development of the Beat System low-frequency cue track for motion picture production sound recording.

1987 Sixtieth Year

Academy Award of Merit (Academy statuette)

BERNARD KÜHL and WERNER BLOCK and OSRAM GMBH RESEARCH AND DEVELOPMENT DEPARTMENT for the invention and the continuing improvement of the OSRAM HMI light source for motion picture photography.

Scientific and Engineering Award (Academy plaque)

WILLI BURTH and KINOTONE CORPORATION for the invention and development of the Non-rewind Platter System for motion picture presentations.

MONTAGE GROUP, LTD., for the development and RONALD C. BARKER and CHESTER L. SCHULER for the invention of the Montage Picture Processor electronic film editing system.

COLIN F. MOSSMAN and RANK FILM LABORATORIES'

DEVELOPMENT GROUP for creating a fully automated, film-handling system for improving productivity of high-speed film processing.

EASTMAN KODAK COMPANY for the development of Eastman Color High-Speed Daylight Negative Film 5297/7297.

EASTMAN KODAK COMPANY for the development of Eastman Color High-Speed SA Negative Film 5295 for blue-screen traveling matte photography.

FRITZ GABRIEL BAUER for the invention and development of the improved features of the Moviecam Camera System.

ZORAN PERISIC of Courier Films, Ltd., for the Zoptic dual-zoom front projection system for visual effects photography.

CARL ZEISS COMPANY for the design and development of a series of superspeed lenses for motion picture photography.

Technical Achievement Award (Academy certificate)

IOAN ALLEN of Dolby Laboratories, Inc., for the Cat. 43 playback-only noise-reduction unit and its practical application to motion picture sound recordings.

JOHN EPPOLITO, WALLY GENTLEMAN, WILLIAM MESA, LES PAUL ROBLEY, and GEOFFREY H. WILLIAMSON for refinements to a dual-screen, front projection, image-compositing system.

JAN JACOBSEN for the application of a dual-screen, front projection system to motion picture special effects photography.

THAINE MORRIS and DAVID PIER for the development of DSC Spark Devices for motion picture special effects.

TADEUZ KRZANOWSKI of Industrial Light and Magic, Inc., for the development of a wire rig model support mechanism used to control the movements of miniatures in special effects.

DAN C. NORRIS and TIM COOK of Norris Film Products for the development of a single-frame exposure system for motion picture photography.

1988 Sixty-first Year

Academy Award of Merit (Academy statuette)

RAY DOLBY and IOAN ALLEN of Dolby Laboratories, Incorporated, for their continuous contributions to motion picture sound through the research and development programs of Dolby Laboratories.

Scientific and Engineering Award (Academy plaque)

ROY W. EDWARDS and the ENGINEERING STAFF OF PHOTO-SONICS, INCORPORATED, for the design and development of the Photo-Sonics 35mm-4ER High-Speed Motion Picture Camera with reflex viewing and video assist.

ARNOLD & RICHTER ENGINEERING STAFF, OTTO BLASCHEK, and ARRIFLEX CORPORATION for the concept and engineering of the Arriflex 35-3 Motion Picture Camera.

BILL TONDREAU of Tondreau Systems; ALVAH MILLER and PAUL JOHNSON of Lynx Robotics; PETER A. REGLA of Elicon; DAN SLATER; BUD ELAM, JOE PARKER, and BILL BRYAN of Interactive Motion Control; and JERRY JEFFRESS, RAY FEENEY, BILL HOLLAND, and KRIS BROWN for their individual contributions and the collective advancements they have brought to the motion picture industry in the field of motion-control technology.

Technical Achievement Award (Academy certificate)

GRANT LOUCKS of Alan Gordon Enterprises, Incorporated, for the design concept and GEOFFREY H. WILLIAMSON of Wilcam for the mechanical and electrical engineering of the Image 300 35mm High-Speed Motion Picture Camera.

MICHAEL V. CHEWEY, III for the development of the motion picture industry's first paper-tape reader incorporating microprocessor technology.

BHP, INC., successor to the Bell & Howell Professional Equipment Division, for the development of a high-speed reader incorporating microprocessor technology for motion picture laboratories.

HOLLYWOOD FILM COMPANY for the development of a high-speed reader incorporating microprocessor technology for motion picture laboratories.

BRUCE W. KELLER and MANFRED G. MICHELSON of Technical Film Systems for the design and development of a high-speed light-valve controller and constant current power supply for motion picture laboratories.

DR. ANTAL LISZIEWICZ and GLENN M. BERGGREN of ISCO-OPTIC GmbH for the design and development of the Ultra-Star series of motion picture lenses.

JAMES K. BRANCH of Spectra Cine, Incorporated, and WILLIAM L. BLOWERS and NASIR J. ZAIDI for the design and development of the Spectra CineSpot one-degree spotmeter for measuring the brightness of motion picture screens.

BOB BADAMI, DICK BERNSTEIN, and BILL BERNSTEIN of Offbeat Systems for the design and development of the Streamline Scoring System, Mark IV, for motion picture music editing.

GARY ZELLER of Zeller International, Limited, for the development of the Zel-Jel fire-protection barrier for motion picture stunt work.

EMANUEL TRILLING of Trilling Resources, Limited, for the development of the Stunt-Gel fire-protection barrier for motion picture stunt work.

PAUL A. ROOS for the invention of a method known as Video Assist, whereby a scene being photographed on motion picture film can be viewed on a monitor and/or recorded on video tape.

1989 Sixty-second Year

Academy Award of Merit (Academy statuette)

None.

Scientific and Engineering Award (Academy plaque)

J. L. FISHER of J. L. Fisher, Inc., for the design and manufacture of the Fisher Model Ten Dolly.

JAMES KETCHAM of JSK Engineering for the engineering of the SDA521 B Advance/Retard system for magnetic-film sound dubbing.

J. NOXON LEAVITT for the invention and ISTEC, INC., for the continuing development of the Wescam Stabilized Camera System.

KLAUS RESCH for the design and ERIC FITZ and FGV SCHMIDLE & FITZ for the development of the Super Panther MS-180 Camera Dolly.

GEOFFREY H. WILLIAMSON of

Wilcam Photo Research, Inc., for the design and development and ROBERT D. AUGUSTE for the electronic design and development of the Wilcam W-7 200-frames-per-second VistaVision Rotating Mirror Reflex Camera.

Technical Achievement Award (Academy certificate)

DR. LEO CATOZZO for the design and development of the CIR-Catozzo Self-Perforating Adhesive Tape Film Splicer.

MAGNA-TECH ELECTRONIC CO. for the introduction of the first remotely controlled advance/retard function for magnetic-film sound dubbing.

1990 Sixty-third Year

Academy Award of Merit (Academy statuette)

EASTMAN KODAK COMPANY for the development of T-grain technology and the introduction of EXR color negative films which utilize this technology.

Scientific and Engineering Award (Academy plaque)

BRUCE WILTON and CARLOS ICINKOFF of Mechanical Concepts; ENGINEERING DEPARTMENT OF ARNOLD & RICHTER; FUJI PHOTO FILM CO., LTD.; MANFRED G. MICHELSON of Technical Film Systems; JOHN W. LANG, WALTER HRASTNIK, and CHARLES J. WATSON of Bell & Howell Company.

Technical Achievement Award (Academy certificate)

WILLIAM L. BLOWERS of Belco Associates and THOMAS F. DENOVE; IAIN NEIL, TAKUO MIYAGISHIMA, and PANAVISION; CHRISTOPHER S. GILMAN and HARVEY HUBERT, JR., of the Diligent Dwarves Effects; JIM GRAVES of J&G Enterprises; BENGT O. ORHALL, KENNETH LUND, BJORN SELIN, and KJELL HOGBERG of AB Film-Teknik; RICHARD MULA and PETE ROMANO of HydroImage; DEDO WEIGERT of Dedo Weigert Film; DR. FRED KOLB, JR., PAUL PREO, PETER BALDWIN, and DR. PAUL KIANKHOOY; and the LIGHTMAKER COMPANY.

1991 Sixty-fourth Year

Academy Award of Merit (Academy statuette)

None.

Scientific and Engineering Award (Academy plaque)

IAIN NEIL for the optical design, ALBERT SAIKI for the mechanical design, and PANAVISION, INC., for the concept and development of the Primo Zoom Lens for 35mm cinematography.

GEORG THOMA for the design and HEINZ FEIERLEIN and the engineering department of SACHTLER AG for the development of a range of fluid tripod heads.

HARRY J. BAKER for the design and development of the first full fluid-action tripod head with adjustable degrees of viscous drag.

GUIDO CARTONI for his pioneering work in developing the technology to achieve selectable and repeatable viscous drag modules in fluid tripod heads.

RAY FEENEY, RICHARD KEENEY, and RICHARD J. LUNDELL for the software development and adaptation of the Solitaire Film Recorder that provides a flexible, cost-effective film recording system.

FAZ FAZAKAS, BRIAN HENSON, DAVE HOUSMAN, PETER MILLER, and JOHN STEPHENSON for the development of the Henson Performance Control System.

MARIO CELSO for his pioneering work in the design, development, and manufacture of equipment for carbon arc and xenon power supplies and igniters used in motion picture projection.

RANDY CARTWRIGHT, DAVID B. COONS, LEM DAVIS, THOMAS HAHN, JAMES HOUSTON, MARK KIMBALL, PETER NYE, MICHAEL SHANTZIS, DAVID F. WOLF, and THE WALT DISNEY FEATURE ANIMATION DEPARTMENT for the design and development of the CAPS production system for feature film animation.

GEORGE WORRALL for the design, development, and manufacture of the Worrall geared camera head for motion picture production.

Technical Achievement Award (Academy certificate)

ROBERT W. STOKER, JR., for the design and development of a cobweb gun for applying nontoxic cobweb effects on motion picture sets with both safety and ease of operation.

JAMES DOYLE for the design and development of the Dry Fogger, which uses liquid nitrogen to produce a safe, dense, low-hanging dry fog.

DICK CAVDEK, STEVE HAMERSKI, and OTTO NEMENZ INTL., INC., for the optomechanical design and development of the Canon/Nemenz Zoom Lens.

KEN ROBINGS and CLAIRMONT CAMERA for the optomechanical design and development of the Canon/Clairmont Camera Zoom Lens.

CENTURY PRECISION OPTICS for the optomechanical design and development of the Canon/Century Precision Optics Zoom Lens.

1992 Sixty-fifth Year

Academy Award of Merit (Academy Statuette)

CHADWELL O'CONNOR of the O'Connor Engineering Laboratories for the concept and engineering of the fluid-damped camera-head for motion picture photography.

Scientific and Engineering Awards (Academy plaque)

LOREN CARPENTER, ROB COOK, ED CATMULL, TOM PORTER, PAT HANRAHAN, TONY APODACA and DARWYN PEACHEY for the development of "RenderMan" software which produces images used in motion pictures from 3D computer descriptions of shape and appearance.

CLAUS WIEDEMANN and ROBERT ORBAN for the design and DOLBY LABORATORIES for the development of the Dolby Labs "Container."

KEN BATES for the design and development of the Bates Decelerator System for accurately and safely arresting the descent of stunt persons in high freefalls.

AL MAYER for the Camera Design; IAIN NEIL and GEORGE KRAEMER for the optical design; HANS SPIRAWSKI and BILL ESLICK for the opto-mechanical design and DON EARL for technical support in developing the Panavision System 65 Studio Sync Sound Reflex Camera for 65mm motion picture photography.

DOUGLAS TRUMBULL for the concept; GEOFFREY H.

WILLIAMSON for the movement design; ROBERT D. AUGUSTE for the electronic design and EDMUND M. DIGIULIO for the camera system design of the CP-65 Showscan Camera System for 65mm motion picture photography.

ARRIFLEX CORPORATION, OTTO BLASCHEK and the ENGINEERING DEPARTMENT OF ARRI, AUSTRIA for the design and development of the Arriflex 765 Camera System for 65mm motion picture photography.

Technical Achievement Awards (Academy certificate)

IRA TIFFEN of the Tiffen Manufacturing Corporation for the production of the Ultra Contrast Filter Series for motion picture photography.

ROBERT R. BURTON of Audio Rents, Incorporated, for the development of the Model S-27 4-Band Splitter/Combiner.

IAIN NEIL for the optical design and KAZ FUDANO for the mechanical design of the Panavision Slant Focus Lens for motion picture photography.

TOM BRIGHAM for the original concept and pioneering work; and DOUGLAS SMYTHE and the COMPUTER GRAPHICS DEPARTMENT OF INDUSTRIAL LIGHT & MAGIC for development and the first implementation in feature motion pictures of the "MORF" system for digital metamorphosis of high resolution images.

DISCONTINUED CATEGORIES

Unique and Artistic Picture

An award for Unique and Artistic Picture was given only the first year. Academy members were asked to nominate "the Producing Company or Producer who produced the most artistic, unique and/or original motion picture without reference to cost or magnitude." As the categories underwent adjustment after the first year, this award was dropped, perhaps because it was scarcely distinguishable from the Best Picture category, which honored "the most outstanding motion picture considering all elements that contribute to a picture's greatness."

1927/28 First Year*

CHANG, Paramount Famous Lasky.
THE CROWD, Metro-Goldwyn-Mayer.
★ SUNRISE, Fox.

*Not given after this year.

Engineering Effects

The Engineering Effects award was given only the first year. It went to the person who "rendered the best achievement in producing effects of whatever character obtained by engineering or mechanical means." The category was dropped after the 1927/28 awards.

1927/28 First Year*

THE JAZZ SINGER, Warner Bros.: NUGENT SLAUGHTER.

THE PRIVATE LIFE OF HELEN OF TROY, First National: RALPH HAMMERAS.

★ WINGS, Paramount: ROY POMEROY.

*Not given after this year.

Assistant Director

Achievement in film directing was recognized from the time of the first Academy Awards. Since directors frequently relied on assistants to direct second units and extras and to help maintain production schedules, a new category honoring assistant directors was announced for the 1932/33 awards.

A multiple award the first year only was given to assistant directors from the seven major studios. The award was continued for four more years and was dropped after 1937.

*1932/33 Sixth Year**

PERCY IKERD, Fox.
★ WILLIAM TUMMEL, Fox.
★ CHARLES DORIAN, Metro-Goldwyn-Mayer.
BUNNY DULL, Metro-Goldwyn-Mayer.
JOHN S. WATERS, Metro-Goldwyn-Mayer.
★ CHARLES BARTON, Paramount.
SIDNEY S. BROD, Paramount.
ARTHUR JACOBSON, Paramount.
EDDIE KILLEY, RKO Radio.
★ DEWEY STARKEY, RKO Radio.
★ FRED FOX, UA.
BENJAMIN SILVEY, UA.
★ SCOTT BEAL, Universal.
JOE MCDONOUGH, Universal.
W. J. REITER, Universal.
AL ALBORN, Warner Bros.
★ GORDON HOLLINGSHEAD, Warner Bros.
FRANK X. SHAW, Warner Bros.

1934 Seventh Year

SCOTT BEAL for *Imitation of Life*. Universal.
CULLEN TATE for *Cleopatra*, Paramount.
★ JOHN WATERS for *Viva Villa*, Metro-Goldwyn-Mayer.

1935 Eighth Year

★ CLEM BEAUCHAMP and PAUL WING for *Lives of a Bengal Lancer*, Paramount.
JOSEPH NEWMAN for *David Copperfield*, Metro-Goldwyn-Mayer.
ERIC STACEY for *Les Miserables*, 20th Century, UA.

1936 Ninth Year

CLEM BEAUCHAMP for *Last of the Mohicans*, Reliance, UA.
WILLIAM CANNON for *Anthony Adverse*, Warner Bros.
JOSEPH NEWMAN for *San Francisco*, Metro-Goldwyn-Mayer.
ERIC G. STACEY for *Garden of Allah*, Selznick, UA.
★ JACK SULLIVAN for *The Charge of the Light Brigade*, Warner Bros.

*Multiple award given this year only.

*1937 Tenth Year**

C. C. COLEMAN, JR., for *Lost Horizon*, Columbia.

RUSS SAUNDERS for *The Life of Emile Zola*, Warner Bros.

ERIC STACEY for *A Star Is Born*, Selznick, UA.

HAL WALKER for *Souls at Sea*, Paramount.

★ ROBERT WEBB for *In Old Chicago*, 20th Century-Fox.

*Not given after this year.

Dance Direction

Awards for Dance Direction, a short-lived category, were given only three times. The 1930s were the golden age of the American film musical, and this award honored the men who designed the memorable and frequently extravagant dance numbers. Ironically, the man most identified with Hollywood musicals of this period, Busby Berkeley, never won this Oscar, although he was nominated in each of the three years the award was given.

In the 1950s the Academy reconsidered an annual award for dancing and choreography. *Variety* noted in 1957 that Academy president George Seaton, in response to a campaign by dance fans, had agreed to form a dance award committee, but nothing came of it. The Academy has instead used honorary awards to publicize achievements in this area. Fred Astaire received an honorary Oscar in 1949, as did Gene Kelly in 1951. *West Side Story* swept the 1961 awards, and director-choreographer Jerome Robbins was given an honorary award. In 1968 Onna White was recognized for her choreography in *Oliver*.

1935 Eighth Year

BUSBY BERKELEY for *Lullaby of Broadway* number from *Gold Diggers of 1935*, Warner Bros.; *The Words Are in My Heart* number from *Gold Diggers of 1935*, Warner Bros.

BOBBY CONNOLLY for *Latin from Manhattan* number from *Go into Your Dance*, Warner Bros.; *Playboy from Paree* number from *Broadway Hostess*, Warner Bros.

★ DAVE GOULD for *I've Got a Feeling You're Fooling* number from *Broadway Melody of 1936*, M-G-M; *Straw Hat* number from *Folies Bergere*, 20th Century, UA.

SAMMY LEE for *Lovely Lady* number from *King of Burlesque*, 20th Century-Fox; *Too Good to Be True* number from *King of Burlesque*, 20th Century-Fox.

HERMES PAN for *Piccolino* number from *Top Hat*, RKO Radio; *Top Hat* number from *Top Hat*, RKO Radio.

LEROY PRINZ for *Elephant Number—It's the Animal in Me* from *Big Broadcast of 1936*, Paramount; *Viennese Waltz* number from *All the King's Horses*, Paramount.

B. ZEMACH for *Hall of Kings* number from *She*, RKO Radio.

1936 Ninth Year

BUSBY BERKELEY for *Love and War* number from *Gold Diggers of 1937*, Warner Bros.

BOBBY CONNOLLY for *1000 Love Songs* number from *Cain and Mabel*, Warner Bros.

★ SEYMOUR FELIX for *A Pretty Girl Is Like a Melody* number from *The Great Ziegfeld*, Metro-Goldwyn-Mayer.

DAVE GOULD for *Swingin' the Jinx* number from *Born to Dance*, Metro-Goldwyn-Mayer.

JACK HASKELL for *Skating Ensemble*

number from *One in a Million*, 20th Century-Fox.

RUSSELL LEWIS for *The Finale* number from *Dancing Pirate*, RKO Radio.

HERMES PAN for *Bojangles* number from *Swing Time*, RKO Radio.

*1937 Tenth Year**

BUSBY BERKELEY for *The Finale* number from *Varsity Show*, Warner Bros.

BOBBY CONNOLLY for *Too Marvelous for Words* number from *Ready, Willing and Able*, Warner Bros.

DAVE GOULD for *All God's Children Got Rhythm* number from *A Day at the Races*, Metro-Goldwyn-Mayer.

SAMMY LEE for *Swing Is Here to Stay* number from *Ali Baba Goes to Town*, 20th Century-Fox.

HARRY LOSEE for *Prince Igor Suite* number from *Thin Ice*, 20th Century-Fox.

★ HERMES PAN for *Fun House* number from *Damsel in Distress*, RKO Radio.

LEROY PRINZ for *Luau* number from *Waikiki Wedding*, Paramount.

*Not given after this year.

Special Effects

In 1938 the Academy Board of Governors voted an honorary award to several individuals who had created the special photographic and sound effects in the Paramount film *Spawn of the North*. By 1939 the category of Special Effects had been officially established as an annual award. Except for three years, 1951 to 1953, it remained an annual award until 1963 when the Academy elected to split the award into two new categories: Special Visual Effects and Sound Effects.

One should note that several achievements listed in the Scientific or Technical awards have contributed to the film industry's ability to produce special effects.

1939 Twelfth Year

GONE WITH THE WIND, Selznick, M-G-M: JOHN R. COSGROVE, FRED ALBIN, and ARTHUR JOHNS.

ONLY ANGELS HAVE WINGS, Columbia: ROY DAVIDSON and EDWIN C. HAHN.

PRIVATE LIVES OF ELIZABETH AND ESSEX, Warner Bros.: BYRON HASKIN and NATHAN LEVINSON.

★ THE RAINS CAME, 20th Century-Fox: E. H. HANSEN and FRED SERSEN.

TOPPER TAKES A TRIP, Roach, UA: ROY SEAWRIGHT.

UNION PACIFIC, Paramount: FARCIOT EDOUART, GORDON JENNINGS, and LOREN RYDER.

THE WIZARD OF OZ, Metro-Goldwyn-Mayer: A. ARNOLD GILLESPIE and DOUGLAS SHEARER.

1940 Thirteenth Year

THE BLUE BIRD, 20th Century-Fox: Photographic: FRED SERSEN; Sound: E. H. HANSEN.

BOOM TOWN, Metro-Goldwyn-Mayer: Photographic: A. ARNOLD GILLESPIE; Sound: DOUGLAS SHEARER.

THE BOYS FROM SYRACUSE, Universal: Photographic: JOHN P. FULTON; Sound: BERNARD B. BROWN and JOSEPH LAPIS.

DR. CYCLOPS, Paramount: Photographic: FARCIOT EDOUART and GORDON JENNINGS; Sound: No credit listed.

FOREIGN CORRESPONDENT, Wanger, UA: Photographic: PAUL EAGLER; Sound: THOMAS T. MOULTON.

THE INVISIBLE MAN RETURNS, Universal: Photographic: JOHN P. FULTON; Sound: BERNARD B. BROWN and WILLIAM HEDGECOCK.

THE LONG VOYAGE HOME, Argosy-Wanger, UA: Photographic: R. T. LAYTON and R. O. BINGER; Sound: THOMAS T. MOULTON.

ONE MILLION B.C., Roach, UA: Photographic: ROY SEAWRIGHT; Sound: ELMER RAGUSE.

REBECCA, Selznick, UA; Photographic: JACK COSGROVE; Sound: ARTHUR JOHNS.

THE SEA HAWK, Warner Bros.: Photographic: BYRON HASKIN; Sound: NATHAN LEVINSON.

SWISS FAMILY ROBINSON, RKO Radio: Photographic: VERNON L. WALKER; Sound: JOHN O. AALBERG.

★ THE THIEF OF BAGDAD, Korda,

UA: Photographic: LAWRENCE BUTLER; Sound: JACK WHITNEY.

TYPHOON, Paramount: Photographic: FARCIOT EDOUART and GORDON JENNINGS; Sound: LOREN RYDER.

WOMEN IN WAR, Republic: Photographic: HOWARD J. LYDECKER, WILLIAM BRADFORD, and ELLIS J. THACKERY; Sound: HERBERT NORSCH.

1941 Fourteenth Year

ALOMA OF THE SOUTH SEAS, Paramount: Photographic: FARCIOT EDOUART and GORDON JENNINGS; Sound: LOUIS MESENKOP.

FLIGHT COMMAND, Metro-Goldwyn-Mayer: Photographic: A. ARNOLD GILLESPIE; Sound: DOUGLAS SHEARER.

★ I WANTED WINGS, Paramount: Photographic: FARCIOT EDOUART and GORDON JENNINGS; Sound: LOUIS MESENKOP.

THE INVISIBLE WOMAN, Universal: Photographic: JOHN FULTON; Sound: JOHN HALL.

THE SEA WOLF, Warner Bros.: Photographic: BYRON HASKIN; Sound: NATHAN LEVINSON.

THAT HAMILTON WOMAN, Korda, UA: Photographic: LAWRENCE BUTLER; Sound: WILLIAM H. WILMARTH.

TOPPER RETURNS, Roach, UA: Photographic: ROY SEAWRIGHT; Sound: ELMER RAGUSE.

A YANK IN THE R.A.F., 20th Century-Fox: Photographic: FRED SERSEN; Sound: E. H. HANSEN.

1942 Fifteenth Year

THE BLACK SWAN, 20th Century-Fox: Photographic: FRED SERSEN; Sound: ROGER HEMAN and GEORGE LEVERETT.

DESPERATE JOURNEY, Warner Bros.: Photographic: BYRON HASKIN; Sound: NATHAN LEVINSON.

FLYING TIGERS, Republic: Photographic: HOWARD LYDECKER; Sound: DANIEL J. BLOOMBERG.

INVISIBLE AGENT, Universal: Photographic: JOHN FULTON; Sound: BERNARD B. BROWN.

JUNGLE BOOK, Korda, UA: Photographic: LAWRENCE BUTLER; Sound: WILLIAM H. WILMARTH.

MRS. MINIVER, Metro-Goldwyn-Mayer: Photographic: A. ARNOLD GILLESPIE and WARREN NEWCOMBE; Sound: DOUGLAS SHEARER.

THE NAVY COMES THROUGH, RKO Radio: Photographic: VERNON L. WALKER; Sound: JAMES G. STEWART.

ONE OF OUR AIRCRAFT IS MISSING, Powell, UA (British): Photographic: RONALD NEAME; Sound: C. C. STEVENS.

PRIDE OF THE YANKEES, Goldwyn, RKO Radio: Photographic: JACK COSGROVE and RAY BINGER; Sound: THOMAS T. MOULTON.

★ REAP THE WILD WIND, Paramount: Photographic: FARCIOT EDOUART, GORDON JENNINGS, and WILLIAM L. PEREIRA; Sound: LOUIS MESENKOP.

1943 Sixteenth Year

AIR FORCE, Warner Bros.: Photographic: HANS KOENEKAMP and REX WIMPY; Sound: NATHAN LEVINSON.

BOMBARDIER, RKO Radio: Photographic: VERNON L. WALKER; Sound: JAMES G. STEWART and ROY GRANVILLE.

★ CRASH DIVE, 20th Century-Fox: Photographic: FRED SERSEN; Sound: ROGER HEMAN.

THE NORTH STAR, Goldwyn, RKO Radio: Photographic: CLARENCE SLIFER and R. O. BINGER; Sound: THOMAS T. MOULTON.

SO PROUDLY WE HAIL, Paramount: Photographic: FARCIOT EDOUART and

GORDON JENNINGS; Sound: GEORGE DUTTON.

STAND BY FOR ACTION, Metro-Goldwyn-Mayer: Photographic: A. ARNOLD GILLESPIE and DONALD JAHRAUS; Sound: MICHAEL STEINORE.

1944 Seventeenth Year

THE ADVENTURES OF MARK TWAIN, Warner Bros.: Photographic: PAUL DETLEFSEN and JOHN CROUSE; Sound: NATHAN LEVINSON.

DAYS OF GLORY, RKO Radio: Photographic: VERNON L. WALKER; Sound: JAMES G. STEWART and ROY GRANVILLE.

SECRET COMMAND, Columbia: Photographic: DAVID ALLEN, RAY CORY, and ROBERT WRIGHT; Sound: RUSSELL MALMGREN and HARRY KUSNICK.

SINCE YOU WENT AWAY, Selznick, UA: Photographic: JOHN R. COSGROVE; Sound: ARTHUR JOHNS.

THE STORY OF DR. WASSELL, Paramount: Photographic: FARCIOT EDOUART and GORDON JENNINGS; Sound: GEORGE DUTTON.

★ THIRTY SECONDS OVER TOKYO, Metro-Goldwyn-Mayer: Photographic: A. ARNOLD GILLESPIE, DONALD JAHRAUS, and WARREN NEWCOMBE; Sound: DOUGLAS SHEARER.

WILSON, 20th Century-Fox: Photographic: FRED SERSEN; Sound: ROGER HEMAN.

1945 Eighteenth Year

CAPTAIN EDDIE, 20th Century-Fox: Photographic: FRED SERSEN and SOL HALPRIN; Sound: ROGER HEMAN and HARRY LEONARD.

SPELLBOUND, Selznick, UA: Photographic: JACK COSGROVE; Sound: No credits listed.

THEY WERE EXPENDABLE, Metro-Goldwyn-Mayer: Photographic: A. ARNOLD GILLESPIE, DONALD JAHRAUS, and R. A. MACDONALD; Sound: MICHAEL STEINORE.

A THOUSAND AND ONE NIGHTS, Columbia: Photographic: L. W. BUTLER; Sound: RAY BOMBA.

★ WONDER MAN, Goldwyn, RKO Radio: Photographic: JOHN FULTON; Sound: A. W. JOHNS.

1946 Nineteenth Year

★ BLITHE SPIRIT, Rank UA (British): Visual: THOMAS HOWARD; Audible: No credits listed.

A STOLEN LIFE, Warner Bros.: Visual: WILLIAM MCGANN; Audible: NATHAN LEVINSON.

1947 Twentieth Year

★ GREEN DOLPHIN STREET, Metro-Goldwyn-Mayer: Visual: A. ARNOLD GILLESPIE and WARREN NEWCOMBE; Audible: DOUGLAS SHEARER and MICHAEL STEINORE.

UNCONQUERED, Paramount: Visual: FARCIOT EDOUART, DEVEREUX JENNINGS, GORDON JENNINGS, WALLACE KELLEY, and PAUL LERPAE; Audible: GEORGE DUTTON.

1948 Twenty-first Year

DEEP WATERS, 20th Century-Fox: Visual: RALPH HAMMERAS, FRED SERSEN, and EDWARD SNYDER; Audible: ROGER HEMAN.

★ PORTRAIT OF JENNIE, The Selznick Studio: Visual: PAUL EAGLER, J. McMILLAN JOHNSON, RUSSELL SHEARMAN, and CLARENCE SLIFER; Audible: CHARLES FREEMAN and JAMES G. STEWART.

1949 Twenty-second Year

★ MIGHTY JOE YOUNG, Cooper, RKO Radio.

TULSA, Walter Wanger Pictures, Eagle-Lion.

1950 Twenty-third Year

★ DESTINATION MOON, George Pal, Eagle-Lion Classics.
SAMSON AND DELILAH, Cecil B. DeMille, Paramount.

*1951 Twenty-fourth Year**

★ WHEN WORLDS COLLIDE, George Pal, Paramount.

1952 Twenty-fifth Year

★ PLYMOUTH ADVENTURE, Metro-Goldwyn-Mayer.

1953 Twenty-sixth Year

★ THE WAR OF THE WORLDS, George Pal, Paramount.

1954 Twenty-seventh Year†

HELL AND HIGH WATER, 20th Century-Fox.
THEM!, Warner Bros.
★ 20,000 LEAGUES UNDER THE SEA, Walt Disney Studios.

1955 Twenty-eighth Year

★ THE BRIDGES AT TOKO-RI, Paramount.
THE DAM BUSTERS, Associated British Picture Corp., Ltd. (British).
THE RAINS OF RANCHIPUR, 20th Century-Fox.

1956 Twenty-ninth Year

FORBIDDEN PLANET, Metro-Goldwyn-Mayer: A. ARNOLD GILLESPIE, IRVING RIES, and WESLEY C. MILLER.
★ THE TEN COMMANDMENTS, Motion Picture Associates, Inc., Paramount: JOHN FULTON.

1957 Thirtieth Year

★ THE ENEMY BELOW, 20th Century-Fox: WALTER ROSSI.
THE SPIRIT OF ST. LOUIS, Leland Hayward-Billy Wilder, Warner Bros.: LOUIS LICHTENFIELD.

1958 Thirty-first Year

★ TOM THUMB, George Pal, M-G-M.: Visual: TOM HOWARD.
TORPEDO RUN, Metro-Goldwyn-Mayer: Visual: A. ARNOLD GILLESPIE; Audible: HAROLD HUMBROCK.

1959 Thirty-second Year

★ BEN-HUR, Metro-Goldwyn-Mayer: Visual: A. ARNOLD GILLESPIE and ROBERT MacDONALD; Audible: MILO LORY.
JOURNEY TO THE CENTER OF THE EARTH, Joseph M. Schenck Enterprises, Inc. & Cooga Mooga Film Prods., Inc., 20th Century-Fox: Visual: L. B. ABBOTT and JAMES B. GORDON; Audible: CARL FAULKNER.

1960 Thirty-third Year

THE LAST VOYAGE, Andrew and Virginia Stone Prod., M-G-M: Visual: A. J. LOHMAN.
★ THE TIME MACHINE, Galaxy Films Prod., M-G-M: Visual: GENE WARREN and TIM BAAR.

1961 Thirty-fourth Year

THE ABSENT-MINDED PROFESSOR, Walt Disney Prods., Buena Vista Dist. Co.: Visual: ROBERT A. MATTEY and EUSTACE LYCETT.
★ THE GUNS OF NAVARONE, Carl Foreman Prod., Columbia: Visual:

*From 1951 through 1953 Special Effects were classified as an "other" award (not necessarily given each year) hence, no nominations.
†Special Effects were again classified as an annual award.

BILL WARRINGTON; Audible: VIVIAN C. GREENHAM.

1962 Thirty-fifth Year

★ THE LONGEST DAY; Darryl F. Zanuck Prods., 20th Century-Fox: Visual: ROBERT MacDONALD; Audible: JACQUES MAUMONT.

MUTINY ON THE BOUNTY, Arcola Prod., M-G-M: Visual: A. ARNOLD GILLESPIE; Audible: MILO LORY.

For the 36th Awards Year (1963), the Academy Board of Governors, in recognition of the fact that the best visual effects and the best audible effects each year did not necessarily occur in the same picture, voted to discontinue the Special Effects Award and created two new Awards: the Special Visual Effects Award and the Sound Effects Award.

Special Visual Effects

The Special Effects award begun in 1939 had recognized persons responsible for both photographic and sound effects on a picture. For the 36th Awards, the Academy voted to eliminate the Special Effects award and create instead two new awards: Special Visual Effects and Sound Effects. This change recognized the fact that the best visual effects and best audible effects each year did not necessarily occur in the same picture. The Sound Effects award was discontinued after 1967, though Special Visual Effects remained an annual award through 1971. After that, recognition in this field came through Special Achievement awards. Special Achievement awards in 1975 and 1977 honored sound effects.

1963 Thirty-sixth Year

THE BIRDS, Alfred J. Hitchcock Prod., Universal: UB IWERKS.

★ CLEOPATRA, 20th Century-Fox Ltd.-MCL Films S.A.-WALWA Films S.A. Prod., 20th Century-Fox: EMIL KOSA, JR.

1964 Thirty-seventh Year

★ MARY POPPINS, Walt Disney Prods.: PETER ELLENSHAW, HAMILTON LUSKE, and EUSTACE LYCETT.

7 FACES OF DR. LAO, Galaxy-Scarus Prod., Metro-Goldwyn-Mayer: JIM DANFORTH.

1965 Thirty-eighth Year

THE GREATEST STORY EVER TOLD, George Stevens Prod., United Artists: J. MCMILLAN JOHNSON.

★ THUNDERBALL, Broccoli-Saltzman-McClory Prod., United Artists: JOHN STEARS.

1966 Thirty-ninth Year

★ FANTASTIC VOYAGE, 20th Century-Fox: ART CRUICKSHANK.

HAWAII, Mirisch Corp. of Delaware Prod., United Artists: LINWOOD G. DUNN.

1967 Fortieth Year

★ DOCTOR DOLITTLE, Apjac Prods., 20th Century-Fox: L. B. ABBOTT.

TOBRUK, Gibraltar Prods.-Corman Company-Universal Prod., Universal: HOWARD A. ANDERSON, JR., and ALBERT WHITLOCK.

1968 Forty-first Year

ICE STATION ZEBRA, Filmways Prod., Metro-Goldwyn-Mayer: HAL MILLAR and J. MCMILLAN JOHNSON.

★ 2001: A SPACE ODYSSEY, Polaris Prod., Metro-Goldwyn-Mayer: STANLEY KUBRICK.

1969 Forty-second Year

KRAKATOA, EAST OF JAVA, American Broadcasting Companies-Cinerama Prod., Cinerama: EUGENE LOURIE and ALEX WELDON.

★ MAROONED, Frankovich-Sturges Prod., Columbia: ROBBIE ROBERTSON.

1970 Forty-third Year

PATTON, 20th Century-Fox: ALEX WELDON.

★ TORA! TORA! TORA!, 20th Century-Fox: A. D. FLOWERS and L. B. ABBOTT.

*1971 Forty-fourth Year**

★ BEDKNOBS AND BROOMSTICKS, Walt Disney Prods., Buena Vista Distribution Company: ALAN MALEY, EUSTACE LYCETT, and DANNY LEE.

WHEN DINOSAURS RULED THE EARTH, A Hammer Film Prod., Warner Bros.: JIM DANFORTH and ROGER DICKEN.

*Special Visual Effects not given as an annual award after 1971.

Sound Effects

1963 Thirty-sixth Year

A GATHERING OF EAGLES, Universal: ROBERT L. BRATTON.

★ IT'S A MAD, MAD, MAD, MAD WORLD, Casey Prod., UA: WALTER G. ELLIOTT.

1964 Thirty-seventh Year

★ GOLDFINGER, Eon Prod., UA: NORMAN WANSTALL.

THE LIVELY SET, Universal: ROBERT L. BRATTON.

1965 Thirty-eighth Year

★ THE GREAT RACE, Patricia-Jalem-Reynard Prod., Warner Bros.: TREGOWETH BROWN.

VON RYAN'S EXPRESS, P-R Prods., 20th Century-Fox: WALTER A. ROSSI.

1966 Thirty-ninth Year

FANTASTIC VOYAGE, 20th Century-Fox: WALTER ROSSI.

★ GRAND PRIX, Douglas-Lewis-John Frankenheimer-Cherokee Prod., M-G-M: GORDON DANIEL.

*1967 Fortieth Year**

★ THE DIRTY DOZEN, MKH Prods., Ltd., M-G-M: JOHN POYNER.

IN THE HEAT OF THE NIGHT, Mirisch Corp. Prod., UA: JAMES A. RICHARD.

*Sound Effects award not given after 1967.

Among the thirty-six founders of the Academy were: (seated, L to R) Louis B. Mayer, Conrad Nagel, Mary Pickford, Douglas Fairbanks, Frank Woods, M. C. Levee, Joseph M. Schenck, and Fred Niblo; (standing, L to R) Cedric Gibbons, J. A. Ball, Carey Wilson, George Cohen, Edwin Loeb, Fred Beetson, Frank Lloyd, Roy Pomeroy, John Stahl, and Harry Rapf.

The first awards were presented at the Academy's second anniversary banquet, held May 16, 1929, in the Blossom Room of Hollywood's Roosevelt Hotel.

Left to Right: M-G-M mogul Louis B. Mayer; Norma Shearer, Best Actress winner for 1929/30; and her husband Irving Thalberg, for whom the Thalberg Award is named. Mayer and Thalberg were two of the thirty-six founders of the Academy.

Vivien Leigh and Hattie McDaniel won the Oscars for Best Actress and best Supporting Actress for their performances in *Gone with the Wind* (1939).

At the first awards, Charlie Chaplin, seen here with Merna Kennedy and Henry Bergman, was given a Special Award "for versatility and genius in writing, acting, directing, and producing *The Circus*." In 1972 Chaplin was again honored by the Academy. Copyrighted photo by permission of Roy Export Co., Est.

A stately D. W. Griffith (right) presents the 1935 Oscars for Best Actor and Actress to Victor McLaglen (*The Informer*) and Bette Davis (*Dangerous*). © Academy of Motion Picture Arts and Sciences.

Dooley Wilson, Humphrey Bogart, and Ingrid Bergman in *Casablanca* (1942). This Best Picture winner also earned Oscars for its director Michael Curtiz and its screenwriters, Julius Epstein, Philip Epstein, and Howard Koch.

Ben Hur won a record eleven awards, including Best Picture, out of twelve nominations.

Katharine Hepburn won her third Best Actress Oscar for *The Lion in Winter* (1968). No performer has matched her record of four Oscars and twelve nominations. © 1968 Haworth Productions Ltd.

Left to Right: Frank Capra, winner of three Oscars for directing; James Cagney, 1942 Best Actor for *Yankee Doodle Dandy*; Darryl Zanuck, who received three Thalberg Awards; and Jack Warner, Academy founder and Thalberg Award winner. © Academy of Motion Picture Arts and Sciences.

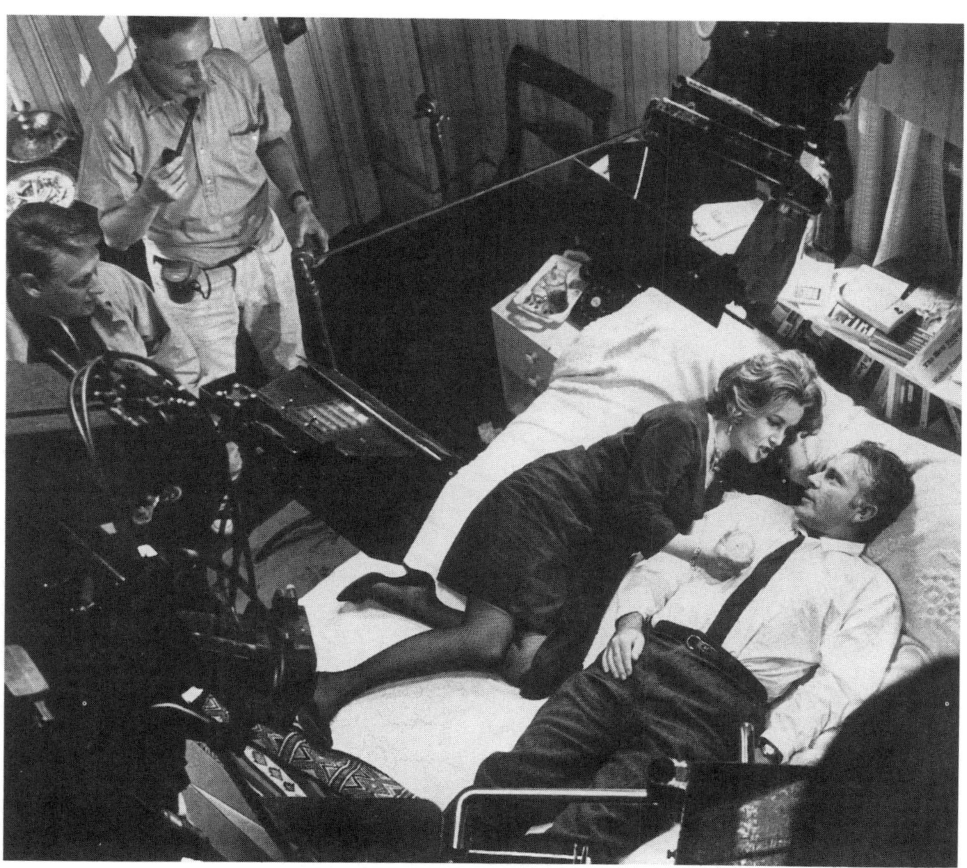

Left to Right: Director Mike Nichols, cinematographer Haskell Wexler, Elizabeth Taylor, and Richard Burton on the set of *Who's Afraid of Virginia Woolf?* (1966). Wexler and Taylor won Oscars for their work. *American Cinematographer* photo.

Cinematographer Freddie Young (left) and director David Lean on location filming *Ryan's Daughter*. Young won three Oscars for Cinematography, all for David Lean pictures. Lean earned ten nominations, including three for writing, and two Oscars for Directing. *American Cinematographer* photo.

Robert Surtees' career as a director of photography included sixteen nominations and three Oscars for Cinematography. *American Cinematographer* photo.

Three legendary directors at the 58th Awards ceremony: Billy Wilder, Akira Kurosawa, and John Huston. Wilder won two directing and three screenwriting Oscars and was nominated twenty times in his career. Huston won two Oscars and received fourteen nominations, including one for Supporting Actor. Kurosawa received a 1989 Honorary Oscar ''for accomplishments that have inspired, delighted, enriched and entertained audiences and influenced filmmakers throughout the world.'' © Academy of Motion Picture Arts and Sciences.

The Silence of the Lambs (1991) became only the third film (after *It Happened One Night* and *One Flew Over the Cuckoo's Nest*) to win Oscars for Best Picture, Actor, Actress, Director, and Screenwriter. Left to Right: screenwriter Ted Tally; Anthony Hopkins; Jodie Foster; producers Edward Saxon, Kenneth Utt, and Ron Bozman; and director Jonathan Demme. © Academy of Motion Picture Arts and Sciences.

II

CHRONOLOGICAL INDEX OF ACADEMY AWARDS

(1927–1992)

FIRST YEAR

1927/28

Awards Ceremony: May 16, 1929
*Hollywood Roosevelt Hotel—Banquet**
(Hosts: Douglas Fairbanks, William C. de Mille)

Best Picture

THE RACKET, The Caddo Company, Paramount Famous Lasky. Howard Hughes, Producer.

7TH HEAVEN, Fox. William Fox, Producer.

⋆ WINGS, Paramount Famous Lasky. Lucien Hubbard, Producer.

Actor

RICHARD BARTHELMESS in *The Noose* and *The Patent Leather Kid*, First National.

⋆ EMIL JANNINGS in *The Last Command* and *The Way of All Flesh*, Paramount Famous Lasky.

Actress

LOUISE DRESSER in *A Ship Comes In*, DeMille Pictures, Pathé.

⋆ JANET GAYNOR in *7th Heaven*, *Street Angel*, and *Sunrise*, Fox.

GLORIA SWANSON in *Sadie Thompson*, Gloria Swanson Productions, UA.

Directing

Comedy Picture (Not given after this year)

⋆ LEWIS MILESTONE for *Two Arabian Knights*, The Caddo Company, UA.

TED WILDE for *Speedy*, Harold Lloyd Corp., Paramount Famous Lasky.

Dramatic Picture

⋆ FRANK BORZAGE for *7th Heaven*, Fox.

HERBERT BRENON for *Sorrell and Son*, Art Cinema, UA.

KING VIDOR for *The Crowd*, Metro-Goldwyn-Mayer.

Writing

Adaptation

ALFRED COHN, *The Jazz Singer*. Warner Bros.

ANTHONY COLDEWAY for *Glorious Betsy*, Warner Bros.

⋆ BENJAMIN GLAZER for *7th Heaven*, Fox.

Original Story

LAJOS BIRO, *The Last Command*, Paramount Famous Lasky.

⋆ BEN HECHT, *Underworld*, Paramount Famous Lasky.

Title Writing (Not given after this year)

GERALD DUFFY, *The Private Life of Helen of Troy*, First National.

⋆ JOSEPH FARNHAM.

GEORGE MARION, JR.

*Awards were for single or multiple achievements or for an entire body of work produced during the qualifying year. For the first year only, those who did not win received Honorable Mention certificates.

Cinematography

GEORGE BARNES, *The Devil Dancer* and *The Magic Flame*, Samuel Goldwyn, UA, and *Sadie Thompson*, Gloria Swanson Productions, UA.

⋆ CHARLES ROSHER, *Sunrise*, Fox.

⋆ KARL STRUSS, *Sunrise*, Fox.

Art Direction

ROCHUS GLIESE, *Sunrise*, Fox.

⋆ WILLIAM CAMERON MENZIES, *The Dove*, Joseph M. Schenck Productions, UA, and *Tempest*, Art Cinema, UA.

HARRY OLIVER, *7th Heaven*, Fox.

Unique and Artistic Picture (Not given after this year)

CHANG, Paramount Famous Lasky.

THE CROWD, Metro-Goldwyn-Mayer.

⋆ SUNRISE, Fox.

Engineering Effects (Not given after this year)

RALPH HAMMERAS.

⋆ ROY POMEROY, *Wings*, Paramount Famous Lasky.

NUGENT SLAUGHTER.

Special Awards

WARNER BROS. for producing *The Jazz Singer*, the pioneer outstanding talking picture, which has revolutionized the industry. (Statuette)

CHARLES CHAPLIN for acting, writing, directing, and producing *The Circus*. (Statuette)*

*The Academy Board of Judges voted unanimously to withdraw Chaplin's name from the competitive categories in order to honor him with a Special Award.

SECOND YEAR

1928/29

Nominations Announced: October 31, 1929
Awards Ceremony: April 3, 1930
*Ambassador Hotel—Banquet**
(Host: William C. de Mille)

Best Picture

ALIBI, Art Cinema, UA. Roland West, Producer.

★ BROADWAY MELODY, Metro-Goldwyn-Mayer. Harry Rapf, Producer.

HOLLYWOOD REVUE, Metro-Goldwyn-Mayer. Harry Rapf, Producer.

IN OLD ARIZONA, Fox. Winfield Sheehan, Studio Head.

THE PATRIOT, Paramount. Ernst Lubitsch, Producer.

Actor

GEORGE BANCROFT in *Thunderbolt*, Paramount Famous Lasky.

★ WARNER BAXTER in *In Old Arizona*, Fox.

CHESTER MORRIS in *Alibi*, Art Cinema, UA.

PAUL MUNI in *The Valiant*, Fox.

LEWIS STONE in *The Patriot*, Paramount Famous Lasky.

Actress

RUTH CHATTERTON in *Madame X*, Metro-Goldwyn-Mayer.

BETTY COMPSON in *The Barker*, First National.

JEANNE EAGELS in *The Letter*, Paramount Famous Lasky.

CORRINNE GRIFFITH in *The Divine Lady*, First National.

BESSIE LOVE in *Broadway Melody*, Metro-Goldwyn-Mayer.

★ MARY PICKFORD in *Coquette*, Pickford, UA.

Directing

LIONEL BARRYMORE for *Madame X*, Metro-Goldwyn-Mayer.

HARRY BEAUMONT for *Broadway Melody*, Metro-Goldwyn-Mayer.

IRVING CUMMINGS for *In Old Arizona*, Fox.

★ FRANK LLOYD for *The Divine Lady*, First National.†

FRANK LLOYD for *Weary River* and *Drag*, First National.

ERNST LUBITSCH for *The Patriot*, Paramount Famous Lasky.

Writing

TOM BARRY, *The Valiant* and *In Old Arizona*, Fox.

*Awards were for single or multiple achievements or for an entire body of work produced during the qualifying year. No nominations were publicized and only the winners' names were revealed, but Academy records indicate that the other names in each category were considered by the Board of Judges.

†Frank Lloyd was nominated for more than one achievement, but his award specified only his work on *The Divine Lady*.

ELLIOTT CLAWSON, *The Leatherneck*, Ralph Block, Pathé; *Sal of Singapore*, Pathé; *Skyscraper* and *The Cop*, DeMille Pictures, Pathé.

★ HANS KRALY, *The Patriot*, Paramount Famous Lasky.*

HANS KRALY, *The Last of Mrs. Cheyney*, Metro-Goldwyn-Mayer.

JOSEPHINE LOVETT, *Our Dancing Daughters*, Cosmopolitan, Metro-Goldwyn-Mayer.

BESS MEREDYTH, *Wonder of Women* and *A Woman of Affairs*, Metro-Goldwyn-Mayer.

Cinematography

GEORGE BARNES, *Our Dancing Daughters*, Cosmopolitan, Metro-Goldwyn-Mayer.

★ CLYDE DEVINNA, *White Shadows in the South Seas*, Cosmopolitan, Metro-Goldwyn-Mayer.

ARTHUR EDESON, *In Old Arizona*, Fox.

ERNEST PALMER, *Four Devils* and *Street Angel*, Fox.

JOHN SEITZ, *The Divine Lady*, First National.

Art Direction

HANS DREIER, *The Patriot*, Paramount Famous Lasky.

★ CEDRIC GIBBONS, *The Bridge of San Luis Rey* and other pictures, Metro-Goldwyn Mayer.

MITCHELL LEISEN, *Dynamite*, Pathé, Metro-Goldwyn-Mayer.

WILLIAM CAMERON MENZIES, *Alibi*, Art Cinema, UA, and *The Awakening*, Samuel Goldwyn, UA.

HARRY OLIVER, *Street Angel*, Fox.

Special Awards

None.

*Hans Kraly was nominated for more than one achievement, but his award specified only his work on *The Patriot*.

1929/30

Nominations Announced: September 19, 1930
Awards Ceremony: November 5, 1930
Ambassador Hotel—Banquet
(Host: Conrad Nagel)

Best Picture

★ ALL QUIET ON THE WESTERN FRONT, Universal. Carl Laemmle, Jr., Producer.

THE BIG HOUSE, Cosmopolitan, Metro-Goldwyn-Mayer. Irving Thalberg, Producer.

DISRAELI, Warner Bros. Darryl F. Zanuck, Producer.

THE DIVORCEE, Metro-Goldwyn-Mayer. Robert Z. Leonard, Producer.

THE LOVE PARADE, Paramount Famous Lasky. Ernst Lubitsch, Producer.

Actor

★ GEORGE ARLISS in *Disraeli*, WARNER BROS.*

GEORGE ARLISS in *The Green Goddess*, Warner Bros.

WALLACE BEERY in *The Big House*, Cosmopolitan, Metro-Goldwyn-Mayer.

MAURICE CHEVALIER in *The Big Pond*, Paramount Publix.

MAURICE CHEVALIER in *The Love Parade*, Paramount Famous Lasky.

RONALD COLMAN in *Bulldog Drummond*, Goldwyn, UA.

RONALD COLMAN in *Condemned*, Goldwyn, UA.

LAWRENCE TIBBETT in *The Rogue Song*, Metro-Goldwyn-Mayer.

Actress

NANCY CARROLL in *The Devil's Holiday*, Paramount.

RUTH CHATTERTON in *Sarah and Son*, Paramount Famous Lasky.

GRETA GARBO in *Anna Christie*, Metro-Goldwyn-Mayer.

GRETA GARBO in *Romance*, Metro-Goldwyn-Mayer.

★ NORMA SHEARER in *The Divorcee*, Metro-Goldwyn-Mayer.†

NORMA SHEARER in *Their Own Desire*, Metro-Goldwyn-Mayer.

GLORIA SWANSON in *The Trespasser*, Kennedy, UA.

Directing

CLARENCE BROWN for *Anna Christie*, Metro-Goldwyn-Mayer.

CLARENCE BROWN for *Romance*, Metro-Goldwyn-Mayer.

ROBERT LEONARD for *The Divorcee*, Metro-Goldwyn-Mayer.

*George Arliss was nominated for work in two films, but his award specified only his performance in *Disraeli*.

†Norma Shearer was nominated for work in two films, but her award specified only her performance in *The Divorcee*.

ERNST LUBITSCH for *The Love Parade*, Paramount Famous Lasky.

★ LEWIS MILESTONE for *All Quiet on the Western Front*, Universal.

KING VIDOR for *Hallelujah*, Metro-Goldwyn-Mayer.

*Writing**

ALL QUIET ON THE WESTERN FRONT, Universal (GEORGE ABBOTT, MAXWELL ANDERSON, and DEL ANDREWS).

★ THE BIG HOUSE, Cosmopolitan, Metro-Goldwyn-Mayer: FRANCES MARION.

DISRAELI, Warner Bros. (JULIAN JOSEPHSON).

THE DIVORCEE, Metro-Goldwyn-Mayer (JOHN MEEHAN).

STREET OF CHANCE, Paramount Famous Lasky (HOWARD ESTABROOK).

*Cinematography**

ALL QUIET ON THE WESTERN FRONT, Universal (ARTHUR EDESON).

ANNA CHRISTIE, Metro-Goldwyn-Mayer (WILLIAM DANIELS).

HELL'S ANGELS, The Caddo Company, UA (GAETANO GAUDIO and HARRY PERRY).

THE LOVE PARADE, Paramount Famous Lasky (VICTOR MILNER).

★ WITH BYRD AT THE SOUTH POLE, Paramount Publix: JOSEPH T. RUCKER and WILLARD VAN DER VEER.

*Art Direction**

BULLDOG DRUMMOND, Samuel Goldwyn, UA (WILLIAM CAMERON MENZIES).

★ KING OF JAZZ, Universal, HERMAN ROSSE.

THE LOVE PARADE, Paramount Famous Lasky (HANS DREIER).

SALLY, First National (JACK OKEY).

THE VAGABOND KING, Paramount Publix (HANS DREIER).

Sound Recording

(New Category)*

★ THE BIG HOUSE, Cosmopolitan, Metro-Goldwyn-Mayer (DOUGLAS SHEARER for MGM Studio Sound Department).

THE CASE OF SERGEANT GRISCHA, RKO Radio (JOHN TRIBBY for the RKO Radio Studio Sound Department).

THE LOVE PARADE, Paramount Famous Lasky (FRANKLIN HANSEN for the Paramount Famous Lasky Studio Sound Department).

RAFFLES, Samuel Goldwyn, UA (OSCAR LAGERSTROM for the United Artists Studio Sound Department).

SONG OF THE FLAME, First National (GEORGE GROVES for the First National Studio Sound Department).

Special Awards

None.

*Nominations for Writing, Cinematography, Art Direction, and Sound Recording were listed by film titles rather than individuals, and only the names of the individuals contributing to the winning films were revealed. Those who contributed to the other films are listed parenthetically.

FOURTH YEAR

1930/31

Nominations Announced: October 5, 1931
Awards Ceremony: November 10, 1931
Biltmore Hotel—Banquet
(MC: Lawrence Grant)

Best Picture

★ CIMARRON, RKO RADIO. William LeBaron, Producer.

EAST LYNNE, Fox. Winfield Sheehan, Studio Head.

THE FRONT PAGE, Caddo, UA. Howard Hughes, Producer.

SKIPPY, Paramount Publix. Adolph Zukor, Studio Head.

TRADER HORN, Metro-Goldwyn-Mayer. Irving Thalberg, Producer.

Actor

★ LIONEL BARRYMORE in *A Free Soul*, Metro-Goldwyn-Mayer.

JACKIE COOPER in *Skippy*, Paramount Publix.

RICHARD DIX in *Cimarron*, RKO Radio.

FREDRIC MARCH in *The Royal Family of Broadway*, Paramount Publix.

ADOLPHE MENJOU in *The Front Page*, Caddo, UA.

Actress

MARLENE DIETRICH in *Morocco*, Paramount Publix.

★ MARIE DRESSLER in *Min and Bill*, Metro-Goldwyn-Mayer.

IRENE DUNNE in *Cimarron*, RKO Radio.

ANN HARDING in *Holiday*, Pathé.

NORMA SHEARER in *A Free Soul*, Metro-Goldwyn-Mayer.

Directing

CLARENCE BROWN for *A Free Soul*, Metro-Goldwyn-Mayer.

LEWIS MILESTONE for *The Front Page*, Caddo, UA.

WESLEY RUGGLES for *Cimarron*, RKO Radio.

★ NORMAN TAUROG for *Skippy*, Paramount Publix.

JOSEF VON STERNBERG for *Morocco*, Paramount Publix.

Writing

Adaptation

★ CIMARRON, RKO Radio: HOWARD ESTABROOK.

THE CRIMINAL CODE, Columbia: SETON MILLER and FRED NIBLO, JR.

HOLIDAY, Pathé: HORACE JACKSON.

LITTLE CAESAR, Warner Bros.: FRANCIS FARAGOH and ROBERT N. LEE.

SKIPPY, Paramount: Publix: JOSEPH MANKIEWICZ and SAM MINTZ.

Original Story

★ THE DAWN PATROL, Warner Bros.-First National: JOHN MONK SAUNDERS.

DOORWAY TO HELL, Warner Bros.-First National: ROWLAND BROWN.

LAUGHTER, Paramount Publix: HARRY D'ABBADIE D'ARRAST, DOUGLAS DOTY, and DONALD OGDEN STEWART.

THE PUBLIC ENEMY, Warner Bros. National: JOHN BRIGHT and KUBEC GLASMON.

SMART MONEY, Warner Bros.: LUCIEN HUBBARD and JOSEPH JACKSON.

Cinematography

CIMARRON, RKO Radio: EDWARD CRONJAGER.

MOROCCO, Paramount Publix: LEE GARMES.

THE RIGHT TO LOVE, Paramount Publix: CHARLES LANG.

SVENGALI, Warners-First National: BARNEY "CHICK" MCGILL.

★ TABU, Paramount Publix: FLOYD CROSBY.

Art Direction

★ CIMARRON, RKO Radio: MAX REE.

JUST IMAGINE, Fox: STEPHEN GOOSSON and RALPH HAMMERAS.

MOROCCO, Paramount Publix: HANS DREIER.

SVENGALI, Warner Bros.: ANTON GROT.

WHOOPEE, Goldwyn, UA: RICHARD DAY.

Sound Recording

METRO-GOLDWYN-MAYER STUDIO SOUND DEPARTMENT.

★ PARAMOUNT PUBLIX STUDIO SOUND DEPARTMENT.

RKO RADIO STUDIO SOUND DEPARTMENT.

SAMUEL GOLDWYN SOUND DEPARTMENT.

Special Awards

None.

Scientific or Technical

(New Category)

Class I

ELECTRICAL RESEARCH PRODUCTS, INC., RCA-PHOTOPHONE, INC., and RKO RADIO PICTURES, INC., for noise-reduction recording equipment.

DuPONT FILM MANUFACTURING CORP. and EASTMAN KODAK CO. for supersensitive panchromatic film.

Class II

FOX FILM CORP. for effective use of synchro-projection composite photography.

Class III

ELECTRICAL RESEARCH PRODUCTS, INC., for moving-coil microphone transmitters.

RKO RADIO PICTURES, INC., for reflex-type microphone concentrators.

RCA-PHOTOPHONE, INC., for ribbon microphone transmitters.

FIFTH YEAR

1931/32

Nominations Announced: October 13, 1932
Awards Ceremony: November 18, 1932
Ambassador Hotel—Banquet
(Host: Conrad Nagel)

Best Picture

ARROWSMITH, Goldwyn, UA. Samuel Goldwyn, Producer.

BAD GIRL, Fox. Winfield Sheehan, Studio Head.

THE CHAMP, Metro-Goldwyn-Mayer. King Vidor, Producer.

FIVE STAR FINAL, First National. Hal B. Wallis, Producer.

★ GRAND HOTEL, Metro-Goldwyn-Mayer. Irving Thalberg, Producer.

ONE HOUR WITH YOU, Paramount Publix. Ernst Lubitsch, Producer.

SHANGHAI EXPRESS, Paramount Publix. Adolph Zukor, Studio Head.

SMILING LIEUTENANT, Paramount Publix. Ernst Lubitsch, Producer.

Actor (tie)

★ WALLACE BEERY in *The Champ*, Metro-Goldwyn-Mayer.

ALFRED LUNT in *The Guardsman*, Metro-Goldwyn-Mayer.

★ FREDRIC MARCH in *Dr. Jekyll and Mr. Hyde*, Paramount Publix.

Actress

MARIE DRESSLER in *Emma*, Metro-Goldwyn-Mayer.

LYNN FONTANNE in *The Guardsman*, Metro-Goldwyn-Mayer.

★ HELEN HAYES in *The Sin of Madelon Clauder*, Metro-Goldwyn-Mayer.

Directing

★ FRANK BORZAGE for *Bad Girl*, Fox.

KING VIDOR for *The Champ*, Metro-Goldwyn-Mayer.

JOSEF VON STERNBERG for *Shanghai Express*, Paramount Publix.

Writing

Adaptation

ARROWSMITH, Goldwyn, UA: SIDNEY HOWARD.

★ BAD GIRL, Fox: EDWIN BURKE.

DR. JEKYLL AND MR. HYDE, Paramount Publix: PERCY HEATH and SAMUEL HOFFENSTEIN.

Original Story

★ THE CHAMP, Metro-Goldwyn-Mayer: FRANCES MARION.

LADY AND GENT, Paramount Publix: GROVER JONES and WILLIAM SLAVENS MCNUTT.

STAR WITNESS, Warner Bros.: LUCIEN HUBBARD.

WHAT PRICE HOLLYWOOD, RKO Radio: ADELA ROGERS ST. JOHN and JANE MURFIN.

Cinematography

ARROWSMITH, Goldwyn, UA: RAY JUNE.

DR. JEKYLL AND MR. HYDE, Paramount Publix: KARL STRUSS.

★ SHANGHAI EXPRESS, Paramount Publix: LEE GARMES.

Art Direction

A NOUS LA LIBERTÉ (French): LAZARE MEERSON.

ARROWSMITH, Goldwyn, UA: RICHARD DAY.

★ TRANSATLANTIC, Fox: GORDON WILES.

Sound Recording

M-G-M STUDIO SOUND DEPARTMENT.

★ PARAMOUNT PUBLIX STUDIO SOUND DEPARTMENT.

RKO RADIO STUDIO SOUND DEPARTMENT.

WARNER BROS.-FIRST NATIONAL STUDIO SOUND DEPARTMENT.

Short Subjects

(New Category)

Cartoons

★ FLOWERS AND TREES, Walt Disney, UA.

IT'S GOT ME AGAIN, Leon Schlesinger, Warner Bros.

MICKEY'S ORPHANS, Walt Disney, Columbia.

Comedy

THE LOUD MOUTH, Mack Sennett.

★ THE MUSIC BOX, Hal Roach, M-G-M (Laurel and Hardy).

SCRATCH-AS-CATCH-CAN, RKO Radio.

Novelty

SCREEN SOUVENIRS, Paramount.

SWING HIGH, Metro-Goldwyn-Mayer (Sport Champion).

★ WRESTLING SWORDFISH, Mack Sennett, Educational (Cannibals of the Deep).

Special Award

WALT DISNEY for the creation of Mickey Mouse. (Statuette)

Scientific or Technical

Class I

None.

Class II

TECHNICOLOR MOTION PICTURE CORP. for their color cartoon process.

Class III

EASTMAN KODAK CO. for the Type II-B Sensitometer.

SIXTH YEAR

1932/33

Nominations Announced: February 26, 1934
Awards Ceremony: March 16, 1934
Ambassador Hotel—Banquet
(MC: Will Rogers)

Best Picture

★ CAVALCADE, Fox. Winfield Sheehan, Studio Head.

A FAREWELL TO ARMS, Paramount. Adolph Zukor, Studio Head.

42nd. STREET, Warner Bros. Darryl F. Zanuck, Producer.

I AM A FUGITIVE FROM A CHAIN GANG, Warner Bros. Hal B. Wallis, Producer.

LADY FOR A DAY, Columbia. Frank Capra, Producer.

LITTLE WOMEN, RKO Radio. Merian C. Cooper, Producer, with Kenneth MacGowan.

THE PRIVATE LIFE OF HENRY VIII, London Films, UA (British). Alexander Korda, Producer.

SHE DONE HIM WRONG, Paramount. William LeBaron, Producer.

SMILIN' THRU, Metro-Goldwyn-Mayer. Irving Thalberg, Producer.

STATE FAIR, Fox. Winfield Sheehan, Studio Head.

Actor

LESLIE HOWARD in *Berkeley Square*, Fox.

★ CHARLES LAUGHTON in *The Private Life of Henry VIII*, London Films, UA (British).

PAUL MUNI in *I Am a Fugitive from a Chain Gang*, Warner Bros.

Actress

★ KATHARINE HEPBURN in *Morning Glory*, RKO Radio.

MAY ROBSON in *Lady for a Day*, Columbia.

DIANA WYNYARD in *Cavalcade*, Fox.

Directing

FRANK CAPRA for *Lady for a Day*, Columbia.

GEORGE CUKOR for *Little Women*, RKO Radio.

★ FRANK LLOYD for *Cavalcade*, Fox.

Assistant Director

(New Category)*

PERCY IKERD, Fox.

★ WILLIAM TUMMEL, Fox.

★ CHARLES DORIAN, Metro-Goldwyn-Mayer.

BUNNY DULL, Metro-Goldwyn-Mayer.

JOHN S. WATERS, Metro-Goldwyn-Mayer.

★ CHARLES BARTON, Paramount.

SIDNEY S. BROD, Paramount.

ARTHUR JACOBSON, Paramount.

EDDIE KILLEY, RKO Radio.

*Multiple award given this year only.

★ DEWEY STARKEY, RKO Radio.
★ FRED FOX, UA.
BENJAMIN SILVEY, UA.
★ SCOTT BEAL, Universal.
JOE MCDONOUGH, Universal.
W. J. REITER, Universal.
AL ALBORN, Warner Bros.
★ GORDON HOLLINGSHEAD, Warner Bros.
FRANK X. SHAW, Warner Bros.

Writing

Adaptation

LADY FOR A DAY, Columbia: ROBERT RISKIN.
★ LITTLE WOMEN, RKO Radio: VICTOR HEERMAN and SARAH Y. MASON.
STATE FAIR, Fox: PAUL GREEN and SONYA LEVIEN.

Original Story

★ ONE WAY PASSAGE, Warner Bros: ROBERT LORD.
THE PRIZEFIGHTER AND THE LADY, Metro-Goldwyn-Mayer: FRANCES MARION.
RASPUTIN AND THE EMPRESS, Metro-Goldwyn-Mayer: CHARLES MACARTHUR.

Cinematography

★ A FAREWELL TO ARMS, Paramount: CHARLES BRYANT LANG, JR.
REUNION IN VIENNA, Metro-Goldwyn-Mayer: GEORGE J. FOLSEY, JR.
SIGN OF THE CROSS, Paramount Publix: KARL STRUSS.

Art Direction

★ CAVALCADE, Fox: WILLIAM S. DARLING.
A FAREWELL TO ARMS, Paramount: HANS DREIER and ROLAND ANDERSON.
WHEN LADIES MEET, Metro-Goldwyn-Mayer: CEDRIC GIBBONS.

Sound Recording

★ A FAREWELL TO ARMS, Paramount, Paramount Studio Sound Department, Franklin B. Hansen, Sound Director.
42ND STREET, Warner Bros., Warner Bros. Studio Sound Department, Nathan Levinson, Sound Director.
GOLDIGGERS OF 1933, Warner Bros., Warner Bros. Studio Sound Department, Nathan Levinson, Sound Director.
I AM A FUGITIVE FROM A CHAIN GANG, Warner Bros., Warner Bros. Studio Sound Department, Nathan Levinson, Sound Director.

Short Subjects

Cartoons

BUILDING A BUILDING, Walt Disney, UA.
THE MERRY OLD SOUL, Walter Lantz, Universal.
★ THE THREE LITTLE PIGS, Walt Disney, UA.

Comedy

MISTER MUGG, Universal. (Comedies)
A PREFERRED LIST, Louis Brock, RKO Radio. (Headliner Series #5)
★ SO THIS IS HARRIS, Louis Brock, RKO Radio. (Special)

Novelty

★ KRAKATOA, Joe Rock, Educational. (Three-reel special)
MENU, Pete Smith, M-G-M. (Oddities)
THE SEA, Educational. (Battle for Life)

Special Awards

None.

Scientific or Technical

Class I

None.

Class II

ELECTRICAL RESEARCH PRODUCTS, INC., for their wide-range recording and reproducing system.

RCA-VICTOR CO., INC., for their high-fidelity recording and reproducing system.

Class III

FOX FILM CORP., FRED JACKMAN and WARNER BROS. PICTURES, INC., and SIDNEY SANDERS of RKO STUDIOS, INC., for their development and effective use of the translucent cellulose screen in composite photography.

SEVENTH YEAR

1934

Nominations Announced: February 5, 1935
Awards Ceremony: February 27, 1935
Biltmore Hotel—Banquet
(MC: Irvin S. Cobb)

Best Picture

THE BARRETTS OF WIMPOLE STREET, Metro-Goldwyn-Mayer. Irving Thalberg, Producer.

CLEOPATRA, Paramount. Cecil B. DeMille, Producer.

FLIRTATION WALK, First National. Jack L. Warner and Hal B. Wallis, Producers, with Robert Lord.

THE GAY DIVORCEE, RKO Radio. Pandro S. Berman, Producer.

HERE COMES THE NAVY, Warner Bros. Lou Edelman, Producer.

THE HOUSE OF ROTHSCHILD, 20th Century, UA. Darryl F. Zanuck, Producer, with William Goetz and Raymond Griffith.

IMITATION OF LIFE, Universal. John M. Stahl, Producer.

★ IT HAPPENED ONE NIGHT, Columbia. Harry Cohn, Producer.

ONE NIGHT OF LOVE, Columbia. Harry Cohn, Producer, with Everett Riskin.

THE THIN MAN, Metro-Goldwyn-Mayer. Hunt Stromberg, Producer.

VIVA VILLA, Metro-Goldwyn-Mayer. David O. Selznick, Producer.

THE WHITE PARADE, Fox. Jesse L. Lasky, Producer.

Actor

★ CLARK GABLE in *It Happened One Night*, Columbia.

FRANK MORGAN in *The Affairs of Cellini*, 20th Century, UA.

WILLIAM POWELL in *The Thin Man*, Metro-Goldwyn-Mayer.

Actress

★ CLAUDETTE COLBERT in *It Happened One Night*, Columbia.

GRACE MOORE in *One Night of Love*, Columbia.

NORMA SHEARER in *The Barretts of Wimpole Street*, Metro-Goldwyn-Mayer.

Directing

★ FRANK CAPRA for *It Happened One Night*, Columbia.

VICTOR SCHERTZINGER for *One Night of Love*, Columbia.

W. S. VAN DYKE for *The Thin Man*, Metro-Goldwyn-Mayer.

Assistant Director

SCOTT BEAL for *Imitation of Life*, Universal.

CULLEN TATE for *Cleopatra*, Paramount.

★ JOHN WATERS for *Viva Villa*, Metro-Goldwyn-Mayer.

Writing

Adaptation

★ IT HAPPENED ONE NIGHT, Columbia: ROBERT RISKIN.

THE THIN MAN, Metro-Goldwyn-Mayer: FRANCES GOODRICH and ALBERT HACKETT.

VIVA VILLA, Metro-Goldwyn-Mayer: BEN HECHT.

Original Story

HIDE-OUT, Metro-Goldwyn-Mayer: MAURI GRASHIN.

★ MANHATTAN MELODRAMA, Metro-Goldwyn-Mayer: ARTHUR CAESAR.

THE RICHEST GIRL IN THE WORLD, RKO Radio: NORMAN KRASNA.

Cinematography

THE AFFAIRS OF CELLINI, 20th Century, UA: CHARLES ROSHER.

★ CLEOPATRA, Paramount: VICTOR MILNER.

OPERATION 13, Metro-Goldwyn-Mayer: GEORGE FOLSEY.

Art Direction

THE AFFAIRS OF CELLINI, 20th Century, UA: RICHARD DAY.

THE GAY DIVORCEE, RKO Radio: VAN NEST POLGLASE and CARROLL CLARK.

★ THE MERRY WIDOW, Metro-Goldwyn-Mayer: CEDRIC GIBBONS and FREDERIC HOPE.

Sound Recording

THE AFFAIRS OF CELLINI, 20th Century, UA: UNITED ARTISTS STUDIO SOUND DEPARTMENT, THOMAS T. MOULTON, Sound Director.

CLEOPATRA, Paramount: PARAMOUNT STUDIO SOUND DEPARTMENT, FRANKLIN HANSEN, Sound Director.

FLIRTATION WALK, First National: WARNER BROS.-FIRST NATIONAL STUDIO SOUND DEPARTMENT, NATHAN LEVINSON, Sound Director.

THE GAY DIVORCEE, RKO Radio: RKO RADIO STUDIO SOUND DEPARTMENT, CARL DREHER, Sound Director.

IMITATION OF LIFE, Universal: UNIVERSAL STUDIO SOUND DEPARTMENT, THEODORE SODERBERG, Sound Director.

★ ONE NIGHT OF LOVE, Columbia: COLUMBIA STUDIO SOUND DEPARTMENT, JOHN LIVADARY, Sound Director.

VIVA VILLA, Metro-Goldwyn-Mayer: MGM STUDIO SOUND DEPARTMENT, DOUGLAS SHEARER, Sound Director.

THE WHITE PARADE, Jesse L. Lasky, Fox: FOX STUDIO SOUND DEPARTMENT, E. H. HANSEN, Sound Director.

Film Editing

(New Category)

CLEOPATRA, Paramount: ANNE BAUCHENS.

★ ESKIMO, Metro-Goldwyn-Mayer: CONRAD NERVIG.

ONE NIGHT OF LOVE, Columbia: GENE MILFORD.

Music

(New Category)*

Score

THE GAY DIVORCEE, RKO Radio Studio Music Department: MAX STEINER, Head; Score by KENNETH WEBB and SAMUEL HOFFENSTEIN.

THE LOST PATROL, RKO Radio Studio Music Department: MAX STEINER, Head; Score by MAX STEINER.

★ ONE NIGHT OF LOVE, Columbia Studio Music Department: LOUIS SILVERS, Head; Thematic music by VICTOR SCHERTZINGER and GUS KAHN.

Song

CARIOCA from *Flying Down to Rio*, RKO Radio: Music by VINCENT

*During the years 1934 through 1937, this was a Music Department Achievement and the award was presented to the departmental head instead of to the composer.

YOUMANS; Lyrics by EDWARD ELISCU and GUS KAHN.

★ THE CONTINENTAL from *The Gay Divorcee*, RKO Radio: Music by CON CONRAD; Lyrics by HERB MAGIDSON.

LOVE IN BLOOM, from *She Loves Me Not*, Paramount: Music by RALPH RAINGER; Lyrics by LEO ROBIN.

Short Subjects

Cartoons

HOLIDAY LAND, Charles Mintz, Columbia.

JOLLY LITTLE ELVES, Universal.

★ THE TORTOISE AND THE HARE, Walt Disney, UA.

Comedy

★ LA CUCARACHA, RKO Radio: (Special)

MEN IN BLACK, Columbia: (Broadway Comedies)

WHAT, NO MEN!, Warner Bros. (Broadway Brevities)

Novelty

BOSOM FRIENDS, Educational. (Treasure Chest)

★ CITY OF WAX, Educational. (Battle for Life)

STRIKES AND SPARES, Metro-Goldwyn-Mayer. (Oddities)

Special Award

SHIRLEY TEMPLE, in grateful recognition of her outstanding contribution to screen entertainment during the year 1934. (Miniature statuette)

Scientific or Technical

Class I

None.

Class II

ELECTRICAL RESEARCH PRODUCTS, INC., for their development of the vertical cut disc method of recording sound for motion pictures (hill-and-dale recording).

Class III

COLUMBIA PICTURES CORP. for their application of the vertical cut disc method (hill-and-dale recording) to actual studio production, with their recording of the sound on the picture *One Night of Love*.

BELL AND HOWELL CO. for their development of the Bell and Howell fully automatic sound and picture printer.

EIGHTH YEAR

1935

Nominations Announced: February 7, 1936
Awards Ceremony: March 5, 1936
Biltmore Hotel—Banquet (Host: Frank Capra)

Best Picture

ALICE ADAMS, RKO Radio. Pandro S. Berman, Producer.

BROADWAY MELODY OF 1936. Metro-Goldwyn-Mayer. John W. Considine, Jr., Producer.

CAPTAIN BLOOD, Warner Bros.-Cosmopolitan. Hal Wallis, Producer, with Harry Joe Brown and Gordon Hollingshead.

DAVID COPPERFIELD, Metro-Goldwyn-Mayer. David O. Selznick. Producer.

THE INFORMER, RKO Radio. Cliff Reid., Producer.

LES MISERABLES, 20th Century, UA. Darryl F. Zanuck, Producer.

LIVES OF A BENGAL LANCER, Paramount. Louis D. Lighton, Producer.

A MIDSUMMER NIGHT'S DREAM, Warner Bros. Henry Blanke, Producer.

★ MUTINY ON THE BOUNTY, Metro-Goldwyn-Mayer. Irving Thalberg, Producer, with Albert Lewin.

NAUGHTY MARIETTA, Metro-Goldwyn-Mayer. Hunt Stromberg, Producer.

RUGGLES OF RED GAP, Paramount. Arthur Hornblow, Jr., Producer.

TOP HAT, RKO Radio. Pandro S. Berman, Producer.

Actor

CLARK GABLE in *Mutiny on the Bounty*, Metro-Goldwyn-Mayer.

CHARLES LAUGHTON in *Mutiny on the Bounty*, Metro-Goldwyn-Mayer.

★ VICTOR MCLAGLEN in *The Informer*, RKO Radio.

FRANCHOT TONE in *Mutiny on the Bounty*, Metro-Goldwyn-Mayer.

Actress

ELISABETH BERGNER in *Escape Me Never*, British & Dominions, UA (British).

CLAUDETTE COLBERT in *Private Worlds*, Paramount.

★ BETTE DAVIS in *Dangerous*, Warner Bros.

KATHARINE HEPBURN in *Alice Adams*, RKO Radio.

MIRIAM HOPKINS in *Becky Sharp*, Pioneer, RKO Radio.

MERLE OBERON in *The Dark Angel*, Goldwyn, UA.

Directing

★ JOHN FORD for *The Informer*, RKO Radio.

HENRY HATHAWAY for *Lives of a Bengal Lancer*, Paramount.

FRANK LLOYD for *Mutiny on the Bounty*, Metro-Goldwyn-Mayer.

Assistant Director (Two winners)

★ CLEM BEAUCHAMP and PAUL WING for *Lives of a Bengal Lancer*, Paramount.

ERIC STACEY for *Les Miserables*, 20th Century, UA.
JOSEPH NEWMAN for *David Copperfield*, Metro-Goldwyn-Mayer.

Writing

Original Story

BROADWAY MELODY OF 1936, Metro-Goldwyn-Mayer: MOSS HART
THE GAY DECEPTION, Lasky, Fox: DON HARTMAN and STEPHEN AVERY.
★ THE SCOUNDREL, Paramount: BEN HECHT and CHARLES MACARTHUR.

Screenplay

★ THE INFORMER, RKO Radio: DUDLEY NICHOLS.
LIVES OF A BENGAL LANCER, Paramount: ACHMED ABDULLAH, JOHN L. BALDERSTON, GROVER JONES, WILLIAM SLAVENS MCNUTT, and WALDEMAR YOUNG.
MUTINY ON THE BOUNTY Metro-Goldwyn-Mayer: JULES FURTHMAN, TALBOT JENNINGS, and CAREY WILSON.

Cinematography

BARBARY COAST, Goldwyn, UA: RAY JUNE.
THE CRUSADES, Paramount: VICTOR MILNER.
LES MISERABLES, 20th Century, UA: GREGG TOLAND.
★ A MIDSUMMER NIGHT'S DREAM, Warner Bros: HAL MOHR.*

Art Direction

★ THE DARK ANGEL, Goldwyn, UA: RICHARD DAY.
LIVES OF A BENGAL LANCER, Paramount: HANS DREIER and ROLAND ANDERSON.
TOP HAT, RKO Radio: CARROLL CLARK and VAN NEST POLGLASE.

Sound Recording

THE BRIDE OF FRANKENSTEIN. Universal: UNIVERSAL STUDIO SOUND DEPARTMENT, GILBERT KURLAND, Sound Director.
CAPTAIN BLOOD Warner Bros: WARNER BROS.-FIRST NATIONAL STUDIO SOUND DEPARTMENT, NATHAN LEVINSON, Sound Director.
THE DARK ANGEL, Goldwyn, UA: UNITED ARTISTS STUDIO SOUND DEPARTMENT, THOMAS T. MOULTON. Sound Director.
I DREAM TOO MUCH. RKO Radio: RKO RADIO STUDIO SOUND DEPARTMENT, CARL DREHER, Sound Director.
LIVES OF A BENGAL LANCER, Paramount: PARAMOUNT STUDIO SOUND DEPARTMENT, FRANKLIN HANSEN, Sound Director.
LOVE ME FOREVER, Columbia: COLUMBIA STUDIO SOUND DEPARTMENT, JOHN LIVADARY, Sound Director.
★ NAUGHTY MARIETTA, M-G-M: M-G-M STUDIO SOUND DEPARTMENT, DOUGLAS SHEARER, Sound Director.
1,000 DOLLARS A MINUTE, Republic: REPUBLIC STUDIO SOUND DEPARTMENT.
THANKS A MILLION, 20th Century-Fox: 20TH CENTURY-FOX STUDIO SOUND DEPARTMENT, E. H. HANSEN, Sound Director.

Film Editing

DAVID COPPERFIELD, Metro-Goldwyn-Mayer: ROBERT J. KERN.

**A Midsummer Night's Dream* was not one of the official nominees. Hal Mohr became the first and only person to win an award as a write-in candidate. The rules were changed the following year to prohibit write-in votes.

THE INFORMER, RKO Radio: GEORGE HIVELY.

LES MISERABLES 20th Century, UA: BARBARA MCLEAN.

LIVES OF A BENGAL LANCER, Paramount: ELLSWORTH HOAGLAND.

★ A MIDSUMMER NIGHT'S DREAM, Warner Bros.: RALPH DAWSON.

MUTINY ON THE BOUNTY, Metro-Goldwyn-Mayer: MARGARET BOOTH.

Music

Score

★ THE INFORMER, RKO Radio Studio Music Department: MAX STEINER, Head; Score by MAX STEINER.

MUTINY ON THE BOUNTY, Metro-Goldwyn-Mayer Studio Music Department: NAT W. FINSTON, Head; Score by HERBERT STOTHART.

PETER IBBETSON, Paramount Studio Music Department: IRVIN TALBOT, Head; Score by ERNST TOCH.

Song

CHEEK TO CHEEK from *Top Hat*, RKO Radio: Music and Lyrics by IRVING BERLIN.

LOVELY TO LOOK AT from *Roberta*, RKO Radio: Music by JEROME KERN; Lyrics by DOROTHY FIELDS and JIMMY MCHUGH.

★ LULLABY OF BROADWAY from *Gold Diggers of 1935*, Warner Bros.: Music by HARRY WARREN; Lyrics by AL DUBIN.

Dance Direction

(New Category)

BUSBY BERKELEY for *Lullaby of Broadway* number from *Gold Diggers of 1935*, Warner Bros.; *The Words Are in My Heart* number from *Gold Diggers of 1935*, Warner Bros.

BOBBY CONNOLLY for *Latin from Manhattan* number from *Go into Your Dance*, Warner Bros: *Playboy from Paree* number from *Broadway Hostess*, Warner Bros.

★ DAVE GOULD for *I've Got a Feeling You're Fooling* number from *Broadway Melody of 1936*, M-G-M; *Straw Hat* number from *Folies Bergere*, 20th Century, UA.

SAMMY LEE for *Lovely Lady* number from *King of Burlesque*, 20th Century-Fox: *Too Good to Be True* number from *King of Burlesque*, 20th Century-Fox.

HERMES PAN for *Piccolino* number from *Top Hat*, RKO Radio: *Top Hat* number from *Top Hat*, RKO Radio.

LEROY PRINZ for *Elephant Number—It's the Animal in Me* from *Big Broadcast of 1936*, Paramount; *Viennese Waltz* number from *All the King's Horses*, Paramount.

BENJAMIN ZEMACH for *Hall of Kings* number from *She*, RKO Radio.

Short Subjects

Cartoons

THE CALICO DRAGON, Harman-Ising, M-G-M.

★ THREE ORPHAN KITTENS, Walt Disney, UA.

WHO KILLED COCK ROBIN?, Walt Disney, UA.

Comedy

★ HOW TO SLEEP, Metro-Goldwyn-Mayer. (Miniature)

OH, MY NERVES, Columbia. (Broadway Comedies)

TIT FOR TAT, Hal Roach, M-G-M. (Laurel and Hardy)

Novelty

AUDIOSCOPIKS, Metro-Goldwyn-Mayer. (Special)

CAMERA THRILLS, Universal. (Special)

★ WINGS OVER MT. EVEREST, Educational. (Special)

Special Award

DAVID WARK GRIFFITH, for his distinguished creative achievements as director and producer and his invaluable initiative and lasting contributions to the progress of the motion picture arts. (Statuette)

Scientific or Technical

Class I

None.

Class II

AGFA ANSCO CORP. for their development of the Agfa infrared film.

EASTMAN KODAK CO. for their development of the Eastman Pola-Screen.

Class III

METRO-GOLDWYN-MAYER STUDIO for the development of antidirectional negative and positive development by means of jet turbulation, and the application of the method to all negative and print processing of the entire product of a major producing company.

WILLIAM A. MUELLER of Warner Bros.-First National Studio Sound Department for his method of dubbing, in which the level of the dialogue automatically controls the level of the accompanying music and sound effects.

MOLE-RICHARDSON CO. for their development of the "Solar-spot" spot lamps.

DOUGLAS SHEARER and METRO-GOLDWYN-MAYER STUDIO SOUND DEPARTMENT for their automatic control system for cameras and sound recording machines and auxiliary stage equipment.

ELECTRICAL RESEARCH PRODUCTS, INC., for their study and development of equipment to analyze and measure flutter resulting from the travel of the film through the mechanisms used in the recording and reproduction of sound.

PARAMOUNT PRODUCTIONS, INC., for the design and construction of the Paramount transparency air-turbine developing machine.

NATHAN LEVINSON, Director of Sound Recording for Warner Bros.-First National Studio, for the method of intercutting variable density and variable area sound tracks to secure an increase in the effective volume range of sound recorded for motion pictures.

NINTH YEAR

1936

Nominations Announced: February 7, 1937
Awards Ceremony: March 4, 1937
Biltmore Hotel—Banquet
(MC: George Jessel)

Best Picture

ANTHONY ADVERSE, Warner Bros. Henry Blanke, Producer.

DODSWORTH, Goldwyn, UA. Samuel Goldwyn, Producer, with Merritt Hulbert.

★ THE GREAT ZIEGFELD, Metro-Goldwyn-Mayer. Hunt Stromberg. Producer.

LIBELED LADY, Metro-Goldwyn-Mayer. Lawrence Weingarten, Producer.

MR. DEEDS GOES TO TOWN, Columbia. Frank Capra, Producer.

ROMEO AND JULIET. Metro-Goldwyn-Mayer. Irving Thalberg, Producer.

SAN FRANCISCO, Metro-Goldwyn-Mayer. John Emerson and Bernard H. Hyman, Producers.

THE STORY OF LOUIS PASTEUR, Warner Bros. Henry Blanke, Producer.

A TALE OF TWO CITIES, Metro-Goldwyn-Mayer. David O. Selznick, Producer.

THREE SMART GIRLS, Universal. Joseph Pasternak, Producer, with Charles R. Rogers.

Actor

GARY COOPER in *Mr. Deeds Goes to Town*, Columbia.

WALTER HUSTON in *Dodsworth*, Goldwyn, UA.

★ PAUL MUNI in *The Story of Louis Pasteur*, Warner Bros.

WILLIAM POWELL in *My Man Godfrey*, Universal.

SPENCER TRACY in *San Francisco*, Metro-Goldwyn-Mayer.

Actress

IRENE DUNNE in *Theodora Goes Wild*, Columbia.

GLADYS GEORGE in *Valiant Is the Word for Carrie*, Paramount.

CAROLE LOMBARD in *My Man Godfrey*, Universal.

★ LUISE RAINER in *The Great Ziegfeld*, Metro-Goldwyn-Mayer.

NORMA SHEARER in *Romeo and Juliet*, Metro-Goldwyn-Mayer.

Supporting Actor

(New Category)

MISCHA AUER in *My Man Godfrey*, Universal.

★ WALTER BRENNAN in *Come and Get It*, Goldwyn, UA.

STUART ERWIN in *Pigskin Parade*, 20th Century-Fox.

BASIL RATHBONE in *Romeo and Juliet*, Metro-Goldwyn-Mayer.

AKIM TAMIROFF in *The General Died at Dawn*, Paramount.

Supporting Actress

(New Category)

BEULAH BONDI in *The Gorgeous Hussy*, Metro-Goldwyn-Mayer.

ALICE BRADY in *My Man Godfrey*, Universal.
BONITA GRANVILLE in *These Three*, Goldwyn, UA.
MARIA OUSPENSKAYA in *Dodsworth*, Goldwyn, UA.
★ GALE SONDERGAARD in *Anthony Adverse*, Warner Bros.

Directing

★ FRANK CAPRA for *Mr. Deeds Goes to Town*, Columbia.
GREGORY LA CAVA for *My Man Godfrey*, Universal.
ROBERT Z. LEONARD for *The Great Ziegfeld*, Metro-Goldwyn-Mayer.
W. S. VAN DYKE for *San Francisco*, Metro-Goldwyn-Mayer.
WILLIAM WYLER for *Dodsworth*, Goldwyn, UA.

Assistant Director

CLEM BEAUCHAMP for *Last of the Mohicans*, Reliance, UA.
WILLIAM CANNON for *Anthony Adverse*, Warner Bros.
JOSEPH NEWMAN for *San Francisco*, Metro-Goldwyn-Mayer.
ERIC G. STACEY for *Garden of Allah*, Selznick, UA.
★ JACK SULLIVAN for *The Charge of the Light Brigade*, Warner Bros.

Writing

Original Story

FURY, Metro-Goldwyn-Mayer: NORMAN KRASNA.
THE GREAT ZIEGFELD, Metro-Goldwyn-Mayer: WILLIAM ANTHONY MCGUIRE.
SAN FRANCISCO, Metro-Goldwyn-Mayer: ROBERT HOPKINS.
★ THE STORY OF LOUIS PASTEUR, Warner Bros.: PIERRE COLLINGS and SHERIDAN GIBNEY.
THREE SMART GIRLS, Universal: ADELE COMMANDINI.

Screenplay

AFTER THE THIN MAN, Metro-Goldwyn-Mayer: FRANCES GOODRICH and ALBERT HACKETT.
DODSWORTH, Goldwyn, UA: SIDNEY HOWARD.
MR. DEEDS GOES TO TOWN, Columbia: ROBERT RISKIN.
MY MAN GODFREY, Universal: ERIC HATCH and MORRIS RYSKIND.
★ THE STORY OF LOUIS PASTEUR, Warner Bros.: PIERRE COLLINGS and SHERIDAN GIBNEY.

Cinematography

★ ANTHONY ADVERSE, Warner Bros.: GAETANO GAUDIO.
THE GENERAL DIED AT DAWN, Paramount: VICTOR MILNER.
THE GORGEOUS HUSSY, Metro-Goldwyn-Mayer: GEORGE FOLSEY.

Art Direction

ANTHONY ADVERSE, Warner Bros.: ANTON GROT.
★ DODSWORTH, Goldwyn, UA: RICHARD DAY.
THE GREAT ZIEGFELD, Metro-Goldwyn-Mayer: CEDRIC GIBBONS, EDDIE IMAZU, and EDWIN B. WILLIS.
LLOYDS OF LONDON, 20th Century-Fox: WILLIAM S. DARLING.
THE MAGNIFICENT BRUTE, Universal: ALBERT S. D'AGOSTINO and JACK OTTERSON.
ROMEO AND JULIET, Metro-Goldwyn-Mayer: CEDRIC GIBBONS, FREDERIC HOPE, and EDWIN B. WILLIS.
WINTERSET, RKO Radio: PERRY FERGUSON.

Sound Recording

BANJO ON MY KNEE, 20th Century-Fox: 20TH CENTURY-FOX STUDIO SOUND DEPARTMENT, E. H. HANSEN. Sound Director.
THE CHARGE OF THE LIGHT BRIGADE, Warner Bros.: WARNER BROS. STUDIO

SOUND DEPARTMENT, NATHAN LEVINSON. Sound Director.

DODSWORTH, Goldwyn. UA: UNITED ARTISTS STUDIO SOUND DEPARTMENT, THOMAS T. MOULTON. Sound Director.

GENERAL SPANKY, Roach. M-G-M: HAL ROACH STUDIO SOUND DEPARTMENT, ELMER A. RAGUSE. Sound Director.

MR. DEEDS GOES TO TOWN, Columbia: COLUMBIA STUDIO SOUND DEPARTMENT, JOHN LIVADARY, Sound Director.

★ SAN FRANCISCO, M-G-M: M-G-M STUDIO SOUND DEPARTMENT, DOUGLAS SHEARER, Sound Director.

THE TEXAS RANGERS. Paramount: PARAMOUNT STUDIO SOUND DEPARTMENT, FRANKLIN HANSEN, Sound Director.

THAT GIRL FROM PARIS, RKO Radio: RKO RADIO STUDIO SOUND DEPARTMENT, J. O. AALBERG, Sound Director.

THREE SMART GIRLS, Universal: UNIVERSAL STUDIO SOUND DEPARTMENT, HOMER G. TASKER, Sound Director.

Film Editing

★ ANTHONY ADVERSE, Warner Bros.: RALPH DAWSON.

COME AND GET IT, Goldwyn, UA: EDWARD CURTISS.

THE GREAT ZIEGFELD, Metro-Goldwyn-Mayer: WILLIAM S. GRAY.

LLOYDS OF LONDON, 20th Century-Fox: BARBARA MCLEAN.

A TALE OF TWO CITIES, Metro-Goldwyn-Mayer: CONRAD A. NERVIG.

THEODORA GOES WILD, Columbia: OTTO MEYER.

Music

Score

★ ANTHONY ADVERSE, Warner Bros. Studio Music Department: LEO FORBSTEIN, Head; Score by ERICH WOLFGANG KORNGOLD.

THE CHARGE OF THE LIGHT BRIGADE, Warner Bros. Studio Music Department: LEO FORBSTEIN, Head; Score by MAX STEINER.

THE GARDEN OF ALLAH, Selznick International Pictures Music Department: MAX STEINER, Head; Score by MAX STEINER.

THE GENERAL DIED AT DAWN, Paramount Studio Music Department: BORIS MORROS, Head; Score by WERNER JANSSEN.

WINTERSET, RKO Radio Studio Music Department: NATHANIEL SHILKRET, Head; Score by NATHANIEL SHILKRET.

Song

DID I REMEMBER from *Suzy*, Metro-Goldwyn-Mayer: Music by WALTER DONALDSON; Lyrics by HAROLD ADAMSON.

I'VE GOT YOU UNDER MY SKIN from *Born to Dance*, Metro-Goldwyn-Mayer: Music and Lyrics by COLE PORTER.

A MELODY FROM THE SKY from *Trail of the Lonesome Pine*, Paramount: Music by LOUIS ALTER; Lyrics by SIDNEY MITCHELL.

PENNIES FROM HEAVEN from *Pennies from Heaven*, Columbia: Music by ARTHUR JOHNSTON; Lyrics by JOHNNY BURKE.

★ THE WAY YOU LOOK TONIGHT from *Swing Time*, RKO Radio: Music by JEROME KERN; Lyrics by DOROTHY FIELDS.

WHEN DID YOU LEAVE HEAVEN from *Sing Baby Sing*, 20th Century-Fox: Music by RICHARD A. WHITING; Lyrics by WALTER BULLOCK.

Dance Direction

BUSBY BERKELEY for *Love and War* number from *Gold Diggers of 1937*, Warner Bros.

BOBBY CONNOLLY for *1000 Love Songs*

number from *Cain and Mabel*, Warner Bros.

★ SEYMOUR FELIX for *A Pretty Girl Is Like a Melody* number from *The Great Ziegfeld*, Metro-Goldwyn-Mayer.

DAVE GOULD for *Swingin' the Jinx* number from *Born to Dance*, Metro-Goldwyn-Mayer.

JACK HASKELL for *Skating Ensemble* number from *One in a Million*, 20th Century-Fox.

RUSSELL LEWIS for *The Finale* number from *Dancing Pirate*, RKO Radio.

HERMES PAN for *Bojangles* number from *Swing Time*, RKO Radio.

Short Subjects

Cartoons

★ COUNTRY COUSIN, Walt Disney, UA.

OLD MILL POND, Harman-Ising, M-G-M.

SINBAD THE SAILOR, Paramount.

One Reel

★ BORED OF EDUCATION, Hal Roach, M-G-M. (Our Gang)

MOSCOW MOODS, Paramount. (Headliners)

WANTED, A MASTER, Pete Smith, M-G-M. (Pete Smith Specialties)

Two Reels

DOUBLE OR NOTHING, Warner Bros. (Broadway Brevities)

DUMMY ACHE, RKO Radio. (Edgar Kennedy Comedies)

★ THE PUBLIC PAYS, Metro-Goldwyn-Mayer. (Crime Doesn't Pay)

Color

★ GIVE ME LIBERTY, Warner Bros. (Broadway Brevities)

LA FIESTA DE SANTA BARBARA, Metro-Goldwyn-Mayer. (Musical Revues)

POPULAR SCIENCE J-6-2, Paramount.

Special Awards

MARCH OF TIME for its significance to motion pictures and for having revolutionized one of the most important branches of the industry—the newsreel. (statuette)

W. HOWARD GREENE and HAROLD ROSSON for the color cinematography of the Selznick International Production, *The Garden of Allah*. (Plaques)

Scientific or Technical

Class I

DOUGLAS SHEARER and the METRO-GOLDWYN-MAYER STUDIO SOUND DEPARTMENT for the development of a practical two-way horn system and a biased Class A push-pull recording system.

Class II

E. C. WENTE and the BELL TELEPHONE LABORATORIES for their multicellular high-frequency horn and receiver.

RCA MANUFACTURING CO., INC., for their rotary stabilizer sound head.

Class III

RCA MANUFACTURING CO., INC., for their development of a method of recording and printing sound records utilizing a restricted spectrum (known as ultraviolet light recording).

ELECTRICAL RESEARCH PRODUCTS, INC., for the ERPI "Type Q" portable recording channel.

RCA MANUFACTURING CO., INC., for furnishing a practical design and specifications for a non-slip printer.

UNITED ARTISTS STUDIO CORP. for the development of a practical, efficient, and quiet wind machine.

TENTH YEAR

1937

Nominations Announced: February 6, 1938
Awards Ceremony: Postponed from March 3 to March 10, 1938, because of flooding
Biltmore Hotel—Banquet
(MC: Bob Burns)

Best Picture

THE AWFUL TRUTH, Columbia. Leo McCarey, Producer, with Everett Riskin.

CAPTAINS COURAGEOUS, Metro-Goldwyn-Mayer. Louis D. Lighton, Producer.

DEAD END, Goldwyn, UA. Samuel Goldwyn, Producer, with Merritt Hulbert.

THE GOOD EARTH, Metro-Goldwyn-Mayer. Irving Thalberg, Producer, with Albert Lewin.

IN OLD CHICAGO, 20th Century-Fox. Darryl F. Zanuck, Producer, with Kenneth MacGowan.

★ THE LIFE OF EMILE ZOLA, Warner Bros. Henry Blanke, Producer.

LOST HORIZON, Columbia. Frank Capra, Producer.

100 MEN AND A GIRL, Universal. Charles R. Rogers, Producer, with Joe Pasternak.

STAGE DOOR, RKO Radio. Pandro S. Berman, Producer.

A STAR IS BORN, Selznick International, UA. David O. Selznick, Producer.

Actor

CHARLES BOYER in *Conquest*, Metro-Goldwyn-Mayer.

FREDRIC MARCH in *A Star Is Born*, Selznick, UA.

ROBERT MONTGOMERY in *Night Must Fall*, Metro-Goldwyn-Mayer.

PAUL MUNI in *The Life of Emile Zola*, Warner Bros.

★ SPENCER TRACY in *Captains Courageous*, Metro-Goldwyn-Mayer.

Actress

IRENE DUNNE in *The Awful Truth*, Columbia.

GRETA GARBO in *Camille*, Metro-Goldwyn-Mayer.

JANET GAYNOR in *A Star Is Born*, Selznick, UA.

★ LUISE RAINER in *The Good Earth*, Metro-Goldwyn-Mayer.

BARBARA STANWYCK in *Stella Dallas*, Goldwyn, UA.

Supporting Actor

RALPH BELLAMY in *The Awful Truth*, Columbia.

THOMAS MITCHELL in *Hurricane*, Goldwyn, UA.

★ JOSEPH SCHILDKRAUT in *The Life of Emile Zola*, Warner Bros.

H. B. WARNER in *Lost Horizon*, Columbia.

ROLAND YOUNG in *Topper*, Roach, M-G-M.

Supporting Actress

★ ALICE BRADY in *In Old Chicago*, 20th Century-Fox.

ANDREA LEEDS in *Stage Door*, RKO Radio.

ANNE SHIRLEY in *Stella Dallas*, Goldwyn, UA.

CLAIRE TREVOR in *Dead End*, Goldwyn, UA.

DAME MAY WHITTY in *Night Must Fall*, Metro-Goldwyn-Mayer.

Directing

WILLIAM DIETERLE for *The Life of Emile Zola*, Warner Bros.

SIDNEY FRANKLIN for *The Good Earth*, Metro-Goldwyn-Mayer.

GREGORY LA CAVA for *Stage Door*, RKO Radio.

★ LEO MCCAREY for *The Awful Truth*, Columbia.

WILLIAM WELLMAN for *A Star Is Born*, Selznick, UA.

Assistant Director

(Not given after this year)

C. C. COLEMAN, JR., for *Lost Horizon*, Columbia.

RUSS SAUNDERS for *The Life of Emile Zola*, Warner Bros.

ERIC STACEY for *A Star Is Born*, Selznick, UA.

HAL WALKER for *Souls at Sea*, Paramount.

★ ROBERT WEBB for *In Old Chicago*, 20th Century-Fox.

Writing

Original Story

BLACK LEGION, Warner Bros.: ROBERT LORD.

IN OLD CHICAGO, 20th Century-Fox: NIVEN BUSCH.

THE LIFE OF EMILE ZOLA, Warner Bros.: HEINZ HERALD and GEZA HERCZEG.

100 MEN AND A GIRL, Universal: HANS KRALY.

★ A STAR IS BORN, Selznick, UA: WILLIAM A. WELLMAN and ROBERT CARSON.

Screenplay

THE AWFUL TRUTH, Columbia: VIÑA DELMAR.

CAPTAINS COURAGEOUS, Metro-Goldwyn-Mayer: MARC CONNOLLY, JOHN LEE MAHIN, and DALE VAN EVERY.

★ THE LIFE OF EMILE ZOLA, Warner Bros.: HEINZ HERALD, GEZA HERCZEG, and NORMAN REILLY RAINE.

STAGE DOOR, RKO Radio: MORRIS RYSKIND and ANTHONY VEILLER.

A STAR IS BORN, Selznick, UA: ALAN CAMPBELL, ROBERT CARSON, and DOROTHY PARKER.

Cinematography

DEAD END, Goldwyn, UA: GREGG TOLAND.

★ THE GOOD EARTH, Metro-Goldwyn-Mayer: KARL FREUND.

WINGS OVER HONOLULU, Universal: JOSEPH VALENTINE.

Art Direction

CONQUEST, Metro-Goldwyn-Mayer: CEDRIC GIBBONS and WILLIAM HORNING.

A DAMSEL IN DISTRESS, RKO Radio: CARROLL CLARK.

DEAD END, Goldwyn, UA: RICHARD DAY.

EVERY DAY'S A HOLIDAY, Major Prods., Paramount: WIARD IHNEN.

THE LIFE OF EMILE ZOLA, Warner Bros.: ANTON GROT.

★ LOST HORIZON, Columbia: STEPHEN GOOSSON.

MANHATTAN MERRY-GO-ROUND, Republic: JOHN VICTOR MACKAY.

THE PRISONER OF ZENDA, Selznick, UA: LYLE WHEELER.

SOULS AT SEA, Paramount: HANS DREIER and ROLAND ANDERSON.
VOGUES OF 1938, Wanger, UA: ALEXANDER TOLUBOFF.
WEE WILLIE WINKIE, 20th Century-Fox: WILLIAM S. DARLING and DAVID HALL.
YOU'RE A SWEETHEART, Universal: JACK OTTERSON.

Sound Recording

THE GIRL SAID NO, Grand National: GRAND NATIONAL STUDIO SOUND DEPARTMENT, A. E. KAYE, Sound Director.
HITTING A NEW HIGH. RKO Radio: RKO RADIO STUDIO SOUND DEPARTMENT, JOHN AALBERG, Sound Director.
★ THE HURRICANE, Goldwyn, UA: UNITED ARTISTS STUDIO SOUND DEPARTMENT, THOMAS T. MOULTON, Sound Director.
IN OLD CHICAGO, 20th Century-Fox: 20TH CENTURY-FOX STUDIO SOUND DEPARTMENT, E. H. HANSEN, Sound Director.
THE LIFE OF EMILE ZOLA, Warner Bros.: WARNER BROS. STUDIO SOUND DEPARTMENT, NATHAN LEVINSON, Sound Director.
LOST HORIZON, Columbia: COLUMBIA STUDIO SOUND DEPARTMENT, JOHN LIVADARY, Sound Director.
MAYTIME, M-G-M: M-G-M STUDIO SOUND DEPARTMENT, DOUGLAS SHEARER, Sound Director.
100 MEN AND A GIRL, Universal: UNIVERSAL STUDIO SOUND DEPARTMENT, HOMER TASKER, Sound Director.
TOPPER, Roach, M-G-M: HAL ROACH STUDIO SOUND DEPARTMENT, ELMER RAGUSE, Sound Director.
WELLS FARGO, Paramount: PARAMOUNT STUDIO SOUND DEPARTMENT, L. L. RYDER, Sound Director.

Film Editing

THE AWFUL TRUTH, Columbia: AL CLARK.
CAPTAINS COURAGEOUS, Metro-Goldwyn-Mayer: ELMO VERNON.
THE GOOD EARTH, Metro-Goldwyn-Mayer: BASIL WRANGELL.
★ LOST HORIZON, Columbia: GENE HAVLICK and GENE MILFORD.
100 MEN AND A GIRL, Universal: BERNARD W. BURTON.

Music

Score

IN OLD CHICAGO, 20th Century-Fox Studio Music Department: LOUIS SILVERS, Head; Score: No composer credit.
THE LIFE OF EMILE ZOLA, Warner Bros. Studio Music Department: LEO FORBSTEIN, Head; Score by MAX STEINER.
LOST HORIZON, Columbia Studio Music Department: MORRIS STOLOFF, Head; Score by DIMITRI TIOMKIN.
THE HURRICANE, Samuel Goldwyn Studio Music Department: ALFRED NEWMAN, Head; Score by ALFRED NEWMAN.
MAKE A WISH, Principal Productions: DR. HUGO RIESENFELD, Musical Director; Score by DR. HUGO RIESENFELD.
MAYTIME, Metro-Goldwyn-Mayer Studio Music Department: NAT W. FINSTON, Head; Score by HERBERT STOTHART.
★ 100 MEN AND A GIRL, Universal Studio Music Department: CHARLES PREVIN, Head; Score: No composer credit.
PORTIA ON TRIAL, Republic Studio Music Department: ALBERTO COLOMBO, Head; Score by ALBERTO COLOMBO.
THE PRISONER OF ZENDA, Selznick International Pictures Music Department: ALFRED NEWMAN, Musical Director; Score by ALFRED NEWMAN.
QUALITY STREET, RKO Radio Studio

Music Department: ROY WEBB, Musical Director; Score by ROY WEBB.

SNOW WHITE AND THE SEVEN DWARFS, Walt Disney Studio Music Department: LEIGH HARLINE, Head; Score by FRANK CHURCHILL, LEIGH HARLINE, and PAUL J. SMITH.

SOMETHING TO SING ABOUT, Grand National Studio Music Department: C. BAKALEINIKOFF, Musical Director; Score by VICTOR SCHERTZINGER.

SOULS AT SEA, Paramount Studio Music Department: BORIS MORROS, Head; Score by W. FRANKE HARLING and MILAN RODER.

WAY OUT WEST, Hal Roach Studio Music Department: MARVIN HATLEY, Head; Score by MARVIN HATLEY.

Song

REMEMBER ME from *Mr. Dodd Takes the Air*, Warner Bros.: Music by HARRY WARREN; Lyrics by AL DUBIN.

★ SWEET LEILANI from *Waikiki Wedding*, Paramount: Music and Lyrics by HARRY OWENS.

THAT OLD FEELING from *Vogues of 1938*, Wanger, UA: Music by SAMMY FAIN; Lyrics by LEW BROWN.

THEY CAN'T TAKE THAT AWAY FROM ME from *Shall We Dance*, RKO Radio: Music by GEORGE GERSHWIN; Lyrics by IRA GERSHWIN.

WHISPERS IN THE DARK from *Artists and Models*, Paramount: Music by FREDERICK HOLLANDER; Lyrics by LEO ROBIN.

Dance Direction

(Not given after this year)

BUSBY BERKELEY for *The Finale* number from *Varsity Show*, Warner Bros.

BOBBY CONNOLLY for *Too Marvelous for Words* number from *Ready, Willing and Able*, Warner Bros.

DAVE GOULD for *All God's Children Got Rhythm* number from *A Day at the Races*, Metro-Goldwyn-Mayer.

SAMMY LEE for *Swing Is Here to Stay* number from *Ali Baba Goes to Town*, 20th Century-Fox.

HARRY LOSEE for *Prince Igor Suite* number from *Thin Ice*, 20th Century-Fox.

★ HERMES PAN for *Fun House* number from *Damsel in Distress*, RKO Radio.

LEROY PRINZ for *Luau* number from *Waikiki Wedding*, Paramount.

Short Subjects

Cartoons

EDUCATED FISH, Paramount.

THE LITTLE MATCH GIRL, Charles Mintz, Columbia.

★ THE OLD MILL, Walt Disney, RKO Radio.

One Reel

A NIGHT AT THE MOVIES, Metro-Goldwyn-Mayer. (Robert Benchley)

★ PRIVATE LIFE OF THE GANNETTS, Educational.

ROMANCE OF RADIUM, Pete Smith, M-G-M. (Pete Smith Specialities)

Two Reels

DEEP SOUTH, RKO Radio. (Radio Musical Comedies)

SHOULD WIVES WORK, RKO Radio. (Leon Errol Comedies)

★ TORTURE MONEY, Metro-Goldwyn-Mayer. (Crime Doesn't Pay)

Color

THE MAN WITHOUT A COUNTRY, Warner Bros. (Broadway Brevities)

★ PENNY WISDOM, Pete Smith, M-G-M. (Pete Smith Specialties)

POPULAR SCIENCE J-7-1, Paramount.

Special Awards

MACK SENNETT, "for his lasting contribution to the comedy technique of the screen, the basic principles of which are as important today as when they were first put into practice, the Academy presents a Special Award to that master of fun, discoverer of stars, sympathetic, kindly, understanding comedy genius—Mack Sennett." (Statuette)

EDGAR BERGEN for his outstanding comedy creation, Charlie McCarthy. (Wooden statuette)

THE MUSEUM OF MODERN ART FILM LIBRARY for its significant work in collecting films dating from 1895 to the present and for the first time making available to the public the means of studying the historical and aesthetic development of the motion picture as one of the major arts. (Scroll certificate)

W. HOWARD GREENE for the color photography of *A Star Is Born*. (This Award was recommended by a committee of leading cinematographers after viewing all the color pictures made during the year.) (Plaque)

Irving G. Thalberg Memorial Award

(New Category)
DARRYL F. ZANUCK.

Scientific or Technical

Class I

AGFA ANSCO CORP. for Agfa Supreme and Agfa Ultra Speed pan motion picture negatives.

Class II

WALT DISNEY PRODS., LTD., for the design and application to production of the Multi-Plane Camera.

EASTMAN KODAK CO. for two fine-grain duplicating film stocks.

FARCIOT EDOUART and PARAMOUNT PICTURES, INC., for the development of the Paramount dual-screen transparency camera setup.

DOUGLAS SHEARER and the METRO-GOLDWYN-MAYER STUDIO SOUND DEPARTMENT for a method of varying the scanning width of variable density sound tracks (squeeze tracks) for the purpose of obtaining an increased amount of noise reduction.

Class III

JOHN ARNOLD and the METRO-GOLDWYN-MAYER STUDIO CAMERA DEPARTMENT for their improvement of the semiautomatic follow focus device and its application to all of the cameras used by the Metro-Goldwyn-Mayer Studio.

JOHN LIVADARY, Director of Sound Recording for Columbia Pictures Corp., for the application of the biplanar light valve to motion picture sound recording.

THOMAS T. MOULTON and the UNITED ARTISTS STUDIO SOUND DEPARTMENT for the application to motion picture sound recording of volume indicators that have peak reading response and linear decibel scales.

RCA MANUFACTURING CO., INC., for the introduction of the modulated high-frequency method of determining optimum photographic processing conditions for variable-width sound tracks.

JOSEPH E. ROBBINS and PARAMOUNT PICTURES, INC., for an exceptional application of acoustic principles to the soundproofing of gasoline generators and water pumps.

DOUGLAS SHEARER and the METRO-GOLDWYN-MAYER STUDIO SOUND DEPARTMENT for the design of the film drive mechanism as incorporated in the ERPI 1010 reproducer.

ELEVENTH YEAR

1938

Nominations Announced: February 12, 1939
Awards Ceremony: February 23, 1939
Biltmore Hotel—Banquet
(Host: Frank Capra)

Best Picture

THE ADVENTURES OF ROBIN HOOD, Warner Bros. Hal B. Wallis, Producer, with Henry Blanke.

ALEXANDER'S RAGTIME BAND, 20th Century-Fox. Darryl F. Zanuck, Producer, with Harry Joe Brown.

BOYS TOWN, Metro-Goldwyn-Mayer. John W. Considine, Jr., Producer.

THE CITADEL, Metro-Goldwyn-Mayer (British). Victor Saville, Producer.

FOUR DAUGHTERS, Warner Bros.-First National. Hal B. Wallis, Producer, with Henry Blanke.

GRAND ILLUSION, R.A.O., World Pictures (French). Frank Rollmer and Albert Pinkovitch, Producers.

JEZEBEL, Warner Bros. Hal B. Wallis, Producer, with Henry Blanke.

PYGMALION, Metro-Goldwyn-Mayer (British). Gabriel Pascal. Producer.

TEST PILOT, Metro-Goldwyn-Mayer. Louis D. Lighton, Producer.

★ YOU CAN'T TAKE IT WITH YOU, Columbia. Frank Capra, Producer.

Actor

CHARLES BOYER in *Algiers*, Wanger, UA.

JAMES CAGNEY in *Angels with Dirty Faces*, Warner Bros.

ROBERT DONAT in *The Citadel*, Metro-Goldwyn-Mayer (British).

LESLIE HOWARD in *Pygmalion*, Metro-Goldwyn-Mayer (British).

★ SPENCER TRACY in *Boys Town*, Metro-Goldwyn-Mayer.

Actress

FAY BAINTER in *White Banners*, Warner Bros.

★ BETTE DAVIS in *Jezebel*, Warner Bros.

WENDY HILLER in *Pygmalion*, Metro-Goldwyn-Mayer (British).

NORMA SHEARER in *Marie Antoinette*, Metro-Goldwyn-Mayer.

MARGARET SULLAVAN in *Three Comrades*, Metro-Goldwyn-Mayer.

Supporting Actor

★ WALTER BRENNAN in *Kentucky*, 20th Century-Fox.

JOHN GARFIELD in *Four Daughters*, Warner Bros.

GENE LOCKHART in *Algiers*, Wanger, UA.

ROBERT MORLEY in *Marie Antoinette*, Metro-Goldwyn-Mayer.

BASIL RATHBONE in *If I Were King*, Paramount.

Supporting Actress

★ FAY BAINTER in *Jezebel*, Warner Bros.

BEULAH BONDI in *Of Human Hearts*, Metro-Goldwyn-Mayer.

BILLIE BURKE in *Merrily We Live*, Roach, M-G-M.

SPRING BYINGTON in *You Can't Take It with You*, Columbia.

MILIZA KORJUS in *The Great Waltz*, Metro-Goldwyn-Mayer.

Directing

★ FRANK CAPRA for *You Can't Take It with You*, Columbia.

MICHAEL CURTIZ for *Angels with Dirty Faces*, Warner Bros.

MICHAEL CURTIZ for *Four Daughters*, Warner Bros.

NORMAN TAUROG for *Boys Town*, Metro-Goldwyn-Mayer.

KING VIDOR for *The Citadel*, Metro-Goldwyn-Mayer.

Writing

Original Story

ALEXANDER'S RAGTIME BAND, 20th Century-Fox: IRVING BERLIN.

ANGELS WITH DIRTY FACES, Warner Bros.: ROWLAND BROWN.

BLOCKADE, Wanger, UA: JOHN HOWARD LAWSON.

★ BOYS TOWN, Metro-Goldwyn-Mayer: ELEANOR GRIFFIN and DORE SCHARY.

MAD ABOUT MUSIC, Universal: MARCELLA BURKE and FREDERICK KOHNER.

TEST PILOT, Metro-Goldwyn-Mayer: FRANK WEAD.

Screenplay

BOYS TOWN, Metro-Goldwyn-Mayer: JOHN MEEHAN and DORE SCHARY.

THE CITADEL, Metro-Goldwyn-Mayer (British): IAN DALRYMPLE, ELIZABETH HILL, and FRANK WEAD.

FOUR DAUGHTERS, Warner Bros.: LENORE COFFEE and JULIUS J. EPSTEIN.

★ PYGMALION, Metro-Goldwyn-Mayer (British): GEORGE BERNARD SHAW; Adaptation by IAN DALRYMPLE, CECIL LEWIS, and W. P. LIPSCOMB.

YOU CAN'T TAKE IT WITH YOU, Columbia: ROBERT RISKIN.

Cinematography

ALGIERS, Wanger, UA: JAMES WONG HOWE.

ARMY GIRL, Republic: ERNEST MILLER and HARRY WILD.

THE BUCCANEER, Paramount: VICTOR MILNER.

★ THE GREAT WALTZ, Metro-Goldwyn-Mayer: JOSEPH RUTTENBERG.

JEZEBEL, Warner Bros.: ERNEST HALLER.

MAD ABOUT MUSIC, Universal: JOSEPH VALENTINE.

MERRILY WE LIVE, Roach, M-G-M: NORBERT BRODINE.

SUEZ, 20th Century-Fox: PEVERELL MARLEY.

VIVACIOUS LADY, RKO Radio: ROBERT DE GRASSE.

YOU CAN'T TAKE IT WITH YOU, Columbia: JOSEPH WALKER.

THE YOUNG IN HEART, Selznick, UA: LEON SHAMROY.

Art Direction

★ THE ADVENTURES OF ROBIN HOOD, Warner Bros.: CARL J. WEYL.

ADVENTURES OF TOM SAWYER, Selznick, UA: LYLE WHEELER.

ALEXANDER'S RAGTIME BAND, 20th Century-Fox: BERNARD HERZBRUN and BORIS LEVEN.

ALGIERS, Wanger, UA: ALEXANDER TOLUBOFF.

CAREFREE, RKO Radio: VAN NEST POLGLASE.

GOLDWYN FOLLIES, Goldwyn, UA: RICHARD DAY.

HOLIDAY, Columbia: STEPHEN GOOSSON and LIONEL BANKS.

IF I WERE KING, Paramount: HANS DREIER and JOHN GOODMAN.

MAD ABOUT MUSIC, Universal: JACK OTTERSON.

MARIE ANTOINETTE, Metro-Goldwyn-Mayer: CEDRIC GIBBONS.

MERRILY WE LIVE, Roach, M-G-M: CHARLES D. HALL.

Sound Recording

ARMY GIRL, Republic: REPUBLIC STUDIO SOUND DEPARTMENT. CHARLES LOOTENS, Sound Director.

* THE COWBOY AND THE LADY, Goldwyn, UA: UNITED ARTISTS STUDIO SOUND DEPARTMENT, THOMAS MOULTON, Sound Director.

FOUR DAUGHTERS, Warner Bros: WARNER BROS. STUDIO SOUND DEPARTMENT, NATHAN LEVINSON. Sound Director.

IF I WERE KING, Paramount: PARAMOUNT STUDIO SOUND DEPARTMENT, L. L. RYDER, Sound Director.

MERRILY WE LIVE, Roach. M-G-M: HAL ROACH STUDIO SOUND DEPARTMENT, ELMER RAGUSE, Sound Director.

SUEZ, 20th Century-Fox: 20TH CENTURY-FOX STUDIO SOUND DEPARTMENT, EDMUND HANSEN, Sound Director.

SWEETHEARTS, M-G-M: M-G-M STUDIO SOUND DEPARTMENT, DOUGLAS SHEARER. Sound Director.

THAT CERTAIN AGE, Universal: UNIVERSAL STUDIO SOUND DEPARTMENT, BERNARD B. BROWN, Sound Director.

VIVACIOUS LADY, RKO Radio: RKO RADIO STUDIO SOUND DEPARTMENT, JAMES WILKINSON, Sound Director.

YOU CAN'T TAKE IT WITH YOU, Columbia: COLUMBIA STUDIO SOUND DEPARTMENT, JOHN LIVADARY, Sound Director.

Film Editing

* THE ADVENTURES OF ROBIN HOOD, Warner Bros.: RALPH DAWSON.

ALEXANDER'S RAGTIME BAND, 20th Century-Fox: BARBARA MCLEAN.

THE GREAT WALTZ, Metro-Goldwyn-Mayer: TOM HELD.

TEST PILOT, Metro-Goldwyn-Mayer: TOM HELD.

YOU CAN'T TAKE IT WITH YOU, Columbia: GENE HAVLICK.

Music

Scoring

* ALEXANDER'S RAGTIME BAND, 20th Century-Fox: ALFRED NEWMAN.

CAREFREE, RKO Radio: VICTOR BARAVALLE.

GIRLS SCHOOL, Columbia: MORRIS STOLOFF and GREGORY STONE.

GOLDWYN FOLLIES, Goldwyn, UA: ALFRED NEWMAN.

JEZEBEL, Warner Bros.: MAX STEINER.

MAD ABOUT MUSIC, Universal: CHARLES PREVIN and FRANK SKINNER.

STORM OVER BENGAL, Republic: CY FEUER.

SWEETHEARTS, Metro-Goldwyn-Mayer: HERBERT STOTHART.

THERE GOES MY HEART, Hal Roach, UA: MARVIN HATLEY.

TROPIC HOLIDAY, Paramount: BORIS MORROS.

THE YOUNG IN HEART, Selznick, UA: FRANZ WAXMAN.

Original Score

* THE ADVENTURES OF ROBIN HOOD, Warner Bros.: ERICH WOLFGANG KORNGOLD.

ARMY GIRL, Republic: VICTOR YOUNG.

BLOCKADE, Walter Wanger, UA: WERNER JANSSEN.

BLOCKHEADS, Hal Roach, UA: MARVIN HATLEY.

BREAKING THE ICE, RKO Radio: VICTOR YOUNG.

THE COWBOY AND THE LADY, Goldwyn, UA: ALFRED NEWMAN.

IF I WERE KING, Paramount: RICHARD HAGEMAN.

MARIE ANTOINETTE, Metro-Goldwyn-Mayer: HERBERT STOTHART.

PACIFIC LINER, RKO Radio: RUSSELL BENNETT.

SUEZ, 20th Century-Fox: LOUIS SILVERS.

THE YOUNG IN HEART, Selznick, UA: FRANZ WAXMAN.

Song

ALWAYS AND ALWAYS from *Mannequin*, Metro-Goldwyn-Mayer: Music by EDWARD WARD; Lyrics by CHET FORREST and BOB WRIGHT.

CHANGE PARTNERS AND DANCE WITH ME from *Carefree*, RKO Radio: Music and Lyrics by IRVING BERLIN.

THE COWBOY AND THE LADY from *The Cowboy and the Lady*, Goldwyn, UA: Music by LIONEL NEWMAN; Lyrics by ARTHUR QUENZER.

DUST from *Under Western Stars*, Republic: Music and Lyrics by JOHNNY MARVIN.

JEEPERS CREEPERS from *Going Places*, Warner Bros.: Music by HARRY WARREN; Lyrics by JOHNNY MERCER.

MERRILY WE LIVE from *Merrily We Live*, Roach, M-G-M: Music by PHIL CRAIG; Lyrics by ARTHUR QUENZER.

A MIST OVER THE MOON from *The Lady Objects*, Columbia: Music by BEN OAKLAND; Lyrics by OSCAR HAMMERSTEIN II.

MY OWN from *That Certain Age*, Universal: Music by JIMMY MCHUGH; Lyrics by HAROLD ADAMSON.

NOW IT CAN BE TOLD from *Alexander's Ragtime Band*, 20th Century-Fox: Music and Lyrics by IRVING BERLIN.

⋆ THANKS FOR THE MEMORY from *Big Broadcast of 1938*, Paramount: Music by RALPH RAINGER; Lyrics by LEO ROBIN.

Short Subjects

Cartoons

BRAVE LITTLE TAILOR, Walt Disney, RKO Radio.

⋆ FERDINAND THE BULL, Walt Disney, RKO Radio.

GOOD SCOUTS, Walt Disney, RKO Radio.

HUNKY AND SPUNKY, Paramount.

MOTHER GOOSE GOES HOLLYWOOD, Walt Disney, RKO Radio.

One Reel

THE GREAT HEART, Metro-Goldwyn-Mayer. (Miniature)

⋆ THAT MOTHERS MIGHT LIVE, Metro-Goldwyn-Mayer. (Miniature)

TIMBER TOPPERS, 20th Century-Fox. (Ed Thorgensen-Sports)

Two Reels

DECLARATION OF INDEPENDENCE, Warner Bros. (Historical Featurette)

SWINGTIME IN THE MOVIES, Warner Bros. (Broadway Brevities)

THEY'RE ALWAYS CAUGHT, Metro-Goldwyn-Mayer. (Crime Doesn't Pay)

Special Awards

DEANNA DURBIN and MICKEY ROONEY for their significant contribution in bringing to the screen the spirit and personification of youth, and as juvenile players setting a high standard of ability and achievement. (Miniature statuette trophies)

HARRY M. WARNER in recognition of patriotic service in the production of historical short subjects presenting significant episodes in the early struggle of the American people for liberty. (Scroll)

WALT DISNEY for *Snow White and the Seven Dwarfs*, recognized as a significant screen innovation that has charmed millions and pioneered a great new entertainment field for the motion picture cartoon. (One statuette—seven miniature statuettes)

OLIVER MARSH and ALLEN DAVEY for the color cinematography of the Metro-Goldwyn-Mayer production, *Sweethearts*. (Plaques)

For outstanding achievement in creating Special Photographic and Sound Effects in the Paramount production, *Spawn of the North*. Special Effects by GORDON JENNINGS, assisted by JAN DOMELA, DEV JENNINGS, IRMIN ROBERTS, and ART SMITH; Transparencies by FARCIOT EDOUART, assisted by LOYAL GRIGGS; Sound Effects by LOREN RYDER, assisted by HARRY MILLS, LOUIS H. MESENKOP, and WALTER OBERST. (Plaques)

J. ARTHUR BALL for his outstanding contributions to the advancement of color in Motion Picture Photography. (Scroll)

Irving G. Thalberg Memorial Award

HAL B. WALLIS.

Scientific or Technical

Class I

None.

Class II

None.

Class III

JOHN AALBERG and the RKO RADIO STUDIO SOUND DEPARTMENT for the application of compression to variable-area recording in motion picture production.

BYRON HASKIN and the SPECIAL EFFECTS DEPARTMENT of WARNER BROS. STUDIO for pioneering the development and for the first practical application to motion picture production of the triple-head background projector.

TWELFTH YEAR

1939

Nominations Announced: February 12, 1940
Awards Ceremony: February 29, 1940
Ambassador Hotel—Banquet
(MC: Bob Hope for last half only)

Best Picture

DARK VICTORY, Warner Bros. David Lewis, Producer.

★ GONE WITH THE WIND, Selznick, M-G-M. David O. Selznick, Producer.

GOODBYE, MR. CHIPS, Metro-Goldwyn-Mayer (British). Victor Saville, Producer.

LOVE AFFAIR, RKO Radio. Leo McCarey, Producer.

MR. SMITH GOES TO WASHINGTON, Columbia. Frank Capra, Producer.

NINOTCHKA, Metro-Goldwyn-Mayer. Sidney Franklin, Producer.

OF MICE AND MEN, Roach, UA. Lewis Milestone, Producer.

STAGECOACH, Wanger, UA. Walter Wanger, Producer.

WIZARD OF OZ, Metro-Goldwyn-Mayer. Mervyn LeRoy, Producer.

WUTHERING HEIGHTS, Goldwyn, UA. Samuel Goldwyn, Producer.

Actor

★ ROBERT DONAT in *Goodbye, Mr. Chips*, Metro-Goldwyn-Mayer (British).

CLARK GABLE in *Gone with the Wind*, Selznick, M-G-M.

LAURENCE OLIVIER in *Wuthering Heights*, Goldwyn, UA.

MICKEY ROONEY in *Babes in Arms*, Metro-Goldwyn-Mayer.

JAMES STEWART in *Mr. Smith Goes to Washington*, Columbia.

Actress

BETTE DAVIS in *Dark Victory*, Warner Bros.

IRENE DUNNE in *Love Affair*, RKO Radio.

GRETA GARBO in *Ninotchka*, Metro-Goldwyn-Mayer.

GREER GARSON in *Goodbye, Mr. Chips*, Metro-Goldwyn-Mayer (British).

★ VIVIEN LEIGH in *Gone with the Wind*, Selznick, M-G-M.

Supporting Actor

BRIAN AHERNE in *Juarez*, Warner Bros.

HARRY CAREY in *Mr. Smith Goes to Washington*, Columbia.

BRIAN DONLEVY in *Beau Geste*, Paramount.

★ THOMAS MITCHELL in *Stagecoach*, Wanger, UA.

CLAUDE RAINS in *Mr. Smith Goes to Washington*, Columbia.

Supporting Actress

OLIVIA DE HAVILLAND in *Gone with the Wind*, Selznick, M-G-M.

GERALDINE FITZGERALD in *Wuthering Heights*, Goldwyn, UA.

★ HATTIE McDANIEL in *Gone with the Wind*, Selznick, M-G-M.

EDNA MAY OLIVER in *Drums along the Mohawk*, 20th Century-Fox.

MARIA OUSPENSKAYA in *Love Affair*, RKO Radio.

Directing

FRANK CAPRA for *Mr. Smith Goes to Washington*, Columbia.

★ VICTOR FLEMING for *Gone with the Wind*, Selznick, M-G-M.

JOHN FORD for *Stagecoach*, Wanger, UA.

SAM WOOD for *Goodbye, Mr. Chips*, Metro-Goldwyn-Mayer (British).

WILLIAM WYLER for *Wuthering Heights*, Goldwyn, UA.

Writing

Original Story

BACHELOR MOTHER, RKO Radio: FELIX JACKSON.

LOVE AFFAIR, RKO Radio: MILDRED CRAM and LEO MCCAREY.

★ MR. SMITH GOES TO WASHINGTON, Columbia: LEWIS R. FOSTER.

NINOTCHKA, Metro-Goldwyn-Mayer: MELCHIOR LENGYEL.

YOUNG MR. LINCOLN, 20th Century-Fox: LAMAR TROTTI.

Screenplay

★ GONE WITH THE WIND, Selznick, M-G-M: SIDNEY HOWARD.

GOODBYE, MR. CHIPS, Metro-Goldwyn-Mayer (British): ERIC MASCHWITZ, R. C. SHERRIFF, and CLAUDINE WEST.

MR. SMITH GOES TO WASHINGTON, Columbia: SIDNEY BUCHMAN.

NINOTCHKA, Metro-Goldwyn-Mayer: CHARLES BRACKETT, WALTER REISCH, and BILLY WILDER.

WUTHERING HEIGHTS, Goldwyn, UA: BEN HECHT and CHARLES MACARTHUR.

Cinematography

Black and White

STAGECOACH, Wanger, UA: BERT GLENNON.

★ WUTHERING HEIGHTS, Goldwyn, UA: GREGG TOLAND.

Color

★ GONE WITH THE WIND, Selznick, M-G-M: ERNEST HALLER and RAY RENNAHAN.

THE PRIVATE LIVES OF ELIZABETH AND ESSEX, Warner Bros.: SOL POLITO and W. HOWARD GREENE.

Art Direction

BEAU GESTE, Paramount: HANS DREIER and ROBERT ODELL.

CAPTAIN FURY, Roach, UA: CHARLES D. HALL.

FIRST LOVE, Universal: JACK OTTERSON and MARTIN OBZINA.

★ GONE WITH THE WIND, Selznick, M-G-M: LYLE WHEELER.

LOVE AFFAIR, RKO Radio: VAN NEST POLGLASE and AL HERMAN.

MAN OF CONQUEST, Republic: JOHN VICTOR MACKAY.

MR. SMITH GOES TO WASHINGTON, Columbia: LIONEL BANKS.

THE PRIVATE LIVES OF ELIZABETH AND ESSEX, Warner Bros.: ANTON GROT.

THE RAINS CAME, 20th Century-Fox: WILLIAM DARLING and GEORGE DUDLEY.

STAGECOACH, Wanger, UA: ALEXANDER TOLUBOFF.

THE WIZARD OF OZ, Metro-Goldwyn-Mayer: CEDRIC GIBBONS and WILLIAM A. HORNING.

WUTHERING HEIGHTS, Goldwyn, UA: JAMES BASEVI.

Sound Recording

BALALAIKA, M-G-M: M-G-M STUDIO SOUND DEPARTMENT, DOUGLAS SHEARER, Sound Director.

GONE WITH THE WIND, Selznick, M-G-M: SAMUEL GOLDWYN STUDIO SOUND DEPARTMENT, THOMAS T. MOULTON, Sound Director.

GOODBYE, MR. CHIPS, M-G-M (British): DENHAM STUDIO SOUND DEPARTMENT, A. W. WATKINS, Sound Director.

THE GREAT VICTOR HERBERT, Paramount: PARAMOUNT STUDIO SOUND DEPARTMENT, LOREN RYDER, Sound Director.

THE HUNCHBACK OF NOTRE DAME. RKO Radio: RKO RADIO STUDIO SOUND DEPARTMENT, JOHN AALBERG, Sound Director.

MAN OF CONQUEST, Republic: REPUBLIC STUDIO SOUND DEPARTMENT, C. L. LOOTENS, Sound Director.

MR. SMITH GOES TO WASHINGTON, Columbia: COLUMBIA STUDIO SOUND DEPARTMENT, JOHN LIVADARY. Sound Director.

OF MICE AND MEN, Roach. M-G-M: HAL ROACH STUDIO SOUND DEPARTMENT, ELMER RAGUSE. Sound Director.

THE PRIVATE LIVES OF ELIZABETH AND ESSEX, Warner Bros.: WARNER BROS. STUDIO SOUND DEPARTMENT, NATHAN LEVINSON, Sound Director.

THE RAINS CAME, 20th Century-Fox: 20TH CENTURY-FOX STUDIO SOUND DEPARTMENT, E. H. HANSEN, Sound Director.

★ WHEN TOMORROW COMES, Universal: UNIVERSAL STUDIO SOUND DEPARTMENT, BERNARD B. BROWN, Sound Director.

Film Editing

★ GONE WITH THE WIND, Selznick, M-G-M: HAL C. KERN and JAMES E. NEWCOM.

GOODBYE, MR. CHIPS, Metro-Goldwyn-Mayer (British): CHARLES FREND.

MR. SMITH GOES TO WASHINGTON, Columbia: GENE HAVLICK and AL CLARK.

THE RAINS CAME, 20th Century-Fox: BARBARA MCLEAN.

STAGECOACH, Wanger, UA: OTHO LOVERING and DOROTHY SPENCER.

Music

Scoring

BABES IN ARMS, Metro-Goldwyn-Mayer: ROGER EDENS and GEORGE E. STOLL.

FIRST LOVE, Universal: CHARLES PREVIN.

THE GREAT VICTOR HERBERT, Paramount: PHIL BOUTELJE and ARTHUR LANGE.

THE HUNCHBACK OF NOTRE DAME, RKO Radio: ALFRED NEWMAN.

INTERMEZZO, Selznick, UA: LOU FORBES.

MR. SMITH GOES TO WASHINGTON, Columbia: DIMITRI TIOMKIN.

OF MICE AND MEN, Roach, UA: AARON COPLAND.

THE PRIVATE LIVES OF ELIZABETH AND ESSEX, Warner Bros.: ERICH WOLFGANG KORNGOLD.

SHE MARRIED A COP, Republic: CY FEUER.

★ STAGECOACH, Walter Wanger; UA: RICHARD HAGEMAN, FRANK HARLING, JOHN LEIPOLD, and LEO SHUKEN.

SWANEE RIVER, 20th Century-Fox: LOUIS SILVERS.

THEY SHALL HAVE MUSIC, Goldwyn, UA: ALFRED NEWMAN.

WAY DOWN SOUTH, Lesser, RKO Radio: VICTOR YOUNG.

Original Score

DARK VICTORY, Warner Bros.: MAX STEINER.

ETERNALLY YOURS, Walter Wanger, UA: WERNER JANSSEN.

GOLDEN BOY, Columbia: VICTOR YOUNG.

GONE WITH THE WIND, Selznick, M-G-M: MAX STEINER.

GULLIVER'S TRAVELS, Paramount: VICTOR YOUNG.
THE MAN IN THE IRON MASK, Small, UA: LUD GLUSKIN and LUCIEN MORAWECK.
MAN OF CONQUEST, Republic: VICTOR YOUNG.
NURSE EDITH CAVELL, RKO Radio: ANTHONY COLLINS.
OF MICE AND MEN, Roach, UA: AARON COPLAND.
THE RAINS CAME, 20th Century-Fox: ALFRED NEWMAN.
★ THE WIZARD OF OZ, Metro-Goldwyn-Mayer: HERBERT STOTHART.
WUTHERING HEIGHTS, Goldwyn, UA: ALFRED NEWMAN.

Song

FAITHFUL FOREVER from *Gulliver's Travels*, Paramount: Music by RALPH RAINGER; Lyrics by LEO ROBIN.
I POURED MY HEART INTO A SONG from *Second Fiddle*, 20th Century-Fox: Music and Lyrics by IRVING BERLIN.
★ OVER THE RAINBOW from *The Wizard of Oz*, Metro-Goldwyn-Mayer: Music by HAROLD ARLEN, Lyrics by E. Y. HARBURG.
WISHING from *Love Affair*, RKO Radio: Music and Lyrics by BUDDY DE SYLVA.

Special Effects

(New Category)
GONE WITH THE WIND, Selznick, M-G-M: JOHN R. COSGROVE, FRED ALBIN, and ARTHUR JOHNS.
ONLY ANGELS HAVE WINGS, Columbia: ROY DAVIDSON and EDWIN C. HAHN.
PRIVATE LIVES OF ELIZABETH AND ESSEX, Warner Bros.: BYRON HASKIN and NATHAN LEVINSON.
★ THE RAINS CAME, 20th Century-Fox: E. H. HANSEN and FRED SERSEN.
TOPPER TAKES A TRIP, Roach, UA: ROY SEAWRIGHT.
UNION PACIFIC, Paramount: FARCIOT EDOUART, GORDON JENNINGS, and LOREN RYDER.
THE WIZARD OF OZ, Metro-Goldwyn-Mayer: A. ARNOLD GILLESPIE and DOUGLAS SHEARER.

Short Subjects

Cartoons

DETOURING AMERICA, Warner Bros.
PEACE ON EARTH, Metro-Goldwyn-Mayer.
THE POINTER, Walt Disney, RKO Radio.
★ THE UGLY DUCKLING, Walt Disney, RKO Radio.

One Reel

★ BUSY LITTLE BEARS, Paramount: (Paragraphics)
INFORMATION PLEASE, RKO Radio.
PROPHET WITHOUT HONOR, Metro-Goldwyn-Mayer. (Miniature)
SWORD FISHING, Warner Bros. (Vitaphone Varieties)

Two Reels

DRUNK DRIVING, Metro-Goldwyn-Mayer. (Crime Doesn't Pay)
FIVE TIMES FIVE, RKO Radio. (Special)
★ SONS OF LIBERTY, Warner Bros. (Historical Featurette)

Special Awards

DOUGLAS FAIRBANKS (Commemorative Award)—recognizing the unique and outstanding contribution of Douglas Fairbanks, first president of the Academy, to the international development of the motion picture. (Statuette)
MOTION PICTURE RELIEF FUND—acknowledging the outstanding services to the industry during the past year of the Motion

Picture Relief Fund and its progressive leadership. Presented to JEAN HERSHOLT, president; RALPH MORGAN, chairman of the Executive Committee; RALPH BLOCK, first vice president; CONRAD NAGEL. (Plaques)

JUDY GARLAND for her outstanding performance as a screen juvenile during the past year. (Miniature statuette)

WILLIAM CAMERON MENZIES for outstanding achievement in the use of color for the enhancement of dramatic mood in the production of *Gone with the Wind*. (Plaque)

TECHNICOLOR COMPANY for its contributions in successfully bringing three-color feature production to the screen. (Statuette)

Irving G. Thalberg Memorial Award

DAVID O. SELZNICK.

Scientific or Technical

Class I

None.

Class II

None.

Class III

GEORGE ANDERSON of Warner Bros. Studio for an improved positive head for sun arcs.

JOHN ARNOLD of Metro-Goldwyn-Mayer Studio for the M-G-M mobile camera crane.

THOMAS T. MOULTON, FRED ALBIN, and the SOUND DEPARTMENT of the SAMUEL GOLDWYN STUDIO for the origination and application of the Delta db test to sound recording in motion pictures.

FARCIOT EDOUART, JOSEPH E. ROBBINS, WILLIAM RUDOLPH, AND PARAMOUNT PICTURES, INC., for the design and construction of a quiet, portable treadmill.

EMERY HUSE AND RALPH B. ATKINSON of Eastman Kodak Co. for their specifications for chemical analysis of photographic developers and fixing baths.

HAROLD NYE of Warner Bros. Studio for a miniature incandescent spot lamp.

A. J. TONDREAU of Warner Bros. Studio for the design and manufacture of an improved sound track printer.

Multiple Award for important contributions in cooperative development of, new, improved process projection equipment:

F. R. ABBOTT, HALLER BELT, ALAN COOK, and BAUSCH & LOMB OPTICAL CO. for faster projection lenses

MITCHELL CAMERA CO. for a new type process projection head

MOLE-RICHARDSON CO. for a new type automatically controlled projection arc lamp

CHARLES HANDLEY, DAVID JOY, and NATIONAL CARBON CO. for improved and more stable high-intensity carbons

WINTON HOCH and TECHNICOLOR MOTION PICTURE CORP. for an auxiliary optical system

DON MUSGRAVE and SELZNICK INTERNATIONAL PICTURES, INC., for pioneering in the use of coordinated equipment in the production of *Gone with the Wind*.

THIRTEENTH YEAR

1940

Nominations Announced: February 10, 1941
Awards Ceremony: February 27, 1941
Biltmore Hotel—Banquet
(Host: Walter Wanger, banquet addressed via radio by President Franklin D. Roosevelt)

Best Picture

ALL THIS, AND HEAVEN TOO, Warner Bros. Jack L. Warner and Hal B. Wallis, Producers, with David Lewis.
FOREIGN CORRESPONDENT, Wanger, UA. Walter Wanger, Producer.
THE GRAPES OF WRATH, 20th Century-Fox. Darryl F. Zanuck, Producer, with Nunnally Johnson.
THE GREAT DICTATOR, Chaplin, UA. Charles Chaplin, Producer.
KITTY FOYLE, RKO Radio. David Hempstead, Producer.
THE LETTER, Warner Bros. Hal B. Wallis, Producer.
THE LONG VOYAGE HOME, Argosy-Wanger, UA. John Ford, Producer.
OUR TOWN, Lesser, UA. Sol Lesser, Producer.
THE PHILADELPHIA STORY, Metro-Goldwyn-Mayer. Joseph L. Mankiewicz, Producer.
★ REBECCA, Selznick International, UA. David O. Selznick, Producer.

Actor

CHARLES CHAPLIN in *The Great Dictator*, Chaplin, UA.
HENRY FONDA in *The Grapes of Wrath*, 20th Century-Fox.
RAYMOND MASSEY in *Abe Lincoln in Illinois*, RKO Radio.
LAURENCE OLIVIER in *Rebecca*, Selznick-UA.
★ JAMES STEWART in *The Philadelphia Story*, Metro-Goldwyn-Mayer.

Actress

BETTE DAVIS in *The Letter*, Warner Bros.
JOAN FONTAINE in *Rebecca*, Selznick, UA.
KATHARINE HEPBURN in *The Philadelphia Story*, Metro-Goldwyn-Mayer.
★ GINGER ROGERS in *Kitty Foyle*, RKO Radio.
MARTHA SCOTT in *Our Town*, Lesser, UA.

Supporting Actor

ALBERT BASSERMANN in *Foreign Correspondent*, Wanger, UA.
★ WALTER BRENNAN in *The Westerner*, Goldwyn, UA.
WILLIAM GARGAN in *They Knew What They Wanted*, RKO Radio.
JACK OAKIE in *The Great Dictator*, Chaplin, UA.
JAMES STEPHENSON in *The Letter*, Warner Bros.

Supporting Actress

JUDITH ANDERSON in *Rebecca*, Selznick, UA.

★ JANE DARWELL in *The Grapes of Wrath*, 20th Century-Fox.
RUTH HUSSEY in *The Philadelphia Story*, Metro-Goldwyn-Mayer.
BARBARA O'NEIL in *All This, and Heaven Too*, Warner Bros.
MARJORIE RAMBEAU in *Primrose Path*, RKO Radio.

Directing

GEORGE CUKOR for *The Philadelphia Story*, Metro-Goldwyn-Mayer.
★ JOHN FORD for *The Grapes of Wrath*, 20th Century-Fox.
ALFRED HITCHCOCK for *Rebecca*, Selznick, UA.
SAM WOOD for *Kitty Foyle*, RKO Radio.
WILLIAM WYLER for *The Letter*, Warner Bros.

Writing

Original Story

★ ARISE, MY LOVE, Paramount: BENJAMIN GLAZER and JOHN S. TOLDY.
COMRADE X, Metro-Goldwyn-Mayer: WALTER REISCH.
EDISON THE MAN, Metro-Goldwyn-Mayer: HUGO BUTLER and DORE SCHARY.
MY FAVORITE WIFE, RKO Radio: LEO MCCAREY, BELLA SPEWACK, and SAMUEL SPEWACK.
THE WESTERNER, Goldwyn, UA: STUART N. LAKE.

Original Screenplay

ANGELS OVER BROADWAY, Columbia: BEN HECHT.
DR. EHRLICH'S MAGIC BULLET, Warner Bros.: NORMAN BURNSIDE, HEINZ HERALD, and JOHN HUSTON.
FOREIGN CORRESPONDENT, Wanger, UA: CHARLES BENNETT and JOAN HARRISON.
THE GREAT DICTATOR, Chaplin, UA: CHARLES CHAPLIN.
★ THE GREAT MCGINTY, Paramount: PRESTON STURGES.

Screenplay

THE GRAPES OF WRATH, 20th Century-Fox: NUNNALLY JOHNSON.
KITTY FOYLE, RKO Radio: DALTON TRUMBO.
THE LONG VOYAGE HOME, Argosy-Wanger, UA: DUDLEY NICHOLS.
★ THE PHILADELPHIA STORY, Metro-Goldwyn-Mayer: DONALD OGDEN STEWART.
REBECCA, Selznick, UA: ROBERT E. SHERWOOD and JOAN HARRISON.

Cinematography

Black and White

ABE LINCOLN IN ILLINOIS, RKO Radio: JAMES WONG HOWE.
ALL THIS, AND HEAVEN TOO, Warner Bros.: ERNEST HALLER.
ARISE, MY LOVE, Paramount: CHARLES B. LANG, JR.
BOOM TOWN, Metro-Goldwyn-Mayer: HAROLD ROSSON.
FOREIGN CORRESPONDENT, Wanger, UA: RUDOLPH MATE.
THE LETTER, Warner Bros.: GAETANO GAUDIO.
THE LONG VOYAGE HOME, Argosy-Wanger, UA: GREGG TOLAND.
★ REBECCA, Selznick, UA: GEORGE BARNES.
SPRING PARADE, Universal: JOSEPH VALENTINE.
WATERLOO BRIDGE, Metro-Goldwyn-Mayer: JOSEPH RUTTENBERG.

Color

BITTER SWEET, Metro-Goldwyn-Mayer: OLIVER T. MARSH and ALLEN DAVEY.
THE BLUE BIRD, 20th Century-Fox: ARTHUR MILLER and RAY RENNAHAN.
DOWN ARGENTINE WAY, 20th Century-Fox: LEON SHAMROY and RAY RENNAHAN.
NORTH WEST MOUNTED POLICE,

Paramount: VICTOR MILNER and W. HOWARD GREENE.

NORTHWEST PASSAGE, Metro-Goldwyn-Mayer: SIDNEY WAGNER and WILLIAM V. SKALL.

★ THE THIEF OF BAGDAD, Korda, UA (British): GEORGE PERINAL.

Art Direction

Black and White

ARISE, MY LOVE, Paramount: HANS DREIER and ROBERT USHER.

ARIZONA, Columbia: LIONEL BANKS and ROBERT PETERSON.

THE BOYS FROM SYRACUSE, Universal: JOHN OTTERSON.

DARK COMMAND, Republic: JOHN VICTOR MACKAY.

FOREIGN CORRESPONDENT, Wanger, UA: ALEXANDER GOLITZEN.

LILLIAN RUSSELL, 20th Century-Fox: RICHARD DAY and JOSEPH C. WRIGHT.

MY FAVORITE WIFE, RKO Radio: VAN NEST POLGLASE and MARK-LEE KIRK.

MY SON, MY SON, Small, UA: JOHN DUCASSE SCHULZE.

OUR TOWN, Lesser, UA: LEWIS J. RACHMIL.

★ PRIDE AND PREJUDICE, Metro-Goldwyn-Mayer: CEDRIC GIBBONS and PAUL GROESSE.

REBECCA, Selznick, UA: LYLE WHEELER.

THE SEA HAWK, Warner Bros.: ANTON GROT.

THE WESTERNER, Goldwyn, UA: JAMES BASEVI.

Color

BITTER SWEET, Metro-Goldwyn-Mayer: CEDRIC GIBBONS and JOHN S. DETLIE.

DOWN ARGENTINE WAY, 20th Century-Fox: RICHARD DAY and JOSEPH C. WRIGHT.

NORTH WEST MOUNTED POLICE, Paramount: HANS DREIER and ROLAND ANDERSON.

★ THE THIEF OF BAGDAD, Korda, UA: VINCENT KORDA.

Sound Recording

BEHIND THE NEWS, Republic: REPUBLIC STUDIO SOUND DEPARTMENT, CHARLES LOOTENS, Sound Director.

CAPTAIN CAUTION. Roach. UA: HAL ROACH STUDIO SOUND DEPARTMENT, ELMER RAGUSE. Sound Director.

THE GRAPES OF WRATH. 20th Century-Fox: 20TH CENTURY-FOX STUDIO SOUND DEPARTMENT, E. H. HANSEN, Sound Director.

THE HOWARDS OF VIRGINIA, Columbia: GENERAL SERVICE STUDIO SOUND DEPARTMENT, JACK WHITNEY, Sound Director.

KITTY FOYLE, RKO Radio: RKO RADIO STUDIO SOUND DEPARTMENT, JOHN AALBERG, Sound Director.

NORTH WEST MOUNTED POLICE, Paramount: PARAMOUNT STUDIO SOUND DEPARTMENT, LOREN RYDER, Sound Director.

OUR TOWN, Lesser, UA: SAMUEL GOLDWYN STUDIO SOUND DEPARTMENT, THOMAS MOULTON, Sound Director.

THE SEA HAWK. Warner Bros.: WARNER BROS. STUDIO SOUND DEPARTMENT, NATHAN LEVINSON, Sound Director.

SPRING PARADE, Universal: UNIVERSAL STUDIO SOUND DEPARTMENT, BERNARD B. BROWN, Sound Director.

★ STRIKE UP THE BAND, M-G-M: M-G-M STUDIO SOUND DEPARTMENT, DOUGLAS SHEARER, Sound Director.

TOO MANY HUSBANDS, Columbia: COLUMBIA STUDIO SOUND DEPARTMENT, JOHN LIVADARY, Sound Director.

Film Editing

THE GRAPES OF WRATH, 20th Century-Fox: ROBERT E. SIMPSON.

THE LETTER, Warner Bros.: WARREN LOW.

THE LONG VOYAGE HOME, Argosy-Wanger, UA: SHERMAN TODD.

★ NORTH WEST MOUNTED POLICE, Paramount: ANNE BAUCHENS.

REBECCA, Selznick, UA: HAL C. KERN.

Music

Scoring

ARISE, MY LOVE, Paramount: VICTOR YOUNG.

HIT PARADE OF 1941, Republic: CY FEUER.

IRENE, Imperadio, RKO Radio: ANTHONY COLLINS.

OUR TOWN, Sol Lesser, UA: AARON COPLAND.

THE SEA HAWK, Warner Bros.: ERICH WOLFGANG KORNGOLD.

SECOND CHORUS, Paramount: ARTIE SHAW.

SPRING PARADE, Universal: CHARLES PREVIN.

STRIKE UP THE BAND, Metro-Goldwyn-Mayer: GEORGIE STOLL and ROGER EDENS.

★ TIN PAN ALLEY, 20th Century-Fox: ALFRED NEWMAN.

Original Score

ARIZONA, Columbia: VICTOR YOUNG.

THE DARK COMMAND, Republic: VICTOR YOUNG.

THE FIGHT FOR LIFE, U.S. Government-Columbia: LOUIS GRUENBERG.

THE GREAT DICTATOR, Chaplin, UA: MEREDITH WILLSON.

THE HOUSE OF SEVEN GABLES, Universal: FRANK SKINNER.

THE HOWARDS OF VIRGINIA, Columbia: RICHARD HAGEMAN.

THE LETTER, Warner Bros.: MAX STEINER.

THE LONG VOYAGE HOME, Argosy-Wanger, UA: RICHARD HAGEMAN.

THE MARK OF ZORRO, 20th Century-Fox: ALFRED NEWMAN.

MY FAVORITE WIFE, RKO Radio: ROY WEBB.

NORTH WEST MOUNTED POLICE, Paramount: VICTOR YOUNG.

ONE MILLION B.C., Hal Roach, UA: WERNER HEYMANN.

OUR TOWN, Sol Lesser, UA: AARON COPLAND.

★ PINOCCHIO, Disney, RKO Radio: LEIGH HARLINE, PAUL J. SMITH, and NED WASHINGTON.

REBECCA, Selznick, UA: FRANZ WAXMAN.

THE THIEF OF BAGDAD, Korda, UA: MIKLOS ROZSA.

WATERLOO BRIDGE, Metro-Goldwyn-Mayer: HERBERT STOTHART.

Song

DOWN ARGENTINE WAY from *Down Argentine Way*, 20th Century-Fox: Music by HARRY WARREN; Lyrics by MARK GORDON.

I'D KNOW YOU ANYWHERE from *You'll Find Out*, RKO Radio: Music by JIMMY MCHUGH; Lyrics by JOHNNY MERCER.

IT'S A BLUE WORLD from *Music in My Heart*, Columbia: Music and Lyrics by CHET FORREST and BOB WRIGHT.

LOVE OF MY LIFE from *Second Chorus*, Paramount: Music by ARTIE SHAW; Lyrics by JOHNNY MERCER.

ONLY FOREVER from *Rhythm on the River*, Paramount: Music by JAMES MONACO; Lyrics by JOHN BURKE.

OUR LOVE AFFAIR from *Strike up the Band*, Metro-Goldwyn-Mayer: Music and Lyrics by ROGER EDENS and GEORGIE STOLL.

WALTZING IN THE CLOUDS from *Spring Parade*, Universal: Music by ROBERT STOLZ; Lyrics by GUS KAHN.

★ WHEN YOU WISH UPON A STAR from *Pinocchio*, Disney, RKO Radio: Music by LEIGH HARLINE; Lyrics by NED WASHINGTON.

WHO AM I? from *Hit Parade of 1941*, Republic: Music by JULE STYNE; Lyrics by WALTER BULLOCK.

Special Effects

THE BLUE BIRD, 20th Century-Fox: Photographic: FRED SERSEN; Sound: E. H. HANSEN.

BOOM TOWN, Metro-Goldwyn-Mayer: Photographic: A. ARNOLD GILLESPIE; Sound: DOUGLAS SHEARER.

THE BOYS FROM SYRACUSE, Universal: Photographic: JOHN P. FULTON; Sound: BERNARD B. BROWN and JOSEPH LAPIS.

DR. CYCLOPS, Paramount: Photographic: FARCIOT EDOUART and GORDON JENNINGS; Sound: No credit listed.

FOREIGN CORRESPONDENT, Wanger, UA: Photographic: PAUL EAGLER; Sound: THOMAS T. MOULTON.

THE INVISIBLE MAN RETURNS, Universal: Photographic: JOHN P. FULTON; Sound: BERNARD B. BROWN and WILLIAM HEDGECOCK.

THE LONG VOYAGE HOME, Argosy-Wanger, UA: Photographic: R. T. LAYTON and R. O. BINGER; Sound: THOMAS T. MOULTON.

ONE MILLION B. C., Roach, UA: Photographic: ROY SEAWRIGHT; Sound: ELMER RAGUSE.

REBECCA, Selznick, UA: Photographic: JACK COSGROVE; Sound: ARTHUR JOHNS.

THE SEA HAWK, Warner Bros.: Photographic: BYRON HASKIN; Sound: NATHAN LEVINSON.

SWISS FAMILY ROBINSON, RKO Radio: Photographic: VERNON L. WALKER; Sound: JOHN O. AALBERG.

★ THE THIEF OF BAGDAD, Korda, UA: Photographic: LAWRENCE BUTLER; Sound: JACK WHITNEY.

TYPHOON, Paramount: Photographic: FARCIOT EDOUART and GORDON JENNINGS; Sound: LOREN RYDER.

WOMEN IN WAR, Republic: Photographic: HOWARD J. LYDECKER, WILLIAM BRADFORD, and ELLIS J. THACKERY; Sound: HERBERT NORSCH.

Short Subjects

Cartoons

★ MILKY WAY, Metro-Goldwyn-Mayer. (Rudolph Ising Series)

PUSS GETS THE BOOT, Metro-Goldwyn-Mayer. (Cat and Mouse Series)

A WILD HARE, Leon Schlesinger, Warner Bros.

One Reel

LONDON CAN TAKE IT, Warner Bros. (Vitaphone Varieties)

MORE ABOUT NOSTRADAMUS, Metro-Goldwyn-Mayer.

★ QUICKER 'N A WINK, Pete Smith, M-G-M.

SIEGE, RKO Radio. (Reelism)

Two Reels

EYES OF THE NAVY, Metro-Goldwyn-Mayer. (Crime Doesn't Pay)

SERVICE WITH THE COLORS, Warner Bros. (National Defense Series)

★ TEDDY, THE ROUGH RIDER, Warner Bros. (Historical Featurette)

Special Awards

BOB HOPE, in recognition of his unselfish services to the Motion Picture Industry. (Special silver plaque)

COLONEL NATHAN LEVINSON for his outstanding service to the industry and the U.S. Army during the past nine years, which has made possible the present efficient mobilization of the motion picture industry facilities for the production of Army Training Films. (Statuette)

Irving G. Thalberg Memorial Award

None.

Scientific or Technical

Class I

20TH CENTURY-FOX FILM CORP. for the design and construction of the 20th Century Silenced Camera, developed by DANIEL CLARK, GROVER LAUBE, CHARLES MILLER, and ROBERT W. STEVENS.

Class II

None.

Class III

WARNER BROS. STUDIO ART DEPARTMENT and ANTON GROT for the design and perfection of the Warner Bros. water ripple and wave illusion machine.

FOURTEENTH YEAR

1941

Nominations Announced: February 9, 1942
Awards Ceremony: February 26, 1942
Biltmore Hotel—Banquet
(MC: Bob Hope, Wendell Willkie was principal speaker)

Best Picture

BLOSSOMS IN THE DUST, Metro-Goldwyn-Mayer. Irving Asher, Producer.

CITIZEN KANE, Mercury, RKO Radio. Orson Welles, Producer.

HERE COMES MR. JORDAN, Columbia. Everett Riskin, Producer.

HOLD BACK THE DAWN, Paramount. Arthur Hornblow, Jr., Producer.

★ HOW GREEN WAS MY VALLEY, 20th Century-Fox. Darryl F. Zanuck, Producer.

THE LITTLE FOXES, Goldwyn, RKO Radio. Samuel Goldwyn, Producer.

THE MALTESE FALCON, Warner Bros. Hal B. Wallis, Producer.

ONE FOOT IN HEAVEN, Warner Bros. Hal B. Wallis, Producer.

SERGEANT YORK, Warner Bros. Jesse L. Lasky and Hal B. Wallis, Producers.

SUSPICION, RKO Radio. Produced by RKO Radio.

Actor

★ GARY COOPER in *Sergeant York*, Warner Bros.

CARY GRANT in *Penny Serenade*, Columbia.

WALTER HUSTON in *All That Money Can Buy*, RKO Radio.

ROBERT MONTGOMERY in *Here Comes Mr. Jordan*, Columbia.

ORSON WELLES in *Citizen Kane*, Mercury, RKO Radio.

Actress

BETTE DAVIS in *The Little Foxes*, Goldwyn, RKO Radio.

OLIVIA DE HAVILLAND in *Hold Back the Dawn*, Paramount.

★ JOAN FONTAINE in *Suspicion*, RKO Radio.

GREER GARSON in *Blossoms in the Dust*, Metro-Goldwyn-Mayer.

BARBARA STANWYCK in *Ball of Fire*, Goldwyn, RKO Radio.

Supporting Actor

WALTER BRENNAN in *Sergeant York*, Warner Bros.

CHARLES COBURN in *The Devil and Miss Jones*, RKO Radio.

★ DONALD CRISP in *How Green Was My Valley*, 20th Century-Fox.

JAMES GLEASON in *Here Comes Mr. Jordan*, Columbia.

SYDNEY GREENSTREET in *The Maltese Falcon*, Warner Bros.

Supporting Actress

SARA ALLGOOD in *How Green Was My Valley*, 20th Century-Fox.

★ MARY ASTOR in *The Great Lie*, Warner Bros.

PATRICIA COLLINGE in *The Little Foxes*, Goldwyn, RKO Radio.
TERESA WRIGHT in *The Little Foxes*, Goldwyn, RKO Radio.
MARGARET WYCHERLY in *Sergeant York*, Warner Bros.

Directing

★ JOHN FORD for *How Green Was My Valley*, 20th Century-Fox.
ALEXANDER HALL for *Here Comes Mr. Jordan*, Columbia.
HOWARD HAWKS for *Sergeant York*, Warner Bros.
ORSON WELLES for *Citizen Kane*, Mercury, RKO Radio.
WILLIAM WYLER for *The Little Foxes*, Goldwyn, RKO Radio.

Writing

Original Story

BALL OF FIRE, Goldwyn, RKO Radio: THOMAS MONROE and BILLY WILDER.
★ HERE COMES MR. JORDAN, Columbia: HARRY SEGALL.
THE LADY EVE, Paramount: MONCKTON HOFFE.
MEET JOHN DOE, Warner Bros.: RICHARD CONNELL AND ROBERT PRESNELL.
NIGHT TRAIN, 20th Century-Fox: GORDON WELLESLEY.

Original Screenplay

★ CITIZEN KANE, Mercury, RKO Radio: HERMAN J. MANKIEWICZ and ORSON WELLES.
THE DEVIL AND MISS JONES, RKO Radio: NORMAN KRASNA.
SERGEANT YORK, Warner Bros.: HARRY CHANDLEE, ABEM FINKEL, JOHN HUSTON, and HOWARD KOCH.
TALL, DARK AND HANDSOME, 20th Century-Fox: KARL TUNBERG and DARRELL WARE.
TOM, DICK AND HARRY, RKO Radio: PAUL JARRICO.

Screenplay

★ HERE COMES MR. JORDAN, Columbia: SIDNEY BUCHMAN and SETON I. MILLER.
HOLD BACK THE DAWN, Paramount: CHARLES BRACKETT and BILLY WILDER.
HOW GREEN WAS MY VALLEY, 20th Century-Fox: PHILIP DUNNE.
THE LITTLE FOXES, Goldwyn, RKO Radio: LILLIAN HELLMAN.
THE MALTESE FALCON, Warner Bros.: JOHN HUSTON.

Cinematography

Black and White

THE CHOCOLATE SOLDIER, Metro-Goldwyn-Mayer: KARL FREUND.
CITIZEN KANE, Mercury, RKO Radio: GREGG TOLAND.
DR. JEKYLL AND MR. HYDE, Metro-Goldwyn-Mayer: JOSEPH RUTTENBERG.
HERE COMES MR. JORDAN, Columbia: JOSEPH WALKER.
HOLD BACK THE DAWN, Paramount: LEO TOVER.
★ HOW GREEN WAS MY VALLEY, 20th Century-Fox: ARTHUR MILLER.
SERGEANT YORK, Warner Bros.: SOL POLITO.
SUN VALLEY SERENADE, 20th Century-Fox: EDWARD CRONJAGER.
SUNDOWN, Wanger, UA: CHARLES LANG.
THAT HAMILTON WOMAN, Korda, UA: RUDOLPH MATE.

Color

ALOMA OF THE SOUTH SEAS, Paramount: WILFRED M. CLINE, KARL STRUSS, and WILLIAM SNYDER.
BILLY THE KID, Metro-Goldwyn-Mayer: WILLIAM V. SKALL and LEONARD SMITH.
★ BLOOD AND SAND, 20th Century-

Fox: ERNEST PALMER and RAY RENNAHAN.
BLOSSOMS IN THE DUST, Metro-Goldwyn-Mayer: KARL FREUND and W. HOWARD GREENE.
DIVE BOMBER, Warner Bros.: BERT GLENNON.
LOUISIANA PURCHASE, Paramount: HARRY HALLENBERGER and RAY RENNAHAN.

Art Direction-Interior Decoration*

Black and White

CITIZEN KANE, Mercury, RKO Radio: PERRY FERGUSON and VAN NEST POLGLASE; Interior Decoration: AL FIELDS and DARRELL SILVERA.
FLAME OF NEW ORLEANS, Universal: MARTIN OBZINA and JACK OTTERSON; Interior Decoration: RUSSELL A. GAUSMAN.
HOLD BACK THE DAWN, Paramount: HANS DREIER and ROBERT USHER; Interior Decoration: SAM COMER.
★ HOW GREEN WAS MY VALLEY, 20th Century-Fox: RICHARD DAY and NATHAN JURAN; Interior Decoration: THOMAS LITTLE.
LADIES IN RETIREMENT, Columbia: LIONEL BANKS; Interior Decoration: GEORGE MONTGOMERY.
THE LITTLE FOXES, Goldwyn, RKO Radio: STEPHEN GOOSSON; Interior Decoration: HOWARD BRISTOL.
SERGEANT YORK, Warner Bros.: JOHN HUGHES; Interior Decoration: FRED MACLEAN.
SON OF MONTE CRISTO, Small, UA: JOHN DUCASSE SCHULZE; Interior Decoration: EDWARD G. BOYLE.
SUNDOWN, Wanger, UA: ALEXANDER GOLITZEN; Interior Decoration: RICHARD IRVINE.
THAT HAMILTON WOMAN, Korda, UA: VINCENT KORDA; Interior Decoration: JULIA HERON.
WHEN LADIES MEET, Metro-Goldwyn-Mayer: CEDRIC GIBBONS and RANDALL DUELL; Interior Decoration: EDWIN B. WILLIS.

Color

BLOOD AND SAND, 20th Century-Fox: RICHARD DAY and JOSEPH C. WRIGHT; Interior Decoration: THOMAS LITTLE.
★ BLOSSOMS IN THE DUST, Metro-Goldwyn-Mayer: CEDRIC GIBBONS and URIE McCLEARY; Interior Decoration: EDWIN B. WILLIS.
LOUISIANA PURCHASE, Paramount: RAOUL PENE DU BOIS; Interior Decoration: STEPHEN A. SEYMOUR.

Sound Recording

APPOINTMENT FOR LOVE, Universal: UNIVERSAL STUDIO SOUND DEPARTMENT, BERNARD B. BROWN, Sound Director.
BALL OF FIRE, Goldwyn, RKO Radio: SAMUEL GOLDWYN STUDIO SOUND DEPARTMENT, THOMAS MOULTON, Sound Director.
THE CHOCOLATE SOLDIER, M-G-M: M-G-M STUDIO SOUND DEPARTMENT, DOUGLAS SHEARER, Sound Director.
CITIZEN KANE, Mercury, RKO Radio: RKO RADIO STUDIO SOUND DEPARTMENT, JOHN AALBERG, Sound Director.
THE DEVIL PAYS OFF, Republic: REPUBLIC STUDIO SOUND DEPARTMENT, CHARLES LOOTENS, Sound Director.
HOW GREEN WAS MY VALLEY, 20th Century-Fox: 20TH CENTURY-FOX STUDIO SOUND DEPARTMENT, E. H. HANSEN, Sound Director.
THE MEN IN HER LIFE, Columbia: COLUMBIA STUDIO SOUND

*Category expanded to include Interior Decorators.

DEPARTMENT, JOHN LIVADARY, Sound Director.

SERGEANT YORK, Warner Bros.: WARNER BROS. STUDIO SOUND DEPARTMENT, NATHAN LEVINSON. Sound Director.

SKYLARK, Paramount: PARAMOUNT STUDIO SOUND DEPARTMENT, LOREN RYDER, Sound Director.

★ THAT HAMILTON WOMAN, Korda, UA: GENERAL SERVICE STUDIO SOUND DEPARTMENT, JACK WHITNEY, Sound Director.

TOPPER RETURNS, Roach, UA: HAL ROACH STUDIO SOUND DEPARTMENT, ELMER RAGUSE, Sound Director.

Film Editing

CITIZEN KANE, Mercury-RKO Radio: ROBERT WISE.

DR. JEKYLL AND MR. HYDE, Metro-Goldwyn-Mayer: HAROLD F. KRESS.

HOW GREEN WAS MY VALLEY, 20th Century-Fox: JAMES B. CLARK.

THE LITTLE FOXES, Goldwyn-RKO Radio: DANIEL MANDELL.

★ SERGEANT YORK, Warner Bros.: WILLIAM HOLMES.

Music

Scoring of a Dramatic Picture

★ ALL THAT MONEY CAN BUY, RKO Radio: BERNARD HERRMANN.

BACK STREET, Universal: FRANK SKINNER.

BALL OF FIRE, Goldwyn, RKO Radio: ALFRED NEWMAN.

CHEERS FOR MISS BISHOP, Rowland, UA: EDWARD WARD.

CITIZEN KANE, Mercury, RKO Radio: BERNARD HERRMANN.

DR. JEKYLL AND MR. HYDE, Metro-Goldwyn-Mayer: FRANZ WAXMAN.

HOLD BACK THE DAWN, Paramount: VICTOR YOUNG.

HOW GREEN WAS MY VALLEY, 20th Century-Fox: ALFRED NEWMAN.

KING OF THE ZOMBIES, Monogram: EDWARD KAY.

LADIES IN RETIREMENT, Columbia: MORRIS STOLOFF and ERNST TOCH.

THE LITTLE FOXES, Goldwyn, RKO Radio: MEREDITH WILLSON.

LYDIA, Korda, UA: MIKLOS ROZSA.

MERCY ISLAND, Republic: CY FEUER and WALTER SCHARF.

SERGEANT YORK, Warner Bros.: MAX STEINER.

SO ENDS OUR NIGHT, Loew-Lewin, UA: LOUIS GRUENBERG.

SUNDOWN, Walter Wanger, UA: MIKLOS ROZSA.

SUSPICION, RKO Radio: FRANZ WAXMAN.

TANKS A MILLION, Roach, UA: EDWARD WARD.

THAT UNCERTAIN FEELING, Lubitsch, UA: WERNER HEYMANN.

THIS WOMAN IS MINE, Universal: RICHARD HAGEMAN.

Scoring of a Musical Picture

ALL AMERICAN CO-ED, Roach, UA: EDWARD WARD.

BIRTH OF THE BLUES, Paramount: ROBERT EMMETT DOLAN.

BUCK PRIVATES, Universal: CHARLES PREVIN.

THE CHOCOLATE SOLDIER, Metro-Goldwyn-Mayer: HERBERT STOTHART and BRONISLAU KAPER.

★ DUMBO, Disney, RKO Radio: FRANK CHURCHILL and OLIVER WALLACE.

ICE CAPADES, Republic: CY FEUER.

THE STRAWBERRY BLONDE, Warner Bros.: HEINZ ROEMHELD.

SUN VALLEY SERENADE, 20th Century-Fox: EMIL NEWMAN.

SUNNY, RKO Radio: ANTHONY COLLINS.

YOU'LL NEVER GET RICH, Columbia: MORRIS STOLOFF.

Song

BABY MINE from *Dumbo*, Disney, RKO Radio: Music by FRANK CHURCHILL; Lyrics by NED WASHINGTON.

BE HONEST WITH ME from *Ridin' on a Rainbow*, Republic: Music and Lyrics by GENE AUTRY and FRED ROSE.

BLUES IN THE NIGHT from *Blues in the Night*, Warner Bros.: Music by HAROLD ARLEN; Lyrics by JOHNNY MERCER.

BOOGIE WOOGIE BUGLE BOY OF COMPANY B from *Buck Privates*, Universal: Music by HUGH PRINCE; Lyrics by DON RAYE.

CHATTANOOGA CHOO CHOO from *Sun Valley Serenade*, 20th Century-Fox: Music by HARRY WARREN; Lyrics by MACK GORDON.

DOLORES from *Las Vegas Nights*, Paramount: Music by LOU ALTER; Lyrics by FRANK LOESSER.

⋆ THE LAST TIME I SAW PARIS from *Lady Be Good*, Metro-Goldwyn-Mayer: Music by JEROME KERN; Lyrics by OSCAR HAMMERSTEIN II.

OUT OF THE SILENCE from *All American Co-Ed*, Roach, UA: Music and Lyrics by LLOYD B. NORLIND.

SINCE I KISSED MY BABY GOODBYE from *You'll Never Get Rich*, Columbia: Music and Lyrics by COLE PORTER.

Special Effects

ALOMA OF THE SOUTH SEAS, Paramount: Photographic: FARCIOT EDOUART and GORDON JENNINGS; Sound: LOUIS MESENKOP.

FLIGHT COMMAND, Metro-Goldwyn-Mayer: Photographic: A. ARNOLD GILLESPIE; Sound: DOUGLAS SHEARER.

⋆ I WANTED WINGS, Paramount: Photographic: FARCIOT EDOUART and GORDON JENNINGS; Sound: LOUIS MESENKOP.

THE INVISIBLE WOMAN, Universal: Photographic: JOHN FULTON; Sound: JOHN HALL.

THE SEA WOLF, Warner Bros.: Photographic: BYRON HASKIN; Sound: NATHAN LEVINSON

THAT HAMILTON WOMAN, Korda, UA: Photographic: LAWRENCE BUTLER; Sound: WILLIAM H. WILMARTH.

TOPPER RETURNS, Roach, UA: Photographic: ROY SEAWRIGHT; Sound: ELMER RAGUSE.

A YANK IN THE R.A.F., 20th Century-Fox: Photographic: FRED SERSEN; Sound: E. H. HANSEN.

Short Subjects

Cartoons

BOOGIE WOOGIE BUGLE BOY OF COMPANY B, Walter Lantz, Universal.

HIAWATHA'S RABBIT HUNT, Leon Schlesinger, Warner Bros.

HOW WAR CAME, Columbia. (Raymond Gram Swing Series)

⋆ LEND A PAW, Walt Disney, RKO Radio.

THE NIGHT BEFORE CHRISTMAS, Metro-Goldwyn-Mayer. (Tom and Jerry Series)

RHAPSODY IN RIVETS, Leon Schlesinger, Warner Bros.

RHYTHM IN THE RANKS, Paramount. (George Pal Puppetoon Series)

THE ROOKIE BEAR, Metro-Goldwyn-Mayer. (Bear Series)

SUPERMAN NO. 1, Paramount.

TRUANT OFFICER DONALD, Walt Disney, RKO Radio.

One Reel

ARMY CHAMPIONS, Pete Smith, M-G-M. (Pete Smith Specialties)

BEAUTY AND THE BEACH, Paramount. (Headliner Series)

DOWN ON THE FARM, Paramount. (Speaking of Animals)

FORTY BOYS AND A SONG, Warner Bros. (Melody Master Series)

KINGS OF THE TURF, Warner Bros. (Color Parade Series)

★ OF PUPS AND PUZZLES, Metro-Goldwyn-Mayer. (Passing Parade Series)

SAGEBRUSH AND SILVER, 20th Century-Fox. (Magic Carpet Series)

Two Reels

ALIVE IN THE DEEP, Woodard Productions, Inc.

FORBIDDEN PASSAGE, Metro-Goldwyn-Mayer. (Crime Doesn't Pay)

THE GAY PARISIAN, Warner Bros. (Miniature Featurette Series)

★ MAIN STREET ON THE MARCH, Metro-Goldwyn-Mayer. (Two-reel special)

THE TANKS ARE COMING, Warner Bros. (National Defense Series)

Documentary

(New Category)

ADVENTURES IN THE BRONX, Film Assocs.

BOMBER, U.S. Office for Emergency Management Film Unit.

CHRISTMAS UNDER FIRE, British Ministry of Information, Warner Bros.

★ CHURCHILL'S ISLAND, Canadian Film Board, UA.

LETTER FROM HOME, British Ministry of Information.

LIFE OF A THOROUGHBRED, 20th Century-Fox.

NORWAY IN REVOLT, March of Time, RKO Radio.

SOLDIERS OF THE SKY, 20th Century-Fox.

WAR CLOUDS IN THE PACIFIC, Canadian Film Board.

Special Awards

REY SCOTT for his extraordinary achievement in producing *Kukan*, the film record of China's struggle, including its photography with a 16mm camera under the most difficult and dangerous conditions. (Certificate)

THE BRITISH MINISTRY OF INFORMATION for its vivid and dramatic presentation of the heroism of the RAF in the documentary film, *Target for Tonight*. (Certificate)

LEOPOLD STOKOWSKI and his associates for their unique achievement in the creation of a new form of visualized music in Walt Disney's production *Fantasia*, thereby widening the scope of the motion picture as entertainment and as an art form. (Certificate)

WALT DISNEY, WILLIAM GARITY, JOHN N. A. HAWKINS, and the RCA MANUFACTURING COMPANY, for their outstanding contribution to the advancement of the use of sound in motion pictures through the production of *Fantasia*. (Certificates)

Irving G. Thalberg Memorial Award

WALT DISNEY.

Scientific or Technical

Class I

None.

Class II

ELECTRICAL RESEARCH PRODUCTS DIVISION OF WESTERN ELECTRIC CO., INC., for the development of the precision integrating sphere densitometer.

RCA MANUFACTURING CO. for the design and development of the MI-3043 Uni-directional microphone.

Class III

RAY WILKINSON and the PARAMOUNT STUDIO LABORATORY for pioneering in the use of and for the first practical application to release printing of fine-grain positive stock.

CHARLES LOOTENS and the REPUBLIC STUDIO SOUND DEPARTMENT for pioneering the use of and for the first practical application to motion picture production of Class B push-pull variable area recording.

WILBUR SILVERTOOTH and the PARAMOUNT STUDIO ENGINEERING DEPARTMENT for the design and computation of a relay condenser system applicable to transparency process projection, delivering considerably more usable light.

PARAMOUNT PICTURES, INC., and 20TH CENTURY-FOX FILM CORP. for the development and first practical application to motion picture production of an automatic scene slating device.

DOUGLAS SHEARER and the METRO-GOLDWYN-MAYER STUDIO SOUND DEPARTMENT, and to LOREN RYDER and the PARAMOUNT STUDIO SOUND DEPARTMENT for pioneering the development of fine-grain emulsions for variable density original sound recording in studio production.

FIFTEENTH YEAR

1942

Nominations Announced: February 8, 1943
Awards Ceremony: March 4, 1943
(MC: Bob Hope) Ambassador Hotel-Banquet
(The custom of presenting the awards at a banquet was discontinued after 1943. Increased attendance made it necessary to switch the ceremonies to theatres.)

Best Picture

THE INVADERS, Ortus, Columbia (British). Michael Powell, Producer.

KINGS ROW, Warner Bros. Hal B. Wallis, Producer.

THE MAGNIFICENT AMBERSONS, Mercury, RKO Radio. Orson Welles, Producer.

★ MRS. MINIVER, Metro-Goldwyn-Mayer. Sidney Franklin, Producer.

THE PIED PIPER, 20th Century-Fox. Nunnally Johnson, Producer.

THE PRIDE OF THE YANKEES, Goldwyn, RKO Radio. Samuel Goldwyn, Producer.

RANDOM HARVEST, Metro-Goldwyn-Mayer. Sidney Franklin, Producer.

THE TALK OF THE TOWN, Columbia. George Stevens, Producer.

WAKE ISLAND, Paramount. Joseph Sistrom, Producer.

YANKEE DOODLE DANDY, Warner Bros. Jack L. Warner and Hal B. Wallis, Producers, with William Cagney.

Actor

★ JAMES CAGNEY in *Yankee Doodle Dandy*, Warner Bros.

RONALD COLMAN in *Random Harvest*, Metro-Goldwyn-Mayer.

GARY COOPER in *The Pride of the Yankees*, Goldwyn, RKO Radio.

WALTER PIDGEON in *Mrs. Miniver*, Metro-Goldwyn-Mayer.

MONTY WOOLLEY in *The Pied Piper*, 20th Century-Fox.

Actress

BETTE DAVIS in *Now, Voyager*, Warner Bros.

★ GREER GARSON in *Mrs. Miniver*, Metro-Goldwyn-Mayer.

KATHARINE HEPBURN in *Woman of the Year*, Metro-Goldwyn-Mayer.

ROSALIND RUSSELL in *My Sister Eileen*, Columbia.

TERESA WRIGHT in *The Pride of the Yankees*, Goldwyn, RKO Radio.

Supporting Actor

WILLIAM BENDIX in *Wake Island*, Paramount.

★ VAN HEFLIN in *Johnny Eager*, Metro-Goldwyn-Mayer.

WALTER HUSTON in *Yankee Doodle Dandy*, Warner Bros.

FRANK MORGAN in *Tortilla Flat*, Metro-Goldwyn-Mayer.

HENRY TRAVERS in *Mrs. Miniver*, Metro-Goldwyn-Mayer.

Supporting Actress

GLADYS COOPER in *Now, Voyager*, Warner Bros.

AGNES MOOREHEAD in *The Magnificent Ambersons*, Mercury, RKO Radio.

SUSAN PETERS in *Random Harvest*, Metro-Goldwyn-Mayer.

DAME MAY WHITTY in *Mrs. Miniver*, Metro-Goldwyn-Mayer.

★ TERESA WRIGHT in *Mrs. Miniver*, Metro-Goldwyn-Mayer.

Directing

MICHAEL CURTIZ for *Yankee Doodle Dandy*, Warner Bros.

JOHN FARROW for *Wake Island*, Paramount.

MERVYN LEROY for *Random Harvest*, Metro-Goldwyn-Mayer.

SAM WOOD for *Kings Row*, Warner Bros.

★ WILLIAM WYLER for *Mrs. Miniver*, Metro-Goldwyn-Mayer.

Writing

Original Story

HOLIDAY INN, Paramount: IRVING BERLIN.

★ THE INVADERS, Ortus, Columbia (British): EMERIC PRESSBURGER.

THE PRIDE OF THE YANKEES, Goldwyn, RKO Radio: PAUL GALLICO.

THE TALK OF THE TOWN, Columbia: SIDNEY HARMON.

YANKEE DOODLE DANDY, Warner Bros.: ROBERT BUCKNER.

Original Screenplay

ONE OF OUR AIRCRAFT IS MISSING, Powell, UA (British): MICHAEL POWELL and EMERIC PRESSBURGER.

THE ROAD TO MOROCCO, Paramount: FRANK BUTLER and DON HARTMAN.

WAKE ISLAND, Paramount: W. R. BURNETT and FRANK BUTLER.

THE WAR AGAINST MRS. HADLEY, Metro-Goldwyn-Mayer: GEORGE OPPENHEIMER.

★ WOMAN OF THE YEAR, Metro-Goldwyn-Mayer: MICHAEL KANIN and RING LARDNER, JR.

Screenplay

THE INVADERS, Ortus, Columbia (British): RODNEY ACKLAND and EMERIC PRESSBURGER.

★ MRS. MINIVER, Metro-Goldwyn-Mayer: GEORGE FROESCHEL, JAMES HILTON, CLAUDINE WEST, and ARTHUR WIMPERIS.

THE PRIDE OF THE YANKEES, Goldwyn, RKO Radio: HERMAN J. MANKIEWICZ and JO SWERLING.

RANDOM HARVEST, Metro-Goldwyn-Mayer: GEORGE FROESCHEL, CLAUDINE WEST, and ARTHUR WIMPERIS.

THE TALK OF THE TOWN, Columbia: SIDNEY BUCHMAN and IRWIN SHAW.

Cinematography

Black and White

KINGS ROW, Warner Bros.: JAMES WONG HOWE.

THE MAGNIFICENT AMBERSONS, Mercury, RKO Radio: STANLEY CORTEZ.

MOONTIDE, 20th Century-Fox: CHARLES CLARKE.

★ MRS. MINIVER, Metro-Goldwyn-Mayer: JOSEPH RUTTENBERG.

THE PIED PIPER, 20th Century-Fox: EDWARD CRONJAGER.

THE PRIDE OF THE YANKEES, Goldwyn, RKO Radio: RUDOLPH MATE.

TAKE A LETTER, DARLING, Paramount: JOHN MESCALL.

THE TALK OF THE TOWN, Columbia: TED TETZLAFF.

TEN GENTLEMEN FROM WEST POINT, 20th Century-Fox: LEON SHAMROY.

THIS ABOVE ALL, 20th Century-Fox: ARTHUR MILLER.

Color

ARABIAN NIGHTS, Wanger, Universal: MILTON KRASNER, WILLIAM V. SKALL, and W. HOWARD GREENE.

★ THE BLACK SWAN, 20th Century-Fox: LEON SHAMROY.

CAPTAINS OF THE CLOUDS, Warner Bros.: SOL POLITO.

JUNGLE BOOK, Korda, UA: W. HOWARD GREENE.

REAP THE WILD WIND, Paramount: VICTOR MILNER and WILLIAM V. SKALL.

TO THE SHORES OF TRIPOLI, 20th Century-Fox: EDWARD CRONJAGER and WILLIAM V. SKALL.

Art Direction-Interior Decoration

Black and White

GEORGE WASHINGTON SLEPT HERE, Warner Bros.: MAX PARKER and MARK-LEE KIRK; Interior Decoration: CASEY ROBERTS.

THE MAGNIFICENT AMBERSONS, Mercury, RKO Radio: ALBERT S. D'AGOSTINO; Interior Decoration: AL FIELDS and DARRELL SILVERA.

THE PRIDE OF THE YANKEES, Goldwyn, RKO Radio: PERRY FERGUSON; Interior Decoration: HOWARD BRISTOL.

RANDOM HARVEST, Metro-Goldwyn-Mayer: CEDRIC GIBBONS and RANDALL DUELL; Interior Decoration: EDWIN B. WILLIS and JACK MOORE.

THE SHANGHAI GESTURE, Arnold, UA: BORIS LEVEN; Interior Decoration: BORIS LEVEN.

SILVER QUEEN, Sherman, UA: RALPH BERGER; Interior Decoration: EMILE KURI.

THE SPOILERS, Universal: JOHN B. GOODMAN and JACK OTTERSON; Interior Decoration: RUSSELL A. GAUSMAN and EDWARD R. ROBINSON.

TAKE A LETTER, DARLING, Paramount: HANS DREIER and ROLAND ANDERSON; Interior Decoration: SAM COMER.

THE TALK OF THE TOWN, Columbia: LIONEL BANKS and RUDOLPH STERNAD; Interior Decoration: FAY BABCOCK.

★ THIS ABOVE ALL, 20th Century-Fox: RICHARD DAY and JOSEPH WRIGHT; Interior Decoration: THOMAS LITTLE.

Color

ARABIAN NIGHTS, Universal: ALEXANDER GOLITZEN and JACK OTTERSON; Interior Decoration: RUSSELL A. GAUSMAN and IRA S. WEBB.

CAPTAINS OF THE CLOUDS, Warner Bros.: TED SMITH; Interior Decoration: CASEY ROBERTS.

JUNGLE BOOK, Korda, UA: VINCENT KORDA; Interior Decoration: JULIA HERON.

★ MY GAL SAL, 20th Century-Fox: RICHARD DAY and JOSEPH WRIGHT; Interior Decoration: THOMAS LITTLE.

REAP THE WILD WIND, Paramount: HANS DREIER and ROLAND ANDERSON; Interior Decoration: GEORGE SAWLEY.

Sound Recording

ARABIAN NIGHTS, Universal: UNIVERSAL STUDIO SOUND DEPARTMENT, BERNARD B. BROWN, Sound Director.

BAMBI, Disney, RKO Radio: WALT DISNEY STUDIO SOUND DEPARTMENT, SAM SLYFIELD, Sound Director.

FLYING TIGERS, Republic: REPUBLIC STUDIO SOUND DEPARTMENT, DANIEL BLOOMBERG, Sound Director.

FRIENDLY ENEMIES, Small, UA: SOUND SERVICE, INC., JACK WHITNEY, Sound Director.

THE GOLD RUSH, Chaplin, UA: RCA SOUND, JAMES FIELDS, Sound Director.

MRS. MINIVER, M-G-M: M-G-M STUDIO SOUND DEPARTMENT, DOUGLAS SHEARER, Sound Director.

ONCE UPON A HONEYMOON, RKO Radio: RKO RADIO STUDIO SOUND DEPARTMENT, STEVE DUNN, Sound Director.

THE PRIDE OF THE YANKEES, Goldwyn, RKO Radio: SAMUEL GOLDWYN STUDIO SOUND DEPARTMENT, THOMAS MOULTON, Sound Director.

ROAD TO MOROCCO, Paramount: PARAMOUNT STUDIO SOUND DEPARTMENT, LOREN RYDER, Sound Director.

THIS ABOVE ALL, 20th Century-Fox: 20TH CENTURY-FOX STUDIO SOUND DEPARTMENT, E. H. HANSEN, Sound Director.

★ YANKEE DOODLE DANDY, Warner Bros.: WARNER BROS. STUDIO SOUND DEPARTMENT, NATHAN LEVINSON, Sound Director.

YOU WERE NEVER LOVELIER, Columbia: COLUMBIA STUDIO SOUND DEPARTMENT, JOHN LIVADARY, Sound Director.

Film Editing

MRS. MINIVER, Metro-Goldwyn-Mayer: HAROLD F. KRESS.

★ THE PRIDE OF THE YANKEES, Goldwyn, RKO Radio: DANIEL MANDELL.

THE TALK OF THE TOWN, Columbia: OTTO MEYER.

THIS ABOVE ALL, 20th Century-Fox: WALTER THOMPSON.

YANKEE DOODLE DANDY, Warner Bros.: GEORGE AMY.

Music

Scoring of a Dramatic or Comedy Picture

ARABIAN NIGHTS, Universal: FRANK SKINNER.

BAMBI, Disney, RKO Radio: FRANK CHURCHILL and EDWARD PLUMB.

THE BLACK SWAN, 20th Century-Fox: ALFRED NEWMAN.

THE CORSICAN BROTHERS, Small, UA: DIMITRI TIOMKIN.

FLYING TIGERS, Republic: VICTOR YOUNG.

THE GOLD RUSH, Chaplin, UA: MAX TERR.

I MARRIED A WITCH, Cinema Guild, UA: ROY WEBB.

JOAN OF PARIS, RKO Radio: ROY WEBB.

JUNGLE BOOK, Korda, UA: MIKLOS ROZSA.

KLONDIKE FURY, Monogram: EDWARD KAY.

★ NOW, VOYAGER, Warner Bros.: MAX STEINER.

THE PRIDE OF THE YANKEES, Goldwyn, RKO Radio: LEIGH HARLINE.

RANDOM HARVEST, Metro-Goldwyn-Mayer: HERBERT STOTHART.

THE SHANGHAI GESTURE, Arnold, UA: RICHARD HAGEMAN.

SILVER QUEEN, Sherman, UA: VICTOR YOUNG.

TAKE A LETTER, DARLING, Paramount: VICTOR YOUNG.

THE TALK OF THE TOWN, Columbia: FREDERICK HOLLANDER and MORRIS STOLOFF.

TO BE OR NOT TO BE, Lubitsch, UA: WERNER HEYMANN.

Scoring of a Musical Picture

FLYING WITH MUSIC, Roach, UA: EDWARD WARD.

FOR ME AND MY GAL, Metro-Goldwyn-Mayer: ROGER EDENS and GEORGIE STOLL.

HOLIDAY INN, Paramount: ROBERT EMMETT DOLAN.

IT STARTED WITH EVE, Universal: CHARLES PREVIN and HANS SALTER.

JOHNNY DOUGHBOY, Republic: WALTER SCHARF.

MY GAL SAL, 20th Century-Fox: ALFRED NEWMAN.

★ YANKEE DOODLE DANDY,

Warner Bros.: RAY HEINDORF and HEINZ ROEMHELD.

YOU WERE NEVER LOVELIER, Columbia: LEIGH HARLINE.

Best Song

ALWAYS IN MY HEART from *Always in My Heart*, Warner Bros.: Music by ERNESTO LECUONA; Lyrics by KIM GANNON.

DEARLY BELOVED from *You Were Never Lovelier*, Columbia: Music by JEROME KERN. Lyrics by JOHNNY MERCER.

HOW ABOUT YOU? from *Babes on Broadway*, Metro-Goldwyn-Mayer: Music by BURTON LANE; Lyrics by RALPH FREED.

IT SEEMS I HEARD THAT SONG BEFORE from *Youth on Parade*, Republic: Music by JULE STYNE; Lyrics by SAMMY CAHN.

I'VE GOT A GAL IN KALAMAZOO from *Orchestra Wives*, 20th Century-Fox: Music by HARRY WARREN; Lyrics by MACK GORDON.

LOVE IS A SONG from *Bambi*, Disney, RKO Radio: Music by FRANK CHURCHILL; Lyrics by LARRY MOREY.

PENNIES FOR PEPPINO from *Flying with Music*, Roach, UA: Music by EDWARD WARD; Lyrics by CHET FORREST and BOB WRIGHT.

PIG FOOT PETE from *Hellzapoppin'*, Universal: Music by GENE DE PAUL; Lyrics by DON RAYE.

THERE'S A BREEZE ON LAKE LOUISE from *The Mayor of 44th Street*, RKO Radio: Music by HARRY REVEL; Lyrics by MORT GREENE.

⋆ WHITE CHRISTMAS from *Holiday Inn*, Paramount: Music and Lyrics by IRVING BERLIN.

Special Effects

THE BLACK SWAN, 20th Century-Fox: Photographic: FRED SERSEN; Sound: ROGER HEMAN and GEORGE LEVERETT.

DESPERATE JOURNEY, Warner Bros.: Photographic: BYRON HASKIN; Sound: NATHAN LEVINSON.

FLYING TIGERS, Republic: Photographic: HOWARD LYDECKER; Sound: DANIEL J. BLOOMBERG.

INVISIBLE AGENT, Universal: Photographic: JOHN FULTON; Sound: BERNARD B. BROWN.

JUNGLE BOOK, Korda, UA: Photographic: LAWRENCE BUTLER; Sound: WILLIAM H. WILMARTH.

MRS. MINIVER, Metro-Goldwyn. Mayer Photographic: A. ARNOLD GILLESPIE and WARREN NEWCOMBE; Sound: DOUGLAS SHEARER.

THE NAVY COMES THROUGH, RKO Radio: Photographic: VERNON L. WALKER; Sound: JAMES G. STEWART.

ONE OF OUR AIRCRAFT IS MISSING, Powell, UA (British): Photographic: RONALD NEAME; Sound: C. C. STEVENS.

PRIDE OF THE YANKEES, Goldwyn, RKO Radio: Photographic: JACK COSGROVE and RAY BINGER; Sound: THOMAS T. MOULTON.

⋆ REAP THE WILD WIND, Paramount: Photographic: FARCIOT EDOUART, GORDON JENNINGS, and WILLIAM L. PEREIRA; Sound: LOUIS MESENKOP.

Short Subjects

Cartoons

ALL OUT FOR V, 20th Century-Fox.

THE BLITZ WOLF, Metro-Goldwyn-Mayer.

⋆ DER FUEHRER'S FACE, Walt Disney, RKO Radio.

JUKE BOX JAMBOREE, Walt Lantz, Universal.

PIGS IN A POLKA, Leon Schlesinger, Warner Bros.

TULIPS SHALL GROW, Paramount. (George Pal Puppetoon)

One Reel

DESERT WONDERLAND, 20th Century-Fox. (Magic Carpet Series)

MARINES IN THE MAKING, Metro-Goldwyn-Mayer. (Pete Smith Specialties)

★ SPEAKING OF ANIMALS AND THEIR FAMILIES, Paramount. (Speaking of Animals)

UNITED STATES MARINE BAND, Warner Bros. (Melody Master Bands)

Two Reels

★ BEYOND THE LINE OF DUTY, Warner Bros. (Broadway Brevities)

DON'T TALK, Metro-Goldwyn-Mayer, (Two-reel special)

PRIVATE SMITH OF THE U.S.A., RKO Radio. (This Is America Series)

*Documentary**

AFRICA, PRELUDE TO VICTORY, March of Time, 20th Century-Fox.

★ BATTLE OF MIDWAY, US Navy, 20th Century-Fox.

COMBAT REPORT, US Army Signal Corps.

CONQUER BY THE CLOCK, Office of War Information, RKO Pathé: FREDERIC ULLMAN, JR.

THE GRAIN THAT BUILT A HEMISPHERE, Coordinator's Office, Motion Picture Society for the Americas: WALT DISNEY.

HENRY BROWNE, FARMER, U.S. Department of Agriculture, Republic.

HIGH OVER THE BORDERS, Canadian National Film Board.

HIGH STAKES IN THE EAST, Netherlands Information Bureau.

INSIDE FIGHTING CHINA, Canadian National Film Board.

IT'S EVERYBODY'S WAR, Office of War Information, 20th Century-Fox.

★ KOKODA FRONT LINE, Australian News and Information Bureau.

LISTEN TO BRITAIN, British Ministry of Information.

LITTLE BELGIUM, Belgian Ministry of Information.

LITTLE ISLES OF FREEDOM, Warner Bros.: VICTOR STOLOFF and EDGAR LOEW.

★ MOSCOW STRIKES BACK, Artkino (Russian).

MR. BLABBERMOUTH, Office of War Information, M-G-M.

MR. GARDENIA JONES, Office of War Information, M-G-M.

NEW SPIRIT, U.S. Treasury Department: WALT DISNEY.

★ PRELUDE TO WAR, U.S. Army Special Services.

THE PRICE OF VICTORY, Office of War Information, Paramount: PINE-THOMAS.

A SHIP IS BORN, U.S. Merchant Marine, Warner Bros.

TWENTY-ONE MILES, British Ministry of Information.

WE REFUSE TO DIE, Office of War Information, Paramount: WILLIAM C. THOMAS.

WHITE EAGLE, Cocanen Films.

WINNING YOUR WINGS, U.S. Army Air Force, Warner Bros.

Special Awards

CHARLES BOYER for his progressive cultural achievement in establishing the French Research Foundation in Los Angeles as a source of reference for the Hollywood Motion Picture Industry. (Certificate)

NOEL COWARD for his outstanding production achievement in *In Which We Serve*. (Certificate)

METRO-GOLDWYN-MAYER STUDIO for its achievement in representing the American Way of

*Four awards were given this year.

Life in the production of the *Andy Hardy* series of films. (Certificate)

Irving G. Thalberg Memorial award

SIDNEY FRANKLIN.

Scientific or Technical

Class I

None.

Class II

CARROLL CLARK, F. THOMAS THOMPSON, and the RKO RADIO STUDIO ART and MINIATURE DEPARTMENTS for the design and construction of a moving cloud and horizon machine.

DANIEL B. CLARK and the 20th CENTURY-FOX FILM CORP. for the development of a lens calibration system and the application of this system to exposure control in cinematography.

Class III

ROBERT HENDERSON and the PARAMOUNT STUDIO ENGINEERING and TRANSPARENCY DEPARTMENTS for the design and construction of adjustable light bridges and screen frames for transparency process photography.

DANIEL J. BLOOMBERG and the REPUBLIC STUDIO SOUND DEPARTMENT for the design and application to motion picture production of a device for marking action negatives for preselection purposes.

SIXTEENTH YEAR

1943

Nominations Announced: February 7, 1944
Awards Ceremony: March 2, 1944
Grauman's Chinese Theatre
(MC: Jack Benny for overseas broadcast)

Best Picture

★ CASABLANCA, Warner Bros. Hal B. Wallis, Producer.

FOR WHOM THE BELL TOLLS, Paramount. Sam Wood, Producer.

HEAVEN CAN WAIT, 20th Century-Fox. Ernst Lubitsch, Producer.

THE HUMAN COMEDY, Metro-Goldwyn-Mayer. Clarence Brown, Producer.

IN WHICH WE SERVE, Two Cities, UA (British). Noel Coward, Producer.

MADAME CURIE, Metro-Goldwyn-Mayer. Sidney Franklin, Producer.

THE MORE THE MERRIER, Columbia. George Stevens, Producer.

THE OX-BOW INCIDENT, 20th Century-Fox. Lamar Trotti, Producer.

THE SONG OF BERNADETTE, 20th Century-Fox. William Perlberg, Producer.

WATCH ON THE RHINE, Warner Bros. Hal B. Wallis, Producer.

Actor

HUMPHREY BOGART in *Casablanca*, Warner Bros.

GARY COOPER in *For Whom the Bell Tolls*, Paramount.

★ PAUL LUKAS in *Watch on the Rhine*, Warner Bros.

WALTER PIDGEON in *Madame Curie*, Metro-Goldwyn-Mayer.

MICKEY ROONEY in *The Human Comedy*, Metro-Goldwyn-Mayer.

Actress

JEAN ARTHUR in *The More the Merrier*, Columbia.

INGRID BERGMAN in *For Whom the Bell Tolls*, Paramount.

JOAN FONTAINE in *The Constant Nymph*, Warner Bros.

GREER GARSON in *Madame Curie*, Metro-Goldwyn-Mayer.

★ JENNIFER JONES in *The Song of Bernadette*, 20th Century-Fox.

Supporting Actor

CHARLES BICKFORD in *The Song of Bernadette*, 20th Century-Fox.

★ CHARLES COBURN in *The More the Merrier*, Columbia.

J. CARROL NAISH in *Sahara*, Columbia.

CLAUDE RAINS in *Casablanca*, Warner Bros.

AKIM TAMIROFF in *For Whom the Bell Tolls*, Paramount.

Supporting Actress

GLADYS COOPER in *The Song of Bernadette*, 20th Century-Fox.

PAULETTE GODDARD in *So Proudly We Hail*, Paramount.

★ KATINA PAXINOU in *For Whom the Bell Tolls*, Paramount.

ANNE REVERE in *The Song of Bernadette*, 20th Century-Fox.
LUCILE WATSON in *Watch on the Rhine*, Warner Bros.

Directing

CLARENCE BROWN for *The Human Comedy*, Metro-Goldwyn-Mayer.
MICHAEL CURTIZ for *Casablanca*, Warner Bros.
HENRY KING for *The Song of Bernadette*, 20th Century-Fox.
ERNST LUBITSCH for *Heaven Can Wait*, 20th Century-Fox.
GEORGE STEVENS for *The More the Merrier*, Columbia.

Writing

Original Story

ACTION IN THE NORTH ATLANTIC, Warner Bros.: GUY GILPATRIC.
DESTINATION TOKYO, Warner Bros.: STEVE FISHER.
★ THE HUMAN COMEDY, Metro-Goldwyn-Mayer: WILLIAM SAROYAN.
THE MORE THE MERRIER, Columbia: FRANK ROSS and ROBERT RUSSELL.
SHADOW OF A DOUBT, Universal: GORDON MCDONNELL.

Original Screenplay

AIR FORCE, Warner Bros.: DUDLEY NICHOLS.
IN WHICH WE SERVE, Two Cities, UA (British): NOEL COWARD.
THE NORTH STAR, Goldwyn, RKO Radio: LILLIAN HELLMAN.
★ PRINCESS O'ROURKE, Warner Bros.: NORMAN KRASNA.
SO PROUDLY WE HAIL, Paramount: ALLAN SCOTT.

Screenplay

★ CASABLANCA, Warner Bros.: JULIUS J. EPSTEIN, PHILIP G. EPSTEIN, and HOWARD KOCH.
HOLY MATRIMONY, 20th Century-Fox: NUNNALLY JOHNSON.
THE MORE THE MERRIER, Columbia: RICHARD FLOURNOY, LEWIS R. FOSTER, FRANK ROSS, and ROBERT RUSSELL.
THE SONG OF BERNADETTE, 20th Century-Fox: GEORGE SEATON.
WATCH ON THE RHINE, Warner Bros.: DASHIELL HAMMETT.

Cinematography

Black and White

AIR FORCE, Warner Bros.: JAMES WONG HOWE, ELMER DYER, and CHARLES MARSHALL.
CASABLANCA Warner Bros.: ARTHUR EDESON.
CORVETTE K-225, Universal: TONY GAUDIO.
FIVE GRAVES TO CAIRO, Paramount: JOHN SEITZ.
THE HUMAN COMEDY, Metro-Goldwyn-Mayer: HARRY STRADLING.
MADAME CURIE, Metro-Goldwyn-Mayer: JOSEPH RUTTENBERG.
THE NORTH STAR, Goldwyn, RKO Radio: JAMES WONG HOWE.
SAHARA, Columbia: RUDOLPH MATE.
SO PROUDLY WE HAIL, Paramount: CHARLES LANG.
★ THE SONG OF BERNADETTE, 20th Century-Fox: ARTHUR MILLER.

Color

FOR WHOM THE BELL TOLLS, Paramount: RAY RENNAHAN.
HEAVEN CAN WAIT, 20th Century-Fox: EDWARD CRONJAGER.
HELLO, FRISCO, HELLO, 20th Century-Fox: CHARLES G. CLARKE and ALLEN DAVEY.
LASSIE COME HOME, Metro-Goldwyn-Mayer: LEONARD SMITH.
★ PHANTOM OF THE OPERA, Universal: HAL MOHR and W. HOWARD GREENE.

THOUSANDS CHEER, Metro-Goldwyn-Mayer: GEORGE FOLSEY.

Art Direction-Interior Decoration

Black and White

FIVE GRAVES TO CAIRO, Paramount: HANS DREIER and ERNST FEGTE; Interior Decoration: BERTRAM GRANGER.

FLIGHT FOR FREEDOM, RKO Radio: ALBERT S. D'AGOSTINO and CARROLL CLARK; Interior Decoration: DARRELL SILVERA and HARLEY MILLER.

MADAME CURIE, Metro-Goldwyn-Mayer: CEDRIC GIBBONS and PAUL GROESSE; Interior Decoration: EDWIN B. WILLIS and HUGH HUNT.

MISSION TO MOSCOW, Warner Bros.: CARL WEYL; Interior Decoration: GEORGE J. HOPKINS.

THE NORTH STAR, Goldwyn, RKO Radio: PERRY FERGUSON; Interior Decoration: HOWARD BRISTOL.

★ THE SONG OF BERNADETTE, 20th Century-Fox: JAMES BASEVI and WILLIAM DARLING; Interior Decoration: THOMAS LITTLE.

Color

FOR WHOM THE BELL TOLLS, Paramount: HANS DREIER and HALDANE DOUGLAS; Interior Decoration: BERTRAM GRANGER.

THE GANG'S ALL HERE, 20th Century-Fox: JAMES BASEVI and JOSEPH C. WRIGHT; Interior Decoration: THOMAS LITTLE.

★ PHANTOM OF THE OPERA, Universal: ALEXANDER GOLITZEN and JOHN B. GOODMAN; Interior Decoration: RUSSELL A. GAUSMAN and IRA S. WEBB.

THIS IS THE ARMY, Warner Bros.: JOHN HUGHES and LT. JOHN KOENIG; Interior Decoration: GEORGE J. HOPKINS.

THOUSANDS CHEER, Metro-Goldwyn-Mayer: CEDRIC GIBBONS and DANIEL CATHCART; Interior Decoration: EDWIN B. WILLIS and JACQUES MERSEREAU.

Sound Recording

HANGMEN ALSO DIE, Pressburger, UA: SOUND SERVICE, INC., JACK WHITNEY, Sound Director.

IN OLD OKLAHOMA, Republic: REPUBLIC STUDIO SOUND DEPARTMENT, DANIEL J. BLOOMBERG, Sound Director.

MADAME CURIE, M-G-M: M-G-M STUDIO SOUND DEPARTMENT, DOUGLAS SHEARER, Sound Director.

THE NORTH STAR, Goldwyn, RKO Radio: SAMUEL GOLDWYN STUDIO SOUND DEPARTMENT, THOMAS MOULTON, Sound Director.

THE PHANTOM OF THE OPERA, Universal: UNIVERSAL STUDIO SOUND DEPARTMENT, BERNARD B. BROWN, Sound Director.

RIDING HIGH, Paramount: PARAMOUNT STUDIO SOUND DEPARTMENT, LOREN L. RYDER, Sound Director.

SAHARA, Columbia: COLUMBIA STUDIO SOUND DEPARTMENT, JOHN LIVADARY, Sound Director.

SALUDOS AMIGOS, Disney, RKO Radio: WALT DISNEY STUDIO SOUND DEPARTMENT C. O. SLYFIELD, Sound Director.

SO THIS IS WASHINGTON, Votion, RKO Radio: RCA SOUND, J. L. FIELDS, Sound Director.

THE SONG OF BERNADETTE, 20th Century-Fox: 20TH CENTURY-FOX STUDIO SOUND DEPARTMENT, E. H. HANSEN, Sound Director.

THIS IS THE ARMY, Warner Bros: WARNER BROS. STUDIO SOUND DEPARTMENT, NATHAN LEVINSON, Sound Director.

★ THIS LAND IS MINE, RKO Radio: RKO RADIO STUDIO SOUND DEPARTMENT, STEPHEN DUNN, Sound Director.

Film Editing

★ AIR FORCE, Warner Bros.: GEORGE AMY.
CASABLANCA, Warner Bros.: OWEN MARKS.
FIVE GRAVES TO CAIRO, Paramount: DOANE HARRISON.
FOR WHOM THE BELL TOLLS, Paramount: SHERMAN TODD and JOHN LINK.
THE SONG OF BERNADETTE, 20th Century-Fox: BARBARA MCLEAN.

Music

Scoring of a Dramatic or Comedy Picture

THE AMAZING MRS. HOLLIDAY, Universal: HANS J. SALTER and FRANK SKINNER.
CASABLANCA, Warner Bros.: MAX STEINER.
THE COMMANDOS STRIKE AT DAWN, Columbia: LOUIS GRUENBERG and MORRIS STOLOFF.
THE FALLEN SPARROW, RKO Radio: C. BAKALEINIKOFF and ROY WEBB.
FOR WHOM THE BELL TOLLS, Paramount: VICTOR YOUNG.
HANGMEN ALSO DIE, Arnold, UA: HANNS EISLER.
HI DIDDLE DIDDLE, Stone, UA: PHIL BOUTELJE.
IN OLD OKLAHOMA, Republic: WALTER SCHARF.
JOHNNY COME LATELY, Cagney, UA: LEIGH HARLINE.
THE KANSAN, Sherman, UA: GERARD CARBONARA.
LADY OF BURLESQUE, Stromberg, UA: ARTHUR LANGE.
MADAME CURIE, Metro-Goldwyn-Mayer: HERBERT STOTHART.
THE MOON AND SIXPENCE, Loew-Lewin, UA: DIMITRI TIOMKIN.
THE NORTH STAR, Goldwyn, RKO Radio: AARON COPLAND.
★ THE SONG OF BERNADETTE, 20th Century-Fox: ALFRED NEWMAN.
VICTORY THROUGH AIR POWER, Disney, UA: EDWARD H. PLUMB, PAUL J. SMITH, and OLIVER G. WALLACE.

Scoring of a Musical Picture

CONEY ISLAND, 20th Century-Fox: ALFRED NEWMAN.
HIT PARADE OF 1943, Republic: WALTER SCHARF.
THE PHANTOM OF THE OPERA, Universal: EDWARD WARD.
SALUDOS AMIGOS, Disney, RKO Radio: EDWARD H. PLUMB, PAUL J. SMITH, and CHARLES WOLCOTT.
THE SKY'S THE LIMIT, RKO Radio: LEIGH HARLINE.
SOMETHING TO SHOUT ABOUT, Columbia: MORRIS STOLOFF.
STAGE DOOR CANTEEN, Lesser, UA: FREDERIC E. RICH.
STAR SPANGLED RHYTHM, Paramount: ROBERT EMMETT DOLAN.
★ THIS IS THE ARMY, Warner Bros.: RAY HEINDORF.
THOUSANDS CHEER, Metro-Goldwyn-Mayer: HERBERT STOTHART.

Song

CHANGE OF HEART from *Hit Parade of 1943*, Republic: Music by JULE STYNE; Lyrics by HAROLD ADAMSON.
HAPPINESS IS A THING CALLED JOE from *Cabin in the Sky*, Metro-Goldwyn-Mayer: Music by HAROLD ARLEN; Lyrics by E. Y. HARBURG.
MY SHINING HOUR from *The Sky's the Limit*, RKO Radio: Music by HAROLD ARLEN; Lyrics by JOHNNY MERCER.
SALUDOS AMIGOS from *Saludos Amigos*, Disney, RKO Radio: Music by CHARLES WOLCOTT; Lyrics by NED WASHINGTON.
SAY A PRAYER FOR THE BOYS OVER THERE from *Hers to Hold*; Universal:

Music by JIMMY MCHUGH; Lyrics by HERB MAGIDSON.

THAT OLD BLACK MAGIC from *Star Spangled Rhythm*, Paramount: Music by HAROLD ARLEN; Lyrics by JOHNNY MERCER.

THEY'RE EITHER TOO YOUNG OR TOO OLD from *Thank Your Lucky Stars*, Warner Bros.: Music by ARTHUR SCHWARTZ; Lyrics by FRANK LOESSER.

WE MUSTN'T SAY GOOD BYE from *Stage Door Canteen*, Lesser, UA: Music by JAMES MONACO; Lyrics by AL DUBIN.

YOU'D BE SO NICE TO COME HOME TO from *Something to Shout About*, Columbia: Music and Lyrics by COLE PORTER.

★ YOU'LL NEVER KNOW from *Hello, Frisco, Hello*, 20th Century-Fox: Music by HARRY WARREN; Lyrics by MACK GORDON.

Special Effects

AIR FORCE, Warner Bros.: Photographic: HANS KOENEKAMP and REX WIMPY; Sound: NATHAN LEVINSON.

BOMBARDIER, RKO Radio: Photographic: VERNON L. WALKER; Sound: JAMES G. STEWART and ROY GRANVILLE.

★ CRASH DIVE, 20th Century-Fox: Photographic: FRED SERSEN; Sound: ROGER HEMAN.

THE NORTH STAR, Goldwyn, RKO Radio: Photographic: CLARENCE SLIFER and R. O. BINGER; Sound: THOMAS T. MOULTON.

SO PROUDLY WE HAIL, Paramount: Photographic: FARCIOT EDOUART and GORDON JENNINGS; Sound: GEORGE DUTTON.

STAND BY FOR ACTION, Metro-Goldwyn-Mayer: Photographic: A. ARNOLD GILLESPIE; and DONALD JAHRAUS; Sound: MICHAEL STEINORE.

Short Subjects

Cartoons

THE DIZZY ACROBAT, Walter Lantz, Universal: WALTER LANTZ, Producer.

THE FIVE HUNDRED HATS OF BARTHOLOMEW CUBBINS, Paramount. (George Pal Puppetoon)

GREETINGS, BAIT, Warner Bros.: LEON SCHLESINGER, Producer.

IMAGINATION, Columbia: DAVE FLEISCHER, Producer.

REASON AND EMOTION, Walt Disney, RKO Radio: WALT DISNEY, Producer.

★ YANKEE DOODLE MOUSE, Metro-Goldwyn-Mayer: FREDERICK QUIMBY, Producer.

One Reel

★ AMPHIBIOUS FIGHTERS, Paramount: GRANTLAND RICE, Producer.

CAVALCADE OF THE DANCE WITH VELOZ AND YOLANDA, Warner Bros.: (Melody Master Bands) GORDON HOLLINGSHEAD, Producer.

CHAMPIONS CARRY ON, 20th Century-Fox: (Sports Reviews) EDMUND REEK, Producer.

HOLLYWOOD IN UNIFORM, Columbia: (Screen Snapshots #1, Series 22) RALPH STAUB, Producer.

SEEING HANDS, Metro-Goldwyn-Mayer: (Pete Smith Specialty).

Two Reels

★ HEAVENLY MUSIC, Metro-Goldwyn-Mayer: JERRY BRESLER and SAM COSLOW, Producers.

LETTER TO A HERO, RKO Radio: (This Is America) FRED ULLMAN, Producer.

MARDI GRAS, Paramount: (Musical Parade) WALTER MACEWEN, Producer.

WOMEN AT WAR, Warner Bros.:

(Technicolor Special) GORDON HOLLINGSHEAD, Producer.

Documentary

Short Subjects

CHILDREN OF MARS, This is America Series, RKO Radio.
★ DECEMBER 7TH, U.S. Navy, Field Photographic Branch, Office of Strategic Services.
PLAN FOR DESTRUCTION, Metro-Goldwyn-Mayer.
SWEDES IN AMERICA, Office of War Information, Overseas Motion Picture Bureau.
TO THE PEOPLE OF THE UNITED STATES, U.S. Public Health Service, Walter Wanger Prods.
TOMORROW WE FLY, U.S. Navy, Bureau of Aeronautics.
YOUTH IN CRISIS, March of Time, 20th Century-Fox.

Features

BAPTISM OF FIRE, U.S. Army, Fighting Men Series.
BATTLE OF RUSSIA, Special Service Division of the War Department.
★ DESERT VICTORY, British Ministry of Information.
REPORT FROM THE ALEUTIANS, U.S. Army Pictorial Service, Combat Film Series.
WAR DEPARTMENT REPORT, Field Photographic Branch, Office of Strategic Services.

Special Awards

GEORGE PAL for the development of novel methods and techniques in the production of short subjects known as Puppetoons. (Plaque)

Irving G. Thalberg Memorial Award

HAL B. WALLIS.

Scientific or Technical

Class I

None.

Class II

FARCIOT EDOUART, EARLE MORGAN, BARTON THOMPSON, and the PARAMOUNT STUDIO ENGINEERING and TRANSPARENCY DEPARTMENTS for the development and practical application to motion picture production of a method of duplicating and enlarging natural color photographs, transferring the image emulsions to glass plates, and projecting these slides by especially designed stereopticon equipment.
PHOTO PRODUCTS DEPARTMENT, E. I. DuPONT DE NEMOURS AND CO., INC., for the development of fine-grain motion picture films.

Class III

DANIEL J. BLOOMBERG and the REPUBLIC STUDIO SOUND DEPARTMENT for the design and development of an inexpensive method of converting Moviolas to Class B push-pull reproduction.
CHARLES GALLOWAY CLARKE and the 20TH CENTURY-FOX STUDIO CAMERA DEPARTMENT for the development and practical application of a device for composing artificial clouds into motion picture scenes during production photography.
FARCIOT EDOUART and the PARAMOUNT STUDIO TRANSPARENCY DEPARTMENT for an automatic electric transparency cueing timer.
WILLARD H. TURNER and the RKO RADIO STUDIO SOUND DEPARTMENT for the design and construction of the phono-cue starter.

SEVENTEENTH YEAR

1944

Nominations Announced: February 5, 1945
Awards Ceremony: March 15, 1945
Grauman's Chinese Theatre
(MCs: John Cromwell and Bob Hope)

Best Picture

DOUBLE INDEMNITY, Paramount. Joseph Sistrom, Producer.

GASLIGHT, Metro-Goldwyn-Mayer. Arthur Hornblow, Jr., Producer.

★ GOING MY WAY, Paramount. Leo McCarey, Producer.

SINCE YOU WENT AWAY, Selznick International, UA. David O. Selznick, Producer.

WILSON, 20th Century-Fox. Darryl F. Zanuck, Producer.

Actor

CHARLES BOYER in *Gaslight*, Metro-Goldwyn-Mayer.

★ BING CROSBY in *Going My Way*, Paramount.

BARRY FITZGERALD in *Going My Way*, Paramount.

CARY GRANT in *None but the Lonely Heart*, RKO Radio.

ALEXANDER KNOX in *Wilson*, 20th Century-Fox.

Actress

★ INGRID BERGMAN in *Gaslight*, Metro-Goldwyn-Mayer.

CLAUDETTE COLBERT in *Since You Went Away*, Selznick, UA.

BETTE DAVIS in *Mr. Skeffington*, Warner Bros.

GREER GARSON in *Mrs. Parkington*, Metro-Goldwyn-Mayer.

BARBARA STANWYCK in *Double Indemnity*, Paramount.

Supporting Actor

HUME CRONYN in *The Seventh Cross*, Metro-Goldwyn-Mayer.

★ BARRY FITZGERALD in *Going My Way*, Paramount.

CLAUDE RAINS in *Mr. Skeffington*, Warner Bros.

CLIFTON WEBB in *Laura*, 20th Century-Fox.

MONTY WOOLLEY in *Since You Went Away*, Selznick, UA.

Supporting Actress

★ ETHEL BARRYMORE in *None but the Lonely Heart*, RKO Radio.

JENNIFER JONES in *Since You Went Away*, Selznick, UA.

ANGELA LANSBURY in *Gaslight*, Metro-Goldwyn-Mayer.

ALINE MACMAHON in *Dragon Seed*, Metro-Goldwyn-Mayer.

AGNES MOOREHEAD in *Mrs. Parkington*, Metro-Goldwyn-Mayer.

Directing

ALFRED HITCHCOCK for *Lifeboat*, 20th Century-Fox.

HENRY KING for *Wilson*, 20th Century-Fox.
★ LEO MCCAREY for *Going My Way*, Paramount.
OTTO PREMINGER for *Laura*, 20th Century-Fox.
BILLY WILDER for *Double Indemnity*, Paramount.

Writing

Original Story

★ GOING MY WAY, Paramount: LEO MCCAREY.
A GUY NAMED JOE, Metro-Goldwyn-Mayer: DAVID BOEHM and CHANDLER SPRAGUE.
LIFEBOAT, 20th Century-Fox: JOHN STEINBECK.
NONE SHALL ESCAPE, Columbia: ALFRED NEUMANN and JOSEPH THAN.
THE SULLIVANS, 20th Century-Fox: EDWARD DOHERTY and JULES SCHERMER.

Original Screenplay

HAIL THE CONQUERING HERO, Paramount: PRESTON STURGES.
THE MIRACLE OF MORGAN'S CREEK, Paramount: PRESTON STURGES.
TWO GIRLS AND A SAILOR, Metro-Goldwyn-Mayer: RICHARD CONNELL and GLADYS LEHMAN.
★ WILSON, 20th Century-Fox: LAMAR TROTTI.
WING AND A PRAYER, 20th Century-Fox: JEROME CADY.

Screenplay

DOUBLE INDEMNITY, Paramount: RAYMOND CHANDLER and BILLY WILDER.
GASLIGHT, Metro-Goldwyn-Mayer: JOHN L. BALDERSTON, WALTER REISCH, and JOHN VAN DRUTEN.
★ GOING MY WAY, Paramount: FRANK BUTLER and FRANK CAVETT.
LAURA, 20th Century-Fox: JAY DRATLER, SAMUEL HOFFENSTEIN, and BETTY REINHARDT.
MEET ME IN ST. LOUIS, Metro-Goldwyn-Mayer: IRVING BRECHER and FRED F. FINKELHOFFE.

Cinematography

Black and White

DOUBLE INDEMNITY, Paramount: JOHN SEITZ.
DRAGON SEED, Metro-Goldwyn-Mayer: SIDNEY WAGNER.
GASLIGHT, Metro-Goldwyn-Mayer: JOSEPH RUTTENBERG.
GOING MY WAY, Paramount: LIONEL LINDON.
★ LAURA, 20th Century-Fox: JOSEPH LASHELLE.
LIFEBOAT, 20th Century-Fox: GLEN MACWILLIAMS.
SINCE YOU WENT AWAY, Selznick, UA: STANLEY CORTEZ and LEE GARMES.
THIRTY SECONDS OVER TOKYO, Metro-Goldwyn-Mayer: ROBERT SURTEES and HAROLD ROSSON.
THE UNINVITED, Paramount: CHARLES LANG.
THE WHITE CLIFFS OF DOVER, Metro-Goldwyn-Mayer: GEORGE FOLSEY.

Color

COVER GIRL, Columbia: RUDY MATE and ALLEN M. DAVEY.
HOME IN INDIANA, 20th Century-Fox: EDWARD CRONJAGER.
KISMET, Metro-Goldwyn-Mayer: CHARLES ROSHER.
LADY IN THE DARK, Paramount: RAY RENNAHAN.
MEET ME IN ST. LOUIS, Metro-Goldwyn-Mayer: GEORGE FOLSEY.
★ WILSON, 20th Century-Fox: LEON SHAMROY.

Art Direction-Interior Decoration

Black and White

ADDRESS UNKNOWN, Columbia: LIONEL BANKS and WALTER HOLSCHER; Interior Decoration: JOSEPH KISH.

THE ADVENTURES OF MARK TWAIN, Warner Bros: JOHN J. HUGHES; Interior Decoration: FRED MACLEAN.

CASANOVA BROWN, International, RKO Radio: PERRY FERGUSON; Interior Decoration: JULIA HERON.

★ GASLIGHT, Metro-Goldwyn-Mayer: CEDRIC GIBBONS and WILLIAM FERRARI; Interior Decoration: EDWIN B. WILLIS and PAUL HULDSCHINSKY.

LAURA, 20th Century-Fox: LYLE WHEELER and LELAND FULLER; Interior Decoration: THOMAS LITTLE.

NO TIME FOR LOVE, Paramount: HANS DREIER and ROBERT USHER; Interior Decoration: SAM COMER.

SINCE YOU WENT AWAY, Selznick, UA: MARK-LEE KIRK; Interior Decoration: VICTOR A. GANGELIN.

STEP LIVELY, RKO Radio: ALBERT S. D'AGOSTINO and CARROLL CLARK; Interior Decoration: DARRELL SILVERA and CLAUDE CARPENTER.

Color

THE CLIMAX, Universal: JOHN B. GOODMAN and ALEXANDER GOLITZEN; Interior Decoration: RUSSELL A. GAUSMAN and IRA S. WEBB.

COVER GIRL, Columbia: LIONEL BANKS and CARY ODELL; Interior Decoration: FAY BABCOCK.

THE DESERT SONG, Warner Bros: CHARLES NOVI; Interior Decoration: JACK MCCONAGHY.

KISMET, Metro-Goldwyn-Mayer: CEDRIC GIBBONS and DANIEL B. CATHCART; Interior Decoration: EDWIN B. WILLIS and RICHARD PEFFERLE.

LADY IN THE DARK, Paramount: HANS DREIER and RAOUL PENE DU BOIS; Interior Decoration: RAY MOYER.

THE PRINCESS AND THE PIRATE, Goldwyn, RKO Radio: ERNST FEGTE; Interior Decoration: HOWARD BRISTOL.

★ WILSON, 20th Century-Fox: WIARD IHNEN; Interior Decoration: THOMAS LITTLE.

Sound Recording

BRAZIL, Republic: REPUBLIC STUDIO SOUND DEPARTMENT, DANIEL J. BLOOMBERG, Sound Director.

CASANOVA BROWN, International, RKO Radio: SAMUEL GOLDWYN STUDIO SOUND DEPARTMENT, THOMAS T. MOULTON, Sound Director.

COVER GIRL, Columbia: COLUMBIA STUDIO SOUND DEPARTMENT, JOHN LIVADARY, Sound Director.

DOUBLE INDEMNITY, Paramount: PARAMOUNT STUDIO SOUND DEPARTMENT, LOREN RYDER, Sound Director.

HIS BUTLER'S SISTER, Universal: UNIVERSAL STUDIO SOUND DEPARTMENT, BERNARD B. BROWN, Sound Director.

HOLLYWOOD CANTEEN, Warner Bros.: WARNER BROS. STUDIO SOUND DEPARTMENT, NATHAN LEVINSON, Sound Director.

IT HAPPENED TOMORROW, Arnold, UA: SOUND SERVICES INC., JACK WHITNEY, Sound Director.

KISMET, M-G-M: M-G-M STUDIO SOUND DEPARTMENT, DOUGLAS SHEARER, Sound Director.

MUSIC IN MANHATTAN, RKO Radio: RKO RADIO STUDIO SOUND DEPARTMENT, STEPHEN DUNN, Sound Director.

VOICE IN THE WIND, Ripley-Monter, UA: RCA SOUND, W. M. DALGLEISH, Sound Director.

★ WILSON, 20th Century-Fox: 20TH CENTURY-FOX STUDIO SOUND DEPARTMENT, E. H. HANSEN, Sound Director.

Film Editing

GOING MY WAY, Paramount: LEROY STONE.

JANIE, Warner Bros: OWEN MARKS.

NONE BUT THE LONELY HEART, RKO Radio: ROLAND GROSS.

SINCE YOU WENT AWAY, Selznick, UA: HAL C. KERN and JAMES E. NEWCOM.

★ WILSON, 20th Century-Fox: BARBARA McLEAN.

Music

Scoring of a Dramatic or Comedy Picture

ADDRESS UNKNOWN, Columbia: MORRIS STOLOFF and ERNST TOCH.

THE ADVENTURES OF MARK TWAIN, Warner Bros: MAX STEINER.

THE BRIDGE OF SAN LUIS REY, Bogeaus, UA: DIMITRI TIOMKIN.

CASANOVA BROWN, International, RKO Radio: ARTHUR LANGE.

CHRISTMAS HOLIDAY, Universal: H. J. SALTER.

DOUBLE INDEMNITY, Paramount: MIKLOS ROZSA.

THE FIGHTING SEABEES, Republic: WALTER SCHARF and ROY WEBB.

THE HAIRY APE, Levey, UA: MICHEL MICHELET and EDWARD PAUL.

IT HAPPENED TOMORROW, Arnold, UA: ROBERT STOLZ.

JACK LONDON, Bronston, UA: FREDERIC E. RICH.

KISMET, Metro-Goldwyn-Mayer: HERBERT STOTHART.

NONE BUT THE LONELY HEART, RKO Radio: C. BAKALEINIKOFF and HANNS EISLER.

THE PRINCESS AND THE PIRATE, Regent, RKO Radio: DAVID ROSE.

★ SINCE YOU WENT AWAY, Selznick, UA: MAX STEINER.

SUMMER STORM, Angelus, UA: KARL HAJOS.

THREE RUSSIAN GIRLS, R & F Prods., UA: FRANKE HARLING.

UP IN MABEL'S ROOM, Small, UA: EDWARD PAUL.

VOICE IN THE WIND, Ripley-Monter, UA: MICHEL MICHELET.

WILSON, 20th Century-Fox: ALFRED NEWMAN.

WOMAN OF THE TOWN, Sherman, UA: MIKLOS ROZSA.

Scoring of a Musical Picture

BRAZIL, Republic: WALTER SCHARF.

★ COVER GIRL, Columbia: CARMEN DRAGON and MORRIS STOLOFF.

HIGHER AND HIGHER, RKO Radio: C. BAKALEINIKOFF.

HOLLYWOOD CANTEEN, Warner Bros: RAY HEINDORF.

IRISH EYES ARE SMILING, 20th Century-Fox: ALFRED NEWMAN.

KNICKERBOCKER HOLIDAY, RCA, UA: WERNER R. HEYMANN and KURT WEILL.

LADY IN THE DARK, Paramount: ROBERT EMMETT DOLAN.

LADY LET'S DANCE, Monogram: EDWARD KAY.

MEET ME IN ST. LOUIS, Metro-Goldwyn-Mayer: GEORGIE STOLL.

THE MERRY MONAHANS, Universal: H. J. SALTER.

MINSTREL MAN, PRC: LEO ERDODY and FERDE GROFÉ.

SENSATIONS OF 1945, Stone, UA: MAHLON MERRICK.

SONG OF THE OPEN ROAD, Rogers, UA: CHARLES PREVIN.

UP IN ARMS, Avalon, RKO Radio: LOUIS FORBES and RAY HEINDORF.

Best Song

I COULDN'T SLEEP A WINK LAST NIGHT from *Higher And Higher*, RKO Radio: Music by JIMMY MCHUGH: Lyrics by HAROLD ADAMSON.

I'LL WALK ALONE from *Follow the Boys*, Universal: Music by JULE STYNE; Lyrics by SAMMY CAHN.

I'M MAKING BELIEVE from *Sweet and Lowdown*, 20th Century-Fox: Music by JAMES V. MONACO; Lyrics by MACK GORDON.

LONG AGO AND FAR AWAY from *Cover*

Girl, Columbia: Music by JEROME KERN; Lyrics by IRA GERSHWIN.

NOW I KNOW from *Up in Arms*, Avalon, RKO Radio: Music by HAROLD ARLEN; Lyrics by TED KOEHLER.

REMEMBER ME TO CAROLINA from *Ministrel Man*, PRC: Music by HARRY REVEL; Lyrics by PAUL WEBSTER.

RIO DE JANEIRO from *Brazil*, Republic: Music by ARY BARROSO; Lyrics by NED WASHINGTON.

SILVER SHADOWS AND GOLDEN DREAMS from *Lady Let's Dance*, Monogram: Music by LEW POLLACK; Lyrics by CHARLES NEWMAN.

SWEET DREAMS SWEETHEART from *Hollywood Canteen*, Warner Bros.: Music by M. K. JEROME; Lyrics by TED KOEHLER.

* SWINGING ON A STAR from *Going My Way*, Paramount: Music by JAMES VAN HEUSEN; Lyrics by JOHNNY BURKE.

TOO MUCH IN LOVE from *Song of the Open Road*, Rogers, UA: Music by WALTER KENT; Lyrics by KIM GANNON.

THE TROLLEY SONG from *Meet Me in St. Louis*, Metro-Goldwyn-Mayer: Music and Lyrics by RALPH BLANE and HUGH MARTIN.

Special Effects

THE ADVENTURES OF MARK TWAIN, Warner Bros.: Photographic: PAUL DETLEFSEN and JOHN CROUSE; Sound: NATHAN LEVINSON.

DAYS OF GLORY, RKO Radio: Photographic: VERNON L. WALKER; Sound: JAMES G. STEWART and ROY GRANVILLE.

SECRET COMMAND, Columbia: Photographic: DAVID ALLEN, RAY CORY, and ROBERT WRIGHT; Sound: RUSSELL MALMGREN and HARRY KUSNICK.

SINCE YOU WENT AWAY, Selznick, UA: Photographic: JOHN R. COSGROVE; Sound: ARTHUR JOHNS.

THE STORY OF DR. WASSELL, Paramount: Photographic: FARCIOT EDOUART and GORDON JENNINGS; Sound: GEORGE DUTTON.

* THIRTY SECONDS OVER TOKYO, Metro-Goldwyn-Mayer: Photographic: A. ARNOLD GILLESPIE, DONALD JAHRAUS, and WARREN NEWCOMBE; Sound: DOUGLAS SHEARER.

WILSON, 20th Century-Fox: Photographic: FRED SERSEN; Sound: ROGER HEMAN.

Short Subjects

Cartoons

AND TO THINK I SAW IT ON MULBERRY STREET, Paramount. (George Pal Puppetoon)

THE DOG, CAT AND CANARY, Columbia. (Screen Gems)

FISH FRY, Universal: WALTER LANTZ, Producer.

HOW TO PLAY FOOTBALL, Walt Disney, RKO Radio: WALT DISNEY, Producer.

* MOUSE TROUBLE, Metro-Goldwyn-Mayer: FREDERICK C. QUIMBY, Producer.

MY BOY, JOHNNY, 20th Century-Fox: PAUL TERRY, Producer.

SWOONER CROONER, Warner Bros.

One Reel

BLUE GRASS GENTLEMEN, 20th Century-Fox: (Sports Review) EDMUND REEK, Producer.

50TH ANNIVERSARY OF MOTION PICTURES, Columbia: (Screen Snapshots #9, Series 23) RALPH STAUB, Producer.

JAMMIN' THE BLUES, Warner Bros.: (Melody Master Bands) GORDON HOLLINGSHEAD, Producer.

MOVIE PESTS, Metro-Goldwyn-Mayer. (Pete Smith Specialty)

* WHO'S WHO IN ANIMAL LAND,

Paramount: (Speaking of Animals) JERRY FAIRBANKS, Producer.

Two Reels

BOMBALERA, Paramount: (Musical Parade) LOUIS HARRIS, Producer.

★ I WON'T PLAY, Warner Bros.: (Featurette) GORDON HOLLINGSHEAD, Producer.

MAIN STREET TODAY, Metro-Goldwyn-Mayer: (Two-reel special) JERRY BRESLER, Producer.

Documentary

Short Subjects

ARTURO TOSCANINI, Motion Picture Bureau, Overseas Branch, Office of War Information.

NEW AMERICANS, This Is America Series, RKO Radio.

★ WITH THE MARINES AT TARAWA, U.S. Marine Corps.

Features

★ THE FIGHTING LADY, 20th Century-Fox and U.S. Navy.

RESISTING ENEMY INTERROGATION, U.S. Army Air Force.

Special Awards

MARGARET O'BRIEN, outstanding child actress of 1944. (Miniature statuette)

BOB HOPE, for his many services to the Academy, a Life Membership in the Academy of Motion Picture Arts and Sciences.

Irving G. Thalberg Memorial Award

DARRYL F. ZANUCK.

Scientific or Technical

Class I

None.

Class II

STEPHEN DUNN and the RKO RADIO STUDIO SOUND DEPARTMENT and RADIO CORPORATION OF AMERICA for the design and development of the electronic compressor-limiter.

Class III

LINWOOD DUNN, CECIL LOVE, and ACME TOOL MANUFACTURING CO. for the design and construction of the Acme-Dunn Optical Printer.

GROVER LAUBE and the 20TH CENTURY-FOX STUDIO CAMERA DEPARTMENT for the development of a continuous-loop projection device.

WESTERN ELECTRIC CO. for the design and construction of the 1126A Limiting Amplifier for variable density sound recording.

RUSSELL BROWN, RAY HINSDALE, and JOSEPH E. ROBBINS for the development and production use of the Paramount floating hydraulic boat rocker.

GORDON JENNINGS for the design and construction of the Paramount nodal point tripod.

RADIO CORPORATION OF AMERICA and the RKO RADIO STUDIO SOUND DEPARTMENT for the design and construction of the RKO reverberation chamber.

DANIEL J. BLOOMBERG and the REPUBLIC STUDIO SOUND DEPARTMENT for the design and development of a multi-interlock selector switch.

BERNARD B. BROWN and JOHN P. LIVADARY for the design and

engineering of a separate soloist and chorus recording room.

PAUL ZEFF, S. J. TWINING, and GEORGE SEID of the Columbia Studio Laboratory for the formula and application to production of a simplified variable area sound negative developer.

PAUL LERPAE for the design and construction of the Paramount traveling matte projection and photographing device.

EIGHTEENTH YEAR

1945

Nominations Announced: January 28, 1946
Awards Ceremony: March 7, 1946
Grauman's Chinese Theatre
(MCs: Bob Hope and James Stewart)

Best Picture

ANCHORS AWEIGH, Metro-Goldwyn-Mayer. Joe Pasternak, Producer.
THE BELLS OF ST. MARY'S, Rainbow, RKO Radio. Leo McCarey, Producer.
★ THE LOST WEEKEND, Paramount. Charles Brackett, Producer.
MILDRED PIERCE, Warner Bros. Jerry Wald, Producer.
SPELLBOUND, Selznick International, UA. David O. Selznick, Producer.

Actor

BING CROSBY in *The Bells of St. Mary's*, Rainbow, RKO Radio.
GENE KELLY in *Anchors Aweigh*, Metro-Goldwyn-Mayer.
★ RAY MILLAND in *The Lost Weekend*, Paramount.
GREGORY PECK in *The Keys of the Kingdom*, 20th Century-Fox.
CORNEL WILDE in *A Song to Remember*, Columbia.

Actress

INGRID BERGMAN in *The Bells of St. Mary's*, Rainbow, RKO Radio.
★ JOAN CRAWFORD in *Mildred Pierce*, Warner Bros.
GREER GARSON in *The Valley of Decision*, Metro-Goldwyn-Mayer.
JENNIFER JONES in *Love Letters*, Wallis, Paramount.
GENE TIERNEY in *Leave Her to Heaven*, 20th Century-Fox.

Supporting Actor

MICHAEL CHEKHOV in *Spellbound*, Selznick, UA.
JOHN DALL in *The Corn Is Green*, Warner Bros.
★ JAMES DUNN in *A Tree Grows in Brooklyn, 20th Century-Fox.*
ROBERT MITCHUM in *G. I. Joe*, Cowan, UA.
J. CARROL NAISH in *A Medal for Benny*, Paramount.

Supporting Actress

EVE ARDEN in *Mildred Pierce*, Warner Bros.
ANN BLYTH in *Mildred Pierce*, Warner Bros.
ANGELA LANSBURY in *The Picture of Dorian Gray*, Metro-Goldwyn-Mayer.
JOAN LORRING in *The Corn Is Green*, Warner Bros.
★ ANNE REVERE in *National Velvet*, Metro-Goldwyn-Mayer.

Directing

CLARENCE BROWN for *National Velvet*, Metro-Goldwyn-Mayer.

ALFRED HITCHCOCK for *Spellbound*, Selznick, UA.

LEO MCCAREY for *The Bells of St. Mary's*, Rainbow, RKO Radio.

JEAN RENOIR for *The Southerner*, Loew-Hakim, UA.

★ BILLY WILDER for *The Lost Weekend*, Paramount.

Writing

Original Story

THE AFFAIRS OF SUSAN, Wallis, Paramount: LASZLO GOROG and THOMAS MONROE.

★ THE HOUSE ON 92ND STREET, 20th Century-Fox: CHARLES G. BOOTH.

A MEDAL FOR BENNY, Paramount: JOHN STEINBECK and JACK WAGNER.

OBJECTIVE-BURMA, Warner Bros.: ALVAH BESSIE.

A SONG TO REMEMBER, Columbia: ERNST MARISCHKA.

Original Screenplay

DILLINGER, Monogram: PHILIP YORDAN.

★ MARIE-LOUISE, Praesens Films (Swiss): RICHARD SCHWEIZER.

MUSIC FOR MILLIONS, Metro-Goldwyn-Mayer: MYLES CONNOLLY.

SALTY O'ROURKE, Paramount: MILTON HOLMES.

WHAT NEXT, CORPORAL HARGROVE?, Metro-Goldwyn-Mayer: HARRY KURNITZ.

Screenplay

G. I. JOE, Cowan, UA: LEOPOLD ATLAS, GUY ENDORE, and PHILIP STEVENSON.

★ THE LOST WEEKEND, Paramount: CHARLES BRACKETT and BILLY WILDER.

MILDRED PIERCE, Warner Bros.: RANALD MACDOUGAL.

PRIDE OF THE MARINES, Warner Bros.: ALBERT MALTZ.

A TREE GROWS IN BROOKLYN, 20th Century-Fox: FRANK DAVIS and TESS SLESINGER.

Cinematography

Black and White

THE KEYS OF THE KINGDOM, 20th Century-Fox: ARTHUR MILLER.

THE LOST WEEKEND, Paramount: JOHN F. SEITZ.

MILDRED PIERCE, Warner Bros.: ERNEST HALLER.

★ THE PICTURE OF DORIAN GRAY, Metro-Goldwyn-Mayer: HARRY STRADLING.

SPELLBOUND, Selznick, UA: GEORGE BARNES.

Color

ANCHORS AWEIGH, Metro-Goldwyn-Mayer: ROBERT PLANCK and CHARLES BOYLE.

★ LEAVE HER TO HEAVEN, 20th Century-Fox: LEON SHAMROY.

NATIONAL VELVET, Metro-Goldwyn-Mayer: LEONARD SMITH.

A SONG TO REMEMBER, Columbia: TONY GAUDIO and ALLEN M. DAVEY.

THE SPANISH MAIN, RKO Radio: GEORGE BARNES.

Art Direction-Interior Decoration

Black and White

★ BLOOD ON THE SUN, Cagney, UA: WIARD IHNEN; Interior Decoration: A. ROLAND FIELDS.

EXPERIMENT PERILOUS, RKO Radio: ALBERT S. D'AGOSTINO and JACK OKEY; Interior Decoration: DARRELL SILVERA and CLAUDE CARPENTER.

THE KEYS OF THE KINGDOM, 20th Century-Fox: JAMES BASEVI and WILLIAM DARLING; Interior Decoration: THOMAS LITTLE and FRANK E. HUGHES.

LOVE LETTERS, Hal Wallis, Paramount: HANS DREIER and ROLAND ANDERSON;

Interior Decoration: SAM COMER and RAY MOYER.

THE PICTURE OF DORIAN GRAY, Metro-Godwyn-Mayer: CEDRIC GIBBONS and HANS PETERS; Interior Decoration: EDWIN B. WILLIS, JOHN BONAR, and HUGH HUNT.

Color

★ FRENCHMAN'S CREEK, Paramount: HANS DREIER and ERNST FEGTE; Interior Decoration: SAM COMER.

LEAVE HER TO HEAVEN, 20th Century-Fox: LYLE WHEELER and MAURICE RANSFORD; Interior Decoration: THOMAS LITTLE.

NATIONAL VELVET, Metro-Goldwyn-Mayer: CEDRIC GIBBONS and URIE MCCLEARY; Interior Decoration: EDWIN B. WILLIS and MILDRED GRIFFITHS.

SAN ANTONIO, Warner Bros.: TED SMITH; Interior Decoration: JACK MCCONAGHY.

A THOUSAND AND ONE NIGHTS, Columbia: STEPHEN GOOSSON and RUDOLPH STERNAD; Interior Decoration: FRANK TUTTLE.

Sound Recording

★ THE BELLS OF ST. MARY'S, Rainbow, RKO Radio: RKO RADIO STUDIO SOUND DEPARTMENT, STEPHEN DUNN, Sound Director.

THE FLAME OF THE BARBARY COAST. Republic: REPUBLIC STUDIO SOUND DEPARTMENT, DANIEL J. BLOOMBERG, Sound Director.

LADY ON A TRAIN, Universal: UNIVERSAL STUDIO SOUND DEPARTMENT, BERNARD B. BROWN, Sound Director.

LEAVE HER TO HEAVEN, 20th Century-Fox: 20TH CENTURY-FOX STUDIO SOUND DEPARTMENT, THOMAS T. MOULTON, Sound Director.

RHAPSODY IN BLUE, Warner Bros.: WARNER BROS. STUDIO SOUND DEPARTMENT, NATHAN LEVINSON, Sound Director.

A SONG TO REMEMBER, Columbia: COLUMBIA STUDIO SOUND DEPARTMENT, JOHN LIVADARY, Sound Director.

THE SOUTHERNER, Loew-Hakim, UA: SOUND SERVICES, INC., JACK WHITNEY, Sound Director.

THEY WERE EXPENDABLE, M-G-M: M-G-M STUDIO SOUND DEPARTMENT, DOUGLAS SHEARER, Sound Director.

THE THREE CABALLEROS, Disney, RKO Radio: WALT DISNEY STUDIO SOUND DEPARTMENT, C. O. SLYFIELD, Sound Director.

THREE IS A FAMILY, Master Productions, UA: RCA SOUND, W. V. WOLFE, Sound Director.

THE UNSEEN, Paramount: PARAMOUNT STUDIO SOUND DEPARTMENT, LOREN L. RYDER, Sound Director.

WONDER MAN, Goldwyn, RKO Radio: SAMUEL GOLDWYN STUDIO SOUND DEPARTMENT, GORDON SAWYER, Sound Director.

Film Editing

THE BELLS OF ST. MARY'S, Rainbow, RKO Radio: HARRY MARKER.

THE LOST WEEKEND, Paramount: DOANE HARRISON.

★ NATIONAL VELVET, Metro-Goldwyn-Mayer: ROBERT J. KERN.

OBJECTIVE-BURMA, Warner Bros.: GEORGE AMY.

A SONG TO REMEMBER, Columbia: CHARLES NELSON.

Music

Scoring of a Dramatic or Comedy Picture

THE BELLS OF ST. MARY'S, Rainbow, RKO Radio: ROBERT EMMETT DOLAN.

BREWSTER'S MILLIONS, Small, UA: LOU FORBES.

CAPTAIN KIDD, Bogeaus, UA: WERNER JANSSEN.

ENCHANTED COTTAGE, RKO Radio: ROY WEBB.

FLAME OF THE BARBARY COAST, Republic: DALE BUTTS and MORTON SCOTT.

G. I. HONEYMOON, Monogram: EDWARD J. KAY.

G. I. JOE, Cowan, UA: LOUIS APPLEBAUM and ANN RONELL.

GUEST IN THE HOUSE, Guest in the House, Inc., UA: WERNER JANSSEN.

GUEST WIFE, Greentree Prods., UA: DANIELE AMFITHEATROF.

THE KEYS OF THE KINGDOM, 20th Century-Fox: ALFRED NEWMAN.

THE LOST WEEKEND, Paramount: MIKLOS ROZSA.

LOVE LETTERS, Wallis, Paramount: VICTOR YOUNG.

MAN WHO WALKED ALONE, PRC: KARL HAJOS.

OBJECTIVE-BURMA, Warner Bros.: FRANZ WAXMAN.

PARIS-UNDERGROUND, Bennett, UA: ALEXANDER TANSMAN.

A SONG TO REMEMBER, Columbia: MIKLOS ROZSA and MORRIS STOLOFF.

THE SOUTHERNER, Loew-Hakim, UA: WERNER JANSSEN.

⋆ SPELLBOUND, Selznick, UA: MIKLOS ROZSA.

THIS LOVE OF OURS, Universal: H. J. SALTER.

VALLEY OF DECISION, Metro-Goldwyn-Mayer: HERBERT STOTHART.

WOMAN IN THE WINDOW, International, RKO Radio: HUGO FRIEDHOFER and ARTHUR LANGE.

Scoring of a Musical Picture

⋆ ANCHORS AWEIGH, Metro-Goldwyn-Mayer: GEORGIE STOLL.

BELLE OF THE YUKON, International, RKO Radio: ARTHUR LANGE.

CAN'T HELP SINGING, Universal: JEROME KERN and H. J. SALTER.

HITCHHIKE TO HAPPINESS, Republic: MORTON SCOTT.

INCENDIARY BLONDE, Paramount: ROBERT EMMETT DOLAN.

RHAPSODY IN BLUE, Warner Bros.: RAY HEINDORF and MAX STEINER.

STATE FAIR, 20th Century-Fox: CHARLES HENDERSON and ALFRED NEWMAN.

SUNBONNET SUE, Monogram: EDWARD J. KAY.

THREE CABALLEROS, Disney-RKO Radio: EDWARD PLUMB, PAUL J. SMITH, and CHARLES WOLCOTT.

TONIGHT AND EVERY NIGHT, Columbia: MARLIN SKILES and MORRIS STOLOFF.

WHY GIRLS LEAVE HOME, PRC.: WALTER GREENE.

WONDER MAN, Beverly, RKO Radio: LOU FORBES and RAY HEINDORF.

Best Song

ACCENTUATE THE POSITIVE from *Here Come the Waves*, Paramount: Music by HAROLD ARLEN; Lyrics by JOHNNY MERCER.

ANYWHERE from *Tonight and Every Night*, Columbia: Music by JULE STYNE; Lyrics by SAMMY CAHN.

AREN'T YOU GLAD YOU'RE YOU from *The Bells of St. Mary's*, Rainbow, RKO Radio: Music by JAMES VAN HEUSEN: Lyrics by JOHNNY BURKE.

THE CAT AND THE CANARY from *Why Girls Leave Home*, PRC: Music by JAY LIVINGSTON; Lyrics by RAY EVANS.

ENDLESSLY from *Earl Carroll Vanities*, Republic: Music by WALTER KENT, Lyrics by KIM GANNON.

I FALL IN LOVE TOO EASILY from *Anchors Aweigh*, Metro-Goldwyn-Mayer: Music by JULE STYNE; Lyrics by SAMMY CAHN.

I'LL BUY THAT DREAM from *Sing Your Way Home*, RKO Radio: Music by ALLIE WRUBEL; Lyrics by HERB MAGIDSON.

IT MIGHT AS WELL BE SPRING from *State Fair*, 20th Century-Fox: Music by RICHARD RODGERS; Lyrics by OSCAR HAMMERSTEIN II.

LINDA from *G. I. Joe*, Cowan, UA: Music and Lyrics by ANN RONELL.

LOVE LETTERS from *Love Letters*, Wallis, Paramount: Music by VICTOR YOUNG; Lyrics by EDWARD HEYMAN.

MORE AND MORE from *Can't Help Singing*, Universal: Music by JEROME KERN; Lyrics by E. Y. HARBURG.

SLEIGHRIDE IN JULY from *Belle of the Yukon*, International, RKO Radio: Music by JAMES VAN HEUSEN; Lyrics by JOHNNY BURKE.

SO IN LOVE from *Wonder Man*, Beverly Prods., RKO Radio: Music by DAVID ROSE; Lyrics by LEO ROBIN.

SOME SUNDAY MORNING from *San Antonio*, Warner Bros.: Music by RAY HEINDORF and M. K. JEROME; Lyrics by TED KOEHLER.

Special Effects

CAPTAIN EDDIE, 20th Century-Fox: Photographic: FRED SERSEN and SOL HALPRIN; Sound: ROGER HEMAN and HARRY LEONARD.

SPELLBOUND, Selznick, UA: Photographic: JACK COSGROVE; Sound: No credits listed.

THEY WERE EXPENDABLE, Metro-Goldwyn-Mayer: Photographic: A. ARNOLD GILLESPIE, DONALD JAHRAUS, and R. A. MACDONALD; Sound: MICHAEL STEINORE.

A THOUSAND AND ONE NIGHTS, Columbia: Photographic: L. W. BUTLER; Sound: RAY BOMBA.

★ WONDER MAN, Goldwyn, RKO Radio: Photographic: JOHN FULTON; Sound: A. W. JOHNS.

Short Subjects

Cartoons

DONALD'S CRIME, Walt Disney, RKO Radio: (Donald Duck) WALT DISNEY, Producer.

JASPER AND THE BEANSTALK, Paramount: (Pal Puppetoon-Jasper Series) GEORGE PAL, Producer.

LIFE WITH FEATHERS, Warner Bros.: (Merrie Melodies) EDDIE SELZER, Producer.

MIGHTY MOUSE IN GYPSY LIFE, 20th Century-Fox: (Terrytoon) PAUL TERRY, Producer.

POET AND PEASANT, Universal: (Lantz Technicolor Cartune) WALTER LANTZ, Producer.

★ QUIET PLEASE, Metro-Goldwyn-Mayer: (Tom and Jerry Series) FREDERICK QUIMBY, Producer.

RIPPLING ROMANCE, Columbia. (Color Rhapsodies)

One Reel

ALONG THE RAINBOW TRAIL, 20th Century-Fox: (Movietone Adventure) EDMUND REEK, Producer.

SCREEN SNAPSHOTS 25TH ANNIVERSARY, Columbia: (Screen Snapshots) RALPH STAUB, Producer.

★ STAIRWAY TO LIGHT, Metro-Goldwyn-Mayer: (John Nesbitt Passing Parade) HERBERT MOULTON, Producer.

STORY OF A DOG, Warner Bros.: (Vitaphone Varieties) GORDON HOLLINGSHEAD, Producer.

WHITE RHAPSODY, Paramount: (Sportlights) GRANTLAND RICE, Producer.

YOUR NATIONAL GALLERY, Universal: (Variety Views) JOSEPH O'BRIEN and THOMAS MEAD, Producers.

Two reels

A GUN IN HIS HAND, Metro-Goldwyn-Mayer: (Crime Does Not Pay) CHESTER FRANKLIN, Producer.

THE JURY GOES ROUND 'N' ROUND, Columbia: (All Star Comedies) JULES WHITE, Producer.

THE LITTLE WITCH, Paramount: (Musical Parade) GEORGE TEMPLETON, Producer.

★ STAR IN THE NIGHT, Warner

Bros.: (Broadway Brevities) GORDON HOLLINGSHEAD, Producer.

Documentary

Short Subjects

★ HITLER LIVES?, Warner Bros.

LIBRARY OF CONGRESS, Overseas Motion Picture Bureau, Office of War Information.

TO THE SHORES OF IWO JIMA, U.S. Marine Corps.

Features

THE LAST BOMB, U.S. Army Air Force.

★ THE TRUE GLORY, Governments of Great Britain and the United States of America.

Special Awards

WALTER WANGER for his six years of service as president of the Academy of Motion Picture Arts and Sciences. (Special plaque)

PEGGY ANN GARNER, outstanding child actress of 1945. (Miniature statuette)

THE HOUSE I LIVE IN, tolerance short subject: produced by Frank Ross and Mervyn LeRoy; directed by Mervyn LeRoy; screenplay by Albert Maltz; song *The House I Live In* music by Earl Robinson, lyrics by Lewis Allen; starring Frank Sinatra; released by RKO Radio. (Statuette)

REPUBLIC STUDIO, DANIEL J. BLOOMBERG, and the REPUBLIC SOUND DEPARTMENT for the building of an outstanding musical scoring auditorium that provides optimum recording conditions and combines all elements of acoustic and engineering design. (Certificates)

Irving G. Thalberg Memorial Award

None.

Scientific or Technical

Class I

None.

Class II

None.

Class III

LOREN L. RYDER, CHARLES R. DAILY, and the PARAMOUNT STUDIO SOUND DEPARTMENT for the design, construction, and use of the first dial-controlled step-by-step sound channel line-up and test circuit.

MICHAEL S. LESHING, BENJAMIN C. ROBINSON, ARTHUR B. CHATELAIN, and ROBERT C. STEVENS of 20th Century-Fox Studio and JOHN G. CAPSTAFF of Eastman Kodak Co. for the 20th Century-Fox film processing machine.

1946

Nominations Announced: February 10, 1947
Awards Ceremony: March 13, 1947
Shrine Civic Auditorium
(MC: Jack Benny)

Best Picture

★ THE BEST YEARS OF OUR LIVES, Goldwyn, RKO Radio. Samuel Goldwyn, Producer.

HENRY V, Rank-Two Cities, UA (British). Laurence Olivier, Producer.

IT'S A WONDERFUL LIFE, Liberty, RKO Radio. Frank Capra, Producer.

THE RAZOR'S EDGE, 20th Century-Fox. Darryl F. Zanuck, Producer.

THE YEARLING, Metro-Goldwyn-Mayer. Sidney Franklin, Producer.

Actor

★ FREDRIC MARCH in *The Best Years of Our Lives*, Goldwyn, RKO Radio.

LAURENCE OLIVIER in *Henry V*, J. Arthur Rank-Two Cities, UA (British).

LARRY PARKS in *The Jolson Story*, Columbia.

GREGORY PECK in *The Yearling*, Metro-Goldwyn-Mayer.

JAMES STEWART in *It's a Wonderful Life*, Liberty Films, RKO Radio.

Actress

★ OLIVIA DE HAVILLAND in *To Each His Own*, Paramount.

CELIA JOHNSON in *Brief Encounter*, Rank, U-I (British).

JENNIFER JONES in *Duel in the Sun*, Selznick International.

ROSALIND RUSSELL in *Sister Kenny*, RKO Radio.

JANE WYMAN in *The Yearling*, Metro-Goldwyn-Mayer.

Supporting Actor

CHARLES COBURN in *The Green Years*, Metro-Goldwyn-Mayer.

WILLIAM DEMAREST in *The Jolson Story*, Columbia.

CLAUDE RAINS in *Notorious*, RKO Radio.

★ HAROLD RUSSELL in *The Best Years of Our Lives*, Goldwyn, RKO Radio.

CLIFTON WEBB in *The Razor's Edge*, 20th Century-Fox.

Supporting Actress

ETHEL BARRYMORE in *The Spiral Staircase*, RKO Radio.

★ ANNE BAXTER in *The Razor's Edge*, 20th Century-Fox.

LILLIAN GISH in *Duel in the Sun*, Selznick International.

FLORA ROBSON in *Saratoga Trunk*, Warner Bros.

GALE SONDERGAARD in *Anna and the King of Siam*, 20th Century-Fox.

Directing

CLARENCE BROWN for *The Yearling*, Metro-Goldwyn-Mayer.

FRANK CAPRA for *It's a Wonderful Life*, Liberty, RKO Radio.

DAVID LEAN for *Brief Encounter*, Rank, U-I (British).

ROBERT SIODMAK for *The Killers*, Hellinger, Universal.

★ WILLIAM WYLER for *The Best Years of Our Lives*, Goldwyn, RKO Radio.

Writing

Original Story

THE DARK MIRROR, Universal-International: VLADIMIR POZNER.

THE STRANGE LOVE OF MARTHA IVERS, Wallis, Paramount: JACK PATRICK.

THE STRANGER, International, RKO Radio: VICTOR TRIVAS.

TO EACH HIS OWN, Paramount: CHARLES BRACKETT.

★ VACATION FROM MARRIAGE, London Films, M-G-M (British): CLEMENCE DANE.

Original Screenplay

THE BLUE DAHLIA, Paramount: RAYMOND CHANDLER.

CHILDREN OF PARADISE, Pathé-Cinema, Tricolore (French): JACQUES PREVERT.

NOTORIOUS, RKO Radio: BEN HECHT.

THE ROAD TO UTOPIA, Paramount: NORMAN PANAMA and MELVIN FRANK.

★ THE SEVENTH VEIL, Rank, Universal (British): MURIEL BOX and SYDNEY BOX.

Screenplay

ANNA AND THE KING OF SIAM, 20th Century-Fox: SALLY BENSON and TALBOT JENNINGS.

★ THE BEST YEARS OF OUR LIVES, Goldwyn, RKO Radio: ROBERT E. SHERWOOD.

BRIEF ENCOUNTER, Rank, U-I (British): ANTHONY HAVELOCK-ALLAN, DAVID LEAN, and RONALD NEAME.

THE KILLERS, Hellinger, U-I: ANTHONY VEILLER.

OPEN CITY, Minerva Films (Italian): SERGIO AMIDEI and F. FELLINI.

Cinematography

Black and White

★ ANNA AND THE KING OF SIAM, 20th Century-Fox: ARTHUR MILLER.

THE GREEN YEARS, Metro-Goldwyn-Mayer: GEORGE FOLSEY.

Color

THE JOLSON STORY, Columbia: JOSEPH WALKER.

★ THE YEARLING, Metro-Goldwyn-Mayer: CHARLES ROSHER, LEONARD SMITH, and ARTHUR ARLING.

Art Direction-Interior Decoration

Black and White

★ ANNA AND THE KING OF SIAM, 20th Century-Fox: LYLE WHEELER and WILLIAM DARLING; Interior Decoration: THOMAS LITTLE and FRANK E. HUGHES.

KITTY, Paramount: HANS DREIER and WALTER TYLER; Interior Decoration: SAM COMER and RAY MOYER.

THE RAZOR'S EDGE, 20th Century-Fox: RICHARD DAY and NATHAN JURAN; Interior Decoration: THOMAS LITTLE and PAUL S. FOX.

Color

CAESAR AND CLEOPATRA, Rank, UA (British): JOHN BRYAN; Interior Decoration: No credits listed.

HENRY V, Rank, UA (British): PAUL SHERIFF and CARMEN DILLON;

Interior Decoration: No credits listed.

★ THE YEARLING, Metro-Goldwyn-Mayer: CEDRIC GIBBONS and PAUL GROESSE; Interior Decoration: EDWIN B. WILLIS.

Sound Recording

THE BEST YEARS OF OUR LIVES, Goldwyn, RKO Radio: SAMUEL GOLDWYN STUDIO SOUND DEPARTMENT, GORDON SAWYER, Sound Director.

IT'S A WONDERFUL LIFE, Liberty, RKO Radio: RKO RADIO STUDIO SOUND DEPARTMENT, JOHN AALBERG, Sound Director.

★ THE JOLSON STORY, Columbia: COLUMBIA STUDIO SOUND DEPARTMENT, JOHN LIVADARY, Sound Director.

Film Editing

★ THE BEST YEARS OF OUR LIVES, Goldwyn, RKO Radio: DANIEL MANDELL.

IT'S A WONDERFUL LIFE, Liberty, RKO Radio: WILLIAM HORNBECK.

THE JOLSON STORY, Columbia: WILLIAM LYON.

THE KILLERS, Hellinger, Universal: ARTHUR HILTON.

THE YEARLING, Metro-Goldwyn-Mayer: HAROLD KRESS.

Music

Scoring of a Dramatic or Comedy Picture

ANNA AND THE KING OF SIAM, 20th Century-Fox: BERNARD HERRMANN.

★ THE BEST YEARS OF OUR LIVES, Goldwyn, RKO Radio: HUGO FRIEDHOFER.

HENRY V, Rank, UA (British): WILLIAM WALTON.

HUMORESQUE, Warner Bros.: FRANZ WAXMAN.

THE KILLERS, Universal: MIKLOS ROZSA.

Scoring of a Musical Picture

BLUE SKIES, Paramount: ROBERT EMMETT DOLAN.

CENTENNIAL SUMMER, 20th Century-Fox: ALFRED NEWMAN.

THE HARVEY GIRLS, Metro-Goldwyn-Mayer: LENNIE HAYTON.

★ THE JOLSON STORY, Columbia: MORRIS STOLOFF.

NIGHT AND DAY, Warner Bros.: RAY HEINDORF and MAX STEINER.

Song

ALL THROUGH THE DAY from *Centennial Summer*, 20th Century-Fox: Music by JEROME KERN; Lyrics by OSCAR HAMMERSTEIN II.

I CAN'T BEGIN TO TELL YOU from *The Dolly Sisters*, 20th Century-Fox: Music by JAMES MONACO; Lyrics by MACK GORDON.

OLE BUTTERMILK SKY from *Canyon Passage*, Wanger, Universal: Music by HOAGY CARMICHAEL; Lyrics by JACK BROOKS.

★ ON THE ATCHISON, TOPEKA AND SANTA FE from *The Harvey Girls*, Metro-Goldwyn-Mayer: Music by HARRY WARREN; Lyrics by JOHNNY MERCER.

YOU KEEP COMING BACK LIKE A SONG from *Blue Skies*, Paramount: Music and Lyrics by IRVING BERLIN.

Special Effects

★ BLITHE SPIRIT, Rank UA (British): Visual: THOMAS HOWARD; Audible: No credit.

A STOLEN LIFE, Warner Bros.: Visual: WILLIAM MCGANN; Audible: NATHAN LEVINSON.

Short Subjects

Cartoons

★ THE CAT CONCERTO, Metro-Goldwyn-Mayer: (Tom and Jerry) FREDERICK QUIMBY, Producer.

CHOPIN'S MUSICAL MOMENTS, Universal: (Musical Miniatures) WALTER LANTZ, Producer.

JOHN HENRY AND THE INKY POO, Paramount: (Puppetoon) GEORGE PAL, Producer.

SQUATTER'S RIGHTS, Disney-RKO Radio: (Mickey Mouse) WALT DISNEY, Producer.

WALKY TALKY HAWKY, Warner Bros.: (Merrie Melodies) EDWARD SELZER, Producer.

One Reel

DIVE-HI CHAMPS, Paramount: (Sportlights) JACK EATON, Producer.

★ FACING YOUR DANGER, Warner Bros.: (Sports Parade) GORDON HOLLINGSHEAD, Producer.

GOLDEN HORSES, 20th Century-Fox: (Movietone Sports Review) EDMUND REEK, Producer.

SMART AS A FOX, Warner Bros.: (Varieties) GORDON HOLLINGSHEAD, Producer.

SURE CURES, Metro-Goldwyn-Mayer: (Pete Smith Specialty) PETE SMITH, Producer.

Two Reels

★ A BOY AND HIS DOG, Warner Bros.: (Featurettes) GORDON HOLLINGSHEAD, Producer.

COLLEGE QUEEN, Paramount: (Musical Parade) GEORGE TEMPLETON, Producer.

HISS AND YELL, Columbia: (All Star Comedies) JULES WHITE, Producer.

THE LUCKIEST GUY IN THE WORLD, Metro-Goldwyn-Mayer: (Two-reel special) JERRY BRESLER, Producer.

Documentary

Short Subjects

ATOMIC POWER, 20th Century-Fox.

LIFE AT THE ZOO, Artkino.

PARAMOUNT NEWS ISSUE #37, Paramount.

★ SEEDS OF DESTINY, U.S. War Department.

TRAFFIC WITH THE DEVIL, Metro-Goldwyn-Mayer.

Features

No Features were nominated this year.

Special Awards

LAURENCE OLIVIER for his outstanding achievement as actor, producer, and director in bringing *Henry V* to the screen. (Statuette)

HAROLD RUSSELL for bringing hope and courage to his fellow veterans through his appearance in *The Best Years of Our Lives*. (Statuette)

ERNST LUBITSCH for his distinguished contributions to the art of the motion picture. (Scroll)

CLAUDE JARMAN, JR., outstanding child actor of 1946. (Miniature statuette)

Irving G. Thalberg Memorial Award

SAMUEL GOLDWYN.

Scientific or Technical

Class I

None.

Class II

None.

Class III

HARLAN L. BAUMBACH and the PARAMOUNT WEST COAST LABORATORY for an improved method for the quantitative determination of hydroquinone and metol in photographic developing baths.

HERBERT E. BRITT for the development and application of formulas and equipment for producing cloud and smoke effects.

BURTON F. MILLER and the WARNER BROS. STUDIO SOUND and ELECTRICAL

DEPARTMENTS for the design and construction of a motion picture arc lighting generator filter.

CARL FAULKNER of the 20th Century-Fox Studio Sound Department for the reversed bias method, including a double bias method for light valve and galvanometer density recording.

MOLE-RICHARDSON CO. for the Type 450 superhigh-intensity carbon arc lamp.

ARTHUR F. BLINN, ROBERT O. COOK, C. O. SLYFIELD, and the WALT DISNEY STUDIO SOUND DEPARTMENT for the design and development of an audio finder and track viewer for checking and locating noise in sound tracks.

BURTON F. MILLER and the WARNER BROS. STUDIO SOUND DEPARTMENT for the design and application of an equalizer to eliminate relative spectral energy distortion in electronic compressors.

MARTY MARTIN and HAL ADKINS of the RKO Radio Studio Miniature Department for the design and construction of equipment providing visual bullet effects.

HAROLD NYE and the WARNER BROS. STUDIO ELECTRICAL DEPARTMENT for the development of the electronically controlled fire and gaslight effect.

1947

Nominations Announced: February 15, 1948
Awards Ceremony: March 20, 1948
Shrine Civic Auditorium
(No MC)

Best Picture

THE BISHOP'S WIFE, Goldwyn, RKO Radio. Samuel Goldwyn, Producer.

CROSSFIRE, RKO Radio. Adrian Scott, Producer.

★ GENTLEMAN'S AGREEMENT, 20th Century-Fox. Darryl F. Zanuck, Producer.

GREAT EXPECTATIONS, Rank-Cineguild, U-I (British). Ronald Neame, Producer.

MIRACLE ON 34TH STREET, 20th Century-Fox. William Perlberg, Producer.

Actor

★ RONALD COLMAN in *A Double Life*, Kanin, U-I.

JOHN GARFIELD in *Body and Soul*, Enterprise, UA.

GREGORY PECK in *Gentleman's Agreement*, 20th Century-Fox.

WILLIAM POWELL in *Life with Father*, Warner Bros.

MICHAEL REDGRAVE in *Mourning Becomes Electra*, RKO Radio.

Actress

JOAN CRAWFORD in *Possessed*, Warner Bros.

SUSAN HAYWARD in *Smash Up—The Story of a Woman*, Wanger, U-I.

DOROTHY MCGUIRE in *Gentleman's Agreement*, 20th Century-Fox.

ROSALIND RUSSELL in *Mourning Becomes Electra*, RKO Radio.

★ LORETTA YOUNG in *The Farmer's Daughter*, RKO Radio.

Supporting Actor

CHARLES BICKFORD in *The Farmer's Daughter*, RKO Radio.

THOMAS GOMEZ in *Ride the Pink Horse*, Universal-International.

★ EDMUND GWENN in *Miracle on 34th Street*, 20th Century-Fox.

ROBERT RYAN in *Crossfire*, RKO Radio.

RICHARD WIDMARK in *Kiss of Death*, 20th Century-Fox.

Supporting Actress

ETHEL BARRYMORE in *The Paradine Case*, Selznick.

GLORIA GRAHAME in *Crossfire*, RKO Radio.

★ CELESTE HOLM in *Gentleman's Agreement*, 20th Century-Fox.

MARJORIE MAIN in *The Egg and I*, Universal-International.

ANNE REVERE in *Gentleman's Agreement*, 20th Century-Fox.

Directing

GEORGE CUKOR for *A Double Life*, Kanin, U-I.

EDWARD DMYTRYK for *Crossfire*, RKO Radio.

★ ELIA KAZAN for *Gentleman's Agreement*, 20th Century-Fox.
HENRY KOSTER for *The Bishop's Wife*, Goldwyn, RKO Radio.
DAVID LEAN for *Great Expectations*, Rank-Cineguild, U-I (British).

Writing

Original Story

A CAGE OF NIGHTINGALES, Gaumont, Lopert Films (French): GEORGES CHAPEROT and RENÉ WHEELER.
IT HAPPENED ON FIFTH AVENUE, Roy Del Ruth, Allied Artists: HERBERT CLYDE LEWIS and FREDERICK STEPHANI.
KISS OF DEATH, 20th Century-Fox: ELEAZAR LIPSKY.
★ MIRACLE ON 34TH STREET, 20th Century-Fox: VALENTINE DAVIES.
SMASH-UP—THE STORY OF A WOMAN, Wanger, U-I: DOROTHY PARKER and FRANK CAVETT.

Original Screenplay

★ THE BACHELOR AND THE BOBBY-SOXER, RKO Radio: SIDNEY SHELDON.
BODY AND SOUL, Enterprise, UA: ABRAHAM POLONSKY.
A DOUBLE LIFE, Kanin Prod., U-I: RUTH GORDON and GARSON KANIN.
MONSIEUR VERDOUX, Chaplin, UA: CHARLES CHAPLIN.
SHOESHINE, Lopert Films (Italian): SERGIO AMIDEI, ADOLFO FRANCI, C. G. VIOLA, and CESARE ZAVATTINI.

Screenplay

BOOMERANG!, 20th Century-Fox: RICHARD MURPHY.
CROSSFIRE, RKO Radio: JOHN PAXTON.
GENTLEMAN'S AGREEMENT, 20th Century-Fox: MOSS HART.
GREAT EXPECTATIONS, Rank-Cineguild, U-I (British): DAVID LEAN, RONALD NEAME, and ANTHONY HAVELOCK-ALLAN.
★ MIRACLE ON 34TH STREET, 20th Century-Fox: GEORGE SEATON.

Cinematography

Black and White

THE GHOST AND MRS. MUIR, 20th Century-Fox: CHARLES LANG, JR.
★ GREAT EXPECTATIONS, Rank-Cineguild, U-I (British): GUY GREEN.
GREEN DOLPHIN STREET, Metro-Goldwyn-Mayer: GEORGE FOLSEY.

Color

★ BLACK NARCISSUS, Rank-Archers, U-I (British): JACK CARDIFF.
LIFE WITH FATHER, Warner Bros.: PEVERELL MARLEY and WILLIAM V. SKALL.
MOTHER WORE TIGHTS, 20th Century-Fox: HARRY JACKSON.

*Art Direction—Set Decoration**

Black and White

THE FOXES OF HARROW, 20th Century-Fox: LYLE WHEELER and MAURICE RANSFORD; Set Decoration: THOMAS LITTLE and PAUL S. FOX.
★ GREAT EXPECTATIONS, Rank-Cineguild, U-I (British): JOHN BRYAN; Set Decoration: WILFRED SHINGLETON.

Color

★ BLACK NARCISSUS, Rank-Archers, U-I (British): ALFRED JUNGE; Set Decoration: ALFRED JUNGE.
LIFE WITH FATHER, Warner Bros.: ROBERT M. HAAS; Set Decoration: GEORGE JAMES HOPKINS.

*Known as Art Direction-Interior Decoration from 1941 to 1946.

Sound Recording

★ THE BISHOP'S WIFE, Goldwyn, RKO Radio: SAMUEL GOLDWYN STUDIO SOUND DEPARTMENT, GORDON SAWYER, Sound Director.

GREEN DOLPHIN STREET, M-G-M: M-G-M STUDIO SOUND DEPARTMENT, DOUGLAS SHEARER, Sound Director.

T-MEN, Reliance Pictures, Eagle-Lion: SOUND SERVICES, INC., JACK WHITNEY, Sound Director.

Film Editing

THE BISHOP'S WIFE, Goldwyn, RKO Radio: MONICA COLLINGWOOD.

★ BODY AND SOUL, Enterprise, UA: FRANCIS LYON and ROBERT PARRISH.

GENTLEMAN'S AGREEMENT, 20th Century-Fox: HARMON JONES.

GREEN DOLPHIN STREET, Metro-Goldwyn-Mayer: GEORGE WHITE.

ODD MAN OUT, Rank-Two Cities, U-I (British): FERGUS MCDONNELL.

Music

Scoring of a Dramatic or Comedy Picture

THE BISHOP'S WIFE, Goldwyn, RKO Radio: HUGO FRIEDHOFER.

CAPTAIN FROM CASTILE, 20th Century-Fox: ALFRED NEWMAN.

★ A DOUBLE LIFE, Kanin, U-I: MIKLOS ROZSA.

FOREVER AMBER, 20th Century-Fox: DAVID RAKSIN.

LIFE WITH FATHER, Warner Bros.: MAX STEINER.

Scoring of a Musical Picture

FIESTA, Metro-Goldwyn-Mayer: JOHNNY GREEN.

★ MOTHER WORE TIGHTS, 20th Century-Fox: ALFRED NEWMAN.

MY WILD IRISH ROSE, Warner Bros.: RAY HEINDORF and MAX STEINER.

ROAD TO RIO, Hope-Crosby, Paramount: ROBERT EMMETT DOLAN.

SONG OF THE SOUTH, Disney, RKO Radio: DANIELE AMFITHEATROF, PAUL J. SMITH, and CHARLES WOLCOTT.

Song

A GAL IN CALICO from *The Time, Place and the Girl*, Warner Bros.: Music by ARTHUR SCHWARTZ; Lyrics by LEO ROBIN.

I WISH I DIDN'T LOVE YOU SO from *The Perils of Pauline*, Paramount: Music and Lyrics by FRANK LOESSER.

PASS THAT PEACE PIPE from *Good News*, Metro-Goldwyn-Mayer: Music and Lyrics by RALPH BLANE, HUGH MARTIN, and ROGER EDENS.

YOU DO from *Mother Wore Tights*, 20th Century-Fox: Music by JOSEF MYROW; Lyrics by MACK GORDON.

★ ZIP-A-DEE-DOO-DAH from *Song of the South*, Disney-RKO Radio: Music by ALLIE WRUBEL; Lyrics by RAY GILBERT.

Special Effects

★ GREEN DOLPHIN STREET, Metro-Goldwyn-Mayer: Visual: A. ARNOLD GILLESPIE and WARREN NEWCOMBE; Audible: DOUGLAS SHEARER and MICHAEL STEINORE.

UNCONQUERED, Paramount: Visual: FARCIOT EDOUART, DEVEREUX JENNINGS, GORDON JENNINGS, WALLACE KELLEY, and PAUL LERPAE; Audible: GEORGE DUTTON.

Short Subjects

Cartoons

CHIP AN' DALE, Walt Disney, RKO Radio: (Donald Duck) WALT DISNEY, Producer.

DR. JEKYLL AND MR. MOUSE, Metro-Goldwyn-Mayer: (Tom and Jerry) FREDERICK QUIMBY, Producer.

PLUTO'S BLUE NOTE, Walt Disney, RKO Radio: (Pluto) WALT DISNEY, Producer.

TUBBY THE TUBA, Paramount: (George Pal Puppetoon) GEORGE PAL, Producer.

★ TWEETIE PIE, Warner Bros.: (Merrie Melodies) EDWARD SELZER, Producer.

One Reel

BROOKLYN, U.S.A., Universal-International: (Variety Series) THOMAS MEAD, Producer.

★ GOODBYE MISS TURLOCK, Metro-Goldwyn-Mayer: (John Nesbitt Passing Parade) HERBERT MOULTON, Producer.

MOON ROCKETS, Paramount: (Popular Science) JERRY FAIRBANKS, Producer.

NOW YOU SEE IT, Metro-Goldwyn-Mayer: PETE SMITH, Producer.

SO YOU WANT TO BE IN PICTURES, Warner Bros.: (Joe McDoakes) GORDON HOLLINGSHEAD, Producer.

Two Reels

CHAMPAGNE FOR TWO, Paramount: (Musical Parade Featurette) HARRY GREY, Producer.

★ CLIMBING THE MATTERHORN, Monogram: (Color) IRVING ALLEN, Producer.

FIGHT OF THE WILD STALLIONS, Universal-International: (Special) THOMAS MEAD, Producer.

GIVE US THE EARTH, Metro-Goldwyn-Mayer: (Special) HERBERT MORGAN, Producer.

A VOICE IS BORN, Columbia: (Musical Featurette) BEN BLAKE, Producer.

Documentary

Short Subjects

★ FIRST STEPS, United Nations Division of Films and Visual Education.

PASSPORT TO NOWHERE, RKO Radio: (This Is America Series) FREDERIC ULLMAN, JR., Producer.

SCHOOL IN THE MAILBOX, Australian News and Information Bureau.

Features

★ DESIGN FOR DEATH, RKO Radio: SID ROGELL, Executive Producer; THERON WARTH and RICHARD O. FLEISCHER, Producers.

JOURNEY INTO MEDICINE, U.S. Department of State, Office of Information and Educational Exchange.

THE WORLD IS RICH, British Information Services: PAUL ROTHA, Producer.

Special Awards

JAMES BASKETTE for his able and heart-warming characterization of Uncle Remus, friend and storyteller to the children of the world. (Statuette)

BILL AND COO, in which artistry and patience blended in a novel and entertaining use of the medium of motion pictures. (Plaque)

SHOE-SHINE—the high quality of this motion picture, brought to eloquent life in a country scarred by war, is proof to the world that the creative spirit can triumph over adversity. (Statuette).

COLONEL WILLIAM N. SELIG, ALBERT E. SMITH, THOMAS ARMAT, and GEORGE K. SPOOR, (one of) the small group of pioneers whose belief in a new medium, and whose contributions to its development, blazed the trail along which the motion picture has progressed, in their lifetime, from obscurity to worldwide acclaim. (Statuettes)

Irving G. Thalberg Memorial Award

NONE.

Scientific or Technical

Class I

None.

Class II

C. C. DAVIS and ELECTRICAL RESEARCH PRODUCTS, DIVISION OF WESTERN ELECTRIC CO., for the development and application of an improved film drive filter mechanism.

C. R. DAILY and the PARAMOUNT STUDIO FILM LABORATORY, STILL and ENGINEERING DEPARTMENTS for the development and first practical application to motion picture and still photography of a method of increasing film speed as first suggested to the industry by E. I. duPont de Nemours & Co.

Class III

NATHAN LEVINSON and the WARNER BROS. STUDIO SOUND DEPARTMENT for the design and construction of a constant-speed sound editing machine.

FARCIOT EDOUART, C. R. DAILY, HAL CORL, H. G. CARTWRIGHT, and the PARAMOUNT STUDIO TRANSPARENCY and ENGINEERING DEPARTMENTS for the first application of a special antisolarizing glass to high-intensity background and spot are projectors.

FRED PONEDEL of Warner Bros. Studio for pioneering the fabrication and practical application to motion picture color photography of large translucent photographic backgrounds.

KURT SINGER and the RCA-VICTOR DIVISION of the RADIO CORPORATION OF AMERICA for the design and development of a continuously variable band elimination filter.

JAMES GIBBONS of Warner Bros. Studio for the development and production of large dyed plastic filters for motion picture photography.

1948

Nominations Announced: February 10, 1949
Awards Ceremony: March 24, 1949
Academy Award Theatre
(MC: Robert Montgomery)

Best Picture

★ HAMLET, Rank-Two Cities, U-I (British). Laurence Olivier, Producer.

JOHNNY BELINDA, Warner Bros. Jerry Wald, Producer.

THE RED SHOES, Rank-Archers, Eagle-Lion (British). Michael Powell and Emeric Pressburger, Producers.

THE SNAKE PIT, 20th Century-Fox. Anatole Litvak and Robert Bassler, Producers.

TREASURE OF SIERRA MADRE, Warner Bros. Henry Blanke, Producer.

Actor

LEW AYRES in *Johnny Belinda*, Warner Bros.

MONTGOMERY CLIFT in *The Search*, Praesens Films, M-G-M (Swiss).

DAN DAILEY in *When My Baby Smiles at Me*, 20th Century-Fox.

★ LAURENCE OLIVIER in *Hamlet*, J. Arthur Rank-Two Cities, U-I (British).

CLIFTON WEBB in *Sitting Pretty*, 20th Century-Fox.

Actress

INGRID BERGMAN in *Joan of Arc*, Sierra, RKO Radio.

OLIVIA DE HAVILLAND in *The Snake Pit*, 20th Century-Fox.

IRENE DUNNE in *I Remember Mama*, RKO Radio.

BARBARA STANWYCK in *Sorry, Wrong Number*, Wallis, Paramount.

★ JANE WYMAN in *Johnny Belinda*, Warner Bros.

Supporting Actor

CHARLES BICKFORD in *Johnny Belinda*, Warner Bros.

JOSÉ FERRER in *Joan of Arc*, Sierra, RKO Radio.

OSCAR HOMOLKA in *I Remember Mama*, RKO Radio.

★ WALTER HUSTON in *Treasure of Sierra Madre*, Warner Bros.

CECIL KELLAWAY in *The Luck of the Irish*, 20th Century-Fox.

Supporting Actress

BARBARA BEL GEDDES in *I Remember Mama*, RKO Radio.

ELLEN CORBY in *I Remember Mama*, RKO Radio.

AGNES MOOREHEAD in *Johnny Belinda*, Warner Bros.

JEAN SIMMONS in *Hamlet*, Rank-Two Cities, U-I (British).

★ CLAIRE TREVOR in *Key Largo*, Warner Bros.

Directing

★ JOHN HUSTON for *Treasure of Sierra Madre*, Warner Bros.

ANATOLE LITVAK for *The Snake Pit*, 20th Century-Fox.
JEAN NEGULESCO for *Johnny Belinda*, Warner Bros.
LAURENCE OLIVIER for *Hamlet*, Rank-Two Cities, U-I (British).
FRED ZINNEMANN for *The Search*, Praesens Films, M-G-M (Swiss).

Writing

Motion Picture Story

THE LOUISIANA STORY, Robert Flaherty, Lopert: FRANCES FLAHERTY and ROBERT FLAHERTY.
THE NAKED CITY, Hellinger, U-I: MALVIN WALD.
RED RIVER, Monterey Productions, UA: BORDEN CHASE.
THE RED SHOES, Rank-Archers, Eagle-Lion (British): EMERIC PRESSBURGER.
★ THE SEARCH, Praesens Films, M-G-M (Swiss): RICHARD SCHWEIZER and DAVID WECHSLER.

Screenplay

A FOREIGN AFFAIR, Paramount: CHARLES BRACKETT, BILLY WILDER, and RICHARD L. BREEN.
JOHNNY BELINDA, Warner Bros.: IRMGARD VON CUBE and ALLEN VINCENT.
THE SEARCH, Praesens Films, M-G-M (Swiss): RICHARD SCHWEIZER and DAVID WECHSLER.
THE SNAKE PIT, 20th Century-Fox: FRANK PARTOS and MILLEN BRAND.
★ TREASURE OF SIERRA MADRE, Warner Bros.: JOHN HUSTON.

Cinematography

Black and White

A FOREIGN AFFAIR, Paramount: CHARLES B. LANG, JR.
I REMEMBER MAMA, RKO Radio: NICHOLAS MUSURACA.
JOHNNY BELINDA, Warner Bros.: TED MCCORD.
★ THE NAKED CITY, Hellinger, U-I: WILLIAM DANIELS.
PORTRAIT OF JENNIE, Selznick Studio: JOSEPH AUGUST.

Color

GREEN GRASS OF WYOMING, 20th Century-Fox: CHARLES G. CLARKE.
★ JOAN OF ARC, Sierra Pictures, RKO Radio: JOSEPH VALENTINE, WILLIAM V. SKALL, and WINTON HOCH.
THE LOVES OF CARMEN, Beckworth Corporation, Columbia: WILLIAM SNYDER.
THE THREE MUSKETEERS, Metro-Goldwyn-Mayer: ROBERT PLANCK.

Art Direction—Set Decoration

Black and White

★ HAMLET, Rank-Two Cities, U-I (British): ROGER K. FURSE; Set Decoration: CARMEN DILLON.
JOHNNY BELINDA, Warner Bros.: ROBERT HAAS; Set Decoration: WILLIAM WALLACE.

Color

JOAN OF ARC, Sierra Pictures, RKO Radio: RICHARD DAY; Set Decoration: EDWIN CASEY ROBERTS and JOSEPH KISH.
★ THE RED SHOES, Rank-Archers, Eagle-Lion (British): HEIN HECKROTH; Set Decoration: ARTHUR LAWSON.

Sound Recording

JOHNNY BELINDA, Warner Bros.: WARNER BROS. SOUND DEPARTMENT.
MOONRISE, Marshall Grant Prods., Republic: REPUBLIC SOUND DEPARTMENT.
★ THE SNAKE PIT, 20th Century-Fox: 20TH CENTURY-FOX SOUND DEPARTMENT.

Film Editing

JOAN OF ARC, Sierra Pictures, RKO Radio: FRANK SULLIVAN.

JOHNNY BELINDA, Warner Bros.: DAVID WEISBART.

★ THE NAKED CITY, Hellinger, U-I: PAUL WEATHERWAX.

RED RIVER, Monterey Prods., UA: CHRISTIAN NYBY.

THE RED SHOES, Rank-Archers, Eagle-Lion (British): REGINALD MILLS.

Music

Scoring of a Dramatic or Comedy Picture

HAMLET, Rank-Two Cities, U-I (British): WILLIAM WALTON.

JOAN OF ARC, Sierra Pictures, RKO Radio: HUGO FRIEDHOFER.

JOHNNY BELINDA, Warner Bros.: MAX STEINER.

★ THE RED SHOES, Rank-Archers; Eagle-Lion (British): BRIAN EASDALE.

THE SNAKE PIT, 20th Century-Fox: ALFRED NEWMAN.

Scoring of a Musical Picture

★ EASTER PARADE, Metro-Goldwyn-Mayer: JOHNNY GREEN and ROGER EDENS.

THE EMPEROR WALTZ, Paramount: VICTOR YOUNG.

THE PIRATE, Metro-Goldwyn-Mayer: LENNIE HAYTON.

ROMANCE ON THE HIGH SEAS, Curtiz, Warner Bros.: RAY HEINDORF.

WHEN MY BABY SMILES AT ME, 20th Century-Fox: ALFRED NEWMAN.

Song

★ BUTTONS AND BOWS from *The Paleface*, Paramount: Music and Lyrics by JAY LIVINGSTON and RAY EVANS.

FOR EVERY MAN THERE'S A WOMAN from *Casbah*, Marston Pictures, U-I: Music by HAROLD ARLEN; Lyrics by LEO ROBIN.

IT'S MAGIC from *Romance on the High Seas*, Curtiz, Warner Bros.: Music by JULE STYNE; Lyrics by SAMMY CAHN.

THIS IS THE MOMENT from *That Lady in Ermine*, 20th Century-Fox: Music by FREDERICK HOLLANDER; Lyrics by LEO ROBIN.

THE WOODY WOODPECKER SONG from *Wet Blanket Policy*, Walter Lantz, UA (Cartoon): Music and Lyrics by RAMEY IDRISS and GEORGE TIBBLES.

Costume Design

(New Category)

Black and White

B. F.'S DAUGHTER, Metro-Goldwyn-Mayer: IRENE.

★ HAMLET, Rank-Two Cities, U-I (British): ROGER K. FURSE.

Color

THE EMPEROR WALTZ, Paramount: EDITH HEAD and GILE STEELE.

★ JOAN OF ARC, Sierra, RKO Radio: DOROTHY JEAKINS and KARINSKA.

Special Effects

DEEP WATERS, 20th Century-Fox: Visual: RALPH HAMMERAS, FRED SERSEN, and EDWARD SNYDER; Audible: ROGER HEMAN.

★ PORTRAIT OF JENNIE, The Selznick Studio: Visual: PAUL EAGLER, J. McMILLAN JOHNSON, RUSSELL SHEARMAN, and CLARENCE SLIFER; Audible: CHARLES FREEMAN and JAMES G. STEWART.

Short Subjects

Cartoons

★ THE LITTLE ORPHAN, Metro-Goldwyn-Mayer; (Tom and Jerry) FRED QUIMBY, Producer.

MICKEY AND THE SEAL, Walt Disney, RKO Radio: (Pluto) WALT DISNEY, Producer.

MOUSE WRECKERS, Warner Bros.: (Looney Tunes) EDWARD SELZER, Producer.

ROBIN HOODLUM, United Productions of America, Columbia: (Fox and Crow) UNITED PRODUCTIONS OF AMERICA, Producer.

TEA FOR TWO HUNDRED, Walt Disney, RKO Radio: (Donald Duck) WALT DISNEY, Producer.

One Reel

ANNIE WAS A WONDER, Metro-Goldwyn-Mayer: (John Nesbitt Passing Parade) HERBERT MOULTON, Producer.

CINDERELLA HORSE, Warner Bros.: (Sports Parade) GORDON HOLLINGSHEAD, Producer.

SO YOU WANT TO BE ON THE RADIO, Warner Bros.: (Joe McDoakes) GORDON HOLLINGSHEAD, Producer.

★ SYMPHONY OF A CITY, 20th Century-Fox: (Movietone Specialty) EDMUND H. REEK, Producer.

YOU CAN'T WIN, Metro-Goldwyn-Mayer: (Pete Smith Specialty) PETE SMITH, Producer.

Two Reels

CALGARY STAMPEDE, Warner Bros.: (Technicolor Special) GORDON HOLLINGSHEAD, Producer.

GOING TO BLAZES, Metro-Goldwyn-Mayer: (Special) HERBERT MORGAN, Producer.

SAMBA-MANIA, Paramount: (Musical Parade) HARRY GREY, Producer.

★ SEAL ISLAND, Walt Disney, RKO Radio: (True Life Adventure Series) WALT DISNEY, Producer.

SNOW CAPERS, Universal-International: (Special Series) THOMAS MEAD, Producer.

Documentary

Short Subjects

HEART TO HEART, Fact Film Organization: HERBERT MORGAN, Producer.

OPERATION VITTLES, U.S. Army Air Force.

★ TOWARD INDEPENDENCE, U.S. Army.

Features

THE QUIET ONE, Mayer-Burstyn: JANICE LOEB, Producer.

★ THE SECRET LAND, U.S. Navy, M-G-M: O. O. DULL, Producer.

Special Awards

MONSIEUR VINCENT (French)—voted by the Academy Board of Governors as the most outstanding foreign language film released in the United States during 1948. (Statuette)

IVAN JANDL, for the outstanding juvenile performance of 1948 in *The Search*. (Miniature statuette)

SID GRAUMAN, master showman, who raised the standard of the exhibition of motion pictures. (Statuette)

ADOLPH ZUKOR, a man who has been called the father of the feature film in America, for his services to the industry over a period of forty years. (Statuette)

WALTER WANGER for distinguished service to the industry in adding to its moral stature in the world community by his production of the picture *Joan of Arc*. (Statuette)

Irving G. Thalberg Memorial Award

JERRY WALD.

Scientific or Technical

Class I

None.

Class II

VICTOR CACCIALANZA, MAURICE AYERS, and the PARAMOUNT STUDIO SET CONSTRUCTION DEPARTMENT for the development and application of "Paralite," a new lightweight plaster process for set construction.

NICK KALTEN, LOUIS J. WITTI, and the 20TH CENTURY-FOX STUDIO MECHANICAL EFFECTS DEPARTMENT for a process of preserving and flame-proofing foliage.

Class III

MARTY MARTIN, JACK LANNON, RUSSELL SHEARMAN, and the RKO RADIO STUDIO SPECIAL EFFECTS DEPARTMENT for the development of a new method of simulating falling snow on motion picture sets.

A. J. MORAN and the WARNER BROS. STUDIO ELECTRICAL DEPARTMENT for a method of remote control for shutters on motion picture arc lighting equipment.

TWENTY-SECOND YEAR

1949

Nominations Announced: February 14, 1950
Awards Ceremony: March 23, 1950
RKO Pantages Theatre
(MC: Paul Douglas)

Best Picture

★ ALL THE KING'S MEN, Rossen, Columbia. Robert Rossen, Producer.

BATTLEGROUND, Metro-Goldwyn-Mayer. Dore Schary, Producer.

THE HEIRESS, Paramount. William Wyler, Producer.

A LETTER TO THREE WIVES, 20th Century-Fox. Sol C. Siegel, Producer.

TWELVE O'CLOCK HIGH, 20th Century-Fox. Darryl F. Zanuck, Producer.

Actor

★ BRODERICK CRAWFORD in *All the King's Men*, Robert Rossen, Columbia.

KIRK DOUGLAS in *Champion*, Screen Plays Corp., UA.

GREGORY PECK in *Twelve O'Clock High*, 20th Century-Fox.

RICHARD TODD in *The Hasty Heart*, Warner Bros.

JOHN WAYNE in *Sands of Iwo Jima*, Republic.

Actress

JEANNE CRAIN in *Pinky*, 20th Century-Fox.

★ OLIVIA DE HAVILLAND in *The Heiress*, Paramount.

SUSAN HAYWARD in *My Foolish Heart*, Goldwyn, RKO Radio.

DEBORAH KERR in *Edward, My Son*, Metro-Goldwyn-Mayer.

LORETTA YOUNG in *Come to the Stable*, 20th Century-Fox.

Supporting Actor

JOHN IRELAND in *All the King's Men*, Rossen, Columbia.

★ DEAN JAGGER in *Twelve O'Clock High*, 20th Century-Fox.

ARTHUR KENNEDY in *Champion*, Screen Plays Corp., UA.

RALPH RICHARDSON in *The Heiress*, Paramount.

JAMES WHITMORE in *Battleground*, Metro-Goldwyn-Mayer.

Supporting Actress

ETHEL BARRYMORE in *Pinky*, 20th Century-Fox.

CELESTE HOLM in *Come to the Stable*, 20th Century-Fox.

ELSA LANCHESTER in *Come to the Stable*, 20th Century-Fox.

★ MERCEDES McCAMBRIDGE in *All the King's Men*, Rossen, Columbia.

ETHEL WATERS in *Pinky*, 20th Century-Fox.

Directing

★ JOSEPH L. MANKIEWICZ for *A Letter to Three Wives*, 20th Century-Fox.

CAROL REED for *The Fallen Idol*, London Films, SRO (British).

ROBERT ROSSEN for *All the King's Men*, Rossen, Columbia.

WILLIAM A. WELLMAN for *Battleground*, Metro-Goldwyn-Mayer.

WILLIAM WYLER for *The Heiress*, Paramount.

Writing

Motion Picture Story

COME TO THE STABLE, 20th Century-Fox: CLARE BOOTHE LUCE.

IT HAPPENS EVERY SPRING, 20th Century-Fox: SHIRLEY W. SMITH and VALENTINE DAVIES.

SANDS OF IWO JIMA, Republic: HARRY BROWN.

★ THE STRATTON STORY, Metro-Goldwyn-Mayer: DOUGLAS MORROW.

WHITE HEAT, Warner Bros.: VIRGINIA KELLOGG.

Screenplay

ALL THE KING'S MEN, A Robert Rossen Prod., Columbia: ROBERT ROSSEN.

THE BICYCLE THIEF, De Sica, Mayer-Burstyn (Italian): CESARE ZAVATTINI.

CHAMPION, Screen Plays Corp., UA: CARL FOREMAN.

THE FALLEN IDOL, London Films, SRO (British): GRAHAM GREENE.

★ A LETTER TO THREE WIVES, 20th Century-Fox: JOSEPH L. MANKIEWICZ.

Story and Screenplay

★ BATTLEGROUND, Metro-Goldwyn-Mayer: ROBERT PIROSH.

JOLSON SINGS AGAIN, Columbia: SIDNEY BUCHMAN.

PAISAN, Roberto Rossellini, Mayer-Burstyn (Italian): ALFRED HAYES, FEDERICO FELLINI, SERGIO AMIDEI, MARCELLO PAGLIERO, and ROBERTO ROSSELLINI.

PASSPORT TO PIMLICO, Rank-Ealing, Eagle-Lion (British): T.E.B. CLARKE.

THE QUIET ONE, Film Documents, Mayer-Burstyn: HELEN LEVITT, JANICE LOEB, and SIDNEY MEYERS.

Cinematography

Black and White

★ BATTLEGROUND, Metro-Goldwyn-Mayer: PAUL C. VOGEL.

CHAMPION, Screen Plays Corp., UA: FRANK PLANER.

COME TO THE STABLE, 20th Century-Fox: JOSEPH LASHELLE.

THE HEIRESS, Paramount: LEO TOVER.

PRINCE OF FOXES, 20th Century-Fox: LEON SHAMROY.

Color

THE BARKLEYS OF BROADWAY, Metro-Goldwyn-Mayer: HARRY STRADLING.

JOLSON SINGS AGAIN, Columbia: WILLIAM SNYDER.

LITTLE WOMEN, Metro-Goldwyn-Mayer: ROBERT PLANCK and CHARLES SCHOENBAUM.

SAND, 20th Century-Fox: CHARLES G. CLARKE.

★ SHE WORE A YELLOW RIBBON, Argosy, RKO Radio: WINTON HOCH.

Art Direction—Set Decoration

Black and White

COME TO THE STABLE, 20th Century-Fox: LYLE WHEELER and JOSEPH C. WRIGHT; Set Decoration: THOMAS LITTLE and PAUL S. FOX.

★ THE HEIRESS, Paramount: JOHN MEEHAN and HARRY HORNER; Set Decoration: EMILE KURI.

MADAME BOVARY, Metro-Goldwyn-Mayer: CEDRIC GIBBONS and JACK MARTIN SMITH; Set Decoration: EDWIN B. WILLIS and RICHARD A. PEFFERLE.

Color

ADVENTURES OF DON JUAN, Warner Bros.: EDWARD CARRERE; Set Decoration: LYLE REIFSNIDER.

★ LITTLE WOMEN, Metro-Goldwyn-Mayer: CEDRIC GIBBONS and PAUL GROESSE; Set Decoration: EDWIN B. WILLIS and JACK D. MOORE.

SARABAND, Rank-Ealing, Eagle-Lion (British): JIM MORAHAN, WILLIAM KELLNER, and MICHAEL RELPH; Set Decoration: No credits listed.

Sound Recording

ONCE MORE, MY DARLING, Neptune Films, U-I: UNIVERSAL-INTERNATIONAL SOUND DEPARTMENT.

SANDS OF IWO JIMA, Republic: REPUBLIC SOUND DEPARTMENT.

★ TWELVE O'CLOCK HIGH, 20th Century-Fox: 20TH CENTURY-FOX SOUND DEPARTMENT.

Film Editing

ALL THE KING'S MEN, Rossen Prod., Columbia: ROBERT PARRISH and AL CLARK.

BATTLEGROUND, Metro-Goldwyn-Mayer: JOHN DUNNING.

★ CHAMPION, Screen Plays Corp., UA: HARRY GERSTAD.

SANDS OF IWO JIMA, Republic: RICHARD L. VAN ENGER.

THE WINDOW, RKO Radio: FREDERIC KNUDTSON.

Music

Scoring of a Dramatic or Comedy Picture

BEYOND THE FOREST, Warner Bros.: MAX STEINER.

CHAMPION, Screen Plays Corp., UA: DIMITRI TIOMKIN.

★ THE HEIRESS, Paramount: AARON COPLAND.

Scoring of a Musical Picture

JOLSON SINGS AGAIN, Sidney Buchman, Columbia: MORRIS STOLOFF and GEORGE DUNING.

LOOK FOR THE SILVER LINING, Warner Bros.: RAY HEINDORF.

★ ON THE TOWN, Metro-Goldwyn-Mayer: ROGER EDENS and LENNIE HAYTON.

Song

★ BABY, IT'S COLD OUTSIDE from *Neptune's Daughter*, Metro-Goldwyn-Mayer: Music and Lyrics by FRANK LOESSER.

IT'S A GREAT FEELING from *It's a Great Feeling*, Warner Bros.: Music by JULE STYNE; Lyrics by SAMMY CAHN.

LAVENDER BLUE from *So Dear to My Heart*, Disney-RKO Radio: Music by ELIOT DANIEL; Lyrics by LARRY MOREY.

MY FOOLISH HEART from *My Foolish Heart*, Goldwyn-RKO Radio: Music by VICTOR YOUNG; Lyrics by NED WASHINGTON.

THROUGH A LONG AND SLEEPLESS NIGHT from *Come to the Stable*, 20th Century-Fox: Music by ALFRED NEWMAN; Lyrics by MACK GORDON.

Costume Design

Black and White

★ THE HEIRESS, Paramount: EDITH HEAD and GILE STEELE.

PRINCE OF FOXES, 20th Century-Fox: VITTORIO NINO NOVARESE.

Color

★ ADVENTURES OF DON JUAN, Warner Bros.: LEAH RHODES, TRAVILLA, and MARJORIE BEST.

MOTHER IS A FRESHMAN, 20th Century-Fox: KAY NELSON.

Special Effects

★ MIGHTY JOE YOUNG, Cooper, RKO Radio.

TULSA, Walter Wanger Pictures, Eagle-Lion.

Short Subjects

Cartoons

★ FOR SCENT-IMENTAL REASONS, Warner Bros.: (Looney Tunes) EDWARD SELZER, Producer.

HATCH UP YOUR TROUBLES, Metro-Goldwyn-Mayer: (Tom and Jerry) FRED QUIMBY, Producer.

MAGIC FLUKE, United Productions of America, Columbia: (Fox and Crow) STEPHEN BOSUSTOW, Producer.

TOY TINKERS, Walt Disney, RKO Radio: WALT DISNEY, Producer.

One Reel

★ AQUATIC HOUSE-PARTY, Paramount: (Grantland Rice Sportlights) JACK EATON, Producer.

ROLLER DERBY GIRL, Paramount: (Pacemaker) JUSTIN HERMAN, Producer.

SO YOU THINK YOU'RE NOT GUILTY, Warner Bros.: (Joe McDoakes) GORDON HOLLINGSHEAD, Producer.

SPILLS AND CHILLS, Warner Bros.: (Black-and-White Sports Review) WALTON C. AMENT, Producer.

WATER TRIX, Metro-Goldwyn-Mayer: (Pete Smith Specialty) PETE SMITH, Producer.

Two Reels

BOY AND THE EAGLE, RKO Radio: WILLIAM LASKY, Producer.

CHASE OF DEATH, Irving Allen Productions: (Color Series) IRVING ALLEN, Producer.

THE GRASS IS ALWAYS GREENER, Warner Bros.: (Black-and-White) GORDON HOLLINGSHEAD, Producer.

SNOW CARNIVAL, Warner Bros.: (Technicolor) GORDON HOLLINGSHEAD, Producer.

★ VAN GOGH, Canton-Weiner: GASTON DIEHL and ROBERT HAESSENS, Producers.

Documentary

Short Subjects (TIE)

A CHANCE TO LIVE, March of Time, 20th Century-Fox: RICHARD DE ROCHEMONT, Producer.

1848, A. F. Films, Inc.: FRENCH CINEMA GENERAL COOPERATIVE, Producer.

THE RISING TIDE, National Film Board of Canada: ST. FRANCIS-XAVIER UNIVERSITY (NOVA SCOTIA), Producer.

★ SO MUCH FOR SO LITTLE, Warner Bros. Cartoons, Inc.: EDWARD SELZER, Producer.

Features

★ DAYBREAK IN UDI, British Information Services: CROWN FILM UNIT, Producer.

KENJI COMES HOME, A Protestant Film Commission Prod.: PAUL F. HEARD, Producer.

Special Awards

THE BICYCLE THIEF (Italian)—voted by the Academy Board of Governors as the most outstanding foreign language film released in the United States during 1949. (Statuette)

BOBBY DRISCOLL, as the outstanding juvenile actor of 1949. (Miniature statuette)

FRED ASTAIRE for his unique artistry and his contributions to the technique of musical pictures. (Statuette)

CECIL B. DEMILLE, distinguished motion picture pioneer, for thirty-seven years of brilliant showmanship. (Statuette)

JEAN HERSHOLT, for distinguished service to the motion picture industry. (Statuette)

Irving G. Thalberg Memorial Award

None.

Scientific or Technical

Class I

EASTMAN KODAK CO. for the development and introduction of an improved safety base motion picture film.

Class II

None.

Class III

LOREN L. RYDER, BRUCE H. DENNEY, ROBERT CARR, and the PARAMOUNT STUDIO SOUND DEPARTMENT for the development and application of the supersonic playback and public address system.

M. B. PAUL for the first successful large-area, seamless, translucent backgrounds.

HERBERT BRITT for the development and application of formulas and equipment producing artificial snow and ice for dressing motion picture sets.

ANDRÉ COUTANT and JACQUES MATHOT for the design of the Eclair Camerette.

CHARLES R. DAILY, STEVE CSILLAG, and the PARAMOUNT STUDIO ENGINEERING, EDITORIAL, and MUSIC DEPARTMENTS for a new precision method of computing variable tempo-click tracks.

INTERNATIONAL PROJECTOR CORP. for a simplified and self-adjusting take-up device for projection machines.

ALEXANDER VELCOFF for the application to production of the infrared photographic evaluator.

TWENTY-THIRD YEAR

1950

Nominations Announced: February 12, 1951
Awards Ceremony: March 29, 1951
RKO Pantages Theatre
(MC: Fred Astaire)

Best Picture

★ ALL ABOUT EVE, 20th Century-Fox. Darryl F. Zanuck, Producer.

BORN YESTERDAY, Columbia. S. Sylvan Simon, Producer.

FATHER OF THE BRIDE, Metro-Goldwyn-Mayer. Pandro S. Berman, Producer.

KING SOLOMON'S MINES, Metro-Goldwyn-Mayer. Sam Zimbalist, Producer.

SUNSET BOULEVARD, Paramount. Charles Brackett, Producer.

Actor

LOUIS CALHERN in *The Magnificent Yankee*, Metro-Goldwyn-Mayer.

★ JOSÉ FERRER in *Cyrano de Bergerac*, Stanley Kramer, UA.

WILLIAM HOLDEN in *Sunset Boulevard*, Paramount.

JAMES STEWART in *Harvey*, Universal-International.

SPENCER TRACY in *Father of the Bride*, Metro-Goldwyn-Mayer.

Actress

ANNE BAXTER in *All about Eve*, 20th Century-Fox.

BETTE DAVIS in *All about Eve*, 20th Century-Fox.

★ JUDY HOLLIDAY in *Born Yesterday*, Columbia.

ELEANOR PARKER in *Caged*, Warner Bros.

GLORIA SWANSON in *Sunset Boulevard*, Paramount.

Supporting Actor

JEFF CHANDLER in *Broken Arrow*, 20th Century-Fox.

EDMUND GWENN in *Mister 880*, 20th Century-Fox.

SAM JAFFE in *The Asphalt Jungle*, Metro-Goldwyn-Mayer.

★ GEORGE SANDERS in *All about Eve*, 20th Century-Fox.

ERICH VON STROHEIM in *Sunset Boulevard*, Paramount.

Supporting Actress

HOPE EMERSON in *Caged*, Warner Bros.

CELESTE HOLM in *All about Eve*, 20th Century-Fox.

★ JOSEPHINE HULL in *Harvey*, Universal-International.

NANCY OLSON in *Sunset Boulevard*, Paramount.

THELMA RITTER in *All about Eve*, 20th Century-Fox.

Directing

GEORGE CUKOR for *Born Yesterday*, Columbia.

JOHN HUSTON for *The Asphalt Jungle*, Metro-Goldwyn-Mayer.

★ JOSEPH L. MANKIEWICZ for *All about Eve*, 20th Century-Fox.
CAROL REED for *The Third Man*, Selznick-London Films, SRO (British).
BILLY WILDER for *Sunset Boulevard*, Paramount.

Writing

Motion Picture Story

BITTER RICE, Lux Films (Italian): GUISEPPE DE SANTIS and CARLO LIZZANI.
THE GUNFIGHTER, 20th Century-Fox: WILLIAM BOWERS and ANDRE DE TOTH.
MYSTERY STREET, Metro-Goldwyn-Mayer: LEONARD SPIGELGASS.
★ PANIC IN THE STREETS, 20th Century-Fox: EDNA ANHALT and EDWARD ANHALT.
WHEN WILLIE COMES MARCHING HOME, 20th Century-Fox: SY GOMBERG.

Screenplay

★ ALL ABOUT EVE, 20th Century-Fox: JOSEPH L. MANKIEWICZ.
THE ASPHALT JUNGLE, Metro-Goldwyn-Mayer: BEN MADDOW and JOHN HUSTON.
BORN YESTERDAY, Columbia: ALBERT MANNHEIMER.
BROKEN ARROW, 20th Century-Fox: MICHAEL BLANKFORT.*
FATHER OF THE BRIDE, Metro-Goldwyn-Mayer: FRANCES GOODRICH and ALBERT HACKETT.

Story and Screenplay

ADAM'S RIB, Metro-Goldwyn-Mayer: RUTH GORDON and GARSON KANIN.
CAGED, Warner Bros.: VIRGINIA KELLOGG and BERNARD C. SCHOENFELD.
THE MEN, Kramer, UA: CARL FOREMAN.
NO WAY OUT, 20th Century-Fox: JOSEPH L. MANKIEWICZ and LESSER SAMUELS.
★ SUNSET BOULEVARD, Paramount: CHARLES BRACKETT, BILLY WILDER, and D. M. MARSHMAN, JR.

Cinematography

Black and White

ALL ABOUT EVE, 20th Century-Fox: MILTON KRASNER.
THE ASPHALT JUNGLE, Metro-Goldwyn-Mayer: HAROLD ROSSON.
THE FURIES, Wallis, Paramount: VICTOR MILNER.
SUNSET BOULEVARD, Paramount: JOHN F. SEITZ.
★ THE THIRD MAN, Selznick-London Films, SRO (British): ROBERT KRASKER.

Color

ANNIE GET YOUR GUN, Metro-Goldwyn-Mayer: CHARLES ROSHER.
BROKEN ARROW, 20th Century-Fox: ERNEST PALMER.
THE FLAME AND THE ARROW, Norma-F.R., Warner Bros.: ERNEST HALLER.
★ KING SOLOMON'S MINES, Metro-Goldwyn-Mayer: ROBERT SURTEES.
SAMSON AND DELILAH, DeMille, Paramount: GEORGE BARNES.

Art Direction—Set Decoration

Black and White

ALL ABOUT EVE, 20th Century-Fox: LYLE WHEELER and GEORGE DAVIS; Set Decoration: THOMAS LITTLE and WALTER M. SCOTT.
THE RED DANUBE, Metro-Goldwyn-

*The Writers Guild of America West now credits blacklisted writer Albert Maltz with the screenplay for *Broken Arrow*; Michael Blankfort, who fronted for Maltz, received the nomination at the time and thus continues to be listed as the official nominee.

Mayer: CEDRIC GIBBONS and HANS PETERS; Set Decoration: EDWIN B. WILLIS and HUGH HUNT.

★ SUNSET BOULEVARD, Paramount: HANS DREIER and JOHN MEEHAN; Set Decoration: SAM COMER and RAY MOYER.

Color

ANNIE GET YOUR GUN, Metro-Goldwyn-Mayer: CEDRIC GIBBONS and PAUL GROESSE; Set Decoration: EDWIN B. WILLIS and RICHARD A. PEFFERLE.

DESTINATION MOON, George Pal, Eagle-Lion Classics: ERNST FEGTE; Set Decoration: GEORGE SAWLEY.

★ SAMSON AND DELILAH, DeMille-Paramount: HANS DREIER and WALTER TYLER; Set Decoration: SAM COMER and RAY MOYER.

Sound Recording

★ ALL ABOUT EVE, 20th Century-Fox: 20TH CENTURY-FOX SOUND DEPARTMENT.

CINDERELLA, Disney, RKO Radio: DISNEY SOUND DEPARTMENT.

LOUISA, Universal-International: UNIVERSAL-INTERNATIONAL SOUND DEPARTMENT.

OUR VERY OWN, Goldwyn, RKO Radio: GOLDWYN SOUND DEPARTMENT.

TRIO, Rank-Sydney Box, PARAMOUNT (British): SOUND DEPARTMENT.

Film Editing

ALL ABOUT EVE, 20th Century-Fox: BARBARA MCLEAN.

ANNIE GET YOUR GUN, Metro-Goldwyn-Mayer: JAMES E. NEWCOM.

★ KING SOLOMON'S MINES, Metro-Goldwyn-Mayer: RALPH E. WINTERS and CONRAD A. NERVIG.

SUNSET BOULEVARD, Paramount: ARTHUR SCHMIDT and DOANE HARRISON.

THE THIRD MAN, Selznick-London Films, SRO (British): OSWALD HAFENRICHTER.

Music

Scoring of a Dramatic or Comedy Picture

ALL ABOUT EVE, 20th Century-Fox: ALFRED NEWMAN.

THE FLAME AND THE ARROW, Norma-F.R., Warner Bros.: MAX STEINER.

NO SAD SONGS FOR ME, Columbia: GEORGE DUNING.

SAMSON AND DELILAH, Paramount: VICTOR YOUNG.

★ SUNSET BOULEVARD, Paramount: FRANZ WAXMAN.

Scoring of a Musical Picture

★ ANNIE GET YOUR GUN, Metro-Goldwyn-Mayer: ADOLPH DEUTSCH and ROGER EDENS.

CINDERELLA, Disney, RKO Radio: OLIVER WALLACE and PAUL J. SMITH.

I'LL GET BY, 20th Century-Fox: LIONEL NEWMAN.

THREE LITTLE WORDS, Metro-Goldwyn-Mayer: ANDRÉ PREVIN.

THE WEST POINT STORY, Warner Bros.: RAY HEINDORF.

Song

BE MY LOVE from *The Toast of New Orleans*, Metro-Goldwyn-Mayer: Music by NICHOLAS BRODSZKY; Lyrics by SAMMY CAHN.

BIBBIDY-BOBBIDI-BOO from *Cinderella*, Disney, RKO Radio: Music and Lyrics by MACK DAVID, AL HOFFMAN, and JERRY LIVINGSTON.

★ MONA LISA from *Captain Carey, USA*, Paramount: Music and Lyrics by RAY EVANS and JAY LIVINGSTON.

MULE TRAIN from *Singing Guns*, Palomar Pictures, Republic: Music and Lyrics by FRED GLICKMAN, HY HEATH, and JOHNNY LANGE.

WILHELMINA from *Wabash Avenue*,

20th Century-Fox: Music by JOSEF MYROW; Lyrics by MACK GORDON.

Costume Design

Black and White

★ ALL ABOUT EVE, 20th Century-Fox: EDITH HEAD and CHARLES LEMAIRE.

BORN YESTERDAY, Columbia: JEAN LOUIS.

THE MAGNIFICENT YANKEE, Metro-Goldwyn-Mayer: WALTER PLUNKETT.

Color

THE BLACK ROSE, 20th Century-Fox: MICHAEL WHITTAKER.

★ SAMSON AND DELILAH, DeMille, Paramount: EDITH HEAD, DOROTHY JEAKINS, ELOIS JENSSEN, GILE STEELE, and GWEN WAKELING.

THAT FORSYTE WOMAN, Metro-Goldwyn-Mayer: WALTER PLUNKETT and VALLES.

Special Effects

★ DESTINATION MOON, George Pal, Eagle-Lion Classics.

SAMSON AND DELILAH, Cecil B. DeMille, Paramount.

Short Subjects

Cartoons

★ GERALD McBOING-BOING, United Productions of America, Columbia: (Jolly Frolics Series) STEPHEN BOSUSTOW, Executive Producer.

JERRY'S COUSIN, Metro-Goldwyn-Mayer: (Tom and Jerry) FRED QUIMBY, Producer.

TROUBLE INDEMNITY, United Productions of America, Columbia: (Mr. Magoo Series) STEPHEN BOSUSTOW, Executive Producer.

One Reel

BLAZE BUSTERS, Warner Bros.: (Vitaphone Novelties) ROBERT YOUNGSON, Producer.

★ GRANDAD OF RACES, Warner Bros.: (Sports Parade) GORDON HOLLINGSHEAD, Producer.

WRONG WAY BUTCH, Metro-Goldwyn-Mayer: PETE SMITH, Producer.

Two reels

★ BEAVER VALLEY, Walt Disney, RKO Radio: (True-Life Adventure) WALT DISNEY, Producer.

GRANDMA MOSES, Falcon Films, Inc., A.F. Films: FALCON FILMS, INC., Producer.

MY COUNTRY 'TIS OF THEE, Warner Bros.: (Featurette Series) GORDON HOLLINGSHEAD, Producer.

Documentary

Short Subjects

THE FIGHT: SCIENCE AGAINST CANCER, NATIONAL FILM BOARD OF CANADA in cooperation with the Medical Film Institute of the Association of American Medical Colleges.

THE STAIRS, Film Documents, Inc.

★ WHY KOREA?, 20th Century-Fox Movietone: EDMUND REEK, Producer.

Features

★ THE TITAN: STORY OF MICHELANGELO, Michelangelo Co., Classics Pictures, Inc.: ROBERT SNYDER, Producer.

WITH THESE HANDS, Promotional Films Co., Inc.: JACK ARNOLD and LEE GOODMAN, Producers.

*Honorary Awards**

GEORGE MURPHY for his services in interpreting the film industry to the country at large. (Statuette)

*From 1927/28 through 1949 known as Special Awards.

LOUIS B. MAYER for distinguished service to the motion picture industry. (Statuette)

THE WALLS OF MALAPAGA (Franco-Italian)—voted by the Board of Governors as the most outstanding foreign language film released in the United States in 1950. (Statuette)

Irving G. Thalberg Memorial Award

DARRYL F. ZANUCK.

Scientific or Technical

Class I

None.

Class II

JAMES B. GORDON and the 20TH CENTURY-FOX STUDIO CAMERA DEPARTMENT for the design and development of a multiple-image film viewer.

JOHN PAUL LIVADARY, FLOYD CAMPBELL, L. W. RUSSELL, and the COLUMBIA STUDIO SOUND DEPARTMENT for the development of a multitrack magnetic recording system.

LOREN L. RYDER and the PARAMOUNT STUDIO SOUND DEPARTMENT for the first studio-wide application of magnetic sound recording to motion picture production.

Class III

None.

TWENTY-FOURTH YEAR

1951

Nominations Announced: February 11, 1952
Awards Ceremony: March 20, 1952
RKO Pantages Theatre
(MC: Danny Kaye)

Best Picture

★ AN AMERICAN IN PARIS, Metro-Goldwyn-Mayer: Arthur Freed, Producer.

DECISION BEFORE DAWN, 20th Century-Fox: Anatole Litvak and Frank McCarthy, Producers.

A PLACE IN THE SUN, Paramount: George Stevens, Producer.

QUO VADIS, Metro-Goldwyn-Mayer: Sam Zimbalist, Producer.

A STREETCAR NAMED DESIRE, Charles K. Feldman Group Prods., Warner Bros.: Charles K. Feldman, Producer.

Actor

★ HUMPHREY BOGART in *The African Queen*, Horizon, UA.

MARLON BRANDO in *A Streetcar Named Desire*, Charles K. Feldman Group Prods., Warner Bros.

MONTGOMERY CLIFT in *A Place in the Sun*, Paramount.

ARTHUR KENNEDY in *Bright Victory*, Universal-International.

FREDRIC MARCH in *Death of a Salesman*, Stanley Kramer, Columbia.

Actress

KATHARINE HEPBURN in *The African Queen*, Horizon, UA.

★ VIVIEN LEIGH in *A Streetcar Named Desire*, Charles K. Feldman Group Prods., Warner Bros.

ELEANOR PARKER in *Detective Story*, Paramount.

SHELLEY WINTERS in *A Place in the Sun*, Paramount.

JANE WYMAN in *The Blue Veil*, Wald-Krasna, RKO Radio.

Supporting Actor

LEO GENN in *Quo Vadis*, Metro-Goldwyn-Mayer.

★ KARL MALDEN in *A Streetcar Named Desire*, Charles K. Feldman Group Prods., Warner Bros.

KEVIN MCCARTHY in *Death of a Salesman*, Kramer, Columbia.

PETER USTINOV in *Quo Vadis*, Metro-Goldwyn-Mayer.

GIG YOUNG in *Come Fill the Cup*, Warner Bros.

Supporting Actress

JOAN BLONDELL in *The Blue Veil*, Wald-Krasna, RKO Radio.

MILDRED DUNNOCK in *Death of a Salesman*, Kramer, Columbia.

LEE GRANT in *Detective Story*, Paramount.

★ KIM HUNTER in *A Streetcar Named Desire*, Charles K. Feldman Group Prods., Warner Bros.

THELMA RITTER in *The Mating Season*, Paramount.

Directing

JOHN HUSTON for *The African Queen*, Horizon, UA.

ELIA KAZAN for *A Streetcar Named Desire*, Charles K. Feldman Group Prods., Warner Bros.

VINCENTE MINNELLI for *An American in Paris*, Metro-Goldwyn-Mayer.

★ GEORGE STEVENS for *A Place in the Sun*, Paramount.

WILLIAM WYLER for *Detective Story*, Paramount.

Writing

Motion Picture Story

THE BULLFIGHTER AND THE LADY, Republic: BUDD BOETTICHER and RAY NAZARRO.

THE FROGMEN, 20th Century-Fox: OSCAR MILLARD.

HERE COMES THE GROOM, Paramount: ROBERT RISKIN and LIAM O'BRIEN.

★ SEVEN DAYS TO NOON, Boulting Bros., Mayer-Kingsley-Distinguished Films (British): PAUL DEHN and JAMES BERNARD.

TERESA, Metro-Goldwyn-Mayer: ALFRED HAYES and STEWART STERN.

Screenplay

THE AFRICAN QUEEN, Horizon, UA: JAMES AGEE and JOHN HUSTON.

DETECTIVE STORY, Paramount: PHILIP YORDAN and ROBERT WYLER.

LA RONDE, Sacha Gordine, Commercial Pictures (French): JACQUES NATANSON and MAX OPHULS.

★ A PLACE IN THE SUN, Paramount: MICHAEL WILSON and HARRY BROWN.

A STREETCAR NAMED DESIRE, Charles K. Feldman Group Prods., Warner Bros.: TENNESSEE WILLIAMS.

Story and Screenplay

★ AN AMERICAN IN PARIS, Metro-Goldwyn-Mayer: ALAN JAY LERNER.

THE BIG CARNIVAL, Paramount: BILLY WILDER, LESSER SAMUELS, and WALTER NEWMAN.

DAVID AND BATHSHEBA, 20th Century-Fox: PHILIP DUNNE.

GO FOR BROKE!, Metro-Goldwyn-Mayer: ROBERT PIROSH.

THE WELL, Popkin, UA: CLARENCE GREENE and RUSSELL ROUSE.

Cinematography

Black and White

DEATH OF A SALESMAN, Kramer, Columbia: FRANK PLANER.

THE FROGMEN, 20th Century-Fox: NORBERT BRODINE.

★ A PLACE IN THE SUN, Paramount: WILLIAM C. MELLOR.

STRANGERS ON A TRAIN, Warner Bros.: ROBERT BURKS.

A STREETCAR NAMED DESIRE, Charles K. Feldman Group Prods., Warner Bros.: HARRY STRADLING.

Color

★ AN AMERICAN IN PARIS, Metro-Goldwyn-Mayer: ALFRED GILKS; Ballet photographed by JOHN ALTON.

DAVID AND BATHSHEBA, 20th Century-Fox: LEON SHAMROY.

QUO VADIS, Metro-Goldwyn-Mayer: ROBERT SURTEES and WILLIAM V. SKALL.

SHOW BOAT, Metro-Goldwyn-Mayer: CHARLES ROSHER.

WHEN WORLDS COLLIDE, Paramount: JOHN F. SEITZ, and W. HOWARD GREENE.

Art Direction—Set Decoration

Black and White

FOURTEEN HOURS, 20th Century-Fox: LYLE WHEELER and LELAND FULLER; Set Decoration: THOMAS LITTLE and FRED J. RODE.

HOUSE ON TELEGRAPH HILL, 20th

Century-Fox: LYLE WHEELER and JOHN DECUIR; Set Decoration: THOMAS LITTLE and PAUL S. FOX.

LA RONDE, Sacha Gordine Prod., Commercial Pictures (French): D'EAUBONNE; Set Decoration: No credits listed.

★ A STREETCAR NAMED DESIRE, Chas. K. Feldman Group Prods., Warner Bros.: RICHARD DAY; Set Decoration: GEORGE JAMES HOPKINS.

TOO YOUNG TO KISS, Metro-Goldwyn-Mayer: CEDRIC GIBBONS and PAUL GROESSE; Set Decoration: EDWIN B. WILLIS and JACK D. MOORE.

Color

★ AN AMERICAN IN PARIS, Metro-Goldwyn-Mayer: CEDRIC GIBBONS and PRESTON AMES; Set Decoration: EDWIN B. WILLIS and KEOGH GLEASON.

DAVID AND BATHSHEBA, 20th Century-Fox: LYLE WHEELER and GEORGE DAVIS; Set Decoration: THOMAS LITTLE and PAUL S. FOX.

ON THE RIVIERA, 20th Century-Fox: LYLE WHEELER and LELAND FULLER; Musical Settings: JOSEPH C. WRIGHT; Set Decoration: THOMAS LITTLE and WALTER M. SCOTT.

QUO VADIS, Metro-Goldwyn-Mayer: WILLIAM A. HORNING, CEDRIC GIBBONS, and EDWARD CARFAGNO; Set Decoration: HUGH HUNT.

TALES OF HOFFMANN, Powell-Pressburger, Lopert (British): HEIN HECKROTH; Set Decoration: No credits listed.

Sound Recording

BRIGHT VICTORY, Universal-International: LESLIE I. CAREY, Sound Director.

★ THE GREAT CARUSO, Metro-Goldwyn-Mayer: DOUGLAS SHEARER, Sound Director.

I WANT YOU, Samuel Goldwyn Prods., Inc., RKO Radio: GORDON SAWYER, Sound Director.

A STREETCAR NAMED DESIRE, Charles K. Feldman Group Prods., Warner Bros.: COL. NATHAN LEVINSON, Sound Director.

TWO TICKETS TO BROADWAY, RKO Radio: JOHN O. AALBERG, Sound Director.

Film Editing

AN AMERICAN IN PARIS, Metro-Goldwyn-Mayer: ADRIENNE FAZAN.

DECISION BEFORE DAWN, 20th Century-Fox: DOROTHY SPENCER.

★ A PLACE IN THE SUN, Paramount: WILLIAM HORNBECK.

QUO VADIS, Metro-Goldwyn-Mayer: RALPH E. WINTERS.

THE WELL, Popkin, UA: CHESTER SCHAEFFER.

Music

Scoring of a Dramatic or Comedy Picture

DAVID AND BATHSHEBA, 20th Century-Fox: ALFRED NEWMAN.

DEATH OF A SALESMAN, Kramer, Columbia: ALEX NORTH.

★ A PLACE IN THE SUN, Paramount: FRANZ WAXMAN.

QUO VADIS, Metro-Goldwyn-Mayer: MIKLOS ROZSA.

A STREETCAR NAMED DESIRE, Charles K. Feldman Prods., Warner Bros.: ALEX NORTH.

Scoring of a Musical Picture

ALICE IN WONDERLAND, Disney, RKO Radio: OLIVER WALLACE.

★ AN AMERICAN IN PARIS, Metro-Goldwyn-Mayer: JOHNNY GREEN and SAUL CHAPLIN.

THE GREAT CARUSO, Metro-Goldwyn-Mayer: PETER HERMAN ADLER and JOHNNY GREEN.

ON THE RIVIERA, 20th Century-Fox: ALFRED NEWMAN.

SHOW BOAT, Metro-Goldwyn-Mayer:

ADOLPH DEUTSCH and CONRAD SALINGER.

Song

★ IN THE COOL, COOL, COOL OF THE EVENING from *Here Comes the Groom*, Paramount: Music by HOAGY CARMICHAEL; Lyrics by JOHNNY MERCER.

A KISS TO BUILD A DREAM ON from *The Strip*, Metro-Goldwyn-Mayer: Music and Lyrics by BERT KALMAR, HARRY RUBY, and OSCAR HAMMERSTEIN II.

NEVER from *Golden Girl*, 20th Century-Fox: Music by LIONEL NEWMAN; Lyrics by ELIOT DANIEL.

TOO LATE NOW from *Royal Wedding*, Metro-Goldwyn-Mayer: Music by BURTON LANE; Lyrics by ALAN JAY LERNER.

WONDER WHY from *Rich, Young and Pretty*, Metro-Goldwyn-Mayer: Music by NICHOLAS BRODSZKY; Lyrics by SAMMY CAHN.

Costume Design

Black and White

KIND LADY, Metro-Goldwyn-Mayer: WALTER PLUNKETT and GILE STEELE.

THE MODEL AND THE MARRIAGE BROKER, 20th Century-Fox: CHARLES LEMAIRE and RENIE.

THE MUDLARK, 20th Century-Fox: EDWARD STEVENSON and MARGARET FURSE.

★ A PLACE IN THE SUN, Paramount: EDITH HEAD.

A STREETCAR NAMED DESIRE, Charles K. Feldman Group Prods., Warner Bros.: LUCINDA BALLARD.

Color

★ AN AMERICAN IN PARIS, Metro-Goldwyn-Mayer: ORRY-KELLY, WALTER PLUNKETT, and IRENE SHARAFF.

DAVID AND BATHSHEBA, 20th Century-Fox: CHARLES LEMAIRE and EDWARD STEVENSON.

THE GREAT CARUSO, Metro-Goldwyn-Mayer: HELEN ROSE and GILE STEELE.

QUO VADIS, Metro-Goldwyn-Mayer: HERSCHEL MCCOY.

TALES OF HOFFMAN, Powell-Pressburger, Lopert (British): HEIN HECKROTH.

Short Subjects

Cartoons

LAMBERT, THE SHEEPISH LION, Walt Disney, RKO Radio: (Special) WALT DISNEY, Producer.

ROOTY TOOT TOOT, United Productions of America, Columbia: (Jolly Frolics) STEPHEN BOSUSTOW, Executive Producer.

★ TWO MOUSEKETEERS, Metro-Goldwyn-Mayer: (Tom and Jerry) FRED QUIMBY, Producer.

One Reel

RIDIN' THE RAILS, Paramount: (Sportlights) JACK EATON, Producer.

THE STORY OF TIME, A Signal Films Production by Robert G. Leffingwell, Cornell Film Company (British).

★ WORLD OF KIDS, Warner Bros.: (Vitaphone Novelties) ROBERT YOUNGSON, Producer.

Two Reels

BALZAC, Les Films du Compass, A.F. Films, Inc. (French): LES FILMS DU COMPASS, Producer.

DANGER UNDER THE SEA, Universal-International: TOM MEAD, Producer.

★ NATURE'S HALF ACRE, Walt Disney, RKO Radio: (True-Life Adventure) WALT DISNEY, Producer.

Documentary

Short Subjects

★ BENJY, made by FRED ZINNEMANN with the cooperation of

Paramount Pictures Corp. for the Los Angeles Orthopaedic Hospital.

ONE WHO CAME BACK (sponsored by the Disabled American Veterans, in cooperation with the United States Department of Defense and the Association of Motion Picture Producers): OWEN CRUMP, Producer.

THE SEEING EYE, Warner Bros.: GORDON HOLLINGSHEAD, Producer.

Features

I WAS A COMMUNIST FOR THE F.B.I., Warner Bros.: BRYAN FOY, Producer.

★ KON-TIKI, An Artfilm Prod., RKO Radio (Norwegian): OLLE NORDEMAR, Producer.

Honorary Awards

GENE KELLY in appreciation of his versatility as an actor, singer, director, and dancer, and specifically for his brilliant achievements in the art of choreography on film. (Statuette)

RASHOMON (Japanese)—voted by the Board of Governors as the most outstanding foreign language film released in the United States during 1951. (Statuette)

Special Effects*

★ WHEN WORLDS COLLIDE, George Pal, Paramount.

Irving G. Thalberg Memorial Award

ARTHUR FREED.

Scientific or Technical

Class I

None.

Class II

GORDON JENNINGS, S. L. STANCLIFFE, and the PARAMOUNT STUDIO SPECIAL PHOTOGRAPHIC and ENGINEERING DEPARTMENTS for the design, construction, and application of a servo-operated recording and repeating device.

OLIN L. DUPY of Metro-Goldwyn-Mayer Studio for the design, construction, and application of a motion picture reproducing system.

RADIO CORPORATION OF AMERICA, VICTOR DIVISION, for pioneering direct positive recording with anticipatory noise reduction.

Class III

RICHARD M. HAFF, FRANK P. HERRNFELD, GARLAND C. MISENER, and the ANSCO FILM DIVISION OF GENERAL ANILINE AND FILM CORP. for the development of the Ansco color scene tester.

FRED PONEDEL, RALPH AYRES, and GEORGE BROWN of Warner Bros. Studio for an air-driven water motor to provide flow, wake, and white water for marine sequences in motion pictures.

GLEN ROBINSON and the METRO-GOLDWYN-MAYER STUDIO CONSTRUCTION DEPARTMENT for the development of a new music wire and cable cutter.

JACK GAYLORD and the METRO-GOLDWYN-MAYER STUDIO CONSTRUCTION DEPARTMENT for the development of balsa falling snow.

CARLOS RIVAS of Metro-Goldwyn-Mayer Studio for the development of an automatic magnetic film splicer.

*From 1951 thru 1953 Special Effects were classified as an "other" Award (not necessarily given each year); hence, there were no nominations.

TWENTY-FIFTH YEAR

1952

Nominations Announced: February 9, 1953
Awards Ceremony: March 19, 1953
RKO Pantages Theatre in Hollywood;
NBC International Theatre in New York
(MC: Bob Hope; MC in New York: Conrad Nagel)
(Academy Awards televised for the first time. For five years—the 25th through 29th Awards—the ceremonies were held simultaneously in Los Angeles and New York.)

Best Picture

★ THE GREATEST SHOW ON EARTH, Cecil B. DeMille, Paramount: Cecil B. DeMille, Producer.

HIGH NOON, Stanley Kramer Prods., UA: Stanley Kramer, Producer.

IVANHOE, Metro-Goldwyn-Mayer: Pandro S. Berman, Producer.

MOULIN ROUGE, Romulus Films, UA: John Huston, Producer.

THE QUIET MAN, Argosy Pictures Corp., Republic: John Ford and Merian C. Cooper, Producers.

Actor

MARLON BRANDO in *Viva Zapata!*, 20th Century-Fox.

★ GARY COOPER in *High Noon*, Stanley Kramer, UA.

KIRK DOUGLAS in *The Bad and the Beautiful*, Metro-Goldwyn-Mayer.

JOSÉ FERRER in *Moulin Rouge*, Romulus Films, UA.

ALEC GUINNESS in *The Lavender Hill Mob*, J. Arthur Rank Presentation-Ealing Studios, U-I (British).

Actress

★ SHIRLEY BOOTH in *Come Back, Little Sheba*, Hal Wallis, Paramount.

JOAN CRAWFORD in *Sudden Fear*, Joseph Kaufman Prods., RKO Radio.

BETTE DAVIS in *The Star*, Bert E. Friedlob, 20th Century-Fox.

JULIE HARRIS in *The Member of the Wedding*, Stanley Kramer, Columbia.

SUSAN HAYWARD in *With a Song in My Heart*, 20th Century-Fox.

Supporting Actor

RICHARD BURTON in *My Cousin Rachel*, 20th Century-Fox.

ARTHUR HUNNICUTT in *The Big Sky*, Winchester, RKO Radio.

VICTOR MCLAGLEN in *The Quiet Man*, Argosy, Republic.

JACK PALANCE in *Sudden Fear*, Kaufman, RKO Radio.

★ ANTHONY QUINN in *Viva Zapata!*, 20th Century-Fox.

Supporting Actress

★ GLORIA GRAHAME in *The Bad and the Beautiful*, Metro-Goldwyn-Mayer.

JEAN HAGEN in *Singin' in the Rain*, Metro-Goldwyn-Mayer.

COLETTE MARCHAND in *Moulin Rouge*, Romulus, UA.

TERRY MOORE in *Come Back, Little Sheba*, Wallis, Paramount.

THELMA RITTER in *With a Song in My Heart*, 20th Century-Fox.

Directing

CECIL B. DEMILLE for *The Greatest Show on Earth*, Cecil B. DeMille, Paramount.

★ JOHN FORD for *The Quiet Man*, Argosy, Republic.

JOHN HUSTON for *Moulin Rouge*, Romulus Films, UA.

JOSEPH L. MANKIEWICZ for *Five Fingers*, 20th Century-Fox.

FRED ZINNEMANN for *High Noon*, Stanley Kramer, UA.

Writing

Motion Picture Story

★ THE GREATEST SHOW ON EARTH, DeMille, Paramount: FREDERIC M. FRANK, THEODORE ST. JOHN, and FRANK CAVETT.

MY SON JOHN, Rainbow, Paramount: LEO MCCAREY.

THE NARROW MARGIN, RKO Radio: MARTIN GOLDSMITH and JACK LEONARD.

THE PRIDE OF ST. LOUIS, 20th Century-Fox: GUY TROSPER.

THE SNIPER, Kramer, Columbia: EDNA ANHALT and EDWARD ANHALT.

Screenplay

★ THE BAD AND THE BEAUTIFUL, Metro-Goldwyn-Mayer: CHARLES SCHNEE.

FIVE FINGERS, 20th Century-Fox: MICHAEL WILSON.

HIGH NOON, Kramer, UA: CARL FOREMAN.

THE MAN IN THE WHITE SUIT, Rank-Ealing, U-I (British): ROGER MACDOUGALL, JOHN DIGHTON, and ALEXANDER MACKENDRICK.

THE QUIET MAN, Argosy, Republic: FRANK S. NUGENT.

Story and Screenplay

THE ATOMIC CITY, Paramount: SYDNEY BOEHM.

BREAKING THE SOUND BARRIER, London Films, UA (British): TERENCE RATTIGAN.

★ THE LAVENDER HILL MOB, Rank-Ealing, U-I (British): T.E.B. CLARKE.

PAT AND MIKE, Metro-Goldwyn-Mayer: RUTH GORDON and GARSON KANIN.

VIVA ZAPATA!, 20th Century-Fox: JOHN STEINBECK.

Cinematography

Black and White

★ THE BAD AND THE BEAUTIFUL, Metro-Goldwyn-Mayer: ROBERT SURTEES.

THE BIG SKY, Winchester, RKO Radio: RUSSELL HARLAN.

MY COUSIN RACHEL, 20th Century-Fox: JOSEPH LASHELLE.

NAVAJO, Bartlett-Foster, Lippert: VIRGIL E. MILLER.

SUDDEN FEAR, Joseph Kaufman, RKO Radio: CHARLES B. LANG, JR.

Color

HANS CHRISTIAN ANDERSEN, Goldwyn, RKO Radio: HARRY STRADLING.

IVANHOE, Metro-Goldwyn-Mayer: F. A. YOUNG.

MILLION DOLLAR MERMAID, Metro-Goldwyn-Mayer: GEORGE J. FOLSEY.

★ THE QUIET MAN, Argosy, Republic: WINTON C. HOCH and ARCHIE STOUT.

THE SNOWS OF KILIMANJARO, 20th Century-Fox: LEON SHAMROY.

Art Direction—Set Decoration

Black and White

★ THE BAD AND THE BEAUTIFUL, Metro-Goldwyn-Mayer: CEDRIC GIBBONS and EDWARD CARFAGNO; Set Decoration:

EDWIN B. WILLIS and KEOGH GLEASON.

CARRIE, Paramount: HAL PEREIRA and ROLAND ANDERSON; Set Decoration: EMILE KURI.

MY COUSIN RACHEL, 20th Century-Fox: LYLE WHEELER and JOHN DECUIR; Set Decoration: WALTER M. SCOTT.

RASHOMON, Daiei, RKO Radio (Japanese): MATSUYAMA; Set Decoration: H. MOTSUMOTO.

VIVA ZAPATA!; 20th Century-Fox: LYLE WHEELER and LELAND FULLER; Set Decoration: THOMAS LITTLE and CLAUDE CARPENTER.

Color

HANS CHRISTIAN ANDERSEN, Goldwyn, RKO Radio: RICHARD DAY and CLAVE; Set Decoration: HOWARD BRISTOL.

THE MERRY WIDOW, Metro-Goldwyn-Mayer: CEDRIC GIBBONS and PAUL GROESSE; Set Decoration: EDWIN B. WILLIS and ARTHUR KRAMS.

★ MOULIN ROUGE, Romulus Films, UA: PAUL SHERIFF; Set Decoration: MARCEL VERTES.

THE QUIET MAN, Argosy, Republic: FRANK HOTALING; Set Decoration: JOHN MCCARTHY, JR., and CHARLES THOMPSON.

THE SNOWS OF KILIMANJARO, 20th Century-Fox: LYLE WHEELER and JOHN DECUIR; Set Decoration: THOMAS LITTLE and PAUL S. FOX.

Sound Recording

★ BREAKING THE SOUND BARRIER, London Films, UA (British): LONDON FILM SOUND DEPARTMENT.

HANS CHRISTIAN ANDERSEN, Goldwyn, RKO Radio: GOLDWYN SOUND DEPARTMENT; GORDON SAWYER, Sound Director.

THE PROMOTER, Rank, Ronald Neame, U-I (British): PINEWOOD STUDIOS SOUND DEPARTMENT.

THE QUIET MAN, Argosy, Republic: REPUBLIC SOUND DEPARTMENT: DANIEL J. BLOOMBERG, Sound Director.

WITH A SONG IN MY HEART, 20th Century-Fox: 20TH CENTURY-FOX SOUND DEPARTMENT, THOMAS T. MOULTON, Sound Director.

Film Editing

COME BACK, LITTLE SHEBA, Wallis, Paramount: WARREN LOW.

FLAT TOP, Monogram: WILLIAM AUSTIN.

THE GREATEST SHOW ON EARTH, DeMille, Paramount: ANNE BAUCHENS.

★ HIGH NOON, Kramer, UA: ELMO WILLIAMS and HARRY GERSTAD.

MOULIN ROUGE, Romulus, UA: RALPH KEMPLEN.

Music

Scoring of a Dramatic or Comedy Picture

★ HIGH NOON, Kramer, UA: DIMITRI TIOMKIN.

IVANHOE, Metro-Goldwyn-Mayer: MIKLOS ROZSA.

MIRACLE OF FATIMA, Warner Bros.: MAX STEINER.

THE THIEF, Fran Prods., UA: HERSCHEL BURKE GILBERT.

VIVA ZAPATA!, 20th Century-Fox: ALEX NORTH.

Scoring of a Musical Picture

HANS CHRISTIAN ANDERSEN, Goldwyn, RKO Radio: WALTER SCHARF.

THE JAZZ SINGER, Warner Bros.: RAY HEINDORF and MAX STEINER.

THE MEDIUM, Transfilm-Lopert (Italian): GIAN-CARLO MENOTTI.

SINGIN' IN THE RAIN, Metro-Goldwyn-Mayer: LENNIE HAYTON.

★ WITH A SONG IN MY HEART,

20th Century-Fox: ALFRED NEWMAN.

Song

AM I IN LOVE from *Son of Paleface*, Paramount: Music and Lyrics by JACK BROOKS.

BECAUSE YOU'RE MINE from *Because You're Mine*, Metro-Goldwyn-Mayer: Music by NICHOLAS BRODSZKY; Lyrics by SAMMY CAHN.

★ HIGH NOON (DO NOT FORSAKE ME, OH MY DARLIN') from *High Noon*, Kramer, UA: Music by DIMITRI TIOMKIN; Lyrics by NED WASHINGTON.

THUMBELINA from *Hans Christian Andersen*, Goldwyn, RKO Radio: Music and Lyrics by FRANK LOESSER.

ZING A LITTLE ZONG from *Just for You*, Paramount: Music by HARRY WARREN; Lyrics by LEO ROBIN.

Costume Design

Black and White

AFFAIR IN TRINIDAD, Beckworth, Columbia: JEAN LOUIS.

★ THE BAD AND THE BEAUTIFUL, Metro-Goldwyn-Mayer: HELEN ROSE.

CARRIE, Paramount: EDITH HEAD.

MY COUSIN RACHEL, 20th Century-Fox: CHARLES LEMAIRE and DOROTHY JEAKINS.

SUDDEN FEAR, Joseph Kaufman, RKO Radio: SHEILA O'BRIEN.

Color

THE GREATEST SHOW ON EARTH, DeMille, Paramount: EDITH HEAD, DOROTHY JEAKINS, and MILES WHITE.

HANS CHRISTIAN ANDERSEN, Goldwyn, RKO Radio: CLAVE, MARY WILLS, and MADAME KARINSKA.

THE MERRY WIDOW, Metro-Goldwyn-Mayer: HELEN ROSE and GILE STEELE.

★ MOULIN ROUGE, Romulus, UA: MARCEL VERTES.

WITH A SONG IN MY HEART, 20th Century-Fox: CHARLES LEMAIRE.

Short Subjects

Cartoons

★ JOHANN MOUSE, Metro-Goldwyn-Mayer: (Tom and Jerry) FRED QUIMBY, Producer.

LITTLE JOHNNY JET, Metro-Goldwyn-Mayer: (M-G-M Series) FRED QUIMBY, Producer.

MADELINE, UPA, Columbia: (Jolly Frolics) STEPHEN BOSUSTOW, Executive Producer.

PINK AND BLUE BLUES, UPA, Columbia: (Mister Magoo) STEPHEN BOSUSTOW, Executive Producer.

ROMANCE OF TRANSPORTATION, National Film Board of Canada (Canadian): TOM DALY, Producer.

One Reel

ATHLETES OF THE SADDLE, Paramount: (Sportlights Series) JACK EATON, Producer.

DESERT KILLER, Warner Bros.: (Sports Parade) GORDON HOLLINGSHEAD, Producer.

★ LIGHT IN THE WINDOW, Art Films Prods., 20th Century-Fox: (Art Series) BORIS VERMONT, Producer.

NEIGHBOURS, National Film Board of Canada (Canadian): NORMAN MCLAREN, Producer.

ROYAL SCOTLAND, Crown Film Unit, BRITISH INFORMATION SERVICES (British).

Two Reels

BRIDGE OF TIME, A London Film Prod., BRITISH INFORMATION SERVICES (British).

DEVIL TAKE US, A Theatre of Life Prod.: (Theatre of Life Series) HERBERT MORGAN, Producer.

THAR SHE BLOWS!, Warner Bros.: (Technicolor Special) GORDON HOLLINGSHEAD, Producer.

★ WATER BIRDS, Walt Disney, RKO Radio: (True-Life Adventure). WALT DISNEY, Producer

Documentary

Short Subjects

DEVIL TAKE US, Theatre of Life Prod.: HERBERT MORGAN, Producer.

THE GARDEN SPIDER (EPEIRA DIADEMA), Cristallo Films, I.F.E. Releasing Corp. (Italian): ALBERTO ANCILOTTO, Producer.

MAN ALIVE!, Made by United Productions of America for the American Cancer Society: STEPHEN BOSUSTOW, Executive Producer.

★ NEIGHBOURS, National Film Board of Canada, Arthur Mayer-Edward Kingsley, Inc. (Canadian): NORMAN McLAREN, Producer.

Features

THE HOAXTERS, Metro-Goldwyn-Mayer: DORE SCHARY, Producer.

NAVAJO, Bartlett-Foster Prod., Lippert Pictures, Inc.: HALL BARTLETT, Producer.

★ THE SEA AROUND US, RKO Radio: IRWIN ALLEN, Producer.

Honorary Awards

GEORGE ALFRED MITCHELL for the design and development of the camera that bears his name and for his continued and dominant presence in the field of cinematography. (Statuette)

JOSEPH M. SCHENCK for long and distinguished service to the motion picture industry. (Statuette)

MERIAN C. COOPER for his many innovations and contributions to the art of motion pictures. (Statuette)

HAROLD LLOYD, master comedian and good citizen. (Statuette)

BOB HOPE for his contribution to the laughter of the world, his service to the motion picture industry, and his devotion to the American premise. (Statuette)

FORBIDDEN GAMES (French)—Best Foreign Language Film first released in the United States during 1952. (Statuette)

Special Effects

PLYMOUTH ADVENTURE, Metro-Goldwyn-Mayer.

Irving G. Thalberg Memorial Award

CECIL B. DeMILLE.

Scientific or Technical

Class I

EASTMAN KODAK CO. for the introduction of Eastman color negative and Eastman color print film.

ANSCO DIVISION, GENERAL ANILINE AND FILM CORP. for the introduction of Ansco color negative and Ansco color print film.

Class II

TECHNICOLOR MOTION PICTURE CORP. for an improved method of color motion picture photography under incandescent light.

Class III

PROJECTION, STILL PHOTOGRAPHIC and DEVELOPMENT ENGINEERING DEPARTMENTS of METRO-GOLDWYN-MAYER STUDIO for an improved method of projecting photographic backgrounds.

JOHN G. FRAYNE and R. R. SCOVILLE and WESTREX CORP.

for a method of measuring distortion in sound reproduction.

PHOTO RESEARCH CORP. for creating the Spectra color temperature meter.

GUSTAV JIROUCH for the design of the Robot automatic film splicer.

CARLOS RIVAS of Metro-Goldwyn-Mayer Studio for the development of a sound reproducer for magnetic film.

TWENTY-SIXTH YEAR

1953

Nominations Announced: February 15, 1954
Awards Ceremony: March 25, 1954
RKO Pantages Theatre in Hollywood; NBC Century Theatre in New York
(MC: Donald O'Connor; MC in New York: Fredric March)

Best Picture

★ FROM HERE TO ETERNITY, Columbia: Buddy Adler, Producer.

JULIUS CAESAR, Metro-Goldwyn-Mayer: John Houseman, Producer.

THE ROBE, 20th Century-Fox: Frank Ross, Producer.

ROMAN HOLIDAY, Paramount: William Wyler, Producer.

SHANE, Paramount: George Stevens, Producer.

Actor

MARLON BRANDO in *Julius Caesar*, Metro-Goldwyn-Mayer.

RICHARD BURTON in *The Robe*, 20th Century-Fox.

MONTGOMERY CLIFT in *From Here to Eternity*, Columbia.

★ WILLIAM HOLDEN in *Stalag 17*, Paramount.

BURT LANCASTER in *From Here to Eternity*, Columbia.

Actress

LESLIE CARON in *Lili*, Metro-Goldwyn-Mayer.

AVA GARDNER in *Mogambo*, Metro-Goldwyn-Mayer.

★ AUDREY HEPBURN in *Roman Holiday*, Paramount.

DEBORAH KERR in *From Here to Eternity*, Columbia.

MAGGIE MCNAMARA in *The Moon Is Blue*, Preminger-Herbert, UA.

Supporting Actor

EDDIE ALBERT in *Roman Holiday*, Paramount.

BRANDON DE WILDE in *Shane*, Paramount.

JACK PALANCE in *Shane*, Paramount.

★ FRANK SINATRA in *From Here to Eternity*, Columbia.

ROBERT STRAUSS in *Stalag 17*, Paramount.

Supporting Actress

GRACE KELLY in *Mogambo*, Metro-Goldwyn-Mayer.

GERALDINE PAGE in *Hondo*, Wayne-Fellows, Warner Bros.

MARJORIE RAMBEAU in *Torch Song*, Metro-Goldwyn-Mayer.

★ DONNA REED in *From Here to Eternity*, Columbia.

THELMA RITTER in *Pickup on South Street*, 20th Century-Fox.

Directing

GEORGE STEVENS for *Shane*, Paramount.

CHARLES WALTERS for *Lili*, Metro-Goldwyn-Mayer.

BILLY WILDER for *Stalag 17*, Paramount.

WILLIAM WYLER for *Roman Holiday*, Paramount.

★ FRED ZINNEMANN for *From Here to Eternity*, Columbia.

Writing

Motion Picture Story

ABOVE AND BEYOND, Metro-Goldwyn-Mayer: BEIRNE LAY, JR.

THE CAPTAIN'S PARADISE, London Films, Lopert-UA (British): ALEC COPPEL.

LITTLE FUGITIVE, Little Fugitive Prod. Co., Joseph Burstyn, Inc.: RAY ASHLEY, MORRIS ENGEL, and RUTH ORKIN.

★ ROMAN HOLIDAY, Paramount: IAN McLELLAN HUNTER.*

Screenplay

THE CRUEL SEA, Rank-Ealing, U-I (British): ERIC AMBLER.

★ FROM HERE TO ETERNITY, Columbia: DANIEL TARADASH

LILI, Metro-Goldwyn-Mayer: HELEN DEUTSCH.

ROMAN HOLIDAY, Paramount: IAN MCLELLAN HUNTER and JOHN DIGHTON.

SHANE, Paramount: A. B. GUTHRIE, JR.

Story and Screenplay

THE BAND WAGON, Metro-Goldwyn-Mayer: BETTY COMDEN and ADOLPH GREEN.

THE DESERT RATS, 20th Century-Fox: RICHARD MURPHY.

THE NAKED SPUR, Metro-Goldwyn-Mayer: SAM ROLFE and HAROLD JACK BLOOM.

TAKE THE HIGH GROUND, Metro-Goldwyn-Mayer: MILLARD KAUFMAN.

★ TITANIC, 20th Century-Fox: CHARLES BRACKETT, WALTER REISCH, and RICHARD BREEN.

Cinematography

Black and White

THE FOUR POSTER, Kramer, Columbia: HAL MOHR.

★ FROM HERE TO ETERNITY, Columbia: BURNETT GUFFEY.

JULIUS CAESAR, Metro-Goldwyn-Mayer: JOSEPH RUTTENBERG.

MARTIN LUTHER, Louis de Rochemont Associates: JOSEPH C. BRUN.

ROMAN HOLIDAY, Paramount: FRANK PLANER and HENRY ALEKAN.

Color

ALL THE BROTHERS WERE VALIANT, Metro-Goldwyn-Mayer: GEORGE FOLSEY.

BENEATH THE TWELVE-MILE REEF, 20th Century-Fox: EDWARD CRONJAGER.

LILI, Metro-Goldwyn-Mayer: ROBERT PLANCK.

THE ROBE, 20th Century-Fox: LEON SHAMROY.

★ SHANE, Paramount: LOYAL GRIGGS.

Art Direction—Set Decoration

Black and White

★ JULIUS CAESAR, Metro-Goldwyn-Mayer: CEDRIC GIBBONS and EDWARD CARFAGNO; Set Decoration: EDWIN B. WILLIS and HUGH HUNT.

MARTIN LUTHER, Louis de Rochemont Assocs.: FRITZ MAURISCHAT and PAUL MARKWITZ; Set Decoration: No credits listed.

THE PRESIDENT'S LADY, 20th Century-Fox: LYLE WHEELER and LELAND FULLER; Set Decoration: PAUL S. FOX.

ROMAN HOLIDAY, Paramount: HAL PEREIRA and WALTER TYLER; Set Decoration: No credits listed.

*The Writers Guild of America West now credits blacklisted writer Dalton Trumbo with the story for *Roman Holiday*. The Oscar was awarded to Ian McLellan Hunter, who acted as a front for Trumbo.

TITANIC, 20th Century-Fox: LYLE WHEELER and MAURICE RANSFORD; Set Decoration: STUART REISS.

Color

KNIGHTS OF THE ROUND TABLE, Metro-Goldwyn-Mayer: ALFRED JUNGE and HANS PETERS; Set Decoration: JOHN JARVIS.

LILI, Metro-Goldwyn-Mayer: CEDRIC GIBBONS and PAUL GROESSE; Set Decoration: EDWIN B. WILLIS and ARTHUR KRAMS.

★ THE ROBE, 20th Century-Fox: LYLE WHEELER and GEORGE W. DAVIS; Set Decoration: WALTER M. SCOTT and PAUL S. FOX.

THE STORY OF THREE LOVES, Metro-Goldwyn-Mayer: CEDRIC GIBBONS, PRESTON AMES, EDWARD CARFAGNO, and GABRIEL SCOGNAMILLO; Set Decoration: EDWIN B. WILLIS, KEOGH GLEASON, ARTHUR KRAMS, and JACK D. MOORE.

YOUNG BESS, Metro-Goldwyn-Mayer: CEDRIC GIBBONS and URIE MCCLEARY Set Decoration: EDWIN B. WILLIS and JACK D. MOORE

Sound Recording

CALAMITY JANE, Warner Bros.: WARNER BROS. SOUND DEPARTMENT, WILLIAM A. MUELLER, Sound Director.

★ FROM HERE TO ETERNITY, Columbia: COLUMBIA SOUND DEPARTMENT, JOHN P. LIVADARY, Sound Director.

KNIGHTS OF THE ROUND TABLE, Metro-Goldwyn-Mayer: A. W. WATKINS, Sound Director.

THE MISSISSIPPI GAMBLER, Universal-International: UNIVERSAL-INTERNATIONAL SOUND DEPARTMENT, LESLIE I. CAREY, Sound Director.

THE WAR OF THE WORLDS, Paramount: PARAMOUNT SOUND DEPARTMENT, LOREN L. RYDER, Sound Director.

Film Editing

CRAZYLEGS, Bartlett, Republic: IRVINE (COTTON) WARBURTON.

★ FROM HERE TO ETERNITY, Columbia: WILLIAM LYON.

THE MOON IS BLUE, Preminger-Herbert, UA: OTTO LUDWIG.

ROMAN HOLIDAY, Paramount: ROBERT SWINK.

WAR OF THE WORLDS, Paramount: EVERETT DOUGLAS.

Music

Scoring of a Dramatic or Comedy Picture

ABOVE AND BEYOND, Metro-Goldwyn-Mayer: HUGO FRIEDHOFER.

FROM HERE TO ETERNITY, Columbia: MORRIS STOLOFF and GEORGE DUNING.

JULIUS CAESAR, Metro-Goldwyn-Mayer: MIKLOS ROZSA.

★ LILI, Metro-Goldwyn-Mayer: BRONISLAU KAPER.

THIS IS CINERAMA, Cinerama Prods. Corp.: LOUIS FORBES.

Scoring of a Musical Picture

THE BANDWAGON, Metro-Goldwyn-Mayer: ADOLPH DEUTSCH.

CALAMITY JANE, Warner Bros.: RAY HEINDORF.

★ CALL ME MADAM, 20th Century-Fox: ALFRED NEWMAN.

5,000 FINGERS OF DR. T., Kramer-Columbia: FREDERICK HOLLANDER and MORRIS STOLOFF.

KISS ME KATE, Metro-Goldwyn-Mayer: ANDRÉ PREVIN and SAUL CHAPLIN.

Song

THE MOON IS BLUE from *The Moon Is Blue*, Preminger-Herbert Prods., UA: Music by HERSCHEL BURKE GILBERT; Lyrics by SYLVIA FINE.

MY FLAMING HEART from *Small Town Girl*, Metro-Goldwyn-Mayer: Music by NICHOLAS BRODSZKY; Lyrics by LEO ROBIN.

SADIE THOMPSON'S SONG (BLUE PACIFIC

BLUES) from *Miss Sadie Thompson*, Beckworth, Columbia: Music by LESTER LEE; Lyrics by NED WASHINGTON.

★ SECRET LOVE from *Calamity Jane*, Warner Bros.: Music by SAMMY FAIN; Lyrics by PAUL FRANCIS WEBSTER.

THAT'S AMORE from *The Caddy*, York Pictures, Paramount: Music by HARRY WARREN; Lyrics by JACK BROOKS.

Costume Design

Black and White

THE ACTRESS, Metro-Goldwyn-Mayer: WALTER PLUNKETT.

DREAM WIFE, Metro-Goldwyn-Mayer: HELEN ROSE and HERSCHEL MCCOY.

FROM HERE TO ETERNITY, Columbia: JEAN LOUIS.

THE PRESIDENT'S LADY, 20th Century-Fox: CHARLES LEMAIRE and RENIE.

★ ROMAN HOLIDAY, Paramount: EDITH HEAD.

Color

THE BAND WAGON, Metro-Goldwyn-Mayer: MARY ANN NYBERG.

CALL ME MADAM, 20th Century-Fox: IRENE SHARAFF.

HOW TO MARRY A MILLIONAIRE, 20th Century-Fox: CHARLES LEMAIRE and TRAVILLA.

★ THE ROBE, 20th Century-Fox: CHARLES LeMAIRE and EMILE SANTIAGO.

YOUNG BESS, Metro-Goldwyn-Mayer: WALTER PLUNKETT.

Short Subjects

Cartoons

CHRISTOPHER CRUMPET, UPA, Columbia: (Jolly Frolics) STEPHEN BOSUSTOW, Producer.

FROM A TO Z-Z-Z-Z-, Warner Bros. Cartoons, Inc., Warner Bros.: (Looney Tunes) EDWARD SELZER, Producer.

RUGGED BEAR, Walt Disney, RKO Radio: (Donald Duck) WALT DISNEY, Producer.

THE TELL TALE HEART, UPA, Columbia: (UPA Cartoon Special) STEPHEN BOSUSTOW, Producer.

★ TOOT, WHISTLE, PLUNK AND BOOM, Walt Disney, Buena Vista Film Distribution Co., Inc.: (Special Music Series) WALT DISNEY, Producer.

One Reel

CHRIST AMONG THE PRIMITIVES, IFE Releasing Corp. (Italian): VINCENZO LUCCI-CHIARISSI, Producer.

HERRING HUNT, NATIONAL FILM BOARD OF CANADA, RKO Pathé, Inc. (Canadian). (Canada Carries on Series)

JOY OF LIVING, Art Film Prods., 20th Century-Fox: (Art Film Series) BORIS VERMONT, Producer.

★ THE MERRY WIVES OF WINDSOR OVERTURE, Metro-Goldwyn-Mayer: (Overture Series) JOHNNY GREEN, Producer.

WEE WATER WONDERS, Paramount: (Grantland Rice Sportlights Series) JACK EATON, Producer.

Two Reels

★ BEAR COUNTRY, Walt Disney, RKO Radio: (True-Life Adventure) WALT DISNEY, Producer.

BEN AND ME, Walt Disney, Buena Vista Film Distribution Co., Inc.: (Cartoon Special Series) WALT DISNEY, Producer.

RETURN TO GLENNASCAUL, DUBLIN GATE THEATRE PROD., Mayer-Kingsley Inc.

VESUVIUS EXPRESS, 20th Century-Fox: (CinemaScope Shorts Series) OTTO LANG, Producer.

WINTER PARADISE, Warner Bros.: (Technicolor Special) CEDRIC FRANCIS, Producer.

Documentary

Short Subjects

★ THE ALASKAN ESKIMO, Walt Disney Prods., RKO Radio: WALT DISNEY, Producer.

THE LIVING CITY, Encyclopaedia Britannica Films, Inc.: JOHN BARNES, Producer.

OPERATION BLUE JAY, U.S. Army Signal Corps.

THEY PLANTED A STONE, World Wide Pictures, British Information Services (British): JAMES CARR, Producer.

THE WORD, 20th Century-Fox: JOHN HEALY and JOHN ADAMS, Producers.

Features

THE CONQUEST OF EVEREST, Countryman Films, Ltd. and Group 3 Ltd., UA (British): JOHN TAYLOR, LEON CLORE, and GRAHAME THARP, Producers.

★ THE LIVING DESERT, Walt Disney Prods., Buena Vista Film Dist. Co., Inc.: WALT DISNEY, Producer.

A QUEEN IS CROWNED, J. Arthur Rank Organization, Ltd., U-I (British): CASTLETON KNIGHT, Producer.

Honorary Awards

PETE SMITH for his witty and pungent observations on the American scene in his series of *Pete Smith Specialties*. (Statuette)

20TH CENTURY-FOX FILM CORPORATION in recognition of their imagination, showmanship, and foresight in introducing the revolutionary process known as CinemaScope. (Statuette)

JOSEPH I. BREEN for his conscientious, open-minded, and dignified management of the Motion Picture Production Code. (Statuette)

BELL AND HOWELL COMPANY for their pioneering and basic achievements in the advancement of the motion picture industry. (Statuette)

Special Effects

THE WAR OF THE WORLDS, Pal, Paramount.

Irving G. Thalberg Memorial Award

GEORGE STEVENS.

Scientific or Technical

Class I

PROFESSOR HENRI CHRETIEN and EARL SPONABLE, SOL HALPRIN, LORIN GRIGNON, HERBERT BRAGG, and CARL FAULKNER of 20th Century-Fox Studios for creating, developing, and engineering the equipment, processes, and techniques known as CinemaScope.

FRED WALLER for designing and developing the multiple photographic and projection systems that culminated in Cinerama.

Class II

REEVES SOUNDCRAFT CORP. for their development of a process of applying stripes of magnetic oxide to motion picture film for sound recording and reproduction.

Class III

WESTREX CORP. for the design and construction of a new film editing machine.

TWENTY-SEVENTH YEAR

1954

Nominations Announced: February 12, 1955
Awards Ceremony: March 30, 1955
RKO Pantages Theatre in Hollywood; NBC Century Theatre in New York
(MC: Bob Hope; MC in New York: Thelma Ritter)

Best Picture

THE CAINE MUTINY, A Stanley Kramer Prod., Columbia: Stanley Kramer, Producer.

THE COUNTRY GIRL, Perlberg-Seaton, Paramount: William Perlberg, Producer.

★ ON THE WATERFRONT, Horizon-American Corp., Columbia: Sam Spiegel, Producer.

SEVEN BRIDES FOR SEVEN BROTHERS, Metro-Goldwyn-Mayer: Jack Cummings, Producer.

THREE COINS IN THE FOUNTAIN, 20th Century-Fox: Sol C. Siegel, Producer.

Actor

HUMPHREY BOGART in *The Caine Mutiny*, Kramer, Columbia.

★ MARLON BRANDO in *On the Waterfront*, Horizon-American, Columbia.

BING CROSBY in *The Country Girl*, Perlberg-Seaton, Paramount.

JAMES MASON in *A Star Is Born*, Transcona, Warner Bros.

DAN O'HERLIHY in *Adventures of Robinson Crusoe*, Dancigers-Ehrlich, UA.

Actress

DOROTHY DANDRIDGE in *Carmen Jones*, Otto Preminger, 20th Century-Fox.

JUDY GARLAND in *A Star Is Born*, Transcona, Warner Bros.

AUDREY HEPBURN in *Sabrina*, Paramount.

★ GRACE KELLY in *The Country Girl*, Perlberg-Seaton, Paramount.

JANE WYMAN in *The Magnificent Obsession*, Universal-International.

Supporting Actor

LEE J. COBB in *On the Waterfront*, Horizon-American, Columbia.

KARL MALDEN in *On the Waterfront*, Horizon-American, Columbia.

★ EDMOND O'BRIEN in *The Barefoot Contessa*, Figaro, UA.

ROD STEIGER in *On the Waterfront*, Horizon-American, Columbia.

TOM TULLY in *The Caine Mutiny*, Kramer, Columbia.

Supporting Actress

NINA FOCH in *Executive Suite*, Metro-Goldwyn-Mayer.

KATY JURADO in *Broken Lance*, 20th Century-Fox.

★ EVA MARIE SAINT in *On the Waterfront*, Horizon-American, Columbia.

JAN STERLING in *The High and the Mighty*, Wayne-Fellows, Warner Bros.

CLAIRE TREVOR in *The High and the*

Mighty, Wayne-Fellows, Warner Bros.

Directing

ALFRED HITCHCOCK for *Rear Window*, Patron, Inc., Paramount.

★ ELIA KAZAN for *On the Waterfront*, Horizon-American, Columbia.

GEORGE SEATON for *The Country Girl*, Perlberg-Seaton, Paramount.

WILLIAM WELLMAN for *The High and the Mighty*, Wayne-Fellows, Warner Bros.

BILLY WILDER for *Sabrina*, Paramount.

Writing

Motion Picture Story

BREAD, LOVE AND DREAMS, Titanus, I.F.E. Releasing Corp. (Italian): ETTORE MARGADONNA.

★ BROKEN LANCE, 20th Century-Fox: PHILIP YORDAN.

FORBIDDEN GAMES, Silver Films, Times Film Corp. (French): FRANÇOIS BOYER.

NIGHT PEOPLE, 20th Century-Fox: JED HARRIS and TOM REED.

THERE'S NO BUSINESS LIKE SHOW BUSINESS, 20th Century-Fox: LAMAR TROTTI.

Screenplay

THE CAINE MUTINY, A Stanley Kramer Prod., Columbia: STANLEY ROBERTS.

★ THE COUNTRY GIRL, Perlberg-Seaton, Paramount: GEORGE SEATON.

REAR WINDOW, Patron Inc., Paramount: JOHN MICHAEL HAYES.

SABRINA, Paramount: BILLY WILDER, SAMUEL TAYLOR, and ERNEST LEHMAN.

SEVEN BRIDES FOR SEVEN BROTHERS, Metro-Goldwyn-Mayer: ALBERT HACKETT, FRANCES GOODRICH, and DOROTHY KINGSLEY.

Story and Screenplay

THE BAREFOOT CONTESSA, A Figaro, Inc., Prod., UA: JOSEPH MANKIEWICZ.

GENEVIEVE, A J. Arthur Rank Presentation-Sirius Prods., Ltd., U-I (British): WILLIAM ROSE.

THE GLENN MILLER STORY, Universal-International: VALENTINE DAVIES and OSCAR BRODNEY.

KNOCK ON WOOD, Dena Prods., Paramount: NORMAN PANAMA and MELVIN FRANK.

★ ON THE WATERFRONT, Horizon-American Corp., Columbia: BUDD SCHULBERG.

Cinematography

Black and White

THE COUNTRY GIRL, Perlberg-Seaton, Paramount: JOHN F. WARREN.

EXECUTIVE SUITE, Metro-Goldwyn-Mayer: GEORGE FOLSEY.

★ ON THE WATERFRONT, Horizon-American Corp., Columbia: BORIS KAUFMAN.

ROGUE COP, Metro-Goldwyn-Mayer: JOHN SEITZ.

SABRINA, Paramount: CHARLES LANG, JR.

Color

THE EGYPTIAN, 20th Century-Fox: LEON SHAMROY.

REAR WINDOW, Patron Inc., Paramount: ROBERT BURKS.

SEVEN BRIDES FOR SEVEN BROTHERS, Metro-Goldwyn-Mayer: GEORGE FOLSEY.

THE SILVER CHALICE, A Victor Saville Prod., Warner Bros.: WILLIAM V. SKALL.

★ THREE COINS IN THE FOUNTAIN, 20th Century-Fox: MILTON KRASNER.

Art Direction—Set Decoration

Black and White

THE COUNTRY GIRL, Perlberg-Seaton, Paramount: HAL PEREIRA and ROLAND ANDERSON; Set Decoration: SAM COMER and GRACE GREGORY.

EXECUTIVE SUITE, Metro-Goldwyn-Mayer: CEDRIC GIBBONS and EDWARD CARFAGNO; Set Decoration: EDWIN B. WILLIS and EMILE KURI.

LE PLAISIR, Stera Film–CCFC Prod., Arthur Meyer-Edward Kingsley (French): MAX OPHULS; Set Decoration: No credits listed.

★ ON THE WATERFRONT, Horizon-American Corp., Columbia: RICHARD DAY; Set Decoration: No credits listed.

SABRINA, Paramount: HAL PEREIRA and WALTER TYLER; Set Decoration: SAM COMER and RAY MOYER.

Color

BRIGADOON, Metro-Goldwyn-Mayer: CEDRIC GIBBONS and PRESTON AMES; Set Decoration: EDWIN B. WILLIS and KEOGH GLEASON.

DESIREE, 20th Century-Fox: LYLE WHEELER and LELAND FULLER; Set Decoration: WALTER M. SCOTT and PAUL S. FOX.

RED GARTERS, Paramount: HAL PEREIRA and ROLAND ANDERSON; Set Decoration: SAM COMER and RAY MOYER.

A STAR IS BORN, A Transcona Enterprises Prod., Warner Bros.: MALCOLM BERT, GENE ALLEN, and IRENE SHARAFF; Set Decoration: GEORGE JAMES HOPKINS.

★ 20,000 LEAGUES UNDER THE SEA, Walt Disney Prods., Buena Vista Film Dist. Co., Inc.: JOHN MEEHAN; Set Decoration: EMILE KURI.

Sound Recording

BRIGADOON, Metro-Goldwyn-Mayer: WESLEY C. MILLER, Sound Director.

THE CAINE MUTINY, Columbia: JOHN P. LIVADARY, Sound Director.

★ THE GLENN MILLER STORY, Universal-International: LESLIE I. CAREY, Sound Director.

REAR WINDOW, Paramount: LOREN L. RYDER, Sound Director.

SUSAN SLEPT HERE, RKO Radio: JOHN O. AALBERG, Sound Director.

Film Editing

THE CAINE MUTINY, A Stanley Kramer Prod., Columbia: WILLIAM A. LYON and HENRY BATISTA.

THE HIGH AND THE MIGHTY, Wayne-Fellows Prod., Inc., Warner Bros.: RALPH DAWSON.

★ ON THE WATERFRONT, Horizon-American Corp., Columbia: GENE MILFORD.

SEVEN BRIDES FOR SEVEN BROTHERS, Metro-Goldwyn-Mayer: RALPH E. WINTERS.

20,000 LEAGUES UNDER THE SEA, Walt Disney Prods., Buena Vista Film Dist. Co., Inc.: ELMO WILLIAMS.

Music

Scoring of a Dramatic or Comedy Picture

THE CAINE MUTINY, A Stanley Kramer Prod., Columbia: MAX STEINER.

GENEVIEVE, A J. Arthur Rank Presentation–Sirius Prods., Ltd., U-I (British): MUIR MATHIESON.*

★ THE HIGH AND THE MIGHTY, Wayne-Fellows Prods., Inc., Warner Bros.: DIMITRI TIOMKIN.

ON THE WATERFRONT, Horizon-American Corp., Columbia: LEONARD BERNSTEIN.

THE SILVER CHALICE, A Victor Saville

*This Academy now recognizes Larry Adler as the composer of *GENEVIEVE*. Adler was blacklisted at the time, and Muir Mathieson was given screen credit for the achievement that earned a nomination.

Prod., Warner Bros.: FRANZ WAXMAN.

Scoring of a Musical Picture

CARMEN JONES, Otto Preminger, 20th Century-Fox: HERSCHEL BURKE GILBERT.

THE GLENN MILLER STORY, Universal-International: JOSEPH GERSHENSON and HENRY MANCINI.

★ SEVEN BRIDES FOR SEVEN BROTHERS, Metro-Goldwyn-Mayer: ADOLPH DEUTSCH and SAUL CHAPLIN.

A STAR IS BORN, A Transcona Enterprises Prod., Warner Bros.: RAY HEINDORF.

THERE'S NO BUSINESS LIKE SHOW BUSINESS, 20th Century-Fox: ALFRED NEWMAN and LIONEL NEWMAN.

Song

COUNT YOUR BLESSINGS INSTEAD OF SHEEP from *White Christmas*, Paramount: Music and Lyrics by IRVING BERLIN.

THE HIGH AND THE MIGHTY from *The High and the Mighty*, Wayne-Fellows Prods., Inc., Warner Bros.: Music by DIMITRI TIOMKIN; Lyrics by NED WASHINGTON.

HOLD MY HAND from *Susan Slept Here*, RKO Radio: Music and Lyrics by JACK LAWRENCE and RICHARD MYERS.

THE MAN THAT GOT AWAY from *A Star Is Born*, A Transcona Enterprises Prod., Warner Bros.: Music by HAROLD ARLEN; Lyrics by IRA GERSHWIN.

★ THREE COINS IN THE FOUNTAIN from *Three Coins in the Fountain*, 20th Century-Fox: Music by JULE STYNE; Lyrics by SAMMY CAHN.

Costume Design

Black and White

THE EARRINGS OF MADAME DE . . . , Franco-London Prods., Arlan Pictures (French): GEORGES ANNENKOV and ROSINE DELAMARE.

EXECUTIVE SUITE, Metro-Goldwyn-Mayer: HELEN ROSE.

INDISCRETION OF AN AMERICAN WIFE, A Vittorio DeSica Prod., Columbia: CHRISTIAN DIOR.

IT SHOULD HAPPEN TO YOU, Columbia: JEAN LOUIS.

★ SABRINA, Paramount: EDITH HEAD.

Color

BRIGADOON, Metro-Goldwyn-Mayer: IRENE SHARAFF.

DESIREE, 20th Century-Fox: CHARLES LEMAIRE and RENE HUBERT.

★ GATE OF HELL, A Daiei Prod., Edward Harrison (Japanese): SANZO WADA.

A STAR IS BORN, A Transcona Enterprises Prod., Warner Bros.: JEAN LOUIS, MARY ANN NYBERG, and IRENE SHARAFF.

THERE'S NO BUSINESS LIKE SHOW BUSINESS, 20th Century-Fox: CHARLES LEMAIRE, TRAVILLA, and MILES WHITE.

Special Effects

(Annual Award again)

HELL AND HIGH WATER, 20th Century-Fox.

THEM!, Warner Bros.

★ 20,000 LEAGUES UNDER THE SEA, Walt Disney Studios.

Short Subjects

Cartoons

CRAZY MIXED UP PUP, Walter Lantz Prods., U-I: WALTER LANTZ, Producer.

PIGS IS PIGS, Walt Disney Prods., RKO Radio: WALT DISNEY, Producer.

SANDY CLAWS, Warner Bros. Cartoons, Inc.: EDWARD SELZER, Producer.

TOUCHÉ, PUSSY CAT, Metro-Goldwyn-Mayer: FRED QUIMBY, Producer.

★ WHEN MAGOO FLEW, United Productions of America, Columbia: STEPHEN BOSUSTOW, Producer.

One Reel

THE FIRST PIANO QUARTETTE, 20th Century-Fox: OTTO LANG, Producer.
THE STRAUSS FANTASY, Metro-Goldwyn-Mayer: JOHNNY GREEN, Producer.
THIS MECHANICAL AGE, Warner Bros.: ROBERT YOUNGSON, Producer.

Two Reels

BEAUTY AND THE BULL, Warner Bros.: CEDRIC FRANCIS, Producer.
JET CARRIER, 20th Century-Fox: OTTO LANG, Producer.
SIAM, Walt Disney Prods., Buena Vista Film Distribution Co., Inc.: WALT DISNEY, Producer.
★ A TIME OUT OF WAR, Carnival Prods.: DENIS SANDERS and TERRY SANDERS, Producers.

Documentary

Short Subjects

JET CARRIER, 20th Century-Fox: OTTO LANG, Producer.
REMBRANDT: A SELF-PORTRAIT, Distributors Corp. of America: MORRIE ROIZMAN, Producer.
★ THURSDAY'S CHILDREN, British Information Services (British): WORLD WIDE PICTURES and MORSE FILMS, Producers.

Features

THE STRATFORD ADVENTURE, National Film Board of Canada, Continental Dist., Inc. (Canadian): GUY GLOVER, Producer.
★ THE VANISHING PRAIRIE, Walt Disney Prods., Buena Vista Film Dist. Co., Inc.: WALT DISNEY, Producer.

Honorary Awards

BAUSCH & LOMB OPTICAL COMPANY for their contributions to the advancement of the motion picture industry. (Statuette)
KEMP R. NIVER for the development of the Renovare Process which has made possible the restoration of the Library of Congress Paper Film Collection. (Statuette)
GRETA GARBO for her unforgettable screen performances. (Statuette)
DANNY KAYE for his unique talents and for his service to the Academy, the motion picture industry, and the American people. (Statuette)
JON WHITELEY for his outstanding juvenile performance in *The Little Kidnappers*. (Miniature statuette)
VINCENT WINTER for his outstanding juvenile performance in *The Little Kidnappers*. (Miniature statuette)
GATE OF HELL (Japanese)—Best Foreign Language Film first released in the United States during 1954. (Statuette)

Irving G. Thalberg Memorial Award

None.

Scientific or Technical

Class I

PARAMOUNT PICTURES, INC., LOREN L. RYDER, JOHN R. BISHOP, and all the members of the technical and engineering staff for developing a method of producing and exhibiting motion pictures known as VistaVision.

Class II

None.

Class III

DAVID S. HORSLEY and the UNIVERSAL-INTERNATIONAL

STUDIO SPECIAL PHOTOGRAPHIC DEPARTMENT for a portable, remote control device for process projectors.

KARL FREUND and FRANK CRANDELL of Photo Research Corp. for the design and development of a direct-reading brightness meter.

WESLEY C. MILLER, J. W. STAFFORD, K. M. FRIERSON, and the METRO-GOLDWYN-MAYER STUDIO SOUND DEPARTMENT for an electronic sound printing comparison device.

JOHN P. LIVADARY, LLOYD RUSSELL, and the COLUMBIA STUDIO SOUND DEPARTMENT for an improved limiting amplifier as applied to sound-level comparison devices.

ROLAND MILLER and MAX GOEPPINGER of Magnascope Corp. for the design and development of a cathode-ray magnetic sound track viewer.

CARLOS RIVAS, G. M. SPRAGUE, and the METRO-GOLDWYN-MAYER STUDIO SOUND DEPARTMENT for the design of a magnetic sound editing machine.

FRED WILSON of the Samuel Goldwyn Studio Sound Department for the design of a variable, multiple-band equalizer.

P. C. YOUNG of the Metro-Goldwyn-Mayer Studio Projection Department for the practical application of a variable focal length attachment to motion picture projector lenses.

FRED KNOTH and ORIEN ERNEST of the Universal-International Studio Technical Department for the development of a hand-portable, electric, dry, oil-fog machine.

TWENTY-EIGHTH YEAR

1955

Nominations Announced: February 18, 1956
Awards Ceremony: March 21, 1956
RKO Pantages Theatre in Hollywood; NBC Century Theatre in New York
(MC: Jerry Lewis: MCs in New York: Claudette Colbert and Joseph L. Mankiewicz)

Best Picture

LOVE IS A MANY-SPLENDORED THING, 20th Century-Fox: Buddy Adler, Producer.

★ MARTY, Hecht and Lancaster's Steven Prods., UA: Harold Hecht, Producer.

MISTER ROBERTS, An Orange Prod., Warner Bros.: Leland Hayward, Producer.

PICNIC, Columbia: Fred Kohlmar, Producer.

THE ROSE TATTOO, Hal Wallis, Paramount: Hal B. Wallis, Producer.

Actor

★ ERNEST BORGNINE in *Marty*, Hecht and Lancaster's Steven Prods., UA.

JAMES CAGNEY in *Love Me or Leave Me*, Metro-Goldwyn-Mayer.

JAMES DEAN in *East of Eden*, Warner Bros.

FRANK SINATRA in *The Man with the Golden Arm*, Preminger, UA.

SPENCER TRACY in *Bad Day at Black Rock*, Metro-Goldwyn-Mayer.

Actress

SUSAN HAYWARD in *I'll Cry Tomorrow*, Metro-Goldwyn-Mayer.

KATHARINE HEPBURN in *Summertime*, Ilya Lopert-David Lean, UA. (Anglo-American)

JENNIFER JONES in *Love Is a Many-Splendored Thing*, 20th Century-Fox.

★ ANNA MAGNANI in *The Rose Tattoo*, Hal B. Wallis, Paramount.

ELEANOR PARKER in *Interrupted Melody*, Metro-Goldwyn-Mayer.

Supporting Actor

ARTHUR KENNEDY in *Trial*, Metro-Goldwyn-Mayer.

★ JACK LEMMON in *Mister Roberts*, An Orange Prod., Warner Bros.

JOE MANTELL in *Marty*, Hecht and Lancaster's Steven Prods., UA.

SAL MINEO in *Rebel without a Cause*, Warner Bros.

ARTHUR O'CONNELL in *Picnic*, Columbia.

Supporting Actress

BETSY BLAIR in *Marty*, Hecht and Lancaster's Steven Prods., UA.

PEGGY LEE in *Pete Kelly's Blues*, A Mark VII Ltd. Prod., Warner Bros.

MARISA PAVAN in *The Rose Tattoo*, Hal Wallis, Paramount.

★ JO VAN FLEET in *East of Eden*, Warner Bros.

NATALIE WOOD in *Rebel without a Cause*, Warner Bros.

Directing

ELIA KAZAN for *East of Eden*, Warner Bros.

DAVID LEAN for *Summertime*, Ilya Lopert-David Lean, UA. (Anglo-American)

JOSHUA LOGAN for *Picnic*, Columbia.

⋆ DELBERT MANN for *Marty*, Hecht and Lancaster's Steven Prods., UA.

JOHN STURGES for *Bad Day at Black Rock*, Metro-Goldwyn-Mayer.

Writing

Motion Picture Story

⋆ LOVE ME OR LEAVE ME, Metro-Goldwyn-Mayer: DANIEL FUCHS.

THE PRIVATE WAR OF MAJOR BENSON, U-I: JOE CONNELLY and BOB MOSHER.

REBEL WITHOUT A CAUSE, Warner Bros.: NICHOLAS RAY.

THE SHEEP HAS 5 LEGS, Raoul Ploquin, United Motion Picture Organization (French): JEAN MARSAN, HENRY TROYAT, JACQUES PERRET, HENRI VERNEUIL, and RAOUL PLOQUIN.

STRATEGIC AIR COMMAND, Paramount: BEIRNE LAY, JR.

Screenplay

BAD DAY AT BLACK ROCK, Metro-Goldwyn-Mayer: MILLARD KAUFMAN.

BLACKBOARD JUNGLE, Metro-Goldwyn-Mayer: RICHARD BROOKS.

EAST OF EDEN, Warner Bros.: PAUL OSBORN.

LOVE ME OR LEAVE ME, Metro-Goldwyn-Mayer: DANIEL FUCHS and ISOBEL LENNART.

⋆ MARTY, Hecht and Lancaster's Steven Prods., UA: PADDY CHAYEFSKY.

Story and Screenplay

THE COURT-MARTIAL OF BILLY MITCHELL, A United States Pictures Prod., Warner Bros.: MILTON SPERLING and EMMET LAVERY.

⋆ INTERRUPTED MELODY, Metro-Goldwyn-Mayer: WILLIAM LUDWIG and SONYA LEVIEN.

IT'S ALWAYS FAIR WEATHER, Metro-Goldwyn-Mayer: BETTY COMDEN and ADOLPH GREEN.

MR. HULOT'S HOLIDAY, Fred Orain Prod., GBD International Releasing Corp. (French): JACQUES TATI and HENRI MARQUET.

THE SEVEN LITTLE FOYS, Hope Enterprises, Inc., and Scribe Prods.: MELVILLE SHAVELSON and JACK ROSE.

Cinematography

Black and White

BLACKBOARD JUNGLE, Metro-Goldwyn-Mayer: RUSSELL HARLAN.

I'LL CRY TOMORROW, Metro-Goldwyn-Mayer: ARTHUR E. ARLING.

MARTY, Hecht and Lancaster's Steven Prods., UA: JOSEPH LASHELLE.

QUEEN BEE, Columbia: CHARLES LANG.

⋆ THE ROSE TATTOO, Hal Wallis, Paramount: JAMES WONG HOWE.

Color

GUYS AND DOLLS, Samuel Goldwyn Prods., Inc., M-G-M: HARRY STRADLING.

LOVE IS A MANY-SPLENDORED THING, 20th Century-Fox: LEON SHAMROY.

A MAN CALLED PETER, 20th Century-Fox: HAROLD LIPSTEIN.

OKLAHOMA!, Rodgers and Hammerstein Pictures, Inc., Magna Theatre Corp.: ROBERT SURTEES.

⋆ TO CATCH A THIEF, Paramount: ROBERT BURKS.

*Art Direction—Set Decoration**

Black and White

BLACKBOARD JUNGLE, Metro-Goldwyn-Mayer: CEDRIC GIBBONS and

*Prior to 1955, Set Decorators were given plaques. Beginning in 1955, Gold Statuettes were also given to Set Decorators.

RANDALL DALL DUELL; Set Decoration: EDWIN B. WILLIS and HENRY GRACE.

I'LL CRY TOMORROW, Metro-Goldwyn-Mayer: CEDRIC GIBBONS and MALCOLM BROWN; Set Decoration: EDWIN B. WILLIS and HUGH B. HUNT.

THE MAN WITH THE GOLDEN ARM, Otto Preminger Prod., UA.: JOSEPH C. WRIGHT; Set Decoration: DARRELL SILVERA.

MARTY, Hecht and Lancaster's Steven Prods., UA: EDWARD S. HAWORTH and WALTER SIMONDS; Set Decoration: ROBERT PRIESTLEY.

★ THE ROSE TATTOO, Hal Wallis, Paramount: HAL PEREIRA and TAMBI LARSEN; Set Decoration: SAM COMER and ARTHUR KRAMS.

Color

DADDY LONG LEGS, 20th Century-Fox: LYLE WHEELER and JOHN DECUIR; Set Decoration: WALTER M. SCOTT and PAUL S. FOX.

GUYS AND DOLLS, Samuel Goldwyn Prods., Inc., M-G-M: OLIVER SMITH and JOSEPH C. WRIGHT; Set Decoration: HOWARD BRISTOL.

LOVE IS A MANY-SPLENDORED THING, 20th Century-Fox: LYLE WHEELER and GEORGE W. DAVIS; Set Decoration: WALTER M. SCOTT and JACK STUBBS.

★ PICNIC, Columbia: WILLIAM FLANNERY and JO MIELZINER; Set Decoration: ROBERT PRIESTLEY.

TO CATCH A THIEF, Paramount: HAL PEREIRA and JOSEPH MCMILLAN JOHNSON; Set Decoration: SAM COMER and ARTHUR KRAMS.

Sound Recording

LOVE IS A MANY-SPLENDORED THING, 20th Century-Fox Studio Sound Department: CARL W. FAULKNER, Sound Director.

LOVE ME OR LEAVE ME, Metro-Goldwyn-Mayer Studio Sound Department: WESLEY C. MILLER, Sound Director.

MISTER ROBERTS, Warner Bros. Studio Sound Department: WILLIAM A. MUELLER, Sound Director.

NOT AS A STRANGER, Radio Corporation of America Sound Department: WATSON JONES, Sound Director.

★ OKLAHOMA!, TODD-AO SOUND DEPARTMENT: FRED HYNES, Sound Director.

Film Editing

BLACKBOARD JUNGLE, Metro-Goldwyn-Mayer: FERRIS WEBSTER.

THE BRIDGES AT TOKO-RI, Perlberg-Seaton, Paramount: ALMA MACRORIE.

OKLAHOMA!, Rodgers and Hammerstein Pictures, Inc., Magna Theatre Corp.: GENE RUGGIERO and GEORGE BOEMLER.

★ PICNIC, Columbia: CHARLES NELSON and WILLIAM A. LYON.

THE ROSE TATTOO, Hal Wallis, Paramount: WARREN LOW.

Music

Scoring of a Dramatic or Comedy Picture

BATTLE CRY, Warner Bros.: MAX STEINER.

★ LOVE IS A MANY-SPLENDORED THING, 20th Century-Fox: ALFRED NEWMAN.

THE MAN WITH THE GOLDEN ARM, Otto Preminger Prod., UA: ELMER BERNSTEIN.

PICNIC, Columbia: GEORGE DUNING.

THE ROSE TATTOO, Hal Wallis, Paramount: ALEX NORTH.

Scoring of a Musical Picture

DADDY LONG LEGS, 20th Century-Fox: ALFRED NEWMAN.

GUYS AND DOLLS, Samuel Goldwyn Prods., Inc., M-G-M: JAY BLACKTON and CYRIL J. MOCKRIDGE.

IT'S ALWAYS FAIR WEATHER, Metro-Goldwyn-Mayer: ANDRÉ PREVIN.
LOVE ME OR LEAVE ME, Metro-Goldwyn-Mayer: PERCY FAITH and GEORGE STOLL.
★ OKLAHOMA!, Rodgers and Hammerstein Pictures, Inc., Magna Theatre Corp.: ROBERT RUSSELL BENNETT, JAY BLACKTON, and ADOLPH DEUTSCH.

Song

I'LL NEVER STOP LOVING YOU from *Love Me or Leave Me*, Metro-Goldwyn-Mayer: Music by NICHOLAS BRODSZKY; Lyrics by SAMMY CAHN.
★ LOVE IS A MANY-SPLENDORED THING from *Love Is a Many-Splendored Thing*, 20th Century-Fox: Music by SAMMY FAIN; Lyrics by PAUL FRANCIS WEBSTER.
(LOVE IS) THE TENDER TRAP from *The Tender Trap*, Metro-Goldwyn-Mayer: Music by JAMES VAN HEUSEN; Lyrics by SAMMY CAHN.
SOMETHING'S GOTTA GIVE from *Daddy Long Legs*, 20th Century-Fox: Music and Lyrics by JOHNNY MERCER.
UNCHAINED MELODY from *Unchained*, Hall Bartlett Prods., Inc., Warner Bros.: Music by ALEX NORTH; Lyrics by HY ZARET.

Costume Design

Black and White

★ I'LL CRY TOMORROW, Metro-Goldwyn-Mayer: HELEN ROSE.
THE PICKWICK PAPERS, Renown Prod., Kingsley International Pictures (British): BEATRICE DAWSON.
QUEEN BEE, Columbia: JEAN LOUIS.
THE ROSE TATTOO, Hal Wallis, Paramount: EDITH HEAD.
UGETSU, Daiei Motion Picture Co., Edward Harrison (Japanese): TADAOTO KAINOSCHO.

Color

GUYS AND DOLLS, Samuel Goldwyn Prods., Inc., M-G-M: IRENE SHARAFF.
INTERRUPTED MELODY, Metro-Goldwyn-Mayer: HELEN ROSE.
★ LOVE IS A MANY-SPLENDORED THING, 20th Century-Fox: CHARLES LEMAIRE.
TO CATCH A THIEF, Paramount: EDITH HEAD.
THE VIRGIN QUEEN, 20th Century-Fox: CHARLES LEMAIRE and MARY WILLS.

Special Effects

★ THE BRIDGES AT TOKO-RI, Paramount.
THE DAM BUSTERS, Associated British Picture Corp., Ltd. (British).
THE RAINS OF RANCHIPUR, 20th Century-Fox.

Short Subjects

Cartoons

GOOD WILL TO MEN, Metro-Goldwyn-Mayer: FRED QUIMBY, WILLIAM HANNA, and JOSEPH BARBERA, Producers.
THE LEGEND OF ROCK-A-BYE-POINT, Walter Lantz Prods., U-I: WALTER LANTZ, Producer.
NO HUNTING, Walt Disney Prods., RKO Radio: WALT DISNEY, Producer.
★ SPEEDY GONZALES, Warner Bros. Cartoons, Inc.: EDWARD SELZER, Producer.

One Reel

GADGETS GALORE, Warner Bros.: ROBERT YOUNGSON, Producer.
★ SURVIVAL CITY, 20th Century-Fox: EDMUND REEK, Producer.
3RD AVE. EL, Carson Davidson Prods., Ardee Films: CARSON DAVIDSON, Producer.
THREE KISSES, Paramount: JUSTIN HERMAN, Producer.

Two Reels

THE BATTLE OF GETTYSBURG, Metro-Goldwyn-Mayer: DORE SCHARY, Producer

★ THE FACE OF LINCOLN, University of Southern California Presentation, Cavalcade Pictures, Inc.: WILBUR T. BLUME, Producer.

ON THE TWELFTH DAY . . . , Go Pictures, Inc., George Brest and Assocs.: GEORGE K. ARTHUR, Producer.

SWITZERLAND, Walt Disney Prods., Buena Vista Film Distribution Co., Inc.: WALT DISNEY, Producer.

24 HOUR ALERT, Warner Bros.: CEDRIC FRANCIS, Producer.

Documentary

Short Subjects

THE BATTLE OF GETTYSBURG, Metro-Goldwyn-Mayer: DORE SCHARY, Producer.

THE FACE OF LINCOLN, University of Southern California Presentation, Cavalcade Pictures, Inc.: WILBUR T. BLUME, Producer.

★ MEN AGAINST THE ARCTIC, Walt Disney Prods., Buena Vista Film Dist. Co., Inc.: WALT DISNEY, Producer.

Features

HEARTBREAK RIDGE, Rene Risacher Prod., Tudor Pictures (French): RENE RISACHER, Producer.

★ HELEN KELLER IN HER STORY, Nancy Hamilton Presentation: NANCY HAMILTON, Producer.

Honorary Award

★ SAMURAI, THE LEGEND OF MUSASHI, (Japanese)—Best Foreign Language Film first released in the United States during 1955. (Statuette)

Irving G. Thalberg Memorial Award

None.

Scientific or Technical

Class I

NATIONAL CARBON CO. for the development and production of a high-efficiency yellow flame carbon for motion picture color photography.

Class II

EASTMAN KODAK CO. for Eastman Tri-X panchromatic negative film.

FARCIOT EDOUART, HAL CORL, and the PARAMOUNT STUDIO TRANSPARENCY DEPARTMENT for the engineering and development of a double-frame, triple-head background projector.

Class III

20TH CENTURY-FOX STUDIO and BAUSCH & LOMB CO. for the new combination lenses for CinemaScope photography.

WALTER JOLLEY, MAURICE LARSON, and R. H. SPIES of 20th Century-Fox Studio for a spraying process that creates simulated metallic surfaces.

STEVE KRILANOVICH for an improved camera dolly incorporating multidirectional steering.

DAVE ANDERSON of 20th Century-Fox Studio for an improved spotlight capable of maintaining a fixed circle of light at constant intensity over varied distances.

LOREN L. RYDER, CHARLES WEST, HENRY FRACKER, and

PARAMOUNT STUDIO for a projection film index to establish proper framing for various aspect ratios.

FARCIOT EDOUART, HAL CORL, and the PARAMOUNT STUDIO TRANSPARENCY DEPARTMENT for an improved dual-stereopticon background projector.

TWENTY-NINTH YEAR

1956

Nominations Announced: February 18, 1957
Awards Ceremony: March 27, 1957
RKO Pantages Theatre in Hollywood; NBC Century Theatre in New York
(MC: Jerry Lewis; MC in New York: Celeste Holm)
(New York ceremony not held after this year)

Best Picture

★ AROUND THE WORLD IN 80 DAYS, The Michael Todd Co., Inc., UA: Michael Todd, Producer.

FRIENDLY PERSUASION, Allied Artists: William Wyler, Producer.

GIANT, Giant Prod., Warner Bros.: George Stevens and Henry Ginsberg, Producers.

THE KING AND I, 20th Century-Fox: Charles Brackett, Producer.

THE TEN COMMANDMENTS, Motion Picture Assocs., Inc., Paramount: Cecil B. DeMille, Producer.

Actor

★ YUL BRYNNER in *The King and I*, 20th Century-Fox.

JAMES DEAN in *Giant*, Giant Prod., Warner Bros.

KIRK DOUGLAS in *Lust for Life*, Metro-Goldwyn-Mayer.

ROCK HUDSON in *Giant*, Giant Prod., Warner Bros.

SIR LAURENCE OLIVIER in *Richard III*, Laurence Olivier Prod., Lopert Films Dist. Corp. (British)

Actress

CARROLL BAKER in *Baby Doll*, A Newtown Prod., Warner Bros.

★ INGRID BERGMAN in *Anastasia*, 20th Century-Fox.

KATHARINE HEPBURN in *The Rainmaker*, Hal Wallis Prods., Paramount.

NANCY KELLY in *The Bad Seed*, Warner Bros.

DEBORAH KERR in *The King and I*, 20th Century-Fox.

Supporting Actor

DON MURRAY in *Bus Stop*, 20th Century-Fox.

ANTHONY PERKINS in *Friendly Persuasion*, Allied Artists.

★ ANTHONY QUINN in *Lust for Life*, Metro-Goldwyn-Mayer.

MICKEY ROONEY in *The Bold and the Brave*, Filmakers Releasing Org., RKO Radio.

ROBERT STACK in *Written on the Wind*, Universal-International.

Supporting Actress

MILDRED DUNNOCK in *Baby Doll*, A Newtown Prod., Warner Bros.

EILEEN HECKART in *The Bad Seed*, Warner Bros.

MERCEDES MCCAMBRIDGE in *Giant*, Giant Prod., Warner Bros.

PATTY MCCORMACK in *The Bad Seed*, Warner Bros.

★ DOROTHY MALONE in *Written on the Wind*, Universal-International.

Directing

MICHAEL ANDERSON for *Around the World in 80 Days*, The Michael Todd Co., Inc., UA.

WALTER LANG for *The King and I*, 20th Century-Fox.

★ GEORGE STEVENS for *Giant*, Giant Prod., Warner Bros.

KING VIDOR for *War and Peace*, A Ponti-DeLaurentiis Prod., Paramount. (Italo-American)

WILLIAM WYLER for *Friendly Persuasion*, Allied Artists.

Writing

Motion Picture Story

★ THE BRAVE ONE, King Bros. Prods., Inc., RKO Radio: ROBERT RICH (pseudonym for DALTON TRUMBO).*

THE EDDY DUCHIN STORY, Columbia: LEO KATCHER.

HIGH SOCIETY, Allied Artists: EDWARD BERNDS and ELWOOD ULLMAN. (withdrawn from final ballot)

THE PROUD AND THE BEAUTIFUL, La Compagnie Industrielle Commerciale Cinematographique, Kingsley International (French): JEAN-PAUL SARTRE.

UMBERTO D., Rizzoli-De Sica-Amato Prod., Harrison and Davidson (Italian): CESARE ZAVATTINI.

Screenplay—Adapted

★ AROUND THE WORLD IN 80 DAYS, The Michael Todd Co., Inc., UA: JAMES POE, JOHN FARROW, and S. J. PERELMAN.

BABY DOLL, A Newtown Prod., Warner Bros.: TENNESSEE WILLIAMS.

FRIENDLY PERSUASION, Allied Artists: (Writer MICHAEL WILSON ineligible under Academy by-laws).

GIANT, Giant Prod., Warner Bros.: FRED GUIOL and IVAN MOFFAT.

LUST FOR LIFE, Metro-Goldwyn-Mayer: NORMAN CORWIN.

Screenplay—Original

THE BOLD AND THE BRAVE, Filmakers Releasing Organization, RKO Radio: ROBERT LEWIN.

JULIE, Arwin Prods., M-G-M: ANDREW L. STONE.

LA STRADA, Ponti-De Laurentiis Prod., Trans-Lux Dist. Corp. (Italian): FEDERICO FELLINI and TULLIO PINELLI.

THE LADY KILLERS, Ealing Studios Ltd., Continental Dist., Inc. (British): WILLIAM ROSE.

★ THE RED BALLOON, Films Montsouris, Lopert Films Dist. Corp. (French): ALBERT LAMORISSE.

Cinematography

Black and White

BABY DOLL, A Newtown Prod., Warner Bros.: BORIS KAUFMAN.

THE BAD SEED, Warner Bros.: HAL ROSSON.

THE HARDER THEY FALL, Columbia: BURNETT GUFFEY.

★ SOMEBODY UP THERE LIKES ME, Metro-Goldwyn-Mayer: JOSEPH RUTTENBERG.

STAGECOACH TO FURY, Regal Films, Inc. Prod., 20th Century-Fox: WALTER STRENGE.

Color

★ AROUND THE WORLD IN 80 DAYS, The Michael Todd Co., Inc., UA: LIONEL LINDON.

THE EDDY DUCHIN STORY, Columbia: HARRY STRADLING.

*Blacklisted screenwriter Trumbo, who wrote the screenplay for *The Brave One* under the pseudonym of Robert Rich, officially received his Oscar on May 2, 1975.

THE KING AND I, 20th Century-Fox: LEON SHAMROY.

THE TEN COMMANDMENTS, Motion Picture Assoc., Paramount: LOYAL GRIGGS.

WAR AND PEACE, A Ponti-De Laurentiis Prod., Paramount (Italo-American): JACK CARDIFF.

Art Direction—Set Decoration

Black and White

THE MAGNIFICENT SEVEN (a.k.a. THE SEVEN SAMURAI), A Toho Prod., Kingsley International (Japanese): TAKASHI MATSUYAMA; Set Decoration: No credits listed.

THE PROUD AND THE PROFANE, The Perlberg-Seaton Prod., Paramount: HAL PEREIRA and A. EARL HEDRICK; Set Decoration: SAMUEL M. COMER and FRANK R. MCKELVY.

THE SOLID GOLD CADILLAC, Columbia: ROSS BELLAH; Set Decoration: WILLIAM R. KIERNAN and LOUIS DIAGE.

* SOMEBODY UP THERE LIKES ME, Metro-Goldwyn-Mayer: CEDRIC GIBBONS and MALCOLM F. BROWN; Set Decoration: EDWIN B. WILLIS and F. KEOGH GLEASON.

TEENAGE REBEL, 20th Century-Fox: LYLE R. WHEELER and JACK MARTIN SMITH; Set Decoration: WALTER M. SCOTT and STUART A. REISS.

Color

AROUND THE WORLD IN 80 DAYS, The Michael Todd Co., Inc., UA: JAMES W. SULLIVAN and KEN ADAM; Set Decoration: ROSS J. DOWD.

GIANT, Giant Prod., Warner Bros.: BORIS LEVEN; Set Decoration: RALPH S. HURST.

* THE KING AND I, 20th Century-Fox: LYLE R. WHEELER and JOHN DECUIR; Set Decoration: WALTER M. SCOTT and PAUL S. FOX.

LUST FOR LIFE, Metro-Goldwyn-Mayer: CEDRIC GIBBONS, HANS PETERS, and PRESTON AMES; Set Decoration: EDWIN B. WILLIS and F. KEOGH GLEASON.

THE TEN COMMANDMENTS, Motion Picture Assocs., Inc., Paramount: HAL PEREIRA, WALTER H. TYLER, and ALBERT NOZAKI; Set Decoration: SAM M. COMER and RAY MOYER.

Sound Recording

THE BRAVE ONE, King Bros. Productions, Inc.: JOHN MYERS, Sound Director.

THE EDDY DUCHIN STORY, Columbia Studio Sound Department: JOHN LIVADARY, Sound Director.

FRIENDLY PERSUASION, Allied Artists, Westrex Sound Services, Inc.: GORDON R. GLENNAN, Sound Director; and Samuel Goldwyn Studio Sound Department: GORDON SAWYER, Sound Director.

* THE KING AND I, 20th Century-Fox Studio Sound Department: CARL FAULKNER, Sound Director.

THE TEN COMMANDMENTS, Paramount Studio Sound Department: LOREN L. RYDER, Sound Director.

Film Editing

* AROUND THE WORLD IN 80 DAYS, The Michael Todd Co., Inc., UA: GENE RUGGIERO and PAUL WEATHERWAX.

THE BRAVE ONE, King Bros. Prods., Inc., RKO Radio: MERRILL G. WHITE.

GIANT, Giant Prod., Warner Bros.: WILLIAM HORNBECK, PHILIP W. ANDERSON, and FRED BOHANAN.

SOMEBODY UP THERE LIKES ME, Metro-Goldwyn-Mayer: ALBERT AKST.

THE TEN COMMANDMENTS, Motion

Picture Assocs., Inc., Paramount: ANNE BAUCHENS.

Music

Scoring of a Dramatic or Comedy Picture

ANASTASIA, 20th Century-Fox: ALFRED NEWMAN.

★ AROUND THE WORLD IN 80 DAYS, The Michael Todd Co., Inc., UA: VICTOR YOUNG.

BETWEEN HEAVEN AND HELL, 20th Century-Fox: HUGO FRIEDHOFER.

GIANT, Giant Prod., Warner Bros.: DIMITRI TIOMKIN.

THE RAINMAKER, A Hal Wallis Prod., Paramount: ALEX NORTH.

Scoring of a Musical Picture

THE BEST THINGS IN LIFE ARE FREE, 20th Century-Fox: LIONEL NEWMAN.

THE EDDY DUCHIN STORY, Columbia: MORRIS STOLOFF and GEORGE DUNING.

HIGH SOCIETY, Sol C. Siegel Prod., M-G-M: JOHNNY GREEN and SAUL CHAPLIN.

★ THE KING AND I, 20th Century-Fox: ALFRED NEWMAN and KEN DARBY.

MEET ME IN LAS VEGAS, Metro-Goldwyn-Mayer: GEORGE STOLL and JOHNNY GREEN.

Song

FRIENDLY PERSUASION (THEE I LOVE) from *Friendly Persuasion*, Allied Artists: Music by DIMITRI TIOMKIN; Lyrics by PAUL FRANCIS WEBSTER.

JULIE from *Julie*, Arwin Prods., M-G-M: Music by LEITH STEVENS; Lyrics by TOM ADAIR.

TRUE LOVE from *High Society*, Sol C. Siegel Prod., M-G-M: Music and Lyrics by COLE PORTER.

★ WHATEVER WILL BE, WILL BE (QUE SERA, SERA) from *The Man Who Knew Too Much*, Hitchcock Prod., Paramount: Music and Lyrics by JAY LIVINGSTON and RAY EVANS.

WRITTEN ON THE WIND from *Written on the Wind*, Universal-International: Music by VICTOR YOUNG; Lyrics by SAMMY CAHN.

Costume Design

Black and White

THE MAGNIFICENT SEVEN (a.k.a. THE SEVEN SAMURAI), A Toho Prod., Kingsley International (Japanese): KOHEI EZAKI.

THE POWER AND THE PRIZE, Metro-Goldwyn-Mayer: HELEN ROSE.

THE PROUD AND THE PROFANE, The Perlberg-Seaton Prod., Paramount: EDITH HEAD.

★ THE SOLID GOLD CADILLAC, Columbia: JEAN LOUIS.

TEENAGE REBEL, 20th Century-Fox: CHARLES LEMAIRE and MARY WILLS.

Color

AROUND THE WORLD IN 80 DAYS, The Michael Todd Co., Inc., UA: MILES WHITE.

GIANT, Giant Prod., Warner Bros: MOSS MABRY and MARJORIE BEST.

★ THE KING AND I, 20th Century-Fox: IRENE SHARAFF.

THE TEN COMMANDMENTS, Motion Picture Assoc., Inc., Paramount: EDITH HEAD, RALPH JESTER, JOHN JENSEN, DOROTHY JEAKINS, and ARNOLD FRIBERG.

WAR AND PEACE, A Ponti-De Laurentiis Prod., Paramount (Italo-American): MARIE DE MATTEIS.

Special Effects

FORBIDDEN PLANET, Metro-Goldwyn-Mayer: A. ARNOLD GILLESPIE, IRVING RIES, and WESLEY C. MILLER.

★ THE TEN COMMANDMENTS, Motion Picture Associates, Inc., Paramount: JOHN FULTON.

Short Subjects

Cartoons

GERALD MCBOING-BOING ON PLANET MOO, UPA Pictures, Columbia: STEPHEN BOSUSTOW, Producer.

THE JAYWALKER, UPA Pictures, Columbia: STEPHEN BOSUSTOW, Producer.

★ MISTER MAGOO'S PUDDLE JUMPER, UPA Pictures, Columbia: STEPHEN BOSUSTOW, Producer.

One Reel

★ CRASHING THE WATER BARRIER, Warner Bros.: KONSTANTIN KALSER, Producer.

I NEVER FORGET A FACE, Warner Bros.: ROBERT YOUNGSON, Producer.

TIME STOOD STILL, Warner Bros.: CEDRIC FRANCIS, Producer.

Two Reels

★ THE BESPOKE OVERCOAT, Romulus Films: GEORGE K. ARTHUR Producer.

COW DOG, Walt Disney Prods., Buena Vista Film Distribution Co., Inc.: LARRY LANSBURGH, Producer.

THE DARK WAVE, 20th Century-Fox: JOHN HEALY, Producer.

SAMOA, Walt Disney Prods., Buena Vista Film Distribution Co., Inc.: WALT DISNEY, Producer.

Documentary

Short Subjects

A CITY DECIDES, Charles Guggenheim and Assocs., Inc. Prod.

THE DARK WAVE, 20th Century-Fox: JOHN HEALY, Producer.

THE HOUSE WITHOUT A NAME, Universal-International: VALENTINE DAVIES, Producer.

MAN IN SPACE, Walt Disney Prods., Buena Vista Film Dist. Co., Inc.: WARD KIMBALL, Producer.

★ THE TRUE STORY OF THE CIVIL WAR, Camera Eye Pictures, Inc.: LOUIS CLYDE STOUMEN, Producer.

Features

THE NAKED EYE, Camera Eye Pictures, Inc.: LOUIS CLYDE STOUMEN, Producer.

★ THE SILENT WORLD, A Filmad-F.S.J.Y.C. Prod., Columbia (French): JACQUES-YVES COUSTEAU, Producer.

WHERE MOUNTAINS FLOAT, Brandon Films, Inc. (Danish): THE GOVERNMENT FILM COMMITTEE OF DENMARK, Producer.

Foreign Language Film Award

(New Category)*

THE CAPTAIN OF KOPENICK, Real-Film (Germany): GYULA TREBITSCH and WALTER KOPPEL, Producers.

GERVAISE, Agnes Delahaie Productions Cinematographiques and Silver Film (France): ANNIE DORFMANN, Producer.

HARP OF BURMA, Nikkatsu Corporation (Japan): MASAYUKI TAKAGI, Producer.

★ LA STRADA, A Ponti-De Laurentiis Production (Italy): DINO DE LAURENTIIS and CARLO PONTI, Producers.

QIVITOQ, A/S Nordisk Films Kompagni (Denmark): O. DALSGAARD-OLSEN, Producer.

Honorary Award

EDDIE CANTOR for distinguished service to the film industry. (Statuette)

Irving G. Thalberg Memorial Award

BUDDY ADLER.

*Prior to 1956 an Honorary Award voted by Board of Governors.

Jean Hersholt Humanitarian Award

(New Category)
Y. FRANK FREEMAN.

Scientific or Technical

Class I

None.

Class II

None.

Class III

RICHARD H. RANGER of Rangertone, Inc., for the development of a synchronous recording and reproducing system for quarter-inch magnetic tape.

TED HIRSCH, CARL HAUGE, and EDWARD REICHARD of Consolidated Film Industries for an automatic scene counter for laboratory projection rooms.

THE TECHNICAL DEPARTMENTS of PARAMOUNT PICTURES CORP. for the engineering and development of the Paramount lightweight horizontal-movement VistaVision camera.

ROY C. STEWART AND SONS of Stewart-Trans Lux Corp., DR. C. R. DAILY, and the TRANSPARENCY DEPARTMENT of PARAMOUNT PICTURES CORP. for the engineering and development of the HiTrans and Para-HiTrans rear projection screens.

THE CONSTRUCTION DEPARTMENT of METRO-GOLDWYN-MAYER STUDIO for a new, hand-portable fog machine.

DANIEL J. BLOOMBERG, JOHN POND, WILLIAM WADE, and the ENGINEERING and CAMERA DEPARTMENTS of REPUBLIC STUDIO for the Naturama adaptation to the Mitchell camera.

THIRTIETH YEAR

1957

Nominations Announced: February 17, 1958
Awards Ceremony: March 26, 1958
RKO Pantages Theatre
(MCs: James Stewart, David Niven, Jack Lemmon, Rosalind Russell, Donald Duck on film, and Bob Hope).

Best Picture

★ THE BRIDGE ON THE RIVER KWAI, A Horizon Picture, Columbia: Sam Spiegel, Producer.

PEYTON PLACE, Jerry Wald Prods., Inc., 20th Century-Fox: Jerry Wald, Producer.

SAYONARA, William Goetz, Prod., Warner Bros.: William Goetz, Producer.

12 ANGRY MEN, Orion-Nova Prod., UA: Henry Fonda and Reginald Rose, Producers.

WITNESS FOR THE PROSECUTION, Edward Small-Arthur Hornblow Prod., UA: Arthur Hornblow, Jr., Producer.

Actor

MARLON BRANDO in *Sayonara*, William Goetz Prod., Warner Bros.

ANTHONY FRANCIOSA in *A Hatful of Rain*, 20th Century-Fox.

★ ALEC GUINNESS in *The Bridge on the River Kwai*, A Horizon Picture, Columbia.

CHARLES LAUGHTON in *Witness for the Prosecution*, Edward Small-Arthur Hornblow Prod., UA.

ANTHONY QUINN in *Wild Is the Wind*, A Hal Wallis Prod., Paramount.

Actress

DEBORAH KERR in *Heaven Knows, Mr. Allison*, 20th Century-Fox.

ANNA MAGNANI in *Wild Is the Wind*, Hal Wallis Prod., Paramount.

ELIZABETH TAYLOR in *Raintree County*, Metro-Goldwyn-Mayer.

LANA TURNER in *Peyton Place*, Jerry Wald Prods. Inc., 20th Century-Fox.

★ JOANNE WOODWARD in *The Three Faces of Eve*, 20th Century-Fox.

Supporting Actor

★ RED BUTTONS in *Sayonara*, William Goetz Prod., Warner Bros.

VITTORIO DE SICA in *A Farewell to Arms*, The Selznick Co., Inc., 20th Century-Fox.

SESSUE HAYAKAWA in *The Bridge on the River Kwai*, A Horizon Picture, Columbia.

ARTHUR KENNEDY in *Peyton Place*, Jerry Wald Prods., Inc., 20th Century-Fox.

RUSS TAMBLYN in *Peyton Place*, Jerry Wald Prods., Inc., 20th Century-Fox.

Supporting Actress

CAROLYN JONES in *The Bachelor Party*, Norma Prod., UA.

ELSA LANCHESTER in *Witness for the*

Prosecution, Edward Small-Arthur Hornblow Prod., UA.

HOPE LANGE in *Peyton Place*, Jerry Wald Prods., Inc., 20th Century-Fox.

★ MIYOSHI UMEKI in *Sayonara*, William Goetz Prod., Warner Bros.

DIANE VARSI in *Peyton Place*, Jerry Wald Prods., Inc., 20th Century-Fox.

Directing

★ DAVID LEAN for *The Bridge on the River Kwai*, A Horizon Picture, Columbia.

JOSHUA LOGAN for *Sayonara*, William Goetz Prod., Warner Bros.

SIDNEY LUMET for *12 Angry Men*, Orion-Nova Prod., UA.

MARK ROBSON for *Peyton Place*, Jerry Wald Prods., Inc., 20th Century-Fox.

BILLY WILDER for *Witness for the Prosecution*, Edward Small-Arthur Hornblow Prod., UA.

Writing*

Screenplay—based on Material from Another Medium

★ THE BRIDGE ON THE RIVER KWAI, A Horizon Picture, Columbia: PIERRE BOULLE, CARL FOREMAN, and MICHAEL WILSON.†

HEAVEN KNOWS, MR. ALLISON, 20th Century-Fox: JOHN LEE MAHIN and JOHN HUSTON.

PEYTON PLACE, Jerry Wald Prods., Inc., 20th Century-Fox: JOHN MICHAEL HAYES.

SAYONARA, William Goetz Prod., Warner Bros.: PAUL OSBORN.

12 ANGRY MEN, Orion-Nova Prod., UA: REGINALD ROSE.

Story and Screenplay—Written Directly for the Screen

★ DESIGNING WOMAN, Metro-Goldwyn-Mayer: GEORGE WELLS.

FUNNY FACE, Paramount: LEONARD GERSHE.

I VITELLONI, Peg Films/Cite Films, API-Janus Films (Italian): Story by FEDERICO FELLINI, ENNIO FLAIANO, and TULLIO PINELLI; Screenplay by FEDERICO FELLINI and ENNIO FLAIANO.

MAN OF A THOUSAND FACES, Universal-International: Story by RALPH WHEELRIGHT; Screenplay by R. WRIGHT CAMPBELL, IVAN GOFF, and BEN ROBERTS.

THE TIN STAR, The Perlberg-Seaton Prod., Paramount: Story by BARNEY SLATER and JOEL KANE; Screenplay by DUDLEY NICHOLS.

Cinematography‡

AN AFFAIR TO REMEMBER, Jerry Wald Prods., Inc., 20th Century-Fox: MILTON KRASNER.

★ THE BRIDGE ON THE RIVER KWAI, A Horizon Picture, Columbia: JACK HILDYARD.

FUNNY FACE, Paramount: RAY JUNE.

PEYTON PLACE, Jerry Wald Prods., Inc., 20th Century-Fox: WILLIAM MELLOR.

SAYONARA, William Goetz Prod., Warner Bros.: ELLSWORTH FREDERICKS.

*Rules were changed this year to two awards for Writing instead of the three awards previously given.

†Boulle, the author of the original novel, neither read nor wrote English but received credit for the screenplay. Foreman and Wilson were the actual screenwriters but were blacklisted at the time and denied onscreen credit; in 1985, the Academy officially recognized their contributions and awarded Oscars to their widows.

‡Rules were changed this year to one Award instead of separate awards for black-and-white and color films.

*Art Direction—Set Decoration**

FUNNY FACE, Paramount: HAL PEREIRA and GEORGE W. DAVIS; Set Decoration: SAM COMER and RAY MOYER.

LES GIRLS, Sol C. Siegel Prods., Inc., M-G-M: WILLIAM A. HORNING and GENE ALLEN; Set Decoration: EDWIN B. WILLIS and RICHARD PEFFERLE.

PAL JOEY, Essex-George Sidney Prod., Columbia: WALTER HOLSCHER; Set Decoration: WILLIAM KIERNAN and LOUIS DIAGE.

RAINTREE COUNTY, Metro-Goldwyn-Mayer: WILLIAM A. HORNING and URIE MCCLEARY; Set Decoration: EDWIN B. WILLIS and HUGH HUNT.

★ SAYONARA, William Goetz Prod., Warner Bros.: TED HAWORTH; Set Decoration: ROBERT PRIESTLEY.

Sound Recording

GUNFIGHT AT THE O.K. CORRAL, Paramount Studio Sound Department: GEORGE DUTTON, Sound Director.

LES GIRLS, Metro-Goldwyn-Mayer Studio Sound Department: DR. WESLEY C. MILLER, Sound Director.

PAL JOEY, Columbia Studio Sound Department: JOHN P. LIVADARY, Sound Director.

★ SAYONARA, WARNER BROS. STUDIO SOUND DEPARTMENT: GEORGE GROVES, Sound Director.

WITNESS FOR THE PROSECUTION, Samuel Goldwyn Studio Sound Department: GORDON SAWYER, Sound Director.

Film Editing

★ THE BRIDGE ON THE RIVER KWAI, A Horizon Picture, Columbia: PETER TAYLOR.

GUNFIGHT AT THE O.K. CORRAL, A Hal Wallis Prod., Paramount: WARREN LOW.

PAL JOEY, Essex-George Sidney Prod., Columbia: VIOLA LAWRENCE and JEROME THOMS.

SAYONARA, William Goetz Prod., Warner Bros.: ARTHUR P. SCHMIDT and PHILIP W. ANDERSON.

WITNESS FOR THE PROSECUTION, Edward Small-Arthur Hornblow Prod., UA: DANIEL MANDELL.

Music†

Scoring

AN AFFAIR TO REMEMBER (Dramatic or Comedy), Jerry Wald Prods., Inc., 20th Century-Fox: HUGO FRIEDHOFER.

BOY ON A DOLPHIN (Dramatic or Comedy), 20th Century-Fox: HUGO FRIEDHOFER.

★ THE BRIDGE ON THE RIVER KWAI (Dramatic or Comedy), A Horizon Picture, Columbia: MALCOLM ARNOLD.

PERRI (Dramatic or Comedy), Walt Disney Prods., Buena Vista Film Dist. Co., Inc.: PAUL SMITH.

RAINTREE COUNTY (Dramatic or Comedy), Metro-Goldwyn-Mayer: JOHNNY GREEN.

Song

AN AFFAIR TO REMEMBER from *An Affair to Remember*, Jerry Wald Prods., Inc., 20th Century-Fox: Music by HARRY WARREN; Lyrics by HAROLD ADAMSON and LEO MCCAREY.

★ ALL THE WAY from *The Joker Is Wild*, A.M.B.L. Prod., Paramount:

*Rules were changed this year to one Award instead of separate awards for black-and-white and color films.

†Rules were changed this year to one Award for Music Scoring instead of separate Awards for Scoring of a Dramatic or Comedy Picture and Scoring of a Musical Picture.

Music by JAMES VAN HEUSEN; Lyrics by SAMMY CAHN.

APRIL LOVE from *April Love*, 20th Century-Fox: Music by SAMMY FAIN; Lyrics by PAUL FRANCIS WEBSTER.

TAMMY from *Tammy and the Bachelor*, Universal-International: Music and Lyrics by RAY EVANS and JAY LIVINGSTON.

WILD IS THE WIND from *Wild Is the Wind*, A Hal Wallis Prod., Paramount: Music by DIMITRI TIOMKIN; Lyrics by NED WASHINGTON.

*Costume Design**

AN AFFAIR TO REMEMBER, Jerry Wald Prods., Inc., 20th Century-Fox: CHARLES LEMAIRE.

FUNNY FACE, Paramount: EDITH HEAD and HUBERT DE GIVENCHY.

★ LES GIRLS, Sol C. Siegel Prods., Inc., M-G-M: ORRY-KELLY.

PAL JOEY, Essex-George Sidney Prod., Columbia: JEAN LOUIS.

RAINTREE COUNTY, Metro-Goldwyn-Mayer: WALTER PLUNKETT.

Special Effects

★ THE ENEMY BELOW, 20th Century-Fox: WALTER ROSSI.

THE SPIRIT OF ST. LOUIS, Leland Hayward-Billy Wilder, Warner Bros.: LOUIS LICHTENFIELD.

Short Subjects†

Cartoons

★ BIRDS ANONYMOUS, Warner Bros.: EDWARD SELZER, Producer.

ONE DROOPY KNIGHT, Metro-Goldwyn-Mayer: WILLIAM HANNA and JOSEPH BARBERA, Producers.

TABASCO ROAD, Warner Bros.: EDWARD SELZER, Producer.

TREES and JAMAICA DADDY, UPA Pictures, Columbia: STEPHEN BOSUSTOW, Producer.

THE TRUTH ABOUT MOTHER GOOSE, Walt Disney Prods., Buena Vista Film Distribution Co., Inc.: WALT DISNEY, Producer.

Live-Action Subjects

A CHAIRY TALE, National Film Board of Canada, Kingsley International Pictures Corp.: NORMAN MCLAREN, Producer.

CITY OF GOLD, National Film Board of Canada, Kingsley International Pictures Corp.: TOM DALY, Producer.

FOOTHOLD ON ANTARCTICA, World Wide Pictures, Lester A. Schoenfeld Films: JAMES CARR, Producer.

PORTUGAL, Walt Disney Prods., Buena Vista Film Distribution Co., Inc.: BEN SHARPSTEEN, Producer.

★ THE WETBACK HOUND, Walt Disney Prods., Buena Vista Film Distribution Co., Inc.: LARRY LANSBURGH, Producer.

Documentary

No Short Subjects nominations voted this year.

Features

★ ALBERT SCHWEITZER, Hill and Anderson Prod., Louis de Rochemont Assocs.: JEROME HILL, Producer.

ON THE BOWERY, Lionel Rogosin Prods., Film Representations, Inc.: LIONEL ROGOSIN, Producer.

TORERO!, Producciones Barbachano Ponce, Columbia (Mexican): MANUEL BARBACHANO PONCE, Producer.

*Rules were changed this year to one Award for Costume Design instead of separate awards for black-and-white and color films.

†Rules were changed this year to two awards for Short Subjects instead of the three previously given.

*Foreign Language Film Award**

THE DEVIL CAME AT NIGHT, Gloria Film (Germany).
GATES OF PARIS, Filmsonor S.A. Production (France).
MOTHER INDIA, Mehboob Productions (India).
★ THE NIGHTS OF CABIRIA, Dino De Laurentiis Production (Italy).
NINE LIVES, Nordsjofilm (Norway).

Honorary Awards

CHARLES BRACKETT for outstanding service to the Academy. (Statuette)
B. B. KAHANE for distinguished service to the motion picture industry. (Statuette)
GILBERT M. ("BRONCHO BILLY") ANDERSON, motion picture pioneer, for his contributions to the development of motion pictures as entertainment. (Statuette)
THE SOCIETY OF MOTION PICTURE AND TELEVISION ENGINEERS for their contributions to the advancement of the motion picture industry. (Statuette)

Irving G. Thalberg Memorial Award

None.

Jean Hersholt Humanitarian Award

SAMUEL GOLDWYN.

Scientific or Technical

Class I

TODD-AO CORP. and WESTREX CORP. for developing a method of producing and exhibiting wide-film motion pictures known as the Todd-AO System.
MOTION PICTURE RESEARCH COUNCIL for the design and development of a high-efficiency projection screen for drive-in theatres.

Class II

SOCIÉTÉ D'OPTIQUE ET DE MÉCHANIQUE DE HAUTE PRECISION for the development of a high-speed vari-focal photographic lens.
HARLAN L. BAUMBACH, LORAND WARGO, HOWARD M. LITTLE, and the UNICORN ENGINEERING CORP. for the development of an automatic printer light selector.

Class III

CHARLES E. SUTTER, WILLIAM B. SMITH, PARAMOUNT PICTURES CORP., and GENERAL CABLE CORP. for the engineering and application to studio use of aluminum, lightweight electrical cable and connectors.

*Rules changed in 1957. The Award is now given to the production company, not to the individual producer.

1958

Nominations Announced: February 23, 1959
Awards Ceremony: April 6, 1959
RKO Pantages Theatre
(MCs: Bob Hope, Jerry Lewis, Mort Sahl, Tony Randall, Sir Laurence Olivier, and David Niven)

Best Picture

AUNTIE MAME, Warner Bros.: Jack L. Warner, Studio Head.

CAT ON A HOT TIN ROOF, Avon Prods., Inc. M-G-M: Lawrence Weingarten, Producer.

THE DEFIANT ONES, Stanley Kramer, UA: Stanley Kramer, Producer.

★ GIGI, Arthur Freed Prods., Inc., M-G-M: Arthur Freed, Producer.

SEPARATE TABLES, Clifton Prods., Inc., US: Harold Hecht, Producer.

Actor

TONY CURTIS in *The Defiant Ones*, Stanley Kramer, UA.

PAUL NEWMAN in *Cat on a Hot Tin Roof*, Avon Prods., Inc., M-G-M.

★ DAVID NIVEN in *Separate Tables*, Clifton Prods., Inc., UA.

SIDNEY POITIER in *The Defiant Ones*, Stanley Kramer, UA.

SPENCER TRACY in *The Old Man and the Sea*, Leland Hayward, Warner Bros.

Actress

★ SUSAN HAYWARD in *I Want to Live!*, Figaro, Inc., UA.

DEBORAH KERR in *Separate Tables*, Clifton Prods., Inc., UA.

SHIRLEY MACLAINE in *Some Came Running*, Sol C. Siegel Prods., Inc., M-G-M.

ROSALIND RUSSELL in *Auntie Mame*, Warner Bros.

ELIZABETH TAYLOR in *Cat on a Hot Tin Roof*, Avon Prods., Inc., M-G-M.

Supporting Actor

THEODORE BIKEL in *The Defiant Ones*, Stanley Kramer, UA.

LEE J. COBB in *The Brothers Karamazov*, Avon Prods., Inc., M-G-M.

★ BURL IVES in *The Big Country*, Anthony-Worldwide Prods., UA.

ARTHUR KENNEDY in *Some Came Running*, Sol C. Siegel Prods., Inc., M-G-M.

GIG YOUNG in *Teacher's Pet*, Perlberg-Seaton, Paramount.

Supporting Actress

PEGGY CASS in *Auntie Mame*, Warner Bros.

★ WENDY HILLER in *Separate Tables*, Clifton Prods., Inc., UA.

MARTHA HYER in *Some Came Running*, Sol C. Siegel Prods., Inc., Metro-Goldwyn-Mayer.

MAUREEN STAPLETON in *Lonelyhearts*, Schary Prods., Inc., UA.

CARA WILLIAMS in *The Defiant Ones*, Stanley Kramer, UA.

Directing

RICHARD BROOKS for *Cat on a Hot Tin Roof*, Avon Prods., Inc., M-G-M.
STANLEY KRAMER for *The Defiant Ones*, Stanley Kramer, UA.
★ VINCENTE MINNELLI for *Gigi*, Arthur Freed Prods., Inc., M-G-M.
MARK ROBSON for *The Inn of the Sixth Happiness*, 20th Century-Fox.
ROBERT WISE for *I Want to Live!*, Figaro, Inc., UA.

Writing

Screenplay—Based on Material from Another Medium

CAT ON A HOT TIN ROOF, Avon Prods., Inc., M-G-M: RICHARD BROOKS and JAMES POE.
★ GIGI, Arthur Freed Prods., Inc., M-G-M: ALAN JAY LERNER.
THE HORSE'S MOUTH, Knightsbridge, UA (British): ALEC GUINNESS.
I WANT TO LIVE!, Figaro, Inc., UA: NELSON GIDDING and DON MANKIEWICZ.
SEPARATE TABLES, Clifton Prods., Inc., UA: TERENCE RATTIGAN and JOHN GAY.

Story and Screenplay—Written Directly for the Screen

★ THE DEFIANT ONES, Stanley Kramer, UA: NATHAN E. DOUGLAS* and HAROLD JACOB SMITH.
THE GODDESS, Carnegie Prods., Inc., Columbia: PADDY CHAYEFSKY.
HOUSEBOAT, Paramount and Scribe, Paramount: MELVILLE SHAVELSON and JACK ROSE.
THE SHEEPMAN, Metro-Goldwyn-Mayer: Story by JAMES EDWARD GRANT; Screenplay by WILLIAM BOWERS and JAMES EDWARD GRANT.
TEACHER'S PET, Perlberg-Seaton, Paramount: FAY KANIN and MICHAEL KANIN.

Cinematography†

Black and White

★ THE DEFIANT ONES, Stanley Kramer, UA: SAM LEAVITT.
DESIRE UNDER THE ELMS, Don Hartman, Paramount: DANIEL L. FAPP.
I WANT TO LIVE!, Figaro, Inc., UA: LIONEL LINDON.
SEPARATE TABLES, Clifton Prods., Inc., UA: CHARLES LANG, JR.
THE YOUNG LIONS, 20th Century-Fox: JOE MACDONALD.

Color

AUNTIE MAME, Warner Bros.: HARRY STRADLING, SR.
CAT ON A HOT TIN ROOF, Avon Prods., Inc., M-G-M: WILLIAM DANIELS.
★ GIGI, Arthur Freed Prods., Inc., M-G-M: JOSEPH RUTTENBERG.
THE OLD MAN AND THE SEA, Leland Hayward, Warner Bros.: JAMES WONG HOWE.
SOUTH PACIFIC, South Pacific Enterprises, Inc., Magna Theatre Corp.: LEON SHAMROY.

Art Direction—Set Decoration

AUNTIE MAME, Warner Bros.: MALCOLM BERT; Set Decoration: GEORGE JAMES HOPKINS.
BELL, BOOK AND CANDLE, Phoenix Prods., Inc., Columbia: CARY ODELL; Set Decoration: LOUIS DIAGE.
A CERTAIN SMILE, 20th Century-Fox: LYLE R. WHEELER and JOHN DECUIR;

*A pseudonym for blacklisted writer Ned Young.
†Rules were changed this year to two awards for Cinematography: one for black-and-white and one for color.

Set Decoration: WALTER M. SCOTT and PAUL S. FOX.

★ GIGI, Arthur Freed Prods., Inc., M-G-M: WILLIAM A. HORNING and PRESTON AMES; Set Decoration: HENRY GRACE and KEOGH GLEASON.

VERTIGO, Alfred J. Hitchcock Prods., Inc., Paramount: HAL PEREIRA and HENRY BUMSTEAD; Set Decoration: SAM COMER and FRANK MCKELVY.

*Sound**

I WANT TO LIVE!, Samuel Goldwyn Studio Sound Department: GORDON E. SAWYER, Sound Director.

★ SOUTH PACIFIC, TODD-AO SOUND DEPARTMENT: FRED HYNES, Sound Director.

A TIME TO LOVE AND A TIME TO DIE, Universal-International Studio Sound Department: LESLIE I. CAREY, Sound Director.

VERTIGO, Paramount Studio Sound Department: GEORGE DUTTON, Sound Director.

THE YOUNG LIONS, 20th Century-Fox Studio Sound Department: CARL FAULKNER, Sound Director.

Film Editing

AUNTIE MAME, Warner Bros.: WILLIAM ZIEGLER.

COWBOY, Phoenix Pictures, Columbia: WILLIAM A. LYON and AL CLARK.

THE DEFIANT ONES, Stanley Kramer, UA: FREDERIC KNUDTSON.

★ GIGI, Arthur Freed Prods., Inc., M-G-M: ADRIENNE FAZAN.

I WANT TO LIVE!, Figaro, Inc., UA: WILLIAM HORNBECK.

Music†

Scoring of a Dramatic or Comedy Picture

THE BIG COUNTRY, Anthony-Worldwide Prods., UA: JEROME MOROSS.

★ THE OLD MAN AND THE SEA; Leland Hayward, Warner Bros.: DIMITRI TIOMKIN.

SEPARATE TABLES, Clifton Prods., Inc., UA: DAVID RAKSIN.

WHITE WILDERNESS, Walt Disney Prods., Buena Vista Film Dist. Co., Inc.: OLIVER WALLACE.

THE YOUNG LIONS; 20th Century-Fox: HUGO FRIEDHOFER.

Scoring of a Musical Picture

THE BOLSHOI BALLET, A Rank Organization Presentation-Harmony Film, Rank Film Distributors of America, Inc. (British): YURI FAIER and G. ROZHDESTVENSKY.

DAMN YANKEES, Warner Bros.: RAY HEINDORF.

★ GIGI, Arthur Freed Prods., Inc., M-G-M: ANDRÉ PREVIN.

MARDI GRAS, Jerry Wald Prods., Inc., 20th Century-Fox: LIONEL NEWMAN.

SOUTH PACIFIC, South Pacific Enterprises, Inc., Magna Theatre Corp.: ALFRED NEWMAN and KEN DARBY.

Song

ALMOST IN YOUR ARMS (LOVE SONG FROM *HOUSEBOAT*) from *Houseboat*, Paramount and Scribe, Paramount: Music and Lyrics by JAY LIVINGSTON and RAY EVANS.

A CERTAIN SMILE from *A Certain Smile*, 20th Century-Fox: Music by SAMMY FAIN; Lyrics by PAUL FRANCIS WEBSTER.

★ GIGI from *Gigi*, Arthur Freed Prods., Inc., M-G-M: Music by FREDERICK LOEWE; Lyrics by ALAN JAY LERNER.

TO LOVE AND BE LOVED from *Some Came Running*, Sol C. Siegel Prods., Inc., M-G-M: Music by JAMES VAN HEUSEN; Lyrics by SAMMY CAHN.

*Category formerly known as Sound Recording.

†Rules were changed this year to two Awards—one for Scoring of a Dramatic or Comedy Picture and one for Scoring of a Musical Picture.

A VERY PRECIOUS LOVE from *Marjorie Morningstar*, Beachwold Pictures, Warner Bros.: Music by SAMMY FAIN; Lyrics by PAUL FRANCIS WEBSTER.

Costume Design

BELL, BOOK AND CANDLE, Phoenix Prods., Inc., Columbia: JEAN LOUIS.
THE BUCCANEER, Cecil B. DeMille, Paramount: RALPH JESTER, EDITH HEAD, and JOHN JENSEN.
A CERTAIN SMILE, 20th Century-Fox: CHARLES LEMAIRE and MARY WILLS.
★ GIGI, Arthur Freed Prods., Inc., M-G-M: CECIL BEATON.
SOME CAME RUNNING, Sol C. Siegel Prods., Inc., M-G-M: WALTER PLUNKETT.

Special Effects

★ TOM THUMB, Pal, M-G-M: Visual: TOM HOWARD.
TORPEDO RUN, Metro-Goldwyn-Mayer: Visual: A. ARNOLD GILLESPIE; Audible: HAROLD HUMBROCK.

Short Subjects

Cartoons

★ KNIGHTY KNIGHT BUGS, Warner Bros.: JOHN W. BURTON, Producer.
PAUL BUNYAN, Walt Disney Prods., Buena Vista Film Distribution Co., Inc.: WALT DISNEY, Producer.
SIDNEY'S FAMILY TREE, Terrytoons, 20th Century-Fox: WILLIAM M. WEISS, Producer.

Live-Action Subjects

★ GRAND CANYON, Walt Disney Prods., Buena Vista Film Distribution Co., Inc.: WALT DISNEY, Producer.
JOURNEY INTO SPRING, British Transport Films, Lester A. Schoenfeld Films: IAN FERGUSON, Producer.
THE KISS, Cohay Prods., Continental Distributing, Inc.: JOHN PATRICK HAYES, Producer.
SNOWS OF AORANGI, New Zealand Screen Board, George Brest Associates.
T IS FOR TUMBLEWEED, Continental Distributing, Inc.: JAMES A. LEBENTHAL, Producer.

Documentary

Short Subjects

★ AMA GIRLS, Walt Disney Prods., Buena Vista Film Dist. Co., Inc.: BEN SHARPSTEEN, Producer.
EMPLOYEES ONLY, Hughes Aircraft Co.: KENNETH G. BROWN, Producer.
JOURNEY INTO SPRING, British Transport Films, Lester A. Schoenfeld Films: IAN FERGUSON, Producer.
THE LIVING STONE, National Film Board of Canada: TOM DALY, Producer.
OVERTURE, United Nations Film Service: THOROLD DICKINSON, Producer.

Features

ANTARCTIC CROSSING, World Wide Pictures, Lester A. Schoenfeld Films: JAMES CARR, Producer.
THE HIDDEN WORLD, Small World Co.: ROBERT SNYDER, Producer.
PSYCHIATRIC NURSING, Dynamic Films Inc.: NATHAN ZUCKER, Producer.
WHITE WILDERNESS, Walt Disney Prods., Buena Vista Film Dist. Co., Inc.: BEN SHARPSTEEN, Producer.

Foreign Language Film Award

ARMS AND THE MAN, H. R. Sokal-P. Goldbaum Production, Bavaria Filmkunst A.G. (Germany).
LA VENGANZA, Guion Producciones Cinematograficas (Spain).
★ MY UNCLE, Specta-Gray-Alter Films in association with Films del Centaure (France).

THE ROAD A YEAR LONG, Jadran Film (Yugoslavia).

THE USUAL UNIDENTIFIED THIEVES, Lux-Vides-Cinecitta (Italy).

Honorary Award

MAURICE CHEVALIER for his contributions to the world of entertainment for more than half a century. (Statuette)

Irving G. Thalberg Memorial Award

JACK L. WARNER.

Jean Hersholt Humanitarian Award

None.

Scientific or Technical

Class I

None.

Class II

DON W. PRIDEAUX, LEROY G. LEIGHTON, and the LAMP DIVISION of GENERAL ELECTRIC CO. for the development and production of an improved 10-kilowatt lamp for motion picture set lighting.

PANAVISION, INC., for the design and development of the Auto Panatar anamorphic photographic lens for 35mm CinemaScope photography.

Class III

WILLY BORBERG of the General Precision Laboratory, Inc., for the development of a high-speed intermittent movement for 35mm motion picture theatre projection equipment.

FRED PONEDEL, GEORGE BROWN, and CONRAD BOYE of the Warner Bros. Special Effects Department for the design and fabrication of a new rapid-fire marble gun.

THIRTY-SECOND YEAR

1959

Nominations Announced: February 22, 1960
Awards Ceremony: April 4, 1960
RKO Pantages Theatre
(MC: Bob Hope)

Best Picture

ANATOMY OF A MURDER, Otto Preminger, Columbia: Otto Preminger, Producer.

★ BEN-HUR, Metro-Goldwyn-Mayer: Sam Zimbalist, Producer.

THE DIARY OF ANNE FRANK, 20th Century-Fox: George Stevens, Producer.

THE NUN'S STORY, Warner Bros.: Henry Blanke, Producer.

ROOM AT THE TOP, Romulus Films, Ltd., Continental Distr., Inc., (British): John Woolf and James Woolf, Producers.

Actor

LAURENCE HARVEY in *Room at the Top*, Romulus Films, Ltd., Continental Dist., Inc. (British)

★ CHARLTON HESTON in *Ben-Hur*, Metro-Goldwyn-Mayer.

JACK LEMMON in *Some Like It Hot*, Ashton Prods. and The Mirisch Co., UA.

PAUL MUNI in *The Last Angry Man*, Fred Kohlmar Prods., Columbia.

JAMES STEWART in *Anatomy of a Murder*, Otto Preminger, Columbia.

Actress

DORIS DAY in *Pillow Talk*, Arwin Prods., Inc., U-I.

AUDREY HEPBURN in *The Nun's Story*, Warner Bros.

KATHARINE HEPBURN in *Suddenly, Last Summer*, Horizon Prod., Columbia.

★ SIMONE SIGNORET in *Room at the Top*, Romulus Films, Ltd., Continental Dist., Inc. (British)

ELIZABETH TAYLOR in *Suddenly, Last Summer*, Horizon Prod., Columbia.

Supporting Actor

★ HUGH GRIFFITH in *Ben-Hur*, Metro-Goldwyn-Mayer.

ARTHUR O'CONNELL in *Anatomy of a Murder*, Otto Preminger, Columbia.

GEORGE C. SCOTT in *Anatomy of a Murder*, Otto Preminger, Columbia.

ROBERT VAUGHN in *The Young Philadelphians*, Warner Bros.

ED WYNN in *The Diary of Anne Frank*, 20th Century-Fox.

Supporting Actress

HERMIONE BADDELEY in *Room at the Top*, Romulus Films, Ltd., Continental Distributing, Inc. (British)

SUSAN KOHNER in *Imitation of Life*, Universal-International.

JUANITA MOORE in *Imitation of Life*, Universal-International.

THELMA RITTER in *Pillow Talk*, Arwin Prods., Inc. U-I.

★ SHELLEY WINTERS in *The Diary of Anne Frank*, 20th Century-Fox.

Directing

JACK CLAYTON for *Room at the Top*, Romulus Films, Ltd., Continental Dist. Inc. (British)

GEORGE STEVENS for *The Diary of Anne Frank*, 20th Century-Fox.

BILLY WILDER for *Some Like It Hot*, Ashton Prods. and The Mirisch Co., UA.

★ WILLIAM WYLER for *Ben-Hur*, Metro-Goldwyn-Mayer.

FRED ZINNEMANN for *The Nun's Story*, Warner Bros.

Writing

Screenplay—Based on Material from Another Medium

ANATOMY OF A MURDER, Otto Preminger, Columbia: WENDELL MAYES.

BEN-HUR, Metro-Goldwyn-Mayer: KARL TUNBERG.

THE NUN'S STORY, Warner Bros.: ROBERT ANDERSON.

★ ROOM AT THE TOP, Romulus Films, Ltd., Continental Dist., Inc. (British): NEIL PATERSON.

SOME LIKE IT HOT, Ashton Prods. and The Mirisch Co., UA: BILLY WILDER and I.A.L. DIAMOND.

Story and Screenplay—Written Directly for the Screen

THE 400 BLOWS, Les Films du Carrosse and SEDIF, Zenith International (French): FRANÇOIS TRUFFAUT and MARCEL MOUSSY.

NORTH BY NORTHWEST, Metro-Goldwyn-Mayer: ERNEST LEHMAN.

OPERATION PETTICOAT, Granart Co., U-I: Story by PAUL KING and JOSEPH STONE; Screenplay by STANLEY SHAPIRO and MAURICE RICHLIN.

★ PILLOW TALK, Arwin Prods., Inc. U-I: Story by RUSSELL ROUSE and CLARENCE GREENE; Screenplay by STANLEY SHAPIRO and MAURICE RICHLIN.

WILD STRAWBERRIES, Svensk Filmindustri, Janus Films (Swedish): INGMAR BERGMAN.

Cinematography

Black and White

ANATOMY OF A MURDER, Otto Preminger, Columbia: SAM LEAVITT.

CAREER, Hal Wallis Prods., Paramount: JOSEPH LASHELLE.

★ THE DIARY OF ANNE FRANK, 20th Century-Fox: WILLIAM C. MELLOR.

SOME LIKE IT HOT, Ashton Prods. and The Mirisch Co., UA: CHARLES LANG, JR.

THE YOUNG PHILADELPHIANS, Warner Bros.: HARRY STRADLING, SR.

Color

★ BEN-HUR, Metro-Goldwyn-Mayer: ROBERT L. SURTEES.

THE BIG FISHERMAN, Rowland V. Lee Prods., Buena Vista Film Dist. Co., Inc.: LEE GARMES.

THE FIVE PENNIES, Dena Prod., Paramount: DANIEL L. FAPP.

THE NUN'S STORY, Warner Bros.: FRANZ PLANER.

PORGY AND BESS, Samuel Goldwyn Prods., Columbia: LEON SHAMROY.

*Art Direction—Set Decoration**

Black and White

CAREER, Hal Wallis Prods., Paramount: HAL PEREIRA and WALTER TYLER; Set

*Rules were changed this year to two awards for Art Direction: one for black-and-white and one for color films.

Decoration: SAM COMER and ARTHUR KRAMS.

★ THE DIARY OF ANNE FRANK, 20th Century-Fox: LYLE R. WHEELER and GEORGE W. DAVIS; Set Decoration: WALTER M. SCOTT and STUART A. REISS.

THE LAST ANGRY MAN, Fred Kohlmar Prods., Columbia: CARL ANDERSON; Set Decoration: WILLIAM KIERNAN.

SOME LIKE IT HOT, Ashton Prods. and The Mirisch Co., UA: TED HAWORTH; Set Decoration: EDWARD G. BOYLE.

SUDDENLY, LAST SUMMER, Horizon Prod., Columbia: OLIVER MESSEL and WILLIAM KELLNER; Set Decoration: SCOT SLIMON.

Color

★ BEN-HUR, Metro-Goldwyn-Mayer: WILLIAM A. HORNING and EDWARD CARFAGNO; Set Decoration: HUGH HUNT.

THE BIG FISHERMAN, Rowland V. Lee Prods., Buena Vista Film Dist. Co., Inc.: JOHN DECUIR; Set Decoration: JULIA HERON.

JOURNEY TO THE CENTER OF THE EARTH, Joseph M. Schenck Enterprises, Inc. and Cooga Mooga Film Prods., Inc., 20th Century-Fox: LYLE R. WHEELER, FRANZ BACHELIN, and HERMAN A. BLUMENTHAL; Set Decoration: WALTER M. SCOTT and JOSEPH KISH.

NORTH BY NORTHWEST, Metro-Goldwyn-Mayer: WILLIAM A. HORNING, ROBERT BOYLE, and MERRILL PYE; Set Decoration: HENRY GRACE and FRANK MCKELVY.

PILLOW TALK, Arwin Prods., Inc., U-I: RICHARD H. RIEDEL; Set Decoration: RUSSELL A. GAUSMAN and RUBY R. LEVITT.

Sound

★ BEN-HUR, METRO-GOLDWYN-MAYER STUDIO SOUND DEPARTMENT: FRANKLIN E. MILTON, Sound Director.

JOURNEY TO THE CENTER OF THE EARTH, 20th Century-Fox Studio Sound Department: CARL FAULKNER, Sound Director.

LIBEL!, Metro-Goldwyn-Mayer London Sound Department (British): A. W. WATKINS, Sound Director.

THE NUN'S STORY, Warner Bros. Studio Sound Department: GEORGE R. GROVES, Sound Director.

PORGY AND BESS, Samuel Goldwyn Studio Sound Department: GORDON E. SAWYER, Sound Director; and Todd-AO Sound Department: FRED HYNES, Sound Director.

Film Editing

ANATOMY OF A MURDER, Otto Preminger, Columbia: LOUIS R. LOEFFLER.

★ BEN-HUR, Metro-Goldwyn-Mayer: RALPH E. WINTERS and JOHN D. DUNNING.

NORTH BY NORTHWEST, Metro-Goldwyn-Mayer: GEORGE TOMASINI.

THE NUN'S STORY, Warner Bros.: WALTER THOMPSON.

ON THE BEACH, Lomitas Prods., UA: FREDERIC KNUDTSON.

Music

Scoring of a Dramatic or Comedy Picture

★ BEN-HUR, Metro-Goldwyn-Mayer: MIKLOS ROZSA.

THE DIARY OF ANNE FRANK, 20th Century-Fox: ALFRED NEWMAN.

THE NUN'S STORY, Warner Bros.: FRANZ WAXMAN.

ON THE BEACH, Lomitas Prods., Inc., UA: ERNEST GOLD.

PILLOW TALK, Arwin Prods., Inc., U-I: FRANK DEVOL.

Scoring of a Musical Picture

THE FIVE PENNIES, Dena Prods., Paramount: LEITH STEVENS.

LI'L ABNER, Panama and Frank, Paramount: NELSON RIDDLE and JOSEPH J. LILLEY.

★ PORGY AND BESS, Samuel Goldwyn Prods., Columbia: ANDRÉ PREVIN and KEN DARBY.

SAY ONE FOR ME, Bing Crosby Prods., 20th Century-Fox: LIONEL NEWMAN.

SLEEPING BEAUTY, Walt Disney Prods., Buena Vista Film Dist. Co., Inc.: GEORGE BRUNS.

Song

THE BEST OF EVERYTHING from *The Best of Everything*, Company of Artists, Inc., 20th Century-Fox: Music by ALFRED NEWMAN; Lyrics by SAMMY CAHN.

THE FIVE PENNIES from *The Five Pennies*, Dena Prods., Paramount: Music and Lyrics by SYLVIA FINE.

THE HANGING TREE from *The Hanging Tree*, Baroda Prods., Inc., Warner Bros.: Music by JERRY LIVINGSTON; Lyrics by MACK DAVID.

★ HIGH HOPES from *A Hole in the Head*, Sincap Prods., UA: Music by JAMES VAN HEUSEN; Lyrics by SAMMY CAHN.

STRANGE ARE THE WAYS OF LOVE from *The Young Land*, C. V. Whitney Pictures, Inc., Columbia: Music by DIMITRI TIOMKIN; Lyrics by NED WASHINGTON.

Costume Design*

Black and White

CAREER, Hal Wallis Prods., Paramount: EDITH HEAD.

THE DIARY OF ANNE FRANK, 20th Century-Fox: CHARLES LEMAIRE and MARY WILLS.

THE GAZEBO, Avon Prod., M-G-M: HELEN ROSE.

★ SOME LIKE IT HOT, Ashton Prods. and The Mirisch Co., UA: ORRY-KELLY.

THE YOUNG PHILADELPHIANS, Warner Bros.: HOWARD SHOUP.

Color

★ BEN-HUR, Metro-Goldwyn-Mayer: ELIZABETH HAFFENDEN.

THE BEST OF EVERYTHING, Company of Artists, Inc., 20th Century-Fox: ADELE PALMER.

THE BIG FISHERMAN, Rowland V. Lee Prods., Buena Vista Film Dist. Co., Inc.: RENIE.

THE FIVE PENNIES, Dena Prod., Paramount: EDITH HEAD.

PORGY AND BESS, Samuel Goldwyn Prods., Columbia: IRENE SHARAFF.

Special Effects

★ BEN-HUR, Metro-Goldwyn-Mayer: Visual: A. ARNOLD GILLESPIE and ROBERT MACDONALD; Audible: MILO LORY.

JOURNEY TO THE CENTER OF THE EARTH, Joseph M. Schenck Enterprises, Inc. and Cooga Mooga Film Prods., Inc., 20th Century-Fox: Visual: L. B. ABBOTT and JAMES B. GORDON; Audible: CARL FAULKNER.

Short Subjects

Cartoons

MEXICALI SHMOES, Warner Bros.: JOHN W. BURTON, Producer.

★ MOONBIRD, Storyboard, Inc.: EDWARD HARRISON and JOHN HUBLEY, Producers.

NOAH'S ARK, Walt Disney Prods., Buena Vista Film Distribution Co., Inc.: WALT DISNEY, Producer.

THE VIOLINIST, Pintoff Prods., Inc., Kingsley International Pictures Corp.: ERNEST PINTOFF, Producer.

*Rules were changed this year to two awards for Costume Design: one for black-and-white and one for color films.

Live-Action Subjects

BETWEEN THE TIDES, British Transport Films, Lester A. Schoenfeld Film (British): IAN FERGUSON, Producer.

★ THE GOLDEN FISH, Les Requins Associés, Columbia (French): JACQUES-YVES COUSTEAU, Producer.

MYSTERIES OF THE DEEP, Walt Disney Prods., Buena Vista Film Distribution Co., Inc.: WALT DISNEY, Producer.

THE RUNNING, JUMPING AND STANDING-STILL FILM, Lion International Films, Ltd., Kingsley-Union Films (British): PETER SELLERS, Producer.

SKYSCRAPER, Joseph Burstyn Film Enterprises, Inc.: SHIRLEY CLARKE, WILLARD VAN DYKE, and IRVING JACOBY, Producers.

Documentary

Short Subjects

DONALD IN MATHMAGIC LAND, Walt Disney Prods., Buena Vista Film Dist. Co., Inc.: WALT DISNEY, Producer.

FROM GENERATION TO GENERATION, Cullen Assocs., Maternity Center Assoc.: EDWARD F. CULLEN, Producer.

★ GLASS, Netherlands Government, George K. Arthur–Go Pictures, Inc. (The Netherlands): BERT HAANSTRA, Producer.

Features

THE RACE FOR SPACE, Wolper, Inc.: DAVID L. WOLPER, Producer.

★ SERENGETI SHALL NOT DIE, Okapia-Film Prod., Transocean Film (German): BERNHARD GRZIMEK, Producer.

Foreign Language Film Award

★ BLACK ORPHEUS, Dispatfilm and Gemma Cinematografica (France).

THE BRIDGE, Fono Film (Germany).

THE GREAT WAR, Dino De Laurentiis Cinematografica (Italy).

PAW, Laterna Film (Denmark).

THE VILLAGE ON THE RIVER, N.V. Nationale Filmproductie Maatschappij (The Netherlands).

Honorary Awards

LEE DE FOREST for his pioneering inventions which brought sound to the motion picture. (Statuette)

BUSTER KEATON for his unique talents which brought immortal comedies to the screen. (Statuette)

Irving G. Thalberg Memorial Award

None.

Jean Hersholt Humanitarian Award

BOB HOPE.

Scientific or Technical

Class I

None.

Class II

DOUGLAS G. SHEARER of Metro-Goldwyn-Mayer, Inc., and ROBERT E. GOTTSCHALK and JOHN R. MOORE of Panavision, Inc., for the development of a system of producing and exhibiting wide-film motion pictures known as Camera 65.

WADSWORTH E. POHL, WILLIAM EVANS, WERNER HOPF, S. E. HOWSE, THOMAS P. DIXON, STANFORD RESEARCH INSTITUTE, and TECHNICOLOR CORP. for the design and development of the Technicolor electronic printing timer.

WADSWORTH E. POHL, JACK ALFORD, HENRY IMUS, JOSEPH SCHMIT, PAUL FASSNACHT, AL

LOFQUIST, and TECHNICOLOR CORP. for the development and practical application of equipment for wet printing.

DR. HOWARD S. COLEMAN, DR. A. FRANCIS TURNER, HAROLD H. SCHROEDER, JAMES R. BENFORD, and HAROLD E. ROSENBERGER of the Bausch & Lomb Optical Co. for the design and development of the Balcold projection mirror.

ROBERT P. GUTTERMAN of General Kinetics, Inc., and the LIPSNER-SMITH CORP. for the design and development of the CF-2 Ultrasonic Film Cleaner.

Class III

UB IWERKS of Walt Disney Prods. for the design of an improved optical printer for special effects and matte shots.

E. L. STONES, GLEN ROBINSON, WINFIELD HUBBARD, and LUTHER NEWMAN of the Metro-Goldwyn-Mayer Studio Construction Department for the design of a multiple-cable remote-controlled winch.

THIRTY-THIRD YEAR

1960

Nominations Announced: February 27, 1961
Awards Ceremony: April 17, 1961
Santa Monica Civic Auditorium
(MC: Bob Hope)

Best Picture

THE ALAMO, Batjac Prod., UA: John Wayne, Producer.

★ THE APARTMENT, The Mirisch Co., Inc., UA: Billy Wilder, Producer

ELMER GANTRY, Burt Lancaster-Richard Brooks Prod., UA: Bernard Smith, Producer.

SONS AND LOVERS, Company of Artists, Inc., 20th Century-Fox: Jerry Wald, Producer.

THE SUNDOWNERS, Warner Bros.: Fred Zinnemann, Producer.

Actor

TREVOR HOWARD in *Sons and Lovers*, Company of Artists, Inc., 20th Century-Fox.

★ BURT LANCASTER in *Elmer Gantry*, Burt Lancaster-Richard Brooks Prod., UA.

JACK LEMMON in *The Apartment*, The Mirisch Company, Inc., UA.

LAURENCE OLIVIER in *The Entertainer*, Woodfall Prod., Continental Dist., Inc. (British)

SPENCER TRACY in *Inherit the Wind*, Stanley Kramer, UA.

Actress

GREER GARSON in *Sunrise at Campobello*, Schary Prod., Warner Bros.

DEBORAH KERR in *The Sundowners*, Warner Bros.

SHIRLEY MACLAINE in *The Apartment*, The Mirisch Co., Inc., UA.

MELINA MERCOURI in *Never on Sunday*, Melinafilm Prod., Lopert Pictures Corp. (Greek)

★ ELIZABETH TAYLOR in *Butterfield 8*, Afton-Linebrook Prod., M-G-M.

Supporting Actor

PETER FALK in *Murder, Inc.*, 20th Century-Fox.

JACK KRUSCHEN in *The Apartment*, The Mirisch Co., Inc., UA.

SAL MINEO in *Exodus*, Carlyle-Alpina S.A. Prod., UA.

★ PETER USTINOV in *Spartacus*, Bryna Prods., Inc., U-I.

CHILL WILLS in *The Alamo*, Batjac Prod., UA.

Supporting Actress

GLYNIS JOHNS in *The Sundowners*, Warner Bros.

★ SHIRLEY JONES in *Elmer Gantry*, Burt Lancaster-Richard Brooks Prod., UA.

SHIRLEY KNIGHT in *The Dark at the Top of the Stairs*, Warner Bros.

JANET LEIGH in *Psycho*, Alfred J. Hitchcock Prods., Paramount.

MARY URE in *Sons and Lovers*, Company of Artists, Inc., 20th Century-Fox.

Directing

JACK CARDIFF for *Sons and Lovers*, Company of Artists, Inc., 20th Century-Fox.

JULES DASSIN for *Never on Sunday*, Melinafilm Prod., Lopert Pictures Corp. (Greek)

ALFRED HITCHCOCK for *Psycho*, Alfred J. Hitchcock Prods., Paramount.

★ BILLY WILDER for *The Apartment*, The Mirisch Co., Inc., UA.

FRED ZINNEMANN for *The Sundowners*, Warner Bros.

Writing

Screenplay—Based on Material from Another Medium

★ ELMER GANTRY, Burt Lancaster-Richard Brooks Prod., UA: RICHARD BROOKS.

INHERIT THE WIND, Stanley Kramer Prod., UA: NATHAN E. DOUGLAS and HAROLD JACOB SMITH.

SONS AND LOVERS, Company of Artists, Inc., 20th Century-Fox: GAVIN LAMBERT and T.E.B CLARKE.

THE SUNDOWNERS, Warner Bros.: ISOBEL LENNART.

TUNES OF GLORY, H.M. Films Limited Prod., Lopert Pictures Corp. (British): JAMES KENNAWAY.

Story and Screenplay—Written Directly for the Screen

THE ANGRY SILENCE, Beaver Films Limited Prod. (British): Story by RICHARD GREGSON and MICHAEL CRAIG; Screenplay by BRYAN FORBES.

★ THE APARTMENT, The Mirisch Co., Inc., UA: BILLY WILDER and I.A.L DIAMOND.

THE FACTS OF LIFE, Panama and Frank Prod., UA: NORMAN PANAMA and MELVIN FRANK.

HIROSHIMA, MON AMOUR, Argos Films-Como Films-Daiei Pictures, Ltd.—Pathé Overseas Prod., Zenith International Film Corp. (French-Japanese): MARGUERITE DURAS.

NEVER ON SUNDAY, Melinafilm Prod., Lopert Pictures Corp. (Greek): JULES DASSIN.

Cinematography

Black and White

THE APARTMENT, The Mirisch Co., UA: JOSEPH LASHELLE.

THE FACTS OF LIFE, Panama and Frank Prod., UA: CHARLES B. LANG, JR.

INHERIT THE WIND, Stanley Kramer Prod., UA: ERNEST LASZLO.

PSYCHO, Alfred J. Hitchcock Prods., Paramount: JOHN L. RUSSELL.

★ SONS AND LOVERS, Company of Artists, Inc., 20th Century-Fox: FREDDIE FRANCIS.

Color

THE ALAMO, Batjac Prod., UA: WILLIAM H. CLOTHIER.

BUTTERFIELD 8, Afton-Linebrook Prod., M-G-M: JOSEPH RUTTENBERG and CHARLES HARTEN.

EXODUS, Carlyle-Alpina S.A. Prod., UA: SAM LEAVITT.

PEPE, G.S.-Posa Films International Prod., Columbia: JOE MACDONALD.

★ SPARTACUS, Bryna Prods., Inc., U-I: RUSSELL METTY.

Art Direction—Set Decoration

Black and White

★ THE APARTMENT, The Mirisch Co., Inc., UA: ALEXANDER TRAUNER; Set Decoration: EDWARD G. BOYLE.

THE FACTS OF LIFE, Panama and Frank Prod., UA: JOSEPH MCMILLAN

JOHNSON and KENNETH A. REID; Set Decoration: ROSS DOWD.

PSYCHO, Alfred J. Hitchcock Prods., Paramount: JOSEPH HURLEY and ROBERT CLATWORTHY; Set Decoration: GEORGE MILO.

SONS AND LOVERS, Company of Artists, Inc., 20th Century-Fox: TOM MORAHAN; Set Decoration: LIONEL COUCH.

VISIT TO A SMALL PLANET, Hall Wallis Prods., Paramount: HAL PEREIRA and WALTER TYLER; Set Decoration: SAM COMER and ARTHUR KRAMS.

Color

CIMARRON, Metro-Goldwyn-Mayer: GEORGE W. DAVIS and ADDISON HEHR; Set Decoration: HENRY GRACE, HUGH HUNT, and OTTO SIEGEL.

IT STARTED IN NAPLES, Paramount and Capri Prod., Paramount: HAL PEREIRA and ROLAND ANDERSON; Set Decoration: SAM COMER and ARRIGO BRESCHI.

PEPE, G.S.-Posa Films International Prod., Columbia: TED HAWORTH; Set Decoration: WILLIAM KIERNAN.

★ SPARTACUS, Bryna Prods., Inc., U-I: ALEXANDER GOLITZEN and ERIC ORBOM; Set Decoration: RUSSELL A. GAUSMAN and JULIA HERON.

SUNRISE AT CAMPOBELLO, Schary Prod., Warner Bros.: EDWARD CARRERE; Set Decoration: GEORGE JAMES HOPKINS.

Sound

★ THE ALAMO, Samuel Goldwyn Studio Sound Department: GORDON E. SAWYER, Sound Director; and Todd-AO Sound Department: FRED HYNES, Sound Director.

THE APARTMENT, Samuel Goldwyn Studio Sound Department: GORDON E. SAWYER, Sound Director.

CIMARRON, Metro-Goldwyn-Mayer Studio Sound Department: FRANKLIN E. MILTON, Sound Director.

PEPE, Columbia Studio Sound Department: CHARLES RICE, Sound Director.

SUNRISE AT CAMPOBELLO, Warner Bros. Studio Sound Department: GEORGE R. GROVES, Sound Director.

Film Editing

THE ALAMO, Batjac Prod., UA: STUART GILMORE.

★ THE APARTMENT, The Mirisch Co., UA: DANIEL MANDELL.

INHERIT THE WIND, Stanley Kramer Prod., UA: FREDERIC KNUDTSON.

PEPE, G.S.-Posa Films International Prod., Columbia: VIOLA LAWRENCE and AL CLARK.

SPARTACUS, Bryna Prods., Inc., U-I: ROBERT LAWRENCE.

Music

Scoring of a Dramatic or Comedy Picture

THE ALAMO, Batjac Prod., UA: DIMITRI TIOMKIN.

ELMER GANTRY, Burt Lancaster-Richard Brooks Prod., UA: ANDRÉ PREVIN.

★ EXODUS, Carlyle-Alpina S.A. Prod., UA: ERNEST GOLD.

THE MAGNIFICENT SEVEN, Mirisch-Alpha Prod., UA: ELMER BERNSTEIN.

SPARTACUS, Bryna Prods., Inc., U-I: ALEX NORTH.

Scoring of a Musical Picture

BELLS ARE RINGING, Arthur Freed Prod., M-G-M: ANDRÉ PREVIN.

CAN-CAN, Suffolk-Cummings Prods., 20th Century-Fox: NELSON RIDDLE.

LET'S MAKE LOVE, Company of Artists, Inc., 20th Century-Fox: LIONEL NEWMAN and EARLE H. HAGEN.

PEPE, G.S.-Posa Films International Prod., Columbia: JOHNNY GREEN.

★ SONG WITHOUT END, Goetz-Vidor Pictures Prod., Columbia:

MORRIS STOLOFF and HARRY SUKMAN.

Song

THE FACTS OF LIFE from *The Facts of Life*, Panama and Frank Prod., UA: Music and Lyrics by JOHNNY MERCER.

FARAWAY PART OF TOWN from *Pepe*, G.S.-Posa Films International Prod., Columbia: Music by ANDRÉ PREVIN; Lyrics by DORY LANGDON.

THE GREEN LEAVES OF SUMMER from *The Alamo*, Batjac Prod., UA: Music by DIMITRI TIOMKIN; Lyrics by PAUL FRANCIS WEBSTER.

★ NEVER ON SUNDAY from *Never on Sunday*, Melinafilm Prod., Lopert Pictures Corp. (Greek): Music and Lyrics by MANOS HADJIDAKIS.

THE SECOND TIME AROUND from *High Time*, Bing Crosby Prods., 20th Century-Fox: Music by JAMES VAN HEUSEN; Lyrics by SAMMY CAHN.

Costume Design

Black and White

★ THE FACTS OF LIFE, Panama and Frank Prod., UA: EDITH HEAD and EDWARD STEVENSON.

NEVER ON SUNDAY, Melinafilm Prod., Lopert Pictures Corp. (Greek): DENNY VACHLIOTI.

THE RISE AND FALL OF LEGS DIAMOND, United States Prod., Warner Bros.: HOWARD SHOUP.

SEVEN THIEVES, 20th Century-Fox: BILL THOMAS.

THE VIRGIN SPRING, Svensk Filmindustri Prod., Janus Films, Inc. (Swedish): MARIK VOS.

Color

CAN-CAN, Suffolk-Cummings Prods., 20th Century-Fox: IRENE SHARAFF.

MIDNIGHT LACE, Ross Hunter-Arwin Prod., U-I: IRENE.

PEPE, G.S.-Posa Films International Prod., Columbia: EDITH HEAD.

★ SPARTACUS, Bryna Prods., Inc., U-I: VALLES and BILL THOMAS.

SUNRISE AT CAMPOBELLO, Schary Prod., Warner Bros.: MARJORIE BEST.

Special Effects

THE LAST VOYAGE, Andrew and Virginia Stone Prod., M-G-M: Visual: A. J. LOHMAN.

★ THE TIME MACHINE, Galaxy Films Prod., M-G-M: Visual: GENE WARREN and TIM BAAR.

Short Subjects

Cartoons

GOLIATH II, Walt Disney Prods., Buena Vista Distribution Co., Inc.: WALT DISNEY, Producer.

HIGH NOTE, Warner Bros.

MOUSE AND GARDEN, Warner Bros.

★ MUNRO, Rembrandt Films, Film Representations, Inc.: WILLIAM L. SNYDER, Producer.

A PLACE IN THE SUN, George K. Arthur-Go Pictures, Inc. (Czechoslovakian): FRANTISEK VYSTRECIL, Producer.

Live-Action Subjects

THE CREATION OF WOMAN, Trident Films, Inc., Sterling World Distributors Corp. (Indian): CHARLES F. SCHWEP and ISMAIL MERCHANT, Producers.

★ DAY OF THE PAINTER, Little Movies, Kingsley-Union Films: EZRA R. BAKER, Producer.

ISLANDS OF THE SEA, Walt Disney Prods., Buena Vista Distribution Co., Inc.: WALT DISNEY, Producer.

A SPORT IS BORN, Paramount: LESLIE WINIK, Producer.

Documentary

Short Subjects

BEYOND SILENCE, United States Information Agency.

A CITY CALLED COPENHAGEN, Statens Filmcentral, Danish Government Film Office. (Danish)

GEORGE GROSZ' INTERREGNUM, Educational Communications Corp.: CHARLES CAREY and ALTINA CAREY, Producers.

★ GIUSEPPINA, James Hill Prod., Lester A. Schoenfeld Films (British): JAMES HILL, Producer.

UNIVERSE, National Film Board of Canada, Lester A. Schoenfeld Films (Canadian): COLIN LOW, Producer.

Features

★ THE HORSE WITH THE FLYING TAIL, Walt Disney Prods., Buena Vista Dist. Co., Inc.: LARRY LANSBURGH, Producer.

REBEL IN PARADISE, Tiare Co.: ROBERT D. FRASER, Producer.

Foreign Language Film Award

KAPO, Vides-Zebrafilm-Cineriz (Italy).

LA VERITÉ, Han Productions (France).

MACARIO, Clasa Films Mundiales, S.A. (Mexico).

THE NINTH CIRCLE, Jadran Film Production (Yugoslavia).

★ THE VIRGIN SPRING, A.B. Svensk Filmindustri (Sweden).

Honorary Awards

GARY COOPER for his many memorable screen performances and the international recognition he, as an individual, has gained for the motion picture industry. (Statuette)

STAN LAUREL for his creative pioneering in the field of cinema comedy. (Statuette)

HAYLEY MILLS for *Pollyanna*, the most outstanding juvenile performance during 1960. (Miniature statuette)

Irving G. Thalberg Memorial Award

None.

Jean Hersholt Humanitarian Award

SOL LESSER.

Scientific or Technical

Class I

None.

Class II

AMPEX PROFESSIONAL PRODUCTS CO. for the production of a well-engineered, multipurpose sound system combining high standards of quality with convenience of control, dependable operation, and simplified emergency provisions.

Class III

ARTHUR HOLCOMB, PETRO VLAHOS, and COLUMBIA STUDIO CAMERA DEPARTMENT for a camera flicker indicating device.

ANTHONY PAGLIA and the 20TH CENTURY-FOX STUDIO MECHANICAL EFFECTS DEPARTMENT for the design and construction of a miniature flak gun and ammunition.

CARL HAUGE, ROBERT GRUBEL, and EDWARD REICHARD of Consolidated Film Industries for the development of an automatic developer replenisher system.

1961

Nominations Announced: February 26, 1962
Awards Ceremony: April 9, 1962
Santa Monica Civic Auditorium
(MC: Bob Hope)

Best Picture

FANNY, Mansfield Prod., Warner Bros: Joshua Logan, Producer.

THE GUNS OF NAVARONE, Carl Foreman Prod., Columbia: Carl Foreman, Producer.

THE HUSTLER, Robert Rossen Prod., 20th Century-Fox: Robert Rossen, Producer.

JUDGMENT AT NUREMBERG, Stanley Kramer Prod., UA: Stanley Kramer, Producer.

★ WEST SIDE STORY, Mirisch Pictures, Inc., and B and P Enterprises, Inc., UA: Robert Wise, Producer.

Actor

CHARLES BOYER in *Fanny*, Mansfield Prod., Warner Bros.

PAUL NEWMAN in *The Hustler*, Robert Rossen Prod., 20th Century-Fox.

★ MAXIMILIAN SCHELL in *Judgment at Nuremberg*, Stanley Kramer Prod., UA.

SPENCER TRACY in *Judgment at Nuremberg*, Stanley Kramer Prod., UA.

STUART WHITMAN in *The Mark*, Raymond Stross-Sidney Buchman Prod., Continental Dist., Inc. (British)

Actress

AUDREY HEPBURN in *Breakfast at Tiffany's*, Jurow-Shepherd Prod., Paramount.

PIPER LAURIE in *The Hustler*, Robert Rossen Prod., 20th Century-Fox.

★ SOPHIA LOREN in *Two Women*, Champion-Les Films Marceau-Cocinor and Société Generale de Cinematographie Prod., Embassy Pictures Corp. (Italo-French)

GERALDINE PAGE in *Summer and Smoke*, Hal Wallis Prod., Paramount.

NATALIE WOOD in *Splendor in the Grass*, NBI Prod., Warner Bros.

Supporting Actor

★ GEORGE CHAKIRIS in *West Side Story*, Mirisch Pictures, Inc., and B and P Enterprises, Inc., UA.

MONTGOMERY CLIFT in *Judgment at Nuremberg*, Stanley Kramer Prod., UA.

PETER FALK in *Pocketful of Miracles*, Franton Prod., UA.

JACKIE GLEASON in *The Hustler*, Robert Rossen Prod., 20th Century-Fox.

GEORGE C. SCOTT in *The Hustler*, Robert Rossen Prod., 20th Century-Fox.

Supporting Actress

FAY BAINTER in *The Children's Hour*, Mirisch-Worldwide Prod., UA.

JUDY GARLAND in *Judgment at Nuremberg*, Stanley Kramer Prod., UA.

LOTTE LENYA in *The Roman Spring of Mrs. Stone*, Seven Arts Presentation, Warner Bros.

UNA MERKEL in *Summer and Smoke*, Hal Wallis Prod., Paramount.

★ RITA MORENO in *West Side Story*, Mirisch Pictures, Inc., and B and P Enterprises, Inc., UA.

Directing

FEDERICO FELLINI for *La Dolce Vita*, Riama Film Prod., Astor Pictures, Inc. (Italian)

STANLEY KRAMER for *Judgment at Nuremberg*, Stanley Kramer Prod., UA.

ROBERT ROSSEN for *The Hustler*, Robert Rossen Prod., 20th Century-Fox.

J. LEE THOMPSON for *The Guns of Navarone*, Carl Foreman Prod., Columbia.

★ ROBERT WISE and JEROME ROBBINS for *West Side Story*; Mirisch Pictures, Inc., and B and P Enterprises, Inc., UA.

Writing

Screenplay—Based on Material from Another Medium

BREAKFAST AT TIFFANY'S, Jurow-Shepherd Prod., Paramount: GEORGE AXELROD.

THE GUNS OF NAVARONE, Carl Foreman Prod., Columbia: CARL FOREMAN.

THE HUSTLER, Robert Rossen Prod., 20th Century-Fox: SIDNEY CARROLL and ROBERT ROSSEN.

★ JUDGMENT AT NUREMBERG, Stanley Kramer Prod., UA: ABBY MANN.

WEST SIDE STORY, Mirisch Pictures, Inc., and B and P Enterprises, Inc., UA: ERNEST LEHMAN.

Story and Screenplay—Written Directly for the Screen

BALLAD OF A SOLDIER, Mosfilm Studio Prod., Kingsley International-M.J.P. Enterprises, Inc. (Russian): VALENTIN YOSHOV and GRIGORI CHUKHRAI.

GENERAL DELLA ROVERE, Zebra and S.N.E. Gaumont Prod., Continental Dist., Inc. (Italian): SERGIO AMIDEI, DIEGO FABBRI, and INDRO MONTANELLI.

LA DOLCE VITA, Riama Film Prod., Astor Pictures, Inc. (Italian): FEDERICO FELLINI, TULLIO PINELLI, ENNIO FLAIANO, and BRUNNELLO RONDI.

LOVER COME BACK, Universal-International-The 7 Pictures Corp., Nob Hill Prods., Inc., Arwin Prods., Inc., U-I: STANLEY SHAPIRO and PAUL HENNING.

★ SPLENDOR IN THE GRASS, NBI Prod., Warner Bros.: WILLIAM INGE.

Cinematography

Black and White

THE ABSENT MINDED PROFESSOR, Walt Disney Prods., Buena Vista Distribution Co., Inc.: EDWARD COLMAN.

THE CHILDREN'S HOUR; Mirisch-Worldwide Prod., UA: FRANZ F. PLANER.

★ THE HUSTLER; Robert Rossen Prod., 20th Century-Fox: EUGEN SHUFTAN.

JUDGMENT AT NUREMBERG, Stanley Kramer Prod., UA: ERNEST LASZLO.

ONE, TWO, THREE, Mirisch Company, Inc., in association with Pyramid Prods., A.G., UA: DANIEL L. FAPP.

Color

FANNY, Mansfield Prod., Warner Bros.: JACK CARDIFF.

FLOWER DRUM SONG, Universal-International-Ross Hunter Prod., in association with Joseph Fields, U-I: RUSSELL METTY.

A MAJORITY OF ONE, Warner Bros.: HARRY STRADLING, SR.

ONE-EYED JACKS, Pennebaker Prod., Paramount: CHARLES LANG, JR.

WEST SIDE STORY, Mirisch Pictures, Inc., and B and P Enterprises, Inc., UA: DANIEL L. FAPP.

Art Direction—Set Decoration

Black and White

THE ABSENT MINDED PROFESSOR, Walt Disney Prod., Buena Vista Distribution Co., Inc.: CARROLL CLARK; Set Decoration: EMILE KURI and HAL GAUSMAN.

THE CHILDREN'S HOUR, Mirisch-Worldwide Prod., UA: FERNANDO CARRERE; Set Decoration: EDWARD G. BOYLE.

★ THE HUSTLER, Robert Rossen Prod., 20th Century-Fox: HARRY HORNER; Set Decoration: GENE CALLAHAN.

JUDGMENT AT NUREMBERG, Stanley Kramer Prod., UA: RUDOLPH STERNAD; Set Decoration: GEORGE MILO.

LA DOLCE VITA, Riama Film Prod., Astor Pictures, Inc. (Italian): PIERO GHERARDI.

Color

BREAKFAST AT TIFFANY'S, Jurow-Shepherd Prod., Paramount: HAL PEREIRA and ROLAND ANDERSON; Set Decoration: SAM COMER and RAY MOYER.

EL CID, Samuel Bronston Prod., in association with Dear Film Prod., Allied Artists: VENIERO COLASANTI and JOHN MOORE.

FLOWER DRUM SONG, Universal-International-Ross Hunter Prod., in association with Joseph Fields, U-I: ALEXANDER GOLITZEN and JOSEPH WRIGHT; Set Decoration: HOWARD BRISTOL.

SUMMER AND SMOKE, Hal Wallis Prod., Paramount: HAL PEREIRA and WALTER TYLER; Set Decoration: SAM COMER and ARTHUR KRAMS.

★ WEST SIDE STORY, Mirisch Pictures, Inc., and B and P Enterprises, Inc., UA: BORIS LEVEN; Set Decoration: VICTOR A. GANGELIN.

Sound

THE CHILDREN'S HOUR, Samuel Goldwyn Studio Sound Department: GORDON E. SAWYER, Sound Director.

FLOWER DRUM SONG, Revue Studio Sound Department: WALDON O. WATSON, Sound Director.

THE GUNS OF NAVARONE, Shepperton Studio Sound Department: JOHN COX, Sound Director.

THE PARENT TRAP, Walt Disney Studio Sound Department: ROBERT O. COOK, Sound Director.

★ WEST SIDE STORY, Todd-AO Sound Department: FRED HYNES, Sound Director; and Samuel Goldwyn Studio Sound Department: GORDON E. SAWYER, Sound Director.

Film Editing

FANNY, Mansfield Prod., Warner Bros.: WILLIAM H. REYNOLDS.

THE GUNS OF NAVARONE, Carl Foreman Prod., Columbia: ALAN OSBISTON.

JUDGMENT AT NUREMBERG, Stanley Kramer Prod., YA: FREDERIC KNUDTSON.

THE PARENT TRAP, Walt Disney Prods., Buena Vista Dist. Co., Inc.: PHILIP W. ANDERSON.

★ WEST SIDE STORY, Mirisch Pictures, Inc., and B and P

Enterprises, Inc., UA: THOMAS STANFORD.

Music

Scoring of a Dramatic or Comedy Picture

★ BREAKFAST AT TIFFANY'S, Jurow-Shepherd Prod., Paramount: HENRY MANCINI.

EL CID, Samuel Bronston Prod., in association with Dear Film Prod., Allied Artists: MIKLOS ROZSA.

FANNY, Mansfield Prod., Warner Bros.: MORRIS STOLOFF and HARRY SUKMAN.

THE GUNS OF NAVARONE, Carl Foreman Prod., Columbia: DIMITRI TIOMKIN.

SUMMER AND SMOKE, Hal Wallis Prod., Paramount: ELMER BERNSTEIN.

Scoring of a Musical Picture

BABES IN TOYLAND, Walt Disney Prods., Buena Vista Dist. Co., Inc.: GEORGE BRUNS.

FLOWER DRUM SONG, Universal-International-Ross Hunter Prod., in association with Joseph Fields, U-I: ALFRED NEWMAN and KEN DARBY.

KHOVANSHCHINA, Mosfilm Studios, Artkino Pictures (Russian): DIMITRI SHOSTAKOVICH.

PARIS BLUES, Pennebaker, Inc., UA: DUKE ELLINGTON.

★ WEST SIDE STORY, Mirisch Pictures, Inc., and B and P Enterprises, Inc., UA: SAUL CHAPLIN, JOHNNY GREEN, SID RAMIN, and IRWIN KOSTAL.

Song

BACHELOR IN PARADISE from *Bachelor in Paradise*, Ted Richmond Prod., M-G-M: Music by HENRY MANCINI; Lyrics by MACK DAVID.

LOVE THEME FROM EL CID (THE FALCON AND THE DOVE) from *El Cid*, Samuel Bronston Prod., in association with Dear Film Prod., Allied, Artists: Music by MIKLOS ROZSA; Lyrics by PAUL FRANCIS WEBSTER.

★ MOON RIVER from *Breakfast at Tiffany's*, Jurow-Shepherd Prod., Paramount: Music by HENRY MANCINI; Lyrics by JOHNNY MERCER.

POCKETFUL OF MIRACLES from *Pocketful of Miracles*, Franton Prod., UA: Music by JAMES VAN HEUSEN; Lyrics by SAMMY CAHN.

TOWN WITHOUT PITY from *Town without Pity*, Mirisch Company in association with Gloria Films, UA: Music by DIMITRI TIOMKIN; Lyrics by NED WASHINGTON.

Costume Design

Black and White

THE CHILDREN'S HOUR, Mirisch-Worldwide Prod., UA: DOROTHY JEAKINS.

CLAUDELLE INGLISH, Warner Bros.: HOWARD SHOUP.

JUDGMENT AT NUREMBERG, Stanley Kramer Prod., UA: JEAN LOUIS.

★ LA DOLCE VITA, Riama Film Prod., Astor Pictures, Inc. (Italian): PIERO GHERARDI.

YOJIMBO, Toho Company, Ltd., and Kurosawa Prod., Toho Company, Ltd. (Japanese): YOSHIRO MURAKI.

Color

BABES IN TOYLAND, Walt Disney Prods., Buena Vista Distribution Co., Inc.: BILL THOMAS.

BACK STREET, Universal-International-Ross Hunter Prods., Inc.-Carrollton, Inc., U-I: JEAN LOUIS.

FLOWER DRUM SONG, Universal-International-Ross Hunter Prod., in association with Joseph Fields, U-I: IRENE SHARAFF.

POCKETFUL OF MIRACLES, Franton Prod., UA: EDITH HEAD and WALTER PLUNKETT.

★ WEST SIDE STORY, Mirisch Pictures, Inc., and B and P

Enterprises, Inc., UA: IRENE SHARAFF.

Special Effects

THE ABSENT MINDED PROFESSOR, Walt Disney Prods., Buena Vista Dist. Co.: Visual: ROBERT A. MATTEY and EUSTACE LYCETT.

★ THE GUNS OF NAVARONE, Carl Foreman Prod., Columbia: Visual: BILL WARRINGTON; Audible: VIVIAN C. GREENHAM.

Short Subjects

Cartoons

AQUAMANIA, Walt Disney Prods., Buena Vista Distribution Co., Inc.: WALT DISNEY, Producer.

BEEP PREPARED, Warner Bros.: CHUCK JONES, Producer.

★ ERSATZ (THE SUBSTITUTE), ZAGREB FILM, Herts-Lion International Corp.

NELLY'S FOLLY, Warner Bros.: CHUCK JONES, Producer.

PIED PIPER OF GUADALUPE, Warner Bros.: FRIZ FRELENG, Producer.

Live-Action Subjects

BALLON VOLE (PLAY BALL!), Ciné-Documents, Kingsley International Pictures Corp.

THE FACE OF JESUS, Dr. John D. Jennings, Harry Stern, Inc.: DR. JOHN D. JENNINGS, Producer.

ROOFTOPS OF NEW YORK, McCarty-Rush Prod., in association with ROBERT GAFFNEY, Columbia.

★ SEAWARDS THE GREAT SHIPS, Templar Film Studios, SCHOENFELD FILMS.

VERY NICE, VERY NICE, National Film Board of Canada, Kingsley International Pictures Corp.

Documentary

Short Subjects

BREAKING THE LANGUAGE BARRIER, United States Air Force.

CRADLE OF GENIUS, Plough Prods., An Irving M. Lesser Film Presentation (Irish): JIM O'CONNOR and TOM HAYES, Producers.

KAHL, Dido-Film-GmbH., AEG-Filmdienst (German).

L'UOMO IN GRIGIO (THE MAN IN GRAY), (Italian): BENEDETTO BENEDETTI, Producer.

★ PROJECT HOPE, MacManus, John and Adams, Inc., Ex-Cell-O Corp., A Klaeger Film Production: FRANK P. BIBAS, Producer.

Features

LA GRANDE OLIMPIADE (OLYMPIC GAMES 1960), dell Istituto Nazionale Luce, Comitato Organizzatore dei Giochi Della XVII Olimpiade: Cineriz (Italian).

★ LE CIEL ET LA BOUE (SKY ABOVE AND MUD BENEATH), Ardennes Films and Michael Arthur Film Prods., Rank Film Distrs., Ltd. (French): ARTHUR COHN and RENÉ LAFUITE, Producers.

Foreign Language Film Award

HARRY AND THE BUTLER, Bent Christensen Production (Denmark).

IMMORTAL LOVE, Shochiku Co., Ltd. (Japan).

THE IMPORTANT MAN, Peliculas Rodriguez, S.A. (Mexico).

PLACIDO, Jet Films (Spain).

★ THROUGH A GLASS DARKLY, A.B. Svensk Filmindustri (Sweden).

Honorary Awards

WILLIAM L. HENDRICKS for his outstanding patriotic service in the conception, writing, and production of the Marine Corps film *A Force in Readiness*, which has brought honor to the Academy and the motion picture industry. (Statuette)

FRED L. METZLER for his dedication and outstanding service to the

Academy of Motion Picture Arts and Sciences. (Statuette)

JEROME ROBBINS for his brilliant achievements in the art of choreography on film. (Statuette)

Irving G. Thalberg Memorial Award

STANLEY KRAMER.

Jean Hersholt Humanitarian Award

GEORGE SEATON.

Scientific or Technical

Class I

None.

Class II

SYLVANIA ELECTRIC PRODUCTS, INC., for the development of a hand-held, high-power photographic lighting unit known as the Sun Gun Professional.

JAMES DALE, S. WILSON, H. E. RICE, JOHN RUDE, LAURIE ATKIN, WADSWORTH E. POHL, H. PEASGOOD, and TECHNICOLOR CORP. for a process of automatic selective printing.

20TH CENTURY-FOX RESEARCH DEPARTMENT, under the direction of E. I. SPONABLE and HERBERT E. BRAGG, and DELUXE LABORATORIES, INC., with the assistance of F. D. LESLIE, R. D. WHITMORE, A. A. ALDEN, ENDEL POOL, and JAMES B. GORDON, for a system of decompressing and recomposing CinemaScope pictures for conventional aspect ratios.

Class III

HURLETRON, INC., ELECTRIC EYE EQUIPMENT DIVISION, for an automatic light-changing system for motion picture printers.

WADSWORTH E. POHL and TECHNICOLOR CORP. for an integrated sound and picture transfer process.

THIRTY-FIFTH YEAR

1962

Nominations Announced: February 25, 1963
Awards Ceremony: April 8, 1963
Santa Monica Civic Auditorium
(MC: Frank Sinatra)

Best Picture

★ LAWRENCE OF ARABIA, Horizon Pictures (G.B.), Ltd.-Sam Spiegel-David Lean Prod., Columbia: Sam Spiegel, Producer.

THE LONGEST DAY, Darryl F. Zanuck Prods., 20th Century-Fox: Darryl F. Zanuck, Producer.

THE MUSIC MAN, Warner Bros.: Morton DaCosta, Producer.

MUTINY ON THE BOUNTY, Arcola Prod., M-G-M: Aaron Rosenberg, Producer.

TO KILL A MOCKINGBIRD, Universal-International-Pakula-Mulligan-Brentwood Prod., U-I: Alan J. Pakula, Producer.

Actor

BURT LANCASTER in *Bird Man of Alcatraz*, Harold Hecht Prod., UA.

JACK LEMMON in *Days of Wine and Roses*, Martin Manulis-Jalem Prod., Warner Bros.

MARCELLO MASTROIANNI in *Divorce—Italian Style*, Lux-Vides-Galatea Film Prod., Embassy Pictures.

PETER O'TOOLE in *Lawrence of Arabia*, Horizon Pictures (G.B.), Ltd.-Sam Spiegel-David Lean Prod., Columbia.

★ GREGORY PECK in *To Kill a Mockingbird*, Universal-International-Pakula-Mulligan-Brentwood Prod., U-I.

Actress

★ ANNE BANCROFT in *The Miracle Worker*, Playfilms Prod., UA.

BETTE DAVIS in *What Ever Happened to Baby Jane?*, Seven Arts-Associates and Aldrich Co. Prod., Warner Bros.

KATHARINE HEPBURN in *Long Day's Journey into Night*, Ely Landau Prods., Embassy Pictures.

GERALDINE PAGE in *Sweet Bird of Youth*, Roxbury Prod., M-G-M.

LEE REMICK in *Days of Wine and Roses*, Martin Manulis-Jalem Prod., Warner Bros.

Supporting Actor

★ ED BEGLEY in *Sweet Bird of Youth*, Roxbury Prod., M-G-M.

VICTOR BUONO in *What Ever Happened to Baby Jane?*, Seven Arts-Associates and Aldrich Co. Prod., Warner Bros.

TELLY SAVALAS in *Bird Man of Alcatraz*, Harold Hecht Prod., UA.

OMAR SHARIF in *Lawrence of Arabia*, Horizon Pictures (G.B.), Ltd.-Sam Spiegel-David Lean Prod., Columbia.

TERENCE STAMP in *Billy Budd*, Harvest Prods., Allied Artists.

Supporting Actress

MARY BADHAM in *To Kill a Mockingbird*, Universal-

International-Pakula-Mulligan-Brentwood Prod., U-I.

★ PATTY DUKE in *The Miracle Worker*, Playfilms Prod., UA.

SHIRLEY KNIGHT in *Sweet Bird of Youth*, Roxbury Prod., M-G-M.

ANGELA LANSBURY in *The Manchurian Candidate*, M.C. Prod., UA.

THELMA RITTER in *Bird Man of Alcatraz*, Harold Hecht Prod., UA.

Directing

PIETRO GERMI for *Divorce—Italian Style*, Lux-Vides-Galatea Film Prod., Embassy Pictures.

★ DAVID LEAN for *Lawrence of Arabia*, Horizon Pictures (G.B.), Ltd.-Sam Spiegel-David Lean Prod., Columbia.

ROBERT MULLIGAN for *To Kill a Mockingbird*, Universal-International-Pakula-Mulligan-Brentwood Prod., U-I.

ARTHUR PENN for *The Miracle Worker*, Playfilms Prod., UA.

FRANK PERRY for *David and Lisa*, Heller-Perry Prods., Continental Dist.

Writing

Screenplay—Based on Material from Another Medium

DAVID AND LISA, Heller-Perry Prods., Continental Distributing: ELEANOR PERRY.

LAWRENCE OF ARABIA, Horizon Pictures (G.B.), Ltd.-Sam Spiegel-David Lean Prod., Columbia: ROBERT BOLT.

LOLITA, Seven Arts Prods., M-G-M: VLADIMIR NABOKOV.

THE MIRACLE WORKER, Playfilms Prod., UA: WILLIAM GIBSON.

★ TO KILL A MOCKINGBIRD, Universal-International-Pakula-Mulligan-Brentwood Prod., U-I: HORTON FOOTE.

Story and Screenplay—Written Directly for the Screen

★ DIVORCE—ITALIAN STYLE, Lux-Vides-Galatea Film Prod., Embassy Pictures: ENNIO DE CONCINI, ALFREDO GIANNETTI, and PIETRO GERMI.

FREUD, Universal-International-John Huston Prod., U-I: Story by CHARLES KAUFMAN; Screenplay by CHARLES KAUFMAN and WOLFGANG REINHARDT.

LAST YEAR AT MARIENBAD, Preceitel-Terra Film Prod., Astor Pictures: ALAIN ROBBE-GRILLET.

THAT TOUCH OF MINK, Universal-International-Granley-Arwin-Nob Hill Prod., U-I.: STANLEY SHAPIRO and NATE MONASTER.

THROUGH A GLASS DARKLY, Svensk Filmindustri Prod., Janus Films: INGMAR BERGMAN.

Cinematography

Black and White

BIRD MAN OF ALCATRAZ, Harold Hecht Prod., UA: BURNETT GUFFEY.

★ THE LONGEST DAY, Darryl F. Zanuck Prods., 20th Century-Fox: JEAN BOURGOIN and WALTER WOTTITZ.

TO KILL A MOCKINGBIRD, Universal-International-Pakula-Mulligan-Brentwood Prod., U-I: RUSSELL HARLAN.

TWO FOR THE SEESAW, Mirisch-Argyle-Talbot Prod., in association with Seven Arts Prods., UA: TED MCCORD.

WHAT EVER HAPPENED TO BABY JANE?, Seven Arts-Associates and Aldrich Co. Prod., Warner Bros.: ERNEST HALLER.

Color

GYPSY, Warner Bros.: HARRY STRADLING, SR.

HATARI!, Malabar Prods., Paramount: RUSSELL HARLAN.

★ LAWRENCE OF ARABIA, Horizon Pictures (G.B.), Ltd.-Sam Spiegel-David Lean Prod., Columbia: FRED A. YOUNG.

MUTINY ON THE BOUNTY, Arcola Prod., M-G-M: ROBERT L. SURTEES.

THE WONDERFUL WORLD OF THE BROTHERS GRIMM, Metro-Goldwyn-Mayer and Cinerama: PAUL C. VOGEL.

Art Direction—Set Decoration

Black and White

DAYS OF WINE AND ROSES, Martin Manulis-Jalem Prod., Warner Bros.: JOSEPH WRIGHT; Set Decoration: GEORGE JAMES HOPKINS.

THE LONGEST DAY, Darryl F. Zanuck Prods., 20th Century-Fox: TED HAWORTH, LEON BARSACO, and VINCENT KORDA; Set Decoration: GABRIEL BECHIR.

PERIOD OF ADJUSTMENT, Marten Prod., M-G-M: GEORGE W. DAVIS and EDWARD CARFAGNO; Set Decoration: HENRY GRACE and DICK PEFFERLE.

THE PIGEON THAT TOOK ROME, Llenroc Prods., Paramount: HAL PEREIRA and ROLAND ANDERSON; Set Decoration: SAM COMER and FRANK R. MCKELVY.

★ TO KILL A MOCKINGBIRD, Universal-International-Pakula-Mulligan-Brentwood Prod., U-I: ALEXANDER GOLITZEN and HENRY BUMSTEAD; Set Decoration: OLIVER EMERT.

Color

★ LAWRENCE OF ARABIA, Horizon Pictures (G.B.), Ltd.-Sam Spiegel-David Lean Prod., Columbia: JOHN BOX and JOHN STOLL; Set Decoration: DARIO SIMONI.

THE MUSIC MAN, Warner Bros.: PAUL GROESSE; Set Decoration: GEORGE JAMES HOPKINS.

MUTINY ON THE BOUNTY, Arcola Prod., M-G-M: GEORGE W. DAVIS and J. MCMILLAN JOHNSON; Set Decoration: HENRY GRACE and HUGH HUNT.

THAT TOUCH OF MINK, Universal-International-Granley-Arwin-Nob Hill Prod., U-I: ALEXANDER GOLITZEN and ROBERT CLATWORTHY; Set Decoration: GEORGE MILO.

THE WONDERFUL WORLD OF THE BROTHERS GRIMM, Metro-Goldwyn-Mayer and Cinerama: GEORGE W. DAVIS and EDWARD CARFAGNO; Set Decoration: HENRY GRACE and DICK PEFFERLE.

Sound

BON VOYAGE, Walt Disney Studio Sound Department: ROBERT O. COOK, Sound Director.

★ LAWRENCE OF ARABIA, Shepperton Studio Sound Department: JOHN COX, Sound Director.

THE MUSIC MAN, Warner Bros. Studio Sound Department: GEORGE R. GROVES, Sound Director.

THAT TOUCH OF MINK, Universal City Studio Sound Department: WALDON O. WATSON, Sound Director.

WHAT EVER HAPPENED TO BABY JANE?, Glen Glenn Sound Department: JOSEPH KELLY, Sound Director.

Film Editing

★ LAWRENCE OF ARABIA, Horizon Pictures (G.B.), Ltd.-Sam Spiegel-David Lean Prod., Columbia: ANNE COATES.

THE LONGEST DAY, Darryl F. Zanuck Prods., 20th Century-Fox: SAMUEL E. BEETLEY.

THE MANCHURIAN CANDIDATE, M.C. Prod., UA: FERRIS WEBSTER.

THE MUSIC MAN, Warner Bros.: WILLIAM ZIEGLER.

MUTINY ON THE BOUNTY, Arcola Prod., M-G-M: JOHN MCSWEENEY, JR.

*Music**

Music Score—Substantially Original

FREUD, Universal-International-John Huston Prod., U-I: JERRY GOLDSMITH.

★ LAWRENCE OF ARABIA, Horizon Pictures (G.B.), Ltd.-Sam Spiegel-David Lean Prod., Columbia: MAURICE JARRE.

MUTINY ON THE BOUNTY, Arcola Prod., M-G-M: BRONISLAU KAPER.

TARAS BULBA, Harold Hecht Prod., UA: FRANZ WAXMAN.

TO KILL A MOCKINGBIRD, Universal-International-Pakula-Mulligan-Brentwood Prod., U-I: ELMER BERNSTEIN.

Scoring of Music—Adaptation or Treatment

BILLY ROSE'S JUMBO, Euterpe-Arwin Prod., M-G-M: GEORGE STOLL.

GIGOT, Seven Arts Prods., 20th Century-Fox: MICHEL MAGNE.

GYPSY, Warner Bros.: FRANK PERKINS.

★ THE MUSIC MAN, Warner Bros.: RAY HEINDORF.

THE WONDERFUL WORLD OF THE BROTHERS GRIMM, Metro-Goldwyn-Mayer and Cinerama: LEIGH HARLINE.

Song

★ DAYS OF WINE AND ROSES from *Days of Wine and Roses*, Martin Manulis-Jalem Prod., Warner Bros.: Music by HENRY MANCINI; Lyrics by JOHNNY MERCER.

LOVE SONG FROM MUTINY ON THE BOUNTY (FOLLOW ME) from *Mutiny on the Bounty*, Arcola Prod., M-G-M: Music by BRONISLAU KAPER; Lyrics by PAUL FRANCIS WEBSTER.

SONG FROM TWO FOR THE SEESAW (SECOND CHANCE) from *Two for the Seesaw*, Mirisch-Argyle-Talbot Prod., in association with Seven Arts Productions, UA: Music by ANDRÉ PREVIN; Lyrics by DORY LANGDON.

TENDER IS THE NIGHT from *Tender Is the Night*, 20th Century-Fox: Music by SAMMY FAIN; Lyrics by PAUL FRANCIS WEBSTER.

WALK ON THE WILD SIDE from *Walk on the Wild Side*, Famous Artists Prods., Columbia: Music by ELMER BERNSTEIN; Lyrics by MACK DAVID.

Costume Design

Black and White

DAYS OF WINE AND ROSES, Martin Manulis-Jalem Prod., Warner Bros.: DON FELD.

THE MAN WHO SHOT LIBERTY VALANCE, John Ford Prod., Paramount: EDITH HEAD.

THE MIRACLE WORKER, Playfilms Prod., UA: RUTH MORLEY.

PHAEDRA, Jules Dassin-Melinafilm Prod., Lopert Pictures: DENNY VACHLIOTI.

★ WHAT EVER HAPPENED TO BABY JANE?, Seven Arts-Associates and Aldrich Co. Prod., Warner Bros.: NORMA KOCH.

Color

BON VOYAGE, Walt Disney Prod., Buena Vista Distribution Co.: BILL THOMAS.

GYPSY, Warner Bros.: ORRY-KELLY.

THE MUSIC MAN, Warner Bros.: DOROTHY JEAKINS.

MY GEISHA, Sachiko Prod., Paramount: EDITH HEAD.

★ THE WONDERFUL WORLD OF THE BROTHERS GRIMM, Metro-Goldwyn-Mayer and Cinerama: MARY WILLS.

Special Effects

★ THE LONGEST DAY, Darryl F. Zanuck Prods., 20th Century-Fox:

*Titles of Music Awards were changed this year.

Visual: ROBERT MACDONALD; Audible: JACQUES MAUMONT.

MUTINY ON THE BOUNTY, Arcola Prod., M-G-M: Visual: A. ARNOLD GILLESPIE; Audible: MILO LORY.

Short Subjects

Cartoons

★ THE HOLE, Storyboard Inc., Brandon Films, Inc.: JOHN HUBLEY and FAITH HUBLEY, Producers.

ICARUS MONTGOLFIER WRIGHT, Format Films, United Artists: JULES ENGEL, Producer.

NOW HEAR THIS, Warner Bros.

SELF DEFENSE—FOR COWARDS, Rembrandt Films, Film Representations, Inc.: WILLIAM L. SNYDER, Producer.

SYMPOSIUM ON POPULAR SONGS, Walt Disney Prods., Buena Vista Distribution Co.: WALT DISNEY, Producer.

Live-Action Subjects

BIG CITY BLUES, Mayfair Pictures Company: MARTINA and CHARLES HUGUENOT VAN DER LINDEN, Producers.

THE CADILLAC, United Producers Releasing Org.: ROBERT CLOUSE, Producer.

THE CLIFF DWELLERS (formerly titled ONE PLUS ONE), Group II Film Prods., Lester A. Schoenfeld Films: HAYWARD ANDERSON, Producer.

★ HEUREUX ANNIVERSAIRE (HAPPY ANNIVERSARY), CAPAC Prods., Atlantic Pictures Corp.: PIERRE ÉTAIX and J. C. CARRIÈRE, Producers.

PAN, Mayfair Pictures Company: HERMAN VAN DER HORST, Producer.

Documentary

Short Subjects

★ DYLAN THOMAS, TWW Ltd., Janus Films (Welsh): JACK HOWELLS, Producer.

THE JOHN GLENN STORY, Department of the Navy, Warner Bros.: WILLIAM L. HENDRICKS, Producer.

THE ROAD TO THE WALL, CBS Films, Inc., Department of Defense: ROBERT SAUDEK, Producer.

Features

ALVORADA (BRAZIL'S CHANGING FACE), MW Filmproduktion (German): HUGO NIEBELING, Producer.

★ BLACK FOX, Image Prods., Inc., Heritage Films, Inc.: LOUIS CLYDE STOUMEN, Producer.

Foreign Language Film Award

ELECTRA, A Michael Cacoyannis Production (Greece).

THE FOUR DAYS OF NAPLES, Titanus-Metro (Italy).

KEEPER OF PROMISES (THE GIVEN WORD), Cinedistri (Brazil).

★ SUNDAYS AND CYBELE, Terra-Fides-Orsay-Trocadero Films (France).

TLAYUCAN, Producciones Matouk, SA (Mexico).

Honorary Awards

None.

Irving G. Thalberg Memorial Award

None.

Jean Hersholt Humanitarian Award

STEVE BROIDY.

Scientific or Technical

Class I

None.

Class II

RALPH CHAPMAN for the design and development of an advanced motion picture camera crane.

ALBERT S. PRATT, JAMES L. WASSELL, and HANS C. WOHLRAB of the Professional Division, Bell & Howell Co., for the design and development of a new and improved automatic motion picture additive color printer.

NORTH AMERICAN PHILIPS CO., INC., for the design and engineering of the Norelco Universal 70/35 mm motion picture projector.

CHARLES E. SUTTER, WILLIAM BRYSON SMITH, and LOUIS C. KENNELL of Paramount Pictures Corp. for the engineering and application to motion picture production of a new system of electric power distribution.

Class III

ELECTRO- VOICE, INC., for a highly directional dynamic line microphone.

LOUIS G. MACKENZIE for a selective sound effects repeater.

THIRTY-SIXTH YEAR

1963

Nominations Announced: February 24, 1964
Awards Ceremony: April 13, 1964
Santa Monica Civic Auditorium
(MC: Jack Lemmon)

Best Picture

AMERICA AMERICA, Athena Enterprises Prod., Warner Bros.: Elia Kazan, Producer.

CLEOPATRA, 20th Century-Fox Ltd.-MCL Films S.A.-WALWA Films S.A. Prod., 20th Century-Fox: Walter Wanger, Producer.

HOW THE WEST WAS WON, Metro-Goldwyn-Mayer and Cinerama: Bernard Smith, Producer.

LILIES OF THE FIELD, Rainbow Prod., UA: Ralph Nelson, Producer.

★ TOM JONES, Woodfall Prod., UA-Lopert Pictures: Tony Richardson, Producer.

Actor

ALBERT FINNEY, in *Tom Jones*, Woodfall Prod., UA-Lopert Pictures.

RICHARD HARRIS in *This Sporting Life*, Julian Wintle-Leslie Parkyn Prod., Walter Reade-Sterling-Continental Dist.

REX HARRISON in *Cleopatra*, 20th Century-Fox Ltd.-MCL Films S.A.-WALWA Films S.A. Prod., 20th Century-Fox.

PAUL NEWMAN in *Hud*, Salem-Dover Prod., Paramount.

★ SIDNEY POITIER in *Lilies of the Field*, Rainbow Prod., UA.

Actress

LESLIE CARON in *The L-Shaped Room*, Romulus Prods., Ltd., Columbia.

SHIRLEY MACLAINE in *Irma La Douce*, Mirisch-Phalanx Prod., UA.

★ PATRICIA NEAL in *Hud*, Salem-Dover Prod., Paramount.

RACHEL ROBERTS in *This Sporting Life*, Julian Wintle-Leslie Parkyn Prod., Walter Reade-Sterling-Continental Dist.

NATALIE WOOD in *Love with the Proper Stranger*, Boardwalk-Rona Prod., Paramount.

Supporting Actor

NICK ADAMS in *Twilight of Honor*, Perlberg-Seaton Prod., M-G-M.

BOBBY DARIN in *Captain Newman, M.D.*, Universal-Brentwood-Reynard, Prod., Universal.

★ MELVYN DOUGLAS in *Hud*, Salem-Dover Prod., Paramount.

HUGH GRIFFITH in *Tom Jones*, Woodfall Prod., UA-Lopert Pictures.

JOHN HUSTON in *The Cardinal*, Gamma Prod., Columbia.

Supporting Actress

DIANE CILENTO in *Tom Jones*, Woodfall Prod., UA-Lopert Pictures.

DAME EDITH EVANS in *Tom Jones*, Woodfall Prod., UA-Lopert Pictures.

JOYCE REDMAN in *Tom Jones*, Woodfall Prod., UA-Lopert Pictures.
★ MARGARET RUTHERFORD in *The V.I.P.s*, Metro-Goldwyn-Mayer.
LILIA SKALA in *Lilies of the Field*, Rainbow Prod., UA.

Directing

FEDERICO FELLINI for *Federico Fellini's 8½*, Cineriz Prod., Embassy Pictures.
ELIA KAZAN for *America America*, Athena Enterprises Prod., Warner Bros.
OTTO PREMINGER for *The Cardinal*, Gamma Prod., Columbia.
★ TONY RICHARDSON for *Tom Jones*, Woodfall Prod., UA-Lopert Pictures.
MARTIN RITT for *Hud*, Salem-Dover Prod., Paramount.

Writing

Screenplay—Based on Material from Another Medium

CAPTAIN NEWMAN, M.D., Universal-Brentwood-Reynard Prod., Universal: RICHARD L. BREEN, PHOEBE EPHRON, and HENRY EPHRON.
HUD, Salem-Dover Prod., Paramount: IRVING RAVETCH and HARRIET FRANK, JR.
LILIES OF THE FIELD, Rainbow Prod., UA: JAMES POE.
SUNDAYS AND CYBELE, Terra-Fides-Orsay-Films Trocadero Prods., Columbia: SERGE BOURGUIGNON and ANTOINE TUDAL.
★ TOM JONES, Woodfall Prod., UA-Lopert Pictures: JOHN OSBORNE.

Story and Screenplay—Written Directly for the Screen

AMERICA AMERICA, Athena Enterprises Prod., Warner Bros.: ELIA KAZAN.
FEDERICO FELLINI'S 8½, Cineriz Prod., Embassy Pictures: FEDERICO FELLINI, ENNIO FLAIANO, TULLIO PINELLI, and BRUNELLO RONDI.
THE FOUR DAYS OF NAPLES, Titanus Prod., M-G-M.: Story by PASQUALE FESTA CAMPANILE, MASSIMO FRANCIOSA, NANNI LOY, and VASCO PRATOLINI; Screenplay by CARLO BERNARI, PASQUALE FESTA CAMPANILE, MASSIMO FRANCIOSA, and NANNI LOY.
★ HOW THE WEST WAS WON, Metro-Goldwyn-Mayer and Cinerama: JAMES R. WEBB.
LOVE WITH THE PROPER STRANGER, Boardwalk-Rona Prod., Paramount: ARNOLD SCHULMAN.

Cinematography

Black and White

THE BALCONY, Walter Reade-Sterling-Allen-Hodgdon Prod., Walter Reade-Sterling-Continental Dist.: GEORGE FOLSEY.
THE CARETAKERS, Hall Bartlett Prod., UA: LUCIEN BALLARD.
★ HUD, Salem-Dover Prod., Paramount: JAMES WONG HOWE.
LILIES OF THE FIELD, Rainbow Prod., UA: ERNEST HALLER.
LOVE WITH THE PROPER STRANGER, Boardwalk-Rona Prod., Paramount: MILTON KRASNER.

Color

THE CARDINAL, Gamma Prod., Columbia: LEON SHAMROY.
★ CLEOPATRA, 20th Century-Fox Ltd.-MCL Films S.A.-WALWA Films S.A. Prod., 20th Century-Fox: LEON SHAMROY.
HOW THE WEST WAS WON, Metro-Goldwyn-Mayer and Cinerama: WILLIAM H. DANIELS, MILTON KRASNER, CHARLES LANG, JR., and JOSEPH LASHELLE.
IRMA LA DOUCE, Mirisch-Phalanx Prod., UA: JOSEPH LASHELLE.
IT'S A MAD, MAD, MAD, MAD WORLD, Casey Prod., UA: ERNEST LASZLO.

Art Direction—Set Decoration

Black and White

★ AMERICA AMERICA, Athena Enterprises Prod., Warner Bros.: GENE CALLAHAN.

FEDERICO FELLINI'S 8½, Cineriz Prod., Embassy Pictures: PIERO GHERARDI.

HUD, Salem-Dover Prod., Paramount: HAL PEREIRA and TAMBI LARSEN; Set Decoration: SAM COMER and ROBERT BENTON.

LOVE WITH THE PROPER STRANGER, Boardwalk-Rona Prod., Paramount: HAL PEREIRA and ROLAND ANDERSON; Set Decoration: SAM COMER and GRACE GREGORY.

TWILIGHT OF HONOR, Perlberg-Seaton Prod., M-G-M: GEORGE W. DAVIS and PAUL GROESSE; Set Decoration: HENRY GRACE and HUGH HUNT.

Color

THE CARDINAL, Gamma Production, Columbia: LYLE WHEELER; Set Decoration: GENE CALLAHAN.

★ CLEOPATRA, 20th Century-Fox Ltd.-MCL Films S.A.-WALWA Films S.A. Prod., 20th Century-Fox: JOHN DeCUIR, JACK MARTIN SMITH, HILYARD BROWN, HERMAN BLUMENTHAL, ELVEN WEBB, MAURICE PELLING, and BORIS JURAGA; Set Decoration: WALTER M. SCOTT, PAUL S. FOX, and RAY MOYER.

COME BLOW YOUR HORN, Essex-Tandem Enterprises Prod., Paramount: HAL PEREIRA and ROLAND ANDERSON; Set Decoration: SAM COMER and JAMES PAYNE.

HOW THE WEST WAS WON, Metro-Goldwyn-Mayer and Cinerama: GEORGE W. DAVIS, WILLIAM FERRARI, and ADDISON HEHR; Set Decoration: HENRY GRACE, DON GREENWOOD, JR., and JACK MILLS.

TOM JONES, Woodfall Production, UA-Lopert Pictures: RALPH BRINTON, TED MARSHALL, and JOCELYN HERBERT; Set Decoration: JOSIE MACAVIN.

Sound

BYE BYE BIRDIE, Columbia Studio Sound Department: CHARLES RICE, Sound Director.

CAPTAIN NEWMAN, M.D., Universal City Studio Sound Department: WALDON O. WATSON, Sound Director.

CLEOPATRA, 20th Century-Fox Studio Sound Department: JAMES P. CORCORAN, Sound Director; and TODD A-O Sound Department: FRED HYNES, Sound Director.

★ HOW THE WEST WAS WON, Metro-Goldwyn-Mayer Studio Sound Department: FRANKLIN E. MILTON, Sound Director.

IT'S A MAD, MAD, MAD, MAD WORLD, Samuel Goldwyn Studio Sound Department: GORDON E. SAWYER, Sound Director.

Film Editing

THE CARDINAL, Gamma Prod., Columbia: LOUIS R. LOEFFLER.

CLEOPATRA, 20th Century-Fox Ltd.-MCL Films S.A.-WALWA Films S.A. Prod., 20th Century-Fox: DOROTHY SPENCER.

THE GREAT ESCAPE, Mirisch-Alpha Picture Prod., UA: FERRIS WEBSTER.

★ HOW THE WEST WAS WON, Metro-Goldwyn-Mayer and Cinerama: HAROLD F. KRESS.

IT'S A MAD, MAD, MAD, MAD WORLD, Casey Prod., UA: FREDERIC KNUDTSON, ROBERT C. JONES, and GENE FOWLER JR.

Music

Music Score—Substantially Original

CLEOPATRA, 20th Century-Fox Ltd.-MCL Films S.A.-WALWA Films

S.A. Prod., 20th Century-Fox: ALEX NORTH.

55 DAYS AT PEKING, Samuel Bronston Prod., Allied Artists: DIMITRI TIOMKIN.

HOW THE WEST WAS WON, Metro-Goldwyn-Mayer and Cinerama: ALFRED NEWMAN and KEN DARBY.

IT'S A MAD, MAD, MAD, MAD WORLD, Casey Prod., UA: ERNEST GOLD.

★ TOM JONES, Woodfall Prod., UA-Lopert Pictures: JOHN ADDISON.

Scoring of Music—Adaptation or Treatment

BYE BYE BIRDIE, Kohlmar-Sidney Prod., Columbia: JOHN GREEN.

★ IRMA LA DOUCE, Mirisch-Phalanx Prod., UA: ANDRÉ PREVIN.

A NEW KIND OF LOVE, Llenroc Prods., Paramount: LEITH STEVENS.

SUNDAYS AND CYBELE, Terra-Fides-Orsay-Films Trocadero Prod., Columbia: MAURICE JARRE.

THE SWORD IN THE STONE, Walt Disney Prods., Buena Vista Distribution Co.: GEORGE BRUNS.

Song

★ CALL ME IRRESPONSIBLE from *Papa's Delicate Condition*, Amro Prods., Paramount: Music by JAMES VAN HEUSEN; Lyrics by SAMMY CAHN.

CHARADE from *Charade*, Universal-Stanley Donen Prod., Universal: Music by HENRY MANCINI; Lyrics by JOHNNY MERCER.

IT'S A MAD, MAD, MAD, MAD WORLD from *It's a Mad, Mad, Mad, Mad World*, Casey Prod., UA: Music by ERNEST GOLD; Lyrics by MACK DAVID.

MORE from *Mondo Cane*, Cineriz Prod., Times Film: Music by RIZ ORTOLANI and NINO OLIVIERO; Lyrics by NORMAN NEWELL.

SO LITTLE TIME from *55 Days at Peking*, Samuel Bronston Prod., Allied Artists: Music by DIMITRI TIOMKIN; Lyrics by PAUL FRANCIS WEBSTER.

Costume Design

Black and White

★ FEDERICO FELLINI'S 8½, Cineriz Prod., Embassy Pictures: PIERO GHERARDI.

LOVE WITH THE PROPER STRANGER, Boardwalk-Rona Prod., Paramount: EDITH HEAD.

THE STRIPPER, Jerry Wald Prods., 20th Century-Fox: TRAVILLA.

TOYS IN THE ATTIC, Mirisch-Claude Prod., UA: BILL THOMAS.

WIVES AND LOVERS, Hal Wallis Prod., Paramount: EDITH HEAD.

Color

THE CARDINAL, Gamma Prod., Columbia: DONALD BROOKS.

★ CLEOPATRA, 20th Century-Fox Ltd.-MCL Films S.A.-WALWA Films S.A. Prod., 20th Century-Fox: IRENE SHARAFF, VITTORIO NINO NOVARESE, and RENIE.

HOW THE WEST WAS WON, Metro-Goldwyn-Mayer and Cinerama: WALTER PLUNKETT.

THE LEOPARD, Titanus Prod., 20th Century-Fox: PIERO TOSI.

A NEW KIND OF LOVE, Llenroc Prods., Paramount: EDITH HEAD.

Special Visual Effects

(New Category)*

THE BIRDS, Alfred J. Hitchcock Prod., Universal: UB IWERKS.

*For the 36th Awards Year, the Academy Board of Governors, in recognition of the fact that the best visual effects and the best audible effects each year did not necessarily occur in the same picture, voted to discontinue the Special Effects Award and created two new awards: The Special Visual Effects Award and the Sound Effects Award.

★ CLEOPATRA, 20th Century-Fox Ltd.-MCL Films S.A.-WALWA Films S.A. Prod., 20th Century-Fox: EMIL KOSA, JR.

Sound Effects

(New Category)

A GATHERING OF EAGLES, Universal: ROBERT L. BRATTON.

★ IT'S A MAD, MAD, MAD, MAD WORLD, Casey Prod., UA: WALTER G. ELLIOTT.

Short Subjects

Cartoons

AUTOMANIA 2000, Halas and Batchelor Prod., Pathé Contemporary Films: JOHN HALAS, Producer.

★ THE CRITIC, Pintoff-Crossbow Prods., Columbia: ERNEST PINTOFF, Producer.

THE GAME (INGRA), Zagreb Film, Rembrandt Films-Film Representations: DUSAN VUKOTIC, Producer.

MY FINANCIAL CAREER, National Film Board of Canada, Walter Reade-Sterling-Continental Distributing: COLIN LOW and TOM DALY, Producers.

PIANISSIMO, Cinema 16: CARMEN D'AVINO, Producer.

Live-Action Subjects

THE CONCERT, James A. King Corp., George K. Arthur-Go Pictures: EZRA BAKER, Producer.

HOME-MADE CAR, BP (North America) Ltd., Lester A. Schoenfeld Films: JAMES HILL, Producer.

★ AN OCCURRENCE AT OWL CREEK BRIDGE, Films du Centaure-Filmartic, Cappagariff-Janus Films: PAUL DE ROUBAIX and MARCEL ICHAC, Producers.

SIX-SIDED TRIANGLE, Milesian Film Prod. Ltd., Lion International Films: CHRISTOPHER MILES, Producer.

THAT'S ME, Stuart Prods., Pathé Contemporary Films: WALKER STUART, Producer.

Documentary

Short Subjects

★ CHAGALL, Auerbach Film Enterprises, Ltd.-Flag Films: SIMON SCHIFFRIN, Producer.

THE FIVE CITIES OF JUNE, United States Information Agency: GEORGE STEVENS, JR., Producer.

THE SPIRIT OF AMERICA, Spotlite News: ALGERNON G. WALKER, Producer.

THIRTY MILLION LETTERS, British Transport Films: EDGAR ANSTEY, Producer.

TO LIVE AGAIN, Wilding, Inc.: MEL LONDON, Producer.

Features

LE MAILLON ET LA CHAINE (THE LINK AND THE CHAIN), Films du Centaure-Filmartic: PAUL DE ROUBAIX, Producer.

★ ROBERT FROST: A LOVER'S QUARREL WITH THE WORLD, WGBH Educational Foundation: ROBERT HUGHES, Producer.

THE YANKS ARE COMING, David L. Wolper Prods.: MARSHALL FLAUM, Producer.

Foreign Language Film Award

★ FEDERICO FELLINI'S 8½, A Cineriz Production (Italy).

KNIFE IN THE WATER, A Kamera Unit of Film Polski Production (Poland).

LOS TARANTOS, Tecisa-Films R.B. (Spain).

THE RED LANTERNS, Th. Damaskinos and V. Michaelides A.E. (Greece).

TWIN SISTERS OF KYOTO, Shochiku Co., Ltd. (Japan).

Honorary Awards

None.

Irving G. Thalberg Memorial Award

SAM SPIEGEL.

Jean Hersholt Humanitarian Award

None.

Scientific or Technical

Class I

None.

Class II

None.

Class III

DOUGLAS G. SHEARER and A. ARNOLD GILLESPIE of Metro-Goldwyn-Mayer Studios for the engineering of an improved background process projection system.

THIRTY-SEVENTH YEAR

1964

Nominations Announced: February 23, 1965
Awards Ceremony: April 5, 1965
Santa Monica Civic Auditorium
(MC: Bob Hope)

Best Picture

BECKET, Hal Wallis Prod., Paramount: Hal B. Wallis, Producer.

DR. STRANGELOVE OR: HOW I LEARNED TO STOP WORRYING AND LOVE THE BOMB, Hawk Films, Ltd. Prod., Columbia: Stanley Kubrick, Producer.

MARY POPPINS, Walt Disney Prods.: Walt Disney and Bill Walsh, Producers.

★ MY FAIR LADY, Warner Bros.: Jack L. Warner, Producer.

ZORBA THE GREEK, Rochley, Ltd. Prod., International Classics: Michael Cacoyannis, Producer.

Actor

RICHARD BURTON in *Becket*, Hal Wallis Prod., Paramount.

★ REX HARRISON in *My Fair Lady*, Warner Bros.

PETER O'TOOLE in *Becket*, Hal Wallis Prod., Paramount.

ANTHONY QUINN in *Zorba the Greek*, Rochley, Ltd. Prod., International Classics.

PETER SELLERS in *Dr. Strangelove or: How I Learned to Stop Worrying and Love the Bomb*, Hawk Films, Ltd. Prod., Columbia.

Actress

★ JULIE ANDREWS in *Mary Poppins*, Walt Disney Prods.

ANNE BANCROFT in *The Pumpkin Eater*, Romulus Films, Ltd. Prod., Royal Films International.

SOPHIA LOREN in *Marriage Italian Style*, Champion-Concordia Prod., Embassy Pictures.

DEBBIE REYNOLDS in *The Unsinkable Molly Brown*, Marten Prod., M-G-M.

KIM STANLEY in *Seance on a Wet Afternoon*, Richard Attenborough-Bryan Forbes Prod., Artixo Prods., Ltd.

Supporting Actor

JOHN GIELGUD in *Becket*, Hal Wallis Prod., Paramount.

STANLEY HOLLOWAY in *My Fair Lady*, Warner Bros.

EDMOND O'BRIEN in *Seven Days in May*, Joel Prods., Paramount.

LEE TRACY in *The Best Man*, Millar-Turman Prod., United Artists.

★ PETER USTINOV in *Topkapi*, Filmways Prod., United Artists.

Supporting Actress

GLADYS COOPER in *My Fair Lady*, Warner Bros.

DAME EDITH EVANS in *The Chalk*

Garden, Quota Rentals, Ltd.-Ross Hunter Prod., Universal.
GRAYSON HALL in *The Night of the Iguana*, Seven Arts Prod., M-G-M.
★ LILA KEDROVA in *Zorba the Greek*, Rochley, Ltd. Prod., International Classics.
AGNES MOOREHEAD in *Hush . . . Hush, Sweet Charlotte*, Associates and Aldrich Co. Prod., 20th Century-Fox.

Directing

MICHAEL CACOYANNIS for *Zorba the Greek*, Rochley, Ltd. Prod., International Classics.
★ GEORGE CUKOR for *My Fair Lady*, Warner Bros.
PETER GLENVILLE for *Becket*, Hal Wallis Prod., Paramount.
STANLEY KUBRICK for *Dr. Strangelove or: How I Learned to Stop Worrying and Love the Bomb*, Hawk Films, Ltd. Prod., Columbia.
ROBERT STEVENSON for *Mary Poppins*, Walt Disney Prods.

Writing

Screenplay—Based on Material from Another Medium

★ BECKET, Hal Wallis Prod., Paramount: EDWARD ANHALT.
DR. STRANGELOVE OR: HOW I LEARNED TO STOP WORRYING AND LOVE THE BOMB, Hawk Films, Ltd. Prod., Columbia: STANLEY KUBRICK, PETER GEORGE, and TERRY SOUTHERN.
MARY POPPINS, Walt Disney Prods.: BILL WALSH and DON DAGRADI.
MY FAIR LADY, Warner Bros.: ALAN JAY LERNER.
ZORBA THE GREEK, Rochley, Ltd. Prod., International Classics: MICHAEL CACOYANNIS.

Story and Screenplay—Written Directly for the Screen

★ FATHER GOOSE, Universal-Granox Prod., Universal: Story by S. H. BARNETT; Screenplay by PETER STONE and FRANK TARLOFF.
A HARD DAY'S NIGHT, Walter Shenson Prod., United Artists: ALUN OWEN.
ONE POTATO, TWO POTATO, Bawalco Picture Prod., Cinema V Distributing: Story by ORVILLE H. HAMPTON; Screenplay by RAPHAEL HAYES and ORVILLE H. HAMPTON.
THE ORGANIZER, Lux-Vides-Mediterranee Cinema Prod., Walter Reade-Sterling-Continental Distributing: AGE, SCARPELLI, and MARIO MONICELLI.
THAT MAN FROM RIO, Ariane-Les Artistes Prod., Lopert Pictures: JEAN-PAUL RAPPENEAU, ARIANE MNOUCHKINE, DANIEL BOULANGER, and PHILIPPE DE BROCA.

Cinematography

Black and White

THE AMERICANIZATION OF EMILY, Martin Ransohoff Prod., M-G-M: PHILIP H. LATHROP.
FATE IS THE HUNTER, Arcola Pictures Prod., 20th Century-Fox: MILTON KRASNER.
HUSH . . . HUSH, SWEET CHARLOTTE, Associates and Aldrich Prod., 20th Century-Fox: JOSEPH BIROC.
THE NIGHT OF THE IGUANA, Seven Arts Prod., M-G-M: GABRIEL FIGUEROA.
★ ZORBA THE GREEK, Rochley, Ltd. Prod., International Classics: WALTER LASSALLY.

Color

BECKET, Hal Wallis Prod., Paramount: GEOFFREY UNSWORTH.
CHEYENNE AUTUMN, John Ford-Bernard Smith Prod., Warner Bros.: WILLIAM H. CLOTHIER.
MARY POPPINS, Walt Disney Prods.: EDWARD COLMAN.
★ MY FAIR LADY, Warner Bros.: HARRY STRADLING.

THE UNSINKABLE MOLLY BROWN, Marten Prod., M-G-M: DANIEL L. FAPP.

Art Direction—Set Decoration

Black and White

THE AMERICANIZATION OF EMILY, Martin Ransohoff Prod., M-G-M: GEORGE W. DAVIS, HANS PETERS, and ELLIOT SCOTT; Set Decoration: HENRY GRACE and ROBERT R. BENTON.

HUSH . . . HUSH, SWEET CHARLOTTE, Associates and Aldrich Prod., 20th Century-Fox: WILLIAM GLASGOW; Set Decoration: RAPHAEL BRETTON.

THE NIGHT OF THE IGUANA, Seven Arts Prod., M-G-M: STEPHEN GRIMES.

SEVEN DAYS IN MAY, Joel Prods., Paramount: CARY ODELL; Set Decoration: EDWARD G. BOYLE.

★ ZORBA THE GREEK, Rochley, Ltd. Prod., International Classics: VASSILIS FOTOPOULOS.

Color

BECKET, Hal Wallis Prod., Paramount: JOHN BRYAN and MAURICE CARTER; Set Decoration: PATRICK MCLOUGHLIN and ROBERT CARTWRIGHT.

MARY POPPINS, Walt Disney Prods.: CARROLL CLARK and WILLIAM H. TUNTKE; Set Decoration: EMILE KURI and HAL GAUSMAN.

★ MY FAIR LADY, Warner Bros.: GENE ALLEN and CECIL BEATON; Set Decoration: GEORGE JAMES HOPKINS.

THE UNSINKABLE MOLLY BROWN, Marten Prod., M-G-M: GEORGE W. DAVIS and PRESTON AMES; Set Decoration: HENRY GRACE and HUGH HUNT.

WHAT A WAY TO GO, Apjac-Orchard Prod., 20th Century-Fox: JACK MARTIN SMITH and TED HAWORTH; Set Decoration: WALTER M. SCOTT and STUART A. REISS.

Sound

BECKET, Shepperton Studio Sound Department: JOHN COX, Sound Director.

FATHER GOOSE, Universal City Studio Sound Department: WALDON O. WATSON, Sound Director.

MARY POPPINS, Walt Disney Studio Sound Department: ROBERT O. COOK, Sound Director.

★ MY FAIR LADY, Warner Bros. Studio Sound Department: GEORGE R. GROVES, Sound Director.

THE UNSINKABLE MOLLY BROWN, Metro-Goldwyn-Mayer Studio Sound Department: FRANKLIN E. MILTON, Sound Director.

Film Editing

BECKET, Hal Wallis Prod., Paramount: ANNE COATES.

FATHER GOOSE, Universal-Granox Prod., Universal: TED J. KENT.

HUSH . . . HUSH, SWEET CHAROLOTTE, Associates and Aldrich Prod., 20th Century-Fox: MICHAEL LUCIANO.

★ MARY POPPINS, Walt Disney Prods.: COTTON WARBURTON.

MY FAIR LADY, Warner Bros.: WILLIAM ZIEGLER.

Music

Music Score—Substantially Original

BECKET, Hal Wallis Prod., Paramount: LAURENCE ROSENTHAL.

THE FALL OF THE ROMAN EMPIRE, Bronston-Roma Prod., Paramount: DIMITRI TIOMKIN.

HUSH . . . HUSH, SWEET CHARLOTTE, Associates and Aldrich Prod., 20th Century-Fox: FRANK DEVOL.

★ MARY POPPINS, Walt Disney Prods.: RICHARD M. SHERMAN and ROBERT B. SHERMAN.

THE PINK PANTHER, Mirisch-G-E Prod., United Artists: HENRY MANCINI.

Scoring of Music—Adaptation or Treatment

A HARD DAY'S NIGHT, Walter Shenson Prod., United Artists: GEORGE MARTIN.

MARY POPPINS, Walt Disney Prods.: IRWIN KOSTAL.

★ MY FAIR LADY, Warner Bros.: ANDRÉ PREVIN.

ROBIN AND THE 7 HOODS, P-C Prod., Warner Bros.: NELSON RIDDLE.

THE UNSINKABLE MOLLY BROWN, Marten Prod., M-G-M: ROBERT ARMBRUSTER, LEO ARNAUD, JACK ELLIOTT, JACK HAYES, CALVIN JACKSON and LEO SHUKEN.

Song

★ CHIM CHIM CHER-EE from *Mary Poppins*, Walt Disney Prods.: Music and Lyrics by RICHARD M. SHERMAN AND ROBERT B. SHERMAN.

DEAR HEART from *Dear Heart*, W.B.-Out-of-Towners Prod., Warner Bros.: Music by HENRY MANCINI; Lyrics by JAY LIVINGSTON and RAY EVANS.

HUSH . . . HUSH, SWEET CHARLOTTE from *Hush . . . Hush, Sweet Charlotte*, Associates and Aldrich Prod., 20th Century-Fox: Music by FRANK DEVOL; Lyrics by MACK DAVID.

MY KIND OF TOWN from *Robin and the 7 Hoods*, P-C Prod., Warner Bros.: Music by JAMES VAN HEUSEN; Lyrics by SAMMY CAHN.

WHERE LOVE HAS GONE from *Where Love Has Gone*, Paramount-Embassy Pictures Prod., Paramount: Music by JAMES VAN HEUSEN; Lyrics by SAMMY CAHN.

Costume Design

Black and White

A HOUSE IS NOT A HOME, Clarence Greene-Russell Rouse Prod., Embassy Pictures: EDITH HEAD.

HUSH . . . HUSH, SWEET CHARLOTTE, Associates and Aldrich Prod., 20th Century-Fox: NORMA KOCH.

KISSES FOR MY PRESIDENT, Pearlayne Prod., Warner Bros.: HOWARD SHOUP.

★ THE NIGHT OF THE IGUANA, Seven Arts Prod., M-G-M: DOROTHY JEAKINS.

THE VISIT, Cinecitta-Dear Film-Les Films du Siècle-P.E.C.S. Prod., 20th Century-Fox: RENE HUBERT.

Color

BECKET, Hal Wallis Prod., Paramount: MARGARET FURSE.

MARY POPPINS, Walt Disney Prods.: TONY WALTON.

★ MY FAIR LADY, Warner Bros.: CECIL BEATON.

THE UNSINKABLE MOLLY BROWN, Marten Prod., M-G-M: MORTON HAACK.

WHAT A WAY TO GO, Apjac-Orchard Prod., 20th Century-Fox: EDITH HEAD and MOSS MABRY.

Special Visual Effects

★ MARY POPPINS, Walt Disney Prods.: PETER ELLENSHAW, HAMILTON LUSKE, and EUSTACE LYCETT.

7 FACES OF DR. LAO, Galaxy-Scarus Prod., Metro-Goldwyn-Mayer: JIM DANFORTH.

Sound Effects

★ GOLDFINGER, Eon Prod., UA: NORMAN WANSTALL.

THE LIVELY SET, Universal: ROBERT L. BRATTON.

Short Subjects

Cartoons

CHRISTMAS CRACKER, NATIONAL FILM BOARD OF CANADA, Favorite Films of California.

HOW TO AVOID FRIENDSHIP, Rembrandt Films, Film Representations: WILLIAM L. SNYDER, Producer.

NUDNIK #2, Rembrandt Films, Film Representations: WILLIAM L. SNYDER, Producer.

★ THE PINK PHINK, Mirisch-Geoffrey Prods., UA: DAVID H. DePATIE and FRIZ FRELENG, Producers.

Live-Action Subjects

★ CASALS CONDUCTS: 1964, Thalia Films, Beckman Film Corp.: EDWARD SCHREIBER, Producer.

HELP! MY SNOWMAN'S BURNING DOWN, Carson Davidson Prods., Pathé Contemporary Films: CARSON DAVIDSON, Producer.

THE LEGEND OF JIMMY BLUE EYES, Robert Clouse Associates, Topaz Film Corp.: ROBERT CLOUSE, Producer.

Documentary

Short Subjects

BREAKING THE HABIT, American Cancer Society, Modern Talking Picture Service: HENRY JACOBS and JOHN KORTY, Producers.

CHILDREN WITHOUT, National Education Association, Guggenheim Productions.

KENOJUAK, National Film Board of Canada.

★ NINE FROM LITTLE ROCK, United States Information Agency, Guggenheim Productions.

140 DAYS UNDER THE WORLD, New Zealand National Film Unit, Rank Film Distributors of New Zealand: GEOFFREY SCOTT and OXLEY HUGHAN, Producers.

Features

THE FINEST HOURS, Le Vien Films, Ltd., Columbia: JACK LE VIEN, Producer.

FOUR DAYS IN NOVEMEMBER, David L. Wolper Prods., UA: MEL STUART, Producer.

THE HUMAN DUTCH, Haanstra Filmproductie: BERT HAANSTRA, Producer.

★ JACQUES-YVES COUSTEAU'S WORLD WITHOUT SUN, Filmad-Les Requins Associés-Orsay-CEIAP, Columbia: JACQUES-YVES COUSTEAU, Producer.

OVER THERE, 1914–18, Zodiac Prods., Pathé Contemporary Films: JEAN AUREL, Producer.

Foreign Language Film Award

RAVEN'S END, AB Europa Film (Sweden).

SALLAH, A Sallah Film Ltd. Production (Israel).

THE UMBRELLAS OF CHERBOURG, A Parc-Madeleine-Beta Films Production (France).

WOMAN IN THE DUNES, A Teshigahara Production (Japan).

★ YESTERDAY, TODAY AND TOMORROW, A Champion-Concordia Production (Italy).

Honorary Award

WILLIAM TUTTLE for his outstanding make-up achievement for *7 Faces of Dr. Lao*. (Statuette)

Irving G. Thalberg Memorial Award

None.

Jean Hersholt Humanitarian Award

None.

Scientific or Technical

Class I

PETRO VLAHOS, WADSWORTH E. POHL, and UB IWERKS for the conception and perfecton of techniques used for color traveling matte composite cinematography.

Class II

SIDNEY P. SOLOW, EDWARD H. REICHARD, CARL W. HAUGE, and JOB SANDERSON of Consolidated Film Industries for the design and development of a versatile, automatic 35mm composite color printer.

PIERRE ANGENIEUX for the development of a ten-to-one zoom lens for cinematography.

Class III

MILTON FORMAN, RICHARD B. GLICKMAN, and DANIEL J. PEARLMAN of ColorTran Industries for advancements in the design and application to motion picture photography of lighting units using quartz iodine lamps.

STEWART FILMSCREEN CORPORATION for a seamless, translucent blue screen for traveling matte color cinematography.

ANTHONY PAGLIA and the 20TH CENTURY-FOX STUDIO MECHANICAL EFFECTS DEPARTMENT for an improved method of producing explosion flash effects for motion pictures.

EDWARD H. REICHARD and CARL W. HAUGE of Consolidated Film Industries for the design of a proximity cue detector and its application to motion picture printers.

EDWARD H. REICHARD, LEONARD L. SOKOLOW, and CARL W. HAUGE of Consolidated Film Industries for the design and application to motion picture laboratory practice of a stroboscopic scene tester for color and black-and-white film.

NELSON TYLER for the design and construction of an improved helicopter camera system.

THIRTY-EIGHTH YEAR

1965

Nominations Announced: February 21, 1966
Awards Ceremony: April 18, 1966
Santa Monica Civic Auditorium
(MC: Bob Hope)

Best Picture

DARLING, Anglo-Amalgamated, Ltd. Prod., Embassy: Joseph Janni, Producer.

DOCTOR ZHIVAGO, Sostar S.A.-Metro-Goldwyn-Mayer British Studios, Ltd. Prod., M-G-M; Carlo Ponti, Producer.

SHIP OF FOOLS, Columbia: Stanley Kramer, Producer.

★ THE SOUND OF MUSIC, Argyle Enterprises Prod., 20th Century-Fox: Robert Wise, Producer.

A THOUSAND CLOWNS, Harrell Prod., United Artists: Fred Coe, Producer.

Actor

RICHARD BURTON in *The Spy Who Came in from the Cold*, Salem Films, Ltd. Prod., Paramount.

★ LEE MARVIN in *Cat Ballou*, Harold Hecht Prod., Columbia.

LAURENCE OLIVIER in *Othello*, B.H.E. Prod., Warner Bros.

ROD STEIGER in *The Pawnbroker*, Ely Landau Prod., American Intl.

OSKAR WERNER in *Ship of Fools*, Columbia.

Actress

JULIE ANDREWS in *The Sound of Music*, Argyle Enterprises Prod., 20th Century-Fox.

★ JULIE CHRISTIE in *Darling*, Anglo-Amalgamated, Ltd. Prod., Embassy.

SAMANTHA EGGAR in *The Collector*, The Collector Company, Columbia.

ELIZABETH HARTMAN in *A Patch of Blue*, Pandro S. Berman-Guy Green Prod., M-G-M.

SIMONE SIGNORET in *Ship of Fools*, Columbia.

Supporting Actor

★ MARTIN BALSAM in *A Thousand Clowns*, Harrell Prod., United Artists.

IAN BANNEN in *The Flight of the Phoenix*, Associates and Aldrich Company Prod., 20th Century-Fox.

TOM COURTENAY in *Doctor Zhivago*; Sostar S.A.-Metro-Goldwyn-Mayer British Studios, Ltd. Prod., M-G-M.

MICHAEL DUNN in *Ship of Fools*, Columbia.

FRANK FINLAY in *Othello*, B.H.E. Prod., Warner Bros.

Supporting Actress

RUTH GORDON in *Inside Daisy Clover*, Park Place Prod., Warner Bros.

JOYCE REDMAN in *Othello*, B.H.E. Prod., Warner Bros.

MAGGIE SMITH in *Othello*, B.H.E. Prod., Warner Bros.

★ SHELLEY WINTERS in *A Patch of*

Blue, Pandro S. Berman-Guy Green Prod., M-G-M.

PEGGY WOOD in *The Sound of Music*, Argyle Enterprises Prod., 20th Century-Fox.

Directing

DAVID LEAN for *Doctor Zhivago*, Sostar S.A.-Metro-Goldwyn-Mayer British Studios, Ltd. Prod., M-G-M.

JOHN SCHLESINGER for *Darling*, Anglo-Amalgamated, Ltd. Prod., Embassy.

HIROSHI TESHIGAHARA for *Woman in the Dunes*, Teshigahara Prod., Pathé Contemporary Films.

★ ROBERT WISE for *The Sound of Music*, Argyle Enterprises Prod., 20th Century-Fox.

WILLIAM WYLER for *The Collector*, The Collector Company, Columbia.

Writing

Screenplay—Based on Material from Another Medium

CAT BALLOU, Harold Hecht Prod., Columbia: WALTER NEWMAN and FRANK R. PIERSON.

THE COLLECTOR, The Collector Company, Columbia: STANLEY MANN and JOHN KOHN.

★ DOCTOR ZHIVAGO, Sostar S.A.-Metro-Goldwyn-Mayer British Studios, Ltd. Prod., M-G-M: ROBERT BOLT.

SHIP OF FOOLS, Columbia: ABBY MANN.

A THOUSAND CLOWNS, Harrell Prod., United Artists: HERB GARDNER.

Story and Screenplay—Written Directly for the Screen

CASANOVA '70, C.C. Champion-Les Films Concordia Prod., Embassy: AGE, SCARPELLI, MARIO MONICELLI, TONINO GUERRA, GIORGIO SALVIONI, and SUSO CECCHI D'AMICO.

★ DARLING, Anglo-Amalgamated, Ltd. Prod., Embassy: FREDERIC RAPHAEL.

THOSE MAGNIFICENT MEN IN THEIR FLYING MACHINES, 20th Century-Fox, Ltd. Prod., 20th Century-Fox: JACK DAVIES and KEN ANNAKIN.

THE TRAIN, Les Prods. Artistes Associés, United Artists: FRANKLIN COEN and FRANK DAVIS.

THE UMBRELLAS OF CHERBOURG, Parc-Madeleine Films Prod., American International: JACQUES DEMY.

Cinematography

Black and White

IN HARM'S WAY, Sigma Prods., Paramount: LOYAL GRIGGS.

KING RAT, Coleytown Prod., Columbia: BURNETT GUFFEY.

MORITURI, Arcola-Colony Prod., 20th Century-Fox: CONRAD HALL.

A PATCH OF BLUE, Pandro S. Berman-Guy Green Prod., M-G-M.: ROBERT BURKS.

★ SHIP OF FOOLS, Columbia: ERNEST LASZLO.

Color

THE AGONY AND THE ECSTASY, International Classics Prod., 20th Century-Fox: LEON SHAMROY.

★ DOCTOR ZHIVAGO, Sostar S.A.-Metro-Goldwyn-Mayer British Studios, Ltd. Prod., M-G-M: FREDDIE YOUNG.

THE GREAT RACE, Patricia-Jalem-Reynard Prod., Warner Bros.: RUSSELL HARLAN.

THE GREATEST STORY EVER TOLD, George Stevens Prod., United Artists: WILLIAM C. MELLOR and LOYAL GRIGGS.

THE SOUND OF MUSIC, Argyle Enterprises Prod., 20th Century-Fox: TED MCCORD.

Art Direction—Set Decoration

Black and White

KING RAT, Coleytown Prod., Columbia: ROBERT EMMET SMITH; Set Decoration: FRANK TUTTLE.

A PATCH OF BLUE, Pandro S. Berman-Guy Green Prod., M-G-M: GEORGE W. DAVIS and URIE MCCLEARY; Set Decoration: HENRY GRACE and CHARLES S. THOMPSON.

★ SHIP OF FOOLS, Columbia: ROBERT CLATWORTHY; Set Decoration: JOSEPH KISH.

THE SLENDER THREAD, Paramount: HAL PEREIRA and JACK POPLIN; Set Decoration: ROBERT BENTON and JOSEPH KISH.

THE SPY WHO CAME IN FROM THE COLD, Salem Films, Ltd. Prod., Paramount: HAL PEREIRA, TAMBI LARSEN, and EDWARD MARSHALL; Set Decoration: JOSIE MACAVIN.

Color

THE AGONY AND THE ECSTASY, International Classics Prod., 20th Century-Fox: JOHN DECUIR and JACK MARTIN SMITH; Set Decoration: DARIO SIMONI.

★ DOCTOR ZHIVAGO, Sostar S.A.-Metro-Goldwyn-Mayer British Studios, Ltd. Prod., M-G-M: JOHN BOX and TERRY MARSH; Set Decoration: DARIO SIMONI.

THE GREATEST STORY EVER TOLD, George Stevens Prod., United Artists: RICHARD DAY, WILLIAM CREBER, and DAVID HALL; Set Decoration: RAY MOYER, FRED MACLEAN, and NORMAN ROCKETT.

INSIDE DAISY CLOVER, Park Place Prod., Warner Bros.: ROBERT CLATWORTHY; Set Decoration: GEORGE JAMES HOPKINS.

THE SOUND OF MUSIC, Argyle Enterprises Prod., 20th Century-Fox: BORIS LEVEN; Set Decoration: WALTER M. SCOTT and RUBY LEVITT.

Sound

THE AGONY AND THE ECSTASY, 20th Century-Fox Studio Sound Department: JAMES P. CORCORAN, Sound Director.

DOCTOR ZHIVAGO, Metro-Goldwyn-Mayer British Studio Sound Department: A. W. WATKINS, Sound Director; and Metro-Goldwyn-Mayer Studio Sound Department: FRANKLIN E. MILTON, Sound Director.

THE GREAT RACE, Warner Bros. Studio Sound Department: GEORGE R. GROVES, Sound Director.

SHENANDOAH, Universal City Studio Sound Department: WALDON O. WATSON, Sound Director.

★ THE SOUND OF MUSIC, 20th Century-Fox Studio Sound Department: JAMES P. CORCORAN, Sound Director; and TODD-AO Sound Department: FRED HYNES, Sound Director.

Film Editing

CAT BALLOU, Harold Hecht Prod., Columbia: CHARLES NELSON.

DOCTOR ZHIVAGO, Sostar S.A.-Metro-Goldwyn-Mayer British Studios, Ltd. Prod., M-G-M: NORMAN SAVAGE.

THE FLIGHT OF THE PHOENIX, Associates and Aldrich Company Prod., 20th Century-Fox. MICHAEL LUCIANO.

THE GREAT RACE, Patricia-Jalem-Reynard Prod., Warner Bros.: RALPH E. WINTERS.

★ THE SOUND OF MUSIC, Argyle Enterprises Prod., 20th Century-Fox: WILLIAM REYNOLDS.

Music

Music Score—Substantially Original

THE AGONY AND THE ECSTASY, International Classics Prod., 20th Century-Fox: ALEX NORTH.

★ DOCTOR ZHIVAGO, Sostar S.A.-Metro-Goldwyn-Mayer British

Studios, Ltd. Prod., M-G-M: MAURICE JARRE.

THE GREATEST STORY EVER TOLD, George Stevens Prod., United Artists: ALFRED NEWMAN.

A PATCH OF BLUE, Pandro S. Berman-Guy Green Prod., M-G-M: JERRY GOLDSMITH.

THE UMBRELLAS OF CHERBOURG, Parc-Madeleine Films Prod., American International: MICHEL LEGRAND and JACQUES DEMY.

Scoring of Music—Adaptation or Treatment

CAT BALLOU, Harold Hecht Prod., Columbia: DEVOL.

THE PLEASURE SEEKERS, 20th Century-Fox: LIONEL NEWMAN and ALEXANDER COURAGE.

★ THE SOUND OF MUSIC, Argyle Enterprises Prod., 20th Century-Fox: IRWIN KOSTAL.

A THOUSAND CLOWNS, Harrell Prod., United Artists: DON WALKER.

THE UMBRELLAS OF CHERBOURG, Parc-Madeleine Films Prod., American International: MICHEL LEGRAND.

Song

THE BALLAD OF CAT BALLOU from *Cat Ballou*, Harold Hecht Prod., Columbia: Music by JERRY LIVINGSTON; Lyrics by MACK DAVID.

I WILL WAIT FOR YOU from *The Umbrellas of Cherbourg*, Parc-Madeleine Films Prod., American International: Music by MICHEL LEGRAND; Lyrics by JACQUES DEMY.

★ THE SHADOW OF YOUR SMILE from *The Sandpiper*, Filmways-Venice Prod., M-G-M: Music by JOHNNY MANDEL; Lyrics by PAUL FRANCIS WEBSTER.

THE SWEETHEART TREE from *The Great Race*, Patricia-Jalem-Reynard Prod., Warner Bros.: Music by HENRY MANCINI; Lyrics by JOHNNY MERCER.

WHAT'S NEW PUSSYCAT? from *What's New Pussycat?*, Famous Artists-Famartists Prod., United Artists: Music by BURT BACHARACH; Lyrics by HAL DAVID.

Costume Design

Black and White

★ DARLING, Anglo-Amalgamated, Ltd. Prod., Embassy: JULIE HARRIS.

MORITURI, Arcola-Colony Prod., 20th Century-Fox: MOSS MABRY.

A RAGE TO LIVE, Mirisch Corp. of Delaware-Araho Prod., United Artists: HOWARD SHOUP.

SHIP OF FOOLS, Columbia: BILL THOMAS and JEAN LOUIS.

THE SLENDER THREAD, Paramount: EDITH HEAD.

Color

THE AGONY AND THE ECSTASY, International Classics Prod., 20th Century-Fox: VITTORIO NINO NOVARESE.

★ DOCTOR ZHIVAGO, Sostar S.A.-Metro-Goldwyn-Mayer British Studios, Ltd. Prod., M-G-M: PHYLLIS DALTON.

THE GREATEST STORY EVER TOLD, George Stevens Prod., United Artists: VITTORIO NINO NOVARESE and MARJORIE BEST.

INSIDE DAISY CLOVER, Park Place Prod., Warner Bros.: EDITH HEAD and BILL THOMAS.

THE SOUND OF MUSIC, Argyle Enterprises Prod., 20th Century-Fox: DOROTHY JEAKINS.

Special Visual Effects

THE GREATEST STORY EVER TOLD, George Stevens Prod., United Artists: J. MCMILLAN JOHNSON.

★ THUNDERBALL, Broccoli-

Saltzman-McClory Prod., United Artists: JOHN STEARS.

Sound Effects

★ THE GREAT RACE, Patricia-Jalem-Reynard Prod., Warner Bros.: TREGOWETH BROWN.

VON RYAN'S EXPRESS, P-R Prods., 20th Century-Fox: WALTER A. ROSSI.

Short Subjects

Cartoons

CLAY OR THE ORIGIN OF SPECIES, Harvard University, Pathé Contemporary Films: ELIOT NOYES, JR., Producer.

★ THE DOT AND THE LINE, Metro-Goldwyn-Mayer: CHUCK JONES and LES GOLDMAN, Producers.

THE THIEVING MAGPIE (LA GAZZA LADRA), Giulio Gianini-Emanuele Luzzati, Allied Artists: EMANUELE LUZZATI, Producer.

Live-Action Subjects

★ THE CHICKEN (LE POULET), Renn Prods., Pathé Contemporary Films: CLAUDE BERRI, Producer.

FORTRESS OF PEACE, Lothar Wolff Prods. for Farner-Looser Films, Cinerama: LOTHAR WOLFF, Producer.

SKATERDATER, Byway Prods., United Artists: MARSHAL BACKLAR and NOEL BLACK, Producers.

SNOW, British Transport Films, in association with Geoffrey Jones (Films) Ltd., Manson Distributing: EDGAR ANSTEY, Producer.

TIME PIECE, Muppets, Inc., Pathé Contemporary Films: JIM HENSON, Producer.

Documentary

Short Subjects

MURAL ON OUR STREET, Henry Street Settlement, Pathé Contemporary Films: KIRK SMALLMAN, Producer.

OUVERTURE, Mafilm Prods., HUNGAROFILM-PATHÉ CONTEMPORARY FILMS.

POINT OF VIEW, Vision Associates Prod., National Tuberculosis Assoc.

★ TO BE ALIVE!, Johnson Wax: FRANCIS THOMPSON, INC., Producer.

YEATS COUNTRY, Aengus Films Ltd. for the Department of External Affairs of Ireland: PATRICK CAREY and JOE MENDOZA, Producers.

Features

THE BATTLE OF THE BULGE . . . THE BRAVE RIFLES, Mascott Prods.: LAURENCE E. MASCOTT, Producer.

★ THE ELEANOR ROOSEVELT STORY, Sidney Glazier Prod., American International: SIDNEY GLAZIER, Producer.

THE FORTH ROAD BRIDGE, Random Film Prods., Ltd., Shell-Mex, and B.P. Film Library: PETER MILLS, Producer.

LET MY PEOPLE GO, Wolper Prods.: MARSHALL FLAUM, Producer.

TO DIE IN MADRID, Ancinex Prods., Altura Films International: FREDERIC ROSSIF, Producer.

Foreign Language Film Award

BLOOD ON THE LAND, Th. Damaskinos and V. Michaelides, A.E.-Finos Film (Greece).

DEAR JOHN, A.B. Sandrew-Ateljeerna (Sweden).

KWAIDAN, A Toho Company, Ltd. Production (Japan).

MARRIAGE ITALIAN STYLE, A Champion-Concordia Production (Italy).

★ THE SHOP ON MAIN STREET, A Ceskoslovensky Film Production (Czechoslovakia).

Honorary Award

BOB HOPE for unique and distinguished service to our industry and the Academy. (Gold medal)

Irving G. Thalberg Memorial Award

WILLIAM WYLER.

Jean Hersholt Humanitarian Award

EDMOND L. DEPATIE.

Scientific or Technical

Class I

None.

Class II

ARTHUR J. HATCH of the Strong Electric Corporation, subsidiary of General Precision Equipment Corporation, for the design and development of an air-blown carbon arc projection lamp.

STEFAN KUDELSKI for the design and development of the Nagra portable ¼ inch tape recording system for motion picture sound recording.

Class III

None.

1966

Nominations Announced: February 20, 1967
Awards Ceremony: April 10, 1967
Santa Monica Civic Auditorium
(MC: Bob Hope)

Best Picture

ALFIE, Sheldrake Films, Ltd. Prod., Paramount: Lewis Gilbert, Producer.

★ A MAN FOR ALL SEASONS, Highland Films, Ltd. Prod., Columbia: Fred Zinnemann, Producer.

THE RUSSIANS ARE COMING! THE RUSSIANS ARE COMING!, Mirisch Corp. of Delaware Prod., UA: Norman Jewison, Producer.

THE SAND PEBBLES, Argyle-Solar Prod., 20th Century-Fox: Robert Wise, Producer.

WHO'S AFRAID OF VIRGINIA WOOLF?, Chenault Prod., Warner Bros.: Ernest Lehman, Producer.

Actor

ALAN ARKIN in *The Russians Are Coming! The Russians Are Coming!*, Mirisch Corp. of Delaware Prod., UA.

RICHARD BURTON in *Who's Afraid of Virginia Woolf?*, Chenault Prod., Warner Bros.

MICHAEL CAINE in *Alfie*, Sheldrake Films, Ltd. Prod., Paramount.

STEVE MCQUEEN in *The Sand Pebbles*, Argyle-Solar Prod., 20th Century-Fox.

★ PAUL SCOFIELD in *A Man for All Seasons*, Highland Films, Ltd. Prod., Columbia.

Actress

ANOUK AIMÉE in *A Man and a Woman*, Les Films 13 Prod., Allied Artists.

IDA KAMINSKA in *The Shop on Main Street*, Ceskoslovensky Film Company Prod., Prominent Films.

LYNN REDGRAVE in *Georgy Girl*, Everglades Prods., Ltd., Columbia.

VANESSA REDGRAVE in *Morgan!*, Quintra Films, Ltd. Prod., Cinema V.

★ ELIZABETH TAYLOR in *Who's Afraid of Virginia Woolf?*, Chenault Prod., Warner Bros.

Supporting Actor

MAKO in *The Sand Pebbles*, Argyle-Solar Prod., 20th Century-Fox.

JAMES MASON in *Georgy Girl*, Everglades Prods., Ltd., Columbia.

★ WALTER MATTHAU in *The Fortune Cookie*, Phalanx-Jalem-Mirisch Corp. of Delaware Prod., UA.

GEORGE SEGAL in *Who's Afraid of Virginia Woolf?*, Chenault Prod., Warner Bros.

ROBERT SHAW in *A Man for All Seasons*, Highland Films, Ltd. Prod., Columbia.

Supporting Actress

★ SANDY DENNIS in *Who's Afraid of Virginia Woolf?*, Chenault Prod., Warner Bros.

WENDY HILLER in *A Man for All Seasons*, Highland Films, Ltd. Prod., Columbia.

JOCELYNE LAGARDE in *Hawaii*, Mirisch Corp. of Delaware Prod., UA.

VIVIEN MERCHANT in *Alfie*, Sheldrake Films, Ltd. Prod., Paramount.

GERALDINE PAGE in *You're a Big Boy Now*, Seven Arts.

Directing

MICHELANGELO ANTONIONI for *Blow-Up*, Carlo Ponti Prod., Premier Productions.

RICHARD BROOKS for *The Professionals*, Pax Enterprises Prod., Columbia.

CLAUDE LELOUCH for *A Man and a Woman*, Les Films 13 Prod., Allied Artists.

MIKE NICHOLS for *Who's Afraid of Virginia Woolf?*, Chenault Prod., Warner Bros.

★ FRED ZINNEMANN for *A Man for All Seasons*, Highland Films, Ltd. Prod., Columbia.

Writing

Screenplay—Based on Material from Another Medium

ALFIE, Sheldrake Films, Ltd. Prod., Paramount: BILL NAUGHTON.

★ A MAN FOR ALL SEASONS, Highland Films, Ltd. Prod., Columbia: ROBERT BOLT.

THE PROFESSIONALS, Pax Enterprises Prod., Columbia: RICHARD BROOKS.

THE RUSSIANS ARE COMING! THE RUSSIANS ARE COMING!, Mirisch Corp. of Delaware Prod., UA: WILLIAM ROSE.

WHO'S AFRAID OF VIRGINIA WOOLF?, Chenault Prod., Warner Bros.: ERNEST LEHMAN.

Story and Screenplay—Written Directly for the Screen

BLOW-UP, Carlo Ponti Prod., Premier Productions: Story by MICHELANGELO ANTONIONI; Screenplay by MICHELANGELO ANTONIONI, TONINO GUERRA, and EDWARD BOND.

THE FORTUNE COOKIE, Phalanx-Jalem-Mirisch Corp. of Delaware Prod., UA: BILLY WILDER and I.A.L. DIAMOND.

KHARTOUM, Julian Blaustein Prod., UA: ROBERT ARDREY.

★ A MAN AND A WOMAN, Les Films 13 Prod., Allied Artists: Story by CLAUDE LELOUCH; Screenplay by PIERRE UYTTERHOEVEN and CLAUDE LELOUCH.

THE NAKED PREY, Theodora Prod., Paramount: CLINT JOHNSTON and DON PETERS.

Cinematography

Black and White

THE FORTUNE COOKIE, Phalanx-Jalem-Mirisch Corp. of Delaware Prod., UA: JOSEPH LASHELLE.

GEORGY GIRL, Everglades Prods., Ltd., Columbia: KEN HIGGINS.

IS PARIS BURNING?, Transcontinental Films-Marianne Prod., Paramount: MARCEL GRIGNON.

SECONDS, The Seconds Company, Paramount: JAMES WONG HOWE.

★ WHO'S AFRAID OF VIRGINIA WOOLF?, Chenault Prod., Warner Bros: HASKELL WEXLER.

Color

FANTASTIC VOYAGE, 20th Century-Fox: ERNEST LASZLO.

HAWAII, Mirisch Corp. of Delaware Prod., UA: RUSSELL HARLAN.

★ A MAN FOR ALL SEASONS,

Highland Films, Ltd. Prod., Columbia: TED MOORE.

THE PROFESSIONALS, Pax Enterprises Prod., Columbia: CONRAD HALL.

THE SAND PEBBLES, Argyle-Solar Prod., 20th Century-Fox: JOSEPH MACDONALD.

Art Direction—Set Decoration

Black and White

THE FORTUNE COOKIE, Phalanx-Jalem-Mirisch Corp. of Delaware Prod., UA: ROBERT LUTHARDT; Set Decoration: EDWARD G. BOYLE.

THE GOSPEL ACCORDING TO ST. MATTHEW, Arco-Lux Cie Cinematografique de France Prod., Walter Reade-Continental Distributing: LUIGI SCACCIANOCE.

IS PARIS BURNING?, Transcontinental Films-Marianne Prod., Paramount: WILLY HOLT; Set Decoration: MARC FREDERIX and PIERRE GUFFROY.

MISTER BUDDWING, DDD-Cherokee Prod., M-G-M: GEORGE W. DAVIS and PAUL GROESSE; Set Decoration: HENRY GRACE and HUGH HUNT.

★ WHO'S AFRAID OF VIRGINIA WOOLF?, Chenault Prod., Warner Bros: RICHARD SYLBERT; Set Decoration: GEORGE JAMES HOPKINS.

Color

★ FANTASTIC VOYAGE, 20th Century-Fox: JACK MARTIN SMITH and DALE HENNESY; Set Decoration: WALTER M. SCOTT and STUART A. REISS.

GAMBIT, Universal: ALEXANDER GOLITZEN and GEORGE C. WEBB; Set Decoration: JOHN MCCARTHY and JOHN AUSTIN.

JULIET OF THE SPIRITS, Rizzoli Films S.P.A. Prod., Rizzoli Films: PIERO GHERARDI.

THE OSCAR, Greene-Rouse Prod., Embassy: HAL PEREIRA and ARTHUR LONERGAN; Set Decoration: ROBERT BENTON and JAMES PAYNE.

THE SAND PEBBLES, Argyle-Solar Prod., 20th Century-Fox: BORIS LEVEN; Set Decoration: WALTER M. SCOTT, JOHN STURTEVANT, and WILLIAM KIERNAN.

Sound

GAMBIT, Universal City Studio Sound Department: WALDON O. WATSON, Sound Director.

★ GRAND PRIX, Metro-Goldwyn-Mayer Studio Sound Department: FRANKLIN E. MILTON, Sound Director.

HAWAII, Samuel Goldwyn Studio Sound Department: GORDON E. SAWYER, Sound Director.

THE SAND PEBBLES, 20th Century-Fox Studio Sound Department: JAMES P. CORCORAN, Sound Director.

WHO'S AFRAID OF VIRGINIA WOOLF?, Warner Bros. Studio Sound Department: GEORGE R. GROVES, Sound Director.

Film Editing

FANTASTIC VOYAGE, 20th Century-Fox: WILLIAM B. MURPHY.

★ GRAND PRIX, Douglas-Lewis-John Frankenheimer-Cherokee Prod., M-G-M: FREDRIC STEINKAMP, HENRY BERMAN, STEWART LINDER, and FRANK SANTILLO.

THE RUSSIANS ARE COMING! THE RUSSIANS ARE COMING!, Mirisch Corp. of Delaware Prod., United Artists: HAL ASHBY and J. TERRY WILLIAMS.

THE SAND PEBBLES, Argyle-Solar Prod., 20th Century-Fox: WILLIAM REYNOLDS.

WHO'S AFRAID OF VIRGINIA WOOLF?, Chenault Prod., Warner Bros.: SAM O'STEEN.

Music

Original Music Score

THE BIBLE, Thalia-A.G. Prod., 20th Century-Fox: TOSHIRO MAYUZUMI.

★ BORN FREE, Open Road Films, Ltd.-Atlas Films, Ltd. Prod., Columbia: JOHN BARRY.

HAWAII, Mirisch Corp. of Delaware Prod., UA: ELMER BERNSTEIN.

THE SAND PEBBLES, Argyle-Solar Prod., 20th Century-Fox: JERRY GOLDSMITH.

WHO'S AFRAID OF VIRGINIA WOOLF?, Chenault Prod., Warner Bros.: ALEX NORTH.

Scoring of Music—Adaptation or Treatment

★ A FUNNY THING HAPPENED ON THE WAY TO THE FORUM, Melvin Frank Prod., United Artists: KEN THORNE.

THE GOSPEL ACCORDING TO ST. MATTHEW, Arco-Lux Cie Cinematografique de France Prod., Walter Reade-Continental Distributing: LUIS ENRIQUE BACALOV.

RETURN OF THE SEVEN, Mirisch Prods., United Artists: ELMER BERNSTEIN.

THE SINGING NUN, Metro-Goldwyn-Mayer: HARRY SUKMAN.

STOP THE WORLD—I WANT TO GET OFF, Warner Bros. Prods., Ltd., Warner Bros.: AL HAM.

Song

ALFIE from *Alfie*, Sheldrake Films, Ltd. Prod., Paramount: Music by BURT BACHARACH; Lyrics by HAL DAVID.

★ BORN FREE from *Born Free*, Open Road Films, Ltd.-Atlas Films, Ltd. Prod., Columbia: Music by JOHN BARRY; Lyrics by DON BLACK.

GEORGY GIRL from *Georgy Girl*, Everglades Prods., Ltd., Columbia: Music by TOM SPRINGFIELD; Lyrics by JIM DALE.

MY WISHING DOLL from *Hawaii*, Mirisch Corp. of Delaware Prod., UA: Music by ELMER BERNSTEIN; Lyrics by MACK DAVID.

A TIME FOR LOVE from *An American Dream*, Warner Bros.: Music by JOHNNY MANDEL; Lyrics by PAUL FRANCIS WEBSTER.

Costume Design

Black and White

THE GOSPEL ACCORDING TO ST. MATTHEW, Arco-Lux Cie Cinematografique de France Prod., Walter Reade-Continental Distributing: DANILO DONATI.

MANDRAGOLA, Europix-Consolidated: DANILO DONATI.

MISTER BUDDWING, DDD-Cherokee Prod., M-G-M: HELEN ROSE.

MORGAN!, Quintra Films, Ltd. Prod., Cinema V: JOCELYN RICKARDS.

★ WHO'S AFRAID OF VIRGINIA WOOLF?, Chenault Prod., Warner Bros.: IRENE SHARAFF.

Color

GAMBIT, Universal: JEAN LOUIS.

HAWAII, Mirisch Corp. of Delaware Prod., UA: DOROTHY JEAKINS.

JULIET OF THE SPIRITS, Rizzoli Films S.P.A. Prod., Rizzoli Films: PIERO GHERARDI.

★ A MAN FOR ALL SEASONS, Highland Films, Ltd. Prod., Columbia: ELIZABETH HAFFENDEN and JOAN BRIDGE.

THE OSCAR, Greene-Rouse Prod., Embassy: EDITH HEAD.

Special Visual Effects

★ FANTASTIC VOYAGE, 20th Century-Fox: ART CRUICKSHANK.

HAWAII, Mirisch Corp. of Delaware Prod., United Artists: LINWOOD G. DUNN.

Sound Effects

FANTASTIC VOYAGE, 20th Century-Fox: WALTER ROSSI.

★ GRAND PRIX, Douglas-Lewis-John Frankenheimer-Cherokee Prod., M-G-M: GORDON DANIEL.

Short Subjects

Cartoons

THE DRAG, National Film Board of Canada, Favorite Films: WOLF KOENIG and ROBERT VERRALL, Producers.

HERB ALPERT AND THE TIJUANA BRASS DOUBLE FEATURE, Hubley Studio, Paramount: JOHN HUBLEY and FAITH HUBLEY, Producers.

THE PINK BLUEPRINT, Mirisch-Geoffrey-DePatie-Freleng, UA: DAVID H. DEPATIE and FRIZ FRELENG, Producers.

Live-Action Subjects

TURKEY THE BRIDGE, Samaritan Prods., Lester A. Schoenfeld Films: DEREK WILLIAMS, Producer.

★ WILD WINGS, British Transport Films, Manson Distributing: EDGAR ANSTEY, Producer.

THE WINNING STRAIN, Winik Films, Paramount: LESLIE WINIK, Producer.

Documentary

Short Subjects

ADOLESCENCE, M.K. Prods.: MARIN KARMITZ and VLADIMIR FORGENCY, Producers.

COWBOY, United States Information Agency: MICHAEL AHNEMANN and GARY SCHLOSSER, Producers.

THE ODDS AGAINST, Vision Associates Prod. for the American Foundation Institute of Corrections: LEE R. BOBKER and HELEN KRISTT RADIN, Producers.

SAINT MATTHEW PASSION, Mafilm Studio, HUNGAROFILM.

★ A YEAR TOWARD TOMORROW, Sun Dial Films, Inc. Prod. for Office of Economic Opportunity: EDMOND A. LEVY, Producer.

Features

THE FACE OF GENIUS, WBZ-TV, Group W, Boston: ALFRED R. KELMAN, Producer.

HELICOPTER CANADA, Centennial Commission, National Film Board of Canada: PETER JONES and TOM DALY, Producers.

LE VOLCAN INTERDIT (THE FORBIDDEN VOLCANO), Cine Documents Tazieff, Athos Films: HAROUN TAZIEFF, Producer.

THE REALLY BIG FAMILY, David L. Wolper, Prod.: ALEX GRASSHOFF, Producer.

★ THE WAR GAME, BBC Prod. for the British Film Institute, Pathé Contemporary Films: PETER WATKINS, Producer.

Foreign Language Film Award

THE BATTLE OF ALGIERS, Igor Film-Casbah Film Production (Italy).

LOVES OF A BLONDE, Barrandov Film Production (Czechoslovakia).

★ A MAN AND A WOMAN, Les Films 13 Production (France).

PHARAOH, Kadr Film Unit Production (Poland).

THREE, Avala Film Production (Yugoslavia).

Honorary Awards

Y. FRANK FREEMAN for unusual and outstanding service to the Academy during his thirty years in Hollywood. (Statuette)

YAKIMA CANUTT for achievements as a stunt man and for developing safety devices to protect stunt men everywhere. (Statuette)

Irving G. Thalberg Memorial Award

ROBERT WISE.

Jean Hersholt Humanitarian Award

GEORGE BAGNALL.

Scientific or Technical

Class I

None.

Class II

MITCHELL CAMERA CORPORATION for the design and development of the Mitchell Mark II 35mm Portable Motion Picture Reflex Camera.

ARNOLD & RICHTER KG for the design and development of the Arriflex 35mm Portable Motion Picture Reflex Camera.

Class III

PANAVISION INCORPORATED for the design of the Panatron Power Inverter and its application to motion picture camera operation.

CARROLL KNUDSON for the production of a composer's manual for motion picture music synchronization.

RUBY RAKSIN for the production of a composer's manual for motion picture music synchronization.

1967

Nominations Announced: February 19, 1968
Awards Ceremony: Postponed from April 8 to April 10, 1968, because of the death of Dr. Martin Luther King, Jr.
Santa Monica Civic Auditorium
(MC: Bob Hope)

Best Picture

BONNIE AND CLYDE, Tatira-Hiller Prod., Warner Bros.-Seven Arts: Warren Beatty, Producer.

DOCTOR DOLITTLE, Apjac Prods., 20th Century-Fox: Arthur P. Jacobs, Producer.

THE GRADUATE, Mike Nichols-Lawrence Turman Prod., Embassy: Lawrence Turman, Producer.

GUESS WHO'S COMING TO DINNER, Columbia: Stanley Kramer, Producer.

★ IN THE HEAT OF THE NIGHT, Mirisch Corp. Prod., United Artists: Walter Mirisch, Producer.

Actor

WARREN BEATTY in *Bonnie and Clyde*, Tatira-Hiller Prod., Warner Bros.-Seven Arts.

DUSTIN HOFFMAN in *The Graduate*, Mike Nichols-Lawrence Turman Prod., Embassy.

PAUL NEWMAN in *Cool Hand Luke*, Jalem Prod., Warner Bros.-Seven Arts.

★ ROD STEIGER in *In the Heat of the Night*, Mirisch Corp. Prod., United Artists.

SPENCER TRACY in *Guess Who's Coming to Dinner*, Columbia.

Actress

ANNE BANCROFT in *The Graduate*, Mike Nichols-Lawrence Turman Prod., Embassy.

FAYE DUNAWAY in *Bonnie and Clyde*, Tatira-Hiller Prod., Warner Bros.-Seven Arts.

DAME EDITH EVANS in *The Whisperers*, Seven Pines Prods., Ltd., United Artists.

AUDREY HEPBURN in *Wait until Dark*, Warner Bros.-Seven Arts.

★ KATHARINE HEPBURN in *Guess Who's Coming to Dinner*, Columbia.

Supporting Actor

JOHN CASSAVETES in *The Dirty Dozen*, MKH Prods., Ltd., Metro-Goldwyn-Mayer.

GENE HACKMAN in *Bonnie and Clyde*, Tatira-Hiller Prod., Warner Bros.-Seven Arts.

CECIL KELLAWAY in *Guess Who's Coming to Dinner*, Columbia.

★ GEORGE KENNEDY in *Cool Hand Luke*, Jalem Prod., Warner Bros.-Seven Arts.

MICHAEL J. POLLARD in *Bonnie and*

Clyde, Tatira-Hiller Prod., Warner Bros.-Seven Arts.

Supporting Actress

CAROL CHANNING in *Thoroughly Modern Millie*, Ross Hunter-Universal Prod., Universal.

MILDRED NATWICK in *Barefoot in the Park*, Hal Wallis Prod., Paramount.

★ ESTELLE PARSONS in *Bonnie and Clyde*, Tatira-Hiller Prod., Warner Bros.-Seven Arts.

BEAH RICHARDS in *Guess Who's Coming to Dinner*, Columbia.

KATHARINE ROSS in *The Graduate*, Mike Nichols-Lawrence Turman Prod., Embassy.

Directing

RICHARD BROOKS for *In Cold Blood*, Pax Enterprises Prod., Columbia.

NORMAN JEWISON for *In the Heat of the Night*, Mirisch Corp. Prod., United Artists.

STANLEY KRAMER for *Guess Who's Coming to Dinner*, Columbia.

★ MIKE NICHOLS for *The Graduate*, Mike Nichols-Lawrence Turman Prod., Embassy.

ARTHUR PENN for *Bonnie and Clyde*, Tatira-Hiller Prod., Warner Bros.-Seven Arts.

Writing

Screenplay—Based on Material from Another Medium

COOL HAND LUKE, Jalem Prod., Warner Bros.-Seven Arts: DONN PEARCE and FRANK R. PIERSON.

THE GRADUATE, Mike Nichols-Lawrence Turman Prod., Embassy: CALDER WILLINGHAM and BUCK HENRY.

IN COLD BLOOD, Pax Enterprises Prod., Columbia: RICHARD BROOKS.

★ IN THE HEAT OF THE NIGHT, Mirisch Corp. Prod., United Artists: STIRLING SILLIPHANT.

ULYSSES, Walter Reade, Jr.-Joseph Strick Prod., Walter Reade-Continental Distributing: JOSEPH STRICK and FRED HAINES.

Story and Screenplay—Written Directly for the Screen

BONNIE AND CLYDE, Tatira-Hiller Prod., Warner Bros.-Seven Arts: DAVID NEWMAN and ROBERT BENTON.

DIVORCE AMERICAN STYLE, Tandem Prods. for National General Prods., Columbia: Story by ROBERT KAUFMAN; Screenplay by NORMAN LEAR.

★ GUESS WHO'S COMING TO DINNER, Columbia: WILLIAM ROSE.

LA GUERRE EST FINIE, Sofracima and Europa-Film Prod., Brandon Films: JORGE SEMPRUN.

TWO FOR THE ROAD, Stanley Donen Films Prod., 20th Century-Fox: FREDERIC RAPHAEL.

Cinematography*

★ BONNIE AND CLYDE, Tatira-Hiller Prod., Warner Bros.-Seven Arts: BURNETT GUFFEY.

CAMELOT, Warner Bros.-Seven Arts: RICHARD H. KLINE.

DOCTOR DOLITTLE, Apjac Prods., 20th Century-Fox: ROBERT SURTEES.

THE GRADUATE, Mike Nichols-Lawrence Turman Prod., Embassy: ROBERT SURTEES.

IN COLD BLOOD, Pax Enterprises Prod., Columbia: CONRAD HALL.

*Rules were changed this year to one Award instead of separate awards for black-and-white and color films.

Art Direction—Set Decoration*

★ CAMELOT, Warner Bros.-Seven Arts: JOHN TRUSCOTT and EDWARD CARRERE; Set Decoration: JOHN W. BROWN.

DOCTOR DOLITTLE, Apjac Prods., 20th Century-Fox: MARIO CHIARI, JACK MARTIN SMITH, and ED GRAVES; Set Decoration: WALTER M. SCOTT and STUART A. REISS.

GUESS WHO'S COMING TO DINNER, Columbia: ROBERT CLATWORTHY; Set Decoration: FRANK TUTTLE.

THE TAMING OF THE SHREW, Royal Films International-Films Artistici Internazionali S.r.L. Prod., Columbia: RENZO MONGIARDINO, JOHN DECUIR, ELVEN WEBB, and GIUSEPPE MARIANI; Set Decoration: DARIO SIMONI and LUIGI GERVASI.

THOROUGHLY MODERN MILLIE, Ross Hunter-Universal Prod., Universal: ALEXANDER GOLITZEN and GEORGE C. WEBB; Set Decoration: HOWARD BRISTOL.

Sound

CAMELOT, Warner Bros.-Seven Arts Studio Sound Department.

THE DIRTY DOZEN, Metro-Goldwyn-Mayer Studio Sound Department.

DOCTOR DOLITTLE, 20th Century-Fox Studio Sound Department.

★ IN THE HEAT OF THE NIGHT, Samuel Goldwyn Studio Sound Department.

THOROUGHLY MODERN MILLIE, Universal City Studio Sound Department.

Film Editing

BEACH RED, Theodora Prods., United Artists: FRANK P. KELLER.

THE DIRTY DOZEN, MKH Prods., Ltd., M-G-M: MICHAEL LUCIANO.

DOCTOR DOLITTLE, Apjac Prods., 20th Century-Fox: SAMUEL E. BEETLEY and MARJORIE FOWLER.

GUESS WHO'S COMING TO DINNER, Columbia: ROBERT C. JONES.

★ IN THE HEAT OF THE NIGHT, Mirisch Corp. Prod., United Artists: HAL ASHBY.

Music

Original Music Score

COOL HAND LUKE, Jalem Prod., Warner Bros.-Seven Arts: LALO SCHIFRIN.

DOCTOR DOLITTLE, Apjac Prods., 20th Century-Fox: LESLIE BRICUSSE.

FAR FROM THE MADDING CROWD, Appia Films, Ltd. Prod., M-G-M: RICHARD RODNEY BENNETT.

IN COLD BLOOD, Pax Enterprises Prod., Columbia: QUINCY JONES.

★ THOROUGHLY MODERN MILLIE, Ross Hunter-Universal Prod., Universal: ELMER BERNSTEIN.

Scoring of Music—Adaptation or Treatment

★ CAMELOT, Warner Bros.-Seven Arts: ALFRED NEWMAN and KEN DARBY.

DOCTOR DOLITTLE, Apjac Productions, 20th Century-Fox: LIONEL NEWMAN and ALEXANDER COURAGE.

GUESS WHO'S COMING TO DINNER, Columbia: DEVOL.

THOROUGHLY MODERN MILLIE, Ross-Hunter-Universal Production, Universal: ANDRÉ PREVIN and JOSEPH GERSHENSON.

VALLEY OF THE DOLLS, Red Lion Prods., 20th Century-Fox: JOHN WILLIAMS.

Song

THE BARE NECESSITIES from *The Jungle Book*, Walt Disney Prods., Buena

*Rules were changed this year to one Award instead of separate awards for black-and-white and color films.

Vista Distribution Co.: Music and Lyrics by TERRY GILKYSON.

THE EYES OF LOVE from *Banning*, Universal: Music by QUINCY JONES; Lyrics by BOB RUSSELL.

THE LOOK OF LOVE from *Casino Royale*, Famous Artists Prods., Ltd., Columbia: Music by BURT BACHARACH; Lyrics by HAL DAVID.

★ TALK TO THE ANIMALS from *Doctor Dolittle*, Apjac Prods., 20th Century-Fox: Music and Lyrics by LESLIE BRICUSSE.

THOROUGHLY MODERN MILLIE from *Thoroughly Modern Millie*, Ross Hunter-Universal Prod., Universal: Music and Lyrics by JAMES VAN HEUSEN and SAMMY CAHN.

*Costume Design**

BONNIE AND CLYDE, Tatira-Hiller Prod., Warner Bros.-Seven Arts: THEADORA VAN RUNKLE.

★ CAMELOT, Warner Bros.-Seven Arts: JOHN TRUSCOTT.

THE HAPPIEST MILLIONAIRE, Walt Disney Prods., Buena Vista Dist. Co.: BILL THOMAS.

THE TAMING OF THE SHREW, Royal Films International-Films Artistici Internazionali S.r.L. Prod., Columbia: IRENE SHARAFF and DANILO DONATI.

THOROUGHLY MODERN MILLIE, Ross Hunter-Universal Prod., Universal: JEAN LOUIS.

Special Visual Effects

★ DOCTOR DOLITTLE, Apjac Prods., 20th Century-Fox: L. B. ABBOTT.

TOBRUK, Gibraltar Prods.-Corman Company-Universal Prod., Universal: HOWARD A. ANDERSON, JR., and ALBERT WHITLOCK.

Sound Effects

(Not given as an Annual Award after this year)

★ THE DIRTY DOZEN, MKH Prods., Ltd., M-G-M: JOHN POYNER.

IN THE HEAT OF THE NIGHT, Mirisch Corp. Prod., UA: JAMES A. RICHARD.

Short Subjects

Cartoons

★ THE BOX, Murakami-Wolf Films, Brandon Films: FRED WOLF, Producer.

HYPOTHESE BETA, Films Orzeaux, Pathé Contemporary Films: JEAN-CHARLES MEUNIER, Producer.

WHAT ON EARTH!, National Film Board of Canada, Columbia: ROBERT VERRALL and WOLF KOENIG, Producers.

Live-Action Subjects

PADDLE TO THE SEA, National Film Board of Canada, Favorite Films: JULIAN BIGGS, Producer.

★ A PLACE TO STAND, T.D.F. Prod. for the Ontario Department of Economics and Development, Columbia: CHRISTOPHER CHAPMAN, Producer.

SKY OVER HOLLAND, John Ferno Prod. for The Netherlands, Seneca International: JOHN FERNO, Producer.

STOP, LOOK AND LISTEN, Metro-Goldwyn-Mayer: LEN JANSON and CHUCK MENVILLE, Producers.

Documentary

Short Subjects

MONUMENT TO THE DREAM, Guggenheim Prods.: CHARLES E. GUGGENHEIM, Producer.

A PLACE TO STAND, T.D.F. Prod. for the Ontario Department of

*Rules were changed this year to one Award for Costume Design instead of separate awards for black-and-white and color films.

Economics and Development: CHRISTOPHER CHAPMAN, Producer.

★ THE REDWOODS, King Screen Prods.: MARK HARRIS and TREVOR GREENWOOD, Producers.

SEE YOU AT THE PILLAR, Associated British-Pathé Prod.: ROBERT FITCHETT, Producer.

WHILE I RUN THIS RACE, Sun Dial Films for VISTA, an Economic Opportunity Program: CARL V. RAGSDALE, Producer.

Features

★ THE ANDERSON PLATOON, French Broadcasting System: PIERRE SCHOENDOERFFER, Producer.

FESTIVAL, Patchke Prods.: MURRAY LERNER, Producer.

HARVEST, United States Information Agency: CARROLL BALLARD, Producer.

A KING'S STORY, Jack Le Vien Prod.: JACK LE VIEN, Producer.

A TIME FOR BURNING, Quest Prods. for Lutheran Film Associates: WILLIAM C. JERSEY, Producer.

Foreign Language Film Award

★ CLOSELY WATCHED TRAINS, Barrandov Film Studio Production (Czechoslovakia).

EL AMOR BRUJO, Films R.B., S.A. Production (Spain).

I EVEN MET HAPPY GYPSIES, Avala Film Production (Yugoslavia).

LIVE FOR LIFE, Les Films Ariane-Les Productions Artistes Associés-Vides Films Production (France).

PORTRAIT OF CHIEKO, Shochiku Co., Ltd. Production (Japan).

Honorary Awards

ARTHUR FREED for distinguished service to the Academy and the production of six top-rated Awards telecasts. (Statuette)

Irving G. Thalberg Memorial Award

ALFRED HITCHCOCK.

Jean Hersholt Humanitarian Award

GREGORY PECK.

Scientific or Technical

Class I

None.

Class II

None.

Class III

ELECTRO-OPTICAL DIVISION of the KOLLMORGEN CORPORATION for the design and development of a series of motion picture projection lenses.

PANAVISION INCORPORATED for a variable-speed motor for motion picture cameras.

FRED R. WILSON of the Samuel Goldwyn Studio Sound Department for an audio level clamper.

WALDON O. WATSON and the UNIVERSAL CITY STUDIO SOUND DEPARTMENT for new concepts in the design of a music scoring stage.

FORTY-FIRST YEAR

1968

Nominations Announced: February 24, 1969
Awards Ceremony: April 14, 1969
Dorothy Chandler Pavilion, Los Angeles County Music Center

Best Picture

FUNNY GIRL, Rastar Prods., Columbia: Ray Stark, Producer.

THE LION IN WINTER, Haworth Prods., Avco Embassy: Martin Poll, Producer.

★ OLIVER!, Romulus Films, Columbia: John Woolf, Producer.

RACHEL, RACHEL, Kayos Prod., Warner Bros.-Seven Arts: Paul Newman, Producer.

ROMEO AND JULIET, B.H.E. Film-Verona Prod.-Dino De Laurentiis Cinematografica Prod., Paramount: Anthony Havelock-Allan and John Brabourne, Producers.

Actor

ALAN ARKIN in *The Heart Is a Lonely Hunter*, Warner Bros.-Seven Arts.

ALAN BATES in *The Fixer*, John Frankenheimer-Edward Lewis Prods., Metro-Goldwyn-Mayer.

RON MOODY in *Oliver!*, Romulus Films, Ltd., Columbia.

PETER O'TOOLE in *The Lion in Winter*, Haworth Prods., Ltd., Avco Embassy.

★ CLIFF ROBERTSON in *Charly*, American Broadcasting Companies-Selmur Pictures Prod., Cinerama.

Actress (tie)

★ KATHARINE HEPBURN in *The Lion in Winter*, Haworth Prods., Ltd., Avco Embassy.

PATRICIA NEAL in *The Subject Was Roses*, Metro-Goldwyn-Mayer.

VANESSA REDGRAVE in *Isadora*, Robert and Raymond Hakim-Universal, Ltd. Prod., Universal.

★ BARBRA STREISAND in *Funny Girl*, Rastar Prods., Columbia.

JOANNE WOODWARD in *Rachel, Rachel*, Kayos Prod., Warner Bros.-Seven Arts.

Supporting Actor

★ JACK ALBERTSON in *The Subject Was Roses*, Metro-Goldwyn-Mayer.

SEYMOUR CASSEL in *Faces*, John Cassavetes Prod., Walter Reade-Continental Distributing.

DANIEL MASSEY in *Star!*, Robert Wise Prod., 20th Century-Fox.

JACK WILD in *Oliver!*, Romulus Films, Ltd., Columbia.

GENE WILDER in *The Producers*, Sidney Glazier Prod., Avco Embassy.

Supporting Actress

LYNN CARLIN in *Faces*, John Cassavetes Prod., Walter Reade-Continental Distributing.

★ RUTH GORDON in *Rosemary's Baby*, William Castle Enterprises Prod., Paramount.

SONDRA LOCKE in *The Heart Is a Lonely Hunter*, Warner Bros.-Seven Arts.

KAY MEDFORD in *Funny Girl*, Rastar Prods., Columbia.
ESTELLE PARSONS in *Rachel, Rachel*, Kayos Prod., Warner Bros.-Seven Arts.

Directing

ANTHONY HARVEY for *The Lion in Winter*, Haworth Prods., Avco Embassy.
STANLEY KUBRICK for 2001: A Space Odyssey, Polaris Prod., Metro-Goldwyn-Mayer.
GILLO PONTECORVO for *The Battle of Algiers*, Igor-Casbah Film Prod., Allied Artists.
⋆ CAROL REED for *Oliver!*, Romulus Films, Columbia.
FRANCO ZEFFIRELLI for *Romeo and Juliet*, B.H.E. Film-Verona Prod.-Dino De Laurentiis Cinematografica Prod., Paramount.

Writing

Screenplay—Based on Material from Another Medium

⋆ THE LION IN WINTER, Haworth Prods., Avco Embassy: JAMES GOLDMAN.
THE ODD COUPLE, Howard W. Koch Prod., Paramount: NEIL SIMON.
OLIVER!, Romulus Films, Columbia: VERNON HARRIS.
RACHEL, RACHEL, Kayos Prod., Warner Bros.-Seven Arts: STEWART STERN.
ROSEMARY'S BABY, William Castle Enterprises Prod., Paramount: ROMAN POLANSKI.

Story and Screenplay—Written Directly for the Screen

THE BATTLE OF ALGIERS, Igor-Casbah Film Prod., Allied Artists: FRANCO SOLINAS and GILLO PONTECORVO.
FACES, John Cassavetes Prod., Walter Reade-Continental Dist.: JOHN CASSAVETES.
HOT MILLIONS, Mildred Freed Albert Prod., Metro-Goldwyn-Mayer: IRA WALLACH and PETER USTINOV.
⋆ THE PRODUCERS, Sidney Glazier Prod., Avco Embassy: MEL BROOKS.
2001: A SPACE ODYSSEY, Polaris Prod., Metro-Goldwyn-Mayer: STANLEY KUBRICK and ARTHUR C. CLARKE.

Cinematography

FUNNY GIRL, Rastar Prods., Columbia: HARRY STRADLING.
ICE STATION ZEBRA, Filmways Prod., Metro-Goldwyn-Mayer: DANIEL L. FAPP.
OLIVER!, Romulus Films, Columbia: OSWALD MORRIS.
⋆ ROMEO AND JULIET, B.H.E. Film-Verona Prod.-Dino De Laurentiis Cinematografica Prod., Paramount: PASQUALINO DE SANTIS.
STAR!, Robert Wise Prod., 20th Century-Fox: ERNEST LASZLO.

Art Direction—Set Decoration

⋆ OLIVER!, Romulus Films, Ltd., Columbia: JOHN BOX and TERENCE MARSH; Set Decoration: VERNON DIXON and KEN MUGGLESTON.
THE SHOES OF THE FISHERMAN, George Englund Prod., Metro-Goldwyn-Mayer: GEORGE W. DAVIS and EDWARD CARFAGNO.
STAR!, Robert Wise Prod., 20th Century-Fox: BORIS LEVEN; Set Decoration: WALTER M. SCOTT and HOWARD BRISTOL.
2001: A SPACE ODYSSEY, Polaris Prod., Metro-Goldwyn-Mayer: TONY MASTERS, HARRY LANGE, and ERNIE ARCHER.
WAR AND PEACE, Mosfilm Prod., Walter Reade-Continental Dist.: MIKHAIL BOGDANOV and GENNADY MYASNIKOV; Set Decoration: G. KOSHELEV and V. UVAROV.

Sound

BULLITT, Warner Bros.-Seven Arts Studio Sound Department.

FINIAN'S RAINBOW, Warner Bros.-Seven Arts Studio Sound Department.

FUNNY GIRL, Columbia Studio Sound Department.

★ OLIVER!, Shepperton Studio Sound Department.

STAR!, 20th Century-Fox Studio Sound Department.

Film Editing

★ BULLITT, Solar Prod., Warner Bros.-Seven Arts: FRANK P. KELLER.

FUNNY GIRL, Rastar Prods., Columbia: ROBERT SWINK, MAURY WINETROBE, and WILLIAM SANDS.

THE ODD COUPLE, Howard W. Koch Prod., Paramount: FRANK BRACHT.

OLIVER!, Romulus Films, Columbia: RALPH KEMPLEN.

WILD IN THE STREETS, American International: FRED FEITSHANS and EVE NEWMAN.

Music

Original Score—for a Motion Picture (not a musical)

THE FOX, Raymond Stross-Motion Pictures International Prod., Claridge Pictures: LALO SCHIFRIN.

★ THE LION IN WINTER, Haworth Prods., Ltd., Avco Embassy: JOHN BARRY.

PLANET OF THE APES, Apjac Prods., 20th Century-Fox: JERRY GOLDSMITH.

THE SHOES OF THE FISHERMAN, George Englund Prod., Metro-Goldwyn-Mayer: ALEX NORTH.

THE THOMAS CROWN AFFAIR, Mirisch-Simkoe-Solar Prod., United Artists: MICHEL LEGRAND.

Score of a Musical Picture (original or adaptation)

FINIAN'S RAINBOW, Warner Bros.-Seven Arts: Adapted by RAY HEINDORF.

FUNNY GIRL, Rastar Prods., Columbia: Adapted by WALTER SCHARF.

★ OLIVER!, Romulus Films, Columbia: Adapted by JOHN GREEN.

STAR!, Robert Wise Prod., 20th Century-Fox: Adapted by LENNIE HAYTON.

THE YOUNG GIRLS OF ROCHEFORT, Mag Bodard-Gilbert de Goldschmidt-Parc Film-Madeleine Films Prod., Warner Bros.-Seven Arts: MICHEL LEGRAND and JACQUES DEMY.

Song

CHITTY CHITTY BANG BANG from *Chitty Chitty Bang Bang*, Warfield Prods., United Artists: Music and Lyrics by RICHARD M. SHERMAN and ROBERT B. SHERMAN.

FOR LOVE OF IVY from *For Love of Ivy*, American Broadcasting Companies-Palomar Pictures International Prod., Cinerama: Music by QUINCY JONES; Lyrics by BOB RUSSELL.

FUNNY GIRL from *Funny Girl*, Rastar Prods., Columbia: Music by JULE STYNE; Lyrics by BOB MERRILL.

STAR! from *Star!*, Robert Wise Prod., 20th Century-Fox: Music by JIMMY VAN HEUSEN; Lyrics by SAMMY CAHN.

★ THE WINDMILLS OF YOUR MIND from *The Thomas Crown Affair*, Mirisch-Simkoe-Solar Prod., United Artists: Music by MICHEL LEGRAND; Lyrics by ALAN BERGMAN and MARILYN BERGMAN.

Costume Design

THE LION IN WINTER, Haworth Prods., Avco Embassy: MARGARET FURSE.

OLIVER!, Romulus Films, Columbia: PHYLLIS DALTON.

PLANET OF THE APES, Apjac Prods., 20th Century-Fox: MORTON HAACK.

★ ROMEO AND JULIET, B.H.E.

Film-Verona Prod.-Dino De Laurentiis Cinematografica Prod., Paramount: DANILO DONATI.

STAR!, Robert Wise Prod., 20th Century-Fox: DONALD BROOKS.

Special Visual Effects

ICE STATION ZEBRA, Filmways Prod., Metro-Goldwyn-Mayer: HAL MILLAR and J. MCMILLAN JOHNSON.

★ 2001: A SPACE ODYSSEY, Polaris Prod., Metro-Goldwyn-Mayer: STANLEY KUBRICK.

Short Subjects

Cartoons

THE HOUSE THAT JACK BUILT, National Film Board of Canada, Columbia: WOLF KOENIG and JIM MACKAY, Producers.

THE MAGIC PEAR TREE, Murakami-Wolf Prods., Bing Crosby Prods.: JIMMY MURAKAMI, Producer.

WINDY DAY, Hubley Studios, Paramount: JOHN HUBLEY and FAITH HUBLEY, Producers.

★ WINNIE THE POOH AND THE BLUSTERY DAY, Walt Disney Prods., Buena Vista Dist.: WALT DISNEY, Producer.

Live-Action Subjects

THE DOVE, Coe-Davis, Schoenfeld Film Dist.: GEORGE COE, SIDNEY DAVIS, and ANTHONY LOVER, Producers.

DUO, NATIONAL FILM BOARD OF CANADA, Columbia.

PRELUDE, Prelude Company, Excelsior Dist.: JOHN ASTIN, Producer.

★ ROBERT KENNEDY REMEMBERED, Guggenheim Prods., National General: CHARLES GUGGENHEIM, Producer.

Documentary

Short Subjects

THE HOUSE THAT ANANDA BUILT, Films Division, Government of India: FALI BILIMORIA, Producer.

THE REVOLVING DOOR, Vision Associates for the American Foundation Institute of Corrections: LEE R. BOBKER, Producer.

A SPACE TO GROW, Office of Economic Opportunity for Project Upward Bound: THOMAS P. KELLY, JR., Producer.

A WAY OUT OF THE WILDERNESS, John Sutherland Prods.: DAN E. WEISBURD, Producer.

★ WHY MAN CREATES, Saul Bass and Associates: SAUL BASS, Producer.

Features

A FEW NOTES ON OUR FOOD PROBLEM, United States Information Agency: JAMES BLUE, Producer.

★ JOURNEY INTO SELF, Western Behavioral Sciences Institute: BILL McGAW, Producer.

THE LEGENDARY CHAMPIONS, Turn of the Century Fights: WILLIAM CAYTON, Producer.

OTHER VOICES, DHS Films: DAVID H. SAWYER, Producer.

YOUNG AMERICANS, The Young Americans Prod.: ROBERT COHN and ALEX GRASSHOFF, Producers.*

Foreign Language Film Award

THE BOYS OF PAUL STREET, Bohgros Films-Mafilm Studio I Production (Hungary).

THE FIREMEN'S BALL, Barrandov Film Studio Production (Czechoslovakia).

THE GIRL WITH THE PISTOL, Documento Film Production (Italy).

*_Young Americans_ won the award, but it was later declared ineligible because it had been released prior to the eligibility year. On May 8, 1969, the first runner-up, _Journey into Self_, was declared the winner.

STOLEN KISSES, Les Films du Carrosse-Les Productions Artistes Associés Production (France).
★ WAR AND PEACE, Mosfilm Production U.S.S.R.

Honorary Awards

JOHN CHAMBERS for his outstanding make-up achievement in *Planet of the Apes*. (Statuette)
ONNA WHITE for her outstanding choreography achievement in *Oliver!*. (Statuette)

Irving G. Thalberg Memorial Award

None.

Jean Hersholt Humanitarian Award

MARTHA RAYE.

Scientific or Technical

Class I

PHILIP V. PALMQUIST of MINNESOTA MINING AND MANUFACTURING CO., DR. HERBERT MEYER of the Motion Picture and Television Research Center, and CHARLES D. STAFFELL of the Rank Organisation for the development of a successful embodiment of the reflex background projection system for composite cinematography.
EASTMAN KODAK COMPANY for the development and introduction of a color reversal intermediate film for motion pictures.

Class II

DONALD W. NORWOOD for the design and development of the Norwood photographic exposure meters.
EASTMAN KODAK COMPANY and PRODUCERS SERVICE COMPANY for the development of a new, high-speed, step-optical reduction printer.
EDMUND M. DiGIULIO, NIELS G. PETERSEN, and NORMAN S. HUGHES of the Cinema Product Development Company for the design and application of a conversion that makes available the reflex viewing system for motion picture cameras.
OPTICAL COATING LABORATORIES, INC., for the development of an improved antireflection coating for photographic and projection lens systems.
EASTMAN KODAK COMPANY for the introduction of a new, high-speed motion picture color negative film.
PANAVISION INCORPORATED for the conception, design, and introduction of a 65mm hand-held motion picture camera.
TODD-AO COMPANY and the MITCHELL CAMERA COMPANY for the design and engineering of the Todd-AO hand-held motion picture camera.

Class III

CARL W. HAUGE and EDWARD H. REICHARD of Consolidated Film Industries and E. MICHAEL MEAHL and ROY J. RIDENOUR of Ramtronics for engineering an automatic exposure control for printing-machine lamps.
EASTMAN KODAK COMPANY for a new direct positive film and to CONSOLIDATED FILM INDUSTRIES for the application of this film to the making of postproduction work prints.

1969

Nominations Announced: February 16, 1970
Awards Ceremony: April 7, 1970
Dorothy Chandler Pavilion, Los Angeles County Music Center

Best Picture

ANNE OF THE THOUSAND DAYS, Hal B. Wallis-Universal Pictures, Ltd. Prod. Universal: Hal B. Wallis, Producer.

BUTCH CASSIDY AND THE SUNDANCE KID, George Roy Hill-Paul Monash Prod., 20th Century-Fox: John Foreman, Producer.

HELLO, DOLLY!, Chenault Productions, 20th Century-Fox: Ernest Lehman, Producer.

★ MIDNIGHT COWBOY, Jerome Hellman-John Schlesinger Prod., United Artists: Jerome Hellman, Producer.

Z, Reggane Films-O.N.C.I.C. Production, Cinema V: Jacques Perrin and Hamed Rachedi, Producers.

Actor

RICHARD BURTON in *Anne of the Thousand Days*, Hal B. Wallis-Universal Pictures, Ltd. Prod., Universal.

DUSTIN HOFFMAN in *Midnight Cowboy*, Jerome Hellman-John Schlesinger Prod., United Artists.

PETER O'TOOLE in *Goodbye, Mr. Chips*, Apjac Prod., Metro-Goldwyn-Mayer.

JON VOIGHT in *Midnight Cowboy*, Jerome Hellman-John Schlesinger Prod., United Artists.

★ JOHN WAYNE in *True Grit*, Hal Wallis Prod., Paramount.

Actress

GENEVIEVE BUJOLD in *Anne of the Thousand Days*, Hal B. Wallis-Universal Pictures, Ltd. Prod., Universal.

JANE FONDA in *They Shoot Horses, Don't They?*, Chartoff-Winkler-Pollack Prod., ABC Pictures Presentation, Cinerama.

LIZA MINNELLI in *The Sterile Cuckoo*, Boardwalk Prods., Paramount.

JEAN SIMMONS in *The Happy Ending*, Pax Films Prod., United Artists.

★ MAGGIE SMITH in *The Prime of Miss Jean Brodie*, 20th Century-Fox Prods., Ltd., 20th Century-Fox.

Supporting Actor

RUPERT CROSSE in *The Reivers*, Irving Ravetch-Arthur Kramer-Solar Prods., Cinema Center Films Presentation, National General.

ELLIOTT GOULD in *Bob & Carol & Ted & Alice*, Frankovich Prods., Columbia.

JACK NICHOLSON in *Easy Rider*, Pando-Raybert Prods., Columbia.

ANTHONY QUAYLE in *Anne of the Thousand Days*, Hal B. Wallis-Universal Pictures, Ltd. Prod., Universal.

★ GIG YOUNG in *They Shoot Horses, Don't They?*, Chartoff-Winkler-Pollack Prod., ABC Pictures Presentation, Cinerama.

Supporting Actress

CATHERINE BURNS in *Last Summer*, Frank Perry-Alsid Prod., Allied Artists.

DYAN CANNON in *Bob & Carol & Ted & Alice*, Frankovich Prods., Columbia.

★ GOLDIE HAWN in *Cactus Flower*, Frankovich Prods., Columbia.

SYLVIA MILES in *Midnight Cowboy*, A Jerome Hellman-John Schlesinger Prod., United Artists.

SUSANNAH YORK in *They Shoot Horses, Don't They?*, Chartoff-Winkler-Pollack Prod., ABC Pictures Presentation, Cinerama.

Directing

COSTA-GAVRAS for Z, Reggane Films-O.N.C.I.C. Prod., Cinema V.

GEORGE ROY HILL for *Butch Cassidy and the Sundance Kid*, George Roy Hill-Paul Monash Prod., 20th Century-Fox.

ARTHUR PENN for *Alice's Restaurant*, Florin Prod., United Artists.

SYDNEY POLLACK for *They Shoot Horses, Don't They?*, Chartoff-Winkler-Pollack Prod., ABC Pictures Presentation, Cinerama.

★ JOHN SCHLESINGER for *Midnight Cowboy*, Jerome Hellman-John Schlesinger Prod., United Artists.

Writing

Screenplay—Based on Material from Another Medium

ANNE OF THE THOUSAND DAYS, Hal B. Wallis-Universal Pictures, Ltd. Prod., Universal: JOHN HALE and BRIDGET BOLAND; Adaptation by RICHARD SOKOLOVE.

GOODBYE, COLUMBUS, Willow Tree Prods., Paramount: ARNOLD SCHULMAN.

★ MIDNIGHT COWBOY, Jerome Hellman-John Schlesinger Prod., United Artists: WALDO SALT.

THEY SHOOT HORSES, DON'T THEY?, Chartoff-Winkler-Pollack Prod., ABC Pictures Presentation, Cinerama: JAMES POE and ROBERT E. THOMPSON.

Z, Reggane Films-O.N.C.I.C. Prod., Cinema V: JORGE SEMPRUN and COSTA-GAVRAS.

Story and Screenplay—Based on Material Not Previously Published or Produced.

BOB & CAROL & TED & ALICE, Frankovich Prods., Columbia: PAUL MAZURSKY and LARRY TUCKER.

★ BUTCH CASSIDY AND THE SUNDANCE KID, George Roy Hill-Paul Monash Prod., 20th Century-Fox: WILLIAM GOLDMAN.

THE DAMNED, Pegaso-Praesidens Film Prod., Warner Bros.: Story by NICOLA BADALUCCO; Screenplay by NICOLA BADALUCCO, ENRICO MEDIOLI, and LUCHINO VISCONTI.

EASY RIDER, Pando-Raybert Prods., Columbia: PETER FONDA, DENNIS HOPPER, and TERRY SOUTHERN.

THE WILD BUNCH, Phil Feldman Prod., Warner Bros.: Story by WALON GREEN and ROY N. SICKNER; Screenplay by WALON GREEN and SAM PECKINPAH.

Cinematography

ANNE OF THE THOUSAND DAYS, Hal B. Wallis-Universal Pictures, Ltd. Prod., Universal: ARTHUR IBBETSON.

BOB & CAROL & TED & ALICE, Frankovich Prods., Columbia: CHARLES B. LANG.

★ BUTCH CASSIDY AND THE SUNDANCE KID, George Roy Hill-Paul Monash Prod., 20th Century-Fox: CONRAD HALL.

HELLO, DOLLY!, Chenault Prods., 20th Century-Fox: HARRY STRADLING.

MAROONED, Frankovich-Sturges Prod., Columbia: DANIEL FAPP.

Art Direction—Set Decoration

ANNE OF THE THOUSAND DAYS, Hal B. Wallis-Universal Pictures, Ltd. Prod., Universal: MAURICE CARTER and LIONEL COUCH; Set Decoration: PATRICK MCLOUGHLIN.

GAILY, GAILY, Mirisch-Cartier Prod., United Artists: ROBERT BOYLE and GEORGE B. CHAN; Set Decoration: EDWARD BOYLE and CARL BIDDISCOMBE.

★ HELLO, DOLLY!, Chenault Prods., 20th Century-Fox: JOHN DeCUIR, JACK MARTIN SMITH, and HERMAN BLUMENTHAL; Set Decoration: WALTER M. SCOTT, GEORGE HOPKINS, and RAPHAEL BRETTON.

SWEET CHARITY, Universal: ALEXANDER GOLITZEN and GEORGE C. WEBB; Set Decoration: JACK D. MOORE.

THEY SHOOT HORSES, DON'T THEY?, Chartoff-Winkler-Pollack Prod., ABC Pictures Presentation, Cinerama: HARRY HORNER; Set Decoration: FRANK MCKELVY.

Sound

ANNE OF THE THOUSAND DAYS, Hal B. Wallis-Universal Pictures, Ltd. Prod., Universal: JOHN ALDRED.

BUTCH CASSIDY AND THE SUNDANCE KID, George Roy Hil-Paul Monash Prod., 20th Century-Fox: WILLIAM EDMUNDSON and DAVID DOCKENDORF.

GAILY, GAILY, Mirisch-Cartier Production, United Artists: ROBERT MARTIN and CLEM PORTMAN.

★ HELLO, DOLLY!, Chenault Productions, 20th Century-Fox: JACK SOLOMON and MURRAY SPIVACK.

MAROONED, Frankovich-Sturges Production, Columbia: LES FRESHOLTZ and ARTHUR PIANTADOSI.

Film Editing

HELLO, DOLLY!, Chenault Prods., 20th Century-Fox: WILLIAM REYNOLDS.

MIDNIGHT COWBOY, Jerome Hellman-John Schlesinger Prod., United Artists: HUGH A. ROBERTSON.

THE SECRET OF SANTA VITTORIA, Stanley Kramer Company Prod., United Artists: WILLIAM LYON and EARLE HERDAN.

THEY SHOOT HORSES, DON'T THEY!, Chartoff-Winkler-Pollack Prod., ABC Pictures Presentation, Cinerama: FREDRIC STEINKAMP.

★ Z, Reggane Films-O.N.C.I.C. Prod., Cinema V: FRANÇOISE BONNOT.

Music

Original Score for a Motion Picture (not a musical)

ANNE OF THE THOUSAND DAYS, Hal B. Wallis-Universal Pictures, Ltd. Prod., Universal: GEORGES DELERUE.

★ BUTCH CASSIDY AND THE SUNDANCE KID, George Roy Hill-Paul Monash Prod., 20th Century-Fox: BURT BACHARACH.

THE REIVERS, Irving Ravetch-Arthur Kramer-Solar Prods., Cinema Center Films Presentation, National General: JOHN WILLIAMS.

THE SECRET OF SANTA VITTORIA, Stanley Kramer Company Prod., United Artists: ERNEST GOLD.

THE WILD BUNCH, Phil Feldman Prod., Warner Bros.: JERRY FIELDING.

Score of a Musical Picture (original or adaptation)

GOODBYE, MR. CHIPS, Apjac Prod., Metro-Goldwyn-Mayer: Music and Lyrics by LESLIE BRICUSSE; Adapted by JOHN WILLIAMS.

★ HELLO, DOLLY!, Chenault Prods.,

20th Century-Fox: Adapted by LENNIE HAYTON and LIONEL NEWMAN.

PAINT YOUR WAGON, Alan Jay Lerner Prod., Paramount; Adapted by NELSON RIDDLE.

SWEET CHARITY, Universal: Adapted by CY COLEMAN.

THEY SHOOT HORSES, DON'T THEY?, Chartoff-Winkler-Pollack Prod., ABC Pictures Presentation, Cinerama: Adapted by JOHN GREEN and ALBERT WOODBURY.

Song

COME SATURDAY MORNING from *The Sterile Cuckoo*, Boardwalk Prods., Paramount: Music by FRED KARLIN; Lyrics by DORY PREVIN.

JEAN from *The Prime of Miss Jean Brodie*, 20th Century-Fox Prods., Ltd., 20th Century-Fox: Music and lyrics by ROD MCKUEN.

★ RAINDROPS KEEP FALLIN' ON MY HEAD from *Butch Cassidy and the Sundance Kid*, George Roy Hill-Paul Monash Prod., 20th Century-Fox: Music by BURT BACHARACH; Lyrics by HAL DAVID.

TRUE GRIT from *True Grit*, Hal Wallis Prod., Paramount: Music by ELMER BERNSTEIN; Lyrics by DON BLACK.

WHAT ARE YOU DOING THE REST OF YOUR LIFE? from *The Happy Ending*, Pax Films Prod., United Artists: Music by MICHEL LEGRAND; Lyrics by ALAN BERGMAN and MARILYN BERGMAN.

Costume Design

★ ANNE OF THE THOUSAND DAYS, Hal B. Wallis-Universal Pictures, Ltd. Prod., Universal: MARGARET FURSE.

GAILY, GAILY, Mirisch-Cartier Prod., United Artists: RAY AGHAYAN.

HELLO, DOLLY!, Chenault Prods., 20th Century-Fox: IRENE SHARAFF.

SWEET CHARITY, Universal: EDITH HEAD.

THEY SHOOT HORSES, DON'T THEY?, Chartoff-Winkler-Pollack Prod., ABC Pictures Presentation, Cinerama: DONFELD.

Special Visual Effects

KRAKATOA, EAST OF JAVA, American Broadcasting Companies-Cinerama Prod., Cinerama: EUGENE LOURIE and ALEX WELDON.

★ MAROONED; Frankovich-Sturges Prod., Columbia: ROBBIE ROBERTSON.

Short Subjects

Cartoons

★ IT'S TOUGH TO BE A BIRD, Walt Disney Prods., Buena Vista Dist.: WARD KIMBALL, Producer.

OF MEN AND DEMONS, Hubley Studios, Paramount: JOHN HUBLEY and FAITH HUBLEY, Producers.

WALKING, National Film Board of Canada, Columbia: RYAN LARKIN, Producer.

Live-Action Subjects

BLAKE, National Film Board of Canada, Vaudeo Inc.: DOUG JACKSON, Producer.

★ THE MAGIC MACHINES, Fly-by-Night Prods., Manson Distributing: JOAN KELLER STERN, Producer.

PEOPLE SOUP, Pangloss Prods., Columbia: MARC MERSON, Producer.

Documentary

Short Subjects

★ CZECHOSLOVAKIA 1968, Sanders-Fresco Film Makers for United States Information Agency: DENIS SANDERS and ROBERT M. FRESCO, Producers.

AN IMPRESSION OF JOHN STEINBECK: WRITER, Donald Wrye Prods. for United States Information Agency: DONALD WRYE, Producer.

JENNY IS A GOOD THING, A.C.I Prod. for Project Head Start: JOAN HORVATH, Producer.

LEO BEUERMAN, Centron Prod.: ARTHUR H. WOLF and RUSSELL A. MOSSER, Producers.

THE MAGIC MACHINES, Fly-by-Night Prods.: JOAN KELLER STERN, Producer.

Features

★ ARTHUR RUBINSTEIN—THE LOVE OF LIFE, Midem Prod.: BERNARD CHEVRY, Producer.

BEFORE THE MOUNTAIN WAS MOVED, Robert K. Sharpe Prods. for the Office of Economic Opportunity: ROBERT K. SHARPE, Producer.

IN THE YEAR OF THE PIG, Emile de Antonio Prod.: EMILE DE ANTONIO, Producer.

THE OLYMPICS IN MEXICO, Film Section of the Organizing Committee for the XIX Olympic Games.

THE WOLF MEN, MGM Documentary: IRWIN ROSTEN, Producer.

Foreign Language Film Award

ADALEN '31, AB Svensk Filmindustri Production (Sweden).

THE BATTLE OF NERETVA, United Film Producers-Igor Film-Eichberg Film-Commonwealth United Production (Yugoslavia).

THE BROTHERS KARAMAZOV, Mosfilm Production (U.S.S.R.).

MY NIGHT AT MAUD'S, Films du Losange-F.F.P-Films du Carrosse-Films des Deux Mondes-Films de la Pleiade-Gueville-Renn-Simar Films Production (France).

★ Z, Reggane-O.N.C.I.C. Production (Algeria).

Honorary Award

CARY GRANT for his unique mastery of the art of screen acting with the respect and affection of his colleagues. (Statuette)

Irving G. Thalberg Memorial Award

None.

Jean Hersholt Humanitarian Award

GEORGE JESSEL.

Scientific or Technical

Class I

None.

Class II

HAZELTINE CORPORATION for the design and development of the Hazeltine Color Film Analyzer.

FOUAD SAID for the design and introduction of the Cinemobile series of equipment trucks for location motion picture production.

JUAN DE LA CIERVA and DYNASCIENCES CORPORATION for the design and development of the Dynalens optical-image motion compensator.

Class III

OTTO POPELKA of Magna-Tech Electronics Co., Inc., for the development of an electronically controlled looping system.

FENTON HAMILTON of Metro-Goldwyn-Mayer Studios for the concept and engineering of a mobile battery power unit for location lighting.

PANAVISION INCORPORATED for the design and development of the Panaspeed Motion Picture Camera Motor.

ROBERT M. FLYNN and RUSSELL HESSY of Universal City Studios, Inc., for a machine-gun modification for motion picture photography.

FORTY-THIRD YEAR

1970

Nominations Announced: February 22, 1971
Awards Ceremony: April 15, 1971
Dorothy Chandler Pavilion, Los Angeles County Music Center

Best Picture

AIRPORT, Ross-Hunter-Universal Prod., Universal: Ross Hunter, Producer.

FIVE EASY PIECES, BBS Prods., Columbia: Bob Rafelson and Richard Wechsler, Producers.

LOVE STORY, The Love Story Company Prod., Paramount: Howard G. Minsky, Producer.

MASH, Aspen Prods., 20th Century-Fox: Ingo Preminger, Producer.

★ PATTON, 20th Century-Fox: Frank McCarthy, Producer.

Actor

MELVYN DOUGLAS in *I Never Sang for My Father*, Jamel Prods., Columbia.

JAMES EARL JONES in *The Great White Hope*, Lawrence Turman Films Prod., 20th Century-Fox.

JACK NICHOLSON in *Five Easy Pieces*, BBS Prods., Columbia.

RYAN O'NEAL in *Love Story*, The Love Story Company Prod., Paramount.

★ GEORGE C. SCOTT in *Patton*, 20th Century-Fox.

Actress

JANE ALEXANDER in *The Great White Hope*, Lawrence Turman Films Prod., 20th Century-Fox.

★ GLENDA JACKSON in *Women in Love*, Larry Kramer-Martin Rosen Prod., United Artists.

ALI MACGRAW in *Love Story*, The Love Story Company Prod., Paramount.

SARAH MILES in *Ryan's Daughter*, Faraway Prods., Metro-Goldwyn-Mayer.

CARRIE SNODGRESS in *Diary of a Mad Housewife*, Frank Perry Films Prod., Universal.

Supporting Actor

RICHARD CASTELLANO in *Lovers and Other Strangers*, ABC Pictures Prod., Cinerama.

CHIEF DAN GEORGE in *Little Big Man*, Hiller Prods., Ltd.-Stockbridge Prods., Cinema Center Films Presentation, National General.

GENE HACKMAN in *I Never Sang for My Father*, Jamel Prods., Columbia.

JOHN MARLEY in *Love Story*, The Love Story Company Prod., Paramount.

★ JOHN MILLS in *Ryan's Daughter*, Faraway Prods., Metro-Goldwyn-Mayer.

Supporting Actress

KAREN BLACK in *Five Easy Pieces*, BBS Prods., Columbia.

LEE GRANT in *The Landlord*, A Mirisch-Cartier II Prod., United Artists.

★ HELEN HAYES in *Airport*, Ross-Hunter-Universal Prod., Universal.

SALLY KELLERMAN in *MASH*, Aspen Prods., 20th Century-Fox.

MAUREEN STAPLETON in *Airport*, Ross Hunter-Universal Prod., Universal.

Directing

ROBERT ALTMAN for *MASH*, Aspen Prods., 20th Century-Fox.

FEDERICO FELLINI for *Fellini Satyricon*, Alberto Grimaldi Prod., United Artists.

ARTHUR HILLER for *Love Story*, The Love Story Company Prod., United Artists.

KEN RUSSELL for *Women in Love*, Larry Kramer-Martin Rosen Prod., United Artists.

★ FRANKLIN J. SCHAFFNER for *Patton*, 20th Century-Fox.

Writing

Screenplay—Based on Material from Another Medium

AIRPORT, Ross Hunter-Universal Prod., Universal: GEORGE SEATON.

I NEVER SANG FOR MY FATHER, Jamel Prods., Columbia: ROBERT ANDERSON.

LOVERS AND OTHER STRANGERS, ABC Pictures Prod., Cinerama: RENEE TAYLOR, JOSEPH BOLOGNA, and DAVID ZELAG GOODMAN.

★ MASH, Aspen Prods., 20th Century-Fox: RING LARDNER, JR.

WOMEN IN LOVE, Larry Kramer-Martin Rosen Prod., United Artists: LARRY KRAMER.

Story and Screenplay—Based on Factual Material or Material Not Previously Published or Produced

FIVE EASY PIECES, BBS Prods., Columbia: Story by BOB RAFELSON and ADRIEN JOYCE; Screenplay by ADRIEN JOYCE.

JOE, Group Prod., Cannon Releasing: NORMAN WEXLER.

LOVE STORY, The Love Story Company Prod., Paramount: ERICH SEGAL.

MY NIGHT AT MAUD'S, Films du Losange-Carrosse-Renn-Deux Mondes-La Gueville-Simar-La Pleiade-F.F.P. Prod., Pathé Contemporary: ERIC ROHMER.

★ PATTON, 20th Century-Fox: FRANCIS FORD COPPOLA and EDMUND H. NORTH.

Cinematography

AIRPORT, Ross Hunter-Universal Prod., Universal: ERNEST LASZLO.

PATTON, 20th Century-Fox: FRED KOENEKAMP.

★ RYAN'S DAUGHTER, Faraway Prods., Metro-Goldwyn-Mayer: FREDDIE YOUNG.

TORA! TORA! TORA!, 20th Century-Fox: CHARLES F. WHEELER, OSAMI FURUYA, SINSAKU HIMEDA, and MASAMICHI SATOH.

WOMEN IN LOVE, Larry Kramer-Martin Rosen Prod., United Artists: BILLY WILLIAMS.

Art Direction—Set Decoration

AIRPORT, Ross Hunter-Universal Prod., Universal: ALEXANDER GOLITZEN and E. PRESTON AMES; Set Decoration: JACK D. MOORE and MICKEY S. MICHAELS.

THE MOLLY MAGUIRES, Tamm Prods., Paramount: TAMBI LARSEN; Set Decoration: DARRELL SILVERA.

★ PATTON, 20th Century-Fox: URIE McCLEARY and GIL PARRONDO; Set Decoration: ANTONIO MATEOS and PIERRE-LOUIS THEVENET.

SCROOGE, Waterbury Films, Ltd. Prod., Cinema Center Films Presentation, National General: TERRY MARSH and BOB CARTWRIGHT; Set Decoration PAMELA CORNELL.

TORA! TORA! TORA!, 20th Century-Fox: JACK MARTIN SMITH, YOSHIRO MURAKI, RICHARD DAY, and TAIZOH KAWASHIMA; Set Decoration:

WALTER M. SCOTT, NORMAN ROCKETT, and CARL BIDDISCOMBE.

Sound

AIRPORT, Ross Hunter-Universal Prod., Universal: RONALD PIERCE and DAVID MORIARTY.

★ PATTON, 20th Century-Fox: DOUGLAS WILLIAMS and DON BASSMAN.

RYAN'S DAUGHTER, Faraway Prods., Metro-Goldwyn-Mayer: GORDON K. MCCALLUM and JOHN BRAMALL.

TORA! TORA! TORA!, 20th Century-Fox: MURRAY SPIVACK and HERMAN LEWIS.

WOODSTOCK, Wadleigh-Maurice, Ltd. Prod., Warner Bros.: DAN WALLIN and LARRY JOHNSON.

Film Editing

AIRPORT, Ross Hunter-Universal Prod., Universal: STUART GILMORE.

MASH, Aspen Prods., 20th Century-Fox: DANFORD B. GREENE.

★ PATTON, 20th Century-Fox: HUGH S. FOWLER.

TORA! TORA! TORA!, 20th Century-Fox: JAMES E. NEWCOM, PEMBROKE J. HERRING, and INOUE CHIKAYA.

WOODSTOCK, Wadleigh-Maurice, Ltd. Prod., Warner Bros.: THELMA SCHOONMAKER.

Music

Original Score

AIRPORT, Ross Hunter-Universal Prod., Universal: ALFRED NEWMAN.

CROMWELL, Irving Allen, Ltd. Prod., Columbia: FRANK CORDELL.

★ LOVE STORY, The Love Story Company Prod., Paramount: FRANCIS LAI.

PATTON, 20th Century-Fox: JERRY GOLDSMITH.

SUNFLOWER, Sostar Prod., Avco Embassy: HENRY MANCINI.

Original Song Score

THE BABY MAKER, Robert Wise Prod., National General: Music by FRED KARLIN; Lyrics by TYLWYTH KYMRY.

A BOY NAMED CHARLIE BROWN, Lee Mendelson-Melendez Features Prod., Cinema Center Films Presentation, National General: Music by ROD MCKUEN and JOHN SCOTT TROTTER; Lyrics by ROD MCKUEN, BILL MELENDEZ, and AL SHEAN; Adapted by VINCE GUARALDI.

DARLING LILI, Geoffrey Prods., Paramount: Music by HENRI MANCINI; Lyrics by JOHNNY MERCER.

★ LET IT BE, Beatles-Apple Prod., United Artists: Music and Lyrics by THE BEATLES.

SCROOGE, Waterbury Films, Ltd. Prod., Cinema Center Films Presentation, National General: Music and Lyrics by LESLIE BRICUSSE; Adapted by IAN FRASER and HERBERT W. SPENCER.

Song

FOR ALL WE KNOW from *Lovers and Other Strangers*, ABC Pictures Prod., Cinerama: Music by FRED KARLIN; Lyrics by ROBB ROYER and JAMES GRIFFIN (a.k.a. ROBB WILSON and ARTHUR JAMES).

PIECES OF DREAMS from *Pieces of Dreams*, RFB Enterprises Prod., United Artists: Music by MICHEL LEGRAND; Lyrics by ALAN BERGMAN and MARILYN BERGMAN.

THANK YOU VERY MUCH from *Scrooge*, Waterbury Films, Ltd. Prod., Cinema Center Films Presentation, National General: Music and Lyrics by LESLIE BRICUSSE.

TILL LOVE TOUCHES YOUR LIFE from *Madron*, Edric-Isracine-Zev Braun Prods., Four Star-Excelsior Releasing: Music by RIZ ORTOLANI; Lyrics by ARTHUR HAMILTON.

WHISTLING AWAY THE DARK from *Darling Lili*, Geoffrey Prods.,

Paramount: Music by HENRI MANCINI; Lyrics by JOHNNY MERCER.

Costume Design

AIRPORT, Ross Hunter-Universal Prod., Universal: EDITH HEAD.

★ CROMWELL, Irving Allen, Ltd. Prod., Columbia: NINO NOVARESE.

DARLING LILI, Geoffrey Prods., Paramount: DONALD BROOKS and JACK BEAR.

THE HAWAIIANS, Mirisch Prods., United Artists: BILL THOMAS.

SCROOGE, Waterbury Films, Ltd. Prod., Cinema Center Films Presentation, National General: MARGARET FURSE.

Special Visual Effects

PATTON, 20th Century-Fox: ALEX WELDON.

★ TORA! TORA! TORA!, 20th Century-Fox: A. D. FLOWERS and L. B. ABBOTT.

Short Subjects

Cartoons

THE FURTHER ADVENTURES OF UNCLE SAM: PART TWO, The Haboush Company, Goldstone Films: ROBERT MITCHELL and DALE CASE, Producers.

★ IS IT ALWAYS RIGHT TO BE RIGHT?, Stephen Bosustow Prods., Lester A. Schoenfeld Films: NICK BOSUSTOW, Producer.

THE SHEPHERD, Cameron Guess and Associates, Brandon Films: CAMERON GUESS, Producer.

Live-Action Subjects

★ THE RESURRECTION OF BRONCHO BILLY, University of Southern California, Department of Cinema, Universal: JOHN LONGENECKER, Producer.

SHUT UP . . . I'M CRYING, Robert Siegler Prods., Lester A. Schoenfeld Films: ROBERT SIEGLER, Producer.

STICKY MY FINGERS . . . FLEET MY FEET, The American Film Institute, Lester A. Schoenfeld Films: JOHN HANCOCK, Producer.

Documentary

Short Subjects

THE GIFTS, Richter-McBride Prods. for the Water Quality Office of the Environmental Protection Agency: ROBERT MCBRIDE, Producer.

★ INTERVIEWS WITH MY LAI VETERANS, Laser Film Corp.: JOSEPH STRICK, Producer.

A LONG WAY FROM NOWHERE, Robert Aller Prods.: BOB ALLER, Producer.

OISIN, An Aengus Film: VIVIEN CAREY and PATRICK CAREY, Producers.

TIME IS RUNNING OUT, Gesellschaft für bildende Filme: HORST DALLMAYR and ROBERT MENEGOZ, Producers.

Features

CHARIOTS OF THE GODS, Terra-Filmkunst GmbH.: DR. HARALD REINL, Producer.

JACK JOHNSON, The Big Fights: JIM JACOBS, Producer.

KING: A FILMED RECORD . . . MONTGOMERY TO MEMPHIS, Commonwealth United Prod.: ELY LANDAU, Producer.

SAY GOODBYE, A Wolper Prod.: DAVID H. VOWELL, Producer.

★ WOODSTOCK, A Wadleigh-Maurice Ltd. Prod.: BOB MAURICE, Producer.

Foreign Language Film Award

FIRST LOVE, Alfa Prods.-Seitz Film Production (Switzerland).

HOA-BINH, Madeleine-Parc-La Gueville-C.A.P.A.C. Production (France).

★ INVESTIGATION OF A CITIZEN ABOVE SUSPICION, Vera Films Production (Italy).

PAIX SUR LES CHAMPS, Philippe Collette-E.G.C. Production (Belgium).

TRISTANA, Forbes Films, Ltd.-United Cineworld-Epoca Films-Talia Film-Les Films Corona-Selenia Cinematografica Production (Spain).

Honorary Awards

LILLIAN GISH for superlative artistry and for distinguished contributions to the progress of motion pictures. (Statuette)

ORSON WELLES for superlative artistry and versatility in the creation of motion pictures. (Statuette)

Irving G. Thalberg Memorial Award

INGMAR BERGMAN.

Jean Hersholt Humanitarian Award

FRANK SINATRA.

Scientific or Technical

Class I

None.

Class II

LEONARD SOKOLOW and EDWARD H. REICHARD of Consolidated Film Industries for the concept and engineering of the color proofing printer for motion pictures.

Class III

SYLVANIA ELECTRIC PRODUCTS, INC., for the development and introduction of a series of compact tungsten halogen lamps for motion picture production.

B. J. LOSMANDY for the concept, design, and application of microminiature, solid-state amplifier modules used in motion picture recording equipment.

EASTMAN KODAK COMPANY and PHOTO ELECTRONICS CORPORATION for the design and engineering of an improved video color analyzer for motion picture laboratories.

ELECTRO SOUND INCORPORATED for the design and introduction of the Series 8000 Sound System for motion picture theatres.

FORTY-FOURTH YEAR

1971

Nominations Announced: February 22, 1972
Awards Ceremony: April 10, 1972
Dorothy Chandler Pavilion, Los Angeles County Music Center
(MCs: Helen Hayes, Alan King, Sammy Davis, Jr., and Jack Lemmon)

Best Picture

A CLOCKWORK ORANGE, A Hawks Films, Ltd. Prod., Warner Bros.: Stanley Kubrick, Producer.

FIDDLER ON THE ROOF, Mirisch-Cartier Prods., UA: Norman Jewison, Producer.

★ THE FRENCH CONNECTION, A Phillip D'Antoni Prod., in association with Schine-Moore Prods., 20th Century-Fox: Philip D'Antoni, Producer.

THE LAST PICTURE SHOW, BBS Prods., Columbia: Stephen J. Friedman, Producer.

NICHOLAS AND ALEXANDRA, A Horizon Pictures Prod., Columbia: Sam Spiegel, Producer.

Actor

PETER FINCH in *Sunday Bloody Sunday*, A Joseph Janni Prod., UA.

★ GENE HACKMAN in *The French Connection*, A Philip D'Antoni Prod., in association with Schine-Moore Prods., 20th Century-Fox.

WALTER MATTHAU in *Kotch*, A Kotch Company Prod., ABC Pictures Presentation, Cinerama.

GEORGE C. SCOTT in *The Hospital*, A Howard Gottfried-Paddy Chayefsky Prod., in association with Arthur Hiller, UA.

TOPOL in *Fiddler on the Roof*, A Mirisch-Cartier Prods., UA.

Actress

JULIE CHRISTIE in *McCabe & Mrs. Miller*, A Robert Altman-David Foster Prod., Warner Bros.

★ JANE FONDA in *Klute*, A Gus Prod., Warner Bros.

GLENDA JACKSON in *Sunday Bloody Sunday*, A Joseph Janni Prod., UA.

VANESSA REDGRAVE in *Mary, Queen of Scots*, A Hal Wallis-Universal Pictures, Ltd. Prod., Universal.

JANET SUZMAN in *Nicholas and Alexandra*, A Horizon Pictures Prod., Columbia.

Supporting Actor

JEFF BRIDGES in *The Last Picture Show*, BBS Prods., Columbia.

LEONARD FREY in *Fiddler on the Roof*, Mirisch-Cartier Prods., UA.

RICHARD JAECKEL in *Sometimes a Great Notion*, A Universal-Newman-Foreman Company Prod., Universal.

★ BEN JOHNSON in *The Last Picture Show*, BBS Prods., Columbia.

ROY SCHEIDER in *The French Connection*, A Philip D'Antoni Prod., in association with Schine-Moore Prods., 20th Century-Fox.

Supporting Actress

ANN-MARGRET in *Carnal Knowledge*, Icarus Prods., Avco Embassy.

ELLEN BURSTYN in *The Last Picture Show*, BBS Prods., Columbia.

BARBARA HARRIS in *Who Is Harry Kellerman, and Why Is He Saying Those Terrible Things about Me?*, A Who Is Harry Kellerman Company Prod., Cinema Center Films Presentation, National General.

★ CLORIS LEACHMAN in *The Last Picture Show*, BBS Prods., Columbia.

MARGARET LEIGHTON in *The Go-Between*, A World Film Services, Ltd. Prod., Columbia.

Directing

PETER BOGDANOVICH for *The Last Picture Show*, BBS Prods., Columbia.

★ WILLIAM FRIEDKIN for *The French Connection*, A Phillip D'Antoni Prod., in association with Schine-Moore Prods., 20th Century-Fox.

NORMAN JEWISON for *Fiddler on the Roof*, Mirisch-Cartier Prods., UA.

STANLEY KUBRICK for *A Clockwork Orange*, A Hawks Films, Ltd., Prod., Warner Bros.

JOHN SCHLESINGER for *Sunday Bloody Sunday*, A Joseph Janni Prod., UA.

Writing

Screenplay—Based on Material from Another Medium

A CLOCKWORK ORANGE, A Hawks Films, Ltd. Prod., Warner Bros.: STANLEY KUBRICK.

THE CONFORMIST, Mars Film Produzione, S.P.A.-Marianne Prods., Paramount: BERNARDO BERTOLUCCI.

★ THE FRENCH CONNECTION, A Philip D'Antoni Prod., in association with Schine-Moore Prods., 20th Century-Fox: ERNEST TIDYMAN.

THE GARDEN OF THE FINZI-CONTINIS, A Gianni Hecht Lucari-Arthur Cohn Prod., Cinema 5, Ltd.: UGO PIRRO and VITTORIO BONICELLI.

THE LAST PICTURE SHOW, BBS Prods., Columbia: LARRY MCMURTRY and PETER BOGDANOVICH.

Story and Screenplay—Based on Factual Material or Material Not Previously Published or Produced

★ THE HOSPITAL, A Howard Gottfried-Paddy Chayefsky Prod., in association with Arthur Hiller, UA: PADDY CHAYEFSKY.

INVESTIGATION OF A CITIZEN ABOVE SUSPICION, A Vera Films, S.P.A. Prod., Columbia: ELIO PETRI and UGO PIRRO.

KLUTE, A Gus Prod., Warner Bros.: ANDY LEWIS and DAVE LEWIS.

SUMMER OF '42, A Robert Mulligan-Richard Alan Roth Prod., Warner Bros.: HERMAN RAUCHER.

SUNDAY BLOODY SUNDAY, A Joseph Janni Prod., UA: PENELOPE GILLIATT.

Cinematography

★ FIDDLER ON THE ROOF, Mirisch-Cartier Prods., UA: OSWALD MORRIS.

THE FRENCH CONNECTION, A Philip D'Antoni Prod., in association with Schine-Moore Prods., 20th Century-Fox: OWEN ROIZMAN.

THE LAST PICTURE SHOW, BBS Prods., Columbia: ROBERT SURTEES.

NICHOLAS AND ALEXANDRA, A Horizon Pictures Prod., Columbia: FREDDIE YOUNG.

SUMMER OF '42, A Robert Mulligan-Richard Alan Roth Prod., Warner Bros.: ROBERT SURTEES.

Art Direction—Set Decoration

THE ANDROMEDA STRAIN, A Universal-Robert Wise Prod., Universal: BORIS

LEVEN and WILLIAM TUNTKE; Set Decoration: RUBY LEVITT.

BEDKNOBS AND BROOMSTICKS, Walt Disney Prods., Buena Vista Distribution Company: JOHN B. MANSBRIDGE and PETER ELLENSHAW; Set Decoration: EMILE KURI and HAL GAUSMAN.

FIDDLER ON THE ROOF, Mirisch-Cartier Prods., UA: ROBERT BOYLE and MICHAEL STRINGER; Set Decoration: PETER LAMONT.

MARY, QUEEN OF SCOTS, A Hal Wallis-Universal Pictures, Ltd. Prod., Universal: TERENCE MARSH and ROBERT CARTWRIGHT; Set Decoration: PETER HOWITT.

★ NICHOLAS AND ALEXANDRA, A Horizon Pictures Prod., Columbia: JOHN BOX, ERNEST ARCHER, JACK MAXSTED, and GIL PARRONDO; Set Decoration: VERNON DIXON.

Sound

DIAMONDS ARE FOREVER, An Albert R. Broccoli-Harry Saltzman Prod., UA: GORDON K. MCCALLUM, JOHN MITCHELL, and ALFRED J. OVERTON.

★ FIDDLER ON THE ROOF, Mirisch-Cartier Prods., UA: GORDON K. McCALLUM and DAVID HILDYARD.

THE FRENCH CONNECTION, A Philip D'Antoni Prod., in association with Schine-Moore Prods., 20th Century-Fox: THEODORE SODERBERG and CHRISTOPHER NEWMAN.

KOTCH, A Kotch Prod., ABC Pictures Presentation, Cinerama: RICHARD PORTMAN and JACK SOLOMON.

MARY, QUEEN OF SCOTS, A Hal Wallis-Universal Pictures, Ltd. Prod., Universal: BOB JONES and JOHN ALDRED.

Film Editing

THE ANDROMEDA STRAIN, A Universal-Robert Wise Prod., Universal: STUART GILMORE and JOHN W. HOLMES.

A CLOCKWORK ORANGE, A Hawks Films, Ltd. Prod., Warner Bros.: BILL BUTLER.

★ THE FRENCH CONNECTION, A Philip D'Antoni Prod., in association with Schine-Moore Prods., 20th Century-Fox: JERRY GREENBERG.

KOTCH, A Kotch Company Prod., ABC Pictures Presentation, Cinerama: RALPH E. WINTERS.

SUMMER OF '42, A Robert Mulligan-Richard Alan Roth Prod., Warner Bros.: FOLMAR BLANGSTED.

Music

Original Dramatic Score

MARY, QUEEN OF SCOTS, A Hal Wallis-Universal Pictures, Ltd. Prod., Universal: JOHN BARRY.

NICHOLAS AND ALEXANDRA, A Horizon Pictures Prod., Columbia: RICHARD RODNEY BENNETT.

SHAFT, Shaft Prods., Ltd., M-G-M: ISAAC HAYES.

STRAW DOGS, A Talent Associates, Ltd.-Amerbroco Films, Ltd. Prod., ABC Pictures Presentation, Cinerama: JERRY FIELDING.

★ SUMMER OF '42, A Robert Mulligan-Richard Alan Roth Prod., Warner Bros.: MICHEL LEGRAND.

Scoring: Adaptation and Original Song Score

BEDKNOBS AND BROOMSTICKS, Walt Disney Prods., Buena Vista Distribution Company: Song Score by RICHARD M. SHERMAN and ROBERT B. SHERMAN; Adapted by IRWIN KOSTAL.

THE BOY FRIEND, A Russflix, Ltd. Prod., M-G-M: Adapted by PETER MAXWELL DAVIES and PETER GREENWELL.

★ FIDDLER ON THE ROOF, Mirisch-Cartier Prods., UA: Adapted by JOHN WILLIAMS.

TCHAIKOVSKY, A Dimitri Tiomkin-Mosfilm Studios Prod.: Adapted by DIMITRI TIOMKIN.

WILLY WONKA AND THE CHOCOLATE FACTORY, A Wolper Pictures, Ltd. Prod., Paramount: Song Score by LESLIE BRICUSSE and ANTHONY NEWLEY; Adapted by WALTER SCHARF.

Song

THE AGE OF NOT BELIEVING from *Bedknobs and Broomsticks*, Walt Disney Prods., Buena Vista Distribution Company: Music and Lyrics by RICHARD M. SHERMAN and ROBERT B. SHERMAN.

ALL HIS CHILDREN from *Sometimes a Great Notion*, A Universal-Newman-Foreman Company Prod., Universal: Music by HENRY MANCINI; Lyrics by ALAN BERGMAN and MARILYN BERGMAN.

BLESS THE BEASTS AND CHILDREN from *Bless the Beasts and Children*, Columbia: Music and lyrics by BARRY DEVORZON and PERRY BOTKIN, JR.

LIFE IS WHAT YOU MAKE IT from *Kotch*, A Kotch Company Production, ABC Pictures Presentation, Cinerama: Music by MARVIN HAMLISCH; Lyrics by JOHNNY MERCER.

★ THEME FROM SHAFT from *Shaft*, Shaft Prods., Ltd., M-G-M: Music and Lyrics by ISAAC HAYES.

Costume Design

BEDKNOBS AND BROOMSTICKS, Walt Disney Prods., Buena Vista Distribution Company: BILL THOMAS.

DEATH IN VENICE, An Alfa Cinematografica-P.E.C.F. Prod., Warner Bros.: PIERO TOSI.

MARY, QUEEN OF SCOTS, A Hal Wallis-Universal Pictures, Ltd. Prod., Universal: MARGARET FURSE.

★ NICHOLAS AND ALEXANDRA, A Horizon Pictures Prod., Columbia: YVONNE BLAKE and ANTONIO CASTILLO.

WHAT'S THE MATTER WITH HELEN?, A Filmways-Raymax Prod., UA: MORTON HAACK.

Special Visual Effects

(Not given as an Annual Award after this year)

★ BEDKNOBS AND BROOMSTICKS, Walt Disney Prods., Buena Vista Distribution Company: ALAN MALEY, EUSTACE LYCETT, and DANNY LEE.

WHEN DINOSAURS RULED THE EARTH, A Hammer Film Prod., Warner Bros.: JIM DANFORTH and ROGER DICKEN.

Short Subjects

*Animated**

★ THE CRUNCH BIRD, Maxwell-Petok-Petrovich Prods., Regency Film Distributing Corp.: TED PETOK, Producer.

EVOLUTION, National Film Board of Canada, Columbia: MICHAEL MILLS, Producer.

THE SELFISH GIANT, Potterton Prods., Pyramid Films: PETER SANDER and MURRAY SHOSTAK, Producers.

Live Action

GOOD MORNING, E/G Films, Seymour Borde and Associates: DENNY EVANS and KEN GREENWALD, Producers.

THE REHEARSAL, A Cinema Verona Prod., Schoenfeld Film Distributing

*The designation of this category was changed from *Cartoons* to *Animated Films*.

Corp.: STEPHEN F. VERONA, Producer.

★ SENTINELS OF SILENCE, Producciones Concord, Paramount: MANUEL ARANGO and ROBERT AMRAM, Producers.

Documentary

Short Subjects

ADVENTURES IN PERCEPTION, Han van Gelder Filmproduktie for Netherlands Information Service: HAN VAN GELDER, Producer.

ART IS . . . , Henry Strauss Associates for Sears Roebuck Foundation: JULIAN KRAININ and DEWITT L. SAGE, JR., Producers.

THE NUMBERS START WITH THE RIVER, A WH Picture for the United States Information Agency: DONALD WRYE, Producer.

★ SENTINELS OF SILENCE, Producciones Concord, Paramount: MANUEL ARANGO and ROBERT AMRAM, Producers.

SOMEBODY WAITING, Snider Prods. for University of California Medical Film Library: HAL RINEY, DICK SNIDER, and SHERWOOD OMENS, Producers.

Features

ALASKA WILDERNESS LAKE, Alan Landsburg Prods.: ALAN LANDSBURG, Producer.

★ THE HELLSTROM CHRONICLE, David L. Wolper Prods., Cinema 5, Ltd.: WALON GREEN, Producer.

ON ANY SUNDAY, Bruce Brown Films-Solar Prods., Cinema 5, Ltd.: BRUCE BROWN, Producer.

THE RA EXPEDITIONS, Swedish Broadcasting Company, Interwest Film Corp.: LENNART EHRENBORG and THOR HEYERDAHL, Producers.

THE SORROW AND THE PITY, Television Rencontre-Norddeutscher Rundfunk-Television Swiss Romande, Cinema 5, Ltd.: MARCEL OPHULS, Producer.

Foreign Language Film Award

DODES'KA-DEN, A Toho Company, Ltd.-Yonki no Kai Production (Japan).

THE EMIGRANTS, A Svensk Filmindustri Production (Sweden).

★ THE GARDEN OF THE FINZI-CONTINIS, A Gianni Hecht Lucari-Arthur Cohn Production (Italy).

THE POLICEMAN, An Ephi-Israeli Motion Picture Studios Production (Israel).

TCHAIKOVSKY, A Dimitri Tiomkin-Mosfilm Studios Production (U.S.S.R.).

Honorary Award

CHARLES CHAPLIN for the incalculable effect he has had in making motion pictures the art form of this century.

Irving G. Thalberg Memorial Award

None.

Jean Hersholt Humanitarian Award

None.

Scientific or Technical

Class I

None.

Class II

JOHN N. WILKINSON of Optical Radiation Corporation for the development and engineering of a system of xenon arc lamphouses for motion picture projection.

Class III

THOMAS JEFFERSON HUTCHINSON, JAMES R. ROCHESTER, and FENTON HAMILTON for the development and introduction of the Sunbrute system of xenon arc lamps for location lighting in motion picture production.

PHOTO RESEARCH, a Division of Kollmorgen Corporation, for the development and introduction of the film-lens-balanced three-color meter.

ROBERT D. AUGUSTE and CINEMA PRODUCTS CO. for the development and introduction of a new crystal-controlled, lightweight motor for the 35mm motion picture Arriflex camera.

PRODUCERS SERVICE CORPORATION and CONSOLIDATED FILM INDUSTRIES; and CINEMA RESEARCH CORPORATION and RESEARCH PRODUCTS, INC., for the engineering and implementation of fully automated blow-up motion picture printing systems.

CINEMA PRODUCTS CO. for a control motor to actuate zoom lenses on motion picture cameras.

FORTY-FIFTH YEAR

1972

Nominations Announced: February 12, 1973
(Song nominations: March 5, 1973)
Awards Ceremony: March 27, 1973
Dorothy Chandler Pavilion, Los Angeles County Music Center
(MCs: Carol Burnett, Michael Caine, Charlton Heston, and Rock Hudson)

Best Picture

CABARET, An ABC Pictures Production, Allied Artists: Cy Feuer, Producer.

DELIVERANCE, Warner Bros.: John Boorman, Producer.

THE EMIGRANTS, A Svensk Filmindustri Production, Warner Bros.: Bengt Forslund, Producer.

* THE GODFATHER, An Albert S. Ruddy Production, Paramount: Albert S. Ruddy, Producer.

SOUNDER, Radnitz/Mattel Productions, 20th Century-Fox: Robert B. Radnitz, Producer.

Actor

* MARLON BRANDO in *The Godfather*, An Albert S. Ruddy Production, Paramount.

MICHAEL CAINE in *Sleuth*, A Palomar Pictures International Production, 20th Century-Fox.

LAURENCE OLIVIER in *Sleuth*, A Palomar Pictures International Production, 20th Century-Fox.

PETER O'TOOLE in *The Ruling Class*, A Keep Films, Ltd. Production, Avco Embassy.

PAUL WINFIELD in *Sounder*, Radnitz/ Mattel Productions, 20th Century-Fox.

Actress

* LIZA MINNELLI in *Cabaret*, An ABC Pictures Production, Allied Artists.

DIANA ROSS in *Lady Sings the Blues*, A Motown-Weston-Furie Production, Paramount.

MAGGIE SMITH in *Travels with My Aunt*, Robert Fryer Productions, Metro-Goldwyn-Mayer.

CICELY TYSON in *Sounder*, Radnitz/ Mattel Productions, 20th Century-Fox.

LIV ULLMANN in *The Emigrants*, A Svensk Filmindustri Production, Warner Bros.

Supporting Actor

EDDIE ALBERT in *The Heartbreak Kid*, A Palomar Pictures International Production, 20th Century-Fox.

JAMES CAAN in *The Godfather*, An Albert S. Ruddy Production, Paramount.

ROBERT DUVALL in *The Godfather*, An Albert S. Ruddy Production, Paramount.

* JOEL GREY in *Cabaret*, An ABC Pictures Production, Allied Artists.

AL PACINO in *The Godfather*, An Albert S. Ruddy Production, Paramount.

Supporting Actress

JEANNIE BERLIN in *The Heartbreak Kid*, A Palomar Pictures International Production, 20th Century-Fox.

★ EILEEN HECKART in *Butterflies Are Free*, Frankovich Productions, Columbia.

GERALDINE PAGE in *Pete 'n' Tillie*, A Universal-Martin Ritt-Julius J. Epstein Production, Universal.

SUSAN TYRRELL in *Fat City*, Rastar Productions, Columbia.

SHELLEY WINTERS in *The Poseidon Adventure*, An Irwin Allen Production, 20th Century-Fox.

Directing

JOHN BOORMAN for *Deliverance*, Warner Bros.

FRANCIS FORD COPPOLA for *The Godfather*, An Albert S. Ruddy Production, Paramount.

★ BOB FOSSE for *Cabaret*, An ABC Pictures Production, Allied Artists.

JOSEPH L. MANKIEWICZ for *Sleuth*, A Palomar Pictures International Production, 20th Century-Fox.

JAN TROELL for *The Emigrants*, A Svensk Filmindustri Production, Warner Bros.

Writing

Screenplay—Based on Material from Another Medium

CABARET, An ABC Pictures Prod., Allied Artists: JAY ALLEN.

THE EMIGRANTS, A Svensk Filmindustri Prod., Warner Bros.: JAN TROELL and BENGT FORSLUND.

★ THE GODFATHER, An Albert S. Ruddy Production, Paramount: MARIO PUZO and FRANCIS FORD COPPOLA.

PETE 'N' TILLIE, A Universal-Martin Ritt-Julius J. Epstein Prod., Universal: JULIUS J. EPSTEIN.

SOUNDER, Radnitz/Mattel Prods., 20th Century-Fox: LONNE ELDER III.

Story and Screenplay—Based on Factual Material or Material Not Previously Published or Produced

★ THE CANDIDATE, A Redford-Ritchie Prod., Warner Bros.: JEREMY LARNER.

THE DISCREET CHARM OF THE BOURGEOISIE, A Serge Silberman Prod., 20th Century-Fox: LUIS BUÑUEL in collaboration with JEAN-CLAUDE CARRIÈRE.

LADY SINGS THE BLUES, A Motown-Weston-Furie Prod., Paramount: TERENCE MCCLOY, CHRIS CLARK, and SUZANNE DE PASSE.

MURMUR OF THE HEART, A Nouvelles Editions de Films-Marianne Productions-Vides Cinematografica-Franz Seitz Filmproduktion, Continental Distributing: LOUIS MALLE.

YOUNG WINSTON, An Open Road Films, Ltd. Prod., Columbia: CARL FOREMAN.

Cinematography

BUTTERFLIES ARE FREE, Frankovich Productions, Columbia: CHARLES B. LANG.

★ CABARET, An ABC Pictures Production, Allied Artists: GEOFFREY UNSWORTH.

THE POSEIDON ADVENTURE, An Irwin Allen Production, 20th Century-Fox: HAROLD E. STINE.

"1776," A Jack L. Warner Production, Columbia: HARRY STRADLING, JR.

TRAVELS WITH MY AUNT, Robert Fryer Productions, Metro-Goldwyn-Mayer: DOUGLAS SLOCOMBE.

Art Direction—Set Decoration

★ CABARET, An ABC Pictures Production, Allied Artists: ROLF ZEHETBAUER and JURGEN

KIEBACH; Set Decoration: HERBERT STRABEL.

LADY SINGS THE BLUES, A Motown-Weston-Furie Production, Paramount: CARL ANDERSON; Set Decoration: REG ALLEN.

THE POSEIDON ADVENTURE, An Irwin Allen Production, 20th Century-Fox: WILLIAM CREBER; Set Decoration: RAPHAEL BRETTON.

TRAVELS WITH MY AUNT, Robert Fryer Productions, Metro-Goldwyn-Mayer: JOHN BOX, GIL PARRONDO, and ROBERT W. LAING.

YOUNG WINSTON, An Open Road Films, Ltd. Production, Columbia: DON ASHTON, GEOFFREY DRAKE, JOHN GRAYSMARK, and WILLIAM HUTCHINSON; Set Decoration: PETER JAMES.

Sound

BUTTERFLIES ARE FREE, Frankovich Prods., Columbia: ARTHUR PIANTADOSI and CHARLES KNIGHT.

★ CABARET, An ABC Pictures Production, Allied Artists: ROBERT KNUDSON and DAVID HILDYARD.

THE CANDIDATE, A Redford-Ritchie Prod., Warner Bros.: RICHARD PORTMAN and GENE CANTAMESSA.

THE GODFATHER, An Albert S. Ruddy Production, Paramount: BUD GRENZBACH, RICHARD PORTMAN, and CHRISTOPHER NEWMAN.

THE POSEIDON ADVENTURE, An Irwin Allen Production, 20th Century-Fox: THEODORE SODERBERG and HERMAN LEWIS.

Film Editing

★ CABARET, An ABC Pictures Production, Allied Artists: DAVID BRETHERTON.

DELIVERANCE, Warner Bros.: TOM PRIESTLEY.

THE GODFATHER, An Albert S. Ruddy Production, Paramount: WILLIAM REYNOLDS and PETER ZINNER.

THE HOT ROCK, A Landers-Roberts Production, 20th Century-Fox: FRANK P. KELLER and FRED W. BERGER.

THE POSEIDON ADVENTURE, An Irwin Allen Production, 20th Century-Fox: HAROLD F. KRESS.

Music

Original Dramatic Score

IMAGES, A Hemdale Group, Ltd.-Lion's Gate Films Prod., Columbia: JOHN WILLIAMS.

★ LIMELIGHT, A Charles Chaplin Prod., Columbia: CHARLES CHAPLIN, RAYMOND RASCH, and LARRY RUSSELL.*

NAPOLEON AND SAMANTHA, A Walt Disney Prods., Buena Vista Distribution Company: BUDDY BAKER.

THE POSEIDON ADVENTURE, An Irwin Allen Production, 20th Century-Fox: JOHN WILLIAMS.

SLEUTH, A Palomar Pictures International Prod., 20th Century-Fox: JOHN ADDISON.

Scoring: Adaptation and Original Song Score

★ CABARET, An ABC Pictures Production, Allied Artists: Adapted by RALPH BURNS.

LADY SINGS THE BLUES, A Motown-Weston-Furie Prod., Paramount: Adapted by GIL ASKEY.

MAN OF LA MANCHA, A PEA Produzioni

*Academy Award eligibility rules require a film to be commercially exhibited in a Los Angeles theater to qualify for Oscar consideration. *Limelight* was made in 1952 but was not shown in Los Angeles until 1972. Thus, its eligibility year fell two decades after its actual year of production.

Europee Associate Prod., UA: Adapted by LAURENCE ROSENTHAL.

Song

BEN from *Ben*, BCP Productions, Cinerama: Music by WALTER SCHARF; Lyrics by DON BLACK.

COME FOLLOW, FOLLOW ME from *The Little Ark*, Robert Radnitz Productions, Ltd., Cinema Center Films Presentation, National General: Music by FRED KARLIN; Lyrics by MARSHA KARLIN.

MARMALADE, MOLASSES & HONEY from *The Life and Times of Judge Roy Bean*, A First Artists Production Company, Ltd. Production, National General: Music by MAURICE JARRE; Lyrics by MARILYN BERGMAN and ALAN BERGMAN.

⋆ THE MORNING AFTER from *The Poseidon Adventure*, An Irwin Allen Production, 20th Century-Fox: Music and Lyrics by AL KASHA and JOEL HIRSCHHORN.

STRANGE ARE THE WAYS OF LOVE from *The Stepmother*, Magic Eye of Hollywood Productions, Crown International: Music by SAMMY FAIN; Lyrics by PAUL FRANCIS WEBSTER.

Costume Design

THE GODFATHER, An Albert S. Ruddy Production, Paramount: ANNA HILL JOHNSTONE.

LADY SINGS THE BLUES, A Motown-Weston-Furie Prod., Paramount: BOB MACKIE, RAY AGHAYAN, and NORMA KOCH.

THE POSEIDON ADVENTURE, An Irwin Allen Production, 20th Century-Fox: PAUL ZASTUPNEVICH.

⋆ TRAVELS WITH MY AUNT, Robert Fryer Prods., Metro-Goldwyn-Mayer: ANTHONY POWELL.

YOUNG WINSTON, An Open Road Films, Ltd. Prod., Columbia: ANTHONY MENDLESON.

Short Subjects

Animated

⋆ A CHRISTMAS CAROL, A Richard Williams Production, American Broadcasting Company Film Services: RICHARD WILLIAMS, Producer.

KAMA SUTRA RIDES AGAIN, Bob Godfrey Films, Ltd., Lion International Films: BOB GODFREY, Producer.

TUP TUP, A Zagreb Film-Corona Cinematografica Production, Manson Distributing Corp.: NEDELJKO DRAGIC, Producer.

Live Action

FROG STORY, Gidron Productions, Schoenfeld Film Distributing Corp.: RON SATLOF and RAY GIDEON, Producers.

⋆ NORMAN ROCKWELL'S WORLD . . . AN AMERICAN DREAM, A Concepts Unlimited Production, Columbia: RICHARD BARCLAY, Producer.

SOLO, Pyramid Films, United Artists: DAVID ADAMS, Producer.

Documentary

Short Subjects

HUNDERTWASSER'S RAINY DAY, an Argos Films-Peter Schamoni Film Prod.: PETER SCHAMONI, Producer.

K-Z, A Nexus Film Production: GIORGIO TREVES, Producer.

SELLING OUT, A Unit Productions Film: TADEUSZ JAWORSKI, Producer.

⋆ THIS TINY WORLD, A Charles Huguenot van der Linden Production: CHARLES and MARTINA HUGUENOT VAN DER LINDEN, Producers.

THE TIDE OF TRAFFIC, A BP-Greenpark Production: HUMPHREY SWINGLER, Producer.

Features

APE AND SUPER-APE, A Bert Haanstra Film Production, Netherlands Ministry of Culture, Recreation, and Social Welfare: BERT HAANSTRA, Producer.

MALCOLM X, A Marvin Worth Production, Warner Bros.: MARVIN WORTH and ARNOLD PERL, Producers.

MANSON, Merrick International Pictures: ROBERT HENDRICKSON and LAURENCE MERRICK, Producers.

★ MARJOE, A Cinema X Production, Cinema 5, Ltd.: HOWARD SMITH and SARAH KERNOCHAN, Producers.

THE SILENT REVOLUTION, A Leonaris Film Production: ECKEHARD MUNCK, Producer.

Foreign Language Film Award

THE DAWNS HERE ARE QUIET, A Gorky Film Studios Production (U.S.S.R.).

★ THE DISCREET CHARM OF THE BOURGEOISIE, A Serge Silberman Production (France).

I LOVE YOU ROSA, A Noah Films Ltd. Production (Israel).

MY DEAREST SEÑORITA, An El Iman Production (Spain).

THE NEW LAND, A Svensk Filmindustri Production (Sweden).

Honorary Awards

CHARLES S. BOREN, leader for thirty-eight years of the industry's enlightened labor relations and architect of its policy of nondiscrimination, with the respect and affection of all who work in films. (Statuette)

EDWARD G. ROBINSON who achieved greatness as a player, a patron of the arts, and a dedicated citizen . . . in sum, a Renaissance man. From his friends in the industry he loves. (Statuette)

Special Achievement Award

(New Category)*

Visual Effects: L. B. ABBOTT and A. D. FLOWERS for *The Poseidon Adventure*, an Irwin Allen Production, 20th Century-Fox.

Irving G. Thalberg Memorial Award

None.

Jean Hersholt Humanitarian Award

ROSALIND RUSSELL.

Scientific or Technical

Class I

None.

Class II

JOSEPH E. BLUTH for research and development in the field of electronic photography and transfer of video tape to motion picture film.

EDWARD H. REICHARD and HOWARD T. LA ZARE of Consolidated Film Industries and EDWARD EFRON of IBM for the engineering of a computerized light-valve monitoring system for motion picture printing.

PANAVISION INCORPORATED for the development and engineering of the Panaflex motion picture camera.

Class III

PHOTO RESEARCH, a Division of Kollmorgen Corporation, and PSC TECHNOLOGY, INC., Acme Products Division, for the Spectra

*Created as an "other" Award—not necessarily given each year and hence no nominations—to honor achievements formerly recognized in the Special Visual Effects and Sound Effects categories.

Film Gate Photometer for motion picture printers.

CARTER EQUIPMENT COMPANY, INC., and RAMTRONICS for the RAMtronics light-valve photometer for motion picture printers.

DAVID DEGENKOLB, HARRY LARSON, MANFRED MICHELSON, and FRED SCOBEY of DeLuxe General Incorporated for the development of a computerized motion picture printer and process control system.

JIRO MUKAI and RYUSHO HIROSE of Canon, Inc., and WILTON R. HOLM of the AMPTP Motion Picture and Television Research Center for development of the Canon Macro Zoom Lens for motion picture photography.

PHILIP V. PALMQUIST and LEONARD L. OLSON of the 3M Company, and FRANK P. CLARK of the AMPTP Motion Picture and Television Research Center for the development of Nextel simulated blood for motion picture color photography.

E. H. GEISSLER and G. M. BERGGREN of Wil-Kin, Inc., for engineering of the Ultra-Vision Motion Picture Theater Projection System.

1973

Nominations Announced: February 19, 1974
Awards Ceremony: April 2, 1974
Dorothy Chandler Pavilion, Los Angeles County Music Center
(MCs: John Huston, David Niven, Burt Reynolds, and Diana Ross)

Best Picture

AMERICAN GRAFFITI, A Universal-Lucasfilm, Ltd.-Coppola Company Prod., Universal: Francis Ford Coppola, Producer; Gary Kurtz, Co-producer.

CRIES AND WHISPERS, A Svenska Filminstitutet-Cinematograph AB Prod., New World Pictures: Ingmar Bergman, Producer.

THE EXORCIST, Hoya Prods., Warner Bros.: William Peter Blatty, Producer.

★ THE STING, A Universal-Bill/Phillips-George Roy Hill Film Prod., Zanuck/Brown Presentation, Universal: Tony Bill, Michael Phillips, and Julia Phillips, Producers.

A TOUCH OF CLASS, Brut Prods., Avco Embassy: Melvin Frank, Producer.

Actor

MARLON BRANDO in *Last Tango in Paris*, A PEA Produzioni Europee Associate S.A.S.-Les Productions Artistes Associés S.A. Prod., UA.

★ JACK LEMMON in *Save the Tiger*, Filmways-Jalem-Cirandinha Prods., Paramount.

JACK NICHOLSON in *The Last Detail*, An Acrobat Films Prod., Columbia.

AL PACINO in *Serpico*, A Produzioni De Laurentiis International Manufacturing Company S.p.A. Prod., Paramount.

ROBERT REDFORD in *The Sting*, A Universal-Bill/Phillips-George Roy Hill Film Prod., Zanuck/Brown Presentation, Universal.

Actress

ELLEN BURSTYN in *The Exorcist*, Hoya Prods., Warner Bros.

★ GLENDA JACKSON in *A Touch of Class*, Brut Prods., Avco Embassy.

MARSHA MASON in *Cinderella Liberty*, A Sanford Prod., 20th Century-Fox.

BARBRA STREISAND in *The Way We Were*, Rastar Prods., Columbia.

JOANNE WOODWARD in *Summer Wishes, Winter Dreams*, A Rastar Pictures Prod., Columbia.

Supporting Actor

VINCENT GARDENIA in *Bang the Drum Slowly*, A Rosenfield Production, Paramount.

JACK GILFORD in *Save the Tiger*, Filmways-Jalem-Cirandinha Prods., Paramount.

★ JOHN HOUSEMAN in *The Paper Chase*, Thompson-Paul Productions, 20th Century-Fox.

JASON MILLER in *The Exorcist*, Hoya Productions, Warner Bros.

RANDY QUAID in *The Last Detail*, An Acrobat Films Prod., Columbia.

Supporting Actress

LINDA BLAIR in *The Exorcist*, Hoya Prods., Warner Bros.
CANDY CLARK in *American Graffiti*, A Universal-Lucasfilm, Ltd.-Coppola Company Prod., Universal.
MADELINE KAHN in *Paper Moon*, A Directors Company Prod., Paramount.
★ TATUM O'NEAL in *Paper Moon*, A Directors Company Prod., Paramount.
SYLVIA SIDNEY in *Summer Wishes, Winter Dreams*, A Rastar Pictures Prod., Columbia.

Directing

INGMAR BERGMAN for *Cries and Whispers*, A Svenska Filminstitutet-Cinematograph AB Prod., New World Pictures.
BERNARDO BERTOLUCCI for *Last Tango in Paris*, A PEA Produzioni Europee Associate S.A.S.-Les Productions Artistes Associés S.A. Prod., UA.
WILLIAM FRIEDKIN for *The Exorcist*, Hoya Prods., Warner Bros.
★ GEORGE ROY HILL for *The Sting*, A Universal-Bill/Phillips-George Roy Hill Film Prod., Zanuck/Brown Presentation, Universal.
GEORGE LUCAS for *American Graffiti*, A Universal-Lucasfilm, Ltd.-Coppola Company Prod., Universal.

Writing

Screenplay—Based on Material from Another Medium

★ THE EXORCIST, Hoya Prods., Warner Bros.: WILLIAM PETER BLATTY.
THE LAST DETAIL, An Acrobat Films Prod., Columbia: ROBERT TOWNE.
THE PAPER CHASE, Thompson-Paul Prods., 20th Century-Fox: JAMES BRIDGES.
PAPER MOON, A Directors Company Prod., Paramount: ALVIN SARGENT.
SERPICO, A Produzioni De Laurentiis International Manufacturing Company S.p.A. Prod., Paramount: WALDO SALT and NORMAN WEXLER.

Story and Screenplay—Based on Factual Material or Material Not Previously Published or Produced

AMERICAN GRAFFITI, A Universal-Lucasfilm, Ltd.-Coppola Company Prod., Universal: GEORGE LUCAS, GLORIA KATZ, and WILLARD HUYCK.
CRIES AND WHISPERS, A Svenska Filminstitutet-Cinematograph AB Prod., New World Pictures: INGMAR BERGMAN.
SAVE THE TIGER, Filmways-Jalem-Cirandinha Prods., Paramount: STEVE SHAGAN.
★ THE STING, A Universal-Bill/Phillips-George Roy Hill Film Prod., Zanuck/Brown Presentation, Universal: DAVID S. WARD.
A TOUCH OF CLASS, Brut Prod., Avco Embassy: MELVIN FRANK and JACK ROSE.

Cinematography

★ CRIES AND WHISPERS, A Svenska Filminstitutet-Cinematograph AB Prod., New World Pictures: SVEN NYKVIST.
THE EXORCIST, Hoya Prods., Warner Bros.: OWEN ROIZMAN.
JONATHAN LIVINGSTON SEAGULL, A JLS Limited Partnership Prod., Paramount: JACK COUFFER.
THE STING, A Universal-Bill/Phillips-George Roy Hill Film Prod., Zanuck/Brown Presentation, Universal: ROBERT SURTEES.
THE WAY WE WERE, Rastar Prods., Columbia: HARRY STRADLING, JR.

Art Direction—Set Decoration

BROTHER SUN, SISTER MOON, Euro International Films-Vic Film (Prods.), Ltd., Paramount: LORENZO MONGIARDINO and GIANNI QUARANTA; Set Decoration: CARMELO PATRONO.

THE EXORCIST, Hoya Prods., Warner Bros: BILL MALLEY; Set Decoration: JERRY WUNDERLICH.

★ THE STING, A Universal-Bill/Phillips-George Roy Hill Film Prod., Zanuck/Brown Presentation, Universal: HENRY BUMSTEAD; Set Decoration: JAMES PAYNE.

TOM SAWYER, An Arthur P. Jacobs Prod., Reader's Digest Presentation, UA: PHILIP JEFFERIES; Set Decoration: ROBERT DE VESTEL.

THE WAY WE WERE, Rastar Prods., Columbia: STEPHEN GRIMES; Set Decoration: WILLIAM KIERNAN.

Sound

THE DAY OF THE DOLPHIN, Icarus Prods., Avco Embassy: RICHARD PORTMAN and LAWRENCE O. JOST.

★ THE EXORCIST, Hoya Prods., Warner Bros.: ROBERT KNUDSON and CHRIS NEWMAN.

THE PAPER CHASE, Thompson-Paul Prods., 20th Century-Fox: DONALD O. MITCHELL and LAWRENCE O. JOST.

PAPER MOON, A Directors Company Prod., Paramount: RICHARD PORTMAN and LES FRESHOLTZ.

THE STING, A Universal-Bill/Phillips-George Roy Hill Film Prod., Zanuck/Brown Presentation, Universal: RONALD K. PIERCE and ROBERT BERTRAND.

Film Editing

AMERICAN GRAFFITI, A Universal-Lucasfilm, Ltd.-Coppola Company Prod., Universal: VERNA FIELDS and MARCIA LUCAS.

THE DAY OF THE JACKAL, Warwick Film Prods., Ltd.-Universal Prods. France S.A., Universal: RALPH KEMPLEN.

THE EXORCIST, Hoya Prods., Warner Bros.: JORDAN LEONDOPOULOS, BUD SMITH, EVAN LOTTMAN, and NORMAN GAY.

JONATHAN LIVINGSTON SEAGULL, A JLS Limited Partnership Prod., Paramount: FRANK P. KELLER and JAMES GALLOWAY.

★ THE STING, A Universal-Bill/Phillips-George Roy Hill Film Prod., Zanuck/Brown Presentation, Universal: WILLIAM REYNOLDS.

Music

Original Dramatic Score

CINDERELLA LIBERTY, A Sanford Prod., 20th Century-Fox: JOHN WILLIAMS.

THE DAY OF THE DOLPHIN, Icarus Prods., Avco Embassy: GEORGES DELERUE.

PAPILLON, A Corona-General Production Company Prod., Allied Artists: JERRY GOLDSMITH.

A TOUCH OF CLASS, Brut Prods., Avco Embassy: JOHN CAMERON.

★ THE WAY WE WERE, Rastar Prods., Columbia: MARVIN HAMLISCH.

Scoring: Original Song Score and/or Adaptation

JESUS CHRIST SUPERSTAR, A Universal-Norman Jewison-Robert Stigwood Prod., Universal: Adapted by ANDRÉ PREVIN, HERBERT SPENCER, and ANDREW LLOYD WEBBER.

★ THE STING, A Universal-Bill/Phillips-George Roy Hill Film Prods., Zanuck/Brown Presentation, Universal: Adapted by MARVIN HAMLISCH.

TOM SAWYER, An Arthur P. Jacobs Prod., Reader's Digest Presentation, UA: Song Score by RICHARD M. SHERMAN and ROBERT B. SHERMAN; Adapted by JOHN WILLIAMS.

Song

ALL THAT LOVE WENT TO WASTE from *A Touch of Class*, Brut Prods., Avco Embassy: Music by GEORGE BARRIE; Lyrics by SAMMY CAHN.

LIVE AND LET DIE from *Live and Let Die*, Eon Prods., UA: Music and Lyrics by PAUL MCCARTNEY and LINDA MCCARTNEY.

LOVE from *Robin Hood*, Walt Disney Prods., Buena Vista Distribution Company: Music by GEORGE BRUNS; Lyrics by FLOYD HUDDLESTON.

★ THE WAY WE WERE from *The Way We Were*, Rastar Prods., Columbia: Music by MARVIN HAMLISCH; Lyrics by ALAN BERGMAN and MARILYN BERGMAN.

NICE TO BE AROUND from *Cinderella Liberty*, A Sanford Prod., 20th Century-Fox: Music by JOHN WILLIAMS; Lyrics by PAUL WILLIAMS.

Costume Design

CRIES AND WHISPERS, A Svenska Filminstitute-Cinematograph AB Prod., New World Pictures: MARIK VOS.

LUDWIG, A Mega Film S.p.A. Prod., Metro-Goldwyn-Mayer: PIERO TOSI.

★ THE STING, A Universal-Bill/Phillips-George Roy Hill Film Prod., Zanuck/Brown Presentation, Universal: EDITH HEAD.

TOM SAWYER, An Arthur P. Jacobs Prod., Reader's Digest Presentation, UA: DONFELD.

THE WAY WE WERE, Rastar Prods., Columbia: DOROTHY JEAKINS and MOSS MABRY.

Short Subjects

Animated

★ FRANK FILM, A Frank Mouris Production: FRANK MOURIS, Producer.

THE LEGEND OF JOHN HENRY, A Stephen Bosustow-Pyramid Films Prod.: NICK BOSUSTOW and DAVID ADAMS, Producers.

PULCINELLA, A Luzzati-Gianini Prod.: EMANUELE LUZZATI and GUILIO GIANINI, Producers.

Live Action

★ THE BOLERO, An Allan Miller Production: ALLAN MILLER and WILLIAM FERTIK, Producers.

CLOCKMAKER, James Street Prods. Ltd: RICHARD GAYER, Producer.

LIFE TIMES NINE, Insight Prods.: PEN DENSHAM and JOHN WATSON, Producers.

Documentary

Short Subjects

BACKGROUND, D'Avino and Fucci-Stone Prods.: CARMEN D'AVINO, Producer.

CHILDREN AT WORK (Paisti Ag Obair), Gael-Linn Films: LOUIS MARCUS, Producer.

CHRISTO'S VALLEY CURTAIN, A Maysles Films Prod.: ALBERT MAYSLES and DAVID MAYSLES, Producers.

FOUR STONES FOR KANEMITSU, A Tamarind Prod.: (Producer credit in controversy).

★ PRINCETON: A SEARCH FOR ANSWERS, Krainin-Sage Prods.: JULIAN KRAININ and DeWITT L. SAGE, JR., Producers.

Features

ALWAYS A NEW BEGINNING, Goodell Motion Pictures: JOHN D. GOODELL, Producer.

BATTLE OF BERLIN, Chronos Film: BENGT VON ZUR MUEHLEN, Producer.

★ THE GREAT AMERICAN COWBOY, Kieth Merrill Associates-Rodeo Film Prods.: KIETH MERRILL, Producer.

JOURNEY TO THE OUTER LIMITS, the

National Geographic Society and Wolper Prods.: ALEX GRASSHOFF, Producer.

WALLS OF FIRE, Mentor Prods.: GERTRUDE ROSS MARKS and EDMUND F. PENNEY, Producers.

Foreign Language Film Award

★ DAY FOR NIGHT, A Les Films du Carrosse-P.E.C.F. (Paris)-P.I.C. (Rome) Production (France).

THE HOUSE ON CHELOUCHE STREET, A Noah Films Production (Israel).

L'INVITATION, A Groupe 5 Geneve-Television Suisse Romande-Citel Films-Planfilm (Paris) Production (Switzerland).

THE PEDESTRIAN, An ALFA Glarus-MFG-Switz-Zev Braun Production (Federal Republic of Germany).

TURKISH DELIGHT, A Rob Houwer Film Production (The Netherlands).

Honorary Awards

HENRI LANGLOIS for his devotion to the art of film, his massive contributions in preserving its past, and his unswerving faith in its future. (Statuette)

GROUCHO MARX in recognition of his brilliant creativity and for the unequalled achievements of the Marx Brothers in the art of motion picture comedy. (Statuette)

Special Achievement Award

None.

Irving G. Thalberg Memorial Award

LAWRENCE WEINGARTEN.

Jean Hersholt Humanitarian Award

LEW WASSERMAN.

Scientific or Technical

Class I

None.

Class II

JOACHIM GERB and ERICH KAESTNER of the Arnold & Richter Company for the development and engineering of the Arriflex 35BL motion picture camera.

MAGNA-TECH ELECTRONIC CO., INC., for the engineering and development of a high-speed, rerecording system for motion picture production.

WILLIAM W. VALLIANT of PSC Technology, Inc., HOWARD F. OTT of Eastman Kodak Company, and GERRY DIEBOLD of the Richmark Camera Service, Inc., for the development of a liquid-gate system for motion picture printers.

HAROLD A. SCHEIB, CLIFFORD H. ELLIS, and ROGER W. BANKS of Research Products Incorporated for the concept and engineering of the Model 2101 optical printer for motion picture optical effects.

Class III

ROSCO LABORATORIES, INC., for the technical advances and the development of a complete system of light-control materials for motion picture photography.

RICHARD H. VETTER of the Todd-AO Corporation for the design of an improved anamorphic focusing system for use in motion picture photography.

FORTY-SEVENTH YEAR

1974

Nominations Announced: February 24, 1975
Awards Ceremony: April 8, 1975
Dorothy Chandler Pavilion, Los Angeles County Music Center
(MCs: Sammy Davis, Jr., Bob Hope, Shirley MacLaine, and Frank Sinatra)

Best Picture

CHINATOWN, A Robert Evans Production, Paramount: Robert Evans, Producer.

THE CONVERSATION, A Directors Company Production, Paramount: Francis Ford Coppola, Producer; Fred Roos, Co-producer.

★ THE GODFATHER PART II, A Coppola Company Production, Paramount: Francis Ford Coppola, Producer; Gray Frederickson and Fred Roos, Co-producers.

LENNY, A Marvin Worth Production, United Artists: Marvin Worth, Producer.

THE TOWERING INFERNO, An Irwin Allen Production, 20th Century-Fox/Warner Bros: Irwin Allen, Producer.

Actor

★ ART CARNEY in *Harry and Tonto*, 20th Century-Fox.

ALBERT FINNEY in *Murder on the Orient Express*, A G.W. Films, Ltd. Production, Paramount.

DUSTIN HOFFMAN in *Lenny*, A Marvin Worth Production, United Artists.

JACK NICHOLSON in *Chinatown*, A Robert Evans Production, Paramount.

AL PACINO in *The Godfather Part II*, A Coppola Company Production, Paramount.

Actress

★ ELLEN BURSTYN in *Alice Doesn't Live Here Anymore*, Warner Bros.

DIAHANN CARROLL in *Claudine*, Third World Cinema Productions in association with Joyce Selznick and Tina Pine, 20th Century-Fox.

FAYE DUNAWAY in *Chinatown*, A Robert Evans Production, Paramount.

VALERIE PERRINE in *Lenny*, A Marvin Worth Production, United Artists.

GENA ROWLANDS in *A Woman under the Influence*, A Faces International Films Production.

Supporting Actor

FRED ASTAIRE in *The Towering Inferno*, An Irwin Allen Production, 20th Century-Fox/Warner Bros.

JEFF BRIDGES in *Thunderbolt and Lightfoot*, A Malpaso Company Film Production, United Artists.

★ ROBERT DE NIRO in *The Godfather Part II*, A Coppola Company Production, Paramount.

MICHAEL V. GAZZO in *The Godfather Part II*, A Coppola Company Production, Paramount.

LEE STRASBERG in *The Godfather Part*

II, A Coppola Company Production, Paramount.

Supporting Actress

★ INGRID BERGMAN in *Murder on the Orient Express*, A G.W. Films, Ltd. Production, Paramount.

VALENTINA CORTESE in *Day for Night*, A Les Films du Carrosse and P.E.C.F., Paris; P.I.C., Rome Production, Warner Bros.

MADELINE KAHN in *Blazing Saddles*, Warner Bros.

DIANE LADD in *Alice Doesn't Live Here Anymore*, Warner Bros.

TALIA SHIRE in *The Godfather Part II*, A Coppola Company Production, Paramount.

Directing

JOHN CASSAVETES for *A Woman under the Influence*, A Faces International Films Production.

★ FRANCIS FORD COPPOLA for *The Godfather Part II*, A Coppola Company Production, Paramount.

BOB FOSSE for *Lenny*, a Marvin Worth Production, United Artists.

ROMAN POLANSKI for *Chinatown*, A Robert Evans Production, Paramount.

FRANÇOIS TRUFFAUT for *Day for Night*, A Les Films du Carrosse and P.E.C.F., Paris; P.I.C., Rome Production, Warner Bros.

Writing

Original Screenplay

ALICE DOESN'T LIVE HERE ANYMORE, Warner Bros.: ROBERT GETCHELL.

★ CHINATOWN, A Robert Evans Production, Paramount: ROBERT TOWNE.

THE CONVERSATION, A Directors Company Production, Paramount: FRANCIS FORD COPPOLA.

DAY FOR NIGHT, A Les Films du Carrosse and P.E.C.F., Paris; P.I.C., Rome Production, Warner Bros.; FRANÇOIS TRUFFAUT, JEAN-LOUIS RICHARD, and SUZANNE SCHIFFMAN.

HARRY AND TONTO, 20th Century-Fox: PAUL MAZURSKY and JOSH GREENFELD.

Screenplay Adapted from Other Material

THE APPRENTICESHIP OF DUDDY KRAVITZ, An International Cinemedia Centre, Ltd. Production, Paramount; MORDECAI RICHLER; Adaptation by LIONEL CHETWYND.

★ THE GODFATHER PART II, A Coppola Company Production, Paramount: FRANCIS FORD COPPOLA and MARIO PUZO.

LENNY, A Marvin Worth Production, United Artists: JULIAN BARRY.

MURDER ON THE ORIENT EXPRESS, A G.W. Films, Ltd. Production, Paramount: PAUL DEHN.

YOUNG FRANKENSTEIN, A Gruskoff/ Venture Films-Crossbow Prods.-Jouer, Ltd. Production, 20th Century-Fox: GENE WILDER and MEL BROOKS.

Cinematography

CHINATOWN, A Robert Evans Production, Paramount: JOHN A. ALONZO.

EARTHQUAKE, A Universal-Mark Robson-Filmakers Group Production, Universal: PHILIP LATHROP.

LENNY, A Marvin Worth Production, United Artists: BRUCE SURTEES.

MURDER ON THE ORIENT EXPRESS, A G.W. Films, Ltd. Production, Paramount: GEOFFREY UNSWORTH.

★ THE TOWERING INFERNO, An Irwin Allen Production, 20th Century-Fox/Warner Bros.: FRED KOENEKAMP and JOSEPH BIROC.

Art Direction—Set Decoration

CHINATOWN, A Robert Evans Production, Paramount: RICHARD

SYLBERT and W. STEWART CAMPBELL; Set Decoration: RUBY LEVITT.

EARTHQUAKE, A Universal-Mark Robson-Filmakers Group Production, Universal: ALEXANDER GOLITZEN and E. PRESTON AMES; Set Decoration: FRANK MCKELVY.

★ THE GODFATHER PART II, A Coppola Company Production, Paramount: DEAN TAVOULARIS and ANGELO GRAHAM; Set Decoration: GEORGE R. NELSON.

THE ISLAND AT THE TOP OF THE WORLD, Walt Disney Productions, Buena Vista Distribution Company: PETER ELLENSHAW, JOHN B. MANSBRIDGE, WALTER TYLER, and AL ROELOFS; Set Decoration: HAL GAUSMAN.

THE TOWERING INFERNO, An Irwin Allen Production, 20th Century-Fox/ Warner Bros.: WILLIAM CREBER and WARD PRESTON; Set Decoration: RAPHAEL BRETTON.

Sound

CHINATOWN, A Robert Evans Production, Paramount: BUD GRENZBACH and LARRY JOST.

THE CONVERSATION, A Directors Company Production, Paramount: WALTER MURCH and ARTHUR ROCHESTER.

★ EARTHQUAKE, A Universal-Mark Robson-Filmakers Group Production, Universal: RONALD PIERCE and MELVIN METCALFE, SR.

THE TOWERING INFERNO, An Irwin Allen Production, 20th Century-Fox/ Warner Bros.: THEODORE SODERBERG and HERMAN LEWIS.

YOUNG FRANKENSTEIN, A Gruskoff/ Venture Films-Crossbow Prods.-Jouer, Ltd. Production, 20th Century-Fox: RICHARD PORTMAN and GENE CANTAMESSA.

Film Editing

BLAZING SADDLES, Warner Bros.: JOHN C. HOWARD and DANFORD GREENE.

CHINATOWN, A Robert Evans Production, Paramount: SAM O'STEEN.

EARTHQUAKE, A Universal-Mark Robson-Filmakers Group Production, Universal: DOROTHY SPENCER.

THE LONGEST YARD, An Albert S. Ruddy Production, Paramount: MICHAEL LUCIANO.

★ THE TOWERING INFERNO, An Irwin Allen Production, 20th Century-Fox/Warner Bros.: HAROLD F. KRESS and CARL KRESS.

Music

Original Dramatic Score

CHINATOWN, A Robert Evans Production, Paramount: JERRY GOLDSMITH.

★ THE GODFATHER PART II, A Coppola Company Production, Paramount: NINO ROTA and CARMINE COPPOLA.

MURDER ON THE ORIENT EXPRESS, A G.W. Films, Ltd. Production, Paramount: RICHARD RODNEY BENNETT.

SHANKS, William Castle Productions, Paramount: ALEX NORTH.

THE TOWERING INFERNO, An Irwin Allen Production, 20th Century-Fox/ Warner Bros.: JOHN WILLIAMS.

Scoring: Original Song Score and/or Adaptation

★ THE GREAT GATSBY, A David Merrick Production, Paramount: Adapted by NELSON RIDDLE.

THE LITTLE PRINCE, A Stanley Donen Enterprises, Ltd. Production, Paramount: Song Score by ALAN JAY LERNER and FREDERICK LOEWE; Adapted by ANGELA MORLEY and DOUGLAS GAMLEY.

PHANTOM OF THE PARADISE, Harbor Productions, 20th Century-Fox: Song Score by PAUL WILLIAMS; Adapted by PAUL WILLIAMS and GEORGE ALICESON TIPTON.

Song

BENJI'S THEME (I FEEL LOVE) from *Benji*, Mulberry Square: Music by EUEL BOX; Lyrics by BETTY BOX.

BLAZING SADDLES from *Blazing Saddles*, Warner Bros.: Music by JOHN MORRIS; Lyrics by MEL BROOKS.

LITTLE PRINCE from *The Little Prince*, A Stanley Donen Enterprises, Ltd. Production, Paramount: Music by FREDERICK LOEWE; Lyrics by ALAN JAY LERNER.

★ WE MAY NEVER LOVE LIKE THIS AGAIN from *The Towering Inferno*, An Irwin Allen Production, 20th Century-Fox/Warner Bros.: Music and Lyrics by AL KASHA and JOEL HIRSCHHORN.

WHEREVER LOVE TAKES ME from *Gold*, Avton Film Productions, Ltd., Allied Artists: Music by ELMER BERNSTEIN; Lyrics by DON BLACK.

Costume Design

CHINATOWN, A Robert Evans Production, Paramount: ANTHEA SYLBERT.

DAISY MILLER, A Directors Company Production, Paramount: JOHN FURNESS.

THE GODFATHER PART II, A Coppola Company Production, Paramount: THEADORA VAN RUNKLE.

★ THE GREAT GATSBY, A David Merrick Production, Paramount: THEONI V. ALDREDGE.

MURDER ON THE ORIENT EXPRESS, A G.W. Films, Ltd. Production, Paramount: TONY WALTON.

Short Films

(Name changed from *Short Subjects*)

Animated

★ CLOSED MONDAYS, Lighthouse Productions: WILL VINTON and BOB GARDINER, Producers.

THE FAMILY THAT DWELT APART, National Film Board of Canada: YVON MALLETTE and ROBERT VERRALL, Producers.

HUNGER, National Film Board of Canada: PETER FOLDES and RENE JODOIN, Producers.

VOYAGE TO NEXT, The Hubley Studio: FAITH HUBLEY and JOHN HUBLEY, Producers.

WINNIE THE POOH AND TIGGER TOO, Walt Disney Productions: WOLFGANG REITHERMAN, Producer.

Live Action

CLIMB, Dewitt Jones Productions: DEWITT JONES, Producer.

THE CONCERT, The Black and White Colour Film Company, Ltd.: JULIAN CHAGRIN and CLAUDE CHAGRIN, Producers.

★ ONE-EYED MEN ARE KINGS, C.A.P.A.C. Productions (Paris): PAUL CLAUDON and EDMOND SECHAN, Producers.

PLANET OCEAN, Graphic Films: GEORGE V. CASEY, Producer.

THE VIOLIN, A Sincinkin, Ltd. Production: ANDREW WELSH and GEORGE PASTIC, Producers.

Documentary

Short Subjects

CITY OUT OF WILDERNESS, Francis Thompson Inc.: FRANCIS THOMPSON, Producer.

★ DON'T, R.A. Films: ROBIN LEHMAN, Producer.

EXPLORATORIUM, A Jon Boorstin Production: JON BOORSTIN, Producer.

JOHN MUIR'S HIGH SIERRA, Dewitt Jones Productions: DEWITT JONES and LESLEY FOSTER, Producers.

NAKED YOGA, A Filmshop Production: RONALD S. KASS and MERVYN LLOYD, Producers.

Features

ANTONIA: A PORTRAIT OF THE WOMAN, Rocky Mountain Productions: JUDY

COLLINS and JILL GODMILOW, Producers.
THE CHALLENGE . . . A TRIBUTE TO MODERN ART, A World View Production: HERBERT KLINE, Producer.
THE 81ST BLOW, A Film by Ghetto Fighters House: JACQUOT EHRLICH, DAVID BERGMAN, and HAIM GOURI, Producers.
★ HEARTS AND MINDS, A Touchstone-Audjeff-BBS Production, Howard Zucker/Henry Jaglom-Rainbow Pictures Presentation: PETER DAVIS and BERT SCHNEIDER, Producers.
THE WILD AND THE BRAVE, E.S.J. Productions, in association with Tomorrow Entertainment, Inc., and Jones/Howard Ltd.: NATALIE R. JONES and EUGENE S. JONES, Producers.

Foreign Language Film Award

★ AMARCORD, An F.C. (Rome)-P.E.C.F. (Paris) Production (Italy).
CATSPLAY, A Hunnia Studio Production (Hungary).
THE DELUGE, A Film Polski Production (Poland).
LACOMBE, LUCIEN, An NEF-UPF (Paris)-Vides Film (Rome)-Hallelujah Film (Munich) Production (France).
THE TRUCE, A Tamames-Zemborain Production (Argentina).

Honorary Awards

HOWARD HAWKS—A master American filmmaker whose creative efforts hold a distinguished place in world cinema. (Statuette)
JEAN RENOIR—a genius who, with grace, responsibility, and enviable devotion through silent film, sound film, feature, documentary, and television, has won the world's admiration. (Statuette)

Special Achievement Award

Visual Effects: FRANK BRENDEL, GLEN ROBINSON, and ALBERT WHITLOCK for *Earthquake*, A Universal-Mark Robson-Filmakers Groups Production, Universal.

Irving G. Thalberg Memorial Award

None.

Jean Hersholt Humanitarian Award

ARTHUR B. KRIM.

Scientific or Technical

Class I

None.

Class II

JOSEPH D. KELLY of Glen Glenn Sound for the design of new audio control consoles that have advanced the state of the art of sound recording and rerecording for motion picture production.
THE BURBANK STUDIOS SOUND DEPARTMENT for the design of new audio control consoles engineered and constructed by the Quad-Eight Sound Corporation.
SAMUEL GOLDWYN STUDIOS SOUND DEPARTMENT for the design of a new audio control console engineered and constructed by the Quad-Eight Sound Corporation.
QUAD-EIGHT SOUND CORPORATION for the engineering and construction of new audio control consoles designed by the Burbank Studios Sound Department and by the Samuel Goldwyn Studios Sound Department.
WALDON O. WATSON, RICHARD J. STUMPF, ROBERT J. LEONARD, and the UNIVERSAL

CITY STUDIOS SOUND DEPARTMENT for the development and engineering of the Sensurround System for motion picture presentation.

Class III

ELEMACK COMPANY, Rome, Italy, for the design and development of the Spyder camera dolly.

LOUIS AMI of the Universal City Studios for the design and construction of a reciprocating camera platform used to photograph special visual effects for motion pictures.

FORTY-EIGHTH YEAR

1975

Nominations Announced: February 17, 1976
Awards Ceremony: March 29, 1976
Dorothy Chandler Pavilion, Los Angeles County Music Center
(MCs: Goldie Hawn, Gene Kelly, Walter Matthau, George Segal, and Robert Shaw)

Best Picture

BARRY LYNDON, A Hawk Films, Ltd. Production, Warner Bros.: Stanley Kubrick, Producer.

DOG DAY AFTERNOON, Warner Bros.: Martin Bregman and Martin Elfand, Producers.

JAWS, A Universal-Zanuck/Brown Production, Universal: Richard D. Zanuck and David Brown, Producers.

NASHVILLE, An ABC Entertainment-Jerry Weintraub-Robert Altman Production, Paramount: Robert Altman, Producer.

★ ONE FLEW OVER THE CUCKOO'S NEST, A Fantasy Films Production, United Artists: Saul Zaentz and Michael Douglas, Producers.

Actor

WALTER MATTHAU in *The Sunshine Boys*, A Ray Stark Production, Metro-Goldwyn-Mayer.

★ JACK NICHOLSON in *One Flew over the Cuckoo's Nest*, A Fantasy Films Production, United Artists.

AL PACINO in *Dog Day Afternoon*, Warner Bros.

MAXIMILIAN SCHELL in *The Man in the Glass Booth*, An Ely Landau Organization Production, AFT Distributing.

JAMES WHITMORE in *Give 'em Hell, Harry!*, A Theatrovision Production, Avco Embassy.

Actress

ISABELLE ADJANI in *The Story of Adele H.*, A Les Films du Carrosse-Les Productions Artistes Associés Production, New World Pictures.

ANN-MARGRET in *Tommy*, A Robert Stigwood Organisation, Ltd. Production, Columbia.

★ LOUISE FLETCHER in *One Flew over the Cuckoo's Nest*, A Fantasy Films Production, United Artists.

GLENDA JACKSON in *Hedda*, A Royal Shakespeare-Brut Productions-George Barrie/Robert Enders Film Production, Brut Productions.

CAROL KANE in *Hester Street*, Midwest Film Productions.

Supporting Actor

★ GEORGE BURNS in *The Sunshine Boys*, A Ray Stark Production, Metro-Goldwyn-Mayer.

BRAD DOURIF in *One Flew over the Cuckoo's Nest*, A Fantasy Films Production, United Artists.

BURGESS MEREDITH in *The Day of the Locust*, A Jerome Hellman Production, Paramount.
CHRIS SARANDON in *Dog Day Afternoon*, Warner Bros.
JACK WARDEN in *Shampoo*, Rubeeker Productions, Columbia.

Supporting Actress

RONEE BLAKLEY in *Nashville*, An ABC Entertainment-Jerry Weintraub-Robert Altman Production, Paramount.
★ LEE GRANT in *Shampoo*, Rubeeker Productions, Columbia.
SYLVIA MILES in *Farewell, My Lovely*, An Elliott Kastner-ITC Production, Avco Embassy.
LILY TOMLIN in *Nashville*, An ABC Entertainment-Jerry Weintraub-Robert Altman Production, Paramount.
BRENDA VACCARO in *Jacqueline Susann's Once Is Not Enough*, A Howard W. Koch Production, Paramount.

Directing

ROBERT ALTMAN for *Nashville*, An ABC Entertainment-Jerry Weintraub-Robert Altman Production, Paramount.
FEDERICO FELLINI for *Amarcord*, An F.C. Productions-P.E.C.F. Production, New World Pictures.
★ MILOS FORMAN for *One Flew over the Cuckoo's Nest*, A Fantasy Films Production, United Artists.
STANLEY KUBRICK for *Barry Lyndon*, A Hawk Films, Ltd. Production, Warner Bros.
SIDNEY LUMET for *Dog Day Afternoon*, Warner Bros.

Writing

Original Screenplay

AMARCORD, an F.C. Productions-P.E.C.F. Production, New World Pictures: FEDERICO FELLINI and TONINO GUERRA.
AND NOW MY LOVE, A Rizzoli Film-Les Films 13 Production, Avco Embassy: CLAUDE LELOUCH and PIERRE UYTTERHOEVEN.
★ DOG DAY AFTERNOON, Warner Bros.: FRANK PIERSON.
LIES MY FATHER TOLD ME, Pentimento Productions, Ltd.-Pentacle VIII Productions, Ltd., Columbia: TED ALLAN.
SHAMPOO, Rubeeker Productions, Columbia: ROBERT TOWNE and WARREN BEATTY.

Screenplay Adapted from Other Material

BARRY LYNDON, A Hawk Films, Ltd. Production, Warner Bros.: STANLEY KUBRICK.
THE MAN WHO WOULD BE KING, An Allied Artists-Columbia Pictures Production, Allied Artists: JOHN HUSTON and GLADYS HILL.
★ ONE FLEW OVER THE CUCKOO'S NEST, A Fantasy Films Production, United Artists: LAWRENCE HAUBEN and BO GOLDMAN.
SCENT OF A WOMAN, A Dean Film Production, 20th Century-Fox: RUGGERO MACCARI and DINO RISI.
THE SUNSHINE BOYS, A Ray Stark Production, Metro-Goldwyn-Mayer: NEIL SIMON.

Cinematography

★ BARRY LYNDON, A Hawk Films, Ltd. Production, Warner Bros.: JOHN ALCOTT.
THE DAY OF THE LOCUST, A Jerome Hellman Production, Paramount: CONRAD HALL.
FUNNY LADY, A Rastar Pictures Production, Columbia: JAMES WONG HOWE.
THE HINDENBURG, A Robert Wise-Filmakers Group-Universal

Production, Universal: ROBERT SURTEES.

ONE FLEW OVER THE CUCKOO'S NEST, A Fantasy Films Production, United Artists: HASKELL WEXLER and BILL BUTLER.

Art Direction—Set Decoration

★ BARRY LYNDON, A Hawk Films, Ltd. Production, Warner Bros.: KEN ADAM and ROY WALKER; Set Decoration: VERNON DIXON.

THE HINDENBURG, A Robert Wise-Filmakers Group-Universal Production, Universal: EDWARD CARFAGNO; Set Decoration: FRANK MCKELVY.

THE MAN WHO WOULD BE KING, An Allied Artists-Columbia Pictures Production, Allied Artists: ALEXANDER TRAUNER and TONY INGLIS; Set Decoration: PETER JAMES.

SHAMPOO, Rubeeker Productions, Columbia: RICHARD SYLBERT and W. STEWART CAMPBELL; Set Decoration: GEORGE GAINES.

THE SUNSHINE BOYS, A Ray Stark Production, Metro-Goldwyn-Mayer: ALBERT BRENNER; Set Decoration: MARVIN MARCH.

Sound

BITE THE BULLET, A Pax Enterprises Production, Columbia: ARTHUR PIANTADOSI, LES FRESHOLTZ, RICHARD TYLER, and AL OVERTON, JR.

FUNNY LADY, A Rastar Pictures Production, Columbia: RICHARD PORTMAN, DON MACDOUGALL, CURLY THIRLWELL, and JACK SOLOMON.

THE HINDENBURG, A Robert Wise-Filmakers Group Universal Production, Universal: LEONARD PETERSON, JOHN A. BOLGER, JR., JOHN MACK, and DON K. SHARPLESS.

★ JAWS, A Universal-Zanuck/Brown Production, Universal: ROBERT L. HOYT, ROGER HEMAN, EARL MADERY, and JOHN CARTER.

THE WIND AND THE LION, A Herb Jaffe Production, Metro-Goldwyn-Mayer: HARRY W. TETRICK, AARON ROCHIN, WILLIAM MCCAUGHEY, and ROY CHARMAN.

Film Editing

DOG DAY AFTERNOON, Warner Bros.: DEDE ALLEN.

★ JAWS, A Universal-Zanuck/Brown Production, Universal: VERNA FIELDS.

THE MAN WHO WOULD BE KING, An Allied Artists-Columbia Pictures Production, Allied Artists: RUSSELL LLOYD.

ONE FLEW OVER THE CUCKOO'S NEST, A Fantasy Films Production, United Artists: RICHARD CHEW, LYNZEE KLINGMAN, and SHELDON KAHN.

THREE DAYS OF THE CONDOR, A Dino De Laurentiis Production, Paramount: FREDRIC STEINKAMP and DON GUIDICE.

Music

Original Score

BIRDS DO IT, BEES DO IT, A Wolper Pictures Production, Columbia: GERALD FRIED.

BITE THE BULLET, A Pax Enterprises Production, Columbia: ALEX NORTH.

★ JAWS, A Universal-Zanuck/Brown Production, Universal: JOHN WILLIAMS.

ONE FLEW OVER THE CUCKOO'S NEST, A Fantasy Films Production, United Artists: JACK NITZSCHE.

THE WIND AND THE LION, A Herb Jaffe Production, Metro-Goldwyn-Mayer: JERRY GOLDSMITH.

Scoring: Original Song Score and/or Adaptation

★ BARRY LYNDON, A Hawk Films, Ltd. Production, Warner Bros.:

Adapted by LEONARD ROSENMAN.

FUNNY LADY, A Rastar Pictures Production, Columbia: Adapted by PETER MATZ.

TOMMY, A Robert Stigwood Organisation, Ltd. Production, Columbia: Adapted by PETER TOWNSHEND.

Original Song

HOW LUCKY CAN YOU GET from *Funny Lady*, A Rastar Pictures Production, Columbia: Music and Lyrics by FRED EBB and JOHN KANDER.

★ I'M EASY from *Nashville*, An ABC Entertainment-Jerry Weintraub-Robert Altman Production, Paramount: Music and Lyrics by KEITH CARRADINE.

NOW THAT WE'RE IN LOVE from *Whiffs*, Brut Productions, 20th Century-Fox: Music by GEORGE BARRIE; Lyrics by SAMMY CAHN.

RICHARD'S WINDOW from *The Other Side of the Mountain*, A Filmways-Larry Peerce-Universal Production, Universal: Music by CHARLES FOX; Lyrics by NORMAN GIMBEL.

THEME FROM MAHOGANY (DO YOU KNOW WHERE YOU'RE GOING TO) from *Mahogany*, A Jobete Film Production, Paramount: Music by MICHAEL MASSER; Lyrics by GERRY GOFFIN.

Costume Design

★ BARRY LYNDON, A Hawk Films, Ltd. Production, Warner Bros.: ULLA-BRITT SODERLUND and MILENA CANONERO.

THE FOUR MUSKETEERS, A Film Trust S.A. Production, 20th Century-Fox: YVONNE BLAKE and RON TALSKY.

FUNNY LADY, A Rastar Pictures Production, Columbia: RAY AGHAYAN and BOB MACKIE.

THE MAGIC FLUTE, A Sveriges Radio A.B. Production, Surrogate Releasing: HENNY NOREMARK and KARIN ERSKINE.

THE MAN WHO WOULD BE KING, An Allied Artists-Columbia Pictures Production, Allied Artists: EDITH HEAD.

Short Films

Animated

★ GREAT, Grantstern Ltd. and British Lion Films Ltd.: BOB GODFREY, Producer.

KICK ME, Robert Swarthe Productions: ROBERT SWARTHE, Producer.

MONSIEUR POINTU, National Film Board of Canada: RENÉ JODOIN, BERNARD LONGPRÉ, and ANDRÉ LEDUC, Producers.

SISYPHUS, Hungarofilms: MARCELL JANKOVICS, Producer.

Live Action

★ ANGEL AND BIG JOE, Bert Salzman Productions: BERT SALZMAN, Producer.

CONQUEST OF LIGHT, Louis Marcus Films Ltd.: LOUIS MARCUS, Producer.

DAWN FLIGHT, Lawrence M. Lansburgh Productions: LAWRENCE M. LANSBURGH and BRIAN LANSBURGH, Producers.

A DAY IN THE LIFE OF BONNIE CONSOLO, Barr Films: BARRY SPINELLO, Producer.

DOUBLETALK, Beattie Productions: ALAN BEATTIE, Producer.

Documentary

Short Subjects

ARTHUR AND LILLIE, Department of Communication, Stanford University: JON ELSE, STEVEN KOVACS, and KRISTINE SAMUELSON, Producers.

★ THE END OF THE GAME, Opus Films Limited: CLAIRE WILBUR and ROBIN LEHMAN, Producers.

MILLIONS OF YEARS AHEAD OF MAN, BASF: MANFRED BAIER, Producer.
PROBES IN SPACE, Graphic Films: GEORGE V. CASEY, Producer.
WHISTLING SMITH, National Film Board of Canada: BARRIE HOWELLS and MICHAEL SCOTT, Producers.

Features

THE CALIFORNIA REICH, Yasny Talking Pictures: WALTER F. PARKES and KEITH F. CRITCHLOW, Producers.
FIGHTING FOR OUR LIVES, A Farm Worker Film: GLEN PEARCY, Producer.
THE INCREDIBLE MACHINE, the National Geographic Society and Wolper Productions: IRWIN ROSTEN, Producer.
★ THE MAN WHO SKIED DOWN EVEREST, A Crawley Films Presentation: F. R. CRAWLEY, JAMES HAGER, and DALE HARTLEBEN, Producers.
THE OTHER HALF OF THE SKY: A CHINA MEMOIR, MacLaine Productions: SHIRLEY MACLAINE, Producer.

Foreign Language Film Award

★ DERSU UZALA, A Mosfilms Studio Production (U.S.S.R.).
LAND OF PROMISE, A Film Polski Production (Poland).
LETTERS FROM MARUSIA, A Conacine Production (Mexico).
SANDAKAN NO. 8, A Toho-Haiyuza Production (Japan).
SCENT OF A WOMAN, A Dean Film Production (Italy).

Honorary Award

MARY PICKFORD in recognition of her unique contributions to the film industry and the development of film as an artistic medium. (Statuette)

Special Achievement Awards

Sound Effects: PETER BERKOS for *The Hindenburg*, A Robert Wise-Filmakers Group-Universal Production, Universal.
Visual Effects: ALBERT WHITLOCK and GLEN ROBINSON for *The Hindenburg*, A Robert Wise-Filmakers Group-Universal Production, Universal.

Irving G. Thalberg Memorial Award

MERVYN LEROY.

Jean Hersholt Humanitarian Award

JULES C. STEIN.

Scientific or Technical

Class I

None.

Class II

CHADWELL O'CONNOR of the O'Connor Engineering Laboratories for the concept and engineering of a fluid-damped camerahead for motion picture photography.
WILLIAM F. MINER of Universal City Studios, Inc., and the WESTINGHOUSE ELECTRIC CORPORATION for the development and engineering of a solid-state, 500-kilowatt, direct-current static rectifier for motion picture lighting.

Class III

LAWRENCE W. BUTLER and ROGER BANKS for the concept of applying low inertia and stepping electric motors to film transport systems and optical printers for motion picture production.
DAVID J. DEGENKOLB and FRED SCOBEY of Deluxe General Incorporated and JOHN C. DOLAN and RICHARD DUBOIS of the Akwaklame Company for the development of a technique for silver recovery from photographic wash-waters by ion exchange.

JOSEPH WESTHEIMER for the development of a device to obtain shadowed titles on motion picture films.

CARTER EQUIPMENT CO., INC., and RAMTRONICS for the engineering and manufacture of a computerized tape-punching system for programming laboratory printing machines.

THE HOLLYWOOD FILM COMPANY for the engineering and manufacture of a computerized tape-punching system for programming laboratory printing machines.

BELL & HOWELL for the engineering and manufacture of a computerized tape-punching system for programming laboratory printing machines.

FREDRIK SCHLYTER for the engineering and manufacture of a computerized tape-punching system for programming laboratory printing machines.

1976

Nominations Announced: February 10, 1977
Awards Ceremony: March 28, 1977
Dorothy Chandler Pavilion, Los Angeles County Music Center
(MCs: Warren Beatty, Ellen Burstyn, Jane Fonda, and Richard Pryor)

Best Picture

ALL THE PRESIDENT'S MEN, A Wildwood Enterprises Production, Warner Bros.: Walter Coblenz, Producer.

BOUND FOR GLORY, The Bound for Glory Company Production, United Artists: Robert F. Blumofe and Harold Leventhal, Producers.

NETWORK, A Howard Gottfried/Paddy Chayefsky Production, Metro-Goldwyn-Mayer/United Artists: Howard Gottfried, Producer.

★ ROCKY, A Robert Chartoff-Irwin Winkler Production, United Artists: Irwin Winkler and Robert Chartoff, Producers.

TAXI DRIVER, A Bill/Phillips Production of a Martin Scorsese Film, Columbia Pictures: MICHAEL PHILLIPS and JULIA PHILLIPS, Producers.

Actor

ROBERT DE NIRO in *Taxi Driver*, A Bill/Phillips Production of a Martin Scorsese Film, Columbia Pictures.

★ PETER FINCH in *Network*, A Howard Gottfried/Paddy Chayefsky Production, Metro-Goldwyn-Mayer/United Artists.

GIANCARLO GIANNINI in *Seven Beauties*, A Medusa Distribuzione Production, Cinema 5, Ltd.

WILLIAM HOLDEN in *Network*, A Howard Gottfried/Paddy Chayefsky Production, Metro-Goldwyn-Mayer/United Artists.

SYLVESTER STALLONE in *Rocky*, A Robert Chartoff-Irwin Winkler Production, United Artists.

Actress

MARIE-CHRISTINE BARRAULT in *Cousin, Cousine,* Les Films Pomereu-Gaumont Production, Northal Film Distributors Ltd.

★ FAYE DUNAWAY in *Network*, A Howard Gottfried/Paddy Chayefsky Production, Metro-Goldwyn-Mayer/United Artists.

TALIA SHIRE in *Rocky,* A Robert Chartoff-Irwin Winkler Production, United Artists.

SISSY SPACEK in *Carrie*, A Redbank Films Production, United Artists.

LIV ULLMANN in *Face to Face*, A Cinematograph A.B. Production, Paramount.

Supporting Actor

NED BEATTY in *Network*, A Howard Gottfried/Paddy Chayefsky Production, Metro-Goldwyn-Mayer/United Artists.

BURGESS MEREDITH in *Rocky*, A Robert

Chartoff-Irwin Winkler Production, United Artists.

LAURENCE OLIVIER in *Marathon Man*, A Robert Evans-Sidney Beckerman Production, Paramount.

★ JASON ROBARDS in *All the President's Men*, A Wildwood Enterprises Production, Warner Bros.

BURT YOUNG in *Rocky*, A Robert Chartoff-Irwin Winkler Production, United Artists.

Supporting Actress

JANE ALEXANDER in *All the President's Men*, A Wildwood Enterprises Production, Warner Bros.

JODIE FOSTER in *Taxi Driver*, A Bill/Phillips Production of a Martin Scorsese Film, Columbia Pictures.

LEE GRANT in *Voyage of the Damned*, An ITC Entertainment Production, Avco Embassy.

PIPER LAURIE in *Carrie*, A Redbank Films Production, United Artists.

★ BEATRICE STRAIGHT in *Network*, A Howard Gottfried/Paddy Chayefsky Production, Metro-Goldwyn-Mayer/United Artists.

Directing

★ JOHN G. AVILDSEN for *Rocky*, A Robert Chartoff-Irwin Winkler Production, United Artists.

INGMAR BERGMAN for *Face to Face*, A Cinematograph A.B. Production, Paramount.

SIDNEY LUMET for *Network*, A Howard Gottfried/Paddy Chayefsky Production, Metro-Goldwyn-Mayer/United Artists.

ALAN J. PAKULA for *All the President's Men*, A Wildwood Enterprises Production, Warner Bros.

LINA WERTMULLER for *Seven Beauties*, A Medusa Distribuzione Production, Cinema 5, Ltd.

Writing

Screenplay—Written Directly for the Screen

COUSIN, COUSINE, Les Films Pomereu-Gaumont Production, Northal Film Distributors Ltd.: JEAN-CHARLES TACCHELLA; Adaptation by DANIELE THOMPSON.

THE FRONT, Columbia Pictures: WALTER BERNSTEIN.

★ NETWORK, A Howard Gottfried/Paddy Chayefsky Production, Metro-Goldwyn-Mayer/United Artists: PADDY CHAYEFSKY.

ROCKY, A Robert Chartoff-Irwin Winkler Production, United Artists: SYLVESTER STALLONE.

SEVEN BEAUTIES, A Medusa Distribuzione Production, Cinema 5, Ltd.: LINA WERTMULLER.

Screenplay Based on Material from Another Medium

★ ALL THE PRESIDENT'S MEN, A Wildwood Enterprises Production, Warner Bros.: WILLIAM GOLDMAN.

BOUND FOR GLORY, The Bound for Glory Production, United Artists: ROBERT GETCHELL.

FELLINI'S CASANOVA, A P.E.A.-Produzioni Europee Associate S.p.A. Production, Universal: FEDERICO FELLINI and BERNADINO ZAPPONI.

THE SEVEN PERCENT SOLUTION, A Herbert Ross Film/Winitsky-Sellers Production, A Universal Release: NICHOLAS MEYER.

VOYAGE OF THE DAMNED, An ITC Entertainment Production, Avco Embassy: STEVE SHAGAN and DAVID BUTLER.

Cinematography

★ BOUND FOR GLORY, The Bound for Glory Company Production,

United Artists: HASKELL WEXLER.

KING KONG, A Dino De Laurentiis Production, Paramount: RICHARD H. KLINE.

LOGAN'S RUN, A Saul David Production, Metro-Goldwyn-Mayer: ERNEST LASZLO.

NETWORK, A Howard Gottfried/Paddy Chayefsky Production, Metro-Goldwyn-Mayer/United Artists: OWEN ROIZMAN.

A STAR IS BORN, A Barwood/Jon Peters Production, First Artists Presentation, Warner Bros.: ROBERT SURTEES.

Art Direction—Set Decoration

★ ALL THE PRESIDENT'S MEN, A Wildwood Enterprises Production, Warner Bros.: GEORGE JENKINS; Set Decoration: GEORGE GAINES.

THE INCREDIBLE SARAH, A Helen M. Strauss-Reader's Digest Films, Ltd. Production, Seymour Borde and Associates: ELLIOT SCOTT and NORMAN REYNOLDS.

THE LAST TYCOON, A Sam Spiegel-Elia Kazan Film Production, Paramount: GENE CALLAHAN and JACK COLLIS; Set Decoration: JERRY WUNDERLICH.

LOGAN'S RUN, A Saul David Production, Metro-Goldwyn-Mayer: DALE HENNESY; Set Decoration: ROBERT DE VESTEL.

THE SHOOTIST, A Frankovich/Self Production, Dino De Laurentiis Presentation, Paramount: ROBERT F. BOYLE; Set Decoration: ARTHUR JEPH PARKER.

Sound

★ ALL THE PRESIDENT'S MEN, A Wildwood Enterprises Production, Warner Bros.: ARTHUR PIANTADOSI, LES FRESHOLTZ, DICK ALEXANDER, and JIM WEBB.

KING KONG, A Dino De Laurentiis Production, Paramount: HARRY WARREN TETRICK, WILLIAM MCCAUGHEY, AARON ROCHIN, and JACK SOLOMON.

ROCKY, A Robert Chartoff-Irwin Winkler Production, United Artists: HARRY WARREN TETRICK, WILLIAM MCCAUGHEY, LYLE BURBRIDGE, and BUD ALPER.

SILVER STREAK, A Frank Yablans Presentations Production, 20th Century-Fox: DONALD MITCHELL, DOUGLAS WILLIAMS, RICHARD TYLER, and HAL ETHERINGTON.

A STAR IS BORN, A Barwood/Jon Peters Production, First Artists Presentation, Warner Bros.: ROBERT KNUDSON, DAN WALLIN, ROBERT GLASS, and TOM OVERTON.

Film Editing

ALL THE PRESIDENT'S MEN, A Wildwood Enterprises Production, Warner Bros.: ROBERT L. WOLFE.

BOUND FOR GLORY, The Bound for Glory Company Production, United Artists: ROBERT JONES and PEMBROKE J. HERRING.

NETWORK, A Howard Gottfried/Paddy Chayefsky Production, Metro-Goldwyn-Mayer/United Artists: ALAN HEIM.

★ ROCKY, A Robert Chartoff-Irwin Winkler Production, United Artists: RICHARD HALSEY and SCOTT CONRAD.

TWO-MINUTE WARNING, A Filmways/Larry Peerce-Edward S. Feldman Film Production, Universal: EVE NEWMAN AND WALTER HANNEMANN.

Music

Original Score

OBSESSION, George Litto Productions, Columbia Pictures: BERNARD HERRMANN.

★ THE OMEN, 20th Century-Fox Productions, Ltd., 20th Century-Fox: JERRY GOLDSMITH.

THE OUTLAW JOSEY WALES, A Malpaso Company Production, Warner Bros.: JERRY FIELDING.

TAXI DRIVER, A Bill/Phillips Production of a Martin Scorsese Film, Columbia Pictures: BERNARD HERRMANN.

VOYAGE OF THE DAMNED, An ITC Entertainment Production, Avco Embassy: LALO SCHIFRIN.

Original Song Score and Its Adaptation or Best Adaptation Score

★ BOUND FOR GLORY, The Bound for Glory Company Production, United Artists: Adapted by LEONARD ROSENMAN.

BUGSY MALONE, A Goodtimes Enterprises, Ltd. Production, Paramount: Song Score and Its Adaptation by PAUL WILLIAMS.

A STAR IS BORN, A Barwood/Jon Peters Production, First Artists Presentation, Warner Bros.: Adapted by ROGER KELLAWAY.

Original Song

AVE SATANI from *The Omen*, 20th Century-Fox Productions, Ltd., 20th Century-Fox: Music and Lyrics by JERRY GOLDSMITH.

COME TO ME from *The Pink Panther Strikes Again*, Amjo Productions, Ltd., United Artists: Music by HENRY MANCINI; Lyrics by DON BLACK.

★ EVERGREEN (LOVE THEME FROM A STAR IS BORN) from *A Star Is Born*, A Barwood/Jon Peters Production, First Artists Presentation, Warner Bros.: Music by BARBRA STREISAND; Lyrics by PAUL WILLIAMS.

GONNA FLY NOW from *Rocky*, a Robert Chartoff-Irwin Winkler Production, United Artists: Music by BILL CONTI; Lyrics by CAROL CONNORS and AYN ROBBINS.

A WORLD THAT NEVER WAS from *Half a House*, Lenro Productions, First American Films: Music by SAMMY FAIN; Lyrics by PAUL FRANCIS WEBSTER.

Costume Design

BOUND FOR GLORY, The Bound for Glory Company Production, United Artists: WILLIAM THEISS.

★ FELLINI'S CASANOVA, A P.E.A.-Produzioni Europee Associate S.p.A. Production, Universal: DANILO DONATI.

THE INCREDIBLE SARAH, A Helen M. Strauss-Reader's Digest Films, Ltd. Production, Seymour Borde and Associates: ANTHONY MENDLESON.

THE PASSOVER PLOT, Coast Industries-Golan-Globus Productions, Ltd., Atlas Films: MARY WILLS.

THE SEVEN PERCENT SOLUTION, A Herbert Ross Film/Winitsky-Sellers Production, A Universal Release: ALAN BARRETT.

Short Films

Animated

DEDALO, A Cineteam Realizzazioni Production: MANFREDO MANFREDI, Producer.

★ LEISURE, A Film Australia Production: SUZANNE BAKER, Producer.

THE STREET, National Film Board of Canada: CAROLINE LEAF and GUY GLOVER, Producers.

Live Action

IN THE REGION OF ICE, An American Film Institute Production: ANDRE GUTTFREUND and PETER WERNER, Producers.

KUDZU, A Short Production: MARJORIE ANNE SHORT, Producer.

THE MORNING SPIDER, The Black and

White Colour Film Company: JULIAN CHAGRIN and CLAUDE CHAGRIN, Producers.
NIGHTLIFE, Opus Films, Ltd.: CLAIRE WILBUR and ROBIN LEHMAN, Producers.
NUMBER ONE, Number One Productions: DYAN CANNON and VINCE CANNON, Producers.

Documentary

Short Subjects

AMERICAN SHOESHINE, Titan Films: SPARKY GREENE, Producer.
BLACKWOOD, National Film Board of Canada: TONY IANZELO and ANDY THOMPSON, Producers.
THE END OF THE ROAD, Pelican Films: JOHN ARMSTRONG, Producer.
* NUMBER OUR DAYS, Community Television of Southern California: LYNNE LITTMAN, Producer.
UNIVERSE, Graphic Films Corp. for NASA: LESTER NOVROS, Producer.

Features

* HARLAN COUNTY, U.S.A., Cabin Creek Films: BARBARA KOPPLE, Producer.
HOLLYWOOD ON TRIAL, October Films/ Cinema Associates Production: JAMES GUTMAN and DAVID HELPERN, JR., Producers.
OFF THE EDGE, Pentacle Films: MICHAEL FIRTH, Producer.
PEOPLE OF THE WIND, Elizabeth E. Rogers Productions: ANTHONY HOWARTH and DAVID KOFF, Producers.
VOLCANO: AN INQUIRY INTO THE LIFE AND DEATH OF MALCOLM LOWRY, National Film Board of Canada: DONALD BRITTAIN and ROBERT DUNCAN, Producers.

Foreign Language Film Award

* BLACK AND WHITE IN COLOR, An Arthur Cohn Production/Société Ivoirienne de Cinema (Ivory Coast).
COUSIN, COUSINE, Les Films Pomereu-Gaumont Production (France).
JACOB, THE LIAR, A VEB/DEFA Production (German Democratic Republic).
NIGHTS AND DAYS, A Polish Corporation for Film-"KADR" Film Unit Production (Poland).
SEVEN BEAUTIES, A Medusa Distribuzione Production (Italy).

Honorary Awards

None.

Special Achievement Awards

Visual Effects: CARLO RAMBALDI, GLEN ROBINSON, and FRANK VAN DER VEER for *King Kong*, A Dino De Laurentiis Production, Paramount.
Visual Effects: L. B. ABBOTT, GLEN ROBINSON, and MATTHEW YURICICH for *Logan's Run*, A Saul David Production, Metro-Goldwyn-Mayer.

Irving G. Thalberg Memorial Award

PANDRO S. BERMAN

Jean Hersholt Humanitarian Award

None.

Scientific or Technical

Class I

None.

Class II

CONSOLIDATED FILM INDUSTRIES and the BARNEBEY-CHENEY COMPANY for the development of a system for the recovery of film-cleaning solvent vapors in a motion picture laboratory.
WILLIAM L. GRAHAM, MANFRED G. MICHELSON, GEOFFREY F. NORMAN, and SIEGFRIED SEIBERT of Technicolor for the

development and engineering of a continuous, high-speed, color, motion picture printing system.

Class III

FRED BARTSCHER of the Kollmorgen Corporation and GLENN BERGGREN of the Schneider Corporation for the design and development of a single-lens magnifier for motion picture projection lenses.

PANAVISION INCORPORATED for the design and development of superspeed lenses for motion picture photography.

HIROSHI SUZUKAWA of Canon and WILTON R. HOLM of AMPTP Motion Picture and Television Research Center for the design and development of superspeed lenses for motion picture photography.

CARL ZEISS COMPANY for the design and development of superspeed lenses for motion picture photography.

PHOTO RESEARCH DIVISION of the KOLLMORGEN CORPORATION for the engineering and manufacture of the spectra TriColor Meter.

FIFTIETH YEAR

1977

Nominations Announced: February 21, 1978
Awards Ceremony: April 3, 1978
Dorothy Chandler Pavilion, Los Angeles County Music Center
(MC: Bob Hope)

Best Picture

★ ANNIE HALL, Jack Rollins-Charles H. Joffe Productions, United Artists: Charles H. Joffe, Producer.

THE GOODBYE GIRL, A Ray Stark Production, Metro-Goldwyn-Mayer/Warner Bros.: RAY STARK, Producer.

JULIA, A Twentieth Century-Fox Production, 20th Century-Fox: RICHARD ROTH, Producer.

STAR WARS, A Twentieth Century-Fox Production, 20th Century-Fox: GARY KURTZ, Producer.

THE TURNING POINT, Hera Productions, 20th Century-Fox: HERBERT ROSS and ARTHUR LAURENTS, Producers.

Actor

WOODY ALLEN in *Annie Hall*, Jack Rollins-Charles H. Joffe Productions, United Artists.

RICHARD BURTON in *Equus*, A Winkast Company, Ltd./P.B., Ltd. Production, United Artists.

★ RICHARD DREYFUSS in *The Goodbye Girl*, A Ray Stark Production, Metro-Goldwyn-Mayer/Warner Bros.

MARCELLO MASTROIANNI in *A Special Day*, A Canafox Films Production, Cinema 5, Ltd.

JOHN TRAVOLTA in *Saturday Night Fever*, A Robert Stigwood Production, Paramount.

Actress

ANNE BANCROFT in *The Turning Point*, Hera Productions, 20th Century-Fox.

JANE FONDA in *Julia*, A Twentieth Century-Fox Production, 20th Century-Fox.

★ DIANE KEATON in *Annie Hall*, Jack Rollins-Charles H. Joffe Productions, United Artists.

SHIRLEY MACLAINE in *The Turning Point*, Hera Productions, 20th Century-Fox.

MARSHA MASON in *The Goodbye Girl*, A Ray Stark Production, Metro-Goldwyn-Mayer/Warner Bros.

Supporting Actor

MIKHAIL BARYSHNIKOV in *The Turning Point*, Hera Productions, 20th Century-Fox.

PETER FIRTH in *Equus*, A Winkast Company, Ltd./P.B., Ltd. Production, United Artists.

ALEC GUINNESS in *Star Wars*, A Twentieth Century-Fox Production, 20th Century-Fox.

★ JASON ROBARDS in *Julia*, A Twentieth Century-Fox Production, 20th Century-Fox.

MAXIMILIAN SCHELL in *Julia*, A

Twentieth Century-Fox Production, 20th Century-Fox.

Supporting Actress

LESLIE BROWNE in *The Turning Point*, Hera Productions, 20th Century-Fox.

QUINN CUMMINGS in *The Goodbye Girl*, A Ray Stark Production, Metro-Goldwyn-Mayer/Warner Bros.

MELINDA DILLON in *Close Encounters of the Third Kind*, Close Encounter Productions, Columbia.

★ VANESSA REDGRAVE in *Julia*, A Twentieth Century-Fox Production, 20th Century-Fox.

TUESDAY WELD in *Looking for Mr. Goodbar*, A Freddie Fields Production, Paramount.

Directing

★ WOODY ALLEN, for ANNIE HALL, Jack Rollins-Charles H. Joffe Productions, United Artists.

GEORGE LUCAS for STAR WARS, A Twentieth Century-Fox Production, 20th Century-Fox.

HERBERT ROSS for THE TURNING POINT, Hera Productions, 20th Century-Fox.

STEVEN SPIELBERG for CLOSE ENCOUNTERS OF THE THIRD KIND, Close Encounter Productions, Columbia.

FRED ZINNEMAN for JULIA, A Twentieth Century-Fox Production, 20th Century-Fox.

Writing

Screenplay—Written Directly for the Screen

★ ANNIE HALL, Jack Rollins-Charles H. Joffe Productions, United Artists: WOODY ALLEN and MARSHALL BRICKMAN.

THE GOODBYE GIRL, A Ray Stark Production, Metro-Goldwyn-Mayer/Warner Bros.: NEIL SIMON.

THE LATE SHOW, A Lion's Gate Film Production, Warner Bros.: Screenplay by ROBERT BENTON.

STAR WARS, A Twentieth Century-Fox Production, 20th Century-Fox: GEORGE LUCAS.

THE TURNING POINT, Hera Productions, 20th Century-Fox: ARTHUR LAURENTS.

Screenplay—Based on Material from Another Medium

EQUUS, A Winkast Company, Ltd./P.B., Ltd. Production, United Artists: PETER SHAFFER.

I NEVER PROMISED YOU A ROSE GARDEN, A Scherick/Blatt Production, New World Pictures: GAVIN LAMBERT and LEWIS JOHN CARLINO.

★ JULIA, A Twentieth Century-Fox Production, 20th Century-Fox: ALVIN SARGENT.

OH, GOD!, A Warner Bros. Production, Warner Bros.: LARRY GELBART.

THAT OBSCURE OBJECT OF DESIRE, A Greenwich-Les Films Galaxie-In Cine Production, First Artists: LUIS BUÑUEL and JEAN-CLAUDE CARRIERE.

Cinematography

★ CLOSE ENCOUNTERS OF THE THIRD KIND, Close Encounter Productions, Columbia: VILMOS ZSIGMOND.

ISLANDS IN THE STREAM, A Peter Bart/Max Palevsky Production, Paramount: FRED J. KOENEKAMP.

JULIA, A Twentieth Century-Fox Production, 20th Century-Fox: DOUGLAS SLOCOMBE.

LOOKING FOR MR. GOODBAR, A Freddie Fields Production, Paramount: WILLIAM A. FRAKER.

THE TURNING POINT, Hera Productions, 20th Century-Fox: ROBERT SURTEES.

Art Direction—Set Decoration

AIRPORT '77, A Jennings Lang Production, Universal: GEORGE C. WEBB; Set Decoration: MICKEY S. MICHAELS.

CLOSE ENCOUNTERS OF THE THIRD KIND,

Close Encounter Productions, Columbia: JOE ALVES and DAN LOMINO; Set Decoration: PHIL ABRAMSON.

THE SPY WHO LOVED ME, Eon Productions, United Artists: KEN ADAM and PETER LAMONT; Set Decoration: HUGH SCAIFE.

★ STAR WARS, A Twentieth Century-Fox Production, 20th Century-Fox: JOHN BARRY, NORMAN REYNOLDS, and LESLIE DILLEY; Set Decoration: ROGER CHRISTIAN.

THE TURNING POINT, Hera Productions, 20th Century-Fox: ALBERT BRENNER; Set Decoration: MARVIN MARCH.

Sound

CLOSE ENCOUNTERS OF THE THIRD KIND, Close Encounter Productions, Columbia: ROBERT KNUDSON, ROBERT J. GLASS, DON MACDOUGALL, and GENE S. CANTAMESSA.

THE DEEP, A Casablanca Filmworks Production, Columbia: WALTER GOSS, DICK ALEXANDER, TOM BECKERT, and ROBIN GREGORY.

SORCERER, A William Friedkin Film Production, Paramount-Universal: ROBERT KNUDSON, ROBERT J. GLASS, RICHARD TYLER, and JEAN-LOUIS DUCARME.

★ STAR WARS, A Twentieth Century-Fox Production, 20th Century-Fox: DON MACDOUGALL, RAY WEST, BOB MINKLER, and DEREK BALL.

THE TURNING POINT, Hera Productions, Twentieth Century-Fox: THEODORE SODERBERG, PAUL WELLS, DOUGLAS O. WILLIAMS, and JERRY JOST.

Film Editing

CLOSE ENCOUNTERS OF THE THIRD KIND, Close Encounter Productions, Columbia: MICHAEL KAHN.

JULIA, A Twentieth Century-Fox Production, 20th Century-Fox: WALTER MURCH and MARCEL DURHAM.

SMOKEY AND THE BANDIT, A Universal/Rastar Production, Universal: WALTER HANNEMANN and ANGELO ROSS.

★ STAR WARS, A Twentieth Century-Fox Production, 20th Century-Fox: PAUL HIRSCH, MARCIA LUCAS, and RICHARD CHEW.

THE TURNING POINT, Hera Productions, 20th Century-Fox: WILLIAM REYNOLDS.

Music

Original Score

CLOSE ENCOUNTERS OF THE THIRD KIND, Close Encounter Productions, Columbia: JOHN WILLIAMS.

JULIA, A Twentieth Century-Fox Production, 20th Century-Fox: GEORGES DELERUE.

MOHAMMAD—MESSENGER OF GOD, A Filmco International Production, Irwin Yablans Company: MAURICE JARRE.

THE SPY WHO LOVED ME, Eon Productions, United Artists: MARVIN HAMLISCH.

★ STAR WARS, A Twentieth Century-Fox Production, 20th Century-Fox: JOHN WILLIAMS.

Original Song Score and Its Adaptation or Best Adaptation Score

★ A LITTLE NIGHT MUSIC, A Sascha-Wien Film Production in association with Elliott Kastner, New World Pictures: Adapted by JONATHAN TUNICK.

PETE'S DRAGON, Walt Disney Productions, Buena Vista Distribution Company; Song Score by AL KASHA and JOEL HIRSCHHORN; Adapted by IRWIN KOSTAL.

THE SLIPPER AND THE ROSE—THE STORY OF CINDERELLA, Paradine Co-Productions, Ltd., Universal: Song Score by RICHARD M. SHERMAN and

ROBERT B. SHERMAN; Adapted by ANGELA MORLEY.

Original Song

CANDLE ON THE WATER from *Pete's Dragon*, Walt Disney Productions, Buena Vista Distribution Company: Music and Lyrics by AL KASHA and JOEL HIRSCHHORN.

NOBODY DOES IT BETTER from *The Spy Who Loved Me*, Eon Productions, United Artists: Music by MARVIN HAMLISCH; Lyrics by CAROLE BAYER SAGER.

THE SLIPPER AND THE ROSE WALTZ (HE DANCED WITH ME/SHE DANCED WITH ME) from *The Slipper and the Rose—The Story of Cinderella*, Pardine Co-Productions, Ltd., Universal: Music and Lyrics by RICHARD M. SHERMAN and ROBERT B. SHERMAN.

SOMEONE'S WAITING FOR YOU from *The Rescuers*, Walt Disney Productions, Buena Vista Distribution Company: Music by SAMMY FAIN; Lyrics by CAROL CONNORS and AYN ROBBINS.

★ YOU LIGHT UP MY LIFE from *You Light up My Life*. The Session Company Production, Columbia: Music and Lyrics by JOSEPH BROOKS.

Costume Design

AIRPORT '77, A Jennings Lang Production, Universal: EDITH HEAD and BURTON MILLER.

JULIA, A Twentieth Century-Fox Production, 20th Century-Fox: ANTHEA SYLBERT.

A LITTLE NIGHT MUSIC, A Sascha-Wien Film Production in association with Elliott Kastner, New World Pictures: FLORENCE KLOTZ.

THE OTHER SIDE OF MIDNIGHT, A Frank Yablans Presentations Production, Twentieth Century-Fox: IRENE SHARAFF.

★ STAR WARS, A Twentieth Century-Fox Production, 20th Century-Fox: JOHN MOLLO.

Visual Effects

(New Category)

CLOSE ENCOUNTERS OF THE THIRD KIND, Close Encounter Productions, Columbia: ROY ARBOGAST, DOUGLAS TRUMBULL, MATTHEW YURICICH, GREGORY JEIN, and RICHARD YURICICH.

★ STAR WARS, A Twentieth Century-Fox Production, 20th Century-Fox: JOHN STEARS, JOHN DYKSTRA, RICHARD EDLUND, GRANT MCCUNE, and ROBERT BLALACK.

Short Films

Animated

THE BEAD GAME, National Film Board of Canada: ISHU PATEL, Producer.

THE DOONESBURY SPECIAL, The Hubley Studio: JOHN HUBLEY, FAITH HUBLEY, and GARRY TRUDEAU, Producers.

JIMMY THE C, A Motionpicker Production: JIMMY PICKER and ROBERT GROSSMAN, Producers.

★ SAND CASTLE, National Film Board of Canada: CO HOEDEMAN, Producer.

Live Action

THE ABSENT-MINDED WAITER, The Aspen Film Society: WILLIAM E. MCEUEN, Producer.

FLOATING FREE, A Trans World International Production: JERRY BUTTS, Producer.

★ I'LL FIND A WAY, National Film Board of Canada: BEVERLY SHAFFER and YUKI YOSHIDA, Producers.

NOTES ON THE POPULAR ARTS, Saul Bass Films: SAUL BASS, Producer.

SPACEBORNE, A Lawrence Hall of Science Production for the Regents of the University of California with the cooperation of NASA: PHILIP DAUBER, Producer.

Documentary

Short Subjects

AGUADA MARTINEZ: OUR PEOPLE, OUR COUNTRY, A Moctesuma Esparza Production: MOCTESUMA ESPARZA, Producer.

FIRST EDITION, D. L. Sage Productions: HELEN WHITNEY and DEWITT L. SAGE, JR., Producers.

★ GRAVITY IS MY ENEMY, A John Joseph Production: JOHN JOSEPH and JAN STUSSY, Producers.

OF TIME, TOMBS AND TREASURE, A Charlie/Papa Production: JAMES R. MESSENGER, Producer.

THE SHETLAND EXPERIENCE, Balfour Films: DOUGLAS GORDON, Producer.

Features

THE CHILDREN OF THEATRE STREET, Mack-Vaganova Company: ROBERT DORNHELM and EARLE MACK, Producers.

HIGH GRASS CIRCUS, National Film Board of Canada: BILL BRIND, TORBEN SCHIOLER, and TONY IANZELO, Producers.

HOMAGE TO CHAGALL—THE COLOURS OF LOVE, A CBC Production: HARRY RASKY, Producer.

UNION MAIDS, A Klein, Reichert, Mogulescu Production: JAMES KLEIN, JULIA REICHERT, and MILES MOGULESCU, Producers.

★ WHO ARE THE DEBOLTS? AND WHERE DID THEY GET NINETEEN KIDS?, Korty Films and Charles M. Schulz Creative Associates in association with Sanrio Films: JOHN KORTY, DAN MCCANN, and WARREN L. LOCKHART, Producers.

Foreign Language Film Award

IPHIGENIA, A Greek Film Centre Production (Greece).

★ MADAME ROSA, A Lira Films Production (France).

OPERATION THUNDERBOLT, A Golan-Globus Production (Israel).

A SPECIAL DAY, A Canafox Films Production (Italy).

THAT OBSCURE OBJECT OF DESIRE, A Greenwich-Les Films Galaxie-In Cine Production (Spain).

Honorary Award

MARGARET BOOTH for sixty-two years of exceptionally distinguished service to the motion picture industry as a film editor.

Medals of Commendation

GORDON E. SAWYER and SIDNEY P. SOLOW in appreciation for outstanding service and dedication in upholding the high standards of the Academy of Motion Picture Arts and Sciences.

Special Achievement Awards

Sound Effects: BENJAMIN BURTT, JR., for the creation of the alien, creature, and robot voices in *Star Wars*, A Twentieth Century-Fox Production, 20th Century-Fox.

Sound Effects Editing Award: FRANK WARNER for *Close Encounters of the Third Kind*, Close Encounter Productions, Columbia.

Irving G. Thalberg Memorial Award

WALTER MIRISCH.

Jean Hersholt Humanitarian Award

CHARLTON HESTON.

Scientific or Technical

Class I

GARRETT BROWN and the CINEMA PRODUCTS CORP. engineering staff, under the supervision of JOHN JURGENS, for the invention and development of Steadicam.

Class II

JOSEPH D. KELLY, BARRY K. HENLEY, HAMMOND H. HOLT, and GLEN GLENN SOUND for the concept and development of a postproduction audio processing system for motion picture films.

PANAVISION, INCORPORATED, for the concept and engineering of the improvements incorporated in the Panaflex Motion Picture Camera.

N. PAUL KENWORTHY, JR., and WILLIAM R. LATADY for the invention and development of the Kenworthy Snorkel Camera System for motion picture photography.

JOHN C. DYKSTRA for the development of the Dykstraflex Camera and to ALVAH J. MILLER and JERRY JEFFRESS for the engineering of the Electronic Motion Control System used in concert for multiple-exposure, visual effects motion picture photography.

EASTMAN KODAK COMPANY for the development and introduction of a new duplicating film for motion pictures.

STEPHAN KUDELSKI of Nagra Magnetic Recorders, Incorporated, for the engineering of the improvements incorporated in the Nagra 4.2L sound recorder for motion picture production.

Class III

ERNST NETTMANN of the Astrovision Division of Continental Camera Systems, Incorporated, for the engineering of its Snorkel Aerial Camera System.

EECO (ELECTRONIC ENGINEERING COMPANY OF CALIFORNIA) for developing a method for interlocking nonsprocketed film and tape media used in motion picture production.

DR. BERNHARD KUHL and WERNER BLOCK of OSRAM, GmbH, for the development of the HMI high-efficiency discharge lamp used for motion picture lighting.

PANAVISION, INCORPORATED, for the design of Panalite, a camera-mounted controllable light for motion picture photography.

PANAVISION, INCORPORATED, for the engineering of the Panahead gearhead for motion picture cameras.

PICLEAR, INC., for originating and developing an attachment to motion picture projectors to improve screen image quality.

FIFTY-FIRST YEAR

1978

Nominations Announced: February 20, 1979
Awards Ceremony: April 9, 1979
Dorothy Chandler Pavilion, Los Angeles County Music Center
(MC: Johnny Carson)

Best Picture

COMING HOME, A Jerome Hellman Enterprises Production, United Artists: Jerome Hellman, Producer.

★ THE DEER HUNTER, An EMI Films/Michael Cimino Film Production, Universal: Barry Spikings, Michael Deeley, Michael Cimino, and John Peverall, Producers.

HEAVEN CAN WAIT, Dogwood Productions, Paramount: Warren Beatty, Producer.

MIDNIGHT EXPRESS. A Casablanca-Filmworks Production, Columbia: Alan Marshall and David Puttnam, Producers.

AN UNMARRIED WOMAN, A Twentieth Century-Fox Production, 20th Century-Fox: Paul Mazursky and Tony Ray, Producers.

Actor

WARREN BEATTY in *Heaven Can Wait*, Dogwood Productions, Paramount.

GARY BUSEY in *The Buddy Holly Story*, An Innovisions-ECA Production, Columbia.

ROBERT DE NIRO in *The Deer Hunter*, An EMI Films/Michael Cimino Film Production, Universal.

LAURENCE OLIVIER in *The Boys from Brazil*, An ITC Entertainment Production, 20th Century-Fox.

★ JON VOIGHT in *Coming Home*, A Jerome Hellman Enterprises Production, United Artists.

Actress

INGRID BERGMAN in *Autumn Sonata*, A Personafilm GmbH Production, Sir Lew Grade-Martin Starger-ITC Entertainment Presentation, New World Pictures.

ELLEN BURSTYN in *Same Time, Next Year*, A Walter Mirisch-Robert Mulligan Production, Mirisch Corporation/Universal Pictures Presentation, Universal.

JILL CLAYBURGH in *An Unmarried Woman*, A Twentieth Century-Fox Production, 20th Century-Fox.

★ JANE FONDA in *Coming Home*, A Jerome Hellman Enterprises Production, United Artists.

GERALDINE PAGE in *Interiors*, A Jack Rollins-Charles H. Joffe Production, United Artists.

Supporting Actor

BRUCE DERN in *Coming Home*, A Jerome Hellman Enterprises Production, United Artists.

RICHARD FARNSWORTH in *Comes a*

Horseman, A Robert Chartoff-Irwin Winkler Production, United Artists.

JOHN HURT in *Midnight Express*, A Casablanca-Filmworks Production, Columbia.

★ CHRISTOPHER WALKEN in *The Deer Hunter*, An EMI Films/Michael Cimino Film Production, Universal.

JACK WARDEN in *Heaven Can Wait*, Dogwood Productions, Paramount.

Supporting Actress

DYAN CANNON in *Heaven Can Wait*, Dogwood Productions, Paramount.

PENELOPE MILFORD in *Coming Home*, A Jerome Hellman Enterprises Production, United Artists.

★ MAGGIE SMITH in *California Suite*, A Ray Stark Production, Columbia.

MAUREEN STAPLETON in *Interiors*, A Jack Rollins-Charles H. Joffe Production, United Artists.

MERYL STREEP in *The Deer Hunter*, An EMI Films/Michael Cimino Film Production, Universal.

Directing

WOODY ALLEN for *Interiors*, A Jack Rollins-Charles H. Joffe Production, United Artists.

HAL ASHBY for *Coming Home*, A Jerome Hellman Enterprises Production, United Artists.

WARREN BEATTY and BUCK HENRY for *Heaven Can Wait*, Dogwood Productions, Paramount.

★ MICHAEL CIMINO for *The Deer Hunter*, An EMI Films/Michael Cimino Film Production, Universal.

ALAN PARKER for *Midnight Express*, A Casablanca-Filmworks Production, Columbia.

Writing

Screenplay Written Directly for the Screen

AUTUMN SONATA, A Personafilm GmbH Production, Sir Lew Grade-Martin Starger-ITC Entertainment Presentation, New World Pictures: INGMAR BERGMAN.

★ COMING HOME, A Jerome Hellman Enterprises Production, United Artists: Story by NANCY DOWD; Screenplay by WALDO SALT and ROBERT C. JONES.

THE DEER HUNTER, An EMI Films/ Michael Cimino Film Production, Universal: Story by MICHAEL CIMINO, DERIC WASHBURN, LOUIS GARFINKLE, and QUINN K. REDEKER; Screenplay by DERIC WASHBURN.

INTERIORS, A Jack Rollins-Charles H. Joffe Production, United Artists: WOODY ALLEN.

AN UNMARRIED WOMAN, A Twentieth Century-Fox Production, 20th Century: PAUL MAZURSKY.

Screenplay Based on Material from Another Medium

BLOODBROTHERS, A Warner Bros. Production, Warner Bros.: WALTER NEWMAN.

CALIFORNIA SUITE, A Ray Stark Production, Columbia: NEIL SIMON.

HEAVEN CAN WAIT, Dogwood Productions, Paramount: ELAINE MAY and WARREN BEATTY.

★ MIDNIGHT EXPRESS, A Casablanca-Filmworks Production, Columbia: OLIVER STONE.

SAME TIME, NEXT YEAR, A Walter Mirisch-Robert Mulligan Production, Mirisch Corporation/Universal Pictures Presentation, Universal: BERNARD SLADE.

Cinematography

★ DAYS OF HEAVEN, An OP Production, Paramount: NESTOR ALMENDROS.

THE DEER HUNTER, An EMI Films/ Michael Cimino Film Production, Universal: VILMOS ZSIGMOND.

HEAVEN CAN WAIT, Dogwood

Productions, Paramount: WILLIAM A. FRAKER.

SAME TIME, NEXT YEAR, A Walter Mirisch-Robert Mulligan Production, Mirisch Corporation/Universal Pictures Presentation, Universal: ROBERT SURTEES.

THE WIZ, A Motown/Universal Pictures Production, Universal: OSWALD MORRIS.

Art Direction - Set Decoration

THE BRINK'S JOB, A William Friedkin Film/Universal Production, Dino De Laurentiis Presentation, Universal: DEAN TAVOULARIS and ANGELO GRAHAM; Set Decoration: GEORGE R. NELSON.

CALIFORNIA SUITE, A Ray Stark Production, Columbia: ALBERT BRENNER; Set Decoration: MARVIN MARCH.

★ HEAVEN CAN WAIT, Dogwood Productions, Paramount: PAUL SYLBERT and EDWIN O'DONOVAN; Set Decoration: GEORGE GAINES.

INTERIORS, A Jack Rollins-Charles H. Joffe Production, United Artists: MEL BOURNE; Set Decoration: DANIEL ROBERT.

THE WIZ, A Motown/Universal Pictures Production, Universal: TONY WALTON and PHILIP ROSENBERG; Set Direction: EDWARD STEWART and ROBERT DRUMHELLER.

Sound

THE BUDDY HOLLY STORY, An Innovisions-ECA Production, Columbia: TEX RUDLOFF, JOEL FEIN, CURLY THIRLWELL, and WILLIE BURTON.

DAYS OF HEAVEN, An OP Production, Paramount: JOHN K. WILKINSON, ROBERT W. GLASS, JR., JOHN T. REITZ, and BARRY THOMAS.

★ THE DEER HUNTER, An EMI Films/Michael Cimino Film Production, Universal: RICHARD PORTMAN, WILLIAM McCAUGHEY, AARON ROCHIN, and DARRIN KNIGHT.

HOOPER, A Warner Bros. Production, Warner Bros.: ROBERT KNUDSON, ROBERT J. GLASS, DON MACDOUGALL, and JACK SOLOMON.

SUPERMAN, A Dovemead, Ltd. Production, Alexander Salkind Presentation, Warner Bros.: GORDON K. MCCALLUM, GRAHAM HARTSTONE, NICOLAS LE MESSURIER, and ROY CHARMAN.

Film Editing

THE BOYS FROM BRAZIL, An ITC Entertainment Production, 20th Century-Fox: ROBERT E. SWINK.

COMING HOME, A Jerome Hellman Enterprises Production, United Artists: DON ZIMMERMAN.

★ THE DEER HUNTER, An EMI Films/Michael Cimino Film Production, Universal: PETER ZINNER.

MIDNIGHT EXPRESS, A Casablanca-Filmworks Production, Columbia: GERRY HAMBLING.

SUPERMAN, A Dovemead, Ltd. Production, Alexander Salkind Presentation, Warner Bros.: STUART BAIRD.

Music

Original Score

THE BOYS FROM BRAZIL, An ITC Entertainment Production, 20th Century-Fox: JERRY GOLDSMITH.

DAYS OF HEAVEN, An OP Production, Paramount: ENNIO MORRICONE.

HEAVEN CAN WAIT, Dogwood Productions, Paramount: DAVE GRUSIN.

★ MIDNIGHT EXPRESS, A

Casablanca-Filmworks Production, Columbia: GIORGIO MORODER.
SUPERMAN, A Dovemead, Ltd. Production, Alexander Salkind Presentation, Warner Bros.: JOHN WILLIAMS.

Original Song Score and Its Adaptation or Best Adaptation Score

★ THE BUDDY HOLLY STORY, An Innovision-ECA Production, Columbia: Adaptation Score by JOE RENZETTI.
PRETTY BABY, A Louis Malle Film Production, Paramount: Adaptation Score by JERRY WEXLER.
THE WIZ, A Motown/Universal Pictures Production, Universal: Adaptation Score by QUINCY JONES.

Original Song

HOPELESSLY DEVOTED TO YOU from *Grease*, A Robert Stigwood/Allan Carr Production, Paramount: Music and Lyrics by JOHN FARRAR.
★ LAST DANCE from *Thank God It's Friday*, A Casablanca-Motown Production, Columbia: Music and Lyrics by PAUL JABARA.
THE LAST TIME I FELT LIKE THIS from *Same Time, Next Year*, A Walter Mirisch-Robert Mulligan Production, Mirisch Corporation/ Universal Pictures Presentation, Universal: Music by MARVIN HAMLISCH; Lyrics by ALAN BERGMAN and MARILYN BERGMAN.
READY TO TAKE A CHANCE AGAIN from *Foul Play*, A Miller-Milkis/Colin Higgins Picture Production, Paramount: Music by CHARLES FOX; Lyrics by NORMAN GIMBEL.
WHEN YOU'RE LOVED from *The Magic of Lassie*, Lassie Productions, The International Picture Show Company: Music and Lyrics by RICHARD M. SHERMAN and ROBERT B. SHERMAN.

Costume Design

CARAVANS, An Ibex Films-F.I.D.C.I. Production, Universal: RENIE CONLEY.
DAYS OF HEAVEN, An OP Production, Paramount: PATRICIA NORRIS.
★ DEATH ON THE NILE, A John Brabourne-Richard Goodwin Production, Paramount: ANTHONY POWELL.
THE SWARM, A Warner Bros. Production, Warner Bros.: PAUL ZASTUPNEVICH.
THE WIZ, A Motown/Universal Pictures Production, Universal: TONY WALTON.

Short Films

Animated

OH MY DARLING, Nico Crama Productions: NICO CRAMA, Producer.
RIP VAN WINKLE, A Will Vinton/Billy Budd Film, Will Vinton Productions: WILL VINTON, Producer.
★ SPECIAL DELIVERY, National Film Board of Canada: EUNICE MACAULAY and JOHN WELDON, Producers.

Live Action

A DIFFERENT APPROACH, A Jim Belcher/ Brookfield Production: JIM BELCHER and FERN FIELD, Producers.
MANDY'S GRANDMOTHER, Illumination Films: ANDREW SUGERMAN, Producer.
STRANGE FRUIT, The American Film Institute: SETH PINSKER, Producer.
★ TEENAGE FATHER, New Visions, Inc., for the Children's Home Society of California: TAYLOR HACKFORD, Producer.

Documentary

Short Subjects

THE DIVIDED TRAIL, A Jerry Aronson Production: JERRY ARONSON, Producer.

AN ENCOUNTER WITH FACES, Films Division, Government of India: K. KAPIL, Producer.

★ THE FLIGHT OF THE GOSSAMER CONDOR, A Shedd Production: JACQUELINE PHILLIPS SHEDD, Producer.

GOODNIGHT MISS ANN, An August Cinquegrana Films Production: AUGUST CINQUEGRANA, Producer.

SQUIRES OF SAN QUENTIN, The J. Gary Mitchell Film Company: J. GARY MITCHELL, Producer.

Features

THE LOVERS' WIND, Ministry of Culture and Arts of Iran: ALBERT LAMORISSE, Producer.

MYSTERIOUS CASTLES OF CLAY, A Survival Anglia Ltd. Production: ALAN ROOT, Producer.

RAONI, A Franco-Brazilian Production: MICHEL GAST, BARRY WILLIAMS, and JEAN-PIERRE DUTILLEUX, Producers.

★ SCARED STRAIGHT!, A Golden West Television Production: ARNOLD SHAPIRO, Producer.

WITH BABIES AND BANNERS: STORY OF THE WOMEN'S EMERGENCY BRIGADE, A Women's Labor History Film Project Production: ANNE BOHLEN, LYN GOLDFARB, and LORRAINE GRAY, Producers.

Foreign Language Film Award

★ GET OUT YOUR HANDKERCHIEFS, A Les Films Ariane-C.A.P.A.C. Production (France).

THE GLASS CELL, A Roxy Film Production (Federal Republic of Germany).

HUNGARIANS, A Dialog Studio Production (Hungary).

VIVA ITALIA!, A Dean Film Production (Italy).

WHITE BIM BLACK EAR, A Central Studio of Films for Children and Youth Production (U.S.S.R.).

Honorary Awards

WALTER LANTZ for bringing joy and laughter to every part of the world through his unique animated motion pictures.

LAURENCE OLIVIER for the full body of his work, for the unique achievements of his entire career, and for his lifetime of contribution to the art of film.

KING VIDOR for his incomparable achievements as a cinematic creator and innovator.

THE MUSEUM OF MODERN ART DEPARTMENT OF FILM for the contribution it has made to the public's perception of movies as an art form.

Medals of Commendation

LINWOOD G. DUNN, LOREN L. RYDER, and WALDON O. WATSON in appreciation for outstanding service and dedication in upholding the high standards of the Academy of Motion Picture Arts and Sciences.

Special Achievement Award

Visual Effects: LES BOWIE, COLIN CHILVERS, DENYS COOP, ROY FIELD, DEREK MEDDINGS, and ZORAN PERISIC for *Superman*, A Dovemead Ltd. Production, Alexander Salkind Presentation, Warner Bros.

Irving G. Thalberg Memorial Award

None.

Jean Hersholt Humanitarian Award

LEO JAFFE.

Scientific or Technical Awards*

Academy Award of Merit (Academy statuette)

EASTMAN KODAK COMPANY for the research and development of a duplicating color film for motion pictures.

STEFAN KUDELSKI of Nagra Magnetic Recorders, Incorporated, for the continuing research, design, and development of the Nagra Production Sound Recorder for motion pictures.

PANAVISION, INCORPORATED, and its engineering staff, under the direction of Robert E. Gottschalk, for the concept, design, and continuous development of the Panaflex Motion Picture Camera System.

Scientific and Engineering Award (Academy plaque)

RAY M. DOLBY, IOAN R. ALLEN, DAVID P. ROBINSON, STEPHEN M. KATZ, and PHILIP S. J. BOOLE of Dolby Laboratories, Incorporated, for the development and implementation of an improved sound recording and reproducing system for motion picture production and exhibition.

Technical Achievement Award (Academy certificate)

KARL MACHER and GLENN M. BERGGREN of Isco Optische Werke for the development and introduction of the Cinelux-ULTRA lens for 35mm motion picture projection.

DAVID J. DEGENKOLB, ARTHUR L. FORD, and FRED J. SCOBEY of DeLuxe General, Incorporated, for the development of a method to recycle motion picture laboratory photographic wash-waters by ion exchange.

KIICHI SEKIGUCHI of CINE-FI International for the development of the CINE-FI Auto Radio Sound System for drive-in theaters.

LEONARD CHAPMAN of Leonard Equipment Company for the design and manufacture of a small, mobile, motion picture camera platform known as the Chapman Hustler Dolly.

JAMES L. FISHER of J. L. Fisher, Incorporated, for the design and manufacture of a small, mobile, motion picture camera platform known as the Fisher Model Ten Dolly.

ROBERT STINDT of Production Grip Equipment Company for the design and manufacture of a small, mobile, motion picture camera platform known as the Stindt Dolly.

*In 1979 the Academy retitled the three categories of the Scientific or Technical Awards. The Class I designation was changed to Academy Award of Merit, Class II to Scientific and Engineering Award, and Class III to Technical Achievement Award.

FIFTY-SECOND YEAR

1979

Nominations Announced: February 25, 1980
Awards Ceremony: April 14, 1980
Dorothy Chandler Pavilion, Los Angeles County Music Center
(MC: Johnny Carson)

Best Picture

ALL THAT JAZZ, A Columbia/ Twentieth Century-Fox Production, 20th Century-Fox: Robert Alan Aurthur, Producer.

APOCALYPSE NOW, An Omni Zoetrope Production, United Artists: Francis Coppola, Producer; Fred Roos, Gray Frederickson, and Tom Sternberg, Co-producers.

BREAKING AWAY, A Twentieth Century-Fox Production, 20th Century-Fox: Peter Yates, Producer.

★ KRAMER VS. KRAMER, Stanley Jaffe Productions, Columbia: Stanley R. Jaffe, Producer.

NORMA RAE, A Twentieth Century-Fox Production, 20th Century-Fox: Tamara Asseyev and Alex Rose, Producers.

Actor

★ DUSTIN HOFFMAN in *Kramer vs. Kramer*, Stanley Jaffe Productions, Columbia.

JACK LEMMON in *The China Syndrome*, A Michael Douglas/IPC Films Production, Columbia.

AL PACINO in ... *And Justice for All*, A Malton Films Limited Production, Columbia.

ROY SCHEIDER in *All That Jazz*, A Columbia/Twentieth Century-Fox Production, 20th Century-Fox.

PETER SELLERS in *Being There*, A Lorimar Film-Und Fernsehproduktion GmbH Production, United Artists.

Actress

JILL CLAYBURGH in *Starting Over*, An Alan J. Pakula/James L. Brooks Production, Paramount.

★ SALLY FIELD in *Norma Rae*, A Twentieth Century-Fox Production. 20th Century-Fox.

JANE FONDA in *The China Syndrome*, A Michael Douglas/IPC Films Production, Columbia.

MARSHA MASON in *Chapter Two*, A Ray Stark Production, Columbia.

BETTE MIDLER in *The Rose*, A Twentieth Century-Fox Production, 20th Century-Fox.

Supporting Actor

★ MELVYN DOUGLAS in *Being There*, A Lorimar Film-Und Fernsehproduktion GmbH Production, United Artists.

ROBERT DUVALL in *Apocalypse Now*, An Omni Zoetrope Production, United Artists.

FREDERIC FORREST in *The Rose*, A

Twentieth Century-Fox Production, 20th Century-Fox.

JUSTIN HENRY in *Kramer vs. Kramer*, Stanley Jaffe Productions, Columbia.

MICKEY ROONEY in *The Black Stallion*, An Omni Zoetrope Production, United Artists.

Supporting Actress

JANE ALEXANDER in *Kramer vs. Kramer*, Stanley Jaffe Productions, Columbia.

BARBARA BARRIE in *Breaking Away*, A Twentieth Century-Fox Production, 20th Century-Fox.

CANDICE BERGEN in *Starting Over*, An Alan J. Pakula/James L. Brooks Production, Paramount.

MARIEL HEMINGWAY in *Manhattan*, A Jack Rollins-Charles H. Joffe Production, United Artists.

★ MERYL STREEP in *Kramer vs. Kramer*, Stanley Jaffe Productions, Columbia.

Directing

★ ROBERT BENTON for *Kramer vs. Kramer*, Stanley Jaffe Productions, Columbia.

FRANCIS COPPOLA for *Apocalypse Now*, An Omni Zoetrope Production, United Artists.

BOB FOSSE for *All That Jazz*, A Columbia/Twentieth Century-Fox Production, 20th Century-Fox.

EDOUARD MOLINARO for *La Cage aux Folles*, A Les Productions Artistes Associés da Ma Produzione SPA Production, United Artists.

PETER YATES for *Breaking Away*, A Twentieth Century-Fox Production, 20th Century-Fox.

Writing

Screenplay Written Directly for the Screen

ALL THAT JAZZ, A Columbia/ Twentieth Century-Fox Production, 20th Century-Fox: ROBERT ALAN AURTHUR and BOB FOSSE.

. . . AND JUSTICE FOR ALL, A Malton Films Limited Production, Columbia: VALERIE CURTIN and BARRY LEVINSON.

★ BREAKING AWAY, A Twentieth Century-Fox Production, 20th Century-Fox: STEVE TESICH.

THE CHINA SYNDROME, A Michael Douglas/IPC Films Production, Columbia: MIKE GRAY, T. S. COOK, and JAMES BRIDGES.

MANHATTAN, A Jack Rollins-Charles H. Joffe Production, United Artists: WOODY ALLEN and MARSHALL BRICKMAN.

Screenplay Based on Material from Another Medium

APOCALYPSE NOW, An Omni Zoetrope Production, United Artists: JOHN MILIUS and FRANCIS COPPOLA.

★ KRAMER VS. KRAMER, Stanley Jaffe Productions, Columbia: ROBERT BENTON.

LA CAGE AUX FOLLES, A Les Productions Artistes Associès da Ma Produzione SPA Production, United Artists: FRANCIS VEBER, EDOUARD MOLINARO, MARCELLO DANON, and JEAN POIRET.

A LITTLE ROMANCE, A Pan Arts Associates Production, Orion Pictures Company: ALLAN BURNS.

NORMA RAE, A Twentieth Century-Fox Production, 20th Century-Fox: IRVING RAVETCH and HARRIET FRANK, JR.

Cinematography

ALL THAT JAZZ, A Columbia/ Twentieth Century-Fox Production, 20th Century-Fox: GIUSEPPE ROTUNNO.

★ APOCALYPSE NOW, An Omni Zoetrope Production, United Artists: VITTORIO STORARO.

THE BLACK HOLE, Walt Disney

Productions, Buena Vista Distribution Company: FRANK PHILLIPS.

KRAMER VS. KRAMER, Stanley Jaffe Productions, Columbia: NESTOR ALMENDROS.

1941, An A-Team/Steven Spielberg Film Production, Universal-Columbia Presentation, Universal: WILLIAM A. FRAKER.

Art Direction—Set Decoration

ALIEN, Twentieth Century-Fox Productions Limited, 20th Century-Fox: MICHAEL SEYMOUR, LES DILLEY, and ROGER CHRISTIAN; Set Decoration: IAN WHITTAKER.

★ ALL THAT JAZZ, A Columbia/Twentieth Century-Fox Production, 20th Century-Fox: PHILIP ROSENBERG and TONY WALTON; Set Decoration: EDWARD STEWART and GARY BRINK.

APOCALYPSE NOW, An Omni Zoetrope Production, United Artists: DEAN TAVOULARIS and ANGELO GRAHAM; Set Decoration: GEORGE R. NELSON.

THE CHINA SYNDROME, A Michael Douglas/IPC Films Production, Columbia: GEORGE JENKINS; Set Decoration: ARTHUR JEPH PARKER.

STAR TREK—THE MOTION PICTURE, A Century Associates Production, Paramount: HAROLD MICHELSON, JOE JENNINGS, LEON HARRIS, and JOHN VALLONE; Set Decoration: LINDA DESCENNA.

Sound

★ APOCALYPSE NOW, An Omni Zoetrope Production, United Artists: WALTER MURCH, MARK BERGER, RICHARD BEGGS, and NAT BOXER.

THE ELECTRIC HORSEMAN, Rastar Films/Wildwood Enterprises/S. Pollack Productions, Columbia: ARTHUR PIANTADOSI, LES FRESHOLTZ, MICHAEL MINKLER, and AL OVERTON.

METEOR, Meteor Productions, American International Pictures: WILLIAM MCCAUGHEY, AARON ROCHIN, MICHAEL J. KOHUT, and JACK SOLOMON.

1941, An A-Team/Steven Spielberg Film Production, Universal-Columbia Presentation, Universal: ROBERT KNUDSON, ROBERT J. GLASS, DON MACDOUGALL, and GENE S. CANTAMESSA.

THE ROSE, A Twentieth Century-Fox Production, 20th Century-Fox: THEODORE SODERBERG, DOUGLAS WILLIAMS, PAUL WELLS, and JIM WEBB.

Film Editing

★ ALL THAT JAZZ, A Columbia/Twentieth Century-Fox Production, 20th Century-Fox: ALAN HEIM.

APOCALYPSE NOW, An Omni Zoetrope Production, United Artists: RICHARD MARKS, WALTER MURCH, GERALD B. GREENBERG, and LISA FRUCHTMAN.

THE BLACK STALLION, An Omni Zoetrope Production, United Artists: ROBERT DALVA.

KRAMER VS. KRAMER, Stanley Jaffe Productions, Columbia: JERRY GREENBERG.

THE ROSE, A Twentieth Century-Fox Production, 20th Century-Fox: ROBERT L. WOLFE and C. TIMOTHY O'MEARA.

Music

Original Score

THE AMITYVILLE HORROR, An American International/Professional Films Production, American International Pictures: LALO SCHIFRIN.

THE CHAMP, A Metro-Goldwyn-Mayer Production, Metro-Goldwyn-Mayer: DAVE GRUSIN.

★ A LITTLE ROMANCE, A Pan Arts Associates Production, Orion Pictures Company: GEORGES DELERUE.

STAR TREK—THE MOTION PICTURE, A Century Associates Production, Paramount: JERRY GOLDSMITH.

10, Geoffrey Productions, Orion Pictures Company: HENRY MANCINI.

Original Song Score and Its Adaptation or Best Adaptation Score

★ ALL THAT JAZZ, A Columbia/ Twentieth Century-Fox Production, 20th Century-Fox: Adaptation Score by RALPH BURNS.

BREAKING AWAY, A Twentieth Century-Fox Production, 20th Century-Fox: Adaptation Score by PATRICK WILLIAMS.

THE MUPPET MOVIE, A Jim Henson Production, Lord Grade/Martin Starger Presentation, AFD (Associated Film Distribution): Original Song Score by PAUL WILLIAMS and KENNY ASCHER; Adapted by PAUL WILLIAMS.

Original Song

★ IT GOES LIKE IT GOES from *Norma Rae*, A Twentieth Century-Fox Production, 20th Century-Fox: Music by DAVID SHIRE; Lyrics by NORMAN GIMBEL.

THE RAINBOW CONNECTION from *The Muppet Movie*, A Jim Henson Production, Lord Grade/Martin Starger Presentation, AFD (Associated Film Distribution): Music and Lyrics by PAUL WILLIAMS and KENNY ASCHER.

SONG FROM 10 (IT'S EASY TO SAY) from *10*, Geoffrey Productions, Orion Pictures Company: Music by HENRY MANCINI; Lyrics by ROBERT WELLS.

THEME FROM ICE CASTLES (THROUGH THE EYES OF LOVE) from *Ice Castles*, An International Cinemedia Center Production, Columbia: Music by MARVIN HAMLISCH; Lyrics by CAROLE BAYER SAGER.

THEME FROM THE PROMISE (I'LL NEVER SAY "GOODBYE") from *The Promise*, A Fred Weintraub-Paul Heller Present./Universal Production, Universal: Music by DAVID SHIRE; Lyrics by ALAN BERGMAN and MARILYN BERGMAN.

Costume Design

AGATHA, A Sweetwall Production in association with Casablanca Filmworks, First Artists Presentation, Warner Bros.: SHIRLEY RUSSELL.

★ ALL THAT JAZZ, A Columbia/ Twentieth Century-Fox Production, 20th Century-Fox: ALBERT WOLSKY.

BUTCH AND SUNDANCE: THE EARLY DAYS, A Twentieth Century-Fox Production, 20th Century-Fox: WILLIAM THEISS.

THE EUROPEANS, Merchant Ivory Productions, Levitt-Pickman: JUDY MOORCROFT.

LA CAGE AUX FOLLES, A Les Productions Artistes Associés da Ma Produzione SPA Production, United Artists: PIERO TOSI and AMBRA DANON.

Visual Effects

★ ALIEN, Twentieth Century-Fox Productions Limited, 20th Century-Fox: H. R. GIGER, CARLO RAMBALDI, BRIAN JOHNSON, NICK ALLDER, and DENYS AYLING.

THE BLACK HOLE Walt Disney Productions, Buena Vista Distribution Company: PETER ELLENSHAW, ART CRUICKSHANK, EUSTACE LYCETT, DANNY LEE, HARRISON ELLENSHAW and JOE HALE.

MOONRAKER, Eon Productions Ltd.,

United Artists: DEREK MEDDINGS, PAUL WILSON, and JOHN EVANS.

1941, An A-Team/Steven Spielberg Film Production, Universal-Columbia Presentation, Universal: WILLIAM A. FRAKER, A. D. FLOWERS, and GREGORY JEIN.

STAR TREK—THE MOTION PICTURE, A Century Associates Production, Paramount: DOUGLAS TRUMBULL, JOHN DYKSTRA, RICHARD YURICICH, ROBERT SWARTHE, DAVE STEWART and GRANT MCCUNE.

Short Films

Animated

DREAM DOLL, Bob Godfrey Films/ Zagreb Films/Halas and Batchelor, Film Wright: BOB GODFREY and ZLATKO GRGIC, Producers.

★ EVERY CHILD, National Film Board of Canada: DEREK LAMB, Producer.

IT'S SO NICE TO HAVE A WOLF AROUND THE HOUSE, AR&T Productions for Learning Corporation of America: PAUL FIERLINGER, Producer.

Live Action

★ BOARD AND CARE, Ron Ellis Films: SARAH PILLSBURY and RON ELLIS, Producers.

BRAVERY IN THE FIELD, National Film Board of Canada: ROMAN KROITOR and STEFAN WODOSLAWSKY, Producers.

OH BROTHER, MY BROTHER, Ross Lowell Productions, Pyramid Films, Inc.: CAROL LOWELL and ROSS LOWELL, Producers.

THE SOLAR FILM, Wildwood Enterprises Inc.: SAUL BASS and MICHAEL BRITTON, Producers.

SOLLY'S DINER, Mathias/Zukerman/ Hankin Productions: HARRY MATHIAS, JAY ZUKERMAN, and LARRY HANKIN, Producers.

Documentary

Short Subjects

DAE, Vardar Film/Skopje.

KORYO CELADON, Charlie/Papa Productions, Inc.

NAILS, National Film Board of Canada.

★ PAUL ROBESON: TRIBUTE TO AN ARTIST, Janus Films, Inc.

REMEMBER ME, Dick Young Productions, Ltd.: DICK YOUNG, Producer.

Features

★ BEST BOY, Only Child Motion Pictures, Inc.: IRA WOHL, Producer.

GENERATION ON THE WIND, More Than One Medium: DAVID A. VASSAR, Producer.

GOING THE DISTANCE, National Film Board of Canada.

THE KILLING GROUND, ABC News Closeup Unit: STEVE SINGER and TOM PRIESTLEY, Producers.

THE WAR AT HOME, Catalyst Films/ Madison Film Production Company: GLENN SILBER and BARRY ALEXANDER BROWN, Producers.

Foreign Language Film Award

THE MAIDS OF WILKO, A Polish Corporation for Film Production (Poland).

MAMA TURNS A HUNDRED, Elias Querejeta P.C. Production (Spain).

A SIMPLE STORY, A Renn Productions/ Sara Films/F.R. 3/Rialto Films Production, Quartet Films (France).

★ THE TIN DRUM, A Franz Seitz Film/Bioskop Film/Artemis Film/ Hallelujah Film/GGB 14.KG/Argos Films Production (Federal Republic of Germany).

TO FORGET VENICE, A Rizzoli Film/ Action Film Production, Quartet Films (Italy).

Honorary Awards

HAL ELIAS for his dedication and distinguished service to the Academy of Motion Picture Arts and Sciences.

ALEC GUINNESS for advancing the art of screen acting through a host of memorable and distinguished performances.

Medals of Commendation

JOHN O. AALBERG, CHARLES G. CLARKE, and JOHN G. FRAYNE in appreciation for outstanding service and dedication in upholding the high standards of the Academy of Motion Picture Arts and Sciences.

Special Achievement Award

Sound Editing: ALAN SPLET for *The Black Stallion*, An Omni Zoetrope Production, United Artists.

Irving G. Thalberg Memorial Award

RAY STARK.

Jean Hersholt Humanitarian Award

ROBERT BENJAMIN.

Scientific or Technical Awards

Academy Award of Merit (Academy statuette)

MARK SERRURIER for the progressive development of the Moviola from the 1924 invention of his father, Iwan Serrurier, to the present Series 20 sophisticated film editing equipment.

Scientific and Engineering Award (Academy plaque)

NEIMAN-TILLAR ASSOCIATES for the creative development and MINI-MICRO SYSTEMS, INCORPORATED, for the design and engineering of an Automated Computer Controlled Editing Sound System (ACCESS) for motion picture postproduction.

Technical Achievement Award (Academy certificate)

MICHAEL V. CHEWEY, WALTER G. EGGERS, and ALLEN HECHT of M-G-M Laboratories for the development of a computer-controlled paper-tape programmer system and its applications in the motion picture laboratory.

IRWIN YOUNG, PAUL KAUFMAN, and FREDRIK SCHLYTER of Du Art Film Laboratories, Incorporated, for the development of a computer-controlled paper-tape programmer system and its applications in the motion picture laboratory.

JAMES S. STANFIELD and PAUL W. TRESTER for the development and manufacture of a device for the repair or protection of sprocket holes in motion picture film.

ZORAN PERISIC of Courier Films, Limited, for the Zoptic Special Optical Effects Device for motion picture photography.

A. D. FLOWERS and LOGAN R. FRAZEE for the development of a device to control flight patterns of miniature airplanes during motion picture photography.

PHOTO RESEARCH DIVISION OF KOLLMORGEN CORPORATION for the development of the Spectra Series II Cine Special Exposure Meter for motion picture photography.

BRUCE LYON and JOHN LAMB for the development of a video animation system for testing motion picture animation sequences.

ROSS LOWELL of Lowel-Light Manufacturing, Incorporated, for the development of compact lighting equipment for motion picture photography.

1980

Nominations Announced: February 17, 1981
Awards Ceremony: Postponed from March 30 to March 31, 1981, due to an assassination attempt on President Ronald Reagan.
Dorothy Chandler Pavilion, Los Angeles County Music Center
(MC: Johnny Carson)

Best Picture

COAL MINER'S DAUGHTER, A Bernard Schwartz-Universal Pictures Production, Universal: Bernard Schwartz, Producer.

THE ELEPHANT MAN, A Brooksfilms, Ltd. Production, Paramount: Jonathan Sanger, Producer.

★ ORDINARY PEOPLE, A Wildwood Enterprises Production, Paramount: Ronald L. Schwary, Producer.

RAGING BULL, A Robert Chartoff-Irwin Winkler Production, United Artists: Irwin Winkler and Robert Chartoff, Producers.

TESS, a Renn-Burrill coproduction with the participation of the Société Française de Production (S.F.P.), Columbia: Claude Berri, Producer; Timothy Burrill, Co-producer.

Actor

★ ROBERT DE NIRO in *Raging Bull*, A Robert Chartoff-Irwin Winkler Production, United Artists.

ROBERT DUVALL in *The Great Santini*, An Orion Pictures-Bing Crosby Production, Orion Pictures.

JOHN HURT in *The Elephant Man*, A Brooksfilms, Ltd. Production, Paramount.

JACK LEMMON in *Tribute*, A Lawrence Turman-David Foster Presentation of a Joel B. Michaels-Garth H. Drabinsky Production, 20th Century-Fox.

PETER O'TOOLE in *The Stunt Man*, Melvin Simon Productions, 20th Century-Fox.

Actress

ELLEN BURSTYN in *Resurrection*, A Universal Pictures Production, Universal.

GOLDIE HAWN in *Private Benjamin*, A Warner Bros. Production, Warner Bros.

MARY TYLER MOORE in *Ordinary People*, A Wildwood Enterprises Production, Paramount.

GENA ROWLANDS in *Gloria*, A Columbia Pictures Production, Columbia.

★ SISSY SPACEK in *Coal Miner's Daughter*, A Bernard Schwartz-Universal Pictures Production, Universal.

Supporting Actor

JUDD HIRSCH in *Ordinary People*, A Wildwood Enterprises Production, Paramount.

★ TIMOTHY HUTTON in *Ordinary*

People, A Wildwood Enterprises Production, Paramount.

MICHAEL O'KEEFE in *The Great Santini*, An Orion Pictures-Bing Crosby Production, Orion Pictures.

JOE PESCI in *Raging Bull*, A Robert Chartoff-Irwin Winkler Production, United Artists.

JASON ROBARDS in *Melvin and Howard*, A Linson/Phillips/Demme-Universal Pictures Production, Universal.

Supporting Actress

EILEEN BRENNAN in *Private Benjamin*, A Warner Bros. Production, Warner Bros.

EVA LE GALLIENNE in *Resurrection*, A Universal Pictures Production, Universal.

CATHY MORIARTY in *Raging Bull*, A Robert Chartoff-Irwin Winkler Production, United Artists.

DIANA SCARWID in *Inside Moves*, A Goodmark Production, AFD (Associated Film Distribution).

★ MARY STEENBURGEN in *Melvin and Howard*, A Linson/Phillips/ Demme-Universal Pictures Production, Universal.

Directing

DAVID LYNCH for *The Elephant Man*, A Brooksfilms, Ltd. Production, Paramount.

ROMAN POLANSKI for *Tess*, A Renn-Burrill Coproduction with the participation of the Société Française de Production (S.F.P.), Columbia.

★ ROBERT REDFORD for *Ordinary People*, A Wildwood Enterprises Production, Paramount.

RICHARD RUSH for *The Stunt Man*, Melvin Simon Productions, 20th Century-Fox.

MARTIN SCORSESE for *Raging Bull*, A Robert Chartoff-Irwin Winkler Production, United Artists.

Writing

Screenplay Written Directly for the Screen (may be based on factual material or on story material not previously published or produced)

BRUBAKER, A Twentieth Century-Fox Production, 20th Century-Fox: Story by W. D. RICHTER and ARTHUR ROSS; Screenplay by W. D. RICHTER.

FAME, A Metro-Goldwyn-Mayer Production, Metro-Goldwyn-Mayer: CHRISTOPHER GORE.

★ MELVIN AND HOWARD, A Linson/Phillips/Demme-Universal Pictures Production, Universal: BO GOLDMAN.

MON ONCLE D'AMERIQUE, A Philippe Dussart-Andrea Films T.F. 1 Production, New World Pictures: JEAN GRUAULT.

PRIVATE BENJAMIN, A Warner Bros. Production, Warner Bros.: NANCY MEYERS, CHARLES SHYER, and HARVEY MILLER.

Screenplay Based on Material from Another Medium

BREAKER MORANT, Produced in association with the Australian Film Commission, the South Australian Film Corporation, and the Seven Network and Pact Productions, New World Pictures/Quartet/Films Incorporated: JONATHAN HARDY, DAVID STEVENS, and BRUCE BERESFORD.

COAL MINER'S DAUGHTER, A Bernard Schwartz-Universal Pictures Production, Universal: TOM RICKMAN.

THE ELEPHANT MAN, A Brooksfilms, Ltd. Production, Paramount: CHRISTOPHER DEVORE, ERIC BERGREN, and DAVID LYNCH.

★ ORDINARY PEOPLE, A Wildwood Enterprises Production, Paramount: ALVIN SARGENT.

THE STUNT MAN, Melvin Simon Productions, 20th Century-Fox: LAWRENCE B. MARCUS; Adaptation by RICHARD RUSH.

Cinematography

THE BLUE LAGOON, A Columbia Pictures Production, Columbia: NESTOR ALMENDROS.

COAL MINER'S DAUGHTER, A Bernard Schwartz-Universal Pictures Production, Universal: RALF D. BODE.

THE FORMULA, A Metro-Goldwyn-Mayer Production, Metro-Goldwyn-Mayer: JAMES CRABE.

RAGING BULL, A Robert Chartoff-Irwin Winkler Production, United Artists: MICHAEL CHAPMAN.

★ TESS, A Renn-Burrill Coproduction with the participation of the Société Française de Production (S.F.P.), Columbia: GEOFFREY UNSWORTH and GHISLAIN CLOQUET.

Art Direction-Set Decoration

COAL MINER'S DAUGHTER, A Bernard Schwartz-Universal Pictures Production, Universal: JOHN W. CORSO; Set Decoration: JOHN M. DWYER.

THE ELEPHANT MAN, A Brooksfilms, Ltd. Production, Paramount: STUART CRAIG and BOB CARTWRIGHT, Set Decoration: HUGH SCAIFE.

THE EMPIRE STRIKES BACK, A Lucasfilm, Ltd. Production, 20th Century-Fox: NORMAN REYNOLDS, LESLIE DILLEY, HARRY LANGE, and ALAN TOMKINS; Set Decoration: MICHAEL FORD.

KAGEMUSHA (THE SHADOW WARRIOR), A Toho Co., Ltd.-Kurosawa Productions, Ltd. Coproduction, 20th Century-Fox: YOSHIRO MURAKI.

★ TESS, A Renn-Burrill Coproduction with the participation of the Société Française de Production (S.F.P.), Columbia: PIERRE GUFFROY and JACK STEVENS.

Sound

ALTERED STATES, A Warner Bros. Production, Warner Bros.: ARTHUR PIANTADOSI, LES FRESHOLTZ, MICHAEL MINKLER, and WILLIE D. BURTON.

COAL MINER'S DAUGHTER, A Bernard Schwartz-Universal Pictures Production, Universal: RICHARD PORTMAN, ROGER HEMAN, and JIM ALEXANDER.

★ THE EMPIRE STRIKES BACK, A Lucasfilm, Ltd. Production, 20th Century-Fox: BILL VARNEY, STEVE MASLOW, GREGG LANDAKER, and PETER SUTTON.

FAME, A Metro-Goldwyn-Mayer, Production, Metro-Goldwyn-Mayer: MICHAEL J. KOHUT, AARON ROCHIN, JAY M. HARDING, and CHRIS NEWMAN.

RAGING BULL, A Robert Chartoff-Irwin Winkler Production, United Artists: DONALD O. MITCHELL, BILL NICHOLSON, DAVID J. KIMBALL, and LES LAZAROWITZ.

Film Editing

COAL MINER'S DAUGHTER, A Bernard Schwartz-Universal Pictures Production; Universal: ARTHUR SCHMIDT.

THE COMPETITION, A Rastar Films Production, Columbia: DAVID BLEWITT.

THE ELEPHANT MAN, A Brooksfilms, Ltd. Production, Paramount: ANNE V. COATES.

FAME, A Metro-Goldwyn-Mayer Production, Metro-Goldwyn-Mayer: GERRY HAMBLING.

★ RAGING BULL, A Robert Chartoff-Irwin Winkler Production, United Artists: THELMA SCHOONMAKER.

Music

Original Score

ALTERED STATES, A Warner Bros. Production, Warner Bros.: JOHN CORIGLIANO.

THE ELEPHANT MAN, A Brooksfilms, Ltd. Production, Paramount: JOHN MORRIS.

THE EMPIRE STRIKES BACK, A Lucasfilm, Ltd. Production, 20th Century-Fox: JOHN WILLIAMS.

★ FAME, A Metro-Goldwyn-Mayer Production, Metro-Goldwyn-Mayer: MICHAEL GORE.

TESS, A Renn-Burrill Coproduction with the participation of the Société Française de Production (S.F.P.), Columbia: PHILIPPE SARDE.

Original Song Score and Its Adaptation or Best Adaptation Score

No nominations.

Original Song

★ FAME from *Fame*, A Metro-Goldwyn-Mayer Production, Metro-Goldwyn-Mayer: Music by MICHAEL GORE; Lyrics by DEAN PITCHFORD.

NINE TO FIVE from *Nine to Five*, A Twentieth Century-Fox Production, 20th Century-Fox: Music and lyrics by DOLLY PARTON.

ON THE ROAD AGAIN from *Honeysuckle Rose*, A Warner Bros. Production, Warner Bros.: Music and Lyrics by WILLIE NELSON.

OUT HERE ON MY OWN, from *Fame*, A Metro-Goldwyn-Mayer Production, Metro-Goldwyn-Mayer: Music by MICHAEL GORE; Lyrics by LESLEY GORE.

PEOPLE ALONE from *The Competition*, A Rastar Films Production, Columbia: Music by LALO SCHIFRIN; Lyrics by WILBUR JENNINGS.

Costume Design

THE ELEPHANT MAN, A Brooksfilms, Ltd. Production, Paramount: PATRICIA NORRIS.

MY BRILLIANT CAREER, A Margaret Fink Films Pty., Ltd. Production, Analysis Film Releasing: ANNA SENIOR.

SOMEWHERE IN TIME, A Rastar-Stephen Deutsch-Universal Pictures Production, Universal: JEAN-PIERRE DORLEAC.

★ TESS, A Renn-Burrill Coproduction with the participation of the Société Française de Production (S.F.P.), Columbia: ANTHONY POWELL.

WHEN TIME RAN OUT, A Warner Bros. Production, Warner Bros.: PAUL ZASTUPNEVICH.

Short Films

Animated

ALL NOTHING, Radio Canada: FREDERIC BACK. Producer.

★ THE FLY, Pannonia Film, Budapest: FERENC ROFUSZ, Producer.

HISTORY OF THE WORLD IN THREE MINUTES FLAT, Michael Mills Productions Ltd.: MICHAEL MILLS, Producer.

Live Action

★ THE DOLLAR BOTTOM, Rocking Horse Films Limited, Paramount: LLOYD PHILLIPS, Producer.

FALL LINE, Sports Imagery, Inc.: BOB CARMICHAEL and GREG LOWE, Producers.

A JURY OF HER PEERS, Sally Heckel Productions: SALLY HECKEL, Producer.

Documentary

Short Subjects

DON'T MESS WITH BILL, John Watson and Pen Densham's Insight

Productions Inc.: JOHN WATSON and PEN DENSHAM.

THE ERUPTION OF MOUNT ST. HELENS, Graphic Films Corporation: GEORGE CASEY, Producer.

IT'S THE SAME WORLD, Dick Young Productions, Ltd.: DICK YOUNG, Producer.

★ KARL HESS: TOWARD LIBERTY, Hallé/Ladue, Inc.: PETER W. LADUE and ROLAND HALLÉ, Producers.

LUTHER METKE AT 94, UCLA Ethnographic Film Program: RICHARD HAWKINS and JORGE PRELORAN, Producers.

Features

AGEE, James Agee Film Project: ROSS SPEARS, Producer.

THE DAY AFTER TRINITY, Jon Else Productions: JON ELSE, Producer.

★ FROM MAO TO MOZART: ISAAC STERN IN CHINA, The Hopewell Foundation: MURRAY LERNER, Producer.

FRONT LINE, David Bradbury Productions: DAVID BRADBURY, Producer.

THE YELLOW STAR—THE PERSECUTION OF EUROPEAN JEWS 1933–45, Chronos Films, BENGT VON ZUR MUEHLEN, Producer.

Foreign Language Film Award

CONFIDENCE, A Mafilm Studios Production (Hungary).

KAGEMUSHA (THE SHADOW WARRIOR), A Toho Co., Ltd.-Kurosawa Productions, Ltd. Coproduction (Japan).

THE LAST METRO, A Les Films du Carrosse Production (France).

★ MOSCOW DOES NOT BELIEVE IN TEARS, A Mosfilm Studio Production (U.S.S.R.).

THE NEST, An A. Punto E.L.S.A. Production (Spain).

Honorary Awards

HENRY FONDA, the consummate actor, in recognition of his brilliant accomplishments and enduring contributions to the art of motion pictures.

Medal of Commendation

FRED HYNES in appreciation for outstanding service and dedication in upholding the high standards of the Academy of Motion Picture Arts and Sciences.

Special Achievement Award

Visual Effects: BRIAN JOHNSON, RICHARD EDLUND, DENNIS MUREN, and BRUCE NICHOLSON, *The Empire Strikes Back*, A Lucasfilm, Ltd. Production, 20th Century-Fox.

Irving G. Thalberg Memorial Award

None.

Jean Hersholt Humanitarian Award

None.

Scientific or Technical Awards

Academy Award of Merit (Academy statuette)

LINWOOD G. DUNN, CECIL D. LOVE, and ACME TOOL AND MANUFACTURING COMPANY for the concept, engineering, and development of the Acme-Dunn Optical Printer for motion picture special effects.

Scientific and Engineering Award (Academy plaque)

JEAN-MARIE LAVALOU, ALAIN MASSERON, and DAVID SAMUELSON of Samuelson Alga Cinema S.A. and Samuelson Film Service, Limited, for the engineering and development of the Louma Camera Crane and remote-control system for motion picture production.

EDWARD B. KRAUSE of Filmline Corporation for the engineering and manufacture of the microdemand drive for continuous motion picture film processors.

ROSS TAYLOR for the concept and development of a system of air guns for propelling objects used in special effects motion picture production.

DR. BERNARD KÜHL and DR. WERNER BLOCK of OSRAM GmbH for the progressive engineering and manufacture of the OSRAM HMI light source for motion picture color photography.

DAVID A. GRAFTON for the optical design and engineering of a telecentric anamorphic lens for motion picture optical effects printers.

Technical Achievement Award (Academy certificate)

CARTER EQUIPMENT COMPANY for the development of a continuous contact, total immersion, additive color motion picture printer.

HOLLYWOOD FILM COMPANY for the development of a continuous contact, total immersion, additive color motion picture printer.

ANDRÉ DeBRIE S.A. for the development of a continuous contact, total immersion, additive color motion picture printer.

CHARLES VAUGHN and EUGENE NOTTINGHAM of Cinetron Computer Systems, Incorporated, for the development of a versatile, general-purpose computer system for animation and optical effects motion picture photography.

JOHN W. LANG, WALTER HRASTNIK, and CHARLES J. WATSON of Bell and Howell Company for the development and manufacture of a modular, continuous contact motion picture film printer.

WORTH BAIRD of LaVezzi Machine Works, Incorporated, for the advanced design and manufacture of a film sprocket for motion picture projectors.

PETER A. REGLA and DAN SLATER of Elicon for the development of a follow focus system for motion picture optical effects printers and animation stands.

FIFTY-FOURTH YEAR

1981

Nominations Announced: February 11, 1982
Awards Ceremony: March 29, 1982
Dorothy Chandler Pavilion, Los Angeles County Music Center
(MC: Johnny Carson)

Best Picture

ATLANTIC CITY, An International Cinema Corporation Production, Paramount: Denis Heroux, Producer.

★ CHARIOTS OF FIRE, Enigma Productions Limited, The Ladd Company/Warner Bros.: David Puttnam, Producer.

ON GOLDEN POND, An ITC Films/IPC Films Production, Universal: Bruce Gilbert, Producer.

RAIDERS OF THE LOST ARK, A Lucasfilm Production, Paramount: Frank Marshall, Producer.

REDS, A J.R.S. Production, Paramount: Warren Beatty, Producer.

Actor

WARREN BEATTY in *Reds*, A J.R.S. Production, Paramount.

★ HENRY FONDA in *On Golden Pond*, An ITC Films/IPC Films Production, Universal.

BURT LANCASTER in *Atlantic City*, An International Cinema Corporation Production, Paramount.

DUDLEY MOORE in *Arthur*, A Rollins, Joffe, Morra, and Brezner Production, Orion.

PAUL NEWMAN in *Absence of Malice*, A Mirage Enterprises Production, Columbia.

Actress

★ KATHARINE HEPBURN in *On Golden Pond*, An ITC Films/IPC Films Production, Universal.

DIANE KEATON in *Reds*, A J.R.S. Production, Paramount.

MARSHA MASON in *Only When I Laugh*, A Columbia Pictures Production, Columbia.

SUSAN SARANDON in *Atlantic City*, An International Cinema Corporation Production, Paramount.

MERYL STREEP in *The French Lieutenant's Woman*, A Parlon Production, United Artists.

Supporting Actor

JAMES COCO in *Only When I Laugh*, A Columbia Pictures Production, Columbia.

★ JOHN GIELGUD in *Arthur*, A Rollins, Joffe, Morra, and Brezner Production, Orion.

IAN HOLM in *Chariots of Fire*, Enigma Productions Limited, The Ladd Company/Warner Bros.

JACK NICHOLSON in *Reds*, A J.R.S. Production, Paramount.

HOWARD E. ROLLINS, JR., in *Ragtime*, A Ragtime Production, Paramount.

Supporting Actress

MELINDA DILLON in *Absence of Malice*, A Mirage Enterprises Production, Columbia.

JANE FONDA in *On Golden Pond*, An ITC Films/IPC Films Production, Universal.

JOAN HACKETT in *Only When I Laugh*, A Columbia Pictures Production, Columbia.

ELIZABETH MCGOVERN in *Ragtime*, A Ragtime Production, Paramount.

★ MAUREEN STAPLETON in *Reds*, A J.R.S. Production, Paramount.

Directing

★ WARREN BEATTY for *Reds*, A J.R.S. Production, Paramount.

HUGH HUDSON for *Chariots of Fire*, Enigma Productions Limited, The Ladd Company/Warner Brothers.

LOUIS MALLE for *Atlantic City*, An International Cinema Corporation Production, Paramount.

MARK RYDELL for *On Golden Pond*, An ITC Films/IPC Films Production, Universal.

STEVEN SPIELBERG for *Raiders of the Lost Ark*, A Lucasfilm Production, Paramount.

Writing

Screenplay Written Directly for the Screen

ABSENCE OF MALICE, A Mirage Enterprises Production, Columbia: KURT LUEDTKE.

ARTHUR, A Rollins, Joffe, Morra, and Brezner Production, Orion: STEVE GORDON.

ATLANTIC CITY, An International Cinema Corporation Production, Paramount: JOHN GUARE.

★ CHARIOTS OF FIRE, Enigma Productions Limited, The Ladd Company/Warner Bros.: COLIN WELLAND.

REDS, A J.R.S. Production, Paramount: WARREN BEATTY and TREVOR GRIFFITHS.

Screenplay Based on Material from Another Medium

THE FRENCH LIEUTENANT'S WOMAN, A Parlon Production, United Artists: HAROLD PINTER.

★ ON GOLDEN POND, An ITC Films/IPC Films Production, Universal: ERNEST THOMPSON.

PENNIES FROM HEAVEN, A Metro-Goldwyn-Mayer/Herbert Ross/Hera Production, Metro-Goldwyn-Mayer: DENNIS POTTER.

PRINCE OF THE CITY, An Orion Pictures/Warner Bros. Production, Orion/Warner Bros.: JAY PRESSON ALLEN and SIDNEY LUMET.

RAGTIME, A Ragtime Production, Paramount: MICHAEL WELLER.

Cinematography

EXCALIBUR, An Orion Pictures Production, Orion: ALEX THOMSON.

ON GOLDEN POND, An ITC Films/IPC Films Production, Universal: BILLY WILLIAMS.

RAGTIME, A Ragtime Production, Paramount: MIROSLAV ONDRICEK.

RAIDERS OF THE LOST ARK, A Lucasfilm Production, Paramount: DOUGLAS SLOCOMBE.

★ REDS, A J.R.S. Production, Paramount: VITTORIO STORARO.

Art Direction - Set Decoration

THE FRENCH LIEUTENANT'S WOMAN, A Parlon Production, United Artists: ASSHETON GORTON; Set Decoration: ANN MOLLO.

HEAVEN'S GATE, Partisan Productions, Ltd., United Artists: TAMBI LARSEN; Set Decoration: JIM BERKEY.

RAGTIME, A Ragtime Production, Paramount: JOHN GRAYSMARK, PATRIZIA VON BRANDENSTEIN, and ANTHONY READING; Set Decoration:

GEORGE DE TITTA, SR., GEORGE DE TITTA, JR., and PETER HOWITT.

★ RAIDERS OF THE LOST ARK, A Lucasfilm Production, Paramount: NORMAN REYNOLDS and LESLIE DILLEY; Set Decoration: MICHAEL FORD.

REDS, A J.R.S. Production, Paramount: RICHARD SYLBERT; Set Decoration: MICHAEL SEIRTON.

Sound

ON GOLDEN POND, An ITC Films/IPC Films Production, Universal: RICHARD PORTMAN and DAVID RONNE.

OUTLAND, A Ladd Company Production, The Ladd Company: JOHN K. WILKINSON, ROBERT W. GLASS, JR., ROBERT M. THIRLWELL, and ROBIN GREGORY.

PENNIES FROM HEAVEN, A Metro-Goldwyn-Mayer/Herbert Ross/Hera Production, Metro-Goldwyn-Mayer: MICHAEL J. KOHUT, JAY M. HARDING, RICHARD TYLER, and AL OVERTON.

★ RAIDERS OF THE LOST ARK, A Lucasfilm Production, Paramount: BILL VARNEY, STEVE MASLOW, GREGG LANDAKER, and ROY CHARMAN.

REDS, A J.R.S. Production, Paramount: DICK VORISEK, TOM FLEISCHMAN, and SIMON KAYE.

Film Editing

CHARIOTS OF FIRE, Enigma Productions Limited, The Ladd Company/Warner Bros.: TERRY RAWLINGS.

THE FRENCH LIEUTENANT'S WOMAN, A Parlon Production, United Artists: JOHN BLOOM.

ON GOLDEN POND, An ITC Films/IPC Films Production, Universal: ROBERT L. WOLFE.

★ RAIDERS OF THE LOST ARK, A Lucasfilm Production, Paramount: MICHAEL KAHN.

REDS, A J.R.S. Production, Paramount: DEDE ALLEN and CRAIG MCKAY.

Music

Original Score

★ CHARIOTS OF FIRE, Enigma Productions Limited, The Ladd Company/Warner Bros.: VANGELIS.

DRAGONSLAYER, A Barwood/Robbins Production, Paramount: ALEX NORTH.

ON GOLDEN POND, An ITC Films/ IPC Films Production, Universal: DAVE GRUSIN.

RAGTIME, A Ragtime Production, Paramount: RANDY NEWMAN.

RAIDERS OF THE LOST ARK, A Lucasfilm Production, Paramount: JOHN WILLIAMS.

Original Song Score and Its Adaptation or Best Adaptation Score

No nominations.

Original Song

★ ARTHUR'S THEME (BEST THAT YOU CAN DO) from *Arthur*, A Rollins, Joffe, Morra, and Brezner Production, Orion: Music and Lyrics by BURT BACHARACH, CAROLE BAYER SAGER, CHRISTOPHER CROSS, and PETER ALLEN.

ENDLESS LOVE from *Endless Love*, A Polygram/Universal Pictures/Keith Barish/Dyson Lovell Production, Universal: Music and Lyrics by LIONEL RICHIE.

THE FIRST TIME IT HAPPENS, from *The Great Muppet Caper*. A Jim Henson/ ITC Film Entertainment Limited Production, Universal: Music and Lyrics by JOE RAPOSO.

FOR YOUR EYES ONLY from *For Your Eyes Only*, An EON Production, United Artists: Music by BILL CONTI; Lyrics by MICK LEESON.

ONE MORE HOUR from *Ragtime*, A Ragtime Production, Paramount:

Music and Lyrics by RANDY NEWMAN.

Costume Design

★ CHARIOTS OF FIRE, Enigma Productions Limited, The Ladd Company/Warner Bros.: MILENA CANONERO.

THE FRENCH LIEUTENANT'S WOMAN, A Parlon Production, United Artists: TOM RAND.

PENNIES FROM HEAVEN, A Metro-Goldwyn-Mayer/Herbert Ross/Hera Production, Metro-Goldwyn-Mayer: BOB MACKIE.

RAGTIME, A Ragtime Production, Paramount: ANNA HILL JOHNSTONE.

REDS, A J.R.S. Production, Paramount: SHIRLEY RUSSELL.

Make-Up

(new category)

★ AN AMERICAN WEREWOLF IN LONDON, A Lycanthrope/Polygram/Universal Pictures Production, Universal: RICK BAKER.

HEARTBEEPS, A Michael Phillips/Universal Pictures Production, Universal: STAN WINSTON.

Visual Effects

DRAGONSLAYER, A Barwood/Robbins Production, Paramount: DENNIS MUREN, PHIL TIPPETT, KEN RALSTON, and BRIAN JOHNSON.

★ RAIDERS OF THE LOST ARK, A Lucasfilm Production, Paramount: RICHARD EDLUND, KIT WEST, BRUCE NICHOLSON, and JOE JOHNSTON.

Short Films

Animated

★ CRAC, Société Radio-Canada: FREDERIC BACK, Producer.

THE CREATION, Will Vinton Productions: WILL VINTON, Producer.

THE TENDER TALE OF CINDERELLA PENGUIN, National Film Board of Canada: JANET PERLMAN, Producer.

Live Action

COUPLES AND ROBBERS, Flamingo Pictures Ltd.: CHRISTINE OESTREICHER, Producer.

FIRST WINTER, National Film Board of Canada: JOHN N. SMITH, Producer.

★ VIOLET, The American Film Institute: PAUL KEMP and SHELLEY LEVINSON, Producers.

Documentary

Short Subjects

AMERICAS IN TRANSITION, Americas in Transition, Inc.: OBIE BENZ, Producer.

★ CLOSE HARMONY, A Noble Enterprise: NIGEL NOBLE, Producer.

JOURNEY FOR SURVIVAL, Dick Young Productions, Inc.: DICK YOUNG, Producer.

SEE WHAT I SAY, Michigan Women Filmmakers Productions: LINDA CHAPMAN, PAM LEBLANC, and FREDDI STEVENS, Producers.

URGE TO BUILD, Roland Hallé Productions, Inc.: ROLAND HALLÉ and JOHN HOOVER, Producers.

Features

AGAINST WIND AND TIDE: A CUBAN ODYSSEY, Seven League Productions, Inc.: SUSANNE BAUMAN and PAUL NESHAMKIN, Producers.

BROOKLYN BRIDGE, Florentine Films: KEN BURNS, Producer.

EIGHT MINUTES TO MIDNIGHT: A PORTRAIT OF DR. HELEN CALDICOTT, The Caldicott Project: MARY BENJAMIN, SUSANNE SIMPSON, and BOYD ESTUS, Producers.

EL SALVADOR: ANOTHER VIETNAM, Catalyst Media Productions: GLENN

SILBER and TETE VASCONCELLOS, Producers.
★ GENOCIDE, Arnold Schwartzman Productions, Inc.: ARNOLD SCHWARTZMAN and RABBI MARVIN HIER, Producers.

Foreign Language Film Award

THE BOAT IS FULL, A Limbo Film AG Production (Switzerland).
MAN OF IRON, A Polish Corporation for Film, Unit "X" Production (Poland).
★ MEPHISTO, A Mafilm-Objektiv Studio and Manfred Durniok Production (Hungary).
MUDDY RIVER, A Kimura Production (Japan).
THREE BROTHERS, An Iter Film (Rome)/ Gaumont (Paris) Production (Italy).

Honorary Awards

BARBARA STANWYCK for superlative creativity and unique contribution to the art of screen acting.

Special Achievement Award

Sound Effects Editing: BENJAMIN P. BURTT, JR., and RICHARD L. ANDERSON for *Raiders of the Lost Ark*, A Lucasfilm Production, Paramount.

Irving G. Thalberg Memorial Award

ALBERT R. "CUBBY" BROCCOLI.

Jean Hersholt Humanitarian Award

DANNY KAYE.

Gordon E. Sawyer Award (new award)

JOSEPH B. WALKER.

Scientific or Technical Awards

Academy Award of Merit (Academy statuette)

FUJI PHOTO FILM COMPANY, LTD., for the research, development, and introduction of a new ultrahigh-speed color negative film for motion pictures.

Scientific and Engineering Award (Academy plaque)

LEONARD SOKOLOW for the concept and design and HOWARD LAZARE for the development of the Consolidated Film Industries' Stroboscan motion picture film viewer.
RICHARD EDLUND and INDUSTRIAL LIGHT AND MAGIC, INCORPORATED, for the concept and engineering of a beam-splitter optical composite motion picture printer.
RICHARD EDLUND and INDUSTRIAL LIGHT AND MAGIC, INCORPORATED, for the engineering of the Empire Motion Picture Camera System.
EDWARD J. BLASKO and DR. RODERICK T. RYAN of the Eastman Kodak Company for the application of the Prostar Microfilm Processor to motion picture title and special optical effects production.
NELSON TYLER for the progressive development and improvement of the Tyler Helicopter motion picture camera platform.

Technical Achievement Award (Academy certificate)

HAL LANDAKER for the concept and ALAN D. LANDAKER for the engineering of the Burbank Studios' Production Sound Department 24-frame color video system.
BILL HOGAN of Ruxton, Ltd., and RICHARD J. STUMPF and DANIEL R. BREWER of Universal City Studios' Production Sound Department for the engineering of a 24-frame color video system.
ERNST F. NETTMANN of Continental Camera Systems, Inc.,

for the development of a pitching lens for motion picture photography.

BILL TAYLOR of Universal Studios for the concept and specifications for a two-format, rotating-head, aerial-image optical printer.

PETER D. PARKS of Oxford Scientific Films for the development of OSF microscopic photography.

DR. LOUIS STANKIEWICZ and H. L. BLACHFORD for the development of Baryfol sound barrier materials.

DENNIS MUREN and STUART ZIFF of Industrial Light and Magic, Incorporated, for the development of a motion picture figure mover for animation photography.

JOHN DEMUTH for the engineering of a 24-frame video system.

1982

Nominations Announced: February 17, 1983
Awards Ceremony: April 11, 1983
Dorothy Chandler Pavilion, Los Angeles County Music Center
(Hosts: Liza Minnelli, Dudley Moore, Walter Matthau, and Richard Pryor)

Best Picture

E.T. THE EXTRA-TERRESTRIAL, A Universal Pictures Production, Universal: Steven Spielberg and Kathleen Kennedy, Producers.

★ GANDHI, An Indo-British Films Production, Columbia: Richard Attenborough, Producer.

MISSING, A Universal Pictures/ Polygram Pictures Presentation of an Edward Lewis Production, Universal: Edward Lewis and Mildred Lewis, Producers.

TOOTSIE, A Mirage/Punch Production, Columbia: Sydney Pollack and Dick Richards, Producers.

THE VERDICT, A Fox-Zanuck/Brown Production, 20th Century-Fox: Richard D. Zanuck and David Brown, Producers.

Actor

DUSTIN HOFFMAN in *Tootsie*, A Mirage/ Punch Production, Columbia.

★ BEN KINGSLEY in *Gandhi*, An Indo-British Films Production, Columbia.

JACK LEMMON in *Missing*, A Universal Pictures/Polygram Pictures Presentation of an Edward Lewis Production, Universal.

PAUL NEWMAN in *The Verdict*, A Fox-Zanuck/Brown Production, 20th Century-Fox.

PETER O'TOOLE in *My Favorite Year*, A Metro-Goldwyn-Mayer/Brooksfilm/ Michael Gruskoff Production, M-G-M/UA.

Actress

JULIE ANDREWS in *Victor/Victoria*, A Metro-Goldwyn-Mayer Production, M-G-M/UA.

JESSICA LANGE in *Frances*, A Brooksfilm/EMI Production, Universal/A.F.D.

SISSY SPACEK in *Missing*, A Universal Pictures/Polygram Pictures Presentation of an Edward Lewis Production, Universal.

★ MERYL STREEP in *Sophie's Choice*, An ITC Entertainment Presentation of a Pakula-Barish Production, Universal/A.F.D.

DEBRA WINGER in *An Officer and a Gentleman*, A Lorimar Production in association with Martin Elfand, Paramount.

Supporting Actor

CHARLES DURNING in *The Best Little Whorehouse in Texas*, A Universal and RKO Pictures Presentation of a Miller-Milkis-Boyett Production, Universal.

★ LOUIS GOSSETT, JR., in *An Officer and a Gentleman*, A Lorimar Production in association with Martin Elfand, Paramount.

JOHN LITHGOW in *The World According to Garp*, A Warner Bros. Production, Warner Bros.

JAMES MASON in *The Verdict*, A Fox-Zanuck/Brown Production, 20th Century-Fox.

ROBERT PRESTON in *Victor/Victoria*, A Metro-Goldwyn-Mayer Production, M-G-M/UA.

Supporting Actress

GLENN CLOSE in *The World According to Garp*, A Warner Bros. Production, Warner Bros.

TERI GARR in *Tootsie*, A Mirage/Punch Production, Columbia.

★ JESSICA LANGE in *Tootsie*, A Mirage/Punch Production, Columbia.

KIM STANLEY in *Frances*, A Brooksfilm/EMI Production, Universal/A.F.D.

LESLEY ANN WARREN in *Victor/Victoria*, A Metro-Goldwyn-Mayer Production, M-G-M/UA.

Directing

★ RICHARD ATTENBOROUGH for *Gandhi*, An Indo-British Films Production, Columbia.

SIDNEY LUMET for *The Verdict*, A Fox-Zanuck/Brown Production, 20th Century-Fox.

WOLFGANG PETERSEN for *Das Boot*, A Bavaria Atelier GmbH Production, Columbia.

SYDNEY POLLACK for *Tootsie*, a Mirage/Punch Production, Columbia.

STEVEN SPIELBERG for *E.T. the Extra-Terrestrial*, A Universal Pictures Production, Universal.

Writing

Screenplay Written Directly for the Screen

DINER, A Jerry Weintraub Production, M-G-M/UA: BARRY LEVINSON.

E.T. THE EXTRA-TERRESTRIAL, A Universal Pictures Production, Universal: MELISSA MATHISON.

★ GANDHI, An Indo-British Films Production, Columbia: JOHN BRILEY.

AN OFFICER AND A GENTLEMAN, A Lorimar Production in association with Martin Elfand, Paramount: DOUGLAS DAY STEWART.

TOOTSIE, A Mirage/Punch Production, Columbia: Story by DON MCGUIRE and LARRY GELBART; Screenplay by LARRY GELBART and MURRAY SCHISGAL.

Screenplay Based on Material from Another Medium

DAS BOOT, A Bavaria Atelier GmbH Production, Columbia: WOLFGANG PETERSEN.

★ MISSING, A Universal Pictures/Polygram Pictures Presentation of an Edward Lewis Production, Universal: COSTA-GAVRAS and DONALD STEWART.

SOPHIE'S CHOICE, An ITC Entertainment Presentation of a Pakula-Barish Production, Universal/A.F.D.: ALAN J. PAKULA.

THE VERDICT, A Fox-Zanuck/Brown Production, 20th Century-Fox: DAVID MAMET.

VICTOR/VICTORIA, A Metro-Goldwyn-Mayer Production, M-G-M/UA: BLAKE EDWARDS.

Cinematography

DAS BOOT, A Bavaria Atelier GmbH Production, Columbia: JOST VACANO.

E.T. THE EXTRA-TERRESTRIAL, A Universal Pictures Production, Universal: ALLEN DAVIAU.

★ GANDHI, An Indo-British Films Production, Columbia: BILLY WILLIAMS and RONNIE TAYLOR.

SOPHIE'S CHOICE, An ITC Entertainment Presentation of a Pakula-Barish Production, Universal/ A.F.D.: NESTOR ALMENDROS.

TOOTSIE, A Mirage/Punch Production, Columbia: OWEN ROIZMAN.

Art Direction—Set Decoration

ANNIE, A Rastar Films Production, Columbia: DALE HENNESY; Set Decoration: MARVIN MARCH.

BLADE RUNNER, A Michael Deeley-Ridley Scott Production, The Ladd Company/Sir Run Run Shaw: LAWRENCE G. PAULL and DAVID L. SNYDER; Set Decoration: LINDA DESCENNA.

★ GANDHI, An Indo-British Films Production, Columbia: STUART CRAIG and BOB LAING; Set Decoration: MICHAEL SEIRTON.

LA TRAVIATA, An Accent Films B.V. Production in association with RAI-Radiotelevisione Italiana, Producers Sales Organization: FRANCO ZEFFIRELLI; Set Decoration: GIANNI QUARANTA.

VICTOR/VICTORIA, A Metro-Goldwyn-Mayer Production, M-G-M/UA: RODGER MAUS, TIM HUTCHINSON, and WILLIAM CRAIG SMITH; Set Decoration: HARRY CORDWELL.

Sound

DAS BOOT, A Bavaria Atelier GmbH Production, Columbia: MILAN BOR, TREVOR PYKE, and MIKE LE-MARE.

★ E.T. THE EXTRA-TERRESTRIAL, A Universal Pictures Production, Universal: ROBERT KNUDSON, ROBERT GLASS, DON DIGIROLAMO, and GENE CANTAMESSA.

GANDHI, An Indo-British Films Production, Columbia: GERRY HUMPHREYS, ROBIN O'DONOGHUE, JONATHAN BATES, and SIMON KAYE.

TOOTSIE, A Mirage/Punch Production, Columbia: ARTHUR PIANTADOSI, LES FRESHOLTZ, DICK ALEXANDER, and LES LAZAROWITZ.

TRON, A Walt Disney Production, Buena Vista Distribution: MICHAEL MINKLER, BOB MINKLER, LEE MINKLER, and JIM LA RUE.

Film Editing

DAS BOOT, A Bavaria Atelier GmbH Production, Columbia: HANNES NIKEL.

E.T. THE EXTRA-TERRESTRIAL, A Universal Pictures Production, Universal: CAROL LITTLETON.

★ GANDHI, An Indo-British Films Production, Columbia: JOHN BLOOM.

AN OFFICER AND A GENTLEMAN, A Lorimar Production in association with Martin Elfand, Paramount: PETER ZINNER.

TOOTSIE, A Mirage/Punch Production, Columbia: FREDRIC STEINKAMP and WILLIAM STEINKAMP.

Music

Original Score

★ E.T. THE EXTRA-TERRESTRIAL, A Universal Pictures Production, Universal: JOHN WILLIAMS.

GANDHI, An Indo-British Films Production, Columbia: RAVI SHANKAR and GEORGE FENTON.

AN OFFICER AND A GENTLEMAN, A Lorimar Production in association with Martin Elfand, Paramount: JACK NITZSCHE.

POLTERGEIST, A Metro-Goldwyn-Mayer/Steven Spielberg Production, M-G-M/UA: JERRY GOLDSMITH.

SOPHIE'S CHOICE, An ITC Entertainment Presentation of a Pakula-Barish Production, Universal/ A.F.D.: MARVIN HAMLISCH.

Original Song Score and Its Adaptation or Best Adaptation Score

ANNIE, A Rastar Films Production, Columbia: Adaptation score by RALPH BURNS.

ONE FROM THE HEART, A Zoetrope Studios Production, Columbia: Song score by TOM WAITS.

★ VICTOR/VICTORIA, A Metro-Goldwyn-Mayer Production, M-G-M/UA: Song score by HENRY MANCINI and LESLIE BRICUSSE; Adapted by HENRY MANCINI.

Original Song

EYE OF THE TIGER from *Rocky III*, A Robert Chartoff-Irwin Winkler/United Artists Production, M-G-M/UA: Music and Lyrics by JIM PETERIK and FRANKIE SULLIVAN III.

HOW DO YOU KEEP THE MUSIC PLAYING? from *Best Friends*, A Timberlane Films Production, Warner Bros.: Music by MICHEL LEGRAND; Lyrics by ALAN BERGMAN and MARILYN BERGMAN.

IF WE WERE IN LOVE from *Yes, Giorgio*, A Metro-Goldwyn-Mayer Production, M-G-M/UA: Music by JOHN WILLIAMS; Lyrics by ALAN BERGMAN and MARILYN BERGMAN.

IT MIGHT BE YOU from *Tootsie*, A Mirage/Punch Production, Columbia: Music by DAVE GRUSIN; Lyrics by ALAN BERGMAN and MARILYN BERGMAN.

★ UP WHERE WE BELONG from *An Officer and a Gentleman*, A Lorimar Production in association with Martin Elfand, Paramount: Music by JACK NITZSCHE and BUFFY SAINTE-MARIE; Lyrics by WILL JENNINGS.

Costume Design

★ GANDHI, An Indo-British Films Production, Columbia: JOHN MOLLO and BHANU ATHAIYA.

LA TRAVIATA, An Accent Films B.V. Production in association with RAI-Radiotelevisione Italiana, Producers Sales Organization: PIERO TOSI.

SOPHIE'S CHOICE, An ITC Entertainment Presentation of a Pakula-Barish Production, Universal/A.F.D.: ALBERT WOLSKY.

TRON, A Walt Disney Production, Buena Vista Distribution: ELOIS JENSSEN and ROSANNA NORTON.

VICTOR/VICTORIA, A Metro-Goldwyn-Mayer Production, M-G-M/UA: PATRICIA NORRIS.

Make-up

GANDHI, An Indo-British Films Production, Columbia: TOM SMITH.

★ QUEST FOR FIRE, An International Cinema Corporation Production, 20th Century-Fox: SARAH MONZANI and MICHELE BURKE.

Visual Effects

BLADE RUNNER, A Michael Deeley-Ridley Scott Production, The Ladd Company/Sir Run Run Shaw: DOUGLAS TRUMBULL, RICHARD YURICICH, and DAVID DRYER.

★ E.T. THE EXTRA-TERRESTRIAL, A Universal Pictures Production, Universal: CARLO RAMBALDI, DENNIS MUREN, and KENNETH F. SMITH.

POLTERGEIST, A Metro-Goldwyn-Mayer/Steven Spielberg Production, M-G-M/UA: RICHARD EDLUND, MICHAEL WOOD, and BRUCE NICHOLSON.

Sound Effects Editing

(new category)

DAS BOOT, A Bavaria Atelier GmbH Production, Columbia: MIKE LE-MARE.

★ E.T. THE EXTRA-TERRESTRIAL, A Universal Pictures Production, Universal: CHARLES L. CAMPBELL and BEN BURTT.

POLTERGEIST, A Metro-Goldwyn-Mayer/Steven Spielberg Production, M-G-M/UA: STEPHEN HUNTER FLICK and RICHARD L. ANDERSON.

Short Films

Animated

THE GREAT COGNITO, Will Vinton Productions: WILL VINTON, Producer.

THE SNOWMAN, Snowman Enterprises Ltd.: JOHN COATES, Producer.

★ TANGO, Film Polski: ZBIGNIEW RYBCZYNAKI, Producer.

Live Action

BALLET ROBOTIQUE, Bob Rogers and Company: BOB ROGERS, Producer.

★ A SHOCKING ACCIDENT, Flamingo Pictures Ltd.: CHRISTINE OESTREICHER, Producer.

THE SILENCE, The American Film Institute: MICHAEL TOSHIYUKI UNO and JOSEPH BENSON, Producers.

SPLIT CHERRY TREE, Learning Corporation of America: JAN SAUNDERS, Producer.

SREDNI VASHIAR, Laurentic Film Productions Ltd.: ANDREW BIRKIN, Producer.

Documentary

Short Subjects

GODS OF METAL, A Richter Productions Film: ROBERT RICHTER, Producer.

★ IF YOU LOVE THIS PLANET, National Film Board of Canada: EDWARD LE LORRAIN, Producer.

THE KLAN: A LEGACY OF HATE IN AMERICA, Guggenheim Productions, Inc.: CHARLES GUGGENHEIM and WERNER SCHUMANN, Producers.

TO LIVE OR LET DIE, American Film Foundation: FREIDA LEE MOCK, Producer.

TRAVELING HOPEFULLY, Arnuthfonyus Films, Inc.: JOHN G. AVILDSEN, Producer.

Features

AFTER THE AXE, National Film Board of Canada: STURLA GUNNARSSON and STEVE LUCAS, Producers.

BEN'S MILL, Public Broadcasting Associates—ODYSSEY: JOHN KAROL and MICHEL CHALUFOUR, Producers.

IN OUR WATER, A Foresight Films Production: MEG SWITZGABLE, Producer.

★ JUST ANOTHER MISSING KID, Canadian Broadcasting Corporation: JOHN ZARITSKY, Producer.

A PORTRAIT OF GISELLE, Wishupon Productions: JOSEPH WISHY, Producer.

Foreign Language Film Award

ALSINO AND THE CONDOR, A Nicaraguan Film Institute Production (Nicaragua).

COUP DE TORCHON (CLEAN SLATE), A Films de la Tour Production (France).

THE FLIGHT OF THE EAGLE, A Bold Productions for the Swedish Film Institute, Swedish Television SVT 2, Svensk Filmindustri, and Norsk Film A/S Production (Sweden).

PRIVATE LIFE, A Mosfilm Studio Production (U.S.S.R.).

★ VOLVER A EMPEZAR (TO BEGIN AGAIN), A Nickel Odeon, S.A. Production (Spain).

Honorary Awards

MICKEY ROONEY in recognition of his sixty years of versatility in a variety of memorable film performances.

Special Achievement Award

None.

Irving G. Thalberg Memorial Award

None.

Jean Hersholt Humanitarian Award

WALTER MIRISCH.

Gordon E. Sawyer Award

JOHN O. AALBERG.

Scientific or Technical Awards

Academy Award of Merit (Academy statuette)

AUGUST ARNOLD and ERICH KAESTNER of Arnold & Richter, GmbH for the concept and engineering of the first operational 35mm, hand-held, spinning-mirror reflex, motion picture camera.

Scientific and Engineering Award (Academy plaque)

COLIN F. MOSSMAN and the RESEARCH AND DEVELOPMENT GROUP OF RANK FILM LABORATORIES, LONDON, for the engineering and implementation of a 4,000-meter printing system for motion picture laboratories.

SANTE ZELLI and SALVATORE ZELLI of Elemack Italia S.r.l., Rome, Italy, for the continuing engineering, design, and development that has resulted in the Elemack Camera Dolly Systems for motion picture production.

LEONARD CHAPMAN for the engineering design, development, and manufacture of the PeeWee Camera Dolly for motion picture production.

DR. MOHAMMAD S. NOZARI of Minnesota Mining and Manufacturing Company for the research and development of the 3M Photogard protective coating for motion picture film.

BRIANNE MURPHY and DONALD SCHISLER of Mitchell Insert Systems, Incorporated, for the concept, design, and manufacture of the MISI Camera Insert Car and Process Trailer.

JACOBUS L. DIMMERS for the engineering and manufacture of the Teccon Enterprises' magnetic transducer for motion picture sound recording and playback.

Technical Achievement Award (Academy certificate)

RICHARD W. DEATS for the design and manufacture of the Little Big Crane for motion picture production.

CONSTANT TRESFON and ADRIAAN DE ROOY of Egripment and ED PHILLIPS and CARLOS DE MATTOS of Matthews Studio Equipment, Incorporated, for the design and manufacture of the Tulip Crane for motion picture production.

BRAN FERREN of Associates and Ferren for the design and development of a computerized lightning effect system for motion picture photography.

CHRISTIE ELECTRIC CORPORATION and LAVEZZI MACHINE WORKS, INCORPORATED, for the design and manufacture of the Ultramittent film transport for Christie motion picture projectors.

FIFTY-SIXTH YEAR

1983

Nominations Announced: February 16, 1984
Awards Ceremony: April 9, 1984
Dorothy Chandler Pavilion, Los Angeles County Music Center
(MC: Johnny Carson)

Best Picture

THE BIG CHILL, A Carson Productions Group Production, Columbia: Michael Shamberg, Producer.

THE DRESSER, A Goldcrest Films/Television Limited/World Film Services Production, Columbia: Peter Yates, Producer.

THE RIGHT STUFF, A Robert Chartoff-Irwin Winkler Production, The Ladd Company through Warner Bros.: Irwin Winkler and Robert Chartoff, Producers.

TENDER MERCIES, An EMI Presentation of an Antron Media Production, Universal/A.F.D.: Philip S. Hobel, Producer.

★ TERMS OF ENDEARMENT, A James L. Brooks Production, Paramount: James L. Brooks, Producer.

Actor

MICHAEL CAINE in *Educating Rita*, An Acorn Pictures Limited Production, Columbia.

TOM CONTI in *Reuben, Reuben*, A Saltair/Walter Shenson Production presented by The Taft Entertainment Company, 20th Century-Fox International Classics.

TOM COURTENAY in *The Dresser*, A Goldcrest Films/Television Limited/World Film Services Production, Columbia.

★ ROBERT DUVALL in *Tender Mercies*, An EMI Presentation of an Antron Media Production, Universal/A.F.D.

ALBERT FINNEY in *The Dresser*, A Goldcrest Films/Television Limited/World Film Services Production, Columbia.

Actress

JANE ALEXANDER in *Testament*, An Entertainment Events Production in association with American Playhouse, Paramount.

★ SHIRLEY MACLAINE in *Terms of Endearment*, A James L. Brooks Production, Paramount.

MERYL STREEP in *Silkwood*, An ABC Motion Pictures Production, 20th Century-Fox.

JULIE WALTERS in *Educating Rita*, An Acorn Pictures Limited Production, Columbia.

DEBRA WINGER in *Terms of Endearment*, A James L. Brooks Production, Paramount.

Supporting Actor

CHARLES DURNING in *To Be or Not to Be*, A Brooksfilms Production, 20th Century-Fox.

JOHN LITHGOW in *Terms of Endearment*, A James L. Brooks Production, Paramount.

★ JACK NICHOLSON in *Terms of Endearment*, A James L. Brooks Production, Paramount.

SAM SHEPARD in *The Right Stuff*, A Robert Chartoff-Irwin Winkler Production, The Ladd Company through Warner Bros.

RIP TORN in *Cross Creek*, A Robert B. Radnitz/Martin Ritt/Thorn EMI Films Production, Universal.

Supporting Actress

CHER in *Silkwood*, An ABC Motion Pictures Production, 20th Century-Fox.

GLENN CLOSE in *The Big Chill*, A Carson Productions Group Production, Columbia.

★ LINDA HUNT in *The Year of Living Dangerously*, A Freddie Fields Presentation of a Metro-Goldwyn-Mayer Production, M-G-M/UA.

AMY IRVING in *Yentl*, A United Artists/Ladbroke Feature/Barwood Production, M-G-M/UA.

ALFRE WOODARD in *Cross Creek*, A Robert B. Radnitz/Martin Ritt/Thorn EMI Films Production, Universal.

Directing

BRUCE BERESFORD for *Tender Mercies*, An EMI Presentation of an Antron Media Production, Universal/A.F.D.

INGMAR BERGMAN for *Fanny and Alexander*, A Cinematograph AB for the Swedish Film Institute/Swedish Television SVT 1, Sweden/Gaumont, France/Personafilm, and Tobis Filmkunst, BRD Production, Embassy.

★ JAMES L. BROOKS for *Terms of Endearment*, A James L. Brooks Production, Paramount.

MIKE NICHOLS for *Silkwood*, An ABC Motion Pictures Production, 20th Century-Fox.

PETER YATES for *The Dresser*, A Gold Crest Film/Television Limited/World Film Services Production, Columbia.

Writing

Screenplay Written Directly for the Screen

THE BIG CHILL, A Carson Productions Group Production, Columbia: LAWRENCE KASDAN and BARBARA BENEDEK.

FANNY AND ALEXANDER, A Cinematograph AB for the Swedish Film Institute/Swedish Television SVT 1, Sweden/Gaumont, France/Personafilm, and Tobis Filmkunst, BRD Production, Embassy: INGMAR BERGMAN.

SILKWOOD, An ABC Motion Pictures Production, 20th Century-Fox: NORA EPHRON and ALICE ARLEN.

★ TENDER MERCIES, An EMI Presentation of an Antron Media Production, Universal/A.F.D.: HORTON FOOTE.

WARGAMES, A United Artists Presentation of a Leonard Goldberg Production, M-G-M/UA: LAWRENCE LASKER and WALTER F. PARKES.

Screenplay Based on Material from Another Medium

BETRAYAL, A Horizon Film Production, 20th Century-Fox International Classics: HAROLD PINTER.

THE DRESSER, A Goldcrest Films/Television Limited/World Film Services Production, Columbia: RONALD HARWOOD.

EDUCATING RITA, An Acorn Pictures Limited Production, Columbia: WILLY RUSSELL.

REUBEN, REUBEN, A Saltair/Walter Shenson Production presented by the Taft Entertainment 20th Century-Fox International Classics: JULIUS J. EPSTEIN.

★ TERMS OF ENDEARMENT, A James L. Brooks Production, Paramount: JAMES L. BROOKS.

Cinematography

★ FANNY AND ALEXANDER, A Cinematograph AB for the Swedish Film Institute/Swedish Television SVT 1, Sweden/Gaumont, France/ Personafilm, and Tobis Filmkunst, BRD Production, Embassy: SVEN NYKVIST.

FLASHDANCE, A Polygram Pictures Production, Paramount: DON PETERMAN.

THE RIGHT STUFF, A Robert Chartoff-Irwin Winkler Production, The Ladd Company through Warner Bros.: CALEB DESCHANEL.

WARGAMES, A United Artists Presentation of a Leonard Goldberg Production, M-G-M/UA: WILLIAM A. FRAKER.

ZELIG, A Jack Rollins and Charles H. Joffe Production, Orion through Warner Bros.: GORDON WILLIS.

Art Direction - Set Decoration

★ FANNY AND ALEXANDER, A Cinematograph AB for the Swedish Film Institute/Swedish Television SVT 1, Sweden/Gaumont, France/ Personafilm, and Tobis Filmkunst, BRD Production, Embassy: ANNA ASP.

RETURN OF THE JEDI, A Lucasfilm Production, 20th Century-Fox: NORMAN REYNOLDS, FRED HOLE, and JAMES SCHOPPE; Set Decoration: MICHAEL FORD.

THE RIGHT STUFF, A Robert Chartoff-Irwin Winkler Production, The Ladd Company through Warner Bros.: GEOFFREY KIRKLAND, RICHARD J. LAWRENCE, W. STEWART CAMPBELL, and PETER ROMERO; Set Decoration: PAT PENDING and GEORGE R. NELSON.

TERMS OF ENDEARMENT, A James L. Brooks Production, Paramount: POLLY PLATT and HAROLD MICHELSON; Set Decoration: TOM PEDIGO and ANTHONY MONDELLO.

YENTL, A United Artists/Ladbroke Feature/Barwood Production, M-G-M/UA: ROY WALKER and LESLIE TOMKINS; Set Decoration: TESSA DAVIES.

Sound

NEVER CRY WOLF, A Walt Disney Production, Buena Vista: ALAN R. SPLET, TODD BOEKELHEIDE, RANDY THOM, and DAVID PARKER.

RETURN OF THE JEDI, A Lucasfilm Production, Twentieth Century-Fox: BEN BURTT, GARY SUMMERS, RANDY THOM, and TONY DAWE.

★ THE RIGHT STUFF, A Robert Chartoff-Irwin Winkler Production, The Ladd Company through Warner Bros.: MARK BERGER, TOM SCOTT, RANDY THOM, and DAVID MACMILLAN.

TERMS OF ENDEARMENT, A James L. Brooks Production, Paramount: DONALD O. MITCHELL, RICK KLINE, KEVIN O'CONNELL, and JIM ALEXANDER.

WARGAMES, A United Artists Presentation of a Leonard Goldberg Production, M-G-M/UA: MICHAEL J. KOHUT, CARLOS DE LARIOS, AARON ROCHIN, and WILLIE D. BURTON.

Film Editing

BLUE THUNDER, A Rastar Features Production, Columbia: FRANK MORRISS and EDWARD ABROMS.

FLASHDANCE, A Polygram Pictures Production, Paramount: BUD SMITH and WALT MULCONERY.

★ THE RIGHT STUFF, A Robert Chartoff-Irwin Winkler Production, The Ladd Company through Warner Bros.: GLENN FARR, LISA FRUCHTMAN, STEPHEN A.

ROTTER, DOUGLAS STEWART and TOM ROLF.

SILKWOOD, An ABC Motion Pictures Production, 20th Century-Fox: SAM O'STEEN.

TERMS OF ENDEARMENT, A James L. Brooks Production, Paramount: RICHARD MARKS.

Music

Original Score

CROSS CREEK, A Robert B. Radnitz/ Martin Ritt/Thorn EMI Films Production, Universal: LEONARD ROSENMAN.

RETURN OF THE JEDI, A Lucasfilm Production, 20th Century-Fox: JOHN WILLIAMS.

★ THE RIGHT STUFF, A Robert Chartoff-Irwin Winkler Production, The Ladd Company through Warner Bros.: BILL CONTI.

TERMS OF ENDEARMENT, A James L. Brooks Production, Paramount: MICHAEL GORE.

UNDER FIRE, A Lions Gate Films Production, Orion: JERRY GOLDSMITH.

Original Song Score and Its Adaptation or Best Adaptation Score

THE STING II, A Jennings Lang/ Universal Pictures Production, Universal; Adaptation score by LALO SCHIFRIN.

TRADING PLACES, An Aaron Russo Production, Paramount: Adaptation score by ELMER BERNSTEIN.

★ YENTL, A United Artists/Ladbroke Feature/Barwood Production, M-G-M/UA: Original song score by MICHEL LEGRAND, ALAN BERGMAN, and MARILYN BERGMAN.

Original Song

★ FLASHDANCE . . . WHAT A FEELING from *Flashdance*, A Polygram Pictures Production, Paramount: Music by GIORGIO MORODER; Lyrics by KEITH FORSEY and IRENE CARA.

MANIAC from *Flashdance*, A Polygram Pictures Production, Paramount: Music and Lyrics by MICHAEL SEMBELLO and DENNIS MATKOSKY.

OVER YOU from *Tender Mercies*, An EMI Presentation of an Antron Media Production, Universal/A.F.D: Music and Lyrics by AUSTIN ROBERTS and BOBBY HART.

PAPA, CAN YOU HEAR ME? from *Yentl*, A United Artists/Ladbroke Feature/ Barwood Production, M-G-M/UA: Music by MICHEL LEGRAND: Lyrics by ALAN BERGMAN and MARILYN BERGMAN.

THE WAY HE MAKES ME FEEL from *Yentl*, A United Artists/Ladbroke Feature/Barwood Production, M-G-M/UA: Music by MICHEL LEGRAND: Lyrics by ALAN BERGMAN and MARILYN BERGMAN.

Costume Design

CROSS CREEK, A Robert B. Radnitz/ Martin Ritt/Thorn EMI Films Production, Universal: JOE I. TOMPKINS.

★ FANNY AND ALEXANDER, A Cinematograph AB for the Swedish Film Institute/Swedish Television SVT 1, Sweden/Gaumont, France/ Personafilm, and Tobis Filmkunst, BRD Production, Embassy: MARIK VOS.

HEART LIKE A WHEEL, An Aurora Film Partners/Twentieth Century-Fox Production, 20th Century-Fox: WILLIAM WARE THEISS.

THE RETURN OF MARTIN GUERRE, A Société Française de Production Cinematographique/ Société de Productions des Films Marcel Dassault—FR 3 Production,

European International Distribution: ANNE-MARIE MARCHAND.

ZELIG, A Jack Rollins and Charles H. Joffe Production, Orion through Warner Bros.: SANTO LOQUASTO.

Make-up

No nominations.

*Visual Effects**

No nominations.

Sound Effects Editing

RETURN OF THE JEDI, A Lucasfilm Production, 20th Century-Fox: BEN BURTT.

★ THE RIGHT STUFF, A Robert Chartoff-Irwin Winkler Production, The Ladd Company through Warner Bros.: JAY BOEKELHEIDE.

Short Films

Animated

MICKEY'S CHRISTMAS CAROL, Walt Disney Productions: BURNY MATTINSON, Producer.

SOUND OF SUNSHINE—SOUND OF RAIN, Hallinan Plus!: EDA GODEL HALLINAN, Producer.

★ SUNDAE IN NEW YORK, Motionpicker Productions: JIMMY PICKER, Producer.

Live Action

★ BOYS AND GIRLS, Atlantis Films Ltd.: JANICE L. PLATT, Producer.

GOODIE-TWO-SHOES, Timeless Films, Paramount Pictures: IAN EMES, Producer.

OVERNIGHT SENSATION, A Bloom Film Production: JON N. BLOOM, Producer.

Documentary

Short Subjects

★ FLAMENCO AT 5:15, National Film Board of Canada: CYNTHIA SCOTT and ADAM SYMANSKY, Producers.

IN THE NUCLEAR SHADOW: WHAT CAN THE CHILDREN TELL US?, Impact Productions: VIVIENNE VERDON-ROE and ERIC THIERMANN, Producers.

SEWING WOMAN, DeepFocus Productions: ARTHUR DONG, Producer.

SPACES: THE ARCHITECTURE OF PAUL RUDOLPH, Eisenhardt Productions, Inc.: ROBERT EISENHARDT, Producer.

YOU ARE FREE (IHR ZEIT FREI), A Brokman/Landis Production: DEA BROKMAN and ILENE LANDIS, Producers.

Features

CHILDREN OF DARKNESS, "Children of Darkness" Productions: RICHARD KOTUK and ARA CHEKMAYAN, Producers.

FIRST CONTACT, Arundel Productions: BOB CONNOLLY and ROBIN ANDERSON, Producers.

★ HE MAKES ME FEEL LIKE DANCIN', Edgar J. Scherick Associates Production: EMILE ARDOLINO, Producer.

THE PROFESSION OF ARMS (War Series Film #3), National Film Board of Canada: MICHAEL BRYANS and TINA VILJOEN, Producers.

SEEING RED, Heartland Productions: JAMES KLEIN and JULIA REICHERT, Producers.

Foreign Language Film Award

CARMEN, An Emiliano Piedra Production (Spain).

ENTRE NOUS, A Partners Production (France).

★ FANNY AND ALEXANDER, A Cinematograph AB for the Swedish Film Institute/Swedish Television SVT 1, Sweden/Gaumont, France/

*Visual Effects were recognized this year by a Special Achievement Award rather than an annual award.

Personafilm, and Tobis Filmkunst, BRD Production (Sweden).

JOB'S REVOLT, A Mafilm Tarsulas Studio/Hungarian Television (Budapest)/ZDF (Mainz) Production (Hungary).

LE BAL, A Cineproduction S.A.-Films A2 (Paris)/Massfilm (Rome)/ O.N.C.I.C. (Alger) Production (Algeria).

Honorary Awards

HAL ROACH in recognition of his unparalleled record of distinguished contributions to the motion picture art form.

Special Achievement Award

Visual Effects: RICHARD EDLUND, DENNIS MUREN, PHIL TIPPETT, KEN RALSTON, for *Return of the Jedi*, A Lucasfilm Production, 20th Century-Fox.

Irving G. Thalberg Memorial Award

None.

Jean Hersholt Humanitarian Award

M. J. FRANKOVICH.

Gordon E. Sawyer Award

DR. JOHN G. FRAYNE.

Scientific or Technical Awards

Academy Award of Merit (Academy statuette)

DR. KURT LARCHE of OSRAM GmbH for the research and development of xenon short-arc discharge lamps for motion picture projection.

Scientific and Engineering Award (Academy plaque)

JONATHAN ERLAND and ROGER DORNEY of Apogee, Incorporated, for the engineering and development of a reverse bluescreen traveling matte process for special effects photography.

GERALD L. TURPIN of Lightflex International Limited for the design, engineering, and development of an on-camera device providing contrast control, sourceless fill light, and special effects for motion picture photography.

GUNNAR P. MICHELSON for the engineering and development of an improved, electronic, high-speed, precision light valve for use in motion picture printing machines.

Technical Achievement Award (Academy certificate)

WILLIAM G. KROKAUGGER of Mole-Richardson Company for the design and engineering of a portable, 12,000-watt, lighting-control dimmer for use in motion picture production.

CHARLES J. WATSON, LARRY L. LANGREHR, and JOHN H. STEINER for the development of the BHP (electromechanical) fader for use on continuous motion picture contact printers.

ELIZABETH D. DE LA MARE of De La Mare Engineering, Incorporated, for the progressive development and continuous research of special-effects pyrotechnics originally designed by Glenn W. De La Mare for motion picture production.

DOUGLAS FRIES, JOHN LACEY, and MICHAEL SIGRIST for the design and engineering of a 35mm reflex conversion camera system for special-effects photography.

JACK CASHIN of Ultra-Stereo Labs, Incorporated, for the engineering and development of a four-channel, stereophonic, decoding system for optical motion picture sound track reproduction.

DAVID J. DEGENKOLB for the design and development of an automated device used in the silver recovery process in motion picture laboratories.

FIFTY-SEVENTH YEAR

1984

Nominations Announced: February 6, 1985
Awards Ceremony: March 25, 1985
Dorothy Chandler Pavilion, Los Angeles County Music Center
(Host: Jack Lemmon)

Best Picture

★ AMADEUS, A Saul Zaentz Company Production, Orion: Saul Zaentz, Producer.

THE KILLING FIELDS, A Goldcrest Films and Television/International Film Investors L.P. Production, Warner Bros.: David Puttnam, Producer.

A PASSAGE TO INDIA, A G.W. Films Limited Production, Columbia: John Brabourne and Richard Goodwin, Producers.

PLACES IN THE HEART, A Tri-Star Pictures Production, Tri-Star: Arlene Donovan, Producer.

A SOLDIER'S STORY, A Caldix Films Production, Columbia: Norman Jewison, Ronald L. Schwary, and Patrick Palmer, Producers.

Actor

★ F. MURRAY ABRAHAM in *Amadeus*, A Saul Zaentz Company Production, Orion.

JEFF BRIDGES in *Starman*, A Columbia Pictures Production, Columbia.

ALBERT FINNEY in *Under the Volcano*, An Ithaca Enterprises Production, Universal.

TOM HULCE in *Amadeus*, A Saul Zaentz Company Production, Orion.

SAM WATERSTON in *The Killing Fields*, A Goldcrest Films and Television/International Film Investors L.P. Production, Warner Bros.

Actress

JUDY DAVIS in *A Passage to India*, A G.W. Films Limited Production, Columbia.

★ SALLY FIELD in *Places in the Heart*, A Tri-Star Pictures Production, Tri-Star.

JESSICA LANGE in *Country*, A Touchstone Films Production, Buena Vista.

VANESSA REDGRAVE in *The Bostonians*, A Merchant Ivory Production, Almi Pictures.

SISSY SPACEK in *The River*, A Universal Pictures Production, Universal.

Supporting Actor

ADOLPH CAESAR in *A Soldier's Story*, A Caldix Films Production, Columbia.

JOHN MALKOVICH in *Places in the Heart*, A Tri-Star Pictures Production, Tri-Star.

NORIYUKI "PAT" MORITA in *The Karate Kid*, A Columbia Pictures Production, Columbia.

★ HAING S. NGOR in *The Killing Fields*, A Goldcrest Films and Television/International Film Investors L.P. Production, Warner Bros.

RALPH RICHARDSON in *Greystoke: The Legend of Tarzan, Lord of the Apes*, A Warner Bros. Production, Warner Bros.

Supporting Actress

★ PEGGY ASHCROFT in *A Passage to India*, A G.W. Films Limited Production, Columbia.

GLENN CLOSE in *The Natural*, A Tri-Star Pictures Production, Tri-Star.

LINDSAY CROUSE in *Places in the Heart*, A Tri-Star Pictures Production, Tri-Star.

CHRISTINE LAHTI in *Swing Shift*, A Warner Bros. Production, Warner Bros.

GERALDINE PAGE in *The Pope of Greenwich Village*, A United Artists-Koch/Kirkwood Production, M-G-M/UA.

Directing

WOODY ALLEN for *Broadway Danny Rose*, A Jack Rollins and Charles H. Joffe Production, Orion.

ROBERT BENTON for *Places in the Heart*, A Tri-Star Pictures Production, Tri-Star.

★ MILOS FORMAN for *Amadeus*, A Saul Zaentz Company Production, Orion.

ROLAND JOFFE for *The Killing Fields*, A Goldcrest Films and Television/International Film Investors L.P. Production, Warner Bros.

DAVID LEAN for *A Passage to India*, A G.W. Films Limited Production, Columbia.

Writing

Screenplay Written Directly for the Screen

BEVERLY HILLS COP, A Don Simpson/Jerry Bruckheimer Production in association with Eddie Murphy Productions, Paramount: Story by DANILO BACH and DANIEL PETRIE, JR.; Screenplay by DANIEL PETRIE, JR.

BROADWAY DANNY ROSE, A Jack Rollins and Charles H. Joffe Production, Orion: WOODY ALLEN.

EL NORTE, An Independent Production, Cinecom International/Island Alive: GREGORY NAVA and ANNA THOMAS.

★ PLACES IN THE HEART, A Tri-Star Pictures Production, Tri-Star: ROBERT BENTON.

SPLASH, A Touchstone Films Production, Buena Vista: Screen story by BRUCE JAY FRIEDMAN; Screenplay by LOWELL GANZ, BABALOO MANDEL, and BRUCE JAY FRIEDMAN; Based on a story by BRIAN GRAZER.

Screenplay Based on Material from Another Medium

★ AMADEUS, A Saul Zaentz Company Production, Orion: PETER SHAFFER.

GREYSTOKE: THE LEGEND OF TARZAN, LORD OF THE APES, A Warner Bros. Production, Warner Bros.: P. H. VAZAK and MICHAEL AUSTIN.

THE KILLING FIELDS, A Goldcrest Films and Television/International Film Investors L.P. Production, Warner Bros.: BRUCE ROBINSON.

A PASSAGE TO INDIA, A G.W. Films Limited Production, Columbia: DAVID LEAN.

A SOLDIER'S STORY, A Caldix Films Production, Columbia: CHARLES FULLER.

Cinematography

AMADEUS, A Saul Zaentz Company Production, Orion: MIROSLAV ONDRICEK.

★ THE KILLING FIELDS, A Goldcrest Films and Television/International Film Investors L.P. Production, Warner Bros.: CHRIS MENGES.

THE NATURAL, A Tri-Star Pictures

Production, Tri-Star: CALEB DESCHANEL.

A PASSAGE TO INDIA, A G.W. Films Limited Production, Columbia: ERNEST DAY.

THE RIVER, A Universal Pictures Production, Universal: VILMOS ZSIGMOND.

Art Direction—Set Decoration

★ AMADEUS, A Saul Zaentz Company Production, Orion: PATRIZIA VON BRANDENSTEIN; Set Decoration: KAREL CERNY.

THE COTTON CLUB, A Totally Independent Production, Orion: RICHARD SYLBERT; Set Decoration: GEORGE GAINES and LES BLOOM.

THE NATURAL, A Tri-Star Pictures Production, Tri-Star: ANGELO GRAHAM, MEL BOURNE, JAMES J. MURAKAMI, and SPEED HOPKINS; Set Decoration: BRUCE WEINTRAUB.

A PASSAGE TO INDIA, A G.W. Films Limited Production, Columbia: JOHN BOX and LESLIE TOMKINS; Set Decoration: HUGH SCAIFE.

2010, A Metro-Goldwyn-Mayer Presentation of a Peter Hyams Film Production, M-G-M/UA: ALBERT BRENNER; Set Decoration: RICK SIMPSON.

Sound

★ AMADEUS, A Saul Zaentz Company Production, Orion: MARK BERGER, TOM SCOTT, TODD BOEKELHEIDE, and CHRIS NEWMAN.

DUNE, A Dino De Laurentiis Corporation Production, Universal: BILL VARNEY, STEVE MASLOW, KEVIN O'CONNELL, and NELSON STOLL.

A PASSAGE TO INDIA, A G.W. Films Limited Production, Columbia: GRAHAM V. HARTSTONE, NICOLAS LE MESSURIER, MICHAEL A. CARTER, and JOHN MITCHELL.

THE RIVER, A Universal Pictures Production, Universal: NICK ALPHIN, ROBERT THIRLWELL, RICHARD PORTMAN, and DAVID RONNE.

2010, A Metro-Goldwyn-Mayer Presentation of a Peter Hyams Film Production, M-G-M/UA: MICHAEL J. KOHUT, AARON ROCHIN, CARLOS DE LARIOS, and GENE S. CANTAMESSA.

Film Editing

AMADEUS, A Saul Zaentz Company Production, Orion: NENA DANEVIC and MICHAEL CHANDLER.

THE COTTON CLUB, A Totally Independent Production, Orion: BARRY MALKIN and ROBERT Q. LOVETT.

★ THE KILLING FIELDS, A Goldcrest Films and Television/ International Film Investors L.P. Production, Warner Bros.: JIM CLARK.

A PASSAGE TO INDIA, A G.W. Films Limited Production, Columbia: DAVID LEAN.

ROMANCING THE STONE, An El Corazon Producciones S.A. Production, 20th Century-Fox: DONN CAMBERN and FRANK MORRISS.

Music

Original Score

INDIANA JONES AND THE TEMPLE OF DOOM, A Lucasfilm Production, Paramount: JOHN WILLIAMS.

THE NATURAL, A Tri-Star Pictures Production, Tri-Star: RANDY NEWMAN.

★ A PASSAGE TO INDIA, A G.W. Films Limited Production, Columbia: MAURICE JARRE.

THE RIVER, A Universal Pictures Production, Universal: JOHN WILLIAMS.

UNDER THE VOLCANO, An Ithaca

Enterprises Production, Universal: ALEX NORTH.

Original Song Score and Its Adaptation or Best Adaptation Score

THE MUPPETS TAKE MANHATTAN, A Tri-Star Pictures Production, Tri-Star: JEFF MOSS.

★ PURPLE RAIN, A Purple Films Company Production, Warner Bros.: PRINCE.

SONGWRITER, A Tri-Star Pictures Production, Tri-Star: KRIS KRISTOFFERSON.

Original Song

AGAINST ALL ODDS (TAKE A LOOK AT ME NOW) from *Against All Odds*, A New Visions Production, Columbia: Music and Lyrics by PHIL COLLINS.

FOOTLOOSE from *Footloose*, A Daniel Melnick Production, Paramount: Music and Lyrics by KENNY LOGGINS and DEAN PITCHFORD.

GHOSTBUSTERS from *Ghostbusters*, A Columbia Pictures Production, Columbia: Music and Lyrics by RAY PARKER, JR.

★ I JUST CALLED TO SAY I LOVE YOU from *The Woman in Red*, A Woman in Red Production, Orion: Music and Lyrics by STEVIE WONDER.

LET'S HEAR IT FOR THE BOY from *Footloose*, A Daniel Melnick Production, Paramount: Music and Lyrics by TOM SNOW and DEAN PITCHFORD.

Costume Design

★ AMADEUS, A Saul Zaentz Company Production, Orion: THEODOR PISTEK.

THE BOSTONIANS, A Merchant Ivory Production, Almi Pictures: JENNY BEAVAN and JOHN BRIGHT.

A PASSAGE TO INDIA, A G.W. Films Limited Production, Columbia: JUDY MOORCROFT.

PLACES IN THE HEART, A Tri-Star Pictures Production, Tri-Star: ANN ROTH.

2010, A Metro-Goldwyn-Mayer Presentation of a Peter Hyams Film Production, M-G-M/UA: PATRICIA NORRIS.

Make-up

★ AMADEUS, A Saul Zaentz Company Production, Orion: PAUL LEBLANC and DICK SMITH.

GREYSTOKE: THE LEGEND OF TARZAN, LORD OF THE APES, A Warner Bros. Production, Warner Bros.: RICK BAKER and PAUL ENGELEN.

2010, A Metro-Goldwyn-Mayer Presentation of a Peter Hyams Film Production, M-G-M/UA: MICHAEL WESTMORE.

Visual Effects

GHOSTBUSTERS, A Columbia Pictures Production, Columbia: RICHARD EDLUND, JOHN BRUNO, MARK VARGO, and CHUCK GASPAR.

★ INDIANA JONES AND THE TEMPLE OF DOOM, A Lucasfilm Production, Paramount: DENNIS MUREN, MICHAEL MCALISTER, LORNE PETERSON, and GEORGE GIBBS.

2010, A Metro-Goldwyn-Mayer Presentation of a Peter Hyams Film Production, M-G-M/UA: RICHARD EDLUND, NEIL KREPELA, GEORGE JENSON, and MARK STETSON.

Sound Effects Editing

No nominations.*

*Sound Effects Editing was recognized this year by a Special Achievement Award rather than an annual award.

Short Films

Animated

★ CHARADE, A Sheridan College Production: JON MINNIS, Producer.

DOCTOR DESOTO, Michael Sporn Animation, Inc.: MORTON SCHINDEL and MICHAEL SPORN, Producers.

PARADISE, National Film Board of Canada: ISHU PATEL, Producer.

Live Action

THE PAINTED DOOR, Atlantis Films Limited in association with the National Film Board of Canada: MICHAEL MACMILLAN and JANICE L. PLATT, Producers.

TALES OF MEETING AND PARTING, The American Film Institute-Directing Workshop for Women: SHARON ORECK and LESLI LINKA GLATTER, Producers.

★ UP, Pyramid Films: MIKE HOOVER, Producer.

Documentary

Short Subjects

THE CHILDREN OF SOONG CHING LING, UNICEF and The Soong Ching Ling Foundation: GARY BUSH and PAUL T. K. LIN, Producers.

CODE GRAY: ETHICAL DILEMMAS IN NURSING, The Nursing Ethics Project/Fanlight Productions: BEN ACHTENBERG and JOAN SAWYER, Producers.

THE GARDEN OF EDEN, Florentine Films: LAWRENCE R. HOTT and ROGER M. SHERMAN, Producers.

RECOLLECTIONS OF PAVLOVSK, Leningrad Documentary Film Studio: IRINA KALININA, Producer.

★ THE STONE CARVERS, Paul Wagner Productions: MARJORIE HUNT and PAUL WAGNER, Producers.

Features

HIGH SCHOOLS, Guggenheim Productions, Inc.: CHARLES GUGGENHEIM and NANCY SLOSS, Producers.

IN THE NAME OF THE PEOPLE, Pan American Films: ALEX W. DREHSLER and FRANK CHRISTOPHER, Producers.

MARLENE, Zev Braun Pictures, Inc./ OKO Film Produktion: KAREL DIRKA and ZEV BRAUN, Producers.

STREETWISE, Bear Creek Productions, Inc.: CHERYL MCCALL, Producer.

★ THE TIMES OF HARVEY MILK, Black Sand Educational Productions, Inc.: ROBERT EPSTEIN and RICHARD SCHMIECHEN, Producers.

Foreign Language Film Award

BEYOND THE WALLS, An April Films Ltd. Production (Israel).

CAMILA, A GEA Cinematografica S.R.L. Production (Argentina).

★ DANGEROUS MOVES, An Arthur Cohn Production (Switzerland).

DOUBLE FEATURE, A Nickel Odeon, S.A. Production (Spain).

WARTIME ROMANCE, An Odessa Film Studio Production (U.S.S.R.).

Honorary Awards

JAMES STEWART for his fifty years of memorable performances and for his high ideals both on and off the screen. With the respect and affection of his colleagues.

NATIONAL ENDOWMENT FOR THE ARTS in recognition of its 20th anniversary and its dedicated commitment to fostering artistic and creative activity and excellence in every area of the arts.

Special Achievement Award

Sound Effects Editing: KAY ROSE for *The River*, A Universal Pictures Production, Universal.

Irving G. Thalberg Memorial Award

None.

Jean Hersholt Humanitarian Award

DAVID L. WOLPER.

Gordon E. Sawyer Award

LINWOOD G. DUNN.

Scientific or Technical Awards

Academy Award of Merit (Academy statuette)

None.

Scientific and Engineering Award (Academy plaque)

DONALD A. ANDERSON and DIANA REINERS of 3M Company for the development of "Cinetrak" Magnetic Film #350/351 for motion picture sound recording.

BARRY M. STULTZ, RUBEN AVILA, and WES KENNEDY of Film Processing Corporation for the development of FPC 200 PB Fullcoat Magnetic Film for motion picture sound recording.

BARRY M. STULTZ, RUBEN AVILA, and WES KENNEDY of Film Processing Corporation for the formulation and application of an improved sound track stripe to 70mm motion picture film, and JOHN MOSELY for the engineering research involved therein.

KENNETH RICHTER of Richter Cine Equipment for the design and engineering of the R-2 Auto-Collimator for examining image quality at the focal plane of motion picture camera lenses.

GÜNTHER SCHAIDT and ROSCO LABORATORIES, INCORPORATED, for the development of an improved, nontoxic fluid for creating fog and smoke for motion picture production.

JOHN WHITNEY, JR., and GARY DEMOS of Digital Productions, Incorporated, for the practical simulation of motion picture photography by means of computer-generated images.

Technical Achievement Award (Academy certificate)

NAT TIFFEN of Tiffen Manufacturing Corporation for the production of high-quality, durable, laminated color filters for motion picture photography.

DONALD TRUMBULL, JONATHAN ERLAND, STEPHEN FOG, and PAUL BURK of Apogee, Incorporated, for the design and development of the "Blue Max" high-power, blue-flux projector for traveling matte composite photography.

JONATHAN ERLAND and ROBERT BEALMEAR of Apogee, Incorporated, for an innovative design for front projection screens and an improved method for their construction.

HOWARD J. PRESTON of Preston Cinema Systems for the design and development of a variable-speed control device with automatic exposure compensation for motion picture cameras.

FIFTY-EIGHTH YEAR

1985

Nominations Announced: February 5, 1986
Awards Ceremony: March 24, 1986
Dorothy Chandler Pavilion, Los Angeles County Music Center
(Hosts: Jane Fonda, Alan Alda, and Robin Williams)

Best Picture

THE COLOR PURPLE, A Warner Bros. Production, Warner Bros.: Steven Spielberg, Kathleen Kennedy, Frank Marshall, and Quincy Jones, Producers.

KISS OF THE SPIDER WOMAN, An H.B. Filmes Production in association with Sugarloaf Films, Island Alive: David Weisman, Producer.

★ OUT OF AFRICA, A Universal Pictures Limited Production, Universal: Sydney Pollack, Producer.

PRIZZI'S HONOR, An ABC Motion Pictures Production, 20th Century-Fox: John Foreman, Producer.

WITNESS, An Edward S. Feldman Production, Paramount: Edward S. Feldman, Producer.

Actor

HARRISON FORD in *Witness*, An Edward S. Feldman Production, Paramount.

JAMES GARNER in *Murphy's Romance*, A Fogwood Films Production, Columbia.

★ WILLIAM HURT in *Kiss of the Spider Woman*, An H.B. Filmes Production in association with Sugarloaf Films, Island Alive.

JACK NICHOLSON in *Prizzi's Honor*, An ABC Motion Pictures Production, 20th Century-Fox.

JON VOIGHT in *Runaway Train*, A Cannon Films Production, Cannon.

Actress

ANNE BANCROFT in *Agnes of God*, A Columbia Pictures Production, Columbia.

WHOOPI GOLDBERG in *The Color Purple*, A Warner Bros. Production, Warner Bros.

JESSICA LANGE in *Sweet Dreams*, An HBO Pictures Production in association with Silver Screen Partners, Tri-Star.

★ GERALDINE PAGE in *The Trip to Bountiful*, A Bountiful Production, Island Pictures.

MERYL STREEP in *Out of Africa*, A Universal Pictures Limited Production, Universal.

Supporting Actor

★ DON AMECHE in *Cocoon*, A Fox/Zanuck-Brown Production, 20th Century-Fox.

KLAUS MARIA BRANDAUER in *Out of Africa*, A Universal Pictures Limited Production, Universal.

WILLIAM HICKEY in *Prizzi's Honor*, An ABC Motion Pictures Production, 20th Century-Fox.

ROBERT LOGGIA in *Jagged Edge*, A

Columbia Pictures Production, Columbia.

ERIC ROBERTS in *Runaway Train*, A Cannon Films Production, Cannon.

Supporting Actress

MARGARET AVERY in *The Color Purple*, A Warner Bros. Production, Warner Bros.

★ ANJELICA HUSTON in *Prizzi's Honor*, An ABC Motion Pictures Production, 20th Century-Fox.

AMY MADIGAN in *Twice in a Lifetime*, A Yorkin Company Production, Bud Yorkin Productions.

MEG TILLY in *Agnes of God*, A Columbia Pictures Production, Columbia.

OPRAH WINFREY in *The Color Purple*, A Warner Bros. Production, Warner Bros.

Directing

HECTOR BABENCO for *Kiss of the Spider Woman*, An H.B. Filmes Production in association with Sugarloaf Films, Island Alive.

JOHN HUSTON for *Prizzi's Honor*, An ABC Motion Pictures Production, 20th Century-Fox.

AKIRA KUROSAWA for *Ran*, A Greenwich Film/Nippon Herald Films/Herald Ace Production, Orion Classics.

★ SYDNEY POLLACK for *Out of Africa*, A Universal Pictures Limited Production, Universal.

PETER WEIR for *Witness*, An Edward S. Feldman Production, Paramount.

Writing

Screenplay Written Directly for the Screen

BACK TO THE FUTURE, An Amblin Entertainment/Universal Pictures Production, Universal: ROBERT ZEMECKIS and BOB GALE.

BRAZIL, An Embassy International Pictures Production, Universal: TERRY GILLIAM, TOM STOPPARD, and CHARLES MCKEOWN.

THE OFFICIAL STORY, A Historias Cinematograficas/Cinemania and Progress Communications Production, Almi Pictures: LUIS PUENZO and AIDA BORTNIK.

THE PURPLE ROSE OF CAIRO, A Jack Rollins and Charles H. Joffe Production, Orion: WOODY ALLEN.

★ WITNESS, An Edward S. Feldman Production, Paramount: Story by WILLIAM KELLEY, PAMELA WALLACE, and EARL W. WALLACE; Screenplay by EARL W. WALLACE and WILLIAM KELLEY.

Screenplay Based on Material from Another Medium

THE COLOR PURPLE, A Warner Bros. Production, Warner Bros.: MENNO MEYJES.

KISS OF THE SPIDER WOMAN, An H.B. Filmes Production in association with Sugarloaf Films, Island Alive: LEONARD SCHRADER.

★ OUT OF AFRICA, A Universal Pictures Limited Production, Universal: KURT LUEDTKE.

PRIZZI'S HONOR, An ABC Motion Pictures Production, 20th Century-Fox: RICHARD CONDON and JANET ROACH.

THE TRIP TO BOUNTIFUL, A Bountiful Production, Island Pictures: HORTON FOOTE.

Cinematography

THE COLOR PURPLE, A Warner Bros. Production, Warner Bros.: ALLEN DAVIAU.

MURPHY'S ROMANCE, A Fogwood Films Production, Columbia: WILLIAM A. FRAKER.

★ OUT OF AFRICA, A Universal Pictures Limited Production, Universal: DAVID WATKIN.

RAN, A Greenwich Film/Nippon Herald Films/Herald Ace Production, Orion Classics: TAKAO SAITO, MASAHARU UEDA, and ASAKAZU NAKAI.

WITNESS, An Edward S. Feldman Production, Paramount: JOHN SEALE.

Art Direction - Set Decoration

BRAZIL, An Embassy International Pictures Production, Universal: NORMAN GARWOOD; Set Decoration: MAGGIE GRAY.

THE COLOR PURPLE, A Warner Bros. Production, Warner Bros.: J. MICHAEL RIVA; Set Decoration: LINDA DE SCENNA.

★ OUT OF AFRICA, A Universal Pictures Limited Production, Universal: STEPHEN GRIMES; Set Decoration: JOSIE MACAVIN.

RAN, A Greenwich Film/Nippon Herald Films/Herald Ace Production, Orion Classics: YOSHIRO MURAKI and SHINOBU MURAKI.

WITNESS, An Edward S. Feldman Production, Paramount: STAN JOLLEY; Set Decoration: JOHN ANDERSON.

Sound

BACK TO THE FUTURE, An Amblin Entertainment/Universal Pictures Production, Universal: BILL VARNEY, B. TENNYSON SEBASTIAN II, ROBERT THIRLWELL, and WILLIAM B. KAPLAN.

A CHORUS LINE, An Embassy Films Associates and Polygram Pictures Production, Columbia: DONALD O. MITCHELL, MICHAEL MINKLER, GERRY HUMPHREYS, and CHRIS NEWMAN.

LADYHAWKE, A Warner Bros. and 20th Century-Fox Production, Warner Bros.: LES FRESHOLTZ, DICK ALEXANDER, VERN POORE, and BUD ALPER.

★ OUT OF AFRICA, A Universal Pictures Limited Production, Universal: CHRIS JENKINS, GARY ALEXANDER, LARRY STENSVOLD, and PETER HANDFORD.

SILVERADO, A Columbia Pictures Production, Columbia: DONALD O. MITCHELL, RICK KLINE, KEVIN O'CONNELL, and DAVID RONNE.

Film Editing

A CHORUS LINE, An Embassy Films Associates and Polygram Pictures Production, Columbia: JOHN BLOOM.

OUT OF AFRICA, A Universal Pictures Limited Production, Universal: FREDRIC STEINKAMP, WILLIAM STEINKAMP, PEMBROKE HERRING, and SHELDON KAHN.

PRIZZI'S HONOR, An ABC Motion Pictures Production, 20th Century-Fox: RUDI FEHR and KAJA FEHR.

RUNAWAY TRAIN, A Cannon Films Production, Cannon: HENRY RICHARDSON.

★ WITNESS, An Edward S. Feldman Production, Paramount: THOM NOBLE.

Music

Original Score

AGNES OF GOD, A Columbia Pictures Production, Columbia: GEORGES DELERUE.

THE COLOR PURPLE, A Warner Bros. Production, Warner Bros.: QUINCY JONES, JEREMY LUBBOCK, ROD TEMPERTON, CAIPHUS SEMENYA, ANDRAE CROUCH, CHRIS BOARDMAN, JORGE CALANDRELLI, JOEL ROSENBAUM, FRED STEINER, JACK HAYES, JERRY HEY, and RANDY KERBER.

★ OUT OF AFRICA, A Universal Pictures Limited Production, Universal: JOHN BARRY.

SILVERADO, A Columbia Pictures Production, Columbia: BRUCE BROUGHTON.

WITNESS, An Edward S. Feldman Production, Paramount: MAURICE JARRE.

Original Song Score

No nominations.

Original Song

MISS CELIE'S BLUES (SISTER) from *The Color Purple*, A Warner Bros. Production, Warner Bros.: Music by QUINCY JONES and ROD TEMPERTON; Lyrics by QUINCY JONES, ROD TEMPERTON, and LIONEL RICHIE.

POWER OF LOVE from *Back to the Future*, An Amblin Entertainment/ Universal Pictures Production, Universal: Music by CHRIS HAYES and JOHNNY COLLA; Lyrics by HUEY LEWIS.

★ SAY YOU, SAY ME from *White Nights*, A New Visions Production, Columbia: Music and Lyrics by LIONEL RICHIE.

SEPARATE LIVES (LOVE THEME FROM *WHITE NIGHTS*) from *White Nights*, A New Visions Production, Columbia: Music and Lyrics by STEPHEN BISHOP.

SURPRISE, SURPRISE from *A Chorus Line*, An Embassy Films Associates and Polygram Pictures Production, Columbia: Music by MARVIN HAMLISCH; Lyrics by EDWARD KLEBAN.

Costume Design

THE COLOR PURPLE, A Warner Bros. Production, Warner Bros.: AGGIE GUERARD RODGERS.

THE JOURNEY OF NATTY GANN, A Walt Disney Pictures and Silver Screen Partners II Production, Buena Vista: ALBERT WOLSKY.

OUT OF AFRICA, A Universal Pictures Limited Production, Universal: MILENA CANONERO.

PRIZZI'S HONOR, An ABC Motion Pictures Production, 20th Century-Fox: DONFELD.

★ RAN, A Greenwich Film/Nippon Herald Films/Herald Ace Production, Orion Classics: EMI WADA.

Make-up

THE COLOR PURPLE, A Warner Bros. Production, Warner Bros.: KEN CHASE.

★ MASK, A Universal Pictures Production, Universal: MICHAEL WESTMORE and ZOLTAN.

REMO WILLIAMS: THE ADVENTURE BEGINS, A Dick Clark/Larry Spiegel/ Mel Bergman Production, Orion: CARL FULLERTON.

Visual Effects

★ COCOON, A Fox/Zanuck-Brown Production, 20th Century-Fox: KEN RALSTON, RALPH MCQUARRIE, SCOTT FARRAR, and DAVID BERRY.

RETURN TO OZ, A Walt Disney Pictures and Silver Screen Partners II Production, Buena Vista: WILL VINTON, IAN WINGROVE, ZORAN PERISIC, and MICHAEL LLOYD.

YOUNG SHERLOCK HOLMES, An Amblin Entertainment Production in association with Henry Winkler/ Roger Birnbaum, Paramount: DENNIS MUREN, KIT WEST, JOHN ELLIS, and DAVID ALLEN.

Sound Effects Editing

★ BACK TO THE FUTURE, An Amblin Entertainment/Universal Pictures Production, Universal: CHARLES L. CAMPBELL and ROBERT RUTLEDGE.

LADYHAWKE, A Warner Bros. and 20th Century-Fox Production, Warner Bros.: BOB HENDERSON and ALAN MURRAY.

RAMBO: FIRST BLOOD PART II, An

Anabasis Investments Production, Tri-Star: FREDERICK J. BROWN.

Short Films

Animated

★ ANNA & BELLA, The Netherlands: CILIA VAN DIJK, Producer.

THE BIG SNIT, National Film Board of Canada: RICHARD CONDIE and MICHAEL SCOTT, Producers.

SECOND CLASS MAIL, National Film and Television School: ALISON SNOWDEN, Producer.

Live Action

GRAFFITI, The American Film Institute: DIANNA COSTELLO, Producer.

★ MOLLY'S PILGRIM, Phoenix Films: JEFF BROWN, Producer.

RAINBOW WAR, Bob Rogers and Company: BOB ROGERS, Producer.

Documentary

Short Subjects

THE COURAGE TO CARE, A United Way Production: ROBERT GARDNER, Producer.

KEATS AND HIS NIGHTINGALE: A BLIND DATE, A Production of the Rhode Island Committee for the Humanities: MICHAEL CROWLEY and JAMES WOLPAW, Producers.

MAKING OVERTURES—THE STORY OF A COMMUNITY ORCHESTRA, A Rhombus Media, Inc. Production: BARBARA WILLIS SWEETE, Producer.

★ WITNESS TO WAR: DR. CHARLIE CLEMENTS, A Skylight Picture Production: DAVID GOODMAN, Producer.

THE WIZARD OF THE STRINGS, A Seventh Hour Production: ALAN EDELSTEIN, Producer.

Features

★ BROKEN RAINBOW, An Earthworks Films Production: MARIA FLORIO and VICTORIA MUDD, Producers.

LAS MADRES—THE MOTHERS OF PLAZA DE MAYO, Sponsored by Film Arts Foundation: SUSANA MUÑOZ and LOURDES PORTILLO, Producers.

SOLDIERS IN HIDING, A Filmworks, Inc. Production: JAPHET ASHER, Producer.

THE STATUE OF LIBERTY, A Florentine Films Production: KEN BURNS and BUDDY SQUIRES, Producers.

UNFINISHED BUSINESS, A Mouchette Films Production: STEVEN OKAZAKI, Producer.

Foreign Language Film Award

ANGRY HARVEST, A CCC-Filmkunst GmbH/Admiral Film Production (Federal Republic of Germany).

COLONEL REDL, A Mafilm-Objektiv Studio/Manfred Durniok/ORF/ZDF Production (Hungary).

★ THE OFFICIAL STORY, A Historias Cinematograficas/ Cinemania and Progress Communications Production (Argentina).

3 MEN AND A CRADLE, A Flach Film Production (France).

WHEN FATHER WAS AWAY ON BUSINESS, A Forum Film Production (Yugoslavia).

Honorary Awards

PAUL NEWMAN in recognition of his many memorable and compelling screen performances and for his personal integrity and dedication to his craft.

ALEX NORTH in recognition of his brilliant artistry in the creation of memorable music for motion pictures.

Medal of Commendation

JOHN H. WHITNEY, SR., for cinematic pioneering.

Special Achievement Award

None.

Irving G. Thalberg Memorial Award

None.

Jean Hersholt Humanitarian Award

CHARLES "BUDDY" ROGERS.

Gordon E. Sawyer Award

None.

Scientific or Technical Awards

Academy Award of Merit (Academy statuette)

None.

Scientific and Engineering Award (Academy plaque)

IMAX SYSTEMS CORPORATION for a method of filming and exhibiting high-fidelity, large-format, wide-angle motion pictures.

ERNST NETTMANN of E. F. Nettmann and Associates for the invention and EDWARD PHILLIPS and CARLOS DEMATTOS of Matthews Studio Equipment, Inc., for the development of the Cam-Remote for motion picture photography.

MYRON GORDIN, JOE P. CROOKHAM, JIM DROST, and DAVID CROOKHAM of Musco Mobile Lighting, Ltd., for the invention of a method of transporting adjustable, high-intensity luminaires and their application to the motion picture industry.

Technical Achievement Award (Academy certificate)

DAVID W. SPENCER for the development of an Animation Photo Transfer (APT) process.

HARRISON AND HARRISON, OPTICAL ENGINEERS, for the invention and development of Harrison Diffusion Filters for motion picture photography.

LARRY BARTON of Cinematography Electronics, Inc., for a precision speed, crystal-controlled device for motion picture photography.

ALAN LANDAKER of the Burbank Studios for the Mark III Camera Drive for motion picture photography.

FIFTY-NINTH YEAR

1986

Nominations Announced: February 11, 1987
Awards Ceremony: March 30, 1987
Dorothy Chandler Pavilion, Los Angeles County Music Center
(Hosts: Chevy Chase, Goldie Hawn, and Paul Hogan)

Best Picture

CHILDREN OF A LESSER GOD, A Burt Sugarman Production, Paramount: Burt Sugarman and Patrick Palmer, Producers.

HANNAH AND HER SISTERS, A Jack Rollins and Charles H. Joffe Production, Orion: Robert Greenhut, Producer.

THE MISSION, A Warner Bros./ Goldcrest and Kingsmere Production, Warner Bros.: Fernando Ghia and David Puttnam, Producers.

★ PLATOON, A Hemdale Film Production, Orion: Arnold Kopelson, Producer.

A ROOM WITH A VIEW, A Merchant Ivory Production, Cinecom: Ismail Merchant, Producer.

Actor

DEXTER GORDON in *'Round Midnight*, An Irwin Winkler Production, Warner Bros.

BOB HOSKINS in *Mona Lisa*, A Palace/ Handmade Production, Island Pictures.

WILLIAM HURT in *Children of a Lesser God*, A Burt Sugarman Production, Paramount.

★ PAUL NEWMAN in *The Color of Money*, A Touchstone Pictures Production in association with Silver Screen Partners II, Buena Vista.

JAMES WOODS in *Salvador*, a Hemdale Film Production, Hemdale Releasing.

Actress

JANE FONDA for *The Morning After*, A Lorimar Motion Pictures Production, 20th Century-Fox.

★ MARLEE MATLIN in *Children of a Lesser God*, A Burt Sugarman Production, Paramount.

SISSY SPACEK in *Crimes of the Heart*, A Crimes of the Heart Production, De Laurentiis Entertainment Group.

KATHLEEN TURNER in *Peggy Sue Got Married*, A Rastar Production, Tri-Star.

SIGOURNEY WEAVER in *Aliens*, A Twentieth Century-Fox Film Production, 20th Century-Fox.

Supporting Actor

TOM BERENGER in *Platoon*, A Hemdale Film Production, Orion.

★ MICHAEL CAINE in *Hannah and Her Sisters*, A Jack Rollins and Charles H. Joffe Production, Orion.

WILLEM DAFOE in *Platoon*, A Hemdale Film Production, Orion.

DENHOLM ELLIOTT in *A Room with a View*, A Merchant Ivory Production, Cinecom.

DENNIS HOPPER in *Hoosiers*, A Carter De Haven Production, Orion.

Supporting Actress

TESS HARPER in *Crimes of the Heart*, A Crimes of the Heart Production, De Laurentiis Entertainment Group.

PIPER LAURIE in *Children of a Lesser God*, A Burt Sugarman Production, Paramount.

MARY ELIZABETH MASTRANTONIO in *The Color of Money*, A Touchstone Pictures Production in association with Silver Screen Partners II, Buena Vista.

MAGGIE SMITH in *A Room with a View*, A Merchant Ivory Production, Cinecom.

★ DIANNE WIEST in *Hannah and Her Sisters*, A Jack Rollins and Charles H. Joffe Production, Orion.

Directing

WOODY ALLEN for *Hannah and Her Sisters*, A Jack Rollins and Charles H. Joffe Production, Orion.

JAMES IVORY for *A Room with a View*, A Merchant Ivory Production, Cinecom.

ROLAND JOFFE for *The Mission*, A Warner Bros./Goldcrest and Kingsmere Production, Warner Bros.

DAVID LYNCH for *Blue Velvet*, A Blue Velvet S.A. Production, De Laurentiis Entertainment Group.

★ OLIVER STONE for *Platoon*, A Hemdale Film Production, Orion.

Writing

Screenplay Written Directly for the Screen

"CROCODILE" DUNDEE, A Rimfire Films Ltd. Production: Story by PAUL HOGAN; Screenplay by PAUL HOGAN, KEN SHADIE, and JOHN CORNELL.

★ HANNAH AND HER SISTERS, A Jack Rollins and Charles H. Joffe Production, Orion: WOODY ALLEN.

MY BEAUTIFUL LAUNDRETTE, A Working Title Ltd./SAF Production for Film Four International, Orion Classics: HANIF KUREISHI.

PLATOON, A Hemdale Film Production, Orion: OLIVER STONE.

SALVADOR, A Hemdale Film Production, Hemdale Releasing: OLIVER STONE and RICHARD BOYLE.

Screenplay Based on Material from Another Medium

CHILDREN OF A LESSER GOD, A Burt Sugarman Production, Paramount: HESPER ANDERSON and MARK MEDOFF.

THE COLOR OF MONEY, A Touchstone Pictures Production in association with Silver Screen Partners II, Buena Vista: RICHARD PRICE.

CRIMES OF THE HEART, A Crimes of the Heart Production, De Laurentiis Entertainment Group: BETH HENLEY.

★ A ROOM WITH A VIEW, A Merchant Ivory Production, Cinecom: RUTH PRAWER JHABVALA.

STAND BY ME, An Act III Production, Columbia: RAYNOLD GIDEON and BRUCE A. EVANS.

Cinematography

★ THE MISSION, A Warner Bros./ Goldcrest and Kingsmere Production, Warner Bros.: CHRIS MENGES.

PEGGY SUE GOT MARRIED, A Rastar Production, Tri-Star: JORDAN CRONENWETH.

PLATOON, A Hemdale Production, Orion: ROBERT RICHARDSON.

A ROOM WITH A VIEW, A Merchant Ivory Production, Cinecom: TONY PIERCE-ROBERTS.

STAR TREK IV: THE VOYAGE HOME, A Harve Bennett Production, Paramount: DON PETERMAN.

Art Direction-Set Decoration

ALIENS, A Twentieth Century-Fox Film Production, 20th Century-Fox: PETER

LAMONT; Set Decoration: CRISPIAN SALLIS.

THE COLOR OF MONEY, A Touchstone Pictures Production in association with Silver Screen Partners II, Buena Vista: BORIS LEVEN; Set Decoration: KAREN A. O'HARA.

HANNAH AND HER SISTERS, A Jack Rollins and Charles H. Joffe Production, Orion: STUART WURTZEL; Set Decoration: CAROL JOFFE.

THE MISSION, A Warner Bros./ Goldcrest and Kingsmere Production, Warner Bros.: STUART CRAIG; Set Decoration: JACK STEPHENS.

★ A ROOM WITH A VIEW, A Merchant Ivory Production, Cinecom: GIANNI QUARANTA and BRIAN ACKLAND-SNOW; Set Decoration: BRIAN SAVEGAR and ELIO ALTRAMURA.

Sound

ALIENS, A Twentieth Century-Fox Film Production, 20th Century-Fox: GRAHAM V. HARTSTONE, NICOLAS LE MESSURIER, MICHAEL A. CARTER, and ROY CHARMAN.

HEARTBREAK RIDGE, A Warner Bros. Production, Warner Bros.: LES FRESHOLTZ, DICK ALEXANDER, VERN POORE, and WILLIAM NELSON.

★ PLATOON, A Hemdale Film Production, Orion: JOHN (DOC) WILKINSON, RICHARD ROGERS, CHARLES (BUD) GRENZBACH, and SIMON KAYE.

STAR TREK IV: THE VOYAGE HOME, A Harve Bennett Production, Paramount: TERRY PORTER, DAVE HUDSON, MEL METCALFE, and GENE S. CANTAMESSA.

TOP GUN, A Don Simpson/Jerry Bruckheimer Production, Paramount: DONALD O. MITCHELL, KEVIN O'CONNELL, RICK KLINE, and WILLIAM B. KAPLAN.

Film Editing

ALIENS, A Twentieth Century-Fox Film Production, 20th Century-Fox: RAY LOVEJOY.

HANNAH AND HER SISTERS, A Jack Rollins and Charles H. Joffe Production, Orion: SUSAN E. MORSE.

THE MISSION, A Warner Bros./ Goldcrest and Kingsmere Production, Warner Bros.: JIM CLARK.

★ PLATOON, A Hemdale Production, Orion: CLAIRE SIMPSON.

TOP GUN, A Don Simpson/Jerry Bruckheimer Production, Paramount: BILLY WEBER, and CHRIS LEBENZON.

Music

Original Score

ALIENS, A Twentieth Century-Fox Film Production, 20th Century-Fox: JAMES HORNER.

HOOSIERS, A Carter De Haven Production, Orion: JERRY GOLDSMITH.

THE MISSION, A Warner Bros./ Goldcrest and Kingsmere Production Warner Bros.: ENNIO MORRICONE.

★ 'ROUND MIDNIGHT, An Irwin Winkler Production, Warner Bros.: HERBIE HANCOCK.

STAR TREK VI: THE UNDISCOVERED COUNTRY, A Harve Bennett Production, Paramount: LEONARD ROSENMAN.

Original Song Score

No nominations.

Original Song

GLORY OF LOVE from *The Karate Kid Part II*, Columbia Pictures Production, Columbia: Music by PETER CETERA and DAVID FOSTER: Lyrics by PETER CETERA and DIANE NINI.

LIFE IN A LOOKING GLASS from *That's Life!*, A Paradise Cove/Ubilam Production, Columbia: Music by

HENRY MANCINI; Lyrics by LESLIE BRICUSSE.

MEAN GREEN MOTHER FROM OUTER SPACE from *Little Shop of Horrors*, A Geffen Company Production, Geffen Company through Warner Bros.: Music by ALAN MENKEN; Lyrics by HOWARD ASHMAN.

SOMEWHERE OUT THERE from *An American Tail*, An Amblin Entertainment Production, Universal: Music by JAMES HORNER, and BARRY MANN; Lyrics by CYNTHIA WEIL.

★ TAKE MY BREATH AWAY from *Top Gun*, A Don Simpson/Jerry Bruckheimer Production, Paramount: Music by GIORGIO MORODER; Lyrics by TOM WHITLOCK.

Costume Design

THE MISSION, A Warner Bros./ Goldcrest and Kingsmere Production Warner Bros.: ENRICO SABBATINI.

OTELLO, A Cannon Production, Cannon: ANNA ANNI.

PEGGY SUE GOT MARRIED, A Rastar Production, Tri-Star: THEADORA VAN RUNKLE.

PIRATES, A Carthago Films Production in association with Accent Cominco, Cannon: ANTHONY POWELL.

★ A ROOM WITH A VIEW, A Merchant Ivory Production, Cinecom: JENNY BEAVAN and JOHN BRIGHT.

Make-up

THE CLAN OF THE CAVE BEAR, A Warner Bros. and PSO Production, Warner Bros.: MICHAEL G. WESTMORE and MICHELE BURKE.

★ THE FLY, A Brooksfilm Ltd. Production, 20th Century-Fox: CHRIS WALAS and STEPHAN DUPUIS.

LEGEND, A Legend Company Production, Universal: ROB BOTTIN, and PETER ROBB-KING.

Visual Effects

★ ALIENS, A Twentieth Century-Fox Film Production, 20th Century-Fox: ROBERT SKOTAK, STAN WINSTON, JOHN RICHARDSON, and SUZANNE BENSON.

LITTLE SHOP OF HORRORS, A Geffen Company Production, Geffen Company through Warner Bros.: LYLE CONWAY, BRAN FERREN, and MARTIN GUTTERIDGE.

POLTERGEIST II: THE OTHER SIDE, A Victor-Grais Production, M-G-M: RICHARD EDLUND, JOHN BRUNO, GARRY WALLER, and WILLIAM NEIL.

Sound Effects Editing

★ ALIENS, A Twentieth Century-Fox Film Production, 20th Century-Fox: DON SHARPE.

STAR TREK IV: THE VOYAGE HOME, A Harve Bennett Production, Paramount: MARK MANGINI.

TOP GUN, A Don Simpson/Jerry Bruckheimer Production, Paramount: CECELIA HALL and GEORGE WATTERS II.

Short Films

Animated

THE FROG, THE DOG, AND THE DEVIL, New Zealand National Film Unit: HUGH MACDONALD and MARTIN TOWNSEND, Producers.

★ A GREEK TRAGEDY, CineTe pvba: LINDA VAN TULDEN and WILLEM THIJSSEN, Producers.

LUXO JR., Pixar Productions: JOHN LASSETER and WILLIAM REEVES, Producers.

Live Action

EXIT, RAI Radiotelevisione Italian/RAI-UNO: STEFANO REALI and PINO QUARTUILO, Producers.

LOVE STRUCK, Rainy Day Productions: FREDDA WEISS, Producer.

★ PRECIOUS IMAGES, Calliope Films Inc.: CHUCK WORKMAN, Producer.

Documentary

Short Subjects

DEBONAIR DANCERS, An Alison Nigh-Strelich Production: ALISON NIGH-STRELICH, Producer.

THE MASTERS OF DISASTER, Indiana University Audio Visual Center: SONYA FRIEDMAN, Producer.

RED GROOMS: SUNFLOWER IN A HOTHOUSE, A Polaris Entertainment Production: THOMAS L. NEFF and MADELINE BELL, Producers.

SAM, A Film by Aaron D. Weisblatt: AARON D. WEISBLATT, Producer.

★ WOMEN—FOR AMERICA, FOR THE WORLD, An Educational Film and Video Project: VIVIENNE VERDON-ROE, Producer.

Features (tie)

★ ARTIE SHAW: TIME IS ALL YOU'VE GOT, A Bridge Film Production: BRIGITTE BERMAN, Producer.

CHILE: HASTA CUANDO?, A David Bradbury Production: DAVID BRADBURY, Producer.

★ DOWN AND OUT IN AMERICA, A Joseph Feury Production: JOSEPH FEURY and MILTON JUSTICE, Producers.

ISAAC IN AMERICA: A JOURNEY WITH ISAAC BASHEVIS SINGER, Film by Amram Nowak Associates: KIRK SIMON, Producer.

WITNESS TO APARTHEID, A Production of Developing News, Inc.: SHARON I. SOPHER, Producer.

Foreign Language Film Award

★ THE ASSAULT, A Fons Rademakers Production B.V. for Cannon Group Holland, Cannon (The Netherlands).

BETTY BLUE, A Gaumont Presentation of a Constellation/Cargo Production, Alive Films (France).

THE DECLINE OF THE AMERICAN EMPIRE, A Corporation Image M&M/National Film Board of Canada Production, Cineplex Odeon (Canada).

MY SWEET LITTLE VILLAGE, A Barrandov Film Studios Production, Circle Films (Czechoslovakia).

38, An Arabella Film/Satel Film Production (Austria).

Honorary Awards

RALPH BELLAMY for his unique artistry and his distinguished service to the profession of acting.

Medal of Commendation

E. M. (AL) LEWIS in appreciation for outstanding service and dedication in upholding the high standards of the Academy of Motion Picture Arts and Sciences.

Special Achievement Award

None.

Irving G. Thalberg Memorial Award

STEVEN SPIELBERG.

Jean Hersholt Humanitarian Award

None.

Gordon E. Sawyer Award

None.

Scientific or Technical Awards

Academy Award of Merit (Academy statuette)

None.

Scientific and Engineering Award (Academy plaque)

BRAN FERREN, CHARLES HARRISON, and KENNETH WISNER of Associates and Ferren for the concept and design of an advanced optical printer.

RICHARD BENJAMIN GRANT and RON GRANT of Auricle Control Systems for their invention of the film composer's time processor.

ANTHONY D. BRUNO and JOHN L. BAPTISTA of Metro-Goldwyn-Mayer Laboratories, Incorporated, and MANFRED G. MICHELSON and BRUCE W. KELLER of Technical Film Systems, Incorporated, for the design and engineering of a continuous-feed printer.

ROBERT GREENBERG, JOEL HYNEK, and EUGENE MAMUT of R/Greenberg Associates, Incorporated, and DR. ALFRED THUMIM, ELAN LIPSCHITZ, and DARRYL A. ARMOUR of the Oxberry Division of Richmark Camera Service, Incorporated, for the design and development of the RGA/Oxberry Compu-Quad Special Effects Optical Printer.

PROFESSOR FRITZ SENNHEISER of Sennheiser Electronic Corporation for the invention of an interference tube directional microphone.

RICHARD EDLUND, GENE WHITEMAN, DAVID GRAFTON, MARK WEST, JERRY JEFFRESS, and BOB WILCOX of Boss Film Corporation for the design and development of a Zoom Aerial (ZAP) 65mm Optical Printer.

WILLIAM L. FREDRICK and HAL NEEDHAM for the design and development of the Shotmaker Elite camera car and crane.

Technical Achievement Award (Academy certificate)

LEE ELECTRIC (LIGHTING) LIMITED for the design and development of an electronic, flicker-free, discharge lamp control system.

PETER D. PARKS of Oxford Scientific Films' Image Quest Division for the development of a live aero-compositor for special effects photography.

MATT SWEENEY and LUCINDA STRUB for the development of an automatic capsule gun for simulating bullet hits for motion picture special effects.

CARL HOLMES of Carl E. Holmes Company and ALEXANDER BRYCE of the Burbank Studios for the development of a mobile DC power supply unit for motion picture production photography.

BRAN FERREN of Associates and Ferren for the development of a laser synchro-cue system for applications in the motion picture industry.

JOHN L. BAPTISTA of Metro-Goldwyn-Mayer Laboratories, Inc., for the development and installation of a computerized silver recovery operation.

DAVID W. SAMUELSON for the development of programs incorporated into a pocket computer for motion picture cinematographers and WILLIAM B. POLLARD for contributing new algorithms on which the programs are based.

HAL LANDAKER and ALAN LANDAKER of the Burbank Studios for the development of the Beat System low-frequency cue track for motion picture production sound recording.

SIXTIETH YEAR

1987

Nominations Announced: February 17, 1988
Awards Ceremony: April 11, 1988
Shrine Civic Auditorium
(Host: Chevy Chase)

Best Picture

BROADCAST NEWS, A Twentieth Century-Fox Production, 20th Century-Fox: James L. Brooks, Producer.

FATAL ATTRACTION, A Jaffe/Lansing Production, Paramount: Stanley R. Jaffe and Sherry Lansing, Producers.

HOPE AND GLORY, A Davros Production Services Limited Production, Columbia: John Boorman, Producer.

★ THE LAST EMPEROR, A Hemdale Film Production, Columbia: Jeremy Thomas, Producer.

MOONSTRUCK, A Patrick Palmer and Norman Jewison Production, M-G-M: Patrick Palmer and Norman Jewison, Producers.

Actor

★ MICHAEL DOUGLAS in *Wall Street*, An Oaxatal Production, 20th Century-Fox.

WILLIAM HURT in *Broadcast News*, A 20th Century-Fox Production, 20th Century-Fox.

MARCELLO MASTROIANNI in *Dark Eyes*, An Excelsior TV and RAI Uno Production, Island Pictures.

JACK NICHOLSON in *Ironweed*, A Taft Entertainment Pictures/Keith Barish Production, Tri-Star.

ROBIN WILLIAMS in *Good Morning, Vietnam*, A Touchstone Pictures Production in association with Silver Screen Partners III, Buena Vista.

Actress

★ CHER in *Moonstruck*, A Patrick Palmer and Norman Jewison Production, M-G-M.

GLENN CLOSE in *Fatal Attraction*, A Jaffe/Lansing Production, Paramount.

HOLLY HUNTER in *Broadcast News*, A 20th Century-Fox Production, 20th Century-Fox.

SALLY KIRKLAND in *Anna*, A Magnus Films Production, Vestron.

MERYL STREEP in *Ironweed*, A Taft Entertainment Pictures/Keith Barish Production, Tri-Star.

Supporting Actor

ALBERT BROOKS in *Broadcast News*, A 20th Century-Fox Production, 20th Century-Fox.

★ SEAN CONNERY in *The Untouchables*, An Art Linson Production, Paramount.

MORGAN FREEMAN in *Street Smart*, A Cannon Films Production, Cannon.

VINCENT GARDENIA in *Moonstruck*, A Patrick Palmer and Norman Jewison Production, M-G-M.

DENZEL WASHINGTON in *Cry Freedom*,

A Marble Arch Production, Universal.

Supporting Actress

NORMA ALEANDRO in *Gaby—A True Story*, A G. Brimmer Production, Tri-Star.

ANNE ARCHER in *Fatal Attraction*, A Jaffe/Lansing Production Paramount.

★ OLYMPIA DUKAKIS in *Moonstruck*, A Patrick Palmer and Norman Jewison Production, M-G-M.

ANNE RAMSEY in *Throw Momma from the Train*, A Rollins, Morra & Brezner Production, Orion.

ANN SOTHERN in *The Whales of August*, An Alive Films Production with Circle Associates, Alive Films.

Directing

★ BERNARDO BERTOLUCCI for *The Last Emperor*, A Hemdale Film Production, Columbia.

JOHN BOORMAN for *Hope and Glory*, A Davros Production Services Limited Production, Columbia.

LASSE HALLSTRÖM for *My Life as a Dog*, A Svensk Filmindustri/ Filmteknik Production, Skouras Pictures.

NORMAN JEWISON for *Moonstruck*, A Patrick Palmer and Norman Jewison Production, M-G-M.

ADRIAN LYNE for *Fatal Attraction*, A Jaffe/Lansing Production, Paramount.

Writing

Screenplay Written Directly for the Screen

AU REVOIR LES ENFANTS (GOODBYE, CHILDREN), An NEF (Paris) Production, Orion Classics: LOUIS MALLE.

BROADCAST NEWS, A 20th Century-Fox Production, 20th Century-Fox: JAMES L. BROOKS.

HOPE AND GLORY, A Davros Production Services Limited Production, Columbia: JOHN BOORMAN.

★ MOONSTRUCK, A Patrick Palmer and Norman Jewison Production, M-G-M: JOHN PATRICK SHANLEY.

RADIO DAYS, A Jack Rollins and Charles H. Joffe Production, Orion: WOODY ALLEN.

Screenplay Based on Material from Another Medium

THE DEAD, A Liffey Films Production, Vestron: Screenplay by TONY HUSTON.

FATAL ATTRACTION, A Jaffe/Lansing Production, Paramount: Screenplay by JAMES DEARDEN.

FULL METAL JACKET, A Natant Production, Warner Bros.: Screenplay by STANLEY KUBRICK, MICHAEL HERR, and GUSTAV HASFORD.

★ THE LAST EMPEROR, A Hemdale Film Production, Columbia: Screenplay by MARK PEPLOE and BERNARDO BERTOLUCCI.

MY LIFE AS A DOG, A Svensk Filmindustri/Filmteknik Production, Skouras Pictures: Screenplay by LASSE HALLSTRÖM, REIDAR JÖNSSON, BRASSE BRÄNNSTRÖM, and PER BERGLUND.

Cinematography

BROADCAST NEWS, A 20th Century-Fox Production, 20th Century-Fox: MICHAEL BALLHAUS.

EMPIRE OF THE SUN, A Warner Bros. Production, Warner Bros.: ALLEN DAVIAU.

HOPE AND GLORY, A Davros Production Services Limited Production, Columbia: PHILIPPE ROUSSELOT.

★ THE LAST EMPEROR, A Hemdale Film Production, Columbia: VITTORIO STORARO.

MATEWAN, A Red Dog Films

Production, Cinecom Pictures: HASKELL WEXLER.

Art Direction - Set Decoration

EMPIRE OF THE SUN, A Warner Bros. Production, Warner Bros.: NORMAN REYNOLDS; Set Decoration: HARRY CORDWELL.

HOPE AND GLORY, A Davros Production Services Limited Production, Columbia: ANTHONY PRATT; Set Decoration: JOAN WOOLLARD.

★ THE LAST EMPEROR, A Hemdale Film Production, Columbia: FERDINANDO SCARFIOTTI; Set Decoration: BRUNO CESARI and OSVALDO DESIDERI.

RADIO DAYS, A Jack Rollins and Charles H. Joffe Production, Orion: SANTO LOQUASTO; Set Decoration: CAROL JOFFE, LES BLOOM, and GEORGE DETITTA, JR.

THE UNTOUCHABLES, An Art Linson Production, Paramount: PATRIZIA VON BRANDENSTEIN; Set Decoration: HAL GAUSMAN.

Sound

EMPIRE OF THE SUN, A Warner Bros. Production, Warner Bros.: ROBERT KNUDSON, DON DIGIROLAMO, JOHN BOYDE, and TONY DAWE.

★ THE LAST EMPEROR, A Hemdale Film Production, Columbia: BILL ROWE and IVAN SHARROCK.

LETHAL WEAPON, A Warner Bros. Production, Warner Bros.: LES FRESHOLTZ, DICK ALEXANDER, VERN POORE, and BILL NELSON.

ROBOCOP, A Tobor Pictures Production, Orion: MICHAEL J. KOHUT, CARLOS DE LARIOS, AARON ROCHIN, and ROBERT WALD.

THE WITCHES OF EASTWICK, A Warner Bros. Production, Warner Bros.: WAYNE ARTMAN, TOM BECKERT, TOM DAHL, and ART ROCHESTER.

Film Editing

BROADCAST NEWS, A 20th Century-Fox Production, 20th Century-Fox: RICHARD MARKS.

EMPIRE OF THE SUN, A Warner Bros. Production, Warner Bros.: MICHAEL KAHN.

FATAL ATTRACTION, A Jaffe/Lansing Production, Paramount: MICHAEL KAHN and PETER E. BERGER.

★ THE LAST EMPEROR, A Hemdale Film Production, Columbia: GABRIELLA CRISTIANI.

ROBOCOP, A Tobor Pictures Production, Orion: FRANK J. URIOSTE.

Music

Original Score

CRY FREEDOM, A Marble Arch Production, Universal: GEORGE FENTON and JONAS GWANGWA.

EMPIRE OF THE SUN, A Warner Bros. Production, Warner Bros.: JOHN T. WILLIAMS.

★ THE LAST EMPEROR, A Hemdale Film Production, Columbia: RYUICHI SAKAMOTO, DAVID BYRNE, and CONG SU.

THE UNTOUCHABLES, An Art Linson Production, Paramount: ENNIO MORRICONE.

THE WITCHES OF EASTWICK, A Warner Bros. Production, Warner Bros.: JOHN T. WILLIAMS.

Original Song Score

No nominations.

Original Song

CRY FREEDOM from *Cry Freedom*, A Marble Arch Production, Universal: Music and Lyrics by GEORGE FENTON and JONAS GWANGWA.

★ (I'VE HAD) THE TIME OF MY LIFE from *Dirty Dancing*, A Vestron Pictures Production in association with Great American Films Limited Partnership, Vestron: Music by

FRANKE PREVITE, JOHN DENICOLA, and DONALD MARKOWITZ; Lyrics by FRANKE PREVITE.

NOTHING'S GONNA STOP US NOW from *Mannequin*, A Gladden Entertainment Production, 20th Century-Fox: Music and Lyrics by ALBERT HAMMOND and DIANE WARREN.

SHAKEDOWN from *Beverly Hills Cop II*, A Don Simpson/Jerry Bruckheimer Production in association with Eddie Murphy Productions, Paramount: Music by HAROLD FALTERMEYER and KEITH FORSEY; Lyrics by HAROLD FALTERMEYER, KEITH FORSEY, and BOB SEGER.

STORYBOOK LOVE from *The Princess Bride*, An Act III Communications Production, 20th Century-Fox: Music and Lyrics by WILLY DEVILLE.

Costume Design

THE DEAD, A Liffey Films Production, Vestron: DOROTHY JEAKINS.

EMPIRE OF THE SUN, A Warner Bros. Production, Warner Bros.: BOB RINGWOOD.

★ THE LAST EMPEROR, A Hemdale Film Production, Columbia: JAMES ACHESON.

MAURICE, A Merchant Ivory Production, Cinecom Pictures: JENNY BEAVAN and JOHN BRIGHT.

THE UNTOUCHABLES, An Art Linson Production, Paramount: MARILYN VANCE-STRAKER.

Make-up

HAPPY NEW YEAR, A Columbia Pictures Production, Columbia: BOB LADEN.

★ HARRY AND THE HENDERSONS, A Universal/Amblin Entertainment Production, Universal: RICK BAKER.

Visual Effects

★ INNERSPACE, A Warner Bros. Production, Warner Bros.: DENNIS MUREN, WILLIAM GEORGE, HARLEY JESSUP, and KENNETH SMITH.

PREDATOR, A 20th Century-Fox Production, 20th Century-Fox: JOEL HYNEK, ROBERT M. GREENBERG, RICHARD GREENBERG, and STAN WINSTON.

Sound Effects Editing

None.*

Short Films

Animated

GEORGE AND ROSEMARY, National Film Board of Canada: EUNICE MACAULAY, Producer.

★ THE MAN WHO PLANTED TREES, Société Radio-Canada/Canadian Broadcasting Corporation: FREDERIC BACK, Producer.

YOUR FACE, Bill Plympton Productions: BILL PLYMPTON, Producer.

Live Action

MAKING WAVES, The Production Pool Ltd.: ANN WINGATE, Producer.

★ RAY'S MALE HETEROSEXUAL DANCE HALL, Chanticleer Films: JONATHAN SANGER and JANA SUE MEMEL, Producers.

SHOESHINE, Tom Abrams Productions: ROBERT A. KATZ, Producer.

Documentary

Short Subjects

FRANCES STELOFF: MEMOIRS OF A BOOKSELLER, A Winterlude Films, Inc., Production: DEBORAH DICKSON, Producer.

IN THE WEE WEE HOURS... University of

*Sound Effects Editing was recognized this year by a Special Achievement Award rather than an annual award.

Southern California School of Cinema/TV: UNIVERSITY OF SOUTHERN CALIFORNIA SCHOOL OF CINEMA/TV.

LANGUAGE SAYS IT ALL, A Tripod Production: MEGAN WILLIAMS, Producer.

SILVER INTO GOLD, Department of Communications, Stanford University: LYNN MUELLER, Producer.

★ YOUNG AT HEART, A Sue Marx Films, Inc., Production: SUE MARX and PAMELA CONN, Producers.

Features

EYES ON THE PRIZE: AMERICA'S CIVIL RIGHTS YEARS/BRIDGE TO FREEDOM 1965, A Blackside, Inc., Production: CALLIE CROSSLEY and JAMES A. DEVINNEY, Producers.

HELLFIRE: A JOURNEY FROM HIROSHIMA, JOHN JUNKERMAN and JOHN W. DOWER, Producers.

RADIO BIKINI, A Production of Crossroads Film Project, Ltd.: ROBERT STONE, Producer.

A STITCH FOR TIME, A Production of Peace Quilters Production Company, Inc.: BARBARA HERBICH and CYRIL CHRISTO, Producers.

★ THE TEN-YEAR LUNCH: THE WIT AND LEGEND OF THE ALGONQUIN ROUND TABLE, An Aviva Films Production: AVIVA SLESIN, Producer.

Foreign Language Film Award

AU REVOIR LES ENFANTS (GOODBYE, CHILDREN), An NEF (Paris) Production (France).

★ BABETTE'S FEAST, A Panorama Film International Production in cooperation with Nordisk Film and the Danish Film Institute (Denmark).

COURSE COMPLETED, A Nickel Odeon Dos Production (Spain).

THE FAMILY, A Massfilm-Cinecittà-Les Films Ariane-Cinemax Production (Italy).

PATHFINDER, A Filmkameratene Production (Norway).

Honorary Awards

No Honorary Awards were given this year.

Special Achievement Award

Sound Effects Editing: STEPHEN FLICK and JOHN POSPISIL for *Robocop*, A Tobor Pictures Production, Orion.

Irving G. Thalberg Memorial Award

BILLY WILDER.

Jean Hersholt Humanitarian Award

None.

Gordon E. Sawyer Award

FRED HYNES.

Scientific or Technical Awards

Academy Award of Merit (Academy statuette)

BERNARD KÜHL and WERNER BLOCK and the OSRAM GMBH RESEARCH AND DEVELOPMENT DEPARTMENT for the invention and the continuing improvement of the OSRAM HM1 light source for motion picture photography.

Scientific and Engineering Award (Academy plaque)

WILLI BURTH and KINOTONE CORPORATION for the invention and development of the Non-rewind Platter System for motion picture presentations.

MONTAGE GROUP, LTD., for the

development and RONALD C. BARKER and CHESTER L. SCHULER for the invention of the Montage Picture Processor electronic film editing system.

COLIN F. MOSSMAN and RANK FILM LABORATORIES' DEVELOPMENT GROUP for creating a fully automated film-handling system for improving productivity of high-speed film processing.

EASTMAN KODAK COMPANY for the development of Eastman Color High Speed Daylight Negative Film 5297/7297.

EASTMAN KODAK COMPANY for the development of Eastman Color High Speed SA Negative Film 5295 for blue-screen traveling matte photography.

FRITZ GABRIEL BAUER for the invention and development of the improved features of the Moviecam Camera System.

ZORAN PERISIC of Courier Films, Ltd., for the Zoptic dual-zoom front projection system for visual effects photography.

CARL ZEISS COMPANY for the design and development of a series of superspeed lenses for motion picture photography.

Technical Achievement Award (Academy certificate)

IOAN ALLEN of Dolby Laboratories, Inc., for the Cat. 43 playback-only noise-reduction unit and its practical application to motion picture sound recordings.

JOHN EPPOLITO, WALLY GENTLEMAN, WILLIAM MESA, LES PAUL ROBLEY, and GEOFFREY H. WILLIAMSON for refinements to a dual-screen, front-projection, image-compositing system.

JAN JACOBSEN for the application of a dual-screen, front-projection system to motion picture special effects photography.

THAINE MORRIS and DAVID PIER for the development of DSC Spark Devices for motion picture special effects.

TADEUZ KRZANOWSKI of Industrial Light and Magic, Inc., for the development of a wire rig model support mechanism used to control the movements of miniatures in special effects.

DAN C. NORRIS and TIM COOK of Norris Film Products for the development of a single-frame exposure system for motion picture photography.

1988

Nominations Announced: February 15, 1989
Awards Ceremony: March 29, 1989
Shrine Civic Auditorium
(MC: None)

Best Picture

THE ACCIDENTAL TOURIST, A Warner Bros. Production, Warner Bros.: Lawrence Kasdan, Charles Okun, and Michael Grillo, Producers.
DANGEROUS LIAISONS, A Lorimar Production, Warner Bros.: Norma Heyman and Hank Moonjean, Producers.
MISSISSIPPI BURNING, A Frederick Zollo Production, Orion: Frederick Zollo and Robert F. Colesberry, Producers.
★ RAIN MAN, A Guber-Peters Company Production, United Artists: Mark Johnson, Producer.
WORKING GIRL, A 20th Century-Fox Production, 20th Century-Fox: Douglas Wick, Producer.

Actor

GENE HACKMAN in *Mississippi Burning*, A Frederick Zollo Production, Orion.
TOM HANKS in *Big*, A 20th Century-Fox Production, 20th Century-Fox.
★ DUSTIN HOFFMAN in *Rain Man*, A Guber-Peters Company Production, United Artists.
EDWARD JAMES OLMOS in *Stand and Deliver*, A Mendez/Musca & Olmos Production, Warner Bros.
MAX VON SYDOW in *Pelle the Conqueror*, A Per Holst/Kaerne Films Production, Miramax Films.

Actress

GLENN CLOSE in *Dangerous Liaisons*, A Lorimar Production, Warner Bros.
★ JODIE FOSTER in *The Accused*, A Jaffe/Lansing Production, Paramount.
MELANIE GRIFFITH in *Working Girl*, A 20th Century-Fox Production, 20th Century-Fox.
MERYL STREEP in *A Cry in the Dark*, A Cannon Entertainment/Golan-Globus Production, Warner Bros.
SIGOURNEY WEAVER in *Gorillas in the Mist*, A Warner Bros. Production, Warner Bros./Universal.

Supporting Actor

ALEC GUINNESS in *Little Dorrit*, A Sands Films Production, Cannon.
★ KEVIN KLINE in *A Fish Called Wanda*, A Michael Shamberg-Prominent Features Production, M-G-M.
MARTIN LANDAU in *Tucker: the Man and His Dream*, A Lucasfilm Production, Paramount.
RIVER PHOENIX in *Running on Empty*, A Lorimar Production, Warner Bros.
DEAN STOCKWELL in *Married to the Mob*, A Mysterious Arts-Demme Production, Orion.

Supporting Actress

JOAN CUSACK in *Working Girl*, A 20th Century-Fox Production, 20th Century-Fox.

★ GEENA DAVIS in *The Accidental Tourist*, A Warner Bros. Production, Warner Bros.

FRANCES MCDORMAND in *Mississippi Burning*, A Frederick Zollo Production, Orion.

MICHELLE PFEIFFER in *Dangerous Liaisons*, A Lorimar Production, Warner Bros.

SIGOURNEY WEAVER in *Working Girl*, A 20th Century-Fox Production, 20th Century-Fox.

Directing

CHARLES CRICHTON for *A Fish Called Wanda*, A Michael Shamberg-Prominent Features Production, M-G-M.

★ BARRY LEVINSON for *Rain Man*, A Guber-Peters Company Production, United Artists.

MIKE NICHOLS for *Working Girl*, A 20th Century-Fox Production, 20th Century-Fox.

ALAN PARKER for *Mississippi Burning*, A Frederick Zollo Production, Orion.

MARTIN SCORSESE for *The Last Temptation of Christ*, A Testament Production, Universal/Cineplex Odeon.

Writing

Screenplay Written Directly for the Screen

BIG, A 20th Century-Fox Production, 20th Century-Fox: GARY ROSS and ANNE SPIELBERG.

BULL DURHAM, A Mount Company Production, Orion: RON SHELTON.

A FISH CALLED WANDA, A Michael Shamberg-Prominent Features Production, M-G-M: Story by JOHN CLEESE and CHARLES CRICHTON; Screenplay by JOHN CLEESE.

★ RAIN MAN, A Guber-Peters Company Production, United Artists: Story by BARRY MORROW; Screenplay by RONALD BASS and BARRY MORROW.

RUNNING ON EMPTY, A Lorimar Production, Warner Bros.: NAOMI FONER.

Screenplay Based on Material from Another Medium

THE ACCIDENTAL TOURIST, A Warner Bros. Production, Warner Bros.: Screenplay by FRANK GALATI and LAWRENCE KASDAN.

★ DANGEROUS LIAISONS, A Lorimar Production, Warner Bros.: Screenplay by CHRISTOPHER HAMPTON.

GORILLAS IN THE MIST, A Warner Bros. Production, Warner Bros./Universal: Screenplay by ANNA HAMILTON PHELAN; Story by ANNA HAMILTON PHELAN and TAB MURPHY.

LITTLE DORRIT, A Sands Films Production, Cannon: Screenplay by CHRISTINE EDZARD.

THE UNBEARABLE LIGHTNESS OF BEING, A Saul Zaentz Company Production, Orion: Screenplay by JEAN-CLAUDE CARRIÈRE and PHILIP KAUFMAN.

Cinematography

★ MISSISSIPPI BURNING, A Frederick Zollo Production, Orion: PETER BIZIOU.

RAIN MAN, A Guber-Peters Company Production, United Artists: JOHN SEALE.

TEQUILA SUNRISE, A Mount Company Production, Warner Bros.: CONRAD L. HALL.

THE UNBEARABLE LIGHTNESS OF BEING, A Saul Zaentz Company Production, Orion: SVEN NYKVIST.

WHO FRAMED ROGER RABBIT, An Amblin Entertainment and

Touchstone Pictures Production, Buena Vista: DEAN CUNDEY.

Art Direction-Set Decoration

BEACHES, A Touchstone Pictures Production in association with Silver Screen Partners III, Buena Vista: ALBERT BRENNER; Set Decoration: GARRETT LEWIS.

★ DANGEROUS LIAISONS, A Lorimar Production, Warner Bros.: STUART CRAIG; Set Decoration: GERARD JAMES.

RAIN MAN, A Guber-Peters Company Production, United Artists: IDA RANDOM; Set Decoration: LINDA DESCENNA.

TUCKER: THE MAN AND HIS DREAM, A Lucasfilm Production, Paramount: DEAN TAVOULARIS; Set Decoration: ARMIN GANZ.

WHO FRAMED ROGER RABBIT, An Amblin Entertainment and Touchstone Pictures Production, Buena Vista: ELLIOT SCOTT; Set Decoration: PETER HOWITT.

Sound

★ BIRD, A Malpaso Production, Warner Bros.: LES FRESHOLTZ, DICK ALEXANDER, VERN POORE, and WILLIE D. BURTON.

DIE HARD, A 20th Century-Fox Production, 20th Century-Fox: DON BASSMAN, KEVIN F. CLEARY, RICHARD OVERTON, and AL OVERTON.

GORILLAS IN THE MIST, A Warner Bros. Production, Warner Bros./Universal: ANDY NELSON, BRIAN SAUNDERS, and PETER HANDFORD.

MISSISSIPPI BURNING, A Frederick Zollo Production, Orion: ROBERT LITT, ELLIOT TYSON, RICHARD C. KLINE, and DANNY MICHAEL.

WHO FRAMED ROGER RABBIT, An Amblin Entertainment and Touchstone Pictures Production, Buena Vista: ROBERT KNUDSON, JOHN BOYD, DON DIGIROLAMO, and TONY DAWE.

Film Editing

DIE HARD, A 20th Century-Fox Production, 20th Century-Fox: FRANK J. URIOSTE and JOHN F. LINK.

GORILLAS IN THE MIST, A Warner Bros. Production, Warner Bros./Universal: STUART BAIRD.

MISSISSIPPI BURNING, A Frederick Zollo Production, Orion: GERRY HAMBLING.

RAIN MAN, A Guber-Peters Company Production, United Artists: STU LINDER.

★ WHO FRAMED ROGER RABBIT, An Amblin Entertainment and Touchstone Pictures Production, Buena Vista: ARTHUR SCHMIDT.

Music

Original Score

THE ACCIDENTAL TOURIST, A Warner Bros. Production, Warner Bros.: JOHN WILLIAMS.

DANGEROUS LIAISONS, A Lorimar Production, Warner Bros.: GEORGE FENTON.

GORILLAS IN THE MIST, A Warner Bros. Production, Warner Bros./Universal: MAURICE JARRE.

★ THE MILAGRO BEANFIELD WAR, A Robert Redford/Moctesuma Esparza Production, Universal: DAVE GRUSIN.

RAIN MAN, A Guber-Peters Company Production, United Artists: HANS ZIMMER.

Original Song Score

No nominations.

Original Song

CALLING YOU from *Bagdad Cafe*, A Pelemele Film Production, Island: Music and Lyrics by BOB TELSON.

★ LET THE RIVER RUN from *Working Girl*, A 20th Century-Fox

Production, 20th Century-Fox: Music and Lyrics by CARLY SIMON.
TWO HEARTS from *Buster*, An N.F.H. Production, Hemdale: Music by LAMONT DOZIER; Lyrics by PHIL COLLINS.

Costume Design

COMING TO AMERICA, An Eddie Murphy Production, Paramount: DEBORAH NADOOLMAN.
★ DANGEROUS LIAISONS, A Lorimar Production, Warner Bros.: JAMES ACHESON.
A HANDFUL OF DUST, A Stage Screen Production, New Line: JANE ROBINSON.
SUNSET, A Hudson Hawk Production, Tri-Star: PATRICIA NORRIS.
TUCKER: THE MAN AND HIS DREAM, A Lucasfilm Production, Paramount: MILENA CANONERO.

Make-up

★ BEETLEJUICE, A Geffen Film Company Production, Geffen/Warner Bros.: VE NEILL, STEVE LA PORTE, and ROBERT SHORT.
COMING TO AMERICA, An Eddie Murphy Production, Paramount: RICK BAKER.
SCROOGED, An Art Linson Production, Paramount: TOM BURMAN and BARI DRIEBAND-BURMAN.

Visual Effects

DIE HARD, A 20th Century-Fox Production, 20th Century-Fox: RICHARD EDLUND, AL DISARRO, BRENT BOATES, and THAINE MORRIS.
★ WHO FRAMED ROGER RABBIT, An Amblin Entertainment and Touchstone Pictures Production, Buena Vista: KEN RALSTON, RICHARD WILLIAMS, EDWARD JONES, and GEORGE GIBBS.
WILLOW, A Lucasfilm Production in association with Imagine Entertainment Production, M-G-M: DENNIS MUREN, MICHAEL MCALISTER, PHIL TIPPETT, and CHRIS EVANS.

Sound Effects Editing

DIE HARD, A 20th Century-Fox Production, 20th Century-Fox: STEPHEN H. FLICK and RICHARD SHORR.
★ WHO FRAMED ROGER RABBIT, An Amblin Entertainment and Touchstone Pictures Production, Buena Vista: CHARLES L. CAMPBELL and LOUIS L. EDEMANN.
WILLOW, A Lucasfilm Production in association with Imagine Entertainment Production, M-G-M: BEN BURTT and RICHARD HYMNS.

Short Films

Animated

THE CAT CAME BACK, National Film Board of Canada: CORDELL BARKER, Producer.
TECHNOLOGICAL THREAT, Kroyer Films, Inc.: BILL KROYER, Producer.
★ TIN TOY, Pixar: JOHN LASSETER, Producer.

Live Action

★ THE APPOINTMENTS OF DENNIS JENNINGS, Schooner Productions, Inc.: DEAN PARISOT and STEVEN WRIGHT, Producers.
CADILLAC DREAMS, Cadillac Dreams Production: MATIA KARRELL, Producer.
GULLAH TALES, Georgia State University: GARY MOSS, Producer.

Documentary

Short Subjects

THE CHILDREN'S STOREFRONT, A Simon and Goodman Picture Company Production: KAREN GOODMAN, Producer.

FAMILY GATHERING, A Lise Yasui Production: LISE YASUI and ANN TEGNELL, Producers.

GANG COPS, Center for Visual Anthropology at the University of Southern California: THOMAS B. FLEMING and DANIEL J. MARKS, Producers.

PORTRAIT OF IMOGEN, A Pacific Pictures Production: NANCY HALE and MEG PARTRIDGE, Producers.

★ YOU DON'T HAVE TO DIE, A Tiger Rose Production in association with Filmworks, Inc.: WILLIAM GUTTENTAG and MALCOLM CLARKE, Producers.

Features

THE CRY OF REASON—BEYERS NAUDE: AN AFRIKANER SPEAKS OUT, A Production of Worldwide Documentaries, Inc.: ROBERT BILHEIMER and RONALD MIX, Producers.

★ HOTEL TERMINUS: THE LIFE AND TIMES OF KLAUS BARBIE, A Production of The Memory Pictures Company: MARCEL OPHULS, Producer.

LET'S GET LOST, A Production of Little Bear Films, Inc.: BRUCE WEBER and NAN BUSH, Producers.

PROMISES TO KEEP, A Production of Durrin Productions, Inc.: GINNY DURRIN, Producer.

WHO KILLED VINCENT CHIN?, A Production of Film News Now Foundation and Detroit Educational Television Foundation: RENEE TAJIMA and CHRISTINE CHOY, Producers.

Foreign Language Film Award

HANUSSEN, An Objektiv Studio/CCC Filmkunst/ZDF/Hungarofilm/MOKEP Production (Hungary).

THE MUSIC TEACHER, An RTBF/K2 One Production (Belgium).

★ PELLE THE CONQUEROR, A Per Holst/Kaerne Films Production (Denmark).

SALAAM BOMBAY!, A Mirabai Production (India).

WOMEN ON THE VERGE OF A NERVOUS BREAKDOWN, An El Deseo/ Laurenfilm Production (Spain).

Honorary Awards

EASTMAN KODAK in recognition of the company's fundamental contributions to the art of motion pictures during the first century of film history.

NATIONAL FILM BOARD OF CANADA in recognition of its fiftieth anniversary and its dedicated commitment to originate artistic, creative, and technological activity and excellence in every area of filmmaking.

Special Achievement Award

Animation Direction: RICHARD WILLIAMS for *Who Framed Roger Rabbit*, An Amblin Entertainment and Touchstone Pictures Production, Buena Vista.

Irving G. Thalberg Memorial Award

None.

Jean Hersholt Humanitarian Award

None.

Gordon E. Sawyer Award

GORDON HENRY COOK.

Scientific or Technical Awards

Academy Award of Merit (Academy statuette)

RAY DOLBY and IOAN ALLEN of Dolby Laboratories, Incorporated, for their continuous contributions to motion picture sound through the research and development programs of Dolby Laboratories.

Scientific and Engineering Award (Academy plaque)

ROY W. EDWARDS and the ENGINEERING STAFF OF PHOTO-SONICS, INCORPORATED, for the design and development of the Photo-Sonics 35mm-4ER High-Speed Motion Picture Camera with reflex viewing and video assist.

The ARNOLD AND RICHTER ENGINEERING STAFF, OTTO BLASCHEK, and ARRIFLEX CORPORATION for the concept and engineering of the Arriflex 35-3 Motion Picture Camera.

BILL TONDREAU of Tondreau Systems; ALVAH MILLER and PAUL JOHNSON of Lynx Robotics; PETER A. REGLA of Elicon; DAN SLATER; BUD ELAM, JOE PARKER, and BILL BRYAN of Interactive Motion Control; and JERRY JEFFRESS, RAY FEENEY, BILL HOLLAND, and KRIS BROWN for their individual contributions and the collective advancements they have brought to the motion picture industry in the field of motion-control technology.

Technical Achievement Award (Academy certificate)

GRANT LOUCKS of Alan Gordon Enterprises, Incorporated, for the design concept and GEOFFREY H. WILLIAMSON of Wilcam for the mechanical and electrical engineering of the Image 300 35mm High-Speed Motion Picture Camera.

MICHAEL V. CHEWEY III for the development of the motion picture industry's first paper-tape reader incorporating microprocessor technology.

BHP, INC., successor to the Bell & Howell Professional Equipment Division, for the development of a high-speed reader incorporating microprocessor technology for motion picture laboratories.

HOLLYWOOD FILM COMPANY for the development of a high-speed reader incorporating microprocessor technology for motion picture laboratories.

BRUCE W. KELLER and MANFRED G. MICHELSON of Technical Film Systems for the design and development of a high-speed light-valve controller and constant current power supply for motion picture laboratories.

DR. ANTAL LISZIEWICZ and GLENN M. BERGGREN of ISCO-OPTIC GmbH for the design and development of the Ultra-Star series of motion picture lenses.

JAMES K. BRANCH of Spectra Cine, Incorporated, and WILLIAM L. BLOWERS and NASIR J. ZAIDI for the design and development of the Spectra CineSpot one-degree spotmeter for measuring the brightness of motion picture screens.

BOB BADAMI, DICK BERNSTEIN, and BILL BERNSTEIN of Offbeat Systems for the design and development of the Streamline Scoring System, Mark IV, for motion picture music editing.

GARY ZELLER of Zeller International Limited for the development of the Zel-Jel fire-protection barrier for motion picture stunt work.

EMANUEL TRILLING of Trilling Resources Limited for the development of the Stunt-Gel fire-protection barrier for motion picture stunt work.

PAUL A. ROOS for the invention of a method known as Video Assist, whereby a scene being photographed on motion picture film can be viewed on a monitor and/or recorded on video tape.

SIXTY-SECOND YEAR

1989

Nominations Announced: February 14, 1990
Awards Ceremony: March 26, 1990
Dorothy Chandler Pavilion, Los Angeles County Music Center
(MC: Billy Crystal)

Best Picture

BORN ON THE FOURTH OF JULY, An A. Kitman Ho and Ixtlan Production, Universal: A. Kitman Ho and Oliver Stone, Producers.

DEAD POETS SOCIETY, A Touchstone Pictures Production in association with Silver Screen Partners IV, Buena Vista: Steven Haft, Paul Junger Witt, and Tony Thomas, Producers.

★ DRIVING MISS DAISY, A Zanuck Company Production, Warner Bros.: Richard D. Zanuck and Lili Fini Zanuck, Producers.

FIELD OF DREAMS, A Gordon Company Production, Universal: Lawrence Gordon and Charles Gordon, Producers.

MY LEFT FOOT, A Ferndale Films Production, Miramax: Noel Pearson, Producer.

Actor

KENNETH BRANAGH in *Henry V*, A Renaissance Films Production in association with BBC, Samuel Goldwyn Company.

TOM CRUISE in *Born on the Fourth of July*, An A. Kitman Ho and Ixtlan Production, Universal.

MORGAN FREEMAN in *Driving Miss Daisy*, A Zanuck Company Production, Warner Bros.

★ DANIEL DAY LEWIS in *My Left Foot*, A Ferndale Films Production, Miramax.

ROBIN WILLIAMS in *Dead Poets Society*, A Touchstone Pictures Production in association with Silver Screen Partners IV, Buena Vista.

Actress

ISABELLE ADJANI in *Camille Claudel*, A Films Christian Fechner-Lilith Films-Gaumont-A2 TV France-Films A2-DD Production, Orion Classics.

PAULINE COLLINS in *Shirley Valentine*, A Lewis Gilbert/Willy Russell Production, Paramount.

JESSICA LANGE in *Music Box*, A Carolco Pictures Production, Tri-Star.

MICHELLE PFEIFFER in *The Fabulous Baker Boys*, A Gladden Entertainment Presentation of a Mirage Production, 20th Century-Fox.

★ JESSICA TANDY in *Driving Miss Daisy*, A Zanuck Company Production, Warner Bros.

Supporting Actor

DANNY AIELLO in *Do the Right Thing*, A Forty Acres and a Mule Filmworks Production, Universal.

DAN AYKROYD in *Driving Miss Daisy*, A Zanuck Company Production, Warner Bros.

MARLON BRANDO in *A Dry White Season*, A Metro-Goldwyn-Mayer Presentation of a Paula Weinstein Production, M-G-M.

MARTIN LANDAU in *Crimes and Misdemeanors*, A Jack Rollins and Charles H. Joffe Production, Orion.

★ DENZEL WASHINGTON in *Glory*, A Tri-Star Pictures Production, Tri-Star.

Supporting Actress

★ BRENDA FRICKER in *My Left Foot*, A Ferndale Films Production, Miramax.

ANJELICA HUSTON in *Enemies, A Love Story*, A Morgan Creek Production, 20th Century-Fox.

LENA OLIN in *Enemies, A Love Story*, A Morgan Creek Production, 20th Century-Fox.

JULIA ROBERTS in *Steel Magnolias*, A Rastar Production, Tri-Star.

DIANNE WIEST in *Parenthood*, An Imagine Entertainment Production, Universal.

Directing

WOODY ALLEN for *Crimes and Misdemeanors*, A Jack Rollins and Charles H. Joffe Production, Orion.

KENNETH BRANAGH for *Henry V*, A Renaissance Films Production in association with BBC, Samuel Goldwyn Company.

JIM SHERIDAN for *My Left Foot*, A Ferndale Films Production, Miramax.

★ OLIVER STONE for *Born on the Fourth of July*, An A. Kitman Ho and Ixtlan Production, Universal.

PETER WEIR for *Dead Poets Society*, A Touchstone Pictures Production in association with Silver Screen Partners IV, Buena Vista.

Writing

Screenplay Written Directly for the Screen

CRIMES AND MISDEMEANORS, A Jack Rollins and Charles H. Joffe Production, Orion: WOODY ALLEN.

★ DEAD POETS SOCIETY, A Touchstone Pictures Production in association with Silver Screen Partners IV, Buena Vista: TOM SCHULMAN.

DO THE RIGHT THING, A Forty Acres and a Mule Filmworks Production, Universal: SPIKE LEE.

SEX, LIES, AND VIDEOTAPE, An Outlaw Production, Miramax: STEVEN SODERBERGH.

WHEN HARRY MET SALLY . . . , A Castle Rock Production, Columbia: NORA EPHRON.

Screenplay Based on Material from Another Medium

BORN ON THE FOURTH OF JULY, An A. Kitman Ho and Ixtlan Production, Universal: OLIVER STONE and RON KOVIC.

★ DRIVING MISS DAISY, A Zanuck Company Production, Warner Bros.: ALFRED UHRY.

ENEMIES, A LOVE STORY, A Morgan Creek Production, 20th Century-Fox: ROGER L. SIMON and PAUL MAZURSKY.

FIELD OF DREAMS, A Gordon Company Production, Universal: PHIL ALDEN ROBINSON.

MY LEFT FOOT, A Ferndale Films Production, Miramax: JIM SHERIDAN and SHANE CONNAUGHTON.

Cinematography

THE ABYSS, A 20th Century-Fox Film Production, 20th Century-Fox: MIKAEL SALOMON.

BLAZE, A Touchstone Pictures Production in association with Silver Screen Partners IV, Buena Vista: HASKELL WEXLER.

BORN ON THE FOURTH OF JULY, An A. Kitman Ho and Ixtlan Production, Universal: ROBERT RICHARDSON.

THE FABULOUS BAKER BOYS, A Gladden Entertainment Presentation of a Mirage Production, 20th Century-Fox: MICHAEL BALLHAUS.

★ GLORY, A Tri-Star Pictures Production, Tri-Star: FREDDIE FRANCIS.

Art Direction-Set Decoration

THE ABYSS, A 20th Century-Fox Film Production, 20th Century-Fox: LESLIE DILLEY: Set Decoration: ANNE KULJIAN.

THE ADVENTURES OF BARON MUNCHAUSEN, A Prominent Features and Laura Film Production, Columbia: DANTE FERRETTI; Set Decoration: FRANCESCA LO SCHIAVO.

★ BATMAN, A Warner Bros. Production, Warner Bros.: ANTON FURST; Set Decoration: PETER YOUNG.

DRIVING MISS DAISY, A Zanuck Company Production, Warner Bros.: BRUNO RUBEO; Set Decoration: CRISPIAN SALLIS.

GLORY, A Tri-Star Pictures Production, Tri-Star: NORMAN GARWOOD; Set Decoration: GARRETT LEWIS.

Sound

THE ABYSS, A 20th Century-Fox Film Production, 20th Century-Fox: DON BASSMAN, KEVIN F. CLEARY, RICHARD OVERTON, and LEE ORLOFF.

★ BLACK RAIN, A Jaffe/Lansing Production in association with Michael Douglas, Paramount: DONALD O. MITCHELL, KEVIN O'CONNELL, GREG RUSSELL, and KEITH A. WESTER.

BORN ON THE FOURTH OF JULY, An A. Kitman Ho and Ixtlan Production, Universal: MICHAEL MINKLER, GREGORY H. WATKINS, WYLIE STATEMAN, and TOD A. MAITLAND.

GLORY, A Tri-Star Pictures Production, Tri-Star: DONALD O. MITCHELL, GREGG C. RUDLOFF, ELLIOT TYSON, and RUSSELL WILLIAMS II.

INDIANA JONES AND THE LAST CRUSADE, A Lucasfilm Ltd. Production, Paramount: BEN BURTT, GARY SUMMERS, SHAWN MURPHY, and TONY DAWE.

Film Editing

THE BEAR, A Renn Production, Tri-Star: NÖELLE BOISSON.

★ BORN ON THE FOURTH OF JULY, An A. Kitman Ho and Ixtlan Production, Universal: DAVID BRENNER and JOE HUTSHING.

DRIVING MISS DAISY, A Zanuck Company Production, Warner Bros.: MARK WARNER.

THE FABULOUS BAKER BOYS, A Gladden Entertainment Presentation of a Mirage Production, 20th Century-Fox: WILLIAM STEINKAMP.

GLORY, A Tri-Star Pictures Production, Tri-Star: STEVEN ROSENBLUM.

Music

Original Score

BORN ON THE FOURTH OF JULY, An A. Kitman Ho and Ixtlan Production, Universal: JOHN WILLIAMS.

THE FABULOUS BAKER BOYS, A Gladden Entertainment Presentation of a Mirage Production, 20th Century-Fox: DAVID GRUSIN.

FIELD OF DREAMS, A Gordon Company Production, Universal: JAMES HORNER.

INDIANA JONES AND THE LAST CRUSADE, A Lucasfilm Ltd. Production, Paramount: JOHN WILLIAMS.

★ THE LITTLE MERMAID, A Walt Disney Pictures Production in association with Silver Screen

Partners IV, Buena Vista: ALAN MENKEN.

Original Song Score

No nominations.

Original Song

AFTER ALL from *Chances Are*, A Tri-Star Pictures Production, Tri-Star: Music by TOM SNOW; Lyrics by DEAN PITCHFORD.

THE GIRL WHO USED TO BE ME from *Shirley Valentine*, A Lewis Gilbert/Willy Russell Production, Paramount: Music by MARVIN HAMLISCH; Lyrics by ALAN BERGMAN, and MARILYN BERGMAN.

I LOVE TO SEE YOU SMILE from *Parenthood*, An Imagine Entertainment Production, Universal: Music and Lyrics by RANDY NEWMAN.

KISS THE GIRL from *The Little Mermaid*, A Walt Disney Pictures Production in association with Silver Screen Partners IV, Buena Vista: Music by ALAN MENKEN; Lyrics by HOWARD ASHMAN.

★ UNDER THE SEA from *The Little Mermaid*, A Walt Disney Pictures Production in association with Silver Screen Partners IV, Buena Vista: Music by ALAN MENKEN; Lyrics by HOWARD ASHMAN.

Costume Design

THE ADVENTURES OF BARON MUNCHAUSEN, A Prominent Features and Laura Film Production, Columbia: GABRIELLA PESCUCCI.

DRIVING MISS DAISY, A Zanuck Company Production, Warner Bros.: ELIZABETH MCBRIDE.

HARLEM NIGHTS, An Eddie Murphy Production, Paramount: JOE I. TOMPKINS.

★ HENRY V, A Renaissance Films Production in association with BBC, Samuel Goldwyn Company: PHYLLIS DALTON.

VALMONT, A Claude Berri and Renn Production, Orion: THEODOR PISTEK.

Make-up

THE ADVENTURES OF BARON MUNCHAUSEN, A Prominent Features and Laura Film Production, Columbia: MAGGIE WESTON and FABRIZIO SFORZA.

DAD, A Universal Pictures/Amblin Entertainment Production, Universal: DICK SMITH, KEN DIAZ, and GREG NELSON.

★ DRIVING MISS DAISY, A Zanuck Company Production, Warner Bros.: MANLIO ROCCHETTI, LYNN BARBER, and KEVIN HANEY.

Visual Effects

★ THE ABYSS, A 20th Century-Fox Film Production, 20th Century-Fox: JOHN BRUNO, DENNIS MUREN, HOYT YEATMAN, and DENNIS SKOTAK.

THE ADVENTURES OF BARON MUNCHAUSEN, A Prominent Features and Laura Film Production, Columbia: RICHARD CONWAY and KENT HOUSTON.

BACK TO THE FUTURE PART II, A Universal Pictures/Amblin Entertainment Production, Universal: KEN RALSTON, MICHAEL LANTIERI, JOHN BELL, and STEVE GAWLEY.

Sound Effects Editing

BLACK RAIN, A Jaffe/Lansing Production in association with Michael Douglas, Paramount: MILTON C. BURROW and WILLIAM L. MANGER.

★ INDIANA JONES AND THE LAST CRUSADE, A Lucasfilm Ltd. Production, Paramount: BEN BURTT and RICHARD HYMNS.

LETHAL WEAPON 2, A Warner Bros.

Production, Warner Bros.: ROBERT HENDERSON and ALAN ROBERT MURRAY.

Short Films

Animated

★ BALANCE, A Lauenstein Production: CHRISTOPH LAUENSTEIN and WOLFGANG LAUENSTEIN, Producers.

COW, The "Pilot" Co-op Animated Film Studio with VPTO Videofilm: ALEXANDER PETROV, Producer.

THE HILL FARM, National Film and Television School: MARK BAKER, Producer.

Live Action

AMAZON DIARY, Determined Productions, Inc.: ROBERT NIXON, Producer.

THE CHILDEATER, Stephen-Tammuz Productions, Ltd.: JONATHAN TAMMUZ, Producer.

★ WORK EXPERIENCE, North Inch Production Ltd.: JAMES HENDRIE, Producer.

Documentary

Short Subjects

FINE FOOD, FINE PASTRIES, OPEN 6 TO 9, A Production of David Petersen, Productions: DAVID PETERSEN, Producer.

★ THE JOHNSTOWN FLOOD, A Production of Guggenheim, Productions, Inc.: CHARLES GUGGENHEIM, Producer.

YAD VASHEM: PRESERVING THE PAST TO ENSURE THE FUTURE, A Ray Errol Fox Production: RAY ERROL FOX, Producer.

Features

ADAM CLAYTON POWELL, A Production of RKB Productions: RICHARD KILBERG and YVONNE SMITH, Producers.

★ COMMON THREADS: STORIES FROM THE QUILT, A Telling Pictures and The Couturie Company Production: ROBERT EPSTEIN and BILL COUTURIE, Producers.

CRACK USA: COUNTY UNDER SIEGE, A Production of Half-Court Productions, Ltd.: VINCE DIPERSIO and WILLIAM GUTTENTAG, Producers.

FOR ALL MANKIND, A Production of Apollo Associates/FAM Productions Inc.: AL REINERT and BETSY BROYLES BREIR, Producers.

SUPER CHIEF: THE LIFE AND LEGACY OF EARL WARREN, A Quest Production: JUDITH LEONARD and BILL JERSEY, Producers.

Foreign Language Film Award

CAMILLE CLAUDEL, A Films Christian Fechner-Lilith Films-Gaumont-A2 TV France-Films A2-DD Production (France).

★ CINEMA PARADISO, A Cristaldifilm/Films Ariane Production (Italy).

JESUS OF MONTREAL, A Max Films/ Gérard Mital Production (Canada).

SANTIAGO, THE STORY OF HIS NEW LIFE, A Dios los Cría Producciones/ Pedro Muñiz Production (Puerto Rico).

WALTZING REGITZE, A Nordisk Film/ Danish Film Institute Production (Denmark).

Honorary Awards

AKIRA KUROSAWA for accomplishments that have inspired, delighted, enriched, and entertained audiences and influenced filmmakers throughout the world.

Special Commendation

The Academy of Motion Picture Arts and Sciences' Board of Governors commends the contributions of the MEMBERS OF THE ENGINEERING COMMITTEES OF

THE SOCIETY OF MOTION PICTURE AND TELEVISION ENGINEERS (SMPTE). By establishing industry standards, they have greatly contributed to making film a primary form of international communication.

Special Achievement Award

None.

Irving G. Thalberg Memorial Award

None.

Jean Hersholt Humanitarian Award

HOWARD W. KOCH.

Gordon E. Sawyer Award

PIERRE ANGENIEUX.

Scientific or Technical Awards

Academy Award of Merit (Academy statuette)

None.

Scientific and Engineering Award (Academy plaque)

J. L. FISHER of J. L. Fisher, Inc., for the design and manufacture of the Fisher Model Ten Dolly.

JAMES KETCHAM of JSK Engineering for the engineering of the SDA521 B Advance/Retard system for magnetic film sound dubbing.

J. NOXON LEAVITT for the invention and ISTEC, INC., for the continuing development of the Wescam Stabilized Camera System.

KLAUS RESCH for the design and ERIC FITZ and FGV SCHMIDLE AND FITZ for the development of the Super Panther MS-180 Camera Dolly.

GEOFFREY H. WILLIAMSON of Wilcam Photo Research, Inc., for the design and development and ROBERT D. AUGUSTE for the electronic design and development of the Wilcam W-7 200-frames per second VistaVision Rotating Mirror Reflex Camera.

Technical Achievement Award (Academy certificate)

DR. LEO CATOZZO for the design and development of the CIR-Catozzo Self-Perforating Adhesive Tape Film Splicer.

MAGNA-TECH ELECTRONIC COMPANY for the introduction of the first remotely controlled advance/retard function for magnetic film sound dubbing.

1990

Nominations Announced: February 13, 1991
Awards Ceremony: March 25, 1991
Shrine Civic Auditorium
(MC: Billy Crystal)

Best Picture

AWAKENINGS, A Columbia Pictures Production, Columbia: Walter F. Parkes and Lawrence Lasker, Producers.

★ DANCES WITH WOLVES, A Tig Production, Orion: Jim Wilson and Kevin Costner, Producers.

GHOST, A Howard W. Koch Production, Paramount: Lisa Weinstein, Producer.

THE GODFATHER PART III, A Zoetrope Studios Production, Paramount: Francis Ford Coppola, Producer.

GOODFELLAS, A Warner Bros. Production, Warner Bros.: Irwin Winkler, Producer.

Actor

KEVIN COSTNER in *Dances with Wolves*, A Tig Production, Orion.

ROBERT DE NIRO in *Awakenings*, A Columbia Pictures Production, Columbia.

GERARD DEPARDIEU in *Cyrano de Bergerac*, A Hachette Premiere Production, Orion Classics.

RICHARD HARRIS in *The Field*, A Granada Production, Avenue Pictures.

★ JEREMY IRONS in *Reversal of Fortune*, A Reversal Films Production, Warner Bros.

Actress

★ KATHY BATES in *Misery*, A Castle Rock Entertainment Production, Columbia.

ANJELICA HUSTON in *The Grifters*, A Martin Scorsese Production, Miramax.

JULIA ROBERTS in *Pretty Woman*, A Touchstone Pictures Production, Buena Vista.

MERYL STREEP in *Postcards from the Edge*, A Columbia Pictures Production, Columbia.

JOANNE WOODWARD in *Mr. & Mrs. Bridge*, A Merchant Ivory Production, Miramax.

Supporting Actor

BRUCE DAVISON in *Longtime Companion*, An American Playhouse Production, Samuel Goldwyn Company.

ANDY GARCIA in *The Godfather Part III*, A Zoetrope Studios Production, Paramount.

GRAHAM GREENE in *Dances with Wolves*, A Tig Production, Orion.

AL PACINO in *Dick Tracy*, A Touchstone Pictures Production, Buena Vista.

★ JOE PESCI in *GoodFellas*, A Warner Bros. Production, Warner Bros.

Supporting Actress

ANNETTE BENING in *The Grifters*, A Martin Scorsese Production, Miramax.

LORRAINE BRACCO in *GoodFellas*, A Warner Bros. Production, Warner Bros.

★ WHOOPI GOLDBERG in *Ghost*, A Howard W. Koch Production, Paramount.

DIANE LADD in *Wild at Heart*, A Polygram/Propaganda Films Production, Samuel Goldwyn Company.

MARY MCDONNELL in *Dances with Wolves*, A Tig Production, Orion.

Directing

FRANCIS FORD COPPOLA for *The Godfather Part III*, A Zoetrope Studios Production, Paramount.

★ KEVIN COSTNER for *Dances with Wolves*, A Tig Production, Orion.

STEPHEN FREARS for *The Grifters*, A Martin Scorsese Production, Miramax.

BARBET SCHROEDER for *Reversal of Fortune*, A Reversal Films Production, Warner Bros.

MARTIN SCORSESE for *Goodfellas*, A Warner Bros. Production, Warner Bros.

Writing

Screenplay Written Directly for the Screen

ALICE, A Jack Rollins and Charles H. Joffe Production, Orion: WOODY ALLEN.

AVALON, A Tri-Star Production, Tri-Star: BARRY LEVINSON.

★ GHOST, A Howard W. Koch Production, Paramount: BRUCE JOEL RUBIN.

GREEN CARD, A Green Card Company Production, Buena Vista: PETER WEIR.

METROPOLITAN, A Westerly Film-Video Production, New Line: WHIT STILLMAN.

Screenplay Based on Material from Another Medium

AWAKENINGS, A Columbia Pictures Production, Columbia: STEVEN ZAILLIAN.

★ DANCES WITH WOLVES, A Tig Production, Orion: MICHAEL BLAKE.

GOODFELLAS, A Warner Bros. Production, Warner Bros.: NICHOLAS PILEGGI and MARTIN SCORSESE.

THE GRIFTERS, A Martin Scorsese Production, Miramax: DONALD E. WESTLAKE.

REVERSAL OF FORTUNE, A Reversal Films Production, Warner Bros.: NICHOLAS KAZAN.

Cinematography

AVALON, A Tri-Star Production, Tri-Star: ALLEN DAVIAU.

★ DANCES WITH WOLVES, A Tig Production, Orion: DEAN SEMLER.

DICK TRACY, A Touchstone Pictures Production, Buena Vista: VITTORIO STORARO.

THE GODFATHER PART III, A Zoetrope Studios Production, Paramount: GORDON WILLIS.

HENRY & JUNE, A Walrus and Associates Production, Universal: PHILIPPE ROUSSELOT.

Art Direction - Set Decoration

CYRANO DE BERGERAC, A Hachette Premiere Production, Orion Classics: EZIO FRIGERIO; Set Decoration: JACQUES ROUXEL.

DANCES WITH WOLVES, A Tig Production, Orion: JEFFREY BEECROFT; Set Decoration: LISA DEAN.

★ DICK TRACY, A Touchstone Pictures Production, Buena Vista:

RICHARD SYLBERT; Set Decoration: RICK SIMPSON.

THE GODFATHER, PART III, A Zoetrope Studios Production, Paramount: DEAN TAVOULARIS; Set Decoration: GARY FETTIS.

HAMLET, An Icon Production, Warner Bros.: DANTE FERRETTI; Set Decoration: FRANCESCA LO SCHIAVO.

Sound

★ DANCES WITH WOLVES, A Tig Production, Orion: RUSSELL WILLIAMS II, JEFFREY PERKINS, BILL W. BENTON, and GREG WATKINS.

DAYS OF THUNDER, A Don Simpson and Jerry Bruckheimer Production, Paramount: CHARLES WILBORN, DONALD O. MITCHELL, RICK KLINE, and KEVIN O'CONNELL.

DICK TRACY, A Touchstone Pictures Production, Buena Vista: THOMAS CAUSEY, CHRIS JENKINS, DAVID E. CAMPBELL, and D. M. HEMPHILL.

THE HUNT FOR RED OCTOBER, A Mace Neufeld/Jerry Sherlock Production, Paramount: RICHARD BRYCE GOODMAN, RICHARD OVERTON, KEVIN F. CLEARY, and DON BASSMAN.

TOTAL RECALL, A Carolco Pictures Production, Tri-Star: NELSON STOLL, MICHAEL J. KOHUT, CARLOS DE LARIOS, and AARON ROCHIN.

Film Editing

★ DANCES WITH WOLVES, A Tig Production, Orion: NEIL TRAVIS.

GHOST, A Howard W. Koch Production, Paramount: WALTER MURCH.

THE GODFATHER PART III, A Zoetrope Studios Production, Paramount: BARRY MALKIN, LISA FRUCHTMAN, and WALTER MURCH.

GOODFELLAS, A Warner Bros. Production, Warner Bros.: THELMA SCHOONMAKER.

THE HUNT FOR RED OCTOBER, A Mace Neufeld/Jerry Sherlock Production, Paramount: DENNIS VIRKLER and JOHN WRIGHT.

Music

Original Score

AVALON, A Tri-Star Production, Tri-Star: RANDY NEWMAN.

★ DANCES WITH WOLVES, A Tig Production, Orion: JOHN BARRY.

GHOST, A Howard W. Koch Production, Paramount: MAURICE JARRE.

HAVANA, A Universal Pictures Limited Production, Universal: DAVID GRUSIN.

HOME ALONE, A 20th Century-Fox Production, 20th Century-Fox: JOHN WILLIAMS.

Original Song Score

No nominations.

Original Song

BLAZE OF GLORY from *Young Guns II*, A Morgan Creek Production, 20th Century-Fox: Music and Lyrics by JON BON JOVI.

I'M CHECKIN' OUT from *Postcards from the Edge*, A Columbia Pictures Production, Columbia: Music and Lyrics by SHEL SILVERSTEIN.

PROMISE ME YOU'LL REMEMBER from *The Godfather Part III*, A Zoetrope Studios Production, Paramount: Music by CARMINE COPPOLA; Lyrics by JOHN BETTIS.

SOMEWHERE IN MY MEMORY from *Home Alone*, A 20th Century-Fox Production, 20th Century-Fox: Music by JOHN WILLIAMS; Lyrics by LESLIE BRICUSSE.

★ SOONER OR LATER (I ALWAYS GET MY MAN) from *Dick Tracy*, A Touchstone Pictures Production, Buena Vista: Music and Lyrics by STEPHEN SONDHEIM.

Costume Design

AVALON, A Tri-Star Production, Tri-Star: GLORIA GRESHAM.

★ CYRANO DE BERGERAC, A Hachette Premiere Production, Orion Classics: FRANCA SQUARCIAPINO.

DANCES WITH WOLVES, A Tig Production, Orion: ELSA ZAMPARELLI.

DICK TRACY, A Touchstone Pictures Production, Buena Vista: MILENA CANONERO.

HAMLET, An Icon Production, Warner Bros.: MAURIZIO MILLENOTTI.

Make-up

CYRANO DE BERGERAC, A Hachette Premiere Production, Orion Classics: MICHÈLE BURKE and JEAN-PIERRE EYCHENNE.

★ DICK TRACY, A Touchstone Pictures Production, Buena Vista: JOHN CAGLIONE, JR., and DOUG DREXLER.

EDWARD SCISSORHANDS, A 20th Century-Fox Production, 20th Century-Fox: VE NEILL and STAN WINSTON.

Visual Effects

None.*

Sound Effects Editing

FLATLINERS, A Stonebridge Entertainment Production, Columbia: CHARLES L. CAMPBELL and RICHARD FRANKLIN.

★ THE HUNT FOR RED OCTOBER, A Mace Neufeld/Jerry Sherlock Production, Paramount: CECELIA HALL and GEORGE WATTERS II.

TOTAL RECALL, A Carolco Pictures Production, Tri-Star: STEPHEN H. FLICK.

Short Films

Animated

★ CREATURE COMFORTS, An Aardman Animations Limited Production: NICK PARK, Producer.

A GRAND DAY OUT, A National Film and Television School Production: NICK PARK, Producer.

GRASSHOPPERS (CAVALLETTE), A Bruno Bozzetto Production: BRUNO BOZZETTO, Producer.

Live Action

BRONX CHEERS, An American Film Institute, Production: RAYMOND DE FELITTA and MATTHEW GROSS, Producers.

DEAR ROSIE, A World's End Production: PETER CATTANEO and BARNABY THOMPSON, Producers.

★ THE LUNCH DATE, An Adam Davidson Production: ADAM DAVIDSON, Producer.

SENZENI NA? (WHAT HAVE WE DONE?), An American Film Institute Production: BERNARD JOFFA and ANTHONY E. NICHOLAS, Producers.

12:01 PM, A Chanticleer Films Production: HILLARY RIPPS and JONATHAN HEAP, Producers.

Documentary

Short Subjects

BURNING DOWN TOMORROW, An Interscope Communications, Inc., Production: KIT THOMAS, Producer.

CHIMPS: SO LIKE US, A Simon and Goodman Picture Company Production: KAREN GOODMAN and KIRK SIMON, Producers.

★ DAYS OF WAITING, A Mouchette Films Production: STEVEN OKAZAKI, Producer.

JOURNEY INTO LIFE: THE WORLD OF THE UNBORN, An ABC/Kane Productions

*Visual Effects were recognized this year by a Special Achievement Award rather than an annual award.

International, Inc., Production: DEREK BROMHALL, Producer.

ROSE KENNEDY: A LIFE TO REMEMBER, A Production of Sanders and Mock Productions and American Film Foundation: FREIDA LEE MOCK and TERRY SANDERS, Producers.

Features

★ AMERICAN DREAM, A Cabin Creek Films Production: BARBARA KOPPLE and ARTHUR COHN, Producers.

BERKELEY IN THE SIXTIES, A Production of Berkeley in the Sixties Production Partnership: MARK KITCHELL, Producer.

BUILDING BOMBS, A Mori/Robinson Production: MARK MORI and SUSAN ROBINSON, Producers.

FOREVER ACTIVISTS: STORIES FROM THE VETERANS OF THE ABRAHAM LINCOLN BRIGADE, A Judith Montell Production: JUDITH MONTELL, Producer.

WALDO SALT: A SCREENWRITER'S JOURNEY, A Waldo Productions, Inc., Production: ROBERT HILLMANN, Producer.

Foreign Language Film Award

CYRANO DE BERGERAC, A Hachette Premiere Production (France).

★ JOURNEY OF HOPE, A Catpics/ Condor Features Production: (Switzerland).

JU DOU, A China Film Co-Production Corporation/Tokuma Shoten Publishing Production: (People's Republic of China).

THE NASTY GIRL, A Production of Sentana Filmproduktion (Germany).

OPEN DOORS, An Erre Produzioni/ Istituto Luce Production (Italy).

Honorary Awards

SOPHIA LOREN—one of the genuine treasures of world cinema who, in a career rich with memorable performances, has added permanent luster to our art form.

MYRNA LOY in recognition of her extraordinary qualities both onscreen and off, with appreciation for a lifetime's worth of indelible performances.

Medals of Commendation

RODERICK T. RYAN, DON TRUMBULL, and GEOFFREY H. WILLIAMSON in appreciation for outstanding service and dedication in upholding the high standards of the Academy of Motion Picture Arts and Sciences.

Special Achievement Award

Visual Effects: ERIC BREVIG, ROB BOTTIN, TIM MCGOVERN, and ALEX FUNKE for *Total Recall*, A Carolco Pictures Production, Tri-Star.

Irving G. Thalberg Memorial Award

RICHARD ZANUCK and DAVID BROWN.

Jean Hersholt Humanitarian Award

None.

Gordon E. Sawyer Award

STEFAN KUDELSKI.

Scientific or Technical Awards

Academy Award of Merit (Academy statuette)

The EASTMAN KODAK COMPANY for the development of T-grain technology and the introduction of EXR color negative films which utilize this technology.

Scientific and Engineering Awards (Academy plaque)

BRUCE WILTON and CARLOS ICINKOFF of Mechanical Concepts;

ENGINEERING DEPARTMENT OF ARNOLD AND RICHTER; FUJI PHOTO FILM COMPANY, LTD.; MANFRED G. MICHELSON of Technical film Systems; and JOHN W. LANG, WALTER HRASTNIK, and CHARLES J. WATSON of Bell & Howell Company.

Technical Achievement Awards (Academy certificate)

WILLIAM L. BLOWERS of Belco Associates and THOMAS F. DENOVE; IAIN NEIL, TAKUO MIYAGISHIMA and PANAVISION; CHRISTOPHER S. GILMAN and HARVEY HUBERT, JR., of the Diligent Dwarves Effects; JIM GRAVES of J&G Enterprises; BENGT O. ORHALL, KENNETH LUND, BJORN SELIN, and KJELL HOGBERG of AB Film-Teknik; RICHARD MULA and PETE ROMANO of HydroImage; DEDO WEIGERT of Dedo Weigert Film; DR. FRED KOLB, JR., PAUL PREO, PETER BALDWIN, and DR. PAUL KIANKHOOY and the LIGHTMAKER COMPANY.

SIXTY-FOURTH YEAR

1991

Nominations Announced: February 5, 1992
Awards Ceremony: March 30, 1992
Dorothy Chandler Pavilion, Los Angeles County Music Center
(MC: Billy Crystal)

Best Picture

BEAUTY AND THE BEAST, A Walt Disney Pictures Production, Buena Vista: Don Hahn, Producer.

BUGSY, A Tri-Star Pictures Production, Tri-Star: Mark Johnson, Barry Levinson, and Warren Beatty, Producers.

JFK, A Camelot Production, Warner Bros.: A. Kitman Ho and Oliver Stone, Producers.

THE PRINCE OF TIDES, A Barwood/Longfellow Production, Columbia: Barbra Streisand and Andrew Karsh, Producers.

★ THE SILENCE OF THE LAMBS, A Strong Heart/Demme Production, Orion: Edward Saxon, Kenneth Utt, and Ron Bozman, Producers.

Actor

WARREN BEATTY in *Bugsy*, A Tri-Star Pictures Production, Tri-Star.

ROBERT DE NIRO in *Cape Fear*, An Amblin Entertainment Production in association with Cappa Films and Tribeca Productions, Universal.

★ ANTHONY HOPKINS in *The Silence of the Lambs*, A Strong Heart/Demme Production, Orion.

NICK NOLTE in *The Prince of Tides*, A Barwood/Longfellow Production, Columbia.

ROBIN WILLIAMS in *The Fisher King*, A Tri-Star Pictures Production, Tri-Star.

Actress

GEENA DAVIS in *Thelma & Louise*, A Pathé Entertainment Production, M-G-M.

LAURA DERN in *Rambling Rose*, A Carolco Pictures Production, Seven Arts/New Line.

★ JODIE FOSTER in *The Silence of the Lambs*, A Strong Heart/Demme Production, Orion.

BETTE MIDLER in *For the Boys*, A 20th Century-Fox Production, 20th Century-Fox.

SUSAN SARANDON in *Thelma & Louise*, A Pathé Entertainment Production, M-G-M.

Supporting Actor

TOMMY LEE JONES in *JFK*, A Camelot Production, Warner Bros.

HARVEY KEITEL in *Bugsy*, A Tri-Star Pictures Production, Tri-Star.

BEN KINGSLEY in *Bugsy*, A Tri-Star Pictures Production, Tri-Star.

MICHAEL LERNER in *Barton Fink*, A Barton Circle Production, 20th Century-Fox.

★ JACK PALANCE in *City Slickers*, A

Castle Rock Entertainment Production, Columbia.

Supporting Actress

DIANE LADD in *Rambling Rose*, A Carolco Pictures Production, Seven Arts/New Line.

JULIETTE LEWIS in *Cape Fear*, An Amblin Entertainment Production in association with Cappa Films and Tribeca Productions, Universal.

KATE NELLIGAN in *The Prince of Tides*, A Barwood/Longfellow Production, Columbia.

* ★ MERCEDES RUEHL in *The Fisher King*, A Tri-Star Pictures Production, Tri-Star.

JESSICA TANDY in *Fried Green Tomatoes*, An Act III Communications in association with Electric Shadow Production, Universal.

Directing

★ JONATHAN DEMME for *The Silence of the Lambs*, A Strong Heart/Demme Production, Orion.

BARRY LEVINSON for *Bugsy*, A Tri-Star Pictures Production, Tri-Star.

RIDLEY SCOTT for *Thelma & Louise*, A Pathé Entertainment Production, M-G-M.

JOHN SINGLETON for *Boyz N the Hood*, A Columbia Pictures Production, Columbia.

OLIVER STONE for *JFK*, A Camelot Production, Warner Bros.

Writing

Screenplay Written Directly for the Screen

BOYZ N THE HOOD, A Columbia Pictures Production, Columbia: JOHN SINGLETON.

BUGSY, A Tri-Star Pictures Production, Tri-Star: JAMES TOBACK.

THE FISHER KING, A Tri-Star Pictures Production, Tri-Star: RICHARD LA GRAVENESE.

GRAND CANYON, A 20th Century-Fox Production, 20th Century-Fox: LAWRENCE KASDAN and MEG KASDAN.

★ THELMA & LOUISE, A Pathé Entertainment Production, M-G-M: CALLIE KHOURI.

Screenplay Based on Material Previously Produced or Published

EUROPA, EUROPA, A CCC-Filmkunst and Les Films de Losange Production, Orion Classics: AGNIESZKA HOLLAND.

FRIED GREEN TOMATOES, An ACT III Communications in association with Electric Shadow Production, Universal: FANNIE FLAGG and CAROL SOBIESKI.

JFK, A Camelot Production, Warner Bros.: OLIVER STONE and ZACHARY SKLAR.

THE PRINCE OF TIDES, A Barwood/ Longfellow Production, Columbia: PAT CONROY and BECKY JOHNSTON.

★ THE SILENCE OF THE LAMBS, A Strong Heart/Demme Production, Orion: TED TALLY.

Cinematography

BUGSY, A Tri-Star Pictures Production, Tri-Star: ALLEN DAVIAU.

★ JFK, A Camelot Production, Warner Bros.: ROBERT RICHARDSON.

THE PRINCE OF TIDES, A Barwood/ Longfellow Production, Columbia: STEPHEN GOLDBLATT.

TERMINATOR 2: JUDGMENT DAY, A Carolco Production, Tri-Star: ADAM GREENBURG.

THELMA & LOUISE, A Pathé Entertainment Production, MGM: ADRIAN BIDDLE.

Art Direction - Set Decoration

BARTON FINK, A Barton Circle Production, 20th Century-Fox:

DENNIS GASSNER; Set Decoration: NANCY HAIGH.

★ BUGSY, A Tri-Star Pictures Production, Tri-Star: DENNIS GASSNER; Set Decoration: NANCY HAIGH.

THE FISHER KING, A Tri-Star Pictures Production, Tri-Star: MEL BOURNE; Set Decoration: CINDY CARR.

HOOK, A Tri-Star Pictures Production, Tri-Star: NORMAN GARWOOD; Set Decoration: GARRETT LEWIS.

THE PRINCE OF TIDES, A Barwood/ Longfellow Production, Columbia: PAUL SYLBERT; Set Decoration: CARYL HELLER.

Sound

BACKDRAFT, A Trilogy Entertainment Group/Brian Grazer Production, Universal: GARY SUMMERS, RANDY THOM, GARY RYDSTROM, and GLENN WILLIAMS.

BEAUTY AND THE BEAST, A Walt Disney Pictures Production, Buena Vista: TERRY PORTER, MEL METCALFE, DAVID J. HUDSON, and DOC KANE.

JFK, A Camelot Production, Warner Bros.: MICHAEL MINKLER, GREGG LANDAKER, and TOD A. MAITLAND.

THE SILENCE OF THE LAMBS, A Strong Heart/Demme Production, Orion: TOM FLEISHMAN and CHRISTOPHER NEWMAN.

★ TERMINATOR 2: JUDGMENT DAY, A Carolco Production, Tri-Star: TOM JOHNSON, GARY RYDSTROM, GARY SUMMERS, and LEE ORLOFF.

Film Editing

THE COMMITMENTS, A Beacon Communications Production, 20th Century-Fox: GERRY HAMBLING.

★ JKF, A Camelot Production, Warner Bros.: JOE HUTSHING and PIETRO SCALIA.

THE SILENCE OF THE LAMBS, A Strong Heart/Demme Production, Orion: CRAIG MCKAY.

TERMINATOR 2: JUDGMENT DAY, A Carolco Production, Tri-Star: CONRAD BUFF, MARK GOLDBLATT, and RICHARD A. HARRIS.

THELMA & LOUISE, A Pathé Entertainment Production, M-G-M: THOM NOBLE.

Music

Original Score

★ BEAUTY AND THE BEAST, A Walt Disney Pictures Production, Buena Vista: ALAN MENKEN.

BUGSY, A Tri-Star Pictures Production, Tri-Star: ENNIO MORRICONE.

THE FISHER KING, A Tri-Star Pictures Production, Tri-Star: GEORGE FENTON.

JFK, A Camelot Production, Warner Bros.: JOHN WILLIAMS.

THE PRINCE OF TIDES, A Barwood/ Longfellow Production, Columbia: JAMES NEWTON HOWARD.

Original Song Score

No nominations.

Original Song

★ BEAUTY AND THE BEAST from *Beauty and the Beast*, A Walt Disney Pictures Production, Buena Vista: Music by ALAN MENKEN; Lyrics by HOWARD ASHMAN.

BELLE from *Beauty and the Beast*, A Walt Disney Pictures Production, Buena Vista: Music by ALAN MENKEN; Lyrics by HOWARD ASHMAN.

BE OUR GUEST from *Beauty and the Beast*, A Walt Disney Pictures Production, Buena Vista: Music by ALAN MENKEN; Lyrics by HOWARD ASHMAN.

(EVERYTHING I DO) I DO IT FOR YOU from *Robin Hood: Prince of Thieves*, A Morgan Creek Production, Warner

Bros.: Music by MICHAEL KAMEN; Lyrics by BRYAN ADAMS and ROBERT JOHN LANGE.

WHEN YOU'RE ALONE from *Hook*, A Tri-Star Pictures Production, Tri-Star: Music by JOHN WILLIAMS; Lyrics by LESLIE BRICUSSE.

Costume Design

THE ADDAMS FAMILY, A Scott Rudin Production, Paramount: RUTH MYERS.

BARTON FINK, A Barton Circle Production, 20th Century-Fox: RICHARD HORNUNG.

★ BUGSY, A Tri-Star Pictures Production, Tri-Star: ALBERT WOLSKY.

HOOK, A Tri-Star Pictures Production, Tri-Star: ANTHONY POWELL.

MADAME BOVARY, An MK2/C.E.D./FR3 Films Production, Samuel Goldwyn Company: CORRINE JORY.

Make-up

HOOK, A Tri-Star Pictures Production, Tri-Star: CHRISTINA SMITH, MONTAGUE WESTMORE, and GREG CANNOM.

STAR TREK VI: THE UNDISCOVERED COUNTRY, A Paramount Pictures Production, Paramount: MICHAEL MILLS, EDWARD FRENCH, and RICHARD SNELL.

★ TERMINATOR 2: JUDGMENT DAY, A Carolco Production, Tri-Star: STAN WINSTON and JEFF DAWN.

Visual Effects

BACKDRAFT, A Trilogy Entertainment Group/Brian Grazer Production, Universal: MIKAEL SALOMON, ALLEN HALL, CLAY PINNEY, and SCOTT FARRAR.

HOOK, A Tri-Star Pictures Production, Tri-Star: ERIC BREVIG, HARLEY JESSUP, MARK SULLIVAN, and MICHAEL LANTIERI.

★ TERMINATOR 2: JUDGMENT DAY, A Carolco Production, Tri-Star: DENNIS MUREN, STAN WINSTON, GENE WARREN, JR., and ROBERT SKOTAK.

Sound Effects Editing

BACKDRAFT, A Trilogy Entertainment Group/Brian Grazer Production, Universal: GARY RYDSTROM and RICHARD HYMNS.

STAR TREK VI: THE UNDISCOVERED COUNTRY, A Paramount Pictures Production, Paramount: GEORGE WATTERS II and F. HUDSON MILLER.

★ TERMINATOR 2: JUDGMENT DAY, A Carolco Production, Tri-Star: GARY RYDSTROM and GLORIA S. BORDERS.

Short Films

Animated

BLACKFLY, A National Film Board of Canada Production: CHRISTOPHER HINTON, Producer.

★ MANIPULATION, A Tandem Films Production: DANIEL GREAVES, Producer.

STRINGS, A National Film Board of Canada Production: WENDY TILBY, Producer.

Live Action

BIRCH STREET GYM, Chanticleer Films Production: STEPHEN KESSLER and T. R. CONROY, Producers.

LAST BREEZE OF SUMMER, American Film Institute Production: DAVID M. MASSEY, Producer.

★ SESSION MAN, Chanticleer Films Production: SETH WINSTON and ROB FRIED, Producers.

Documentary

Short Subjects

BIRDNESTERS OF THAILAND (A.K.A. SHADOW HUNTERS), Antenne 2/

National Geographic Society/M.D.I./ Wind Horse Production: ERIC VALLI and ALAIN MAJANI, Producers.

★ DEADLY DECEPTION: GENERAL ELECTRIC, NUCLEAR WEAPONS AND OUR ENVIRONMENT, Women's Educational Media, Inc., Production: DEBRA CHASNOFF, Producer.

A LITTLE VICIOUS, Film and Video Workshop, Inc., Production: IMMY HUMES, Producer.

THE MARK OF THE MAKER, McGowan Film and Video, Inc.: DAVID MCGOWAN, Producer.

MEMORIAL: LETTERS FROM AMERICAN SOLDIERS, Couturie Company Production: BILL COUTURIE and BERNARD EDELMAN, Producers.

Features

DEATH ON THE JOB, Half-Court Pictures, Ltd., Production: VINCE DIPERSIO and WILLIAM GUTTENTAG, Producers.

DOING TIME: LIFE INSIDE THE BIG HOUSE, Video Verité Production: ALAN RAYMOND and SUSAN RAYMOND, Producers.

★ IN THE SHADOW OF THE STARS, Light-Saraf Films Production: ALLIE LIGHT and IRVING SARAF, Producers. (First Run Features).

THE RESTLESS CONSCIENCE: RESISTANCE TO HITLER WITHIN GERMANY 1933–1945, Hava Kohav Beller Production: HAVA KOHAV BELLER, Producer.

WILD BY LAW, Florentine Films Production: LAWRENCE HOTT and DIANE GAREY, Producers.

Foreign Language Film Award

CHILDREN OF NATURE, An Icelandic Film Corporation Ltd./Max Film (Berlin)/Metro Film (Oslo) Production (Iceland).

THE ELEMENTARY SCHOOL, A Barrandov Film Studio Production (Czechoslovakia).

★ MEDITERRANEO, A Pentafilm S.p.A./A.M.A. Film S.r.l. Film Production, Miramax (Italy).

THE OX, A Sweetland Films AB/Jean Doumanian Production (Sweden).

RAISE THE RED LANTERN, An ERA International (HK) Ltd. Presentation in association with China Film Co-production Corporation Production, Orion Classics (Hong Kong).

Honorary Awards

SATYAJIT RAY for his rare mastery of the art of motion pictures and for his profound humanitarian outlook, which has had an indelible influence on filmmakers and audiences throughout the world.

Medals of Commendation

RICHARD J. STUMPF and JOSEPH WESTHEIMER in appreciation for outstanding service and dedication in upholding the high standards of the Academy of Motion Picture Arts and Sciences.

Award of Commendation (Special plaque)

PETE COMANDINI, RICHARD T. DAYTON, DONALD HAGANS, and RICHARD T. RYAN of YCM Laboratories for the creation and development of a motion picture film restoration process using liquid gate and registration correction on a contact printer.

Special Achievement Award

None.

Irving G. Thalberg Memorial Award

GEORGE LUCAS.

Jean Hersholt Humanitarian Award

None.

Gordon E. Sawyer Award

RAY HARRYHAUSEN.

Scientific or Technical Awards

Academy Award of Merit (Academy statuette)

None.

Scientific and Engineering Award (Academy plaque)

IAIN NEIL for the optical design, ALBERT SAIKI for the mechanical design, and PANAVISION, INC., for the concept and development of the Primo Zoom Lens for 35mm cinematography.

GEORG THOMA for the design and HEINZ FEIERLEIN and the engineering department of SACHTLER AG for the development of a range of fluid tripod heads.

HARRY J. BAKER for the design and development of the first full fluid-action tripod head with adjustable degrees of viscous drag.

GUIDO CARTONI for his pioneering work in developing the technology to achieve selectable and repeatable viscous drag modules in fluid tripod heads.

RAY FEENEY, RICHARD KEENEY, and RICHARD J. LUNDELL for the software development and adaptation of the Solitaire Film Recorder which provides a flexible, cost-effective film recording system.

FAZ FAZAKAS, BRIAN HENSON, DAVE HOUSMAN, PETER MILLER, and JOHN STEPHENSON for the development of the Henson Performance Control System.

MARIO CELSO for his pioneering work in the design, development, and manufacture of equipment for carbon arc and xenon power supplies and igniters used in motion picture projection.

RANDY CARTWRIGHT, DAVID B. COONS, LEM DAVIS, THOMAS HAHN, JAMES HOUSTON, MARK KIMBALL, PETER NYE, MICHAEL SHANTZIS, DAVID F. WOLF, and THE WALT DISNEY FEATURE ANIMATION DEPARTMENT for the design and development of the "CAPS" production system for feature film animation.

GEORGE WORRALL for the design, development, and manufacture of the Worrall geared camera head for motion picture production.

Technical Achievement Award (Academy certificate)

ROBERT W. STOKER, JR., for the design and development of a cobweb gun for applying nontoxic cobweb effects on motion picture sets with both safety and ease of operation.

JAMES DOYLE for the design and development of the Dry Fogger, which uses liquid nitrogen to produce a safe, dense, low-hanging dry fog.

DICK CAVDEK, STEVE HAMERSKI, and OTTO NEMENZ INTERNATIONAL, INC., for the optomechanical design and development of the Canon/Nemenz Zoom Lens.

KEN ROBINGS and CLAIRMONT CAMERA for the optomechanical design and development of the Canon/Clairmont Camera Zoom Lens.

CENTURY PRECISION OPTICS for the optomechanical design and development of the Canon/Century Precision Optics Zoom Lens.

SIXTY-FIFTH YEAR

1992

Nominations Announced: February 17, 1993
Awards Ceremony: March 29, 1993
Dorothy Chandler Pavilion, Los Angeles County Music Center
(MC: Billy Crystal)

Best Picture

THE CRYING GAME, A Palace Pictures Production, Miramax: Stephen Wooley, Producer.

A FEW GOOD MEN, A Castle Rock Entertainment Production, Columbia: David Brown, Rob Reiner, and Andrew Scheinman, Producers.

HOWARDS END, A Merchant Ivory Production, Sony Pictures Classics: Ismail Merchant, Producer.

SCENT OF A WOMAN, A Universal Pictures Production, Universal: Martin Brest, Producer.

★ UNFORGIVEN, A Warner Bros. Production, Warner Bros.: Clint Eastwood, Producer.

Actor

ROBERT DOWNEY, JR. in *Chaplin*, A Carolco Pictures Production, Tri-Star.

CLINT EASTWOOD in *Unforgiven*, A Warner Bros. Production, Warner Bros.

★ AL PACINO in *Scent of a Woman*, A Universal Pictures Production, Universal.

STEPHEN REA in *The Crying Game*, A Palace Pictures Production, Miramax.

DENZEL WASHINGTON in *Malcolm X*, A By Any Means Necessary Cinema Production, Warner Bros.

Actress

CATHERINE DENEUVE in *Indochine*, A Paradis Films/La Générale d'Images/BAC Films/Orly Films/Ciné Cinq Production, Sony Pictures Classics.

MARY MCDONNELL in *Passion Fish*, An Atchafalaya Films Production, Miramax.

MICHELLE PFEIFFER in *Love Field*, A Sanford/Pillsbury Production, Orion.

SUSAN SARANDON in *Lorenzo's Oil*, A Kennedy Miller Films Production, Universal.

★ EMMA THOMPSON in *Howards End*, A Merchant Ivory Production, Sony Pictures Classics.

Supporting Actor

JAYE DAVIDSON in *The Crying Game*, A Palace Pictures Production, Miramax.

★ GENE HACKMAN in *Unforgiven*, A Warner Bros. Production, Warner Bros.

JACK NICHOLSON in *A Few Good Men*, A Castle Rock Entertainment Production, Columbia.

AL PACINO in *Glengarry Glen Ross*, A Stephanie Lynn Production, New Line.

DAVID PAYMER in *Mr. Saturday Night*, A Castle Rock Entertainment Production, Columbia.

Supporting Actress

JUDY DAVIS in *Husbands and Wives*, A Tri-Star Pictures Production, Tri-Star.

JOAN PLOWRIGHT in *Enchanted April*, A BBC Films Production in association with Greenpoint Films, Miramax.

VANESSA REDGRAVE in *Howards End*, A Merchant Ivory Production, Sony Pictures Classics.

MIRANDA RICHARDSON in *Damage*, A SKREBA/Damage/NEF/Le Studio Canal + Production, New Line.

★ MARISA TOMEI in *My Cousin Vinny*, A 20th Century-Fox Production, 20th Century-Fox.

Directing

ROBERT ALTMAN for *The Player*, An Avenue Pictures Production, Fine Line.

MARTIN BREST for *Scent of a Woman*, A Unversal Pictures Production, Universal.

★ CLINT EASTWOOD for *Unforgiven*, A Warner Bros. Production, Warner Bros.

JAMES IVORY for *Howards End*, A Merchant Ivory Production, Sony Pictures Classics.

NEIL JORDAN for *The Crying Game*, A Palace Pictures Production, Miramax.

Writing

Screenplay Written Directly for the Screen

★ THE CRYING GAME, A Palace Pictures Production, Miramax: Written by NEIL JORDAN.

HUSBANDS AND WIVES, A Tri-Star Pictures Production, Tri-Star: Written by WOODY ALLEN.

LORENZO'S OIL, A Kennedy Miller Films Production, Universal: Screenplay by GEORGE MILLER and NICK ENRIGHT.

PASSION FISH, An Atchafalaya Films Production, Miramax: Written by JOHN SAYLES.

UNFORGIVEN, A Warner Bros. Production, Warner Bros.: Written by DAVID WEBB PEOPLES.

Screenplay Based on Material Previously Produced or Published

ENCHANTED APRIL, A BBC Films Production in association with Greenpoint Films, Miramax: Screenplay by PETER BARNES.

★ HOWARDS END, A Merchant Ivory Production, Sony Pictures Classics: Screenplay by RUTH PRAWER JHABVALA.

THE PLAYER, An Avenue Pictures Production, Fine Line: Screenplay by MICHAEL TOLKIN.

A RIVER RUNS THROUGH IT, A Columbia Pictures Production, Columbia: Screenplay by RICHARD FRIEDENBERG.

SCENT OF A WOMAN, A Universal Pictures Production, Universal: Screenplay by BO GOLDMAN.

Cinematography

HOFFA, A 20th Century-Fox Production, 20th Century-Fox: STEPHEN H. BURUM.

HOWARDS END, A Merchant Ivory Production, Sony Pictures Classics: TONY PIERCE-ROBERTS.

THE LOVER, A Renn Production/Burrill Productions/Films A2, MGM/UA: ROBERT FRAISSE.

★ A RIVER RUNS THROUGH IT, A Columbia Pictures Production, Columbia: PHILIPPE ROUSSELOT.

UNFORGIVEN, A Warner Bros. Production, Warner Bros: JACK N. GREEN.

Art Direction - Set Decoration

BRAM STOKER'S DRACULA, A Columbia Pictures Production, Columbia: THOMAS SANDERS; Set Decoration: GARRETT LEWIS.

CHAPLIN, A Carolco Pictures Production, Tri-Star: STUART CRAIG; Set Decoration: CHRIS A. BUTLER.

★ HOWARDS END, A Merchant Ivory Production, Sony Pictures Classics: LUCIANA ARRIGHI; Set Decoration: IAN WHITTAKER.

TOYS, A 20th Century-Fox Production, 20th Century-Fox: FERDINANDO SCARFIOTTI; Set Decoration: LINDA DESCENNA.

UNFORGIVEN, A Warner Bros. Production, Warner Bros.: HENRY BUMSTEAD, Set Decoration: JANICE BLACKIE-GOODINE.

Sound

ALADDIN, A Walt Disney Pictures Production, Buena Vista: TERRY PORTER, MEL METCALFE, DAVID J. HUDSON, and DOC KANE.

A FEW GOOD MEN, A Castle Rock Entertainment Production, Columbia: KEVIN O'CONNELL, RICK KLINE, and BOB EBER.

★ THE LAST OF THE MOHICANS, A 20th Century-Fox Production, 20th Century-Fox: CHRIS JENKINS, DOUG HEMPHILL, MARK SMITH, and SIMON KAYE.

UNDER SIEGE, A Northwest Production, Warner Bros.: DON MITCHELL, FRANK A. MONTANO, RICK HART, and SCOTT SMITH.

UNFORGIVEN, A Warner Bros. Production, Warner Bros.: LES FRESHOLTZ, VERN POORE, DICK ALEXANDER, and ROB YOUNG.

Film Editing

BASIC INSTINCT, A Carolco Production, Tri-Star: FRANK J. URIOSTE.

THE CRYING GAME, A Palace Pictures Production, Miramax: KANT PAN.

A FEW GOOD MEN, A Castle Rock Entertainment Production, Columbia: ROBERT LEIGHTON.

THE PLAYER, An Avenue Pictures Production, Fine Line: GERALDINE PERONI.

★ UNFORGIVEN, A Warner Bros. Production, Warner Bros.: JOEL COX.

Music

Original Score

★ ALADDIN, A Walt Disney Pictures Production, Buena Vista: ALAN MENKEN.

BASIC INSTINCT, A Carolco Production, Tri-Star: JERRY GOLDSMITH.

CHAPLIN, A Carolco Pictures Production, Tri-Star: JOHN BARRY.

HOWARDS END, A Merchant Ivory Production, Sony Pictures Classics: RICHARD ROBBINS.

A RIVER RUNS THROUGH IT, A Columbia Pictures Production, Columbia: MARK ISHAM.

Original Song Score

No nominations.

Original Song

BEAUTIFUL MARIA OF MY SOUL from *The Mambo Kings*, A Northwest Production, Warner Bros.: Music by ROBERT KRAFT; Lyrics by ARNE GLIMCHER.

FRIEND LIKE ME from *Aladdin*, A Walt Disney Pictures Production, Buena Vista: Music by ALAN MENKEN; Lyrics by HOWARD ASHMAN.

I HAVE NOTHING from *The Bodyguard*, A Warner Bros. Production, Warner Bros.: Music by DAVID FOSTER; Lyrics by LINDA THOMPSON.

RUN TO YOU from *The Bodyguard*, A Warner Bros. Production, Warner

Bros.: Music by JUD FRIEDMAN; Lyrics by ALLAN RICH.

★ WHOLE NEW WORLD from *Aladdin*, A Walt Disney Pictures Production, Buena Vista: Music by ALAN MENKEN; Lyrics by TIM RICE.

Costume Design

★ BRAM STOKER'S DRACULA, A Columbia Pictures Production, Columbia: EIKO ISHIOKA.

ENCHANTED APRIL, A BBC Films Production in association with Greenpoint Films, Miramax: SHEENA NAPIER.

HOWARDS END, A Merchant Ivory Production, Sony Pictures Classics: JENNY BEAVAN and JOHN BRIGHT.

MALCOLM X, A By Any Means Necessary Cinema Production, Warner Bros.: RUTH CARTER.

TOYS, A 20th Century-Fox Production, 20th Century-Fox: ALBERT WOLSKY.

Make-up

BATMAN RETURNS, A Warner Bros. Production, Warner Bros.: VE NEILL, RONNIE SPECTER, and STAN WINSTON.

★ BRAM STOKER'S DRACULA, A Columbia Pictures Production, Columbia: GREG CANNOM, MICHÈLE BURKE, and MATTHEW W. MUNGLE.

HOFFA, A 20th Century-Fox Production, 20th Century-Fox: VE NEILL, GREG CANNOM, and JOHN BLAKE.

Visual Effects

ALIEN[3], A 20th Century-Fox Production, 20th Century-Fox: RICHARD EDLUND, ALEC GILLIS, TOM WOODRUFF, JR., and GEORGE GIBBS.

BATMAN RETURNS, A Warner Bros. Production, Warner Bros.: MICHAEL FINK, CRAIG BARRON, JOHN BRUNO, and DENNIS SKOTAK.

★ DEATH BECOMES HER, A Universal Pictures Production, Universal: KEN RALSTON, DOUG CHIANG, DOUG SMYTHE, and TOM WOODRUFF.

Sound Effects Editing

ALADDIN, A Walt Disney Pictures Production, Buena Vista: MARK MANGINI.

★ BRAM STOKER'S DRACULA, A Columbia Pictures Production, Columbia: TOM C. MCCARTHY and DAVID E. STONE.

UNDER SIEGE, A Northwest Production, Warner Bros.: JOHN LEVEQUE and BRUCE STAMBLER.

Short Films

Animated

ADAM, An Aardman Animations Ltd. Production: PETER LORD, Producer.

★ MONA LISA DESCENDING A STAIRCASE, A Joan C. Gratz Production: JOAN C. GRATZ, Producer.

ŘEČI, ŘEČI, ŘEČI . . . (WORDS, WORDS, WORDS), A Krátký Film Production: MICHAELA PAVLÁTOVÁ, Producer.

THE SANDMAN, A Batty Berry Mackinnon Production: PAUL BERRY, Producer.

SCREEN PLAY, A Bare Boards Film Production: BARRY J.C. PURVES, Producer.

Live Action

(Not given after this year.)

CONTACT, A Chanticleer Films, Inc. Production: JONATHAN DARBY and JANA SUE MEMEL, Producers.

CRUISE CONTROL, A Palmieri Pictures Production: MATT PALMIERI, Producer.

THE LADY IN WAITING, A Taylor Made Films Production: CHRISTIAN M. TAYLOR, Producer.

★ OMNIBUS, A Lazennec tout court/

Le C.R.R.A.V. Production: SAM KARMANN, Producer.

SWAN SONG, A Renaissance Films PLC Production: KENNETH BRANAGH, Producer.

Documentary

Short Subjects

(Not given after this year.)

AT THE EDGE OF CONQUEST: THE JOURNEY OF CHIEF WAI-WAI, A Realis Pictures, Inc. Production: GEOFFREY O'CONNOR, Producer.

BEYOND IMAGINING: MARGARET ANDERSON AND THE "LITTLE REVIEW," A Wendy L. Weinberg Production: WENDY L. WEINBERG, Producer.

THE COLOURS OF MY FATHER: A PORTRAIT OF SAM BORENSTEIN, An Imageries P.B. Ltd. Production in coproduction with the National Film Board of Canada: RICHARD ELSON and SALLY BOCHNER, Producers.

★ EDUCATING PETER, A State of the Art, Inc. Production: THOMAS C. GOODWIN and GERARDINE WURZBURG, Producers.

WHEN ABORTION WAS ILLEGAL: UNTOLD STORIES, A Concentric Media Production: DOROTHY FADIMAN, Producer.

Features

CHANGING OUR MINDS: THE STORY OF DR. EVELYN HOOKER, An Intrepid Production: DAVID HAUGLAND, Producer.

FIRES OF KUWAIT, A Black Sun Films, Ltd./IMAX Corporation Production: SALLY DUNDAS, Producer.

LIBERATORS: FIGHTING ON TWO FRONTS IN WORLD WAR II, A Miles Educational Film Productions, Inc. Production: WILLIAM MILES and NINA ROSENBLUM, Producers.

MUSIC FOR THE MOVIES: BERNARD HERRMANN, An Alternate Current Inc./Les Films d'Ici Production: MARGARET SMILOV and ROMA BARAN, Producers.

★ THE PANAMA DECEPTION, An Empowerment Project Production: BARBARA TRENT and DAVID KASPER, Producers.

Foreign Language Film Award

CLOSE TO EDEN, A Camera One-Hachette premiere et Compagnie/ UGC Images (France)/Studio Trite (URSS) Production (Russia).

DAENS, A Favourite Films/Films Dérives/Titane & Shooting Star Filmcompany Production (Belgium).

★ INDOCHINE, A Paradis Films/La Générale d'Images/BAC Films/Orly Films/Ciné Cinq Production (France).

A PLACE IN THE WORLD, An Adolfo Aristarain/Osvaldo Papaleo/Mirna Rosales Production (Uruguay).*

SCHTONK, A Bavaria Film GmbH Production (Germany).

Honorary Awards

FEDERICO FELLINI in appreciation of one of the screen's master storytellers.

Medal of Commendation

PETRO VLAHOS in appreciation for outstanding service and dedication in upholding the high standards of the Academy of Motion Picture Arts and Sciences.

Special Achievement Award

None.

Irving G. Thalberg Memorial Award

None.

*Disqualified after the nominations were announced.

Jean Hersholt Humanitarian Award

AUDREY HEPBURN
ELIZABETH TAYLOR

Gordon E. Sawyer Award

ERICH KAESTNER

Scientific or Technical Awards

Academy Award of Merit (Oscar)

CHADWELL O'CONNOR of the O'Connor Engineering Laboratories for the concept and engineering of the fluid-damped camera-head for motion picture photography.

Scientific and Engineering Awards (Academy plaque)

LOREN CARPENTER, ROB COOK, ED CATMULL, TOM PORTER, PAT HANRAHAN, TONY APODACA and DARWYN PEACHEY for the development of "RenderMan" software which produces images used in motion pictures from 3D computer descriptions of shape and appearance.

CLAUS WIEDEMANN and ROBERT ORBAN for the design and DOLBY LABORATORIES for the development of the Dolby Labs "Container."

KEN BATES for the design and development of the Bates Decelerator System for accurately and safely arresting the descent of stunt persons in high freefalls.

AL MAYER for the Camera Design; IAIN NEIL and GEORGE KRAEMER for the optical design; HANS SPIRAWSKI and BILL ESLICK for the opto-mechanical design and DON EARL for technical support in developing the Panavision System 65 Studio Sync Sound Reflex Camera for 65mm motion picture photography.

DOUGLAS TRUMBULL for the concept; GEOFFREY H. WILLIAMSON for the movement design; ROBERT D. AUGUSTE for the electronic design and EDMUND M. DIGIULIO for the camera system design of the CP-65 Showscan Camera System for 65mm motion picture photography.

ARRIFLEX CORPORATION, OTTO BLASCHEK and the ENGINEERING DEPARTMENT OF ARRI, AUSTRIA for the design and development of the Arriflex 765 Camera System for 65mm motion picture photography.

Technical Achievement Award (Academy certificate)

IRA TIFFEN of the Tiffen Manufacturing Corporation for the production of the Ultra Contrast Filter Series for motion picture photography.

ROBERT R. BURTON of Audio Rents, Incorporated, for the development of the Model S-27 4-Band Splitter/Combiner.

IAIN NEIL for the optical design and KAZ FUDANO for the mechanical design of the Panavision Slant Focus Lens for motion picture photography.

TOM BRIGHAM for the original concept and pioneering work; and DOUGLAS SMYTHE and the COMPUTER GRAPHICS DEPARTMENT OF INDUSTRIAL LIGHT & MAGIC for development and the first implementation in feature motion pictures of the "MORF" system for digital metamorphosis of high resolution images.

APPENDICES

APPENDIX I

Academy Founders

On the evening of January 11, 1927, thirty-six persons who represented a cross section of the film industry held a dinner at the Ambassador Hotel in Los Angeles to discuss the formation of an organization that would benefit the motion picture industry. These people became the founders of the Academy of Motion Picture Arts and Sciences.

The branch of the Academy that each member joined is indicated after the name.

J. ARTHUR BALL (1895–1951) Technicians Branch. Pioneer color film engineer. Cameraman and later technical director of Technicolor.

RICHARD BARTHELMESS (1895–1963) Actors Branch. Leading man for First National whose most memorable films were *Broken Blossoms* and *Tol'able David.* Formed his own company in 1921.

FRED BEETSON (1879–1953) Producers Branch. Came to Hollywood in 1923 at the request of Will Hays. An officer of the Association of Motion Picture Producers for nearly twenty years, also organizer and president of the Central Casting Corporation and a founder and vice-president of the Motion Picture Relief Fund.

CHARLES H. CHRISTIE (1880–1955) Producers Branch. Coproducer with brother Al of the Christie Comedies. Vice president and general manager of Christie Studios.

GEORGE W. COHEN (1895–1971) Special member. Known as the "father of motion picture contracts." As a member of the law firm of Loeb, Walker, and Loeb, he represented several studios and, with Edwin Loeb, drew up the constitution and by-laws of the Academy.

CECIL B. DEMILLE (1881–1959) Directors Branch. Pioneer Hollywood producer and director. In 1913, with Jesse Lasky, Samuel Goldwyn, and Arthur Friend, formed the Jesse L. Lasky Feature Play Company. Later founded his own production company. Active in the Association of Motion Picture Producers.

DOUGLAS FAIRBANKS, SR. (1883–1939) Actors Branch. Swashbuckling leading man. Began film career in 1914 with D. W. Griffith. In 1919, with Mary Pickford, Charlie Chaplin, and Griffith, formed United Artists. Married Pickford in 1920. First president of the Academy of Motion Picture Arts and Sciences.

JOSEPH WHITE FARNHAM (1884–1931) Writers Branch. After a career as writer, independent exhibitor, and advertising manager for Lubin, came to Hollywood as a free-lance editor and writer. In 1924 joined MGM as title writer and editor.

CEDRIC GIBBONS (1895–1960) Technicians Branch. Came to Hollywood with the Goldwyn Company. Became head of MGM's art department when Goldwyn merged with Metro.

BENJAMIN F. GLAZER (1888–1956)

Writers Branch. Screenwriter who worked for several studios including Paramount, Fox, and MGM. In 1928 became head of production for Pathé.

SID GRAUMAN (1879–1950) Producers Branch. Veteran movie exhibitor. Built the Million Dollar Theatre in Los Angeles, also the Metropolitan, Egyptian, and Chinese. Credited by *Variety* with originating the gala Hollywood premiere.

MILTON E. HOFFMAN (1880–1952) Producers Branch. Started with Paramount in 1916, later worked for MGM and for Cecil B. DeMille. In 1924 became executive studio manager for Paramount.

JACK HOLT (1888–1951) Actors Branch. Broke into pictures as a stunt man in 1913, eventually became a star for Columbia.

HENRY KING (1888–1982) Directors Branch. Entered films as an actor for the Lubin Co., in 1912. Began directing in 1916 for Pathé. In the 1920s directed for First National, Paramount, Goldwyn, and United Artists. From 1930 on directed for Fox.

JESSE L. LASKY (1880–1958) Producers Branch. In 1913, with DeMille, Goldwyn, and Arthur Friend, formed Jesse L. Lasky Feature Play Company. Became vice president in charge of production after merger with Adolph Zukor's Famous Players in 1916.

M. C. LEVEE (1891–1972) Producers Branch. Began with Fox in 1917. Senior executive with Paramount, vice president of United Studios, then vice president and executive business manager of First National. First treasurer of the Academy of Motion Picture Arts and Sciences.

FRANK LLOYD (1889–1960) Directors Branch. Began directing in 1913. Formed his own production company in 1923 and worked as a producer-director releasing through First National.

HAROLD LLOYD (1893–1971) Actors Branch. Comedian best known for perilous comic situations involving dangerous stunts. Began film work in 1916. First contract was with Hal Roach. Formed his own production company in 1923.

EDWIN LOEB (1887–1970) Special member. Founder of a law firm widely known for motion picture contract work. In 1927 the Academy expressed its indebtedness to Loeb and George Cohen of Loeb, Walker, and Loeb "for their untiring and able services, voluntarily tendered in drafting the Constitution and By-laws, and for other legal work and advice."

JEANIE MACPHERSON (1887–1946) Writers Branch. Began as an actress with Florence Lawrence and Mary Pickford. Later had her own unit at Universal where she wrote, directed, and acted in two-reelers. Fired for taking seven days on a production. Hired by Cecil B. DeMille and became best known as a screenwriter for him.

LOUIS B. MAYER (1885–1957) Producers Branch. Vice president in charge of production for MGM. Began producing films in 1916. Formed his own company which he merged with Loew's Metro and Goldwyn's company to form MGM in 1924.

BESS MEREDYTH (1890–1969) Writers Branch. Started as an extra for Biograph. Began writing screenplays for Griffith in 1913, later worked for several studios. Co-scripted (with Carey Wilson) *Ben Hur* for MGM.

CONRAD NAGEL (1897–1970) Actors Branch. Leading man for MGM. Active in Actors' Equity and then the Academy in trying to negotiate a standard contract for actors.

FRED NIBLO (1874–1948) Directors Branch. After much stage experience, entered films in 1917 as actor, director, and producer. Directed *The Mark of Zorro*, *Blood and Sand*, *Ben Hur*. Became one of MGM's top directors in the 1920s. First vice president of the Academy of Motion Picture Arts and Sciences.

MARY PICKFORD (1893–1979) Producers Branch. Started in films with Griffith at Biograph. Organized her own company in 1916 and became an independent producer in 1918. The following year she founded United Artists with Fairbanks, Chaplin, and Griffith.

ROY J. POMEROY (1893–1947) Technicians Branch. Joined Lasky in 1922 and became head of special photographic effects department for Paramount. Parted the Red Sea for DeMille's *Ten Commandments*. Later worked on sound production and directed Paramount's first all-talking picture, *Interference*.

HARRY RAPF (1881–1949) Producers Branch. Joined Mayer in 1924 and became producer, later production executive for MGM.

JOSEPH M. SCHENCK (1878–1961) Producers Branch. Veteran showman and movie mogul. In 1924 became chairman of the board of United Artists. Later founded Twentieth Century Productions.

MILTON SILLS (1882–1930) Actors Branch. Leading man for First National. One of the founders of Actors' Equity.

JOHN M. STAHL (1886–1950) Directors Branch. Began directing films in 1914. Directed for First National, then MGM in the 1920s. In 1928 became vice president supervising production for Tiffany-Stahl Productions.

IRVING G. THALBERG (1899–1936) Producers Branch. Started with Universal in 1917, became studio manager at age twenty-one. Became head of production for Louis B. Mayer's company in 1923. When MGM was formed, became second only to Mayer in charge of production.

RAOUL WALSH (1887–1980) Directors Branch. Joined Biograph in 1912 as an actor and assistant to D. W. Griffith. Directed films for various companies including Fox and Paramount.

HARRY WARNER (1881–1958) Producers Branch. Eldest of the four Warner brothers. Named president when the studio was founded in 1923.

JACK L. WARNER (1892–1978) Producers Branch. Youngest of the four Warner brothers. Active in film exhibition and distribution from 1905. Began film production with brother Sam in 1912. Named vice president in charge of production when Warner Brothers Studio was founded in 1923.

CAREY WILSON (1889–1962) Writers Branch. Top screenwriter for Thalberg at MGM. Co-scripted (with Bess Meredyth) *Ben Hur* and many other MGM hits.

FRANK WOODS (1860–1939) Writers Branch. Film critic for the New York *Dramatic Mirror*. In 1911 joined D. W. Griffith as a story editor. Convinced Griffith to film *The Clansman*. Became scenario chief at Famous Players-Lasky. First secretary of the Academy of Motion Picture Arts and Sciences.

APPENDIX II

Academy Presidents

Douglas Fairbanks, Sr.	May 4, 1927–October 1929
William C. DeMille	October 1929–October 1931
M. C. Levee	October 1931–October 1932
Conrad Nagel (resigned)	October 1932–April 1933
J. Theodore Reed	April 1933–October 1934
Frank Lloyd	October 1934–October 1935
Frank Capra (no elections held 1936/37 and 1937/38)	October 1935–December 1939
Walter Wanger	December 1939–October 1941
Bette Davis (resigned)	October 1941–December 1941
Walter Wanger	December 1941–October 1945
Jean Hersholt	October 1945–May 1949
Charles Brackett	May 1949–May 1955
George Seaton	June 1955–May 1958
George Stevens	June 1958–May 1959
B. B. Kahane (died in office)	June 1959–September 1960
Valentine Davies (died in office)	September 1960–July 1961
Wendell R. Corey	August 1961–May 1963
Arthur Freed	June 1963–May 1967
Gregory Peck	June 1967–May 1970
Daniel Taradash	June 1970–May 1973
Walter Mirisch	June 1973–May 1977
Howard W. Koch	June 1977–July 1979
Fay Kanin	July 1979–July 1983
Gene Allen	July 1983–July 1985
Robert Wise	July 1985–July 1988
Richard Kahn	July 1988–July 1989
Karl Malden	July 1989–August 1992
Robert Rehme	August 1992–Present

APPENDIX III

Directors of Best Picture

Year	*Film*	*Director*
1927/28	Wings	William A. Wellman
1928/29	Broadway Melody	Harry Beaumont
1929/30	All Quiet on the Western Front	Lewis Milestone*
1930/31	Cimarron	Wesley Ruggles
1931/32	Grand Hotel	Edmund Goulding
1932/33	Cavalcade	Frank Lloyd*
1934	It Happened One Night	Frank Capra*
1935	Mutiny on the Bounty	Frank Lloyd
1936	The Great Ziegfeld	Robert Z. Leonard
1937	The Life of Emile Zola	William Dieterle
1938	You Can't Take It with You	Frank Capra*
1939	Gone with the Wind	Victor Fleming*
1940	Rebecca	Alfred Hitchcock
1941	How Green Was My Valley	John Ford*
1942	Mrs. Miniver	William Wyler*
1943	Casablanca	Michael Curtiz*
1944	Going My Way	Leo McCarey*
1945	The Lost Weekend	Billy Wilder*
1946	The Best Years of Our Lives	William Wyler*
1947	Gentlemen's Agreement	Elia Kazan*
1948	Hamlet	Laurence Olivier
1949	All the King's Men	Robert Rossen
1950	All About Eve	Joseph L. Mankiewicz*
1951	An American in Paris	Vincente Minnelli
1952	The Greatest Show on Earth	Cecil B. DeMille
1953	From Here to Eternity	Fred Zinnemann*
1954	On the Waterfront	Elia Kazan*
1955	Marty	Delbert Mann*
1956	Around the World in Eighty Days	Michael Anderson
1957	The Bridge on the River Kwai	David Lean*

*Also won Oscar for Directing.

DIRECTORS OF BEST PICTURE

Year	*Film*	*Director*
1958	Gigi	Vincente Minnelli*
1959	Ben-Hur	William Wyler*
1960	The Apartment	Billy Wilder*
1961	West Side Story	Robert Wise,* Jerome Robbins*
1962	Lawrence of Arabia	David Lean*
1963	Tom Jones	Tony Richardson*
1964	My Fair Lady	George Cukor*
1065	The Sound of Music	Robert Wise*
1966	A Man for All Seasons	Fred Zinnemann*
1967	In the Heat of the Night	Norman Jewison
1968	Oliver	Carol Reed*
1969	Midnight Cowboy	John Schlesinger*
1970	Patton	Franklin J. Schaffner*
1971	The French Connection	William Friedkin*
1972	The Godfather	Francis Ford Coppola
1973	The Sting	George Roy Hill*
1974	The Godfather II	Francis Ford Coppola*
1975	One Flew over the Cuckoo's Nest	Milos Forman*
1976	Rocky	John G. Avildsen*
1977	Annie Hall	Woody Allen*
1978	The Deer Hunter	Michael Cimino*
1979	Kramer vs. Kramer	Robert Benton*
1980	Ordinary People	Robert Redford*
1981	Chariots of Fire	Hugh Hudson
1982	Gandhi	Richard Attenborough*
1983	Terms of Endearment	James L. Brooks*
1984	Amadeus	Milos Forman*
1985	Out of Africa	Sydney Pollack*
1986	Platoon	Oliver Stone*
1987	The Last Emperor	Bernardo Bertolucci*
1988	Rain Man	Barry Levinson*
1989	Driving Miss Daisy	Bruce Beresford
1990	Dances with Wolves	Kevin Costner*
1991	The Silence of the Lambs	Jonathan Demme*
1992	Unforgiven	Clint Eastwood*

Selected Bibliography

The following list includes books published by the Academy of Motion Picture Arts and Sciences, books specifically about the Oscars, and those film histories, biographies, and other works that mention the Academy in a significant way.

For articles on specific Oscar shows, the reader is encouraged to check the specific dates of the presentations and then consult the major Hollywood trade papers such as *Variety* or the *Hollywood Reporter* and newspapers such as the *Los Angeles Times* and *New York Times*. Indexes such as *Film Literature Index*, *Reader's Guide to Periodical Literature*, and databases such as InfoTrac will lead the researcher to long lists of citations on the Academy and the awards. (InfoTrac's General Periodicals Index comes in both a Public Library version and an Academic Library version; it is wise to consult both.)

Books

Academy of Motion Picture Arts and Sciences. *Academy War Film Library Catalog of Prints: May 1942–May 1944*. Hollywood, CA: AMPAS, 1944. 109 pp., indexed. A list of over four hundred films from the United States, Great Britain, Canada, Australia, and Belgium that the Academy collected during the war "primarily as an aid to studio production."

———. *Motion Picture Sound Engineering*. New York: Van Nostrand, 1938. 547 pp., indexed. Reprint of lectures sponsored by the Research Council. Updates the Academy's 1931 book on sound and includes an appendix list of members who served on Research Council committees.

———. *Press Clippings File on the Senate Sub-Committee War Film Hearings, Volume One, August 1–October 15, 1941*. 294 pp., indexed. Fascinating collection of cartoons and clippings from newspapers, studio press releases, trade papers, and the Congressional Record concerning the investigation by Senate isolationists who complained of Hollywood war propaganda. Limited edition of 175 copies printed.

Altman, Richard. *And the Envelope, Please*. New York: J. B. Lippincott, 1978. 160 pp., illustrated. A quiz book on the Academy Awards with lots of stumpers to entertain trivia buffs who enjoy this sort of sport.

Bergan, Ronald, Graham Fuller, and David Malcolm. *Academy Award Winners*. New York: Crescent Books, 1986. 312 pp., indexed. As the title implies, winners are listed but not nominees. Lots of nicely reproduced photos. Brief, informative commentary on each year through the 58th Awards (1985).

Brown, Peter. *The Real Oscar: The Story behind the Academy Awards*. Westport, CT: Arlington House, 1981. 240 pp., indexed. Carefully researched and stylishly written account of Oscar's darker side—stories the Academy probably wishes everyone would forget. The author is a veteran Hollywood reporter with solid credentials.

Brown, Peter, and Jim Pinkston. *Oscar Dearest: Six Decades of Scandal, Politics and Greed behind Hollywood's Academy Awards 1927–1986*. New York: Harper & Row, 1987. 306 pp., indexed. An updated edition of Brown's *The Real Oscar*. The authors include a good annotated bibliography and an interesting final chapter listing who won but shouldn't have, who should have won but didn't, and who won for the wrong reasons.

Capra, Frank. *The Name above the Title*. New York: Macmillan, 1971. 562 pp., indexed. Autobiography of the director who won three Oscars and served as president of the Academy from 1935 to 1939. An insider's view of the most crisis-ridden period in the Academy's history.

Clark, Henry. *Academy Award Diary: 1928–1955*. New York: Pageant Press, 1959. 188 pp., no index. Year-by-year account of the awards with little analysis or critical comment. The design of the book makes the material nearly inaccessible.

Cohen, Daniel, and Susan Cohen. *History of the Oscars*. London: Bison Books, 1986. 192 pp., indexed. Emphasis is on pictures rather than text. Nominees listed only for the major categories. Similar to *Academy Award Winners* by Bergan, Fuller, and Malcolm.

Cowan, Lester, ed. *Recording Sound for Motion Pictures*. New York: McGraw-Hill, 1931. 404 pp., indexed. Reprint of lectures first published in the Academy's Technical Digest series. In his preface, Academy president William de Mille wrote: "[I]f the Academy had not been organized to make such cooperation [between studio sound technicians] possible, this book would never have been written, and we offer it to the craft with a certain paternal glow."

Crowther, Bosley. *Hollywood Rajah: The Life and Times of Louis B. Mayer*. New York: Henry Holt, 1960. 339 pp., indexed. Some brief references to the founding of the Academy.

Dodds, John C., and Morris B. Holbrook. "What's an Oscar Worth? An Empirical Estimation of the Effects of Nominations and Awards on Movie Distribution and Revenues." *Current Research in Film: Audiences, Economics, and Law, Vol. 4*. Ed. Bruce Austin. Norwood, New Jersey: Ablex, 1988. Pp. 72–88. Using box office data from 1975 to 1984, the authors provide empirical evidence supporting the conventional wisdom that says an Oscar nomination or award increases a film's distribution and ticket sales.

Eder, Shirley. *Not This Time, Cary Grant!* New York: Doubleday, 1973. 295 pp., no index. A short section called "Oscar Memories" is a personal glimpse of the 1971 Awards by a veteran Hollywood gossip columnist.

Edmonds, I. G., and Reiko Mimura. *The Oscar Directors*. Cranbury, New Jersey: A. S. Barnes, 1980. 253 pp., illustrations, indexed. Interesting and informative profiles of Oscar-winning directors from Lewis Milestone and Frank Borzage (1927/28) to Robert Benton (1979).

Frederick, Nathalie. *The New Hollywood and the Academy Awards*. Beverly Hills, CA: Hollywood Awards Publications, 1971. 208 pp., no index. Heavily illustrated paperback reference. Emphasis is on the Best Picture and Acting awards with all other winners listed after each decade. The major shortcoming is the failure to include an index and the names of the nominees. Now quite dated.

Hayes, R. M. *Trick Cinematography: The Oscar Special Effects Movies*. Jefferson, NC: McFarland, 1986. 370 pp., indexed. Organized chronologically, the book lists the nominees and winners for Special Visual Effects (later Visual Effects) and Scientific or Technical award winners in the visual effects field. Each entry includes a brief commentary, complete credits for all nominated films, and a list of other nominations the films received.

Holden, Anthony. *Behind the Oscar. The Secret History of the Academy Awards*. New York: Simon & Schuster, 1992. 672 pp.

Koszarski, Richard. *An Evening's Entertainment: The Age of the Silent Feature Picture 1915–1928*. Vol. 3 of *History of the American Cinema*, Charles Harpole, ed. New York: Charles Scribner's Sons, 1990. 395 pp., indexed. The final chapter, titled "The Envelope, Please," covers the founding of the Academy. The author devotes much of the chapter to a defense of *Sunrise*, winner of the Oscar for Unique and Artistic Picture. He speculates on why this category was eliminated after the first year and accuses the Academy of revisionist history that accords *Sunrise* a status much lower than intended by the original voters.

Levy, Emanuel. *And the Winner is . . . The History and Politics of the Oscar Awards*. New York: Frederick Ungar, 1987. 390 pp., indexed. A carefully documented exploration of the connections between the Oscar and its political, social, and cultural settings. The book is reviewed in some depth by Ira S. Jaffe in *Literature/Film Quarterly* 16.2 (1988): 137 and by Mickie Edwardson in the *Journal of Popular Film & Television* 16.3 (Fall 1988): 131.

Libby, Bill. *They Didn't Win the Oscars*. Westport, CT: Arlington House, 1980. 236 pp., indexed. More substantial than the title would imply. Chapters are divided by genre, actors, actresses, and directors. The author concludes that "it is the pictures and the performances that count, not the Awards."

Likeness, George. *The Oscar People: From Wings to My Fair Lady*. Mendota, IL: Wayside Press, 1965. 432 pp., indexed but does not include all the winners' names. The Best Picture and Acting awards are emphasized at the expense of the other categories. Very little history or explanation of the categories.

Manfull, Helen, ed. *Additional Dialogue: Letters of Dalton Trumbo, 1942–1962*. New York: Evans, 1970. 576 pp., indexed. Includes some fascinating letters on the Academy's role during the blacklist period.

Michael, Paul. *Academy Awards: A Pictorial History*, 3d rev. ed. New York: Crown, 1988.

Michael, Paul, ed. *The American Movies Reference Book: The Sound Era*. Englewood Cliffs, NJ: Prentice-Hall, 1969. The section called "The Awards" is useful for comparing Oscar-winning achievements with the awards from several other groups including the New York Film Critics, *Film Daily*, *Photoplay*, and the National Board of Review.

Osborne, Robert. *50 Golden Years of Oscar: The Official History of the Academy of Motion Picture Arts and Sciences*. La Habra, CA: ESE California, 1978. A richly illustrated, lavish volume with all the nominees and winners of the first fifty years.

———. *Sixty Years of the Oscar: The Official History of the Academy Awards*. New York: Abbeville, 1989. 319 pp., indexed. An updated and improved version with more photos and a very substantial text. Incorporates research by Academy historian Patrick Stockstill that corrects some misconceptions about the early years. Essential reading.

Perry, Louis B., and Richard S. Perry. *A History of the Los Angeles Labor Movement, 1911–1941*. Berkeley: University of California Press, 1963. 622 pp., indexed. The chapter on "Union Success in the Movie Industry" is a detailed account of the labor relations with which the Academy involved itself for the first decade of its existence. The authors conclude that the Academy was established by the producers as a means of frustrating the bargaining attempts by the talent groups and forestalling unionization.

Pickard, Roy. *The Oscar Movies from A to Z*. London: Frederick Muller Ltd., 1978. 252 pp., indexed. Alphabetical listings of every feature film to win an Oscar in any category. Short films and documentaries are not included. Honorary and other Oscars are listed in an appendix. Other appendices include a list of one hundred famous films that received no Oscar nominations and a separate list of nominated films that won no awards.

Reed, Rex. *Conversations in the Raw*. New York: World Publishing, 1969. 312 pp., no index. One small section includes an amusing, vitriolic, and jaundiced account of the 40th Awards ceremony, which the author calls "a night of back-stabbing and utter stupidity."

Ross, Murray. *Stars and Strikes: Unionization of Hollywood*. New York: Columbia University Press, 1941. 233 pp., indexed. Essential reading for anyone interested in learning how the motion picture industry became unionized. Includes many references to the role played by the Academy in this struggle.

Sands, Pierre Norman. *A Historical Study of the Academy of Motion Picture Arts and Sciences (1927–1947)*. New York: Arno Press, 1973. 262 pp., no index. Reprint of a 1966 University of Southern California Ph.D. dissertation. A very comprehensive study of the Academy's early history, though the material lacks any critical objectivity and is arranged to please a committee of academicians rather than a general readership. An index would have made this book far more valuable.

Simonet, Thomas, and the Editors of the Associated Press. *Oscar: A Pictorial History of the Academy Awards*. Chicago: Contemporary Books, 1983. 266 pp., indexed. As the title implies, the book focuses on photos rather than text. Nominees are listed for some but not all categories.

Sklar, Robert. *Movie-Made America: A Cultural History of American Movies*. New York: Random House, 1975. 340 pp., indexed. Calls the Academy a company union set up by the producers in response to Equity's drive to organize actors. Mentions the Academy's role in the 1933 bank holiday studio crisis and the work of the Research Council in World War II. Many other minor references to the Academy.

Steinberg, Cobbett. *Film Facts*. New York: Facts on File, Inc., 1980. 476 pp., indexed. A useful reference book on all aspects of film. Part 6 on Awards covers the Oscars through 1979 and offers comparisons with other major film prizes.

Who Wrote the Movie and What Else Did He Write? An Index of Screenwriters and Their Film Works, 1936–1969. Los Angeles, CA: Academy of Motion Picture Arts and Sciences and the Writers Guild of America-West, 1970. 491 pp., indexed. The Awards index includes the Oscar winners and nominees for writing and the awards of the Screen Writers' Guild. A good, useful research tool.

Wiley, Mason, and Damien Bona. *Inside Oscar: The Unofficial History of the Academy Awards*. New York: Ballantine, 1988. 928 pp., indexed. Contains an astonishing amount of information including presenters as well as winners and nominees. Lists rule changes, historical background, and eligible films and songs that failed to get nominations. A fascinating blend of scholarship and fan magazine trivia. Essential reading.

Articles

"Abandoned Oscar." *Newsweek* 11 April 1949: 90. This brief article says the decision by the five major studios to withdraw financial support for the Oscar ceremonies was not a hasty reaction to the British film *Hamlet* winning Best Picture but was decided months before the awards.

"Academy Talent Up in Arms." *Motion Picture Herald* III 29 April 1933: 10. Trade paper account of the Academy talent groups' opposition to the producers' proposed Artists' Service Bureau. Says the Academy champions the workers' cause against the producers.

"The Academy Writer-Producer Agreement . . . Another Attempt to Destroy the Guild." *Screen Guilds' Magazine* 2 (October 1935): 1–2. Militant accusation by the actors' and writers' guilds that the Academy is a company union and tool of the producers. Academy founder Frank Woods confirmed some allegations, corrected others in an article in the following issue (see below).

Alpert, Hollis. "A Matter of Opinion." *Saturday Review* 11 April 1935: 55. A brief complaint that the Oscars reflect "an inability to distinguish between the pretentious and the real, a nostalgia for the past, a fear of the future." Mentions the general dismay registered when *The Greatest Show on Earth* was named Best Picture over *High Noon*.

American Premiere. March 1982. A special section on the Academy Awards with several very brief, basic, not particularly useful articles.

Architectural Digest. The April 1990 and April 1992 issues are titled Academy Awards Collector's Editions. As one might expect, the primary focus is on the architectural and interior design of the homes of Oscar-winning stars and directors from Hollywood's golden age; other articles include Richard Schickel on D. W. Griffith, Michael Webb on Cedric Gibbons and the MGM Style, and pieces on George Hurrell, William Wellman, and many more. Beautifully illustrated.

Arlen, Michael J. "The Big Parade." *New Yorker* 30 April 1979: 122–24. The magazine's TV critic ruminates on the question of whether television has overwhelmed the Oscar ceremony. He suggests we view the annual awards program not as a theatrical event but as a ceremonial parade.

"An Award Worth Winning." *The Screen Guilds' Magazine* 3 (March 1936): 1. A reprint of screennwriter Dudley Nichols' letter to the Academy refusing his Oscar for *The Informer*.

Bart, Peter. "The Paranoia Pageant." *Variety* 23 March 1992: 5, 10. To the TV viewers, the Oscar show is a slick celebration, but, says the author, "on the occasions when I've hovered back stage or mingled with the nominees, . . . I've witnessed a vastly more surreal spectacle—a pageant of panic and paranoia."

Beaton, Welford. "Industry Fashioning Weapon of Defence." *The Film Spectator* III 28 May 1927: 3. Laudatory editorial noting the formation of the Academy as a means for the motion picture industry to answer unjust criticism with a unified voice.

———. "Is Entitled to the Support of All." *The Film Spectator* III 28 May 1927:4. More praise for the newly founded Academy. Quotes at length the declaration of aims printed on the invitations to the Academy's organizational banquet.

Bickerstaff, Isaac. "The Oscars—By Radio." *Films in Review* 3 (April 1952): 164–70. Useless account of listening to the 1952 Oscar ceremony on the radio.

"Black Wins Best Actor Oscar Only Once in 62 Years." *Jet* 16 April 1990: 54+. "In reality, so few roles are written for Blacks that could lead to Oscar consideration, it is not surprising that Blacks are underrepresented when it comes to taking home the statuettes." The article is minor but includes a helpful list of all Black actor/actress nominees from 1939 to 1989.

Bogdanovich, Peter. "Oscar at Fifty." *Esquire* 22 April 1978. The evolution of the awards from a private party among friends to "the movies' biggest promotional event, a kind of yearly election with a good deal of political thinking required."

Bower, Anthony. "Academy Awards." *Nation* 152 (15 March 1941): 305. Some historical background but mostly an account of the 1940 Awards banquet which was addressed via radio by President Franklin Roosevelt.

Canby, Vincent. "Actresses and the Oscar Race." *New York Times* 24 Jan 1988: 19, 25. "Since clearly it's impossible to compare the kind of performance that, say, Judy Garland gives in 'A Star Is Born' to Grace Kelly's in 'The Country Girl,' the all important deciding factors in such contests must be arbitrary though not irrelevant."

———. "Ah, How Fickle the Ways of the Oscar." *New York Times* 13 April 1980: Sec. 2: 21. Thoughts of a veteran Oscar-watcher.

———. "Devaluation Overtakes the Oscar for Best Foreign Film." *New York Times* 7 April 1985: Sec. 2: C19–20. Complaining of mediocre choices and the limited voter pool, he yearns for the old days when this was an "other" award chosen by the Board of Governors.

———. "In the Afterglow of the Oscars." *New York Times* 16 April 1978: Sec. 2: 15. "The Oscars are too easy to knock over, like old people on upper Broadway. There's no sport in it anymore."

———. "Oscar Night Casts Its Magic Spell." *New York Times* 23 March 1986: Sec. 2: 21. Quotes liberally from anecdotes in *Inside Oscar* by Wiley and Bona.

———. "Spotting Winners in a Clouded Crystal Ball." *New York Times* 28 March 1982: 20, 24. A good example of the prediction article. Canby picked winners in ten categories (and got half correct).

———. "The Stories behind the Oscars." *New York Times* 5 April 1987: C23. Brief, thoughtful post-ceremony observations. Six examples are cited with Canby's interpretation of the subtext and sometimes sub-subtext.

———. "Why We Watch the Academy Awards." *New York Times* 30 March 1989: Sec. 2: 1, 17. Canby compares the awards ceremony to "taking an extremely slow Seventh Avenue Local to heaven. It's a very long ride, and overcrowded, and the arrival—by which time one is exhausted—is always a bit of an anticlimax. Yet one simply cannot afford to miss it." A thoughtful, interesting essay.

Carlson, Timothy. "Vote Counter Frank Johnson: Nobody Knows the Totals He's Seen." *Washington Post* 15 April 1980: Sec. 2: 1. An entertaining profile of the Price Waterhouse accountant who knows the winners long before anyone else does.

Champlin, Charles. "The Academy at Fifty." *American Film* March 1978: 16–19. A look at the Academy's year-round activities.

———. "Brando and the Offer He Refused." *Los Angeles Times* 30 March 1973: Calendar. He calls Sacheen Littlefeather's refusal speech "the night's best performance by far." Champlin feels most would agree with the reasons that prompted Brando's refusal of the Oscar, but he feels, "The gesture also belongs to a uniquely American tradition which believes that publicity itself solves problems, or which is prepared to believe that problems are as simple and as easily solved as the publicity makes them out to be."

———. "Craft over Content: An Oscar Tradition." *Los Angeles Times* 2 April 1978: Calendar: 1, 40. Champlin says the Oscars "define exactly where the movies were, comfortably and safely, in their year. There is hardly a wobble off center, politically speaking.... Anger, cynicism, and reproach do not loom large in 50 years' worth of Best Pictures."

———. Oscar: The Tale That Wags the Film Academy." *Los Angeles Times* 24 February 1980: Calendar: 27. To eliminate in-breeding and in-fighting, Champlin advocates opening up more nominations to the whole Academy rather than the individual branches. "The difficulties occur in the so-called technical branches, which tend to be small, elderly, and close-knit. They have a clubhouse flavor and a genuine pride in traditional craftsmanship which is, however, hard on innovation and new boys in town."

Chandler, Raymond. "Oscar Night in Hollywood." *Atlantic* 181 (March 1948): 24–27. Stylish, iconoclastic piece which characterizes the Oscar ceremony as a "grotesque ritual." "If we permit noise, ballyhoo, and bad theatre to influence us in the selection of the people who are to run the country, why should we object to the same methods in the selection of meritorious achievement in the film business."

———. "Oscar Night in Hollywood." *Sight and Sound* 19 (June 1950): 157–61. Identical to Chandler's 1948 *Atlantic* article.

Cohn, Lawrence. "Oscar Choices/Omissions Reflect Quirky Voting Rules." *Variety* 18 February 1991: 5, 14, 16. An interesting summary of some nomination anomalies of the past few years. Worthy achievements are sometimes disqualified by the "quirky" rules.

———. "Rules of Oscar Game: Grand Illusion?" *Variety* 14 March 1990: 5. The author argues that the foreign language film nomination procedure is out of sync with reality. He offers some suggestions for this and other categories.

Culhane, John. "With Help from Friends, Oscar's a Wit and Raconteur." *New York Times* 10 April 1988: Sec. 2: 46. A behind-the-scenes look at how producer Samuel Goldwyn, Jr., and writer Ernest Lehman create an Oscar show.

Curry, Jack. "Skip the Envelope, Please." *TV Guide* 12 April 1980: 19. A brief look at voting patterns and how they may be used to predict winners.

Daily Variety. 1933–present. Major trade paper in Hollywood and a constant source of news about the Academy and the motion picture industry.

Duka, John. "Spurning an Oscar." *New York Times* 28 March 1982: Sec. 2: 20. Very minor piece reminding us that Dudley Nichols, George C. Scott, and Marlon Brando are the only winners to refuse an Oscar.

Ebert, Roger, and Gene Siskel. "Oscar, the Grouch." *Premiere* April 1992: 78. Some thoughts on how the Oscars are chosen.

Edwardson, Mickie. "Oscar's Law and Other Patterns in Choices of Motion Picture Academy Award Winners." *Journal of Popular Film & Television* 15.1 (Spring 1987): 16–25. "Oscar's Law," says the author, states that "a nominee has a better chance to win if nominated for work on one of the Best Picture award candidates." This rule appears statistically valid for eight categories. Other voter patterns are also explored.

———. "Patterns in Choosing Oscar-Winning Best Pictures." *Journal of Popular Film &*

Television 17.4 (Winter 1990): 130–138. A follow-up to her 1987 article. Ten long-standing and stable voter patterns are identified as predictors for the Best Picture award.

Elkin, Stanley. "In Darkest Hollywood." *Harper's* December 1989: 51–61. A rambling, first-person account of attending the Oscar ceremonies. The author, a novelist, has an eye for detail but spends much of the essay discussing his own background and illness.

Elliott, Paul. "Looking over the Oscars." *Atlantic* 174 (August 1944): 103–7. Inconsequential; mostly a complaint about *Casablanca* winning the Best Picture award.

Fairbanks, Jr., Douglas. ". . . the Envelope Please." *Time* 11 April 1983: 45–56. Part of a special advertising section sponsored by Buick. The son of the Academy's first president weaves his own memories into a brief, anecdotal summary of Oscar highlights.

Farber, Stephen. "Janet Gaynor Recalls the First Awards." *New York Times* 28 March 1982: Sec. 2: 19. Brief, though interesting, reminiscence by the recipient of the first Best Actress award.

Gabler, Neal. "The Bare Facts." *Video Review* April 1991: 21–23. Sees the Oscars as an expression of nostalgia for the old Hollywood. "Put simply, the Academy celebrates not the virtues for which most of us go to the movies: speed, action, romance, glamour, thrills. These are the things that earn Hollywood money but of which it is ashamed. Instead, . . . it purveys those trusty middlebrow values: sentimentality, high-mindedness, sobriety. These are the yardsticks by which Hollywood wants to be reckoned." Gabler's sidebar on "Handicapping the Oscars" is full of insight and advice on how to pick the big winners.

Garringer, Nelson E. "Academy Award Nominations." *Films in Review* 8 (March 1957): 111–15. Oscar trivia culled from the nominations lists; too dated to be of value.

Gledhill, Donald. "The Motion Picture Academy, A Cooperative in Hollywood." *Journal of Educational Sociology* 13 (January 1940). Brief overview of Academy achievements by the organization's executive secretary. Part of a special issue on "Some Educational Aspects of Motion Pictures."

———. "Screen Academy and the Field It Covers." *Hollywood Spectator* 1 March 1940. Virtually identical to Gledhill's article in the *Journal of Educational Sociology* published two months earlier.

Goldman, William. "The Big Picture: Capos and Indians." *New York* 25 March 1991: 21.

———. "The Big Picture: Pushing the Envelope." *New York* 30 March 1992: 22.

———. "The Big Picture: Scoping the Oscars." *New York* 26 March 1990: 26. In each article, the author, an Oscar-winning screenwriter, comments on the principal nominees and, after narrowing the field, offers the conventional wisdom on possible winners. For example, he lists compelling reasons "Why Jessica Tandy Will Win" and follows with compelling reasons "Why Jessica Tandy Won't Win."

Grant, Lee. "Musical Oscar: Some Sweet and Sour Notes." *Los Angeles Times* 8 April 1979: Calendar: 34, 42–47. Excellent exploration of the controversies surrounding the Academy's Musical Branch. (The author is a *Times* staff writer, not the actress.)

Halliday, David Graham. "Supporting Actors: They Get No Respect." *Variety* 22 March 1989: 5. An excellent argument to change the nominating rules. "What is lost in handing supporting nominations to actors who are billed above the title is recognition for performers who bolster a good film or stand out in features gone wrong."

Harmetz, Aljean. "An Award May Bring Up to $20 Million More." *New York Times* 28 March 1982: Sec. 2: 19. "Winning an Academy Award means more than glory. It also means hard cash."

———. "Do Ads Buy Nominations for Oscars?" *New York Times* 28 February 1980: Sec. 2: 17.

———. "The Expensive Oscar-Nomination Manipulations." *New York Times* 30 March 1989: C22. Studios spend from $60,000 to $150,000 per movie to get nominations. Continues the author's long-term exploration of the financial strategies surrounding the Oscars.

———. "Hollywood, Hoopla Over, Now the Wait for Oscars." *New York Times* 3 April 1979: Sec. 3: 7.

———. "How to Win an Oscar Nomination." *New York Times* 5 April 1970: Sec. 2: 11.

———. "The Oscar Chase: A Peek behind the Screen." *New York Times* 8 April 1984: Sec. 2: 1. Explores the studio campaigns to get nominations and the potential return on the investment.

Harvey, Brett. "Oh, God, So Many People to Thank!" *Village Voice* 31 March 1987: 51–52. A review essay on *Oscar Dearest* by Brown and Pinkston, *And the Winner Is...* by Levy, and *Inside Oscar* by Wiley and Bona. He casts his vote for *Inside Oscar*.

Hersholt, Jean. "The Academy Speaks." *Atlantic* 181 (May 1948): 43–45. The president of the Academy responds to Raymond Chandler's anti-Academy article that appeared two months earlier. Hersholt describes the other Academy activities besides the Oscars and defends the Academy against charges of arbitrary voting, politicking, and discrimination against foreign films.

Heston, Charlton. "Critical Analysis." Letter. *American Film* June 1990: 6. The actor offers an amusing, sarcastic response to the April 1990 article "If Critics Picked the Oscars." (See McGilligan below.)

Hollywood Reporter. 1930–present. Another major Hollywood trade paper that regularly reports the news of the Academy and the movie industry.

Hubler, Richard. G. "Pulitzer Prize for Motion Pictures." *Screenwriter* 2 (January 1947): 7–10. A plea from a screenwriter for an impartial judge outside the industry to bestow awards of merit for motion picture achievement. Complains that the "inbred praise and inhibited exhibitionism" of the Academy Awards lower the standards of movies.

Hurd, Reggie, Jr. "Academy Award Mistakes." *Films in Review* 6 (May 1955): 209–15. Lists performances that should have won Oscars but didn't. Nearly everyone who scans the winners' lists plays this game sooner or later.

Jennings, C. Robert. "Oscar and the Generation Gap." *Los Angeles Times* 7 April 1968: West Magazine: 9, 12–14. Is the old guard ready for the New Hollywood? The author looks at the nominations and thinks not: "That such clunkers as [*Dr.*] *Dolittle*, [*Guess Who's Coming to*] *Dinner*, and something called *Beach Red*—did anyone see it?—were nominated for Best Achievement in Film Editing, and such brilliant edit jobs as *Bonnie and Clyde*, *Two for the Road*, and *In Cold Blood* were not, is a spleen-busting travesty."

Joseph, Robert. "Re: Unions in Hollywood." *Films* 1 (Summer 1940): 35–40. Claims that the founding of the Academy was a plot by the producers "to sell the talent groups down the river." Characterizes the Academy's involvement in labor relations as "a twelve year history of chicanery and malfeasance, broken faith and double crossing."

Kaufer, Scott. "Buying an Oscar." *Film Comment* March/April 1981: 54. Amusing account of the annual Oscar hucksterism in the Hollywood trade papers. The author contends that the ads are frequently better than the movies—"handsomer, better executed, easier to fathom."

Kerr, Walter. "All about the Oscars." *New York Times* 28 March 1982: Sec. 2: 1, 20. Brief introductory essay (one of six Oscar articles in this issue of the *Times*).

Kline, Herbert. "Academy's Last Supper." *New Theatre* 3 (April 1936): 32–33. An account of the tumultuous battle by Hollywood talent groups to win recognition and bargaining power from the producers. The title refers to the successful boycott of the Awards banquet in 1936 by the Screen Actors' and Screen Writers' Guilds.

Knight, Arthur. "Academy Moves to Encourage Excellence." *Los Angeles Times* 7 April 1974: Calendar: 18, 31, 69. A useful summary of Academy reforms, especially the efforts to attract new, younger members and to provide such services and projects as film preservation.

Lavery, Emmet. "Mr. Shakespeare's Earthquake: Much Ado about the Oscars." *Saturday Review* 16 April 1949: 13. The author, a member of the Academy Board of Governors, contends that by picking *Hamlet* as Best Picture, Academy voters have demonstrated that the balloting is free from studio influence and Hollywood chauvinism.

Lees, David, and Stan Berkowitz. "A Race for Fame and Money." *Los Angeles Times* 8 April 1979: Calendar: 4–7. Several brief, insightful articles on Academy membership, myths, and how to orchestrate an Oscar campaign.

Levy, Shawn. "The Very 'Best.' " *American Film* March 1991: 66–69. The author asks what becomes a "Best Picture" most? "Best pictures are telling barometers of American culture, economics, and morality, representing, as they do, the consensus of the Hollywood creative community at a given moment in history." Eight winners are offered as the most representative.

Lindsay, Robert. "Oscars Make and Break Careers." *New York Times* 28 March 1982: Sec. 2: 19. Calls winning an Oscar "perhaps one of the most pervasive of national fantasies, at least comparable to pitching a no-hitter for the Yankees or being elected America's first female President."

Logan, Somerset. "The Battle of Hollywood." *New Republic* 59 (7 August 1929): 308. A pro-Actors' Equity article about the attempt to unionize actors. The Academy is not mentioned.

———. "Revolt in Hollywood." *Nation* 129 (17 July 1929): 61. Cites poor conditions for actors and their need for a union. No mention of the Academy. "Equity will prevail in Hollywood."

McGilligan, Pat, and Mark Rowland. "Can 80 Critics Be Wrong?" *American Film* April 1991: 28–33. The second annual critic's poll again offers the reader a chance to compare the choices of the Academy voters to those of the film critics.

———. "If Critics Picked the Oscars . . . " *American Film* April 1990: 26–31. Eighty critics are polled. A sidebar on "There Oughta Be a Category" offers some unsung achievements. See the June 1990 letters to the editor for Charlton Heston's reponse.

Meisel, Myron. "Who Picks the Oscars?" *Film Comment* March/April 1982: 53. An exploration of the Academy's nominating process and membership requirements. The author notes some occasional rule-bending in certain categories.

"The Menace of the Academy." *The Screen Player* 1 (15 April 1934): 1. Editorial published by the Screen Actors Guild claiming the producer-controlled Academy is trying to destroy the Guild.

Musto, Michael. "La Dolce Musto." *Village Voice* 26 April 1988: 46. A hilarious and wicked account of the author's trip to the Oscars.

———. "Up the Academy." *Village Voice* 8 April 1986: 59. Oscar-bashing at its funniest.

Myers, Edith D. "Oscar Computes." *Datamation* 15 April 1986: 68. Focuses mostly on the Medal of Commendation for John Whitney, pioneer computer special-effects wizard. Good sidebar on how the nominations for the Scientific or Technical Awards are solicited and how the recipients are chosen.

New York Times 21 April 1933: 24. Brief news story of Conrad Nagel's resignation as AMPAS president in the stormy aftermath of Hollywood's 1933 salary-cut crisis. "Created originally by the film executives to protect themselves from Actors Equity and the A.F. of L. [the Academy] has risen to the defense of the actors and now finds itself in the ironical position of opposing the producers who have given it their financial support."

Niver, Kemp R. "From Film to Paper to Film." *Quarterly Journal of the Library of Congress* 21 (October 1964): 248–64. Excellent article on the restoration of the paper prints collection, a joint project of the Academy and the Library of Congress.

"Organized Hosts." *Screen Guilds' Magazine* 3 (March 1936): 3. "The fight of the Guilds against the Academy is a fight between honest employees' organizations and a company union." Calls for the Academy to be destroyed and forgotten.

"Oscar." *Films and Filming* 1 (June 1955): 3. Worthless article purportedly on the history of the Academy Awards.

"Oscar on TV." *Life* 30 March 1953: 39+. A mostly pictorial essay on the first Awards show to be televised. Wryly notes that television "bought the right to the ceremony for $100,000, used it for a one and a half hour show which presumably kept millions of TV-viewers from going to the movies that night."

Pierson, Frank. "The Starstruck, Center Stage: Hollywood's Self-inflicted Paean in the Neck." *Washington Post* 15 April 1980: Sec. 2: 1. The author, an Oscar-winning screenwriter, characterizes the Academy Awards as a room cloud of hype, notes the near religious tone of the Oscar ceremony, and confesses he remains starstruck by it all.

Powers, Charles. "Jack Lemmmon: The Long Wait before Oscar." *Los Angeles Times* 7 April 1974: Calendar: 1, 20–22. A lengthy, interesting profile of how an Oscar-winning star prepares for the big night when he is again favored to win the prize.

Roderick, Kyle. "A Star Is Poured." *Premiere* April 1991: 66–67. How Chicago's R. S. Owens and Company manufactures the Oscar statuette.

Rodman, Howard A. "Doing Oscar." *Village Voice* 21 March 1989: 64. Brief, interesting account of how the Academy prepares for the nomination announcements.

Rosenfield, Paul. "Oscar at 50: You've Come a Long Way, Baby." *Los Angeles Times* 2 April 1978: Calendar: 1, 38. An entertaining overview of the first half century. "Oscar has survived a streaker, two crashers, an AFTRA strike, a sunken podium, and Sacheen Littlefeather."

Rubenstein, L., and Dan Georgakas. "I Am Now and Have Always Been..." *Cineaste* 8.1 (Summer 1977): 26–28, 58. An interview with Oscar.

"Sadder but Braver." *Nation* 188 (24 January 1959): 62. Brief item noting the Academy's repeal of its controversial "blacklist" amendment that prevented suspected Communists from receiving Oscar recognition. See also *Daily Variety* 14 January 59.

Sarris, Andrew. "Academy Leaders." *Film Comment* March/April 1980: 15. The author notes that the Academy voters over the years have favored tears to laughter, heaviness to lightness.

———. "The Big Oscar Hangover." *Village Voice* 26 April 1983: 47. Sarris, who seldom has much good to say about the choices of Academy voters, suggests that "the Oscar ceremony is now intentionally designed to inflict as much pain and suffering as possible on both its participants and its viewers. Pain and suffering are the indispensible ingredients of its ever more popular mystique. Its fluffs and fiascoes are as much a part of its legend as its infrequent felicities."

———. "The Five Nominees and How They Grew." *Film Comment* March/April 1989: 8. Interesting background and nominating procedures for the Foreign Language Film Award.

———. "The Importance of Winning Oscar." *Film Comment* March/April 1979. Sarris observes the choices of Academy voters over the years and concludes, "In the aesthetic war between 'blanc' and 'noir' the Academy has always gone 'blanc.' "

———. "Rip Van Winkle Handicaps the Oscars." *Village Voice* 12 March 1985: 43. Typical of Sarris's prediction articles. He rates in order *all* nominees in *all* categories. Throughout the 1980s, Sarris would generally write an article making his predictions and after the Oscar ceremony publish a postmortem listing his winning percentage.

Schickel, Richard. "Measuring Oscar." *American Film* March 1978: 3. Observes that Academy voters, despite some lapses, have honored some memorable achievements in the past fifty years. If the awards "don't quite represent the ultimate in motion picture achievement as their industry apologists and hired flacks annually insist, they are not quite the monument to bad taste and faulty judgment that their critics insist on telling us each spring."

Schulberg, Budd. "How My Daddy Won the Oscar (Or, What a Difference 42 Years Makes)." *Los Angeles Times* 13 April 1969: West Magazine: 47, 54–55. The author, an Oscar-winning screenwriter and novelist, recalls how B. P. Schulberg played his hunches and won the first Best Picture award for *Wings*. Concludes with the memory of all the Oscar winners his father helped "who were always out when he called or never bothered to answer his letters when fortunes were reversed."

Simon, John. "Oscars . . . They Shun the Best, Don't They?" *New York Times* 1 March 1970: Sec. 2: 1. Complains that the Academy is not a suitable judge. He favors a small jury to select the winners rather than a "large, unwieldy, semi-autonomous and influenceable body." See *New York Times* 5 April 70: Sec. 2: 11 for several rebuttals.

Skolsky, Sidney. "What Goes On at the Academy Awards." *McCalls* (April 1962): 74. Entertaining reminiscences of memorable Oscar ceremonies by a veteran observer of the Hollywood scene. It is in this article that Skolsky defends his claim that he, not Margaret Herrick or Bette Davis, named the statuette "Oscar."

Stanley, Fred M. "Oscar: His Life and Times." *New York Times Magazine* 18 March 1945: 18. Explodes some myths, such as the story that Cedric Gibbons sketched the Oscar design on a tablecloth, but perpetuates other inaccuracies.

Thalberg, Irving. "Technical Activities of the Academy of Motion Picture Arts and Sciences." *Journal of the Society of Motion Picture Engineers* 15 (July 1930): 3–16. A good summary of the projects of the Academy's Producers-Technicians Committee that supervised AMPAS technical activities before the Research Council was founded.

"That's Me." *Newsweek* 26 January 1959: 25. As soon as the Academy repealed its blacklist amendment, screenwriter Dalton Trumbo identified himself as the "Robert Rich" who had won the 1956 Oscar for writing *The Brave One*.

Thompson, Ben. "Oscars Wild." *New Statesman & Society* 29 March 1991: 27. Short, amusing British view of the Oscars. "Hollywood's annual climax of vulgarity tends to be viewed with a peculiarly British mix of condescension and envy, the blend dictated by how well we do."

Travers, Peter. "Oscar-Bashing: Memo to the Academy on Its 64th Birthday: Retire or Reform." *Rolling Stone* 2 April 1992: 39. In his yearly ritual of constructive criticism, the author offers further advice on how the Academy might improve its awards.

———. "Oscar-Bashing." *Rolling Stone* 5 April 1990: 37. "When innovative new talents are shut out of the race, they are being shut out by their own peers. Whatever the excuse—envy, fear, ignorance—Oscar deserves to be trounced for its sins of omission."

———. "Oscar-Bashing." *Rolling Stone* 4 April 1991: 62. Excoriates the Academy for its neglect of women directors, bias against independent films, and unwillingness to vote for actors in unsympathetic roles.

Trumbo, Dalton. "The Graven Image." *Theatre Arts* 34 (July 1950): 32–35. Humorous tongue-in-cheek account of awards (not just Oscars) bestowed in Hollywood.

Wald, Jerry, and Norman Krasna. "Oscar Fever." *Films in Review* 3 (March 1952): 102–4. A very minor piece advocating greater use of original scripts rather than adaptations.

Warga, Wayne. "Academy Spadework a Long Row to Hoe." *Los Angeles Times* 28 February 1971: Calendar: 1, 59. Interesting background piece on the Academy staff that works all night under *tight* security to prepare the nomination announcements.

———. "A Half Century of Movie Arts, Survival." *Los Angeles Times* 8 May 1977: Calendar: 1, 20–21. The author offers some history and visits with a few of the surviving participants of the Academy's first banquet held on May 11, 1927. Among those interviewed are Henry King, Norman Taurog, and King Vidor.

Westerbeck, Colin. "Star Warts: And the Winner is . . . " *Commonweal* 8 May 1981: 275. The author sees Oscar night as an overproduced and pathetic spectacle—"TV's annual put-down of the whole idea of movies and movie stars."

"What Makes Simon Snicker?" *New York Times* 5 April 1970: Sec. 2: 11. Several letters to the editor responding to film critic John Simon's March 1, 1970 piece criticizing the Oscars. Simon then replies to all of his critics.

Wiley, Mason. "The Oscar Chase: A Peek behind the Screen." *New York Times* 8 April 1984: Sec. 2: 1, 24. An excellent article on the Academy's membership policies.

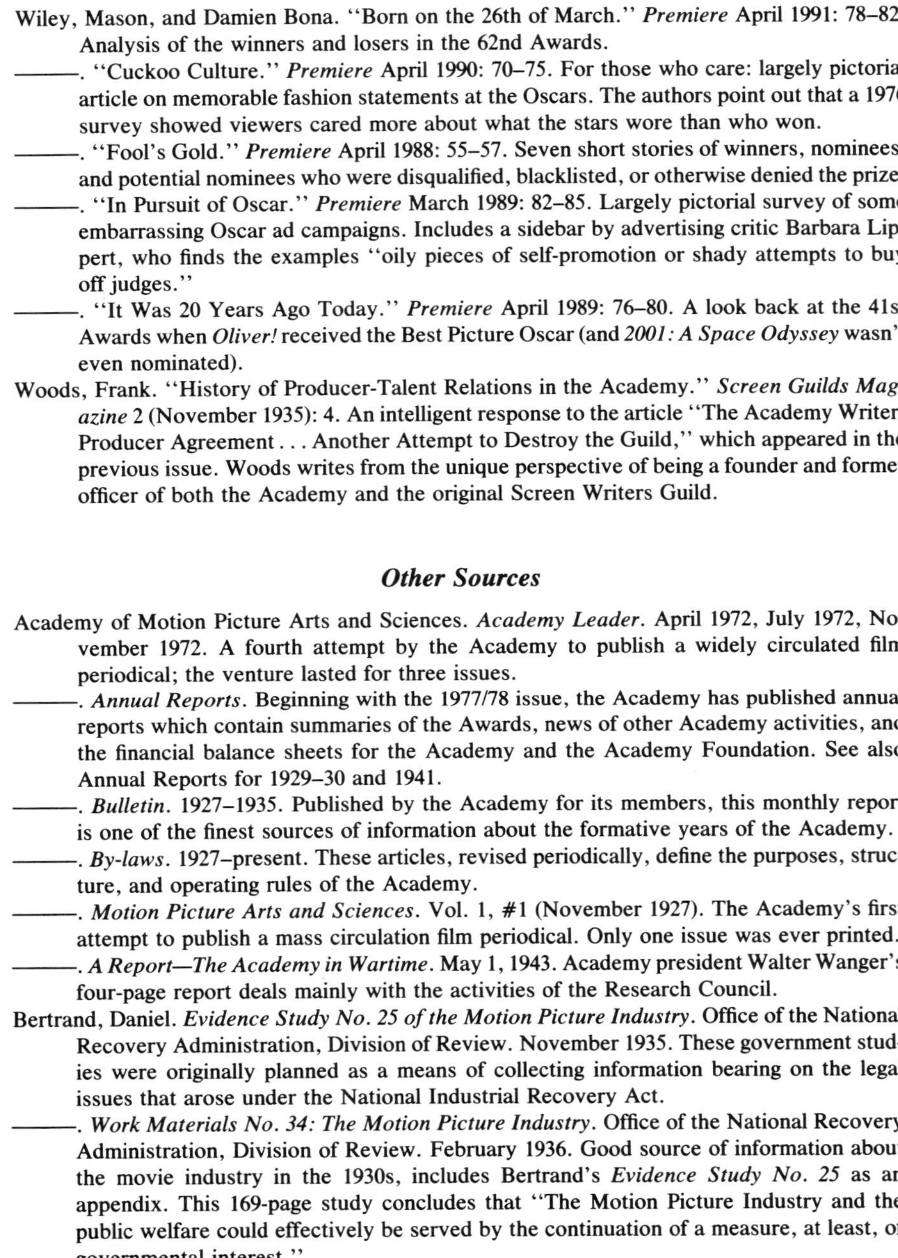

Wiley, Mason, and Damien Bona. "Born on the 26th of March." *Premiere* April 1991: 78–82. Analysis of the winners and losers in the 62nd Awards.

———. "Cuckoo Culture." *Premiere* April 1990: 70–75. For those who care: largely pictorial article on memorable fashion statements at the Oscars. The authors point out that a 1976 survey showed viewers cared more about what the stars wore than who won.

———. "Fool's Gold." *Premiere* April 1988: 55–57. Seven short stories of winners, nominees, and potential nominees who were disqualified, blacklisted, or otherwise denied the prize.

———. "In Pursuit of Oscar." *Premiere* March 1989: 82–85. Largely pictorial survey of some embarrassing Oscar ad campaigns. Includes a sidebar by advertising critic Barbara Lippert, who finds the examples "oily pieces of self-promotion or shady attempts to buy off judges."

———. "It Was 20 Years Ago Today." *Premiere* April 1989: 76–80. A look back at the 41st Awards when *Oliver!* received the Best Picture Oscar (and *2001: A Space Odyssey* wasn't even nominated).

Woods, Frank. "History of Producer-Talent Relations in the Academy." *Screen Guilds Magazine* 2 (November 1935): 4. An intelligent response to the article "The Academy Writer-Producer Agreement . . . Another Attempt to Destroy the Guild," which appeared in the previous issue. Woods writes from the unique perspective of being a founder and former officer of both the Academy and the original Screen Writers Guild.

Other Sources

Academy of Motion Picture Arts and Sciences. *Academy Leader*. April 1972, July 1972, November 1972. A fourth attempt by the Academy to publish a widely circulated film periodical; the venture lasted for three issues.

———. *Annual Reports*. Beginning with the 1977/78 issue, the Academy has published annual reports which contain summaries of the Awards, news of other Academy activities, and the financial balance sheets for the Academy and the Academy Foundation. See also Annual Reports for 1929–30 and 1941.

———. *Bulletin*. 1927–1935. Published by the Academy for its members, this monthly report is one of the finest sources of information about the formative years of the Academy.

———. *By-laws*. 1927–present. These articles, revised periodically, define the purposes, structure, and operating rules of the Academy.

———. *Motion Picture Arts and Sciences*. Vol. 1, #1 (November 1927). The Academy's first attempt to publish a mass circulation film periodical. Only one issue was ever printed.

———. *A Report—The Academy in Wartime*. May 1, 1943. Academy president Walter Wanger's four-page report deals mainly with the activities of the Research Council.

Bertrand, Daniel. *Evidence Study No. 25 of the Motion Picture Industry*. Office of the National Recovery Administration, Division of Review. November 1935. These government studies were originally planned as a means of collecting information bearing on the legal issues that arose under the National Industrial Recovery Act.

———. *Work Materials No. 34: The Motion Picture Industry*. Office of the National Recovery Administration, Division of Review. February 1936. Good source of information about the movie industry in the 1930s, includes Bertrand's *Evidence Study No. 25* as an appendix. This 169-page study concludes that "The Motion Picture Industry and the public welfare could effectively be served by the continuation of a measure, at least, of governmental interest."

Campbell, R. Wright. *Killer of Kings*. New York: Bobbs-Merrill, 1979. A thriller written by a veteran screenwriter and novelist. A gang plans to kidnap, ransom, and assassinate stars on Oscar night at the Dorothy Chandler Pavilion. (The author's screenplay for *Man of a Thousand Faces* was nominated for an Oscar in 1957.)

Emanuel, Itzhak. *A Descriptive History of the Academy of Motion Picture Arts and Sciences*

Annual Awards: The Television Productions, 1953–1970. 416 pp., no index. A 1971 UCLA Master's thesis. Extremely detailed and technical, with charts, illustrations, and thirty-six appendices. Unpublished.

Hayes, Helen, and Thomas Chastain. *Where the Truth Lies*. New York: William Morrow, 1988. A murder mystery novel set at the Academy Awards. Cowritten by a two-time Oscar winning actress.

Oscar's Greatest Moments 1971–91 (Videotape). Produced and directed by Jeff Margolis; written by Stephen Pouliot and Hal Kanter. Hosted by Karl Malden. Two decades of Award ceremony highlights. Two more tapes are scheduled: 1953–1970 and 1927–1952.

Sale, Richard. *The Oscar*. New York: Simon & Schuster, 1963. A novel about the quest for the big prize. Made into an undistinguished film in 1966.

U.S. Congress, House. Committee on Appropriations. *Hearings before the Subcommittee of the Committee on Appropriations, House of Representatives, 86th Congress, 1st Session, 1960*. Brief discussion of funding for the restoration of the Library of Congress Paper Print Collection, a project with which the Academy was greatly involved.

U.S. Congress, Senate. *Investigation of Concentration of Economic Power. Monograph No. 43: The Motion Picture Industry—A Pattern of Control*. Temporary National Economic Committee, 76th Congress, 3rd Sessions, 1941. This 92-page pamphlet, written by the committee's administrative assistant Daniel Bertrand, covers such issues as block booking, blind selling, and overbuying.

Index

Aalberg, John, 150–52, 154–55, 292, 301, 305, 341, 373, 377, 385, 388, 393, 395, 399, 432, 457, 473, 618, 636
Abbott, F. R., 305, 390
Abbott, George, 83, 356
Abbott, L. B., 295, 344, 346–47, 502, 549, 564, 576, 599
Abdullah, Achmed, 84, 368
Abe Lincoln in Illinois, 33, 111, 391–92
Above and Beyond, 91, 185, 467–68
Abraham, F. Murray, 39, 643
Abramson, Phil, 143, 603
Abroms, Edward, 173, 639
Absence of Malice, 39, 68, 104, 625–26
Absent Minded Professor, The, 118, 137, 344, 511–12, 514
Absent-Minded Waiter, The, 253, 604
Abyss, The, 125, 146, 163, 233, 675–77
Academy Award Theatre, 13, 440
Academy of Motion Picture Arts and Sciences (AMPAS): Academy Foundation, 8–9; Academy Leader, 8; Academy Players Directory, 8; Annual Index of Motion Picture Credits, 8; Aperture Committee, 6; Blacklist, 5; Center for Motion Picture Study, 9; College Affairs Committee, 7; Conciliation Committee, 5; Don and Gee Nicholl Fellowships, 9; Dues, 14; Emergency Committee, 3; Founding, 1; George Pal Lecture, 9; George Stevens Lecture, 9; Jack Oakie Lecture, 9; Labor Relations, 2, 4–5; Margaret Herrick Library, 9; Marvin Borowsky Memorial Lectureship, 9; Membership, 14; Military Personnel Selection Committee, 7; National Film Information Service, 7; Producers–Technicians Joint Committee, 6; Publications and Educational Activities, 7–9; Reorganization Committee, 5; Research Council, 6–7, 302; Samuel Goldwyn Theater, 9; Screen Achievements Records Bulletin, 8; Screen Illumination Committee, 6; Statement of Aims, 2; Statuette, 12–13; Student Film Awards, 9; Technical Activities, 6–7; Visiting Artists Program, 7, 9; Voting and Nominating procedures, 9–10
"Accentuate the Positive," 202, 427
Accidental Tourist, The, 29, 70, 107, 197, 667–69
Accused, The, 51, 667
Acheson, James, 226, 664, 670
Achtenberg, Ben, 273,647
Ackland, Rodney, 87, 405
Ackland–Snow, Brian, 146, 657
Acme Tool and Manufacturing Company, 307, 324, 422, 623
Action in the North Atlantic, 87, 412
Actors Equity Association, 3
Actress, The, 217, 469
Adair, Tom, 205, 486
Adalen '31, 279, 560
Adam, Ken, 135, 143, 485, 591, 603
Adam, 257, 695
Adam Clayton Powell, 275, 678
Adams, Bryan, 215, 689
Adams, David, 252, 575, 581
Adams, John, 261, 470
Adams, Nick, 56, 522
Adamson, Harold, 199–202, 205, 373, 414, 420, 491
Adam's Rib, 90, 451
Addams Family, The, 226, 689
Addison, John, 188, 192, 525, 574
Address Unknown, 130, 181, 418, 420
Adjani, Isabelle, 48, 51, 589, 674
Adkins, Hal, 309, 434
Adler, Buddy, 22, 298, 466, 477, 487
Adler, Larry, 185 n, 473 n
Adler, Peter Herman, 184, 457
Adolescence, 265, 544
Adventures in Perception, 267, 570
Adventures in the Bronx, 258, 402
Adventures of Baron Munchausen, The, 146, 226, 229, 233, 676–77
Adventures of Don Juan, 132, 216, 447
Adventures of Mark Twain, The, 130, 181, 343, 419–21
Adventures of Robin Hood, The, 19, 127, 165, 178, 381–83
Adventures of Robinson Crusoe, 35, 471
Adventures of Tom Sawyer, 127, 382
Affair in Trinidad, 217
Affairs of Cellini, 32, 111, 127, 149, 364–65
Affairs of Susan, The, 88, 425
Affair to Remember, An, 117, 186, 205, 219, 490–92
"Affair to Remember, An," 205, 491
Africa, Prelude to Victory, 258, 409
African Queen, The, 34, 45, 74, 91, 455–56
"After All," 214, 677
After the Axe, 272, 635
After the Thin Man, 84, 372
Against All Odds, 213, 646
"Against All Odds (Take A Look At Me Now)," 213, 646
Against Wind and Tide: A Cuban Odyssey, 271, 628
Agatha, 224, 616
Age, 97, 529, 535
Agee, James, 91, 456
Agee, 271, 623
"Age of Not Believing, The," 209, 569
Agfa Ansco Corporation, 303–4
Aghayan, Ray, 222–23, 559, 575, 592
Agnes of God, 50, 69, 196, 649–51
Agony and the Ecstasy, The, 120, 140, 157, 189, 221, 535–37
Agueda Martinez: Our People, Our Country, 270, 605
Aherne, Brian, 53, 386
Ahnemann, Michael, 265, 544
Aiello, Danny, 61, 674
Aimee, Anouk, 47, 540
Air Force, 87, 113, 166, 342, 412, 414–15
Airport, 25, 67, 99, 121, 141, 158, 170, 190, 222, 561–64

Airport '77, 143, 224, 602, 604
Akst, Albert, 168, 485
Aladdin, 164, 197, 215, 235, 694–95
Alamo, The, 23, 56, 118, 156, 169, 187, 206, 505–8
Alaskan Eskimo, The, 261, 470
Alaska Wilderness Lake, 267, 470, 570
Albert, Eddie, 55, 58, 466, 572
Albert Schweitzer, 262, 492
Albertson, Jack, 57, 551
Albin, Fred, 305, 341, 389, 390
Alborn, Al, 337, 362
Alcott, John, 122, 590
Alda, Alan, 649
Alden, A. A., 315, 515
Aldred, John, 158–59, 558, 568
Aldredge, Theoni V., 223, 586
Aleandro, Norma, 69, 662
Alekan, Henry, 116, 467
Alexander, Dick, 160–64, 597, 603, 633, 651, 657, 663, 669, 694
Alexander, Gary, 162, 651
Alexander, Jane, 48, 50, 68, 561, 596, 614, 637
Alexander, Jim, 161–62, 621, 639
Alexander's Ragtime Band, 19, 85, 128, 166, 177, 200, 381–84
Alfie, 24, 36, 66, 97, 208, 540–41, 543
"Alfie," 208, 543
Alford, Jack, 314, 503
Algiers, 32, 53, 111, 128, 381–82
Ali Baba Goes to Town, 340, 378
Alibi, 17, 31, 126, 353–54
Alice, 108, 681
Alice Adams, 18, 43, 367
Alice Doesn't Live Here Anymore, 48, 67, 101, 583–84
Alice in Wonderland, 184, 457
Alice's Restaurant, 77, 557
Alien, 144, 231, 615–16
Aliens, 51, 145, 162, 173, 196, 232, 235, 655–58
Alien 3, 233, 695
Alive in the Deep, 239, 402
All About Eve, 17, 22, 55, 64, 74, 90, 115, 132, 154, 167, 184, 450–53, 707
All American Co-Ed, 179, 201, 400–401
Allan, Ted, 101, 590
Allder, Nick, 231, 616
Allen, David, 232, 343, 421, 652
Allen, Dede, 171–72, 591, 627
Allen, Gene, 135–36, 139, 473, 491, 530, 705
Allen, Ioan R., 323, 330, 612, 666, 672
Allen, Irving, 242–43, 438, 448
Allen, Irwin, 26, 261, 464, 583
Allen, Jay Presson, 100, 104, 573, 626
Allen, Peter, 212, 627
Allen, Reg, 142, 574
Allen, Woody, 38, 78–80, 102–3, 105–9, 601–2, 608, 614, 644, 650, 656, 662, 675, 681, 693, 708
Aller, Bob, 267, 564
"All God's Children Got Rhythm," 340, 378
Allgood, Sara, 63, 397
"All His Children," 209, 569
All Nothing, 254, 622
All Out for V, 239, 408
All Quiet on the Western Front, 17, 71, 83, 110, 355–56, 707
All That Jazz, 27, 39, 78, 103, 123, 144, 172, 194, 224, 613–16
"All That Love Went to Waste," 209, 581
All That Money Can Buy, 33, 179, 397, 400
All the Brothers Were Valiant, 116, 467
All the King's Horses, 339, 369
All the King's Men, 21, 34, 55, 64, 74, 90, 167, 445–47, 707
All the President's Men, 26, 59, 68, 78, 102, 143, 160, 171, 595–97
"All the Way," 205, 491
All This, and Heaven Too, 20, 63, 112, 391–92
"All Through the Day," 203, 432
Almendros, Nestor, 122–23, 608, 615, 621, 633
"Almost in Your Arms (Love Song From Houseboat)," 206, 496
Aloma of the South Seas, 112, 342, 398, 401
Along the Rainbow Trail, 241, 428
Alonzo, John, 122, 584
Alper, Bud, 160, 162, 597, 651
Alphin, Nick, 162, 645
Alsino and the Condor, 281, 635
Alter, Louis, 199, 201, 373, 401
Altered States, 161, 194, 621–22
Altman, Robert, 26, 77–78, 81, 562, 589–90, 693
Alton, John, 116, 456
Altramura, Elio, 146, 657
Alves, Joe, 143, 603
Alvorada (Brazil's Changing Face), 264, 520
"Always and Always," 200, 384
Always a New Beginning, 268, 581
Always in My Heart, 201, 408
"Always in My Heart," 201, 408
Amadeus, 28, 39–40, 79, 106, 124, 145, 162, 173, 225, 228, 643–46, 708
Ama Girls, 263, 497
Amarcord, 78, 101, 280, 587, 590
Amazing Mrs. Holliday, The, 180, 414
Amazon Diary, 256, 678
Ambassador Hotel, 1, 13, 353, 355, 359, 361, 386, 404, 701
Ambler, Eric, 92, 467
Ameche, Don, 60, 649
Ament, Walton C., 243, 448
America, America, 24, 76, 96, 138, 522–24
American Dream (1990 documentary), 275, 684
American Dream, An (1966), 208, 543
American Graffiti, 25, 67, 77, 101, 171, 578–80
American in Paris, An, 22, 74, 91, 116, 133, 167, 184, 217, 455– 58, 707
Americanization of Emily, The, 119, 139, 529–30
American Shoeshine, 269, 599
American Society of Cinematographers, 6
American Tail, An, 213, 658
American Werewolf in London, An, 228, 628
Americas in Transition, 271, 628
Ames, Preston, 133–34, 136, 139, 141–42, 457, 468, 473, 485, 496, 530, 562, 585
Amfitheatrof, Daniele, 182–83, 427, 437
Ami, Louis, 320, 558
Amidei, Sergio, 89–90, 96, 431, 436, 446, 511
"Am I In Love," 204, 463
Amityville Horror, The, 194, 615
AMPAS. See Academy of Motion Picture Arts and Sciences
Ampex Professional Products Company, 315, 509
Amphibious Fighters, 240, 415
Amran, Robert, 251, 267, 570
Amy, George, 166, 407, 414, 426
Anastasia, 46, 186, 483, 486
Anatomy of a Murder, 23, 35, 56, 95, 118, 168, 499–501
Anchors Away, 21, 33, 114, 182, 202, 424–25, 427
Ancilotto, Alberto, 261, 464
Anderson, Carl, 136, 142, 501, 574
Anderson, Dave, 313, 481
Anderson, Donald A., 327, 648
Anderson, George, 305, 390
Anderson, Gilbert M. (Broncho Billy), 290, 493
Anderson, Hayward, 248, 520
Anderson, Hesper, 106, 656
Anderson, Howard A., Jr., 346, 549
Anderson, John, 145, 651
Anderson, Judith, 62, 391
Anderson, Maxwell, 83, 356
Anderson, Michael, 74, 484, 707
Anderson, Philip W., 168–69, 485, 491, 512

Anderson, Richard L., 234, 296, 629, 635
Anderson, Robert, 95, 99, 500, 562
Anderson, Robin, 271, 641
Anderson, Roland, 127–31, 133–35, 137–39, 362, 368, 377, 393, 406, 425, 462, 473, 507, 512, 518, 524
Anderson Platoon, The, 266, 550
. . . And Justice for All, 39, 103, 613, 614
And Now My Love, 101, 590
André DeBrie S.A., 324, 624
Andrews, Del, 83, 356
Andrews, Julie, 47, 50, 528, 534, 631
Andromeda Strain, The, 142, 170, 567–68
And to Think I Saw It on Mulberry Street, 240, 421
Andy Hardy Films, 287, 410
Angel and Big Joe, 252, 592
Angels over Broadway, 86, 392
Angels with Dirty Faces, 32, 72, 85, 381–82
Angenieux, Pierre, 301, 316, 533, 679
Angry Harvest, 282, 653
Angry Silence, The, 95, 506
Anhalt, Edna, 90–91, 451, 461
Anhalt, Edward, 90–1, 97, 451, 461, 529
Anna, 51, 661
Anna and Bella, 255, 653
Anna and the King of Siam, 63, 88, 114, 131, 183, 430–32
Anna Christie, 42, 71, 110, 355–56
Annakin, Ken, 97, 535
Annenkov, Georges, 218, 474
Anne of the Thousand Days, 25, 37, 47, 57, 99, 121, 141, 158, 190, 222, 556–59
Anni, Anna, 225, 658
Annie, 144, 195, 633–34
Annie Get Your Gun, 115, 133, 167, 184, 451–52
Annie Hall, 26, 38, 49, 78, 102, 601–2, 708
Annie Was a Wonder, 242, 443
Ann-Margret, 48, 67, 567, 589
A Nous la Liberté, 127, 360
Ansco Film Division, General Aniline and Film Corp., 311, 459, 464
Anstey, Edgar, 250, 264, 526, 538, 544
Antarctic Crossing, 263, 497
Anthony Adverse, 19, 62, 111, 127, 165, 176, 337, 371–73
Antonia: A Portrait of the Woman, 269, 586
Antonioni, Michelangelo, 76, 98, 541
"Anywhere," 202, 427
Apartment, The, 23, 35, 46, 56, 75, 95, 118, 137, 156, 169, 505–7, 708
Ape and Super-Ape, 268, 576
Apocalypse Now, 27, 59, 78, 103, 123, 144, 160, 172, 613–15
Apodaca, Tony, 333, 697
Applebaum, Louis, 182, 427
Appointment for Love, 152, 399
Appointments of Dennis Jennings, The, 256, 670
Apprenticeship of Duddy Kravitz, The, 101, 584
April Love, 205, 492
"April Love," 205, 492
Aquamania, 248, 514
Aquatic House Party, 243, 448
Arabian Nights, 113, 130, 152, 180, 406–7
Arango, Manuel, 251, 267, 570
Arbogast, Roy, 231, 604
Archer, Anne, 70, 662
Archer, Ernie, 141–42, 552, 568
Arden, Eve, 63, 424
Ardolino, Emile, 272, 641
Ardrey, Robert, 98, 541
"Aren't You Glad You're You," 202, 427
Arise, My Love, 85, 112, 128, 178, 392–94
Arizona, 128, 179, 393–94
Arkin, Alan, 36–37, 540, 551
Arlen, Alice, 105, 638
Arlen, Harold, 200–203, 205, 389, 401, 414–15, 421, 427, 442
Arling, Arthur, 114, 117, 431, 478
Arliss, George, 31, 355
Armat, Thomas, 288, 438
Armbruster, Robert, 188, 531
Armour, Darryl A., 329, 660
Arms and the Man, 278, 497
Armstrong, John, 269, 599
Army Champions, 239, 401
Army Girl, 111, 150, 178, 382–83
Arnaud, Leo, 188, 531
Arnold, August, 326, 636
Arnold, Jack, 261, 453
Arnold, John, 304–5, 379, 390
Arnold, Malcolm, 186, 491
Arnold & Richter Engineering Staff, 330, 672; Engineering Department, 332, 685
Arnold & Richter KG, 317, 545
Aronson, Jerry, 270, 610
Around the World in 80 Days, 22, 74, 93, 117, 168, 186, 218, 483–86, 707
ARRI, Austria, Engineering Department, 334, 697
Arriflex Corporation, 330, 334, 672, 697
Arrighi, Luciana, 147, 694
Arrowsmith, 17, 83, 110, 127, 359–60
Arthur, George K., 246, 481, 487
Arthur, Jean, 44, 411
Arthur, 39, 59, 104, 212, 625–27
Arthur and Lillie, 269, 592
Arthur Rubinstein—The Love of Life, 267, 560
"Arthur's Theme (Best That You Can Do)," 212, 627
Artie Shaw: Time Is All You've Got, 274, 659
Art Is . . . , 267, 570
Artists and Models, 200, 378
Artkino, 409, 433
Artman, Wayne, 163, 663
Arturo Toscanini, 259, 442
Ascher, Kenny, 194, 211, 616
Ashby, Hal, 78, 170, 542, 548, 608
Ashcroft, Peggy, 69, 644
Asher, Irving, 20, 397
Asher, Japhet, 273, 653
Ashley, Ray, 91, 467
Ashman, Howard, 12, 213–15, 658, 677, 688, 694
Ashton, Don, 142, 574
Askey, Gil, 192, 574
Asp, Anna, 145, 639
Asphalt Jungle, The, 55, 74, 90, 115, 450–51
Assault, The, 282, 659
Asseyev, Tamara, 27, 613
Association of Motion Picture Producers, 6–7
Astaire, Fred, 58, 289, 339, 448, 450, 583
Astin, John, 250, 554
Astor, Mary, 63, 397
Athaiya, Bhanu, 225, 634
Athletes of the Saddle, 244, 463
Atkin, Laurie, 315, 515
Atkinson, Ralph B., 305, 390
Atlantic City, 27, 39, 50, 79, 104, 625–26
Atlas, Leopold, 88, 425
Atomic City, The, 91, 461
Atomic Power, 260, 433
Attenborough, Richard, 27, 79, 631–32, 708
At the Edge of Conquest: The Journey of Chief Wai-Wai, 276, 696
Audioscopiks, 237, 369
Auer, Mischa, 53, 371
August, Joseph, 115, 441
Auguste, Robert D., 319, 332, 334, 571, 679, 697
Auntie Mame, 23, 46, 65, 118, 136, 168, 494–96
Aurel, Jean, 265, 532
Au Revoir Les Enfants (Goodbye, Children), 107, 282, 662, 665
Aurthur, Robert Alan, 27, 103, 613–14
Austin, John, 140, 542
Austin, Michael, 106, 644
Austin, William, 167, 462
Australian News and Information Bureau, 259–60, 409, 438
Automania 2000, 249, 526

Autry, Gene, 201, 401
Autumn Sonata, 49, 103, 607–8
Avalon, 108, 125, 197, 226, 681–83
Avery, Margaret, 69, 650
Avery, Stephen, 84, 368
"Ave Satani," 210, 598
Avila, Ruben, 327, 648
Avildsen, John G., 78, 272, 596, 635, 708
Awakening, The, 126, 354
Awakenings, 29, 41, 108, 680–81
Awful Truth, The, 19, 43, 53, 72, 85, 165, 375–77
Axelrod, George, 95, 511
Ayers, Maurice, 309, 444
Aykroyd, Dan, 61, 675
Ayling, Denys, 231, 616
Ayres, Lew, 34, 440
Ayres, Ralph, 311, 459

Baar, Tim, 344, 508
Babcock, Fay, 130–31, 406, 419
Babenco, Hector, 79, 650
Babes in Arms, 33, 178, 386, 388
Babes in Toyland, 187, 220, 513
Babes on Broadway, 201, 408
Babette's Feast, 282, 665
Baby Doll, 45, 64, 93, 117, 483–84
"Baby It's Cold Outside," 203, 447
Baby Maker, The, 191, 563
"Baby Mine," 201, 401
Bacalov, Luis Enrique, 189, 543
Bach, Danilo, 105, 644
Bacharach, Burt, 190, 208, 212, 537, 543, 549, 558–59, 627
Bachelin, Franz, 137, 501
Bachelor and the Bobby-Soxer, The, 89, 436
Bachelor in Paradise, 206, 513
"Bachelor in Paradise," 206, 513
Bachelor Mother, 85, 387
Bachelor Party, The, 65, 489
Back, Frederic, 254, 256, 622, 628, 664
Backdraft, 164, 233, 235, 688–89
Background, 268, 581
Backlar, Marshal, 249, 538
Back Street (1941), 179, 400
Back Street (1961), 220, 513
Back to the Future, 106, 162, 213, 234, 650–52
Back to the Future Part II, 233, 677
Badalucco, Nicola, 99, 557
Badami, Bob, 331, 672
Bad and the Beautiful, The, 34, 64, 91, 116, 133, 217, 460–61, 463
Bad Day at Black Rock, 35, 74, 93, 477–78
Baddeley, Hermione, 65, 499
Bad Girl, 17, 72, 83, 359
Badham, Mary, 65, 516
Bad Seed, The, 46, 64–65, 117, 483–84
Bagdad Cafe, 214, 669
Bagnall, George, 299, 545
Baier, Manfred, 269, 593
Bainter, Fay, 11, 43, 62, 65, 381, 510
Baird, Stuart, 172, 174, 609, 669
Baird, Worth, 325, 624
Bakaleinikoff, C., 177, 180–82, 378, 414, 420
Baker, Buddy, 192, 574
Baker, Carroll, 45, 483
Baker, Ezra, 248–49, 508, 526
Baker, Harry J., 332, 691
Baker, Mark, 256, 678
Baker, Rick, 228–29, 628, 646, 664, 670
Baker, Suzanne, 253, 598
Balalaika, 151, 387
Balance, 256, 678
Balcony, The, 119, 523
Balderston, John L., 84, 88, 368, 418
Baldwin, Peter, 332, 685
Ball, Derek, 160, 603
Ball, J. Arthur, 286, 385, 701
Ballad of a Soldier, 96, 511
"Ballad of Cat Ballou," 207, 537
Ballard, Carroll, 266, 550
Ballard, Lucien, 119, 523
Ballard, Lucinda, 217, 458
Ballet Robotique, 254, 635
Ballhaus, Michael, 124–25, 662, 676
Ball of Fire, 44, 86, 152, 179, 397–400
Ballon Vole (Play Ball!), 248, 514
Balsam, Martin, 57, 534
Balzac, 244, 458
Bambi, 152, 180, 201, 406–8
Bancroft, Anne, 46–47, 49–50, 516, 528, 546, 601, 649
Bancroft, George, 31, 353
Band Wagon, The, 92, 185, 217, 467–69
Bang the Drum Slowly, 58, 578
Banjo on My Knee, 149, 372
Banks, Lionel, 128–31, 321, 382, 387, 393, 399, 406, 418
Banks, Roger, 320, 582, 593
Bannen, Ian, 57, 534
Banning, 208, 549
Baptism of Fire, 259, 416
Baptista, John L., 328–29, 660
Baran, Roma, 276, 696
Baravalle, Victor, 177, 383
Barbary Coast, 111, 368
Barber, Lynn, 229, 677
Barbera, Joseph, 246, 480, 492
Barclay, Richard, 252, 575
Barefoot Contessa, The, 55, 92, 471–72
Barefoot in the Park, 66, 547
"Bare Necessities, The," 208, 548
Barker, Cordell, 256, 670
Barker, Ronald C., 329, 666
Barker, The, 42, 353
Barkleys of Broadway, The, 115, 446
Barnebey–Cheney Company, 321, 599
Barnes, George, 110, 112, 114–15, 352, 354, 392, 425, 451
Barnes, John, 261, 470
Barnes, Peter, 109, 693
Barnett, S. H., 97, 529
Barrault, Marie–Christine, 49, 595
Barrett, Alan, 224, 598
Barretts of Wimpole Street, The, 18, 43, 364
Barrie, Barbara, 68, 614
Barrie, George, 209–10, 581, 592
Barron, Craig, 233, 695
Barroso, Ary, 202, 421
Barry, John (art director), 143, 603
Barry, John (music), 189–91, 196–98, 208, 543, 553, 568, 651, 682, 694
Barry, Julian, 101, 584
Barry, Tom, 83, 353
Barry Lyndon, 26, 78, 101, 122, 143, 193, 223, 589–92
Barrymore, Ethel, 63–64, 417, 430, 435, 445
Barrymore, Lionel, 32, 71, 353, 357
Barsacq, Leon, 138, 518
Barthelmess, Richard, 9, 31, 351, 701
Bartlett, Hall, 261, 464
Barton, Charles, 337, 361
Barton, Larry, 328, 654
Barton Fink, 61, 147, 226, 686–87, 689
Bartscher, Fred, 321, 600
Baryshnikov, Mikhail, 59, 601
Basevi, James, 128, 130–31, 387, 393, 413, 425
Basic Instinct, 174, 198, 694
Baskette, James, 288, 438
Bass, Ronald, 107, 668
Bass, Saul, 253–54, 266, 554, 604, 617
Basserman, Albert, 53, 391
Bassler, Robert, 21, 440
Bassman, Don, 158, 163, 563, 669, 676, 682
Bates, Alan, 37, 551
Bates, Jonathan, 161, 633
Bates, Kathy, 51, 680
Bates, Ken, 333, 697
Batista, Henry, 168, 473
Batman, 146, 676
Batman Returns, 230, 233, 695
Battle Cry, 185, 479
Battleground, 21, 55, 74, 90, 115, 167, 445–47
Battle of Algiers, The, 76, 99, 279, 544

Battle of Berlin, 268, 581
Battle of Gettysburg, The, 246, 262, 481
Battle of Midway, 259, 409
Battle of Neretva, The, 279, 560
Battle of Russia, 259, 416
Battle of the Bulge, . . . The Brave Rifles, The, 265, 538
Bauchens, Anne, 165–68, 365, 394, 462, 486
Bauer, Fritz Gabriel, 330, 666
Bauman, Susanne, 271, 628
Baumbach, Harlan L., 308, 313, 433, 493
Bausch & Lomb Optical Company, 290, 305, 312, 390, 475, 481
Baxter, Anne, 45, 63, 430, 450
Baxter, Warner, 31, 353
Beaches, 146, 669
Beach Red, 170, 548
Bead Game, The, 253, 604
Beal, Scott, 337, 362, 364
Bealmear, Robert, 328, 648
Bear, Jack, 222, 564
Bear, The, 174, 676
Bear Country, 245, 469
Beatles, The, 191, 563
Beaton, Cecil, 139, 219, 221, 497, 530–31
Beattie, Alan, 252, 592
Beatty, Ned, 59, 595
Beatty, Warren, 24, 27, 29, 36, 38–39, 41, 78–79, 101, 103–4, 546, 590, 595, 607–8, 625–26, 686
Beauchamp, Clem, 337, 367, 372
Beau Geste, 53, 128, 386–87
Beaumont, Harry, 71, 353, 707
"Beautiful Maria Of My Soul," 215, 694
Beauty and the Beach, 239, 401
Beauty and the Beast, 29, 164, 197, 214–15, 686, 688
"Beauty and the Beast," 214, 688
Beauty and the Bull, 245, 475
Beavan, Jenny, 225–27, 646, 658, 664, 695
Beaver Valley, 244, 453
Because You're Mine, 204, 463
"Because You're Mine," 204, 463
Bechir, Gabriel, 138, 518
Beckert, Tom, 160, 163, 603, 663
Becket, 24, 36, 57, 76, 97, 120, 139, 157, 169, 188, 221, 528–31
Becky Sharp, 43, 367
Bedknobs and Broomsticks, 142, 191, 209, 222, 346, 568–69
Beecroft, Jeffrey, 146–47, 681
Beep Prepared, 248, 514
Beery, Wallace, 31–32, 355
Beetlejuice, 229, 670
Beetley, Samuel E., 169–70, 518, 548
Beetson, Fred, 1, 701
Before the Mountain Was Moved, 267, 560
Beggs, Richard, 160, 615
Begley, Ed, 56, 516
Behind the News, 151, 393
"Be Honest with Me," 201, 401
Being There, 39, 59, 613
Belcher, Jim, 253, 610
Bel Geddes, Barbara, 63, 440
Belgian Ministry of Information, 259, 409
Bell, John, 233, 677
Bell, Madeline, 273, 659
Bell, Book and Candle, 136, 219, 495, 497
Bellah, Ross, 135, 485
Bellamy, Ralph, 53, 293, 375, 659
Bell and Howell Company, 289, 303, 321, 366, 470, 593
"Belle," 215, 688
Belle of the Yukon, 182, 203, 427–28
Beller, Hava Kohav, 276, 690
Bells Are Ringing, 187, 507
Bells of St. Mary's, The, 21, 33, 44, 73, 153, 166, 182, 202, 424–27
Bell Telephone Laboratories, 304, 374
Belt, Haller, 305, 390
"Be My Love," 204, 452,
Ben, 209, 575
"Ben," 209, 575
Ben and Me, 245, 469
Bendix, William, 54, 404
Beneath the Twelve Mile Reef, 116, 467
Benedek, Barbara, 105, 638
Benedetti, Benedetto, 264, 514
Benford, James R., 314, 504
Ben Hur (1959), 17, 23, 35, 56, 75, 95, 118, 136, 156, 168, 187, 219, 344, 499–502, 708
Bening, Annette, 70, 681
Benjamin, Mary, 272, 628
Benjamin, Robert, 297, 300, 618
Benji, 210, 586
"Benji's Theme (I Feel Love)," 210, 586
Benjy (documentary), 261, 458
Bennett, Charles, 86, 392
Bennett, Richard Rodney, 189, 191–92, 548, 568, 585
Bennett, Robert Russell, 186, 480
Bennett, Russell, 178, 384
Benny, Jack, 411, 430
Ben's Mill, 272, 635
Benson, Joseph, 255, 635
Benson, Sally, 88, 431
Benson, Suzanne, 232, 658
Benton, Bill W., 163, 682
Benton, Robert (set decorator), 138–40, 524, 530, 536, 542
Benton, Robert (writer-director), 78–79, 98, 102–3, 105, 547, 602, 614, 644, 708
Benz, Obie, 271, 628
"Be Our Guest," 215, 688
Berenger, Tom, 60, 655
Beresford, Bruce, 79, 104, 620, 638, 708
Bergen, Candice, 68, 614
Bergen, Edgar, 13, 286, 379
Berger, Fred W., 171, 574
Berger, Mark, 160, 162, 615, 639, 645
Berger, Peter E., 174, 663
Berger, Ralph, 129, 406
Berggren, Glenn, 319, 321, 323, 331, 577, 600, 612, 672
Berglund, Per, 107, 662
Bergman, Alan, 195, 208–14, 553, 559, 563, 569, 575, 581, 610, 616, 634, 640, 677
Bergman, David, 269, 587
Bergman, Ingmar, 25, 77–79, 95–96, 101, 103, 105, 298, 500, 517, 565, 578–79, 596, 608, 638
Bergman, Ingrid, 42, 44, 46, 49, 62, 67, 411, 417, 424, 440, 483, 584, 607
Bergman, Marilyn, 195, 208–14, 553, 559, 563, 569, 575, 581, 610, 616, 634, 640, 677
Bergner, Elisabeth, 43, 367
Bergren, Eric, 104, 620
Berkeley, Busby, 339–40, 369, 373, 378
Berkeley in the Sixties, 275, 684
Berkeley Square, 32, 361
Berkey, Jim, 144, 626
Berkos, Peter, 295, 593
Berlin, Irving, 85–86, 199–202, 205, 369, 382, 389, 405, 408, 432, 474
Berlin, Jeanne, 67, 573
Berman, Brigitte, 274, 659
Berman, Henry, 170, 542
Berman, Pandro S., 18–19, 22, 298, 364, 367, 375, 450, 460, 599
Bernard, James, 91, 456
Bernari, Carlo, 97, 523
Bernds, Edward, 82, 93, 484
Bernstein, Bill, 331, 672
Bernstein, Dick, 331, 672
Bernstein, Elmer, 185, 187–89, 195, 207–8, 210, 479, 507, 513, 519, 543, 548, 559, 586, 640
Bernstein, Leonard, 185, 473
Bernstein, Walter, 102, 596
Berri, Claude, 27, 249, 538, 619
Berry, David, 232, 652
Berry, Paul, 257, 695
Bert, Malcolm, 135–36, 473, 495
Bertolucci, Bernardo, 77, 80, 100, 107, 567, 579, 662, 708
Bertrand, Robert, 159, 580
Bespoke Overcoat, The, 246, 487
Bessie, Alvah, 88, 425
Best, Marjorie, 216, 218, 220–21, 447, 486, 508, 537

Best Boy, 271, 617
Best Friends, 212, 634
Best Little Whorehouse in Texas, The, 60, 631
Best Man, The, 57, 528
Best of Everything, The, 206, 219, 502
"Best of Everything, The," 206, 502
Best Things in Life Are Free, The, 186, 486
Best Years of Our Lives, The, 21, 33, 54, 73, 88, 154, 167, 183, 288, 430–33, 707
Betrayal, 105, 638
Bettis, John, 214, 682
Betty Blue, 282, 659
Between Heaven and Hell, 186, 486
Between the Tides, 247, 503
Beverly Hills Cop, 105, 644
Beverly Hills Cop II, 214, 664
Beyond Imagining: Margaret Anderson and the "Little Review," 276, 696
Beyond Silence, 263, 508
Beyond the Forest, 183, 447
Beyond the Line of Duty, 240, 409
Beyond the Walls, 281, 647
B. F.'s Daughter, 216
BHP, Inc., 331, 672
Bibas, Frank P., 264, 514
"Bibbidy-Bobbidi-Boo," 204, 452
Bible, The, 189, 543
Bickford, Charles, 54, 411, 435, 440
Bicycle Thief, The, 90, 289, 446, 448
Biddiscombe, Carl, 141, 558, 563
Biddle, Adrian, 125, 687
Big, 107, 667–68
Big Broadcast of 1936, 339, 369
Big Broadcast of 1938, 200, 384
Big Carnival, The, 91, 456
Big Chill, The, 28, 69, 105, 637–38
Big City Blues, 248, 520
Big Country, The, 56, 186, 494, 496
Big Fisherman, The, 118, 137, 219, 500–502
Biggs, Julian, 250, 549
Big House, The, 17, 31, 83, 148, 355–56
Big Pond, The, 32, 355
Big Sky, The, 55, 116, 460–61
Big Snit, The, 255, 653
Bikel, Theodore, 56, 494
Bilheimer, Robert, 274, 671
Bilimoria, Fali, 266, 554
Bill, Tony, 26, 578
Bill and Coo, 288, 438
Billy Budd, 56, 516
Billy Rose's Jumbo, 188, 519
Billy the Kid, 112, 398
Biltmore Hotel, 2, 13, 357, 364, 367, 371, 375, 381, 391, 397
Binger, R. O., 341–42, 395, 408, 415
Birch Street Gym, 257, 689
Bird, 163, 669
Bird Man of Alcatraz, 36, 56, 65, 119, 516–17
Birdnesters of Thailand (a.k.a. Shadow Hunters), 276, 689
Birds, The, 346, 525
Birds Anonymous, 246, 492
Birds Do It, Bees Do It, 192, 591
Birkin, Andrew, 255, 635
Biro, Lajos, 82, 351
Biroc, Joseph, 119, 122, 529, 584
Birth of the Blues, 180, 400
Bishop, John R., 312, 475
Bishop, Stephen, 213, 652
Bishop's Wife, The, 21, 73, 154, 167, 183, 435–37
Bite the Bullet, 159, 193, 591
Bitter Rice, 90, 451
Bitter Sweet, 112, 128, 392–93
Biziou, Peter, 124, 668
Blachford, H. L., 325, 630
Black, Don, 208–10, 543, 559, 575, 586, 598
Black, Karen, 67, 561
Black, Noel, 249, 538
Black and White in Color, 280, 599
Blackboard Jungle, 93, 117, 168, 478–79
Blackfly, 257, 689
Black Fox, 264, 520
Black Hole, The, 123, 231, 614, 616
Blackie-Goodine, Janice, 147, 694
Black Legion, 84, 376
Black Narcissus, 114, 132, 436
Black Orpheus, 278, 503
Black Rain, 163, 235, 676–77
Black Rose, The, 216, 453
Black Stallion, The, 59, 172, 296, 614–15, 618
Black Swan, The, 113, 180, 342, 406–8
Blackton, J. Stuart, 9
Blackton, Jay, 185–86, 479–80
Blackwood, 269, 599
Blade Runner, 144, 232, 633–34
Blair, Betsy, 64, 477
Blair, Linda, 67, 579
Blake, Ben, 242, 438
Blake, John, 230, 695
Blake, Michael, 108, 681
Blake, Yvonne, 223, 569, 592
Blake, 251, 559
Blakley, Ronee, 67, 590
Blalack, Robert, 231, 604
Blane, Ralph, 202–3, 421, 437
Blangsted, Folmar, 171, 568
Blanke, Henry, 18–19, 21, 23, 367, 371, 375, 381, 440, 499
Blankfort, Michael, 90, 451
Blaschek, Otto, 330, 334, 672, 697
Blasko, Edward J., 325, 629
Blatty, William Peter, 26, 100, 578–79
Blaze, 125, 675
Blaze Busters, 243, 453
"Blaze of Glory," 214, 682
Blazing Saddles, 67, 171, 210, 584–86
"Blazing Saddles," 210, 586
Bless the Beasts and Children, 209, 569
"Bless the Beasts and Children," 209, 569
Blewitt, David, 172, 621
Blinn, Arthur F., 309, 434
Blithe Spirit, 343, 432
Blitz Wolf, The, 239, 408
Block, Ralph, 287, 408
Block, Werner, 322, 324, 329, 606, 624, 665
Blockade, 85, 178, 382–83
Blockheads, 178, 383
Blondell, Joan, 64, 455
Blood and Sand (1941), 112, 129, 398–99
Bloodbrothers, 103, 608
Blood on the Land, 278, 538
Blood on the Sun, 131, 425
Bloom, Harold Jack, 92, 467
Bloom, John, 172–73, 627, 633, 651
Bloom, Jon N., 255, 641
Bloom, Les, 145–46, 645, 663
Bloomberg, Daniel, 152–53, 155, 288, 307–8, 313, 342, 406–8, 410, 413, 416, 419, 422, 426, 429, 462, 488
Blossoms in the Dust, 20, 44, 112, 129, 397, 399
Blowers, William L., 331, 332, 672, 685
Blow-Up, 76, 98, 541
Blue, James, 266, 554
Blue Bird, The (1940), 112, 341, 392, 395
Blue Dahlia, The, 88, 431
Blue Grass Gentlemen, 240, 421
Blue Lagoon, The, 123, 621
Blues in the Night, 201, 401
"Blues in the Night," 201, 401
Blue Skies, 183, 203, 432
Blue Thunder, 173, 639
Blue Veil, The, 45, 64, 455
Blue Velvet, 80, 656
Blume, Wilbur T., 246, 262, 481
Blumenthal, Herman A., 137, 139, 141, 501, 524, 558
Blumoff, Robert F. 26, 595
Bluth, Joseph E., 319, 576
Blyth, Ann, 63, 424
Board and Care, 254, 617
Boardman, Chris, 196, 651
Boates, Brent, 233, 670
Boat Is Full, The, 281, 629

Bob & Carol & Ted & Alice, 57, 66, 99, 121, 556–57
Bobker, Lee R., 265–66, 544, 554
Bochner, Sally, 276, 696
Bode, Ralf D., 123, 621
Body and Soul, 34, 89, 167, 435–37
Bodyguard, The, 215, 694
Boehm, David, 87, 418
Boehm, Sydney, 91, 461
Boekelheide, Jay, 234, 641
Boekelheide, Todd, 161–62, 639, 645
Boemler, George, 168, 479
Boetticher, Budd, 90, 456
Bogart, Humphrey, 33–35, 411, 455, 471
Bogdanov, Mikhail, 141, 552
Bogdanovich, Peter, 77, 100, 567
Bohanan, Fred, 168, 485
Bohlen, Anne, 270, 611
Boisson, Noelle, 174, 676
"Bojangles," 340, 374
Boland, Bridget, 99, 557
Bold and the Brave, The, 56, 93, 483–84
Bolero, The, 252, 581
Bolger, John A., Jr., 159, 591
Bologna, Joseph, 99, 562
Bolshoi Ballet, The, 186, 496
Bolt, Robert, 96–98, 517, 535, 541
Bomba, Ray, 343, 428
Bombalera, 240, 422
Bombardier, 342, 415
Bomber, 258, 402
Bonar, John, 131, 426
Bond, Edward, 98, 541
Bondi, Beulah, 62, 371, 381
Bonicelli, Vittorio, 100, 567
Bon Jovi, Jon, 214, 682
Bonnie and Clyde, 24, 36, 47, 57, 66, 76, 98, 120, 222, 546–47, 549
Bonnot, Francoise, 170, 558
Bon Voyage, 157, 220, 518–19
Boogie Woogie Bugle Boy of Company B, 239, 401
"Boogie Woogie Bugle Boy of Company B," 201, 401
Boole, Philip S. J., 323, 612
Boomerang!, 89, 436
Boom Town, 112, 341, 392, 395
Boorman, John, 25, 28, 77, 80, 107, 572–73, 661–62
Boorstin, Jon, 269, 586
Booth, Charles G., 88, 425
Booth, Margaret, 165, 292, 369, 605
Booth, Shirley, 45, 460
Bor, Milan, 161, 633
Borberg, Willy, 314, 498
Borders, Gloria S., 235, 689
Bored of Education, 237, 374
Boren, Charles S., 291, 576
Borgnine, Ernest, 35, 477
Born Free, 189, 208, 543
"Born Free," 208, 543
Born on the Fourth of July, 29, 40, 80, 108, 125, 163, 174, 197, 674–76
Born to Dance, 199, 339, 373–74
Born Yesterday, 22, 45, 74, 90, 216, 450–51, 453
Bortnik, Aida, 106, 650
Borzage, Frank, 71–72, 351, 359
Bosom Friends, 237, 366
Bostonians, The, 50, 225, 643, 646
Bosustow, Nick, 251, 564, 581
Bosustow, Stephen, 243–47, 261, 448, 453, 458, 463–64, 469, 475, 487, 492
Botkin, Perry, Jr., 209, 569
Bottin, Rob, 229, 296, 658, 684
Boulanger, Daniel, 97, 529
Boulle, Pierre, 6, 93 n, 94, 490, 490 n
Bound for Glory, 26, 102, 122, 171, 193, 223, 595–98
Bourgoin, Jean, 119, 517
Bourguignon, Serge, 96, 523
Bourne, Mel, 144–45, 147, 609, 645, 688
Boutelje, Phil, 178, 181, 388, 414
Bowers, William, 90, 94, 451, 495
Bowie, Les, 295, 611
Box, Betty, 210, 586
Box, Euel, 210, 586
Box, John, 138, 140–42, 145, 518, 536, 552, 568, 645
Box, Muriel, 88, 431
Box, Sydney, 88, 431
Box, The, 250, 549
Boxer, Nat, 160, 615
Boy and His Dog, A, 242, 433
Boy and the Eagle, 243, 448
Boyd, John, 163, 669
Boyde, John, 163, 663
Boye, Conrad, 314, 498
Boyer, Charles, 32–33, 36, 287, 375, 381, 409, 417, 510
Boyer, François, 92, 472
Boy Friend, The, 191, 568
Boyle, Charles, 114, 425
Boyle, Edward G., 129, 136–37, 139–41, 399, 501, 506, 512, 530, 542, 558
Boyle, Richard, 106, 656
Boyle, Robert, 137, 141–43, 501, 558, 568, 597
Boy Named Charlie Brown, A, 191, 563
Boy on a Dolphin, 186, 491
Boys and Girls, 255, 641
Boys from Brazil, The, 38, 172, 194, 607, 609
Boys from Syracuse, The, 128, 341, 393, 395
Boys of Paul Street, The, 279, 554
Boys Town, 19, 32, 72, 85, 381–82
Boyz N the Hood, 81, 108, 687
Bozman, Ron, 29, 686
Bozzetto, Bruno, 256, 683
Brabourne, John, 25, 28, 551, 643
Bracco, Lorraine, 70, 681
Bracht, Frank, 170, 553
Brackett, Charles, 21–23, 85–86, 88–90, 92, 290, 387, 398, 424–25, 431, 441, 450–51, 467, 483, 493, 705
Bradbury, David, 271, 274, 623, 659
Bradford, William, 342, 395
Brady, Alice, 62, 372, 376
Bragg, Herbert, 311, 315, 470, 515
Bramall, John, 158, 563
Bram Stoker's Dracula, 147, 226, 230, 235, 694–95
Branagh, Kenneth, 40, 80, 257, 674–75, 696
Branch, James K., 331, 672
Brand, Millen, 89, 441
Brandauer, Klaus Maria, 60, 649
Brando, Marlon, 11, 31, 34–35, 37, 61, 455, 460, 466, 471, 489, 572, 578, 675
Brannstrom, Brasse, 107, 662
Bratton, Robert L., 348, 526, 531
Braun, Zev, 273, 647
Brave Little Tailor, 238, 384
Brave One, The, 5–6, 93, 155, 168, 484–85
Bravery in the Field, 254, 617
Brazil, 106, 145, 153, 182, 202, 419–21, 650–51
Bread, Love and Dreams, 92, 472
Breaker Morant, 104, 620
Breakfast at Tiffany's, 46, 95, 137, 187, 206, 510–13
Breaking Away, 27, 68, 78, 103, 194, 613–14, 616
Breaking the Habit, 264, 532
Breaking the Ice, 178, 384
Breaking the Language Barrier, 263, 514
Breaking the Sound Barrier, 91, 155, 461–62
Brecher, Irving, 88, 418
Breen, Joseph, 289, 470
Breen, Richard, 89, 92, 96, 441, 467, 523
Bregman, Martin, 26, 589
Breir, Betsy Broyles, 275, 678
Brendel, Frank, 295, 587
Brennan, Eileen, 68, 620
Brennan, Walter, 53–54, 371, 381, 391, 397
Brenner, Albert, 143, 145–46, 591, 603, 609, 645, 669
Brenner, David, 174, 676
Brenon, Herbert, 71, 351
Breschi, Arrigo, 137, 507
Bresler, Jerry, 240–42, 415, 422, 433
Brest, Martin, 30, 81, 692–93
Bretherton, David, 171, 574

Bretton, Raphael, 139, 141–43, 530, 558, 574, 585
Brevig, Eric, 233, 296, 684, 689
Brewer, Daniel R., 325, 629
Brewster's Millions, 182, 426
Brickman, Marshall, 102–3, 602, 614
Bricusse, Leslie, 189–91, 195, 208–9, 213–15, 548–49, 558, 563, 569, 634, 658, 682, 689
Bride of Frankenstein, The, 149, 368
Bridge, Joan, 222, 543
Bridge, The, 278, 503
Bridge of San Luis Rey, The (1929), 126, 354
Bridge of San Luis Rey, The (1944), 181, 420
Bridge of Time, 244, 463
Bridge on the River Kwai, The, 6, 23, 35, 56, 75, 94, 117, 168, 186, 489–91, 707
Bridges, James, 101, 103, 578, 614
Bridges, Jeff, 40, 58, 566, 583, 643
Bridges at Toko-Ri, The, 168, 344, 479–80
Brief Encounter, 44, 73, 88, 430–31
Brigadoon, 134, 155, 218, 473–74
Brigham, Tom, 334, 697
Bright, John (costume designer), 225–27, 646, 658, 664, 695
Bright, John (writer), 83, 358
Bright Victory, 34, 154, 455, 457
Briley, John, 104, 632
Brind, Bill, 270, 605
Brink, Gary, 144, 615
Brink's Job, The, 143, 609
Brinton, Ralph, 139, 524
Bristol, Howard, 129–31, 134–35, 138, 141, 399, 406, 413, 419, 462, 479, 512, 548, 552
British Information Services, 244, 260, 448, 463
British Ministry of Information, The, 258–59, 287, 402, 409, 416
Britt, Herbert, 308, 310, 433, 449
Brittain, Donald, 270, 599
Britton, Michael, 254, 617
Broadcast News, 28, 40, 51, 60, 107, 124, 174, 661–63
Broadway Danny Rose, 79, 105, 664
Broadway Hostess, 339, 369
Broadway Melody, 17, 42, 71, 353, 707
Broadway Melody of 1936, 18, 84, 339, 367–69
Broccoli, Albert R. ("Cubby"), 298, 629
Brock, Louis, 237, 362
Brod, Sidney S., 337, 361
Brodine, Norbert, 111, 115, 382, 456
Brodney, Oscar, 92, 472
Brodszky, Nicholas, 204–5, 452, 458, 463, 468, 480
Broidy, Steve, 299, 520
Broken Arrow, 55, 90, 115, 450–51
Broken Lance, 64, 92, 471–72
Broken Rainbow, 273, 653
Brokman, Dea, 272, 641
Bromhall, Derek, 275, 684
Bronx Cheers, 256, 683
Brooklyn, U.S.A., 242, 438
Brooklyn Bridge, 272, 628
Brooks, Albert, 60, 661
Brooks, Donald, 220, 222, 525, 554, 564
Brooks, Jack, 203–5, 432, 463, 469
Brooks, James L., 28, 79, 105, 107, 637–39, 661–62, 708
Brooks, Joseph, 211, 604
Brooks, Mel, 99, 101, 210, 552, 584, 586
Brooks, Richard, 75–76, 93–95, 98, 478, 495, 506, 541, 547
Brothers Karamazov, The (USA), 56, 494
Brothers Karamazov, The (USSR), 279, 560
Brother Sun, Sister Moon, 142, 580
Broughton, Bruce, 196, 651
Brown, Barry Alexander, 271, 617
Brown, Bernard B., 151–53, 308, 341–42, 383, 388, 393, 395, 399, 406, 408, 413, 419, 422, 426
Brown, Bruce, 268, 570
Brown, Clarence, 21, 71, 73, 355, 357, 411–12, 424, 431
Brown, David, 26, 28, 30, 297–98, 589, 631, 684, 692
Brown, Frederick J., 235, 653
Brown, Garret, 322, 606
Brown, George, 311, 314, 459, 498
Brown, Harry, 89, 91, 446, 456
Brown, Harry Joe, 18–19, 367, 381
Brown, Hilyard, 139, 524
Brown, Jeff, 255, 653
Brown, John W., 140, 548
Brown, Kenneth, 263, 497
Brown, Kris, 330, 672
Brown, Lew, 200, 378
Brown, Malcolm F., 135, 479, 485
Brown, Rowland, 83, 85, 357, 382
Brown, Russell, 308, 422
Brown, Tregoweth, 348, 538
Browne, Leslie, 68, 602
Brubaker, 103, 620
Brun, Joseph C., 116, 467
Bruno, Anthony D., 328, 660
Bruno, John, 232–33, 646, 658, 677, 695
Bruns, George, 187–88, 210, 502, 513, 525, 581
Bryan, Bill, 330, 672
Bryan, John, 132, 139, 431, 436, 530
Bryans, Michael, 272, 641
Bryce, Alexander, 329, 660
Brynner, Yul, 35, 483
Buccaneer, The (1938), 111, 382
Buccaneer, The (1958), 219, 497
Buchman, Sidney, 85–87, 90, 387, 398, 405, 446
Buckner, Robert, 86, 405
Buck Privates, 180, 201, 400–401
Buddy Holly Story, The, 38, 160, 194, 607, 609–10
Buff, Conrad, 174, 688
Bugsy, 29, 41, 61, 80, 108, 125, 147, 197, 226, 686–89
Bugsy Malone, 193, 598
Building a Building, 236, 362
Building Bombs, 275, 684
Bujold, Genevieve, 47, 556
Bulldog Drummond, 32, 126, 355–56
Bull Durham, 107, 668
Bullfighter and the Lady, 90, 456
Bullitt, 158, 170, 553
Bullock, Walter, 199, 201, 373, 395
Bumstead, Henry, 136, 138, 142, 147, 496, 518, 580, 694
Bunuel, Luis, 100, 102, 573, 602
Buono, Victor, 56, 516
Burbank Studios Sound Department, 320, 587
Burbridge, Lyle, 160, 597
Burk, Paul, 328, 648
Burke, Billie, 62, 382
Burke, Edwin, 83, 359
Burke, Johnny, 199–200, 202–3, 373, 394, 421, 427–28
Burke, Marcella, 85, 382
Burke, Michele, 228–30, 634, 658, 683, 695
Burks, Robert, 115–17, 120, 456, 472, 478, 535
Burman, Tom, 229, 670
Burnett, Carol, 572
Burnett, W. R., 87, 405
Burning Down Tomorrow, 275, 683
Burns, Allan, 103, 614
Burns, Bob, 375
Burns, Catherine, 66, 557
Burns, George, 58, 589
Burns, Ken, 272–73, 628, 653
Burns, Ralph, 192, 194–95, 574, 616, 634
Burnside, Norman, 86, 392
Burrill, Timothy, 27, 619
Burrow, Milton C., 235, 677
Burstyn, Ellen, 48–49, 67, 567, 578, 583, 595, 607, 619
Burth, Willi, 329, 665
Burton, Bernard W., 165, 377

Burton, John W., 247, 497, 502
Burton, Richard, 34, 36–38, 55, 460, 466, 528, 534, 540, 556, 601
Burton, Robert R., 334, 697
Burton, Willie D., 160–63, 609, 621, 639, 669
Burtt, Benjamin, 163, 234–35, 634, 639, 641, 670, 676–77
Burtt, Benjamin, Jr., 295–96, 605, 629
Burum, Stephen H., 125, 693
Busch, Niven, 84, 376
Busey, Gary, 38, 607
Bush, Gary, 273, 647
Bush, Nan, 275, 671
Bus Stop, 55, 483
Buster, 214, 670
Busy Little Bears, 238, 389
Butch and Sundance: The Early Days, 224, 616
Butch Cassidy and the Sundance Kid, 25, 76, 99, 121, 158, 190, 208, 556–59
Butler, Bill, 122, 170, 568, 591
Butler, Chris A., 147, 694
Butler, David, 102, 596
Butler, Frank, 86–88, 405, 418
Butler, Hugo, 86, 392
Butler, Lawrence, 321, 342–43, 395, 401, 408, 593
Butterfield 8, 46, 118, 505–6
Butterflies Are Free, 67, 121, 159, 573–74
Buttons, Red, 56, 489
"Buttons and Bows," 203, 442
Butts, Dale, 182, 427
Butts, Jerry, 253, 604
Bye Bye Birdie, 157, 188, 524–25
Byington, Spring, 62, 382
Byrne, David, 196, 663

Caan, James, 58, 572
Cabaret, 25, 48, 58, 77, 100, 121, 142, 171, 159, 192, 572–74
Cabin in the Sky, 201, 414
Caccialanza, Victor, 309, 444
Cacoyannis, Michael, 24, 76, 97, 528–29
Cactus Flower, 66, 557
Caddy, The, 205, 469
Cadillac, The, 248, 520
Cadillac Dreams, 256, 670
Cady, Jerome, 87, 418
Caesar, Adolph, 60, 643
Caesar, Arthur, 84, 365
Caesar and Cleopatra, 132, 431
Caged, 45, 64, 90, 450–51
Cage of Nightingales, A, 89, 436
Caglione, John, Jr., 229, 683
Cagney, James, 4, 32–33, 35, 381, 404, 477
Cagney, William, 20, 404
Cahn, Sammy, 201–10, 408, 420, 427, 442, 447, 452, 458, 463, 474, 480, 486, 492, 496, 502, 508, 513, 525, 531, 549, 553, 581, 592
Cain and Mabel, 339, 374
Caine, Michael, 36–37, 39, 60, 540, 572, 637, 655
Caine Mutiny, The, 22, 35, 55, 92, 155, 168, 185, 471–73
Calamity Jane, 155, 185, 204, 468–69
Calandrelli, Jorge, 196, 651
Calgary Stampede, 243, 443
Calhern, Louis, 34, 450
Calico Dragon, The, 237, 369
California Reich, The, 269, 593
California Suite, 68, 103, 143, 608–9
Callahan, Gene, 137–39, 143, 512, 524, 597
"Calling You," 214, 669
"Call Me Irresponsible," 207, 525
Call Me Madam, 185, 207, 468–69
Cambern, Donn, 173, 645
Camelot, 121, 122, 140, 158, 189, 547–49
Camera Thrills, 237, 369
Cameron, John, 192, 580
Camila, 281, 647
Camille, 43, 375
Camille Claudel, 51, 282, 674, 678
Campanile, Pasquale Festa, 97, 523
Campbell, Alan, 85, 376
Campbell, Charles L., 234–35, 634, 652, 670, 683
Campbell, David E., 163, 682
Campbell, Floyd, 310, 454
Campbell, R. Wright, 94, 490
Campbell, W. Stewart, 142–43, 145, 585, 591, 639
Canadian Film Board, 258–59, 402, 409. *See also* National Film Board of Canada
Can Can, 187, 219, 507–8
Candidate, The, 100, 159, 573–74
"Candle on the Water," 211, 604
Cannom, Greg, 229–30, 689, 695
Cannon, Dyan, 66, 68, 253, 557, 599, 608
Cannon, Vince, 253, 599
Cannon, William, 327, 372
Canonero, Milena, 223–26, 592, 628, 652, 670, 683
Cantamessa, Gene, 159–62, 574, 585, 603, 615, 633, 645, 657
Can't Help Singing, 182, 203, 427–28
Cantor, Eddie, 290, 487
Canutt, Yakima, 291, 544
Canyon Passage, 203, 432
Cape Fear (1991), 41, 70, 686–87
Capra, Frank, 18–21, 71–73, 361, 364, 367, 371–72, 375, 381–82, 386–87, 430–31, 705, 707
Capstaff, John G., 308, 429
Captain Blood, 18, 149, 367–68
Captain Carey, U.S.A., 204, 452
Captain Caution, 151, 393
Captain Eddie, 343, 428
Captain from Castile, 183, 437
Captain Fury, 128, 387
Captain Kidd, 182, 427
Captain Newman, M.D., 56, 96, 157, 522–24
Captain of Kopenick, The, 277, 487
Captains Courageous, 19, 32, 85, 165, 375–77
Captains of the Clouds, 113, 130, 406
Captain's Paradise, The, 91, 467
Cara, Irene, 212, 640
Caravans, 224, 610
Carbonara, Gerard, 181, 414
Cardiff, Jack, 75, 114, 117–18, 436, 485, 506, 511
Cardinal, The, 57, 76, 119, 139, 169, 220, 522–25
Career, 118, 136, 219, 500, 502
Carefree, 128, 177, 200, 382–84
Caretakers, The, 119, 523
Carey, Altina, 263, 509
Carey, Charles, 263, 509
Carey, Harry, 53, 386
Carey, Leslie, 154–56, 457, 468, 473, 496
Carey, Patrick, 265, 267, 538, 564
Carey, Vivien, 267, 564
Carfagno, Edward, 133–34, 136, 138, 141, 143, 457, 461, 467–68, 473, 501, 518, 552, 591
"Carioca," 199, 365
Carlin, Lynn, 66, 551
Carlino, Lewis John, 102, 602
Carl Zeiss Company, 321, 330, 600, 666
Carmen, 281, 641
Carmen Jones, 45, 185, 471–72, 474
Carmichael, Bob, 254, 622
Carmichael, Hoagy, 203–4, 432, 458
Carnal Knowledge, 67, 567
Carney, Art, 38, 583
Caron, Leslie, 45, 47, 466, 522
Carpenter, Claude, 131, 133, 419, 425, 462
Carpenter, Loren, 333, 697
Carr, Cindy, 147, 688
Carr, James, 247, 261, 263, 470, 492, 497
Carr, Robert, 310, 449
Carradine, Keith, 210, 592
Carrere, Edward, 132, 137, 140, 447, 507, 548
Carrere, Fernando, 137, 512
Carrie (1952), 133, 217, 462–63
Carrie (1976), 49, 68, 595–96
Carriere, J. C., 248, 520
Carriere, Jean-Claude, 100, 102, 107, 573, 602, 668
Carroll, Diahann, 48, 583
Carroll, Nancy, 42, 355
Carroll, Sidney, 95, 511

Carson, Johnny, 13, 607, 613, 619, 625, 637
Carson, Robert, 85, 376
Carter, John, 159, 591
Carter, Maurice, 139, 141, 530, 558
Carter, Michael A., 162, 645, 657
Carter, Ruth, 227, 695
Carter Equipment Company, 319, 321, 324, 577, 594, 624
Cartoni, Guido, 332, 691
Cartwright, H. G., 309, 439
Cartwright, Randy, 333, 691
Cartwright, Robert, 139, 141–42, 144, 530, 562, 568, 621
Casablanca, 20, 33, 54, 73, 87, 113, 166, 180, 411–12, 414, 707
Casals Conducts: 1964, 249, 532
Casanova Brown, 130, 153, 181, 419–20
Casanova '70, 97, 535
Casbah, 203, 442
Case, Dale, 251, 564
Case of Sgt. Grischa, The, 148, 356
Casey, George, 252, 269, 271, 586, 593, 623
Cashin, Jack, 327, 642
Casino Royale, 208, 549
Cass, Peggy, 65, 494
Cassavetes, John, 57, 77, 99, 546, 552, 584
Cassel, Seymour, 57, 551
Castellano, Richard, 58, 561
Castillo, Antonio, 223, 569
"Cat and the Canary, The," 202, 427
Cat Ballou, 36, 97, 169, 189, 207, 534–37
Cat Came Back, The, 256, 670
Cat Concerto, The, 241, 432
Cathcart, Daniel, 130–31, 413, 419
Catmull, Ed, 333, 697
Cat on a Hot Tin Roof, 23, 35, 46, 75, 94, 118, 494–95
Catozzo, Dr. Leo, 332, 679
Catsplay, 280, 587
Cattaneo, Peter, 256, 683
Causey, Thomas, 163, 682
Cavalcade, 18, 43, 72, 127, 361–62, 707
Cavalcade of the Dance with Veloz and Yolanda, 240, 415
Cavdek, Dick, 333, 691
Cavett, Frank, 88–90, 418, 436, 461
Cayton, William, 266, 554
Celso, Mario, 333, 691
Centennial Summer, 183, 203, 432
Century Precision Optics, 333, 691
Cerny, Karel, 145, 645
Certain Smile, A, 136, 206, 219, 495–97
"Certain Smile, A," 206, 496
Cesari, Bruno, 146, 663
Cetera, Peter, 213, 657
Chagall, 264, 526
Chagrin, Claude, 252–53, 586, 599
Chagrin, Julian, 252–53, 586, 599
Chairy Tale, A, 247, 492
Chakiris, George, 56, 510
Chalk Garden, The, 66, 528
Challenge . . . A Tribute to Modern Art, The, 269, 587
Chalufour, Michel, 272, 635
Chambers, John, 291, 555
Champ, The (1931), 17, 32, 72, 83, 359
Champ, The (1979), 194, 615
Champagne for Two, 242, 438
Champion, 34, 55, 90, 115, 167, 184, 445–47
Champions Carry On, 240, 415
Chan, George B., 141, 558
Chances Are, 214, 677
Chance to Live, A, 260, 448
Chandlee, Harry, 86, 398
Chandler, Jeff, 55, 450
Chandler, Michael, 173, 645
Chandler, Raymond, 88, 418, 431
Chang, 355, 352
"Change of Heart," 201, 414
"Change Partners and Dance with Me," 200, 384
Changing Our Minds: The Story of Dr. Evelyn Hooker, 276, 696
Channing, Carol, 66, 547
Chaperot, Georges, 89, 436
Chaplin, Charlie, 12, 20, 33, 86, 89, 191, 285, 291, 352, 391–92, 436, 570, 574
Chaplin, Saul, 184–87, 457, 468, 474, 486, 513
Chaplin, 41, 147, 198, 692, 694
Chapman, Christopher, 250, 266, 550
Chapman, Leonard, 323, 326, 612, 636
Chapman, Linda, 271, 628
Chapman, Michael, 123, 621
Chapman, Ralph, 315, 520
Chapter Two, 49, 613
Charade (1984, animation), 255, 647
Charade (1963), 207, 525
"Charade," 207, 525
Charge of the Light Brigade, The, 149, 176, 337, 372–74
Chariots of Fire, 27, 59, 79, 104, 172, 194, 224, 625–28, 708
Chariots of the Gods, 267, 564
Charles Guggenheim and Associates, 262, 487
Charlie/Papa Productions, 271, 617
Charly, 37, 551
Charman, Roy, 160–62, 591, 609, 627, 657
Chartoff, Robert, 26–28, 595, 619, 637
Chase, Borden, 89, 441
Chase, Chevy, 655, 661
Chase, Ken, 229, 652
Chase of Death, 243, 448
Chasnoff, Debra, 276, 690
Chatelain, Arthur B., 308, 429
"Chattanooga Choo Choo," 201, 401
Chatterton, Ruth, 42, 353, 355
Chayefsky, Paddy, 93–94, 100, 102, 478, 495, 567, 596
"Cheek to Cheek," 199, 369
Cheers for Miss Bishop, 179, 400
Chekhov, Michael, 54, 424
Chekmayan, Ara, 272, 641
Cher, 51, 69, 638, 661
Chetwynd, Lionel, 101, 584
Chevalier, Maurice, 32, 290, 355, 498
Chevry, Bernard, 267, 560
Chew, Richard, 171–72, 591, 603
Chewey, Michael V., 323, 618
Chewey, Michael V., III, 331, 672
Cheyenne Autumn, 120, 529
Chiang, Doug, 233, 695
Chiari, Mario, 140, 548
Chicken, The (Le Poulet), 249, 538
Chikaya, Inoue, 170, 563
Childeater, The, 256, 678
Children at Work, 268, 581
Children of a Lesser God, 28, 40, 50, 69, 106, 655–56
Children of Darkness, 272, 641
Children of Mars, 259, 416
Children of Nature, 283, 690
Children of Paradise, 88, 431
Children of Soong Ching Ling, The, 272, 647
Children of Theatre Street, The, 270, 605
Children's Hour, The, 65, 118, 137, 157, 220, 510–13
Children's Storefront, The, 274, 659
Children Without, 264, 532
Chile: Hasta Cuando?, 274, 659
Chilvers, Colin, 295, 611
"Chim Chim Cher-ee," 207, 531
Chimps: So Like Us, 275, 683
China Syndrome, The, 39, 49, 103, 144, 613–15
Chinatown, 26, 38, 48, 77, 101, 122, 142, 159, 171, 192, 223, 583–86
Chip an' Dale, 242, 437
Chitty Chitty Bang Bang, 208, 553
"Chitty Chitty Bang Bang," 208, 553
Chocolate Soldier, The, 112, 152, 180, 398–99
Chopin's Musical Moments, 241, 433
Chorus Line, A, 162, 173, 213, 651–52

Choy, Christine, 275, 671
Chretien, Professor Henri, 311, 470
Christ Among the Primitives, 245, 469
Christian, Roger, 143–44, 603, 615
Christie, Charles, 701
Christie, Julie, 47–48, 534, 566
Christie Electric Corporation, 326, 636
Christmas Carol, A, 251, 575
Christmas Cracker, 249, 532
Christmas Holiday, 181, 420
Christmas Under Fire, 258, 402
Christo, Cyril, 274, 665
Christopher, Frank, 273, 647
Christopher Crumpet, 245, 469
Christo's Valley Curtain, 268, 581
Chukhrai, Grigori, 96, 511
Churchill, Frank, 177, 180, 201, 378, 400–401, 407–8
Churchill's Island, 258, 402
Cilento, Diane, 65, 522
Cimarron (1931), 17, 32, 43, 71, 83, 111, 127, 357–58, 707
Cimarron (1960), 137, 156, 507
Cimino, Michael, 27, 78, 103, 607–8, 708
Cinderella, 154, 184, 204, 452
Cinderella Horse, 242, 443
Cinderella Liberty, 48, 192, 210, 578, 580–1
Cine-Documents, 248, 514
Cinema Paradiso, 282, 678
Cinema Product Development Company, 317, 555
Cinema Products Corporation, 319, 321, 571, 606
Cinema Research Corporation, 319, 571
Cinquegrana, August, 270, 611
Circus, The, 285, 352
Citadel, The, 19, 32, 72, 85, 381–82
Citizen Kane, 20, 33, 73, 86, 112, 129, 152, 166, 179, 397–400
City Called Copenhagen, A, 263, 509
City Decides, A, 262, 487
City of Gold, 247, 492
City of Wax, 237, 366
City Out of Wilderness, 268, 586
City Slickers, 61, 686
Clairmont Camera, 333, 691
Clan of the Cave Bear, 229, 658
Clark, Al, 165–69, 377, 388, 447, 496, 507
Clark, Candy, 67, 579
Clark, Carroll, 127, 130–31, 137, 139, 307, 365, 368, 376, 410, 413, 419, 512, 530
Clark, Chris, 100, 573
Clark, Daniel, 306–7, 396, 410
Clark, Frank P., 319, 577
Clark, James B., 166, 400
Clark, Jim, 173, 645, 657
Clarke, Arthur C., 99, 552
Clarke, Charles G., 113, 115, 292, 307, 405, 412, 416, 441, 446, 618
Clarke, Malcolm, 274, 671
Clarke, Shirley, 247, 503
Clarke, T.E.B., 90, 91, 95, 446, 461, 506
Clatworthy, Robert, 137–41, 507, 518, 536, 548
Claudelle Inglish, 220, 513
Claudine, 48, 583
Claudon, Paul, 252, 586
Clave, 217, 462–63
Clawson, Elliott, 83, 354
Clay, or the Origin of Species, 249, 538
Clayburgh, Jill, 49, 607, 613
Clayton, Jack, 75, 500
Cleary, Kevin F., 163, 669, 676, 682
Cleese, John, 107, 668
Cleopatra (1934), 18, 111, 149, 165, 337, 364–65
Cleopatra (1963), 24, 36, 119, 139, 157, 188, 346, 522–26
Cliff Dwellers, The, 248, 520
Clift, Montgomery, 34, 56, 440, 455, 466, 510
Climax, The, 131, 419
Climb, 252, 586
Climbing the Matterhorn, 242, 438
Cline, Wilfred M., 112, 398
Clockmaker, 252, 581
Clockwork Orange, A, 25, 77, 100, 170, 566–68
Cloquet, Ghislain, 123, 621
Clore, Leon, 262, 470
Close, Glenn, 51, 69, 632, 638, 644, 661, 667
Closed Mondays, 252, 586
Close Encounters of the Third Kind, 68, 78, 122, 143, 160, 172, 193, 231, 295, 602–5
Close Harmony, 271, 628
Closely Watched Trains, 279, 550
Close To Eden, 283, 696
Clothier, William H., 118, 120, 506, 529
Clouse, Robert, 248–49, 520, 532
Coal Miner's Daughter, 27, 49, 104, 123, 144, 161, 172, 619–21
Coates, Anne, 169, 172, 518, 530, 621
Coates, John, 254, 635
Cobb, Irwin S., 13, 364
Cobb, Lee J., 55–56, 471, 494
Coblenz, Walter, 26, 595
Coburn, Charles, 8, 54, 397, 411, 430
Cocanen Films, 259, 409
Coco, James, 59, 625
Cocoon, 60, 232, 649, 652
Code Gray: Ethical Dilemmas In Nursing, 273, 647
Coe, Fred, 24, 534
Coe, George, 250, 554
Coen, Franklin, 97, 535
Coffee, Lenore, 85, 382
Cohen, George W., 701
Cohn, Alfred, 82, 351
Cohn, Arthur, 264, 275, 514, 684
Cohn, Harry, 18, 364
Cohn, Robert, 266, 554
Colasanti, Veniero, 138, 512
Colbert, Claudette, 43–44, 364, 367, 417, 477
Coldeway, Anthony, 82, 351
Coleman, C. C., Jr., 338, 376
Coleman, Cy, 190, 559
Coleman, Dr. Howard S., 314, 504
Colesberry, Robert F., 29, 667
Colla, Johnny, 213, 652
Collector, The, 47, 76, 97, 534–35
College Queen, 242, 433
Collinge, Patricia, 63, 398
Collings, Pierre, 84, 372
Collingwood, Monica, 167, 437
Collins, Anthony, 178–80, 389, 394, 400
Collins, Judy, 269, 587
Collins, Pauline, 51, 674
Collins, Phil, 213–14, 646, 670
Collis, Jack, 143, 597
Colman, Edward, 118, 120, 511, 529
Colman, Ronald, 32–34, 355, 404, 435
Colombo, Alberto, 177, 377
Colonel Redl, 282, 653
Color of Money, The, 40, 69, 106, 146, 655–57
Color Purple, The, 28, 50, 69, 106, 124, 145, 196, 213, 225, 229, 649–52
Colours of My Father: A Portrait of Sam Borenstein, 276, 696
Columbia Pictures Corporation, 237, 239–41, 303, 366, 369, 401, 421, 428; Camera Department, 315, 509; Sound Department, 149–58, 310, 312, 365, 368, 373, 377, 383, 388, 393, 399, 407, 413, 419, 426, 432, 454, 468, 476, 485, 491, 507, 524, 553
Comandini, Pete, 294, 690
Combat Report, 259, 409
Comden, Betty, 92–93, 467, 478
Come and Get It, 53, 165, 371, 373
Come Back, Little Sheba, 45, 64, 167, 460, 462
Come Blow Your Horn, 139, 524
Come Fill the Cup, 55, 455
"Come Follow, Follow Me," 209, 575
Comer, Sam, 129, 131–39, 399, 406, 419, 426, 431, 452, 473, 479, 485, 491, 496, 501, 507, 512, 518, 524

Comes a Horseman, 59, 607
"Come Saturday Morning," 208, 559
"Come to Me," 210, 598
Come to the Stable, 45, 64, 89, 115, 132, 204, 445–47
Coming Home, 26, 38, 49, 59, 68, 78, 103, 172, 607–9
Coming to America, 226, 229, 670
Commandini, Adele, 84, 372
Commandos Strike at Dawn, The, 180, 414
Commitments, The, 174, 688
Common Threads: Stories from the Quilt, 275, 678
Competition, The, 172, 212, 621–22
Compson, Betty, 42, 353
Comrade X, 85, 392
Concert, The (1963 short), 249, 526
Concert, The (1974), 252, 586
Condemned, 32, 355
Condie, Richard, 255, 653
Condon, Richard, 106, 650
Coney Island, 181, 414
Confidence, 281, 623
Conformist, The, 100, 567
Conley, Renie, 224, 610. *See also* Renie
Conn, Pamela, 274, 665
Connaughton, Shane, 108, 675
Connell, Richard, 86–87, 398, 418
Connelly, Joe, 92, 478
Connelly, Marc, 85, 376
Connery, Sean, 60, 661
Connolly, Bob (documentary), 272, 641
Connolly, Bobby, 339–40, 369, 373, 378
Connolly, Myles, 88, 425
Connors, Carol, 210–11, 598, 604
Conquer by the Clock, 259, 409
Conquest, 32, 127, 375–76
Conquest of Everest, The, 261, 470
Conquest of Light, 252, 592
Conrad, Con, 199, 366
Conrad, Scott, 171, 597
Conroy, Pat, 109, 687
Conroy, T. R., 257, 689
Considine, John W., Jr., 18, 19, 367, 381
Consolidated Film Industries, 318–19, 321, 555, 571, 599
Constant Nymph, The, 44, 411
Contact, 257, 695
Conti, Bill, 39, 195, 210, 212, 598, 627, 640
Conti, Tom, 39, 637
"Continental, The," 199, 366
Conversation, The, 26, 101, 159, 583–85
Conway, Lyle, 232, 658
Conway, Richard, 233, 677
Cook, Alan, 305, 390
Cook, Gordon Henry, 301, 671
Cook, Rob, 333, 697
Cook, Robert O., 157, 309, 434, 512, 518, 530
Cook, Tim, 330, 666
Cook, T. S., 103, 614
Cool Hand Luke, 37, 57, 98, 189, 546–48
Coons, David B., 333, 691
Coop, Denys, 295, 611
Cooper, Gary, 4, 31–34, 290, 371, 397, 404, 411, 460, 509
Cooper, Gladys, 63, 66, 405, 411, 528
Cooper, Jackie, 32, 357
Cooper, Merian C., 18, 22, 289, 460, 464
Cop, The, 83, 354
Copland, Aaron, 178–79, 181, 184, 388–89, 394, 414, 447
Coppel, Alec, 91, 467
Coppola, Carmine, 192, 214, 585, 682
Coppola, Francis Ford, 25–27, 29, 77–78, 80, 100–101, 103, 562, 573, 578, 583–84, 613–14, 680–81, 708
Coquette, 42, 353
Corby, Ellen, 63, 440
Corcoran, James P., 157–58, 524, 536, 542
Cordell, Frank, 190, 563
Cordwell, Harry, 145–46, 633, 663
Corey, Wendell, 705
Corigliano, John, 194, 622
Corl, Hal, 309, 312–13, 481–82
Cornell, John, 106, 656
Cornell, Pamela, 141, 562
Corn Is Green, The, 54, 63, 424
Corsican Brothers, The, 180, 407
Corso, John W., 144, 621
Cortese, Valentina, 67, 584
Cortez, Stanley, 113–14, 405, 418
Corvette K-225, 113, 412
Corwin, Norman, 93, 484
Cory, Ray, 343, 421
Cosgrove, Jack, 341–43, 408, 428
Cosgrove, John R., 341, 343, 389, 395, 421
Coslow, Sam, 240, 415
Costa-Gavras, 76, 99, 105, 557, 632
Costello, Dianna, 255, 653
Costner, Kevin, 29, 41, 80, 680–81, 708
Cotton Club, The, 144, 173, 645
Couch, Lionel, 137, 141, 507, 558
Couffer, Jack, 122, 579
Country, 50, 643
Country Cousin, 237, 374
Country Girl, The, 22, 35, 45, 74, 92, 116, 134, 471–73
"Count Your Blessings Instead of Sheep," 205, 474
Coup De Torchon (Clean Slate), 281, 635
Couples and Robbers, 254, 628
Courage, Alexander, 189–90, 537, 548
Courage to Care, The, 273, 653
Course Completed, 282, 665
Courtenay, Tom, 39, 57, 534, 637
Court Martial of Billy Mitchell, The, 93, 478
Cousin, Cousine, 49, 102, 280, 595, 599
Cousteau, Jacques-Yves, 247, 262, 265, 487, 503, 532
Coutant, Andre, 310, 449
Couturie, Bill, 275–76, 678, 690
Cover Girl, 114, 131, 153, 202, 418–20
Cow, 256, 678
Coward, Noel, 21, 87, 287, 409, 411–12
Cowboy (1958), 168, 496
Cowboy (1966), 265, 544
Cowboy and the Lady, The, 150, 178, 200, 303, 384
"Cowboy and the Lady, The," 200, 384
Cow Dog, 246, 487
Cox, Joel, 175, 694
Cox, John, 157, 512, 518, 530
Crabe, James, 123, 621
Crac, 254, 628
Crack USA: County Under Seige, 275, 678
Cradle of Genius, 264, 514
Craig, Michael, 95, 506
Craig, Phil, 200, 384
Craig, Stuart, 144–47, 621, 633, 657, 669, 694
Crain, Jeanne, 45, 445
Cram, Mildred, 85, 387
Crama, Nico, 253, 610
Crandell, Frank, 312, 476
Crash Dive, 342, 415
Crashing the Water Barrier, 246, 487
Crawford, Broderick, 34, 445
Crawford, Joan, 44–45, 424, 435, 460
Crawley, F. R., 269, 593
Crazylegs, 168, 468
Crazy Mixed up Pup, 245, 474
Creation, The, 254, 628
Creation of Woman, The, 248, 508
Creature Comforts, 256, 683
Creber, William, 140, 142–43, 536, 574, 585
Crichton, Charles, 80, 107, 668
Cries and Whispers, 25, 77, 101, 121, 223, 578–79, 581
Crimes and Misdemeanors, 61, 80, 108, 675
Crimes of the Heart, 51, 69, 107, 655–56
Criminal Code, The, 83, 357

Crisp, Donald, 54, 397
Cristiani, Gabriella, 174, 663
Critchlow, Keith, 269, 593
Critic, The, 248, 526
"Crocodile" Dundee, 106, 656
Cromwell, John, 417
Cromwell, 190, 222, 563–64
Cronenweth, Jordan, 124, 656
Cronjager, Edward, 111–14, 116, 358, 398, 405–6, 412, 418, 467
Cronyn, Hume, 54, 417
Crookham, David, 328, 654
Crookham, Joe P., 328, 654
Crosby, Bing, 11, 33, 35, 417, 424, 471
Crosby, Floyd, 111, 358
Cross, Christopher, 212, 627
Cross Creek, 60, 69, 195, 225, 638, 640
Crosse, Rupert, 57, 556
Crossfire, 21, 54, 63, 73, 89, 435–36
Crossley, Callie, 274, 665
Crouch, Andrae, 196, 651
Crouse, John, 343, 421
Crouse, Lindsay, 69, 644
Crowd, The, 71, 335, 351–52
Crowley, Michael, 273, 653
Cruel Sea, The, 92, 467
Cruickshank, Art, 231, 346, 543, 616
Cruise, Tom, 40, 674
Cruise Control, 257, 695
Crump, Owen, 261, 459
Crunch Bird, The, 251, 569
Crusades, The, 111, 368
Cry Freedom, 61, 196, 213, 661, 663
"Cry Freedom," 213, 663
Crying Game, The, 29, 41, 61, 81, 109, 174, 692–94
Cry in the Dark, A, 51, 667
Cry of Reason—Beyers Naude: An Afrikaner Speaks Out, The, 274, 671
Crystal, Billy, 13, 674, 680, 686, 692
Csillag, Steve, 310, 449
Cukor, George, 72–74, 76, 361, 392, 435, 450, 529, 708
Cullen, Edward F., 263, 503
Cummings, Irving, 71, 353
Cummings, Jack, 22, 471
Cummings, Quinn, 68, 602
Cundey, Dean, 125, 669
Curtin, Valerie, 103, 614
Curtis, Tony, 35, 494
Curtiss, Edward, 165, 373
Curtiz, Michael, 72–73, 382, 405, 412, 707
Cusack, Joan, 70, 668
Cyrano de Bergerac (1950), 34, 41, 450
Cyrano de Bergerac (1990), 146, 226, 229, 282, 680–81, 683–84
Czechoslovakia 1968, 266, 559
DaCosta, Morton, 24, 516
Dad, 229, 677
Daddy Long Legs, 185, 205, 479–80
Dae, 271, 617
Daens, 283, 696
Dafoe, Willem, 60, 655
D'Agostino, Albert S., 127, 129–31, 372, 406, 413, 419, 425
DaGradi, Don, 97, 529
Dahl, Tom, 163, 663
Dailey, Dan, 34, 440
Daily, Charles R., 308–10, 313, 429, 439, 449, 488
Daisy Miller, 223, 586
Dale, James, 315, 515
Dale, Jim, 208, 543
Dalgleish, William, 153, 419
Dall, John, 54, 424
Dallmayr, Horst, 267, 564
Dalrymple, Ian, 85, 382
Dalton, Phyllis, 221–22, 226, 537, 553, 677
Dalva, Robert, 172, 615
Daly, Tom, 244, 247, 249, 263, 265, 463, 492, 497, 526, 544
Damage, 70, 693
Dam Busters, The, 344, 480
D'Amico, Suso Cecchi, 97, 535
Damned, The, 99, 557
Damn Yankees, 186, 496
Damsel in Distress, A, 127, 340, 376, 378
Dances with Wolves, 29, 41, 61, 70, 80, 108, 125, 146, 163, 174, 197, 226, 680–83, 708
Dancing Pirate, 340, 374
Dandridge, Dorothy, 45, 471
Dane, Clemence, 88, 431
Danevic, Nena, 173, 645
Danforth, Jim, 346–47, 531, 569
Dangerous, 43, 367
Dangerous Liaisons, 29, 51, 70, 107, 146, 197, 226, 667–70
Dangerous Moves, 281, 647
Danger under the Sea, 244, 458
Daniel, Eliot, 204, 447, 458
Daniel, Gordon, 348, 544
Daniels, William, 110, 115, 118, 119, 356, 441, 495, 523
Danish Government Film Office, 263, 487, 509
Danon, Ambra, 224, 616
Danon, Marcello, 103, 614
D'Antoni, Philip, 25, 566
Darby, Jonathan, 257, 695
Darby, Ken, 186–89, 486, 496, 502, 513, 525, 548
Darin, Bobby, 56, 522
Dark Angel, The, 43, 127, 149, 367–68
Dark at the Top of the Stairs, The, 65, 505
Dark Command, 128, 179, 393–94
Dark Eyes, 40, 661
Dark Mirror, The, 88, 431
Dark Victory, 19, 43, 178, 386, 388
Dark Wave, The, 246, 262, 487
Darling, William, 127–28, 130–31, 362, 372, 377, 387, 413, 425, 431
Darling, 24, 47, 76, 97, 221, 534–35, 537
Darling Lili, 191, 209, 222, 563–64
D'Arrast, Harry d'Abbadie, 83, 357
Darwell, Jane, 62, 392
Das Boot, 79, 105, 123, 161, 173, 234, 632–34
Dassin, Jules, 75, 95, 506
Dauber, Philip, 253, 605
Davey, Allen, 112–14, 286, 385, 392, 412, 418, 425
Daviau, Allen, 123–25, 632, 650, 662, 681, 687
David, Hal, 208, 537, 543, 549, 559
David, Mack, 204, 206–8, 452, 502, 513, 519, 525, 531, 537, 543
David and Bathsheba, 91, 116, 133, 184, 217, 456–58
David and Lisa, 75, 96, 517
David Copperfield, 18, 165, 337, 367–68
Davidson, Adam, 256, 683
Davidson, Carson, 243, 249, 480, 532
Davidson, Jaye, 61, 692
Davidson, Roy, 341, 389
Davies, Jack, 97, 535
Davies, Peter Maxwell, 191, 568
Davies, Tessa, 145, 639
Davies, Valentine, 6, 89, 92, 262, 436, 446, 472, 487, 705
D'Avino, Carmen, 249, 268, 526, 581
Davis, Bette, 11–12, 42–46, 367, 381, 386, 391, 397, 404, 417, 450, 460, 516, 705
Davis, C. C., 309, 439
Davis, Frank, 88, 97, 425, 535
Davis, Geena, 51, 70, 668, 686
Davis, George W., 132–35, 137–41, 451, 457, 468, 479, 491, 501, 507, 518, 524, 530, 536, 542, 552
Davis, Judy, 50, 70, 643, 693
Davis, Lem, 333, 691
Davis, Peter, 269, 587
Davis, Sammy, Jr., 566, 583
Davis, Sidney, 250, 554
Davison, Bruce, 61, 680
Dawe, Tony, 162–63, 639, 663, 669, 676
Dawn, Jeff, 229, 689
Dawn Flight, 252, 592
Dawn Patrol, The, 83, 357
Dawns Here Are Quiet, The, 280, 576
Dawson, Beatrice, 218, 480

Dawson, Ralph, 165, 168, 369, 373, 383, 473
Day, Doris, 46, 499
Day, Ernest, 124, 645
Day, Richard, 127–30, 132–34, 140–41, 358, 360, 365, 368, 372, 376, 382, 393, 399, 406, 431, 441, 457, 462, 473, 536, 562
Day After Trinity, The, 271, 623
Day at the Races, A, 340, 378
Daybreak in Udi, 260, 448
Day for Night, 67, 77, 101, 280, 582, 584
Day in the Life of Bonnie Consolo, A, 253, 592
Day of the Dolphin, The, 159, 192, 580
Day of the Jackal, The, 171, 580
Day of the Locust, The, 58, 122, 590
Day of the Painter, 248, 508
Days of Glory, 343, 421
Days of Heaven, 122, 160, 194, 224, 608–10
Days of Thunder, 163, 682
Days of Waiting, 275, 683
Days of Wine and Roses, 36, 46, 138, 207, 220, 516, 518–19
"Days of Wine and Roses," 207, 519
Dayton, Richard T., 294, 690
Dead, The, 107, 226, 662, 664
Dead End, 19, 62, 111, 127, 375–76
Deadly Deception: General Electric, Nuclear Weapons and Our Environment, 276, 690
Dead Poets Society, 29, 40, 80, 108, 674–75
Dean, James, 35, 477, 483
Dean, Lisa, 147, 681
de Antonio, Emile, 267, 560
Dearden, James, 107, 662
Dear Heart, 207, 531
"Dear Heart," 207, 531
Dear John, 279, 538
"Dearly Beloved," 201, 408
Dear Rosie, 256, 683
Death Becomes Her, 233, 695
Death in Venice, 222, 569
Death of a Salesman, 34, 55, 64, 115, 184, 455–57
Death on the Job, 276, 690
Death on the Nile, 224, 610
Deats, Richard W., 326, 636
D'Eaubonne, 133, 457
Debonair Dancers, 273, 659
De Broca, Philippe, 97, 529
December 7th, 259, 416
Decision Before Dawn, 22, 167, 455, 457
Declaration of Independence, 238, 384
Decline of the American Empire, 282, 659
De Concini, Ennio, 96, 517
DeCuir, John, 133–37, 139–41, 457, 462, 479, 485, 495, 501, 524, 536, 548, 558
Dedalo, 253, 598
Deeley, Michael, 27, 607
Deep, The, 160, 603
Deep South, 238, 378
Deep Waters, 343, 442
Deer Hunter, The, 26, 38, 59, 68, 78, 103, 122, 160, 172, 607–9, 708
De Felitta, Raymond, 256, 683
Defiant Ones, The, 6, 23, 35, 56, 65, 75, 94, 117, 168, 494–96
De Forest, Lee, 290, 503
Degenkolb, David J., 319, 321, 323, 327, 577, 593, 612, 642
De Givenchy, Hubert, 219, 492
de Grasse, Robert, 111, 382
de Havilland, Olivia, 42, 44–45, 62, 386, 397, 430, 440, 445
Dehn, Paul, 91, 101, 456, 584
De La Cierva, Juan, 318, 560
De La Mare, Elizabeth D., 327, 642
Delamare, Rosine, 218, 474
de Larios, Carlos, 162–63, 639, 645, 663, 682
Delerue, Georges, 190, 192–94, 196, 558, 580, 603, 616, 651
Deliverance, 25, 77, 171, 572–74
dell'Instituto Nazionale Luce, 264, 514
Delmar, Vina, 85, 376
Deluge, The, 280, 587
Deluxe Laboratories, Inc., 315, 515
De Matteis, Marie, 219, 486
De Mattos, Carlos, 326, 328, 636, 654
Demerest, William, 54, 430
De Mille, Cecil B., 18, 22–23, 74, 289, 297, 364, 448, 460–61, 464, 483, 701, 707
de Mille, William, 351, 353, 705
Demme, Jonathan, 80, 687, 708
Demos, Gary, 327, 648
De Muth, John, 325, 630
Demy, Jacques, 97, 189–90, 207, 535, 537, 553
Deneuve, Catherine, 52, 692
Denham Studio Sound Department, 151, 388
DeNicola, John, 214, 664
De Niro, Robert, 38–39, 41, 58, 583, 595, 607, 619, 680, 686
Denmark Government Film Committee, 262, 487
Denney, Bruce H., 310, 449
Dennis, Sandy, 66, 541
Denove, Thomas F., 332, 685
Densham, Pen, 252, 271, 581, 623
Depardieu, Gerard, 41, 680
de Passe, Suzanne, 100, 573
DePatie, David, 249–50, 532, 544
DePatie, Edmond L., 299, 539
De Paul, Gene, 201, 408
Der Fuehrer's Face, 239, 408
Dern, Bruce, 59, 607
Dern, Laura, 51, 686
De Rochemont, Richard, 260, 448
De Rooy, Adriaan, 326, 636
De Roubaix, Paul, 249, 264, 526
Dersu Uzala, 280, 593
De Santis, Giuseppe, 90, 451
De Santis, Pasqualino, 121, 552
DeScenna, Linda, 144–47, 615, 633, 651, 669, 694
Deschanel, Caleb, 123–24, 639, 645
Desert Killer, 244, 463
Desert Rats, The, 92, 467
Desert Song, The, 131, 419
Desert Victory, 259, 416
Desert Wonderland, 239, 409
De Sica, Vittorio, 56, 489
Desideri, Osvaldo, 146, 663
Design for Death, 260, 438
Designing Woman, 94, 490
Desiree, 134, 218, 473–74
Desire Under the Elms, 117, 495
Desperate Journey, 342, 408
Destination Moon, 133, 344, 452–53
Destination Tokyo, 87, 412
De Sylva, Buddy, 200, 389
Detective Story, 45, 64, 74, 91, 455–56
De Titta, George, Jr., 144, 146, 627, 663
De Titta, George, Sr., 144, 627
Detlefson, Paul, 343, 421
Detlie, John S., 128, 393
De Toth, Andre, 90, 451
Detouring America, 238, 389
Deutsch, Adolph, 184–86, 452, 458, 468, 474, 480
Deutsch, Helen, 92, 467
DeVestel, Robert, 142–43, 580, 597
Devil and Miss Jones, The, 54, 86, 397–98
Devil Came at Night, The, 277, 493
Devil Dancer, The, 110, 352
DeVille, Willy, 214, 664
Devil Pays Off, The, 152, 399
Devil's Holiday, The, 42, 355
Devil Take Us, 244, 261, 463–64
De Vinna, Clyde, 110, 354
Devinney, James A., 274, 665
DeVol, Frank, 187–90, 207, 501, 530–31, 537, 548
DeVore, Christopher, 104, 620
DeVorzon, Barry, 209, 569
De Wilde, Brandon, 55, 466
Diage, Louis, 135–36, 485, 491, 495
Diamond, I.A.L., 95, 98, 500, 506, 541
Diamonds Are Forever, 158, 568

Diary of a Mad Housewife, 48, 561
Diary of Anne Frank, The, 23, 56, 65, 75, 118, 136, 187, 219, 499–502
Diaz, Ken, 229, 677
Dicken, Roger, 347, 569
Dickinson, Thorold, 263, 497
Dickson, Deborah, 274, 664
Dick Tracy, 61, 125, 147, 163, 214, 226, 229, 680–83
"Did I Remember," 199, 373
Diebold, Gerry, 320, 582
Die Hard, 163, 233, 235, 669–70
Diehl, Gaston, 243, 448
Dieterle, William, 72, 376, 707
Dietrich, Marlene, 42, 357
Different Approach, A, 253, 610
Dighton, John, 91–92, 461, 467
Digirolamo, Don, 161, 163, 633, 663, 669
Digiulio, Edmund M., 317, 334, 555, 697
Dilley, Leslie, 143–44, 146, 603, 615, 621, 627, 676
Dillinger, 88, 425
Dillon, Carmen, 132, 431, 441
Dillon, Melinda, 68, 602, 626
Dimmers, Jacobus L., 326, 636
Diner, 104, 632
Dior, Christian, 218, 474
DiPersio, Vince, 275–76, 678, 690
Dirka, Karel, 273, 647
Dirty Dancing, 213, 663
Dirty Dozen, The, 57, 158, 170, 348, 546, 548–49
DiSarro, Al, 233, 670
Discreet Charm of the Bourgeoisie, The, 100, 280, 573, 576
Disney, Walt, 13, 24, 236–48, 250, 259, 261–63, 285–87, 297, 360, 362, 366, 369, 374, 378, 384–85, 389, 401–2, 408, 415, 421, 428, 433, 437–38, 443, 448, 453, 458, 464, 469–70, 474–75, 480–81, 487, 492, 497, 502–3, 508, 514, 520, 528, 554
Disney Sound Department. *See* Walt Disney Productions; Sound Department
Disraeli, 17, 31, 83, 355–56
Dive Bomber, 112, 399
Dive-Hi Champs, 241, 433
Divided Trail, The, 270, 610
Divine Lady, The, 42, 71, 110, 353–54
Divorce American Style, 98, 547
Divorcee, The, 17, 42, 71, 83, 355–56
Divorce-Italian Style, 36, 75, 96, 516–17
Dix, Richard, 32, 357
Dixon, Thomas P., 314, 503
Dixon, Vernon, 141–43, 552, 568, 591
Dizzy Acrobat, The, 240, 415
Dmytryk, Edward, 73, 435
Dockendorf, David, 158, 558
Doctor Desoto, 255, 647
Doctor Dolittle, 24, 121, 140, 158, 170, 189–90, 208, 346, 546–49
Doctor Zhivago, 24, 57, 76, 97, 120, 140, 157, 169, 189, 221, 534–37
Dodes'ka-den, 279, 570
Dodsworth, 19, 32, 62, 72, 84, 127, 150, 371–73
Dog, Cat and Canary, The, 240, 421
Dog Day Afternoon, 26, 38, 58, 78, 101, 171, 589–91
Doherty, Edward, 87, 418
Doing Time: Life Inside the Big House, 276, 690
Dolan, John C., 321, 593
Dolan, Robert Emmett, 180–83, 400, 407, 414, 420, 426–27, 432, 437
Dolby, Ray, 323, 330, 612, 672
Dolby Laboratories, 333, 697
Dollar Bottom, The, 254, 622
Dolly Sisters, The, 203, 432
"Dolores," 201, 401
Domela, Jan, 286, 385
Donald Duck, 489
Donald in Mathmagic Land, 263, 503
Donald's Crime, 241, 428
Donaldson, Walter, 199, 373
Donat, Robert, 32–33, 381, 386
Donati, Danilo, 221–23, 543, 549, 554, 598
Donfeld, 222–23, 225, 559, 581, 652. *See also* Feld, Don
Dong, Arthur, 272, 641
Donlevy, Brian, 53, 386
Donovan, Arlene, 28, 643
Don't, 269, 586
Don't Mess with Bill, 271, 622
Don't Talk, 240, 409
Doonesbury Special, The, 253, 604
Doorway to Hell, 83, 357
Dorian, Charles, 337, 361
Dorleac, Jean-Pierre, 224, 622
Dorney, Roger, 326, 642
Dornhelm, Robert, 270, 605
Dorothy Chandler Pavilion, 13, 551, 556, 561, 566, 572, 578, 583, 589, 595, 601, 607, 613, 619, 625, 631, 637, 643, 649, 655, 674, 686, 692
Dot and the Line, The, 249, 538
Do the Right Thing, 61, 108, 674–75
Doty, Douglas, 83, 357
Double Feature, 281, 647
Double Indemnity, 21, 44, 73, 88, 113, 153, 181, 417–20
Double Life, A, 34, 73, 89, 183, 435–37
Double or Nothing, 237, 374
Doubletalk, 253, 592
Douglas, Everett, 168, 468
Douglas, Haldane, 130, 413
Douglas, Kirk, 34–35, 445, 460, 483
Douglas, Melvyn, 37, 57, 59, 522, 561, 613
Douglas, Michael, 26, 40, 589, 661
Douglas, Nathan (Ned Young), 6, 94–95, 495, 506
Douglas, Paul, 445
Dourif, Brad, 58, 589
Dove, The (1928), 126, 352
Dove, The (1968), 250, 554
Dowd, Nancy, 103, 608
Dowd, Ross J., 135, 137, 485, 507
Dower, John W., 274, 665
Down and Out in America, 274, 659
Down Argentine Way, 112, 128, 200, 392–94
"Down Argentine Way," 200, 394
Downey, Robert, Jr., 41, 692
Down on the Farm, 239, 401
Doyle, James, 333, 691
Dozier, Lamont, 214, 670
Drag, 71, 353
Drag, The (short film), 250, 544
Dragic, Nedeljko, 251, 575
Dragon, Carmen, 182, 420
Dragon Seed, 63, 113, 417–18
Dragonslayer, 195, 232, 627–28
Drake, Geoffrey, 142, 574
Dratler, Jay, 88, 418
Dr. Cyclops, 341, 395
Dream Doll, 254, 617
Dream Wife, 217, 469
Dreher, Carl, 149, 365, 368
Dr. Ehrlich's Magic Bullet, 86, 392
Drehsler, Alex W., 273, 647
Dreier, Hans, 126–31, 133, 354, 356, 358, 362, 368, 377, 383, 387, 393, 399, 406, 413, 419, 425–26, 431, 452
Dresser, Louise, 42, 351
Dresser, The, 28, 39, 79, 105, 637–38
Dressler, Marie, 42–43, 357, 359
Drexler, Doug, 229, 683
Dreyfuss, Richard, 38, 601
Drieband-Burman, Bari, 229, 670
Driscoll, Bobby, 289, 448
Driving Miss Daisy, 29, 40, 51, 61, 108, 146, 174, 226, 229, 674–77, 708
Dr. Jekyll and Mr. Hyde (1932), 32, 83, 111, 359–60
Dr. Jekyll and Mr. Hyde (1941), 112, 166, 179, 398, 400
Dr. Jekyll and Mr. Mouse, 242, 437
Drost, Jim, 328, 654

Dr. Strangelove, or: How I Learned to Stop Worrying and Love the Bomb, 24, 36, 76, 97, 528–29
Drumheller, Robert, 144, 609
Drums Along the Mohawk, 62, 387
Drunk Driving, 238, 389
Dryer, David, 232, 634
Dry White Season, A, 61, 675
Dubin, Al, 199, 202, 369, 378, 415
Dublin Gate Theatre Prod., 469
DuBois, Raoul Pene, 129, 131, 399, 419
DuBois, Richard, 321, 593
Ducarme, Jean–Louis, 160, 603
Dudley, George, 128, 387
Duel in the Sun, 44, 63, 430
Duell, Randall, 129, 135, 399, 406, 479
Duffy, Gerald, 12, 82, 351
Dukakis, Olympia, 70, 662
Duke, Patty, 65, 517
Dull, Bunny, 337, 361
Dull, O. O., 260, 443
Dumbo, 180, 201, 400–401
Dummy Ache, 237, 374
Dunaway, Faye, 47–49, 546, 583, 595
Duncan, Robert, 270, 599
Dundas, Sally, 276, 696
Dune, 162, 645
Duning, George, 184–86, 447, 452, 468, 486
Dunn, James, 54, 424
Dunn, Linwood G., 292, 301, 307, 324, 346, 422, 543, 611, 623, 648
Dunn, Michael, 57, 534
Dunn, Steve, 152–53, 307, 407, 413, 419, 422, 426
Dunne, Irene, 43, 45, 357, 371, 375, 386, 440
Dunne, Philip, 86, 91, 398, 456
Dunning, John, 167–68, 447, 501
Dunnock, Mildred, 64, 455, 483
Duo, 250, 554
DuPont de Nemours and Co.,Inc., Photo Products Division, 307, 416
DuPont Film Manufacturing Corp., 302, 358
Dupuis, Stephen, 229, 658
Dupy, Olin L., 311, 459
Duras, Marguerite, 95, 506
Durbin, Deanna, 286, 384
Durham, Marcel, 172, 603
Durning, Charles, 60, 631, 637
Durrin, Ginny, 275, 671
"Dust," 200, 384
Dutilleux, Jean–Pierre, 270, 611
Dutton, George, 156, 343, 415, 421, 437, 491, 496
Duvall, Robert, 39, 58–59, 572, 613, 619, 637
Dwyer, John M., 144, 621
Dyer, Elmer, 113, 412
Dykstra, John, 231–32, 322, 604, 606, 617
Dylan Thomas, 264, 520
Dynamite, 126, 354
Dynasciences Corporation, 318, 560

Eagels, Jeanne, 42, 353
Eagler, Paul, 341, 343, 395, 442
Earl, Don, 333, 697
Earl Carroll Vanities, 202, 427
Earrings of Madame De . . . , The, 218, 474
Earthquake, 122, 142, 159, 171, 295, 584–85, 587
Easdale, Brian, 183, 442
Easter Parade, 183, 442
East Lynne, 17, 357
Eastman Kodak Company, 293, 302–4, 310–12, 317–18, 322, 330, 332, 358, 360, 370, 379, 449, 464, 481, 555, 565, 606, 612, 666, 670, 684
East of Eden, 35, 64, 74, 93, 477–78
Eastwood, Clint, 30, 41, 81, 692–93, 708
Easy Rider, 57, 99, 556–57
Eaton, Jack, 241, 243–45, 433, 448, 458, 463, 469
Ebb, Fred, 210, 592
Eber, Bob, 164, 694
Eddy Duchin Story, The, 93, 117, 155, 186, 484–86
Edelman, Bernard, 276, 690
Edelman, Lou, 18, 364
Edelstein, Alan, 273, 653
Edemann, Louis L., 235, 670
Edens, Roger, 178–80, 183–84, 200, 203, 388, 394, 407, 437, 442, 447, 452
Edeson, Arthur, 110, 113, 354, 356, 412
Edison the Man, 85, 392
Edlund, Richard, 231–33, 296, 325, 329, 604, 623, 628–29, 634, 642, 646, 658, 660, 670, 695
Edmundson, William, 158, 558
Edouart, Farciot, 8, 286, 304–5, 307, 309, 312–13, 341–43, 379, 385, 389–90, 395, 401, 408, 415–16, 421, 437, 439, 481–82
Educated Fish, 238, 378
Educating Peter, 276, 696
Educating Rita, 39, 50, 105, 637–38
Educational, 237–38, 362, 366, 369, 378
Edward, My Son, 45, 445
Edwards, Blake, 105, 632
Edwards, Roy W., 330, 672
Edward Scissorhands, 229, 683
Edzard, Christine, 107, 668
EECO (Electronic Engineering Company of California), 322, 606
Efron, Edward, 319, 576
Egg and I, The, 63, 435
Eggar, Samantha, 47, 534
Eggers, Walter, 323, 618
Egyptian, The, 116, 472
Ehrenborg, Lennart, 268, 570
Ehrlich, Jacquot, 269, 587
E. I. DuPont de Nemours and Company. *See* DuPont de Nemours and Co., Inc.
8½. See Federico Fellini's 8½
1848, 260, 448
Eight Minutes to Midnight: A Portrait of Dr. Helen Caldicott, 272, 628
81st Blow, The, 269, 587
Eisenhardt, Robert, 272, 641
Eisler, Hanns, 181, 414, 420
Elam, Bud, 330, 672
El Amor Brujo, 279, 550
El Cid, 138, 187, 206, 512–13
Elder, Lonne III, 100, 573
Eleanor Roosevelt Story, The, 265, 538
Electra, 278, 520
Electrical Research Products Inc., 302–4, 358, 363, 366, 370, 374, 402. *See also* Western Electric Company
Electric Horseman, The, 160, 615
Electro Sound Incorporated, 318, 565
Electro–Voice, Inc., 315, 521
Elemack Company, 320, 588
Elementary School, The, 283, 690
Elephant Man, The, 27, 39, 78, 104, 144, 172, 194, 224, 619–22
"Elephant Number—It's the Animal In Me," 339, 369
Elfand, Martin, 26, 589
Elias, Hal, 292, 618
Eliscu, Edward, 199, 366
Ellenshaw, Harrison, 231, 616
Ellenshaw, Peter, 142, 231, 346, 531, 568, 585, 616
Ellington, Duke, 187, 513
Elliot, Denholm, 60, 655
Elliott, Jack, 189, 531
Elliott, Walter G., 348, 526
Ellis, Clifford H., 320, 582
Ellis, John, 232, 652
Ellis, Ron, 254, 617
Elmer Gantry, 23, 35, 65, 95, 187, 505–7
El Norte, 105, 644
El Salvador: Another Vietnam, 272, 628
Else, Jon, 269, 271, 592, 623
Elson, Richard, 276, 696
Emerson, Hope, 64, 450
Emerson, John, 19, 371
Emert, Oliver, 138, 518
Emes, Ian, 255, 641

Emigrants, The, 25, 48, 77, 100, 279, 570, 572–73
Emma, 43, 359
Emperor Waltz, The, 183, 216, 442
Empire of the Sun, 124, 146, 163, 174, 196, 226, 662–64
Empire Strikes Back, The, 144, 161, 194, 296, 621–23
Employees Only, 263, 497
Enchanted April, 70, 109, 226, 693, 695
Enchanted Cottage, 182, 427
Encounter with Faces, An, 270, 611
Endless Love, 212, 627
"Endless Love," 212, 627
"Endlessly," 202, 427
End of the Game, The, 269, 592
End of the Road, The, 269, 599
Endore, Guy, 88, 425
Enemies, A Love Story, 70, 108, 675
Enemy Below, The, 344, 492
Engel, Jules, 248, 520
Engel, Morris, 91, 467
Engelen, Paul, 228, 646
Enright, Nick, 109, 693
Entertainer, The, 35, 505
Entre Nous, 281, 641
Ephron, Henry, 96, 523
Ephron, Nora, 105, 108, 638, 675
Ephron, Phoebe, 96, 523
Eppolito, John, 330, 666
Epstein, Julius J., 85, 87, 100, 105, 382, 412, 573, 638
Epstein, Philip G., 87, 412
Epstein, Robert, 273, 275, 647, 678
Equity, 3
Equus, 38, 59, 102, 601–2
Erdody, Leo, 182, 420
Erland, Jonathan, 326, 328, 642, 648
Ernest, Orien, 312, 476
Ersatz, 248, 514
Erskine, Karin, 223, 592
Eruption of Mount St. Helens, 271, 623
Erwin, Stuart, 53, 371
Escape Me Never, 43, 367
Eskimo, 165, 365
Eslick, Bill, 333, 697
Esparza, Moctesuma, 270, 605
Estabrook, Howard, 83, 356–57
Estus, Boyd, 272, 628
Etaix, Philip, 248, 520
Eternally Yours, 178, 388
Etherington, Hal, 160, 597
E. T. The Extra-Terrestrial, 27, 79, 104, 123, 161, 173, 195, 232, 234, 631–34
Europa, Europa, 109, 687
Europeans, The, 224, 616
Evans, Bruce A., 107, 656
Evans, Chris, 233, 670
Evans, Dame Edith, 47, 65–66, 522, 528, 546
Evans, Denny, 251, 569
Evans, John, 231, 617
Evans, Ray, 202–7, 427, 442, 452, 486, 492, 496, 531
Evans, Robert, 26, 583
Evans, William, 314, 503
"Evergreen (Love Theme from A Star Is Born)," 210, 598
Every Child, 254, 617
Every Day's a Holiday, 127, 376
"(Everything I Do) I Do It For You," 215, 688
Evolution, 251, 569
Excalibur, 123, 626
Executive Suite, 64, 116, 134, 218, 471–74
Exit, 255, 658
Exodus, 56, 118, 187, 505–7
Exorcist, The, 26, 48, 58, 67, 77, 100, 122, 142, 159, 171, 578–80
Experiment Perilous, 131, 425
Exploratorium, 269, 586
Eychenne, Jean-Pierre, 229, 683
"Eye of the Tiger," 212, 634
"Eyes of Love, The," 208, 549
Eyes of the Navy, 239, 395
Eyes on the Prize: America's Civil Rights Years/Bridge to Freedom 1965, 274, 665
Ezaki, Kohei, 218, 486

Fabbri, Diego, 96, 511
Fabulous Baker Boys, The, 51, 125, 174, 197, 674, 676
Face of Genius, The, 265, 544
Face of Jesus, The, 248, 514
Face of Lincoln, The, 246, 262, 481
Faces, 57, 66, 99, 551–52
Face to Face, 49, 78, 595–96
Facing Your Danger, 241, 433
Facts of Life, The, 95, 118, 137, 206, 219, 506, 508
"Facts of Life, The," 206, 508
Fadiman, Dorothy, 276, 696
Faier, Yuri, 186, 496
Fain, Sammy, 200, 205–7, 209–11, 378, 469, 480, 492, 496–97, 519, 575, 598, 604
Fairbanks, Douglas, Sr., 2, 287, 351, 389, 701, 705
Fairbanks, Jerry, 240, 242, 422, 438
Faith, Percy, 185, 480
"Faithful Forever," 200, 389
Falcon Films, 244, 453
Falk, Peter, 56, 505, 510
Fallen Idol, The, 74, 90, 446
Fallen Sparrow, The, 180, 414
Fall Line, 254, 622
Fall of the Roman Empire, The, 188, 530
Faltermeyer, Harold, 214, 664
Fame, 103, 161, 172, 194, 211–12, 620–22
"Fame," 211, 622
Family, The, 282, 665
Family Gathering, 274, 671
Family That Dwelt Apart, The, 252, 586
Fanny, 23, 36, 118, 169, 187, 510–13
Fanny and Alexander, 79, 105, 123, 145, 225, 281, 638–41
Fantasia, 287, 402
Fantastic Voyage, 120, 140, 170, 346, 348, 540, 542–44
Fapp, Daniel L., 117–21, 495, 500, 511–12, 530, 552, 558
Faragoh, Francis, 83, 357
"Faraway Part of Town," 206, 508
Farewell My Lovely, 67, 590
Farewell to Arms, A (1932), 18, 111, 127, 149, 361–62
Farewell to Arms, A (1957), 56, 489
Far from the Madding Crowd, 189, 548
Farmer's Daughter, The, 44, 54, 435
Farnham, Joseph White, 83, 351, 701
Farnsworth, Richard, 59, 607
Farr, Glenn, 173, 639
Farrar, John, 211, 610
Farrar, Scott, 232–33, 652, 689
Farrow, John, 73, 93, 405, 484
Fassnacht, Paul, 314, 503
Fatal Attraction, 28, 51, 70, 80, 107, 174, 661–63
Fat City, 67, 573
Fate Is the Hunter, 119, 529
Father Goose, 97, 157, 169, 529–30
Father of the Bride (1950), 22, 34, 90, 450–51
Faulkner, Carl, 155–56, 308, 311, 344, 434, 470, 479, 485, 496, 501, 502
Fawcett, George, 9
Fazakas, Faz, 333, 691
Fazan, Adrienne, 167–68, 457, 496
Federico Fellini's 8½, 76, 96, 138, 220, 278, 523–26
Feeney, Ray, 330, 332, 672, 691
Fegte, Ernst, 130–31, 133, 413, 419, 426, 452
Fehr, Kaja, 173, 651
Fehr, Rudi, 173, 651
Feierlein, Heinz, 332, 691
Fein, Joel, 160, 609
Feitshans, Fred, 170, 553
Feld, Don, 220, 519. *See also* Donfeld
Feldman, Charles K., 21, 455
Feldman, Edward S., 28, 649
Felix, Seymour, 339, 374
Fellini, Federico, 75–78, 89–90,

93–94, 96, 101–2, 294, 431, 446, 484, 490, 511, 523, 562, 590, 596, 696
Fellini Satyricon, 77, 562
Fellini's Casanova, 102, 223, 596, 598
Fenton, George, 195–97, 213, 633, 663, 669, 688
Ferdinand the Bull, 238, 384
Ferguson, Ian, 247, 263, 497, 503
Ferguson, Perry, 127, 129–30, 372, 399, 406, 413, 419
Ferno, John, 250, 549
Ferrari, William, 130, 139, 419, 524
Ferren, Bran, 232, 326, 328–29, 636, 658, 660
Ferrer, Jose, 34, 54, 440, 450, 460
Ferretti, Dante, 146–47, 676, 682
Fertik, William, 252, 581
Festival, 266, 550
Fettis, Gary, 147, 682
Feuer, Cy, 25, 177–80, 383, 388, 394, 400, 572
Feury, Joseph, 274, 659
Few Good Men, A, 29, 61, 164, 175, 692, 694
Few Notes on Our Food Problem, A, 266, 554
FGV Schmidle and Fitz, 331, 679
Fiddler on the Roof, 25, 37, 58, 77, 121, 142, 158, 191, 566–69
Field, Fern, 253, 610
Field, Roy, 296, 611
Field, Sally, 42, 49, 50, 613, 643
Field, The, 41, 680
Fielding, Jerry, 190–91, 193, 558, 568, 598
Field of Dreams, 29, 108, 197, 674–76
Fields, A. Roland, 131, 425
Fields, Al, 129, 399, 406
Fields, Dorothy, 199, 369, 373
Fields, James L., 152–53, 406, 413
Fields, Verna, 171, 591
Fierlinger, Paul, 254, 617
Fiesta, 183, 437
50th Anniversary of Motion Pictures, 240, 421
55 Days at Peking, 188, 207, 525
Fight for Life, The, 179, 394
Fighting for Our Lives, 269, 593
Fighting Lady, The, 260, 422
Fighting Seabees, The, 181, 420
Fight: Science Against Cancer, The, 261, 453
Fight of the Wild Stallions, 242, 438
Figueroa, Gabriel, 120, 529
Film Associates, 258, 402
Film Documents, Inc., 261, 453
"Finale, The" (1936), 340, 374
"Finale, The" (1937), 340, 378
Finch, Peter, 12, 37–38, 566, 595
Fine, Sylvia, 204, 206, 468, 502
Fine Food, Fine Pastries, Open 6 to 9, 275, 678
Finest Hours, The, 265, 532
Finian's Rainbow, 158, 190, 553
Fink, Michael, 233, 695
Finkel, Abem, 86, 398
Finkelhoffe, Fred F., 88, 418
Finlay, Frank, 57, 534
Finney, Albert, 36, 38–40, 522, 583, 637, 643
Finston, Nat W., 176–77, 369, 377
Firemen's Ball, The, 279, 554
Fires of Kuwait, 276, 696
First Contact, 272, 641
First Edition, 270, 605
First Love (1939), 128, 178, 387–88
First Love (1970, Swiss), 279, 564
First National Studio Sound Department, 148, 356
First Piano Quartette, The, 245, 475
First Steps, 260, 438
"First Time It Happens, The," 212, 627
First Winter, 254, 628
Firth, Michael, 269, 599
Firth, Peter, 59, 601
Fish Called Wanda, A, 61, 80, 107, 667–68
Fisher, James L., 323, 331, 612, 679
Fisher, Steve, 87, 412
Fisher King, The, 41, 70, 108, 147, 197, 686–88
Fish Fry, 240, 421
Fitchett, Robert, 266, 550
Fitz, Eric, 331, 679
Fitzgerald, Barry, 11, 31, 33, 54, 417
Fitzgerald, Geraldine, 62, 386
Five Cities of June, The, 264, 526
Five Easy Pieces, 25, 37, 67, 99, 561–62
Five Fingers, 74, 91, 461
Five Graves to Cairo, 113, 130, 166, 412–14
Five Hundred Hats of Bartholomew Cubbins, The, 240, 415
Five Pennies, The, 118, 187, 206, 219, 500–502
"Five Pennies, The," 206, 502
Five Star Final, 18, 359
5000 Fingers of Dr. T., 185, 468
Five Times Five, 238, 389
Fixer, The, 37, 551
Flagg, Fannie, 109, 687
Flaherty, Frances, 89, 441
Flaherty, Robert, 89, 441
Flaiano, Ennio, 94, 96, 490, 511, 523
Flame and the Arrow, The, 115, 184, 451–52
Flamenco at 5:15, 272, 641
Flame of New Orleans, 129, 399
Flame of the Barbary Coast, The, 153, 182, 426–27
Flannery, William, 135, 479
Flashdance, 123, 173, 212, 639–40
"Flashdance . . . What a Feeling," 212, 640
Flatliners, 235, 683
Flat Top, 167, 462
Flaum, Marshall, 264–65, 526, 538
Fleischer, Dave, 240, 415
Fleischer, Richard O., 260, 438
Fleischman, Tom, 161, 164, 627, 688
Fleishman, Tom, 164, 688
Fleming, Thomas B., 274, 670
Fleming, Victor, 72, 387, 707
Fletcher, Louise, 49, 589
Flick, Stephen Hunter, 234–35, 296, 635, 665, 670, 683
Flight Command, 342, 401
Flight for Freedom, 130, 413
Flight of the Eagle, The, 281, 635
Flight of the Gossamer Condor, The, 270, 611
Flight of the Phoenix, The, 57, 169, 534, 536
Flirtation Walk, 18, 149, 364–65
Floating Free, 253, 604
Florio, Maria, 273, 653
Flournoy, Richard, 87, 412
Flower Drum Song, 118, 138, 157, 187, 220, 512–13
Flowers, A. D., 231, 295, 324, 347, 564, 576, 617–18
Flowers and Trees, 236, 360
Fly, The (1980 animation), 254, 622
Fly, The (1986), 229, 658
Flying Down to Rio, 199, 365
Flying Tigers, 152, 180, 342, 406–8
Flying with Music, 180, 201, 407–8
Flynn, Robert M., 318, 560
Foch, Nina, 64, 471
Fog, Stephen, 328, 648
Foldes, Peter, 252, 586
Folies Bergere, 339, 369
Follow the Boys, 202, 420
Folsey, George, 111, 113–14, 116, 119, 362, 365, 372, 413, 418, 431, 436, 461, 467, 472, 523
Fonda, Henry, 23, 33, 39, 292, 391, 489, 623, 625
Fonda, Jane, 42, 48–50, 68, 556, 566, 595, 601, 607, 613, 626, 649, 655
Fonda, Peter, 99, 557
Foner, Naomi, 107, 668
Fontaine, Joan, 44, 391, 397, 411
Fontanne, Lynn, 43, 359
Foote, Horton, 96, 105–6, 517, 638, 650
Foothold on Antarctica, 247, 492
Footloose, 213, 646
"Footloose," 213, 646

For All Mankind, 275, 678
"For All We Know," 209, 563
Forbes, Bryan, 95, 506
Forbes, Louis, 178, 182–83, 185, 388, 420, 426–27, 468
Forbidden Games, 92, 289, 464, 472
Forbidden Passage, 239, 402
Forbidden Planet, 344, 486
Forbstein, Leo, 176–77, 373, 377
Force in Readiness, A, 290, 514
Ford, Arthur L., 323, 612
Ford, Harrison, 40, 649
Ford, John, 20, 22, 71–74, 367, 386, 391–92, 398, 460–61, 707
Ford, Michael, 144–45, 621, 627, 639
Foreign Affair, A, 89, 115, 441
Foreign Correspondent, 20, 53, 86, 112, 128, 341, 391–93, 395
Foreman, Carl, 6, 23, 90–91, 93 n, 94–95, 100, 446, 451, 461, 490, 490 n, 510–111, 573
Foreman, John, 25, 28, 556, 649
Forever Activists: Stories from the Veterans of the Abraham Lincoln Brigade, 275, 684
Forever Amber, 183, 437
"For Every Man There's a Woman," 203, 442
Forgency, Vladimir, 265, 544
For Love of Ivy, 208, 553
"For Love of Ivy," 208, 553
Forman, Milos, 78–79, 590, 644, 708
Forman, Milton, 316, 533
For Me and My Gal, 180, 407
Formula, The, 123, 621
Forrest, Chet, 200–201, 394, 408
Forrest, Frederic, 59, 613
For Scent-Imental Reasons, 243, 448
Forsey, Keith, 212, 214, 640, 664
Forslund, Bengt, 25, 100, 572–73
For the Boys, 51, 686
Forth Road Bridge, The, 265, 538
Fortress of Peace, 249, 538
Fortune Cookie, The, 57, 98, 120, 140, 540–42
Forty Boys and a Song, 239, 401
42nd Street, 18, 149, 361–62
For Whom the Bell Tolls, 20, 33, 44, 54, 63, 113, 130, 166, 181, 411–14
For Your Eyes Only, 212, 627
"For Your Eyes Only," 212, 627
Fosse, Bob, 77–78, 103, 573, 584, 614
Foster, David, 213, 215, 657, 694
Foster, Jodie, 42, 51, 68, 596, 667, 686
Foster, Lesley, 269, 586
Foster, Lewis R., 85, 87, 387, 412
Fotopoulos, Vassilis, 139, 530
Foul Play, 211, 610
Four Daughters, 19, 53, 72, 85, 150, 381–83
Four Days in November, 265, 532
Four Days of Naples, The, 96, 278, 520, 523
Four Devils, 110, 354
400 Blows, The, 95, 500
Four Musketeers, The, 223, 592
Four Poster, The, 116, 467
Four Stones for Kanemitsu, 268, 581
Fourteen Hours, 133, 456
Fowler, Gene, Jr., 169, 524
Fowler, Hugh S., 170, 563
Fowler, Marjorie, 170, 548
Fox, Charles, 210–11, 592, 610
Fox, Fred, 337, 362
Fox, Paul S., 132–36, 139, 431, 436, 446, 457, 462, 467–68, 473, 479, 485, 496, 524
Fox, Ray Errol, 275, 678
Fox, William, 17, 351
Fox, The, 190, 553
Foxes of Harrow, The, 132, 436
Fox Film Corporation, 3, 302–3, 358, 363
Fox Studio Sound Department, 149, 365
Foy, Bryan, 261, 459
Fracker, Henry, 313, 481
Fraisse, Robert, 125, 693
Fraker, William, 602, 609, 615, 617, 639, 650
Fraker, William A., 122–24, 231, 617
Frances, 50, 69, 631–32
Frances Steloff: Memoirs of a Bookseller, 274, 664
Franci, Adolfo, 89, 436
Franciosa, Anthony, 35, 489
Franciosa, Massimo, 96–97, 523
Francis, Alec, 10
Francis, Cedric, 245–46, 469, 475, 481, 487
Francis, Freddie, 118, 125, 506, 676
Frank, Frederic M., 91, 461
Frank, Harriet, Jr., 96, 103, 523, 614
Frank, Melvin, 26, 88, 92, 95, 101, 431, 472, 506, 578–79
Frank Film, 252, 581
Franklin, Chester, 241, 428
Franklin, Richard, 235, 683
Franklin, Sidney, 20–21, 72, 297, 376, 386, 404, 410–11, 430
Frankovich, M. J., 300, 642
Fraser, Ian, 191, 563
Fraser, Robert D., 263, 509
Frayne, John G. (Dr.), 292, 301, 311, 464, 618, 642
Frazee, Logan R., 324, 618
Frears, Stephen, 80, 681
Fredericks, Ellsworth, 117, 490
Frederickson, Gray, 26–27, 583, 613
Frederix, Marc, 140, 542
Fredrick, William L., 329, 660
Freed, Arthur, 22–23, 291, 297, 455, 459, 494, 550, 705
Freed, Ralph, 201, 408
Freeman, Charles, 343, 442
Freeman, Morgan, 40, 61, 661, 674
Freeman, Y. Frank, 291, 299, 488, 544
Free Soul, A, 32, 43, 71, 357
Freleng, Friz, 248–50, 514, 532, 544
French, Edward, 229, 689
French Cinema General Cooperative, 260, 448
French Connection, The, 25, 37, 58, 77, 100, 121, 159, 170, 566–68, 708
French Lieutenant's Woman, The, 50, 104, 144, 224, 625–28
Frenchman's Creek, 131, 426
Frend, Charles, 166, 388
Fresco, Robert, 267, 559
Fresholtz, Les, 158–64, 558, 580, 591, 597, 615, 621, 633, 651, 657, 663, 669, 694
Freud, 96, 188, 517, 519
Freund, Karl, 111–112, 312, 376, 398–99, 476
Frey, Leonard, 58, 566
Friberg, Arnold, 219, 486
Fricker, Brenda, 70, 675
Fried, Gerald, 192, 591
Fried, Rob, 257, 689
Friedenberg, Richard, 109, 693
Fried Green Tomatoes, 70, 109, 687
Friedhofer, Hugo, 182–83, 185–86, 427, 432, 437, 442, 468, 486, 491, 496
Friedkin, William, 77, 567, 579, 708
Friedman, Bruce Jay, 105, 644
Friedman, Jud, 215, 695
Friedman, Sonya, 273, 659
Friedman, Stephen J., 25, 566
"Friend Like Me," 215, 694
Friendly Enemies, 152, 406
Friendly Persuasion, 5, 22, 55, 75, 93, 155, 205, 483–86
"Friendly Persuasion (Thee I Love)," 205, 486
Frierson, K. M., 312, 476
Fries, Douglas, 327, 642
Frigerio, Ezio, 146, 681
Froeschel, George, 87, 405
Frogmen, The, 90, 115, 456
Frog, the Dog, and the Devil, The, 255, 658
Frog Story, 251, 575
From A to Z-Z-Z-Z, 245, 469
From Generation to Generation, 263, 503
From Here to Eternity, 22, 34, 45, 55, 64, 74, 92, 116, 155, 168, 185, 217, 466–69, 707

From Mao to Mozart: Isaac Stern in China, 271, 623
Front, The, 102, 596
Front Line, 271, 623
Front Page, The (1931), 17, 32, 71, 357
Fruchtman, Lisa, 172–74, 615, 639, 682
Fuchs, Daniel, 92–93, 478
Fudano, Kaz, 334, 697
Fuji Photo Film Company, Ltd., 325, 332, 629, 685
Full Metal Jacket, 107, 662
Fuller, Charles, 106, 644
Fuller, Leland, 131, 133–34, 419, 456–57, 462, 467, 473
Fullerton, Carl, 229, 652
Fulton, John, 341–44, 395, 401, 408, 428, 486
"Fun House," 340, 378
Funke, Alex, 296, 684
Funny Face, 94, 117, 136, 219, 490–92
Funny Girl, 24, 47, 66, 121, 158, 170, 190, 208, 551–53
"Funny Girl," 208, 553
Funny Lady, 122, 159, 193, 210, 223, 590–92
Funny Thing Happened on the Way to the Forum, A, 189, 543
Furies, The, 115, 451
Furness, John, 223, 586
Furse, Margaret, 217, 221–22, 458, 531, 553, 559, 564, 569
Furse, Roger K., 132, 216, 441–42
Furst, Anton, 146, 676
Further Adventures of Uncle Sam: Part Two, The, 251, 564
Furthman, Jules, 84, 368
Furuya, Osami, 121, 562
Fury, 84, 372

Gable, Clark, 32–33, 364, 367, 386
Gaby—A True Story, 69, 662
Gadgets Galore, 246, 480
Gaffney, Robert, 248, 514
Gaily, Gaily, 141, 158, 222, 558–59
Gaines, George, 143, 145, 591, 597, 609, 645
Galati, Frank, 107, 668
Gale, Bob, 106, 650
"Gal in Calico, A," 203, 437
Gallico, Paul, 86, 405
Galloway, James, 171, 580
Gambit, 140, 158, 221, 542–43
Game, The, 248, 526
Gamley, Douglas, 192, 585
Gandhi, 27, 39, 79, 104, 123, 144, 161, 173, 195, 225, 228, 631–34, 708
Gang Cops, 274, 671
Gangelin, Victor A., 131, 138, 419, 512
Gang's All Here, The, 130, 413
Gannon, Kim, 201–2, 408, 421, 427
Ganz, Armin, 146, 669
Ganz, Lowell, 105, 644
Garbo, Greta, 42–43, 290, 355, 375, 386, 474
Garcia, Andy, 61, 680
Gardenia, Vincent, 58, 61, 578, 661
Garden of Allah, 177, 286, 337, 372–74
Garden of Eden, The, 273, 647
Garden of the Finzi-Continis, The, 100, 279, 567, 570
Garden Spider, The (Epeira Diadema), 261, 464
Gardiner, Bob, 252, 586
Gardner, Ava, 45, 466
Gardner, Herb, 97, 535
Gardner, Robert, 273, 653
Garey, Diane, 276, 690
Garfield, John, 34, 53, 381, 435
Garfinkle, Louis, 103, 608
Gargan, William, 53, 391
Garity, William, 287, 402
Garland, Judy, 45, 65, 287, 390, 471, 511
Garmes, Lee, 111, 114, 118, 358, 360, 418, 500
Garner, James, 40, 649
Garner, Peggy Ann, 288, 429
Garr, Teri, 69, 632
Garson, Greer, 43–44, 46, 386, 397, 404, 411, 417, 424, 505
Garwood, Norman, 145–47, 651, 676, 688
Gaslight, 21, 33, 44, 63, 88, 114, 130, 417–19
Gaspar, Chuck, 232, 646
Gassner, Dennis, 147, 688
Gast, Michel, 270, 611
Gate of Hell, 218, 290, 474–75
Gates of Paris, 278, 493
Gathering of Eagles, A, 348, 526
Gaudio, Gaetano "Tony," 110–14, 356, 372, 392, 412, 425
Gausman, Hal, 137, 139, 142, 146, 512, 530, 568, 585, 663
Gausman, Russell A., 129–31, 137, 399, 406, 413, 419, 501, 507
Gawley, Steve, 233, 677
Gay, John, 94, 495
Gay, Norman, 171, 580
Gay Deception, The, 84, 368
Gay Divorcee, The, 18, 127, 149, 176, 199, 364–66
Gayer, Richard, 252, 581
Gaylord, Jack, 311, 459
Gaynor, Janet, 42–43, 351, 375
Gay Parisian, The, 239, 402
Gazebo, The, 219, 502
Gazzo, Michael V., 58, 583
Geissler, E. H., 319, 577
Gelbart, Larry, 102, 105, 602, 632
General Cable Corp., 314, 493
General Della Rovere, 96, 511
General Died at Dawn, The, 53, 111, 177, 371–73
General Electric Co. (lamp division), 314, 498
General Service Studio Sound Department, 152, 393, 400
General Spanky, 150, 373
Generation on the Wind, 271, 617
Genevieve, 92, 185, 472–73
Genn, Leo, 55, 455
Genocide, 272, 629
Gentleman, Wally, 330, 666
Gentleman's Agreement, 21, 34, 44, 63, 73, 89, 167, 435–37, 707
George, Chief Dan, 58, 561
George, Gladys, 43, 371
George, Peter, 97, 529
George, William, 233, 664
George and Rosemary, 256, 664
George Grosz' Interregnum, 263, 509
George Washington Slept Here, 129, 406
Georgy Girl, 47, 57, 120, 208, 540–41, 543
"Georgy Girl," 208, 543
Geraghty, Tom, 10
Gerald McBoing-Boing, 243, 453
Gerald McBoing-Boing on the Planet Moo, 246, 487
Gerb, Joachim, 320, 582
Germi, Pietro, 75, 96, 517
Gershe, Leonard, 94, 490
Gershenson, Joseph, 185, 190, 474, 548
Gershwin, George, 200, 378
Gershwin, Ira, 200, 202, 205, 378, 421, 474
Gerstad, Harry, 167, 447, 462
Gervaise, 277, 487
Gervasi, Luigi, 141, 548
Getchell, Robert, 101–2, 584, 596
Get Out Your Handkerchiefs, 280, 611
Gherardi, Piero, 137–38, 140, 220, 222, 512–13, 524–25, 542–43
Ghia, Fernando, 28, 655
Ghost, 29, 70, 108, 174, 197, 680–82
Ghost and Mrs. Muir, The, 114, 436
Ghostbusters, 213, 232, 646
"Ghostbusters," 213, 646
Gianini, Guilio, 252, 581
Giannetti, Alfredo, 96, 517
Giannini, Giancarlo, 38, 595
Giant, 22, 35, 65, 75, 93, 136, 168, 186, 218, 483–86
Gibbons, Cedric, 8–9, 12, 126–36, 354, 362, 365, 372, 376, 383, 387, 393, 399, 406, 413, 419, 426, 432, 446–47, 452, 457, 461–62, 467–68, 473, 478–79, 485, 701
Gibbons, James, 309, 439

Gibbs, George, 232–33, 646, 670, 695
Gibney, Sheridan, 84, 372
Gibson, William, 96, 517
Giddings, Nelson, 94, 495
Gideon, Ray, 252, 575
Gideon, Raynold, 107, 656
Gielgud, John, 57, 59, 528, 625
Gifts, The, 267, 564
Giger, H. R., 231, 616
Gigi, 17, 23, 75, 94, 118, 136, 168, 186, 206, 216, 219, 494–97, 708
"Gigi," 206, 496
Gigot, 188, 519
G. I. Honeymoon, 182, 427
G. I. Joe, 54, 88, 182, 203, 424–25, 427–28
Gilbert, Bruce, 27, 625
Gilbert, Herschel Burke, 184–85, 204, 462, 468, 474
Gilbert, Lewis, 24, 540
Gilbert, Ray, 203, 437
Gilford, Jack, 58, 578
Gilks, Alfred, 116, 456
Gilkyson, Terry, 208, 549
Gillespie, A. Arnold, 316, 341–45, 389, 395, 401, 408, 415, 421, 428, 437, 486, 496, 502, 520, 527
Gilliam, Terry, 106, 650
Gilliatt, Penelope, 100, 567
Gillis, Alec, 233, 695
Gilman, Christopher S., 332, 685
Gilmore, Stuart, 169–70, 507, 563, 568
Gilpatric, Guy, 87, 412
Gimbel, Norman, 210–11, 592, 610, 616
Ginsberg, Henry, 23, 483
Girl Said No, The, 150, 377
Girls School, 177, 383
"Girl Who Used to Be Me, The," 214, 677
Girl with the Pistol, The, 279, 544
Gish, Lillian, 63, 285, 291, 430, 565
Giuseppina, 263, 509
Give 'Em Hell, Harry!, 38, 589
Give Me Liberty, 237, 374
Give Us the Earth, 242, 438
Glasgow, William, 139, 530
Glasmon, Kubec, 83, 358
Glass, Robert J., 160–61, 597, 603, 609, 615, 633
Glass, Robert W., Jr., 160–61, 609, 627
Glass, 263, 503
Glass Cell, The, 280, 611
Glatter, Lesli Linka, 255, 647
Glazer, Benjamin, 82, 85, 351, 392, 701
Glazier, Sidney, 265, 538
Gleason, Jackie, 56, 510
Gleason, James, 54, 397
Gleason, Keogh, 133–36, 457, 462, 468, 473, 485, 496
Gledhill, Donald, 8
Glengarry Glen Ross, 61, 692
Glen Glenn Sound, 157, 322, 518, 606
Glennan, Gordon R., 155, 485
Glenn Miller Story, The, 92, 155, 185, 472–74
Glennon, Bert, 112, 387, 399
Glenville, Peter, 76, 529
Glickman, Fred, 204, 452
Glickman, Richard B., 316, 533
Gliese, Rochus, 126, 352
Glimcher, Arne, 215, 694
Gloria, 49, 619
Glorious Betsy, 82, 351
Glory, 61, 125, 146, 163, 174, 675–76
"Glory of Love," 213, 657
Glover, Guy, 253, 262, 475, 598
Gluskin, Lud, 178, 389
Go-Between, The, 67, 567
Goddard, Paulette, 11, 63, 411
Goddess, The, 94, 495
Godfather, The, 11, 25, 37, 58, 77, 100, 159, 171, 223, 572–75, 708
Godfather, Part II, The, 26, 38, 58, 67, 77, 101, 142, 192, 223, 583–86, 708
Godfather, Part III, The, 29, 61, 80, 125, 147, 174, 214, 680–82
Godfrey, Bob, 251–52, 254, 575, 592, 617
Godmilow, Jill, 269, 587
Gods of Metal, 272, 635
Goeppinger, Max, 312, 476
Goetz, William, 18, 23, 364, 489
Goff, Ivan, 94, 490
Goffin, Gerry, 210, 592
Go for Broke!, 91, 456
Going My Way, 11, 21, 33, 54, 73, 87–88, 114, 166, 202, 417–19, 421, 707
Going Places, 200, 384
Going the Distance, 271, 617
Going to Blazes, 243, 443
Go into Your Dance, 339, 369
Gold, Ernest, 187–88, 190, 207, 501, 507, 525, 558
Gold, 210, 586
Goldberg, Whoopi, 50, 70, 649, 681
Goldblatt, Mark, 174, 688
Goldblatt, Stephen, 125, 687
Golddiggers of 1933, 149, 362
Golddiggers of 1935, 199, 339, 369
Golddiggers of 1937, 339, 373
Golden Boy, 178, 388
Golden Fish, The, 247, 503
Golden Girl, 204, 458
Golden Horses, 241, 433
Goldfarb, Lyn, 270, 611
Goldfinger, 348, 531
Goldman, Bo, 102, 104, 109, 590, 620, 693
Goldman, James, 98, 552
Goldman, Les, 249, 538
Goldman, William, 99, 102, 557, 596
Gold Rush, The, 152, 180, 406
Goldsmith, Jerry, 188–96, 198, 210, 519, 537, 543, 553, 563, 580, 585, 591, 598, 609, 616, 633, 640, 657, 694
Goldsmith, Martin, 91, 461
Goldwyn, Samuel, 17, 19–21, 297, 299, 359, 371, 375, 386, 397, 404, 430, 433, 435, 493
Goldwyn Follies, 128, 177, 382–83
Goldwyn Sound Department. *See* Samuel Goldwyn Studio Sound Department
Goliath II, 248, 508
Golitzen, Alexander, 128–31, 137–38, 140–42, 393, 399, 406, 413, 419, 507, 512, 518, 542, 548, 558, 562, 585
Gomberg, Sy, 90, 451
Gomez, Thomas, 54, 435
Gone with the Wind, 19, 33, 43, 62, 72, 85, 112, 128, 151, 166, 178, 287, 306, 341, 386–90, 707
"Gonna Fly Now," 210, 598
Goodbye Columbus, 99, 557
Goodbye Girl, The, 26, 38, 49, 68, 102, 601–2
Goodbye Miss Turlock, 242, 438
Goodbye, Mr. Chips (1939), 19, 33, 43, 72, 85, 166, 386–88
Goodbye, Mr. Chips (1969), 37, 190, 556, 558
Good Earth, The, 19, 43, 72, 111, 165, 375–77
Goodell, John D., 268, 581
GoodFellas, 29, 61, 70, 80, 108, 174, 680–82
Goodie-Two-Shoes, 255, 641
Goodman, David, 273, 653
Goodman, David Zelag, 99, 562
Goodman, John B., 128–31, 383, 406, 413, 419
Goodman, Karen, 274–75, 670, 683
Goodman, Lee, 261, 453
Goodman, Richard Bryce, 163, 682
Good Morning, 251, 569
Good Morning, Vietnam, 40, 661
Good News, 203, 437
Goodnight Miss Ann, 270, 611
Goodrich, Frances, 84, 90, 92, 365, 372, 451, 472
Good Scouts, 238, 384
Good Will to Men, 246, 480
Goodwin, Richard, 28, 643
Goodwin, Thomas C., 276, 696
Goosson, Stephen, 127–29, 131, 358, 376, 382, 399, 426
Gordin, Myron, 328, 654
Gordon, Charles, 29, 674
Gordon, Dexter, 40, 655

Gordon, Douglas, 270, 605
Gordon, James B., 310, 315, 344, 454, 502, 515
Gordon, Lawrence, 29, 674
Gordon, Mack, 200–204, 394, 401, 408, 415, 420, 432, 437, 447
Gordon, Ruth, 66, 89–91, 436, 451, 461, 534, 551
Gordon, Steve, 104, 626
Gore, Christopher, 104, 620
Gore, Lesley, 212, 622
Gore, Michael, 194–95, 211–12, 622, 640
Gorgeous Hussy, The, 62, 111, 371–72
Gorillas in the Mist, 51, 107, 163, 174, 197, 667–69
Gorog, Laszlo, 88, 425
Gorton, Assheton, 144, 626
Gospel According to St. Matthew, The, 140, 189, 221, 542–43
Goss, Walter, 160, 603
Gossett, Jr., Louis, 60, 632
Gottfried, Howard, 26, 595
Gottschalk, Robert E., 314, 503
Gould, Dave, 339–40, 369, 374, 378
Gould, Elliott, 57, 556
Goulding, Edmund, 707
Gouri, Haim, 269, 587
Grace, Henry, 135–40, 479, 496, 501, 507, 518, 524, 530, 536, 542
Graduate, The, 24, 37, 47, 66, 76, 98, 121, 546–47
Graffiti, 255, 653
Grafton, David, 324, 329, 624, 660
Graham, Angelo, 142–45, 585, 609, 615, 645
Graham, William L., 321, 599
Grahame, Gloria, 63–64
Grain That Built a Hemisphere, The, 259, 409
Grandad of Races, 243, 453
Grand Canyon (1958 short), 247, 497
Grand Canyon (1991), 108, 687
Grand Day Out, A, 256, 683
Grand Hotel, 18, 359, 707
Grand Illusion, 19, 381
Grandma Moses, 244, 453
Grand National Studio Sound Department, 150, 377
Grand Prix, 158, 170, 348, 542–44
Granger, Bertram, 130, 413
Grant, Cary, 33, 291, 397, 417, 560
Grant, James Edward, 94, 495
Grant, Lawrence, 357
Grant, Lee, 64, 67–68, 455, 561, 590, 596
Grant, Richard Benjamin, 328, 660
Grant, Ron, 328, 660
Granville, Bonita, 62, 372
Granville, Roy, 342–43, 415, 421
Grapes of Wrath, The, 20, 33, 62, 72, 86, 151, 166, 391–93
Grashin, Mauri, 84, 365
Grasshoff, Alex, 266, 268, 544, 554, 582
Grasshoppers (Cavallette), 256, 683
Grass Is Always Greener, The, 243, 448
Gratz, Joan C., 257, 695
Grauman, Sid, 9–10, 288, 443, 702
Grauman's Chinese Theatre, 13, 411, 417, 424
Graves, Ed, 141, 548
Graves, Jim, 332, 685
Gravity Is My Enemy, 270, 605
Gray, Lorraine, 270, 611
Gray, Maggie, 145, 651
Gray, Mike, 103, 614
Gray, William S., 165, 373
Graysmark, John, 142, 144, 574, 626
Grazer, Brian, 105, 644
Grease, 211, 610
Great, 252, 592
Great American Cowboy, The, 268, 581
Great Britain, government, 260, 429
Great Caruso, The, 155, 184, 217, 457–58
Great Cognito, The, 254, 635
Great Dictator, The, 20, 33, 54, 86, 179, 391–92, 394
Great Escape, The, 169, 524
Greatest Show on Earth, The, 22, 74, 91, 167, 217, 460–63, 707
Greatest Story Ever Told, The, 120, 140, 189, 221, 346, 535–37
Great Expectations, 21, 73, 89, 114, 132, 435–36
Great Gatsby, The, 192, 223, 585–86
Great Heart, The, 238, 384
Great Lie, The, 63, 397
Great McGinty, The, 86, 392
Great Muppet Caper, The, 212, 627
Great Race, The, 120, 157, 169, 207, 348, 535–38
Great Santini, The, 39, 59, 619–20
Great Victor Herbert, The, 151, 178, 388
Great Waltz, The, 62, 111, 166, 382–83
Great War, The, 278, 503
Great White Hope, The, 37, 48, 561
Great Ziegfeld, The, 19, 43, 72, 84, 127, 165, 339, 371–74, 707
Greaves, Daniel, 257, 689
Greek Tragedy, A, 255, 658
Green, Adolph, 92–93, 467, 478
Green, Guy, 114, 436
Green, Jack N., 125, 693
Green, Johnny, 183–84, 186–88, 190, 245, 437, 442, 457, 469, 475, 486, 491, 507, 513, 525, 553, 559
Green, Paul, 84, 362
Green, Walon, 99, 268, 557, 570
Greenberg, Jerry, 170, 172, 568, 615
Greenberg, Richard, 233, 664
Greenberg, Robert M., 233, 328, 660, 664
Greenburg, Adam, 125, 687
Green Card, 108, 681
Green Dolphin Street, 114, 154, 167, 343, 436–37
Greene, Clarence, 91, 95, 456, 500
Greene, Danford B., 170–71, 563, 585
Greene, Graham (actor), 61, 680
Greene, Grahame (writer), 90, 446
Greene, Mort, 201, 408
Greene, Sparky, 269, 599
Greene, W. Howard, 112–13, 116, 286, 374, 379, 387, 393, 399, 406, 412, 456
Greene, Walter, 183, 427
Greenfeld, Josh, 101, 584
Green Goddess, The, 31, 355
Green Grass of Wyoming, 115, 441
Greenham, Vivian C., 345, 514
Greenhut, Robert, 28, 655
"Green Leaves of Summer, The," 206, 508
Greenstreet, Sydney, 54, 397
Greenwald, Ken, 251, 569
Greenwell, Peter, 191, 568
Greenwood, Don, Jr., 139, 524
Greenwood, Trevor, 266, 550
Green Years, The, 54, 114, 430–31
Greetings, Bait, 240, 415
Gregory, Carl, 8
Gregory, Grace, 134, 138, 473, 524
Gregory, Robin, 160–61, 603, 627
Gregson, Richard, 95, 506
Grenzbach, Charles (Bud), 159, 162, 574, 585, 657
Gresham, Gloria, 226, 683
Grey, Harry, 242–43, 438, 443
Grey, Joel, 58, 572
Greystoke: The Legend of Tarzan, Lord of the Apes, 60, 106, 228, 644, 646
Grgic, Zlatko, 254, 617
Griffin, Eleanore, 85, 382
Griffin, James, 209, 563
Griffith, Corrinne, 42, 353
Griffith, D. W., 9, 285–86, 370
Griffith, Hugh, 56–57, 499, 522
Griffith, Melanie, 51, 667
Griffith, Raymond, 18, 364

Griffiths, Mildred, 131, 426
Griffiths, Trevor, 104, 626
Grifters, The, 51, 70, 80, 108, 680–81
Griggs, Loyal, 116–17, 120, 286, 385, 467, 485, 535
Grignon, Lorin, 311, 470
Grignon, Marcel, 120, 541
Grillo, Michael, 29, 667
Grimes, Stephen, 139, 142, 145, 530, 580, 651
Groesse, Paul, 128, 130, 132–34, 138–40, 393, 413, 432, 447, 452, 457, 462, 468, 518, 524, 542
Grofé, Ferde, 182, 420
Gross, Matthew, 256, 683
Gross, Roland, 166, 420
Grossman, Robert, 253, 604
Grot, Anton, 127–28, 306, 358, 372, 376, 387, 393, 396
Groves, George, 148, 156–58, 356, 491, 501, 507, 518, 530, 536, 542
Gruault, Jean, 104, 620
Grubel, Robert, 315, 509
Gruenberg, Louis, 179–80, 394, 400, 414
Grusin, Dave, 194–95, 197, 212, 609, 615, 627, 634, 669, 676, 682
Grzimek, Bernhard, 263, 503
Guaraldi, Vince, 191, 563
Guardsman, The, 32, 43, 359
Guare, John, 104, 626
Guerra, Tonino, 97–98, 101, 535, 541, 590
Guess, Cameron, 251, 564
Guess Who's Coming to Dinner, 24, 37, 47, 57, 66, 76, 98, 141, 170, 190, 546–48
Guest in the House, 182, 427
Guest Wife, 182, 427
Guffey, Burnett, 116–17, 119–20, 467, 484, 517, 535, 547
Guffroy, Pierre, 140, 144, 542, 621
Guggenheim, Charles, 250, 266, 272–73, 275, 549, 554, 635, 647, 678
Guidice, Don, 171, 591
Guinness, Alec, 34–35, 59, 61, 94, 292, 460, 489, 495, 601, 618, 667
Guiol, Fred, 93, 484
Gullah Tales, 256, 670
Gulliver's Travels, 178, 200, 389
Gunfight at the O.K. Corral, 156, 168, 491
Gunfighter, The, 90, 451
Gun in His Hand, A, 241, 428
Gunnarsson, Sturla, 272, 635
Guns of Navarone, The, 23, 75, 95, 157, 169, 187, 344, 510–14
Guthrie, A. B., Jr., 92, 467
Gutman, James, 269, 599
Guttentag, William, 274–76, 671, 678, 690
Gutteridge, Martin, 232, 658
Gutterman, Robert P., 314, 504
Guttfreund, Andre, 253, 598
Guy Named Joe, A, 87, 418
Guys and Dolls, 117, 185, 218, 478–80
Gwangwa, Jonas, 196, 213, 663
Gwenn, Edmund, 54–55, 435, 450
Gypsy, 119, 188, 220, 517, 519

Haack, Morton, 221–23, 531, 553, 569
Haanstra, Bert, 263, 265, 268, 503, 532, 576
Haas, Robert M., 132, 436, 441
Hackett, Albert, 84, 90, 92, 365, 372, 451, 472
Hackett, Joan, 68, 626
Hackford, Taylor, 254, 610
Hackman, Gene, 37, 40, 57–58, 61, 546, 561, 566, 667, 692
Hadjidakis, Manos, 206, 508
Haessens, Robert, 243, 448
Hafenrichter, Oswald, 167, 452
Haff, Richard M., 311, 459
Haffenden, Elizabeth, 219, 222, 502, 543
Haft, Steven, 29, 674
Hagans, Donald, 294, 690
Hageman, Richard, 178–80, 388, 394, 400, 407
Hagen, Earle H., 187, 507
Hagen, Jean, 64, 460
Hager, James, 269, 593
Hahn, Don, 29, 686
Hahn, Edwin C., 341, 389
Hahn, Thomas, 333, 691
Haigh, Nancy, 147, 688
Hail the Conquering Hero, 87, 418
Haines, Fred, 98, 547
Hairy Ape, The, 181, 420
Hajos, Karl, 181–82, 420, 427
Halas, John, 249, 526
Hale, Joe, 231, 616
Hale, John, 99, 557
Hale, Nancy, 274, 671
Half a House, 210, 598
Hall, Alexander, 73, 398
Hall, Allen, 233, 689
Hall, Cecelia, 235, 658, 683
Hall, Charles D., 128, 383, 387
Hall, Conrad, 121–22, 124, 535, 542, 547, 557, 590, 668
Hall, David, 127, 140, 377, 536
Hall, Grayson, 66, 529
Hall, John, 342, 401
Halle, Roland, 271, 623, 628
Hallelujah, 71, 356
Hallenberger, Harry, 113, 399
Haller, Ernest, 111–12, 114–15, 119, 382, 387, 392, 425, 451, 517, 523
Hallinan, Eda Godel, 255, 641
"Hall of Kings," 339, 369
Hallstrom, Lasse, 80, 107, 662
Halprin, Sol, 311, 343, 428, 470
Hal Roach Studio Sound Department, 150–52, 373, 377, 383, 388, 393, 400
Halsey, Richard, 171, 597
Ham, Al, 189, 543
Hambling, Gerry, 172, 174, 609, 621, 669, 688
Hamerski, Steve, 333, 691
Hamilton, Arthur, 209, 563
Hamilton, Fenton, 318–19, 560, 570
Hamilton, Nancy, 262, 481
Hamlet (1948), 13, 21, 34, 64, 73, 132, 183, 216, 440–42, 707
Hamlet (1990), 147, 226, 682–83
Hamlisch, Marvin, 192–93, 195, 209–11, 213–14, 569, 580–81, 603–4, 610, 616, 633, 652, 677
Hammeras, Ralph, 127, 336, 343, 352, 358, 442
Hammerstein, Oscar, II, 200–201, 203–4, 401, 428, 432, 458
Hammett, Dashiell, 87, 412
Hammond, Albert, 214, 664
Hampton, Christopher, 107, 668
Hampton, Orville H., 97, 529
Hancock, Herbie, 196, 657
Hancock, John, 251, 564
Handford, Peter, 162–63, 651, 669
Handful of Dust, A, 226, 670
Handley, Charles, 306, 390
Haney, Kevin, 229, 677
Hanging Tree, The, 206, 502
"Hanging Tree, The," 206, 502
Hangmen Also Die, 152, 181, 413–14
Hankin, Larry, 254, 617
Hanks, Tom, 40, 667
Hanna, William, 246, 480, 492
Hannah and Her Sisters, 28, 60, 69, 80, 106, 146, 173, 655–57
Hannemann, Walter, 172, 597, 603
Hanrahan, Pat, 333, 697
Hans Christian Andersen, 116, 133, 155, 184, 204, 217, 461–63
Hansen, E. H., 149–53, 341–42, 365, 368, 372, 377, 383, 388–89, 393, 395, 399, 401, 407, 413, 419
Hansen, Franklin, 148–50, 356, 362, 365, 368, 373
Hanussen, 282, 671
Happiest Millionaire, The, 222, 549
"Happiness Is a Thing Called Joe," 201, 414
Happy Ending, The, 48, 209, 556, 559
Happy New Year, 229, 664
Harburg, E. Y., 200–201, 203, 389, 414, 428

Hard Day's Night, A, 97, 188, 529, 531
Harder They Fall, The, 117, 484
Harding, Ann, 43, 357
Harding, Jay M., 161, 621, 627
Hardy, Jonathan, 104, 620
Harlan, Russell, 116–17, 119–20, 461, 478, 517–18, 535, 541
Harlan County, U.S.A., 269, 599
Harlem Nights, 226, 677
Harline, Leigh, 177, 179–81, 188, 200, 378, 394, 407–8, 414, 519
Harling, Frank, 178, 388, 420
Harling, W. Franke, 177, 181, 378
Harman-Ising, 237, 369, 374
Harmon, Sidney, 86, 405
Harp of Burma, 277, 487
Harper, Tess, 69, 656
Harris, Barbara, 67, 567
Harris, Jed, 92, 472
Harris, Julie (actress), 45, 460
Harris, Julie (costume designer), 216, 221, 537
Harris, Leon, 144, 615
Harris, Louis, 240, 422
Harris, Mark, 266, 550
Harris, Richard (actor), 36, 41, 522, 680
Harris, Richard (film editor), 174, 688
Harris, Vernon, 98, 552
Harrison, Charles, 328, 660
Harrison, Doane, 166–67, 414, 426, 452
Harrison, Edward, 247, 502
Harrison, Joan, 86, 392
Harrison, Rex, 36, 522, 528
Harrison and Harrison, Optical Engineers, 328, 654
Harry and the Butler, 278, 514
Harry and the Hendersons, 229, 664
Harry and Tonto, 38, 101, 583–84
Harryhausen, Ray, 301, 690
Hart, Bobby, 212, 640
Hart, Moss, 84, 89, 368, 436
Hart, Rick, 164, 694
Harten, Charles, 118, 506
Hartleben, Dale, 269, 593
Hartman, Don, 84, 86, 368
Hartman, Elizabeth, 47, 534
Hartstone, Graham, 160, 162, 609, 645, 657
Harvest, 266, 550
Harvey, Anthony, 76, 552
Harvey, Laurence, 35, 499
Harvey, 34, 64, 450
Harvey Girls, The, 183, 203, 432
Harwood, Ronald, 105, 638
Hasford, Gustav, 107, 662
Haskell, Jack, 339, 374
Haskin, Byron, 305, 341–42, 385, 389, 395, 401, 408
Hasty Heart, The, 34, 445
Hatari!, 119, 518
Hatch, Arthur J., 316, 539
Hatch, Eric, 84, 372
Hatch Up Your Troubles, 243, 448
Hatful of Rain, A, 35, 489
Hathaway, Henry, 72, 367
Hatley, Marvin, 177–78, 378, 383
Hauben, Lawrence, 102, 590
Hauge, Carl, 313, 315–16, 318, 488, 509, 533, 555
Haugland, David, 276, 696
Havana, 197, 682
Havelock-Allan, Anthony, 25, 88–89, 431, 436, 551
Havlick, Gene, 165–66, 377, 383, 388
Hawaii, 66, 120, 158, 189, 208, 221, 346, 541–43
Hawaiians, The, 222, 564
Hawkins, John N. A., 287, 402
Hawkins, Richard, 271, 623
Hawks, Howard, 73, 292, 398, 587
Hawn, Goldie, 49, 66, 557, 589, 619, 655
Haworth, Edward S. "Ted," 135–39, 479, 491, 501, 507, 518, 530
Hayakawa, Sessue, 56, 489
Hayes, Alfred, 90–91, 446, 456
Hayes, Chris, 213, 652
Hayes, Helen, 43, 62, 67, 359, 561, 566
Hayes, Isaac, 191, 209, 568–69
Hayes, Jack, 189, 196, 531, 651
Hayes, John Michael, 92, 94, 472, 490
Hayes, John Patrick, 247, 497
Hayes, Raphael, 97, 529
Hayes, Tom, 264, 514
Hays, Will, 3
Hayton, Lennie, 183–84, 190, 432, 442, 447, 462, 553, 559
Hayward, Leland, 22, 477
Hayward, Susan, 44–46, 435, 445, 460, 477, 494
Hazeltine Corporation, 318, 560
Head, Edith, 216–24, 442, 447, 458, 463, 469, 474, 480, 486, 492, 497, 502, 508, 513, 519, 525, 531, 537, 543, 559, 564, 581, 592, 604
Healy, John, 246, 261–62, 470, 487
Heap, Jonathan, 257, 683
Heard, Paul F., 261, 448
Heartbeeps, 228, 628
Heartbreak Kid, The, 58, 67, 572–73
Heartbreak Ridge (1955 documentary), 262, 481
Heartbreak Ridge (1986), 162, 657
Heart Is a Lonely Hunter, The, 37, 66, 551
Heart like a Wheel, 225, 640
Hearts and Minds, 269, 587
Heart to Heart, 260, 443
Heath, Hy, 204, 452
Heath, Percy, 83, 359
Heaven Can Wait (1943), 20, 73, 113, 122, 411–12
Heaven Can Wait (1978), 27, 38, 59, 68, 78, 103, 143, 194, 607–9
Heaven Knows, Mr. Allison, 46, 94, 489–90
Heavenly Music, 240, 415
Heaven's Gate, 144, 626
Hecht, Allen, 323, 618
Hecht, Ben, 82, 84–86, 88, 351, 365, 368, 387, 392, 431
Hecht, Harold, 22–23, 477, 494
Heckart, Eileen, 64, 67, 483, 573
Heckel, Sally, 254, 622
Heckroth, Hein, 132–33, 217, 441, 457–58
Hedda, 49, 589
Hedgecock, William, 341, 395
Hedrick, A. Earl, 135, 485
Heerman, Victor, 84, 362
Heflin, Van, 54, 404
Hehr, Addison, 137, 139, 507, 524
Heim, Alan, 171–72, 597, 615
Heindorf, Ray, 180–86, 188, 190, 203, 408, 414, 419, 427–28, 432, 437, 442, 447, 452, 462, 468, 474, 496, 519, 553
Heiress, The, 21, 45, 55, 74, 115, 132, 184, 216, 445–47
Held, Tom, 166, 383
Helen Keller in Her Story, 262, 481
Helicopter Canada, 265, 544
Hell and High Water, 344, 474
Heller, Caryl, 147, 688
Hellfire: A Journey from Hiroshima, 274, 665
Hellman, Jerome, 25–26, 556, 607
Hellman, Lillian, 86–87, 398, 412
Hello Dolly!, 25, 121, 141, 158, 170, 190, 222, 556, 558–59
Hello Frisco, Hello, 113, 202, 412, 415
Hell's Angels, 110, 356
Hellstrom Chronicle, The, 267, 570
Hellzapoppin', 201, 408
Help! My Snowman's Burning Down, 249, 532
Helpern, David, 269, 599
He Makes Me Feel Like Dancin', 272, 641
Heman, Roger, 159, 161, 342–43, 408, 415, 421, 428, 442, 591, 621
Hemingway, Mariel, 68, 614
Hemphill, D. M., 163, 682
Hemphill, Doug, 164, 694
Hempstead, David, 20, 391
Henderson, Charles, 182, 427
Henderson, Robert, 235, 652, 678
Henderson, Robert (sci-tech.), 307, 410
Hendricks, William L., 264, 290, 514, 520

Hendrickson, Robert, 268, 576
Hendrie, James, 256, 678
Henley, Barry K., 322, 606
Henley, Beth, 107, 656
Hennesy, Dale, 140, 143–44, 542, 597, 633
Henning, Paul, 96, 511
Henry, Buck, 78, 98, 547, 608
Henry, Justin, 59, 614
Henry & June, 125, 681
Henry Browne, Farmer, 259, 409
Henry V (1946), 21, 33, 132, 183, 277, 288, 430–33
Henry V (1989), 40, 80, 226, 674–75, 677
Henson, Brian, 333, 691
Henson, Jim, 250, 538
Hepburn, Audrey, 45–47, 300, 466, 471, 499, 510, 546, 697
Hepburn, Katharine, 42–47, 50, 361, 367, 391, 404, 455, 477, 483, 499, 516, 546, 551, 625
Herald, Heinz, 84–86, 376, 392
Herb Alpert and the Tijuana Brass Double Feature, 250, 544
Herbert, Jocelyn, 139, 524
Herbich, Barbara, 274, 665
Herczeg, Geza, 84–85, 376
Herdan, Earle, 170, 558
Here Come the Waves, 202, 427
Here Comes Mr. Jordan, 20, 33, 54, 73, 86, 112, 397–98
Here Comes the Groom, 90, 204, 456, 458
Here Comes the Navy, 18, 364
Herman, Al, 128, 387
Herman, Justin, 243, 246, 448, 480
Heron, Julia, 129–30, 137, 399, 406, 419, 501, 507
Heroux, Denis, 27, 625
Herr, Michael, 107, 662
Herrick, Margaret, 12
Herring, Pembroke, 170–71, 173, 563, 597, 651
Herring Hunt, 245, 469
Herrmann, Bernard, 179, 183, 193, 400, 432, 597, 598
Herrnfeld, Frank P., 311, 459
Hersholt, Jean, 277, 287, 289, 299, 390, 448, 705. *See also* Jean Hersholt Humanitarian Award
Hers to Hold, 202, 414
Hertzbrun, Bernard, 128, 382
Hessy, Russell, 318, 560
Hester Street, 49, 589
Heston, Charlton, 35, 300, 499, 572, 605
Heureux Anniversaire (Happy Anniversary), 248, 520
Hey, Jerry, 196, 651
Heyerdahl, Thor, 268, 570
Heyman, Edward, 203, 428
Heyman, Norma, 29, 665
Heymann, Werner, 179–80, 182, 394, 400, 407, 419
Hiawatha's Rabbit Hunt, 239, 401
Hickey, William, 60, 649
Hidden World, The, 263, 497
Hide-Out, 84, 365
Hi Diddle Diddle, 414
Hier, Rabbi Marvin, 272, 629
Higgins, Ken, 120, 541
High and the Mighty, The, 64, 74, 168, 185, 205, 471–74
"High and the Mighty, The," 205, 474
Higher and Higher, 182, 202, 420
High Grass Circus, 270, 605
"High Hopes," 206, 502
High Noon, 22, 34, 74, 91, 167, 184, 204, 460–63
"High Noon (Do Not Forsake Me, Oh My Darling)," 204, 463
High Note, 248, 508
High over the Borders, 259, 409
High Schools, 273, 647
High Society (Allied Artists), 82, 93, 484
High Society (MGM), 82, 205, 486
High Stakes in the East, 259, 409
High Time, 206, 508
Hildyard, David, 159, 568, 574
Hildyard, Jack, 117, 490
Hill, Elizabeth, 85, 382
Hill, George Roy, 76–77, 557, 579, 708
Hill, Gladys, 102, 590
Hill, James, 249, 263, 509, 526
Hill, Jerome, 263, 492
Hiller, Arthur, 77, 562
Hiller, Wendy, 43, 65–66, 381, 494, 541
Hill Farm, The, 256, 678
Hillmann, Robert, 276, 684
Hilton, Arthur, 167, 432
Hilton, James, 87, 405
Himeda, Sinsaku, 121, 562
Hindenburg, The, 122, 143, 159, 295, 590–91, 593
Hinsdale, Ray, 308, 422
Hinton, Christopher, 257, 689
Hirose, Ryusho, 319, 577
Hiroshima, Mon Amour, 95, 506
Hirsch, Judd, 59, 619
Hirsch, Paul, 172, 603
Hirsch, Ted, 313, 488
Hirschhorn, Joel, 193, 209–11, 575, 586, 603–4
His Butler's Sister, 153, 419
Hiss and Yell, 242, 433
History of the World in Three Minutes Flat, The, 254, 622
Hitchcock, Alfred, 72–75, 298, 392, 417, 425, 472, 506, 550, 707
Hitchhike to Happiness, 182, 427
Hitler Lives?, 260, 429
Hit Parade of 1941, 178, 200, 394–95
Hit Parade of 1943, 181, 201, 414
Hitting a New High, 150, 377
Hively, George, 165, 369
Ho, A. Kitman, 29, 674, 686
Hoa-Binh, 279, 564
Hoagland, Elsworth, 165, 369
Hoaxters, The, 261, 464
Hobel, Philip S., 28, 637
Hoch, Winton, 115–16, 306, 390, 441, 446, 461
Hoedeman, Co, 253, 604
Hoffa, 125, 230, 693, 695
Hoffe, Monckton, 86, 398
Hoffenstein, Samuel, 83, 88, 176, 359, 365, 418
Hoffman, Al, 204, 452
Hoffman, Dustin, 37–40, 546, 556, 583, 613, 631, 667
Hoffman, Milton E., 702
Hogan, Bill, 325, 629
Hogan, Paul, 106, 656–56
Hogberg, Kjell, 332, 685
Holcomb, Arthur, 315, 509
Hold Back the Dawn, 20, 44, 86, 112, 129, 179, 397–400
Holden, William, 34, 38, 450, 466, 595
"Hold My Hand," 205, 474
Hole, Fred, 145, 639
Hole, The, 248, 520
Hole in the Head, A, 206, 502
Holiday (1930), 43, 83, 357
Holiday (1938), 128, 382
Holiday Inn, 86, 180, 201, 405, 407–8
Holiday Land, 237, 366
Holland, Agnieszka, 109, 687
Holland, Bill, 330, 672
Hollander, Frederick, 180, 185, 200, 203, 378, 407, 442, 468
Holliday, Judy, 45, 450
Hollingshead, Gordon, 18, 240–44, 261, 337, 362, 367, 415–16, 421–22, 428–29, 433, 438, 443, 448, 453, 459, 463–64
Holloway, Stanley, 57, 528
Hollywood (Magazine), 8
Hollywood Canteen, 153, 182, 202, 419–21
Hollywood Film Company, 321, 324, 331, 594, 624, 672
Hollywood in Uniform, 240, 415
Hollywood on Trial, 269, 599
Hollywood Revue, 17, 353
Hollywood Roosevelt Hotel, 351
Holm, Celeste, 63–64, 435, 445, 450, 483
Holm, Ian, 59, 625
Holm, Wilton R., 319, 321, 577, 600
Holmes, Carl, 329, 660
Holmes, John W., 170, 568
Holmes, Milton, 88, 425
Holmes, William, 166, 400

Holscher, Walter, 130, 136, 418, 491
Holt, Hammond H., 322, 606
Holt, Jack, 702
Holt, Willy, 140, 542
Holy Matrimony, 87, 412
Homage to Chagall—The Colours of Love, 270, 605
Home Alone, 197, 214, 682
Home in Indiana, 114, 418
Home-Made Car, 249, 526
Homulka, Oscar, 54, 440
Hondo, 64, 466
Honeysuckle Rose, 212, 622
Hook, 147, 215, 226, 229, 233, 688–89
Hooper, 160, 609
Hoosiers, 60, 196, 656–57
Hoover, John, 271, 628
Hoover, Mike, 255, 647
Hope, Bob, 13, 287–89, 291, 299, 386, 395, 397, 404, 417, 422, 424, 460, 464, 471, 489, 494, 499, 503, 505, 510, 528, 534, 538, 540, 546, 583, 601
Hope, Frederic, 127, 365, 372
Hope and Glory, 28, 80, 107, 124, 146, 661–63
"Hopelessly Devoted to You," 211, 610
Hopf, Werner, 314, 503
Hopkins, Anthony, 41, 686
Hopkins, George James, 130, 132–33, 135–41, 413, 436, 457, 473, 495, 507, 518, 530, 536, 542, 558
Hopkins, Miriam, 43, 367
Hopkins, Robert, 84, 372
Hopkins, Speed, 145, 645
Hopper, Dennis, 60, 99, 557, 656
Hornbeck, William, 167–68, 432, 457, 485, 496
Hornblow, Arthur, Jr., 18, 20–21, 23, 367, 397, 417, 489
Horner, Harry, 132, 137, 141, 446, 512, 558
Horner, James, 196–97, 213, 657–58, 676
Horning, William, 127–28, 133, 136–37, 376, 387, 457, 491, 496, 501
Hornung, Richard, 226, 689
Horse's Mouth, The, 94, 495
Horse with the Flying Tail, The, 263, 509
Horsley, David S., 312, 475
Horvath, Joan, 266, 560
Hoskins, Bob, 40, 655
Hospital, The, 37, 100, 566–67
Hotaling, Frank, 134, 462
Hotel Terminus: The Life and Times of Klaus Barbie, 275, 671
Hot Millions, 99, 552
Hot Rock, The, 171, 574
Hott, Lawrence R., 273, 276, 647, 690
Houseboat, 94, 206, 495–96
House I Live In, The, 288, 429
House Is Not a Home, A, 531, 221
Houseman, John, 22, 58, 466, 578
House of Rothschild, The, 18, 364
House of Seven Gables, The, 179, 394
House on 92nd Street, The, 88, 425
House on Chelouche Street, The, 280, 582
House on Telegraph Hill, 133, 456
House That Ananda Built, The, 266, 554
House That Jack Built, The, 250, 554
House Without a Name, The, 262, 487
Housman, Dave, 333, 691
Houston, James, 333, 691
Houston, Kent, 233, 677
"How About You?," 201, 408
Howard, James Newton, 197, 688
Howard, John C., 171, 585
Howard, Leslie, 32, 361, 381
Howard, Sidney, 83–85, 359, 372, 387
Howard, Thomas, 343, 432
Howard, Tom, 344, 497
Howard, Trevor, 35, 505
Howards End, 30, 52, 70, 81, 109, 125, 147, 198, 227, 692–95
Howards of Virginia, The, 151, 179, 393–94
Howarth, Anthony, 270, 599
"How Do You Keep the Music Playing?," 212, 634
Howe, James Wong, 111–13, 117–20, 122, 382, 392, 405, 412, 478, 495, 523, 541, 590
Howells, Barry, 269, 593
Howells, Jack, 264, 520
How Green Was My Valley, 20, 54, 63, 73, 86, 112, 129, 152, 166, 397–400, 707
Howitt, Peter, 142, 144, 146, 568, 627, 669
"How Lucky Can You Get," 210, 592
Howse, S. E., 314, 503
How the West Was Won, 24, 97, 119, 139, 157, 169, 188, 221, 522–25
How to Avoid Friendship, 249, 532
How to Marry a Millionaire, 217, 469
How to Play Football, 240, 421
How to Sleep, 237, 369
How War Came, 239, 401
Hoyt, Robert L., 159, 591
Hrastnik, Walter, 325, 332, 624, 685
Hubbard, Lucien, 17, 83, 351, 358–59
Hubbard, Winfield, 314, 504
Hubert, Harvey, Jr., 332, 685
Hubert, Rene, 218, 221, 474, 531
Hubley, Faith, 248, 250–53, 520, 544, 554, 559, 586, 604
Hubley, John, 247–48, 250–53, 502, 520, 544, 554, 559, 586, 604
Hud, 36, 47, 57, 76, 96, 119, 138, 533–24
Huddleston, Floyd, 210, 581
Hudson, David, 162, 164, 657, 688, 694
Hudson, Hugh, 79, 626, 708
Hudson, Rock, 35, 483, 572
Hughan, Oxley, 265, 532
Hughes, Frank E., 131, 425, 431
Hughes, Howard, 17, 351, 357
Hughes, John, 129–30, 399, 413, 419
Hughes, Norman S., 317, 555
Hughes, Robert, 264, 526
Hulbert, Merrit, 19, 371, 375
Hulce, Tom, 40, 643
Huldschinsky, Paul, 130, 419
Hull, Josephine, 64, 450
Human Comedy, The, 21, 33, 73, 87, 113, 411–12
Human Dutch, The, 265, 532
Humbrock, Harold, 344, 497
Humes, Immy, 276, 690
Humoresque, 183, 432
Humphreys, Gerry, 161–62, 633, 651
Hunchback of Notre Dame, The, 151, 178, 388
Hundertwasser's Rainy Day, 268, 575
Hungarians, 280, 611
Hungarofilm, 265, 544
Hungarofilm-Pathe Contemporary Films, 265, 538
Hunger, 252, 586
Hunky and Spunky, 238, 384
Hunnicutt, Arthur, 55, 460
Hunt, Hugh, 130–31, 133–40, 413, 426, 452, 457, 467, 479, 491, 501, 507, 518, 524, 530, 542
Hunt, Linda, 69, 638
Hunt, Marjorie, 273, 647
Hunter, Holly, 51, 661
Hunter, Ian McLellan, 91 n, 92, 467, 467 n
Hunter, Kim, 64, 455
Hunter, Ross, 25, 561
Hunt for Red October, The, 163, 174, 235, 682–83
Hurletron, Inc., 315, 515
Hurley, Joseph, 137, 507
Hurricane, The, 53, 150, 177, 375, 377
Hurst, Ralph S., 136, 485

Hurt, John, 39, 59, 608, 619
Hurt, William, 40, 649, 655, 661
Husbands and Wives, 70, 109, 693
Huse, Emery, 305, 390
Hush Hush, Sweet Charlotte, 66, 119, 139, 169, 188, 207, 221, 529–31
"Hush Hush, Sweet Charlotte," 207, 531
Hussey, Ruth, 62, 392
Hustler, The, 11, 23, 36, 46, 56, 75, 95, 118, 137, 510–12
Huston, Anjelica, 51, 69–70, 650, 675, 680
Huston, John, 22, 57, 73–74, 79, 86, 89–91, 94, 102, 392, 398, 440–41, 450–51, 456, 460–61, 490, 522, 578, 590, 650
Huston, Tony, 107, 662
Huston, Walter, 32–33, 54–55, 371, 397, 404, 440
Hutchinson, Thomas Jefferson, 319, 570
Hutchinson, Tim, 145, 633
Hutchinson, William, 142, 574
Hutshing, Joe, 174, 676, 688
Hutton, Timothy, 59, 619
Huyck, Willard, 101, 579
Hyer, Martha, 65, 494
Hyman, Bernard H., 19, 371
Hymns, Richard, 235, 670, 677, 689
Hynek, Joel, 233, 328, 660, 664
Hynes, Fred, 155–58, 292, 301, 479, 496, 501, 507, 512, 524, 536, 623, 665
Hypothese Beta, 250, 549

I Am a Fugitive from a Chain Gang, 18, 32, 149, 361–62
Ianzelo, Tony, 269–70, 599, 605
Ibbetson, Arthur, 121, 557
"I Can't Begin to Tell You," 203, 432
Icarus Montgolfier Wright, 248, 520
Ice Capades, 180, 400
Ice Castles, 211, 616
Ice Station Zebra, 121, 346, 552, 554
Ichac, Marcel, 249, 526
Icinkoff, Carlos, 332, 684
"I Couldn't Sleep a Wink Last Night," 202, 420
"I'd Know You Anywhere," 200, 394
I Dream Too Much, 149, 368
Idress, Ramey, 203, 442
I Even Met Happy Gypsies, 279, 550
"I Fall in Love Too Easily," 202, 427
If I Were King, 53, 128, 150, 178, 381, 383–84
"If We Were In Love," 212, 634
If You Love This Planet, 272, 635
"I Have Nothing," 215, 694
Ihnen, Wiard, 127, 131, 376, 419, 425
"I Just Called To Say I Love You," 213, 646
Ikerd, Percy, 337, 361
"I'll Buy That Dream," 202, 427
I'll Cry Tomorrow, 45, 117, 218, 477–80
I'll Find a Way, 253, 604
I'll Get By, 184, 452
"I'll Never Stop Loving You," 205, 480
"I'll Walk Alone," 202, 420
"I Love to See You Smile," 214, 677
I Love You Rosa, 280, 576
Images, 191, 574
Imagination, 240, 415
I Married a Witch, 180, 407
IMAX Systems Corporation, 328, 654
Imazu, Eddie, 127, 372
"I'm Checkin' Out," 214, 682
"I'm Easy," 210, 592
Imitation of Life (1934), 18, 149, 337, 364–65
Imitation of Life (1959), 65, 499
"I'm Making Believe," 202, 420
Immortal Love, 278, 514
Important Man, The, 278, 514
Impression of John Steinbeck: Writer, An, 267, 560
Imus, Harry, 314, 503
Incendiary Blonde, 182, 427
In Cold Blood, 76, 98, 121, 189, 547–48
Incredible Machine, The, 269, 593
Incredible Sarah, The, 143, 223, 597
Indiana Jones and the Last Crusade, 163, 197, 235, 676–77
Indiana Jones and the Temple of Doom, 195, 232, 645–46
Indiscretion of an American Wife, 218, 474
Indochine, 52, 283, 692, 696
Industrial Light and Magic, Incorporated, 325, 629; Computer Graphics Department, 334, 697
I Never Forget a Face, 246, 487
I Never Promised You a Rose Garden, 102, 602
I Never Sang for My Father, 37, 58, 99, 561–62
Information Please, 238, 389
Informer, The, 11, 18, 32, 72, 82, 84, 165, 176, 367–69
Inge, William, 96, 511
Inglis, Tony, 143, 591
In Harm's Way, 120, 535
Inherit the Wind, 35, 95, 118, 169, 505–7
Innerspace, 232, 664
Inn of the Sixth Happiness, The, 75, 495
In Old Arizona, 17, 31, 71, 83, 110, 353–54
In Old Chicago, 19, 62, 84, 150, 177, 338, 375–77, 413
In Old Oklahoma, 152, 181, 414
In Our Water, 271, 635
Inside Daisy Clover, 66, 140, 221, 534, 536–37
Inside Fighting China, 259, 409
Inside Moves, 68, 620
Interiors, 49, 68, 78, 103, 143, 607–9
Intermezzo, 178, 388
International Projector Corp., 310, 449
Interrupted Melody, 45, 93, 218, 477–78, 480
Interviews with My Lai Veterans, 267, 564
"In the Cool, Cool, Cool of the Evening," 204, 458
In the Heat of the Night, 24, 37, 76, 98, 158, 170, 348, 546–49, 708
In the Name of the People, 273, 647
In the Nuclear Shadow: What Can the Children Tell Us?, 272, 641
In the Region of Ice, 253, 598
In the Shadow of the Stars, 276, 690
In the Wee Wee Hours . . ., 274, 664
In the Year of the Pig, 267, 560
Introduction to the Photoplay, 7
Invaders, The, 20, 86–87, 404–5
Investigation of a Citizen Above Suspicion, 100, 279, 564, 567
Invisible Agent, 342, 408
Invisible Man Returns, The, 341, 395
Invisible Woman, The, 342, 401
In Which We Serve, 21, 87, 287, 409, 411–12
Iphigenia, 280, 605
"I Poured My Heart into a Song," 200, 389
Ireland, John, 55, 445
I Remember Mama, 45, 54, 63, 115, 440–41
Irene, 179, 216, 220, 394, 442, 508
Irish Eyes Are Smiling, 182, 420
Irma La Douce, 47, 119, 188, 522–23, 525
Irons, Jeremy, 41, 680
Ironweed, 40, 51, 661
Irvine, Richard, 129, 399
Irving, Amy, 69, 638
Irving G. Thalberg Memorial Award, 13, 297
Isaac in America: A Journey with Isaac Bashevis Singer, 274, 659
Isadora, 47, 551

Isham, Mark, 198, 694
Ishioka, Eiko, 226, 695
Is It Always Right to Be Right?, 251, 564
Island at the Top of the World, The, 142, 585
Islands in the Stream, 122, 602
Islands of the Sea, 248, 508
Is Paris Burning?, 120, 140, 541–42
Istec, Inc., 331, 679
"It Goes Like It Goes," 211, 616
It Happened One Night, 18, 32, 43, 72, 84, 364, 707
It Happened on Fifth Avenue, 89, 436
It Happened Tomorrow, 153, 181, 419–20
It Happens Every Spring, 89, 446
"It Might As Well Be Spring," 203, 428
"It Might Be You," 212, 634
"It's a Blue World," 200, 394
It's a Great Feeling, 203, 447
"It's a Great Feeling," 203, 447
It's Always Fair Weather, 93, 185, 478, 480
It's a Mad, Mad, Mad, Mad World, 119, 157, 169, 188, 207, 348, 523–26
"It's a Mad, Mad, Mad, Mad World," 207, 525
It's a Wonderful Life, 21, 34, 73, 154, 167, 430–32
"It Seems I Heard That Song Before," 201, 408
It's Everybody's War, 259, 409
It's Got Me Again, 236, 360
It Should Happen to You, 218, 474
"It's Magic," 203, 442
It's So Nice to Have a Wolf Around the House, 254, 617
It Started in Naples, 137, 507
It Started with Eve, 180, 407
It's the Same World, 271, 623
It's Tough to Be a Bird, 250, 559
Ivanhoe, 22, 116, 184, 460–62
"I've Got a Feeling You're Fooling," 339, 369
"I've Got a Gal in Kalamazoo," 201, 408
"I've Got You Under My Skin," 199, 373
"(I've Had) The Time of My Life," 213, 663
Ives, Burl, 56, 494
I Vitelloni, 94, 490
Ivory, James, 80–81, 656, 693
I Wanted Wings, 342, 401
I Want to Live!, 46, 75, 94, 117, 156, 168, 494–96
I Want You, 155, 457
I Was a Communist for the F.B.I., 261, 459
Iwerks, Ub, 314, 316, 346, 504, 525, 533
"I Will Wait for You," 207, 537
"I Wish I Didn't Love You So," 203, 437
I Won't Play, 240, 422

Jabara, Paul, 211, 610
Jack Johnson, 267, 564
Jack London, 181, 420
Jackman, Fred, 303, 363
Jackson, Calvin, 189, 531
Jackson, Doug, 251, 559
Jackson, Felix, 85, 387
Jackson, Glenda, 42, 48–49, 561, 566, 578, 589
Jackson, Harry, 114, 436
Jackson, Horace, 83, 357
Jackson, Joseph, 83, 358
Jacob, the Liar, 280, 599
Jacobs, Arthur, 24, 546
Jacobs, Henry, 264, 532
Jacobs, Jim, 267, 564
Jacobsen, Jan, 330, 666
Jacobson, Arthur, 337, 361
Jacoby, Irving, 247, 503
Jacqueline Susann's Once Is Not Enough, 67, 590
Jacques-Yves Cousteau's World Without Sun, 265, 532
Jaeckel, Richard, 58, 566
Jaffe, Leo, 300, 611
Jaffe, Stanley R., 27–28, 613, 661
Jaffe, Sam, 55, 450
Jagged Edge, 60, 649
Jagger, Dean, 55, 445
Jahraus, Donald, 343, 415, 421, 428
James, Arthur, 209, 563
James, Gerard, 146, 669
James, Peter, 142–43, 574, 591
Jammin' the Blues, 240, 421
Jandl, Ivan, 288, 443
Janie, 166, 419
Jankovics, Marcell, 252, 592
Janni, Joseph, 24, 534
Jannings, Emil, 31, 351
Janson, Len, 250, 549
Janssen, Werner, 177–78, 182, 373, 383, 388, 427
Janus Films, 271, 617
Jarman, Claude, Jr., 288, 433
Jarre, Maurice, 188–89, 193, 196–97, 209, 519, 525, 537, 575, 603, 645, 652, 669, 682
Jarrico, Paul, 86, 398
Jarvis, John, 134, 468
Jasper and the Beanstalk, 241, 428
Jaworski, Tadeusz, 268, 575
Jaws, 26, 159, 171, 193, 589, 591
Jaywalker, The, 246, 487
Jazz Singer, The (1927), 82, 148, 285, 336, 351–52
Jazz Singer, The (1953), 184, 462
Jeakins, Dorothy, 216–17, 219–23, 226, 442, 463, 486, 513, 519, 531, 537, 543, 581, 664
"Jean," 208, 559
Jean Hersholt Humanitarian Award, 299
"Jeepers Creepers," 200, 384
Jefferies, Philip, 142, 580
Jeffress, Jerry, 322, 329–30, 606, 660, 672
Jein, Gregory, 231, 604, 617
Jenkins, Chris, 162–64, 651, 682, 694
Jenkins, George, 143–44, 597, 615
Jennings, Devereaux, 286, 343, 385, 437
Jennings, Gordon, 286, 308, 310, 341–43, 385, 389, 395, 401, 408, 415, 421–22, 437, 459
Jennings, Joe, 144, 615
Jennings, John D., 248, 514
Jennings, Talbot, 84, 88, 368, 431
Jennings, Wilbur, 212, 622
Jennings, Will, 212, 634
Jenny Is a Good Thing, 267, 560
Jensen, John, 219, 486, 497
Jenson, George, 232, 646
Jenssen, Elois, 217, 225, 634
Jerome, M. K., 202–3, 421, 428
Jerry's Cousin, 243, 453
Jersey, Bill, 266, 275, 550, 678
Jessel, George, 299, 371, 560
Jessup, Harley, 233, 664, 689
Jester, Ralph, 218–19, 486, 497
Jesus Christ Superstar, 192, 580
Jesus of Montreal, 282, 678
Jet Carrier, 245, 262, 475
Jewison, Norman, 24–25, 28–29, 76–77, 80, 540, 547, 566–7, 643, 661–62, 708
Jezebel, 19, 43, 62, 111, 177, 381–83
JFK, 29, 61, 81, 109, 125, 164, 174, 197, 686–88
Jhabvala, Ruth Prawer, 107, 109, 656, 693
Jimmy the C, 253, 604
Jirouch, Gustav, 311, 465
Joan of Arc, 44, 54, 115, 132, 167, 183, 216, 289, 440–42
Joan of Paris, 180, 407
Job's Revolt, 281, 642
Jodoin, Rene, 252, 586, 592
Joe, 99, 562
Joffa, Bernard, 256, 683
Joffe, Carol, 146, 657, 663
Joffe, Charles, 26, 601
Joffe, Roland, 79–80, 644, 656
Johann Mouse, 244, 463
John Glenn Story, The, 264, 520
John Henry and the Inky Poo, 241, 433
John Muir's High Sierra, 269, 586
Johnny Belinda, 21, 34, 45, 54, 63, 73, 89, 115, 132, 154, 167, 183, 440–42
Johnny Come Lately, 181, 414

Johnny Doughboy, 180, 407
Johnny Eager, 54, 404
Johns, A. W., 343, 428
Johns, Arthur, 341, 343, 389, 395, 421
Johns, Glynis, 65, 505
Johnson, Ben, 58, 566
Johnson, Brian, 231–32, 296, 616, 623, 628
Johnson, Celia, 44, 430
Johnson, Joseph McMillan, 135, 137–38, 343, 346, 442, 479, 507, 518, 537, 554
Johnson, Larry, 158, 563
Johnson, Mark, 29, 667, 686
Johnson, Nunnally, 20, 86–87, 391–92, 404, 412
Johnson, Paul, 330, 672
Johnson, Tom, 164, 688
Johnston, Arthur, 199, 373
Johnston, Becky, 109, 687
Johnston, Clint, 98, 541
Johnston, Joe, 232, 628
Johnstone, Anna Hill, 223, 225, 575, 628
Johnstown Flood, The, 275, 678
Joker Is Wild, The, 205, 491
Jolley, Stan, 145, 651
Jolley, Walter, 313, 481
Jolly Little Elves, 237, 366
Jolson Sings Again, 90, 115, 184, 446–47
Jolson Story, The, 34, 54, 114, 154, 167, 183, 430–32
Jonathan Livingston Seagull, 122, 171, 579–80
Jones, Bob, 159, 568
Jones, Carolyn, 65, 489
Jones, Chuck, 248–49, 514, 538
Jones, Dewitt, 252, 269, 586
Jones, Edward, 233, 670
Jones, Eugene, 269, 587
Jones, Grover, 83–84, 359, 368
Jones, Harmon, 167, 437
Jones, James Earl, 37, 561
Jones, Jennifer, 44–45, 63, 411, 417, 424, 430, 477
Jones, Natalie, 269, 587
Jones, Peter, 265, 544
Jones, Quincy, 28, 189, 194, 196, 208, 213, 549, 553, 610, 651–52
Jones, Robert C., 103, 169–71, 524, 548, 597, 608
Jones, Shirley, 65, 505
Jones, Tommy Lee, 61, 686
Jones, Watson, 155, 479
Jonsson, Reidar, 107, 662
Jordan, Neil, 81, 109, 693
Jory, Corrine, 226, 689
Joseph, John, 270, 605
Josephson, Julian, 83, 356
Jost, Jerry, 160, 603
Jost, Lawrence O., 159, 580, 585
Journey for Survival, 271, 628
Journey into Life: The World of the Unborn, 275, 683
Journey into Medicine, 260, 438
Journey into Self, 258, 266, 554, 554 n
Journey into Spring, 247, 263, 497
Journey of Hope, 282, 684
Journey of Natty Gann, 225, 652
Journey to the Center of the Earth, 137, 156, 344, 501, 502
Journey to the Outer Limits, 268, 581
Joy, David, 306, 390
Joyce, Adrian, 99, 562
Joy of Living, 245, 469
Juarez, 53, 386
Judgment at Nuremberg, 23, 36, 56, 65, 75, 95, 118, 137, 169, 220, 510–13
Ju Dou, 282, 684
Juke Box Jamboree, 239, 408
Julia, 26, 49, 59, 68, 78, 102, 122, 172, 193, 224, 601–4
Julie, 93, 205, 484, 486
"Julie," 205, 486
Juliet of the Spirits, 140, 222, 542–43
Julius Caesar, 22, 34, 116, 134, 185, 466–68
June, Ray, 111, 117, 360, 368, 490
Junge, Alfred, 132, 134, 436, 468
Jungle Book, The (1942), 113, 130, 180, 342, 406–8
Jungle Book, The (1967), 208, 548
Junkerman, John, 274, 665
Jurado, Katy, 64, 471
Juraga, Boris, 139, 524
Juran, Nathan, 129, 132, 399, 431
Jurgens, John, 322, 606
Jury Goes Round 'n' Round, The, 241, 428
Jury of Her Peers, A, 254, 622
Just Another Missing Kid, 272, 635
Just for You, 204, 463
Justice, Milton, 274, 659
Just Imagine, 127, 358

Kaestner, Erich, 301, 320, 326, 582, 636, 697
Kagemusha (The Shadow Warrior), 144, 281, 621, 623
Kahane, B. B., 290, 493, 705
Kahl, 264, 514
Kahn, Gus, 176, 199–200, 365–66, 394
Kahn, Madeline, 67, 579, 584
Kahn, Michael, 172, 174, 603, 627, 663
Kahn, Richard, 705
Kahn, Sheldon, 171, 173, 591, 651
Kainoscho, Tadaoto, 218, 480
Kalinina, Irina, 273, 647
Kalmar, Bert, 204, 458
Kalser, Konstantin, 246, 487
Kalten, Nick, 310, 444
Kama Sutra Rides Again, 251, 575
Kamen, Michael, 215, 689
Kaminska, Ida, 47, 540
Kander, John, 210, 592
Kane, Carol, 49, 589
Kane, Doc, 164, 688, 694
Kane, Joel, 94, 490
Kanin, Fay, 94, 495, 705
Kanin, Garson, 89–91, 436, 451, 461
Kanin, Michael, 87, 94, 405, 495
Kansan, The, 181, 414
Kaper, Bronislau, 180, 185, 188, 207, 400, 468, 519
Kapil, K., 270, 611
Kaplan, William B., 162, 651, 657
Kapo, 278, 509
Karate Kid, The, 60, 643
Karate Kid Part II, The, 213, 657
Karinska, Madame, 216–17, 442, 463
Karl Hess: Toward Liberty, 271, 623
Karlin, Fred, 191, 208–9, 559, 563, 575
Karlin, Marsha, 209, 575
Karmann, Sam, 257, 696
Karmitz, Marin, 265, 544
Karol, John, 272, 635
Karrell, Matia, 256, 670
Karsh, Andrew, 29, 686
Kasdan, Lawrence, 29, 105, 107–8, 638, 667–68, 687
Kasdan, Meg, 108, 687
Kasha, Al, 193, 209–11, 575, 586, 603–4
Kasper, David, 276, 696
Kass, Ronald, 269, 586
Katcher, Leo, 93, 484
Katz, Gloria, 101, 579
Katz, Robert A., 256, 664
Katz, Stephen M., 323, 612
Kaufman, Boris, 116–17, 472, 484
Kaufman, Charles, 96, 517
Kaufman, Millard, 92–93, 467, 478
Kaufman, Paul, 323, 618
Kaufman, Philip, 107, 668
Kaufman, Robert, 98, 547
Kawashima, Taizoh, 141, 562
Kay, Edward, 179–80, 182, 400, 407, 420, 427
Kaye, A. E., 150, 377
Kaye, Danny, 290, 300, 455, 474, 629
Kaye, Simon, 161–62, 164, 627, 633, 657, 694
Kazan, Elia, 24, 73–74, 76, 96, 436, 456, 472, 478, 522–23, 707
Kazan, Nicholas, 108, 681
Keaton, Buster, 290, 503
Keaton, Diane, 49–50, 601, 625
Keats and His Nightingale: A Blind Date, 273, 653
Kedrova, Lila, 66, 529
Keeney, Richard, 332, 691

Keeper of Promises (The Given Word), 278, 520
Keitel, Harvey, 61, 686
Kellaway, Cecil, 55, 57, 440, 546
Kellaway, Roger, 193, 598
Keller, Bruce W., 328, 331, 660, 672
Keller, Frank P., 170–71, 548, 553, 574, 580
Kellerman, Sally, 67, 561
Kelley, Wallace, 343, 437
Kelley, William, 106, 650
Kellner, William, 132, 136, 447, 501
Kellogg, Virginia, 90, 446, 451
Kelly, Gene, 33, 289, 339, 424, 459, 589
Kelly, Grace, 45, 64, 466, 471
Kelly, Joseph, 157, 320, 322, 518, 587, 606
Kelly, Nancy, 46, 483
Kelly, Thomas P., Jr., 266, 554
Kelman, Alfred R., 265, 544
Kemp, Paul, 254, 628
Kemplen, Ralph, 167, 170–71, 462, 553, 580
Kenji Comes Home, 261, 448
Kennaway, James, 95, 506
Kennedy, Arthur, 34, 55–56, 445, 455, 477, 489, 494
Kennedy, George, 57, 546
Kennedy, Kathleen, 27–28, 631, 649
Kennedy, Wes, 327, 648
Kennell, Louis C., 315, 521
Kenojuak, 264, 532
Kent, Ted J., 169, 530
Kent, Walter, 202, 421, 427
Kentucky, 53, 381
Kenworthy, N. Paul, Jr., 322, 606
Kerber, Randy, 196, 651
Kern, Hal C., 166, 388, 394, 420
Kern, Jerome, 182, 199, 201–3, 369, 373, 401, 408, 421, 427–28, 432
Kern, Robert J., 165–66, 368, 426
Kernochan, Sarah, 268, 576
Kerr, Deborah, 45–46, 445, 466, 483, 489, 494, 505
Kessler, Stephen, 257, 689
Ketcham, James, 331, 679
Key Largo, 64, 440
Keys of the Kingdom, The, 33, 114, 131, 182, 424–25, 427
Khartoum, 98, 541
Khouri, Callie, 108, 687
Khovanshchina, 187, 513
Kiankhooy, Dr. Paul, 332, 685
Kick Me, 252, 592
Kiebach, Jurgen, 142, 574
Kiernan, William R., 135–37, 140, 142, 485, 491, 501, 507, 542, 580
Kilberg, Richard, 275, 678
Killers, The, 73, 89, 167, 183, 431–32
Killey, Eddie, 337, 361
Killing Fields, The, 28, 40, 60, 79, 106, 124, 173, 643–45
Killing Ground, The, 271, 617
Kimball, David J., 161, 621
Kimball, Mark, 333, 691
Kimball, Ward, 250, 262, 487, 559
Kind Lady, 217, 458
King, Alan, 566
King, Frank and Maurice, 6
King, Henry, 9, 73, 412, 418, 702
King, Paul, 95, 500
King: A Filmed Record . . . Montgomery to Memphis, 267, 564
King and I, The, 23, 35, 46, 74, 117, 136, 156, 186, 218, 483–86
King Kong (1976), 122, 160, 295, 597, 599
King of Burlesque, 339, 369
King of Jazz, 126, 356
King of the Zombies, 179, 400
King Rat, 120, 139, 535
Kingsley, Ben, 39, 61, 631, 686
Kingsley, Dorothy, 92, 472
Kings of the Turf, 239, 402
King Solomon's Mines, 22, 115, 167, 450–52
Kings Row, 20, 73, 113, 404–5
King's Story, A, 266, 550
Kinotone Corporation, 329, 665
Kirk, Mark-Lee, 128–29, 131, 393, 406, 419
Kirkland, Geoffrey, 145, 639
Kirkland, Sally, 51, 661
Kish, Joseph, 130, 132, 137, 139–40, 418, 441, 501, 536
Kismet, 114, 131, 153, 181, 418–20
Kiss, The, 247, 497
Kisses for My President, 221, 531
Kiss Me Kate, 185, 468
Kiss of Death, 54, 89, 435–36
Kiss of the Spider Woman, 28, 40, 79, 106, 649–50
"Kiss the Girl," 214, 677
"Kiss to Build a Dream, A," 204, 458
Kitchell, Mark, 275, 684
Kitty, 131, 431
Kitty Foyle, 20, 44, 72, 86, 151, 391–93
Klan, A Legacy of Hate in America, The, 272, 635
Kleban, Edward, 213, 652
Klein, James, 270, 272, 605, 641
Kline, Herbert, 269, 587
Kline, Kevin, 61, 667
Kline, Richard C., 163, 669
Kline, Richard H., 121, 122, 547, 597
Kline, Rick, 162–64, 639, 651, 657, 682, 694
Klingman, Lynzee, 171, 591
Klondike Fury, 180, 407
Klotz, Florence, 224, 604
Klute, 48, 100, 566–67
Knickerbocker Holiday, 182, 420
Knife in the Water, 278, 526
Knight, Castleton, 262, 470
Knight, Charles, 159, 574
Knight, Darrin, 160, 609
Knight, Shirley, 65, 505, 517
Knights of the Round Table, 134, 155, 468
Knighty Knight Bugs, 247, 497
Knock on Wood, 92, 472
Knoth, Fred, 312, 476
Knox, Alexander, 33, 417
Knudson, Carroll, 317, 545
Knudson, Robert, 159–61, 163, 574, 597, 603, 609, 615, 633, 663, 669
Knudtson, Frederic, 167–69, 447, 496, 501, 507, 512, 524
KNX Radio, 13
Koch, Howard (writer), 86–87, 398, 412
Koch, Howard W. (producer), 300, 679, 705
Koch, Norma, 220–21, 223, 519, 531, 575
Koehler, Ted, 202–3, 421, 428
Koenekamp, Fred J., 121–22, 562, 584, 602
Koenekamp, Hans, 342, 415
Koenig, Lt. John, 130, 413
Koenig, Wolf, 250, 544, 549, 554
Koff, David, 270, 599
Kohlmar, Fred, 22, 477
Kohn, John, 97, 535
Kohner, Frederick, 85, 382
Kohner, Susan, 65, 499
Kohut, Michael J., 161–63, 615, 621, 627, 639, 645, 663, 682
Kokoda Front Line, 259, 409
Kolb, Dr. Fred, Jr., 332, 685
Kollmorgen Corporation: Electro-Optical Division, 317, 319, 550; Photo Research Division, 319, 321, 324, 571, 576, 600, 618
Kon Tiki, 261, 459
Kopelson, Arnold, 28, 655
Kopple, Barbara, 269, 275, 599, 684
Korda, Alexander, 18, 361
Korda, Vincent, 128–30, 138, 393, 399, 406, 518
Korjus, Miliza, 62, 382
Korngold, Erich Wolfgang, 176, 178–79, 373, 383, 388, 394
Korty, John, 264, 270, 532, 605
Koryo Celadon, 271, 617
Kosa, Emil, Jr., 346, 526
Koshelev, G., 141, 552
Kostal, Irwin, 187–89, 191, 193, 513, 531, 537, 568, 603
Koster, Henry, 73, 436
Kotch, 37, 159, 170, 209, 566, 568–69
Kotuk, Richard, 272, 641

Kovacs, Steven, 269, 592
Kovic, Ron, 108, 675
Kraemer, George, 333, 697
Kraft, Robert, 215, 694
Krainin, Julian, 267–68, 570, 581
Krakatoa, 237, 362
Krakatoa: East of Java, 346, 559
Kraly, Hans, 83, 85, 354, 376
Kramer, Larry, 99, 562
Kramer, Stanley, 22–24, 75–76, 298, 460, 471, 494–95, 510–11, 515, 534, 546–47
Kramer vs. Kramer, 27, 39, 59, 68, 78, 103, 123, 172, 613–15, 708 Krams, Arthur, 134–38, 462, 468, 479, 501, 507, 512
Krasker, Robert, 115, 451
Krasna, Norman, 84, 86–87, 365, 372, 398, 412
Krasner, Milton, 113, 115–17, 119, 406, 451, 472, 490, 523, 529
Krause, Edward B., 324, 624
Krepela, Neil, 232, 646
Kress, Carl, 171, 585
Kress, Harold F., 166–67, 169, 171, 400, 407, 432, 524, 574, 585
Krilanovich, Steve, 313, 481
Krim, Arthur B., 299, 587
Kristofferson, Kris, 196, 646
Kroitor, Roman, 254, 617
Krokaugger, William G., 327, 642
Kroyer, Bill, 256, 670
Kruschen, Jack, 56, 505
Krzanowski, Tadeuz, 330, 666
Kubrick, Stanley, 24–26, 76–78, 97, 99–101, 107, 346, 528–29, 552, 554, 566–67, 589–90, 662
Kuchel, Thomas, 8
Kudelski, Stefan, 301, 316, 322, 539, 606, 612, 684
Kudzu, 253, 598
Kuhl, Dr. Bernhard, 322, 324, 329, 606, 624, 665
Kukan, 287, 402
Kuljian, Anne, 146, 676
Kureishi, Hanif, 106, 656
Kuri, Emile, 129, 132–35, 137, 139, 142, 406, 446, 462, 473, 512, 530, 568
Kurland, Gilbert, 149, 368
Kurnitz, Harry, 88, 425
Kurosawa, Akira, 79, 293, 650, 678
Kurtz, Gary, 25–26, 578, 601
Kusnick, Harry, 343, 421
Kwaidan, 279, 538
Kymry, Tylwyth, 191, 563
K-Z, 268, 575

La Cage aux Folles, 78, 103, 224, 614, 616
La Cava, Gregory, 72, 372, 376
Lacey, John, 327, 642
Lacombe, Lucien, 280, 587
La Cucaracha, 237, 366
Ladd, Diane, 67, 70, 584, 681, 687
Laden, Bob, 229, 664
Ladies in Retirement, 129, 179, 399–400
La Dolce Vita, 75, 96, 137, 220, 511–13
Ladue, Peter W., 271, 623
Lady and Gent, 83, 359
Lady Be Good, 201, 401
Lady Eve, The, 86, 398
Lady for a Day, 18, 43, 72, 83, 361–62
Ladyhawke, 162, 234, 651–52
Lady in the Dark, 114, 131, 182, 418–20
Lady in Waiting, The, 257, 695
Lady Killers, The, 93, 484
Lady Let's Dance, 182, 202, 420–21
Lady Objects, The, 200, 384
Lady of Burlesque, 181, 414
Lady on a Train, 153, 426
Lady Sings the Blues, 48, 100, 192, 223, 572–75
Laemmle, Carl, 297
Laemmle, Carl, Jr., 17, 355
La Fiesta de Santa Barbara, 237, 374
La Fuite, Rene, 264, 514
Lagarde, Jocelyne, 66, 541
Lagerstrom, Oscar, 148, 356
La Grande Olympiade (Olympic Games 1960), 264, 514
La Gravenese, Richard, 108, 687
La Guerre Est Finie, 98, 547
Lahti, Christine, 69, 644
Lai, Francis, 191, 563
Laing, Robert W., 142, 145, 574, 633
Lake, Stuart N., 86, 392
Lamb, Derek, 254, 617
Lamb, John, 324, 618
Lambert, Gavin, 95, 102, 506, 602
Lambert, The Sheepish Lion, 244, 458
Lamont, Peter, 142–43, 145, 568, 603
Lamorisse, Albert, 94, 270, 484, 611
Lancaster, Burt, 34–36, 39, 466, 505, 516, 625
Lanchester, Elsa, 64–65, 445, 489
Landaker, Alan, 325, 328–29, 629, 654, 660
Landaker, Gregg, 161, 164, 621, 627, 688
Landaker, Hal, 325, 329, 629, 660
Landau, Ely, 267, 564
Landau, Martin, 61, 667, 675
Landis, Ilene, 272, 641
Landlord, The, 67, 561
Land of Promise, 280, 593
Landsburg, Alan, 267, 570
Lane, Burton, 201, 204, 408, 458
Lang, Charles B., Jr., 111–15, 116–19, 121, 358, 362, 392, 398, 412, 418, 436, 441, 461, 472, 478, 495, 500, 506, 512, 523, 557, 573
Lang, John W., 325, 332, 624, 685
Lang, Otto, 245, 262, 469, 475
Lang, Walter, 74, 484
Langdon, Dory, 206–7, 508, 519
Lange, Arthur, 178, 181–82, 388, 414, 420, 427
Lange, Harry, 141, 144, 552, 621
Lange, Hope, 65, 490
Lange, Jessica, 11, 50–51, 62, 69, 631–32, 643, 649, 674
Lange, Johnny, 204, 452
Lange, Robert John, 215, 689
Langlois, Henri, 291, 582
Langrehr, Larry L., 327, 642
Language Says It All, 274, 665
Lannon, Jack, 310, 444
Lansburgh, Brian, 253, 592
Lansburgh, Larry, 246–47, 263, 487, 492, 509
Lansburgh, Lawrence M., 253, 592
Lansbury, Angela, 63, 65, 417, 424, 517
Lansing, Sherry, 28, 661
Lantieri, Michael, 233, 677, 689
Lantz, Walter, 237, 239, 240–41, 245–46, 292, 362, 401, 408, 415, 421, 428, 433, 474, 480, 611
Lapis, Joseph, 341, 395
La Porte, Steve, 229, 670
Larche, Dr. Kurt, 326, 642
Lardner, Ring, Jr., 87, 99, 405, 562
Larkin, Ryan, 251, 559
Larner, Jeremy, 100, 573
La Ronde, 91, 133, 456–57
Larsen, Tambi, 135, 138, 140–41, 144, 479, 524, 536, 562, 626
Larson, Harry, 319, 577
Larson, Maurice, 313, 481
La Rue, Jim, 161, 633
La Shelle, Joseph, 114–20, 418, 446, 461, 478, 500, 506, 523, 541
Lasker, Lawrence, 29, 105, 638, 680
Lasky, Jesse L., 18, 20, 364, 397, 702
Lasky, William, 243, 448
Las Madres—The Mothers of Plaza de Mayo, 273, 653
Lassally, Walter, 120, 529
Lasseter, John, 255–56, 658, 670
Lassie Come Home, 113, 412
Last Angry Man, The, 35, 136, 499, 501
Last Bomb, The, 260, 429
Last Breeze of Summer, 257, 689
Last Command, The, 31, 82, 351
"Last Dance," 211, 610

Last Detail, The, 38, 58, 101, 578–79
Last Emperor, The, 17, 29, 80, 107, 124, 146, 163, 174, 196, 226, 661–64, 708
Last Metro, The, 281, 623
Last of Mrs. Cheyney, The, 83, 354
Last of the Mohicans (1936), 337, 372
Last of the Mohicans (1992), 164, 694
Last Picture Show, The, 25, 58, 67, 77, 100, 121, 566–67
La Strada, 93, 277, 484, 487
Last Summer, 66, 557
Last Tango in Paris, 37, 77, 578–79
Last Temptation Of Christ, The, 80, 668
"Last Time I Felt Like This, The," 211, 610
"Last Time I Saw Paris, The," 201, 401
Last Tycoon, The, 143, 597
Last Voyage, The, 344, 508
Last Year at Marienbad, 96, 517
Las Vegas Nights, 201, 401
Laszlo, Ernest, 118–22, 506, 511, 523, 535, 541, 552, 562, 597
Latady, William R., 322, 606
Late Show, The, 102, 602
Lathrop, Philip, 119, 122, 529, 584
"Latin from Manhattan," 339, 369
La Traviata, 145, 225, 633–34
Laube, Grover, 306, 308, 396, 422
Lauenstein, Christoph, 256, 678
Lauenstein, Wolfgang, 256, 678
Laughter, 83, 357
Laughton, Charles, 32, 35, 361, 367, 489
Laura, 73, 88, 114, 130, 417–19
Laurel, Stan, 290, 509
Laurents, Arthur, 26, 102, 601–2
Laurie, Piper, 46, 68–69, 510, 596, 656
Lavalou, Jean-Marie, 324, 623
"Lavender Blue," 204, 447
Lavender Hill Mob, The, 34, 91, 460–61
La Venganza, 278, 497
La Verite, 278, 509
Lavery, Emmet, 93, 478
LaVezzi Machine Works, Incorporated, 326, 636
Lawrence, Jack, 205, 474
Lawrence, Richard J., 145, 639
Lawrence, Robert, 169, 507
Lawrence, Viola, 168–69, 491, 507
Lawrence of Arabia, 23, 36, 56, 75, 96, 119, 138, 157, 169, 188, 516–19, 708
Lawson, Arthur, 132, 441
Lawson, John Howard, 85, 382
Lay, Beirne, Jr., 91, 93, 467, 478
Layton, R. T., 341, 395
La Zare, Howard T., 319, 325, 576, 629
Lazarowitz, Les, 161, 621, 633
Leachman, Cloris, 67, 567
Leaf, Caroline, 253, 598
Lean, David, 73–76, 79, 88–89, 106, 173, 431, 436, 478, 490, 517, 535, 644–45, 707–8
Lear, Norman, 98, 547
Leatherneck, The, 83, 354
Leave Her to Heaven, 44, 114, 131, 153, 424–26
Leavitt, J. Noxon, 331, 679
Leavitt, Sam, 117–18, 495, 500, 506
Le Bal, 281, 642
Le Baron, William, 17–18, 357, 361
Lebenthal, James, 247, 497
Lebenzon, Chris, 173, 657
LeBlanc Pam, 271, 628
LeBlanc, Paul, 228, 646
Le Ciel et La Boue (The Sky Above and Mud Beneath), 264, 514
Lecuona, Ernesto, 201, 408
Leduc, Andre, 252, 592
Lee, Danny, 231, 347, 569, 616
Lee, Lester, 204, 469
Lee, Peggy, 64, 477
Lee, Robert N., 83, 357
Lee, Sammy, 339–40, 369, 378
Lee, Spike, 108, 675
Lee Electric (Lighting) Limited, 329, 660
Leeds, Andrea, 62, 376
Leeson, Mick, 212, 627
Leffingwell, Robert G., 244, 458
Le Gallienne, Eva, 68, 620
Legend, 229, 658
Legendary Champions, The, 266, 554
Legend of Jimmy Blue Eyes, The, 249, 532
Legend of John Henry, The, 252, 581
Legend of Rock-A-Bye Point, The, 246, 480
Legrand, Michel, 189–91, 195, 207–9, 212–13, 537, 553, 559, 563, 568, 634, 640
Lehman, Ernest, 24–25, 92, 95, 98, 472, 500, 511, 540–41, 556
Lehman, Gladys, 87, 418
Lehman, Robin, 253, 269, 586, 592, 599
Leigh, Janet, 65, 505
Leigh, Vivien, 42, 45, 386, 455
Leighton, Leroy G., 314, 498
Leighton, Margaret, 67, 567
Leighton, Robert, 175, 694
Leipold, John, 178, 388
Leisen, Mitchell, 126, 354
Leisure, 253, 598
Le Lorrain, Edward, 272, 635
Lelouch, Claude, 76, 98, 101, 541, 590
Le Maillon et la Chaine (The Link and the Chain), 264, 526
Le Maire, Charles, 216–19, 458, 463, 469, 474, 480, 486, 492, 497, 502
Le-Mare, Mike, 161, 234, 633–34
Le Messurier, Nicolas, 160, 162, 609, 645, 657
Lemmon, Jack, 31, 35–36, 38–39, 55, 477, 489, 499, 505, 516, 522, 566, 578, 613, 619, 631, 643
Lend a Paw, 239, 401
Lengyel, Melchior, 85, 387
Lennart, Isobel, 93, 95, 478, 506
Lenny, 26, 38, 48, 77, 101, 122, 583–84
Lenya, Lotte, 65, 511
Leo Beuerman, 267, 560
Leonard, Harry, 343, 428
Leonard, Jack, 91, 461
Leonard, Judith, 275, 678
Leonard, Robert J., 320, 587
Leonard, Robert Z. (director), 17, 71–72, 355, 372, 707
Leondopoulos, Jordan, 171, 580
Leopard, The, 221, 525
Le Plaisir, 134, 473
Lerner, Alan Jay, 91, 94, 97, 192, 204, 206, 210, 456, 458, 495–96, 529, 586
Lerner, Michael, 61, 686
Lerner, Murray, 266, 271, 550, 623
Le Roy, Mervyn, 20, 73, 298, 386, 405, 593
Lerpae, Paul, 308, 343, 423, 437
Les Films du Compass, 244, 458
Les Girls, 136, 156, 219, 491–92
Leshing, Michael, 308, 429
Leslie, F. D., 315, 515
Les Miserables, 18, 111, 165, 337, 367–69
Lesser, Sol, 20, 299, 391, 509
Lethal Weapon, 163, 663
Lethal Weapon 2, 235, 677
Let It Be, 191, 563
Let My People Go, 265, 538
Let's Get Lost, 275, 671
"Let's Hear It for the Boy," 213, 646
Let's Make Love, 187, 507
Letter, The (1929), 42, 353
Letter, The (1940), 20, 43, 54, 72, 112, 166, 179, 391–92, 394
Letter from Home, 258, 402
Letters from Marusia, 280, 593
Letter to a Hero, 240, 415
Letter to Three Wives, A, 21, 74, 90, 445–46
"Let the River Run," 214, 669
Levee, M. C. (Mike), 2, 702, 705
Leven, Boris, 128–29, 136, 138,

140–42, 146, 382, 406, 485, 512, 536, 542, 552, 568, 657
Leventhal, Harold, 26, 595
Leveque, John, 235, 695
Leverett, George, 342, 408
Le Vien, Jack, 265–66, 532, 550
Levien, Sonya, 84, 93, 362, 478
Levinson, Barry, 29, 80, 103–4, 108, 614, 632, 668, 681, 686–87, 708
Levinson, Nathan, 149–55, 287, 304, 309, 341–43, 362, 365, 368, 370, 373, 377, 383, 388–89, 393, 395, 400–401, 407–8, 413, 415, 419, 421, 426, 432, 439, 457
Levinson, Shelley, 254, 628
Levitt, Helen, 90, 446
Levitt, Ruby R., 137, 140, 142, 501, 536, 568, 585
Le Volcan Interdit (The Forbidden Volcano), 265, 544
Levy, Edmond, 265, 544
Lewin, Albert, 18–19, 367, 375
Lewin, Robert, 93, 484
Lewis, Andy, 100, 567
Lewis, Cecil, 85, 382
Lewis, Daniel Day, 40, 674
Lewis, Dave, 100, 567
Lewis, David (producer), 19–20, 386, 391
Lewis, E. M. (Al), 293, 659
Lewis, Edward, 27, 631
Lewis, Garrett, 146–47, 669, 676, 688, 694
Lewis, Herbert Clyde, 89, 436
Lewis, Herman, 158–59, 563, 574, 585
Lewis, Huey, 213, 652
Lewis, Jerry, 477, 483, 494
Lewis, Juliette, 70, 687
Lewis, Mildred, 27, 631
Lewis, Russell, 340, 374
Libel!, 156, 501
Libeled Lady, 19, 371
Liberators: Fighting on Two Fronts in World War II, 276, 696
Library of Congress, 429; Paper Prints Collection, 8
Lichtenfield, Louis, 344, 492
Lies My Father Told Me, 101, 590
Life and Times of Judge Roy Bean, The, 209, 575
Life at the Zoo, 260, 433
Lifeboat, 73, 87, 114, 417–18
"Life in a Looking Glass," 213, 657
"Life Is What You Make It," 209, 569
Life of a Thoroughbred, 258, 402
Life of Emile Zola, The, 19, 32, 53, 72, 84–85, 127, 150, 177, 338, 375–77, 707
Life Times Nine, 252, 581
Life with Father, 34, 114, 132, 183, 435–37
Life with Feathers, 241, 428
Light, Allie, 276, 690
Light in the Window, 244, 463
Lightmaker Company, 332, 685
Lighton, Louis D., 18–19, 367, 375, 381
Li'l Abner, 187, 502
Lili, 45, 74, 92, 116, 134, 185, 466–68
Lilies of the Field, 24, 36, 66, 96, 119, 522–23
Lilley, Joseph J., 187, 502
Lillian Russell, 128, 393
Limelight, 12, 191, 574, 574 n
Lin, Paul T. K., 273, 647
"Linda," 203, 428
Linder, Stewart, 170, 542
Linder, Stu, 174, 669
Lindon, Lionel, 114, 117, 418, 484, 495
Link, John, 166, 414
Link, John F. (film editor), 174, 669
L'Invitation, 280, 582
Lion in Winter, The, 25, 37, 47, 76, 98, 190, 222, 551–53
Lipschitz, Elan, 329, 660
Lipscomb, W. P., 85, 382
Lipsky, Eleazar, 89, 436
Lipsner-Smith Corporation, 314, 504
Lipstein, Harold, 117, 478
Listen to Britain, 259, 409
Lisziewicz, Dr. Antal, 331, 672
Lithgow, John, 60, 632, 638
Litt, Robert, 163, 669
Little, Howard M., 313, 493
Little, Thomas, 129–34, 399, 406, 413, 419, 425–26, 431, 436, 446, 451, 456–57, 462
Little Ark, The, 209, 575
Little Belgium, 259, 409
Little Big Man, 58, 561
Little Caesar, The, 83, 357
Little Dorrit, 61, 107, 667–68
Little Foxes, The, 20, 44, 63, 73, 86, 129, 166, 179, 397–400
Little Fugitive, 91, 467
Little Isles of Freedom, 259, 409
Little Johnny Jet, 244, 463
Little Kidnappers, The, 290, 475
Little Match Girl, The, 238, 378
Little Mermaid, The, 197, 214, 676
Little Night Music, A, 193, 224, 603–4
Little Orphan, The, 242, 442
Little Prince, 192, 210, 585–86
"Little Prince," 210, 586
Little Romance, A, 103, 194, 614–15
Little Shop of Horrors, 213, 232, 658
Littleton, Carol, 173, 633
Little Vicious, A, 276, 690
Little Witch, The, 241, 428
Little Women (1933), 18, 72, 83, 132, 361–62
Little Women (1949), 115, 446–47
Littman, Lynne, 269, 599
Litvak, Anatole, 22, 73, 440–41, 455
Livadary, John P., 149–56, 304, 308, 310, 312, 365, 368, 373, 377, 379, 383, 388, 393, 400, 407, 413, 419, 422, 426, 432, 454, 468, 473, 476, 485, 491
Live and Let Die, 209, 581
"Live and Let Die," 209, 581
Live for Life, 279, 550
Lively Set, The, 348, 531
Lives of a Bengal Lancer, 18, 72, 84, 127, 149, 165, 337, 367–69
Living City, The, 261, 470
Living Desert, The, 262, 470
Livingston, Jay, 202–7, 427, 442, 452, 486, 492, 496, 531
Livingston, Jerry, 204, 206–7, 452, 502, 537
Living Stone, The, 263, 497
Lizzani, Carlo, 90, 451
Lloyd, Frank, 10, 71–72, 353, 361, 367, 702, 705, 707
Lloyd, Harold, 289, 464, 702
Lloyd, Mervyn, 269, 586
Lloyd, Michael, 232, 652
Lloyd, Russell, 171, 591
Lloyds of London, 127, 165, 372–73
Locke, Sondra, 66, 551
Lockhart, Gene, 53, 381
Lockhart, Warren L., 270, 605
Loeb, Edwin, 702
Loeb, Janice, 90, 260, 443, 446
Loeb, Walker, and Loeb, 701, 702
Loeffler, Louis, 168–69, 501, 524
Loesser, Frank, 201–4, 401, 415, 437, 447, 463
Loew, Edgar, 259, 409
Loewe, Frederick, 192, 206, 210, 496, 585–86
Lofquist, Al, 314, 504
Logan, Joshua, 23, 74–75, 478, 490, 510
Logan's Run, 122, 143, 295, 597, 599
Loggia, Robert, 60, 649
Loggins, Kenny, 213, 646
Lohman, A. J., 344, 508
Lolita, 96, 517
Lombard, Carole, 43, 371
Lomino, Dan, 143, 603
London, Mel, 264, 526
London Can Take It, 239, 395
London Film Sound Department, 155, 462
Lonelyhearts, 65, 494
Lonergan, Arthur, 140, 542

"Long Ago and Far Away," 202, 420
Long Day's Journey into Night, 46, 516
Longenecker, John, 251, 564
Longest Day, The, 23, 119, 137, 169, 345, 516–18
Longest Yard, The, 171, 585
Longpre, Bernard, 252, 592
Longtime Companion, 61, 680
Long Voyage Home, The, 20, 86, 112, 166, 179, 341, 391–92, 394–95
Long Way from Nowhere, A, 267, 564
Look for the Silver Lining, 184, 447
Looking for Mr. Goodbar, 68, 122, 602
"Look of Love, The," 208, 549
Lootens, Charles, 150–52, 306, 383, 388, 393, 399, 403
Loquasto, Santo, 146, 225, 641, 663
Lord, Peter, 257, 695
Lord, Robert, 18, 84, 362, 364, 376
Loren, Sophia, 46–47, 293, 510, 528, 684
Lorenzo's Oil, 52, 109, 692–93
Lorring, Joan, 63, 424
Lory, Milo, 344–45, 502, 520
Los Angeles County Music Center. *See* Dorothy Chandler Pavilion
Lo Schiavo, Francesca, 146–47, 676, 682
Losee, Harry, 340, 378
Losmandy, B. J., 318, 565
Los Tarantos, 278, 526
Lost Horizon (1937), 19, 53, 127, 150, 165, 177, 338, 375–77
Lost Patrol, The, 176, 365
Lost Weekend, The, 21, 33, 73, 88, 114, 166, 182, 424–27, 707
Lottman, Evan, 171, 580
Loucks, Grant, 331, 672
Loud Mouth, The, 236, 360
Louis, Jean, 216–22, 463, 469, 474, 480, 486, 492, 497, 513, 537, 543, 549
Louisa, 154, 452
Louisiana Purchase, 113, 129, 399
Louisiana Story, The, 89, 441
Lourie, Eugene, 346, 559
Love, Bessie, 42, 353
Love, Cecil, 307, 324, 442, 623
"Love," 210, 581
Love Affair, 19, 43, 62, 85, 128, 200, 386–87, 389
"Love and War," 339, 373
Love Field, 52, 692
"Love in Bloom," 199, 366
Love Is a Many Splendored Thing, 22, 45, 117, 155, 185, 205, 218, 477–80
"Love Is a Many Splendored Thing," 205, 480
"Love Is a Song," 201, 408
"(Love Is) The Tender Trap," 205, 480
Lovejoy, Ray, 173, 657
Love Letters, 44, 131, 182, 203, 424–25, 427–28
"Love Letters," 203, 428
"Lovely Lady," 339, 369
"Lovely To Look At," 199, 369
Love Me Forever, 149, 368
Love Me or Leave Me, 35, 92–93, 155, 185, 205, 477–80
"Love of My Life," 200, 394
Love Parade, The, 17, 32, 71, 110, 126, 148, 355–56
Lover, Anthony, 250, 554
Lover, The, 125, 693
Lover Come Back, 96, 511
Lovering, Otho, 166, 388
Lovers and Other Strangers, 58, 99, 209, 561–63
Lovers' Wind, The, 270, 611
Loves of a Blonde, 279, 544
Loves of Carmen, The, 115, 441
"Love Song from Mutiny on the Bounty (Follow Me)," 207, 519
Love Story, 25, 37, 48, 58, 77, 99, 191, 561–63
Love Struck, 255, 658
"Love Theme from *El Cid* (The Falcon and the Dove)," 206, 513
Lovett, Josephine, 83, 354
Lovett, Robert Q., 173, 645
Love with the Proper Stranger, 47, 97, 119, 138, 220, 522–25
Low, Colin, 249, 263, 509, 526
Low, Warren, 166–68, 394, 462, 479, 491
Lowe, Greg, 254, 622
Lowell, Carol, 254, 617
Lowell, Ross (short films), 254, 617
Lowell, Ross (sci-tech.), 324, 618
Loy, Myrna, 294, 684
Loy, Nanni, 97, 523
L-Shaped Room, The, 47, 522
"Luau," 340, 378
Lubbock, Jeremy, 196, 651
Lubitsch, Ernst, 17–18, 20, 71, 73, 288, 353, 355–56, 359, 411–12, 433,
Lucas, George, 77–78, 101–2, 298, 579, 602, 690
Lucas, Marcia, 171–72, 580, 603
Lucas, Steve, 272, 635
Lucci-Chiarissi, Vincenzo, 245, 469
Luce, Clare Booth, 89, 446
Luciano, Michael, 169–71, 530, 536, 548, 585
Luck of the Irish, The, 55, 440
Luckiest Guy in the World, The, 242, 433
Ludwig, Otto, 168, 468
Ludwig, William, 93, 478
Ludwig, 223, 581
Luedtke, Kurt, 104, 106, 626, 650
Lukas, Paul, 33, 411
"Lullaby of Broadway," 199, 339, 369
Lumet, Sidney, 75, 78–79, 104, 490, 590, 596, 626, 632
Lunch Date, The, 256, 683
Lund, Kenneth, 332, 685
Lundell, Richard J., 332, 691
Lunt, Alfred, 32, 359
L'Uomo In Grigio (The Man in Gray), 264, 514
Luske, Hamilton, 346, 531
Lust for Life, 35, 56, 93, 136, 483–85
Luthardt, Robert, 140, 542
Luther Metke at 94, 271, 623
Luxo Jr., 255, 658
Luzzati, Emanuele, 249, 252, 538, 581
Lycett, Eustace, 231, 344, 346–47, 514, 531, 569, 616
Lydecker, Howard J., 342, 395, 408
Lydia, 179, 400
Lynch, David, 78, 80, 104, 620, 656
Lyne, Adrian, 80, 662
Lyon, Bruce, 324, 618
Lyon, Francis, 167, 437
Lyon, William A., 167–68, 170, 432, 468, 473, 479, 496, 558

Mabry, Moss, 218, 221, 223, 486, 531, 537, 581
Macario, 278, 509
MacArthur, Charles, 84–85, 362, 368, 387
Macaulay, Eunice, 253, 256, 610, 664
MacAvin, Josie, 139–40, 145, 524, 536, 651
Maccari, Ruggero, 102, 590
MacDonald, Hugh, 255, 658
MacDonald, Joe, 117–18, 120, 495, 506, 542
MacDonald, R. A., 343, 428
MacDonald, Robert, 344–45, 502, 520
MacDougall, Don, 160–61, 591, 603, 609, 615
MacDougall, Ranald, 88, 425
MacDougall, Roger, 91, 461
MacEwen, Walter, 240, 415
MacGowan, Kenneth, 18–19, 361, 375
MacGraw, Ali, 48, 561
Macher, Karl, 323, 612
Mack, Earle, 270, 605
Mack, John, 159, 591
MacKay, Jim, 250, 554

MacKay, John Victor, 127–28, 376, 387, 393
Mackendrick, Alexander, 91, 461
MacKenzie, Louis G., 316, 521
Mackie, Bob, 223–24, 575, 592, 628
MacLaine, Shirley, 46–47, 49–50, 269, 494, 505, 522, 583, 593, 601, 637
MacLean, Fred, 129–30, 140, 399, 419, 536
MacMahon, Aline, 63, 417
MacMillan, David, 162, 639
MacMillan, Michael, 255, 647
Macpherson, Jeannie, 702
Macrorie, Alma, 168, 479
MacWilliams, Glen, 114, 418
Mad About Music, 111, 128, 177, 382–83
Madame Bovary (1949), 132, 446
Madame Bovary (1991), 132, 226, 689
Madame Curie, 21, 33, 44, 113, 130, 153, 181, 411–14
Madame Rosa, 280, 605
Madame X, 42, 71, 353
Maddow, Ben, 90, 451
Madeline, 244, 463
Madery, Earl, 159, 591
Madigan, Amy, 69, 650
Madron, 209, 563
Magic Flame, The, 110, 352
Magic Fluke, 243, 448
Magic Flute, The, 223, 592
Magic Machines, The, 251, 266, 559–60
Magic of Lassie, The, 211, 610
Magic Pear Tree, The, 250, 554
Magidson, Herb, 199, 202–3, 366, 415, 427
Magnani, Anna, 45–46, 477, 489
Magna-Tech Electronic Co., Inc., 320, 332, 582, 679
Magne, Michel, 188, 519
Magnificent Ambersons, The, 20, 63, 113, 129, 404–6
Magnificent Brute, The, 127, 372
Magnificent Obsession, 45, 471
Magnificent Seven, The (Japanese), 135, 218, 485–86
Magnificent Seven, The (U.S.A.), 187, 507
Magnificent Yankee, The, 34, 216, 450, 453
Mahin, John Lee, 94, 376, 490
Mahogany, 210, 592
Maids of Wilko, The, 281, 617
Main, Marjorie, 63, 435
Main Street on the March, 239, 402
Main Street Today, 241, 422
Maitland, Tod A., 163–64, 676, 688
Majani, Alain, 276, 690
Majority of One, A, 119, 512
Make a Wish, 177, 377
Making Overtures—The Story of a Community Orchestra, 273, 653
Making Waves, 256, 664
Mako, 57, 540
Malcolm X (1972), 268, 576
Malcolm X (1992), 41, 227, 692, 695
Malden, Karl, 55, 455, 471, 705
Maley, Alan, 347, 569
Malkin, Barry, 173–74, 645, 682
Malkovich, John, 60, 643
Malle, Louis, 79, 100, 107, 573, 626, 662
Mallette, Yvon, 252, 586
Malley, Bill, 142, 580
Malmgren, Russell, 343, 421
Malone, Dorothy, 65, 484
Maltese Falcon, The, 20, 54, 86, 397–98
Maltz, Albert, 88, 90 n, 425, 451n
Mama Turns a Hundred, 281, 617
Mambo Kings, The, 215, 694
Mamet, David, 105, 632
Mamut, Eugene, 328, 660
Man Alive!, 261, 464
Man and a Woman, A, 47, 76, 98, 279, 540–41, 544
Man Called Peter, A, 117, 478
Manchurian Candidate, The, 65, 169, 517–18
Mancini, Henry, 185, 187–88, 191, 194–95, 206–11, 213, 474, 513, 519, 525, 531, 537, 563–64, 569, 598, 616, 634, 658
Mandel, Babaloo, 105, 644
Mandel, Johnny, 207–8, 537, 543
Mandell, Daniel, 165–69, 400, 407, 432, 491, 507
Mandragola, 221, 543
Mandy's Grandmother, 253, 610
Man for All Seasons, A, 24, 36, 57, 66, 76, 98, 120, 222, 540–41, 543, 708
Manfredi, Manfredo, 253, 598
Manger, William L., 235, 677
Mangini, Mark, 235, 658, 695
Manhattan, 68, 103, 614
Manhattan Melodrama, 84, 365
Manhattan Merry Go Round, 127, 376
"Maniac," 212, 640
Man in Space, 262, 487
Man in the Glass Booth, The, 38, 589
Man in the Iron Mask, The, 178, 389
Man in the White Suit, The, 91, 461
Manipulation, 257, 689
Mankiewicz, Don, 94, 495
Mankiewicz, Herman J., 86–87, 398, 405
Mankiewicz, Joseph, 20, 74, 77, 83, 90, 92, 357, 391, 445–46, 451, 461, 707
Mann, Abby, 95, 97, 511, 535
Mann, Barry, 213, 658
Mann, Delbert, 74, 478, 707
Mann, Stanley, 97, 535
Mannequin, 200, 214, 384, 664
Mannheimer, Albert, 90, 451
Man of a Thousand Faces, 94, 490
Man of Conquest, 128, 151, 178, 387–89
Man of Iron, 281, 629
Man of La Mancha, 192, 574
Mansbridge, John B., 142, 568, 585
Manson, 268, 576
Mantell, Joe, 55, 477
"Man That Got Away, The," 205, 474
Man Who Knew Too Much, The (1956), 205, 486
Man Who Planted Trees, The, 256, 664
Man Who Shot Liberty Valance, The, 220, 519
Man Who Skied Down Everest, The, 269, 593
Man Who Walked Alone, 182, 427
Man Who Would Be King, The, 102, 143, 171, 223, 590–92
Man Without a Country, The, 238, 378
Man with the Golden Arm, The, 35, 135, 185, 477, 479
Marathon Man, 59, 596
March, Fredric A., 4, 31–34, 357, 359, 375, 430, 455, 466
March, Marvin, 143–44, 591, 603, 609, 633
Marchand, Anne-Marie, 225, 641
Marchand, Colette, 64, 460
March of Time, 258–59, 286, 374, 402, 409, 416
Marcus, Lawrence B., 104, 621
Marcus, Louis, 252, 268, 581, 592
Mardi Gras (1943), 240, 415
Mardi Gras (1958), 186, 496
Margadonna, Ettore, 92, 472
Mariani, Giuseppe, 141, 548
Marie Antoinette, 43, 53, 128, 178, 381, 383
Marie-Louise, 88, 425
Marines in the Making, 239, 409
Marion, Frances, 83–84, 356, 359, 362
Marion, George, Jr., 83, 351
Marischka, Ernst, 88, 425
Marjoe, 268, 576
Marjorie Morningstar, 206, 497
Mark, The, 36, 510
Marker, Harry, 166, 426
Mark of the Maker, The, 227, 690
Mark of Zorro, The (1940), 179, 394
Markowitz, Donald, 214, 664

Marks, Daniel J., 274, 671
Marks, Gertrude Ross, 268, 582
Marks, Owen, 166, 414, 419
Marks, Richard, 172–74, 615, 640, 663
Markwitz, Paul, 134, 467
Marlene, 273, 647
Marley, John, 58, 561
Marley, Peverell, 111, 114, 382, 436
"Marmalade, Molasses and Honey," 209, 575
Marooned, 121, 158, 346, 558–59
Marquet, Henri, 93, 478
Marriage Italian Style, 47, 279, 528, 538
Married to the Mob, 61, 667
Marsan, Jean, 92, 478
Marsh, Oliver, 112, 286, 385, 392
Marsh, Terence, 140–42, 536, 552, 562, 568
Marshal, Alan, 27, 607
Marshall, Charles, 113, 412
Marshall, Edward "Ted," 139–40, 524, 536
Marshall, Frank, 27–28, 625, 649
Marshman, D. M., Jr., 90, 451
Martin, George, 188, 531
Martin, Hugh, 202–3, 421, 437
Martin, Marty, 309–10, 434, 444
Martin, Robert, 158, 558
Martin Luther, 116, 134, 467
Marty, 22, 35, 55, 64, 74, 93, 117, 135, 477–79, 707
Marvin, Johnny, 200, 384
Marvin, Lee, 36, 534
Marx, Groucho, 291, 582
Marx, Sue, 274, 665
Mary, Queen of Scots, 48, 142, 159, 191, 222, 566, 568–69
Mary Poppins, 24, 47, 76, 97, 120, 139, 157, 188, 207, 221, 346, 528–31
Maschwitz, Eric, 85, 387
Mascott, Lawrence, 265, 538
MASH, 25, 67, 77, 99, 170, 561–63
Mask, 229, 652
Maslow, Steve, 161–62, 621, 627, 645
Mason, James, 35, 57, 60, 471, 540, 632
Mason, Marsha, 48–50, 578, 601, 613, 625
Mason, Sarah Y., 84, 362
Masser, Michael, 210, 592
Masseron, Alain, 324, 623
Massey, Daniel, 57, 551
Massey, David M., 257, 689
Massey, Raymond, 33, 391
Masters, Tony, 141, 552
Masters of Disaster, The, 273, 659
Mastrantonio, Mary Elizabeth, 69, 656
Mastroianni, Marcello, 36, 38, 516, 601, 661
Mate, Rudolph, 112–13, 392, 398, 405, 412
Mateos, Antonio, 141, 562
Matewan, 124, 662
Mathias, Harry, 254, 617
Mathieson, Muir, 185, 473
Mathison, Melissa, 104, 632
Mathot, Jacques, 310, 449
Mating Season, The, 64, 456
Matkosky, Dennis, 212, 640
Matlin, Marlee, 50, 655
Matsuyama, Takashi, 133, 135, 462, 485
Mattey, Robert A., 344, 514
Matthau, Walter, 37–38, 57, 540, 566, 589, 631
Mattinson, Burny, 255, 641
Matz, Peter, 193, 592
Maumont, Jacques, 345, 520
Maurice, Bob, 267, 564
Maurice, 226, 664
Maurischat, Fritz, 134, 467
Maus, Rodger, 145, 633
Maxsted, Jack, 142, 568
May, Elaine, 103, 608
Mayer, Al, 333, 697
Mayer, Louis B., 1, 2, 289, 297, 454, 702
Mayes, Wendell, 95, 500
Mayor of 44th Street, The, 201, 408
Maysles, Albert, 268, 581
Maysles, David, 268, 581
Maytime, 150, 177, 377
Mayuzumi, Toshiro, 189, 543
Mazursky, Paul, 27, 99, 101, 103, 108, 557, 584, 607–8, 675
McAlister, Michael, 232–33, 646, 670
McBride, Elizabeth, 226, 677
McBride, Robert, 267, 564
McCabe and Mrs. Miller, 48, 566
McCall, Cheryl, 273, 647
McCallum, Gordon K., 159, 160, 563, 568, 609
McCambridge, Mercedes, 64–65, 445, 483
McCann, Dan, 270, 605
McCarey, Leo, 19, 21, 73, 85–87, 91, 205, 375–76, 386–87, 392, 417–18, 424–25, 461, 491, 707
McCarthy, Frank, 22, 25, 455, 561
McCarthy, John, 134, 140, 462, 542
McCarthy, Kevin, 55, 455
McCarthy, Tom C., 235, 695
McCartney, Linda, 210, 581
McCartney, Paul, 210, 581
McCaughey, William, 160–61, 591, 597, 609, 615
McCleary, Urie, 129, 131, 136, 139, 141, 399, 426, 468, 491, 536, 562
McCloy, Terence, 100, 573
McConaghy, Jack, 131, 419, 426
McCord, Ted, 115, 119–20, 441, 517, 535
McCormack, Patty, 65, 483
McCoy, Herschel, 217, 458, 469
McCune, Grant, 231–32, 604, 617
McDaniel, Hattie, 62, 387
McDonell, Gordon, 87, 412
McDonnell, Fergus, 167, 437
McDonnell, Mary, 52, 70, 681, 692
McDonough, Joe, 337, 362
McDormand, Frances, 70, 668
McEuen, William E., 253, 604
McGann, William, 343, 432
McGaw, Bill, 266, 554
McGill, Barney "Chick," 111, 358
McGovern, Elizabeth, 69, 626
McGovern, Tim, 296, 684
McGowan, David, 276, 690
McGuire, Don, 104, 632
McGuire, Dorothy, 44, 435
McGuire, William Anthony, 84, 372
McHugh, Jimmy, 199–200, 202, 369, 394, 415, 420
McKay, Craig, 172, 174, 627, 688
McKelvy, Frank R., 135–38, 141–43, 485, 496, 501, 518, 558, 585, 591
McKeown, Charles, 106, 650
McKuen, Rod, 191, 208, 559, 563
McLaglen, Victor, 32, 55, 367, 460
McLaren, Norman, 244, 247, 261, 463–64, 492
McLean, Barbara, 165–67, 369, 373, 383, 388, 414, 420, 452
McLoughlin, Patrick, 139, 141, 530, 558
McMurtry, Larry, 100, 567
McNamara, Maggie, 45, 466
McNutt, William Slavens, 83–84, 359, 368
McQuarrie, Ralph, 232, 652
McQueen, Steve, 36, 540
McSweeney, John, Jr., 169, 518
Mead, Thomas, 241–44, 428, 438, 443, 458
Meahl, E. Michael, 318, 555
"Mean Green Mother from Outer Space," 213, 658
Medal for Benny, A, 54, 88, 424–25
Meddings, Derek, 231, 296, 611, 617
Medford, Kay, 66, 552
Medioli, Enrico, 99, 557
Mediterraneo, 283, 690
Medium, The, 184, 462
Medoff, Mark, 106, 656
Meehan, John, 83, 85, 132–33, 135, 356, 382, 446, 452, 473
Meerson, Lazare, 127, 360

Meet John Doe, 86, 398
Meet Me in Las Vegas, 186, 486
Meet Me in St. Louis, 88, 114, 182, 202, 418, 420–21
Melendez, Bill, 191, 563
Mellor, William, 115, 117–18, 120, 456, 490, 500, 535
"Melody from the Sky, A," 199, 373
Melvin and Howard, 59, 68, 104, 620
Member of the Wedding, 45, 460
Memel, Jana Sue, 256–57, 664, 695
Memorial: Letters from American Soldiers, 276, 690
Men, The, 90, 451
Men Against the Arctic, 262, 481
Menegoz, Robert, 267, 564
Men in Black, 237, 366
Men in Her Life, The, 152, 399
Mendleson, Anthony, 223, 575, 598
Mendoza, Joe, 265, 538
Menges, Chris, 124, 644, 656
Menjou, Adolphe, 32, 357
Menken, Alan, 197, 213–15, 658, 677, 688, 694–95
Menotti, Gian-Carlo, 184, 462
Menu, 237, 362
Menville, Chuck, 250, 549
Menzies, William Cameron, 126, 287, 352, 354, 356, 390
Mephisto, 281, 629
Mercer, Johnny, 191, 200–209, 394, 401, 408, 414–15, 427, 432, 458, 480, 508, 513, 519, 525, 537, 563–64, 569
Merchant, Ismail, 28, 30, 248, 508, 655, 692
Merchant, Vivien, 66, 541
Mercouri, Melina, 46, 505
Mercy Island, 179, 400
Meredith, Burgess, 58–59, 590, 595
Meredyth, Bess, 9, 83, 354, 702
Merkel, Una, 65, 511
Merrick, Lawrence, 268, 576
Merrick, Mahlon, 182, 420
Merrill, Bob, 208, 553
Merrill, Keith, 268, 581
Merrily We Live, 62, 111, 128, 150, 200, 382–84
"Merrily We Live," 200, 384
Merry Monahans, The, 182, 420
Merry Old Soul, The, 237, 362
Merry Widow, The, 127, 134, 217, 365, 462–63
Merry Wives of Windsor Overture, The, 245, 469
Mersereau, Jacques, 130, 413
Merson, Marc, 251, 559
Mesa, William, 330, 666
Mescall, John, 113, 405
Mesenkop, Louis H., 286, 342, 385, 401, 408
Messel, Oliver, 136, 501
Messenger, James R., 270, 605
Metcalfe, Mel, 162, 164, 657, 688, 694
Metcalfe, Melvin, Sr., 159, 585
Meteor, 160, 615
Metro-Goldwyn-Mayer (MGM), 7, 236–40, 259–60, 287, 297, 303, 366, 369, 370, 374, 378, 384, 389, 395, 401–2, 408–9, 415–16, 421, 428, 433; Camera Department, 304, 379; Construction Department, 311, 313, 459, 488; Development Engineering Department, 311, 464; London Sound Department, 501, 536; Projection Department, 311, 464; Sound Department, 148–58, 303–6, 312, 356, 358, 360, 365, 368, 370, 373–74, 377, 379, 380, 383, 387, 393, 399, 403, 407, 413, 419, 426, 437, 476, 479, 491, 501, 507, 524, 530, 536, 542, 548; Still Photographic Department, 311, 464
Metropolitan, 108, 681
Metty, Russell, 119, 506, 512
Metzler, Fred L., 290, 514
Meunier, Charles, 250, 549
Mexicali Shmoes, 247, 502
Meyer, Dr. Herbert, 317, 555
Meyer, Nicholas, 102, 596
Meyer, Otto, 165–66, 373, 407
Meyers, Nancy, 104, 620
Meyers, Sidney, 90, 446
Meyjes, Menno, 106, 650
MGM. *See* Metro-Goldwyn-Mayer
Michael, Danny, 163, 669
Michaels, Mickey S., 141, 143, 562, 602
Michelet, Michel, 181, 420
Michelson, Gunnar P., 327, 642
Michelson, Harold, 144–45, 615, 639
Michelson, Manfred, 319, 321, 328, 331–32, 577, 599, 660, 672, 685
Mickey and the Seal, 242, 443
Mickey Mouse, 236, 285, 360
Mickey's Christmas Carol, 255, 641
Mickey's Orphans, 236, 360
Midler, Bette, 49, 613, 686
Midnight Cowboy, 25, 37, 66, 77, 99, 170, 556–58, 708
Midnight Express, 27, 59, 78, 103, 172, 194, 607–9
Midnight Lace, 220, 508
Midsummer Night's Dream, A, 18, 111, 165, 367–69
Mielziner, Jo, 135, 479
Mighty Joe Young, 343, 447
Mighty Mouse in Gypsy Life, 241, 428
Milagro Beanfield War, 197, 669
Mildred Pierce, 21, 44, 63, 88, 114, 424–25
Miles, Christopher, 249, 526
Miles, Sarah, 48, 561
Miles, Sylvia, 66–67, 557, 590
Miles, William, 276, 696
Milestone, Lewis, 20, 71, 351, 356–57, 386, 707
Milford, Gene, 165, 168, 365, 377, 473
Milford, Penelope, 68, 608
Milius, John, 103, 614
Milky Way, 238, 395
Milland, Ray, 33, 424
Millar, Hal, 346, 554
Millard, Oscar, 90, 456
Millenotti, Maurizio, 226, 683
Miller, Allan, 252, 581
Miller, Alvah, 322, 330, 606, 672
Miller, Arthur, 112–14, 392, 398, 405, 412, 425, 431
Miller, Burton (costume designer), 224, 604
Miller, Burton F. (sci-tech.), 309, 433–34
Miller, Charles, 306, 396
Miller, Ernest, 111, 382
Miller, F. Hudson, 235, 689
Miller, George, 109, 693
Miller, Harley, 130, 413
Miller, Harvey, 104, 620
Miller, Jason, 58, 578
Miller, Peter, 333, 691
Miller, Roland, 312, 476
Miller, Seton, 83, 86, 357, 398
Miller, Virgil E., 116, 461
Miller, Wesley C., 155–56, 312, 344, 473, 476, 479, 486, 491
Million Dollar Mermaid, 116, 461
Millions of Years Ahead of Man, 269, 593
Mills, Harry, 286, 385
Mills, Hayley, 290, 509
Mills, Jack, 139, 524
Mills, John, 58, 561
Mills, Michael (animated short), 251, 254, 569, 622
Mills, Michael (make-up), 229, 689
Mills, Peter, 265, 538
Mills, Reginald, 167, 442
Milner, Victor, 110–13, 115, 356, 365, 368, 372, 382, 393, 406, 451
Milo, George, 137–38, 507, 512, 518
Milton, Franklin E., 156–58, 501, 507, 524, 530, 536, 542
Min and Bill, 42, 357
Mineo, Sal, 55–56, 477, 505
Miner, William F., 321, 593
Mini-Micro Systems, Incorporated, 323, 618

Minker, Bob, 160–61, 603, 633
Minkler, Lee, 161, 633
Minkler, Michael, 160–64, 615, 621, 651, 676, 688
Minnelli, Liza, 48, 556, 572, 631
Minnelli, Vincente, 74–75, 456, 495, 707–8
Minnesota Mining and Manufacturing Co., 317, 555
Minnis, Jon, 255, 647
Minsky, Howard G., 25, 561
Minstrel Man, 182, 202, 420–21
Mintz, Charles, 237–38, 366, 378
Mintz, Sam, 83, 357
Miracle of Fatima, 184, 462
Miracle of Morgan's Creek, The, 87, 418
Miracle on 34th Street, 21, 54, 89, 435–36
Miracle Worker, The, 46, 65, 75, 96, 220, 516–17, 519
Mirisch, Walter, 23, 298, 300, 546, 605, 636, 705
Misener, Garland C., 311, 459
Misery, 51, 680
"Miss Celie's Blues (Sister)," 213, 652
Missing, 27, 39, 50, 105, 631–32
Mission, The, 28, 80, 124, 146, 173, 196, 225, 655–58
Mission to Moscow, 130, 413
Mississippi Burning, 29, 40, 70, 80, 124, 163, 174, 667–69
Mississippi Gambler, The, 155, 468
Miss Sadie Thompson, 204, 469
Mister Buddwing, 140, 221, 542–43
Mister 880, 55, 450
Mister Magoo's Puddle Jumper, 246, 487
Mister Mugg, 237, 362
Mister Roberts, 22, 55, 155, 477, 479
"Mist Over the Moon, A," 200, 384
Mitchell Camera Corporation, 306, 317–18, 390, 545, 555
Mitchell, Donald, 160, 164, 597, 694
Mitchell, Donald O., 159, 161–63, 580, 621, 639, 651, 657, 676, 682
Mitchell, George Alfred, 289, 464
Mitchell, J. Gary, 270, 611
Mitchell, John, 158, 162, 568, 645
Mitchell, Robert, 251, 564
Mitchell, Sidney, 199, 373
Mitchell, Thomas, 53, 375, 386
Mitchum, Robert, 54, 424
Mix, Ronald, 274, 671
Miyagishima, Takuo, 332, 685
Mnouchkine, Ariane, 97, 529
Mock, Freida Lee, 272, 275, 635, 684
Mockridge, Cyril J. 185, 479
Model and the Marriage Broker, The, 217, 458
Moffat, Ivan, 93, 484
Mogambo, 45, 64, 466
Mogulescu, Miles, 270, 605
Mohammad—Messenger of God, 193, 603
Mohr, Hal, 111, 113, 116, 368, 412, 467
Mole-Richardson Co., 303, 306, 309, 370, 390, 434
Molinaro, Edouard, 78, 103, 614
Mollo, Ann, 144, 626
Mollo, John, 224–25, 604, 634
Molly Maguires, The, 141, 562
Molly's Pilgrim, 255, 653
Monaco, James, 200, 202–3, 394, 415, 420, 432
Mona Lisa, 40, 655
"Mona Lisa," 204, 452
Mona Lisa Descending a Staircase, 257, 695
Monaster, Nate, 96, 517
Mondello, Anthony, 145, 639
Mondo Cane, 207, 525
Mongiardino, Lorenzo, 141, 142, 548, 580
Monicelli, Mario, 97, 529, 535
Mon Oncle d'Amerique, 104, 620
Monroe, Thomas, 86, 88, 398, 425
Monsieur Pointu, 252, 592
Monsièur Verdoux, 89, 436
Monsieur Vincent, 288, 443
Montage Group, Ltd., 329, 665
Montage (magazine), 8
Montanelli, Indro, 96, 511
Montano, Frank A., 164, 694
Montell, Judith, 275, 684
Montgomery, George, 129, 399
Montgomery, Robert, 32–33, 375, 397, 440
Monument to the Dream, 266, 549
Monzani, Sarah, 228, 634
Moody, Ron, 37, 551
Moon and Sixpence, The, 181, 414
Moonbird, 247, 502
Moon Is Blue, The, 45, 168, 204, 466, 468
"Moon Is Blue, The," 204, 468
Moonjean, Hank, 29, 667
Moonraker, 231, 616
Moonrise, 154, 441
"Moon River," 206, 513
Moon Rockets, 242, 438
Moonstruck, 29, 51, 61, 70, 80, 107, 661–62
Moontide, 113, 405
Moorcroft, Judy, 224–25, 616, 646
Moore, Dudley, 39, 625, 631
Moore, Grace, 43, 364
Moore, Jack D., 129, 132–34, 141, 406, 447, 457, 468, 558, 562
Moore, John (art director), 138, 512
Moore, John R. (sci-tech.), 314, 503
Moore, Juanita, 65, 499
Moore, Mary Tyler, 49, 619
Moore, Ted, 120, 542
Moore, Terry, 64, 460
Moorehead, Agnes, 63, 66, 417, 440, 529
Morahan, Jim, 132, 447
Morahan, Tom, 137, 507
Moran, A. J., 310, 444
Moraweck, Lucien, 178, 389
"More," 207, 525
More About Nostradamus, 239, 395
"More and More," 203, 428
Moreno, Rita, 65, 511
More the Merrier, The, 21, 44, 54, 73, 87, 411–12
Morey, Larry, 201, 204, 408, 447
Morgan, Earle, 307, 416
Morgan, Frank, 4, 32, 54, 364, 404
Morgan, Herbert, 242–44, 250, 261, 438, 443, 463–64
Morgan, Ralph, 287, 390
Morgan!, 47, 221, 540, 543
Mori, Mark, 275, 684
Moriarty, Cathy, 68, 620
Moriarty, David, 158, 563
Morita, Noriyuki "Pat," 60, 643
Morituri, 120, 221, 535, 604
Morley, Angela, 192–93, 585, 604
Morley, Robert, 53, 381
Morley, Ruth, 220, 519
Morning After, The, 50, 655
"Morning After, The," 209, 575
Morning Glory, 43, 361
Morning Spider, The, 253, 598
Morocco, 42, 72, 111, 127, 357–58
Moroder, Giorgio, 194, 212–13, 610, 640, 658
Moross, Jerome, 186, 496
Morricone, Ennio, 194, 196–97, 609, 657, 663, 688
Morris, Chester, 31, 353
Morris, John, 194, 210, 586, 622
Morris, Oswald, 121–23, 552, 567, 609
Morris, Thaine, 233, 330, 666, 670
Morriss, Frank, 173, 639, 645
Morros, Boris, 177, 373, 378, 383
Morrow, Barry, 107, 668
Morrow, Douglas, 89, 446
Morse, Susan E., 173, 657
Morse Films, 262, 475
Moscow Does Not Believe in Tears, 281, 623
Moscow Moods, 237, 374
Moscow Strikes Back, 259, 409
Mosher, Bob, 92, 478
Moss, Gary, 256, 670
Moss, Jeff, 196, 646
Mosser, Russell A., 267, 560
Mossman, Colin F., 326, 329, 636, 666

Mother Goose Goes Hollywood, 238, 384
Mother India, 278, 493
Mother Is a Freshman, 216, 447
Mother Wore Tights, 114, 183, 203, 436–37
Motion Picture and Television Research Center, 317, 555
Motion Picture Arts and Sciences (magazine), 7
Motion Picture Country Day Home, 299
Motion Picture Relief Fund, 287, 299, 389
Motion Picture Research Council, 7, 313, 493
Motion Picture Sound Engineering (book), 7
Motion Picture and Television Research Center, 317, 555
Motion Picture Country Day Home, 299
Motsumoto, H., 133, 462
Moulin Rouge, 22, 34, 64, 74, 134, 167, 217, 460–63
Moulton, Herbert, 241–42, 428, 438, 443
Moulton, Thomas, 149–55, 305, 341–42, 365, 368, 373, 377, 379, 383, 388, 390, 393, 395, 399, 407–8, 413, 415, 419, 426, 462
Mouris, Frank, 252, 581
Mourning Becomes Electra, 34, 44, 435
Mouse and Garden, 248, 508
Mouse Trouble, 240, 421
Mouse Wreckers, 242, 443
Moussy, Marcel, 95, 500
Movie Pests, 240, 421
Moyer, Ray, 131–36, 138–40, 419, 426, 431, 452, 473, 485, 491, 512, 524, 536
Mr. & Mrs. Bridge, 51, 680
Mr. Blabbermouth, 259, 409
Mr. Deeds Goes to Town, 19, 32, 72, 84, 150, 371–73
Mr. Dodd Takes the Air, 199, 378
Mr. Gardenia Jones, 259, 409
Mr. Hulot's Holiday, 93, 478
Mr. Saturday Night, 61, 693
Mr. Skeffington, 44, 54, 417
Mrs. Miniver, 20, 33, 44, 54, 63, 73, 87, 113, 152, 166, 342, 404–5, 407–8, 707
Mr. Smith Goes to Washington, 20, 33, 53, 72, 85, 128, 151, 166, 178, 386–88
Mrs. Parkington, 44, 63, 417
Mudd, Victoria, 273, 653
Muddy River, 281, 629
Mudlark, The, 217, 458
Mueller, Lynn, 274, 665
Mueller, William A., 155, 303, 370, 468, 479
Muggleston, Ken, 141, 552
Mukai, Jiro, 319, 577
Mula, Richard, 332, 685
Mulconery, Walt, 173, 639
"Mule Train," 204, 452
Mulligan, Robert, 75, 517
Munck, Eckehard, 268, 576
Mungle, Matthew W., 230, 695
Muni, Paul, 4, 31–32, 35, 353, 361, 371, 375, 499
Munoz, Susana, 273, 653
Munro, 248, 508
Muppet Movie, The, 194, 211, 616
Muppets Take Manhattan, The, 196, 646
Murakami, James J., 145, 645
Muraki, Jimmy, 250, 554
Muraki, Shinobu, 145, 651
Muraki, Yoshiro, 141, 144–45, 220, 513, 562, 621, 651
Mural on Our Street, 265, 538
Murch, Walter, 159–60, 172, 174, 585, 603, 615, 682
Murder, Inc., 56, 505
Murder on the Orient Express, 38, 67, 101, 122, 192, 223, 583–86
Muren, Dennis, 232–33, 296, 325, 623, 628, 630, 634, 642, 646, 652, 664, 670, 677, 689
Murfin, Jane, 83, 359
Murmur of the Heart, 100, 573
Murphy, Brianne, 326, 636
Murphy, George, 289, 453
Murphy, Richard, 89, 92, 436, 467
Murphy, Shawn, 163, 676
Murphy, Tab, 107, 668
Murphy, William B., 170, 542
Murphy's Romance, 40, 124, 649–50
Murray, Alan, 235, 652, 678
Murray, Don, 55, 483
Museum of Modern Art, Department of Film, The, 292, 611
Museum of Modern Art Film Library, 286, 379
Musgrave, Don, 306, 390
Music Box, 51, 360, 674
Music Box, The (1931/32), 236, 360
Music for Millions, 88, 425
Music for the Movies: Bernard Hermann, 276, 696
Music in Manhattan, 153, 419
Music in My Heart, 200, 394
Music Man, The, 24, 138, 157, 169, 220, 516, 518–19
Music Teacher, The, 282, 671
Musuraca, Nicholas, 115, 441
Mutiny on the Bounty (1935), 18, 32, 72, 84, 138, 165, 176, 367–69, 707
Mutiny on the Bounty (1962), 24, 119, 169, 188, 207, 345, 516, 518–20
Myasnikov, Gennady, 141, 552
My Beautiful Laundrette, 106, 656
My Boy, Johnny, 240, 421
My Brilliant Career, 224, 622
My Country 'Tis of Thee, 244, 453
My Cousin Rachel, 55, 116, 133, 217, 460–63
My Cousin Vinny, 70, 693
My Dearest Senorita, 280, 576
Myers, John, 155, 485
Myers, Richard, 205, 474
Myers, Ruth, 226, 689
My Fair Lady, 24, 36, 57, 66, 76, 97, 120, 139, 157, 169, 221, 528–31, 708
My Favorite Wife, 86, 128, 179, 392–94
My Favorite Year, 39, 631
My Financial Career, 249, 526
"My Flaming Heart," 204, 468
My Foolish Heart, 45, 445, 447
"My Foolish Heart," 204, 447
My Gal Sal, 130, 180, 406, 407
My Geisha, 220, 519
"My Kind of Town," 207, 531
My Left Foot, 29, 40, 70, 80, 108, 674–75
My Life as a Dog, 80, 107, 662
My Man Godfrey, 32, 43, 53, 62, 72, 84, 371–72
My Night at Maud's, 99, 279, 560, 562
"My Own," 200, 384
Myrow, Josef, 203–4, 437
"My Shining Hour," 201, 414
My Sister Eileen, 44, 404
My Son, My Son, 128, 393
My Son John, 91, 461
Mysteries of the Deep, 247, 503
Mysterious Castles of Clay, 270, 611
Mystery Street, 90, 451
My Sweet Little Village, 282, 659
My Uncle, 278, 497
My Wild Irish Rose, 183, 437
"My Wishing Doll," 208, 543

Nabokov, Vladimir, 96, 517
Nadoolman, Deborah, 226, 670
Nagel, Conrad, 1, 3, 4, 277, 287, 355, 359, 390, 460, 702, 705
Nails, 271, 617
Naish, J. Carrol, 54, 411, 424
Nakai, Asakazu, 124, 651
Naked City, The, 89, 115, 167, 441–42
Naked Eye, The, 262, 487
Naked Prey, The, 98, 541
Naked Spur, The, 92, 467
Naked Yoga, 269, 586
Napier, Sheena, 227, 695
Napoleon and Samantha, 191, 574
Narrow Margin, The, 91, 461
Nashville, 26, 67, 78, 210, 589–90

Nasty Girl, The, 283, 684
Natanson, Jacques, 91, 456
National Carbon Co., 306, 312, 390, 481
National Education Association, 264, 532
National Endowment for the Arts, 293, 647
National Film Board of Canada, 245, 249–50, 261, 264, 271, 293, 453, 469, 514, 532, 554, 617, 671
National Industrial Recovery Act, 4
National Recovery Administration, 4; NRA Motion Picture Code, 4
National Tuberculosis Assoc., 265, 538
National Velvet, 63, 73, 114, 131, 166, 424–26
Natural, The, 69, 124, 145, 195, 644–45
Nature's Half Acre, 244, 458
Natwick, Mildred, 66, 547
Naughton, Bill, 97, 541
Naughty Marietta, 18, 149, 367–68
Nava, Gregory, 105, 644
Navaho, 116, 261, 461, 464
Navy Comes Through, The, 342, 408
Nazarro, Ray, 90, 456
NBC Century Theatre, 466, 471, 477, 483
NBC International Theatre, 460
Neal, Patricia, 47, 522, 551
Neame, Ronald, 21, 88–89, 342, 408, 431, 435–36
Needham, Hal, 329, 660
Neff, Thomas L., 273, 659
Negulesco, Jean, 73, 441
Neighbors, 244, 261, 463–64
Neil, Iain, 332–34, 685, 691, 697
Neil, William, 232, 658
Neill, Ve, 229–30, 670, 683, 695
Neiman-Tillar Associates, 323, 618
Nelligan, Kate, 70, 687
Nelly's Folly, 248, 514
Nelson, Andy, 163, 669
Nelson, Bill, 163, 663
Nelson, Charles, 167–69, 426, 479, 536
Nelson, George R., 142–45, 585, 609, 615, 639
Nelson, Greg, 229, 677
Nelson, Kay, 216, 447
Nelson, Ralph, 24, 522
Nelson, William, 162, 657
Nelson, Willie, 212, 622
Neptune's Daughter, 203, 447
Nervig, Conrad, 165, 167, 365, 373, 452
Neshamkin, Paul, 271, 628
Nest, The, 281, 623
Netherlands Information Bureau, 259, 409
Nettmann, Ernst, 322, 325, 328, 606, 629, 654
Network, 12, 26, 38, 49, 59, 68, 78, 102, 122, 171, 595–97
Neumann, Alfred, 87, 418
"Never," 204, 458
Never Cry Wolf, 161, 639
Never on Sunday, 46, 75, 95, 206, 219, 505–6, 508
"Never on Sunday," 206, 508
New Americans, 259, 422
Newcom, James E., 166–67, 170, 388, 420, 452, 563
Newcombe, Warren, 342–43, 408, 421, 437
Newell, Norman, 207, 525
New Kind of Love, A, 188, 221, 525
New Land, The, 280, 576
Newley, Anthony, 191, 569
Newman, Alfred, 177–90, 204, 206, 377, 383, 388–89, 394, 400, 407, 414, 420, 427, 432, 437, 442, 447, 452, 457, 463, 468, 474, 479, 486, 496, 501–2, 513, 525, 537, 548, 563
Newman, Charles, 202, 421
Newman, Christopher, 159, 161–62, 164, 568, 574, 580, 621, 645, 651, 688
Newman, David, 98, 547
Newman, Emil, 180, 400
Newman, Eve, 170, 172, 553, 597
Newman, Joseph, 337, 368, 372
Newman, Lionel, 184–87, 189–90, 200, 204, 452, 458, 474, 486, 496, 502, 507, 537, 548, 559
Newman, Luther, 314, 504
Newman, Paul, 25, 36–37, 39–40, 293, 494, 510, 522, 546, 551, 625, 631, 653
Newman, Randy, 195, 197, 212, 214, 627–28, 645, 677, 682
Newman, Walter, 91, 97, 103, 456, 535, 608
New Spirit, The, 259, 409
New Zealand Screen Board, 247, 497, 532
Ngor, Haing S., 60, 643
Niblo, Fred, 1, 2, 703
Niblo, Fred, Jr., 83, 357
"Nice To Be Around," 210, 581
Nicholas, Anthony E., 256, 683
Nicholas and Alexandra, 25, 48, 121–22, 142, 191, 566–69
Nichols, Dudley, 5, 11, 82, 84, 86–87, 94, 368, 392, 412, 490
Nichols, Mike, 76, 79–80, 541, 547, 638, 668
Nicholson, Bill, 161, 621
Nicholson, Bruce, 232, 296, 623, 628, 634
Nicholson, Jack, 37–38, 40, 57, 60–61, 556, 561, 578, 583, 589, 625, 638, 649, 661, 692
Niebeling, Hugo, 264, 520
Nigh-Strelich, Alison, 273, 659
Night and Day, 183, 432
Night at the Movies, A, 238, 378
Night Before Christmas, The, 239, 401
Nightlife, 253, 599
Night Must Fall, 32, 62, 375–76
Night of the Iguana, The, 66, 120, 139, 221, 529–31
Night People, 92, 472
Nights and Days, 280, 599
Nights of Cabiria, The, 278, 493
Night Train, 86, 398
Nikel, Hannes, 173, 633
Nine from Little Rock, 264, 532
Nine Lives, 278, 493
1941, 123, 161, 231, 615
Nine to Five, 212, 622
"Nine to Five," 212, 622
Nini, Diane, 213, 657
Ninotchka, 20, 43, 85, 386–87
Ninth Circle, The, 278, 509
Nitzsche, Jack, 193, 195, 212, 591, 633–34
Niven, David, 489, 494, 578
Niver, Kemp, 8, 290, 475
Nixon, Robert, 256, 678
Noah's Ark, 247, 502
Noble, Nigel, 271, 628
Noble, Thom, 173–74, 651, 688
"Nobody Does It Better," 211, 604
No Hunting, 246, 480
Nolte, Nick, 41, 686
None But the Lonely Heart, 33, 63, 166, 181, 417, 420
None Shall Escape, 87, 418
Noose, The, 31, 351
Nordemar, Olle, 261, 459
Noremark, Henny, 223, 592
Norlind, Lloyd B., 201, 401
Norman, Geoffrey F., 321, 599
Norman Rockwell's World... An American Dream, 252, 575
Norma Rae, 27, 49, 103, 211, 613–14, 616
Norris, Dan C., 330, 666
Norris, Patricia, 224–26, 610, 622, 634, 646, 670
Norsch, Herbert, 342, 395
North, Alex, 184–90, 192–93, 195–96, 205, 293, 457, 462, 479–80, 486, 507, 525, 536, 543, 553, 585, 591, 627, 646, 653
North, Edmund H., 100, 562
North American Philips Co. Inc., 315, 521
North by Northwest, 95, 137, 169, 500–501
North Star, The, 87, 113, 130, 153, 181, 342, 412–15
North West Mounted Police, 112, 128, 151, 166, 179, 392–94

Northwest Passage, 112, 393
Norton, Rosanna, 225, 634
Norway in Revolt, 258, 402
Norwood, Donald W., 317, 555
No Sad Songs for Me, 184, 452
Not as a Stranger, 155, 479
Notes on the Popular Arts, 253, 604
"Nothing's Gonna Stop Us Now," 214, 664
No Time for Love, 131, 419
Notorious, 54, 88, 430–31
Nottingham, Eugene, 324, 624
Novarese, Vittorio Nino, 216, 221–22, 447, 525, 537, 564
Novi, Charles, 131, 419
Novros, Lester, 269, 599
Now, Voyager, 44, 63, 180, 404–5, 407
No Way Out, 90, 451
Now Hear This, 248, 520
"Now I Know," 202, 421
"Now It Can Be Told," 200, 384
"Now That We're in Love," 210, 592
Now You See It, 242, 438
Noyes, Eliot, Jr., 249, 538
Nozaki, Albert, 136, 485
Nozari, Dr. Mohammad S., 326, 636
Nudnik #2, 249, 532
Nugent, Frank S., 91, 461
Number One, 253, 599
Number Our Days, 269, 599
Numbers Start with the River, The, 267, 570
Nun's Story, The, 23, 46, 75, 95, 118, 156, 169, 187, 499–501
Nurse Edith Cavell, 178, 389
Nyberg, Mary Ann, 217–18, 469, 474
Nyby, Christian, 167, 442
Nye, Harold, 305, 309, 390, 434
Nye, Peter, 333, 691
Nykvist, Sven, 122, 123–24, 579, 639, 668

Oakie, Jack, 54, 391
Oakland, Ben, 200, 384
Oberon, Merle, 43, 367
Oberst, Walter, 286, 385
Objective-Burma, 88, 166, 182, 425–27
O'Brien, Edmond, 55, 57, 471, 528
O'Brien, Joseph, 241, 428
O'Brien, Liam, 90, 456
O'Brien, Margaret, 288, 422
O'Brien, Sheila, 217, 463
Obsession, 193, 597
Obzina, Martin, 128–29, 387, 399
Occurrence at Owl Creek Bridge, An, 249, 526
O'Connell, Arthur, 55–56, 477, 499
O'Connell, Kevin, 162–64, 639, 645, 651, 657, 676, 682, 694
O'Connor, Chadwell, 320, 333, 593, 697
O'Connor, Donald, 466
O'Connor, Geoffrey, 276, 696
O'Connor, Jim, 264, 514
Odd Couple, The, 98, 170, 552–53
Odd Man Out, 167, 437
Odds Against, The, 265, 544
Odell, Carey, 131, 136, 139, 495, 530
Odell, Robert, 128, 387
O'Donoghue, Robin, 161, 633
O'Donovan, Edwin, 143, 609
Oestreicher, Christine, 254, 628, 635
Officer and a Gentleman, An, 50, 60, 104, 173, 195, 212, 631–34
Official Story, The, 106, 282, 650, 653
Off the Edge, 269, 599
Of Human Bondage, 11
Of Human Hearts, 62, 381
Of Men and Demons, 251, 559
Of Mice and Men (1939), 20, 151, 178, 386, 388–89
Of Pups and Puzzles, 239, 402
Of Time, Tombs, and Treasure, 270, 605
Oh, God!, 102, 602
Oh, My Nerves, 237, 369
O'Hara, Karen A., 146, 657
Oh Brother, My Brother, 254, 617
O'Herlihy, Dan, 35, 471
Oh My Darling, 253, 610
Oisin, 267, 564
Okazaki, Steven, 273, 275, 653, 683
O'Keefe, Michael, 59, 620
Okey, Jack, 126, 131, 356, 425
Oklahoma!, 117, 168, 155, 185, 478–80
Okun, Charles, 29, 667
Old Man and the Sea, The, 35, 118, 186, 494–96
Old Mill, The, 238, 378
Old Mill Pond, 237, 374
"Ole Buttermilk Sky," 203, 432
Olin, Lena, 70, 675
Oliver, Edna May, 62, 387
Oliver, Harry, 126, 352, 354
Oliver!, 25, 37, 57, 76, 98, 121, 141, 158, 170, 190, 222, 291, 551–53, 708
Olivier, Laurence, 21, 31, 33–38, 59, 277, 288, 292, 386, 391, 430, 433, 440–41, 483, 494, 505, 534, 572, 596, 607, 611, 707
Oliviero, Nino, 207, 525
Olmos, Edward James, 40, 525
Olson, Leonard L., 319, 577
Olson, Nancy, 64, 450
Olympics in Mexico, The, 267, 560
O'Meara, C. Timothy, 172, 615
Omen, The, 193, 210, 598
Omens, Sherwood, 267, 570
Omnibus, 257, 695
On Any Sunday, 268, 570
Once More, My Darling, 154, 447
Once upon a Honeymoon, 152, 407
Ondricek, Miroslav, 124, 626, 644
One, Two, Three, 118, 511
O'Neal, Ryan, 37, 561
O'Neal, Tatum, 62, 67, 579
One Droopy Night, 246, 492
One-Eyed Jacks, 119, 512
One-Eyed Men Are Kings, 252, 586
One Flew Over the Cuckoo's Nest, 26, 38, 49, 58, 78, 102, 122, 171, 193, 589–91, 708
One Foot in Heaven, 20, 397
One from the Heart, 195, 634
One Hour with You, 18, 359
140 Days Under the World, 264, 532
100 Men and a Girl, 19, 85, 150, 165, 177, 375–77
O'Neil, Barbara, 63, 392
One in a Million, 340, 374
One Million B.C., 179, 341, 394–95
"One More Hour," 212, 627
One Night of Love, 18, 43, 72, 149, 165, 176, 303, 364–66
One of Our Aircraft Is Missing, 86, 342, 405, 408
One Potato, Two Potato, 97, 529
1,000 Dollars a Minute, 149, 368
One Way Passage, 84, 362
One Who Came Back, 261, 459
On Golden Pond, 27, 39, 50, 68, 79, 104, 123, 161, 172, 195, 625–27
Only Angels Have Wings, 341, 389
"Only Forever," 200, 394
Only When I Laugh, 50, 59, 68, 625–26
"On the Atchison, Topeka, and Santa Fe," 203, 432
On the Beach, 169, 187, 501
On the Bowery, 263, 492
On the Riviera, 133, 184, 457
"On the Road Again," 212, 622
On the Town, 184, 447
On the Twelfth Day . . ., 246, 481
On the Waterfront, 22, 35, 55, 64, 74, 92, 116, 134, 168, 185
Open City, 89, 431
Open Doors, 283, 684
Operation Blue Jay, 261, 470
Operation Petticoat, 95, 500
Operation 13, 111, 365
Operation Thunderbolt, 280, 605
Operation Vittles, 260, 443
Ophuls, Marcel, 268, 275, 570, 671
Ophuls, Max, 91, 134, 456, 473

Oppenheimer, George, 87, 405
Optical Coating Laboratories Inc., 317, 555
Orban, Robert, 333, 697
Orbom, Eric, 137, 507
Orchestra Wives, 201, 408
Ordinary People, 27, 49, 59, 78, 104, 619–20, 708
Oreck, Sharon, 255, 647
Organizer, The, 97, 529
Organizing Committee for the XIX Olympic Games, 267, 560
Orhall, Bengt O., 332, 685
Orkin, Ruth, 91, 467
Orloff, Lee, 163–64, 676, 688
Orry-Kelly, 216–17, 219–20, 458, 492, 502, 519
Ortolani, Riz, 207, 209, 525, 563
Osbiston, Alan, 169, 512
Osborn, Paul, 93–94, 478, 490
Osborne, John, 96, 523
Oscar, The, 140, 222, 542–43
OSRAM GmbH Research and Development Department, 329, 624, 665
O'Steen, Sam, 170–71, 173, 542, 585, 640
Otello, 225, 658
Othello (1965), 36, 57, 66, 534
Other Half of the Sky: A China Memoir, The, 269, 593
Other Side of Midnight, The, 224, 604
Other Side of the Mountain, The, 210, 592
Other Voices, 266, 554
O'Toole, Peter, 36–37, 39, 516, 528, 551, 556, 572, 619, 631
Ott, Howard F., 320, 582
Otterson, Jack, 127–30, 372, 377, 383, 387, 393, 399, 406
Otto Nemenz International, Inc., 333, 691
Our Dancing Daughters, 83, 110, 354
"Our Love Affair," 200, 394
Our Town, 20, 44, 128, 151, 179, 391, 393–94
Our Very Own, 154, 452
Ouspenskaya, Maria, 62, 372, 387
"Out Here On My Own," 212, 622
Outland, 161, 627
Outlaw Josey Wales, The, 193, 598
Out of Africa, 28, 50, 60, 79, 106, 124, 145, 162, 173, 196, 649–52, 708
"Out of the Silence," 201, 401
Ouverture, 265, 538
Overnight Sensation, 255, 641
"Over the Rainbow," 200, 389
Over There, 1914–18, 265, 532
Overton, Al, 160–61, 163, 615, 627, 669
Overton, Al, Jr., 159, 591
Overton, Alfred J., 158, 568
Overton, Richard, 163, 669, 676, 682
Overton, Tom, 160, 597
Overture, 263, 497
"Over You," 212, 640
Owen, Alun, 97, 529
Owens, Harry, 199, 378
Ox, The, 283, 690
Ox-Bow Incident, The, 21, 411

Pacific Liner, 178, 384
Pacino, Al, 11, 38, 39, 41, 58, 61, 572, 578, 583, 589, 613, 680, 692
Paddle to the Sea, 250, 549
Page, Geraldine, 46, 49–50, 64, 66–67, 69, 466, 510, 516, 541, 573, 607, 649, 644
Paglia, Anthony, 315–16, 509, 533
Pagliero, Marcello, 90, 446
Paint Your Wagon, 190, 559
Painted Door, The, 255, 647
Paisan, 90, 446
Paix sur les Champs, 279, 565
Pakula, Alan J., 23, 78, 105, 516, 596, 632
Pal, George, 241–42, 288, 428, 433, 438
Palance, Jack, 55, 61, 460, 466, 686
Paleface, The, 203, 442
Pal Joey, 136, 156, 168, 219, 491–92
Palmer, Adele, 219, 502
Palmer, Ernest, 110, 112, 115, 354, 399, 451
Palmer, Patrick, 28–29, 643, 655, 661
Palmieri, Matt, 257, 695
Palmquist, Philip V., 317, 319, 555, 577
Pan, 249, 520
Pan, Hermes, 339–40, 369, 374, 378
Pan, Kant, 174, 694
Panama, Norman, 88, 92, 95, 431, 472, 506
Panama Deception, The, 276, 696
Panavision, Inc., 314, 317–19, 321–23, 332, 498, 545, 550, 555, 560, 576, 600, 606, 612, 685, 691
Panic in the Streets, 90, 451
"Papa, Can You Hear Me?," 212, 640
Papa's Delicate Condition, 207, 525
Paper Chase, The, 58, 159, 578–80
Paper Moon, 67, 101, 159, 579–80
Papillon, 192, 580
Paradine Case, The, 63, 435
Paradise, 255, 647
Paramount Famous Lasky Sound Department, 148, 356
Paramount News Issue #37, 260, 433
Paramount Pictures, Inc., 3, 7, 236–40, 260, 304–6, 309, 312–13, 370, 374, 378–79, 384, 389–90, 401–3, 409, 415, 421, 433, 439, 475, 482, 488, 493; Editorial Department, 310, 449; Engineering Department, 306–7, 309–10, 403, 410, 416, 439, 449, 459; Music Department, 310, 449; Set Construction Department, 309, 444; Sound Department, 149–56, 306, 308, 310, 362, 365, 368, 373, 377, 383, 388, 393, 400, 403, 407, 413, 419, 426, 429, 449, 452, 454, 468, 485, 491, 496; Special Photographic Department, 310–11, 459; Still Department, 309, 439; Transparency Department, 307, 309, 312–13, 410, 416, 439, 481–82, 488; West Coast Laboratory, 308, 433
Paramount Publix Sound Department, 148, 358, 360
Parenthood, 70, 214, 675, 677
Parent Trap, The, 157, 169, 512
Paris Blues, 187, 513
Parisot, Dean, 256, 670
Paris-Underground, 182, 427
Park, Nick, 256, 683
Parker, Alan, 78, 80, 608, 668
Parker, Arthur Jeph, 143–44, 597, 615
Parker, David, 161, 639
Parker, Dorothy, 85, 89, 376, 436
Parker, Eleanor, 45, 450, 455, 477
Parker, Joe, 330, 672
Parker, Max, 129, 406
Parker, Ray, Jr., 213, 646
Parkes, Walter F., 29, 105, 269, 593, 638, 680
Parks, Larry, 34, 430
Parks, Peter D., 325, 329, 630, 660
Parrish, Robert, 167, 437, 447
Parrondo, Gil, 141–42, 562, 568, 574
Parsons, Estelle, 66, 547, 552
Parton, Dolly, 212, 622
Partos, Frank, 89, 441
Partridge, Meg, 274, 671
Pascal, Gabriel, 19, 381
Passage to India, 28, 50, 69, 79, 106, 124, 145, 162, 173, 195, 225, 643–46
Passion Fish, 52, 109, 692–93
Passover Plot, The, 223, 598
Passport to Nowhere, 260, 438
Passport to Pimlico, 90, 446
"Pass That Peace Pipe," 203, 437
Pasternak, Joseph, 19, 21, 371, 375, 424
Pastic, George, 252, 586
Pat and Mike, 91, 461

Patch of Blue, A, 47, 66, 120, 139, 189, 534–37
Patel, Ishu, 253, 255, 604, 647
Patent-Leather Kid, The, 31, 351
Paterson, Neil, 95, 500
Pathfinder, 282, 665
Patrick, Jack, 88, 431
Patriot, The, 17, 31, 71, 83, 126, 353–54
Patrono, Carmelo, 142, 580
Patton, 11, 25, 37, 77, 100, 121, 141, 158, 170, 191, 347, 561–64, 708
Paul, Edward, 181, 420
Paul, M. B., 310, 449
Paul Bunyan, 247, 497
Paul Robeson: Tribute to an Artist, 271, 617
Paull, Lawrence G., 144, 633
Pavan, Marisa, 64, 477
Pavlatova, Michaela, 257, 695
Paw, 278, 503
Pawnbroker, The, 36, 534
Paxinou, Katina, 63, 411
Paxton, John, 89, 436
Paymer, David, 61, 693
Payne, James, 139–40, 142, 524, 542, 580
Peace on Earth, 238, 389
Peachey, Darwyn, 333, 697
Pearce, Donn, 98, 547
Pearcy, Glen, 269, 593
Pearlman, Daniel J., 316, 533
Pearson, Noel, 29, 674
Peasgood, H., 315, 515
Peck, Gregory, 33–34, 36, 299, 424, 430, 435, 445, 516, 705
Peckinpah, Sam, 99, 557
Pedestrian, The, 280, 582
Pedigo, Tom, 145, 639
Pefferle, Richard, 131–33, 136, 138, 419, 446, 452, 491, 518
Peggy Sue Got Married, 51, 124, 225, 655–56, 658
Pelle the Conqueror, 40, 282, 667, 671
Pelling, Maurice, 139, 524
Pending, Pat, 145, 639
Penn, Arthur, 75–77, 517, 547, 557
Penney, Edmund F. 268, 582
"Pennies for Peppino," 201, 408
Pennies from Heaven, 104, 161, 199, 224, 373, 626–28
"Pennies from Heaven," 199, 373
Penny Serenade, 33, 397
Penny Wisdom, 238, 378
"People Alone," 212, 622
People of the Wind, 270, 599
Peoples, David Webb, 109, 693
People Soup, 251, 559
Pepe, 118, 137, 156, 169, 187, 206, 220, 506–8
Peploe, Mark, 107, 662
Pereira, Hal, 133–40, 462, 467, 473, 479, 485, 491, 496, 500, 507, 512, 518, 524, 536, 542
Pereira, William L., 342, 408
Perelman, S. J., 93, 484
Perils of Pauline, The, 203, 437
Perinal, George, 112, 393
Period of Adjustment, 138, 518
Perisic, Zoran, 232, 296, 324, 330, 611, 618, 652, 666
Perkins, Anthony, 55, 483
Perkins, Frank, 188, 519
Perkins, Jeffrey, 163, 682
Perl, Arnold, 268, 576
Perlberg, William, 20–22, 411, 435, 471
Perlman, Janet, 254, 628
Peroni, Geraldine, 175, 694
Perret, Jacques, 92, 478
Perri, 186, 491
Perrin, Jacques, 25, 556
Perrine, Valerie, 48, 583
Perry, Eleanor, 96, 517
Perry, Frank, 75, 517
Perry, Harry, 110, 356
Pesci, Joe, 59, 61, 620, 680
Pescucci, Gabriella, 226, 677
Pete Kelly's Blues, 64, 477
Pete 'n' Tillie, 67, 100, 573
Peter Ibbetson, 176, 369
Peterik, Jim, 212, 634
Peterman, Don, 123–24, 639, 656
Peters, Don, 98, 541
Peters, Hans, 131, 133–34, 136, 139, 426, 452, 468, 485, 530
Peters, Susan, 63, 405
Petersen, David, 275, 678
Petersen, Niels G., 317, 555
Petersen, Wolfgang, 78, 105, 632
Peterson, Leonard, 159, 591
Peterson, Lorne, 232, 646
Peterson, Robert, 128, 393
Pete's Dragon, 193, 211, 603–4
Petok, Ted, 251, 569
Petri, Elio, 100, 567
Petrie, Daniel, Jr., 105, 644
Petrov, Alexander, 256, 678
Peverall, John, 27, 607
Peyton Place, 23, 46, 56, 65, 75, 94, 117, 489–90
Pfeiffer, Michelle, 51–52, 70, 668, 674, 692
Phaedra, 220, 519
Phantom of the Opera (1943), 113, 130, 153, 181, 412–14
Phantom of the Paradise, 192, 585
Pharaoh, 279, 544
Phelan, Anna Hamilton, 107, 668
Philadelphia Story, The, 20, 33, 44, 62, 72, 86, 391–92
Phillips, Edward, 326, 328, 636, 654
Phillips, Frank, 123, 615
Phillips, Julia, 26, 578, 595
Phillips, Lloyd, 254, 622
Phillips, Michael, 26, 578, 595
Phoenix, River, 61, 667
Photo Electronics Corporation, 318, 565
Photo Research Corporation, 311, 465
Photo-Sonics, Incorporated, Engineering Staff, 330, 672
Pianissimo, 249, 526
Piantadosi, Arthur, 158–61, 558, 574, 591, 597, 615, 621, 633
"Piccolino," 339, 369
Picker, Jimmy, 253, 255, 604, 641
Pickford, Mary, 42, 292, 353, 593, 703
Pickup on South Street, 64, 466
Pickwick Papers, The, 218, 480
Piclear, Inc., 322, 606
Picnic, 22, 55, 74, 135, 168, 185, 477–79
Picture of Dorian Gray, The, 63, 114, 131, 424–26
Pidgeon, Walter, 33, 404, 411
Pieces of Dreams, 209, 563
"Pieces of Dreams," 209, 563
Pied Piper, The, 20, 33, 113, 404–5
Pied Piper of Guadalupe, 248, 514
Pier, David, 330, 666
Pierce, Ronald, 158–59, 563, 580, 585
Pierce-Roberts, Tony, 124–25, 656, 693
Pierson, Frank R., 97–98, 101, 535, 547, 590
Pigeon That Took Rome, The, 138, 518
"Pig Foot Pete," 201, 408
Pigs in a Polka, 239, 408
Pigs Is Pigs, 245, 474
Pigskin Parade, 53, 371
Pileggi, Nicholas, 108, 681
Pillow Talk, 46, 65, 95, 137, 187, 499–501
Pillsbury, Sarah, 254, 617
Pinelli, Tullio, 93–94, 96, 484, 490, 511, 523
Pinewood Studios Sound Department, 155, 462
Pink and Blue Blues, 244, 463
Pink Blueprint, The, 250, 544
Pinkovich, Albert, 19, 381
Pink Panther, The, 188, 210, 531
Pink Panther Strikes Again, The, 210, 598
Pink Phink, The, 249, 532
Pinky, 45, 64, 445
Pinney, Clay, 233, 689
Pinocchio, 179, 200, 394
Pinsker, Seth, 253, 610
Pinter, Harold, 104–5, 626, 638
Pintoff, Ernest, 247, 249, 502, 526
Pirate, The, 183, 442
Pirates, 226, 658
Pirosh, Robert, 90–91, 446, 456
Pirro, Ugo, 100, 567

Pistek, Theodor, 225–26, 646, 677
Pitchford, Dean, 211, 213–14, 622, 646, 677
Place in the Sun, A, 5, 22, 34, 45, 74, 91, 115, 167, 184, 217, 455–58
Place in the Sun, A (animated short), 248, 508
Place in the World, A, 283, 696
Places in the Heart, 28, 50, 60, 69, 79, 105, 225, 643–44, 646
Place to Stand, A, 250, 266, 549
Placido, 278, 514
Planck, Robert, 114–16, 425, 441, 446–47
Planer, Frank, 115–16, 446, 456, 467
Planer, Franz, 118, 500, 511
Planet Ocean, 252, 586
Planet of the Apes, 190, 222, 291, 553
Plan for Destruction, 259, 416
Platoon, 28, 60, 80, 106, 124, 162, 173, 655–57, 708
Platt, Janice L., 255, 641, 647
Platt, Polly, 145, 639
"Playboy from Paree," 339, 369
Player, The, 81, 109, 175, 693–94
Pleasure Seekers, The, 189, 537
Ploquin, Raoul, 93, 478
Plowright, Joan, 70, 693
Plumb, Edward H., 180–81, 183, 407, 414, 427
Plunkett, Walter, 216–21, 458, 469, 492, 497, 513, 525
Pluto's Blue Note, 242, 438
Plymouth Adventure, 344, 464
Plympton, Bill, 256, 664
Pocketful of Miracles, 56, 206, 220, 510, 513
"Pocketful of Miracles," 206, 513
Poe, James, 93–94, 96, 99, 484, 495, 523, 557
Poet and Peasant, 241, 428
Pohl, Wadsworth E., 314–16, 503, 515, 533
Pointer, The, 238, 389
Point of View, 265, 538
Poiret, Jean, 103, 614
Poitier, Sidney, 35–36, 494, 522
Polanski, Roman, 77–78, 99, 552, 584, 620
Polglase, Van Nest, 127–29, 365, 368, 382, 387, 393, 399
Policeman, The, 279, 570
Polito, Sol, 112–13, 387, 398, 406
Poll, Martin, 25, 551
Pollack, Lew, 202, 421
Pollack, Sydney, 27–28, 77, 79, 557, 631–32, 649–50, 708
Pollard, Michael J., 57, 546
Pollard, William, B., 329, 660
Pollyanna, 290, 509
Polonsky, Abraham, 89, 436
Poltergeist, 195, 232, 234, 633–35, 658
Poltergeist II: The Other Side, 232, 658
Pomeroy, Roy, 336, 352, 703
Ponce, Manuel Barbachano, 263, 492
Pond, John, 313, 488
Ponedel, Fred, 309, 311, 314, 439, 459, 498
Pontecorvo, Gillo, 76, 99, 552
Ponti, Carlo, 24, 487, 534
Pool, Endel, 315, 515
Poore, Vern, 162–64, 651, 657, 663, 669, 694
Popelka, Otto, 318, 560
Pope of Greenwich Village, The, 69, 644
Poplin, Jack, 140, 536
Popular Science J-6-2, 237, 374
Popular Science J-7-1, 238, 378
Porgy and Bess, 118, 156, 187, 219, 500–502
Porter, Cole, 82, 199, 201–2, 205, 373, 401, 415, 486
Porter, Terry, 162, 164, 657, 688, 694
Porter, Tom, 333, 697
Portia on Trial, 177, 377
Portillo, Lourdes, 273, 653
Portman, Clem, 158, 558
Portman, Richard, 159–62, 558, 568, 574, 580, 585, 591, 609, 621, 627, 645
Portrait of Chieko, 279, 550
Portrait of Giselle, A, 272, 635
Portrait of Imogen, 274, 671
Portrait of Jennie, 115, 343, 441–42
Portugal, 247, 492
Poseidon Adventure, The, 67, 121, 142, 159, 171, 192, 209, 223, 295, 573–76
Pospisil, John, 296, 665
Possessed, 44, 435
Postcards from the Edge, 51, 214, 680, 682
Potter, Dennis, 104, 626
Powell, Anthony, 216, 223–24, 226, 575, 610, 622, 658, 689
Powell, Michael, 20–21, 86, 404–5, 440
Powell, William, 32, 34, 364, 371, 435
Power and the Prize, The, 218, 486
"Power of Love," 213, 652
Poyner, John, 348, 549
Pozner, Vladimir, 88, 431
Pratolini, Vasco, 97, 523
Pratt, Albert S., 315, 520
Pratt, Anthony, 146, 663
Precious Images, 255, 659
Predator, 233, 664
Preferred List, 237, 362
Preloran, Jorge, 271, 623
Prelude, 250, 554
Prelude to War, 259, 409
Preminger, Ingo, 25, 561
Preminger, Otto, 23, 73, 76, 418, 499, 523
Preo, Paul, 332, 685
President's Lady, The, 134, 217, 467, 469
Presnell, Robert, 86, 398
Pressburger, Emeric, 21, 86–87, 89, 405, 440–41
Preston, Howard J., 328, 648
Preston, Robert, 60, 632
Preston, Ward, 143, 585
Pretty Baby, 194, 610
"Pretty Girl Is Like a Melody, A," 339, 374
Pretty Woman, 51, 680
Prevert, Jacques, 88, 431
Previn, Andre, 184–88, 190, 192, 206–7, 468, 480, 496, 502, 507–8, 519, 525, 531, 548, 580
Previn, Charles, 177–80, 182, 377, 383, 388, 394, 400, 407, 420, 452
Previn, Dory, 208, 559
Previte, Franke, 214, 664
Price, Richard, 107, 656
Price of Victory, The, 259, 409
Price Waterhouse and Company, 3, 12
Pride and Prejudice, 128, 393
Prideaux, Don W., 314, 498
Pride of St. Louis, The, 91, 461
Pride of the Marines, 88, 425
Pride of the Yankees, The, 20, 33, 44, 86–87, 113, 129, 152, 166, 180, 342, 404–8
Priestley, Robert, 135–36, 479, 491
Priestley, Tom (documentary), 271, 617
Priestley, Tom (film editor), 171, 574
Prime of Miss Jean Brodie, The, 48, 208, 556, 559
Primrose Path, 63, 392
Prince, 196, 646
Prince, Hugh, 201, 401
"Prince Igor Suite," 340, 378
Prince of Foxes, 115, 216, 446–47
Prince of the City, 104, 626
Prince of Tides, The, 29, 41, 70, 109, 125, 147, 197, 686–88
Princess and the Pirate, The, 131, 181, 419–20
Princess Bride, The, 214, 664
Princess O'Rourke, 87, 412
Princeton: A Search For Answers, 268, 581
Prinz, Leroy, 339–40, 369, 378
Prisoner of Zenda, The, 127, 177, 376–77
Private Benjamin, 49, 68, 104, 619–20
Private Life, 281, 635
Private Life of Helen of Troy, The, 82, 336, 351

Private Life of Henry VIII, The, 18, 32, 361
Private Life of the Gannets, 238, 378
Private Lives of Elizabeth and Essex, The, 112, 128, 151, 178, 341, 387–89
Private Smith of the U.S.A., 240, 409
Private War of Major Benson, The, 92, 478
Private Worlds, 43, 367
Prizefighter and the Lady, The, 84, 362
Prizzi's Honor, 28, 40, 60, 69, 79, 106, 173, 225, 649–52
Probes in Space, 269, 593
Producers, The, 57, 99, 551–52
Producers' Association. *See* Association of Motion Picture Producers
Producers Service Company, 317, 319, 555, 571
Producers-Technicians Joint Committee, 302
Professionals, The, 76, 98, 120, 541–42
Profession of Arms, The, 272, 641
Project Hope, 264, 514
Promise, The, 211, 616
"Promise Me You'll Remember," 214, 682
Promises to Keep, 275, 671
Promoter, The, 155, 462
Prophet Without Honor, 238, 389
Proud and the Beautiful, The, 93, 484
Proud and the Profane, The, 135, 218, 485–86
Pryor, Richard, 595, 631
PSC Technology Inc., 319, 576
Psychiatric Nursing, 263, 497
Psycho, 65, 75, 118, 137, 505–7
Public Enemy, The, 83, 358
Public Pays, The, 237, 374
Puenzo, Luis, 106, 650
Pulcinella, 252, 581
Pumpkin Eater, The, 47, 528
Purple Rain, 196, 646
Purple Rose of Cairo, The, 106, 650
Purves, Barry J. C., 257, 695
Puss Gets the Boot, 238, 395
Puttnam, David, 27–28, 607, 625, 643, 655
Puzo, Mario, 100–101, 573, 584
Pye, Merrill, 137, 501
Pygmalion, 19, 32, 43, 85, 381–82
Pyke, Trevor, 161, 633

Qivitoq, 277, 487
Quad-Eight Sound Corporation, 320, 587
Quaid, Randy, 58, 579
Quality Street, 177, 377
Quaranta, Gianni, 142, 145–46, 580, 633, 657
Quartuilo, Pino, 255, 658
Quayle, Anthony, 57, 556
Queen Bee, 117, 218, 478, 480
Queen Is Crowned, A, 262, 470
Quenzer, Arthur, 200, 384
Quest for Fire, 228, 634
Quicker 'n a Wink, 239, 395
Quiet Man, The, 22, 55, 74, 91, 116, 134, 155, 460–62
Quiet One, The, 90, 260, 443, 446
Quiet Please, 241, 428
Quimby, Fred, 240–46, 415, 421, 428, 432, 437, 442, 448, 453, 458, 463, 474, 480
Quinn, Anthony, 35–36, 55–56, 460, 483, 489, 528
Quo Vadis, 22, 55, 116, 133, 167, 184, 217, 455–58

Race for Space, The, 263, 503
Rachedi, Hamed, 25, 556
Rachel, Rachel, 25, 47, 66, 551–52
Rachmil, Lewis J., 128, 393
Racket, The, 17, 351
Radin, Helen Kristt, 265, 544
Radio Bikini, 274, 665
Radio Corporation of America, 307–9, 422, 479. *See also* RCA
Radio Days, 107, 146, 662–63
Radnitz, Robert B., 25, 572
Ra Expeditions, The, 268, 570
Rafelson, Bob, 25, 99, 561–62
Raffles, 148, 356
Raft, George, 4
Rage to Live, A, 221, 537
Raging Bull, 26–27, 39, 59, 68, 79, 123, 161, 172, 619–21, 627–28
Ragsdale, Carl V., 266, 550
Ragtime, 6, 60, 69, 104, 123, 144, 195, 212, 225, 625
Raguse, Elmer A., 150–52, 341–42, 373, 377, 383, 388, 393, 395
Raiders of the Lost Ark, 27, 79, 123, 144, 161, 172, 195, 232, 296, 625–29
"Rainbow Connection, The," 211, 616
Rainbow War, 255, 653
"Raindrops Keep Falin' on My Head," 208, 559
Raine, Norman Reilly, 85, 376
Rainer, Luise, 42–43, 371, 375
Rainger, Ralph, 199–200, 366, 389
Rainmaker, The, 46, 186, 483, 486
Rain Man, 29, 40, 80, 107, 124, 146, 174, 197, 667–69, 708
Rains, Claude, 53–54, 386, 411, 417, 430
Rains Came, The, 128, 151, 166, 178, 341, 387–89
Rains of Ranchipur, The, 344, 480
Raintree County, 46, 136, 186, 219, 489, 491–92
Raise the Red Lantern, 283, 690
Raksin, David, 183, 186, 437, 496
Raksin, Ruby, 317, 545
Ralston, Ken, 232–33, 296, 628, 642, 652, 670, 677, 695
Rambaldi, Carlo, 231–33, 295, 599, 616, 634
Rambeau, Marjorie, 63–64, 392, 466
Rambling Rose, 51, 70, 686–87
Rambo: First Blood Part II, 235, 652
Ramin, Sid, 187, 513
Ramsey, Anne, 70, 662
Ramtronics, 318–19, 321, 555, 577, 594
Ran, 79, 124, 145, 225, 650–52
Rand, Tom, 224, 628
Randall, Tony, 494
Random, Ida, 146, 669
Random Harvest, 20, 33, 63, 73, 87, 129, 180, 404–7
Ranger, Richard H., 313, 488
Rank Film Laboratories' Development Group, 329–30, 666
Rank Organisation, 317, 555
Ransford, Maurice, 131–32, 134, 426, 436, 468
Raoni, 270, 611
Rapf, Harry, 17, 353, 703
Raphael, Frederic, 97–98, 535, 547
Raposo, Joe, 212, 627
Rappeneau, Jean-Paul, 97, 529
Rasch, Raymond, 12, 191, 574
Rashomon, 133, 289, 459, 462
Rasky, Harry, 270, 605
Rasputin and the Empress, 84, 362
Rathbone, Basil, 53, 371, 381
Rattigan, Terence, 91, 94, 461, 495
Raucher, Herman, 100, 567
Raven's End, 278, 532
Ravetch, Irving, 96, 103, 523, 614
Rawlings, Terry, 172, 627
Ray, Nicholas, 92, 478
Ray, Satyajit, 294, 690
Ray, Tony, 27, 607
Raye, Don, 201, 401, 408
Raye, Martha, 299, 555
Raymond, Alan, 276, 690
Raymond, Susan, 276, 690
Ray's Male Heterosexual Dance Hall, 256, 664
Razor's Edge, The, 21, 54, 63, 430–31
RCA Manufacturing Company, Inc., 287, 304–6, 374, 379, 402
RCA-Photophone, Inc., 302–3, 358
RCA Sound, 152–55, 406, 413, 419, 426

RCA-Victor Co., Inc., 303, 309, 311, 363, 439, 459
Rea, Stephen, 41, 692
Reading, Anthony, 144, 626
Ready, Willing and Able, 340, 378
"Ready to Take a Chance Again," 211, 610
Reali, Stefano, 255, 658
Really Big Family, The, 266, 544
Reap the Wild Wind, 113, 130, 342, 406, 408
Rear Window, 74, 92, 116, 155, 472–73
Reason and Emotion, 240, 415
Rebecca, 20, 33, 44, 62, 72, 86, 112, 128, 166, 179, 341, 391–95, 707
Rebel in Paradise, 263, 509
Rebel Without a Cause, 55, 64, 92, 477–78
Řeči, Řeči, Řeči . . . (Words, Words, Words), 257, 695
Recollections of Pavlovsk, 273, 647
Recording Sound for Motion Pictures (book), 7
Red Balloon, The, 93, 484
Red Danube, The, 133, 451
Redeker, Quinn K., 103, 608
Redford, Robert, 38, 78, 578, 620, 708
Red Garters, 135, 473
Redgrave, Lynn, 47, 540
Redgrave, Michael, 34, 435
Redgrave, Vanessa, 47–48, 50, 68, 70, 540, 551, 566, 602, 643, 693
Red Grooms: Sunflower in a Hothouse, 273, 659
Red Lanterns, The, 278, 526
Redman, Joyce, 65–66, 523, 534
Red River, 89, 167, 441–42
Reds, 27, 39, 50, 60, 69, 79, 104, 123, 144, 161, 172, 225, 625–28
Red Shoes, The, 21, 89, 132, 167, 183, 440–42
Redwoods, The, 266, 550
Ree, Max, 127, 358
Reed, Carol, 74, 76, 446, 451, 552, 708
Reed, Donna, 64, 466
Reed, J. Theodore, 4, 705
Reed, Tom, 92, 472
Reek, Edmund, 240–41, 243, 246, 261, 415, 421, 428, 433, 443, 453, 480
Reeves, William, 255, 658
Reeves Soundcraft Corp., 312, 470
Reeves, William, 255, 658
Regla, Peter A., 325, 330, 624, 672
Rehearsal, The, 251, 569
Rehme, Robert, 705
Reichard, Edward, 313, 315–16, 318–19, 488, 509, 533, 555, 565, 576
Reichert, Julia, 270, 272, 605, 641
Reid, Cliff, 18, 367
Reid, Kenneth A., 137, 507
Reifsnider, Lyle, 132, 447
Reiner, Rob, 30, 692
Reiners, Diana, 327, 648
Reinert, Al, 275, 678
Reinhardt, Betty, 88, 418
Reinhardt, Wolfgang, 96, 517
Reinl, Dr. Harald, 267, 564
Reisch, Walter, 85, 88, 92, 387, 392, 418, 467
Reiss, Stuart, 134–36, 139–41, 468, 485, 501, 530, 542, 548
Reiter, W. J., 337, 362
Reitherman, Wolfgang, 252, 586
Reitz, John T., 160, 609
Reivers, The, 57, 190, 556, 558
Relph, Michael, 132, 447
Rembrandt: A Self Portrait, 262, 475
Remember Me, 271, 617
"Remember Me," 199, 378
"Remember Me to Carolina," 202, 421
Remick, Lee, 46, 516
Remo Williams: The Adventure Begins, 229, 652
Renie, 217, 219, 221, 458, 469, 502, 525. *See also* Conley, Renie
Rennahan, Ray, 112–14, 387, 392, 399, 412, 418
Renoir, Jean, 73, 292, 425, 587
Renovare Process, 8, 290, 475
Renzetti, Joe, 194, 610
Report from the Aleutians, 259, 416
Report on Incandescent Illumination (book), 7
Republic Studios, 288, 429; Camera Departments, 313, 488; Engineering Department, 313, 488; Sound Department, 149–55, 288, 306–8, 368, 383, 388, 393, 399, 403, 406, 410, 413, 416, 419, 422, 426, 429, 441, 447, 462
Resch, Klaus, 331, 679
Rescuers, The, 211, 604
Research and Development Group of Rank Film Laboratories, London, 326, 636
Research Products, Inc., 319, 571
Resisting Enemy Interrogation, 260, 422
Restless Conscience: Resistance to Hitler Within Germany 1933–45, 276, 690
Resurrection, 49, 68, 619–20
Resurrection of Broncho Billy, The, 251, 564
Return of Martin Guerre, The, 225, 640
Return of the Jedi, 145, 161, 195, 234, 296, 639–42
Return of the Seven, 189, 543
Return to Glennascaul, 245, 469
Return to Oz, 232, 652
Reuben, Reuben, 39, 105, 637–38
Reunion in Vienna, 111, 362
Revel, Harry, 201–2, 408, 421
Revere, Anne, 63, 412, 424, 435
Reversal of Fortune, 41, 80, 108, 680, 681
Revolving Door, The, 266, 554
Revue Studio Sound Department, 157, 512
Reynolds, Burt, 578
Reynolds, Debbie, 47, 528
Reynolds, Norman, 143–46, 597, 603, 621, 627, 639, 663
Reynolds, William, 169–72, 512, 536, 542, 558, 574, 580, 603
Rhapsody in Blue, 154, 182, 426, 427
Rhapsody in Rivets, 239, 401
Rhodes, Leah, 216, 447
Rhythm in the Ranks, 239, 401
Rhythm on the River, 200, 394
Rice, Charles, 156–57, 507, 524
Rice, Grantland, 240–41, 415, 428
Rice, H. E., 315, 515
Rice, Tim, 215, 695
Rich, Allan, 215, 695
Rich, Frederic E., 181, 414, 420
Rich, Robert, 5–6, 82, 93, 484, 484 n. *See also* Trumbo, Dalton
Rich, Young, and Pretty, 204, 458
Richard, James A., 348, 549
Richard, Jean-Louis, 101, 584
Richards, Beah, 66, 547
Richards, Dick, 27, 631
Richardson, Henry, 173, 651
Richardson, John, 232, 658
Richardson, Miranda, 70, 693
Richardson, Ralph, 55, 60, 445, 644
Richardson, Robert, 125, 656, 676, 687
Richardson, Tony, 23, 76, 522–23, 708
"Richard's Window," 210, 592
Richard III, 35, 483
Richest Girl in the World, The, 84, 365
Richie, Lionel, 212–13, 627, 652
Richler, Mordecai, 101, 584
Richlin, Maurice, 95, 500
Richter, Kenneth, 327, 648
Richter, Robert, 272, 635
Richter, W. D., 103, 620
Rickards, Jocelyn, 221, 543
Rickman, Tom, 104, 620
Riddle, Nelson, 187–88, 190, 192, 502, 507, 531, 559, 585
Ridenour, Roy J., 318, 555
Ride the Pink Horse, 54, 435
Riding High, 153, 413
Ridin' on a Rainbow, 201, 401

Ridin' the Rails, 244, 458
Riedel, Richard H., 137, 501
Ries, Irving, 344, 486
Riesenfeld, Dr. Hugo, 177, 377
Right Stuff, The, 27, 60, 123, 145, 162, 173, 195, 234, 637–41
Right to Love, The, 111, 358
Riney, Hal, 267, 570
Ringwood, Bob, 226, 664
"Rio de Janeiro," 202, 421
Rippling Romance, 241, 428
Ripps, Hillary, 257, 683
Rip Van Winkle, 253, 610
Risacher, Rene, 262, 481
Rise and Fall of Legs Diamond, The, 219, 508
Risi, Dino, 102, 590
Rising Tide, The, 260, 448
Riskin, Everett, 18–20, 375, 397
Riskin, Robert, 83–85, 90, 362, 364, 372, 382, 456
Ritt, Martin, 76, 523
Ritter, Thelma, 64–65, 450, 456, 461, 466, 471, 499, 517
Riva, J. Michael, 145, 651
Rivas, Carlos, 311–12, 459, 465, 476
River, The, 50, 124, 162, 196, 296, 643, 645, 647
River Runs Through It, A, 109, 125, 198, 693–94
RKO Pantages Theatre, 13, 450, 445, 455, 460, 466, 471, 477, 483, 489, 494, 499
RKO Radio Pictures, 3, 7, 20, 236–40, 259, 302, 358, 363, 366, 374, 378, 389, 395, 397, 409, 416, 422; Art Department, 307, 410; Miniature Department, 307, 410; Sound Department, 148–55, 305, 307–8, 356, 358, 360, 365, 368, 373, 376, 383, 385, 388, 393, 399, 407, 413, 416, 419, 422, 426, 432; Special Effects Department, 310, 444
Roach, Hal, 236–37, 293, 369, 374, 642
Roach, Janet, 106, 650
Road a Year Long, The, 278, 498
Road to Morocco, The, 86, 152, 405, 407
Road to Rio, 183, 437
Road to the Wall, The, 264, 520
Road to Utopia, The, 88, 431
Robards, Jason, 59, 596, 601, 620
Robbe-Grilet, Alain, 96, 517
Robbins, Ayn, 210–11, 598, 604
Robbins, Jerome, 75, 291, 339, 511, 515, 708
Robbins, Joseph E., 305, 308, 379, 390, 422
Robbins, Richard, 198, 694
Robb-King, Peter, 229, 658
Robe, The, 22, 34, 116, 134, 217, 466–69
Robert, Daniel, 144, 609
Roberta, 199, 369
Robert Frost: A Lover's Quarrel with the World, 264, 526
Robert Kennedy Remembered, 250, 554
Roberts, Austin, 212, 640
Roberts, Ben, 94, 490
Roberts, (Edwin) Casey, 129–30, 132, 406, 441
Roberts, Eric, 60, 650
Roberts, Irmin, 286, 385
Roberts, Julia, 51, 70, 675, 680
Roberts, Rachael, 47, 522
Roberts, Stanley, 92, 472
Robertson, Cliff, 37, 551
Robertson, Hugh A., 170, 558
Robertson, Robbie, 346, 559
Robin, Leo, 199–200, 203–4, 366, 378, 389, 428, 437, 442, 463, 468
Robin and the Seven Hoods, 188, 207, 531
Robings, Ken, 333, 691
Robin Hood, 210, 581
Robin Hood: Prince of Thieves, 215, 688
Robin Hoodlum, 242, 443
Robinson, Benjamin C., 308, 429
Robinson, Bruce, 106, 644
Robinson, David P., 323, 612
Robinson, Edward G., 291, 576
Robinson, Edward R., 129, 406
Robinson, Glen, 295, 311, 314, 459, 504, 587, 593, 599
Robinson, Jane, 226, 670
Robinson, Phil Alden, 108, 675
Robinson, Susan, 275, 684
Robley, Les Paul, 330, 666
Robocop, 163, 174, 296, 663, 665
Robson, Flora, 63, 430
Robson, Mark, 75, 490, 495
Robson, May, 43, 361
Rocchetti, Manlio, 229, 677
Rochester, Art, 163, 663
Rochester, Arthur, 159, 585
Rochester, James R., 319, 570
Rochin, Aaron, 159–63, 591, 597, 609, 615, 621, 639, 645, 663, 683
Rock, Joe, 237, 362
Rockett, Norman, 140–41, 536, 563
Rocky, 26, 38, 49, 59, 78, 102, 160, 171, 210, 595–98, 708
Rocky III, 212, 634
Rode, Fred J., 133, 456
Roder, Milan, 177, 378
Rodgers, Aggie Guerard, 225, 652
Rodgers, Richard, 203, 428
Roelofs, Al, 142, 585
Roemheld, Heinz, 180, 400, 408
Rofusz, Ferenc, 254, 622
Rogell, Sid, 260, 438
Rogers, Bob, 254–55, 635, 653
Rogers, Charles "Buddy," 300, 654
Rogers, Charles R., 19, 371, 375
Rogers, Ginger, 44, 391
Rogers, Richard, 162, 657
Rogers, Will, 13, 361
Rogosin, Lionel, 263, 492
Rogue Cop, 116, 472
Rogue Song, The, 32, 355
Rohmer, Eric, 100, 562
Roizman, Morrie, 262, 475
Roizman, Owen, 122–23, 567, 579, 597, 633
Rolf, Tom, 173, 640
Rolfe, Sam, 92, 467
Roller Derby Girl, 243, 448
Rollins, Howard E., 60, 625
Rollmer, Frank, 19, 381
Romance, 42, 71, 355
Romance of Radium, 238, 378
Romance of Transportation, 244, 463
Romance on the High Seas, 183, 203, 442
Romancing the Stone, 173, 645
Roman Holiday, 22, 45, 55, 74, 91 n, 92, 116, 134, 168, 217, 466–69
Romano, Pete, 332, 639, 685
Roman Spring of Mrs. Stone, The, 65, 511
Romeo and Juliet (1936), 19, 43, 53, 127, 371–72
Romeo and Juliet (1968), 25, 76, 121, 222, 551–53
Romero, Peter, 145, 639
Rondi, Brunello, 96, 511, 523
Ronell, Ann, 182, 203, 427–28
Ronne, David, 161–62, 627, 645, 651
Rooftops of New York, 248, 514
Rookie Bear, The, 239, 401
Room at the Top, 23, 35, 46, 65, 75, 95, 499–500
Room with a View, A, 28, 60, 69, 80, 107, 124, 146, 226, 655–58
Rooney, Mickey, 33, 56, 59, 286, 293, 384, 386, 411, 483, 614, 635
Roos, Fred, 26–27, 583, 613
Roos, Paul A., 331, 673
Roosevelt, Franklin D., 4, 391
Root, Alan, 270, 611
Rooty Toot Toot, 244, 458
Rosco Laboratories, Inc., 320, 327, 582, 648
Rose, Alex, 27, 613
Rose, David, 181, 203, 420, 428
Rose, Fred, 201, 401
Rose, Helen, 217–19, 221, 458, 463, 469, 474, 480, 486, 502, 543
Rose, Jack, 93–94, 101, 478, 495, 579
Rose, Kay, 296, 647
Rose, Reginald, 23, 94, 489–90
Rose, William, 92, 93, 98, 472, 484, 541, 547

Rose, The, 49, 59, 161, 172, 613, 615
Rose Kennedy: A Life to Remember, 275, 684
Rosemary's Baby, 66, 98, 551–52
Rosenbaum, Joel, 196, 651
Rosenberg, Aaron, 24, 516
Rosenberg, Philip, 144, 609, 615
Rosenberger, Harold E., 314, 504
Rosenblum, Nina, 276, 696
Rosenblum, Steven, 174, 676
Rosenman, Leonard, 193, 195–96, 592, 598, 640, 657
Rosenthal, Laurence, 188, 192, 530, 575
Rose Tattoo, The, 22, 45, 64, 117, 135, 168, 185, 218, 477, 479, 480
Rosher, Charles, 9, 110–11, 114–16, 352, 365, 418, 431, 451, 456
Ross, Angelo, 172, 603
Ross, Arthur, 103, 620
Ross, Diana, 48, 572, 578
Ross, Frank (producer), 22, 466
Ross, Frank (writer), 87, 412
Ross, Gary, 107, 668
Ross, Herbert, 26, 78, 601–2
Ross, Katherine, 66, 547
Ross, Murray, 2, 4
Rosse, Herman, 126, 356
Rossellini, Roberto, 90, 446
Rossen, Robert, 21, 23, 74–75, 90, 95, 418, 445–46, 510–11, 707
Rossi, Walter, 344, 348, 492, 538, 544
Rossif, Frederic, 265, 538
Rosson, Harold, 112, 114–15, 117, 286, 374, 392, 451, 484
Rosten, Irwin, 267, 269, 560, 593
Rota, Nino, 192, 585
Roth, Ann, 225, 646
Roth, Richard, 26, 601
Rotha, Paul, 260, 438
Rotter, Stephen A., 173, 639–640
Rotunno, Giuseppe, 123, 614
'Round Midnight, 40, 196, 655, 657
Rouse, Russell, 91, 95, 456, 500
Rousselot, Philippe, 124–25, 662, 681, 693
Rouxel, Jacques, 146, 681
Rowe, Bill, 163, 663
Rowlands, Gena, 48–49, 583, 619
Royal Family of Broadway, The, 32, 357
Royal Scotland, 244, 463
Royal Wedding, 204, 458
Royer, Robb, 209, 563
Rozhdestvensky, G., 186, 496
Rozsa, Miklos, 179–85, 187, 206, 394, 400, 407, 420, 427, 432, 437, 457, 462, 468, 501, 513
Rubeo, Bruno, 146, 676
Rubin, Bruce Joel, 108, 681
Ruby, Harry, 204, 458
Rucker, Joseph T., 110, 356
Ruddy, Albert S., 25, 572
Rude, John, 315, 515
Rudloff, Gregg C., 163, 676
Rudloff, Tex, 160, 609
Rudolph, William, 305, 390
Ruehl, Mercedes, 70, 687
Rugged Bear, 245, 469
Ruggiero, Gene, 168, 479, 485
Ruggles, Wesley, 71, 357, 707
Ruggles of Red Gap, 18, 367
Ruling Class, The, 37, 572
Runaway Train, 40, 60, 173, 649–51
Running, Jumping, and Standing Still Film, The, 247, 503
Running on Empty, 61, 107, 667–68
"Run to You," 215, 694
Rush, Richard, 79, 104, 620–21
Russell, Bob, 208, 549, 553
Russell, Greg, 163, 676
Russell, Harold, 54, 288, 430, 433
Russell, John L., 118, 506
Russell, Ken, 77, 562
Russell, Larry, 12, 191, 574
Russell, Lloyd, 310, 312, 454, 476
Russell, Robert, 87, 412
Russell, Rosalind, 44, 46, 299, 404, 430, 435, 489, 494, 576
Russell, Shirley, 224–25, 616, 628
Russell, Willy, 105, 638
Russians Are Coming! The Russians Are Coming!, The, 24, 36, 98, 170, 540–42
Rutherford, Margaret, 66, 523
Rutledge, Robert, 234, 652
Ruttenberg, Joseph, 111–14, 116–18, 382, 392, 398, 405, 412, 418, 467, 484, 495, 506
Ryan, Dr. Roderick T., 294, 325
Ryan, Richard T., 294, 690
Ryan, Robert, 54, 435
Ryan, Roderick T., 325, 629, 684
Ryan's Daughter, 48, 58, 121, 158, 561–63
Rybczynaki, Zbigniew, 254, 635
Rydell, Mark, 79, 626
Ryder, Loren L., 150–56, 286, 292, 306, 308, 310, 312–13, 341–42, 376, 383, 385, 388–89, 393, 395, 400, 403, 407, 413, 419, 426, 429, 449, 454, 468, 473, 475, 481, 485, 611
Rydstrom, Gary, 164, 235, 688–89
Ryskind, Morris, 84–85, 372, 376

Sabbatini, Enrico, 225, 658
Sabrina, 45, 74, 92, 116, 134, 218, 471–74
Sachtler AG, 332, 691
Sadie Thompson, 42, 110, 351–52
"Sadie Thompson's Song (Blue Pacific Blues)," 204, 468
Sage, Dewitt L., Jr., 267–68, 270, 570, 581, 605
Sagebrush and Silver, 239, 402
Sager, Carole Bayer, 211–12, 604, 616, 627
Sahara, 54, 113, 153, 411–13
Sahl, Mort, 494
Said, Fouad, 318, 560
Saiki, Albert, 332, 691
Saint, Eva Marie, 74, 471
Sainte-Marie, Buffy, 212, 634
St. Francis-Xavier University, 260, 448
St. John, Adela Rogers, 83, 359
St. John, Theodore, 91, 461
Saint Matthew Passion, 265, 544
Saito, Takao, 124, 651
Sakamoto, Ryuichi, 196, 663
Salaam Bombay!, 282, 671
Salinger, Conrad, 184, 458
Sallah, 278, 532
Sallis, Crispian, 145–46, 657, 676
Sally, 126, 356
Sal of Singapore, 83, 354
Salomon, Mikael, 125, 233, 675, 689
Salt, Waldo, 99, 101, 103, 557, 579, 608
Salter, Hans J., 180–82, 407, 414, 420, 427
Salty O'Rourke, 88, 425
Saludos Amigos, 153, 181, 201, 413–14
"Saludos Amigos," 201, 414
Salvador, 40, 106, 655–56
Salvioni, Giorgio, 97, 535
Salzman, Bert, 252, 592
Sam, 273, 659
Samba-Mania, 243, 443
Same Time, Next Year, 49, 103, 123, 211, 607–8, 610
Samoa, 246, 487
Samson and Delilah, 115, 133, 184, 217, 344, 451–53
Samuel Goldwyn Studio Sound Department, 148, 151–58, 301, 305, 317, 320, 358, 388, 390, 393, 399, 407, 413, 419, 426, 432, 437, 452, 462, 485, 491, 496, 501, 507, 512, 524, 542, 548, 550, 587
Samuels, Lesser, 90–91, 451, 456
Samuelson, David, 324, 329, 623, 660
Samuelson, Kristine, 269, 592
Samurai: The Legend of Musashi, 290, 481
San Antonio, 131, 203, 426, 428
Sand, 115, 446
Sandakan No. 8, 280, 593
Sand Castle, 253, 604
Sander, Peter, 251, 569
Sanders, Denis, 245, 267, 475, 559
Sanders, George, 55, 450
Sanders, Sidney, 303, 363
Sanders, Terry, 245, 275, 475, 684
Sanders, Thomas, 147, 694
Sanderson, Job, 316, 533

Sandman, The, 257, 695
Sand Pebbles, The, 24, 36, 57, 120, 140, 158, 170, 189, 540, 542–43
Sandpiper, The, 207, 537
Sands, William, 170, 553
Sands of Iwo Jima, 34, 89, 154, 167, 445–47
Sandy Claws, 245, 474
San Francisco, 19, 32, 72, 84, 150, 337, 371–73
Sanger, Jonathan, 27, 256, 619, 664
Santa Monica Civic Auditorium, 13, 505, 510, 516, 522, 528, 534, 540, 546
Santiago, Emilio, 218, 469
Santiago, The Story of His New Life, 282, 678
Santillo, Frank, 170, 542
Saraband, 132, 447
Saraf, Irving, 276, 690
Sarah and Son, 42, 355
Sarandon, Chris, 58, 590
Sarandon, Susan, 50–52, 625, 686, 692
Saratoga Trunk, 63, 430
Sarde, Philippe, 194, 622
Sargent, Alvin, 101–2, 104, 579, 602, 620
Saroyan, William, 87, 412
Sartre, Jean-Paul, 93, 484
Satlof, Ron, 252, 575
Satoh, Masamichi, 121, 562
Saturday Night Fever, 38, 601
Saudek, Robert, 264, 520
Saunders, Brian, 163, 669
Saunders, Jan, 255, 635
Saunders, John Monk, 83, 357
Saunders, Russ, 338, 376
Savage, Norman, 169, 536
Savalas, Telly, 56, 516
Savegar, Brian, 146, 657
Save the Tiger, 38, 58, 101, 578–79
Saville, Victor, 19, 381, 386
Sawley, George, 130, 133, 406, 452
Sawyer, David H., 266, 554
Sawyer, Gordon, 154–58, 292, 301, 426, 432, 437, 457, 462, 485, 491, 496, 501, 507, 512, 524, 542, 605
Sawyer, Joan, 273, 647
Saxon, Edward, 29, 686
"Say a Prayer for the Boys Over There," 201, 414
Say Goodbye, 267, 564
Sayles, John, 109, 693
Sayonara, 23, 35, 56, 65, 75, 94, 117, 136, 156, 168, 489–91
Say One for Me, 187, 502
"Say You, Say Me," 213, 652
Scaccianoce, Luigi, 140, 542
Scaife, Hugh, 143–45, 603, 621, 645
Scalia, Pietro, 174, 688
Scared Straight, 270, 611
Scarfiotti, Ferdinando, 146–47, 663, 694
Scarpelli, 97, 529, 535
Scarwid, Diana, 68, 620
Scent of a Woman (1975), 102, 280, 590, 593
Scent of a Woman (1992), 30, 41, 81, 109, 692, 693
Schaeffer, Chester, 167, 457
Schaffner, Franklin, 77, 562, 708
Schaidt, Gunther, 327, 648
Schamoni, Peter, 268, 575
Scharf, Walter, 179–82, 184, 190–91, 209, 400, 407, 414, 420, 462, 553, 569, 575
Schary, Dore, 21, 85–86, 246, 261–62, 382, 392, 445, 464, 481
Scheib, Harold A., 320, 582
Scheider, Roy, 39, 58, 566, 613
Scheinman, Andrew, 30, 692
Schell, Maximilian, 36, 38, 59, 510, 589, 601
Schenck, Joseph M., 289, 464, 703
Schermer, Jules, 87, 418
Schertzinger, Victor, 72, 176–77, 364–65, 378
Schiffman, Suzanne, 101, 584
Schiffrin, Simon, 264, 526
Schifrin, Lalo, 189–90, 193–95, 212, 548, 553, 598, 615, 622, 640
Schildkraut, Joseph, 53, 375
Schindel, Morton, 255, 647
Schioler, Torben, 270, 605
Schisgal, Murray, 105, 632
Schisler, Donald, 326, 636
Schlesinger, John, 76–77, 535, 557, 567, 708
Schlesinger, Leon, 236, 238–40, 395, 401, 408, 415
Schlosser, Gary, 265, 544
Schlyter, Fredrik, 321, 323, 594, 618
Schmidt, Arthur, 167–68, 172, 174, 452, 491, 621, 669
Schmiechen, Richard, 273, 647
Schmit, Joseph, 314, 503
Schnee, Charles, 91, 461
Schneider, Bert, 269, 587
Schoenbaum, Charles, 115, 446
Schoendoerffer, Pierre, 266, 550
Schoenfeld, Bernard C., 90, 451
Schoenfeld Films, 248, 514, 520
School in the Mailbox, 260, 438
Schoonmaker, Thelma, 170, 172, 174, 563, 621, 682
Schoppe, James, 145, 639
Schrader, Leonard, 106, 650
Schreiber, Edward, 249, 532
Schroeder, Barbet, 80, 681
Schroeder, Harold H., 314, 504
Schtonk, 283, 696
Schulberg, Budd, 92, 472
Schuler, Chester L., 329, 666
Schulman, Arnold, 97, 99, 523, 557
Schulman, Tom, 108, 675
Schulze, John DuCasse, 128–29, 393, 399
Schumann, Werner, 272, 635
Schwartz, Arthur, 202–3, 415, 437
Schwartz, Bernard, 27, 619
Schwartzman, Arnold, 272, 629
Schwary, Ronald L., 27–28, 619, 643
Schweizer, Richard, 88–89, 425, 441
Schwep, Charles F., 248, 508
Scobey, Fred, 319, 321, 323, 577, 593, 612
Scofield, Paul, 36, 540
Scognamillo, Gabriel, 134, 468
Scorsese, Martin, 79–80, 108, 620, 668, 681
Scott, Adrian, 21, 435
Scott, Allan, 87, 412
Scott, Cynthia, 272, 641
Scott, Elliot, 139, 143, 146, 530, 597, 669
Scott, Geoffrey, 265, 532
Scott, George C., 11, 37, 56, 499, 510, 561, 566
Scott, Martha, 44, 391
Scott, Michael, 255, 269, 593, 653
Scott, Morton, 182, 427
Scott, Rey, 287, 402
Scott, Ridley, 80, 687
Scott, Tom, 162, 639, 645
Scott, Walter M., 133–37, 139–41, 451, 457, 462, 468, 473, 479, 485, 496, 501, 524, 530, 536, 542, 548, 552, 558, 563
Scoundrel, The, 84, 368
Scoville, R. R., 311, 464
Scratch-As-Catch-Can, 236, 360
Screen Actors Guild, 4
Screen Guilds' Magazine, The, 4
Screen Play, 257, 695
Screen Snapshots 25th Anniversary, 241, 428
Screen Souvenirs, 236, 360
Screen Writers Guild, 4, 5, 82
Scrooge, 141, 191, 209, 222, 562–64
Scrooged, 229, 670
Sea, The, 237, 362
Sea Around Us, The, 261, 464
Sea Hawk, The, 128, 151, 179, 341, 393–95
Seale, John, 124, 651, 668
Seal Island, 243, 443
Seance on a Wet Afternoon, 47, 528
Search, The, 34, 73, 89, 288, 440–41
Seaton, George, 5, 74, 87, 89, 92, 99, 299, 339, 412, 436, 472, 515, 562, 705

Seawards the Great Ships, 248, 514
Sea Wolf, The, 342, 401
Seawright, Roy, 341–42, 389, 395, 401
Sebastian, B. Tennyson, II, 162, 651
Sechan, Edmond, 252, 586
Second Chorus, 179, 200, 394
Second Class Mail, 255, 653
Second Fiddle, 200, 389
Seconds, 120, 541
"Second Time Around, The," 206, 508
Secret Command, 343, 421
Secret Land, The, 260, 443
"Secret Love," 204, 469
Secret of Santa Vittoria, The, 170, 190, 558
Seeds of Destiny, 260, 433
Seeing Eye, The, 261, 459
Seeing Hands, 240, 415
Seeing Red, 272, 641
See What I Say, 271, 628
See You at the Pillar, 266, 550
Segal, Erich, 99, 562
Segal, George, 57, 540, 589
Segall, Harry, 86, 398
Seger, Bob, 214, 664
Seibert, Siegfried, 321, 599
Seid, George, 308, 423
Seirton, Michael, 144–45, 627, 633
Seitz, John, 110, 113–16, 354, 412, 418, 425, 451, 456, 472
Sekiguchi, Kiichi, 323, 612
Self Defense—for Cowards, 248, 520
Selfish Giant, The, 251, 569
Selig, Colonel William N., 288, 438
Selin, Bjorn, 332, 685
Sellers, Peter, 36, 39, 247, 503, 528, 613
Selling Out, 268, 575
Selzer, Edward, 241–43, 245–46, 260, 428, 433, 438, 443, 448, 469, 474, 480, 492
Selznick, David O., 18–21, 297, 364, 367, 371, 375, 386, 390–91, 417, 424
Selznick International Pictures Inc., 306, 390
Sembello, Michael, 212, 640
Semenya, Caiphus, 196, 651
Semler, Dean, 125, 681
Semprun, Jorge, 98–99, 547, 557
Senior, Anna, 224, 622
Sennett, Mack, 236, 285–86, 378
Sennheiser, Prof. Fritz, 329, 660
Sensations of 1945, 182, 420
Sentinels of Silence, 11, 236, 251, 258, 267, 570
Senzemi Na? (What Have We Done?), 256, 683
"Separate Lives (Love Theme from White Nights)," 213, 652
Separate Tables, 23, 35, 46, 65, 94, 117, 186, 494–96
Serengeti Shall Not Die, 263, 503
Sergeant York, 20, 33, 54, 63, 73, 86, 112, 129, 152, 166, 179, 397–400
Serpico, 38, 101, 578–79
Serrurier, Mark, 323, 618
Sersen, Fred, 341–43, 389, 395, 401, 408, 415, 421, 428, 442
Service with the Colors, 239, 395
Session Man, 257, 689
Seven Beauties, 38, 78, 102, 280, 595–96, 599
Seven Brides for Seven Brothers, 22, 92, 116, 168, 185, 471–74
Seven Days in May, 57, 139, 528, 530
Seven Days to Noon, 90, 456
7 Faces of Dr. Lao, 291, 346, 531–32
Seven Little Foys, The, 93, 478
Seven Percent Solution, The, 102, 224, 596, 598
1776, 121, 573
Seventh Cross, The, 54, 417
7th Heaven, 17, 42, 71, 82, 126, 351–52
Seven Thieves, 219, 508
Seventh Veil, The, 88, 431
Sewing Woman, 272, 641
sex, lies, and videotape, 108, 675
Seymour, Michael, 144, 615
Seymour, Stephen A., 129, 399
Sforza, Fabrizio, 229, 677
Shadie, Ken, 106, 656
Shadow of a Doubt, 87, 412
"Shadow of Your Smile, The," 207, 537
Shaffer, Beverly, 253, 604
Shaffer, Peter, 102, 106, 602, 644
Shaft, 191, 209, 568–69
Shagan, Steve, 101–2, 579, 596
"Shakedown," 214, 664
Shall We Dance, 200, 378
Shamberg, Michael, 28, 637
Shampoo, 58, 67, 101, 143, 590–91
Shamroy, Leon, 111–20, 382, 392, 405, 418, 425, 446, 456, 461, 467, 472, 478, 485, 495, 500, 523, 535
Shane, 22, 55, 74, 92, 116, 466–67
Shanghai Express, 18, 72, 111, 359–60
Shanghai Gesture, The, 129, 180, 406–7
Shankar, Ravi, 195, 633
Shanks, 192, 585
Shanley, John Patrick, 107, 662
Shantzis, Michael, 333, 691
Shapiro, Arnold, 270, 611
Shapiro, Stanley, 95–96, 500, 511, 517
Sharaff, Irene, 135, 216–22, 224, 458, 469, 473–74, 480, 486, 502, 508, 513–14, 525, 543, 549, 559, 604
Sharif, Omar, 56, 516
Sharpe, Don, 235, 658
Sharpe, Robert K., 267, 560
Sharpless, Don K., 159, 591
Sharpsteen, Ben, 247, 263, 492, 497
Sharrock, Ivan, 163, 663
Shavelson, Melville, 93–94, 478, 495
Shaw, Artie, 179, 200, 394
Shaw, Frank X., 337, 362
Shaw, George Bernard, 85, 382
Shaw, Irwin, 87, 405
Shaw, Robert, 57, 540, 589
She, 339, 369
Shean, Al, 191, 563
Shearer, Douglas, 148–55, 303–6, 314, 316, 341–43, 356, 365, 368, 370, 373–74, 377, 379–80, 383, 387, 389, 393, 395, 399, 401, 403, 407–8, 413, 419, 421, 426, 437, 457, 503, 527
Shearer, Norma, 42–43, 355, 357, 364, 371, 381
Shearman, Russell, 310, 343, 442, 444
Shedd, Jacqueline Phillips, 270, 611
She Done Him Wrong, 18, 361
Sheehan, Winfield, 17–18, 357, 359, 361
Sheep Has Five Legs, The, 92, 478
Sheepman, The, 94, 495
Sheldon, Sidney, 89, 436
She Loves Me Not, 199, 366
Shelton, Ron, 107, 668
She Married a Cop, 178, 388
Shenandoah, 157, 536
Shepard, Sam, 60, 638
Shepherd, The, 251, 565
Shepperton Studio Sound Department, 157–58, 512, 518, 530, 553
Sheridan, Jim, 80, 675
Sheriff, Paul, 132, 134, 431, 462
Sheriff, R. C., 85, 387
Sherman, Richard M., 188, 191–93, 207–9, 211, 531, 553, 568–69, 580, 603–4, 610
Sherman, Robert B., 188, 191–92, 194, 207–9, 211, 531, 553, 568–69, 580, 604, 610
Sherman, Roger M., 273, 647
Sherwood, Robert E., 86, 88, 392, 431
Shetland Experience, The, 270, 605
She Wore a Yellow Ribbon, 115, 446
Shilkret, Nathaniel, 177, 373
Shingleton, Wilfred, 132, 436

Ship Comes In, A, 42, 351
Ship Is Born, A, 259, 409
Ship of Fools, 24, 36, 47, 57, 97, 120–21, 139, 534–37
Shire, David, 211, 616
Shire, Talia, 49, 67, 584, 595
Shirley, Anne, 62, 376
Shirley Valentine, 51, 214, 674, 677
Shocking Accident, A, 254, 635
Shoe-shine (foreign language film), 89, 277, 288, 436, 438
Shoeshine (short), 256, 664
Shoes of the Fisherman, The, 141, 190, 552–53
Shootist, The, 143, 597
Shop on Main Street, The, 47, 279, 538, 540
Shorr, Richard, 235, 670
Short, Marjorie Anne, 253, 598
Short, Robert, 229, 670
Shostak, Murray, 251, 569
Shostakovich, Dimitri, 187, 513
Should Wives Work, 238, 378
Shoup, Howard, 219–21, 502, 508, 513, 531, 537
Show Boat (1951), 116, 184, 456–57
Shrine Civic Auditorium, 13, 430, 435, 661, 667, 680
Shuftan, Eugen, 118, 511
Shuken, Leo, 178, 189, 388, 531
Shut Up . . . I'm Crying, 251, 564
Shyer, Charles, 104, 620
Siam, 245, 475
Sickner, Roy N., 99, 557
Sidney, Sylvia, 67, 579
Sidney's Family Tree, 247, 497
Siege, 239, 395
Siegel, Otto, 137, 507
Siegel, Sol C., 21–22, 445, 471
Siegler, Robert, 251, 564
Sign of the Cross, 111, 362
Signoret, Simone, 46–47, 499, 534
Sigrist, Michael, 327, 642
Silber, Glenn, 271–72, 617, 629
Silence, The, 254, 635
Silence of the Lambs, The, 29, 41, 51, 90, 109, 164, 174, 686–88, 708
Silent Revolution, The, 268, 576
Silent World, The, 262, 487
Silkwood, 50, 69, 79, 105, 173, 637–38, 640
Silliphant, Sterling, 98, 547
Sills, Milton, 703
Silly Symphonies, 236
Silvera, Darrell, 129–31, 135, 141, 399, 406, 413, 419, 425, 479, 562
Silverado, 162, 196, 651
Silver Chalice, The, 116, 185, 472–73
Silver Into Gold, 274, 665
Silver Queen, 128, 180, 406–7
Silvers, Louis, 176–78, 365, 377, 388
"Silver Shadows and Golden Dreams," 202, 421
Silverstein, Shel, 214, 682
Silver Streak, 160, 597
Silvertooth, Wilbur, 306, 403
Silvey, Benjamin, 337, 362
Simmons, Jean, 48, 64, 440, 556
Simon, Carly, 214, 670
Simon, Kirk, 274–75, 659, 683
Simon, Neil, 98, 102–3, 552, 590, 602, 608
Simon, Roger L., 108, 675
Simon, S. Sylvan, 22, 450
Simonds, Walter, 135, 479
Simoni, Dario, 138, 140–41, 518, 536, 548
Simple Story, A, 281, 617
Simpson, Claire, 173, 657
Simpson, Rick, 145, 147, 645, 682
Simpson, Robert E., 166, 393
Simpson, Susanne, 272, 628
Sinatra, Frank, 35, 55, 299, 466, 477, 516, 565, 583
Sinbad the Sailor, 237, 374
"Since I Kissed My Baby Goodbye," 201, 401
Since You Went Away, 21, 44, 54, 63, 114, 131, 166, 417–21
Sing Baby Sing, 199, 373
Singer, Kurt, 309, 439
Singer, Steve, 271, 617
Singing Guns, 204, 452
Singing Nun, The, 189, 543
Singin' in the Rain, 64, 184, 460, 462
Singleton, John, 81, 108, 687
Sing Your Way Home, 202, 427
Sin of Madelon Claudet, The, 43, 359
Siodmak, Robert, 73, 431
Sister Kenny, 44, 430
Sistrom, Joseph, 20–21, 404, 417
Sisyphus, 252, 592
Sitting Pretty, 34, 440
Six-Sided Triangle, 249, 526
Skala, Lilia, 66, 523
Skall, William V., 112–16, 393, 398, 406, 436, 441, 456, 472
Skaterdater, 249, 538
"Skating Ensemble," 339, 374
Skiles, Marlin, 183, 427
Skinner, Frank, 177, 179–80, 383, 394, 400, 407, 414
Skippy, 17, 32, 72, 83, 357
Sklar, Zachary, 109, 687
Skolsky, Sidney, 12
Skotak, Dennis, 233, 677, 695
Skotak, Robert, 232–33, 658, 689
Skylark, 152, 400
Sky Over Holland, 250, 549
Skyscraper, 83, 247, 354, 503
Sky's the Limit, The, 181, 201, 414
Slade, Bernard, 103, 608
Slater, Barney, 94, 490
Slater, Dan, 325, 330, 624, 672
Slaughter, Nugent, 336, 352
Sleeping Beauty, 187, 502
"Sleighride in July," 203, 428
Slender Thread, The, 140, 221, 535, 537
Slesin, Aviva, 274, 665
Slesinger, Tess, 88, 425
Sleuth, 37, 77, 192, 572–74
Slifer, Clarence A., 342–43, 415, 442
Slimon, Scot, 136, 501
Slipper and the Rose—The Story of Cinderella, The, 193, 211, 603–4
"Slipper and the Rose Waltz, The (He Danced with Me/She Danced with Me)," 211, 604
Slocombe, Douglas, 121–23, 573, 602, 626
Sloss, Nancy, 273, 647
Slyfield, C. O. (Sam), 152–54, 309, 406, 413, 426, 434
Smallman, Kirk, 265, 538
Small Town Girl, 204, 468
Smart as a Fox, 241, 433
Smart Money, 83, 358
Smash-Up: The Story of a Woman, 44, 89, 435–36
Smiling Lieutenant, 18, 359
Smilin' Thru, 18, 361
Smilov, Margaret, 276, 696
Smith, Albert E., 288, 438
Smith, Art, 286, 438
Smith, Bernard, 23–24, 505, 522
Smith, Bud, 171, 173, 580, 639
Smith, Christina, 229, 689
Smith, Dick, 228–29, 646, 677
Smith, Harold Jacob, 6, 94–95, 495, 506
Smith, Howard, 268, 576
Smith, Jack Martin, 132, 135, 139–41, 446, 485, 524, 530, 536, 542, 548, 558, 562
Smith, John N., 254, 628
Smith, Kenneth F., 232–33, 634, 664
Smith, Leonard, 112–14, 398, 412, 425, 431
Smith, Maggie, 48, 66, 68–69, 534, 556, 572, 608, 656
Smith, Mark, 164, 694
Smith, Oliver, 135, 479
Smith, Paul J., 177, 179, 181, 183–84, 186, 378, 394, 414, 427, 437, 452, 491
Smith, Pete, 237–39, 242–44, 289, 362, 374, 378, 395, 401, 433, 438, 443, 448, 453, 470
Smith, Robert Emmet, 139, 535
Smith, Scott, 164, 694
Smith, Shirley W., 89, 446
Smith, Ted, 130–31, 406, 426
Smith, Tom, 228, 634

Smith, William B., 313, 315, 493, 521
Smith, William Craig, 145, 633
Smith, Yvonne, 275, 678
Smokey and the Bandit, 172, 603
Smythe, Douglas, 233, 334, 695, 697
Snake Pit, The, 21, 45, 73, 89, 154, 183, 440–42
Snell, Richard, 229, 689
Snider, Dick, 267, 570
Sniper, The, 91, 461
Snodgress, Carrie, 48, 561
Snow, Tom, 213–14, 646, 677
Snow, 249, 538
Snow Capers, 243, 443
Snow Carnival, 243, 448
Snowden, Alison, 255, 653
Snowman, The, 254, 635
Snows of Aorangi, 247, 497
Snows of Kilimanjaro, The, 116, 134, 461–62
Snow White and the Seven Dwarfs, 13, 177, 286, 378, 385
Snyder, David L., 144, 633
Snyder, Edward, 343, 442
Snyder, Robert, 261, 263, 453, 497
Snyder, William, 112, 115, 398, 441, 446
Sobieski, Carol, 109, 687
Société d'Optique et de Mécanique de Haute Precision, 313, 493
Society of Motion Picture and Television Engineers (SMPTE), The, 290, 493; Engineering Committees, 293, 678–79
So Dear to My Heart, 204, 447
Soderberg, Theodore, 149, 159, 160–61, 365, 568, 574, 585, 603, 615
Soderbergh, Steven, 108, 675
Soderlund, Ulla-Britt, 223, 592
So Ends Our Night, 179, 400
"So In Love," 203, 428
Sokolove, Richard, 99, 557
Sokolow, Leonard, 316, 318, 325, 533, 565, 629
Solar Film, The, 254, 617
Soldier's Story, A, 28, 60, 106, 643–44
Soldiers in Hiding, 273, 653
Soldiers of the Sky, 258, 402
Solid Gold Cadillac, The, 135, 218, 485–86
Solinas, Franco, 99, 552
"So Little Time," 207, 525
Solly's Diner, 254, 617
Solo, 252, 575
Solomon, Jack, 158–61, 558, 568, 591, 597, 609, 615
Solow, Sidney P., 292, 316, 533, 605
Somebody Up There Likes Me, 117, 135, 168, 484–85
Somebody Waiting, 267, 570
Some Came Running, 46, 56, 65, 206, 219, 494, 496–97
Some Like It Hot, 35, 75, 95, 118, 136, 219, 499–502
"Someone's Waiting for You," 211, 604
"Some Sunday Morning," 203, 428
"Something's Gotta Give," 205, 480
Something to Shout About, 181, 202, 414–15
Something to Sing About, 177, 378
Sometimes a Great Notion, 58, 209, 566, 569
"Somewhere in My Memory," 214, 682
Somewhere in Time, 224, 622
"Somewhere Out There," 213, 658
So Much for So Little, 260, 448
Sondergaard, Gale, 62–63, 372, 430
Sondheim, Stephen, 214, 682
"Song from *10* (It's Easy to Say)," 211, 616
"Song from *Two for the Seesaw* (Second Chance)," 207, 519
Song of Bernadette, The, 21, 44, 54, 63, 73, 87, 113, 130, 153, 166, 181, 411–14
Song of the Flame, 148, 356
Song of the Open Road, 182, 202, 420–21
Song of the South, 183, 203, 437
Song to Remember, A, 33, 88, 114, 154, 167, 182, 424–27
Song Without End, 187, 507
Songwriter, 196, 646
Son of Monte Cristo, 129, 399
Son of Paleface, 204, 463
Sons and Lovers, 23, 35, 65, 75, 95, 118, 137, 505–7
Sons of Liberty, 238, 389
"Sooner Or Later (I Always Get My Man)," 214, 682
Sopher, Sharon I., 274, 659
Sophie's Choice, 50, 105, 123, 195, 225, 631–34
So Proudly We Hail, 11, 63, 87, 113, 342, 411–12, 415
Sorcerer, 160, 603
Sorrell and Son, 71, 351
Sorrow and the Pity, The, 268, 570
Sorry, Wrong Number, 45, 440
Sothern, Ann, 70, 662
So This Is Harris, 237, 362
So This Is Washington, 153, 413
Souls at Sea, 127, 177, 338, 376–78
Sounder, 25, 37, 48, 66, 100, 572–73
Sound of Music, The, 24, 47, 76, 120, 140, 158, 169, 189, 221, 534–37, 708
Sound of Sunshine—Sound of Rain, 255, 641
Sound Service, Inc., 152–54, 406, 413, 419, 426, 437
Southern, Terry, 97, 99, 529, 557
Southerner, The, 73, 154, 182, 425–27
South Pacific, 118, 156, 186, 495–96
So You Think You're Not Guilty, 243, 413
So You Want to Be in Pictures, 242, 438
So You Want to Be on Radio, 242, 442
Spaceborne, 253, 605
Spacek, Sissy, 49–51, 595, 619, 631, 643, 655
Spaces: The Architecture of Paul Rudolph, 272, 641
Space to Grow, A, 266, 554
Spanish Main, The, 114, 425
Spartacus, 56, 118, 137, 169, 187, 220, 505–8
Spawn of the North, 286, 341, 385
Speaking of Animals and Their Families, 239, 409
Spears, Ross, 271, 623
Special Day, A, 38, 280, 601, 605
Special Delivery, 253, 610
Specter, Ronnie, 230, 695
Speedy, 71, 351
Speedy Gonzales, 246, 480
Spellbound, 21, 54, 73, 114, 182, 343, 424–25, 427–28
Spencer, David W., 328, 654
Spencer, Dorothy, 166–67, 169, 171, 388, 457, 524, 585
Spencer, Herbert, 191–92, 563, 580
Sperling, Milton, 93, 478
Spewack, Bella, 86, 392
Spewack, Samuel, 86, 392
Spiegel, Sam, 22–23, 25, 298, 471, 489, 516, 527, 566
Spielberg, Anne, 107, 668
Spielberg, Steven, 27–28, 78–79, 298, 602, 626, 631–32, 649, 659
Spies, R. H., 313, 481
Spigelgass, Leonard, 90, 451
Spikings, Barry, 27, 607
Spills and Chills, 243, 448
Spinello, Barry, 253, 592
Spiral Staircase, The, 63, 430
Spirawski, Hans, 333, 697
Spirit of America, The, 264, 526
Spirit of St. Louis, The, 344, 492
Spivack, Murray, 158, 558, 563
Splash, 105, 644
Splendor in the Grass, 46, 96, 510–11
Splet, Alan, 161, 296, 618, 639
Split Cherry Tree, 255, 635

Spoilers, The, 129, 406
Sponable, Earl, 311, 315, 470, 515
Spoor, George K., 288, 438
Sporn, Michael, 255, 647
Sport Is Born, A, 248, 508
Sprague, Chandler, 87, 418
Sprague, G. M., 312, 476
Springfield, Tom, 208, 543
Spring Parade, 112, 151, 179, 200, 392–94
Spy Who Came in from the Cold, The, 36, 140, 534, 536
Spy Who Loved Me, The, 143, 193, 211, 603–4
Squarciapino, Franca, 226, 683
Squatter's Rights, 241, 433
Squires, Buddy, 273, 653
Squires of San Quentin, 270, 611
Sredni Vashtar, 255, 635
Stacey, Eric, 337–38, 368, 372, 376
Stack, Robert, 56, 483
Staffell, Charles D., 317, 555
Stafford, J. W., 312, 476
Stagecoach, 20, 53, 72, 112, 128, 166, 178, 386–88
Stagecoach to Fury, 117, 484
Stage Door, 19, 62, 72, 85, 375–76
Stage Door Canteen, 181, 202, 414–15
Stahl, John, 18, 364, 703
Stairs, The, 261, 453
Stairway to Light, 241, 428
Stalag 17, 34, 55, 74, 466
Stallone, Sylvester, 38, 102, 595–96
Stambler, Bruce, 235, 695
Stamp, Terence, 56, 516
Stancliffe, S. L., 310, 459
Stand and Deliver, 40, 667
Stand By for Action, 343, 415
Stand By Me, 107, 656
Stanfield, James S., 324, 618
Stanford, Thomas, 169, 513
Stanford Research Institute, 314, 503
Stankiewicz, Dr. Louis, 325, 630
Stanley, George, 12
Stanley, Kim, 47, 69, 528, 632
Stanwyck, Barbara, 43–45, 292, 375, 397, 417, 440, 629
Stapleton, Maureen, 65, 67–69, 494, 562, 608, 626
Star!, 57, 121, 141, 158, 190, 208, 221, 551–54
"Star!," 208, 553
Star, The, 45, 460
Star in the Night, 241, 428
Star Is Born, A (1937), 19, 32, 43, 72, 85, 286, 338, 375–76, 379
Star Is Born, A (1954), 35, 45, 135, 185, 205, 218, 471, 473–74
Star Is Born, A (1976), 122, 160, 193, 210, 597–98
Stark, Ray, 24, 26, 298, 551, 601, 618
Starkey, Dewey, 337, 362
Starman, 40, 643
Stars and Strikes, 2
Star Spangled Rhythm, 181, 202, 414–15
Starting Over, 49, 68, 613–14
Star Trek—The Motion Picture, 144, 194, 231, 615–16
Star Trek IV: The Voyage Home, 124, 162, 235, 656–58
Star Trek VI: The Undiscovered Country, 196, 229, 236, 689
Star Wars, 26, 59, 78, 102, 143, 160, 172, 193, 224, 231, 295, 601–5
Star Witness, 83, 359
State Fair, 18, 84, 182, 203, 361–62, 427–28
Stateman, Wylie, 163, 676
Statue of Liberty, The, 273, 653
Staub, Ralph, 240–41, 415, 421, 428
Stears, John, 231, 346, 538, 604
Steele, Gile, 216–17, 442, 447, 458, 463
Steel Magnolias, 70, 675
Steenburgen, Mary, 68, 620
Steiger, Rod, 36–37, 55, 471, 534, 546
Stein, Jules C., 300, 593
Steinbeck, John, 87–88, 91, 418, 425, 461
Steiner, Fred, 196, 651
Steiner, John H., 327, 642
Steiner, Max, 176–85, 365, 369, 373, 377, 383, 388, 394, 400, 407, 414, 420, 427, 432, 437, 442, 447, 452, 462, 473, 479
Steinkamp, Fredric, 170–71, 173, 542, 558, 591, 633, 651
Steinkamp, William, 173–74, 633, 651, 676
Steinore, Michael, 343, 415, 428, 437
Stella Dallas, 43, 62, 375–76
Stensvold, Larry, 162, 651
Stephani, Frederick, 89, 419
Stephens, Jack, 146, 657
Stephenson, James, 54, 391
Stephenson, John, 333, 691
Step Lively, 131, 419
Stepmother, The, 209, 575
Sterile Cuckoo, The, 48, 208, 556–59
Sterling, Jan, 64, 471
Stern, Joan Keller, 251, 267, 559–60
Stern, Stewart, 91, 98, 456, 552
Sternad, Rudolph, 130–31, 137, 406, 426, 512
Sternberg, Tom, 27, 613
Stetson, Mark, 232, 646
Stevens, C. C., 342, 408
Stevens, David, 104, 620
Stevens, Freddi, 271, 628
Stevens, George, 8, 20–23, 73–75, 297, 404, 411–12, 455–56, 466, 470, 483–84, 499–500, 705
Stevens, George, Jr., 264, 526
Stevens, Jack, 144, 621
Stevens, Leith, 187–88, 205, 486, 501, 525
Stevens, Robert C., 308, 429
Stevens, Robert W., 306, 396
Stevenson, Edward, 217, 219, 458, 508
Stevenson, Philip, 88, 425
Stevenson, Robert, 76, 529
Stewart, Dave, 232, 617
Stewart, Donald, 105, 632
Stewart, Donald Ogden, 83, 86, 357, 392
Stewart, Douglas, 173, 640
Stewart, Douglas Day, 104, 632
Stewart, Edward, 144, 609, 615
Stewart, James, 33–35, 293, 386, 391, 424, 430, 450, 489, 499, 647
Stewart, James G. (sound), 342–43, 408, 415, 421, 442
Stewart, Roy C. and Sons, 313, 488
Stewart Filmscreen Corporation, 316, 533
Sticky My Fingers . . . Fleet My Feet, 251, 564
Stillman, Whit, 108, 681
Stindt, Robert, 323, 612
Stine, Harold E., 121, 573
Sting, The, 26, 38, 77, 101, 122, 142, 159, 171, 192, 223, 578–81, 708
Sting II, The, 195, 640
Stitch for Time, A, 274, 665
Stockwell, Dean, 61, 667
Stoker, Robert W., Jr., 333, 691
Stokowski, Leopold, 287, 402
Stolen Kisses, 279, 555
Stolen Life, A, 343, 432
Stoll, George E., 178–80, 182, 185–86, 188, 200, 388, 394, 407, 420, 427, 480, 486, 519
Stoll, John, 138, 518
Stoll, Nelson, 162–63, 645, 682
Stoloff, Morris, 177, 179–87, 377, 383, 400, 407, 414, 420, 427, 432, 447, 468, 486, 508, 513
Stoloff, Victor, 259, 409
Stolz, Robert, 181, 200, 394, 420
Stone, Andrew L., 93, 484
Stone, David E., 235, 695
Stone, Gregory, 177, 383
Stone, Joseph, 95, 500
Stone, Leroy, 166, 419
Stone, Lewis, 31, 353
Stone, Oliver, 29, 80–81, 103, 106, 108–9, 608, 656, 674–75, 686–87, 708
Stone, Peter, 97, 529
Stone, Robert, 274, 665

Stone Carvers, The, 273, 647
Stones, E. L., 314, 504
Stop, Look, and Listen, 250, 549
Stoppard, Tom, 106, 650
Stop the World—I Want to Get Off, 189, 543
Storaro, Vittorio, 123–25, 614, 626, 662, 681
Storm over Bengal, 177, 383
"Storybook Love," 214, 664
Story of Adele H., The, 48, 589
Story of a Dog, 241, 428
Story of Dr. Wassell, The, 343, 421
Story of Louis Pasteur, The, 19, 32, 84, 371–72
Story of Three Loves, The, 134, 468
Story of Time, The, 244, 458
Stothart, Herbert, 176–82, 369, 377, 383, 389, 394, 400, 407, 414, 420, 427
Stoumen, Louis Clyde, 262, 264, 487, 520
Stout, Archie, 116, 461
Strabel, Herbert, 142, 574
Stradling, Harry, Sr., 113–21, 412, 425, 446, 456, 461, 478, 484, 495, 500, 512, 517, 529, 552, 558
Stradling, Harry, Jr., 121–22, 573, 579
Straight, Beatrice, 68, 596
"Strange Are the Ways of Love" (1959), 206, 502
"Strange Are the Ways of Love" (1972), 209, 575
Strange Fruit, 253, 610
Strange Loves of Martha Ivers, The, 88, 431
Stranger, The, 88, 431
Strangers on a Train, 115, 456
Strasburg, Lee, 58, 583
Strategic Air Command, 93, 478
Stratford Adventure, The, 262, 475
Stratton Story, The, 89, 446
Strauss, Robert, 55, 466
Strauss Fantasy, The, 245, 475
Strawberry Blonde, The, 180, 400
Straw Dogs, 191, 568
"Straw Hat," 339, 369
Streep, Meryl, 50–51, 68, 608, 614, 625, 631, 637, 649, 661, 667, 680
Street, The, 253, 598
Street Angel, 42, 110, 126, 351, 354
Streetcar Named Desire, A, 22, 34, 45, 64, 74, 91, 115, 133, 155, 184, 217, 455–58
Street of Chance, 83, 356
Street Smart, 61, 661
Streetwise, 273, 647
Streisand, Barbra, 29, 42, 47–48, 210, 551, 578, 598, 686
Strenge, Walter, 117, 484
Strick, Joseph, 98, 267, 547, 564
Strikes and Spares, 237, 366
Strike Up the Band, 151, 179, 200, 393–94
Stringer, Michael, 142, 568
Strings, 256, 689
Strip, The, 204, 458
Stripper, The, 220, 525
Stromberg, Hunt, 18–19, 364, 367, 371
Strub, Lucinda, 329, 660
Struss, Karl, 8, 110–12, 352, 360, 362, 398
Stuart, Mel, 265, 532
Stuart, Walker, 249, 526
Stubbs, Jack, 135, 479
Studio Basic Agreement, 1
Stultz, Barry M., 327, 648
Stumpf, Richard J., 294, 320, 325, 587, 629, 690
Stunt Man, The, 39, 79, 104, 619–21
Sturges, John, 74, 478
Sturges, Preston, 86–87, 392, 418
Sturtevant, John, 140, 541
Stussy, Jan, 270, 605
Styne, Jule, 201–5, 208, 395, 408, 414, 420, 427, 442, 447, 474, 553
Su, Cong, 196, 663
Subject Was Roses, The, 47, 57, 551
Sudden Fear, 45, 55, 116, 217, 460–61, 463
Suddenly, Last Summer, 46, 136, 499, 501
Suez, 111, 150, 178, 382–83
Sugarman, Burt, 28, 655
Sugerman, Andrew, 253, 610
Sukman, Harry, 187, 189, 508, 513, 543
Sullavan, Margaret, 43, 381
Sullivan, Frank (film editor), 167, 442
Sullivan, Frankie, III (music), 212, 634
Sullivan, Jack, 337, 372
Sullivan, James W., 135, 485
Sullivan, Mark, 233, 689
Sullivans, The, 87, 418
Summer and Smoke, 46, 65, 138, 187, 510–13
Summer of '42, 100, 121, 171, 191, 567–68
Summers, Gary, 162–64, 639, 676, 688
Summer Storm, 181, 420
Summertime, 45, 74, 477–78
Summer Wishes, Winter Dreams, 48, 67, 578–79
Sunbonnet Sue, 182, 427
Sundae in New York, 255, 641
Sunday Bloody Sunday, 37, 48, 77, 100, 566–67
Sundays and Cybele, 96, 188, 278, 520, 523, 525
Sundown, 112, 129, 179, 398–400
Sundowners, The, 23, 46, 65, 75, 95, 505–6
Sunflower, 191, 563
Sunny, 180, 400
Sunrise, 42, 110, 126, 335, 351–52
Sunrise at Campobello, 46, 137, 156, 220, 505, 507–8
Sunset, 226, 670
Sunset Boulevard, 22, 34, 45, 55, 64, 74, 90, 115, 133, 167, 184, 450–52
Sunshine Boys, The, 38, 58, 102, 143, 589–91
Sun Valley Serenade, 112, 180, 201, 398, 400–401
Super Chief: The Life and Legacy of Earl Warren, 275, 678
Superman, 160, 172, 194, 296, 609–11
Superman No. 1, 239, 401
Sure Cures, 241, 433
"Surprise, Surprise," 213, 652
Surtees, Bruce, 122, 584
Surtees, Robert, 114–23, 418, 451, 456, 461, 478, 500, 518, 547, 567, 579, 597, 602, 609
Survival City, 246, 480
Susan Slept Here, 155, 205, 473–74
Suspicion, 20, 44, 179, 397, 400
Sutter, Charles E., 313, 315, 493, 521
Sutton, Peter, 161, 621
Suzman, Janet, 48, 566
Suzukawa, Hiroshi, 321, 600
Suzy, 199, 373
Svengali, 111, 127, 358
Swanee River, 178, 388
Swanson, Gloria, 42, 45, 351, 355, 450
Swan Song, 257, 696
Swarm, The, 244, 610
Swarthe, Robert, 232, 252, 592, 617
Swedes in America, 259, 416
Sweeney, Matt, 329, 660
Sweet and Lowdown, 202, 420
Sweet Bird of Youth, 46, 56, 65, 516–17
Sweet Charity, 141, 190, 222, 558–59
Sweet Dreams, 50, 649
"Sweet Dreams Sweetheart," 202, 421
Sweete, Barbara Willis, 273, 653
Sweethearts, 150, 177, 286, 383, 385
"Sweetheart Tree, The," 207, 537
"Sweet Leilani," 199, 378
Swerling, Jo, 87, 405
Swing High, 236, 360
"Swinging on a Star," 202, 421

"Swingin' the Jinx," 339, 374
"Swing Is Here to Stay," 340, 378
Swingler, Humphrey, 268, 576
Swing Shift, 69, 644
Swing Time, 199, 340, 373–74
Swingtime in the Movies, 238, 384
Swink, Robert, 168, 170, 172, 468, 553, 609
Swiss Family Robinson, 341, 395
Switzerland, 246, 481
Switzgable, Meg, 272, 635
Swooner Crooner, 240, 421
Sword Fishing, 238, 389
Sword in the Stone, The, 188, 525
Sylbert, Anthea, 223–24, 586, 604
Sylbert, Paul, 143, 147, 609
Sylbert, Richard, 140, 142–45, 147, 542, 585, 591, 627, 645, 682, 688
Sylvania Electric Products, Inc., 315, 318, 515, 565
Symansky, Adam, 272, 641
Symphony of a City, 243, 443
Symposium on Popular Songs, 248, 520

Tabasco Road, 246, 492
Tabu, 111, 358
Tacchella, Jean-Charles, 102, 596
Tajima, Renee, 275, 671
Take a Letter, Darling, 113, 129, 180, 405–7
"Take My Breath Away," 213, 658
Take the High Ground, 92, 467
Talbot, Irvin, 176, 369
Tale of Two Cities, A, 19, 165, 371, 373
Tales of Hoffman, 133, 217, 457–58
Tales of Meeting and Parting, 255, 647
Talk of the Town, The, 20, 86–87, 113, 129, 166, 180, 404–7
"Talk to the Animals," 208, 549
Tall, Dark, and Handsome, 86, 398
Tally, Ted, 109, 687
Talsky, Ron, 223, 592
Tamblyn, Russ, 56, 489
Taming of the Shrew, The, 141, 222, 548–49
Tamiroff, Akim, 53–54, 371, 411
Tammuz, Jonathan, 256, 678
"Tammy," 205, 492
Tammy and the Bachelor, 205, 492
Tandy, Jessica, 51, 70, 674, 687
Tango, 254, 635
Tanks a Million, 179, 400
Tanks Are Coming, The, 239, 402
Tansman, Alexander, 182, 427
Taradash, Daniel, 11, 92, 467, 705
Taras Bulba, 188, 519
Target for Tonight, 287, 402
Tarloff, Frank, 97, 529
Tasker, Homer G., 150, 373, 377
Tate, Cullen, 337, 364
Tati, Jacques, 93, 478
Taurog, Norman, 72, 357, 382
Tavoularis, Dean, 142–44, 146–47, 585, 609, 615, 669, 682
Taxi Driver, 26, 38, 68, 193, 595–96, 598
Taylor, Bill, 325, 630
Taylor, Christian M., 257, 695
Taylor, Elizabeth, 42, 46–47, 300, 489, 494, 499, 505, 540, 697
Taylor, John, 261, 470
Taylor, Peter, 168, 491
Taylor, Renee, 99, 562
Taylor, Ronnie, 123, 632
Taylor, Ross, 324, 624
Taylor, Samuel, 92, 472
Tazieff, Haroun, 265, 544
Tchaikovsky, 191, 279, 569–70
Teacher's Pet, 56, 94, 494–95
Tea for Two Hundred, 242, 442
Technical Threat, 256, 670
Technicolor Motion Picture Corp., 287, 303, 306, 311, 314–15, 360, 390, 464, 503–4, 515
Teddy, the Rough Rider, 239, 395
Teenage Father, 253, 610
Teenage Rebel, 135, 218, 485–86
Tegnell, Ann, 274, 671
Tell Tale Heart, The, 245, 469
Telson, Bob, 214, 669
Temperton, Rod, 196, 213, 651–52
Tempest, The, 126, 352
Temple, Shirley, 285, 366
Templeton, George, 241–42, 428, 433
10, 194, 211, 616
Ten Commandments, The (1956), 23, 117, 136, 156, 168, 218, 344, 484, 485–86
Tender Is the Night, 207, 519
"Tender Is the Night," 207, 519
Tender Mercies, 28, 39, 79, 105, 212, 637–38, 640
Tender Tale of Cinderella Penguin, The, 254, 628
Tender Trap, The, 205, 480
Ten Gentlemen from West Point, 113, 405
Ten-Year Lunch: The Wit and Legend of the Algonquin Round Table, 274, 665
Tequila Sunrise, 124, 668
Teresa, 91, 456
Terminator 2: Judgment Day, 125, 164, 174, 229, 233, 235, 687–89
Terms of Endearment, 28, 50, 60, 79, 105, 145, 173, 195, 637–40, 708
Terr, Max, 180, 407
Terry, Paul, 240–41, 421, 428
Teshigahara, Hiroshi, 76, 535
Tesich, Steve, 103, 614
Tess, 27, 78, 123, 144, 194, 224, 619–22
Testament, 50, 637
Test Pilot, 19, 85, 166, 381–83
Tetrick, Harry Warren, 159–60, 591, 597
Tetzlaff, Ted, 113, 405
Texas Rangers, The, 150, 373
Thackery, Ellis J., 342, 395
Thalberg, Irving G., 17–19, 297, 355, 357, 359, 361, 364, 367, 371, 375, 703. *See also* Irving G. Thalberg Memorial Award
Than, Joseph, 87, 418
Thank God It's Friday, 211, 610
Thanks a Million, 149, 368
"Thanks for the Memory," 200, 384
Thank Your Lucky Stars, 202, 415
"Thank You Very Much," 209, 563
Tharp, Grahame, 262, 470
Thar She Blows!, 244, 464
That Certain Age, 150, 200, 383–84
That Forsyte Woman, 217, 453
That Girl from Paris, 150, 373
That Hamilton Woman, 112, 129, 152, 342, 398–401
That Lady in Ermine, 203, 442
That Man from Rio, 97, 529
That Mothers Might Live, 238, 384
That Obscure Object of Desire, 102, 280, 602, 605
"That Old Black Magic," 202, 415
"That Old Feeling," 199, 378
"That's Amore," 205, 469
That's Life, 213, 657
That's Me, 249, 526
That Touch of Mink, 96, 138, 157, 517–18
That Uncertain Feeling, 179, 400
Their Own Desire, 42, 355
Theiss, William, 223–25, 598, 616, 640
Thelma & Louise, 51, 80, 108, 125, 174, 686–88
Them!, 344, 474
"Theme from *Ice Castles* (Through the Eyes of Love)," 211, 616
"Theme from *Mahogany* (Do You Know Where You're Going To)," 210, 592
"Theme from *Shaft*," 209, 569
"Theme from *The Promise* (I'll Never Say Goodbye)," 211, 616
Theodora Goes Wild, 43, 165, 371, 373
There Goes My Heart, 177, 383
"There's a Breeze on Lake Louise," 201, 408

There's No Business Like Show Business, 92, 185, 218, 472, 474
These Three, 62, 372
Thevenet, Pierre-Louis, 141, 562
"They Can't Take That Away from Me," 200, 378
They Knew What They Wanted, 53, 391
They Planted a Stone, 261, 470
They're Always Caught, 238, 384
"They're Either Too Young or Too Old," 202, 415
They Shall Have Music, 178, 388
They Shoot Horses, Don't They?, 48, 57, 66, 77, 99, 141, 170, 190, 222, 556–59
They Were Expendable, 154, 343, 426, 428
Thief, The, 184, 462
Thief of Bagdad, The, 112, 128, 179, 341, 393–95
Thiermann, Eric, 272, 641
Thieving Magpie, The (La Gazza Ladra), 249, 538
Thijssen, Willem, 255, 658
Thin Ice, 340, 378
Thin Man, The, 18, 32, 72, 84, 364–65
3rd Avenue El, 246, 480
Third Man, The, 74, 115, 167, 451–52
Thirlwell, Robert M. "Curly," 159–62, 591, 609, 627, 645, 651
38, 282, 659
Thirty Million Letters, 264, 526
Thirty Seconds over Tokyo, 114, 343, 418, 421
This Above All, 113, 130, 152, 166, 405–7
This Is Cinerama, 185, 468
This Is the Army, 130, 153, 181, 413–14
"This Is the Moment," 203, 442
This Land Is Mine, 153, 413
This Love of Ours, 182, 427
This Mechanical Age, 245, 475
This Sporting Life, 36, 47, 522
This Tiny World, 268, 575
This Woman Is Mine, 179, 400
Thom, Randy, 161–62, 164, 639, 688
Thoma, Georg, 332, 691
Thomas, Anna, 105, 644
Thomas, Barry, 160, 609
Thomas, Bill, 219–22, 508, 513, 519, 525, 537, 549, 564, 569
Thomas, Jeremy, 29, 661
Thomas, Kit, 275, 683
Thomas, Tony, 29, 674
Thomas, William C., 259, 409
Thomas Crown Affair, The, 190, 208, 553
Thompson, Andy, 269, 599
Thompson, Barnaby, 256, 683
Thompson, Barton, 307, 416
Thompson, Charles, 134, 139, 462, 536
Thompson, Daniele, 102, 596
Thompson, Emma, 52, 692
Thompson, Ernest, 104, 626
Thompson, F. Thomas, 307, 410
Thompson, Francis, 265, 268, 538, 586
Thompson, J. Lee, 75, 511
Thompson, Linda, 215, 694
Thompson, Robert E., 99, 557
Thompson, Walter, 166, 169, 407, 501
Thoms, Jerome, 168, 491
Thomson, Alex, 123, 626
Thorne, Ken, 189, 543
Thoroughly Modern Millie, 66, 141, 158, 189–90, 208, 222, 547–49
"Thoroughly Modern Millie," 208, 549
Those Magnificent Men in Their Flying Machines, 97, 535
Thousand and One Nights, A, 131, 343, 426, 428
Thousand Clowns, A, 24, 57, 97, 189, 534–35, 537
1,000 Dollars a Minute, 149, 368
"1000 Love Songs," 339, 373
Thousands Cheer, 113, 130, 181, 413–14
Three, 279, 544
Three Brothers, 281, 629
Three Caballeros, The, 154, 183, 426–27
Three Coins in the Fountain, 22, 116–117, 205, 471–72, 474
"Three Coins in the Fountain," 205, 474
Three Comrades, 43, 381
Three Days of the Condor, 171, 591
Three Faces of Eve, The, 46, 489
Three Is a Family, 154, 426
Three Kisses, 246, 480
Three Little Pigs, The, 237, 362
Three Little Words, 184, 452
3 Men and a Cradle, 282, 653
Three Musketeers, The (1948), 115, 441
Three Orphan Kittens, 237, 369
Three Russian Girls, 181, 420
Three Smart Girls, 19, 84, 150, 371–73
Through a Glass Darkly, 96, 278, 514, 517
"Through a Long and Sleepless Night," 204, 447
Throw Mama From The Train, 70, 662
"Thumbelina," 204, 463
Thumim, Dr. Alfred, 329, 660
Thunderball, 346, 537
Thunderbolt, 31, 353
Thunderbolt and Lightfoot, 58, 583
Thursday's Children, 262, 475
Tibbett, Lawrence, 32, 355
Tibbles, George, 203, 442
Tide of Traffic, The, 268, 576
Tidyman, Ernest, 100, 567
Tierney, Gene, 44, 424
Tiffen, Ira, 334, 697
Tiffen, Nat, 327, 648
Tilby, Wendy, 257, 689
"Till Love Touches Your Life," 209, 563
Tilly, Meg, 69, 650
Timber Toppers, 238, 384
Time, Place, and the Girl, The, 203, 437
Time for Burning, A, 266, 550
"Time for Love, A," 208, 543
Time Is Running Out, 267, 564
Time Machine, The, 344, 508
Time Out of War, A, 245, 475
Time Piece, 250, 538
Times of Harvey Milk, The, 273, 647
Time Stood Still, 246, 487
Time to Love and a Time to Die, A, 156, 496
Tin Drum, The, 281, 617
Tin Pan Alley, 179, 394
Tin Star, The, 94, 490
Tin Toy, 256, 670
Tiomkin, Dimitri, 177–78, 180–81, 184–88, 191, 204–7, 377, 388, 407, 414, 420, 447, 462–63, 473–74, 486, 492, 496, 502, 507–8, 513, 525, 530, 569
Tippett, Phil, 232–33, 296, 628, 642, 670
Tipton, George Aliceson, 192, 586
T Is for Tumbleweed, 247, 497
Titan: The Story of Michelangelo, The, 261, 453
Titanic, 92, 134, 467–68
Tit for Tat, 237, 369
Tlayucan, 278, 520
T-Men, 154, 437
Toast of New Orleans, The, 204, 452
Toback, James, 108, 687
To Be Alive!, 265, 538
To Be Or Not To Be (1942), 180, 407
To Be Or Not To Be (1983), 60, 637
Tobruk, 346, 549
To Catch a Thief, 117, 135, 218, 478–80
Toch, Ernst, 176, 181, 369, 400, 420
Todd, Michael, 22, 483
Todd, Richard, 34, 445
Todd, Sherman, 166, 394, 414
Todd-AO Corp., 313, 318, 493, 555; Sound Department, 155–58, 479, 496, 501, 507, 512, 524, 536
To Die in Madrid, 265, 538

To Each His Own, 44, 88, 430–31
To Forget Venice, 281, 617
To Kill a Mockingbird, 24, 36, 65, 75, 96, 119, 138, 188, 516–19
Toland, Gregg, 111–12, 368, 387, 392, 398
Toldy, John S., 85, 392
To Live Again, 264, 526
To Live or Let Die, 272, 635
Tolkin, Michael, 109, 693
"To Love and Be Loved," 206, 496
Toluboff, Alexander, 127–28, 377, 382, 387
Tom, Dick, and Harry, 86, 398
Tomasini, George, 169, 501
Tomei, Marisa, 70, 693
Tom Jones, 24, 36, 57, 65, 76, 96, 139, 188, 522–25, 708
Tomkins, Alan, 144, 621
Tomkins, Leslie, 145, 639, 645
Tomlin, Lily, 67, 590
Tommy, 48, 193, 589, 592
Tomorrow We Fly, 259, 416
Tompkins, Joe I., 225–26, 640, 677
Tom Sawyer, 142, 192, 223, 580–81
Tom Thumb, 344, 497
Tondreau, A. J., 305, 390
Tondreau, Bill, 330, 672
Tone, Franchot, 32, 367
Tonight and Every Night, 183, 202, 427
"Too Good to Be True," 339, 369
"Too Late Now," 204, 458
Too Many Husbands, 151, 393
"Too Marvelous for Words," 340, 378
"Too Much in Love," 202, 421
Toot, Whistle, Plunk, and Boom, 245, 469
Tootsie, 27, 39, 69, 79, 104, 123, 161, 173, 212, 631–34
Too Young to Kiss, 133, 457
Top Gun, 162, 173, 213, 235, 657–58
Top Hat, 19, 127, 199, 339, 367–69
"Top Hat," 339, 369
Topkapi, 57, 528
Topol, 37, 566
Topper, 53, 150, 375, 377
Topper Returns, 152, 342, 400–401
Topper Takes a Trip, 341, 389
Tora! Tora! Tora!, 121, 141, 158, 170, 347, 562–64
Torch Song, 64, 466
Torero!, 263, 492
Torn, Rip, 60, 638
Torpedo Run, 344, 497
Tortilla Flat, 54, 404
Tortoise and the Hare, The, 237, 366
Torture Money, 238, 378
Tosi, Piero, 221–25, 525, 569, 581, 616, 634
Total Recall, 163, 235, 296, 682–84
To the People of the United States, 259, 416
To the Shores of Iwo Jima, 260, 429
To the Shores of Tripoli, 113, 406
Touche, Pussy Cat, 245, 474
Touch of Class, A, 26, 48, 101, 192, 209, 578–81
Tover, Leo, 112, 115, 398, 446
Toward Independence, 260, 443
Towering Inferno, The, 26, 58, 122, 143, 159, 171, 192, 210, 583–86
Towne, Robert, 101, 579, 584, 590
Townsend, Martin, 255, 658
Townshend, Peter, 193, 592
Town Without Pity, 206, 513
"Town Without Pity," 206, 513
Toys, 147, 227, 694–95
Toys in the Attic, 220, 525
Toy Tinkers, 243, 448
Tracy, Lee, 57, 528
Tracy, Spencer, 31–32, 34–37, 371, 375, 381, 450, 477, 494, 505, 510, 546
Trader Horn, 17, 357
Trading Places, 195, 640
Traffic with the Devil, 260, 433
Trail of the Lonesome Pine, 199, 373
Train, The, 97, 535
Transatlantic, 127, 360
Trauner, Alexander, 137, 143, 506, 591
Traveling Hopefully, 272, 635
Travels with My Aunt, 48, 121, 142, 223, 572–75
Travers, Henry, 54, 404
Travilla, 216–18, 220, 447, 469, 474, 525
Travis, Neil, 174, 682
Travolta, John, 38, 601
Treasure of Sierra Madre, 21, 55, 73, 89, 440–41
Tree Grows in Brooklyn, A, 54, 88, 424
Trees and Jamaica Daddy, 246, 492
Trent, Barbara, 276, 696
Tresfon, Constant, 326, 636
Trespasser, The, 42, 355
Trester, Paul W., 324, 618
Treves, Giorgio, 268, 575
Trevor, Claire, 62, 64, 376, 440, 471
Trial, 55, 477
Tribby, John, 148, 356
Tribute, 39, 619
Trilling, Emanuel, 331, 673
Trio, 154, 452
Trip to Bountiful, The, 50, 106, 649–50
Tristana, 279, 565
Trivas, Victor, 88, 431
Troell, Jan, 77, 100, 573
"Trolley Song, The," 202, 421
Tron, 161, 225, 633–34
Tropic Holiday, 177, 383
Trosper, Guy, 91, 461
Trotter, John Scott, 191, 563
Trotti, Lamar, 21, 85, 87, 92, 387, 411, 418, 472
Trouble Indemnity, 243, 453
Troyat, Henry, 92–93, 478
Truant Officer Donald, 239, 401
Truce, The, 280, 587
Trudeau, Garry, 253, 604
True Glory, The, 260, 429
True Grit, 37, 208, 556, 559
"True Grit," 208, 559
"True Love," 205, 486
True Story of the Civil War, The, 262, 487
Truffaut, François, 77, 95, 101, 500, 584
Trumbo, Dalton, 5, 6, 82, 86, 91 n, 93, 93 n, 392, 467 n, 484, 484 n
Trumbull, Donald, 294, 327, 648, 684
Trumbull, Douglas, 231–32, 333, 604, 617, 634, 694
Truscott, John, 140, 222, 548–49
Truth About Mother Goose, The, 247, 492
Tubby the Tuba, 242, 438
Tucker, Larry, 99, 557
Tucker: The Man and His Dream, 61, 146, 226, 667, 669–70
Tudal, Antoine, 96, 523
Tulips Shall Grow, 239, 409
Tully, Tom, 55, 471
Tulsa, 344, 448
Tummel, William, 337, 361
Tunberg, Karl, 86, 95, 398, 500
Tunes of Glory, 95, 506
Tunick, John, 193, 603
Tuntke, William H., 139, 142, 530, 568
Tup Tup, 251, 575
Turkey the Bridge, 250, 544
Turkish Delight, 280, 582
Turman, Lawrence, 24, 546
Turner, Dr. A. Francis, 314, 504
Turner, Kathleen, 51, 655
Turner, Lana, 46, 489
Turner, Willard H., 307, 416
Turning Point, The, 26, 49, 59, 68, 78, 102, 122, 143, 160, 172, 601–3
Turpin, Gerald L., 326, 642
Tuttle, Frank, 131, 139–40, 426, 535, 548
Tuttle, William, 291, 532
Tweetie Pie, 242, 438
12 Angry Men, 23, 75, 94, 489–90

Twelve O'Clock High, 21, 34, 55, 154, 445, 447
12:01 P.M., 256, 683
Twentieth (20th) Century-Fox, 7, 238–39, 258, 260, 289, 306–7, 312, 384, 396, 402–3, 408–10, 422, 433, 470, 481; Camera Department, 307–8, 310, 416, 422, 454; Mechanical Effects Department, 310, 315–16, 444, 509, 533; Research Department, 315, 515; Sound Department, 149–58, 368, 372, 377, 383, 388, 393, 399, 407, 413, 419, 426, 441, 447, 452, 462, 479, 485, 496, 501, 524, 536, 542, 548, 553
24 Hour Alert, 246, 481
Twenty-One Miles, 259, 409
20,000 Leagues Under the Sea, 135, 168, 344, 473–74
Twice in a Lifetime, 69, 650
Twilight of Honor, 56, 138, 522, 524
Twining, S. J., 308, 423
Twin Sisters of Kyoto, 278, 526
Two Arabian Nights, 71, 351
Two for the Road, 98, 547
Two for the Seesaw, 119, 207, 517, 519
Two Girls and a Sailor, 87, 418
"Two Hearts," 214, 670
Two-Minute Warning, 172, 597
Two Mouseketeers, 244, 458
2001: A Space Odyssey, 76, 99, 141, 346, 552, 554
2010, 145, 162, 225, 228, 232, 645–46
Two Tickets to Broadway, 155, 457
Two Women, 46, 510
Tyler, Nelson, 316, 325, 533, 629
Tyler, Richard, 159–61, 591, 597, 627
Tyler, Walter, 132–34, 136–38, 142, 431, 452, 467, 473, 485, 500, 507, 512, 585
Typhoon, 342, 395
Tyrrell, Susan, 67, 573
Tyson, Cicely, 48, 572
Tyson, Elliot, 163, 669, 676

Ueda, Masaharu, 124, 651
Ugetsu, 218, 480
Ugly Duckling, The, 238, 389
Uhry, Alfred, 108, 675
Ullman, Elwood, 93, 484
Ullman, Fred, 240, 415
Ullman, Frederick, Jr., 259–60, 409, 438
Ullmann, Liv, 48–49, 572, 595
Ulysses, 98, 547
Umberto D., 93, 484
Umbrellas of Cherbourg, The, 97, 189, 207, 278, 532, 535, 537
Umeki, Miyoshi, 65, 490
Unbearable Lightness of Being, The, 107, 124, 668
Unchained, 205, 480
"Unchained Melody," 205, 480
Unconquered, 343, 437
Under Fire, 195, 640
Under Seige, 164, 235, 694–95
"Under the Sea," 214, 677
Under the Volcano, 40, 196, 643, 645
Under Western Stars, 200, 384
Underworld, 82, 351
Unfinished Business, 273, 653
Unforgiven, 30, 41, 61, 81, 109, 125, 147, 164, 175, 692–94, 708
Unicorn Engineering Corp., 313, 493
Uninvited, The, 114, 418
Union Maids, 270, 605
Union Pacific, 341, 389
United Artists Studio Corp., 304, 374; Sound Department, 148–50, 305, 356, 365, 368, 373, 377, 379, 383
United Nations, Division of Films and Visual Education, 260, 438
United Productions of America, 242, 433
United States: Air Force, 263, 514; Army; 259–60, 416, 443; Army Air Force, 259–60, 409, 422, 429, 443; Army Pictorial Services, 259, 416; Army Signal Corps, 259, 261, 409, 470; Army Special Services, 259, 409; Department of Agriculture, 259, 409; Department of State, 260, 438; government, 260, 429; Information Agency, 263–64, 508, 532; Marine Band, 239, 409; Marine Corps, 260, 422, 429; Merchant Marine, 259, 489; Navy, 259–60, 409, 416, 422; Office for Emergency Management Film Unit, 258, 402; Office of Strategic Services, 259, 416; Office of War Information, 259–60, 409, 416, 422, 429; Public Health Service, 259, 416; War Department, 260, 433; War Department, Office of Special Services, 259, 416
Universal-International: Sound Department, 154–56, 447, 452, 468, 496; Special Photographic Department, 312, 475
Universal Studios, 3, 237, 362, 366, 369; Sound Department, 149–53, 157–58, 317, 320, 365, 368, 373, 383, 388, 393, 399, 406, 413, 419, 426, 518, 524, 530, 536, 542, 548, 550, 587
Universe (1960), 263, 509
Universe (1976), 269, 599
University of Southern California, 7; School of Cinema/TV, 274, 665
Unmarried Woman, An, 27, 49, 103, 607–8
Uno, Michael Toshiyuki, 255, 635
Unseen, The, 154, 426
Unsinkable Molly Brown, The, 47, 120, 139, 157, 188, 221, 528, 530–31
Unsworth, Geoffrey, 120, 121–23, 529, 573, 584, 621
Untouchables, The, 60, 146, 196, 226, 661, 663–64
Up, 255, 647
Up in Arms, 182, 202, 420–21
Up in Mabel's Room, 181, 420
"Up Where We Belong," 212, 634
Ure, Mary, 65, 506
Urge to Build, 271, 628
Urioste, Frank J., 174, 663, 669, 694
Usher, Robert, 128–29, 131, 393, 399, 419
Ustinov, Peter, 55–57, 99, 455, 505, 528, 552
Usual Unidentified Thieves, The, 278, 498
Utt, Kenneth, 29, 686
Uvarov, V., 141, 552
Uytterhoeven, Pierre, 98, 101, 541, 590

Vacano, Jost, 123, 632
Vacation from Marriage, 88, 431
Vaccaro, Brenda, 67, 590
Vachlioti, Denny, 219–20, 508, 519
Vagabond King, The, 126, 356
Valentine, Joseph, 111–12, 115, 376, 382, 392, 441
Valiant, The, 31, 83, 353
Valiant Is the Word for Carrie, 43, 371
Valiant, The, 31, 83, 353
Valles, 217, 220, 508
Valley of Decision, The, 44, 182, 424, 427
Valley of the Dolls, 190, 548
Valli, Eric, 276, 690
Valliant, William W., 320, 582
Vallone, John, 144, 615
Valmont, 226, 677
Vance–Straker, Marilyn, 226, 664
Van Der Horst, Herman, 249, 520
Van Der Linden, Charles Huguenot, 248, 268, 520, 575
Van Der Linden, Martina, 248, 268, 520, 575
Van Der Veer, Frank, 295, 599
Van Der Veer, Willard, 110, 356
Van Dijk, Cilia, 255, 653
Van Druten, John, 88, 418
Van Dyke, W. S., 5, 72, 364, 372
Van Dyke, Willard, 247, 503
Van Enger, Richard, 167, 447

Van Every, Dale, 85, 376
Van Fleet, Jo, 64, 477
Van Gelder, Han, 570, 267
Vangelis, 195, 627
Van Gogh, 243, 448
Van Heusen, James, 202–3, 205–8, 421, 427–28, 480, 492, 496, 502, 508, 513, 525, 531, 549, 553
Vanishing Prairie, The, 262, 475
Van Runkle, Theadora, 222–23, 225, 549, 586, 658
Van Tulden, Linda, 255, 658
Vardar Film, 271, 617
Vargo, Mark, 232, 646
Varney, Bill, 161–62, 621, 627, 645, 651
Varsi, Diane, 65, 490
Varsity Show, 340, 378
Vasconcellos, Tete, 272, 629
Vassar, David A., 271, 617
Vaughn, Charles, 324, 624
Vaughn, Robert, 56, 499
Vazak, P. H. (pseudonym for Robert Towne), 106, 644
Veber, Francis, 103, 614
Veiller, Anthony, 85, 89, 376, 431
Velcoff, Alexander, 310, 449
Verdict, The, 27, 39, 60, 79, 105, 631–32
Verdon-Roe, Vivienne, 272–73, 641, 659
Vermont, Boris, 244–45, 463, 469
Verneuil, Henri, 93, 478
Vernon, Elmo, 165, 377
Verona, Stephen F., 251, 570
Verrall, Robert, 250, 252, 544, 549, 586
Vertes, Marcel, 134, 217, 462–63
Vertigo, 136, 156, 496
Very Nice, Very Nice, 248, 514
"Very Precious Love, A," 206, 497
Vesuvius Express, 245, 469
Vetter, Richard H., 320, 582
Victor/Victoria, 50, 60, 69, 105, 145, 195, 225, 631–34
Victory Through Air Power, 181, 414
Vidor, King, 17, 71–72, 75, 292, 351, 356, 359, 382, 484, 611
"Viennese Waltz," 339, 369
Viljoen, Tina, 272, 641
Village on the River, The, 278, 503
Vincent, Allen, 89, 441
Vinton, Will, 232, 252–54, 586, 610, 628, 635, 652
Viola, C. G., 89, 436
Violet, 254, 628
Violin, The, 252, 586
Violinist, The, 247, 502
V.I.P.'s, The, 66, 523
Virgin Queen, The, 218, 480
Virgin Spring, The, 219, 278, 508
Virkler, Dennis, 174, 682
Visconti, Luchino, 99, 557
Visit, The, 221, 531
Visit to a Small Planet, 137, 507
Vivacious Lady, 111, 151, 382–83
Viva Italia!, 280, 611
Viva Villa, 18, 84, 149, 337, 364–65
Viva Zapata!, 34, 55, 91, 133, 184, 460–62
Vlahos, Petro, 294, 315–16, 509, 533, 696
Vogel, Paul C., 115, 119, 446, 518
Vogues of 1938, 127, 199, 377-78
Voice in the Wind, 153, 181, 419–20
Voice Is Born, A, 242, 438
Voight, Jon, 37–38, 40, 556, 607, 649
Volcano: An Inquiry into the Life and Death of Malcolm Lowry, 270, 599
Volck, A. George, 10
Volver A Empezar (To Begin Again), 281, 635
Von Brandenstein, Patrizia, 144–46, 626, 645, 663
Von Cube, Irmgard, 89, 441
Von Ryan's Express, 348, 538
Von Sternberg, Joseph, 72, 357, 359
Von Stroheim, Erich, 55, 450
Von Sydow, Max, 40, 667
Von Zur Muehlen, Bengt, 268, 271, 581, 623
Vorisek, Dick, 161, 627
Vos, Marik, 219, 223, 225, 581, 640
Vowell, David H., 267, 564
Voyage of the Damned, 68, 102, 193, 596, 598
Voyage to Next, 252, 586
Vucotic, Dusan, 249, 526
Vystrecil, Frantisek, 248, 508

Wabash Avenue, 204, 452
Wada, Emi, 225, 652
Wada, Sanzo, 218, 474
Wade, William, 313, 488
Wagner, Jack, 88, 393, 425
Wagner, Paul, 273, 647
Wagner, Sidney, 112–13, 418
Waikiki Wedding, 199, 340, 378
Waits, Tom, 195, 634
Wait Until Dark, 47, 546
Wake Island, 20, 54, 73, 87, 404–5
Wakeling, Gwen, 217, 453
Walas, Chris, 229, 658
Wald, Jerry, 21, 23, 297, 424, 440, 443, 489, 505
Wald, Malvin, 89, 441
Wald, Robert, 163, 663
Waldo Salt: A Screenwriter's Journey, 275, 684
Walken, Christopher, 59, 608
Walker, Algernon G., 264, 526
Walker, Don, 189, 537
Walker, Hal, 338, 376
Walker, Joseph B., 111–12, 114, 301, 382, 398, 431, 629
Walker, Roy, 143, 145, 591, 639
Walker, Vernon L., 341–43, 395, 408, 415, 421
Walking, 251, 559
Walk on the Wild Side, 207, 519
"Walk on the Wild Side," 207, 519
Walky Talky Hawky, 241, 433
Wallace, Earl W., 106, 650
Wallace, Oliver, 180–81, 184, 186, 400, 414, 452, 457, 496
Wallace, Pamela, 106, 650
Wallace, William, 132, 441
Wallach, Ira, 99, 552
Waller, Fred, 311, 470
Waller, Garry, 232, 658
Wallin, Dan, 158, 160, 563, 597
Wallis, Hal B., 18–23, 25, 297, 359, 361, 364, 367, 381, 385, 391, 397, 404, 411, 477, 528, 556
Walls, Howard, 8
Walls of Fire, 268, 582
Walls of Malapaga, The, 289, 454
Wall Street, 40, 661
Walsh, Bill, 23, 97, 528–29
Walsh, Raoul, 703
Walt Disney Productions, 304, 379; Feature Animation Department, 333, 691; Sound Department, 152–54, 157, 309, 406, 413, 426, 434, 452, 512, 518, 530
Walters, Charles, 74, 466
Walters, Julie, 50, 637
Walton, Tony, 144, 221, 223–24, 531, 586, 609–10, 615
Walton, William, 183, 432, 442
"Waltzing in the Clouds," 200, 394
Waltzing Regitze, 282, 678
Wanger, Walter, 8, 20, 24, 288–89, 386, 391, 429, 443, 522, 705
Wanstall, Norman, 348, 531
Wanted, A Master, 237, 374
War Against Mrs. Hadley, The, 87, 405
War and Peace (USA), 75, 117, 219, 484–86
War and Peace (USSR), 141, 279, 552, 555
War at Home, The, 271, 617
Warburton, Irvine (Cotton), 168–69, 468, 530
War Clouds in the Pacific, 258, 402
Ward, David, 101, 579
Ward, Edward, 179–81, 200–201, 400, 407–8, 414
Warden, Jack, 58–59, 590, 608
War Department Report, 259, 416
Ware, Darrell, 86, 398

War Game, The, 266, 544
Wargames, 105, 123, 162, 638–39
Wargo, Lorand, 313, 493
Warner, Frank, 295, 605
Warner, H. B., 53, 375
Warner, Harry M., 3, 286, 384, 703
Warner, Jack L., 18, 20, 23–24, 298, 364, 391, 404, 494, 498, 528, 703
Warner, Mark, 174, 676
Warner Brothers-First National Studio Sound Department, 149, 360, 368
Warner Brothers Pictures, 3, 237–40, 248, 260, 285, 303, 352, 363, 366, 374, 378, 384, 389, 395, 401–2, 409, 421, 429, 508, 520; Art Department, 306, 396; Electrical Department, 308–10, 433–34, 444; Sound Department, 149–58, 308–9, 362, 365, 372, 377, 383, 388, 393, 400, 407, 413, 419, 426, 433–34, 439, 441, 468, 479, 491, 501, 507, 518, 530, 536, 542, 548, 553; Special Effects Department, 305, 385
Warner Bros.-Seven Arts Studio Sound Department, 158, 553
War of the Worlds, The, 155, 168, 344, 468, 470
Warren, Diane, 214, 664
Warren, Gene, 344, 508
Warren, Gene, Jr., 233, 689
Warren, Harry, 199–205, 369, 378, 394, 401, 408, 415, 432, 463, 469, 491
Warren, John F., 116, 472
Warren, Leslie Ann, 69, 632
Warrington, Bill, 345, 514
Warth, Theron, 260, 438
Wartime Romance, 282, 647
Washburn, Deric, 103, 608
Washington, Denzel, 41, 61, 661, 675, 692
Washington, Ned, 179, 200–202, 204–7, 394, 401, 414, 421, 447, 463, 469, 474, 492, 502, 513
Wassell, James L., 315, 520
Wasserman, Lew, 299, 582
Watch on the Rhine, 21, 33, 63, 87, 411–12
Water Birds, 244, 464
Waterloo Bridge, 112, 179, 392, 394
Waters, Ethel, 64, 445
Waters, John S. (assistant director), 337, 361, 364
Waterston, Sam, 40, 643
Water Trix, 243, 448
Watkin, David, 124, 650
Watkins, A. W., 151, 155–57, 388, 468, 501, 536
Watkins, Gregory H., 163, 676, 682
Watkins, Peter, 266, 544
Watson, Charles J., 325, 327, 332, 624, 642, 685
Watson, John, 252, 271, 581, 623
Watson, Lucile, 63, 412
Watson, Waldon O., 158, 292, 317, 320, 512, 518, 524, 530, 536, 542, 550, 587, 611
Watters, George, II, 235, 658, 683, 689
Waxman, Franz, 178–79, 182–85, 187–88, 383, 394, 400, 427, 432, 452, 457, 474, 501, 519
Way Down South, 178, 388
"Way He Makes Me Feel, The," 213, 640
Wayne, John, 23, 34, 37, 445, 505, 556
Way of All Flesh, The, 31, 351
Way Out of the Wilderness, A, 266, 554
Way Out West, 177, 378
Way We Were, The, 48, 122, 142, 192, 210, 223, 578–81
"Way We Were, The," 210, 581
"Way You look Tonight, The," 199, 373
Wead, Frank, 85, 382
Weary River, 71, 353
Weatherwax, Paul, 167–68, 442, 485
Weaver, Sigourney, 11, 51, 62, 70, 655, 667–68
Webb, Clifton, 34, 54, 417, 430, 440
Webb, Elven, 139, 141, 524, 548
Webb, George C., 140–41, 143, 542, 548, 558, 602
Webb, Ira S., 130–31, 406, 413, 419
Webb, James R., 97, 523
Webb, Jim, 160–61, 597, 615
Webb, Kenneth, 176, 365
Webb, Robert, 338, 376
Webb, Roy, 177, 179–82, 378, 394, 407, 414, 420, 427
Webber, Andrew Lloyd, 192, 580
Weber, Billy, 173, 657
Weber, Bruce, 275, 671
Webster, Ferris, 168–69, 479, 518, 524
Webster, Paul Francis, 202, 205–10, 469, 480, 486, 492, 496–97, 508, 513, 519, 525, 537, 543, 575, 598
Wechsler, David, 89, 441
Wechsler, Richard, 25, 561
Wee Water Wonders, 245, 469
Wee Willie Winkie, 127, 377
Weigert, Dedo, 332, 685
Weil, Cynthia, 213, 658
Weill, Kurt, 182, 420
Weinberg, Wendy L., 276, 696
Weingarten, Lawrence, 19, 23, 298, 371, 494, 582
Weinstein, Lisa, 29, 680
Weintraub, Bruce, 145, 645
Weir, Peter, 80, 108, 650, 675, 681
Weisbart, David, 167, 442
Weisblatt, Aaron D., 273, 659
Weisburd, Dan E., 266, 554
Weisman, David, 28, 649
Weiss, Fredda, 255, 658
Weiss, William M., 247, 497
Weld, Tuesday, 68, 602
Weldon, Alex, 346–47, 559, 564
Weldon, John, 253, 610
Well, The, 91, 167, 456–57
Welland, Colin, 104, 626
Weller, Michael, 104, 626
Welles, Orson, 20, 33, 73, 86, 291, 397–98, 404, 565
Wellesley, Gordon, 86, 398
Wellman, William, 72, 74, 85, 376, 446, 472, 707
Wells, George, 94, 490
Wells, Paul, 160–61, 603, 615
Wells, Robert, 211, 616
Wells Fargo, 150, 377
Welsh, Andrew, 252, 586
"We May Never Love Like This Again," 210, 586
"We Mustn't Say Goodbye," 202, 415
Wente, E. C., 304, 374
We Refuse to Die, 259, 409
Werner, Oskar, 36, 534
Werner, Peter, 253, 598
Wertmuller, Lina, 78, 102, 596
West, Charles, 313, 481
West, Claudine, 85, 87, 387, 405
West, Kit, 232, 628, 652
West, Mark, 329, 660
West, Ray, 160, 603
West, Roland, 17, 353
Wester, Keith A., 163, 676
Western Electric Co., 308, 422; Electrical Research Products Division, 306, 309, 439
Westerner, The, 53, 86, 128, 391–93
Westheimer, Joseph, 294, 321, 594, 690
Westinghouse Electric Corporation, 321, 593
Westlake, Donald E., 108, 681
Westmore, Michael G., 229, 646, 652, 658
Westmore, Montague, 229, 689
Weston, Maggie, 229, 677
West Point Story, The, 184, 452
Westrex Corp., 311–13, 464, 470
Westrex Sound Service, 156, 485
West Side Story, 17, 23, 56, 65, 75, 95, 119, 138, 157, 169, 187, 220, 339, 510–13, 708
Wetback Hound, The, 247, 492
Wet Blanket Policy, 203, 442
Wexler, Haskell, 120, 122, 125, 541, 591, 597, 663, 675
Wexler, Jerry, 194, 610

Wexler, Norman, 99, 101, 562, 579
Weyl, Carl, 127, 130, 382, 413
Whales of August, The, 70, 662
What, No Men!, 237, 366
What Are You Doing the Rest of Your Life?, 209, 559
What a Way to Go, 139, 221, 530–31
Whatever Happened to Baby Jane?, 46, 56, 119, 157, 220, 516–19
"Whatever Will Be Will Be (Que Sera, Sera)," 205, 486
What Next, Corporal Hargrove?, 88, 425
What on Earth!, 250, 549
What Price Hollywood, 83, 359
What's New Pussycat?, 208, 537
"What's New Pussycat?," 208, 537
What's the Matter with Helen?, 223, 569
Wheeler, Charles F., 121, 562
Wheeler, Lyle, 127–28, 131–39, 376, 382, 387, 393, 419, 426, 431, 436, 446, 451, 456–57, 462, 467–68, 473, 479, 485, 495, 501, 524
Wheeler, Rene, 89, 436
Wheelwright, Ralph, 94, 490
When Abortion Was Illegal: Untold Stories, 276, 696
"When Did You Leave Heaven," 199, 373
When Dinosaurs Ruled the Earth, 347, 569
When Father Was Away On Business, 282, 653
When Harry Met Sally . . ., 108, 675
When Ladies Meet (1933), 127, 362
When Ladies Meet (1941), 129, 399
When Magoo Flew, 245, 475
When My Baby Smiles at Me, 34, 183, 440, 442
When Time Ran Out, 224, 622
When Tomorrow Comes, 151, 388
When Willie Comes Marching Home, 90, 451
When Worlds Collide, 116, 344, 456, 459
"When You're Alone," 215, 689
"When You're Loved," 211, 610
"When You Wish upon a Star," 200, 394
Where Love Has Gone, 207, 531
"Where Love Has Gone," 207, 531
Where Mountains Float, 262, 487
"Wherever Love Takes Me," 210, 586
Whiffs, 210, 592
While I Run This Race, 266, 550
Whisperers, The, 47, 546
"Whispers in the Dark," 200, 378
"Whistling Away the Dark," 209, 563
Whistling Smith, 269, 593
White, George, 167, 437
White, Jules, 241–42, 428, 433
White, Merrill G., 168, 485
White, Miles, 217–18, 463, 474, 486
White, Onna, 291, 339, 555
White Banners, 43, 381
White Bim Black Ear, 280, 611
White Christmas, 205, 474
"White Christmas," 201, 408
White Cliffs of Dover, The, 114, 418
White Eagle, 259, 409
White Heat, 90, 446
Whiteley, Jon, 290, 475
Whiteman, Gene, 329, 660
White Nights, 213, 652
White Parade, The, 18, 149, 364, 365
White Rhapsody, 241, 428
White Shadows in the South Seas, 110, 354
White Wilderness, 186, 263, 496–97
Whiting, Richard A., 199, 373
Whitlock, Albert, 295, 346, 549, 587, 593
Whitlock, Tom, 213, 658
Whitman, Stuart, 36, 510
Whitmore, James, 38, 55, 445, 589
Whitmore, R. D., 315, 515
Whitney, Helen, 270, 605
Whitney, Jack, 151–54, 342, 393, 395, 400, 406, 413, 419, 426, 437
Whitney, John, Jr., 327, 648
Whitney, John H., Sr., 293, 653
Whittaker, Ian, 144, 147, 615, 694
Whittaker, Michael, 216, 453
Whitty, Dame May, 62–63, 376, 405
"Who Am I?," 200, 395
Who Are the DeBolts? And Where Did They Get Nineteen Kids?, 270, 605
Who Framed Roger Rabbit, 124, 146, 163, 174, 233, 235, 296, 668–71
Who Is Harry Kellerman, and Why Is He Saying Those Terrible Things About Me?, 67, 567
Who Killed Cock Robin?, 237, 369
Who Killed Vincent Chin?, 275, 671
"Whole New World," 215, 695
Whoopee, 127, 358
Who's Afraid of Virginia Woolf?, 24, 36, 47, 57, 66, 76, 98, 120, 140, 158, 170, 189, 221, 540–43
Who's Who in Animal Land, 240, 421
Who Wrote the Movie and What Else Did He Write? (book), 8
Why Girls Leave Home, 183, 202, 427
Why Korea?, 261, 453
Why Man Creates, 266, 554
Wick, Douglas, 29, 667
Widmark, Richard, 54, 435
Wiedemann, Claus, 333, 697
Wiest, Dianne, 69–70, 656, 675
Wilborn, Charles, 163, 682
Wilbur, Claire, 253, 269, 592, 599
Wilcox, Bob, 329, 660
Wild, Harry, 111, 382
Wild, Jack, 57, 551
Wild and the Brave, The, 269, 587
Wild At Heart, 70, 681
Wild Bunch, The, 99, 190, 557–58
Wild By Law, 276, 690
Wilde, Cornel, 33, 424
Wilde, Ted, 71, 351
Wilder, Billy, 23, 73–75, 85–86, 88–92, 95, 98, 298, 387, 398, 418, 425, 441, 451, 456, 466, 472, 490, 500, 505–6, 541, 665, 707–8
Wilder, Gene, 57, 101, 551, 584
Wild Hare, A, 238, 395
Wild in the Streets, 170, 553
Wild Is the Wind, 35, 46, 205, 489, 492
"Wild Is the Wind," 205, 492
Wild Strawberries, 95, 500
Wild Wings, 250, 544
Wiles, Gordon, 127, 360
"Wilhelmina," 204, 452
Wilkinson, James, 151, 383
Wilkinson, John (Doc), 162, 657
Wilkinson, John K., 160–61
Wilkinson, John N., 319, 570, 609, 627
Wilkinson, Ray, 306, 402
Williams, Barry, 270, 611
Williams, Billy, 121, 123, 562, 626, 632
Williams, Cara, 65, 495
Williams, Derek, 250, 544
Williams, Douglas, 158, 160–61, 563, 597, 603, 615
Williams, Elmo, 167–68, 462, 473
Williams, Glenn, 164, 688
Williams, J. Terry, 170, 542
Williams, John, 190–97, 210, 212, 214–15, 548, 558, 569, 574, 580–81, 585, 591, 603, 610, 622, 627, 633–34, 640, 645, 663, 669, 676, 682, 688–89
Williams, Megan, 274, 665
Williams, Patrick, 194, 616
Williams, Paul, 192–94, 210–11, 581, 585–86, 598, 616

Williams, Richard, 233, 251, 295–96, 575, 670–71
Williams, Robin, 40–41, 649, 661, 674, 686
Williams, Russell, II, 163, 676, 682
Williams, Tennessee, 91, 93, 456, 484
Williamson, Geoffrey H., 294, 330–31, 333–34, 666, 672, 679, 684, 694
Willingham, Calder, 98, 547
Willis, Edwin B., 126–27, 129–36, 372, 399, 406, 413, 419, 426, 432, 446–47, 452, 457, 462, 467–68, 473, 479, 485, 491
Willis, Gordon, 124, 125, 639, 681
Willkie, Wendell, 397
Willow, 233, 235, 670
Wills, Chill, 56, 505
Wills, Mary, 217–20, 223, 463, 480, 486, 497, 502, 519, 598
Willson, Meredith, 179, 394, 400
Willy Wonka and the Chocolate Factory, 191, 569
Wilmarth, William H., 342, 401, 408
Wilson, Carey, 84, 368, 703
Wilson, Fred, 312, 317, 476, 550
Wilson, Jim, 29, 680
Wilson, Michael, 5–6, 82, 91, 93, 93 n, 94, 456, 461, 484, 490, 490n
Wilson, Paul, 231, 617
Wilson, Robb, 209, 563
Wilson, S., 315, 515
Wilson, 21, 33, 73, 87, 114, 131, 153, 166, 181, 343, 417–21
Wilton, Bruce, 332, 684
Wimperis, Arthur, 87, 405
Wimpy, Rex, 342, 415
Wind and the Lion, The, 159, 193, 591
"Windmills of Your Mind, The," 208, 553
Window, The, 167, 447
Windy Day, 250, 554
Winetrobe, Maury, 170, 553
Winfield, Paul, 37, 572
Winfrey, Oprah, 69, 650
Wing, Paul, 337, 367
Wing and a Prayer, 87, 418
Wingate, Ann, 256, 664
Winger, Debra, 50, 631, 637
Wingrove, Ian, 232, 652
Wings, 17, 336, 351–52, 707
Wings Over Honolulu, 111, 376
Wings Over Mt. Everest, 237, 369
Winik, Leslie, 248, 250, 508, 544
Winkler, Irwin, 26–29, 595, 619, 637, 680
Winnie the Pooh and the Blustery Day, 250, 554
Winnie the Pooh and Tigger Too, 252, 586
Winning Strain, The, 250, 544
Winning Your Wings, 259, 409
Winston, Seth, 257, 689
Winston, Stan, 228–30, 232–33, 628, 658, 664, 683, 689, 695
Winter, Vincent, 290, 475
Winter Paradise, 245, 469
Winters, Ralph E., 167–69, 171, 452, 457, 473, 501, 536, 568
Winters, Shelley, 45, 62, 65–67, 455, 500, 534, 573
Winterset, 127, 177, 372–73
Wise, Robert, 23–24, 75–76, 166, 298, 400, 495, 510–11, 534–35, 540, 544, 705, 708
"Wishing," 200, 389
Wishy, Joseph, 272, 635
Wisner, Kenneth, 328, 660
Witches of Eastwick, The, 163, 196, 663
With a Song in My Heart, 45, 64, 155, 184, 217, 460–63
With Babies and Banners: Story of the Women's Emergency Brigade, 270, 611
With Byrd at the South Pole, 110, 356
With the Marines at Tarawa, 260, 422
With These Hands, 261, 453
Witness, 28, 40, 80, 106, 124, 145, 173, 196, 649–52
Witness for the Prosecution, 23, 35, 65, 75, 156, 168, 489–91
Witness to Apartheid, 274, 659
Witness to War: Dr. Charlie Clements, 273, 653
Witt, Paul Junger, 29, 674
Witti, Louis J., 310, 444
Wives and Lovers, 220, 525
Wiz, The, 123, 144, 194, 224, 609–10
Wizard of Oz, The, 20, 128, 178, 200, 341, 386–87, *389*
Wizard of the Strings, The, 273, 653
Wodoslawsky, Stefan, 254, 617
Wohl, Ira, 271, 617
Wohlrab, Hans C., 315, 520
Wolcott, Charles, 181, 183, 201, 414, 427, 437
Wolf, Arthur H., 267, 560
Wolf, David F., 333, 691
Wolf, Fred, 250, 549
Wolfe, Robert L., 171–72, 597, 615, 627
Wolfe, W. V., 154, 426
Wolff, Lothar, 249, 538
Wolf Men, The, 267, 560
Wolpaw, James, 273, 653
Wolper, David L., 263, 300, 503, 648
Wolsky, Albert, 224–27, 616, 634, 652, 689, 695
Woman in Red, The, 213, 646
Woman in the Dunes, 76, 278, 532, 535
Woman in the Window, 182, 427
Woman of Affairs, A, 83, 354
Woman of the Town, 181, 420
Woman of the Year, 44, 87, 404–5
Woman Under the Influence, A, 48, 77, 583–84
Women—For America, For the World, 273, 659
Women at War, 240, 415
Women in Love, 48, 77, 121, 561–62
Women in War, 342, 395
Women on the Verge of a Nervous Breakdown, 282, 671
Wonder, Stevie, 213, 646
Wonderful World of the Brothers Grimm, The, 119, 138, 188, 220, 518–19
Wonder Man, 154, 183, 203, 343, 426–28
Wonder of Women, 83, 354
"Wonder Why," 204, 458
Wood, Michael, 232, 634
Wood, Natalie, 46–47, 64, 477, 510, 522
Wood, Peggy, 66, 535
Wood, Sam, 20, 72–73, 387, 392, 405, 411
Woodard, Alfre, 69, 638
Woodard Productions, 239, 402
Woodbury, Albert, 190, 559
Woodruff, Tom, 233, 695
Woodruff, Tom, Jr., 233, 695
Woods, Frank, 2, 703
Woods, James, 40, 655
Woodstock, 158, 170, 267, 563–64
Woodward, Joanne, 46–48, 51, 489, 551, 578, 680
"Woody Woodpecker Song, The," 203, 442
Woolf, James, 23, 499
Woolf, John, 23–24, 499, 551
Woollard, Joan, 146, 663
Woolley, Monty, 33, 54, 404, 417
Woolley, Stephen, 29, 692
Word, The, 261, 470
"Words Are in My Heart, The," 339, 369
Work Experience, 256, 678
Working Girl, 29, 51, 70, 81, 214, 667–69
Workman, Chuck, 255, 659
World According to Garp, The, 60, 69, 632
World Is Rich, The, 260, 438
World of Kids, 244, 458
"World That Never Was, The," 210, 598
World Wide Pictures, 262, 475
Worrall, George, 333, 691
Worth, Marvin, 26, 268, 576, 583
Wottitz, Walter, 119, 517
Wrangell, Basil, 165, 377
Wrestling Swordfish, 236, 360
Wright, Robert, 200–201, 343, 394, 408, 421

Wright, John, 174, 682
Wright, Joseph C., 128–30, 132–33, 135, 138, 393, 399, 406, 413, 446, 457, 479, 512, 518
Wright, Steven, 256, 670
Wright, Teresa, 11, 44, 62–63, 398, 404–5
Writers Guild of America, 8
Written on the Wind, 56, 65, 205, 483–84, 486
"Written on the Wind," 205, 486
Wrong Way Butch, 244, 453
Wrubel, Allie, 203, 427, 437
Wrye, Donald, 267, 560, 570
Wunderlich, Jerry, 142–43, 580, 597
Wurtzel, Stuart, 146, 657
Wurzburg, Gerardine, 276, 696
Wuthering Heights, 20, 33, 62, 72, 85, 112, 128, 178, 386–87, 389
Wycherly, Margaret, 63, 398
Wyler, Robert, 91, 456
Wyler, William, 21–22, 71–76, 298, 372, 387, 392, 398, 405, 431, 445–46, 456, 466–67, 483–84, 500, 535, 539, 707–8
Wyman, Jane, 44–45, 430, 440, 455, 471
Wynard, Diana, 43, 361
Wynn, Ed, 56, 499

Yad Vashem: Preserving the Past to Ensure the Future, 275, 678
Yankee Doodle Dandy, 20, 33, 54, 73, 86, 152, 166, 180, 404–5, 407–8
Yankee Doodle Mouse, 240, 415
Yank in the R.A.F., A, 342, 401
Yanks Are Coming, The, 264, 526
Yasui, Lise, 274, 671
Yates, Peter, 27–28, 78–79, 613–14, 637–38
Yearling, The, 21, 34, 44, 73, 114, 132, 167, 430–32
Year of Living Dangerously, The, 69, 638
Year Toward Tomorrow, A, 265, 544
Yeatman, Hoyt, 233, 677
Yeats Country, 265, 538
Yellow Star: The Persecution of European Jews 1933–45, The, 271, 623
Yentl, 69, 145, 195, 212–13, 638–40
Yes, Giorgio, 212, 634
Yesterday, Today, and Tomorrow, 278, 532
Yojimbo, 220, 513
Yordan, Philip, 88, 91–92, 425, 456, 472
York, Susannah, 66, 557
Yoshida, Yuki, 253, 604
Yoshov, Valentin, 96, 511
You Are Free (Ihr Zent Frei), 272, 641
You Can't Take It with You, 19, 62, 72, 85, 111, 151, 165, 381–83, 707
You Can't Win, 243, 443
"You'd Be So Nice to Come Home To," 202, 415
"You Do," 203, 437
You Don't Have to Die, 274, 671
"You Keep Coming Back Like a Song," 203, 432
You Light up My Life, 211, 604
"You Light up My Life," 211, 604
You'll Find Out, 200, 394
You'll Never Get Rich, 180, 201, 400–401
"You'll Never Know," 202, 415
Youmans, Vincent, 199, 366
Young, Burt, 59, 596
Young, Dick, 271, 617, 623, 628
Young, Freddie, 116, 119–21, 461, 518, 535, 562, 567
Young, Gig, 55–57, 455, 494, 557
Young, Irwin, 323, 618
Young, Loretta, 44–45, 435, 445
Young, Ned (pseudonym for Nathan Douglas), 6, 94 n, 495 n
Young, P. C., 312, 476
Young, Peter, 146, 676
Young, Rob, 164, 694
Young, Roland, 53, 375
Young, Victor, 178–84, 186, 203–5, 383, 388–89, 394, 400, 407, 414, 427–28, 442, 447, 452, 486
Young, Waldemar, 84, 368
Young Americans, 258, 266, 554, 554 n
Young at Heart, 274, 665
Young Bess, 134, 218, 468–69
Young Frankenstein, 101, 159, 584–85
Young Girls of Rochefort, The, 190, 553
Young Guns II, 214, 682
Young in Heart, The, 111, 178, 382–83
Young Land, The, 206, 502
Young Lions, The, 117, 156, 186, 495–96
Young Mr. Lincoln, 85, 387
Young Philadelphians, The, 56, 118, 219, 499–500, 502
Young Sherlock Holmes, 232, 652
Youngson, Robert, 243–46, 453, 458, 475, 480, 487
Young Winston, 100, 142, 223, 573–75
You're a Big Boy Now, 66, 541
You're a Sweetheart, 127, 377
Your Face, 256, 664
Your National Gallery, 241, 428
Youth in Crisis, 259, 416
Youth on Parade, 201, 408
You Were Never Lovelier, 152, 180, 201, 407–8
Yuricich, Matthew, 231, 295, 599, 604
Yuricich, Richard, 231–32, 604, 617, 634

Z, 25, 76, 99, 170, 279, 556–58, 560
Zaentz, Saul, 26, 28, 589, 643
Zagreb Film, 248, 514
Zaidi, Nasir J., 331, 672
Zaillian, Steven, 108, 681
Zamparelli, Elsa, 226, 683
Zanuck, Darryl F., 3, 7–8, 17–23, 28, 297, 355, 361, 364, 367, 375, 379, 381, 391, 397, 417, 422, 430, 435, 445, 450, 454, 516
Zanuck, Lili Fini, 29, 674
Zanuck, Richard D., 26, 29, 297–98, 589, 631, 674, 684
Zapponi, Bernadino, 102, 596
Zaret, Hy, 205, 480
Zaritsky, John, 272, 635
Zastupnevich, Paul, 223–24, 575, 610, 622
Zavattini, Cesare, 89–90, 93, 436, 446, 484
Zeff, Paul, 308, 423
Zeffirelli, Franco, 76, 145, 552, 633
Zehetbauer, Rolf, 142, 573
Zelig, 124, 225, 639, 641
Zeller, Gary, 331, 672
Zelli, Salvatore, 326, 636
Zelli, Sante, 326, 636
Zemach, B., 339, 369
Zemeckis, Robert, 106, 650
Ziegler, William, 168–69, 496, 518, 530
Ziff, Stuart, 325, 630
Zimbalist, Sam, 22–23, 450, 455, 499
Zimmer, Hans, 197, 669
Zimmerman, Don, 172, 609
"Zing a Little Zong," 204, 463
Zinneman, Fred, 23–24, 73–77, 261, 441, 458, 461, 467, 500, 505–6, 540–41, 602, 707, 708
Zinner, Peter, 171–73, 574, 609, 633
"Zip-a-Dee-Do-Dah," 203, 437
Zollo, Frederick, 29, 667
Zoltan, 229, 652
Zorba the Greek, 24, 36, 66, 76, 97, 120, 139, 528–30
Zsigmond, Vilmos, 122, 124, 602, 608, 645
Zucker, Nathan, 263, 497
Zukerman, Jay, 254, 617
Zukor, Adolph, 17–18, 288, 357, 359, 361, 443

About the Author

RICHARD SHALE is a Professor of English at Youngstown State University, Youngstown, Ohio, and an adjunct faculty member of the Department of Human Values in Medicine at the Northeastern Ohio University College of Medicine, Rootstown, Ohio. His publications include *Donald Duck Joins Up: The Walt Disney Studio During World War II* (1982) and numerous articles on aspects of film and popular culture.

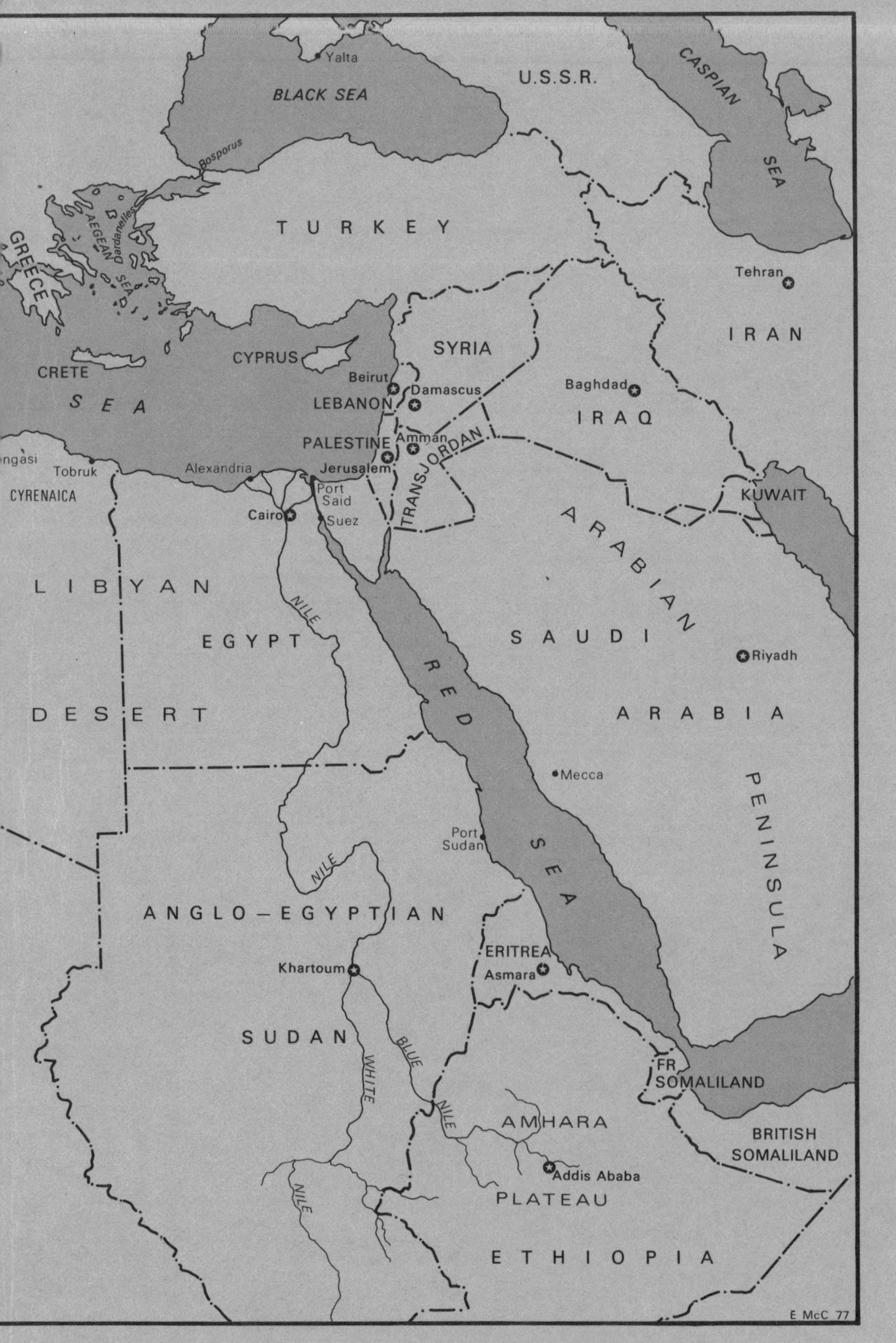
Yalta
BLACK SEA
U.S.S.R.
CASPIAN SEA
Bosporus
Dardanelles
AEGEAN SEA
GREECE
TURKEY
Tehran
IRAN
CYPRUS
SYRIA
CRETE
SEA
Beirut
Damascus
LEBANON
Baghdad
IRAQ
PALESTINE
Amman
Jerusalem
TRANSJORDAN
Tobruk
Alexandria
CYRENAICA
Port Said
Cairo
Suez
KUWAIT
ARABIAN
LIBYAN
NILE
EGYPT
SAUDI
Riyadh
RED SEA
DESERT
ARABIA
Mecca
PENINSULA
Port Sudan
NILE
ANGLO-EGYPTIAN
ERITREA
Khartoum
Asmara
SUDAN
BLUE
WHITE
FR SOMALILAND
NILE
AMHARA
BRITISH SOMALILAND
Addis Ababa
NILE
PLATEAU
ETHIOPIA
E McC 77

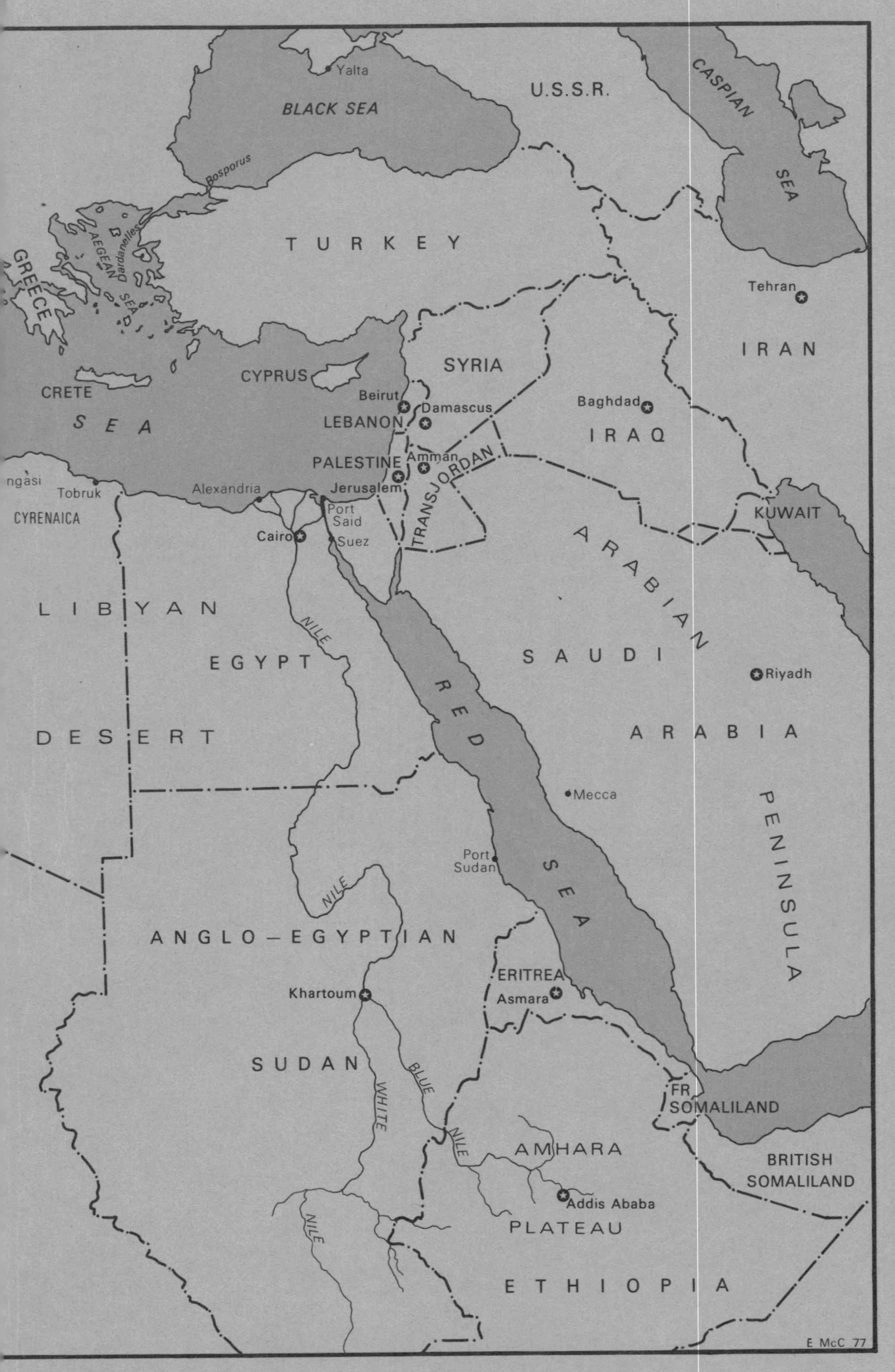

Yalta
BLACK SEA
U.S.S.R.
CASPIAN
SEA
Bosporus
Dardanelles
AEGEAN
SEA
GREECE
T U R K E Y
Tehran
I R A N
CYPRUS
SYRIA
CRETE
Beirut
Damascus
Baghdad
S E A
LEBANON
I R A Q
PALESTINE
Amman
TRANSJORDAN
ngasi
Tobruk
Alexandria
Jerusalem
CYRENAICA
Port Said
KUWAIT
Cairo
Suez
A R A B I A N
L I B Y A N
NILE
S A U D I
E G Y P T
Riyadh
R E D
D E S E R T
A R A B I A
Mecca
P E N I N S U L A
Port Sudan
S E A
NILE
A N G L O – E G Y P T I A N
ERITREA
Khartoum
Asmara
S U D A N
BLUE
WHITE
NILE
FR SOMALILAND
A M H A R A
BRITISH SOMALILAND
Addis Ababa
NILE
PLATEAU
E T H I O P I A
E McC 77